OUTSTANDING POETS OF 1998

OUTSTANDING POETS OF 1998

The National Library of Poetry

Leah Parker, Editor

Outstanding Poets of 1998

Library of Congress
Cataloging in Publication Data

ISBN 1-58235-072-8

Manufactured in The United States of America by
Watermark Press
One Poetry Plaza, Suite D
Owings Mills, MD 21117

FOREWORD

Throughout life, we store information collected from experiences and try in some way to make sense of it. When we are not able to fully understand the things which occur in our lives, we often externalize the information. By doing this, we are afforded a different perspective, thus allowing us to think more clearly about difficult or perplexing events and emotions. Art is one of the ways in which people choose to externalize their thoughts.

Within the arts, modes of expression differ, but poetry is a very powerful tool by which people can share sometimes confusing, sometimes perfectly clear concepts and feelings with others. Intentions can run the gamut as well: the artists may simply want to share something that has touched their lives in some way, or they may want to get help to allay anxiety or uncertainty. The poetry within *Outstanding Poets of 1998* is from every point on the spectrum: every topic, every intention, every event or emotion imaginable. Some poems will speak to certain readers more than others, but it is always important to keep in mind that each verse is the voice of a poet, of a mind which needs to make sense of this world, of a heart which feels the effects of every moment in this life, and perhaps of a memory which is striving to surface. Nonetheless, recalling our yesterdays gives birth to our many forms of expression.

Melisa S. Mitchell
Editor

Editor's Note

Suppose you want to write
of a woman braiding
another woman's hair—
straight down, or with beads and shells
in three-strand plaits or corn-rows—
you had better know the thickness
the length   the pattern
why she decides to braid her hair
how it is done to her
what country it happens in
what else happens in that country

You have to know these things
                    —Adrienne Rich, "North American Time"

The poet's writing a poem has often been compared to the painter's painting a picture: The influential Roman poet Horace wrote, "*Ut pictura poesis*," meaning, "as in a picture, so in poetry." Both painting and poetry employ a creative medium to reflect, to interpret, and to represent the intersection of the artist's inner workings and the reality of the world around him. The painter may notice a beautiful mountain landscape or a stray dog on a city corner, and the thoughts and emotions evoked by his experience drive him to try to communicate his feelings to others around him. While he absorbs the picturesque view or the seemingly ordinary, everyday scene that confronts him, the creative impulse begins to come into play. The painter must decide the colors to use, the various textures to incorporate, the number of clouds to include in the sky, as well as the area of the background necessary in order to portray accurately his interpretation of the scene onto a canvas. All of these previous decisions are vital to the final outcome of the painting—its composition, perspective, and depth, among other elements.

In the same way, the poet must make creative decisions as well, using words as his palette. What imagery or metaphor is necessary to communicate his innate understanding to his audience? What details are critical to the description of the mountain's peak, or superfluous in the rendering of the dog's solitary stance on the corner? Adrienne Rich examines these choices in the above excerpt from her poem "North American Time." Not only are the specific details of the braiding of a woman's hair relevant,

straight down, or with beads and shells
in three-strand plaits or corn-rows—
you had better know the thickness
the length   the pattern,

but the larger, more expansive contextual issues as well. It is important to know all of the particulars that comprise the overall picture, whether it is a stream running next to the mountain, or a pedestrian sitting on a park bench watching the dog. Carefully choosing which words to use is a monumental part of writing a poem. Knowing which images accurately represent the poet's emotional stake in the work is also key. All of these elements factor into the overall message that the artist intends to communicate through his art.

Rich points out that to write about something as seemingly prosaic as "a woman braiding / another woman's hair," the poet must address larger issues as well. Fundamental to the poem are issues such as the country in which it occurs and that country's current political and socio-economic situation. It may be that the braiding is a ritual in a certain area of that country, or that the braids represent a political statement. Possibly, the braiding is merely for aesthetic purposes, but if the poet does not know all of this, his picture will be incomplete and its impact lessened as a result. Just as the painter selects which elements of the background to incorporate into his painting, the poet must also decide what is important in communicating his message. Rich stresses, "You have to know these things," because it is only in the full knowledge of the entire portrayal that the poet can accurately and justly "paint his picture."

As you read through *Outstanding Poets of 1998*, enjoy the pictures that the poets herein paint. Through the words these poets choose, hear their messages. In contemplating the components that they choose to include, as well as what they choose to leave out, perhaps you may even share somewhat in their experiences.

Angela C. Hughes
Editor

The production of *Outstanding Poets of 1998* has been a culmination of the efforts of many individuals. Editors, assistant editors, customer service representatives, data entry administrators, and office personnel have all contributed to the publication of this anthology. Thank you to all involved; I am grateful for your creativity, ingenuity, hard work, and support.

Howard Ely, Managing Editor

Golden Hours

Some of summer's golden hours
Can be spent among the golden flowers.
Black-eyed Susans and mustard grow
Where the wetlands overflow.
Among the flowers are golden birds,
Flying about in little herds.
Gold finches, gold as they can be,
Swoop from flower to flower and then tree to tree.
What a lovely golden group
To find where the finches swoop.

　　Mary L. Fogg

Friendship's Fire

Old friends have passed away,
New friends have come to stay
But, only for a while,
To laugh and make you smile
The time is short, indeed,
Do not display your greed
Take a moment to give,
Each day that you may live
Hold a hand, hug a heart,
Before your friends depart
Speak of simple pleasures,
Seek those faded treasures
Share the tears and sorrows,
Search for great tomorrows
Learn to say "I love you!"
Before the morning dew
In the night, death may come,
The Lord will gather some
An angel will appear, in shining midnight clear,
Good-byes are laid to rest; few will reap Heaven's best.

　　Beverly Withee

Gone, Our Sea of Grass

To the drought-stricken ranchers of West Texas
Wrinkled and cracked is the Earth's shriveled face,
Hostile and brooding in the sun's summer blaze.
Windswept and desperate, it stares back at me,
That which once was a bountiful sea.
Green shoots and petaled blooms once knew the kiss of spring,
But I have almost forgotten its yearly capricious fling.
Now, only dust and limestone thrive in this thirsty land of mine.
Yes, I can always pray, but I will never whine.
The good years and the bad years
Are a cross the rancher bears,
For his much loved land entwines his soul,
Holding him captive in his rancher's role.
Today, I gaze upward to a world far away,
And I cry out with urgent voice to say:
"I have prayed, dear Lord, it seems in vain,
So please let Your tears fall as blessed rain."

　　Margauerite I. Wilkinson

Beautiful Elaina

Mirror, mirror on the wall, please show me what love is.
Is it the happiness in this aging skin?
Is it contentment with my soft, not-so-thick brown hair?
Or maybe love is appreciating the
Voluptuous figure that dances by herself at times.

Elaina, look deep into the hazel eyes staring back at you.
Understand the innocence almost lost.
Recognize you're alone in thinking no one
Appreciates your full, candy apple lips.
The talents that lie beneath your fingertips
And deep within your heart are looked upon and admired.

Love, Elaina, is being proud of the beauty in the mirror.

　　Elaina Norman

The Wind

I can't see you; there is no face,
but I can hear you every place.
Sometimes you're gentle as can be;
sometimes your force can move a tree.

The whole world knows of your sweet grace,
your soft caress upon their face.
In springtime when the blossoms bloom,
you blow about their sweet perfume.

Up in the air, you hold a kite
and blow a bird with all your might.
When summer comes with skies of blue,
you toss around a cloud or two.

Some of them are fleecy white
like little lambs that run in flight.
The other ones are dust and sand
from lack of water on the land.

Now into fall you press your luck,
and from gay trees their beauty pluck.
I heard you whistle; I saw you sway
bright Goldenrod along your way.

　　Emma Noon Reed

Marriage

In the little gazebo by the riverside
Stood the nervous groom and the blushing bride.
They pledged their all to become husband and wife,
And sunshine sparkled on their brand new life.
Time will bring great happiness, disappointments, too;
Handle each with loving care and God will see it though.
Have patience and understanding, with humor tucked inside,
And don't forget the gazebo by the riverside.

Marriage is not fifty-fifty, as others may lament;
Each should give lovingly, one hundred percent.
Talk things over in a calm and loving way.
Never go to bed angry, take the time to pray.
God will guide you and be there at your side,
As he was in the gazebo by the riverside.
Make each tomorrow better than today,
Remembering the love you shared on your wedding day.
When he was a handsome groom and she a lovely bride,
In the gazebo by the riverside.

　　Mary R. Stanley

Stranger in the Night

To my friends, Alberta and Angel Hough
You invaded the stillness of my darkened room,
Quietly appearing like a cloud of gloom.
Devil or angel, friend or foe?
Hail from Heaven or Hades below?

You appeared as bold as Armored Knight,
Dream a-fleeting, a phantom, a light.
You seemed so near, yet miles away,
As separate as night is from the day.

An intruder you were, unwelcome guest,
The essence of gentility at gracious best.
Respectful silence lifted the clouds of gloom
That accompanied your presence to my darkened room.

With bravery, I struggled to glimpse your face,
But at last I lost, so delicate the race.
Devil or angel, friend or foe?
A God from Olympia on a mission below?

As quietly you appeared in the darkness of night,
So slowly you vanished from mortal sight.
Stranger in the night, friend or foe?
Hail from Heaven or Hades below?

　　Jean Manning

Happiness

They constantly fight to be together
Through clear and stormy weather.
We push their love to the limit,
Yet they go on believing in it.
As the obstacles pile toward the sky,
They stand, hand in hand, wondering why.
How much more can they possibly take
Before their hearts break?
Is true happiness such an impossible feat
That we become so susceptible to defeat?

Jennifer Brown

The Waves

The waves rush over
the abandoned seal.
This young seal cries with a piercing sound
that affects all who know him.
The onlookers watch as this child's fears are made real.
He is lost, cold,
and no one will help.
Does this say something about our devastated society?
We will stand by while the young and defenseless
fall prey to their greatest fears,
being lost, alone, and unwanted,
while we stand by and care only if it affects us!

Mandee Thomas

Chocolate Dreams

To my loving parents
The picture of the chocolate goddess manipulating
The elaborate dreams of innocent children sleeping,
Soft moon rays beaming upon their annual worship,
Prayers spoken under tongue while they are dreaming—
No child can escape her clutches, even those who try hiding.

When a child falls into a sleep of frantic
Captured in a slumber-like cell that holds a maniac,
Chocolate goddess grabs them with her dark fingertips.
The child forever in her keep, like guarding a lunatic,
Until the morning light causes her to panic.

Slumbering children should beware, beware,
For, while sleeping, take care, take care.
From her sugary shoes to her chocolate lips,
The chocolate goddess awaits for you there,
To lead you slowly to her lair.

Ingrid Schultz

Little, Empty Shoes

One, two little empty shoes left lying on the ground,
The little wearer of them wasn't anywhere around.
One, two little fresh-shed socks left tagging close behind—
Where, oh, where now did she go, that little girl of mine?

She must have gone out searching for a furry kitty-cat
And forgot I wanted her to hurry right on back.
Little shoeless, dimpled feet, oh, where now did you go?
You must have hurried right on past my open-eyed window.

How I wish old Father Time could just roll back those years,
Let me kiss and hug her tight, banish all her fears.
Why, she could have a dozen cats, a dog and rabbit, too,
If only she could hurry back for just a day or two.

How I miss that little girl with her sunny smile,
Tossing natural golden curls, laughing all the while,
And those eyes, so wide and blue, just like the deep blue sea.
I wish that she could hurry home to Daddy and to me.

Those two little, empty shoes still long for dimpled feet.
My two arms are aching just to rock her back to sleep.
The rope swing, still and empty now, hangs on in memory,
Waiting for that little girl who played beneath my tree.

Nell Campbell

My Closest Friend

I'd like to thank my mother for all that she has done
I've loved her for a while now since my time has begun
She's always been there for me through thick and through thin
Even through our fights, she always seems to win
She's always there with me through good times and bad
She always stays by my side even though I make her mad
I love her very much and will until the end
She's not just my mother she's my closest friend

Sabrina Hayko

Legacy

Time is swiftly passing by
And all of us will surely die.
We leave behind our legacy,
For most of us a memory.
Some are remembered for good deeds done.
Some are remembered for victories won.
When my time comes to die and leave,
Who will be left behind to grieve?
What did I accomplish here on Earth?
Will I leave any memory of worth?
Maybe I made someone happy one day.
Maybe chased some gloom away.
Maybe I dried a tear or two.
Maybe I helped a smile show through.
These are the things that truly last.
When our future is gone, all that's left is our past.

Eileen Combest

Romance Novels

I read romance novels and wish it was me,
I've always wanted to be swept off my feet for everyone to see.
In my books people are always happy and so much in love,
I wish I had someone to love and to dream of
All I've had is heartaches and lots of loneliness to bear,
I can't seem to find anyone to love me and care.
All I find are men who just want to be a one night stand.
To take me out to eat, then wham, bam, thank-you, ma'am.
I did find men, I've been married four times, divorced three,
But, I just can't seem to make them be there for me.
After all these years I fell in love and I know he's Mr. Right
And he knows how I feel and I hate to let him out of my sight.
We love each other but, we can't be together.
Because his married to someone else and he's still with her.
He won't leave her for me, even though he tells me that he loves me,
I just can't seem to be the reason to set him free.
I would give anything for us to just go away together
And make a new life before it's too late for us forever.

Susan E. Messinger

Happiness Is

Happiness is knowing,
That you are truly loved,
But that someone special.

Knowing that you are secure,
With the person you are,
Is also happiness.

Happiness is knowing,
That you have learned,
To believe, trust and most of all,
Love yourself, for the person that you are.

Having accomplished all that is needed,
To be a complete person on the inside,
Only then, can we be truly happy.

Being happy with ourselves,
We are ready to accept the happiness,
That awaits us in our lifetime
And that is the greatest happiness of all.

Roxanne M. Linville

My Realistic Mother

Composed within nineteen seventy-three,
Sixty-four lines explicitly to thee.
Intentional obscuration by me,
Prevarication, instantly I see.

Disregarding human essentialism,
While craving passionate nominalism,
Quickly abandon reflective idealism,
Albeit, receiving abusive realism.

Never hurling fists', switches' or slaps' away,
Nauseating substance you would say.
Requirement: continually to obey!
Prolonged existence; emotional dismay.

Antagonistic weaponry, quiet sigh,
Lacking perfection: bloodly: I did cry!
Unsuccessfully warned! "I'll break these ties'!"
Memories: your numerous tears! "Good-bye."

You mother; God deliberately sought,
To admonishing love his small tot!
For mama's love, I continually fought!
Condone child abuse . . . I think not!

Tara Katrena

Familiar

There are paths and persons known to each other
Since the couple began to date one another.
Her hair to flow over his shoulder used to rejoice;
And how sweet did sound the sweetheart's voice!

Unexpected chats, though without themes, were bright
And thus continued endlessly, night after night.
The gates usually were not shut at that section:
Unchained dogs followed us, barking to no objection.

Covering her sight from the dazzle with a small hand,
There was a school girl with homework gone bland.
Innermost stirrings in her virginal soul of a gal,
She seemed to dream a moment of some future pal.

Here tonight to this old path, familiar since along ago,
We are coming back to revive our youth glow.
Husband and wife, at dogs' barking and running after,
Look at one another, convulsed with laughter.

Were our love in those green days left to disappear,
How could we have our easy mind in this night sphere?
We walk on the old path of familiarity permanent
And embrace in our four arms the wide firmament. . . .

Nhuan Xuan Le

The Daydreamer

With my philosophy book my burden,
With the autumn pulse of a forest's heart
Throbbing about me, I sat myself down
On a golden throne of leaves, leaned my back
Against a tree's, and, gazing past treetops
Fronting a pasture sky, watched purer sheep
Than I wander by. On wild, winsome wings,
The wind, her fingers running through my hair,
Came flitting past my face, her breath fresh, free.
She kissed a lone leaf. I watched it sigh, die,
Then begin its joyful journey to join
Its fallen brothers waiting on the ground.
And then I gazed at other leaves and saw
Not frail multicolored fragility
But the stiff cold of black and white; and saw
Not artless Nature's intricate veinings
But words like Plato and Pythagoras,
Socrates and Aristotle. My eyes
Returned to treetops, then to sky beyond,
Where purer sheep than I yet wandered by.

Richard G. Rinker

The Heart's Haven

Adrift upon a lonely sea,
I searched for you and you for me.
I looked for love that would not cease,
For strength and friendship's joyous peace.
When 'cross the teeming waves of night
I saw the beacon of your light.
I heard the music of your song
And knew you were where I belong.
To reach you then I gave my best
Till in your haven I found rest.
Now anchored forever on your shore,
I've found my peace.
I search no more.

DeAnna Drake Sampson

Can We Say

I woke up this morning with Jesus on my mind,
With a prudent heart not to be unkind,
No harsh words from my lips today
To anyone I happen to see on my way.

Lord, help me to let Your love shine anew,
For I don't know what others are going through.
Don't let me be the cause of someone's hurt
By the wrong tone of voice or a misplaced word.

I want to forgive those who have done wrong to me,
For without God's forgiveness, where would I be?
We have all made mistakes and come short of His grace,
So that makes us all equal, regardless of race.

Create within me the right spirit, Lord,
Clean hands and a pure heart, according to Your Word.
Then I know You will hear me when I pray,
If a heart full of love I keep all the way.

There is a way, and only one way,
That all these things we can truly say.
It's every day, Lord, we must yield to You
And let the Holy Spirit lead us in all we do.

Doris T. Bowie

Dreaming of You

I dreamt of you, handsome, standing there
The moon on the water casting gold on your hair
Your uplifted arms, pulling me to your side,
The motion of water, drifting out with the tide.
I yearned for your lips, crushing mine, and still,
Feeling your love, your touch, such a thrill,
Enveloping my soul, night down to my heels.
Casting prudence to the wind, your lips I could feel,
Burning, inviting, seeking feelings, I employed,
Never leave me, stay forever, it's you I adore.
We were happy as lovers with a family of seven
A marriage that lasted, I thought made in Heaven.
But, alas, the awakening meant another day dawned,
Instead of a wife, I was another woman wronged,
And I cried, for the outcome wasn't all I desired.
My life changed completely, I was no longer inspired.
Till I realized my children meant all I could hold,
And to me were more precious than all the world's gold.
Yes, at times I miss you, but I tell you this, my dear,
I had the best of you and I'm happy to be here.

Elizabeth E. O'Donnell

Golden Splendor

Autumn leaves as they float on a breeze,
Like monarch butterflies in a whirl of color
Quietly surrender summer
To await the blanket of winter,
A time for reflection, beauties of the season.

Monique Sirois

As If

Bluelight sadness fog ascends
up from an ocean . . . oceans away
Shale thin beauty falls
away a hidden mountain canyon

Anger
as if an abandoned ships
whose ghosts could not survive
disappear on watercolor seas . . .
still alive

Fear
as if a shadow's sight
deserts the darkness now to see
it is safe upon the edge of night's
division morning light

As I an apparition now the sun's horizon birth
it is sorrow's final breath at last . . .
color finds the earth

As if I know it's true
As if I look
Into the eyes of you

Mark Patrick Acuna

I Thought I Was Patient, Lord

I thought I was patient, Lord,
Until I watched the little flowers.
They took weeks and months,
Instead of minutes and hours.

The seeds took days, sometimes weeks,
Before they began to slowly peek
Above the soil and in the air
To discover what was going on up there.

The blooming time was put off longer,
Until the roots and stems became much stronger
To give support where the blossoms would grow.
Then the need for patience was a little more.

I thought I was patient, Lord,
Until I came close to Thee
And observed the seeds, flowers, and trees,
The clouds, stars, ants, the birds, and bees.

I studied again salvation's plan
And the way you deal with sinful man.
I thought I was patient, Lord,
Until your love drew me close to Thee.

Odessa Lockley

True Friends

As the flower grows from a tiny seed
to a magnificent rainbow of color,
Our friendship grows.
As the lighthouse guides the brave ships
through fierce storms in the darkest of nights,
Our friendship shines and guides.
As the weary soldiers lay down their lives
for their comrades in battle,
Our friendship is loyal and steadfast.
As a mother cares and nurtures her child
through life's lessons,
Our friendship is caring and nurturing.
As the oceans flow to the seas and the
tides are ever constant,
Our friendship is never ending.
We are separate, yet we are one.
We are individual, but very much alike.
We are on different journeys,
but we have a common goal.
We are true friends!

Deborah J. Redding

Simply

Because all that you are
can be enough,
is enough
to get you through this life.
Just give all that you are and fulfillment
will make you see
that you are more than enough
in every way.

Leizel Ching

Once Again

To my friend, Willie
Once again we met,
Once again we loved, once again we are separated.
Alone, I live for our measured reunions.
I memorize your total being.
Your warm eyes, your broad smile, your deep laughter and . . .
Your penetrating love.
I replay our conversations over and over again.
It's as if . . . they are the only records my mind recognizes
Or . . . my ears elect to hear.
I write letters and poems to you,
Which, more often than not, find themselves rejected
By my own censorship.
They seem too shallow or too deep, too weak or too strong,
Not acceptable in my own mind for your eyes to read . . .
Or for your soul to digest.
Once again the depression of separation sets in,
Leaving me painfully sad.
Fighting the tears that force themselves
Down the hollows of my aging cheeks,
Once again I think of you, once again I smile.

Sarah Kirk Oden

To Be a Star . . .

To my dear wife Eupema on her 70th birthday
You will go far
faster than in new speeding car
when you trust Lord, what don't have par
with hope, life is not a closed jar
and not sour, like vinegar
listen more to a guitar
count truly your days, in your calendar
feel good and proud, like a husar
and you will be strong, like a jaguar
because you will graduate high, from each life's seminar
be a golden star
and go far . . .

Frank Z. Glinski

My Love Is Forever

You came into my life you
touched my heart you showered
me with kindness there are so
many ways that you showed me you care

I want to give back for the things
you've done for me I want to be
there for you so I'll tell you that
my love is forever

The only tears I want to see falling
are tears of joy and happiness never sadness

I know that you don't really show
your emotions but deep down I know
you've cried silently this is true
because I've been there too

I'm really glad that I've found
trust in you it's not easy spilling
out your heart to just anyone so for
now and forever my love shall be

Michele Masi

Thoughts of Mother

To my ever-loving mother, Raquel Nunez Santos
When we think of our mothers we think of the one,
Who's provided best care for her daughter or son.
They've been there from the start, from the day of our birth.
When we think of their love, we can't question its worth.
Their clinging concern will always be there.
In times of much gladness or in times of despair.
Their worrisome ways is just part of their being.
At times drive you crazy, at times make you scream.
When they think they've annoyed you,
    they'll be back with some charm.
They just meant to prevent the absorption of harm.
So the next time you think of your great mother's ways,
Ask dear God to uphold her for many more days.

  Edward Santos

The Rose, the Breeze, and the Rain

To Susan, with whom I have shared these wonders
I've seen the beauty of a perfect rose,
Its glory for all to see,
Its scent reaching out to penetrate
My heart—it has the key.

I've felt the whisper of a soft, summer breeze
Dusting my soul with a love,
Releasing my heart of life's many dismays
So soft, as the coo of a dove.

I've felt the drops of a warm, summer rain
Cleansing my soul with its touch,
Feeling renewed in the great miracle
Of everyday life full of such.

These wonders God gives us day by day
If only we don't disdain
To notice along our walk in life
The rose, the breeze, and the rain.

  Mildred Kelley

Thinking of You

I sit and think of you, wondering what you're doing
right now, hoping you are safe and well.
I think of you at different times of the day
whether I hear a song or you just drift into
my thoughts because I love the warm feeling I
get when that happens.
I think of you at night and wish that you
are here holding me.
I love thinking about you and I hope you
think about me too.

  Kimberly Gelineau

Angels

I know that Angels are watching over us,
trying to correct the mistakes we make,
wishing they could discuss
the bond we must take.

This bond connects us to one another,
to see each other when our time is done,
realizing that we are sister and brother,
knowing that we are one.

I know our Angels listen
when we say our prayers at night,
that they are watching us glow and glisten,
knowing that everything will be all right.

Your Angel is with you now
and loves you in such a way;
I can not even begin to tell you how
just count your blessings everyday.

  Sarah Cortez

Morning Splendor

At five a.m. the moon was high
A perfect circle in the sky
An orange globe above the trees
That wavered in the morning breeze.

I feasted on that morning scene
The beauty there was clear and keen
But duty called; I must prepare
For daily tasks. What should I wear?

The minutes passed, the moon was gone
Yet dew was glistening on the lawn
While in the east the sun rose high
Another feast for human eye.

Refreshed and filled with dawn's delight
Those minutes at the end of night
Would help me face the day ahead
While I was earning daily bread.

How great the God Who made it all
And gave us minds that can recall
The beauties that we see each day
And for such bounty asks no pay.

  Dorothy Howard Adler

We Thought to Us We Did Belong

In a garden down nearby the sea,
I beheld your face come close to me,
And I dreamed you took me by the hand
And then pledged to me a golden band.

Music swelled in the unfettered air
As we sat alone amidst the square
And so thought to think ourselves in love
Until we should reach our home above.

Birds were singing in the tops of trees,
Giving credence to the honey bees,
And as you and I devoured their song,
It so seemed to us we did belong.

We sure thought to us we did belong,
As we heard a melody of song
Of our nature's symphony so rare,
Out there where our love we'd freely share.

  Reagan Murff

Courage Personified

Brave and hearty a man was he;
Joined the Marines, flew over the sea.
Years of battle, shot down in war,
Returned a hero, now a legend of yore.

His life moved on in a brand new struggle,
Vocation now chosen, other burdens to juggle.
Director of many; honest, fair and strong,
Loved, respected by employees; he helped them along.

The best husband and father, loving and kind;
Shouldered responsibility, helped anyone in a bind.
When serious illness approached, faced it head on,
Another conquest defeated by one so strong.

An unsung hero, this warrior of life,
Whose armor of strength vanquished all of world's strife.

  Mary Christensen

Black Brigand

They say he came from the lake of fire,
Where all is death and evil desire.
They call him a renegade, the devil's steed.
They say he came from a demon's seed.
He is black as death and all men fear
When in his dreams this steed appears.

  Sharon Nottestad

The Signs of Times

The snow's still sitting in the yard,
And I'm wishing awfully hard
That it would melt and go away
And spring could really come to stay!

Wishing doesn't always make it so,
But one day it will really go.
And then the grass and flowers grow;
The lawn we will have to mow!

The cycle always starts again.
The sun will shine, then comes the rain.
It gets real hot, and we'll complain
Until the snow comes back again.

So then the years go slipping by.
Things happen! Then we laugh or cry.
The snow still comes. The sun still shines.
We cannot change the signs of times!

Auda M. Heaton

Ride the Storm

To my precious daughter, Kim Berko
Ride the storm, for you're not alone.
I'm with you through it all.
To comfort and encourage you, I know; I've been there too.
Although you can't see through the darkness,
And the strong winds keep you down;
You're a survivor, and your faith will revive you.
Saddle up and ride the storm.
Though hurricanes blow, and hard rains fall,
When you're through it all you shall stand tall.
Fear not my child; hold tight the reins.
This trial will pass; just ride the storm.

Aurelia C. Connolly

My Peace Pond at Six A.M.

My heart needs quieting and refilling.
Thank You, God, for this peace-generating place!

Here I find "quiet waters,"
a symphony of color,
graceful ducks and their children,
a family of eloquent swans,
birds and frogs competing in song,
gentle breezes cooling my brow,
friendly sun announcing the dawn.
Your creation speaks peace to me.

But there is another world out there . . .
a world of hate and fear,
of hunger and greed,
of beatings and killings,
of knives and guns,
of inner and outer wars.

Empower me to engage this second world.

Atlee Beechy

Naked Ladies

Blooming in December
After all else has blossomed,
When the earth is drought-stricken,
The hills sunburnt,
Up come a clump against the grape-stake fence
With their thick, tubular stems
Sucking moisture from some unexpected depth.

There is a defiance in me
That admires these ladies,
Bright in their muted landscape.
There is a defiance in me
That admires
Whatever is strong and delicate.

Diana Vance

Reincarnation

Who was I? Where was I born?
When did I begin? Was I male or female?
Did I live before? If so, when did I die?
Where did I live? What did I do?
A vicious circle? How do we know?
We are told if we look into our rear view mirrors,
We are seeing our future.
Or is it the past?
Is it true that our past is our future?
If so, am I going to where I have been before?
What does life hold in store for me?
Should I review what I have done, or look ahead
To what I can do?
How long will it take me to reach my future?
Which way do I go? What will it be?
How will I know if I am there?
Maybe tomorrow if I am there?
Maybe tomorrow I will know.
But for now, I am content to be here, or is it there?
Only time will tell and I have plenty of that. Or do I?

Philomena Rossi

I Hide Them Well

My faults are mine; I hide them well;
I push them back from other's views.
They gnaw at me, but I won't tell.
They're not substantial, not front page news.

But Someone does, He sees and hears
The fright within this frame of mine,
And gently heals with healing tears
The wounds my soul cannot define.

Oh, yes, the faults are mine—I hide them well.
But thank you, God, in me You dwell,
And I shall try, day by day,
To lose my faults along the way.

Margaret Gamber

Good-bye

Don't go in front of me, I may not follow.
Don't come behind me, I may not lead.
Don't cry for me, do not fill with sorrow.
My tortured soul has been set free.
Don't mourn for me the tears of tomorrow.
Don't weep for me, though your heart may bleed.
Rejoice for me, my soul no longer hollow,
My captive tears have now been freed.
Don't judge me, my sins are many.
Don't pity me, my cross too heavy to bear.
Just remember me, even though this parting
In your heart creates a tear.
Don't go in front of me, too tired to follow.
Don't come behind me, the blind leading the blind.
Just remember me this day and tomorrow,
No longer in front, no longer behind.
Good-bye, loved alls, good-bye.

Shalaina A. Pinkney

A Blessed Friendship

In memory of my special friend, Mary Hawkins-Baker
Our acquaintance ignited, electrifying the world.
A natural bond unfolded, a social highway
of unclassified information.
Changes erupted, on a pleasant note.
Sharing, caring, and other elements of love.
A stable and steady relationship was so long endured.
Tears of joy and laughter and sadness, too.
A sudden separation, no warning, no clue.
Time fades memories and creates eternal personal shrines.
A friendship that's blessed is cherished forever.

Marsha Bingham

On Growing Old

Compassion have when you see in me
faltering steps or strain to hear;
forgive me when I fail to see
a loyal friend whom I hold dear.

My ears are wrecked; my eyes are dim;
and steady hands do tremble now,
so look away when I spill my gin—
spare me remorse and troubled brow.

You've noticed that response is slow,
that remembrance is seldom there;
alas, my mind you will never know
for the tide is out; the rocks are bare.

　　Friend, dwell not on how I now behave,
　　but what I did with the life God gave.
　　　Harold Corey

The Lotus

Your beauty is spread over watery miles
History refreshes your background from the Nile
Fairies danced upon your evergreen floor
Sniffing the sweetness from your magic door—of petals

Nymphs so lightly swept the breeze
Through this saga of waved, on beautied sea
Danced they through the magic of the night
While their moon friend played his roly-poly game of flight

Across scalloped seas of cloud, over each head
Scented breath stemming from the bleakness of its bed
Enchanting nymph or fairy in its path
Of silent beauty stirring here

Stepped they lightly on their toes—so gay
To dance here in the lily pond 'til day
Soars its sweet aroma in silvery leaves of magic, mystic wind
On a diamond-studded sea—of mirrored eternal time

Waiting for fairy or nymph to jump and play
Concealing them within their beauty always
The lily pad their stool of heavenly rest
This sacred flower forever here is blessed
　　　Rita W. Moody

Every Child

A child's eyes are so big and bright,
So full of love and pure delight.
They make you wonder what they see
When they play so happily.
I love the way that children are,
When they are near and when they are far.
When you are sad, they know what to say,
Either "it's all right" or "it's okay."
In this world, they are my light,
Even when all they do is fight.
A child can always brighten my day,
Even when I have to pay.
　　　Christy M. Rand

Storms of Life Haiku

the woman of strength
yearning to be held with care
had to serve instead

I have understood that women
have traditionally "done what has to be done."
So, before, during, and after the flood
of 1997 in Grand Forks, North Dakota,
many women of various ages
were working along side the men. Stress? Yes.
Scared? Definitely! But, doing what had to be done.
　　　Phyllis Sue Newnam Sand

Like Kopopelli

Kopopelli, the lost Anasazi Indian,
Was a hunchback, giver of good luck and health,
Who dressed in feathers, danced, and played the flute.
Kopopelli, thought to bring well-being to all.

Perhaps a mere dreamer of his times,
His drawing discovered by the Navajos
Dated back one thousand years ago.
Thus, an irony of a giver of well-being thus stands.
Dejavu, a giver of well-being, who took the fall,
Who disappeared, feathers, dreams, flute and all.

But one thousand years cannot erase
His human spirit from Earth's embrace.
Is Kopopelli alive today,
In some dimension, in some few way?

Sit back quietly, start dreaming, and face the winds.
Relax your mind, your soul, your being.
Listen closely for ancient sounds and dreams.
Kopopelli's melodic flute can still be heard.
He's bonded with us; his dreams are yours and mine,
For dreamers' dreams are infinite in time.
　　　Carlos Torres

The Tale of the Roasted Pig

There once was a pig that boasted:
"I swear I'll never get roasted!
I may get toasted—
But NEVER ROASTED!
I'm too pretty and pink
I can oink in a wink!

I don't know why they call people pigs.
They'll never be like me, strong and big.
They insult my name,
Me, they defame!!
I'm a very beautiful pink pig!
I'll NEVER get roasted
—Not even toasted!

Ouch! Put that fire out!
You've burned my SNOUT!
I guess I'm delicious,
Maybe it's auspicious!
I make gourmets happy,
These people are SAPPY!!!"
The pink pig w-a-i-l-e-d.
And that's the end of his tale.
　　　Rosalind Pinto

Escape

Dedicated to the memory of Cecil and Kennedy
She fluttered momentarily on the edge of time,
Singing and warbling—in tune with all mankind.
One day this one of beauty was caught in a cruel cage,
her wings beat against unrelenting bars
until they were bruised and broken,
seeking to escape, struggling to be free.
Free from tightening bands that pressed the
very life from one so frail and slight.
Free from all that clutched her soul
and kept it imprisoned in dark night,
when it longed to wing its way through the
golden rays of dawn that promised eternal light.

One day the door of the cage was somehow left unlocked,
and with her remaining strength, she weakly pushed
the door ajar, and silently slipped away.
Now she was free—free to search the Great Beyond,
her lithesome spirit could no more be caged in bars.
Her soul soared upward to heights unknown,
broken wings now healed and strong.
Let there be no grief, for she has found Escape!
　　　Mary Bagley

Peace

To my loving mother, Susie Hawkins
Peace . . . what can we do to obtain it?
Does anyone know how to gain it?
Man alone cannot do it, although he has tried.
Money can't buy it. For it, many have died.
A price must be paid, so it says in the Word.
The Prince of Peace will come, Jesus, the Lord.
Many years have passed; the time is at hand
When things must change on this land.
Some will be left, not heeding the call.
They were deceived by Satan, that's all.
Turn to Jesus now, your head humbly bowed.
He will bring peace and contentment now.

Ruby M. Cerutti

My Dreams Crossed the Miles

Last night when I closed my eyes to go to sleep,
You lay heavy on my mind
This morning when I woke up you were right where
I left you last night but in the mean time
My dreams crossed the miles between
Us and I was there loving you in the night
Your arms were holding me, your lips were touching
mine and everything was so right
You were saying all the things I wanted
you to say then someone called your name
and you drifted away
I gotta go now and face the day before me,
but I'll see you tonight when
I close my eyes to go to sleep
and once again my dreams run wild and free

Martha Welfel

God's Blessings

God loves me. How do I know?
He gives flowers in spring,
And the sun's golden glow.
He gives me hills clad in green, glossy coats.
He gives sweet, gentle music
In the bird's liquid notes.
He gives me trees, both rugged and tall,
Laden with fruit, both summer and fall.
He gives me my garden, both fragrant and fair,
And snow white lilies that bloom by the wall.
In winter he gives me pure, white snow,
And bright candles burning
While the yule logs glow.
He gives me both family and friends
To cherish and love, while peace wraps my heart
Like the wings of a dove.

Eva Darrington Rule

Wonders of the Lord

When we look up at the sky
And watch a little bird flying by,
How does it use its wings to float along,
Feeling the wind with nothing going wrong?
How does it build its nest with work so complete,
That when it has finished, its nest is so neat?
How does it know to feed and give its babies love?
Don't we know, its intelligence comes from the Lord above?

When winter comes and the trees seem dead,
They begin to bud in spring, and in summer leaves spread.
The Lord has them painted in hues of green,
Just one of His beauties that we have ever seen.
The flowers begin to bloom into colors so bright
That all they need to live is rain and the Lord's light.
The world is filled with our Lord's love,
And everything we have comes from above.

Janis B. Drinnon

Can I Help You?

A voice heard when I push my button:
"Can I help you?" . . . said over and over again
Not always would the same aide come in
To give me a bedpan, drink of water then

Run out, leaving my things out of reach
Me upset, distressed, depressed, I can't get the pen
To write my thank you notes to each
Person who thoughtfully surprised me with a gift when

In walked the doctor . . . "Let me examine you."
He felt the right side: "Do you have pains?"
"Yes, doctor. Is there anything you can do?"
"Time will heal. You'll be able to walk again."

Days go by as I lie in bed
"Can I help you?" constantly goes through my head.

Peggy Raduziner

THE OLD SOFA

Dear old sofa—the secrets you hold:
    you've held our babies
      and many old souls;

     The tears you've heard
      and laughter of many,
Along with stories and secrets of plenty;

     You've held our sick children
      and watched TV, too,
And without a complaint, you've worn out too;

     With baby spills and coffee stains
      you've soaked it all in
With all our love and the love of our kin.

     Thank you for your precious time,
May you hold up under more of the same kind,
    And thanks, again, for sharing our prayers
     And for the secrets we won't always share.

Colleen Harmon

A Chance

As shadows linger and pass on the night,
a homeless cat or dog faces the same plight.

Seen, but not often cared about,
As through the streets and alleys they filter in and out.

Lost or abandoned often their story,
if only we help, it is to our glory.

A chance to really stand tall,
by answering a helpless animal's call.

And this I found to be true:
you will never love them as much as they love you.

Richard A. Granholm

Gargoyle

With loving appreciation to the angel of his presence
I ambled down the country lane, then it came into view,
The old Gothic church and its gabled gate, too.
I ran over the flagstones, smelled heavy moss air
To see if Gargoyle, grotesque, on the spout was still there.
There he was, after all these years,
Protecting the sacred through history's tears.
"I'm back again," I called up with a shout.
(Would an old, childhood game still have any clout?)
So I turned my head—in a nonchalant way . . .
Surveying the fields . . . and the time of day . . .
Then I swung abruptly, to catch him off guard
As he statuesquely looked down on the verdant courtyard.
I jerked back to eye Gargoyle as fast as a blink,
And the ancient friend flashed me a "welcome back" wink.

Carolyn Gray

Betty

Thank you for a million things that somehow I forgot
That you give to me each day since we tied the knot;
For without them I would be a nothing that I know,
Without a place to just sit down or a place to go.
Thank you for the beauty that your presence brings to me,
For you are the everything for all the world to see;
You have added meaning to my life (you may not know),
Staying ever by my side where'er we had to go.
Thank you for understanding when things were filled with fear,
And there seemed no answer to things that were so near;
For you helped me find the way though the sky was grey,
And you helped me gather strength along our chosen way.
Thank you for our yesterdays that were so filled with love,
And for everything we have that graced us from above;
For you stayed by my side though I stumble and I fell,
And helped me to rise again and made sure that I was well.
Thank you for tomorrows that are always a new theme,
And are part of everything that we will ever dream;
But the thing that's best of all I'll say before I'm through:
Thank you for all the things that are a part of you.

Merle C. Hansen

Chrysalis

Yon caterpillar on a thorn,
A lowly worm with visions high,
Royal-robed and tractor-borne,
His goal: to mount the arching sky.

But first, the sleep in sculptured tomb
Upon a sapling sparsely-boughed,
Until Time's slowly-turning loom
Has woven strands to form a shroud.

When howling winds and icy blasts
Are soothed by mild-eyed Spring,
This metamorphic stage shall pass.
Behold! a Monarch's spreading wings.

And what of man? More curious still,
Wrought from the dust where worms abide.
He, too, shall sleep within a shell,
Awaiting visions ere he died,

Until the hour when Time shall cease,
When Voice and Trump shall sound: "Ye saints, arise!"
And our chambered chrysalis
Awakes, bursts forth with Crown of Life!

Rush T. Morrow

A Maiden's Goblet

Specter's silent hour of the immortal heavens
Blesses creation with the fruition of morning'
Flame, scattering tastes of fortune's music upon
A banquet of faded flowers and sorrowful tears.

Maiden's once enchanted goblets are lost in the
light of day, shining on blighted leaves tread
By sacred spirits, at life's insane dance, in
Ardor's temple high above Earth's distant orbit.

Birth's luster unfurls the dawn of a clear sun,
Echoing sweet songs of pleasure's moments intoned
By joy's proclamation, to crown gardens with vast
Boughs of grace and fearless blooms of shame.

Shedding plumage of foliage falls down upon the
deathless ground, breathing life's quick glances
and flashes, to pledge an innocent cup's delight
For the harmony of dream's melody in golden souls.

Sky's beams juvenate the bower of the globe's
Fantasy ornaments, chained by new daylight to the
Wreath of nature in the awakening branches of ivy,
Whose alluring stalks cascade and expire beneath.

Donald M. McIntyre

Dear Sis

Sharing laughter, tears, and pain,
Sisters, hands held down the lane,
Moments shadowed by real life,
You and I felt arrows bite.

I hear your voice, whispered thoughts.
You heard me when others scoffed.
I see your hands and busy feet
In play, in serious work you seek.

Together, no one could detain
Rapture, happiness, and our gains.
We soared above the petty strife;
Head on, we met the needs of life.

I thank you, Sis, for being there
To comfort, nurture, and to care.
What life has given us was true.
It strengthened and supported both me and you.

Our love, together and alone,
Enough to turn the well-tossed stone,
Today we treasure all we are:
Sisters following the brightest star!

Patricia L. Purrett

The Arms of Life

The moment I opened my eyes to life, to be,
I saw the two graceful arms
Of a great man of wisdom who gave life to me,
A man that is ample with love.

As a toddler, I aggressed in many frays,
Yet never had a single foe,
And those arms of love were with me every day.
Still, whose they were I do not know.

Though my family always picked me up as I
Giggled with joy, smiled with fun,
Most of all, when sadness approached and I'd cry,
They were the hands of a man, just one.

As I mature and move on to bigger things,
I have realized those loving arms,
I've come to conclude, those arms will always bring
My life and I away from harm.

The moment I opened my eyes to life, to be,
The arms that so took me aboard,
The loving arms that were reaching out for me,
Were the loving arms of the Lord.

Jessica Lindsey

Return from Paradise

I watch the millions of wave tops
Glittering and dancing along the surface.
The sea is enchanting and intriguing.
It makes me feel insignificant and little.
In the back of my mind, I still hear you.
Your voice echoes, your pleas and sobs intertwine.
Only now with these hundreds of miles between us
Can I feel hope and love growing inside me.
Now the sun is sinking and I am thinking
That there will be brighter days in our future.
This beauty of nature gives me hope.
It plants the seeds of happiness and love inside me,
Replacing the wilting roses that bind us.
I will be leaving in a few days from tonight
And returning to my life and you, my love.
I will cry when I part with this beauty,
But I will return home to you not alone.
I will run for your arms wholeheartedly
And share with you all the love and beauty
That this paradise has instilled in me.

Melody Hartke

One Life, One Song

One life, like a song sung softly to the spheres,
Makes music to the ears of one who listens and who hears.
Discordant notes and harmony together make the sound,
But the space between notes is where true meaning is found.
A life maybe as brief as just one note on a page
Or as long as the longest symphony ever played.
But long or short, the melody has meaning though unfinished,
And for those ears who hear it, the meaning is undiminished.
Somewhere the song continues its sweetly sung praise.
The music lives forever, not just for earthbound days.
One life, like a song sung softly to the spheres,
Makes beautiful music to the ears of one who listens and who hears.

I'm listening, Mom.
     Beni Bonucchi

Untitled

To feel secure for the time you're here,
To know that you will always have someone near.

To be special in your own certain way,
To be told, "I love you," every day.

To have friends that really do care,
To remember all the good times you share.

To feel the love that will grow inside,
To follow the rules that you must abide.

To have faith in everything that you do,
To believe that his love will always be true.

To the world that may never understand,
To the person who will always be there to hold your hand.
     Lisa A. Zimmerman

Mother

To my brother, Pierre
Death do not fear
Mother said, combing her hair into a knot
Airplane's haunting drone above us
Calm and silent—holding hand
Mother and father by my side
Down the stairs we went, seeking shelter
Around us, bombs without end
Houses crumbling, death so near
Mother's whisper, Pierre, Pierre
The only human sound
     Daisy Friedman

I Watched the Pieces Moving

I watch the pieces moving . . .
Your queen, his rook, your pawn
Sliding across the squares

And then the knight moves in to take you . . .
His strategy deceiving,
unlike the pawns so swiftly outmaneuvered by Your Grace

Such a glorious lady . . .
Dignified and proud . . .
Thrust into mortal danger

They say you play the same game that your
Father played so long ago
As you hid behind the sofa, watching the pieces go one by one
Into the wet glass by the board . . .
Unable to change to course

If I could only change the rules, I'd give her far more power
And no knight could touch her with his mighty halberd . . .
Felling her into the empty glass
Reflected in the tearing eyes behind the sofa

Watching the pieces move
     Nannette Sexton Gunn

The Last Painting

In memory of my daughter, Karen Shelia Kniceley
The old painter sat, with a picture in mind,
Of a love he once had for a very long time.
But as he started to paint, he took only one stroke.
His hands shook with age; his paint brush he broke.

He looked toward the sky, screaming with pain,
"Please Lord, let me paint just one picture again."
Her face is fading from my feeble mind;
My memories have faded and dimmed with time.

I barely remember her sea green eyes,
Her auburn hair, and sparkling smile.
She was a beauty, my very own life.
For sixty years, she was my beautiful wife.

They found him at sunrise, his brush in hand.
His heart had stopped, but he had painted again.
The face on the canvas was one of a kind.
He'll never know, he left a masterpiece behind.
     Wanda Wade

Reckless Heart

I told you once, I told you twice
Breaking my heart isn't very nice
Now it's time for me to get even
You don't need to ask for the reason
Since you broke my sensible heart
Now I'm going to tear yours apart
It's going to hurt you more than you can measure
Your pain will be my ultimate pleasure
The pain you have caused me will never heal
You just don't know what was real
You were only after some cheap thrill
Boy, did you find it in the wrong place
Now everything's just turned around and slapped you in the face
Someday, someone will treat you this way
Then you'll realize that having a reckless
Heart is a hard price you have to pay
     Sarin Van

Waiting

Waiting, waiting all my life
Sure that there was more than woe and strife
Prayers, regrets and longing nights
Find me at the end of life
Waiting, waiting for the light.
     Hazel Chipman

Cherished One

I hear the screams of a dying woman
It is far away, but still I hear it
Pathos echoing in my dreams
As if she is being violated daily and the
onslaught never stops, or so it seems

I sense something of immense significance
is happening and can almost taste impending doom
In my dreams the woman takes the form of a panther
and is majestically draped observing her kingdom
through golden eyes that spark against the emerald gloom

Her court is lively
skittering through the trees
slithering about her lofty throne
Their movement and unearthly vocalization
is haunting and surreal

Suddenly the chorus stops and the golden slits of
her eyes open wide—the court has vanished
Rain forest cherished one
Proud beauty still wearing only a diadem of sky
     Marcia Vinson Arnold

The Journey of a Rainbow
Jose and James, my rainbow
There rainbows all our lives
They appear in different colors
We may not see them with our naked eyes
We may not know it exists

This rainbow is God, He's all around us
His message is love, His colors are the heart and a breath
As confusion persists upon this Earth
He surrounds us with love

We must learn to walk away from it
The key is master your inner strengths—that is Divine
Just let all peace within prevail
Silence is the language of love

Whisper unto your friends there might be just one
Believe deep within, for you're guided by spiritual energies
Nothing is hidden for clouds disappearing
Left are the breezes in your deep and responsive heart

All the grays disappeared as love filled all the gaps
Laughters of an immense as rains have come, erased all your pains
The sun once again shines and a rainbow stands journeying
Filling all your hearts with more love
Minerva A. Garcia

Happy Forty
Do you remember when first you met
So happy, in love, quite content
In May, 1958, both were young
You were united in marriage as one

Later added was a bundle of joy
Proud father on the phone says, "It is a boy"
David Allen, first of the family tree
All were as happy as could be

As years roll around two girls came along
Debra Sue and Diane Marie
This completes the family tree

What is a home without grandchildren
Yours and know are your joy
It surely better be, for there are six boys
To hold, to love, to have fun and enjoy

God has blessed you these forty years
Some laughter, some tears
I'm sure there were time when it was tough
But He was always in touch

Forty years later there a mother's eyes
You are still happy, in love, very wise
I am proud you are my family
Leota Todd

Responsibility
Tear at perforation, fold at the crease
Don't lubricate with oil if there is grease
Marinate with white wine, season to taste
Use edible garnish so there is no waste

Educate the ignorant feed the down and out
Punish the guilty as long as there's no doubt
Penetrate the perimeter without crossing the line
Brush after eating, if you have the time

Tame all the tyrants, free all the oppressed
Gather all the nudists and make them get dressed
Substantiate the evidence, eradicate the crime
Speed up the computer so there's no line

Always exit in a timely and ordered fashion
Express all your emotions with sincere compassion
Drive for the other guy, cross at the light
Never ever give up without putting up a fight
Robert Wormington

The Seductive Wave
The seductive wave with its gentle touch,
It is a feeling I like very much.
The wave wraps its watery arms around you;
The feeling of excitement will astound you.
The seductive wave kisses your body ever so lightly
As the moon shines down on the waves so brightly.
It is such a titillating feeling;
It sends your heart reeling.
As the waves take you in their watery arms,
They fill you with their seductive charms.
The seductive wave whispers in my ear;
It tells me I have nothing to fear
As the waves crash into shore.
Then the seductive wave carries me
Out to sea once more.
Margie Chisom

The Heart of God
The heart of Almighty God has no
boundary lines nor extinction barriers.
Mine human eyes gazed with amazement
upon the beautiful sunset last evening.
Likeness appeared in glorious array
"Of" God's colorful tapestry of ornate
weavings and highest mountain tops
where quietness and confidence abideth.
"And" we can forever regain perspective "Selah."
The heart of God Almighty is all loving
and forever abiding in the bosom of
Jesus Christ, our Gardener, Ab'ba.
Anne Rivett

Forever Strangers
Let us remain forever . . . strangers
Bypass all emotional dangers,
Of treading the tightrope of a relationship,
To which neither of us wish to commit.

Before the fires of our lust begin to burn, lips touch,
Our passion-filled bodies begin to yearn,
Before our hearts beat with a sudden rush,
Our skin take on a sensational flush,
Before untamed (unchained) desire directs its call,
Before we cling to each other as if that moment were all,
Before we lose ourselves to thrills or emotion that lingers,
Maybe we should remain forever . . . strangers.

Honesty, sincerity, trust, and understanding
Certainly, would be too demanding,
So, before we begin, we must let it end,
To assure we avoid all the dangers,
We are as we've remained forever . . . strangers.
Olivia McDougald-Jones

The Last Trail Drive
The old cowhand sat at the end of the day
And gazed across the plains to yesterday.
Through dim misty eyes, he saw the big herd
And cattle as far as the eye could see . . .
Clouds of dust, Old Blaze, and me.
Once more, the herd would cross the stream
As the old cowhand sat and daydreamed.
We kept that herd moving up the trail
And there in plain view were some of the boys he once knew:
Dan, Ben, Tom, and Joe.
They were so real, he whispered, "Hello,"
As he slowly rocked to and fro.
Then it became many years ago.
There would be a reunion by and by, somewhere in the western sky.
A tear filled his old misty eye
As the herd slowly drifted out of sight.
Twilight descended into night and once again rode in the great parade.
Leoma C. Allen

Gentleness

When waves of war o'er the Earth are swelling,
When hate in the heart of man is dwelling,
When bells for the dead are loudly knelling,
Is gentleness found?

When the wounds of Earth are deep and long,
When the meek are crushed by the will of the strong,
When strife and greed sing together in song,
Is gentleness found?

Search in the love between a child and mother.
Search in the trust of a man for his brother.
Search where the aged care for each other.
Gentleness lives.

Lindsay Cooper Calhoun

In Memory of Daddy

In loving memory of daddy, Jeffie Lee Mitchell
He was a very good provider for me and my sister
And also a good husband to our mother.

As well as buying food for us to eat,
He shared with other children and adults also.

Daddy made sure that we had clothes
When we needed them and not what we wanted.
Where we wanted them. He said it is better
To give than to receive,
So he bought for other people
When they needed, when he could.

When Daddy was very sick,
He was still concerned about all of us.
Now that he had to leave us,
I hope he is feeling better
And in Heaven with God.

Norma Jean Mitchell

Lover's Sonnet

If every thought I had of you
Was changed into a flower
I could walk amidst an eternal garden
And fill a million bower

If every kiss I save for thee
Was sent into the sky
The light from them would dwarf the stars
And the sun would fade on high

And if every tear I shed for you
Were to flow into the seas
The world would flood in a moment's time
And would drown the lands for thee

For thee alone do own my heart
Through time and tide, we shall not part

Angela Bray

All Different

We are all different
Our shape, color, and size
We think of ourselves
Living for ourselves
We're living next to each other
For each other
Your difference builds your personality
Sets you apart from other people
Everyone is unique and special in their own way
There are gifts of the mind we are given
To live in the wild world
We can never live without difference
The difference is supposed to be cherished
But some people throw it away

Emily Vernon

The Restless Sea

No matter if the sea's waves crash or gently lap the shore,
Its power keeps on calling me—I must come back for more.
An early morning storm at sea wails and churns the surf.
The howling wind is like a mother crying out at birth.
Thunder cracks its whip of steel. It speaks with power and might.
The demons in the deep all rise to wonder at the sight.
Predawn darkness instantly turns to bright midday.
Moments freeze with strobes of light ere vanishing away.
A small boat tosses like a toy in the unrelenting waves.
Its unknown crew will find its peace in watery, unmarked graves.
Storm clouds hide the horizon and obliterate the sun.
But then, first hints of dawn reveal the waves still on the run.
It's almost over. But, there's still a blowing rain,
As it spits and sputters till the end with a last word of disdain.
The storm subsides; the sun comes out as rain clouds drift apart,
Giving life another chance, granting us another start.
The ocean's roar still goes on and keeps on calling me.
I'll return again to see my friend—the restless, endless sea.

Richard McGauley

Grandma's Stories

Grandma's stories that she would tell
Of her childhood and her life and the hard road ahead.
She would tell us about Heaven and God,
And the Devil and Hell and how
Great-grandma got married at twelve.
Back then, she said, that wasn't young.
You got married, had children, that was
How it was done.
She told us how Great-grandma died,
How they buried her on a hillside.
She said, Life has its ups and downs,
But that doesn't mean we have to frown.
Go around happy with a smile on your face,
Love makes this world a better place.
Now I am old and turning gray,
I find myself telling stories to
My grandchildren in just the same way.

Linda Smith

Life

Life
Amidst a churning of feelings, hopes, and dreams
Cascading truths, deception, and unforeseen occurrences
We ride along unaware of our own reality
Afraid of that which we do not know, the path we do not see
Bubbling with excitement
Gazing upon a reflection
Of an undecided life
A life that changes with every moment
Yet time has taught us well
Direction and determination draws us closer
To the calmer waters of today
So we may discover and attain
Reality as we see it

Ellen Hai

Life's Continuing Presence

To walk across the floors of old houses,
To hear the floor boards creak beneath my feet,
To wonder who has crossed these boards before me,
To wonder if our souls will ever meet,

The creaking boards seem to tell a story.
A window pane reflects a painful view.
The smells I smell hold presence of those before me;
The stillness whispers of their lives so true.

Their book of life will remain a quiet secret,
As forever within these walls will hold
A story that will for all earthly time remain hidden,
A story that silent memories will not unfold.

Georgia Elizabeth Pate

He Watches Me

I caught a glimpse
From the corner of my eye,
Of him watching me
As I passed by.
I stopped and smiled,
Then continued moving about the room,
Dusting, folding clothes, and running the vacuum.
All the while watching him, watching me.
There is a faint smile on his lips
That still touches me
Like a warm embrace,
And a slight glint in his eyes,
As if to ask, why?
He cannot speak, or feel, or touch, or move,
Yet he watches me from his corner of the room.
He watches like a guardian angel, as I sit or sleep
Or move about the room.
He is surrounded by glass and wood,
Now held tightly by a picture frame.

    Shirley Bundridge

Let's Talk

Shall we. Communicate. The topic for today is. . . .
We hear it many times a day. We all do it.
Yak, yak, yak, let's talk.
Words alone are empty.
Together, words change lives, increase knowledge,
break hearts, or damage souls.
The cut of words lasts a lifetime;
the cuts of knives heal and fade away.
"We need to talk" starts shivers and palpitations.
Talking over coffee, over drinks, sometimes over our heads.
All generations, all societies,
talk, talk, talk.
The key to all this babble is listening,
with the heart and mind as well as the ears.
So the next time you hear, "let's talk,"
hope it is followed by a smile.

    Melanie K. Graves

God Saw the Need To Take Mom Home

To my loving mother, Louisa Wilson Adkins
When God saw the need to take mom home,
I felt so desperate and so all alone;
I could not understand how could this
Be; most of all why would God take
My only mom away from me?

I would cry at night, sometimes till the break of dawn.
I missed hearing her gentle voice speaking
To me while she held me in her arms.

As the days pass on, even though I miss her still,
My sorrows are now easier for I believe
I will see her again one day when
I go where Jesus lives.

    Imogene Adkins Gaffney

Lotta Kids

We gotta lotta kids, mine and his and step ones too.
Little ones and big ones just to name a few.
Some are getting older and some seem very small
But just to have them any age we've really got it all.

I'd like to have a great big house and a yard of many acres
So each could know one another for childhood is so sacred.
We have blondes and brunettes, redheads too,
Some are tall, some short, some round but any size will do.
We will always love them, each and every one
'Tis what life is all about when all is said and done.

    Betty G. Bruce

A Good Life after All

Sometimes we think our lives aren't what we want
But God says "leave it all up to Him"
Think you want someone else's life
God will keep you from too much strife!
Put your trust in Him
Choosing others' shoes to wear
May be more than you can bear

The grass always seems greener on the other side
Until you get over there and find out, the best was your side!
Being content with what we have may sound to simple
But you don't really grow
Until you follow that very example

Put your trust in God instead of mankind
It's a better solution, you will find!

    Lorraine Vincent

From the Eyes of an Eagle

Ascending high in the sky,
surveying his domain from above,
the majestic eagle beholds
the devastation and destruction
that Man has caused.

And his heart breaks.

Forests burning, lakes and streams polluted.
The air no longer clean.
The skies no longer pristine.

What has Mankind done to his kingdom?
What has he done to himself?

The eagle's eyes fill with tears.

Only Man can save his planet,
and only Man can save humanity.
But will he?

And is it already too late?

    Norma Boyd

Conquer Life

Dramatized feelings inside
unspoken words heart that is broken
whispered I'll always be there
my imperative plea I'll keep pitching conquering life
My faith revolves around the sun
gravitation opens my windows to Heaven
hard experiences will pass away my light is love
creative ingenuity is my strength conquer life
saturate my mind peaceful quietness
my confidence based on solid foundation
acquaint thyself obstacles overcome
hold together conquer life
ambitions are opportunities
I believe in myself attuned
in harmony throughout the universe
I can conquer life survey my burning
desires content with whatever
comes conquers life

    Barbara Thomas

Offspring

In pain and joy, I gave birth to thee,
Nurtured and cared for the human to be.
In pain and joy, I set you free
To find the person you are meant to be.
I pray that in joy you will set yourself free
Of those sins visited on you by me.
Then, true to yourself you will be—
But your child will remain with me.

    Dorothy S. Rice

Grown So Fast

To Staci, with all my love
You are my firstborn grandchild
A sweet, young girl, not meek or mild
You speak your mind; you share your thoughts
You've learned the lessons the world has taught
You're smart and pretty and full of zest
You make me proud as you pass each test
Could it be no longer than a year
You took your first step; you showed no fear
Was it a year ago, surely no more
You started school, became a cheerleader
Now there are boys knocking at your door
Yes, my granddaughter, the years have flown
Now you start high school; my, how you've grown
You're fourteen, going on twenty
When I say this, you think it's funny
You have your mother's smile, your father's eyes
What is in your heart and mind will make you wise
Always be happy; that's what life is for; stay in school
Be kind and loving—I could ask for no more
You've grown into a lovely lady, but you'll always be Mimi's baby

Dorothy Wise

Progress

A number code replaced the knob to open the hotel door.
A simple brass doorknob: what stories it could tell!
It opened the door to king and commoner alike,
To days of sorrow, days of happiness or celebration.
From the newly wedded beginning their life as one
To those with many years of happiness together,
This place will linger long for them in memory.
Here to the weary traveler sought welcome rest,
The troubled ones adapting to a changing world,
A grieving widow seeking healing for her shattered dreams—
All found here a sanctuary from life's adversities.
Every day another tale was told behind that closed door,
A tale of memories, of love, of sadness, of joy.
The brass knob kept the tales within and kept the world outside.
Now the knob no longer guards the hotel door;
It is a paper weight sitting alone upon a desk.
Somehow it seems enclosed within its heart,
Are all the tales and secrets guarded through the years.
It still remains a symbol of gracious living from another time.
We shall not ever see its like again.

Nellie L. Truxal

No Introduction

To my grandmother, Mattie, her children, James, Shirley, Fred, Vivian
He needs no introduction
We should all know who he is
He gave his only son
Who died for all our sins

There is nothing too great or small
That we could not bring to him.
Yes, he is a powerhouse
When all else seems so dim.

Our place on Earth is only but . . . for a little while
And when we feel we can't go on . . .
Look up, take his hand . . .
He will carry you that extra mile.

She leaves behind four children
Who will miss her each passing day.
Our father's house, she is at peace
And this is where she will stay.

My family keep on bended knees
And your head up toward the sky
A light in use will always shine
There are no more good-byes.

Karen Birdsong

A Grown-up Mountaineer's Look Back

He was born in a city called Asheville,
Affectionately called, "The land of the sky."
A stone's throw from the village of Biltmore,
In walking distance of his school, Oakley High.
He came to be in the Blue Ridge Mountains,
Where he began his unique kind of life,
Delivered by some country house doctor,
But under the critical eye of a midwife.
The family, in the midst of Depression years
And with "a-doin' better" as their goal,
Moved out to live in a country place,
Where farming and hard work took its toll.
The good country life for him was Utopia,
Spending carefree days before grade school
And really getting to know his brother, Buck,
Swimming for hours in a creek-made swimming pool.
This mountaineer's best days were yet to come
At his school where the children would gather.
Thanking his Lord for his determined teachers,
And an unyielding principal, tough as leather.

Harvey Taylor

Most Blessed of All

To Eric Earnes, my greatest inspiration, I love you always
I believe that for everything that happens
there is a reason for it to be.
Perhaps it's already all planned out,
or perhaps we infer our own destiny.

Thinking of this, my mind wanders.
I consider my life and what I've achieved,
and I can't imagine what I've done to deserve
this wonderful reward that I have received.

I whisper, "Thank you, I'm so grateful,"
and tilt my eyes to Heaven above.
God saw a reason to bless me with
the most true and greatest love.

For all eternity I will be thankful
that my destiny is you,
because you are more than I asked for;
you are my every dream come true.

And if I never again receive
another gift in all my life,
I am still most blessed of all
because I am blessed to be your wife.

Rebecca Robinette

Proud To Be a Colored Child

Yes, proud to be, I am a colored child.
As you know, I get up in the morning with a natural glow.

I don't have much money,
Rich with brown sugar and honey.

No college education,
No money for a summer vacation,

Yes, proud I remain.
I can handle all the pain.

Scorned for the color of my skin,
But when you see me you will see my grin.

Challenged by a dysfunctional life,
That is why I must state my plight.

Yes, proud I remain.
I can handle all the pain

Steadfast with God, a way for me to stand tall,
The Creator who made me sees me through it all.

Yes, proud to be a colored child.

Tanya Mason

Daydream

If I could have just one more day.
To watch my baby boy at play,
We'd build a snow man, ride a sled,
Maybe go for a swim instead.

Perhaps we'd play a game of catch.
He'd watch his mother try to match,
His natural skill that came with ease.
He'd laugh, of course, and then would tease.

Sometimes we'd line up tiny cars,
Search night skies for familiar stars,
Run with the dog or play in sand.
Looking back, life seemed so grand.

Oh, what love and joy he brought,
When he arrived, a tiny tot,
With big blue eyes and skin so fair,
Framed by lovely golden hair.

And then the years sped swiftly by.
No more is he my "little guy."
He's all grown up and proud are we
Of the fine young man he grew to be.

Laverne E. Cowles

Torture: Great Mental Suffering; Agony

To the Goddess that changed my life, Christine Vanhyfte
The faces of no one twist and distort into surreal lunacy
Palindromes of reality melt and disperse eternal chaos
Remnants of substantiated truth scatter echoes of time
Thoughts of the last tortured life fade into shades of blood-gray

Lost . . .
Subconscious fathoms reach to be felt,
melding, molding, maligning hell,
disdaining memory and distinguishing hate,
sealing the only survivors fate.

Damned . . .
Miscellaneous excerpts of trysts long broken left behind
Fragmented mirror images of Pandora's last captive
Epochs of Armageddon sprung towards trapped naivete
Barren wastelands line horizons of spheres soon forgotten

Executed . . .
Ten and two years prior then
Death refuses admittance of him
Gnarled ice continues its tread
It seems that Job has come again

Please . . .

Jason Stowell

Listen Close

Listen close to the rain
It sounds just like a mandolin,
Music falling to the water upon the sea
As if it's playing just for you and me.
Listen to the wind chime in
Banjo sounds all through the air,
Look, into my eyes
Can't you see how much I care.
Walking along the shore of the beach
While the summer storm plays a melody,
The chill in the air don't bother me
While I'm right here in your arms.
Hey, let's make our own kind of storm.
Together we will make beautiful music
That will echo all throughout the land
While we play and roll about in the sand.
A wonderful feeling from deep inside
I promise that my love, I will never hide
Because you've reached beyond into my heart,
And went straight, deep into my soul.

Kimberlee Jenca

Filled with Music

I have often been warned of the loneliness
On this path I must traverse.
But as I walk alone,
On this weary road,
I hear sparrows in the trees
Whistling
Just for my ears;
I am filled with music.
I see toads
Jumping in the thicket,
An ornate dance only for my eyes.
And I feel pensive over a limping rabbit;
Survival of the fittest has determined its fate.
But before it fades from memory
I have learned compassion.
At the end of the road
This beauty could only have come
From my solitude.

Matti Baldassari

Mama's Rocking Chair

Is that my mama's rocking chair leaned up against that wall?
And draped across the arm I see mama's old blue shawl.
I can almost see her sitting there holding out her arms.
Waiting to rock a bye, rock a bye, sing please don't cry,
I will keep you safe and warm in my old blue shawl.

Mama's gone to Heaven—been gone these long, long years,
But every time I see that chair, I can't hold back the tears.
We rocked for many hours wrapped in that old blue shawl
Rocked away the tears, the fears, and finally the years.

I'm sure she has a new shawl,
Perhaps it's lined with gold.
To rock those baby angels in,
Just like our days of old.

Mama's rocking chair with her old blue shawl,
Rocking silently.
Always there for me.
Mama's rocking chair.

Louise Platt

Evening Symphonies

In Oklahoma, August's setting sun
is splashing symphonies across the sky.
The haze of evening's fiery theme begun,
clouds echo blending hues of red, and vie

For ever-brighter notes. This weaving tone
of colors plays the gently moving strain,
and shades of crimson, lilac, yellow—blown
so softly—harmonize in rich refrain.

A jet stream threads its way across the blue
and pinks, its low-pitched, delicate accord.
The tune goes on when sun's long out of view.
I stay to see the last melodic chord.

"Bravo," respond my silent accolades
as evening's colorful recital fades.

Constance Pollock

Me and the Car

No payments are due; we're faithful to you.
Our model's been axed; odometer's maxed.
Our head-lamps are sagging; back ends are dragging.
Worn tread still rolling; ignition's still tolling.
Our finish is chipped, and our seats are all ripped.
Our water boils; patience toils.
Our engines keep running, but a day is soon coming
When you'll push to the floor, and we'll answer no more.
You'll know that we're dead, but you'll fix us instead,
With your time and invention, persuasive attention,
Like a truce in a war.
See ya, and buy a new car!

Nora T. Day

Time

Apart from yesterday, now never dies,
Although, in essence, time certainly flies.
Forever ageless, never growing old,
This marching father always moving bold.
Unending motion, seasons warm and cold,
Eternally going, time's undying hold.
Conclusion lacking, stories will unfold.

Robin Ramsey

Dear Dadda

Today, we come to honor and to pay our last respects
To a devoted man of God who was a good father to us all,
A loving husband, family and beloved friend to many.
Your love, generosity, and courage we will treasure in our hearts.

Our hearts are filled with pain and sorrow.
God, help us dry our weepy eyes.
Dear Dadda, you held your head up high as you traveled
Through life's trials and tribulations.
In spite of this, you were always there to lend a helping hand.
Your presence, strength, and determination will be remembered
And sorely missed.
But I seek comfort in the fact that I know
Your spirit is peacefully up above.

The journey has been a long one, dear Dadda.
Lay down your sleepy head.
Dear Dadda, we deeply love you and miss you.
God rest your weary soul.

Bernice A. Wherry-Smith

For You

I want to be there for you
To cry when you cry, to smile when you smile
To scream when you scream, to cherish what you cherish
To share the memories you have
To relive the steps you've already taken

I want to be there for you
When you need me the most
So you can look at me the way I secretly look at you
So I can be your first thought when you get up
And your last thought when you go to bed

I want to be there for you
Because I worry and I care
But most of all, just because
I love you

Dawn Durbin

Close to Nature

Faded sun going down,
yellow August evening,
red robins on the ground,
soon they will be leaving,
flying locust in the trees,
their sound mechanisms loudly screaming.

Listen carefully,
hear the calves crying,
lost from their mothers.
My orange pumpkins
that are scattered across the yard.
Without names, I know not one from the other.
The white bee hive,
where my bees thrive, is definitely a wonder.

In the center of the yard
is my tall cedar tripod.
With long bared arms,
my yellow peace rose fans.
And all around
the tall trees close me in.

Millard G. Pendergraph

The Question

Sand swirled across a desert in profusion
Like the moments of a lifetime, unknown.
It erased every step of a weary traveler
As he faltered, then continued on, alone.

He walked toward a house on the horizon,
Dark and worn as the ark after the storm
That sheltered generations of believers
Until materialism subjected faith to scorn.

Steps up to the porch were a challenge;
He proceeded for commitment was clear.
His presence brought sudden recognition;
Silence hovered in the wake of awe and fear.

His bearded face was wet with perspiration;
Sun-tinged hair framed vivid eyes of blue;
Scarred hands called back historic malice;
A flowing robe of white was fresh as new.

He spoke, then asked, "Am I an ornament?"
Truth became the question answered no.
He asked again and said, "I thought I was."
Dreams often show us what we know is so.

Louise Wright

That Wintry Feeling

On the ground, a pristine white, snow has fallen overnight
With the morning sun, it's sparkling just like diamonds
While the children all dressed warm, the walking arm and arm
To break the chill of the northwest wind a-blowing

It brings back memories of coal-fed chimneys
Smoke rising from, the houses all around us
Momma rising from her bed, to greet six lil' sleepy-heads
All tiptoeing on the cold floor to the kitchen

Dad with coffee all brewed up, he was pouring in our cups
With the milk and sugar, we would drink to warm us
The drafts coming through the floors, and the matching drafty doors
Bundled up like teddy bears, Momma brushing out our hair

The cold walk we'd make to school, teachers thought I had on rouge
On my windburned face, with soap that were just a scrubbing
While they tried to call my mom, just get through that party line
I'm recalling, as I get that wintry feeling

Home again safe and sound, just a scooting all around
Momma's cooking, her homemade soup a stirring
Scent fills the air didn't have a care, more coal dad's shoveling
Water heated, baths done touch my memory, as I get that wintry feeling

Lillian Heigle Ridlen

Garden of Wonders

A garden of wonders, a dream come true
Vegetation so green, sky so blue

As Heaven dawns, it's a beautiful sight
To see it grow in the sun so bright

A garden of wonders, well-tended with care
Vegetation so green and beauty so rare

Beans, corn, tomatoes, and greens
A springtime joy, a gardener's dream

And flowering plants to bloom in the spring
What beautiful artistry they will bring

So they'll dig the soil and pull the weeds
Then plant and water the garden seeds

And watch it grow amid the sun
A garden of wonders, so delightful and fun

As it sweetens and grows within the field
What wonderful harvest it will yield

A garden of wonders, with beauty so bright
Blossoming in the sun's golden light

Alice Gmiterek Ryden

My Prison

My prison is only made of what I think I cannot do;
My prison is my mind.
My prison has no bars or locks;
My prison is my body.
My prison has no boundaries, no limits;
My prison is my soul.

My boundaries are limitless
Unless I think otherwise;
I will escape from this prison of fear,
And I will be free so long as I believe.

As long as I have hope I can never be caught;
As long as have freedom I will never be imprisoned.
As long as have my cross I will never be alone;
As long as I have faith in the Lord I will always be free.

Harrison Rhodes

The Past Is Gone

Alone, I stood on the hilltop,
my curls flying in the breeze.
I watched as the Ford roadster slowly drove away.
Would he stop and say good-bye?
The man I loved so much.
I was only nine, but now my heart felt old.
Just before the bend, he stopped and waved.
I knew it was the end.
Slowly, I walked back to the house;
now it seemed so empty.
My lovely young mother, quiet.
She knew too the past was gone
and tears would never flow.
Time would go on.

Grace Palmer Alex

Ladybug

To my loving husband

Oh, ladybug, with fingertips I trace around the blackened stains
Spots like falling ink jets, I plunge into your pool
Thick and bottomless, alone without a sound
It spits me out

I climb into the crimson red flames of sun-wrap
Fields of burning trees, a showy red
Orange and scarlet glowing tongues of light
Spreading arms around each other, impassioned flush with glow
Breathing in, the flame goes out

Oh, ladybug, where do you go?
Take me with you
I'll sit upon your wings, wire webs protecting me
Feeling warm, a cage to wrap about my soul

Dr. Susan Cangurel

The Pigskinner

Little time remained in this pivotal game
This struggle he felt was his to win
His chance came on the last play of the game
As he scooped up an errant fumble
He looked up field as he set his resolve
Confident was he in this last-ditch rumble
More than confident he—hasn't He already scored three
Early touchdown in this hard fought bout?
So away he flees on his fateful flight—in disdain
For the others present. They'll not catch him tonight
For he must score in this last and final minute.
Then the field before him faded as he carried
The ball to the goal. (As easy as tracking a mole)
It amazes me still—when I see that sheer will
Is the force that can settle an issue
And as often as not—it's the same guy on the spot
Who ultimately makes and is the difference

Alvin J. Kuppenbender

Earth, My Home

"Dear Sis," I wrote to her who helped me to grow
From infancy through my teen years and so on;
Wherever she went I was allowed to go.
"I miss you so much. When are you coming home?"

"Dear Gal, though halfway around the world from you,
You all are seldom far from my mind and heart.
Will you give my love to the family too?
Though separated, we're never far apart."

Her spouse was teaching the Arabs how to weld
In the oil fields of Dhahran at that time.
"Even dry, sun-drenched old Arabia held
Its fair share of attraction for me and mine.

I love the turquoise gulf with its beaches clean,
Shadowy date groves that for miles one can see.
Roving flocks of goats tended by men serene,
In old, biblical robes, who give smiles free.

Straggling camels graze like cattle as they roam,
Humps sharply outlined against the brassy sky.
Where could I go on this Earth and not be home?"
Heavenly Father made it for us, that's why!

Thelma Jo Parker

June Days

"What is so rare as a day in June?", a poet asked one day.
I wonder what makes it rarer than one in April or in May?
Is it because the sky's more blue,
Or the grass more green, the colors more true?

Do the birds sing sweeter as they soar in the sky?
Does the sun shine brighter when it meets the eye?
Are the breezes more gentle, the flowers more sweet?
Does the dust feel softer on a child's bare feet?

Oh, what is the magic of the days in June
That makes one sing a more joyous tune?
There's no real secret . . . the reason is clear:
June's the month of beginnings in the middle of the year!

Graduation time's here and life's filled with zest,
Vacations bring travel, reunions, and rest.
Then wedding bells ring and true vows are made.
New homes are begun and foundations are laid.

Yes, June brings wonderful days indeed,
When cares are forgotten and from worries we're freed.
So celebrate June and give God the praise
For granting us a month so filled with rare days!

Elizabeth Thornton Watkins

Wings of an Eagle

How high can an eagle fly?
Does it climb to the heights and soar
Free through the air,
Before it falls, only to die?

How wide is its wingspan?
How far can it see?
Can its heart hold someone as dear
As you are to me?

Can it love? Does it feel?
With life's blows,
Can it deal?

If all of this can be true of a mere bird,
My love, then my call
Above it must be heard.

For I, because of you, my dear,
To the heights do soar,
And it is my call you hear,
As it is I who am the eagle!

Patricia A. Ur

The Rock of the World

Foundations of petrified rock
Connected by columns of sapphire gold
Cast by serpentine fire.
A place that's taken an eternity to build
By the rock of the world.

Carbon dating cannot determine the rock's origin,
Yet it has revealed its image on a burial cloth.
For millenniums the rock has communicated
Through the creation of souls that become
Pebbles of the rock of the world.

These pebbles will dwell
In a place that's taken an eternity to build
Faith in the rock establishes a covenant forever.
Foundations of petrified rock
Dwarf mountains of adversity from the rock:

Only through columns of sapphire faith
Can still waters from the rock
Purify the soul.
The goal is to become a pebble
The pebble is where the rock of the world is.
            Timothy L. White

Denise

To God's most precious gift, my loving daughter, Denise Freeman
Free to go, free to reign, but stay awhile, remain the same
My baby girl is growing
Your life almost your own
Choices made for your future, while seventeen years have flown
My heart is always with you
Each breath you take, my own
Each happy moment shared with you
You'll never be alone
Each pain you feel, I also feel
Each scrape along the way
A kiss to help your boo-boos heal
And sent back out to play
Your loving eyes and gentle smile
A pleasure to behold
Your wit and wisdom, an astonishment
Your actions sometimes bold
You are my shining star at night
My sunshine through each day
Through thick and thin, I love you
My love is here to stay
            Diane M. Hubiak

First Rose

A mystical rose,
Transcended only by the heavens,
Planted lovingly before time,
Waiting for a morning to break,
To reach for the warmth of the sun
As it radiates,
Unashamed and without conditions . . .

Man and woman take their first stroll.
Naked before the world, gingerly they step,
Viewing the lushness dripping
From every pore of nature.

The rose stands out,
Beseeching them to come closer,
Tantalizing them with its pungent fragrance,
Its singular beauty;
Each syllable of color and texture displayed its perfection.

They stopped and breathed in its splendor,
Then left, carrying with them the
Knowledge and feeling of harmony
With their world, with their God.
            Sharon M. Swain

In Remembrance of Ollivant, Rita, and Ollivant Jr.

Surely, there is no subtlety in death, and,
For a season, little pleasure in the lives left behind.

But, rest assured. All will be well.
We will live again with memories
Of the love that we can still feel,
Of the gentle spirits that we still enjoy.

Despite the absence of the lives themselves,
There remains a Presence with us
That brings comfort and rest.

From the one who knows our every thought,
Sees our most awful fears,
Senses our deepest pain,
And exceeds our highest expectations.

We must remember Him now, trust in Him now,
Because He knows the purposes of all
And fashions all to His pleasure.
He knows the pain we feel.
He feel it with us.

And, in God's perfect time, He will heal us
That we may live, laugh, and love again.
            Kristi Yvette Jordan

Only God Can

Only God can put those clouds like cotton
Floating in the sky of blue
Only God can have the birds singing
In a beautiful morning for me and you

Only God can paint the beautiful blossoms
That bloom on the trees
Only God can paint the beauty of fall
The beautiful color of the leaves

Only God can paint the beautiful flowers
That brings beauty everywhere
Only God can give the sunshine and rain
To make the flowers grow, it takes his care

Only God can paint the beautiful rainbow
And place it in the sky
Only God can paint a perfect sunset
As each beautiful day passes by

Only God can build a place called Heaven
And mansions to behold
Where the flowers will bloom forever
And the streets are paved with gold
            David Lee Knepp

Waiting

Watch with me
As the last patches of snow begin to go,
For they carry with them the barren ways
Of the past, colorless days,
Days that were needed
To help a few of us to see.
When the heart of the tree ceased to beat,
All dreams were not blown away
Without a chance to show their colors a future day.
Bare branches were not the end,
For when they were able to bend
In the autumn of their life,
They sent their whirling messengers down to earth
To work their way into the memories of the past.
These new seeds of life
Do not fall into silent graves
That will be soon forgotten:
But nestled in the blanket
Of past summer days,
Wait for the first signs of spring.
            Lawrence Bergman

Design of Expression

My senses are wandering in the alabaster clouds,
With unsaid words and thundering phrases
Waiting to be released into an atmosphere
Of receptive souls holding endowed daydreams.

Let me create mind pictures of landscape gems,
Coloring the horizon with a vivid coral sunset,
A mental canvas displaying rainbow imagery,
A floral gallery of brilliant impressions.

The tall amethyst mountains of sculptured beliefs,
The vision of a reflecting river and sapphire skies,
Shaded trees of jade in lavish foliage
Painting with pastels of the printed word.

Barbara Ann Schick

Rocking Chair

An outstretched arm cradles you as you sleep through the night.
Its comforting embrace soothes you and gives you warmth
in the quiet of darkness.
Suddenly, you awake!
The arm is gone and you are alone.
Your head lies on a fluffy pillow as you listen to the
stark silence and slowly drift off again to sleep.
At dawn, you stir again, to find a friend whose outstretched
arm surrounds you and holds you close.
You are surprised—the arm is your own!
You have learned to love yourself, to ease your own loneliness.
and rock yourself caringly throughout the night. . . .

Elaine P. Millen

Sadness Strikes Again

It waits around the corner near
Something you cannot taste, see, or hear

It wraps itself around, as you pass the corner by
Showing no mercy, ignoring your cry

Its grasp is of a parasite type
Like glue on paper so white

A struggle ensues to find an escape
No one knows how long it will take

It comes like a virus, no cure in sight
It matters not how hard you fight

And when the release finally comes
Is after all the damage is done

Bernie Lawrence

Jigsaw Puzzle Friendships

I started at the picture on the box,
Illustrated was a well defined picture,
Small, interlocking, colorful images,
Its assembly a time consuming adventure.

A kaleidoscope of vivid illustrations,
Captivated my attention,
Carefully, I removed the pieces from the box,
Examining each piece's dimension.

Each piece so unique had its own place,
I envisioned them as endearing friends,
The symmetry of the pieces shared with one another,
The connectedness of friendships that did not end.

These pieces complex and well defined,
Friendships diverse, yet complimentary,
Each piece represented a friend I had known,
Enriching and redefining my life's journey.

These puzzle pieces are an extension of myself,
The dependency of interrelationships between others now clear,
The whole is still the sum of its parts,
The jigsaw puzzle of friendships treasured and dear.

Iva J. Cooper

Blessings beyond Measure

I thank you, Lord, that I can see,
For some cannot see the tiny bee.
I thank You, too, for ears to hear
Sweet sounds of home so very dear.
For a voice bursting forth to sing
Praises to You for the little things,
Feet to walk on life's highway,
Arms to enfold loved ones every day,
So many blessings sent from above
Showing the measure of Your "great love."
Lord, please forgive, when I fail to say,
"Thank you, Father, for each new day."

Joline Faye Wood

Canyon Sunrise

Stars rear back
to accommodate a ripple of light
blazing over the cliffs, tangled
in the pines where smokeless beauty roars.
Blood red-orange spills its dancing stain,
all shimmering with sensual desire.

A spiral of purple cavorts within
the scarlet flame and a drumbeat
crescendos, while violins weep without sorrow
for the daydreamer to awaken in a pool of gold.

A symphony of silent passion
boldly echoes off canyon walls to steal
your breath away and you stay and wait until
the steady vibrations become a patter
and then merely the lick
of a whisper that endures forever.

Bree Gale

The Phases of Friendship

A friend is like a precious gem,
forever sparks when times are dim.

A friend is loyal, loving and true
always there when you are down and blue.

A friend is one not to be bought with a price
always ready to make a sacrifice.

A friend is one rarely found
until the end, he is loyally bound.

A friend is there in a heavy flow of tears,
though they've been there for months it seems like years.

A friend is there through thick and thin.
that's why friendship can last to the end.

A friend is there when your world has no wealth,
but at the sight of silence they will be there until the death.

Bernita Addison

Why

Did you ever stop to wonder why,
The blue's so blue up in the sky?
And the big soft clouds so fleecy white,
Take shape and form, then fade from sight?
And the way the trees turn green in spring,
Then in winter shed everything?
And why the rivers' gentle flow get so big
And madly grow to waves so big they
Beat the shore, then recede and be calm once more?
Did you ever stop to meditate on all the things
He did create? The heavens and Earth and much more too,
In us, the faith and love and courage to do
All the things we know are right
To help us be a guiding light?

Ruth Phillips

Passion Plants a Fostering Crop

Cultivate a heart with patience and kindness
And harvest forgiveness and mercy.
Bring hope to a table of bitter menu,
And the hungry shall eat sweetness.
Give water of faith to the thirsty
And look upon the blossom of Peace.
Shop in the store of Love.
And come home with the bounties of . . .
Life.

Marion Murphy

Broken

You slowly turn away from me
Without a care, without a glance.
When I get mad and all I want to do is scream,
You see me as a passing storm.
I try to tell you.
I try to show you.
Yet, when you hear me, you don't really listen.
You are blind to everyone around you.
Well, almost.
You have changed so much, yet you do not see.
I thought it was forever.
I guess I thought wrong.

Catherine K. Thompson

Butterfly

Lackadaisical chrysalis hanging like a silky balloon,
Waiting for imago metamorphosis from your cocoon.

Like an organist's fingers pressing keys for chiming,
Slowly, slowly emerging forth in nature's rhythmic timing.

Lepidoptera, picturesque wings, regal butterfly,
Knowing not of the dangerous world darting by.

Philanthropic, from flower to flower you're flitting,
Ambitious pollination with each drop of nectar sipping.

Making this world a much bountiful place,
Lepidoptera, with your beauty and charming grace.

Unaware of any catastrophic untimely ending,
From egg, to larvae, to pupa, to adult ascending.

June Serviss

A Father's Love

In loving memory of my father, William Curtis Lang
The smile of pride upon your face,
There's nothing in the world to take its place.
The very first man a little girl loves,
One of God's great gifts from above.

You helped me stand, when I could only crawl.
You gave me guidance, when I felt I was up against a wall.
You never faltered to meet our needs,
Watching us grow, and hoping we'd succeed.

You taught me of our history and taught me all that I could be.
We used to sit and talk and even share a quiet walk.
As I grew into womanhood,
You taught me all things, strong and good.

You taught me to overcome my fears.
You showed me even a strong man can shed tears.
You showed me love in all its forms.
You were there from conception to the minute we were newborns.

Your wealth was not in silver or gold;
You felt richer with each child you were able to hold.
When you felt the end was near,
You called each person to whom you felt dear.
The day God called you up above,
Was the day I lost that special father's love.

Deborah Lang

My Baby's Blocks

I see them scattered on the floor,
My baby's blocks,
Across the rug, behind the door,
In little flocks.

And when I seek with weary feet
My rocking chair,
Upon its soft be-cushioned seat,
I find them there.

Long after she has gone to bed,
Her Blocks Remain
And tell me mutely where her curly head
This day has been.

I cannot miss her when she sleeps,
For all about,
The toys she leaves where'er she creeps—
Her presence shout.

The smudges of her tiny hands upon the wall,
The soldier waiting her commands, her dollies all.

I cannot miss my little girl, where'er she be,
For every corner holds a toy that peaks to me.

Margaret J. Wagner

Star of Destiny

To my most loved niece, Ma. Ceres Roxanne B. Posadas
June 12, 1973 . . . the day your frail cry echoed your birth.
A sweet angel you are to the family who love you so much:
A darling grandchild to Daddy and Mang;
A sweet little sister to Uncles and Aunts,
A very responsible daughter to Mama and Papa,
A loving "Manang" to sister Anne and brother Patrick.

"Tweet-tweet" you are fondly called by all;
Forever in our hearts we shall continue you to call.
Your sweet smiles, your crunchy laughs, and funny jokes,
Your serene thoughts and inspiring words of hope,
Your faith and Godly views of life that kept you strong,
Your love for everyone you endlessly have shown—
Now everything lies so futile, still undone.

October 23, 1997 . . . the day that took away all dreams to share,
A day that shook our hearts to know our dearest "Tweet-Tweet" gone.
Hearts that mourn the loss of a most loved child,
So untimely, no chance to bid good-bye,
Now reunited with Daddy, a dream you always dreamed.
In our hearts, a star you shall forever shine,
"Tweet-Tweet," our star of destiny and a princess of the family.

Remedious H. Badiang

Enigma

Every page is filled with details,
lines and lines of untold lies.
Deception, description, memories
haunted in dreams, and sometimes
just the plain truth.

Characters raped with roles,
"Burning with desire by his lingering eyes,
The endurance between them was too intense,"
and, like us,
"'I'm sorry I woke you way after midnight,'
your voice lingers, a coy laughter,
a soft intimate shyness.
'In truth upon my heart,
I didn't incline to tell you I loved you.'"

Jotting down a line in thought,
"His ponderous features looked down on her,
almost alarmed to ask: Why?"
As I ask myself: Why?
In truth to love you: Why?

Colleen Dawn

There Was a Room

There was a room.
A room darkened, with walls lit only by
The candle of her heart.
Within this room, shadows hung upon the walls
As pictures, where she was found pacing in empty circles,
Paralyzed by all other extremities.
There were no words from her.
Her lips were cold and still, as if she were dead;
For what she had to say
Could be heard only by her heart's bittersweet love.
Though longing,
She would be heard never on Earth,
For he who would listen walks Earth forever no more.
A mystic trance, almost enchanting, consumes her,
And her will, full of truth and purity,
Dances to its song.
With each day passing and every night that at birth is a memory,
She waits patiently for her time to come,
Knowing that the rain will soon bring a new tomorrow.
There was a room.

   Lacy Ann Mills

Raindrops

Raindrops fall in sleet and hail.
It makes one wonder, why do we fail?
Raindrops fall when the sky is clear.
Why does this happen?
Maybe to increase our fear.

Raindrops fall when the sky is gray.
Raindrops fall, it seems like every day.
Raindrops fall in hurt and in pain.
It makes one wonder, what will they gain?

Sometimes it's light.
Sometimes it's not.
Sometimes we fight
And then wonder why we fought.

Raindrops falling everyday.
One day.
Someday.
It will go away.

   Moira Sweeting

The Vet

There he stands in a moment of silence,
Before a wall of fallen buddies.
A tear trickles down a well-weathered cheek
As he tries to forget the screams of the wounded
And the hurt of those he left behind.
Will the scar it has left ever fade?
Will he ever be able to laugh aloud
Without feeling the pain tugging at his heart,
Reminding him of those that will come no more?

   Florence S. Cowell

Eddie Flick—My One True Love

I love it when you hold me tight,
Making me feel everything is all right;
Sincerity and love reflect on my face,
As you hold me tight in your warm embrace.

My love for you is true and strong;
With you by my side nothing is wrong;
Your smile, your laugh, your tears, your touch,
I want you to know that I love you so much.

Your memory, our love, I'll hold in my heart,
Until the next time that we are apart,
But love like ours will never end,
For all my love to you I send.

   Stacia Glenn

Traces of Acceptance

Inside my soul there are many hidden things
thoughts that are silently overpowering
My love for the arts is outweighed by my apathy
is outweighed by my apathy
my hate for violence
is overcome by my rage

I have no aspirations
just to be content is all I ask for
Insults are easier to believe
than love offered in words

I suffer the plague of silent hate
it is consuming intoxicating
and it poisons my soul

I have so many emotions
I turn numb

   Angela Merriman

Aimless Souls

Breaking pieces fall to the floor,
Remnants of a broken heart.
Still it seems she comes back for more,
Just to be torn apart.

Living a life empty and meaningless,
Comfort seems so far away.
Walking into the night endless,
Maybe finding her someday.

It seems the two souls should meet
To remove the endless pain.
Then, as one, their hearts could beat
As friendship and love is gained.

Never will one see the other,
Never wanting another lover,
Aimless souls wonder through empty fields,
Tightly holding up their metal shields.

   Misty Jones

A Peaceful Place

Walking through a prayer garden
Close to Johnson's Spring,
Searching inwardly, the soul communes
With the Father amidst the noisy chatter.
Uttering the heartfelt prayer,
The petitioner expresses thanks
Or pleads for burdens to be released.
A master's infinite wisdom
Listens and responds,
"My child, allow me space within.
Press on to a greater calling;
Ignore the noisiness now about;
Listen and learn of me through the fresh spring
Splashing o'er the rocks.
Feel my power through cool, gentle breezes;
Observe miraculous creations
Whether gigantic or minute."

   Patricia Cruzan

Celebration of Spring

A breeze blows across the freshly cut grass
The smell of nature—flowers and sunshine—
Fills the air; she throws off her coat and dances
Arms and legs waving madly among the bright
Colors of spring. Insects buzz around her
Glad to be free from the cold of winter
Trees blossom merrily as buds sprout from
Their winter darkened branches; people
Emerge from their houses to watch her dance
Her dance—a celebration of spring

   Amanda Sedlak

Sunken Treasure

Rippling waves forevermore,
Cover the vastness of the ocean's floor.
Sunken treasures of many past histories
Shrouded in cryptic stories and mysteries.
Rippling waves forevermore.
Great sailing ships sent out by Spain,
Tossed by blowing winds and torrential rains.
Unknown hazards and charts not true,
Sinking to the ocean floor beneath the sea of blue.
Washing up ancient relics from the ocean deck,
Prized memorabilia of the ships that wrecked.
Rippling waves forevermore.
Following a cadence for the far off shore.
A watery cover made by the wind,
Hiding the resting places where the ships did end.
Rippling waves forevermore, forevermore, forevermore.

   Dr. R. W. Nelson

Last Act

She turned us away once, but now we're invited to see
a stranger who seems to be her, but just couldn't be.
Sad to view, a long, gaunt rack of bones and skeleton
where once the blush of skin and muscle had been.
Was it an alien's body lying cold and still,
alive, yet motionless like a broken Jack and Jill?
This proud bird perched on a wrinkled bed was not fowl,
yet on her neck was a skull with piercing eyes of an owl.
Her thin lips were smiling; she shone with inner light,
as her heart welcomed a vision of his most holy site
Then, finally, this stranger told us not to miss her in the calm,
courageous whisper of my dying sister.

   Ralph Haworth

The Human Touch

Will your imagination be dulled away
As you sit on the Internet to shoot and play?
Will you watch the land, the sea, and the sky
Go through your screen and just flit by?

Is this what life is meant to be—
Plastic and metal and technology?
No human touch or talk or love,
It's all directed to the monitor above.

How blind we are to our real needs
To embrace humanity with good deeds,
For people in anguish and bitter with grief
Need someone to bring them comfort and relief.

Technology used right will always be
Answers to problems for you and me.
But we must not lose the human touch
To live a real life which means so much.

   Viola Ainslie

Barry

I am as a parched field of wilted grain,
Awaiting and longing for a soaking rain.

I reach for the heavens and look to the sky,
And ask the unanswerable question—why?

Your lips do not answer—your eyes no longer see.
You are in another dimension—faraway from me.

Why did it happen and why did you die?
I know in my heart you are not where you lie.

On the wings of an eagle, your spirit flies free,
But I still feel your heart beat deep within me.

The tears I have shed have returned to me as rain,
But do little to extinguish the awful, burning pain.

We sow what we reap—I know this to be true;
From the roots of my being, I'll always love you.

   Lucille Krista

Tracy

I breathe deeply and savor the quiet,
this peaceful time before the sun devours the day.
I open her door and gaze with wonder, because
there nothing more beautiful than Tracy in the
morning when she's sleeping.

The sun rises and the house awakens. I listen
for her footsteps. My body braces against the
anger that will mark our day.
This small tyrant who rules our world . . .
why does she beat her fists against life?
Then she smiles and the angels sing.

I watch her closely to see what battles will
be waged today. I will win some, so will she—
but the war is never won.
I again breathe deeply and hold it in hopes
that she will find the peace that we need.

The house sleeps and again I gaze with wonder
as an angel rests, for there's nothing more
beautiful than Tracy in the evening when
she's sleeping.

   Irene M. Evans

The Perfect Couple

Geoff and Charlene Bell, don't give up on your Love
You both look, oh, so cute,
I knew this day would come.
You met over four years ago,
And you've been together, since then, as one.

I know you both are happy,
By the way you both do shine.
I can't get over how cute you look,
Even in the morning time.

You make her, oh, so happy; you make him glow inside.
I don't know how you did it,
But you made your love combine.
Was it magic, or even a charm, or maybe a wish upon a star,
A prayer from God is mighty nice,
Or even someone's lucky advice.

No, it must have been the first day you met,
The sparks in your eyes, the love in your hearts.
You two met over four years ago,
Now you plan to spend the rest of your life
Together Forever!

   Desiree T. Figueroa

Leery Eye

To brother, Lindsay Blake, now recovered from cancer
Awake no more, oh, leery eyes
Be ever where unrise!
Stay thy breath in own mean breast
Forbidden thee unsleep unrest

Awake no more in tender love
Unmeasured treasure from above
Unheard forever, be freeze!
Never resurrect in please passing breeze

Where nor luscious gold, spry diamond
There be easy sleeping sound
Looks so merry, no nearby found
Be wane of life's fecund ground

Opaque, oblique unrule glad sky
More never weep, never cry
Heaveness face, happiness sun
Tenderness to never done

Cease encumbering life's peaceful valley
Cease nightingale singing melancholy
Nor light behind heaviness hill
Sleep! never rise in merriness will

   Osbourne C. Blake

Why?

A time to laugh, a time to cry
Is given each of us
Throughout the ages, we've asked "why?"
When we in God do trust . . .
If on this day we chance to weep
Comfort will come our way
When God's instructions we do keep
And to Him daily pray . . .
Our prayer should be filled with our praise
And thanks to God above
In spite of all our burdens now
We're kept within His love . . .

Our joy will come when He sees fit
To lift our present load
By taking sorrow to Himself
As we journey life's road . . .
Then maybe we will cease asking
"Why, Lord, did this occur?"
He does indeed know what is best
Of that I am quite sure . . .

Dorothy B. Crosby

Weak in Life, but Strong in Love

Over sixty-five, a new beginning has just begun.
Maybe we're in our Senior years, but still having fun.
From experience we know what life is all about.
Now we can love each other and leave the nonsense out.

We may not be popular nor sophisticated.
But one thing for sure, our lives are not outdated.
We may not always have a lot of thrills.
But we can let the world know, we ain't over the hill.

So you talk about love, it is old as the beginning.
When you look at us and see we are still winning.
Through the fire and the flood as the ages ring.
To the end of our lives, we will still have a fling.

Some people may say, we are forgetful and to old
But they don't know, true love will never grow cold.
We touch, we laugh, we hug, and feel each other's pain.
And through all hardships, our true love still remains.

When God put us together, He said we would always abound.
So He hasn't stopped us from loving, He just slowed us down.
Maybe we're sliding down hill with our wheels spinning.
But we are truly in love, with a new beginning.

Lois N. Moss

Speak to Me

Speak to me of the wind,
Gusting the truth in my face.

Speak to me of the moon,
Waning, only to fill again.

Speak to me of the stars,
Reflecting the wisdom of the ages.

Speak to me of the sea,
Kissing the sand and rolling away.

Speak to me of the trees,
Shaking their leaves in agreement with fall.

Speak to me of the birds,
Gliding on the thermals of the wind.

Speak to me of children,
Crying out for an open heart.

Speak to me of then and now.
Speak to me.

Lynnette Schuepbach

The Warmth of Your Embrace

To Tom for touching my heart in a special way
Oh, what a feeling from the warmth of your embrace.
Just the touch of your body next to mine,
My heart so full of joy, all because of your touch.
All you need to do, is just hold me.
Just wrap your arms around me,
And I feel that an Angel has me in his arms.
Oh, what a special feeling to feel the embrace of Heaven
wrapped around you.
Just because of your touch,
There is a magic that I can't explain.
For it's soothing, calming, peaceful, and so very joyful,
All because of the warmth of your embrace.
What a special gift from God.
That I get to have someone to make me feel this way.
That Heaven's arms are wrapped around me, holding me close.
Oh, the comfort, the strength,
Oh, what joy there is in that feeling.
Thank you father, for this special friend,
This friend that you have blessed me with.
Oh, what a feeling to feel the warmth of your embrace.

Velma Carpenter

Family Reunion, 1998

Gazing upon this sea of courtly countenances
causes me to ponder
Precious is the symmetry of souls to whom I am akin—
what a wonder!
For certain there is a kindred spirit abiding,
stirring my heart
Dynamic is the perceptive ambience of bonding gaiety,
igniting events to start
Vibrant expectancy permeates the room
in anticipation of what shall be!
Conversing are new and renewed
relationships, united intrinsically
Lineage from past generations warmly
connecting with present posterity
Desirous of future regathering
in solemnity, yet, with a hint of hilarity

Muriel G. Singleton

Reflections in a Dreamer's Eye

I sat alone upon the hill gazing at the waters
down below, and watched the whitecaps kiss the
hungry shore with their ebb and flow.
Graceful eucalyptus trees upon the gentle hill
waved their pleasure, on the ocean's dauntless chill.
Majestic were the mountains above the water's edge.
The cypress bent in stoic silence upon a pillowed ledge.
The "Golden Gate" stood, rigidly abrupt, each side
planted firmly in the Earth, and, like a magic carpet,
it spanned the restless ocean's girth.
Gallant sails gliding in full regalia as they passed,
Colors gaily flying on the wind, prideful of their masts.
Coquettish, brilliant little stars peeking provocatively
through the twilight's twinkling light,
sparkling in anticipation to delight a lover's night.
In the distance, a radiant orange glow filled the apathetic
sky and melted at the shoreline with the evening tide,
trimmed in gold and mauve restraint to fill a dreamer's eye.

Leonka Boxer

Our Little Angel

You are a little angel the Lord has sent to me,
And we love you so.
We will keep you safe and happy and watch you grow.
We promise to love and to guide you in the right way.
We know not what you will grow up to be,
But we will help you to be the best that you can be,
For now you are part of our family.

Mary B. Taylor

Untitled

How can there be those fools who say,
A love like ours lasts but a day
In this infinite measure known as time?

This tender warmth that fills my being
Must still exist when eyes stop seeing
To warm the chilling endlessness of time.

Could all the joy of your dear face
Be lost to view and leave no trace
Within the boundless flow of time?

Oh, no, dear God, and God there be,
I know my love will share with me
This limitless eternity of time.

Patricia N. Worsham

What Happened Between

He read his lines the best he could
What happened between was his life.

Silent eyes look out from a child's face
Seeing much more than young eyes should see.

The depth, the knowing, the pain, the growing.

The shadowy, unforeseen events that sear
And form the child's soul.

Being without a catalyst to translate
His experiences into words, however, knowing intuitively.

The child assimilates the impressions until
They become a constant, nebulous companion
Influencing his every thought and deed.

All the while, he read his lines the best he could
What happened between was his life.

Wanda Simpson

There's No Other

A mother will always be there,
To show how much she'll always care.
A mother will show you all the right ways,
To help you through good or bad days.
Even when she's sick she'll see,
To her best that you're happy.
If mother has no man,
She'll still do the best she can,
To be mother, and father, protector, provider.
Do what you can and stick close beside her.
Help her out by doing what she may ask,
That shouldn't be a very hard task.
After all there's no other,
Like your very own mother.

Shareen Widder

An Angel's Dream

To my parents for showing me how to see the world through their eyes
An angel's dust in sparkling rays long ago were laid
The ocean's endless enchanting praise as purple waves fade
Crystal eyes of blue rise with the morning light
Finding things exciting and new, waking from her endless night
Stars set deep within her soul
A child exuberating from her sweet slumber
Playful smiles evoke a man to love her
A radiant glow holds her dreams of gold
Once a child for her father to mold
Now the refreshing reflection of her mother
Sharing the light of her brother
Somehow still a priceless jewel
A diamond in the rough shining through
With dreams reaching for the heavens above
Dreaming dreams of endless love.

Colleen O'Brien

True Sight

I write about God . . . so much these days.
Something has leaped in my soul.
I use my words . . . to write for you.
Maybe for me, that's God's goal.

Yet, I sometimes wonder: what took me so long?
Did I have the gift all along?
When I write the words upon my paper,
Sometimes it sounds like a song.

I believe that God has touched my heart,
For me to express the views I see.
Though it may not be a pretty sight,
I pray my words . . . will set somebody free.

If I can touch . . . just one person's heart
Through the words I write,
Maybe, just maybe, I could open their eyes,
For them . . . to have "true sight."

Susan Kline

The Artist, Prince

To a visionary, The Artist, Prince—Peace, be wild
The artist formerly known as Prince,
has taught us through the years to respect ourselves
and ignore those who try to disillusion us.
Don't ever look back to the past.
The future should be your main focus!
Don't rush into sex; when you find that irresistible person,
you will know and it will last forever.
He has taught us so much, I could go on and on,
but trouble is, I only get to write 20 lines!
So, in closing, I just would like to say
thank you to the artist, Prince.
You truly are my lucky star,
that shines down on me and gives me hope
that one day, I too can be a star!

Rebecca Ann Pinson

Sybil of This Millennium

Sage Sybil, heiress of prognostic sight,
Entranced in prescient ecstasy, foresee
The coming days, that which we must rewrite!

"Blithe querent, can you bear my prophecy?
That which all your cultures have achieved
Lies threatened by one lost strategic key:

Technology's a prize, but not enough
Without Compassion, Conscience, Beauty.
So much you value in this time's mere slough!

Reprise of ruined Rome you need not be:
Humaneness must sign all humanity."

Ann Trinita Sohm

Theater

The stage is bare, the props all rolled away.
In childhood I dreamed this ghostly place
where drifting shadows mouth their soundless lines
and search in vain for partners to the dance.

Vacant rows, seats folded back, the curtain drawn,
this hollow shell of life, this fragile soul,
awaits a word, a footstep, an embrace,
awaits an incarnation to become.

Musicians take with them the pulsing breath,
and actors slipping through the backstage door
carry off the meaning and applause
that make conception whole unto itself.

Then who will love this lonely nothingness,
this empty echo silent as a stone?
Perhaps the one that turns off the last light,
the one who lifts the playbills off the floor.

Bianca C. Stewart

For You

For you, I listen when you speak
For you, I stay humble and meek
For you, I sacrifice hopes and dreams
For you, I listen to all your schemes
For you, I please things I'd rather not
For you, I give that which I have not
For you, I miss that which I should see
For you and I to always be
For me, you speak when you should listen
For me, you scowl when you should be forgiving
For me, you keep your dreams inside
For me, your plans you always hide
For me, you do as you well please
For me, you feel not at ease
For me, you go your own way
For me, I hope you see someday
For you, I give my undying love
For you, I will miss all the above

Louise M. Bistrick

To Charles

I love you more than you can ever know.
Until you say the word, I promise, I won't go.

Just as the sun sets and the moon shines,
I want you to always be mine.

Every breathe I take, I think of you,
It is only those times we are apart that I am blue.

I know someone said, "All good things must come to an end."
Well dear, that's definitely one rule I'm willing to bend.

While I fantasize rolling with you in the sand,
It's crazy, but I'm happy just to hold your hand.

I love you more than anything else.
It is to you that I give all of myself.

Angela Brock

The Seasons

Sweet scented perfume fills the morning air
And warbling birds are pleasant to my ear.
'Tis spring, the season called by all most fair,
But they know not the one I hold most dear.

The summer eve's afloat on gentle breeze.
A thousand stars illuminate the sky.
The moon, still orange, slowly climbs the trees,
But lovelier, the one that holds me nigh.

The autumn leaves a panoply display
And wild excitement fills the crisp fall air.
The low hung sun portends the short'ning day.
No matter, I am with my love most fair.

The winter trees, in coats of icy lace
Are naught, whene'er I see my love's sweet face.

Jack C. Page

Forget Thee Not

As I journey through my valley of life with heavenly
    Mountains within my sight,
I wonder, will I be able to climb that mountain, to
    See the world in a different light?
There's nothing wrong with the valley, but it's not
    Where I want to be.
I want to climb that mountain—there's so much more to see.
I'll see that very same valley—the one where I no
    Longer fit.
Although I'll be above, I'll not look down on it.
I'll always remember where I came from—that valley
    So far below,
And, I'll help them sow their seeds, so the fruits of
    Their labor can grow.

Stanley N. Harrison

Aslan's Hope

My Creator has granted the hope;
Why, the salvation of Aslan's hope is hope.
Clap your hands: Hope is Aslan!
He died for man: Only God is Aslan!
Clap your hands: Prayer is Aslan!
He died for Man: Eternity is Aslan!
My lines are the written Hope;
Why, the time of Aslan's hope is hope!
Praise and shout: Aslan is hope!
Praise and shout: The Lamb is hope!
Praise and shout: Man now has hope!
My signs of love are your salvation of hope.
My lines above is your revelation of hope.
Aslan's hope is hope of hope.
Aslan's hope is hope I wrote.
Aslan's hope is hope of Pope.
I write Aslan's hope for all creation.
I write Aslan's hope for man's salvation.
He who has hope, pray for all nations.
He who has hope, praise God's creation.

Timothy A. Wik

Elizabeth Dale Gross

Evening star, bright and shining in the Western sky,
Lyric of hearth and home with a lilt of a lullaby,
Integrity and immortal youth embellish every scene.
Zephyr, the gentle wind are you, soft and ever serene.

Angelic presence and charm define your life sublime.
Beauty, too, never fading with the passage of time.
Enchanting you'll be by your unassuming caring way;
Torrents of good fortune will come to you some day.

Happiness in full measure you'll have all your life;
Divine guidance secures you full freedom from strife.
An able lawyer, having the highest ethics and skills,
Law's prestigious positions you'll attain at will.

Endowed with many gifts of a bountiful heart and mind,
Gem of the purest ray serene, ever so hard to find,
Rose of wondrous roses rare, forever in full bloom.
Openhearted and friendly, you enliven every room.

Surely you're that perfect woman by Him nobly planned,
Sweetly to love, praise, blame, comfort, and command.

Elijah E. Jhirad

My Life's Reflection

Now as I reflect back on my life
I've gone through many joys, trials and strife
There's been a number of deaths in my family
I didn't understand but God has his plan for me

Then I had to deal with lots of bitterness
There was a time I was overcome by stress
I went through a period of depression
It affected my thoughts and expression

There was a time when too much alcohol I'd drink
It affected my actions and my ability to think
There was a time I struggled with unforgiveness.
God says if we don't forgive then he can't bless

There was a time when the pastor anointed me
From that medical problem I was set free
I've felt the awesome power of prayer
And I've also felt God's love and care

There are times I falter along the way
He gently nudges me as I start to stray
He chastises and guides me along life's path I trod
Through all this I've had a closer walk with God

Marcia Kay Miller

Paths

Seeking peace on the bank of a stream rain forgot
Not swallowing the thought, "You're all that you have got"
That, "The truth is but a lie, there really is no wrong"
"It doesn't weigh which way's turned or what road's gone on"
But I know when there's water, streams flow just one way
But this stream's been dry so long, none can dare say
If "the water goes right" or "left it will flow"
Some say, "It will choose which way is correct to go"
They say, "Choose any path or go beat out one new"
"No one cares where you go or what you choose to do"
"Keep on, on your path, and go past each turning bend"
"If you keep on going, you'll reach the flat world's end"
Heeding to my heart and the dust at the stream's base
That chants and proclaims, "Popular claims aren't the case!"
This divine intuition, taken as a text
States that any road is not as good as the next
"We all are equal; there's no Heaven, there's no Hell"
"Go to the right or the left; each one's just as well"
But I fancy there's One place I'm supposed to be
I take the truth in step, all streams lead to the sea

　　Josie Tibbitts

Ode to a Seal

I've frolicked in the summer sun
Along the sandy beach.
I've teased the many sea birds
That came within my reach.
I've swam along the coral reef,
Dived to the ocean bed.
I've played among the seaweed
That swirled around my head.
I've napped upon the arctic ice
And rode the dolphin's wake.
I've tasted all life's pleasures
That were there for me to take.
I've watched the seasons come and go,
My time has served me well.
The years, they are so many,
It's hard for me to tell.
But now, alas, my life is spent,
My time has all but gone.
I'm counting down the hours, the minutes,
Now there's none.

　　Margaret Kohler

Cherokees from Oklahoma Summer of '78

We're Cherokees from the state of Oklahoma.
Our parents moved us there to see money grow our trees.
They forgot to warn us about the Birds and the Bees.
Now they all grow "pot" in sunny California.
They make their living way back in the hills,
While me and my family work in the mills.
We built our house in the country. "It's nice,"
But the damn pot growers are thicker than mice.
The weed they grow are for big bucks we're told.
The pot they grow is a plant to behold:
They have big sticky buds and they're all for sale.
Camp gets some, "Growers, ask someone to go get my bail."
We're Cherokees from Oklahoma territory.
We have a lot of grief to carry, a lot of worry,
'Cause there's camouflage figures behind every tree,
And, with their rifles aimed, they'll shoot you and me.
After smoking their buds, "they're higher than a kite."
Just keep moving my friend, they're here for the night.
Drive on down the road and don't turn around—
They shoot to kill, and it's not a pretty sight
When they leave you on the ground.

　　Verna Freeman

Natus Est

The Christmas bells ring joyously,
And carols fill the air.
　　Angels singing Glorias
　　Made olden shepherds stare.

The Christmas lights are twinkling
On houses, stores, and trees.
　　A star shone bright on Bethlehem
　　And three kings on their knees.

The Christmas tree is lovely,
Clad in gold, and green, and red.
　　Once a Child in swaddling clothes
　　Lay in a manger bed.

Christmas brings so many joys,
Family, friends, and fun.
　　Let's not forget that ancient Cause—
　　The birth of God's own Son.

　　Eileen M. Miller

The Fire of Life

Where can you find a key for a lock of hair?
Fond memories of a friend forever we can share.

I lie down to rest, there's no more violence,
Now I hear nothing but silence.

I picture a bed of flowers for that they pose,
The brightest one of them all is the queen I suppose.

Five dozen rubies, ten diamond rings,
One white dove with pure golden wings.

A thought in my mind I hold to treasure.
With joy, with love, and with pleasure.

The younger I think, the older I get.
The fire of life will always be lit.

　　Alicia Loughrey

Jessica

Jessica, Jessica, dear sweet Jessica,
my child of love, of anger, of tears.
In you, I placed such store.

To meet your eyes and hear your voice
would do my heart much good.

With anxious fear I remember the hour God
chose to raise His hand.
The days of anger, the nights of tears,
the hatred of men and mothers.

The dream to die and retrieve
my child from the fate of some—not others.

The cry, the kiss, the tear,
the smile . . . of you my senses wonder.
To feel your flesh and know your mind,
kept from me all these years;

I often sit and ask myself—what woman
would have grown from this child I'd never hold?

　　Linda M. Young

Forgotten Tears

When did the laughter of the children die?
When did the little ones start to cry?
Did it die when the bread and the milk went dry?
Did it die when Mommy and Daddy no longer tried
To give love to each other and no longer cared
What happened to babies so little and scared?
When did the laughter of the children die?
It died when nobody cared if they cried

　　Pierrette Pancrazi

The Blessing

To my true father, Henry Syverson
In '95 my heart went bad.
Seventy percent left was all I had.
In '97 my kidneys quit.
I just said, "the Hell with it!"
I sat down and plain gave up.
I could see the bottom of life's cup.
But slowly, I began to realize,
That my physical malfunctions were not a curse.
But for the Grace of God, I could be worse.
I also finally saw another benefit.
A good thing had come out of it.
Instead of rushing on my way through life,
I had slowed down, and I had lost my strife.
I could finally gaze at Nature for hours.
I had finally stopped to smell the flowers.

Alan Anderson

A Summer Storm

The day was lovely, sunny, and warm,
When all at once a summer storm came boiling up;
Black clouds came billowing across the sky,
Blown by a west wind and riding high.
Lightning streaked in a jigsaw design,
And the willow bowed to the stately pine
As the wind tossed her branches in violet rage,
And from the hills came the scent of sage.
The sky grew dark; the lightning flashed.
The limbs on the trees tossed and thrashed.
Great drops of rain came pelting down
And the creek turned muddy and brown.
As suddenly as the rain had begun,
The rain stopped and out come the sun
And it benevolently smiled on a rain-washed world.
While across the sky, a rainbow unfurled
Her colors in a pastel display.
And sighing softly, the wind blew the last cloud away.

Leeora Jacobe

The Tree

There's a beautiful tree beside the road
It's straight and tall
It's the prettiest one of all

I named it Martha Howard
You see, she died there from a fall
The Lord put it there for us all
Look for it as you drive along
It will stand out, so pretty and strong

Look for her on 135 West
Her spirit has gone on to rest
Beside the tree is where she was put to death

So next time you drink and drive
Think of the crime
And her killer doing time
Cry for her son
For his only memory is from the tree

Laverne Howard

A Little Visitor

Did you seen a glowing green figure
at the foot of your bed,
looking straight at you,
then jumping on your bed?

Did you ever pat a Little Green Alien,
learning how strangely soft it feels,
yet very frightened?

Did you ever watch him
gently gliding across the nightly jeweled sky
on his two little green feet?

Richard Rios

Chasing

My live goes on without you.
On the outside, it seems I live, going through
the routines of my life.
While inside my heart things stand still as
if death has taken over.
Trying to piece together my soul, yet your ghost
still lingers near, preventing me from doing so.

I see your ghost around every corner, constantly
lingering nearby, just close enough to be seen out
of the corner of my eye.

To chase it away seems an endless game—creating
new memories with ones of new.
Yet finding only peace and freedom is short lived
for your ghost is strong, stronger than I.
What to do? To continue chasing away your ghost in
hopes that one day I will succeed, thus ending my pain and torment—
the loss of you in my life.

Elizabeth Huie-Norris

Puppy Love

I've never felt this way before
And it happened right after you open the door
We walk from class to class each day
From November up till May

So I watched you March in the cymbal line
I saw that you were very kind
And as we laugh and talk and play around
You never let me fall on the wet, muddy ground (hee, hee!)

You came up to me and took me by surprise
Then I looked deep into your eyes
As I look into your eyes I see
That we were truly meant to be

Even if we are only friends forever
It would truly be a pleasure
But after sometime of being together
I hope that we will stay together forever

Shantelle Moses

Reflections of the Heart

For Jim, your love has made me whole again
Look back with me,
and through my heart.
Take that long journey,
and never shall we be apart.

Our souls have touched,
they now are joined.
One person we've become,
our lives together have now begun.

They said the odds were very slim
that our love would ever really win.
Obstacles, they will come and go,
but never will they stop love's flow.

Someday we'll reflect on what used to be,
to early beginnings of you and me.
We'll look back to our yesterdays,
and find that we were always meant to be.

Barbara McGinley

All Alone

All alone in this shell of mine,
A casing for effect,
Wondering what it is all about,
This earthly journey of mine.
Alone in this vastness of time,
A bargain by all accounts.
When will I rise in glory,
My maker to behold?
When will I find out what it is all about,
Alone in this shell of mine?

Elizabeth Klumpp

When the Swallows Go

In memory of my mother, Natalie Mae Thayer
There are signs of Fall about the country side.
The well-groomed swallows gather on the wires.
When all their band has mustered
        They will leave
The autumn chilliness of northern air
And take their flight above
        The purple hills
To winter in the gay, exotic South.
Perhaps they will return to Capistrano
Or to other tropic gardens
Where the flowers bloom gayly
And the sun-kissed air is warm.
We love to watch the swallow congregation
Balancing side by side
With perfect grace.
But now we feel a little sad at parting.
The wires will seem empty
        When they go.
    Mildred N. Thayer

The Memory of Love

We always remember the spring of love
when our hearts were aglow with joy,
and everything we did seemed magic
through our love for that girl or boy.

The autumn of love finds us happy
and content with the one we love.
We know each other's faults or virtues
and accept these as part of our love.

The winter of love tests us greatly.
It pulls and it strains, but it holds.
True love come through like a champion.
Its strength and its caring unfolds.

But now I hear a voice calling.
It sounds so familiar to me.
I think it's the voice of my true love
saying: "Come! Here and now! This is me."
    Evelyn M. Strom

Reflectors

As late autumnal leaves separate
and free float from one singularity
to another, mulch to loam, and there on
to smaller still, so too, does this tiny flake
I hold. A human shard yet eroding?
Is this spot where a tear dried? Did a joy
begin here? Will life with it be made again?
What part of a jot will my moment scar?
Its heartfelt bursts of joy or sadness stain?
If this flake dissevers to what I breathe,
is it mirroring my own endlessness?
These things I crave to know as truth so I
can imprint the slag of my life upon
these splinters structuring eternity;
until, perhaps, somehow I am again.
    Milton Foster

Wishes

For Hunter E. Wickersham, aged two months
May peace rain down upon you
From the heavens above
May your soul know joy
And your heart love
May tomorrow's dreams be yours to hold
And may they all be laced with white and gold
And all your days
Blessed in every way
For this is the wish
That I have wished for you
    Brian K. Green

For Loula

I pledge as I weep at your funeral
To frolic whenever I can,
To gift each celebration
With flowers and laughter and song.

I promise to plant seeds for tomorrow
And saplings to grace the new day,
That children will play in the garden
With sunshine warming their way.

Tired and trembling, friends follow your casket
To Oak Hill, where John and Harriette lie.
The ritual lends strength to the pilgrims
Who wonder why butterflies die.

Magnolias are burgeoning with blossoms
Trailing fragrance from past to now,
Turning thoughts and dreams to green pastures
With angels singing nearby.
    Gladys Wallace

The Loss of My Child

In memory of my five-year-old son, Billy
Sometimes you feel an emptiness that no one can explain.
The feelings from within your heart may never be the same.
I love my son and now he's gone they say it's meant to be
but how on Earth, sometimes I think, could this have happened to me.

We never can imagine the pain we feel inside until we've lost
someone we love and emptiness will rise.
So as I move ahead each day, I wonder how
and why so now I come to realize on my baby I do rely.
    Tammie Wilson

Eulogy

He was a big man, who stood tall and proud,
And even to illness he remained unbowed.
When he became confined to a wheelchair,
His demeanor denied that it was even there.
Yes, even in sitting he still stood tall,
So one wasn't aware of the chair at all.
He drew respect and love from all who knew him,
And his inner strength would let nothing subdue him.
Though he was wont to disclaim words of honor and praise,
He made our lives richer in so many ways.
Selfishly we mourn his passing with a deep sense of loss,
Forgetting how gallantly he bore his cross.
While his death to us is a thing of disaster,
He has risen from his chair to walk with the Master.
    Esther B. Knott

How Exciting

It will be exciting to see,
What God holds in Heaven for thee,
With Jesus, His shining hands and feet of gold,
No worries of being young or old,
All pain removed, both body and soul,
No hatred, bitterness, or feeling cold.
Yes, it's going to be exciting to see,
Our heavenly Father reaching out to thee.
How high our spirits will soar.
Never will we want for anything more.
There will only be tears of joy
For every man, woman, girl, and boy.
Oh, how exciting it will be,
Musical harps and angels singing with glee.
As God showers us with His adorning love,
We will rise with Jesus and snowy white doves.
Our days are going to be full of delight.
Nights will twinkle with Heaven's glittery light.
Gold streets, silver mansions, and He . . .
An exciting, beautiful sight we shall see.
    Norma J. Avery

The Case for Antioxidants

To Dr. Antonio Caracta, Sustainer of Life and Hope
The unreality of reality
  spins a web that purveys me to contemplate
  on the Richter scale—how do I rate
my finicky weaknesses . . . my weather worn stresses!
Past history can't be demured—how now to be insured!
        against a corpus
whose aches and pains come into focus!

From life's chance serendipity or odd crass asymmetry
blueprints of heredity
predetermine some part of our destiny

Even that genius Kasparov, learned that humility
follows human frailty
imperfections of mortality
Can we find a lesson to be learned?

That Deep Blue computer had choice of millions of positions
we humans have simpler requisitions
As for me, seeking remedies
in diet, vitamins, holistic simplicities . . .

Here's for Rejuvenation! Resuscitation!
Maybe that last solution is Reincarnation!
    Shulamith Lukrec

The Angel

No guarding ghost, illusive as the air,
Dumb and invisible, no seraph caught,
Down from the millions Heaven has to spare—
The angel that is shadow to my lot.

Of clay divine, I follow in her face,
A stronger light than Heaven's highest star,
And mold the noblest virtues from her grace,
Because I see and know them as they are.

The sinew of my arm, the heart that beats
Behind my purpose, and the saintly voice
Above my deed and daring, she repeats
Herself in me, my chooser and my choice.

Not as a seraph, humbled from the grace
Of Zion, was my guardian sent to me,
But as an angel who had found a place
Of love and comfort in my heart came she.

Not as a babe I took her, all unknown;
Denied the right to summon and prefer
The guardian angel that I call my own,
I had a portion in selecting her!
    Walter C. Bruno

The Gift of Love

True love is a gift of God.
Just as He freely loves us,
So must our love be freely given.
It cannot come with a price-tag,
One must never expect to give
And to receive love in equal amounts.
Nor can one demand their love be returned.
Love can only be repaid with freely-given love.
If, unfortunately, that isn't to be,
The wise will walk away, having enjoyed the giving,
If only for a moment, or for a lifetime.
Close the account! Write it off!
This is a lesson of life to be learned,
To be nourished, eventually to keep as a cherished memory.
Slowly one heals, and gently awakens
To a vibrant filling of innocent hope,
As the greater wisdom of experience floods the soul.
Only then will the joy of loving again be possible
The human heart becomes divine
When touched by love, it defies time.
    Jeanne Rafferty

He Is Risen

Our Lord, Jesus Christ, He is Risen from the dead.

He lived in Jerusalem. He prayed for the
sick. He healed a woman had been sick
twelve long years. He opened blinded
eyes and turned water to wine and,
the dead began to rise when he prayed for them.

He is Risen; He is Risen.

Our Lord, Jesus Christ, He is Risen from the dead.

All the little flowers are now sleeping
in the cold winter bed. When the
sun beam bright came peeping from
the blue sky over head. Wake up,
little dear; do not waste the
morning off. Happy Easter time is here.
So he woke up one and all, so the
flower hill told the story all along the
way, for the risen Lord of glory. Christ,
He came on Easter day.

He is Risen; He is Risen.

Our Lord Jesus Christ, He is Risen from the dead.
    Jennie A. Maxwell

The Roads of My Village

The roads of my village entered the city and got lost
Lost in the crowd of desires
Humbled by the boisterous lane

The roads of my village were shy; were quiet
Adored with the golden dust of virtues
Singing the hymns of tradition
The roads of my village were cultured

Stretched lazily under the shade of the Gulmohar tree
Living in present, bare to the seasons
Happy without reasons
The roads of my village accompanied many a feet to destination

The roads of my village were desirous
Were ambitious, they walked up to the city and got lost
Lost in the future, now searching for the present
Tired under the weight of tires and countless feet, sad at heart

The roads of my village want to come back to the village
Want to rest under the shade of the Gulmohar tree
Want to hear the taps of feet
Want to stretch till night and wait for the chirping day

The roads of my village want to be happy, happy once again
    Anubha Sharma

It Is Raining, My Dear

My dear, it is raining,
And the night is passing
With the same monotonous, incessant tempo of the day.

The windows are perspiring
From the glare of the street lights,
And the intermittent drops remind me
Of people dropping dead everywhere.

The world moves dizzily through space
Like an uncontrolled vehicle,
And the tides of time lay at the street curbs,
Reinforced by every passing auto.

Life then, my dear, is only the backwash
Of time and space, the ever-constant.

This world moving ever, turns our days into decay,
And drives like a constant, unremitting avenger
Through the darkness that blinds our reason,
And the time and space that dulls our passions.
    George W. French

Canvasing the Globe—Color Stop—Bali

To Alan, always and all ways
If I filled a carpet bag with cotton,
and carried a large roll of canvas,
If I had a big brush within my bag, and a thin box of colors,
I could start to make a Balinese sky.
If I tore the cotton into balls, and added grey,
I could float the clouds with shadows.
If I added purple for the high mountain, and a streak of gold,
I could blaze the sun.
If I mixed twenty greens, I could lay the banana leaf,
and the palms, and the rice fields.
If I speckled yellow with white, I could polka-dot
the petals of the plumeria, and scent the valleys.
If I added browns, I could flow the rivers,
and dot the rice fields with sticks and flags.
If I could sift the browns and whites through my fingers,
I could sprinkle sand.
If I could pour watered white, to cream the sand,
and trickle rivulets of foamy blue from my brush,
to make a Bali sea, I could float peacefully away on my palette,
and wade into paradise.

Marjorie Weigel Hyman

A Stepmother's Dream

I am not your mother, I dare not pretend
All I really wanted was to be your friend
It was that way before they day
Your Dad and I were engaged

I always wanted a daughter of my own
I knew my boys would someday leave me alone
It seemed that way before the day
Your Dad and I were engaged

I took you for glasses and had your teeth checked
Replaced your shoes when you said they were wrecked
That was the way before the day
Your Dad and I were engaged

Someday, you'll see that I meant no harm
I've shown my love with many a charm
Can friendship stay like before the day
Your Dad and I were engaged

I may have tried to control you some time
Moms have that right, for friends it's a crime?
But love continues the way before the day
Your Dad and I were engaged

Louise E. Szerzo

Thinking of You, Dad

I'd like to take a moment
Because I have some things to say
There couldn't be a better time
Now that it's Father's Day.

You're a special person in my life
God planned it just that way
You're always filled with so much love
And then you turn and give it all away.

I'd like to thank you for your patience
For your endless hours of care
And for your influence on my life
That only you and I can share.

Thank you Dad for all you are
And for all you've given me
You have filled my life with memories
That I now share with my own family.

Yes, Dad, I'm thinking of you
And my heart just fills with pride
Because you're special, one of a kind
And I'll always be proud when you're by my side.

Jane Johnson

What Will We Become

To the Palmyra Eagle graduating class of 1998
As we moved throughout these past years,
we have shared laughter and some of us tears.
Now the day has come that we say good-bye,
the tears come back as many of us cry.
We are to become adults and live on our own,
the thought that scares us is that we are alone.
Many memories come back as I think of the past,
our lives are changing so mysteriously fast.
We will see new faces and have many new friends,
our high school years have now come to an end.
Have we learned from our mistakes, the past they came from?
I hope they will influence what we will become.

Maegan J. Sankey

Daddy

He lay quietly in his home that he'd always loved,
Hands folded atop the sheet,
Shallow, regular breathing,
Eyelids fluttered now and then.

From time to time,
He'd wake to look around and smile.
He talked of two men who were friends.
No, they weren't in the room, they were outside the room.
He talked of going home.

No pain was evident, just serene quietness.
Once, being an artist, he tried to draw,
His last and final picture,
With a blue pencil on paper with an American flag in the corner.

Breathing stopped, then started again, peacefully.
We all knelt and held him, told him he could go along without us.
We'd miss him terribly, but we couldn't go this time.
A favorite poem recited by his faithful wife of 55 years, he smiled.

No breathing, breathing again,
In the stillness, he left quietly,
Our Daddy died.

Wanda Sigler

Dead Battery

A car can go eight miles on empty
But I can go 800
This strength
Was brought by six pounds and some odd ounces
Of tears, sleep, and surprise

His eyes of dark blue candy
Flash to the rhythm of his lemon mouth
And his fists of cream
Squeeze the fear from my thumb

The gentle scratch
Of his tiny nails . . .
It has scarred my heart forever

Dana Lobelle

Dancing Water

Dancing water, at your best,
Dancing water, when do you rest?
Here, there, you tumble and fall,
On your way, from mountain tall.
A ripple, a fall, a pool too,
These are nothing new to you.
You dance, twirl and even run wild,
You swing and sway and slow awhile.
Then off you go, at a wild pace,
Through trees and meadows, to that far off place.
When at last, your goal you reach.
You will be dancing on a beach.
Dancing water, at your best,
Dancing water, when do you rest?

Harold E. Lehfeldt

True Love

Fever, chills
pleasure, pain
love, hate, love, hate
round and round until they are inseparable
you infiltrate me with a sideways smile
and whenever I feel ready to break free
you're back
but when I need you
you vanish
I'm stripped of confidence and beauty
I hate everything without you
dependent
uninspired
a hamster running nowhere on your wheel
I just want the carnival to stop

    Chrissy Kasap

Life's Voice

Endings and beginnings,
Beginnings and endings.
Now, I understand the voice of life
always telling;
we begin, we middle, we end.
Beginnings,
encircle my spirit with joyous anticipation
of the freedom in newness.
Middles,
stretching to learn the strength in shadows,
seeking to know the harmony of clearness.
Endings,
permeate my soul with the stillness of silent terror.
After fresh touches, comforting growth and deafening pain,
I now hear life's voice vibrating in my center;
Haunting and strong,
Always chanting,
Endings and beginnings,
Beginnings and endings.

    Donna Blanc

Day of Joy

Behind God's veil of heavenly sight,
The light of day shines through
In perfect rhythm with the night.
A day of joy comes true.

It fills my heart with thankfulness,
Thankful for beauty to see
Wonderful gifts of God's design
Deep—as deep as the sea.

I will rejoice
For this mighty world 'neath God's command!
I will rejoice
For the lifeline joining every man!
For this day of joy
I will rejoice!

This is a day the Lord has blest;
This is a day to be glad.
All of my thoughts will be joyful thoughts,
This is no day to be sad.

    Katherine Flynn

Dreams

I look at my dreams through curious eyes
And wonder up at star-filled skies
And think of what that dream might bring;
I'm sure it's filled with wondrous things.
Stars, moons, tombs, and dooms,
it's all the same so wake up soon.
Don't want to miss that bright morning sun,
Where rainbows are,
When I follow my own star.

    Kattia Mitchell

On Being Assertive

It's hard to speak up
When you're feeling depressed
You mumble the words
You want to express

They see that you're weak
If your tears start to flow
But if you lash out in anger
"You're out of control"

You lose sight of the point
That your mind wants to make
When your emotions crowd in
And your mind just goes blank

So brain, please, don't fail me now
Just help me to speak those words somehow

Don't let this pain get in my way
Just let me mean the words that I say

    Nancy Jessup

Shall the Heavens Fall?

If the night sky rose with the sun
and set with the eve
If time's spindle unraveled all which is past
If hope rested in chance
and chanced to believe
And no future would ever last

Would the heavens fall?
If dreams played our reality
and our reality only dreams
If mankind embraced its fall
and fell to repent
If we could accept our ignorance unseen
and yet remain content

Shall the heavens fall?
If tomorrow never became today
If faith was always broken
If hopes were given away
If emotions were only token
Would the heavens fall?

    Adam Bach

Going My Way?

They talk of what lies in their future,
years and years ahead.
I think of only the upcoming minute,
second by second instead.
Some say I have no foresight,
others, I have no dreams.
But they're not looking deep enough,
for all is not as it seems.
I live my life for each second,
every minute of every day.
Look too far to the future,
and your life just slips away.
My life is a journey, I'm enjoying the ride,
and the sites along the way.
I don't waste time worrying and waiting.
I'm living my life away.

    Misty Dawn Fogle

Friendship

Oh, the comfort of friendship is worth more than money.
It is worth more than bees for honey.
Happy is the person who finds a friend,
Having neither to weigh thoughts nor measure them—but
Being honest, open, and free.
To be silent of discussions,
Not having to be careful of what you say,
Listen with a breath of kindness and blow the rest away.
Friends remember friends for many a day.

    Bernice Erman

Untitled

My soul is an ocean,
An endless churning tide,
Holding all the thoughts and feelings
That I wish to hide.
Some spots are dark and stormy,
As oppressive as can be,
Answer, pride, and hateful thoughts
Dwell amongst that sea.
Yet, some spots are calm and breezy,
A tropical place of rest,
All my good things I keep in there,
Like creativity, intelligence, morality, my best.
One I love so dearly,
Won't you please set sail?
So many things in life
Just die and fade away,
But my love for you
Is forever here to stay.

Steven Johnson

Angels Are with Us

Have you seen an angel today?
Or would you know if one came your way?
Angels come in many ways
They come to help us not to stray

Have you seen an angel today?
Did you meet someone and sincerely say
May I be of any help in any way?
Or did you just go your own way?

Have you seen an angel today?
Be sure to thank the Lord for angels when you pray
Even without our knowing, with us angels stay
So have you seen an angel today?

Patricia Isenman

An Exploding Bomb Broke America's Heart

From the back of a truck that was rented,
A bomb exploded while the Ryder truck was unattended,
It took only a few seconds for the homemade bomb to blow
Apart the huge, Alfred P. Murray Federal Building, we now know.

In Oklahoma City, Oklahoma, the rubble was widespread,
One hundred sixty plus persons were dead,
Hundreds of persons injured also,
To the scene many volunteer rescuers did go.

The bomb blast shook towns several miles away,
More importantly it shook this nation on that fatal day,
Because of a few evil men our nation will never be the same,
Hundreds of onlookers came.

The image of the bombed-out federal building will remain,
In our minds forever and about those who are to blame,
Each person praying and doing their part,
When the exploding bomb, "broke America's heart."

Geneva Stockton Norrell

Savior

Nail-pierced hands and a spear in his side . . .
While up on the cross, he wept and died.
To show his love, he withstood the pain,
So that we could be cleansed and born again.
Upon his head was a crown of thorns,
But under his skin, his heart was torn.
His withered body spilled out blood.
Still on the cross, he died with love.
Though he was born of Heaven, he was despised.
And he willingly traded his soul for our lives:
His eyes full of glory and his arms open wide.
Embracing the heavens, while stepping inside.

Lauren King

Sunshine and Rain

Riches in life we relate to sunshine
and the rain is our doubt and tears;
we always pray for sun-filled days,
but why is it the rain that many fear?
My being is a lovely garden
that God implanted many years ago;
the seeds of love He bestowed on me
with the sunshine and rain will grow.
Too much sunshine will wither the flower,
too much rain will drown the hope,
but together, if given in harmony,
gardens of life soon learn to cope.
Ofttimes I've trod the hollows of life
and the last import I wanted was rain;
I'd whisper a prayer, the sun shone through,
and, lo, I started to blossom again.
I know when my days on Earth are o'er,
as I pass from this life and pain,
I'll thank the Lord for the sun-filled days,
but I couldn't have grown without the rain.

Eileen M. Caszatt

Dream by Day, Dream by Night

Which do I profess to be the best.
May I say that rarely do night time dreams
Please nor, do they soothe thy soul.
For they ask me not what I like,
Or what my emotions need.
Not even what my desires and feelings convey.
At times nightly dreams can be cruel,
Even brutal, but then again they can
Somehow solve troubling problems.
I know not why, but at time they do.
Rarely do I recall night time dreams in lustrous color.
Or awe-inspiring beauty, but in dull black
And white with overcasting gray.
Yet for the most part, I recall not at all.
But when I dream by day, the wondrous
Choice is all my very own to pick and choose at will.
One can dream in all the glory
Of heavenly colors so bright and cheerful,
With the most profuse array of delightful events I desire.
May we all have our choice to dream by day—dream by night.

Eugene A. Schmitt

The Parable of Life

*To my namesake and loving granddaughter,
Jennifer Claire McPherson*
He knew me before He formed me
in my mother's womb and had a plan for me.
All flesh is as grass that withers
and flowers that fade, as the vapors
that appear for a little while and are gone.
We fulfill our mission and move on,
as others born soon take our
place on the stage of life.
Each generation makes it own place
in history and the scheme of life.
So let it be! So let it be!

Irma McPherson

Ponder the Moment

This statue carved of stone,
cold, alone, yet naked,
vulnerable to the world,
with a warmth and beauty to behold
stirring at the depth of the soul . . .

By all those who gaze upon its
unique grace and alluring charisma,
a sense of peace, a serenity, unfolds,
waiting, waiting to unfold, the magic of stone.

Shirley E. Sargent

New Love

To Rodney Mullinix, who'd open up my heart again
Cherries are red, berries are blue,
There's no one I know truer than you.
From the things you say, to the things you do,
Lets me know you feel the same way too.
I want you to know how much I care.
I think we make a pretty good pair.
A gentle touch of your hand
Lets me know you care to understand.
Your gentle words I love to hear
Make me smile from ear to ear.
A twinkle in your eye, a smile on your face
Make me tingle all over the place.
A gentle kiss from your lips
Makes my body want to flip.
I love the way you hold me tight;
It makes me feel so secure at night.
Seven weeks have gone by so fast;
It makes me forget about the past.
Cherries are red, berries are blue,
You're the best thing for me and I hope I am for you.

Trina M. Early

Bleeding Hearts

Each time I see thee, bleeding hearts,
A wave of tender feeling starts

That takes me back across the years
To childhood days of smiles and tears.

I see a garden, quaint and fair,
With Grandma tending flowers there.

Your heart-shaped pendants, row on row,
The purest pink and white did show.

They seemed so real, so pure, so sweet;
Their lifeblood flowed with every beat!

Dear bleeding hearts, I've loved you so,
Through all the years from long ago.

For in your pretty forms I see
Those days long past, that seem to be.

Cecilia Tyne

We Didn't Belong

You never did belong to me,
Nor I to you.
But there was something in your smile
That seemed so good and true.
I'll always hold you in my heart,
And wish upon a star
That one day, someway, you'll be the angel
That I believe you are.
But after all these silent days,
The score remains the same,
And, probably, your passing thoughts
Never say or think my name.
When your glory days are over,
And you're done the things you must do,
If, by chance, you happen back my way,
I'll be here, waiting for you.

Robert L. Bray

Dream Worker

We stretch and yawn and rub our eyes.
Little do we know the dream worker has just passed by.
When good nights have been said and we are dressed in our p.j.'s,
We climb in and snuggle in our nice, warm beds.
We yawn again and close our eyes, and drift
Off to sleep, not knowing the "dream worker" just passed by.

Julia K. Clayton

Search

I came awake one night to find
That I was trapped within my mind,
And I walked along strange paths unknown to men.
I had no other choice at all,
Forward walk or backward fall,
For my exit must be sought for deep within.

While in my silent mind I trod,
Beside the dead (or living) Rod,
And watched the chaos that surrounds each would-be soul,
I found the silence (strangely bright),
Slicing at me through the night,
And I could be, if I would be, either dead or young or old.

I found, at last, I had returned,
But my would-be soul still burned.
So I seek, and always shall, that unkind view.
For my restless would-be soul
Drives me through the naked cold,
Ever drives me to be seeking for the lie that would be true.

Dan F. Buzzarde

Forbidden Fruit

To those with eyes to see and ears to hear
God's Worth is the real power behind all creation
But secular science worships Darwinism without much hesitation

Man was made in the image and likeness of God
His special creation to rule this earthly sod

But a serpent possessed appeared on the scene
Controlled by Satan who had devised an evil scheme

Eve and Adam he tempted to sin
To eat the forbidden fruit denied by Him

Knowledge of good and evil came with that first bite
Knowing they had sinned, they hurriedly took flight

Sins roots from that day did rapidly branch out
And polluted all creation round about

But kind Providence sent a Saviour to redeem
His shed blood only can make you clean

One day this sin sick world will pass away
Than a new Heaven and Earth with rule the day

Utopia will then become a living reality
When sin is banished for all eternity

Than all will be as it was meant to be
Before our first parents partook of that tree

Andy Beckman

Angel Baby

To my darling angel baby, Marcella Rawlings, love Mom, XO
Sometimes wishes really do come true
I prayed so hard and God sent me you
A precious, darling, wee baby girl
With dimpled smile and strawberry curls
A miracle sent from God above
An angel baby to love
I have watched you grow through the passing years
Through scraps and bumps, your saddest tears
Now here you are, sweet sixteen
A lovely, charming beauty queen
Still in my heart you will always be
An angel baby to me
Though Daddy is so far away
He is smiling down on you this day
He sends to you from his home above
His ever lasting love
For you will always be
An angel baby to him . . . to me

Lillian M. Rawlings

For the Love of Stacie

Every man has his wrongs,
The things the world will never know.
But you have saved my soul
From the plague that threatened my sanity.

I have not sinned by saying you're divine,
Because only God himself could have sent you to me.
You are a goddess in my eyes,
And I will never know what I have done
To deserve your love.

I will repay your kindness and love;
I will place my head on the chopping block
And bare my back to the whip.
I would walk into the fire of hell
And fight the beast with my own hand
To carry you to the gates of paradise.
You are deserving of no punishment,
And no punishment will I allow you to receive.
My love for you is greater than the heavens,
And I will cherish you always.

Gary Vetro

Seasons

Spring is full of exuberance and life.
Mountain streams are running wild and rife.
A spirit of new life responds eagerly to the dare
Of old man winter, reluctant to let go
And let spring have her way and melt the snow.

September and October are very beautiful in their way,
When trees don their autumn colors, so vibrant and gay.
Such exquisite beauty should cause our hearts to sing,
But, alas! Summer is gone, birds are on the wing.
And so, a feeling of nostalgia may then pervade the mind,
When we realize that winter is not far behind.

Winter may steal in softly with just a few flakes of snow,
But then, once more, the world is covered with a mantle of white.
No more sound of crickets, birds, or bees to break the quiet,
Only the pristine, silent cold and chill winds that blow.

Irma Blase Senkbeil

Back to Reality

Ray, I hope it's not an affront
To mention your back,
But lately you've been reclining in the sack.
Your figure that once stood tall,
Is now like the Northridge Mall;
Shaking like a baby in a crib,
Or a dancer in an ad-lib;
But, Ray, though your stature is tarnished
With this latest fall,
You'll surely recover
Like a bouncing ball;
Pain from the rear
Is not easy to face,
Yet we know you can do it
With a great deal of grace;
So get on the court,
Don't be taken aback,
Stand on your feet,
And stay out of the sack.

Bernard Holtzman

Profound Sound

A few of the most beautiful sounds I've ever
Heard are the laughter of children, a saxophone
And violin, church bells and falling rain,
The sighs of my love and his beating heart,
The song of angels and a mother's prayer.
These wonders God gave us, this sense of sound,
These blessings bestowed: He is profound.

Billie Lou Pike-Moss

Cold

The chill of the night brings memories of old,
when I was a child and I was so cold.

The wintry weather bristled outside,
my feet hurt so bad, I thought I would cry.

The pot bellied stove, all chucked full of wood,
with a blanket around me, that's where I stood.

I remember praying, don't let the fire die down,
for the rest of the house was cold all around.

I knew I could get warm with the sunrise, but
that would be hours, could I survive?

I guess that I made it, for now I am old,
but I'll never forget what it is to be cold.

Mike Jacobs

War

As I sit here, men around me die
My rifle sits there beside me
But upon my knees I fell
For when will you tell
Dear Lord, what is the meaning of this
I miss my wife, my children's kiss
How can you put me on this
Earth to take another's life
Leaving at home a waiting wife?
In the good book, you said
Love thy neighbor
To kill, a sin
Yet here I am, getting ready to do it again
Here, I point my rifle, not worrying about next of kin
I'm trying to save my own skin
Please, get me home
To the land of apple pie
To the blue skies
Of Indiana

Steven Dant

As for Me . . .

I have built my house on the mountain top
Open to the light of the sun
Where fresh breezes blow by day and by night
Far from all earthly bounds
I've cast away cares as an outmoded robe
And donned the garment of praise
In honor of Him who leads the way
By the light of love's pure rays

Come, come with me now
And drown in the Joys
Of dancing with stars, diving through Clouds
Swimming in crystal seas
Come, come sing with me now
Sing with the Choirs of Heaven and Earth
United at last, one with the music of the spheres

When we've danced and sung praises through eons of time
We'll find that we've only begun
So let us merge our sparks of love now
With that great flame of Love
Which burns eternally

Blossom Blake Hammond

Redemption

I am part of your past
To think of me is a crime
Therefore, to acknowledge me, a sin
Thoughts of me bring upon guilt and shame
You wish you could forget
But to forget you must first forgive yourself

Melissa Lehtinen

The Five and Ten

Sadie, Sadie, me scrub lady, me scribe
I pondered thee would not come to for me
'Tis a fluke 'twas in me think 'tis Sadie, Sadie me missing link
In a blink of me eye I feel I must write
Me script 'tis known me writing pen knows which words will do
I don't sweat the small stuff when I'm in the mood
For in this no time I could not find me happiness
Than I met a female eagle not a ten but a five
She stems from reality's Heckathorn tribe
Called Nadine The Eagle Serene
With sincerity she asked
Are are broke
Yes I replied
Feeling like the child
In that moment of honesty I stated
But you just fixed me
By putting me inner most thoughts into words
You expressed me to me
I healed
She used a power that's a ten not a five

Derry Martin

Robin

I saw someone the other day
Who was righting the wrongs of a few.
She explained, "Two wrongs don't make a right,"
She reminded me of you.

I watched someone the other day,
Demanding credit be given where due.
As she determinedly tried to balance the scales,
How quickly my thoughts turned to you.

And I saw someone the other day
Whose heart was painted blue.
She was crying because souls were dying,
For a moment, I thought it was you.

I remember a nurse, one long ago day,
Who brought me a life, so brand new,
And kindly placed it in my opened arms.
I looked down, and it was you.

And since that day, though some dreams slipped away,
And faith faltered heavily, too,
Every true thing I found that didn't let down,
With joy reminded me of you.

Barbara L. Painter

I Remember Love

To my loving daughters, April and CoCo
Not unlike our mothers and fathers
Who cared for us, with such tender joy,
All our pain and suffering would cease
Because they were there to give us peace.

I remember not so long ago,
A phone call from my mom.
A laugh or two, we shared that day
We love you, dear daughter, come what may.

Today, I have children and grandchildren too,
What a pleasure to know that my love for them is true.
The sound of a bell, the clock is ticking
My God grant us knowledge, and stop bickering.

We put things together, and take them apart,
And sit down to a table, it's love a la carte
Love is a simple word, expressed from East to West,
Sometimes, it is weak, not at its best.

The world is the same, only people are changing.
Drugs, disease and pestilence is here.
Is there a future? I hope and pray,
For the power of love is the only way.

Arnetta Moore

Heaven

There is this most wonderful place
It's not Earth or in outer space
It's a place that lies deep in your heart
It's always been there even from the start
In this place, angels sing
Songs of joy to His throne they bring
The streets there are made with gold
Always to be there and never to be sold
Beside the street, there lies a crystal sea
I dream of it now, but one day I will see
When I'm there, I'll lay crowns at his feet
Then surely Christ I shall meet
I shall see the scars on His body
And just think He died for me and everybody
There, I shall meet friends from the past
Then surely I will be happy at last
On Earth I shall stay
Till the trumpet sounds one glorious day

Tracy Estes

The Loneliest Girl in Town

To my loving mother, Rose Singleton, a true English Rose
In the cafes downtown
I am known as a clown
How happy I seem to be
But at the back of those smiles
There lies tears all the while
And heartaches that no one can see
The life that I lead is not real
A lonely girl and here is just how I feel.
I've rings on my fingers and heartaches inside
I'm the loneliest girl in town
I'm everyone's buddy but nobody's joy.
I'm the loneliest girl in town
Too many parties that bring me no fun
Too many bright lights instead of the sun
To many sweethearts but not the right one
I'm the loneliest girl in town

Rosemary Singleton

Running Out of Gas

The unyielding pressure to form yourself,
to become one with the life you live is crucial.
And then you pause, not suddenly as confident.

I slip away into a battle where the outcome is already assumed.
No one sees, or is it that everyone but me sees?

Back in the beginning, I elevated the struggle
to become certain at the expense of a simple, normal life.

And the funny thing about it is that each trail
I might have selected ends in the same way.

Essentially, everyone is confused;
everybody has weaknesses which betray them.
And the more difficulty you have in affirming
the only reality you can ever know, the longer the delay. . . .

Mike McNair

Emeralds

To my loving mother, Gloria, yes, dreams do come true
He looks deep into my soul with piercing, emerald eyes.
I see a violent storm lying in wait behind his dark lashes.
As he enchants me with his stare,
I become frightened knowing that he will possess me.
His voice a gentle ringing in my ear,
A promise of love caressing my heart,
And with that there is no fear.
Evil is he, this warlock, and his unholy wants.
How my skin burns with his every touch.
I have waited throughout my lifetime
For him to come back to me.
Alas, 'tis only a dream . . . yet he comes.

Diane Cortez

paper and ink as coursing veins

Sitting on the floor indigenous style
I file through humorous cards intended
To make a graduate momentarily forget
That they are trading a piece of paper
With calligraphic best wishes scrolled on it
For 1-2-3-4 a year relationships
That will eternally change levels
The second the applause decrescendos

I naively attempt expediency
As each card's individual scent
Wafts forth and inhabits me
Making the year's past events fertile
And the developing emptiness frighteningly real

I cry on the inside and put the three perfect cards
That took me half an hour to find back
Before rising and leaving them for later
Midnight madness provides the perfect excuse
For not letting go just yet

christopher michael mclamb

Lights

I comprehend the lights in the night
Gently they float in the air, gliding
They call awaking souls to the light
Sweet souls of the unborn are drawn to the colors
They call to the lost souls to dance left and right
Burning in the shadows, glowing with warmth
The lights are like ghosts playing tag in the night,
While they shine there are no new deaths
The grim reaper is amused at the sight
Their glory is like falling fire, burning slowly
I wish I could fall into the well of lights
Pretty lights, beautiful lights, delightful lights.

Dominick Chianese

Despairity

Oh, but mortal being that I,
Who cannot live, who cannot die.
This feeble body is bound by thee.
And only my soul shall remain free.

My boggled mind a massive mess,
My body held captive by subtle stress.
My head bowed low, amid despair,
My heart so heavy, it has no care.

This ole mortal being, must one day rest.
When loosed from the slavery of life's morbid test.
Bow down, bow down!
Old retched body, bow down!
Till one day, when rest will be bliss,
And peace thou soul, shall not resist

Joyce Matlock Porter

Be with Me

Trust in me—let me be your rock.
Believe in me, and hand and hand we will walk.
Reach for me—I will hold on tight.
Yearn for me, and I'll love with all my might.
Laugh with me—let me brighten your day.
Cry with me—let me feel your dismay.
Yell for me—I will come to your side.
Love with me—we have nothing to hide.
Live for me, as I live for you.
Show the world our love is forever true.
Grow with me, both strong and tall.
Be with me, and we'll get through it all.
Remember that we fought brave and strong
To be together, where we belong.

Leah James

Good-bye, Old Friend

Today I had to say "good-bye"
To my friend of many years.
But the presence of him will stay with me.
I'll miss him and shed many tears.

He was always with me wherever I went;
His love complete and true.
He didn't ask for much in life—
Only my love, and understanding too.

Whenever a problem came into my life,
He always understood.
And he was always there for me.
He'd share them, if he could.

I knew that I would lose him,
That his time would come "someday."
But it came too soon, unexpected,
And he could no longer stay.

He was everything a friend should be,
And he didn't want to go.
But, in spirit, he'll always be with me.
I loved him—my dog named "Bo."

Vivian McElfresh

Sands of Time

In memory of Mama, I still miss your face
Glancing through the windows of sand
Drifting along endless spaces of the existence
Thoughts and dreams and memories of the past
Standing idly in one place, alone again, naturally
Reflecting on yesterday, today, and tomorrow
Loves lost and found and lost again
A cycle of life spinning along like the spokes on my old bike
The sun peeking through scattered clouds
Darkness looming in the distance
Mom's sweet soul cooking tickling the essence of my thought process
Hearing my sister calling out my name in fun
Wondering if I am in trouble again
Pondering, pondering, drifting along like the sands of time
Flowing along in the breeze of a swift autumn wind
along a beautifully decorated Jamaican shore
Pretty blue water so clear, your reflection
radiates everything in the pathway
The sands of my time, like grains slowly slipping away
Where they are going no one really knows
Like the hourglass going, going, almost gone . . .

Kemmie L. Conway

Mother.Wonderful.Com.

To my wonderful and beautiful mother, Clara Barron
M is for the many nights you held me close.
O is for only you could calm my fears.
T is for the many times you wiped away my nightmarish tears.
H is for the hours you worked so hard.
E is for each day you taught me to pray.
R is for the radiance you always display.
Together these letters may only spell mother,
But they mean so much more.
You were the one my eyes first beheld,
That painful OCT day when Venus lined with Mars.
Whether I was chasing butterflies on a sunny day,
Running from acid rain or making castles of clay;
You were always there to lift my spirits,
As your gorgeous blue eyes sparkled,
A halo above your head pulsated and aura of gold and blue,
Sending me on a spiritual journey!
Hours enveloped days, days enveloped years,
While computers send out messages of worldly strife,
Yet Mother.Wonderful.Com.
Remains the light of my life.

Glenda Jordan

Miss You

I have halted my footfall midair.
Listened, vainly straining
To hear the nearness of you.
Yet I know you are there,
For the early morning sun scatters diamonds
Over my dew-strewn lawn
And the mocking bird, full-throated,
Fills the sky with his inimitable arias.
I long to experience the brightness of you.
Miss your distinctive handwriting
That spells my name.
Yet, somehow, I am assured all is well.
Mary Francis is busy with her pageant girls!
"Be humble, be sincere, be serene."
"We Southern Girls are born to preen."
And forthwith,
At the touch of her inspiration coaching,
True beauty unfolds.

Eugene C. Michel

Life

Life is a reason to wake up and see
What's going on around you, what the day will be

Take a deep breath, and open your eyes
Don't take a chance and let life slip you by

So many people in so many ways
Just sit around day after day

They never have lived, or even tried
Until it's too late and life's passed them by

There's an old saying, and I believe it's true
Be all you can be, and do all you can do

Don't be foolish and let life slip away
Live all you can live, and live for each day

Memories are something you have to earn
It comes from living, and knowledge you've learned

There's nothing worse, I've heard it said
To never have lived just walk around dead

So take some advice from the middle age class
Live for the future, don't dwell in the past

Wake up each morning and see what you can see
Live for each day, and be all you can be!

Deborah J. McGill

A Talent for Living

My days fly by in a dizzy whirl,
My garden is never tended.
It seems I'm always much too rushed,
To see that our clothes get mended.

My house doesn't look like a magazine ad,
My children all look tumbled.
I'm fighting desperately to mend
The birthday cake that crumbled.

Still I always have time for a victory shout,
Or a good soft shoulder to cry on.
When my husband or child needs a listening ear,
I'm the one they rely on.

Poetry just isn't my art,
Nor music, nor writing, nor painting.
I'm afraid I'm just a simple maid,
With only a talent for living.

But if you offered me a choice
Of all that the world has for giving,
I'd pass on all those other things,
And take the talent for living.

Celia Miller

The Sea, My Love

At times when she's most ugly,
She is still a wondrous sight.
As the moon throws beams across her body,
She shimmers in the night.

The contours of her body
Never seem to stay the same;
Her swells and dips keep changing
So we never know her game.

Many men have crossed her;
Many have lost their life.
None have ever tried to boss her,
Or asked her to be his wife.

With all her beauty, charm, and wit,
Many men have loved her well.
While in the dip, they kissed her,
And fondled at her swell.

A blustery affair at best, I say,
Is all that can be had.
When the tides of love keep changing,
Surely men go mad.

Michael K. Roper

The Isle of Carlos

Jewel of Pacifica, thine kings did I once know,
For at their feet I did learn the secrets of the deep.
The phosphorous ripples in the waves did guide thee
O'er the reefs in search of other isles across the watery graves.

David Olsen

The Music Box

Play, little music box, your soul is so sweet.
After a few notes, your song will repeat.
But I do not mind; I love to hear it.
I find it comforting just to be near it.
Why do I enjoy the sound so much?
Perhaps it is because it keeps me in touch
With a time long ago, when life was kinder
And I did not have a constant reminder
To hurry up and run here and there,
But to take a moment just to share
A daydream or two, a pleasant thought,
Before happiness was something to be bought.
So play, little music box, play your song well.
I will listen and remember, but try not to dwell
On a time that was, but is no more,
And I will look for the good and for what is in store.

Carolyn Waller Fabian

Music

life is a cast combination of today
and yesterday the song of the wing
leads the trained light of the trees
the twisted tonic of reason thrives upon uncertainty
the ambiguity of tonight's twilight
lends lizards to fortune's fearlessness
its voice mends the mellow moon, meandering melodically
perfection's faces are forward behind
the bellowing blisters of stillness
swamp-driven nephew, nurture, notice, be no longer notorious
mementos defy moments, they don't them define
sweetness of simple time is its innocence, its soul
sweetness sleeping symbolically senses its sound
it soothes (seethes in) its seed
swallow me, it murmurs, muss me
master my mistakes, my muse muses on the moor
moving the moss that there moves with melancholy
creating cobwebs, callously they coat crimson

Jessica Tobacman

Carbon Copy

Take a moment of your life,
Take a good look around you, turn yourself completely around,
Take a good look in the mirror at yourself,
Tell me, "What do you see?"
I see the memories of my past,
I see my present life, what's happening to me now,
I see what the future holds for me.

Try to hold on to the memories of your past
As long as you can.
Hold those memories close to your heart,
For no one can take those memories away.

The present, you make your life as you want it,
You can be anyone you choose to be or you can be "just you."

The future you see, these are your dreams, hold on to them.
For, as I see you in the past, present, and the future,
I see you as a carbon copy of me.
Take a moment of your life.
Take a good look around you,
Turn yourself completely around,
Take a good look in the mirror at yourself.

Dawn M. Regalla

Lord, Hold My Hand

Hold my hand, Lord, I am Your child,
If you don't, Lord, I will surely die.
I thought I could walk this journey all by myself;
Sorry to say, I can't do it at all.

The mountains are awfully high;
Oh! Those valleys are so deep.
The nights are dark and scary.
Hold my hand, Lord, help me to stand.

The enemies are roaring like a lion,
Trying, trying to get in.
Hold my hand, Lord, I promise You I won't cry.

Forget me not, Lord, when the sun goes down,
The moon stands still;
And the stars cease to shine.
Hold my hand, Lord, I can't do this alone.

When the morning comes and the light begins
To shine; life is okay.
Oh! What a beautiful day.
Hold my hand, Lord, I want You to stay.
Hold my hand, Lord, don't ever go away.

Cassandra Mitchum

Sprouts

To grandpa Peter, Uncle Bills, Arthur's and Robert Frost's memory
The girl in the Mirror inside the vacuum
Silent, incensed minding the house I'll leave
If invented mirage is the mother of dim
Sunlight of the sky roasting peanuts on the hard street.
Tiffany days of fab kisses the night of doom
Which breaks even following Civil War haunted house seats.
Science calms the free eagles in the East Room
Where reform rotates on the ceiling's hungry glaze.
Wise airfare rattles the cars without enough ka-boom.
Cool on the airwaves, Ava Maria's daze
Wanders across the nation to the Red room.
Cafes back home, in the Blue Room is Sammy Nut-Out,
Inventor honored with loop frame spectacles
And air purifier. Ozone observers don't pout
For sultans can't believe what they read in the ports.
Uptown in New York on Broadway are the sprouts
Growing a city on the sea mount in Manhattan.
Running on the balcony and bagels is girl,
Union on the American way of white pearls.
Mae West's squad car chases Thomas Edison.

Billy C. Samer

Quiet

To my love, John Johnson, the first is the best
Quiet, but for the rain outside,
I lie by the fire in your arms.
You fill the endless abyss crying out for love.
You replace the faceless lovers
Of countless hopeful dreams—
The cabins, summer evenings,
And brave adventures in white,
Yet you cannot find your heroes.

Quiet, you are he, ever hero to my heart:
He who dared confront my fears and see me in my eyes.
Through all my poems, days, and nights,
You alone are precious
Like one kind, courageous dragon
Or a star which never sets.
You fill my senses, fill my dreams.
Do not weep, be quiet.

Jennifer Green

Angel Light

Many years ago, when my age was only three years,
My father's death brought forth the tears.
And my mom, in her great sorrow,
Was forced to begin a new tomorrow.

A young, former country girl, she began anew;
She immediately took over life's new view
To provide all necessities, and worked to excess
Protecting with care her blessed.

As companions in life, we remained each day,
Until World War II military took me away,
And a second angel came into my life
To alleviate and diminish the daily strife.

A small town girl soon came my way,
With smiles and laughter to brighten the day,
Who, before the war, became my wife,
And who continues today in our happy life.

While problems are daily for all in life,
I can thank my mom and my wife
For the glory and angel's light
They brought together to my sight.

Edmund C. Bowie

Dilemma . . . Arrived

*To my grandchildren Georgie, Priscilla,
Michael, Emelie, John, and Caitlin*
Government great as meant, created in bull sessions freedom bent
Must have study and update to keep pace with tech progress rate

Cohorts in update session as recreation find tort a vexation
Tort, satisfied not on word list forbidden, explore gist, hidden
Tort, a misdeed by morals need, training a faulty weed or no heed

In a concept ill fraught, parents held liable for child's tort
A concept, grave, but worry nix, if it ain't broke, don't fix

To break it now runs by booze, dope, TV, film, knives, and guns
To law brought, likely bought, all by a terrible dilemma caught
Law rules, justice bent, compliance or punishment, great but late.

Law, a must, but, more must is guidance, opportunity, and trust
Child, vehicle of life, must be right or guide—restrain tight
Parents not training sound must be found to guide a turnaround

New task for all, lawmakers have more work, heed a new call
Can't heed until rid of effort stealing reelection is done deed

We need one ten year term for house, senate, and executive spot
After ten years elect one fifth every two years, sequence by lot

Lobby conned lawmakers see no truth, academicians bare the truth
Build D.C. City Deluxe for their rotation to give Lawmakers truth
The vote, people's tool, needs age for smarts and cool, Amen.

George K. Marshall

Dear Little Teddy Bear

Dear little teddy bear, fuzzy and stout,
I'll bet you'll never know what this is about—
That to a little girl you are a delight.
She looks up at you, her eyes shining bright.
You are my helper too, gratefully I say.
You are her companion all through the day.
To her you are someone to hold, love, and squeeze,
Someone to play with, to coax, and to tease.
Dear little teddy bear, almost worn out,
That she loves you, there is no doubt.
She kisses you; I kiss you, too,
Something that only for her I would do.
Nighttime finds you cuddled in bed
Next to a sweet little sleepy head,
A pair of loving arms holding you tight—
Little girl, teddy bear, goodnight.

Maria G. Alonzo

I'm Remembering

Collections of thoughts and emotions seem pointless
Now that you've gone, catfish nibbling at the lines,
Campfire roaring with the blowing of the west winds . . .
Doves vocally welcoming the coming of dawn with song
You in a fetal position on the sleeping bag
Aroma of Maxwell House scents the air
While being poured from thermos to cup
You crack open one eye and then the other
Face stained with salt, I'm remembering your belly button
Warming in the sun, after we've drank of each other
"Until the last drop" then the season changes
It's outerwear once more

Charles E. Hampton

I'm Not Your Ordinary Woman

I'm not your ordinary woman, though I might have been
Competing with other women to select amongst men.
I have heard the magic words, shared time and time again,
Only to discover they enchanted my closest friend.
Is it worth the time to share from the heart,
When someone else may be in the shadow, ready to take charge?
My goal may be set high, out of sight for most guys,
But that is where I want it to be
If there is satisfaction for me.
Men want to be cool, without an interest in school,
Always searching for Miss Right to quench their appetite.
You ask me where I work and the number of years
I have been there. Is this my home and do I care to share?
No! I'm not your ordinary woman.

Pearl Quimbley

Pieces

Leaves float slowly, softly to the bottom,
Filling a heart with hurt.
Happiness sets in, blowing away
Pieces of ache only for a
Fleeting moment. They
Always settle down,
Fall into a place carved out by some past pain.
Nothing can rid the bleeding hurt away.
Hope soothes pain, love helps, but really
Just pushed it away, buries it
In some corner to be forgotten
Until the past is dredged up.
A spark sets it all on fire, burning a
Hole. Searing hotness.
Helpless. Desperately
Searching. Light.
A way to escape soon closes up,
Burning itself,
Drowning in waves of its own pain

Kristy Witkowski

The Runaway

The snow falls,
As a tiny girl sits
In the midst of a field.
She has run away,
Away from her fears, her happiness, sadness, and memories.
She asks the Lord what she should do.
He answers her plea,
But she cannot hear, see, or feel
The warmth all around her.
She is blinded by her sorrow.
She dare not cry,
For fear the tears will freeze,
Not only onto her, but onto her soul.
She yells to the Lord,
And He answers,
But she cannot hear Him.
She cries to Him this time, infuriated by her own stupidity.
And then she answers herself.
The small girl stands, brushes off the snow,
And leaves the field.

Laura Wandel

Missing You

I'm counting the days that you are away
I'm saying the words that I really want to say
I'm counting the times when it was only us two
I'm saving the kisses gene that's only for you

I'm thinking about the togetherness we were allowed
I'm wishing that you were here with me now
I'm thinking about the times when we went here and there
I'm wishing that you could give me to the love we used to share

I'm trying to understand that it was for the best
I'm hoping that you slow down and get plenty of rest
I'm trying to cope without you the best I can
I'm hoping that you will always be my man

I'm wanting to touch your human flesh so much
I'm remembering how much we both used to touch
I'm wanting to remember the nights both of our loves grew
I'm remembering how much I will always will be "missing you!"

Jennifer Eastman

Me

What a unique being I have here—me.
Kind, conceited, conspicuous, some of my personalities.
Compassionate, doubtful, compulsive, oh my!
All my friends and enemies: me, myself, and I.
There are times I have to protect myself from you, she, and he.
But then I have to guard and protect myself from me!
Sometimes on me I lie on, or lie to.
Then in secret my mind admits you lied on you!
There are goods; there's bad all stirred up in the mix.
The good, not bad, trying to protect me from the tricks.
Hot one minute, cold the next,
Sometimes these compelling conditions make me a mess!
Good is good to you; bad will use you.
You pray, Lord! Lord! By then you confuse you!
I do tend to myself both night and day.
And I do get compensated with self-sitters pay.
When I try to take control, by God's perfect Grace,
To try and keep my personalities in their place.

Vivian Noisette

Rainbows

I'm trying now like never before to understand life.
Meanings flash by but seeking true happiness is slowly aroused.
You find just one day to be precious as gold,
But tomorrow it slips through your fingers only as sand.
I'm trying to understand you and myself, collecting illusive rainbows.

Karen Yokley

Angels

I peak out my window every night,
Before I lay in bed.
The moon and stars fill the sky;
They create the dreams in my head.
I believe the stars to be guardian angels,
Smiling back at me;
They're glowing bright all up in Heaven,
Glowing softly and beautifully.
I can hear them singing very softly
And, flying among the clouds,
They're sending us messages from God himself,
Though they're not speaking that loud.
I see them spread their wings out wide;
It's their way of giving hugs.
They hold me very very close to them;
They hold me very snug.
They say "sweet dreams" to me every night,
Before I lay in bed.
I fall asleep and I'm flying with them;
Throughout my dreams I am lead.

Christine Rees

Intimacy

To my loving angel
A tender kiss, a warm embrace,
A flirting glance, my heart does race,
A moonlight walk, hand-in-hand,
A midnight chat, woman to man,
A romantic movie, sharing one chair,
Talking and laughing, while brushing your hair,
Dancing real slow to an oldies tune,
Counting the stars around the moon,
Intimacy comes in many ways,
During long, summer nights, or cold, winter days,
But I'm just happy that I could share
This wonderful moment with a woman so fair.

Dale Mentor

I Love You

I love you in so many ways
and for so many reasons.
I love you when you confide in me
because I can see the honesty in your eyes.
I love you when I'm feeling sad
because you know exactly
how to cheer me up.
I love you when you smile at me
because you make my heart smile with you.
I love you when you hug me
because your arms make me feel
like nothing can ever hurt me.
I even love you when you're stubborn
because you stand up for what you
believe in and I hope you'll always
remember that I believe in you.

Jodi E. Pretekin

This Pain Is Called Love

Death happens so quickly to one's soul,
that people confide in it so frequently.
Take my grandpa for example:
He shot himself to ease the pain,
even though the minute he pulled the trigger
it would kill him instantly, yet cause more pain,
which is coming to great depth at this point.
The pain is so strong, it can bring two others' hearts together
instantly and tear them apart a minute later.
This pain is called love.
People don't realize the risk you take
when you rupture the love that someone has for you,
even though this pain called love will never end.

Meghan A. McHaney

Everlasting

Bombardments of memories rusting through perceptual barriers
Sensations twisting on perpetual pendulums
From a higher power we connect in spirit
Elapsing in fear, control and anger
Branches of light and grandiose vibes
Riding the corridor above and beyond
From inner self to outer reality to depths of hidden mind thoughts
Glorious and beauteous gestures of the holistic avenue
Healing wings flying higher and farther
Touching the souls of all who wander
In fractured moments that are stolen and sold
In battered kingdoms with pampered visitors
See how God is getting our attention
With nature's forces that are devastating
Christ's tender hands rejuvenating
So do not give into fear this calls for true faith
For with a human heart and with a human soul
The Holy Spirit is unmasking
Because of the Father and because of the Son,
Hope is infinite and everlasting

George Rivera

Another Realm

Dare to dream, the poets say,
and so I slowly drift away.
Within my head, a secret place,
where few have access through the gate,
credentials of integrity, we advocate.

Better Homes and Gardens eager to cover,
space so unique and novel, captivating yet free,
abounding with charm and creativity.
Never ending delight to the eye,
where souls can meet and never die.

A place where God and angels feel at home,
joyfully linger and freely roam.
For who in his right mind abandons Heaven,
love and loyalty, humor and laughter,
the intricate allure of being forgiven?

Peace untold and comfort enfolding,
floating through space among the stars,
celestial sounds, heavenly fragrance,
unblemished slate, pure reverence,
where no one has claim to disturb or desecrate.

Louise Segit

Life's Garden

Today, I went walking in Life's Garden of my mind.
Valleys of discouragement tried to destroy this garden so fine.
Weeds of distrusting God and thistles of sin wanted to grow,
While seeds of disobedience the enemy daily tried to sow.

A devastating storm came into the garden, unaware,
Crushing the garden until the cry of grief filled the air.
With broken and wounded branches, it wept through the night;
Gently, God cradled it with mercy and love until the light.

From out of the deep wounds, many strong branches grew,
Producing flowers of sweet fragrance, more than it ever knew.
For the garden's roots were planted in the river of God's Word
And were nourished by His promises, which it daily heard.

Healthy trees and flowers in this garden depend on me,
Whether I allow God to be the Master Gardener, you see.
He tills, prunes, weeds, and sends blessings of sun and rain
Until the best comes forth, bringing glory to His name.

Today, I went walking in Life's Garden of my mind
And watched God's hand at work until it was refined.
Lovingly, He embraced and molded the garden in His hands;
Thankful, the garden bowed in praise for God's Holy plan!

Jean L. Lake

The Mountain Rests

High above the foothills
the mountain stands majestically
With heavy snow-capped arms lifted up
attempting to embrace the sun
Reaching hoards of dark uncaring clouds
that push down and burst like heavy water-filled balloons
Stretching every mineral every ounce of dirt every blade of grass
the mountain undauntedly breaks through then stops
Until the morning sun draws near enough
to see its shining face and feel its warmth
Until the fresh waters of melting snow
pass down over every rock and through every hidden crevice
Until its heavy arms are light enough to reach again . . .
the mountain rests

Janet Nicholson Swann

I'm Blessed

After having six children, I hardly get any rest.
But through it all, I do my best.
If it hadn't been for my dear Bob,
I would not have this kind of job.
I work, cook, and do the rest,
And through it all, I still say I'm blessed.
All of these kids God gave to me,
I ask myself: How could this be?
Could it be just a test?
Thank you, Lord. I'm really blessed.
One last thing I wanna say:
I thank you, Lord, in every way.

Brenda L. Edwards

The Debate

The soul and the spirit were conversing one day
When the soul blurted out: I don't see it that way.
I do as I please and please what I do
And answer to no one, especially you.

The spirit spoke softly:
You're way out of synch.
Pleasing yourself
Is beginning to stink.

The flesh spoke up, arrogant and tall:
You'll always answer my beck and call.
I put you through such passion and pain.
I can drive the strongest soul insane.

The spirit spoke softly, as it did before:
Flesh, you're the worst and most loathsome whore.
There's nothing that you won't peddle or price.
You deceive the soul with every cunning device.

Now hold on, spoke soul, who was caught in the middle:
There must be an answer to this troublesome riddle.
There is, said spirit, polite and nice:
His name is Jesus; His surname is Christ.

Rosemary Shaw

To My Loving and Wonderful Boyfriend, Jason

I want to hold you in my loving arms forever.
I'm gonna be there for you until the end.
When I'm around you, I feel as light as a feather,
And that's the way it should have always been.
I feel so very safe when I'm around you.
You let me know I will never be harmed.
In a bad situation, you let me know exactly what to do.
Just let you know, and I'll be armed.
I'll be armed with the love of a man
Who lets me know I'm as special as it gets.
You always make me as happy as you can.
That's why I want to tell you
I've loved you since the day we met.

Sandy Coulter

My Appeal and Prayer by Pen

To my beloved wife, Gening Bunyi
The world of Media today, control the Internet Power,
Competitions of Web site, the business firms may suffer.
Bit Networks on Internet, put million dollar investment
Not to gain much, but to block, and attract million Web users.

While the world of Humanity, Human right is not exercise,
Due to material desire, for money, drug and sex abuses;
Kidnapping, violence were rampant, immorality exists,
Love and Care for their children, lessen by broken families.

Why is it, forbidden desire, since the creation of the Earth,
All forbidden things are sweet, tempted to test, hunger to eat.
Even the King lost their throne, for the enchantment to sex,
So with the greatest warrior, became weakened and defeated.

On the news . . . how many nieces were raped by their stepfathers?
How many needy employees were harassed by their employers?
How many secretaries were victimized by their leaders?
How many children were abused, assaulted, raped, and murdered?

Only God knows . . . Oh, Lord! Please hear . . . my appeal
    and prayer by Pen,
On behalf of those families mournings for their beloved victims.
To expunge their depth sorrow, on their heartbreak suffering
Hang those abusers to death! And cast them to Hell forever.

Porfirio A. Mariano

Beeloved

Today I climbed a big tall tree
To find the hive of my favorite Bee
I spotted it there, way out on a limb
And waited for her to invite me in

I saw her peeking out the door
And buzzing her wings across the floor
She wanted to tidy up the hive
Before her honey stepped inside

I gave her pollen and her face beamed red
She took me straight to her honeycomb bed
She was soft and gentle, pure and sweet
The sexiest Bee you would ever meet

It was then I wanted the world to see
How much I loved my Honey Bee
I gave her flowers from a honeysuckle vine
As I dropped to my knees and said, "Bee mine."

Bill Wied

Envelopes

My heart is not an organ
that plays to the duets of life
but rather a series of cells
in the shape of envelopes:
some are sealed to be opened
only upon demise of the carnal anatomy,

Some colored bright with hope, some faded the edges worn,
some filled with sorrow of past events,
some with edges frayed left with remnants of feelings.

There are a few envelopes of cellophane,
some you can see through with bits and pieces of ideas,
wishes, desires, fragmented dreams
though forgotten, difficult to conjure up.

My breathing comes every once in a while;
yet, I cannot utter a sound
as I learn not to make my presence known
since no one listens anyhow.
Now, the covered flap drops over my head like a shroud;
My throat is dry, I cannot utter a word.

Death overcomes my countenance.

Alyx Jen

God Is in Armenia

He's there and also here with me
His love is given to all and is free
In Yerevan, I encountered his love from on high
There were no ABC's on which to rely
Words that I didn't understand were spoken
Still, He came through in love unbroken

The eyes of love, the caring ways
Made me know God is there in all our days
Miles, differing cultures, language do not alter
God's love is there and it cannot falter
God made us all fascinating and unique
No matter how we look or the language we speak

Sharing that love in a far-off land
Brings joy and peace, a holy band
All creation, each soul is precious and good
When touched with a holy spiritual food
Thank you Father, Lord of all, You care for all
Nations who heed your call

Thank You for giving to the world Your Son
The world means each and every one!

Donna Henn

Soul Searching

As we find ourselves going through the turns
and twists that life hands us,
we find ourselves searching within our
inner selves for answers.
Searching for peace within our souls,
but searching too hard to where the trials and
tribulations get even more confusing.
Life is something that is said to be so simple,
but yet we send ourselves into a tailspin
trying to find the answers.
When all the time the answers come from our
hearts, not really our minds.
Barriers and limitations that we cause
within our own thoughts.
When peace and acceptance is at our fingertips,
the sky is endless and the clouds are many.
But to find that silver lining
comes from putting our spirits to the test
and reaching for the stars and the moon.
The powers are endless.

Betty Ortiz

The Autumn Colors

It is my lunchtime.
I look out the window of my office
and gaze at the green hill,
my friend from the summer.

I see the trees changed:
wearing a new dress.
So colorful and charming.
They change me into a bird.

I fly and touch their heads.
I fall in their arms: waving and bouncing.
Like them, I too feel the chill of change;
experiencing a childish happiness.

I then fly away from them higher and higher.
Hoping to touch the clouds and kiss them in their blue bed.

A squad of guards, emerging
from the western tomb, gently lead them away.
Girls in black veils laugh at me and fly.

A group of angels in long, transparent dress
pour cups of champagne on my face.
Drunk. I see God's perfection in beauty.

Musa M. Maroofi

Weak Outer Shell

This weak outer shell that we call our own bodies
is a complex and intricate system
with many delicate balances
that enable the body to function and perform.

We ask, "Why me, Lord?" when our bodies start to fail,
but we aren't always thankful when we sail!
Perhaps we need to stop and count our blessings
and give praise to the Father up above.

We seem to forget that beyond this life
awaits Heaven and the presence of Christ,
our Savior and King who will end all pain and strife.
Then we will be made complete in that beautiful life.

If we truly understood what was to come
then we would not fight so hard for our earthly life.
We can await the great day of being with our Lord
while we live for Him during our stay in this world.

Instead of being upset about our outer shell deteriorating
we need to turn our eyes to Jesus and realize
He gave us a blessing—life itself.
Our bodies are truly His—not our own.

Angela P. Sorrell

To Bryan

Sometimes when I look at you
I stare in awe, because it seems
That God must have created light
So it could shine forth through your eyes
And He must have created the sea
So it could be your gentle touch
And He must have created the wind
So it could be your softest breath
And He must have created the sunshine
So it could glow in your smile
And He must have created the trees
To dance in the wind with your laughter
And He must have created the crashing waves
To be the pounding of your heart
And He must have created the sunset
To be the beautiful magic of your love
And He must have created me
To love you all my life

Elizabeth Mongillo

One Last Time

To my parents, whom I am very proud of and love
A shadow falls across the land
As a brilliant color flashes across the sky.
A cry shatters the air like an eagle in flight . . .
A gust of wind
Like two giant wings beating together.
A shadow falls.
The ancient dragon is flying one last . . . time.

Jaimi Bradburn

To My Love

When we are not together I miss you so much, not being
able to keep myself from wanting to feel your touch.

There are so many reasons why I love you,
If one day I decided to tell you I'd be talking
the whole day through.

The nights we are together I never want them to end
because you are such a beautiful sight, just like our
song says you were wonderful tonight.

When I think of you a smile comes to my face, knowing
that no one will ever be able to take your place.

I have never ever loved someone the way that I love you,
I just want you to know Eric you are my dream come true.

Candice Bryson

Truth

Truth will set you free and at ease
Truth is like a floating spirit in deep sleep
Truth is a labor of love, like sleep never ceasing
Truth is a labor of love, the music
Truth is an abode of love, like sound is peace
Truth was when there was nothing, always well be
Truth is in the sound of music and in the light of the world
Truth is an essence of what lies beyond
Truth is what lies beyond and to fellowship divine
Truth is a fellowship with essence till we shine
Truth lies into the self of man and with self-withdrawal
Truth is changeless, given to all
Truth is like the fleeting wind, never ceasing
Truth is an essence of words fully alchemized
Truth is a word loving, hurting like the wind
Truth is in your inner self, now and forever
Truth was created for life, creative life
Truth lies in the creator of life
Truth is in the beholder who holds the truth
Truth is in the beholder, truth is everywhere you find it

Mary C. Delozier

Would I Die If I Didn't See You?

To my beloved mother, Mary
Would I die if I didn't see you?
Would the Earth stop spinning around?
Would the birds cease chirping their songs?
Would the clouds stop swirling ahead?
Would the rain fall, or would I be dead?
Or is it all in my head?
I don't know, because, as you said,
I'm coming down in an hour or two—
And I know you mean four or five.
Hurry up, I think I'm alive.

Fran Sapser

Pretense

Hanging low and saying they're high
Seems to be an alibi
For doing some of the things they do,
To keep from crying and losing their cool.

They drink and dance and socialize;
They listen to each other lie.
Their egos say that they don't care;
They can't get caught in the human snare.

And they laugh and joke and fool around
And drink to wash the sadness down.

Dianna L. Beaudry

The Great Divide

Easier the open door to take
When the bitter soul is blind to what's at stake
How to stop the hurts the heart does know
The ills of disillusion hidden deep below
Long ago in a different dream before the weeping and the screams
A veiled face and white lace could boast of a love worth telling

Oh, but the heart then young and swelling
Fragrant as roses in open air
Sweet and pure as a child's prayer
Soft the whispers of pride when the coo of doves did guide
Grim and hopeless now, the sighs devoid of grace
Easier an open door to face than mend the vows that did command
Two now one shall walk hand in hand
The worn fabrics of black and white thread
Unravel and leave the young voices for dead
A new generation rapidly multiplied
Rising up confused and angry in the great divide
Easier the open door to take
When the bitter soul is blind to what's at stake

Loraine L. Bishop

Halloween Night

To my grandson, David W. Penny
Halloween night is here at last;
The midnight hour is about to pass.
Tiny little figures draped in white,
Chanting and dancing in the night.
A gust of wind and swirling leaves;
And eerie echoes through the trees.
Ghosts and goblins coming to call,
Creepy shadows on the garden wall.
Jack O Lanterns illuminating the night;
Black cats stalking, what a fright!
The rustle of leaves in the evening breeze;
A hooty owl in the old oak tree.
Witches on broomsticks flying high,
Bats on wing zooming by—
Scary things left unseen
Are images of Halloween.

Betty J. Kabbe

Shouts and Whispers

I love America, this land of the free;
For places of beauty, there is much to see.

There is beauty that shouts, like the mountains and the shores.
And beauty, the message is a but a whisper, one must "listen" more.

My home is on the prairie, in these hills of grass and sand;
Beauty here is but a whisper, one of the quietest in the land.

One can see it in the sunrise, glowing orange in the east.
For beauty, some may call a famine—to me, here is a feast.

The wind sends the breezes that cause the grasses to sway,
Then the hills become an ocean . . . green and brown are the waves.

The colors that amass here are of every shade and hue.
The pinks are found in a wild rose; prairie violets have the blues.

Other flowers here are red, yellow, purple, white, and even green;
Visit in the spring or summer and you'll see just what I mean.

Wildlife abounds here, such as the pheasants, grouse, and deer;
The eagles, hawks, and coyotes are the predators they fear.

Another beauty is the cattle, our livelihood in this sandhill land;
Watching calves frisking in the grass, you'll see a Master's hand.

For He alone created this America, land of our birth;
With all its shouts and whispers, nothing's like it on this Earth!

Terri Licking

One Dozen Silk Roses

To my husband, Steve—My Love
My love gave me silk roses today
and as he placed them gently in my hand
he said they'd mean much more than any real bouquet
and that soon I'd understand

One dozen silk roses were wrapped with such care
in fine paper colored in green
And although no buds or thorns appeared
they had the prettiest red petals I've seen

And when I put them in a vase on a shelf up above
suddenly everything seemed so clear
I knew he wanted these silk roses to be a token of his love
and that this token would always be there

But then as my eye shed a tear he said honey don't cry
instead smile at this beauty so still
and feel the joy of knowing down deep inside
that I love you and I always will

And if these roses keep on touching your heart
just like a sunset does in the sky
I want you to know that they'll never grow apart
and like my love for you they'll never die

Margaret J. Pulkowski

A Winter's Day by the Lake

I sit on this shore,
in the midst of February.
The weather is damp,
yet unusually warm.
Yesterday's sun melted the snow, reduced to piles of sand,
and today's cold rain beats down on the road.

Lady Highland is silent,
her voice muffled by her shroud.
The cloak chokes her rhythmic song,
but cannot support a man.

The gulls squabble for perches,
and the wind moans off the lake.
Next to this and my pencil, no noises dwell here.

The landscape is lifeless,
save myself and the gulls,
and the loneliness surrounds me.

The lady is quiet,
as I sit here to write,
and the gulls fight for perches
and the world goes on.

Adam Seidl

An Inspirational Love

With such passion, he reveled in her beauty.
A chance meeting, it must have been fate.
Hearts intertwined as their eyes met,
it was love at first glance, a moment they'd not forget.
Two souls surrendered to a force much stronger than will.
They dared to think, in a moment, a future could've been built.
Vowing to someday return, he left. Off to war he went.
Saddened, his country he had to defend; both felt assured
in spite of all that was said they'd never meet again.
Nine years came, went, so much time and space in between.
Could those feelings, the attraction stirred,
be just a dream or was it more than what it had seemed?
Destiny touched their lives twice when, by chance, they met again.
and, like the breeze that catches the embers of a quiet fire,
their souls were torched, windblown with desire.
Meet once, twice, marry to have a family together—forty-four years,
still growing strong through all the laughter and all the tears.
An inspirational love story, one to be admired,
one not uncommon to their era—yet one to be desired.

Eileen M. Maher

Where Are You?

To my best friend and loving mother, Denise Seely
On the day you left me, I asked, "Why?"
Why wasn't I given a chance to say good-bye?
You were taken away.
I didn't have a choice.
There was no warning, no sign, nothing
to let me know that you were leaving.

Where are you now?
I wish I knew wherever you are; I hope
if offers you a view of the world,
full of the places and things you wanted to see and do.

I hope to see you again someday.
I will see you when I pass away.
But, it won't be now; I must be patient.
For I still have many lessons to learn and teach.

I will be able to reach you, and I will be in
your reach through the prayers that I will say
to and for you every night.

So wherever you are, I hope to reunited
with you again,
my dear Mother, my best friend.

Nicolle Burke

Senior Citizen's Plea

When you look at me once,
   you see white hair and makeup carefully applied,
But take the time to look again; discover the real me inside.

My sparkling eyes top cheeks a little fat,
That support a friendly smile and lips that love to chat.

Those hands covered with sun spots can still do their part
To create intricate designs and watercolor art.

And play the piano, though not in concert style,
But quite enough to entertain an interested, sweet grandchild.

Hands are the leading force that helps me when I play
At golf and bowling and horseshoes or whatever comes my way.

These legs don't look the same as they did in the long ago,
But there is still a joyous bounce in my step-just a little slow!

It takes more than one look to see a loving heart,
But it is there reaching out attempting to do its part.

So take another look—put initial judgement aside.
You may be quite surprised at the real me inside.

Hilda Gentry McKnight

Time

Time, oh time, where did you go?
Could it be that my steps are too slow?
You race ahead; the clock ticks away.
Before I know it, it's the end of the day.

Time, oh time, you really click away.
For each lost moment, there's no replay.
You move along waiting on no one!
Nothing stops you not even the setting sun.

I must somehow find a better plan,
a plan to move along with that clock's hand.
Yes, I know that you move swiftly ahead.
It will soon be time for me to go to bed.

Bedtime comes, I look back at my day.
So much work is left, I am sorry to say.
This body moved too slow, time didn't wait.
I'll have to close my day in a way that I hate.

Tomorrow comes the dawn, a new day begun.
I'll move faster from dawn to setting sun.
I know I can't return to that lost day.
For each wasted moment, there is no replay.

Barbara Alverson

The Nursing Home

I stopped by a local nursing home the other day,
And there in the lobby sat a little lady, old and gray.
She said, "I'm waiting for my son to come, and
He should be here before the day is done."

The nurse behind the desk quickly raised her head
And sadly whispered, "He won't be coming, for he is dead."
I realized then the lady was living in years past;
Probably her best years and she was trying to make them last.

I smiled and said, "Be patient, sweet one,
For soon the Lord will take you to your son."
She nodded as if to say she understood me,
And for her sake I asked the Lord to come quickly.

As I visited in the rooms of the other residents there,
I asked the Lord to be with those who had no one to care.
And to impress upon others like me
To stop by and give them some company.

These folks who have reached their sunset years,
Have borne many burdens and shed many tears.
These fathers, mothers and others dear
Whose lives will soon be over here.

Judy L. O'Neal

What Value Success

I was born one day without a thought,
Only a cry to deny any silence.
What was the purpose of my arrival?
No one knew about this little boy,
Except I was someone's pride and joy.

Neither did I ask if life was fair,
For this is also a subjective fare,
And how could I ever know
What price or worth is my name,
For price and worth mean the same?

And now I see that life is a journey
For one to enjoy in all its glory
And not to judge in the universe,
For who is to judge my life's success?
Does it matter in a century, priceless or worthless?

And life is neither brief nor lengthy.
It is eternal in every sense
As we watch the shinier stars on darker nights
And think of brighter thoughts on darker days.
Live life to brighten lives, to enlighten one's own ways!

Richard Y. Segawa

Untitled

I feel your presence late into the night,
And I know you are not too far out of my sight.
I can sense your smiles and your radiant glow;
As I feel you watching me sleep, all my tears flow.

There once was a time when you were so near,
And my life was so great, I needn't have one fear.
But now you're gone, and I can't see you with my eyes.
Memories come of how there was never an exchange of good-byes.

Just seeing your body lie there, still and cold . . .
One last look from your eyes I never got to behold.
Because now you're gone and never coming back,
All my days are dreary and black.

This is all because some guy wanted a pleasant-filled evening;
His punishment now is being locked up, but he is still seeing.
He gets a free room with lots of good food,
And soon he'll get off because of a good attitude.

This is how our court systems work now:
He'll be out with a smile and a bow.
While your body will lie in the ground forever,
He will be thinking that he was so very clever.

Stacie Greenwald

The Bowman Archer

Beneath the pale rim of a curious moon,
I ventured the forest near old Barsoom.
When an unerring shadow whispered its lot,
I fore hastened my passage, rather than not.
A bevy of spirits and serpentine beings
Enthralled a threshold of senseless fleeing.
Then, ever so slight, drifting, upwards rising,
Crept odors of decadence awesomely despising.
Run rapid my breathing in fathomless sighs,
Attuned with Sagittarius and stalking cat eyes.

Best be to illuminate dark rhymes of thee,
Of hollow worlds roared a beast unto me.
I strung my bow and sped forth a fatal wrath,
To reckon with this specter that forged my path.
Grasp he did, my fiery shaft, within a wispy hand,
Hawklike the flight of an arrow,
Flung back to where I stand.
And all is a still,
A still in the chilly air of quiet . . .
For truly, all seasons becometh winter.

Gary Brakefield

Chaos

In the middle of the chaos that is my life,
I wander through the wreckage of my past
Trying to reach a destination
That continually eludes my every effort
To make sense of it all,
To find a peace of mind, of soul, and
A balance in my life.

But, I wonder, will I recognize it?
This uncertain future, this unknown happiness,
Something I have never known
But for brief moments
Here and there.

But, perhaps that is the mystery,
The great secret to it all.
Maybe we are only meant
To catch a glimpse now and then,
So we can appreciate
Those briefly shining moments
In the stark reality
Of our everyday lives.

Beverly Anya Chesanek

Will My Loved One Be Around

Aloaha'oe, Dorothy Papu Aquino
When the evening sun goes down.
Will my loved one be around.
Dreaming of her through the nights.
Of holding on to her so tight.
Will my loved one be around.

Night goes by; it's early morn'.
Dreams forgotten, now it's dawn.
She's lighting up her sweet, sweet smile.
For I'll be holding her tonight.
Will my loved one be around.

Dreamer's come and dreamer's go.
Like the sun, the moon, the rose.
All that memories that we hold.
Never, never letting go.

For, I'll be holding her tonight.
Under twinkling stars so tight.
Promises to always be around.
Lighting up her smile so bright, tonight.
Will my loved one be around.

Stan Aquino

The Golden Bauhinia of Hong Kong

The Golden Bauhinia at the water front,
facing Kowloon Peninsular and overlooking Victoria Harbor,
is a replica of Bauhinia Blakeana,
the flora album of "Hong Kong" The Fragrant Harbor.

It's here, at the square of the Convention Center;
majestically, she stands watching vessels and cargoes
steaming in and out of the bustling harbor,
enhancing trade and prosperity in this prestigious land,
proudly know as "The Pearl Of The Orient!"

It's here, at this landmark square, visitors and residents
flock in front of this golden replica to pose
and to witness the glamorous glare
of the return of the precious pearl to her mother shell.

For this glamorous replica is a special, precious gift
of love, and honor, from the motherland,
in celebrating the happy family union, so jubilant,
and in enhancing the well-being and prosperity of this
"Precious Pearl of the Orient!"
Blessed shall "The Fragrant Harbor" forever prosper!
Blessed shall "The Pearl of The Orient" shine with even greater pride!

Yukwor Lee

Me and You

For the love of my life, Terra Fisher
The time I've spent with you
Has made my heart grow warm and near.
All the things I've done with you,
And with everything that we've been through,
Now I can finally see clear.

I can see the visions in my head
Of me and you together, forever.
Always holding hands, making love in the sand.
Sitting around watching movies
While the kids are upstairs in bed.

We'll be living a life of dreams and fantasies.
Everything you could imagine will come true
'Cause, forever and ever, it will be me and you.

Eric Ferriss

My Beautiful Bride

I think of you when I see beauty;
A rainbow in the sky.
Birds singing or winging
An arc to distant places.

I think of you when I see poppy fields,
Or a lonely flower swaying gently in
A capricious summer breeze.

I think of you when the first light of day
Sparkles with a million beads,
Brilliant, on the meadow wet with dew.

I think of you when I walk alone,
On sun drenched, sandy shore,
Where beauty blends with stony point.

I think of you, lovely you, gracious you.
I always think of you when I see beauty.

Alfonso San Miguel

School Is Out

She awoke with a grin,
Then she began to giggle.
As I tickled her toes,
She started to wiggle.
Gramma, don't, she laughed with glee.
I hugged her and asked, do you love me?
Farther than the moon and the stars above,
Was her cheerful reply, so filled with love.
Come on, get dressed, we have to scurry.
Eat you breakfast, dear, please hurry.
Stop! Don't tease your sister.
Don't be cruel.
There's your bus; now go to school.
As the yellow bus pulls away,
I have a special prayer I say.
Thank you, God, for days like this
That fill my life with loving bliss.
Today I think I'll give a shout.
Today school is finally out!

Virginia Wagner

To a Mourning Dove

Why are you mourning, my little dove?
Is it yet another case of unrequited love?
Or is it the growing scarcity of safe water to drink,
And the supply of choice worms and bugs continues to shrink?
(Blasted parking lots!)
Is it because of the rotten, stinking air you must breathe?
Or the sounds of gunshots in the streets far beneath
(Without rhyme or reason and not just in dove season)?
Oh, why are you grieving, my little turtle?
Surely not because it's the end of Urkel!
(Did I say that?)

Helen Kampschroeder

Clouds in the Sky

High in the sky I see with my eyes.
Clouds forming, sunrise morning.
Fast moving breeze, clouds float by.
Different shapes clouds make.
Traveling through the sky.
In and out of clouds, planes fly.
Puff clouds white, change its sight
To deep dark gray, like night.
Oh! Oh! Rain! Rain coming down.
After the rain, dark clouds left town.
Sunshine broke out bright
Until sunshine fades, to bring in the night,
As the evening dark surrounds the clouds
With sparkling silver stars of tiny lights
Delightfully shows proud
Where the clouds are now.
Good night old evening clouds
Until the morning brings the dawn,
New beginnings, shapes to form,
Eyes open and mouths yawn.

Mary Pernorio

Precious Little Lamb

To my beloved son, Sean, and daughter-in-law, Marni
Precious little lamb, what a miracle thou art!
Sent from God our Father, directly from His heart.

Precious little lamb, fresh from Heaven above.
Sent to us, from God Himself, an expression of His love.

Precious little lamb, how innocent, so fair!
God's unique creation, entrusted to our care.

Precious little lamb, we're glad you've come to stay.
We'll love and laugh together, we'll work and learn and play.

Precious little lamb, how we've waited for this day!
To see your blessed, tiny face, to look at you and say . . .

Oh, precious little lamb, the great Shepherd sent you here.
And even though you're now with us, He's forever near.

He'll never leave you or forsake you. He'll be with you every day.
He'll bid the angels to watch over you, to guide you on your way.

He's always there to listen—don't hesitate to call!
And always, please remember, He loves you most of all!

And precious little lamb, please forgive us when we err;
Teach us to be mindful and to go to God in prayer.

Now, precious little lamb, we hear the angels sing
To celebrate your birthday, a wondrous holy thing!

Judith Ann Crawford

Realm of Existence

All that is dark and veiled,
billowing in the winds of pain.
The sighs of children covering like clouds the moon.
When adrenaline becomes the drug of choice
and we jump into pools of night.
Running so fervently into the labyrinth of greenness
into our eternal life.
Dressed in black to hide our hearts
we wail our songs of tears.
Content to exist in our fantasy world,
happy to live within our own deaths.
Eternal darkness with eyes glowing bright,
clashes of thunder to pervade our eternal thoughts.
With strobe and flame our only day
to light us through our night.
Dancing in crystalline droplets of rain intermingling with our drug.
In grotesque beauty we exist; only our world and the sky above.
This is our realm
Come see our fall into ecstasy
As we come to life.

Candi Terry

Bennet's Love

God sent this angel down from Heaven above.
He sent him down for us to love.
God said to take good care of this little boy.
I said there was no problem; he is a bundle of joy.

Bennett, you were brought to our home one fine day.
You were so wonderful in every way.
You brightened up everyone in this house,
Even when you slept and were quiet as a mouse.

We loved you so and wished you could stay,
But knew you would have to leave one day.
You need to grow up with your sister and brother
And have a young, energetic father and mother.

We have no doubts you will grow up fine.
You have a personality divine.
Everyone loves your flirty eyes
And the wonderful smile you use so wise.

Living with you has been such a pleasure.
Many memories we will always treasure.
And now, as you will be leaving our home,
You will always be in our hearts no matter where you roam.

Ruth Whiting

Wondering

Do you . . .
Feel the warmth from the sun on your shoulders?
See how the light strikes the roadside boulders?
Smell the aroma that fills the spring air?
Oh, darling, I know that you care.

Do you . . .
Help the neighbor down the road with his chores?
He's been laid up and doesn't go outdoors.
When the neighbors all lend a helping hand,
Oh, darling, a day's work is grand.

Do you . . .
Set goals before dawn, each day of your life
Conquering fear and overcoming strife?
Think of me as you accomplish each task.
Oh, darling, I will never ask.

Do you . . .
Know I'll be by your side throughout the day,
Maybe only in your thoughts, when you pray?
When all is said and done, at day's end,
Oh, darling, you just say "Amen."

Donna J. Moore

This Crazy World

The Jesus of love, the devil of hate
Working on the same planet where fools congregate
Where mountains are climbed, men and women destroyed
Just to brighten a cause that's so pure null and void

This crazy square world where people get high
Where robbers kill daily at the blink of an eye
Where power is great in both black and white
With conflicts resolved but not always right

This crazy round world so full of despair
Where pain and hate seems to grow everywhere
Where spirits abound in the name of supreme
And fools follow fools in search of a dream

This crazy blue world where God is the light
But Satan comes up each day for a fight
Where gambling is wrong in the world of redeem
But money comes first in a world of esteem

While deserts are quiet, rivers storm right ahead
With heavy winds threatening to wake up the dead
Where raging volcanos spew out fire from Hell
But here in my soul, all is well, all is well

James Weldon Lane

A Train in the Distance

The sounds of children playing carefree and gay
Fill the air on a warm summer's day.

The sun is setting; dusk mutes every sound,
Only a dog barking and wild life moving 'round.

The same time each night the sleepy town does know,
In the distance, they will hear a train whistle blow.

Another place bustles with city noise and clatter,
A train whistle blows, to a city does it matter?

The wide open plains dressed with cactus and briar,
Sounds ring out from the birds perched on barbed wire.

Across the flat terrain the mighty iron rolls by,
In a cabin, the whistles pervade the air and die.

Each time the whistle blows and fills the air,
A childlike heart wonders, the train is going where?

It is a reminder; our small world is only a piece,
Of a larger world with experiences to release.

Places with different people, customs and styles.
Roadways and highways that go on for miles.

A train in the distance is going to these new places,
On tracks that connect miles to discover new faces.

Joyce Maria Paes

I Win

Don't lay me out in some casket
for people to walk by and stare.

That was only the house I lived in,
and I'm most certainly not there.

I have no regrets about my life,
for my steps I could not change.

I've no bitterness towards anyone
I loved whether or not it came back in exchange.

I have had so many days and nights
that I hungered so for love,

And now my hunger is satisfied
for I fly free like a dove.

No longer can people judge me
by the house I walked in . . .

It's passed away forever!
I'm free!
I win!

Brenda Gail Eaton

Daddy's Little Girl

He picked me up when I fell down
He knew exactly when I needed to be held
He spoiled me with lots of love
And made me feel safe
I was Daddy's little girl

He's always there when I need help
He gives me total support, no matter what
With every goal I make, he cheers me on
And with every accomplishment, you can see how proud he is
I'm still Daddy's little girl

He'll give me away in marriage one day
His wisdom and advice I will carry on with me
I will cherish all the memories we've shared
Nothing could ever destroy our special bond
I'll always be Daddy's little girl

With his constant love, I will succeed
No matter how old I am, he'll always be there
I love him for everything he's given me
And for being the wonderful man that he is
I was, am, and always will be Daddy's little girl

Laura Bridges

My True Love

The one good man that I have found
Makes my mind spin round and round.
I don't know what I am doing anymore;
I just want to be with the man I adore!
Why do I fall in love so fast?
Memories that will forever last!
Why don't you love me, like I love you?
My feelings are forever true.
Why does it hurt so bad when you say,
"I don't want a relationship, but don't go away."
Although I may never catch your heart,
I am unhappy when we are apart.
A gentle hug and a kiss good-bye,
I will wait for you until I die.

Becky Nastansky

Ode to Norsemen

Scandinavia, Scandinavia,
your roots impregnate my soul.
Your singing, dining, dancing, dressing,
my habits and appetites reflect what you uphold.

Famous for your forestry, fishing, and northern fauna,
also your work ethic and perseverance.
They all lend admiration for your contributions
to this earthly planet and my life experience.

Blond is beautiful and,
accompanied by blue eyes, is a superlative unbeatable.
Rosy cheeks and pearly smiles
make all ethnic jokes non-tarnishable.

Known for your glaciers, fjords, akvavit,
most ancient mountains, and Lutheran souls.
Your scientists, explorers and inventors have brought
the world Saab, Scandia, dynamite and trolls.

You have Stockholm, Copenhagen, Oslo and Helsinki,
also Amundsen, Trygve Lie, and Hammarskjold.
Why shouldn't I be prideful as product of your mould?

Nile B. Norton

Beauty beyond Measure

Snow flakes are dancing around me
All shapes and sizes, all beautiful to see
Each unique but resembling each other
They dance, flutter, and touch one another
As they touch the grass and cover the land
United together, all working hand in hand
The trees bend low with a burden of snow
From glistening hills to the valleys below
All is possible as a cooperative venture
They created this beauty beyond measure
Little by little, each flake started to fall
But it couldn't be done without one and all

Nancy Ouellette

This Old Man

This old man was tiny and frail,
his body weak, his mind sharp as a nail.
There are many memories of this old man,
that through the ages are etched in the sand.

In his diary, he wrote
of beautiful things he saw each day,
from the glistening morning frost
and rising of the sun,
to all the things that day he had done.

He loved to tell stories of old,
which in my heart I will forever hold.
He reminisced of the good and bad.
This old man, my Dad.

Shirley Lyle

Misty Dreams

Surreal and misty is the dream:
Fairy rings and bright moonbeams,
Unicorns prance on silver hooves,
Golden saddles on great gray wolves,
Wine red tapestries with golden cords,
Trolls in their caves with a treasure horde,
Blue satin dresses with pearly tassels,
Maids asleep and enchanted castles,
Dragon wings in the nighttime sky,
Magic reigns in a blueberry pie,
Fairies fly over the morning dew,
Rainbows come in every hue.
Lightly falls the snow in an icy frost . . .
On the morning, the dream is lost.

Ann Boehm

The Sideways Stairs

The sideways stairs, going nowhere.
Neither up nor down, neither here nor there.

Having no place, no reason or rhyme.
Out of synch, out of step, out of place, out of time.

Going full circle, curving left till it's right.
Head meeting tail, it's a puzzling sight.

Life's made like that, of impossible dreams.
Unending circles without any seams.

So where do I start, and where do I stop?
On the sideways stairs, without bottom or top!

Larry P. Zimmerman

A Career Is What You Are

Clyde is his name, which signifies "a light of hope."
He has worked patiently to achieve, and not to stand
In the shadows and mope.
The university held a wisdom for him to accomplish.
It was there, so he took the reins to drive on to
Expectant fluency.
The pace was slow, but success was on its way,
An electrical engineers diploma was received,
Which opened the door to go in rapid mobility.
The computer age will make things faster.
However, engineering is a careful precise calculation
That fits into everything, that he masters.
He will walk in wisdom with all that he loves and cherishes.
With great success, his ability to stay on top of
His pinnacle in life has progressed.

God is there to support every success,
As retirement may come in five years or less.

Gladys N. Ginter

Misled along the Way

Down long, dark tunnels, over vast open vales
Along the waters of a sea-blue ocean
With the wind whispering again another way
They carry me with them, wherever it is they may go
Though I can see the light
I am misled along the way
I struggle to be free
But not with chains am I held
No, they keep me close by temptation of the soul
They know my being well—they are the prisoner's keep
Though with fire and light, I fight
Darkness keeps me misled along the way
Wind, water, darkness, dust
It makes a muddled river
Though branches of relief I sight
They extend only too short of my reach
Yet a weapon have I at my side
If only the chance of time should come
I could free myself to be
No longer misled along the way

Shannon Santos

Fallen

To Katrin, my heart will never forget you
I am still falling . . . I will soon hit rock bottom
and once again I will rise and your painful ride
will blend with my past . . . I inhaled every part of you
just like the nicotine in your cigarettes
my lungs are stained with a touch of hate
sometimes I tend to forget . . . I long to reach out for you
and all I find is this empty space
should I continue to reload my emotional gun . . .
point to my head and play Russian roulette?
I will no longer be so weak . . . my feelings grow stale
but I still remain your emotional slave
every night the thought of you sleeps by my side
I am constantly stabbed on my back
when the morning comes I find traces
of tears fresh on my face
take a second and contemplate what is around you
try to digest every word I write to you
I will be falling besides you
while your eyes remain closed
and my torn emotions crash with the floor

Madelein Ruiz

His Amazing Grace

As I gaze up into the moonlight
I can't believe the spectacle that I'm seeing
And then I begin to ask myself
What's the reason for my being?

There are times we ask ourselves
What is our true worth?
And I ask myself over and over
Why has God kept me on this Earth?

He has kept me here
In spite of my own self
I know that there would be no more me
If from my side he left

They say things aren't always
What they and we think it seems
But I just want to thank you, Lord
For allowing me to live out my dream

I can only hope that one day
I will be able to look into his face
But I do know the only reason I still live
It's only by his amazing grace

Oscar Frazier

Faith

The road of life we travel often varies
Sometimes it is short, sometimes it tarries

To a mission on Earth we all have been sent
When that's accomplished, then death is the event

Death does not mean ashes and dust and the end
It's living the next life, world without end

God, for a son, a carpenter he chose
His life on Earth to understand our woes

In my father's house are many mansions, he said
Which proves that we have another life ahead

I go to prepare a place for you
That's what I believe is true

If we give love and help to others in need
It makes our lives richer and better indeed

If we are kind to others, I am sure we won't fail
That is the moral of this little tale

So keep your faith and give your love
And God will bless you from above

Henrietta Gumpert

My Sunday Angel

I started for church on Sunday morning
And knew something was wrong with my driving
And I, to really ponder begun
Had a flat tire to add to my chagrin

Drove to the gas station round the corner
But the compressor does not work says the owner
Preparing to call AAA on the phone
I ask a stranger do I dial one for the tone

He says do you have problems with your car
I say flat tire, oh! Yah
He swings his car to the gas station
And there knelt down before the nation

He dug out my tools from beneath the book pack
And says where is that missing jack
He lugs out the spare from the front dickey
And fixes that car in a jiffy

He would not accept from me a gift
But only said say a prayer for my soul's uplift
He said his name was Emmanuel
But he was indeed my Sunday Angel

Elizabeth Kythail

Christmas Long Ago

Gather around, my little children, for
A story I'm going to tell.
When I was just a wee one, I remember it so well.
I sat upon my father's knee, all safe and warm was I.
While outside winter's first snowfall
Was falling from the sky.
Father told of a little babe who was
Born this very night,
In a cold and drafty stable underneath
A star so bright.
His mother gently laid him on a warm bundle of hay,
While Joseph stood by Mary and thanked
God for guiding their way.
The tiny babe lay sleeping while heavenly angels
Told of His birth,
To shepherds on a hillside who were asleep upon the Earth.
They hurried and knelt while beholding the tiny king,
Not knowing of the salvation that He would someday bring.
Father told me Jesus was the reason Christmas came to be,
To save a world from sin and with grace He would set us free.

Cheryl Dianne Mathis

As Truths Unfold

Reality shattered; new perceptions unfold
As life experiences of others are told.
Actual beliefs begin to unwind
Because imperfections exist in mankind.

Each reality has to be realigned;
Emotions, perceptions, beliefs intertwined.
Truths can be buried: escape, elude.
Or truths can be faced with hope renewed.

Today is the first day life begins
Even as the past is unravelin'.
Painful truths and feelings bottled up inside
From authority of others we did abide.

You cannot control any past event.
You can only make choices today, the present.
Accept and face the pain and feelings of the past
So these do not control, but offer guidance at last.

You will never forget past events and pain.
Forgiving is not forgetting: the feelings and pain remain.
Forgiving means living life without these in control,
No longer acting a part, but acknowledging the whole.

Linda Morrow

The Voice

The night wind rustles through the leaves.
There is a faint voice singing in the distance.
The voice is clearer now.
The wind rushes through the trees, and an angel appears.

The wind is calling out, wanting you to follow the angel.
It is too late, though; fog surrounds the angel.
The voice gets fainter and fades.

Clouds cover the moon; you can't see.
Suddenly, a great light explodes in front of you.
The wind swirls around the light.
You hear the beautiful voice again.

The light changes into the angel.
She holds her hand out to you.
Reach for her hand.

Jamie Kathryn Heil

Energy

Life's energy is like fire
Whose flame leaps joyfully and effortlessly
Higher and higher,
Crackling, dancing, warming.

But when life is doused
By the torrent of body crisis,
The continuous drizzle of chronic pain,
Or the showers of old age,

The wood of our life cannot dance
And we lie like embers in the fireplace,
Unable to reignite,
Just glowing from the memory of the flame.

Helen Hunter

An Innocent Baby

An innocent baby was born,
Waiting for the big clashing of a thunderstorm.
It's the night that's very cold and wispy.
Some babies tend to be unhappy:
An innocent baby who didn't ask to be here,
And the baby is the one who cries those tears.
Why does that baby cry?
The more you think, the more you wonder why.
An innocent baby who's alone in the dark . . .
The baby starts to develop roughness like bark.
Some babies were developed by people who don't care,
And some parents don't promise to always be there.
An innocent baby was born.
That baby will go through life with many thorns.
The innocent baby deserves love
And freeness to fly like a dove.

Pamela Wyman

A Musing Misery

Deep into a dark world,
You were the one who gave me light,
My eyes were weak,
But my heart was strong,
I never imagined I'd find delight from pain,
Within my appeasement lies a dolorous tribulation,
I can do nothing but absorb your entirety,
Deep within my tragic soul,
The silhouette of you I cannot hold,
I lie alone, but thoughts are of you,
Ascending through Heaven,
Adjoining souls of two fade away,
Giving my contribution for a glorious aspiration,
With this there's nothing except my entirety,
When will I a vow to my fate,
Erato lies within fatiguing my pallid state,
Now you've become my muse for eternity,
A musing misery.

Jimmy Mills

Unicorn?

To great-granddaughter, Christyle Dawn, who loves unicorns
A thing of beauty is a unicorn,
And yet, he's only a myth.
With beauteous body, uniform,
He can perform mysteries with.

He's purported to return affection
To any worthy of respect,
Who are going in a sure direction,
And one another's differences expect.

With love that asks no recompense,
No return of favor, or gain,
Keeping no count of any expense,
Only offering love without pain.

Have you heard of these qualities before
In a person of mercy, power, and praise?
I trust your thought will return and adore
The great I am, who is the Ancient of days.

Who sits on a throne in Paradise,
Forgives all sin when it's confessed,
The one Eternal Lord, all wise,
Who one day, will our works assess.

Dawn P. Ware

Twenty-One

Twenty-first birthday, 1998 is the year
This special day should be filled with gleeful cheer
When all your friends gather 'round
And make that most silly sound:
"Happy Birthday to you! Happy Birthday to you!"
Embarrassed by now what else can you do?

Look at the cake and the candles
And consider the new responsibilities for you to handle
Blow out the candles and make a wish
And dream of the things you will accomplish
Then put a smile back onto your face
And unwrap your gifts at a frantic pace

Happiness and joy are in the air
No other birthday could quite compare
A million images race through your mind
Of the childhood you have now left behind
Not everyday do you have so much fun
Then again, not everyday do you turn twenty-one

Aaron Wright

I Wait for Dark

Hooded figures that shuffle by day,
With shielded eyes that seem to say,
"I'm not here, you can't see me,
I wait for dark, so leave me be.

Alone at night, I steal, I fight,
Not hampered by dawn's bright light.
So leave me be. Alone in fear,
The end of life seems so near.

So leave me be, I don't need you.
I am me and you are you.
Our worlds are different, so far apart.
So leave me be, I wait for dark.

No one sees how my heart bleeds.
No one cares for all my needs.
So leave me be. I wait for dark."
"I wait for dark," is what they say.

They need to find the Light, the Way
Christ Jesus says, "Come unto Me."
So please, dear friends, don't leave them be,
Or they will find the Dark.

Ronald A. Josephsen

Stand Up for Yourself

To my deceased daughter, Racquel Steer, and my son, Frank Brady
What! You fold up!
Hold-up the publisher who paid you short.
Pen them a letter;
You better
Pierce them through for nought.
Listen to me,
A lawsuit, I will lay at your door, for prompt delivery.
They say, "no!"
I don't think so.
Dial up my lawyer,
Settle this by a judge's order.
Court-date is set.
Ready for confrontation? You bet!
Took three-weeks to deliberate:
The judge rules reparate
A hundred-thousand dollars to her account.
Publisher now press to handout.
My lawyer digged and I settle the dust.
Stand-up for yourself.

   Louise Brady

Me Without Lee

In Memory of Shelton Lee
In 1977 I was living my life of
Happiness and alcohol free, just
Feeling so proud of myself,
And what the Lord had done for me.

Then as if a miracle there came into my life wonderful "Lee"
I really knew a true blessing and
All that came after were life's
Fulfillment of love, joy and companionship,
That there was a radiance just
Looking at me all could plainly see.

We traveled, explored worldly wonders
Far and near, I thought this would
Last a lifetime, until a sudden stop
Came so unexpectedly.
Now I just look back on the happy times
The Lord had given me.
And now I walk not alone today,
Although none can see
I can still feel the blessed presence of Lee.

   Lenora A. Brownlee

Oh, Robert

Hey little Robert, are you having fun
Are you busy making us, another sun
Will the sky burn brighter
Will we feel the heat
Of your "Little Boy"
Ensuring their defeat

Hey little Robert, are you helping us to win
Will you spread the enemy, a bit too thin
Will they evaporate
Will they have time to run
Is there another way
To say that we have won

Oh, Robert, what have you done
Fortitudes of nightmares
To subdue the "Rising Sun"
No more sunsets, no more free skies
No one wonders, no more than I
Of our dreams yet to come
Oh, Robert, what have we done

   Brett Lassa

In the Night

Late at night, when it's dark and quiet,
everyone sleeps but me.
I'm thinking of him, I cannot deny it,
if only my thoughts could be.
Seeing his face, even for a moment,
takes me through the day.
Hearing his voice, the little time spent,
is more than words can say.
I was told to follow my heart;
things would go right one day.
I'm told now that we should part,
but God knows I need you to stay.
Dreams often are made true
for those who will wait.
My dreams are taken unused,
and it's almost too late.
One last thought I'm thinking of
as I close my eyes tonight:
Why is it wrong to dream and love
if you know inside that it's right?

   Daniella Norris

Ode to Billy T

To Billy, forever in my heart
Who is this little man to be,
So new, so fresh, so cuddly.
I smell your cheeks and hold you close,
And stroke your arms and kiss your toes,
I rock and sing sweet lullabies,
And whisper love into your eyes,
Eyes that open wide and twinkle,
Tiny little fingers wrinkled.
You know not yet the love you give,
But soon you'll know, each day you live.
And so the generations grow,
You're blessed with love and this I know.
I'll watch you spread your little wings,
And dream for you, all life's good things.
I take my tender thoughts, and pen,
Of cherished love, what God has sent,
Sweet babe who brings such joy to me,
To whom I write love's ode to thee,
For who is this little man to be,
He's my new great nephew, He's Billy "T".

   Trudy A. Lee

My Grandma

In loving memory of Edna B. Garrison
You are the kindest person I know
Spreading love everywhere you go

You are always there with open ears
Hugging me tightly, reducing my fears

You stand beside me whatever I choose
Supporting me whether I win or lose

You helped me through my toughest hour
Cheering me on, giving me power

It's clear you have a heart of gold
After you, God broke the mold

You are an Angel, it is easy to see
God sent you here to watch over me

You have planted a seed deep in my heart
So I know our souls will not part

For our connection is forever and ever
And I will forget you never

   Tammi S. Schuchard

Hello, I'm Glad You Came

Hello, I'm glad you came
When you're with me, it's never the same,
Smile for me and tell me it's all right
And I'll hold on to you with all my might.

I ache inside to feel your very presence
I want to feel you very essence,
Why do I feel so much torture and pain
It's when we're finally together, it will all be gain.

Waiting seems to be the hardest part
Because you are the only one holding my heart,
Let's get away from life's heavy trials
Consuming each other for a many a miles.

Knowing with you, I will survive
You make me feel so much more alive,
When you're gone, I count each passing minute
Because of my very existence, you are in it.

Christopher S. Armes

Who Are You

Who are you, I know you.
From the moment you walked into the room,
I saw your face and looked into your eyes,
I recognized in them, a soul I have known before.
My heart sang with joy, when first, we kissed,
To the depths of my being, did my love soar
With our first union.

Who are you, I know you.
They say real love knows no boundary of time,
This must be true, for I feel as though I have
Loved you before through many lifetimes.
I know I love you now, as much as I did then,
And will forever and always, for soul mates are we,
There is no ending to our love.
Who are you,
I know who you are.

Tracey Daly

The Sailor

Oh, see what you've done to this fair Irish lady?
A sailor you are and a man you've become
Confident leader of seafaring traders
Forgetting the past with a gallon of rum
Shipping from island to island by ocean
Warring with pirates and thieves all the same
Learning the wrath and the trials of the sailor
Round and about is the way of the game
A young Irish lad and the bride he abandoned
He left the young girl to live on the land
She would have sailed for a year or a hundred
I reckon she'd linger on every command
Return yourself to her and keep her forever
The waves will be waiting if marriage has failed
Yet one should know that a sailor belongs there
He won't go home 'til the last ship is sailed

Alexandra Brooke

Why

The sullen rain, falling down,
A small child with a tear and a frown,
Big brown eyes, looking up to the sky,
The only question on his mind is why.
They took his mother, and father, too,
And now this small child doesn't know what to do.
Where will he stay; who will he love?
The rain just keeps falling from up above.
It's the tears of the angels, as they cry.
For this frightened little child doesn't know why.
His Mommy and Daddy would want him to be brave,
As he looks at them for the last time, lying in their grave.
He knows they'll always be with him, though buried under stone,
But now this small child is all alone.
With big brown eyes, looking to the sky,
The only thing he doesn't know is why.

Kelly Marron

If Only You Were Here

So many pages in the book of life have now turned.
So many times in my walk of strife have I yearned
To have you on my side in life and teach me what you learned.
If only you were here. If only I were there.

The many things I've so patiently waited to tell you.
The many things I've so anxiously waited to show you.
The many questions I've forever waited to ask you.
If only you were here. If only I were there.

To see everyone and how they are so different.
To feel everything and express your wonderment.
To touch everyone with your magical enchantment.
If only you were here. If only I were there.

I would often write to you when I was just a child.
Whether it was a card or a note, it somehow always made you smile.
So I write to you now, even though we're separated
  by more than a mile.
If only you were here. If only I were there.

Tawnie L. Mayer

One Song

To my deceased father, Johnnie Luna
What if we all sing one song of love?
Would everything look good from above?
What if we all sing one song of peace?
Would all violence cease?
What if one song would make all our troubles cease?
Would my father still be deceased?

What would this one hymn do to the world?
Would everyone know world peace?
What would one theme do for us?
Would it make the world come to a hush?

Could the people of the world all have one hope?
Could there be any more ropes?
Could we all share one dream?
Without the dirty schemes?

What would tomorrow bring if we all sing one song?

Jill Luna

Season Thoughts

To my entire supportive family
The days are longer each day I arise.
The flowers are blooming, I see through these eyes.
The trees are stretching high to the sky,
As days get warmer, each that go by.
The seasons are different in each of their ways;
The colors of change make way for new days.
The weather does the drastic extreme.
Like the frozen water melts, gurgles the stream,
The land that was blanketed so white and so pure
Melts away, leaving new shoots of life there.
So the sun rises higher each day,
Warming the earth, changing its way.
So winter, it goes; spring, it begins.
The summer gets hot so we look for the rains.
And fall will return as colors, they change.
The leaves will fall all over again.

Lois A. Cicairos

Heavenly Lights

To my mother, Ruth N. Streetman, with love
Oh, Lord! We are like a shooting star!
We are on a journey through Your heavenly lights,
getting closer and closer to where you are.
Not for worldly profit or fame, but for our
love for You and Your Son's Holy name.
Your Word, Your Love, Your Spirit are our light.
Every time we come close to them, they are
a guide to our souls and we are confirmed
that our directions are right.
Like beacons they shine along life's stormy way
and the lights, if we follow them, will lead us
to you, forever to stay

Robert O. Streetman

To My Mom

Who's always been there for me.
Who's always cared for me, always loved me.
When times were hard, you're there to comfort and protect.
You've always loved me for who I was and nothing less.
Though I've done so much wrong and caused you so much pain.
You stand by my side. I can't tell you how much I love you,
Because it wouldn't be right. For I love you more.

Momma, you're so special to me, you're all I really got,
then again you're all I really want. To my mom.

Though we are only human, to me you perform miracles,
you're there for me, Zachary, and James.
Literally holding a family together.
Everyone fails to realize that without you, there would be nothing.
You've helped me grow and helped me know.
We've had our good times, and our bad times;
they all sit in my memories in bliss.
If I could only go back, I'd be the greatest son,
the greatest mother ever had.
Despite the things I've done you still see me as such.
Momma, I love you more than all the world.

    Chad Farris

Elegy of a Rose

The rose doth bend down this day
In her garden, so forlorn.
For a storm hath left her leaves in disarray
And her beautiful petals torn.

The rose doth bend down this day,
And silently she mourns,
For the one who nurtured her in the sun's warm rays
Hath gone and will ne'er return.

Oh, the rose doth bend down this day.
Her scented tears fall to the earthen floor,
And those tears they flow in vain, do they
For the one who will toil there no more.

Oh, the rose this day doth downward bend
In mourning, beneath the skies of gray.
For the angels came on the morning wind
And led thee
Gently
Away.

    Melanie Crane

Dream Apparition

In came an invasion of my sight.
So weak am I.
Slowly.
Weaker.
The sight of him,
Him,
Him—so real and breathing and whole.
His elusive structure, encompassed by
Generously textured skin, bent before me.
His head was within my reach, only looking
So soft, so warm, so vulnerable.
He was strong, full, and complete.
I struggled so passionately not to comfort him,
Not to touch him.
Then my mind's eye noticed the all-knowing,
Mechanical eye of "Big Brother," hung abruptly
On the wall, which stopped me,
Forcing me into a rationale of reality.
I turned, and he disappeared instantaneously.
He was a dream apparition of mine, many moons ago.

    Jean Antinarelli

The Tune Up

To my loving husband and grandpa, George Elfond
A rusty wheel, an old frame,
Worn out seat, broken chain,
No tires, horn not working,
Looking into his grandfathers eyes,
The little one, trustingly, said
"Grandpa, can you fix it?"
Grandpa's warm, tender eyes,
Studied the frame and worn out parts,
"'Tis worth it," he said, finally
Then with sure, but old and wrinkled hands,
He painstakingly began his work
From a broken old pile of junk
Stood a proud replica of an old time bike.
"Grandpa, Grandpa," called the grandson
"You fixed it, you fixed it, it looks like"
Something in the old times movies
"Only better, 'cause you fixed it!"
Those words made the struggle worthwhile.

    Virginia Elfond

Somebody's Grandpa

I watched him from my window, taking his daily walk
And once from my garden, we did exchange some talk
He said he came to visit, but the spends his time alone
I suspect he has a family, security, and loving home,
Some questions gave way to answers, some seemed to drift away
One thing I know, he's lonely; we could meet another day.
Yes he's somebody's grandpa and ninety years old.
Enjoys telling stories, many yet to be told,
He has held many a child in the years that passed on by
His lap became their throne, words of comfort soothed their cry.
He became their grandpa, his ways were warm and kind,
Each child loved him dearly, for grandpas were hard to find.
He says he lost some weight from what we used to be,
But he walks steady with a walker, a delight to see.
Just to hear him talk brings a sparkle to one's eyes,
From a heart of compassion, he's strengthened many ties.
Life's travels have not aged him, his mind remains strong
He loves everything around him, remembers those that are gone.
On he's somebodies grandpa, could be yours or mine,
Only love and faith have kept him, God's gift from another time.

    Elsie M. Westrick

Time beneath the Sands

Our bodies are held here in time and space,
To what we call the human race.
But my spirit soars outside of me,
And dreams of who I want to be.
For you may not understand
What has gone beneath the sands,
For time is but a fragment of the whole of outer space,
And we must accept the fact we are among the human race.
For, oh! Those threads, those threads that hold our fragile fate,
For here we hold the keys to change our altered state.
Oh! Bonds of time now do not blind me with your clouded views,
For I do not wish to say or do the things that you do.
For he holds his silver blade as sharp as a razor's edge,
As we walk upon this, our fragile ledge.
But I cannot stay beneath these bonds, no!
For time has called for me.
For I must stretch beyond my limits and allow my spirit to be freed.
Oh! Bonds of time, now do not blind thyself with thy clouded views,
For it is you who must decide now! For it is your turn to choose!

    Diane Doris Schmiege

Lunarcy

To amuse the newest muse, my friend, Amy Hinz
Night washes over,
   a strange delightful dirge,
   an anonymous deluge for the despairing.
Music, moonlit muses
   tangling with strings of memories,
   strumming spells tinged with mystery
   that rise and fall to the rhythm
   of slowly breathing river fog.

Their sorcery swirls
   wrapping woven intricacies,
   detailed intimacies of a lover gone mad.
Solitary ravishings to sanity
   invite these lunar seductions
   that penetrate time's shifting, shallow veil,
   diluting present realities revealed
   as proof to the distillation of will.

    Keith E. Nobles

To Season

Wild onions scented sunshine
Pepper in the nose
A welcome perfume in June
As ladybugs lit
On the nascent Rose of Sharon.

A red-winged blackbird found contentment in his field.
The lanky heron searched.
Water would lead to delicacies:
Crawfish and tadpoles
Sacrificing their innocence.

Marsh, field, and stream
Riverbank celebrate summer's metamorphosis
Stalwart passengers of the planet
Benchmarks
Statuary in mud and thatch
Fertile home to spice
Islands in the mind.

    Michele Pinet

Serenity

Noble sun peers in and touches my heart
With colors of pink and blue and green
Fluttering out from unlit corners
Drifting to the melody of a carousel
Elegant crystal displays her masterly art

Engulfing me with memories of you
Lying tenderly beside me
Fingertips pulse to the rhythm
Dancing on delicate nooks inside my arm
Music of your voice soothing without trepidation
Intimate euphoria in the peace we share

Quietly the corners of my mouth
Turn slightly upward, my lips
Part and are moist because
You are on my mind
Held in anticipation
Of when we next touch

    Jennifer Singleton

The Perfect Woman

Through his eyes, I wonder how he sees me.
Does he see me as I really am
or does he see a perfect woman?
That, I could never be.
My heart sees him as he is and I wonder
if his heart is like mine
or is his heart afraid to love
the perfect woman I will never be?

    Tammy Flanigan

Blessed Assurance

Up each winding pathway
Past each corridor of life.
Rest assured God's watching.
He stands—By your side.

Changing minds, points of view
He gives you Rest when each day's through.
The Glory in each Blessed Day—
Through rain or shine the path's the same.

His Spirit Renews you all day long.
Comforts you when things go wrong.
Shapes you for the things you do.
Assists the life that God renews.

Don't give way when life is tough.
Lean on God—He'll show the way.
Each day is known, its number too.
The Throne awaits each heart that's true.

    Verna Emerson

The Old Man

I saw an old man walking down the road;
His back was humped and his feet were slow.

My friend, I said, where are you bound?
I'm headed for a city not made by man.

A city where there is no night,
Where everything is beautiful and bright.

We won't have to worry about anything,
For everything has been taken care of, in his name.

I stood there with my head bowed low.
Tell me, sir, I do not know
How to get to Heaven's city fair,
Where everything is beyond compare.

The old man looked at me through tear-stained eyes.
Look to the middle man on the cross.
He's the one that paid the cost.

    Edith F. Gosnell

Since You've Been Gone

In memory of my loving husband, Leroy Poindexter
Since you've been gone
The days are lonely
The nights are so long
It seems as though the morning will never come
The telephone doesn't ever ring.
And now the birds don't even sing
Your friends don't come by anymore
No one ever knocks at the door
We miss you walking across the floor
The house is as quiet as can be
There's no one home most of the time but me
No one to tell me good morning or good night
No one to say don't worry everything is all right
No one to talk to when I am lonely or blue
No one to smile at me and say I love you
No one to greet me when I come home
Oh, how I've missed you since you've been gone.

    Ophelia Poindexter

Alone

He's an old man that's lonely
for he loved himself only
sits in his room night after night
wonders what happened with his life
nobody sees or cares why he cries
always running, deceit and those lies
old woman cries night after night
remembers the love she lost with no fight
tired of giving and trying, wasn't right
at least she loved and lived
maybe he tried but had nothing to give

    Sandra Zang

Tempt Not Thy God

The rich man moved West and bragged as he went,
"I build where I want and what I desire!"
He lost his grand California home when God sent him
earthquakes with mud slides and fire.

"So I lost a house—that's nothing!" said he.
"I'll move to Tampa. That's using my brain!"
But his mansion was blown far out to sea
When God sent him His wildest hurricane.

He built a new place, an Iowa farm.
His cattle and pigs were buried in mud.
His crops were all drowned, his barns washed away
When God showed His strength with one mighty flood.

He stood in the rain by his Northern lodge
And bragged, "To me, here's nothing frightening.
No hurricanes, floods, nor earthquakes with fires."
He was struck down by one bolt of lightning.

Yvonne M. Visnaw

Midnight

From the dream, the nightmare waits
Pulling the sleeper inside these gates
Where sound is distorted by wind and trees
Freezing the dreamer down to his knees
Frozen there among the stones
Only scant feet from the bones
The bones that could tell, but don't
The meaning of the dream, but won't
Or of the path of escape
Back safely to sanity's gate
For the nightmare rules this place and hour
From behind the stones, the dreamer can only cower
And wait and pray for light's relief
To take him from the darkly grief
Until that final dream of the reaper
When fate leaves the eternal sleeper
Where the nightmare is no longer found
Beneath the stone that marks the ground

Mark Neel

Night Skies

The gentle tapping of rain on the street
makes the darkness of night feel gentle and sweet.
As the wind rustles leaves while
we keep, and the night noises
rock you gently to sleep, and fireflies
flash sparks in the night,
all is quiet at the sight.
After the rain, the sky gets a glow,
as thousands of stars light up for show.
The moon, looking bright on a
fresh-groomed night, throws shadows
around and out of sight.
And in the center square, the
clock is striking twelve o'clock
for peace everywhere.
Oh, beautiful night, star-studded
night, with wind blowing slow, keep
us safe till the Lord makes his show.

Alola J. Reuter

Without You

Have you ever heard the lonesome sound
of a coyote's cry?

Have you ever seen a single star
that shines in a cloudy sky?

It's an elderly man who sits all alone,
alone in his rocking chair.

I know it's the feeling that I will have
when you are so longer.

Anthony Tingelstad

Seed of an Oak Tree

I'm a seed, watered and free
To bloom as a leaf on the branch of a big oak tree.
Here comes the lumberjack to cut me down.
I look in the sky, so beautiful you see.
I say, "Lord, please help me."
He says, "Hold on, my mighty tree.
When they cut you down,
Your wood will be used for purposes of many,
But your mighty soul shall dwell with me for all to see . . .
The seed of a tree."

Gregory Wilson

You Just Stand

When you cannot find money for church tithing
When you have been talked about lied on, cheated, misused
When you have been called everything
but a "child" of God you just stand
Sticks and stones may break your bones
but words will not hurt you
But you just stand when you cannot find words
To carry you through you just stand

Stand for holiness
Stand on God's words
Just ask Him
He will see you through

Sylvia L. Wilborns

The Crossroad of Life

Standing and watching at the crossroad,
I try not to fantasize;
I look and wonder, how many have crossed here?
This is not a new route to my surprise.

The road I choose determines many things;
Only I am given the choice to see,
Positives and negatives of this world;
And what I may turn out to be.

Which road should I take?
Should I cross here or should I cross there,
In life there are not any signs, posted;
Saying traveler you better beware.

We have only been given directions;
In a book teaching us what is right,
Ten commandments were given on a mountain top;
Only for justice you still have to fight.

So I'll stand and watch at the crossroad;
There are so many vices to adhere,
When you get to your crossroad in life, remember;
To please travel with God not fear.

Raymond C. Christian

Unwanted Excuse

What will I tell her?
How will I tell her?
She's so young, so pure.
I can't tell her.
But later on she'll want to know.
Then what?
What will I say when she asks?
When she asks.
I'll tell her.
Then I'll hear her deny it.
She'll call me a liar and begin to cry.
I'll hear her scream from inside her room.
It's my duty to tell her.
And when it happens, I'll be ready.
Ready to tell her everything.
Beginning with why her father did it.

Hannah Miller

A Special Child

A special child was born today,
So perfect and precious in every way.

The miracle of birth is hard to perceive.
Can you comprehend? Can you believe?

A man, a woman, a family now three,
The blessing of life has created a "We."

How quickly life changes just overnight;
Little fingers now hold yours so tight.

Hold him close, now quietly speak,
And touch his smooth, rosy cheek.

Softly sing and hear the new sounds;
A tiny heart now beats and resounds.

Take a minute to smile and to share,
Accept the joy from all who care.

Yes, this special child that you now hold
Is yours forever, to love and to mold.

Jan Eckmann

Special Stray

I hadn't been home a minute or two.
You and the crew were nowhere in view.
You had been winning me over in your own special way
and we looked forward to seeing each other each day.

You had been adopting me slowly, one day at a time.
Your trust was growing; you thought I was kind.
As I again looked to check on the crew,
I couldn't believe what I saw was you!

I rushed to your side as you lay in the street,
cried uncontrollably as I got to my feet.
The breeze couldn't dry the tears on my face.
Oh, how I'll cherish our last embrace.

We each handle grief in our own special way—
some of us cry and some of us pray.
I don't know how to handle my grief,
for crying and praying bring no relief.

I am the only soul on Earth who knew your ways,
could pet your coat, and give you praise.
Now no longer part of the crew,
I pray God wanted a kitten—you!

Ronald "Tosie" Ragan

Why Must I Fight?

Oh, how lonely my heart can be
When my sweetheart's away from me.
But though this is true,
I have no reason to be blue.

I joined the Corps,
To fight in a war.
To Vietnam I went
And, there, a year I spent.

Hardships were far from being few,
But we faced them, because we knew
That if we fought in this war-torn hell,
People at home would live peaceful and well.

But while men are dying,
And, back home, wives are crying,
I know to the world we're showing
That even through hell, we'll keep going.

We'll keep on going, into the jaws of death,
On through the mouth of hell,
Till one thing on Earth is left:
Peace to all and freedom, as well.

Andrew Boyko

Cut Glass Frames

Cut glass frames
the garden of wildflowers,
the brilliant array of color
all placed in its spot in nature's perfect way.
A forest of green encircles it.
A meadow of loveliness
placed in a hidden area
of danger just ahead of it,
a select few may view
its loveliness in all its glory.

Many a path will lead astray;
only its wrath will be in the way.

Sonja Ann Zofrea

A Woman's Point of View

You may caress me in your arms with delicate ease;
But why am I always down begging on my knees?

To you, it may seem you are my only protection;
But you aren't the only man supplying sweet care and affection.

You touch and you hold me while playing with my mind;
And when you get closer, my feelings unwind.

You use me, abuse me, you hurt and misuse me;
But deep down inside, you don't want to lose me.

I'm sick and I'm tired of being mistreated;
I want to go where I know I am needed.

With me, you acted so mean and so cruel;
Figuring I was for sure living under your rule.

Hey baby, let me tell you that ain't cool.
I ain't nobody's flunky and nobody's fool.

Now while realizing you've lost a good thing;
The love I gave to you, never again will I ever bring.

Oh love, I prayed for memories that we'd both gladly treasure;
For now they're just traces of a dream; gone always and forever.

Pamela Faye Yancey

I Ask of Thee

These things I ask of Thee:
Give me grace to show courage in the face of fear
The presence of mind to remain calm while walls of security
Are tore down around me.
Give me faith to be true to the inner voice of consequence
For my actions, my thoughts, my deeds.
Give me strength to walk forward instead of turning back
The presence of heart to respond to a situation in need.
Give me Your wisdom to choose my battles carefully
With humility and fortitude,
The humanity to face fear fairly and not flaunt victory
And fight the good fight 'til it's done.

Debra Yergen

Stardust

Like bright fires burning deep in the cosmic blackness,
Galaxies glittering and glowing,
Ageless mystery forever destined
To be beyond our knowing,
The wonder of the night sky
Lured me from afar.
Enthralled, I lingered, that I might see
The splendor of the dawn.
I scaled the lofty peaks of Earth
That I might touch a star,
But when it turned to dust within my outstretched hand,
I knew
It was the realm of God
I had encroached upon!

Phyllis Burchfield Fulton

With

You with hazel eyes, that captivates my mind
You with silken lips, that caress mine two so kind
You with velvet hands, that thrill my every nerve
You with milky breasts, that lean with perfect curve
You with gentle laugh, that's music to my ears
You with pretty smile, that chase away my fears
You with raven hair, that frames your pretty face
You with open arms, that held our deep embrace
You with passion soul, that flames a burning heart
You with someone else, mere that keeps us apart

Michael R. Lee

Old Age

'Tis a saddened time in life,
when old one does become,
from his home he must move on
until he does succumb.

Hearing is getting difficult.
Seeing not quite as far, but
there is always someone around
who tells you where you are.

This time in life we must all accept
until God calls us home.
We must remember to be thankful
we are not left alone.

There are so many things to be thankful for,
many activities are planned.
We can enjoy all of these
and do as many as we can.

Remember your Creator;
He never leaves you alone.
Even in the darkest hours,
He still calls you His own.

Norma M. Dubinsky

Symphony of Wonder

Tear-filled eyes, shivers rippling
music exquisite, beautifully enchanting
masterful, teen musicians extraordinaire
focused passion, harmonic fanfares

River of life pulsing to the tempo
weaving through each other, flowing so gentle
audience moved, crying with emotion
beautiful music, sensitive teens, dedicated devotion

Sue Nosker

Nostalgia

A sandy beach that I walked upon,
Where the waves came in from the emerald sea,
And a mother, who planted daffodils,
Still live today in my memory.
When the sun is warm, in the early June,
With hydrangeas and iris all in bloom,
It calls to mind the home of my youth,
And the vine by the back door, with sweet perfume.
Today, I miss those days of old,
And that sandy beach, where I walk no more;
But in my yard, purple iris bloom,
While my mother grows daffodils on Heaven's shore.
As I've grown mature through experience,
And I've traveled the miles on this planet Earth,
Some things stand out in mind today,
Those things that really have great worth.
My mother's faith in the word of God
Has abided in me for these many years;
It comforts me when I'm feeling sad,
And delivers me from all my fears.

Jewell Clark

Enigma

The stork brings its burden of life
purpose pursued a meaning sought after
Misunderstanding.   Dragon's fire destroys
A friendship of life obliterated
tears fall to soak the ground as cold eyes stare

The ladder is climbed the golden ring snatched
innocence lost, victory rings hollow
A junkie weeps his compass lie broken
Death wears a smile as happiness laments
pestilence walks the land and you know its face

Romance, laughter, joy, loathing, mistrust, rage . . .
Truth can be found in the bloom of a rose

Craig Toczko

Who Is This Man Called Jesus?

Who is this man called Jesus?
Does He have any part in your life?
Who is this man called Jesus?
He banishes all pain and strife.
Who is this man called Jesus?
Wonderful counselor and friend.
Who is this man called Jesus?
Lord of all mankind is He,
Giver of so great salvation—salvation full and free.
'Tis always so sweet to kneel at His feet;
These old earthly cares we bring.
Through it all, trials great and small,
Ever giving thanks and praise to God, our King,
Surrendering to Him your life
Because He paid the supreme sacrifice.
Whatever your need, He will supply.
As you open your heart, He draweth nigh.
When you've given your very best,
Through fiery trials you passed the test,
Then you will know just who Jesus is.

Norma L. Daughtry

Rule of Life

When life is up against the wall
When troubles get you down
When nothing goes right

Something is always there to pull you through
Whether it's the love of your family
Or your faith in the Lord

'Cause nothing is out of reach
Nothing is too hard
Nothing can't be solved

'Cause love is the answer
God is the key
To all your hopes and dreams

Shannon Becker

Stardust

Have you ever experienced passion?
True romance?
Ever felt love? A love that manipulates your senses
Like that first lick of ice cream?
It feels heavenly and too-good-to-be-true.
It makes you unable to sleep
And causes your heart to soar.
Have you ever experienced a night
That was absolutely perfect,
So full of magic that the stardust never fully wore off?

These moments that go by so quickly
Make life even more exciting and worthwhile.
No matter how much you wish for these moments to last forever,
They never will.
They disappear when the time is up,
Yet the stardust lasts forever.

Selina Bennett

The Guardian

Old man, I warn thee:
Beware of dark demons frothing of death's stench.
Horned and plenty they come out of the trench.
Up, up, up, up from his hole,
They're sent by Hell to help harvest your soul!
Say you don't believe?
Now how can this be?
You didn't come here to worship,
But you bent your knees!
Precious few sands remain in the glass,
So I beseech you, and you must react
To love and accept him,
For your time has passed.

Larry Spencer

Winter 1967

The quiet hum of the tires on the clear, dry road.
The brilliance of the moonlight on the snow-covered fields.
The pale green of the dash lights reflecting softly inside the car.
The huddled bundle of a fluffy, yellow-gold coat
in the opposite corner of the front seat.
And the liquid, warm glow of cheerful, blue-grey eyes
peeping out from the yellow fluff that rings a familiar face.

The quiet conversation of "small talk" as the two—
one nervously, one smilingly—pass the time.
The sound of her gentle laugh as her soft voice
dispels the quiet of the night
and creates an all-consuming ache in his heart.

Alan H. Packard

Benefits of Pets

One's close association and love for a pet reduces stress
and strife and often adds to one's life.
While the selection of a pet is normally a dog
or a cat, similar benefits may be derived from a pet hog or rat.
Contrary to some human relations over time,
the love for one's pet does not fade away
and cease; instead, they bring on more joy and peace.
Pet's provide unconditional love that during lifetime
is there to stay and does not go away.
Pets are particularly beneficial to older adults,
since they provide companionship and stimulate healthful results.
In a study of a one-year survival rate of heart attack victims,
a pet ownership relation was found to be the most
significant indication.

Currently, both Canada and the United States are resorting
more to pet therapy to speed up and enhance human ailment recovery.
The pets, many of which routinely participate in pet therapy,
are taken to hospitals, nursing homes,
and other institutions, to enhance human ailment restitution.

Charles W. Morton

You're Gone

You're gone, and I'm left all alone
You're gone, and I'm here by the phone
I'm wondering where you can be
And just who you went to see
The nights seem so dreary and long
Come back—you were right, I was wrong
Here is where you ought to be
Here and near, close to me
I remember you at my side
And your voice, there's just no place to hide
I was wrong, you were right
And I died when you left me that night
I was wrong, I was wrong
Now you're gone, now you're gone, now you're gone
You're gone, you're gone, you're gone

Bert D. Dolerhie

Desert Sonata

To Sherry Heinlerling, friend, wife, God bless you
Your lips play delicious tricks with mine, parked
here in this wasteland, overlooking desert lights,
Phoenix bright, rising from ashes before our very
eyes, the perfume of your indulgence entices me
to further regrets, anticipating wilderness, I almost
forget that you are a girlfriend of mine, I don't think
you ever understood me, but we must have tried,
three years is a long while to lay with romance
and style, of changing hearts and minds, changing
climates and times, I will look at you from a
distance, a special reminder of youth gone by, this
desert sonata playing in my mind.

Brett A. Holloway

The Old Windmill

Beyond the river, beyond the seas
there lives a man who is eighty-three.
He lives on a farm along with his wife
and on this farm there is a windmill
that has been there all his life.

If you look beyond the mountains,
if you look beyond the fields,
you'll see the man who is eighty-three
who goes by the name of Shields.

The windmill was built when he was born
although it is now old and torn.
The man still lives on a farm with his wife
along with the windmill that has
been there all of his life.

Keara Monahan

Searching

The older I get, the more I begin to see
that life just repeats itself
over and over until eternity.
You find yourself in a place, in which
you never thought you would be
climbing and scratching against a wall
that seems so impenetrable and immovable
What is one to do?
When your back is up against a brick wall
and every place your turn
you only see a corner of that same wall.
I have asked myself this question so many times before
but still no answer has been revealed
but the one I already know,
And that is to depend on the Lord
so that he can see you through.
I have yet to understand the mystery of this life
but I will still look and search for the answer
until I can find my peace of mind that lies in mankind.

Victoria Jones

My Sweet Grandmaw

To my grandmother Beatrice Hill who taught love and compassion
My grandmaw would hold me on the cold and winter nights;
She soothed away my sorrows by the early morning light.
She loved to teach me all the things she held so dear;
And when all the world despised me it was she who really cared.

My grandmaw always told me about all the things she knew;
And I never heard her grumble though her luxuries were few.
Her hands were worn and calloused but so many were the times;
She would come and find me weeping and would slip a hand in mine.

My grandmaw, she would tuck me in my soft old single bed;
She would wrap me in the covers, place a pillow 'neath my head.
And her soul was sweet and gentle and her voice was soft and low;
How I wish that she could hold me as she did so long ago.

Rachael-Rebekah E. Purpel

Shelter

Closed in by walls of my own creation
I hear the voices of others around me
yet I cannot see the speaker

To them, I am invisible, hidden from view
and the world knows not of my existence
Soundlessly, my cries live on unanswered
and my prayers go unheeded

My unguarded eyes plead
for understanding and comfort
Still, no one reaches out to me,
no arms surround me, protect me

Drifting then, I wait in the shadows
hoping for, longing for
just a touch—
to bring me to shelter

Valerie Field

Written Love

All the words about and lovers
Ever written cover with litter
Our helpless globe. The garbage smothers
Every glowing coal of true feeling.

They would tell us, "Love is a snare.
Love is an action; love is a feeling.
Lovers see beauty everywhere.
Love turns night to day, Hell to Heaven."

Though the words I swallowed with a gulp,
Chewing carefully to aid digestion,
I did not recognize the pulp
As love, when at last love seized my soul.

No written word ever prepared me
For the unconquerable, trembling
Way I feel, powerful and weak-kneed,
Whenever your eyes look into mine.

Jessica Andelin

No More

I ain't gonna do nothin', nothin' no more
My boat has been a sailin' on a dried up old shore
I been pushing these old oars as hard as I can . . .
Only to end up on dry river's bend
So, put down the anchor
Ain't no place no more
A dried up riverbed and a dried up old shore
My boat ain't a-floatin' . . .
And there ain't no shore
My boat is deadlocked on a dried up old floor
So, put down the anchor
She will float no more
How can she go on with a dried up old shore . . . dry riverbed
No water no more . . .
So, put down the anchor, put down the oar
My feet are crusty, no water no more
Dried up river and a dried up shore
So, put down the anchor, put down the oar . . . what for?
Ain't no water left in this river no more

Carolyn S. Sax

God's Signature

With an array of color
It arches across the sky
Reminding us of a promise
That He will never again destroy the world
A beautiful rainbow
The signature of God's promise

Lisa Van Noord

A Melody Lost

The world goes much faster.
Our friends depart,
But that's the way things have been from the start.
Buildings get taller.
Computers get smaller.
For sure, I can't stop it; still I'd like to know—
Where, oh where, did our music go?
Why do scenes from the past seem somehow much better,
Like the girl at the dance the first time you met her,
Like the cheesecake at Lindy's after the show—
Where, oh where, did our music go?

There was Perry and Frank and Ella and Satchmo,
Memories, sweet memories—
Where did our music go?
My fervent hope when I leave this sphere
Is that I can say . . .
"Hey, my music's here!"

Ed Jordan

The Hidden Effect

Every word you mutter, everything you do
Even when the wall seems the only to care,
Chalk dust on your hands, emotions ringing true
You're on center stage so you need to be aware

That teenage eyes are focused on you
Judging each move you make
Learning first hand what to do
Knowing that you rarely make a mistake.

Teenage eyes are scrutinizing you
Searching for an ulterior motive
Checking a peer response or two
Building trust with each smile that you give.

Teenage eyes are pondering with you
Measuring how much they've grown
Hoping that someday they'll be just like you
Dreaming of a bright future of their own.

Joyce L. Griggs

Morning Dream

Early one morning as I lie in bed,
With the one I love there by my side.
I awake from a deep sleep
As she gently touches my arm,
Her fingers slowly caressing,
Tender, soft, and warm.

As reality reaches my mind
And my conscience comprehends the quietness,
I hear the sound of a mocking bird,
Singing out so beautiful, piercing the morning air.
Such a wonderful peace envelopes me
And it seems I can feel the sound I hear.

Like seeing the sound as rainbow colors
   it floods my mind, clear the bright.
This sound heard in Heaven, think I might.
Could I really describe the sound,
A beautiful bird singing, this wonderful feeling
Early one morning, deep in my mind?

Jimmy James Tatum

On Bended Knee

On bended knee, I come to thee.
In our love, only you can humble me.
Within our love, I have come to find the real me.
Only through your love has brought me strength and courage.
My love for thee shines for others to see.
For your spirit and love is what I hope, all will ever be!
Remember, only your love can break my heart.
Only you love can mend it.

Robert E. Shepherd

The Old Apple Tree

The old apple tree was there for me.
Of the many years I spent,
climbing and eating some of the fruits
were very sweet to me.

The days I came, I climbed your branches
to look for the ripest fruits,
but every one that I ever took was a delicious
juicy fruit.

I sat upon your branches and wondered, every time,
if you would yield those lovely fruits as you
did so many times.
"You do not have to worry, son.
I'll keep it fresh each year, especially for such
a lovely boy who has been to school each day."

Thank you, dear, sweet apple tree.
Your fruits were sweet and free.
For the many years I remember you,
you were always good to me.

Cleveland Fletcher

To You and Me

To Dawn, see what your love does to me!
In stillness, a warm, sheltering embrace,
when the moon glides past a starless face.
The wind whispers so gently,
as a quiet voice reaches me.

Of sorrows faced when all was lost,
and dreams were shattered beyond cost.
Of lonely roads and lonelier miles,
dark asphalt scattered through green miles.

Of forests stretching endlessly
too many to count, the eyes can't see
How start of tree meets end of grass,
just like this, all life must pass.

And so it whispered within my soul,
where few can reach, but One can go.
And He it is whose voice last heard,
in gentle tones, my mind did burn,

As He opened my heart so easily,
And in stepped one who's love filled me.
Then voices whispered, joyous and free!
Of the love God gave to you and me!

Raymond S. Bell

The Way To Go

Love to my three wives
Up or down
Swim or drown.
Walk and run
Both well done.
Promises keep
So people won't weep.
Speak the truth
From basement to roof
Always be clean
So you're fit to be seen
Walk real tall
Then you won't appear small
Love everyone as yourself
Put all your troubles on the shelf.
Accept nature and all its glory
Mornings will follow without a worry
Give God thanks for everything
Winter, fall, summer, and spring
Now you are ready for another new day
To tackle any troubles that might come your way.

George Mixell

I'm a Dreamer

Please know that I'm a dreamer, always thinking what could be.
This imperfect world casts shadows that light will never see.

Progress doesn't always have to be replacing the old with new.
Holding on to parts of the past
Can enrich the present as well as the future, too.

Instead of throwing the past away, why not fix it up, add touches?
We can change the whole meaning of progress if we steal it
Away from greed's clutches.

Our world will always be imperfect, casting shadows here and there.
Working to escape the shadows, we'll find others who dare.

Progress could mean adding values to abandoned goals,
Avoiding some shadows and lessening our tolls.

Fame or fortune doesn't have to be the definition of success.
Why not happiness and peace of mind, lasting rewards nonetheless?

Being a dreamer opens doors, but reality closes some, too.
Progress and success should be for all to reach
When one wants to stop and start anew.

Joan Wilson

Guide Us

Our shameless leaders lead in sin
Our country sinks in trials dim
With loathsome pride and idle prattle
We do not hear of death's dark rattle

We kill our babies ere they're born
And look on them in utter scorn
We have no conscience, it is plain
The world of pleasure our only pain

Dear Lord, you've seen the depths we've gone
You've seen the hurts we travel on
We look to thee to bring us through
We know Your love that makes us new

Our sin is on us night and day
And yet you love us when we stray
We have a faith, we know You care
Your love is with us everywhere

And now it's time to go with You
Our serving days are all too few
Your loving greeting we hear now
Dear Loving Lord, to Thee I bow

John W. Roach

Dreamer

An artist never rests, but even in repose
works, planning the next creation,
hoping to momentarily coax soul awareness
to remembrance.

On pigment-colored palette,
the painter's brush dances,
blending shades of hues
which take the breath away.

Mesmerized in melody,
the composer dares to feel inspired,
evoking emotions only imagined
to be long dead.

Deep into the night, the poet stares
for hours at a single line,
striving to transmute—through mere words—
the essence of love.

An artists never sleeps
but forever dreams, transcending
imaginary limitations, ascending
to the boundless realm of the soul.

Nila Dury

House

To my special and loving husband, Howard Short Jr.
The house that has no face . . .
If you go inside this house with no face,
It will swallow you up and spit you out.
The mouth of this house is dark and scary,
With long winding stairs and doors everywhere.
Where do I go?
What do I do?
Run or stay?
If I stay, the house will swallow me up;
If I leave, it will be angry with me.
So what do I do with the house with no face?
Should I stay or should I go?
Which door to open?
Which not?
"How much can I take from the house with no face?"

Nancy Carol Short

Death Is Dying

Death stares me in the face,
Growling its deep ferocious growl,
Asking me, begging me to try.
I stall, thinking
Life is good in a good life
But life is hated in a bad life.
Stalling, thinking.
Death over life?
Life over death.
I attack, grabbing death by the throat,
Fighting with more than I ever had in my life,
Strangling with all my strength,
Done.
Death is dying beside me.
I lay beside death, gasping for air.
Life over death.
Victory over death.

Karly Zoe Becker

See and Wait

For Nitza
A single glance from you not so long ago,
the new moon could not have seen
the several dancers of Yam Ha'melach.
Like a waxing, engorged Diana rising at dusk
pursued by a hungry, inflamed Aurora at dawn,
your visage, ever-remembered, grew and filled mind and heart.
Not to illumine my entire world but constantly
your nearness, magnetic buoy to the spirit,
now you are not here.
Diana is waning thin of late at night,
and fat Aurora hangs colorless today.
I try to hold the image.
The thought is the synaptic endorphonic.
Like a blind one, I wait for the sound telephonic
to reminds me to ask myself
Oh, when shall I see again a glance from you?

John C. Ohrenschall

My Dream

The other night I had a dream; it was as clear as day;
there were people all around, each finding their own way.
There were no children on the streets;
they were tucked safe in bed at home.
There were smiles on friendly faces, and no parents were alone.
As I went about my travels, much to my surprise,
I saw no tears of hunger, or fear in no one's eyes.
The world as we've known it no longer did exist;
the world's population, for peace and security did persist.
I did not see one person in my entire dream
who was intent on murder or aiming to demean.
I awoke feeling happy, and I pondered what it might mean
to live in a world as filled with love,
as the one I visited in my dream.

Cathy A. Bellah

Only You

I sit here, all alone,
And I think of you.
What can I do?
I can only watch and wait and pray.
They ask if you want a DNR,
If you want to live.
There is no answer.
Undying devotion from your children,
Your grandchildren, and your husband—
I hope it is enough to help you live on.
My Nana, all alone. I know you are scared.
Now there is silence,
And all I can do is think of you.

Kiralina Fix

My Heart

This is my heart, the sum of me.
Take it apart and what do you see?
An ode to the wind, a meadow, a bee,
A splashy sail on a choppy sea,
Thoughts about flowers, compassion for birds,
Silent and hushed poems without words.

This is my heart; it operates me.
Its vital parts let me continue to be.
It makes me alive, in complete locomotion.
It governs me and gives me emotion—
Emotion that sometimes strains at the core,
Causes distress, makes my being sore.

This is my heart; it generates love,
Enraptures my soul—a gift from above.
As sure as it beats and throbs in my chest,
God's in His Heaven. Believe! It's no jest.
A petal pops forth and the early spring
Scores deep in this heart, makes tinkling bells ring.

Marjorie Rateau Lanza

Take a Step

Take a step, as your feet touch the earth,
it is not time gone by,
but more like a cosmic bond, a new birth.

For, I am you, as you are me.
We are one heart and soul,
as we shall always be.

I will still hold you, even after I die,
for everything is connected,
the sun, the moon, the Earth, and the sky.

To you I will show love and much respect,
since we are one and the same.
As I take care of you, it is also myself I protect.

I hope you understand what I'm talking about—
of all things in this universe that are part of me
you're the one thing I cannot live without.

Dennis King

Alone

Illuminating the sky, the heavenly starlight
above looks into my inner being trying to
find a blaze like its own but, to its dismay,
finds nothing of the sort.
I myself cannot fathom its reasons for doing
something so like a lost person of its
own conscious, glare, and beauty.
"Why?" I ask, but only a deafening silence answers.
Pondering all that cannot even be imagined,
I sit here in the darkness letting my mind wander
along endless paths that only one who is alone can travel.

Samantha Willis

The Clay

You are the potter, we are the clay,
Shaping and molding, day after day.
Trials and triumphs strengthen and clean,
So someday we'll glow with that heavenly sheen.

Don't let us complain, Lord,
When things hurt too much.
You're turning the wheel
With Your Master touch.

And when things are going smooth,
Don't let us turn bland,
We'll need much more molding
From Your Potter's hand.

You know what is needed
To become what we must,
So in You, heavenly Father,
We are putting our trust.

We need to learn, Lord,
How to obey,
So You can make vessels
Out of this clay!

Sharon Ostrander

On the Wings of a Butterfly

To my loving mother, Adeline Harvis—I love you
I have given you life.
I have toiled to give you bread.
I have prayed to God to guide you through.
I have prepared you to be strong.
I have given you a gift to last forever (love).
My life was not an easy one,
But still I smiled,
And still I prayed.
You were my only child,
A child whom I've fed from my breast.
I have rocked you.
I have cuddled you.
I have loved you.
If I could, I would have given you the sun, moon, and stars.
Before I leave this Earth,
I'll say a prayer, I'll call your name.
I'll fly away, way up high above the sky.
I will return upon the wings of a butterfly.
Should you see a butterfly fluttering around,
It would be me, your mother, "On the Wings of a Butterfly."

Doris Gadpaille

Parents

They've been there since I was born,
They've fed me my peas and corn,
And even when my heart is torn,
They won't let me mourn.

They taught me to ride a bike,
Bought me a dog named Spike,
Given me two brothers whom I like,
They treated me well even as a bad little tike.

They've been with me through the rough,
They've helped make me tough,
Always told me I was "buff,"
And for this I cannot ever thank them enough.

They are there through good and bad,
Make me happy when I am sad,
Cool me down when I am mad,
I don't know where I'd be without Mom and Dad.

In closing, I'd like to say,
That they are the greatest pair today,
Without them, I'd never be okay,
They will always be a ray of sun on a cloudy day.

Daniel Nelson

What Is Love?

To my precious aunt, Nita Mullen
What is love? What is love?
I asked my Father, what is love?
And He said to me,
Look my child toward calvary.
He gave His life that I might live,
He promised His all He would give.
What is love? What is love?
I asked my Father what is love?
As I looked toward calvary and His redemption plan.
I said to my Father help me to understand.
Then He said to me it was His greatest sacrifice
As His son bore our sins at calvary and gave His life.
That was love. That was love. Sent from our Father above.
That was love. That was love.
And then he turned and looked at me
And I heard my Father say, My child . . .
Walk in love, walk in love, you must walk in love all of your days
You must love, you must love in all of your ways.
You must love, you must love.

Diana Rogers

Farewell to Ashely Dusten

To my loving wife and friend for life, Sue
Standing on the pier, I think back to the age of five
When our smiles first met. We were very much alive.

Looking at you now, or what's left in this vase,
Oh, Ashely, my dear friend, I see time end its chase.
Seems life is mostly vapor with a remainder so slight
To remind us of Earth's dearth without water, air, and light.

Is there not some cosmic scribe who records all goodness found,
Our shining moments, and joy shipped by light, waves, and sound?
One could only hope for a receiver so supreme.
Alas, the waves breaking on the shore awaken me from my dream.

'Twas your dying wish; you said, "No human landfill for me.
Let the body be burned. Return the remnant to the sea."

Leaning o'er the leeward rail, abetting the restless wind,
I upend the insensate urn and cast its contents in.
Watching as the watery tongues lap your residue up,
There's nothing left to see now. They've had their one more sup.

What fitting epitaph for you, my disinterred friend,
Can I engrave in air to mark your stone-less end?
Though some may feel I violate a friend's undying trust,
Yet voice it I must, 'Ashely to ashes. Dusten to dust.'

Ronald Sherrod

To Celebrate My Mother

To my angel—my mom—Juanita Lund
A mother is a special thing,
That nothing can replace.
Everything she does means so much,
In many different ways.
From gifts little or big.
A mother always gives anything she can.
She's always there to listen.
She's always there to care.
A mother is an angel sent by God.
To guide her child to be the best that they can be.
To bring out their potential.
To teach them to explore.
To show them there are many wonders,
Behind each and every door.
We should celebrate each and every day,
The angel that is our mother,
There to guide our way.
When I was born I was truly blessed;
I was given to you.

Trish Lund

Confused Weather

To the creator, my true father and mother
Mother Earth is getting so old
Yet, she continues to rebirth . . . so I am told
Her weather unpredictable, a woman
In her changes
Her weather is extreme
In the scales and ranges
The wind, the rain, the heat, and the cold
Where it once was . . . differently unfolds
People uprooting to new, safer locations
Chancing the new with some reservation?
You cannot run from the earthly, climatic upsets
Hide and flee to where you won't fret?
Weathering is a part of everyday living
Make peace with yourselves
Learn the pattern of receiving and giving
When all is in balance in the areas of love
Weathered perfection will bless you
From the within and above
    Marguerite Baldasaro

Those Who Can, Teach

Writers can teach and teachers can write,
But who is to say the other is slight?

Some can do one, while others, still both.
But, who here among us can honestly gloat

That of all the passersby, both women and men,
Not one of them left a word inscribed without pen?

Who tilled and who seeded in hopes it just might
Help the toil to yield its strength before the world's blight

Could have a chance at choking off those precious few germs
That without care would fall away, sustenance for worms.

Bridging gaps and paving roads that most of us walk,
Could it be true some things we learn need not come through chalk?

I tell you, Sir, Miss, Madam, Dear, you really should come to know
A book will never say, "Very good!" or recognize the glow

Of a fire burning deep in mind, a heart, and in a soul
That with a little care and fanning can burn much longer than coal.

So, now I'll tell all you doubting-Toms, whose hands must be shown,
That books alone surely can't suffice: What grows must be grown.
    James W. Post

What I'll Forever Miss

If only I could submerge the sun
Into the dark and deepest oceans
Just bring the stars and Moon to Earth
All and further more I wish I could
To find the love I lost I would
Just walk over the seas and fly up yonder
To build on the farthest star a berth
Where I could moor our ship away from Earth.
There are outside a thousand raindrops dancing
And in my mind there were a million thoughts pounding my head
Just like those raindrops that were drenching the soil
So were the rolling down tears showering my soul
Bring back I beg that smile that made my life before
Now that my broken heart despise feeling its cool.
You said you just didn't want to hurt my feelings
How could that be when long ago you left them ailing
Like in a cool dark alley so merciless for them to die
Please bring the sunshine back into my life I beg of you
Now that my world is crumbling and my heart's hurting for you
I will forever miss so saddened those times
    Dake Munoz

Mama

To my loving mom, Christie Eargle
All of my life—you have been here.
When needed you're always full of love and care.
Your love is always here for me.
It costs not a thing—yes, it is free.

As I sit here I realize life's not just fun,
But bad times pass by and are done.
And because of you I can see
That I can be anything I want to be.

You help me with school, piano, and dance.
Without you I wouldn't have a chance—
Of being successful at anything,
So thanks for all the gifts you help bring.

You are so very, very special to me.
And this I hope for you is easy to see!
    Lizzi Eargle

The Day

The day I took the time to notice the world,
I took the time to remember the little girl,
The one with the ponytails and dirt on her face,
The one in the memories that I try to misplace.

When I looked into the porcelain veil,
I could remember the mask that I displayed well.
I could remember the sights that I saw long ago,
And I could remember the feelings I tried not to show.

When I sat beside that long-forgotten stream,
I remember the dream that I often did dream.
I thought he was my loving embrace,
But in teenage innocence, I took a fall from grace.

As I sit under this tree with unending shade,
I remember the mistake that I almost made.
I remember looking down the dark tunnel
    that almost ruptured my world.
I stopped when something in my mind softly purled.

I don't understand why I am here.
Little happiness shines through my tears.
A smile on my face hides inside my shadow.
To myself I never want to go.
    Kimberly Schriver

My Darling

My Darling,
We haven't known each other for very long,
But I feel a bond between us.

I love to be near you, to smell you, to feel your touch.
The day you came into my life was a blessing.

Without you, I feel like a part of me is missing;
I miss your smile, and the way you look at me.
I miss our little "chats" about everything, and nothing.
Did you know?

I want to share my dreams with you, and I want to know yours.
I want you to understand my passions, and calm my fears.

I want you to be proud of my achievements,
Knowing that you believe in me helps me strive harder to
Reach my goals.

I want you to know who I am when I'm alone.
Did you know?

There is so much that I want to say to you,
But I am Afraid.
"Some things are better left unsaid", they say.
Did you know . . . That I love you?
    Lisa A. Gerstenberger

Wake Up, America

In memory of husband, James Penn
We are living in a world of turmoil and strife.
Some may say that's life, but if we let everything go,
Nothing will come out right.

America, wake up!
Do not let the Dream that became reality die.
It took so long to get where we are.

Life is not a joy ride.
It's also not about having to choose sides.
It's a new day, and a few individuals do not have it their way.

Let's all come together.
Destroy hate; embrace love as we walk side by side,
Trusting in the One above.

The Dreamer is gone,
But the Dream shall live on.
    Odella Jones Penn

My Beloved

I would not trade the happiness of loving you
To escape the pain of loosing you

Nor shall I allow this dark time
To cast its shadow on memories of yesterday's sunlight

For in time the darkness will fade
And morning will come again.

Until then, I shall hold to the dream . . .
That someday we will be together again
    Diane Helferich

Two Hearts, One Vow

To Lori King, the love of my life, my trouble
Destiny has brought two hearts finally together . . .
together to be as one for all eternity . . .
for till to the end they always will be as one.
Two hearts, who first when they met . . . were friends . . .
but now to be lovers.
They will now bring together their souls and their lives . . .
to commit to each other the love they have.
Together now . . . they must swear a solemn vow to one
another . . . that no matter the pains and sorrows that may arise,
that love will never leave or be destroyed,
because the true love that's from within, will always be there.
So now as these two hands hold each other . . . just as
they hold each others' hearts . . . they will be joined in an
everlasting partnership, which will always be and never to end.
To honor . . . to cherish you . . . to love and to obey,
this I will promise and vow to keep . . . as long as we live.
To you, my everlasting love.
    Anthony Taitano

Teddy Bear's Plea

In memory of my granddaughter, Jody C. Patterson
There was a Teddy Bear in a corner bedroom floor,
all alone and, oh, so sad of a life he once had,
with a little girl that is no more.
She cuddled him at night and loved him all the time.
Never will they be together again, he looked across the room,
the empty bed, tears rolled down his fuzzy cheeks,
a lump formed in his throat.
She was sick, there is nothing left,
his friend is no more.
Why the Lord did not let Teddy Bears walk or talk,
the things that they could tell.

He knows what is next, perhaps a box, an attic floor,
where he will be collecting dust, just thrown aside,
with no one left to love.
    Isabell G. Rossa

Until Then

To my best friend, Joe Pennington
In looking back across the years
I dream a thousand dreams
In retrospect, the flow of tears
is erased, or so it seems

A flow of tears that served to
cleanse all hurt, and pain, and sorrow
. . . and in return brought
back to life the joy of each tomorrow

A joy which was to free the heart
of each life that is traced
as if by sunshine, rain, sleet, and snow
with strength the life was braced.

Fortified to look ahead with vision
energy, and might . . .
renewed in spirit to surge
on, toward a guiding light
. . . a light that grows brighter each and everyday,
a Beacon that directs us all along the way . . . and until then—
    Suzy Williams

Artichoke

To my special sixth grade English teacher, Mrs. Nieh
In fields of happiness, beauty, and life,
My friends and I used to live.
Every day, our master used to water us.
Ah, what a cool, refreshing feeling.

An enormous truck entered the fields of joy
And took us all away in our sadness.

As we enter the store, we feel sad and lonely
as we are separated.

Our gorgeous layers of green leaves
show off our beauty.

Showers of water pour down on me,
like an ocean wave ready to crash.

As I roll down the fast moving conveyer belt
I am happy and scared at the same time,
for as I make a wonderful family happy,
I am losing my own life.

Picking my leaves
as if I am a dead tree,
stirred in a huge pot
and put to my own death. . . .
    Elizabeth M. Magner

From Daddy's Girl

To Reverend Charles Joseph Britt
As far as I know, you never held me in your arms
Or told me that you loved me.
You never brought me a birthday card or a Christmas present.
You weren't there to comfort me when my second-grade
May-Day Forget-Me-Not performance was rained-out.
You were not there when I was seven and the lightning bolt
Struck me and electrified my whole body.
You weren't there to protect me when Mrs. Todd would
Release her German Shepherd to chase me on my way to the store.
You weren't there to be proud of me when I was a keystone safety,
Played the flute, and sang in the glee club in elementary school.
You weren't there when I was a color guard,
Played the autoharp, and sang in the chorus in junior high.
You were not there to be proud of me when I was a majorette,
Played volleyball, sang in the choir and graduated high school.
No, Daddy,
You were not there in body because God had called you home.
But you were there in spirit, my special angel,
And I never felt alone.
I love you, Daddy.
    Maisha Dorrah Britt

Ah, Retirement

"How do you like retirement?" they ask.
Remember those years preparing?
Make wise investments now.
Where will we live?
What trips should we take?
What kind of volunteer work would I like to do?
Then, one day, it's here!
Well, it's not the Golden Years advertisers hype,
That's for sure.
There are problems—new problems,
Just like any other stage of life you've been through already.
With one difference:
You're lucky to have made it this far,
But this is the last stage of your life on this Earth.
That's sobering.
A new dimension to consider,
Don't waste it!
Use it wisely.
With imagination, patience, discipline, enthusiasm,
You'll finish the course.

Carol Paton McNitt

God Only Knows

Zachary is his name,
For God only knows his fame,
For God only knows why he came.
He's filled our hearts with joy and laughter.
He fills our lives with only running after.
Oh, but that doesn't matter,
For God only knows that
Zachary got in there, batter.

Judith Hartmann

Anything, Anything

Eyes like starlight,
glistening, glistening . . .
Ears like emptiness,
listening, listening . . .
Tears like the sky,
moistening, moistening . . .
Mind like loneliness,
poisoning, poisoning . . .
Dream like a symphony painted in pale blue.
Dream like a memory coming into view.
I like starlight,
glistening, glistening . . .
You like emptiness,
listening, listening . . .
They like the sky,
bringing back memories
of when they could see
anything, anything . . .

Stephen Wederski

A Puddle of Memories

A puddle of memories pooled at my feet.
The depths unknown, the bottom unreachable.
Silence has overcome his rhythmic beat,
Words left unspoken are now unspeakable.

There is nothing left to do, nothing left to see,
But to return to our lives and live in our memories.
What we see and what we hear now is from the past.
To the future we must look, for it comes and goes so fast.

Our daily lives are spied on by a watchful eye,
Guiding us through our petty decisions.
Watching from the soft pillows of the sky,
And offering advice with cutting incisions.

He will forever be with us, in our hearts and souls,
And shall be greatly missed by one and all.

Brian Messer

Verbally Superfluous

To Mrs. T., the quintessential teacher
Allegorically, metaphorically, free verse reigns
Most categorically.
Multi-syllables, in word-salad,
Deign to validate our
Self-appointed genius.

Once, pentameter iambic,
Idiom, disguised in limerick,
Paradigm for 'the old way,'
Caveats, so none will stray,
Critics dissect the impervious.

Wax rhetorical, wane grammatical,
Piques the id and strokes the ego.
Ephemeral attempts defy symmetrical.
Flagrant, participles dangling,
Nouns and adjectives, akimbo!

When verb and pronoun blend in concert.
Symphony (or worse) cacophony results
Rare indeed, albeit true, when
Simplicity and prose conjoin
And clarity ensues.

Maureen E. Opal

Alone

I fell off the bridge,
landing in the crashing sea.
I ran from my life,
the wall slamming me in the face.
I cried alone,
drowning myself in wet tears.
I looked for you,
seeing no one around me.
I lied to them,
leaving the truth behind.
I believed their words,
straining my thoughts and mind to the limit.
I screamed for help,
only my voice echoed loudly.
I dreamt in my sleep,
of never waking up again.
I tried to live,
but it was never enough.
I died that night,
did you even notice?

Debra Kruger

These Golden Years?

Those golden years have finally come,
And you wonder what that really means.
Who ever thought to give such a name
To those old years of such misery and pain?

You have false teeth that can't chew a steak
And eyeglasses that don't help you see.
Your hair has grown thin and turned to dull gray—
And you wonder whatever happened to me?

Your steps have grown feeble; you must watch every step
To make sure you don't end up on the floor.
You have to be careful and plan every move,
So you don't have more aches and pains to endure.

It seems that the best of these years are just
To eat soup and sit in a chair,
And if you can't get up by yourself
In time, there'll be somebody there,
To help you get up, and hand you your cane,
And rub your back with Ben Gay.
Now ain't that a pleasant thought to endure
And to help make the most of each day?

Ruth Detrick

True Love

What one fears the most, could also be
what the one wants the most of, a feeling so genuine and pure,
yet fierce and brutal as a lion, the feeling of love.
However, this cannot be tamed or captured in haste,
it is invisible to the hunter, and soon he will give up,
becoming the hunted, only to be caught by another.

Tripping the snare, and getting caught in a cage
of happiness and hurt, joy and pain, the hunter
seeing that this is not love, and letting one go, tears in the rain.
The hunter then learns true love cannot be tricked and caught,
and it can't be seen, but is only found deep in one's heart,
waking the hunter from his lonely dream.

Christopher James Key

Me and Immortality

Me and immortality strolled quietly down the lane,
A tormented soul, long since passed who seemed to share my pain,
He hastened me to sit with him, this hollowed mystic shroud,
I heard his words inside my head, but none were spoke aloud,
He shared with me his own remorse of life and love gone by,
He told me of his dreadfulness, and how he came to die,
He put to me the questions that I dared not ask myself,
Of where my tempest soul was bound, for Heaven or for Hell,
He told me many tales of woe, of lovers come and gone,
He sang to me of lonesome sorrow, a sad yet touching song,
It seemed as if we had talked for days when we ended conversation,
And we rose and turned to part our ways, two different destinations,
A drop of pity touched my heart, as I watched him walk away,
And I thanked him for the precious gift he gave to me that day,
The choice to yield as his companion was mine to contemplate,
I could find my mortal happiness, or walk his lonesome fate.

Melinda Jones

Mara's Song

From the first moment that I held you in my arms
I knew I'd be forever a prisoner of your charms.
And as years have passed, some in joy, some in strife
You've always been a warm light in my life.
Cliches? Yes, but what else can I do when
Everything's been said a thousand times or two?
And by much better poets than me or you.
Be that as it may, all the cliches on Earth
Can't express how I felt on the day of your birth.
My heart started to flutter, my head began to whirl
As the nurse said to me, "You have a baby girl."
I watched you grow, shared your joys and your tears,
Answered your questions, and helped banish your fears.
Now, all too soon it seems, my little girl has grown
And is out in the world making a life of her own.
But that's as it should be and as I write this today
There is just one final thing to you I must say.
That no matter what, come Hell or high water,
I'll always be proud to say, "You are my daughter."

Gary L. Privitt

Love Power

A strange essence between woman and man
Draws them closer, they don't understand
Happens like a thief in the night
Creeps into the mind even if you put up a fight
Catches you off guard
Beginning before realizing it starts
One partner usually wants to be closer to the other
Reminding of the scenario with fire and water
One releases, the other pushes harder
One feels powerful like a raging storm
The other appears to be a calm
Love power is controlled at last
When the storm ceases, calmness begins to burn
just a little and . . . it begins to rain.

Mary Ann Wilson

The Mutt

Triumphant parade of canines assemble
from ferocious German shepherds to elegant French poodles,
displaying pure varieties all proudly lined up,
ignoring the despised, isolated mutt.

Discriminated minorities segregate into communities,
alienating those of racial diversity.
The ethnic mixture has no specific people for support
to wipe the struggling tears in need of comfort.

I don't have my mother's appearance.
I'm a rejected foreigner in my father's land.
My identity is torn between two continents,
separated by the cruel Pacific.

I am a victim of a silent world war,
fearfully sensing the hatred on both sides burn
as dark eyes pierce through my white skin,
jeering attacks, "You're a child of abominating sin!"

They arm themselves with insults,
refusing to know my true self,
a confused, hurt soul that painfully bleeds.
I'm a human being too, not just a half-breed.

Amanda Rose Taulbee

Living

Time I shared. Life I captured.
Years displayed my hold on living.
I cried, smiled and at time felt the rips
that tried to tear me apart.
Time just kept on giving.

I captured living, every day was mine I felt.
Forever I would live. One day I looked straight ahead.
Time had made its run, youth took its place.
Reasoning was at hand. I could hear, it's your health.

I had not towel to throw in.
Just captured life and kept on living.
My trail was well beaten. As I looked over my shoulder,
I saw so many smiles . . . a sparkle in the little one's eyes.
I saw tears rolling of joys with extended arms.
I found that the gift of life was giving.

I let no dust settle. Captured life, had to live.
Couldn't recall a bad day I could see all of those past struggles,
The end runs to make ends meet.
I saw all of the hardships and couldn't raise a frown.
I felt no hate . . . You see, living is forgiving.

Donnell Linthecome

Copper to Gold

To Sedrach "Popeye" Diaz, my partner in life
You are the rock upon which I stand
and yours is the heart I carry, so carefully, in my hands.
You remind me of an uncharted, blue-green sea,
wherein, as Pisces (the sign of the fish), I came to belong and be,
whose calm waters, near shore, underscore—
further out to sea—passionate, dominant, beguiling waves,
and the forceful pull of your duality.
Dear Gemini of mine (sign of the twins),
as you let me win or have the draw
in the always unequal battles of a sometimes bittersweet war,
and the feel of me, of all my senses in the immenseness,
I came to realize, in the hypnotic warmth of those waters
and, in the scope of our beginning in your vast and unknown sea,
that it was also that which made the special-ness in you and me
into the wonderful team of "We."
Now, we are under God's brilliant sight,
a man and his wife who are blessed by each other
for living a lifetime: he as a friend, she as his lover
two halves which made a whole,
copper pieces turned to gold.

Susan Lauren Fields

Keep in Mind

Life is a school that's never out
A process never ending
Learning is what it's all about
It's closure always pending
For man did eat of the knowledge tree
And yet we still are learning
So use your gifts to the best of your ability
And keep your desire burning
Yes we all must go to great lengths
To gather all we desire
So with your knowledge and your strengths
Go set the world on fire
But with this knowledge does come power
And all that pursue
For in your finest hour
A debt will come due
To lead the stray
And the blind
To light up the way
For the future of mankind
> *Lynne Grant*

The Roaring Twenties

To my cherished daughter, Patricia L. Chandler
In the roaring twenties the girls were called "Flappers,"
They wore "tomboy" skirts, you might call them trappers.

The hems of their skirts were above their knees,
Their wind blown haircuts were great in a breeze.

The boys were called Sheiks and Jelly Beans too,
Valentino was their Sheik with his hair full of goo.

The boys wore bell bottom pants, with color matched shoes.
They could drive their dad's car, if they didn't drink booze.

The Charleston dance gave them plenty of action.
The fox trot was popular if you shield from traction.

"Yes, Sir, that's my baby" was the song of the times,
You could dance until midnight with just a few dimes.

The horse and buggy had long been passe,
But the autos and radios, were here to stay.
> *Frances E. Adams*

Slow Me Down

To Troy Osborne, grandson
Slow me down like a rocking chair
So I can think of things I have missed
Like a book at the end of a chapter in your life
Slowly comes to an end so I can move on
Rocking a new chapter in rocking in a slump
Having dreams of all my passed
Friends, loved ones of long ago
I open my eyes, they fade from sight
Slowly rocking, thinking of things to be
Hoping my rocking chair won't be broke
Slowly looking down beside me
A little red rocking chair
Two big, brown eyes looking at me
Rock faster, Grandma
I think, oh, what a rocking
Chapter this is going to be
> *Shirley Easter*

A Joyous Rebirth

Long shadows are cast on the mothering ground,
While the sun plots its course in a song without sound.
The birds keep on singing their brilliant song,
And small ones learn what's right and what's wrong.
The cold winter's done, and it's time for rebirth.
Every song that's now sung revives Mother Earth.
> *Meghan Garn*

My Dearest One

Your deepest, kindest, truest heart
Goes often un-admired
Your generous good nature
That survived the funeral fires

Your gracious, proud demeanor
Always steadfast in a storm
And your candles always burning
Like a beacon, safe and warm

There are those who won't embrace you
Though your longing arms reach out
There are those who can't replace you
And of that, please have no doubt

You're the guidance of our family
As our matriarch, you reign
Like a pilot, guiding slowly
Through the random hurricane

You're my love, my friend, my dearest one
My confidant, my Muse
Forever deep within my heart
My love you'll never lose
> *Kim Redder*

Field Trip

Our lunch bags were packed with bread and fruits.
We grabbed our sweaters and put on boots.
Out into our car, labelled simply, Mopar.
She would take us up to the hills, not far.
And there, we would witness such vistas and views,
store them in memory for future muse.
Upon the foothills, the beast chugged to a halt.
The climb would decide who was worth their salt.
So peaceful and quiet, aside from the crows,
the paths were littered with signs full of noes.
No littering, loitering, smoking, camping,
no glass, no hunting, trapping, or tramping.
Up away we went, until winded and spent,
and a rest we did take where the trail bent.
Wandering a bit, as I often desire,
I found some evidence of a campfire.
Lush green grass was covered with bottles from beer.
Oh, how could this be with nature so near?
Sadness and anger rose within me.
This was not what we had come to see.
> *Cindy J. Adsit*

Just a Country Girl

I was just a country girl
Raised down on the farm,
Where everyone was neighbor
And all was peaceful and calm.
Our food came from the garden—
The melons from the vine,
Our fruit from the orchard.
To us, they were really fine.

With wide open spaces and rolling hills
And corn waving on the stalk,
With nice sloping meadows
And goldenrod wherever you walk,
We would climb the big, tall poplars
And sing to our heart's delight.
We went to church on Sunday,
Serving the Lord with all our might.

As I look back on those former years,
It brings one to the verge of tears,
For our ways of pleasure will be no more.
They're gone forever with the days of yore.
> *Trula Hewitt*

A Promise

To my loving husband, Donald Jay Wagner
I'm learning to live with Sanity
Ever since you pulled me in.
My mind is filled with strange ideas.
It's like a fish who's found its fins.

Are we cartoon people leading cartoon lives
Sending signals to worlds beyond?
Lost souls losing fear, intervene,
Two rights never make a wrong.

See, stupidity rains on simple minds,
That's where it always starts.
Something ventured, nothing gained,
Dripping sounds from ripped out hearts.

Seems now we're living fiction lives
Made up as we go along.
Insanity might be a much safer place,
But it's not where I belong.

Deep feelings we have bring deeper thoughts.
It's something that can't be learned.
Put your hand in flames just one time,
I promise you won't get burned.

    Teresa Wagner

We at Her

It started to rain when you left,
the white blossoms wet.
Between their legs, I caught a tiny shadow of us,
slightly violet, walking together in the grass
of a morning that pasted a Sunday and a half
like sharp, orange lightning, like a dance of the daring,
the young and the hushed.

    Ursula Villarreal

Life's Shadows

In memory of my son, Roland C. Moore, in the spirit of his goodness
I am standing and seeing the play
Of life's shadows in an illusive flight and play.

Where is the candor that life has to teach?
Each one on a different path,
of right and wrong it is not to say,
these are just lessons of the day.

So take your journey with an open heart,
as we all are one and apart.
In life's shadows we grow
to come and to know.

    Elise Thrasher

Maine

Have you experienced Maine?
The bright, sunny, cool summers.
The harsh winters,
The beautiful, colorful autumns,
The not-so-nice late springs.

Summer in Maine is weather to dream of,
Life in Maine is peaceful, safe, vigorous, and hard.
You may ask—how is this so?
But once you've experienced Maine, you will know.
For it is kind, but it can be harsh,
It is beautiful, but can be ugly on a stormy winter's night.

Maine provides skiing, snowmobiling, sledding, fresh
air, climbing, hiking, horseback riding, like riding
Kayaking, pottery, antiques—and a host of other things.

But until you visit—you cannot say,
"I have experienced Maine!
Because no one can describe the unlimited beauty
Until you have experienced Maine.

    Juanita A. Maddox

Innocence

Through the eyes of a child,
the world is a wonderful place.
Full of excitement and awe,
the explorations are fantastic.

Through the eyes of a child,
innocence is plentiful.
Truths are told how it is—
not sugarcoated—and lies do not exist.

Life is pure and simple,
etched out by the experiences gone through—
some filled with joy and happiness . . .
others filled with hate and darkness.

A child can be made into an adult too soon,
but the child's love for hope is strong,
Strong to survive the adult life forced upon thee,
To once again live the pure and simple ways lost long ago.

    Cristita Mae Sanchez

Desert Beach

Burnt feet from the hot sun
Beating on the sand on a white desert beach
Waves splashing up are on the run
Further and further out they reach

The soothing coolness of the ocean
Calling with a lulling roar
Setting shells in motion
Like an opening closing door

It's hypnotic rhythm beckons
With a placid tranquility
Crashing the waves in seconds
Breaking back to reality

The sun amid sky gets hotter
Scorching the land with its heat
Causing its path to totter
But it does not defeat

    Pamela Ritchie

I Quest

On the shelf of life,
My deeds lay ,for all to focus on . . .
Some great, some small,
All making a difference.
Special touches . . . Opening Doors . . . Touching hearts!

But still in the hours before dawn,
When night is at its darkest,
I awaken and lay wondering has
The dreaming and hoping,
The reaching and Believing,
The sharing of Enthusiasm, Energies and Talents
Been enough?

And yet, I forge onward . . . continuing the Quest
To ensure that
The life I live
Will reflect
The vision held in my heart.

    Lisa P. Files

Giving, Sharing Our Souls

Give a hand to those in help reaching the stars.
Give a shoulder to those who need one to cry on.
Listen to those who cry out for help.
Share your love with those who don't receive enough
Share a smile with those who need their grey skies brighten
Give kindness to those who feel unwanted and try to
make them feel wanted again.
Share your souls with the world to
make it more beautiful and peaceful without war.

    Brindicy Alcaraz

The Enigma

In the beginning
the dawning light
revealed your truths
High Priests knew you well

Death came

You stand alone on the silent plain
deaf and mute, the quiet mist enfolds you
In awe, strangers gaze upon you
What are you, they wonder
Touching, looking,
they claim you're a god

You're alone, mystical and aloof
naked, revealing
An enigma of the ages

A new breed walks among you
Are you really god, they ask
Brains and eyes probe your secrets
You are mute, no more
You are not a god
You know the sun and moon

Claude Shaver

The Spring

To my English teacher, Dr. McCaffrey, who inspires me to write
When sleep hovers near and my soul is almost content,
my thought are of him.
Years have come and gone, but he is fresh in my mind.
Thinking of him is like sitting in a park
on a pretty and peaceful day in the middle of Fall.

Yet I long to be at that special
place where I first discovered love.
Everything was new and enticing like the Spring.

Now I feel as though Fall allows
me to remember the beauty of the spring.

The seasons will change, but
Spring will never come again.

Gone is my love, and gone is my youth.
Without him, there is no Spring.

But in the fall, I remember,
and I cherish the scenery that unfolds within my mind.

Stephanie Gifford

I Am Aware

Mine and God's:
Sights of dogwood,
Maple, and oak,
Stands of spruce,
Of cedar, arbor vitae, fir;
Rugs of myrtle, sundry moss
Cover the ground.

Embroidering with pendants,
The lilies of the valleys droop
Among the midget iris
And moist violets.

All these are blanketed
Within the songs of life.
Sounds spring from robins, sparrows,
Cardinals, and mockingbirds,
Drowning out the scolding blue jays
With their song.
From sunrise to bright sunset,
I listen to their serenade
And, in my soul, rejoicing, I also sing along.

Esther T. Ryder

Last Night

Last night a thought of you crossed my mind
So I decided to send you a few lines;
Tell you all about my life,
The times I've forgotten how to laugh or smile but when
I think of the cross you had to bear,
Everything seems just fine.

Wouldn't it be nice to sit and chat,
Maybe talk about this or that,
Or how everyone got old and fat?
What about meeting in a back alley
Like two stray cats?

Just a funny idea that passed through my head—
Guess I'll talk to you in church instead.
Sometimes it's hard to follow your path considering
The life I've led.
Maybe this time I'll find the wisdom to make it
Through the night like a few wise men said.

Antonio P. Johnson

To Me

To me, you are a very special lady.
One in a million, you are a breath
of fresh air and sweet as a lilac in the spring.
I know there are some who may think
different—they have their right.
To me, you are my star, and there were one star
that outshined you . . . it was on Jesus' birth.
You carry me for the time of my birth.
You walk with me and you feed me, you love me.
Giving birth, knowing the responsibility,
the long authority of being a mother.
Giving your care and freedom for the time
for me, making me the centerpiece of your love and life.
To me, how could I not feel all this love
and knowing words alone is not enough . . .
Only if my heart could speak.

Mary Chubb

Procrastination's Pull

I, wanting, wanted not.
Lived in fantasy's applaud;
Applaud all my fantasies
Dreamed dreams of knighted glories, deeds.
Played not the knighted part,
Sought not the glory deed. . . .

My head, a visionary stage,
Proclaimed me author of the page.
With singleness of sight,
Converted audiences to sing my praise.
In reality, raised not to center stage . . .
Nor the spotlight's illuminating rays.

I thought I wanted, and would,
Tomorrow . . .
Step out of self.
Counted not on Procrastination's pull,
Found like Rip Van Winkle . . .
I, more the fool.

Betty Wyeth

Speak Softly

I speak to my spirit everyday for a spiritual cleansing.
I speak softly to my spirit to close the holes devoured by stress.
I speak softly to my spirit to nourish a mature growth in God.
I speak softly to my spirit to learn from my mistakes.
I speak softly to my spirit to learn from other folks' mistakes.
I speak softly to my spirit to purge negative thoughts when they
    infiltrate my mind.
I speak softly to my spirit with a healing love shared with others.
I speak softly to my spirit in an elegance befitting God.
I speak softly to my spirit for others to see the glory of the Lord.

Delma M. Webb

Lost Water

At first I fall from the sky in the form of rain
I then become a wet weather stream as I go down the long drain
Down the road, I am joined by a few more streams
And become a branch
I now provide drinking water for cattle as I go through a ranch
Next, I will meet another branch after about a week
When this happens, I will become a creek
Later, I will get hit by another creek which will cause
My water to shake and shiver
I will become very large and my new will be river
After a month or so, I will then find a sea or an ocean
The sun will then evaporate me
And put the whole cycle back into motion
As a result, I feel lost and alone
Because I will never have a steady home

     Brent Stevenson

Far and Near

You came here from far
To a distant land
A land unknown to you
A land as unfamiliar as the past
You came here seeking for something new
Something that would be true
Here I am, in front of you
Waving my hands frantically
Yet you do not see me
Because I have been there from the beginning
Watching out for you
Caring, loving, with an empty heart
Hoping one day that you will see me
Standing there in front of you
And your eyes will be opened
Like rays of sun through the clouds
Like an angel in the sky
Holding my hands out to you
Hoping that you will embrace me
With nothing but your heart

     Christopher Fuller

A Message for Jim

To my dear friend James Hamilton of Ragley, LA
Dear Jim,
I was watching the clouds in the sky today;
So many formations put me in a daze.
To my amazement—and I know what I saw—
Was the formation of a beautiful dog.
He sent a message as I stared at him.
He said, "I am the dog who belongs to Jim.
Tell him not to be sad that I have gone away,
For I am happy here in Heaven this day.
Tell him to look up. God will let him know
That I am well and safe and watch over him below.
We will be together when God says when,
So please be happy until we meet again."
May this message fill you with God's love within,
To know your faithful friend now dwells with him.

     Jeannie L. McKinstry

Inspiration

In memory of my father, a caring man, Eugene Pippins
The pen in my hand awakes and comes alive,
When I think a thought that could survive.
I start to feel inspired with only a word in mind;
I go from there to see what else I can find.
If the line doesn't appear to properly fit,
I search until it arrives and I don't quit.
I know the inspiration the soul can achieve,
So I let my pen go and just believe.
Before I know, 'tis true—it finally appears.
A poem is written and to be read for years.

     Kathy D. Gulledge

Time to Myself

I sit here alone, thinking of you,
The things that we've done,
The things we've been through.
Sometimes I think the bad outweighs the good.
Our love seems to work in reverse,
Not as it should.

Is it right to stay by your side,
Hoping one day to be your bride?
You're still deciding what you want out of life.
You're not thinking about having a wife.

The fighting is common.
Most of the time we don't speak.
It leaves us both angry, our emotions weak.
Is our love strong enough to survive,
Or am I clinging to dreams, keeping hope alive?

Sometimes I want to talk to you,
But I won't swallow my pride.
I just sit in my room . . . alone and hide.

     Maria A. J. Giron

Who Am I?

For my loving and supportive husband, Robert, and loving parents
I am a daughter of a strong woman,
With pride and grace, who is full of love.
Who am I?

I am a sister to some, some proud and strong,
Others are outspoken but still full of love.
Who am I?

I am a mother to my children who are witty, gay,
Outspoken, happy, joyous and full of love.
Who am I?

I am a wife to my husband who makes me happy.
He is strong, supportive and makes me feel loved.
Who am I?

I am a woman, strong, loved, loving with more to give.
I am a woman reborn through love and knowing that.
That is who I am.

     Tonia J. Shabazz

The Lonely Sea

Why do your crests fall down so heavily?
Your crashing curses permeate my ears.
Your trenchant arms strain to encompass me,
But nothing touches me . . . except your tears.
Your curls do take the lives of many men.
I'd think that you'd be satisfied by now.
But no! Devouring them all ten by ten,
Your mean heart ne'er stops its eternal vow.
I don't know why you feel so desolate,
For deep inside your awesome assemblage
A hidden world of life, a world fully wet,
Longs for you to quiet your own rampage.
Your company is really what they crave.
The fauna does honor your every wave.

     Erika Gamst

Pressure

What is pressure is called the dark side of life,
the side of life where people can't cope because
they have too many stresses. Too many stresses in life
cause people to do crazy things; like trying to commit
suicide. But in reality they are just people crying out.
What are they crying out for? Well, one might say they were
crying out for help, the help they need because they are unable
to handle the problems of every day life.
So what is pressure? It's not only the dark side of life; it's
people crying.

     Deanna Noel

The Death of a Princess

The inner beauty of its purpose
Radiates its outside beauty
Of Princess Diana that everyone admires
By the entire commoners of the commonwealth

Princess Diana, the commoner's aspiration
A bridge that inter-links to the monarchy
From its wedding day you've seen
To its saddened demise, interment

Thy subjects, Princess Diana, they grieve
You deserve for you are their princess
In popularity as well as in beauty
That is irreplaceable in Buckingham Palace

Thy smiling face captivates everyone
And thy handshake a credo of goodwill
A radical change is being seen
A prince is co-mingling with the crowds

Thy subjects have came far and near
Bringing flowers, a symbol of empathy
The British Royals were grieving privately
Accepted flowers from a grieving nation

Ismael O. Peralta

Evening Sky

In the evening of the dark,
The brightness of the moon, spotlight the stars
In the sky, to shine with a spark
For you and I to find, where they are.
Hidden in the sky, stars come out to cling
Sparkling up a tune, as if to sing
After the clouds all leave,
Clearing the sky free.
In the sky, its beauty brings,
Appearing stars, delightfully to see . . .
But ever so far,
These little stars
In the sky, where they are pinned
Like on royal silk, crystal studs fastened.
Dark evening gown's silver tone sequins
Shine up the town's night frequent,
Way in the sky, shimmering bright,
Celebrating holiday lights,
Until sky waves its magic wand
For dawn and all is gone.

Josephine Pernorio

The Crutches of Reason

The other night I had a dream;
A dream to show me the way, it seems.
This dream carried me to another land,
The land where I'll make my final stand.

Where your ears can see, and your eyes can hear,
and laughter's your last defense for fear.
Your stomach knows more than your heart or your brain.
And the crutches of reason will drive you insane.

I call it a dream because there are no words
to describe the things that I've seen and heard.
But words aren't the only way to express
the patterns behind the chaotic mess.

And if your mind is weak, and your heart is strong,
like me, you'll face terror with a song.
Time is short—don't waste your breath.
Your lifetime companion . . . is your death!

When my death takes me by the hand,
I hope for the strength to make my last stand.
With true intent, my spirit strong,
I'll rally my power for my last song.

John Chris Cowling

Beyond My Reach

Just a chance, was all that I asked,
A chance to show that we could last.

A brief encounter was all we had,
And with just a phone call it all went bad.

A lasting memory held dear to my heart,
A love from your past is what tore us apart.

I will love you always, my Georgia Peach,
But I realized today you are beyond my reach.

I will wait for you, a day, a month, a year
Just say the word because I am yours, I am here.

Search your heart, you'll find me there,
Call my name, I am always near.

I love you, today, tomorrow, forever,
A love lasting, leaving you never.

Sharyl Klawitter

I Love Thee as No Man Hath Ever Before

I love thee as no man hath ever before
Loved a woman, or you, with depth of heart
Unearthed when thou explored my virgin store
And discovered this wellspring I impart.
I love thee as thou always wished to be,
Overwhelmed by a zealous, transparent soul
Attentive to thy self through constancy,
Neglecting not in part thy given whole.
I love thee as I ofttimes thought ideal,
With honest, tender longing blossomed forth
From fate's mysterious nature, to reveal
Life's harvested treasures and timely worth.
My love is nothing more than I aspired
To grasp for nothing less than you desired.

Randy D. Geiger

A Dream

She lived in the city
with all it's noises—
ambulances, police cars, fire engines, sirens,
loud music, and impatient people.
When she walked in the streets
with her mother,
she looked nervously around.
Was she safe or not?
Always on guard.
But one day she visited a tranquil place,
full of fireflies
displaying their art of light,
birds chirping sweetly,
so green and quiet,
so peaceful!
She felt: This was home.

Anne Marfey

Mother's Last Words

My sons, you know I'll soon be gone,
But I won't have to cross Jordan alone,
For off in the distance, I can already see
A great band of angels coming for me.

No matter how deep, and no matter how wide,
They'll carry me safely to the other side,
Where God will comfort and watch over me
And keep me safe through Eternity.

So boys, I ask you to please understand:
I'll soon be living in God's Promised land,
Where I'll always be happy and safe in His keeping,
And I'll never be dead . . . I'll only be sleeping.

Dean Sellers

Many Lives Are Gone, A Holocaust Poem

Many lives are gone,
because all they have done wrong.
They took the young to their deaths,
where lives were to end in one last breath.
They killed them for all to see,
but others could not flee.
They were killed time by time,
their deaths were an ultimate crime.

Sarah Rosenman

Memories of Home

Rolling green fields and galloping colts.
My favorite mare's soft whinny at night,
Announcing the arrival of her first foal
And perfect birth at dawn's first light.

Apple blossoms, busy bees, an eager wait
To gather and grind—it's cider time.
My front yard sale by the grass
To friends and neighbors, just a dime.

My daddy's quiet patience while underfoot,
As he answered questions of "Why" and "How."
Mama's soft lap as she dried my tears,
When my small problems brought on despair.

So very special was the evening meal,
A leisurely time for laughter and sharing,
Telling the things we'd done that day.
No greater blessing than parents caring.

V. Jane Brummitt

Forever Youthful, Forever Free

Our daughters are together in Heaven above,
Touching our hearts, flying away like a dove.
Their love stayed behind as a piece of our hearts,
And, with that in mind, we never shall part.

My daughter, she passed on many years ago.
She lives in my heart; she's part of my soul.
She's happier now and plays all day long;
She draws pretty pictures as she sings me a song.

Sent to watch over me, she's an angel of love,
As is your daughter too up in Heaven above.
They'll learn and they'll grow as they watch over us;
They're living their lives through our gentle touch.

Our guardian angels, together they'll be.
Forever they're youthful; forever they're free.
They watch over you, they watch over me,
And, someday hereafter, together we'll be.

Pamela K. Berkhiem

Save the Children

Children murdering children
What has happened to our children
A tortured life they must lead
Imagine the depth of their despair

Their anger has turned to rage
Why are they so filled with rage
Some say it's their drugs or alcohol
Others say it's their music or lack of discipline
Still others say it's all of the above.

They must have some values
What of love respect responsibility
Where is the value of human life

We must save our children
These children are our future
Our country's future

Patricia Fisher

Time Gone By

To my loving children, LaToya and Tre
Sometimes I question the time that's passed,
As to how it's gone by so very fast.
One day my kids are not yet born . . .
The next they're gone leaving my heart torn.

Games of run, catch, jump, and fall
Made me feel so very small.
Football games and marching band
Always caused my chest to span.

Life must go on without a doubt,
And I'm sure that's what life's about.
But I surely miss the special things,
The young growing family only brings.

Hoyte Phifer Jr.

Paradoxo's Jeopardy

As an avenging angel, the silent vestige presence appeared
with eighth power; it destroyed her satisfied mind,
awoke ill favored vultures of guilt, beset her conscience
judiciary of behavior, hid in the passage of time.
Kaleidoscope shadow shapes in tortuous rhythm, seemingly
sail a vindictive circle over a catacomb of buried memories.
An entity of remorse stabs a heart filled with tears,
tears she dare not release;
opening the floodgate of profound regret
would most surely drown her in grief.
Love never shown, love never known,
heartache remnant of a mistake made long ago,
limb of a stranger, progeny she never knew,
life discarded without appraisal at the hands of a fool.
Flip a coin in life's highway at the fork in the road,
a wrong turn in judgement; the result a lost soul.
Speed 90 miles an hour down Donner Summitt's mountain curves
assures a ticket to hell on the river of no return.

Betty B. Holmes

Images, Beliefs, and Film

Images, ideas, and beliefs are pictures
stored in the mind's deep interior;
they need expression by word and deed
to come to light and into play.
Like film needs light and correct exposure
to reveal images by processing,
ideas and beliefs, too, need exposure,
repetition, and correct nurturing.
Or else they become dim, dull,
and lose their powerful qualities,
fade away from the conscious mind,
and just become old memories.
Like old film, with not enough light,
or right amount of exposure
which quickly loses its luster, quality,
and sensitivity needed for film or play,
ideas and beliefs, too, lose their power
and appeal and if unused, quickly fade away.

Patricia McQueen

A Love of Beautiful Things

In my fantasy, perhaps I should have taken
Some unpardonable gross liberty, perhaps even
Lightly touched with a single finger that
Warm vulnerable bone fluttered down in one's shoulder
That superbly rotates an arm in an arc,
Or perhaps given one careful glance at your hands?

But I didn't—I swear I didn't—I merely
Allowed my glance to wander onto some one
Perfect jewel in your beautiful face—I've since
Forgotten specifically which—and
May I be forgiven, for I too love beautiful things.

Cathe Jefferson

A Sonnet for W.S.

Bill sat on the steps under the gargoyles.
He had just finish'd a scribning session.
Repos'd and pond'rous of his midnight toils
He took a break, respite from his ambition.
Well, he knew he would finish successfully.
The story was complete: except for the end.
He needed time to think just how it would be;
The trick? To send the plot 'round the final bend.
His mind soar'd searching for inspiration.
Wearily, he worried about the length,
His brow wet from constant perspiration:
Ever vigilant and resolv'd, his strength.
  He'd done it before, near times double a score;
  This time, as pen laid down, he'd write no more.
    Benjamin D. Loudermilk

Euclid

To my dear mother, Gladys Parrish Priddy
Born of the wild wind,
Searching, searching, searching!
Oh! Lonely heart, please quit beating.
Oh! Time is forever; wait! Wait! Wait!
Time! Time! Time!
My youth! Give me back my youth.
Old man with heart of stone,
Oh! Time. You did stop for me.
While I laid down to rest
Safe at last on the beautiful shore,
Safe from the deep foam,
Never to toss any more.
Safe in the arms of dear Jesus at last,
Beautiful beyond scripture,
The pearly gates past.
    Bobby Lindon Priddy

Rocking Horse of Time

Two lives joined to work as one;
Circumstance, challenge, intimidate the mind.
Perseverance, trust your soul's truest run;
Webs of thoughts intertwine.
This antique horse preserved with care,
Rocked by hands with emotional touch,
Reminds us life, special relationships are rare;
Mind-set determines life as such.
Strong-willed compromise with unique balance
Sets the foundation you must build,
Like this horse with its starred glance
Shows fortitude, determination, and will.
Push gently this rocking horse of time,
Remembering your love will set the pace.
Preservation defeats the clock, character matures like wine;
Hold the reins firm—this is your race.
    Michael Gielarowski

Under Capricorn

Years ago I avoided the high afternoon
in Salsipuedes, drank what was left to drink
of the wines of the midday meal, reserving a stitch
of time for the sobremesa, no doubt, but soon

took refuge between cool sheets,
slept the canonical siesta, and arose before
sundown, so as to share in the lore
and rite of yerba mate. But now, free

as only the old can be free, I stay with the sun,
watch every cloud that sweeps away its heat
(if just for the nonce) and every beam of bright

that restores it—like an old song in a new tongue,
like the passage from season to season, and quite
like the stream down which our lives are flung.
    J. David Danielson

The Hiding Place

Foxxy is the name of the Pomeranian,
Who is a happy-go-lucky five-year-old.
He lives with a Golden Retriever named Max,
Whose concern for his friend is a sight to behold.

The ten-year-old has a protective quality
That showed when Foxxy had pink eye and couldn't see.
Big golden Max knew his friend had a swollen eye;
And Foxxy sat still while Max was licking his eye.

Max showed compassion beyond the realm of friendship.
The boys are as close as two peas in a pod;
Except when it comes to sharing their rawhide;
Foxxy has a habit of hiding the bones.

Once the hole is dug and filled in with his nose,
And the dirt matches the soil on his toes;
Foxxy keeps an eye on his friend, when Max moves . . .
And his burial place for the rawhide bones.

But Max, in his wisdom, knows what just took place;
He couldn't miss the dirt on Foxxy's face;
While he pretends to ignore Foxxy's mischief
And the trips back and forth to the hiding place.
    Rosemary Brenner

Watching Me

To the one I love most, James Campbell
I feel it, someone's watching me.
I look around, you're all I see.
For a moment we just sit and stare,
Wondering how much the others cares.
Then ashamed you quickly glance the other way.
If you asked me about it you know what I'd say.
I'm lost in these feelings that I know you share.
I think a you a fool, for not letting on how much you care.
Turning back to my paper, I pick up my pen.
Full of emotions, I start to write again,
And once more someone watches me,
And once again it's you that I see.
When will you tell me what I already know?
I love you so much, I might never let go.
Since I know that you love me too,
Forever I'll stay here and wait for you,
And we're staring at each other once again,
Knowing in our hearts we're more than just friends.
    Desirea MacBride

The Touch

Dedicated to the finest friends life has to offer
Came the moment,
Encouraged by age and mindful stirrings.
History stood ground,
Anxiously anticipating the nudge.
Have courage. Touch! Push!
Swinging open, light blanketed the heartland,
Over thoughts and questions stumbling.
Who? What goes there? Why? Pretend childhood or abject reality?

Assertive—searching, the odyssey began.
Illuminating recesses deep within the soul,
Kindled dark and dirty memories.
Normal chameleoned into anomaly,
As disquieting answers sought the glow.
Without warning, the unthinkable appeared.

Damned Secrets!
Truth stripped the past of fiction,
Planting seeds of passionate and solemn vow.
Exposed, life's lineage gave no comfort—only lies.
But for a family of friends, came riches
Of belief and deliverance—not ties.
    Carol Rose

Missing

To my love, Antoine Young
Tick-tock times go on without you in my arms, aching for your kiss.
My lips run dry, my blood has run cold without your warmth.
Needing you is all I think of day in day out.
Without you there in my life,
    my heart has stopped beating without your love.
I need you more than I ever knew.
Now without you I ache in every part of my body.
Waiting for eternity to come, maybe see you again someday
if you ever come back from where you've gone—may not be far
but it feels like forever since you've touched me like that.
Just the sound of your name makes me want to cry for what
I may never have again.
Always in my mind, body, and soul there you stay forever,
eternally yours.

Philena Primmer

The Kiss

The first glow of dawn
Is giving promise to the awaiting day . . .

The morning glories
Are just beginning to unfurl . . . are they heavenly blue?

The persistently rushing waves
Are advancing, about to strike cymbals with the cliffs . . .

The restless audience
Suddenly hushes—the conductor's wand is raised!

The freshly baked, wondrous smelling bread
Is almost to your watering mouth . . .

How all these moving, breath-holding moments
Mirror the tender, passionate, beautiful, exciting,
Deliciously sweet anticipation of lips for—the kiss!

Deborah Jones

A Philosophy of Life

There comes a time where I stop and ask myself:
Why do I do the things I do?
Why am I so helpful and why am I so nice?
Why do I care so much? Why do I have a conscience?
But no answer came from my mouth, I did not bother to answer
Every day comes and goes, I still treat everyone
The way I want to be treated
With no worries in the world about the consequences
I know it will work out
But a couple of things still go through my head:
Why do you care so much and why do you go out of your way to help?
Are you dumb, are you stupid, or are you just plan crazy? No!
The question was just answered—God!
He cares for everyone, yes, you and me
And there's nothing I wouldn't do for him
He did everything for you and me
To give back my thanks for all he has done
I will live my life for him until the end, because I have already won!

Twila Black

Pier Sunset

To all who encourage me and my writing career
at the end of a pier is where you will spot me
just watching a magical sunset
and the beautiful colors over the sea,
colors which you wish to capture
but which remain just out of reach
purple, pink, orange, red
all the colors not usually associated with the beach,
the sun has gone but just before twilight appears
I make a secret wish
that in the morning, the bright sun reappears!

Kamylle Santiago

A Sleeping Bag for 2

Time, the fire
stands soon settles down,
two logs crumble rolling over
for the last time in their sleep . . .
to support one another one last time
for flames flicker away the lingering luminescence of day,
the ambers of burning bruises
failed promises the misgivings of
lessons needed be learned,
an order through disorder, I don't know
the teachings of piled history books
look, the discern differentiates and someday declines time.
she can either rush us rust us or fail and freeze,
the seduction of inside reverses forces more
difficult to understand more depth than destiny.
so face to face together again the smiles
the laughter, the blues and browns (sometimes also green)
We stand and kindle thesis love this kind flame with fiery hope
as One united dream two dream.

Nathan Hayward

On Life in America

The hills so high—they reach the sky
The fields so green as you've ever seen—
With cities and towns sprinkled around
A finer land there never has been

The land is grand—as God had planned
Full of people you know—with whom you grow—
Life is good, but troubles come your way
Just say a prayer, the answer is there—soon you will know

Whatever you do—to yourself be true
To your children show love—it's up to you
Be kind to your friends and neighbors all—
Make America the land of love—let's heed the call

And when you are old—with aches and pains
Look back on the good—recall your gains—
Did you make the grade and run the race
With your heart and soul, and a happy face?

Your reward is due—the time is at hand
To say good-bye to this fair land
Family, friends—all have been special to you
America, the greatest, long may she live—free and true

Thelma E. Lent

My Precious Miranda

To my beautiful daughter, Miranda Darrielle Clark
When I held your tiny body for the very first time,
And saw your beautiful face.
I knew what I was feeling at that moment,
Was something I could never replace.

I was so proud when I looked at you,
It's hard to believe I was a dad.
And when I think of how the Lord blessed your mother
And I, it makes me so glad.

I look so forward to the days ahead,
Just watching you grow and learn different things.
And inside my heart and soul, it's such a special love this brings.

My sweet and beautiful daughter Miranda I love you so much,
You keep me so alive. And if I didn't have you in my life,
I think I would probably just die.
So, my precious Miranda,
As father and daughter
I pray we will always be together.

'Cause God knows how I feel
For you, and he knows that I want
This to last forever.

Jeffrey Scott Clark

Kari

The summer breeze whispered in my ear
Telling me a secret I was longing to hear
That during my wandering you would appear
And draw my desires poignantly near
The weather was blistering at that time of year
Like the heat in my heart which would instantly sear
For in but a moment you were christened, my dear
And my plans for that summer started to veer
New goals and intentions became perfectly clear
You paved the roadway down which I would steer
When we were close, my emotions would cheer
When we were apart, my eyes dropped a tear
But our plans for the future were never in fear
For this wasn't a fling or some jaunt cavalier
Something genuine and special was happening here
At least that's what the summer breeze whispered into my ear

Andrew T. Collier

Our Love Endures

The warmth of sunsets on summer's eves,
The joy of the jaybird as winter leaves,
Blossoming buds as springtime blooms,
Reflections on snow of winter's full moon . . .
So is our love like the beauty of the seasons—
With rhythm and rhyme and infinite reasons.
Ever as powerful and ever just as sure
As the rolling of the Earth—our love endures.

Deborah L. Scranton

We Don't Even Care

Are we to blind to see, is it easier to look away
The problem is still there
Or is it, we don't even care

And our planet we are hurting, we're just too hard on her
We're not playing very fair
Or is it, we don't even care.

Let's look through the window, and see the damage we've done
So will we take that dare
Or is it, we don't ever care.

And yes we better hurry, before it becomes too late
She's showing a lot of wear
Or is it, we don't even care

Well we've taken so much, can't we put a little back
We've just stripped her bare
Or is it, we don't even care.

Time is going to run out, we better open up our eyes
And we better start to care
Or we'll look, and there'll be nothing there

George Soderquist

My Heart Dances to the Beat of a Distant Drummer

My heart dances to the beat of the distant drummer, oceans away
King, queens, you say?
Purple, orange, red, and green
Wondrous life for many a teen
Bejeweled of riches from the land of home
Adventurous sights rival that of Rome
Denying the truth whence we come?
Boldness, talented, gifted for sure
A race that once was solid and pure
Though threads that bonded, formed an instant cure
Sometimes flowed a silent tear
Even when skies were blue and clear
Remembering the songs that readjusted our fear
Oh God, my people, how they persevere!
Ah, yes, my heart dances to the beat of a distant drummer
Oceans away, Kings, Queens . . . I say!

Yvonne H. Cannon

Ghetto

The sounds of siren
made me scream
as I stood and observed
the twisted lane of the ghetto
which had been abandoned by prosperity.
The sight of the garbage
in the gutters that stink,
along with thoughts of police brutality,
tingled at my integrity. . . .
The lanes are embanked
by fleets of rusty zinc fences
which conceal the reality of its poverty.
Children wander, scantily dressed,
hate to stay at home—
it's like a rat's nest. . . .
Took to the streets seeking better,
but endangering their lives momentarily.

Barrington Brown

Never Give Up

Once you've started, don't give up.
When you're almost about to succeed, don't give up.
When something goes wrong, don't give up.
If you're having doubts about yourself, don't give up.
Even if you haven't even started, don't give up.
Never Give Up!

Jessica Tenney

Caseload

Let the old man out
Look to see
Look to see
Look to see what was seen
Stay with the caseload
Don't trip over your tracks
Before you make them
But allow some drift
With the driftwood
Only as far is necessary
To gain full focus, to feed thought power
As to do so allows you
To level square
Staying straight as flight of an arrow
Without benefit of wings of a sparrow
This holds tightly
To the happy and sad
And the tensely leaning toward mad
To withhold brightness, by day or night

George B. Gassert

Song of My Youth

Far away, under a clear blue sky,
Seats my native country, near the sea.
It is a beautiful Island, simple and shy,
I often visit! I love to see!

Hand by hand, my memories and I,
Walk the familiar narrow streets,
Where a "Pale Song," like "A Note" from the sky,
Whispers in my ears, "Youthful Dreams."

I hear the "Note Of Youth" of another time . . .
The "Song Of Youth," that was mine . . .
And haunts me still, when I am there . . .
Although painful, I do care.

That "Note Of Youth," comes from everywhere!
From the sea, from the sky, from the air.
From the mountains, the trees, the birds that singing . . .
From my "Deep Memory," when I am thinking.
But suddenly, "The Elusions Of Youth" disappear.
Then I feel "Lonely!" the "Loneliness" I fear . . .

Julie Poriazi Kaldis

Looking over My Shoulder

Dedicated to my late father, Harry B. Vevle
When I was old enough to know fear,
you scared my very soul
because you were so strict.
When I was seventeen, I no longer feared you,
because I felt nothing but hate towards you.
I did not understand.
As I became a wife and, eventually, a mother,
I started thinking in the terms of a wife and a mother,
and, slowly, I began to understand.
You did your best for me and looked after me
and gave me credit, when no one else did.
In the end, it meant so much to me that
we got a chance to say one more last "I love you."
But now, some years have passed,
and I wish you were here to look over my shoulder!
I miss you!

Carol Rafferty

Marianna

In loving memory of my grandmother, Marianna Scroglieri
She was a small, delicate Italian girl
Uprooted in 1907 from homeland, family, and the graves of two babies
By her young husband.

She said, "I will survive." She did.

"America is the place to live," he told her.
The words echoed as she became violently ill
In the immigrant steerage.

She said, "I will survive." She did.

Across the continent, she followed her husband . . .
Frightened, pregnant, and with a baby in her arms.
Neither knew how to communicate in English.

She said, "I will survive." She did.

Planting gardens, taking in boarders, raising chickens,
Working from dawn to dusk,
She raised nine children and buried four in the Colorado soil.

She said, "I will survive." She did.

Eventually, her body rebelled against
Washing tons of laundry, kneading countless loves of bread,
Scrubbing too many floors, birthing eleven children. Cancer!

She said, "I will survive." She did not.

Shirley Weston

Safely Home

They found him in the morning, lying in the street,
cold and stiff, yet he looked so peacefully asleep.

He was old, and worn and ragged were his clothes,
but his face shown with an inner glow, it was beautiful in repose.

The curious crowd sneered, with their scornful gaze,
cursing, as they grumbled, no great loss, take the bum away.

Oh! My pity for humanity, for they will never know,
that he was unique among them, flawless—pure as purest gold.

He gave up all his worldly goods, to help more needy souls.
He had ambitions in the past and many human goals,
but abandoned them as a man, in his search for truth,
as he came to realize, they were the foolish dreams of youth.

He truly loved the one who had made the sacrifice,
so, all mankind, good or evil, could find eternal life.

An angel came for him one cold and lonely night,
to carry him to Heaven, up through the star-filled skies,
where he would meet his "Lord" and forever with Him abide.

He knelt before the "King" who sat upon His golden throne,
and knew that he was blessed, for he was safely home.

Lillian Stepney

Inspiration

The joy of creating is a delight,
While observing the full moon at night.

Colorful sunsets are glorious,
As the changing scene is victorious.

Flowers blooming in the Spring
Make the atmosphere ring.

Discover the majestic mountains,
Or reflections in ancient fountains.

Curiosity produces pleasant designs,
When one ventures into nature's confines.

Studying the wonders of the world brings sighs,
While observing with curious eyes.

Deep feelings fill the heart
Producing wonderful works of art.

No matter how mysterious it may seem,
The urge to create is like a dream.

Donald O. Williams

Lida, My Sweet, My Valentine

I know I'm tired in all that is,
Of love and hatred, of godliness.
I long for the day when I'm to meet
Jesus, our Lord, the King of kings.

Whence come thine presence
In my despair.
Mine heart seeks thee, though love as pair.
I thank thee much for thine sweet love
And weave my heart with thou like glove.

To this great day, my life I thank.
Thou precious love in mine arms length.
I'm happy to know now thou art mine,
To love and hold 'til the end of time.

Lida, my sweet, my valentine,
I thee am coming to make you mine.
Fear not our future, for it is sealed.
With God the Father, we will prevail.

Meng T'ang

Echoes of Love

To my husband John, with love
Do you know how it feels to be in love?
Then just look at the world that surrounds you!
Everything tells you, you're in love
When your love has his arms around you:
The sunshine beams; the birds fly high;
The raindrops gleam; the clouds drift by;
The horses prance; the trees sway low;
The flowers dance; and now you know;
Your heart whispers, I love you!
The bells all chime; the moon glows light;
The oceans calm; the stars shine bright.
Your heart opens up to the songs of love;
It's paradise shared; that's how it goes.
The heavens smile, and now you know;
The breeze echoes, "I love you."

Betty Seyfferle

Moods in Blue

He popped in, as quickly as he left.
Sadness always leads its path to me.
I'll survive, I always do!
A beautiful year burns the pages into my memory book,
never to be forgotten.
"Sad Eyes" plays on the radio and
somehow it rings true!

Dana D. Smith

The Strongest One

To my best friend, Norma Castleman, you're the strongest one
Strength was once present,
But slightly disappeared as cancer struck
Rough days and sleepless nights
Lay in store for the strongest one
Sitting in the darkness longing
For her friends and family
Denial came as quick as lightning
And left as quick as thunder
Within a few weeks
The stormy days became a part of history
Rejoicing began as the results
Were heard
The cancer had not spread
And she would survive
Strength appeared not only in her,
But in everyone she knew
The strongest one is the
Woman who overcame the darkness
Set out to destroy her!

  Jennie Jobe

You Gave Me the Key to Love

To my hero, my role model, my mom, Marcia Iacchei
When a tidal wave crashes onto the shore,
Her hand reaches out to calm the rough sea.
As my petals fall,
They are caught with her spirit of comfort.
Occasionally trees collapse and block my path,
But her strength clears the way.
When rain pours down darkening my day,
I am enlightened by her sunrise.
When tears roll down my cheek;
Through fear, rejection, pain, or sorrow,
Her arms of compassion are sure to embrace me.
But when it is time to let go,
Though reluctant and scared for me,
She waves good-bye,
Keeping memories of our past,
And prayers for my future.
But now I can step outside with confidence.
Because my mom gave me the key to love.
Thanks, Mom.

  Nicole Iacchei

Winter Horizon

My core has become like ice cold and hard

I will not become like the bird in winter snow that
Shuts his eyes and pulls within himself
For warmth and security.

Let the wind whip through me
Like that of hot water falling upon Earth's frozen ground

In the sharp bitter cold of winter is where my soul will be
My musing will be my comfort
Alone I shall withstand the perils of this arduous torment

Let the snow upon my feet, hands, and face freeze
I shall not be afraid or scared for I am numb
My unwilling though enduring consciousness
Will provide me with the warmth needed
To keep my heart pounding
For in the future I am sure to once again see and feel the sun
And melt from the warmth of another soul

Only, for now, when you look into my eyes and you speak to me
Do not become alarmed the chill you feel is soon to pass
It will return home . . . to me.

  Andrea Thomas-Powell

A Love Message for My Children

This "special" poem is dedicated to all my children
Before your birth I prayed for you.
God answered by having me give birth.
I thank Him everyday for His gifts.
Do continue keeping God in your heart.
Everyday of your life do give thanks.
Thanking Him is all He ever wants.
And remember He will always love you.
Some "thoughts" for you to live by:
Learn to live by the 10 commandments.
Accept the "golden rule" as your guide.
Keep your Bible close, read it often.
"Readings" may seem very difficult to follow,
One wording is "turn the other cheek."
Mothers do it everyday; you can too!
Thank you my children for reading this.
There aren't "enough" thanks for your "love!"
You prove your love in many ways.
Mom always did, always will love you.
I'm proud to say "I'm your Mom."

  Eve Westaby

Eternally Yours?

When I die, don't box me up and put me away.
Lay me down in a great forest so I will be
able to live some other day.

Lay me down and leave me as I was when I came
into this world—naked and free.
Then give me your blessing and take a last look,
remembering me as I was; then, as quickly
as you came, leave, happily.

Continue on with your life and don't worry about me, I'll be fine.
And if you ever need to be reassured, just look to the skyline.

I'll always be with you and watch over you wherever you go,
No matter if it is your memory of me to warm you
on a cold day or if it is a cool breeze to
make it easier on a sweltering day, I'm with
you wherever you go.

Whenever you look into my midst for comfort and to be near me

Please respect me and hold me gently, cherishing
the moment at hand, because everything is on
its way to somewhere else, even though it is
not always clear to see.

  Mason W. Schmidt III

The President Can Love

You have a human quality
and presidential behavior
other men don't have.
This behavior towards me is so special.

A man like you I want,
a man with style
that never loses his touch,
because his personality is demanded.

I swear that I will give you my love in every way.
I will shower you with caressing love
any time of the day and any time of the night
like no one has ever given to you.

I don't care if you're President of this nation;
you have the right to feel for me
that great big passion,
and I want the whole world to know
that the President is loved by me.
I want the world to know that he has
a caring heart and he can love.

  Olga Batista

Ninety-Seven, Summer of Loss

To Almighty Allah, Lord of all the worlds
Here stood the mother of the poor and wretched mass.
There stood the princess of the common class.

There above them sat the high and mighty, rich and royal mounted,
Firmly seated, but slipping fast.

And the people know their leaders,
Not those of means and power, for they will quickly pass.

And who will be left to pay the cost
In this, the strange summer of loss?

The princess and the mother both gone,
On our hearts their names embossed.

Their capacity to love, did they ever exhaust?
Tried and true examples of maternity,
Both walking on the shining waters of humanity.

Now walking one behind the other into history,
But facing more importance in eternity.

   Shahid Abdul Haqq

You Are Perfection

On hot summer days I dream of being cooled by your touch.
A cool breeze whispers your name through the trees.
You are perfection from your caramel-colored skin,
To the beauty of your face, to the soul within.
You remind me of an angel with your heavenly glow.
You are my other half; I want to get to know.

You are perfection 'cause I can find no faults.
When you are near, all words seem to halt.
When God made you He had perfection on his mind;
Girls like you in this world are too hard to find.
Maybe one day I'll get my wish;
Only you can send me to this world of bliss.

Yes, you are perfection, a little bird told me,
From the highest mountain to the deepest sea.
I hope one day we could be together,
Me and you together forever.
You are as beautiful as a dove.
You are perfection; you are love.

   Thomas Floyd Jr.

Thank You

To Ed Gil Christ, whose friendship I cherish
Thank you for being my friend and always being there.
Your friendship is a treasure, indeed a gift most rare.
Thank you for all the joy you have brought into my life,
where your presence alone makes it free from strife.
Thank you for the tenderness of your touch; your warmth,
patience, and understanding mean so very much.
Thank you for all the simple pleasures and precious
time that we have shared,
where love and laughter reigned supreme and we dared dream
of a world few have ever known: a pasture
rich in memories we have sown.
Yes, you have filled a special place within my heart,
and there you will remain forever and a day.
What more can I say, except thank you again for
being my friend and all the kind things that you do. With all
my heart I sincerely say there could never be another you.

   Iris B. Dillon

The Frozen Rose

My teardrops fell spurned
Upon the spirals of a beautiful red rose.
Some glistening petals fell.
My love burned.
The red rose froze.

   Connie J. Moyes

Wake Up, Little Sister

Wake up, little sister, sleeping beauty,
I pray for the prince to pierce your darkness.
Is your coma a consuming echo
Or a deafening stillness where spirits walk?
Are you caught in some wide chasm dangling
Between Earth and Heaven, afraid to choose?
Are you a guest on some great odyssey,
Awaiting the transcending finale?
Are you embraced by some euphoric dream
That ensnares you in rapture and splendor?
Please do not succumb to this sleeping death.

But, my dearest little sister,
Dress in your soul's richest garments
And your invincible spirit.
Awake, see daybreak's new dawning,
Touch the soothing satin of sheets,
Smell the rare perfume of roses,
Hear the welcome of our voices,
Taste the sweetness of communion
And promise of resurrection.

   June Nash

A Parable of Purpose

Down in the garden
a persimmon tree grew,
but for what purpose
we never knew.
From its branches
it produced no fruit,
only absorbed the strength
of earth through its root.
To our judgement
it was for no use,
for no visible fruit
did it ever produce.

Near by was grape vine
from which much fruit grew.
It served its purpose,
this we surely knew.
But as it grew larger
and began to expand,
it reached out as to grasp a hand.
Through the branches of the tree it gently wound.

   Doris Parsons Weaver

To

To everyone who has given me a hand
when I was down on my luck
and helped me on my feet to land
your memory has since been stuck.
I'd like to say thank you.

To everyone who has been a friend
and helped me pass the days
who always had a laugh to send
as we walked through life's maze.
I'd like to say I love you.

To everyone I've never met,
although we may have passed by
but conversation never let
for this I know not why.
I'd like to say hello.

To everyone who laughs at me
because we're not the same
you chuckle because of what you see,
must I take all the blame?
I'd like to say you cant hurt me . . . but you can.

   Jason Siscoe

Jasper for Your Soul

For dusty Rosebud and Goo-Goo, I love you always
before me lies a parade of a thousand faces:
bloo fluke, pepur, fli and drat,
liper, finkle, and nate are but a few.
dancing tiptoe, in and out, in and out.
feathers swaying, makeup dripping.
in then out and back in again.
curling backwards and sideways but never forward.
hooking the floor board desperate not to fall through.
a thousand faces, a thousand fold
I know.

white and shining, soothing and calming.
deep and penetrable, filling and feeling.
say it like you mean it.
whisper it to me, tell me what it is.
"JASPER"
know that I am your Jasper.

Roxanne Manolesco

Commandment

To Jessica, who inspires me in her own way
I knew that the second I picked up my pen
to write this poem, it was sin.

Although this hot blue ink smears paper in a way
that suggests longing, my stagnant imagination
cannot even begin to think of words
that would satisfy Aphrodite,
words that could build an archway
over our understanding of each other:
the way heroes understand courage,
the way villains understand wickedness,
the way kings understand power.

The only way to give justice to these thoughts
is to write them in your heart instead.
That you can look in to your heart and know me,
that would make time and distance fall away,
the way a petal would fall off a rose.

Cynthia Cabral

Life's Stream

My life flows on unto the sea.
Along the way it changes me.
Once a carefree, happy stream,
I thought of nothing but to dream,
But varied currents pressed my run.

Rocks appeared to thwart my course,
And frightening whirlpools spent my force.
What once were happy days, are fraught with apprehension.
I am forced to twist and turn,
Regardless of intention.

What lies ahead! Around the bend!
A falls, a cataract?
Oh, would it were a peaceful sea
Opening its arms to me.

Ruth Keating

Hollow Halls

In the darkness alone, I am lost
I reach for you, I find nothing
In the darkness without you, I am empty
All that I have done, meaningless
I stand alone
The door to the castle stands open
It is empty, hollow
Halls once filled with joy
Echo with grief
The princess has gone
The warrior stands alone, his heart wailing
His refuge broken he waits
For the princess to return

David D. Holtze Jr.

Let Me Know

Lord, let me know the way I should go.
Clear up all of this confusion and pain.
Instead, replace it with Heaven's bright glow,
To shine through the fog and rain.
Lord, I listen for songs from above
Singing to me words of wisdom and peace
And promises of an everlasting love,
That no sin or neglect could change or cease.
Lord, right now my heart is full of sorrow,
Not sure of my purpose or long term plan,
In search of the desires of tomorrow,
With many memories still in command.
Lord, please help let me know the reasons why;
Give me the strength to give life one more try.

Robin A. Kennon

Mother

On your face, always a smile,
Always willing to talk awhile.
You take the time to show you care
When on your nerves we know we wear.
You give us wings
And the little things,
Like manners and morals,
Dresses of florals.
You teach us grace
And how to save face.
From diapers to dances,
Your presence enhances
Our hours and days,
Our mights and mays.
We're happy that you are our mother.
We'd never settle for any other.
And though sometimes we don't show our love,
Know that we worship you as God above.

Maria C. Janoski

Song of a Free Bird

Ever hear the song of a free bird?
"Ain't no telling—
theyz seldom ever heard."

Tell me about her words and her music.
"Theyz played in way we just don't understand."

So to love her is to free her?
"She gots to be moving on."

When men see her they want her
"and take her to dere room!"
But their beds cannot be
"hers with a canopy!"

She belongs up with the winds!
"Fer her changes never end."
The song of a free bird
is seldom ever heard.

Misti Poulos

Grimmy Bunt

Although I've only known you for a year and a few,
You are the only person I give my secrets to.

I burden you with problems, that are always on the rise,
And of course for this, I could never fully apologize.

Your strength has seen me through the worst of all my days,
Because of that, in you my friendship lays.

For all the times you stood by me, no matter how pathetic.
I know I sometimes I bother you,
but you somehow just don't let it.

Be careful what you wish for and with whom you coincide,
But in case you ever need me,
I'll be by your side.

Kelly Mastracchio

The Sign

In memory of my lovely daughter, Cynthia
I stood weeping by her lonely resting-place,
Shrouded in a grief too harsh for me to face.

"Where is she?" I cried aloud. "Is she—forever—dead?
Or does she live in spirit, as the preacher said?"

"Look for a sign," He'd consoled me.
"You know she's in heavenly attire,
Wearing a brilliant halo, no doubt, and singing with the choir."

My senses failed to note, at first, the sweetness in the air
Or the gathering clouds of golden mist that formed a winding stair.

Waves of ethereal music filled the stillness of the scene.
I trembled in euphoric awe; amazed at what it could mean.

And then—a luminous white feather, unlike any of this land,
Softly floated—out of nowhere—and settled in my hand.

Larue Lennen

Poetry

Tonight, all I need is the moonlight
For if I want to write a true poem
I have to learn to trust nature
And everything it holds
I don't need a lamp to see if I am
Writing my poetry right
All I need is to keep my poetry in my heart
A place were I know no one can steal it
A place were I cannot lose what I have written down
For it will stay with me forever
And no one can take that away from me
Poetry is not just something someone scribbles
On a piece of paper
It is what they feel inside
For me, writing poetry is like having a door open
But to everyone else, I just scribble things on paper

Samantha Shelton

True Love

What makes one think they might find love
When looking at the beautiful full moon above
And sitting by God's ocean that is, oh, so blue
Wishing for a lover who would be true?

Would one be asking God for way too much?
Moon above, ocean blue, true love, and such
I know God made our world for woman and man
So that one may find love on his land

There must be surely someone around
Which could be found with true love abound
So all one needs to do is keep looking around
Then someday their love will be found

Then one could have love that is so true
While viewing God's ocean that is, oh, so blue
And his beautiful full moon shining above
Our God made all this so we might find love

Marjorie Marie Privett

Unforgiveness

Unforgiveness is the pain we love to bear,
The banner we carry, the standard we share.
It hardens our hearts; it perverts our souls.
Unforgiveness, the salve that heals our pain.

But the enemy is a liar; he has deceived us all!
The perversion backfires,
Destroying our ability to see
That the walls we have built
Never set us free.

The enemy is a liar; why can't we see?
Forgiveness is the key that sets us free,
Free to tear down the walls, set the captives free!
As I look in the mirror, that captive is me.

Wandamarie B. Crawford

Scars

Perfection can never be achieved.
There will always be a Flaw somewhere.
Scars are everywhere:
In our Minds,
In our Souls,
In our Bodies.
I have Scars everywhere.
My Mind is scattered in a million different directions
because I can't let things go unanswered.
Sometimes the answers Hurt.
My soul is Scarred because someone felt the need
to damage the innocence of a Child.
My Body carries Scars because I've been Harmed.
Everyone has Scars, they just don't always show.
So no one can ever be Perfect.
Perfection cannot be Achieved.
Everyone is Different.
How can Perfection be defined?
Is there a definition? No!
There is only One who can be Perfect . . . God!

Sherrie Golden

Of Primary Importance

To my loving parents, Peter and Frances
From the ginger of the seed can be found not a sound
As if in anger of stagnation the sound
Of an explosion fills the void
The message to the seeds of time
Whispered from the first divine
Hatred's an erosion to avoid

The words were all but overturned
Save only by the gentle brood who strived
Whose quiet love still softly burned

While disquieting tones continued to survive

As amber flame of candle faintly glows
And clarifies the picture of the night
The light of love shines freely as it goes
Amid the ruins of hatred's fading sight

Though hatred's nature is corrupt and vile
And seeks to overcome the best of us
Disallowing it to consume our domicile
May one day soon become the test of us.

Thomas G. Raffa

Close Your Eyes and Feel the Season

The creaking of tall fir limbs
yields to the gentle mountain breeze
kissing the meadow the sun warms with ease
The eagle, he glides overhead
calling to his mate; the sunlight dims

Green to yellow to orange and red
changing colors show summer's end
Through the evergreen, the cottontail, mule deer, and elk
prepare for the season ahead
Strength and will to survive with God's guiding hand

Soft, white flakes begin to coat the forest floor
as crisp air kisses all it touches
The lake held motionless, though life below goes on evermore
A beautiful blanket sparkles with the sun's light
grows deadly cold through the long night

Nature's babies all shapes and sizes playfully begin anew
colorful flowers, pink and purple and blue
The eagle returns her chicks loudly calling
scented wild lilac's sweet, fresh and true

Virginia A. Ferguson

Winter Tree

O', what majesty the sunrise reveals,
A breathtaking brilliance of color
Splashed across the blue winter sky,
An explosion of yellows, orange, and pinks.
Reflections of sunlight from the icebound winter tree,
Stark branches silhouetted against the sky,
And sculpture of man and nature merged together,
Symphony of tinkling, crackling, falling ice,
Wine glasses shattered in the stone hearth,
The exhilaration of reaching lofty peaks,
A fleeting moment in time quickly vanishing forever,
Never to be recaptured again—
As the sun sets beyond the piercing white clouds,
The kaleidoscope of color hues rapidly changes
To yellows, deep orange, and raging fire red,
Soon to vanish in the darkness beyond twilight.
The winter trees immersed in the pale moonlight,
With a mystical veil from another world,
Returning the forest to a strange, silent retreat,
As man contemplates his fate in the journey through life.

　　Walter P. Lemiech

Untitled

Every day was tough,
Never being good enough.
While a child, 'twas seeded,
Lacking the love she needed,
Safe refuge to hide,
God planted faith deep inside.
Doing all she could,
Always striving to be good
As child and as wife,
The empty feeling—the strife—
Her faith had insured.
Deep inside, her hope endured.
Now, arising fear
Emanated by his leer,
Uncontrolled temper,
He was coming after her.
Her body was used, beaten, battered, and abused.
His fists continued punching, smashing—he ensued.
Last tear shed—now dead,
With the nodding of her head.

　　Annette K. Sonnenberg

Eternal Kingdom

England, strong with power,
Must maintain a tower.
Babel was to fall;
Its kingdom had no call.

Man's kingdom makes demands,
Servants to beat the band.
Pyramiding castles in the sand
Possess large parcels of land.

Names blazing in the spotlight,
Attracting pleasures of the night.
Triumph of the restless young,
Their shallow kingdom, too soon sung.

The magic kingdom exists;
Tiny tots love its bliss.
Dream of the heart, this fairyland,
Cascades into adult's hands.

Good seed, sewn inside,
Grows a kingdom within that gives pride.
Kingdoms and kings may fade away,
But the kingdom of God is the eternal, radiant ray.

　　Rhoda W. Brown

Heaven's in the Air

In memory of a loving man, Glenwood Shorey
Tears fall as a man is given away
the heavens open their gates
the smell of wood can be taken
in with the autumn sorrow

Everything crawls out of my grasp
the air freezes my lungs
as the winter earth swallows my lonely tears

Giggles from happy children
carried by the wind
spring flowers arise for he is still alive

I sit on the porch
and think how life slowly drips away
while all along he had filled the summer air

　　Elysia Melendez

Truthfully Be

Every adult ever states we should always think of children.
They should not be subject to sexuality, rudeness, or violence.
And so this should truthfully be.

Why do we not uphold the words we speak,
Rather than be an example of all we should not be?
And so this should truthfully be.

Imprinted words on movie or TV screens say,
"Parental guidance suggested because of adult language or scenes."
Adults should reflect the truth as to how an adult should be:
Loving, caring, and respectable to all children, by speaking
A language without vulgarity.

By setting an example of purity and morality,
Eliminate scenes of explicit sexuality
And let imagination return for prosperity.
And so this should truthfully be.

　　John R. Kaselnak

Endless

but I never reached the top
I climbed till every bone ached
till every muscle burned
till my vision blurred
and my head pounded as loud as my heart.
Something happened . . .
I lost my grip
I lost my strength
I lost the will . . .
or was it all stolen from me . . .
by the shear force of the rigid mountain,
by its endless life,
its stillness.
It laughed as I cried
and grew as I fell.
And when I hit bottom
I got up,
began my climb again,
but I never reached the top.

　　Daniel Grussgott

The Nobleman

A knight in shining armor,
A'flight on a sweet, swift mare,
Gallops off into battle.
With his trumpet in hand,
Bow in another, he strides off, gallantly
Fearless, into the maw
Of fighting and discord, the endless yell
Of an ancient, years old dispute.

　　Jennifer Kempkes

Recovery

To Rob
I've seen you hurting, lived your pain.
I consoled you to make it better
And found my life close to insane.
You didn't have drive to make yourself well,
And you continued to live a life of hell.
It hurts me so to see you suffer,
For I wish I could take your pain away.
The love we shared was so dear to me
And will always forever be.
Now you've started to see the light;
Give your life a new start, give it all your might.
You are forever in my thoughts and prayers,
And I wish nothing but the best,
For you are worth every effort to make it last.
Recovery, a tough task, Lord knows you're worth the chance,
To give yourself all life has to offer
And to dance the dance.
With or without you, forever in my heart,
Is where you will be from here on out.

Traci Lynn Edwards

Dancin' in Paris

I be awerkin' at fixin' dinner,
and my man, he be awerkin' in the fields,
and well, I just startin' inta dreamin'
'bout me a'dancin' in Paris.

I be wearin' sparkly shoes with high, skinny
heels, and one o' them slinky gowns. I'm a'drinkin'
that bubbly stuff outin' a one-legged glass.
Lotsa good-lookin' men be astin' me ta dance.

Then my man comes home, clumpin' in muddy
boots, his shirt and pants dirty and dusty.
He be a mess! Ceptin' his eyes—they be warm
'n brown like new-plowed fields, and his voice
be like a river a'flowin', so deep and smooth.
"Dinner ready yet, sugar bun?"

His hand touches my hair right gentle—
like the breeze of a summer night a'mussin'
the leaves o' the willer tree. 'Long about then,
my heart feels like velvet cushins be a'pressin'
agin' it. Well, I startin' inta thinkin' . . .
who wants ta be dancin' in Paris anyhow?

Mary Naylor

Knowing

Worry in your darkness
and Bleed in your tears,
for not understanding
hurts most of All.
You notice what other don't,
and it could be your Paranoid State,
yet it could be more.
And you just don't understand,
and the bleeding intensifies,
for what lies beneath the skin
could change you.
Could this all be in your Head?
Could all the thinking damage more?
Could you forget and the problem go away?
Or would it grow in your blindness?
Will you die in your darkness?

Or will the body change
and, with it, sanity?
For what is not known pierces the skin
far deeper then the Truth!

Etana Holowinko

My Mother

For my mother, Helen Livingston Hughes
My mother died this year
Her delicacy frayed by complexities of life
She found peace, whole and absolute
Touched by tranquility of spirit
A whisper of God
Transcending all limitations
I quietly watched
Spiritual love before unseen
My heart understood
It seemed a perfect wisdom
The grace of compassion
She spoke to me in ways I had never known
A love so sweet and sure
The sense of spirit unending
My heart she held, I finally knew
My mother died this year
And I was born again and again
Overwhelmed by the spirit of grace and goodness

Judy Tyson

My Mother's Daughters

In memory of my mother, Mary L. Carmichael
She had one son, then a daughter was born
Her life with her mother was short, only six hours.
My mother said that she was heartbroken and forlorn
But that God eventually comforted her
With six more daughters, one by one.
She loved and cared for these daughters
As if each were the only one.
She taught them about the great love of God
And how every problem He could solve.
And as my Mother aged in years
She became even more dear to her daughters.
She taught them to hold onto God's unchanging hand
For He always had a plan, for each daughter.
And even at age eighty-three when she became bedridden
The daughters had not forgotten
Together all six cared for their loving Mother
Until she left them, to be with her first daughter.

Martha J. Currington

Child of Three

I am a child
Innocent and pure
I am on this Earth for a reason I am sure.
Angels watch over me day and night,
For they will never take flight.

Please listen.
I have a story to tell,
A story about mommy and me.
Rage, hatred, beatings, and neglect,
For no food bears our cupboards,
Until that knock at our door.
For, my mommy has crack
breakfast, lunch, and supper.
Alcohol and drugs are her lover.
Off in a corner, watching and listening,
Waiting for the rage, then comes the beating!
For, this is my day.

No one will listen, no one does see,
For I am only a child of three.

Leigh Jarrell

Grandpa

A plain, gold wedding band.
Thick, solid, and strong. A 14K gold masterpiece
symbolizing the love and loyalty of the man who once wore it.
Baby fine scratches mar this band, but never diminish its beauty.
Its strength shines in the light, mirroring all of his honor.
The magical power of his love can still be felt embracing your finger,
and his smile often winks at you as the band turns upon your hand.
His never ending circle of love . . . I know Grandpa is always with me.

Diana Niedholdt

The Jukebox Playing

I am now sitting in a bar room alone
Listening to the jukebox playing,
Saying something about love is all gone,
And about love has all come to an end.

My eyes are red, my head's in a spin,
For you see my heart has been broken again.
Oh, baby, what an awful shape I'm in,
And to think I promise never to do this again.

But there are tears that must be cried,
Until there's no more tears to fall,
Till there's less hurt way deep inside.
For one more beer was the cause of it all.

Now the jukebox playing with all my quarters,
And I will sit here, until last quarter is played
And let tears run down my cheek like water,
For you said we will now be only friends.

Alice Bertrand

Walking Dream

I took a walk tonight. And not for the first time, but, yet again,
I noticed the magnificence of the planet
that we are privileged to dwell upon.
I watched the yellow-bright sun dismount slowly
from its low perch in the light blue sky.
The paling sky displayed a tapestry of light
and dark clouds sketched across its breadth;
interlaced with pink and lavender hues peeking through their threads.
The sun wrapped golden ribbon around the package
of clouds nearest its dimming glow.
The sea, slate gray tonight instead of its usual bright blue,
beckons temptingly to Jack Frost.
Looking skyward, in perfect timing with Mother Nature,
I am treated to one of her beautiful treasures, creating a glorious memory.
Upon an invisible cue from their captain,
a jagged group of seabirds form their legendary vee
and wing off in beautiful, inspiring harmony across the sunset.
The unexpected sight of such raw nature in action,
especially so near human habitat, stopped me in my tracks.
No National Geographic this! This is real-time. Now. Mine. Stunning!

Gina Osher

Jesus, Our Example

Wasn't God good to send Jesus to show us the way we should walk?
Wasn't God good to send Jesus to show us the talk we should talk?

God sent His son, our example, to show how we all should live,
To show how to love one another and how many times to forgive,

Seventy times seven is many, but that is the number He gave.
Whatever the problem, large or small, forgive and a friendship you'll save.

Life can be sweet or sad with grief that makes life hard to bear,
But the challenge to overcome trials is the test to show us God's "care."

"All things are possible," Jesus said, "to him that can believe."
He is willing to give the power, through our faith,
So our goals we'll achieve.

Life is a race that goes on and on. One day at a time we're to live.
Only God knows when our end will be,
So, 'til then, I'll feel free to forgive.

So wasn't God good to send Jesus, our brother, our Savior, our friend?
He showed us by His example how to live 'til the very end.

Rue Ceil Graves

Lord, Help Me

"In as much as ye have done it unto one of
the least of these my brethren, ye have done it unto me."
Matthew 25:40

"Rejoice with them that do rejoice, and weep with them that weep."
Romans 12:15

Today I walked among mankind, wept with the sorrowful,
    served poor and ill,

Invited a stranger into my home, visited in a prisoner's cell. . . .

Yet, when I encountered one whom wealth and fame had touched,
    my voice

And hands powerless became! Lord, help me: I can weep,
    but not rejoice!

Mary Earle Lowry Curry

Conscience of Decency

Conscience of decency is within each of us.
One sometimes tries to go around it,
but it keeps coming back like an old bus.
One may hang around the corner trying to push it away,
but when it's there, it is there to stay.
One may even shuffle it about with a bad act or two.
"Lo and behold," we say, "this is not the thing to do."
So gathering our precious selves with scoldings 'til we are blue, our
conscience of decency prevails, and we become once again like new.
One will sense proudness when one carries their laurels high.
The feeling inspires other good deeds
which, in turn, creates a bond and tie.
Fortunate are we to understand the
difference between good and bad.
Thus moving on to better things,
making each past moment the best we ever had.

Mary Rubino Andreatta

The Ancient Tribes

They were the ones that came before, opening up the door.

Escape the persecution, slavery; being set free,
Make the long voyage across a vast, untamed sea,
To land on some strange foreign shore and plant a seed,
Watch it grow and the world that will come to be.

Future generations, descendants from the ancient tribes,
Living deep inside the exploited wilderness,
Awaken in mysterious night by the barking dogs.
Where do we now stand in the Universe?
Who are you in this life? A resident in the mockery of light.

Knowledge lost from the moon and sun,
"Old and wise satyr," grand creator,
Give us one last time to perfect our art,
Give us wisdom in a darker hour.

"Monsters of skin", the master of sin,
Lost in violence, sex, and worldly games of desire, reckless and wild;
Warmed by the presence of the old, ancient fire.

Stuart L. Spanier

Smiles

Sometimes words are not enough
To communicate our feelings deep inside our souls;
It's difficult to express our innermost thoughts.
Sometimes it takes a touch, a handclasp.

It can bring about understanding that alludes us otherwise.
When we gaze into each other's eyes,
Instant recognition and hope arise.
Out of confusion, understanding's the prize.

I hope I've met and answered a lonely need, if only with a smile.
A stranger smiled at me one ragged day, and I recall it made me glad.
It has lent contentment to my day.
So, I smile on my way.

Frances Mundy

Memories

To my wife, Miriam F. Cook
Though our hearts may yearn for loved ones and we long to
have them near,
Separated as we are, we cling to memories dear.

For time has mellowed all of us and we think of days gone by
When we were younger, full of life, but time just seemed to fly.

Now, gone are the carefree dreams we had; with truth we face each day.
Echoes of children laughing, scurrying to and fro in play . . .

Wonderful, beautiful memories yet and we'd trade with not one soul.
Each thought a treasure beyond compare; our lives have been so full!

    Herbert N. Cook

My Butterfly

You came into this world, so delicate and small,
More of color and cuddlesome of them all,
And as I watched each day, dependent little thing
Before I could take a breath, you had sprouted tiny wings.
You grew beautiful, broad wings in every imaginable color
And there were splashes throughout your wings in all shades of yellow,
Winging your way from here to there, lighting each thing you touched.
And everything seem to glow, they loved you very much,
And as the years went swiftly past, strong winds began to blow.
You fought so hard to keep in flight, pressure on your wings did show.
But time was a disadvantage, the wind didn't subside.
It pounded harder and harder, your wings couldn't glide.
And then one day God said, "Enough, wild wing, be still."
He took my butterfly to rest in peace, in eternity, was His will.

    Gloria M. Little

Sounds from the Womb

To all expectant mothers who are contemplating abortion
Mommy, do you hear me? I did not ask you and daddy to make
me. You and daddy had a night of pleasure while out on the
town; and mommy, you found yourself carrying me around.
Then one day you said: "I cannot afford this child." So you
and daddy conspired to end my life long before I had the chance
to catch a glimpse of the beautiful world outside. I will try to run
away from the doctor's attack weapon, but mommy where will I
run to? Who will be there to plead my case and to rescue me
from the sharp instrument that will so viciously snatch my life
away from me? I will scream, I will scream to the top of my voice.
Mommy, will you hear me? Do you hear me mommy? Mommy
please, all I want is the same chance you and daddy had: to live,
to move, to crawl, to walk, to run, to play, to be nurtured, to give
unconditional love and to be loved. Mommy, I want to live!
Never will I get the chance to go to school or to Disney World
like the other little children. Oh, mommy, what did I do wrong?
Can't you just give me to a loving couple who so desperately
want a child to love, to cherish and to care for? Mommy, why
are you doing this to me? Mommy dear, what did I do to
deserve capital punishment? What you and daddy did was not
my fault. You must have hated me a bunch mommy, because
within a few minutes, you will have me murdered. Mommy, you
and daddy wanted the pleasure, but you just did not want to
bear the pain.

    Frankie P. Futrell

Me Too, You

Was it those eyes or the look you always had?
Or maybe it was the way you held my head.
It doesn't really matter, as we reflect on all those years;
That you're ten years my senior was never here nor there.
But the thought of not having you was more than I could bear.
Guess we'll never know, was it those eyes or your fingers in my hair.
Then you kiss and you whisper; "me too, you" was all I needed to hear.
But those eyes, so mysterious and blue,
When you enter our room, my only thoughts—"Me too, You."

    Janet K. Thomas

The Ponderer

At conception I did swim so very swift and fast,
But, one day, not long ago, I wondered why I hadn't finished last.
I thought about what had happened to the rest,
And why they had let me race ahead of them.
Were they too slow, or did they know I was chosen for the test?

Had I been sent from above, and angel in disguise,
A special little person, with blondish hair and big blue eyes?
Was I returned to Earth to take the place
Of someone journeying back through space?

Could it have been the beggar,
   with a countenance so forlorn and grim,
Departed now from his corner on the walk,
Old and sick, following his friend's departure before him?
Or the gambler with his stack of cards,
Clutched too tightly in his hand, with a look of fright on his frozen face,
When they pried him from the sand?

No one will ever know the reason they were selected,
But through all the joy and trials and sorrows, we carry on,
Because unanimously, we were elected.

    Sondra Middletown

Heart of America

In memory of Benjamin Marino, M.P. second World War
Heart of America, I hear your heart beat.
It's time to make our vows, to be good soldiers, for we can't be beat.
We must have vigilance and patiently pray, when we can, let's be
strong and be proud Americans. Respect our leaders with esteem;
they know what's best for our American dreams. Our leader, our
military across the sea, they're on patrol for you and me. When
you hear news that makes history, don't get upset, for our world
is very complex. Our Presidents have done their best. Many
changes have been made, and many changes there will be. Let's
respect our laws, for this is a great country. Wars of the past,
they're hard to forget. Service men that were brave so we could
be free, and yet the ones that can't be found and the ones
resting. The Marines, the first on the beat, fighting for our
freedom, this our Great country: Men of land and sea, and men
or renown. America, I hear your heart beat. It's peace and
freedom that's our fight. Fight with your intellect and make your
vows with your heart and make them now. Just our government,
their history in time. Let's be good soldiers and give our heart
time and be proud as can be. For, time given is cherished, but
never forgotten. Not now, ever in time. God bless our country
and all the rest. Heart of America, we're on the beat, be vigilant
soldiers and help keep peace and freedom in our great country.

    Agnes Hardy

A Needed Gift, the Mind

To my children, Pete, Pamela,
Grandchildren, Nathan, Danielle, Travis
Your mind is what you feed it, so feed it well; it must
Last your lifetime, so nourish every cell.
Without a strong mind, your body goes stale; don't
Waste a great mind that has a lot to tell.
Whether you are female or you are male, never allow
Your mind or your body to begin to gel.

Feed the mind daily with the best of materials, and
Never allow it to become weak or dizzy.
Read books on real life, enjoy sweet poems, is a few
Ideas to keep your mind busy.
Exercise the mind with intelligent happenings of life;
It's the mind that helps the body function so nice.

Keep the mind sober with long nights of rest, so it may
Surpass any daytime test.
Our mind is a treasure, a jewel with a crest, so give
It good care as time goes by, and it will give back to you
Its very best—a peaceful mind awakens with a
Fruitfulness and fullness of zest.

So I say to you, tutor it and school it with all your
Might, and it will connect with your brain to become a beacon of light.

    Joie L. Bullock

Faith

All my life I've believed that God is love
And we are all His children, bar none.
Through my faith, it's Christ, my Lord, who reigns from Heaven above.
He reassures me that he is with me—that my prayers are heard
and answered, especially when day is done.

If I falter as I travel down life's highway,
I pray that Christ's forgiveness prevails.
For God and Christ understand and are with us all,
to hear our pleas about our frailties and such.
That are brought to the fore and solved by prayer,
prayer that never fails.
I give thanks to my Lord, constant companion, judge,
guard and guide—a feeling that He is my Midas touch.

No matter what I humbly bring before Him,
all will be good with blessings bestowed as well.
Yes, I know His presence is with me. He is my help and my friend.
His compassion supports my well being.
He is a just God and so I write. The whole world to tell.
Therefore, thank you Father, for your love and understanding
and all else that I am receiving.

Donald A. Richards

Rejoice with Jesus

What if Mary had told the angel Gabriel to be on his way?
Mary had a hectic schedule, people to see and places to go on that day.
What if Joseph's heart had been filled with vengeance,
Hate, and arrogant pride?
Legally, he could have Mary stoned;
Instead, he took her as his loving bride.
What if the innkeeper had refused Mary and Joseph shelter
   in the manger?
With an inn full of travelers, he didn't want his reputation
   put in danger.

Without the birth of Jesus, why celebrate—
   what would our destiny be?
We would have no source of hope and our souls lost eternally.
Mary was a true, obedient servant of God, our heavenly Father.
She gave birth to Jesus Christ, our Lord,
   without any complaints of bother.

Accepting Him as Savior is each individual's choice.
With Him, you have every reason to celebrate and rejoice!
Without Jesus as Lord, what will your true meaning of Christmas be?
Gifts, food, friends, and family all satisfy, but only temporarily.

Invite Jesus, right now, to live in your heart.
Have true hope, joy, and peace right from the start.
With Jesus, you will never be alone—Jesus is always near.
Now, you will truly have a blessed Christmas and Happy New Year!

Virginia Rhodes

Voices of War

Many men fought for our freedom
Some knew nothing of wars and their deceit
We greeted the decorated heroes,
   murderers of mothers and small children
The real heroes left in Vietnam with unexplainable diseases
And missing body parts
Our minds wash away the horror of Iwo Jima
The bodies scored and unnecessary lives lost
Why do we make so many mothers cry in vain?
We all were put here to live as one
Let's do that before it's all said and done
It's not over, it's just begone
The fight for world freedom, for all nations, creeds, and colors
The answer is not separation, but unity
To uncover the injustices done not to one, but all
Speak as a unit and all the wrongs will be righted without slight
There will be no oversights, just peace and harmony
For all to see and live within for eternity!

Andrea R. Martin

The Message/Generation X

The ghetto is still the same as it was yesterday, today:
Thousand of lives still wasting away.

People looking for satisfaction in the labels that they wear,
Only to find none there.

Education being taken for granted; I can't understand it.
Generation X: "Wake up! Can't you see the conspiracy?"
Materialist, virtue reality.

All must be put in the proper prospect. "Don't neglect."

For wisdom and knowledge always reign supreme
   in achieving one's dreams.

Charles Robinson

Dreams

While I am in a deep slumber, comfortable and cozy,
images of my past come to my vision.
Images that I do not want to remember come to me, haunt me.
Stress, fear, anger, and any other emotions God has put in name to us
strangle me, torture me, until I can no longer breathe.
I lay there in my bed thinking about heartbreaks, divorce, depression.
I try to think of the times when I was little.
No worries, but all those times are memories now,
memories that are fading away.
My life is like a growing beautiful flower,
freezing from the cold night air,
Times are changing, feelings have change, the world has changed.
But for the better? Only time will tell.
When I am in a deep slumber, comfortable and cozy,
images of my past comes to my vision.
Images that I do not want to remember come to me,
are washed away by a gentle kiss upon lips
that comes present in the morning.
I see light shining brightly from between the curtains
and realize it was a dream.
For a kiss and love is stronger than any bad dream.

Tina Marie Cook

Recognition

To Mrs. Marsha Tower and Mrs. Julie G.
Today is yesterday, tomorrow will be today. The dreams I pray
will not go away. The hands I shook, the smiles returned was
a beginning into a new life. Day after day, I walked the same path,
stagnated in yesterday. Trying to cope with tomorrow only
brought me sorrow. My world came tumbling down when I
realized I was on a merry-go-round. Repeated actions of
yesterday confirmed I was not ready for today. Down on
myself, mad at the world, striving to run away, I realized there is
a tomorrow and we start from yesterday. These hands I once shook
gave me a hug, smiled tenderly, picked me up, gave me a new
tomorrow to see. Now I am set free. I will always be grateful to
these special ladies, their love and trust they had in me. I will
always be grateful for that special attention of educating me.
God bless you, my friends, now it is possible, what I dreamed of
yesterday will be possible today.

Phyllis Datta Gupta

Somewhere in Between

I can't always be sunny side up; 'twould be an impossible task.
So what kind of egg am I is a question that now I ask.

For one deems me fragile, another tough. Which side of me prevails?
If I were tossed in the air like a coin, would I land heads or tails?

If were as fragile as an uncooked egg, I'd be afraid to ramble.
If I should meet Humpty Dumpty's fate, like Humpty I'd be scrambled.

If I were as tough as a hard-boiled egg, neither pain nor joy I'd feel.
Even if my shell should crack, inside my feelings are sealed.

Therefore, a perfect place to be is somewhere in between,
Fragile enough to feel—tough enough to endure—
A three minute egg I would seem.

Carolyn Rogers Hudson

To Preserve

To Mum, Daisy LeBoutillier Bishop
The conserve is first an imperfect attempt,
like burnt ice, fractured.
The boiling crystallized sweetness doesn't age,
is never even born.
I imagine my duty is not, after all,
To pass on the faces of your amazing essence,
Yet my eyes tear as I clasp your gnarled finger
curled tenderly around my breath.

Then, I see
Your sand grain sized eyes stare as
Dusty airs whirl beseeching closer,
Shifting with the growing heat of a sunburn night.
Your history, faces in time,
Seem aline the rim of a vast silver mirror hinging the stars.
They gaze, hung to dry, perfect shadows, each almost like one another,
Faces, now cast out, yet lovingly cooled,
And finally calm.
And I know to kiss your marbleized forehead, your lips
Filled, full, all knowing.
And I will preserve the sugared honey of your soul.

      Elaine B. Politis

Out in Left Field

Sometimes I feel like a motherless child; but I remember God.
When I didn't need the constant resentment about your consent.

I'm hanging around with just a frown, nothing more or nothing less,
I confess.

Sometimes I feel like a fatherless child, but I remember God.
When I get confused about my identity.
Certainly not knowing whose needs are greater.

My mother for loving my dad too much or my dad for not knowing
I would be born as a result.

Sometimes I feel like a homeless child, but I remember God.
When I was controlled by the streets and roam the back alley
for a handout from anyone I tend to meet or greet.
I may live in a shelter or seek refuge at a mission.
I dwelled in a place and survive the wrath.
Sometimes I feel like a helpless child, but I remember God.
When I was contained by fear and driven by knowing one day,
I will have better days ahead. Instead of out in left field, I pray.

You just want to beat the odds of life that all people need
all believed in justifying their will to live in God's watchful eyes.

      Patricia Dian Nunn

The Faces of Love

To my father and personal cheer leader, David Christians Sr.
Liars and thieves speak of love all the time
it drips from their lips like nectar from a flower.
Poets and writers define love without experience
as the clearest brightest star in all the heavens.
While the true lovers struggle with the single syllable
trying feebly to express the fire within their hearts.
Seductively the liar calls upon his prey
to begin their part in his masquerade.
Silently the poet watches so he may write
the story of this unforgettable night.
All alone the lover waits knowing he cannot tempt the hands of fate.
In rush the thieves to do their part and steal away the innocence of love.
At this point to the writers take over and try to explain the fear of loss.
While in the darkness the lover sits gaining his courage and strength.
Now the liars and thieves have slipped away
with the night at the break of day.
The poets and writers lay down their pens
always knowing they shall be picked up again.
Now the lover speaks, without their demands
and is rewarded by the life placed in his hands.

      Fonda J. Christians

The Boatman's Fare

For those who have faith and dare to dream—believe
Gods created mortals weak and insecure, gift from Olympus is
newborn innocent and pure; entombed in soil
   are seeds plum, cherry, peach, apricot
Imprisoned by mortals' ignorance, greed, and lustful desires are psyche
and love—freedom viciously sought;
Folly of youth is to rape tree before the harvest and ripened fruit,
selfishly indulging forbidden pursuits;
Chained to craving of lust, an unforgiving God,
slave begins journey foretold,
Bloodied hearts hang as mementos, trophies of fool's gold;

Future certain as one falls from grace, tumbling down gauntlet
blackened by fate, life desperately grasps at emptiness
of past unable to save face;
Searching and finding a soul mate now a matter for luck,
dice rolled by gods, Aphrodite has last say as who will and will not;
Venturing forth blind in faith and conviction,
pilgrim makes offering of gratitude for what little is possessed,
hope from box gift to Pandora cherished above the rest;
Mortal seeks counsel in matters of love and soul, finding not virtue
or truth until boatman tells one to return to where they came for
traveler unable to pay toll.

      Norman A. Cloutier

The Wake-Up Call

Earnestly the Lord speaks to me with a message that is most clear.
He whispers, "My child, sound the alarm; make ready for my time
cometh; you must now prepare!"

You ask, "what alarm do you speak of?
Why do you talk in such a way?"
   Kindly lend me an ear, and I will tell you
What I see, all these signs have to say.

His word says in the end times all will be shaken that can be,
the Earth will rock to and fro. Floods, drought,
sickness and famine will spread o'er the land.
Disobedience, self-love, strife will arise
and the hearts of men shall grow cold.

Today wickedness surrounds us, violence walks down every street
Rampant AIDS kills thousands, while safety,
even in the womb may not be found.
Rains bring floods, sun brings drought, fires rage across the land
Crops wither, they drown, they burn,
surely there's a curse upon the ground!

Many say these signs are nothing why worry, they've heard it all before
But those who see, who understand, have oil in their lamp
and keep their eyes on that far eastern shore.

      Elaine Ridley

The Sensitive Plant

A palomar-onyx tendril of white-gloaming light
Rising from the dark-horizoned, Vedic-shadowed dune
In vermilion-jade exaltations of auburn-streaming
Jonquils and red-glowing zinnias a cypress-wombed
Filament of eternity cascading into myrmidon-membraned
Dreams of asphodel-fountained seas a mirabelle-sage
Lotus-aureole soaring in ancient-hermetic, Giverny-effulgent silences
A Promethean-scarred, autumnal-helixed plant more powerful
Than marble-surging omens of ocean waves more subliminal
Than phoenix-sceptered mantras of sea gull-alabaster
Sabbaths crying soft-splashing tears of a lost figure
Along the mistral-dewed shore of perpetual twilight
Crying mandolin-echoes of Magellan-wandering terns
Listening to the jasmine-willow incandescence of wind
Shaping the anemone-veined sky in luminous-orange
Matrices of cobalt-Diaspora dawns in lilac-tessera,
Saffron-pealing resonances of ivory-sibylline,
Lemon-lazuli light.

      Hugo Walter

Always in My Heart . . .

Do you remember the first time we've touched?
We held our hands not saying too much
We felt fire of love as it raged through our hearts
The time when you saw me forever by your side?

Do you remember the time when all was just right?
No matter how you looked at me—I was your type
You saw me handsome, charming and funny as one can be
You promised in your prayers you'd never-ever let me leave?

Do you remember the dark cloud that obscured our sun one-day?
We both worried a bit but paid no attention to it yet
That could would stick around for while then refused to go
Dumping cold rains—killing the fire of love in us both?

Do you remember praying to God to make that cloud disappear?
To push it away from our sights before it submerged us in fear
To let sun come out and shine its light on our lives once again
While we grew cold, distant—stranger with each passing day?

The morning came and I wish I wouldn't wake up at all
Watching you box your dresses, take pictures down from the wall
You removed the key from your key ring—and I thought I'd die
As you left our house, our castle, our nest—as you left my heart . . .

Milan F. Sabata

Help, Please Help

Once again I went to work, and once again I felt like a jerk.
Why, oh, why am I not able to stay, things are not working out my way.

My first night alone, eleven to seven.
Life was a nightmare, but everybody said it should have been heaven.

Looking around at the alarms on the wall,
Listening to footsteps going down the hall.

Eight different codes on a cardboard sign
Looking around, what else do I find.

TV cameras, emergency phone, computers, and numbers galore,
Cover the walls from the ceiling to the floor.

The phone on the desk would ring, and break the silent of the night.
This goes on and on until the morning light.

This little room is an important place,
But I feel like I'm shut up in a small case.

This work is not what I'm put here to do.
Please forgive me when I give it back to you.

Glenda Nichols

Dismissed

Silently the tears roll down, the cheeks that love once kissed.
Silently she watches them and knows that she's not missed.
They know it all, they do not ask the simple question, "Why?"
The answers she gave so long ago, gave them wings to fly.

The hours of their birth are gone, the pain a distant past,
As once she wished, it is all done, the childhood didn't last.
The diapers that she often changed, the fevers she kissed away,
Forgotten now except by her, upon this lonely day.

The friends she hates, the troubled games, the shrill demands that hurt.
The feelings she keeps so deep inside, when they become so curt.
The screaming voice that has replaced the baby's screaming cries.
The anger that now she cannot soothe with kisses she dare not try.

They race outside, they run away, she stands there left behind,
Never again to hold her child, she knows their love is blind.
For now they look to their own needs, they only indulge their cravings.
They cannot see someday they'll need her steadfast strength and loving.

She tries her best to hide the hurt, the pain that leaves no peace.
She keeps the feelings to herself, they need not fear to see.
Time will replace their disregard, perhaps in time she will be missed,
But for now the tears kiss silently the cheeks love has dismissed.

Barbara Deacon

July's God is a Blue Heron on a Blue Lake

July busts wide the blue she must ;
Combusts her blue around us ;
Thrusts her **blazing** - blue into **blinking** eye, & **boundless** sky ;
Encrusts it's kingly countenance In celestial   hue ;
Entrusts her baby - blue to careless earth .
Sweeps her bouncing - blue into summer's girth ;
Steeps the world in flame ;Keeps blue - on - blue in array ,
As, quietly, it came ; came conundrum of connate display ;
Came the jubilee , in silence , eerie ; came herons on the lake today ;
Secretive , & calm , as if , in holiness , embalmed .
Thus, in silence , did ravishing revival pray .
What each apostle knew , not any sound would say ;
'Til it's ending - dance begun , & multitudes were one;
Bodies blending ; ascending into sun .
Thus , did it's nations , now, withdraw ;
Dissolve in desolations maw ;
Become , in relentless - blue, effaced ;
Telling all, In their going ;
Compelling, by the showing of it's race,
The O m n i s c i e n c i a of the Knowing Face .

Janice Takata

Remember . . . When?

The child in her keeps searching for happy memories of yesterday.
Some she wishes to cherish and make them stay,
others she just must erase forever.
To play in the sunlight with laughter, not a care in the world.
Not knowing pain nor sorrow only looking forward to tomorrow
for another day of play.
As she walks through the grassy fields searching for spring flowers,
picking more than her small hands can hold.
Now running, she speeds up the pace
   clutching the freshly picked bouquet,
thinking and hoping of the joy it will bring to a loved ones face.
The garden covered with strawberries, raspberries,
apple, plum and cherry trees,
she anxiously awaits the season to give her reason
to taste all that is new and savor each bite with great delight.
It is now time for the journey home,
with backpacks and baskets of freshly picked fruits.
She wants to help, to wash, to peel, to slice, to dice,
how to preserve all with just the right spice.
As the night descends upon her,
   tired and exhaustingly happy from the day,
with a child's prayer and the gentle hands that tuck her in,
make her believe that tomorrow will be even better than today.

Christina Nelson

Philip Milgrom, "Mr. Insurance Man"

You walked in icy rain, in darkest night, in deepest snow.
You walked where others feared to go.
You walked in torrid heat, in burning sun.
You toiled endlessly, while others had their fun. . . .

You served with honesty and pride
Those from whom you made for daily bread.
How terribly unjust that already you lie
Beneath the Earth's hard cold bed. . . .

So great were your dreams of things yet to be,
So close the horizon you were readying to see;
But indeed, God must have loved you
Not to let you know that, with your cherished goal within your grasp,
Life would abruptly go. . . .

I saw it, and I live it,
But it never will seem true
That you did go, and leave behind the one who leaned on you!

Oh Lord, why did you take that strong and vibrant tree,
And leave behind, so cruelly behind, the weak and suffering me! . . .
God Rest Your Soul, Philip Milgrom,
Mr. Insurance Man, "To tall and small. . . ."

Phyllis Milgrom

Storm

For the ones who bring sunshine into the lives of others,
The Zablothy
It was a cold tempestuous day, chaos occurred this way.
The surging waves crashed rigorously upon the shore.
Causing the earth to tremble once more.
It bruised the land and threw mist in the air,
Causing onlookers to shake as they stare.
It slowly made the wearisome bodies fall.
Like dying shadows down a long, lonely hall.
The chuckling wind howled at night,
Causing small children to dash with fright.
What a dire predicament the storm must be,
To make onlookers shake at the sights they may see.
A tormenting storm just as scary to hear,
Draws a tear to each person who slowly comes near,
As they listen to voices screaming with fear,
Their mangled bodies now washed onto the shore.
The tainted, pale skin like never before.
The splendor is gone and nothing is there,
It washes away dreams to fill the mind with despair.
The roaring wind finally lets go, as if only to warn that life goes by slow
A storm quickly brews again on the land,
Covering the bodies with brown, coarse sand.

Christina Steinbrecher

Spirit So Strong

To the man God has chosen for me to be my husband
We looked in each others eyes with a strong glaring look
Wondering what he is thinking reading my mind so it seemed,
     at the time.
Is he telling me something in those glaring looks?
As the minutes go by, I feel his spirit talking to me,
Without him saying a word.
The only thing that stands in the way
is the classroom that keeps us apart.
I thought we had a common ground.
Those mind-reading glares, as he moves across the room,
I still feel something real in my spirit.
Yet I'm not sure if I'm right or wrong.
Can my thinking be so wrong, with my spirit so strong?
It's okay to be wrong if that is the case.
Though it would be nice if I knew.
I hate this guessing game that is being played in my mind.
The position he holds needs to be considered in this world
Of revenge, not really sure if anything should be said.
Maybe he just needed to see if I was for real,
Waiting for someone so special.
Time is too short to be wasted on prayers that don't get answered.

Donna Marie Krupa

Between

All cuddly in blue, like a little puff of air from the great sky above.
So fragile, it seemed as if he would break at the touch
of mighty loving hands.
Hands of protection, balance, and peace.
The love which guides along the confusing path of existence.
One point stop,
No turn signal, no lights.
Free thought, free words,
The wind not so gentle,
All the air so thick, suffocating.
Behind locked doors weeps mother next to father,
Both so still, statuesque.
The red flame twisting as it breathes,
Sucking life into confusion and dismay.
Deep in the bowels of the heart,
a faint ticking of natures healing touch.
My child, my love, my son.
Bring him peace, bless his soul,
His heart is good, his flame will dim.
You are not alone, soon you will understand.

Jessie Haase

Walt Whitman Revisits Grand Central Station

Benched in solitude, slouched and disheveled, he sits
watching with an eye too bright, too interested, the mirage
and motion of unknowns surfacing, merging, dividing,
vanishing—automatons riding invisible tracks to inscrutable ends—
random, fathomless, locked into programs of private purpose,
unseen and unseeing, impersonal however animated, discursive,
dismissive, appearing, dispersing and gone, lost in the
non-commemorative trot and trance—a transient market place,
a vacuity except for him, alone, watching with the too-bright eye,
animate of mien and emotion, taking it all in, embracing each,
diverting, extracting, humanizing, imagining acquaintance,
celebrating encounter, immortalizing a look, a gesture, a greeting,
drawing back to revel and exult and recall—this solitary
sitter in the midst of emptiness, possessing nothing, bereft
of child, family, lover, wealth, approval—paying spontaneous
homage to all, living vicariously upon the endless
disjunctive bearers of non-knowing, emitting to them and for them
the unheeded cry for stillness, for hearing, for speech, for plain talk,
for something resonant, honorable and clean—in him, the solitary,
the sacred, the dispossessed meet and merge and close.

David L. Hyde

My Nature

To my Justin, who makes my life complete
I went to the mountains where the stillness wrapped
around me like a soft caress. . . .
It helped me to endure the strangle hold that had gripped me,
full of stress. . . .
The night air was full of tiny bits of golden light . . .
that changed my attitude from I couldn't to I might.

The gurgling stream flowed softly around and over the stones. . . .
It made me relax, feel weightless, right down to my bones. . . .
The air was fragrant as it whispered through the pines. . . .
I knew all of this was given to me, the mountains,
the trees, the birds, all mine.

The chirps of the birds as they were flitting to feed their young . . .
I knew there were many, many songs still out there, yet to be sung. . . .
Nature is on no schedule, not scurrying all about. . . .
They all have a purpose, and its their time table, without a doubt.

The sun when it's setting with its soft blue and rose hue . . .
Is only there for a minute and not seen by a multitude;
it's just there for a few.
As the faint golden light sinks lower in the sky . . .
I find, I turn to listen to the day saying good-bye.

Angela D. Redman

Our Milestone

For our love misplaced, yet never lost, C.
In this place so frantic, marked with loneliness and fear, where
hopes seem meant to sink, one day I whispered so bold a prayer,
and he came to me with wings, I think. It seems a lifetime later I
endure this test, asking above the how's and why's that I could
deserve, and so too he, this blessing sought unwillingly. Two
lives which together touched a place unknown and left loneliness
behind on their path, now humbly allow the arms of fate to lift
the pain of this heavy destiny's wrath. But I will not stand by
recklessly and shatter these memories that complete me. This I
promise, a lifetime long, so that maybe then he'll see that inside
of his mind, locked deep in his soul, there's a truth known, will
last; what lies ahead tomorrow for us is no battle for our past.
For a soul mate found in friendship through Hell, a love that
can't wear thin, is what lonely souls whisper to God for as they
trade in all their sins. I know not when our eyes will meet, and I
doubt I'll know again his touch, but my heart will hold a place
for him, my friend whom I love so very much. In this moment's
end I plea for something that would bound him to my heart, but
nothing more, not said nor done, can spare me from this part.
His time to fly has come once more, and my time, too, to let him
know that, with one last kiss to stain his lips, I remove my hand
and let him go. I have no magic left to throw . . .
my love, I love you, so I'll let go.

Christen Sherman

A Special Person Is What You Are to Me

To all of my special friends
A special person is there when you hurt and shares a moment or two.
A special person is there when you smile and laughs as loud as you.

A special person stands by you and walks by your side
on sunshine or rainy days.
A special person walks hand in hand and shares your many ways.

A special person listens and learns when you have something to say.
A special person comments and cares no matter what time of the day.

A special person is what you are to me, now and for the future.
I dream that special person so kind and wonderful
flows through to me like a stream.

So know that you are special to me, and know that I care for you.
Because you changed my cloudy days to days
   with skies so bright, so blue.

May this mean as much to you as it does to me, and may you
always be that wonderful and special person you really are.

   Timothy Herrick

October Snowstorm

She awakened to the sunshine softly framing her face
Unaware and without forethought, she strolled to the window
Disbelief engulfed her as she peered out through the glass pane
Beauty and devastation completely and mysteriously intertwined
Sparkling white crystals quietly conceal everything in white
Icicles shimmer from rooftops and reflect a rainbow of color
While the sidewalks and streets are covered in a blanket of debris
The severed limbs lay twisted and broken
Some just dangle perilously from the treetops waiting for their demise
One can hear the crackling sound resonate through the streets
As another limb breaks and falls to its death
The branches seem to cry out in agonizing pain
   as they begin their descent
Ghoulishly carved pumpkins sit frozen and crystallized
   on various doorsteps
A burst of sunshine gives warmth where needed
As the first tear of many slides down her cheek
The mourning for what once was
. . . Has only just begun

   Theresa K. Allgood

The Undying Indian Spirit

The soldiers swept across the plains like an army of locusts
Pillaging and destroying the Indian States
Seizing their land in the name of progress
In reality for their own selfish, national gain

Blood and tears soaked the verdant grounds
Tree and shrub alike—the tribal men and women were defoliated
Stripped of their own personal belongings
And the children, fragile little flowers of the prairie
Were trampled and forcibly torn from their youthful innocence

Though families were cruelly destroyed
And their rich customs mercilessly mocked
America neither weeps nor mourns, but seeks to forget
Purging the lingering guilt from her collective conscience

Though the vanquished Lakota, Blackfeet, and Apache, to name a few
Were driven into concentration camps
Squalid reservations of poverty and disease
With little realistic hope of survival . . . they would not die!

Though they still labor under history's cruel fate
And the "perfect" American nation still seeks to assimilate them
The Indian Spirit, like the phoenix, is undying and enduring
Awaiting the day when it again will arise and the Indians will be able
To shape and mold their own lives and destiny

   William Sutherland

Beware of Their Voice and the Mask They Put On

"Beware of their voice and the mask they put on."
With his or her lips the hater makes herself or himself unrecognizable,
But inside of her or him, she or he puts on deception.

Although she or he makes her or his voice gracious,
Do not believe in her or him.
For there are seven detestable things in her or his heart.
Hatred is covered over by deceit and a fake smile.

Her or his badness will one day be uncovered.
"Watch out," for the mask they put on! While they give gifts.
"Watch out," for what they tell you in secret behind a closed door.

When expose in the near future.
Beware of their voice and the hand that is swearing on the Bible.
For the wicked do that to cover over their lie.
For they fear not. So "beware of their voice and the mask they put on."

   Sanda May Benlien

My Poetry

My poetry is nonetheless my voice to the world.
Through it I laugh, I cry, I rejoice,
I speak, and, in the end, with it
I will ultimately die.
With my poetry I speak what is thought,
but too afraid to be spoken.
My poetry,
my voice,
my endless, yet beautiful, meaning.
I smile, for I know that my poetry brings comfort to the tired
and weary soul, inspiration to the one without words,
and, often times, love to the heart that thought it had forgotten how.
If I capture the heart or mind, or even free the soul,
then I have done my job,
achieved my dream . . .
true and final expression.

   Randrea Majors

Over to Tom's House

When the family gets together for whatever occasion.
We always go over to Tom's house.

Tom's house is a very unique part of family history.
There you can always be yourself.
Many of the world as well as local affairs are solved at Tom's house.
It's not many places in the world where you can voice your opinion
and be highly respected.

From a youngster to adulthood, I've seen nothing but unity,
love, honor, and mutual respect at Tom's house.

Always a hand shake and a smile,
a place to let your hair down.

A tall, lean husband, father, brother, uncle, friend,
and so much more at Tom's house.
I guess you know where I'm going—Over to Tom's House.

   Lawrence A. Johnson

Our Lives

We travel through our lives wondering what will happen to us,
who we will meet, but we don't always get an answer. We think
that things can't get any worse, but they always do. We cry
ourselves to sleep because we have lost a friend, but we have
also gained friends. We look at people and wonder what they
think of us, and we know inside that they are wondering the
same thing. We spend our entire lives searching for our
purpose, and when we think that we have found it, our purpose
has changed. We carry our burdens with us denying ourselves
the peace of releasing them to God. Holding on to the
past, we never look to our future. We wander through this brutal life
fighting off verbal assaults and mental attacks from this unforgiving world only to find ourselves at the end of our lives. But
looking toward Heaven, we see our future, our eternity with
Christ, and a sense of peace falls upon us.

   Nathan C. Washington

A Spiritual Message

God has laid upon my heart a message
I believe He wants me to impart
For all of you whom I believe.
He is our Redeemer and Savior, as well we
Can see with all the disasters and tragedy going on in our world today.
In our St. James' Bible version,
God speaks of Men and Scientists that He gives them the knowledge
For greater things to come,
But in their desire they use this knowledge to delve,
Too far into God's works that when the end of the world shall come.
Our political world is in a whirl,
People so confused, as with our "Christian World"
Which denomination to believe?
God does not care about denomination,
Only what is in our "heart and soul"
So let's come together—Roman Catholics, Protestants.
Show all the world how compatible
We can be.

Viola B. Jelinek

Memories

Memories, what are memories, what do I remember?
A chair in the corner of our kitchen, mama's arms held me tight
Was there a kiss as well, did I know then that soon those arms
would never hold me again
The living room holds the casket,
   the mourners who patted me on the head
Poor child they said, I was only seven.
Papa holding me on his lap, his tears flow down my face
His love is gone, but papa, I am here, but his love is gone.

My dear daughter, oh, how the pains have diminished him
My strong, handsome brother, what is cancer, I am only 10.
What is this sickness that reduced to a skeleton what once was my
brother straight and tall, papa, oh, papa, hold your eldest, as he
breathes his last, another casket looms, flowers, I hate their smell.

A few years pass, what is this awful feeling
Stopping suddenly in the middle of the sidewalk, what is wrong?
All the relatives are there, I hear crying, my papa is gone.
A casket looms again, I hate my house, the sight never leaves.
The years pass and time has a way of fading the silhouettes
but memories, ah, in that part we call memory, love never fades.

Anne Brockmeier

Thought?

I never thought you'd do that, you hurt me, oh, so bad.
I never thought you'd do that, you made me feel so sad.

I feel as though you've reached down through the curtains of my eyes.
You went into my heart, tore it up, then let it die.

The vision I once had of you is now completely shattered.
The memories I have are very scarcely scattered.

I opened up to you, to show you who I am.
Then you read me like a book to all of your friends.

Slowly, day by day, I'm losing self-control.
This situation I'm going through is getting way too old.

Well, I just sit back and smile through a thousand tears,
The same thing I've been doing for about a thousand years.

I'm tired of wasting my time on people like you,
Listening to stories that aren't at all true.

I can't believe you did that; sometimes I wish you dead.
Unfortunately, the thoughts of you still linger in my head.

I'll try to go to sleep and try not to dream of you,
Try not to think of all the mean things that you like to do.

I still never thought you'd do that, you hurt me, oh, so bad.
I still never thought you'd do that, you made me feel so sad.

Melissa Marshall

Me and New Orleans

Please take me to New Orleans.
I hear that there are women standing on the corner waiting
for a little something with the little cash that you have.
Please take me to a place that has the best drunken men
that one could ever talk to.

Maybe, someday, we will go together.
Maybe, someday, we will be together.
Just maybe we will see each other way down in New Orleans.

Please take me to New Orleans where the men dance in the
streets with their best Sunday suits on.
Please take me where my mom said every dying child goes to play.

Maybe, someday, we will see it all.
Maybe this night in New Orleans will never end.

Please take me to New Orleans where the nightingale sings so sweet.
Please take me down where the food is so spicy
that you have to drink an ocean to quench your thirst.

Maybe, someday, we will be standing side by side
   way down in New Orleans.

Robin Whitt

One American Eagle's View

The councils of men of earthly clay could never bring to stay,
answers or solutions solving the sweeping quandaries of today.

Nor could the brooding clouds bring forth Tyranny's child
of ominous hue to long remain in power's seat, with torturous plans
enslaving me and you.

For centuries of earthly years greed did spawn in minds of certain
men, passing on their evil plots all men to master and control.

Yet freedom's song, newborn in our republic, rang loud and clear,
sung by honest hearts, liberty to proclaim,
and equality for each and all, body and soul.

Though men of Satan's ignoble brood may gain control under
a black blanket of deceit and dishonesty,

And their plots, all men to conquer, now cover the Earth
with crushing nets of their Satanic dynasty;

Still, fear not, oh righteous of heart and soul,
tho' bounded by the sin-swept depths of dreaded demonic dominance,

But rejoice in the sure truth of the Word of God, which our hearts in
certainty enfold in blessed confidence.

For, our beloved Saviour, as it is written in His Word,
will, at His own appointed time, all evil dismantle and destroy;

And together, then, we shall live with Him forever in His glorious love.

Doris E. McClure

Myself

We give myself to you,
Although I am afraid.
I know how much she yearns for you;
To me, it's just a phase.
We are selfish when it comes to her—
She is the essence of our heart,
Her beauty is our soul.
We spent our lives protecting her
From the world's tainted bowel.

As we give myself to you,
I ask that you in turn
Be good and patient with her,
Change nothing of her ways.
When you decide to pierce her, be prepared to stay.
Let her give herself willingly and you will surely be amazed:
Her softness can relinquish any man's domain.
Enjoy her blissful nature,
But her spirit must be left untamed.
Remember—to me, she is the only person I ever want to be . . . myself.

Nita Ford

Would You Still Remember Me?

So it was told,
God blesses each who has their own
everything else was either bought or sold.
Possibly stolen or wrong, what if you have nothing?
Meek words are all I have to offer,
not like anything else but it's something.
My praises and humblings are now softer.
Who says I'm not suppose to be blessed?
Am I not suppose to be recognized because I'm one who has less?
Left countless in numbers, must my heart be circumcised
so that my name is remembered?
And if I had plenty would it matter if I not shared any?
If I thought I was better I'd have everything I need or maybe just about.
Because I'd rather not give but receive, others are just left out.
Would you still remember Me?

Pamela Denise Singletary

Trail's End

Lying upon his blanket, his saddle for a pillow,
Listening to teardrops falling from a nearby weeping willow.
Sunset yielding to gloaming hour . . . fireflies darting in the dusk
Wondering where his trail will end as, someday, he knows it must.

Whiling away the lonely hours . . . from twilight into night,
The moon comes out a slender disc . . . stars are glittering bright.
A coyote's yelp, a wolf's sad call, the night is nigh-well spent,
The morning sun comes peeping out, casting it's rosy tint.

Dawn has come, darkness flown, another day at hand,
Where will his long trail lead him as he roams this thirsty land?
Gazing o'er the valley from the lofty mountain height . . .
Miles-upon-miles of swaying grass—My, what a lonely sight!

Galloping on through the purple sage . . . wind blowing in his face
Weaving the shimmering, golden sand, like a shuttle weaving
  lace. Riding, riding, ever riding . . . will his trail never end?
Endless days, endless nights . . . dreaming of what might have been.

Riding, riding, ever riding . . . will his wand'rings never cease?
Not 'til on the Lone Prairie . . . a gravestone marked—
"YOUR TRAIL HAS ENDED . . .
REST IN PEACE!"

Elga Haymon White

Voices

Just to think of it hurts my soul.
Candle lights shine brighter than my heart.
My courageous persona is the lesson learned tomorrow.

Seeping through my pillow is the truth.
Faraway winds are blowing. Slumber in my bed.
June is my summer. Autumn is my friend.
Hurt is the word I express under and over again.

Now, if I let you peer into the center of my heart,
You would understand the rumors of the wind coming in and out again.

Secrets, shades of laughter, praying lips tremble under the light.
I may wander into the myriad lights feeling alone and soiled in spirit,
But none can see the labor of my destiny.

Shauna R. Davis

Mid-Morning Trance

It was a dark, sullen night. It had finally stopped raining outside.
The dampness rattled through my bones.
I felt extremely uneasy. My mind wandered endlessly.
My thoughts flowed through me like a drug on a mission.
My depression grew deeper. I wallowed in my own pain.
Is it really worth it?
From the powers within I become who I really am.
Should they force their way out of me, I hold no responsibility.
I christen your injustice; the feeling is mutual.
This evening I share with you. The two of us are fakes.
Pawns if you will. Will this delirium ever halt?

Dublin M. Puglia

Woodcarving

I love to carve in many woods—Butternut, White Pine, and Ash,
Tupelo, Poplar, and Red Cedar I use, but Basswood I like the best.

Many tools I need to use, V-tools, U-tools and chisels.
Many different kinds of knives that have to be very sharp.
Pencils put patterns on wood, rulers keep edges straight.
Carving gloves and finger protectors keep Band-Aids away from me.

Dogs and cats and frogs are animals I like to carve,
Cardinals, Blue Jays, and even wolves, dolphins, and ducks and geese.
My people are three inches high, are caricatures of young and old.
Large Trolls and Nissen and faces of all, a challenge for me to do.

Christmas ornaments of Santas and angels and children on sleds,
Crosses and bells and a Star of David decorate my tree each year.
Chip carving is my favorite for ornaments and plates.
I carved two music boxes and gave them to my girls.

When the carving is done I sand it and sand it and sand it,
Then stain or paint is added in layers and varnish on top of that.
Some carvings have special settings and others will stand alone.
Some lay on the ground just waiting for me
  to put them where they belong.

I keep them in boxes and shelves
  and display them at wood carving shows.
But mostly I like to just give them away to family and all my friends.

Jackie Webb

Sea of Grey

The once brilliant glowing glittering gold of the imperial
Throne now has sadly been cast into Medusan stone
Long since overthrown are the good old days like a flag flown
At half mast; dried up and as dead as a fossilized bone
To atone for the lost souls sold for a piece of the promiscuous
Past we find ourselves condemned to reap the demons we have sown

Turning a blind eye and/or a deaf ear on insignificant minute
Flaws the treasured American dream now is beginning to fray
Treating the symptoms and not the cause suddenly our systems are
Spiraling into alarming disarray paving the way for more urban decay
With our leaders above and beyond the laws
  and worshiping heroes with feet
Molded of clay led by renegade outlaws
  anarchy is the new order of the day

Existing in a blight infested world where the crystalline structure
Between right and wrong is no longer in black and white
Carrying on with no guiding light to direct us left or right it's
A trial and error search through the beacon-less night
Trapped in a heaven versus hell tug of war plight to recapture
The lost magic of the majestic Renaissancian limelight
It's going to take Superman summoning up all his Herculean might to
Break us free from the parasitic stronghold
  of the Apocalyptic Kryptonite

John C. Franklin

Angel

Grandpa you taught me everything I needed to know,
so why didn't you tell me I was going to have to let you go?

Day after day I know I will be O.K., with my guardian angel by my side.
When I go to bed at night you look down upon me
from above and whisper you turned out all right.
As the sunsets and the day ends, the last breeze
that sweeps through is you, tucking me in for the night.
Every star in the night sky is a kiss from me to you.
The rain that falls are the tears that fall from your face,
so I try to kiss each drop.
The moon in the night sky that shines so bright,
is the warmth of your smile that covers me each and every night.
You watched me grow from the little girl I use to be,
to the young lady I am today.
I miss you more and more every day!

Stephanie Caton

Where Has Tomorrow Gone

Tomorrow is the best of days; it's the day of hopes and dreams.
When life goes bad and things go wrong, it's never as bad as it seems,
Because they'll always be tomorrow, to right our every wrong.
And if the tune turns ugly, tomorrow will have a new song.
Tomorrow is the day, when all our dreams come true.
It's the day we've planned forever, our whole life through and through.
We filled our lives with plans, with steps we would take each day,
But we've missed so many tomorrows, the steps have crumbled away.
The goals we set seemed easy, when the tomorrow's were easy to find,
But as we all got older, the tomorrows have left us behind.
Now we watch as our dreams grow dim
   and wonder if our dreams are dead.
Where has tomorrow gone? Alas, it's just a day ahead.

Donald W. Bivens

Mother

To my devoted, loving, caring, nourishing mother, Herminia G. Gomez
Mother, you are the sun that rises and shines
   above the skies every morning.
You are the light that guides my path through this ever-winding world.
You are the sedative that soothes and coats all my insecurities and
worries and turns them from mountains into molehills.
Finally, Mother, you are the sole existence for my life.
I thank you for your sacrifice in having me.
I hope I am the apple of my child's eyes as you are mine.

Dora Elva Gomez

Part We Shall

There comes a day when all shall part, to leave this world of beauty
The forests and flower and all Earth's wonder will disappear;
Our deepest memories are awakened on this trembling day
Sleeping, a deep, deep sleep; yet, I will experience, this very thing.

For, I shall call upon death, as it calls upon me
the end to all beginning shall be with sorrow;
yet, I must except great departure for some beings
this shall be the means for the beginning
Departure is forever, the privacy is sacred to the immortal.

For worthy of a new beginning is yet to come.
It worrying-ness was among being
Heaven shall be a new beginning, yet a time will come
When all shall part, I surrender to this
For the ending in exchange I will experience great wonder.

For, part we shall the ending, for a new beginning.
For, worthy of a new being to me is unknown.

Lorna Lassick

How Much More?

God sees the sparrow when it falls from the sky,
Also the raven, who for its food cries,
As we go to the ant, and thus are made wise,
Or look to the eagle, whose path we can't fly.
How much more for us will He share, if only to him will we go in prayer.

The sparrow has a house, and the swallow a nest,
And the wily old fox has a hole for his rest.
Consider the lily, in its glorious array,
And remember the bees, as they dart and sway.
How much more for us will he bear, if only to him will we go in prayer.

Blessings even for life we find in the dew,
And after the rain storm, the rainbow breaks through.
Though the son of man had no place for his head,
He shall care for his flock, and see that their fed.
How much more for us will he care, if only to him will we go in prayer.

Close to his bosom, will he carry his sheep,
And by the still waters, he'll watch as they sleep.
Up the mountains he'll guide them, and through the valleys below,
And then when he calls them, his voice they will know.
How much more for us will he bear? He settled it at calvary;
He bore it all there.

Dorothy M. Kelley

Through the Eyes of a Child

To Mother who held me up
The closet monsters are real;
They lurk behind the acorn teeth and waxy mustache
Of every sales man who tried to pawn off swampland in Florida.
The basement demons live.
They inhabit the shifting eyes and faulty stories
Of every immoral preacher that was dragged to court by his
chorus-boys.
The under-the-bed insanity
Hides in the dark laugh and possessed stare
Of all the murderers who did it for pleasure.
And the boogie man reigns
In every dark alley, death row, and rioting mob,
That dare to scare the heroes.

LeEtta Gross

Yellow Rose

My other self . . .
my guiding light . . .
my inspiration . . .
my friend!

Throughout the years,
Your shadow blends with mine
And we become united;
Two spirits tumbling in the same direction through the tunnels of life
Until we meet the blinding ray of light at the end of the journey
Where I can only weep with thankfulness
To have this yellow rose by me until the end of time
This rose . . . this yellow rose,
Is friendship,
The most blessed gift of life.

Quyen Vu

To the Girl in My Dreams

Even though she lives next door to me, she just gives me so
many rest'less nights. As I reach out to her through my own
thoughts, as her sleek body slides next to mine, as I pour out my
heart to her with all of my desires, I don't know when it happened, but I fell in love with her. I find myself thinking about her
all the time. Every time I am near her, I just want to take her by
the hands, and lead her into a paradise of hot passion, which
would fulfill both of our dreams. But all of those
dangerous temptations keep coming out, that I feel for her,
which I can't control. They will always be there every time I see
her, but I never got the chance to know her. Now that she has
moved on, I will never know how she felt about me. It will be
hard for me to let go, but I will always cherish, those memories of
her with me, no matter where she is. If only I could find her in
real life, and not through my own dreams.

Terry R. Cook

Camp Salmon

The morning light is pink and blue, you wipe your eyes and
grab a brew. No time to eat—there's too much fun, you must
be out before the sun. Water rushing through the grass,
around the rocks it hits with a splash—white bubbles from
moving so fast, the bottom dark as tinted glass. A cast, a whiz,
a line drawn tight from the water rushing as if in flight. At once
a flash of pink and white and the line is not pulling so awfully
tight.It turns and moves as if upstream, and excitement builds as
you start to scream. "I got one—I got one," and you know it's
not a dream. It seems as if the time flies by, the kick and pull of a
little caught fly. You see the eyes and then a gill and you reach
down thinking you'll get your fill. Triumphant! Triumphant!
You hold it up high and you see the proud look in your father's
eye. Dinner will be good tonight as it sizzles and snaps in the
fading twilight. You eat and you eat and crawl off to bed, the
dream of it all again in your head. Tomorrow will be another fun
day, so you sleep well knowing all is O.K. The morning light is
pink and blue, you wipe your eyes and grab a brew. . . .

Holly Denig

Our Environment

The trees are down, the grass has gone,
No more mossy paths to walk upon.
No soil, rich enough to grow
The seeds that the wind doth sow.
No stream running cool and clear over the rocks.
No woods to hide the frightened fox.
The woods are gone, where is the game?
The way man strips the Earth is a shame.
Wherever spraying has been, tho' birds and butterflies are seldom seen.
Many small animals have left because of man's greedy theft.
Most of the land that once was green,
Now only buildings can be seen.
Soon the Earth will be robed in black.
Will cover the world like a sack.
The lakes and streams near the road
Will soon be unclean by the overload
Of gasoline fumes and acid rain,
Never to be sweet and pure again.
Man is not mindless, he must know
That he has gone about as far as it is safe to go.

Elsie Audrey Dean

Autumn Shadows

The days are short, the colors gold,
my thoughts adrift as night grows cold.
The fire flames as shadows loom,
its cracklings pierce the silent room.
Old quilted chair do comfort me with brass
tipped cane against my knee.
My trusted friends lay at my feet,
their eyes now closed, contented sleep.
As memories rise from days gone by,
to withered shape, no longer tied.
To love once seen with blinded eyes,
his heart called out, not heard the cries.
Obscure the clues to beast untamed,
his love withdrawn from whence it came.
Too late life's veil revealed to see my one true love, cruel irony.
He's lost in time without a trace, left glimpse reflections of his face.
Dark brown hair, steel eyes of blue, his warming smile and heart so true.
Escape in dreams from mortal bounds that I might find him far beyond.
Until that day when one will be, the autumn shadows blanket me.

Shayne Maxwell

I'm Sorry

Have I ever told you how sorry I am
For acting the way that I have been?

I didn't mean to make you feel like I didn't care
That I didn't appreciate the time you did spend here

But it was hard to admit to myself I was really caring about you
Because it's when they know you care they'll break your heart in two

I loved every minute we spent together
I loved the way we held each other

I'm sorry I didn't show it before, I hope you understand
But it takes a while for a broken heart to mend

I like the way we fought over the remote control
We were just like a married couple

I love when you laugh—it made me laugh, too
I'm so sorry it took this to express my feelings for you

You notice a good thing when they've left
But how was I to know you weren't like the rest?

I made a mistake, I had no clue
I didn't realize how much I'd miss you

Ten thousand I'm sorry's, I wish I could go back in time and erase it all
Because then I'd look forward to fighting over the remote control

Rikki Vander Meer

Gratitude

Why should I be thoughtful and grateful for my loved ones,
relatives, my job, coworkers, boss, and home?
Why must I ask blessings for every member of my family,
friends, neighbors, and all people?
I give thanks, I am grateful, I am alive, and I have been borne,
Thus, I can see the beauty of the mornings
in the sunrise, and a glorious sunset.
To see God's beauty, in the surroundings, all beauties of nature.
The starry heavens, the lovely eyes of your child,
The adoring eyes of your bird, cat or dog.
To have seen all the riches around you,
To smell the sweet fragrance of the flowers or the new-mown grass,
To see the snow-clad mountains,
    scintillating like diamonds on a sunny day.
To hear the music of the spheres.
Listen to bands concerts, operas, pianos, and violins.
Be always grateful for anything and everything.
Great numbers of people are in misery and poverty,
by their lack of gratitude!

As Shakespeare said, "O Lord who lends me life,
lend me a heart replete with thankfulness."

Mila Rodrigues

Keeper's Pupil

Once again, the cool comfort of darkness comes to blanket me.
Here in this vast plain where time cannot be measured.

No clocks to tick away the years, the secret is revealed.
My senses now are sharp and keen, awakened to the things
even my eyes have not seen.

I've journeyed to many different worlds, past, present and future.
The cosmic expanse, ageless and endless,
    flows around and through me.

The passage I travel a constant one, eternal through space and time.
To fulfill the stint a die is cast, the bonding of flesh to soul.

A bargain made not end or stay beyond the designated moment.
The dread of being sent again for lessons incomplete.

To repeat or be promoted, the results are kept obscured.
My essence rushed toward the light, as the body wrap encloses.

The trauma so acute, forgetting all that was before,
I howl and scream and weep out loud, my loss I will endure!

Teresa Ann Haight

The Friendship

The growth of a friendship that seemed to bloom
Like a delicate flower under the light of the moon
The birth of a friendship that would be challenged soon
For a destiny that could be doomed

If only they knew that becoming closer would benefit the most
Yet the passing of another day; would bring them close
How would they exactly know what was in store for them down the road

Would they have know what they would mean
To one another; they became the Angels they both need
Who would have known their friendship would last
Or even if it would have grown so very fast

They looked after each other day after day
They took care of each other in every way
They became the breath of air that they relied on every single day

Somehow they helped satisfy each others needs
But though everything all they could do was wait and see
If the love they had could possibly succeed

Even though their relationship began to deplete
    and it seemed as if it was defeat
Their friendship that was so unique would exist for all of eternity

And in the end they will always be linked,
    until the day they meet again . . .

Stephanie ReAnn Ball

Facing the Storm

I saw the dark clouds gathering in the distance.
I'm not sure when they converged and threatened to overtake us.
The rumbling of the thunder has become louder
until it is nearly deafening.
Flashes of lightning are coming more frequently.
I'm frightened by the intensity of the storm
and the lightning bolts tearing through the air around me.
I can't show fear. If I do, more storms will come
with greater force until I am held captive and we are both destroyed.
Little girls may run and hide, not mothers.
Even when the wind takes my breath away
and the rain stings my face, I will stand steadfast,
ready to embrace you until the storm is over, if you'll let me.

Cheryl Salisbury Carroll

He's Only a Man!

We expect too much from a government official.
Can one expect an evening alone,
Without receiving an international call via the telephone?
The rush of the primaries are in effect.
We slide between booths, wondering, "Who should I elect?"

Choices have been made; foundations have been laid,
Directions they have been giving,
Entering the White House for easy living;
The man has a wife and a daughter,
Binoculars and cameras for a simple glass of water.

It just doesn't seem fair, that paparazzi are everywhere,
Disappointments on every hand,
Our fault! Due to the trust we've put in a man;
The minute his eyes shift away from his wife,
The media rushes in to mess up his life,
Dragging the man from the White House to court,
This thing is such a norm, you could call it a sport.
Namely, he's only a man; checking his agenda and looking for things,
Please check out his back shoulder, he hasn't grown wings,
    he's only man!

Iris Hailu

Adnil's Mom

Enduring "alien" chatter with an indulgent smile.
Verses of "Found a Peanut" sung in that slightly off-key style.
A meal of macaroni—transformed into elegant fare.
Softly whispered reassurances for the child that's had a scare.

Humorous attempts to speak quietly, so as to be a lady.
The ever-perfect hairstyle, made famous by Carol Brady.
Dark nights in the desert, hoping to glimpse UFO's.
The careful refrigeration of a daughter's first prom rose.

These memories, and millions more, are lodged in a daughter's heart.
A jumble of warm, safe, feelings that will never, ever, part.
But, of all these many memories, perhaps one stands out the most:
A faux stern admonishment of "girls . . . eat that toast!"

Linda Hamblin

Gutters

Trees stretch their skeleton fingertips into the gloom,
Branches bending and blowing
With the wind that howls around corners
And by windows where eager noses are pressed.
As the wind lifts brown, leathery leaves over treetops and rooftops
Where birds hide in gutters and wait
In their nests of twine and twigs and threads of tinsel lost from a tree,
All gathered on some nicer day,
Some day when the trees praised the sky's blue,
When the wind turned young cheeks and noses a brisk, rosy red
As it lifted crisp leaves over rooftops
Where they gently glided into gutters
And mingled with bird nests
Made with threads from the clothes line,
Where clothes danced with the wind.

Amy D'Amico

You Wrapped Me in Tenderness

To my Boaz, with all my heart
I'm beginning to believe the sun will rise
To trust Your touch, to believe You are mine
For so long I've been waiting for You to knock me to the ground
I'm scared that just when I believe it won't, that blow will come around

You took away the world I had built
You refused to condemn me in spite of my guilt
I was so afraid of Your mighty hand
Then You touched me in a way my heart could understand

And I spat on Your Mercies, made doormat of Your Grace
I tried so hard to make You give up
But You cupped my chin in Your hands
    and wiped the tears from my face
You showed me what it means to be loved

You wrapped me in tenderness, wooed me with Your Light
And even when it wasn't easy, You were there by my side
You are the greatest romancer I have ever known
You wrapped me in tenderness, You are my Love, my Lord

Suzanne Emry

The Last of September

They said it was windy that night, the last of September. They said the waves were high, the water cold, and the night full of shadows. They said that they shouldn't have been out there. And I want to know where his guardian angel was that night. I want to know who held his hand to ease his fear.

On the first of October it was windy still. The waves were still high, the water still cold, and the night would remain full of shadows. The night we heard, we gathered, tearfully, silently, closely knit together in a circle of friends. Some wondered how one night could so viciously change the rest of our lives, while others held onto some shred of hope.

We stood on the shoreline, watching the water foam at our feet, and hoping to catch a glimpse of something that would make it all easier. Facing the wind with an unrealistic sadness, we watched each other silhouetted against the backdrop of a dark night. And some called out his name with cries that were carried to him by the swell of the waves.

And on this night we remained as one, held together by memories, and finding the strength to smile within a single chuckle that echoed in our hearts. And this beauty that eased our troubled souls was begotten by the knowledge that one dear man was loved by so many, joining us all in this unbroken bond of friendship, and sometimes almost coming close to compensating for the loss.

Sue Capuano

Angel in My Eyes

She's the fire in my heart, she's the apple of my eye
Some people call her granny but, she's an angel in disguise
Always helping others with her big heart open wide
Seventy years long a working with the good Lord by her side

I can still remember the way it used to be
We would sit and rock for hours back when I was three
She would pick me up and hug me and fix my skinned knee
Some people call her granny but, she's an angel to me

Oh, some people call her granny but she's an angel in disguise
Always helping others with her big heart open wide
Seventy years long a working with the good Lord by her side
Some people call her granny but she an angel in my eyes

She goes to church every Sunday and works down at the day care
Loves all her grandchildren and wished that they were there
I wrote this here poem for her to let her know we love and still care
Some people call her granny I just wished that I was there

Ray Williams

I Dream

To Tyra Brett—you'll always be my heart and soul
I dream of the one who I never got to know.
It's still hard for me to believe that you had to go.
I dream of the person you could have grown up to be.
The images of the life you should have had are easy to see.

I dream of the fun we could have had with each other.
I wonder if we'd have been birds of a feather.
I dream of the family that we should have been.
I haven't felt this much sorrow since I can't remember when.

I dream of the family that you could have had.
It's hard to believe that life can be so cruel and sad.
I dream of the brother or sister, father or mother
That you might have been; your life, out so short, seems to me a sin.
Sometimes I wonder if you were actually real.
Your heartbeat and your laughter I could almost feel.

Walter L. Winters

Tango of the Wind

Across the garden, the evening breeze comes from out of the west
Branches of the birch tree sway is cadence with the changing gusts
Down low, their motion to and fro goes slow, slow
But near the top, the smaller branches go quick, quick
Capricious wind now commands that all go slow
Another gust stirs the tree once more and again I see
Slow, slow, quick, quick, slow
The motion of the tango dancer's feet
Now memory speaks of other places, other times
Where tall prairie grasses swayed slow, slow, quick, quick, slow
Wavelets lapping on the shore of a mountain lake
   slow, slow, quick, quick, slow
Or are these scenes just silent echoes running through my mind?
Dreams of romance, the rapture of dance
   with a beautiful lady in my arms?
Heard in the recorded music I just played, Tango of the Roses. . . .

John E. Partanen

Home

Newspaper rolled inside a dirty rag . . . a place to lay his head.
A cardboard box on a concrete slab . . . space the old man called his bed.
He wore no socks . . . and through the crudely tied, torn plastic bags
One could glimpse his crusted feet.
There was a dirty purple heart tacked on his tattered coat
As he lay exposed on the dirty, snowy street.
People stopped to mingle . . . whisper, and to stare . . .
Their full attention now they gave.
Tomorrow's papers would say a word or two
Of the nameless hero . . . now placed in a potter's grave.
And we the people . . . we shall go to bed tonight
'Neath blankets warm, and soft, clean sheets.
Few of us will even think to morn the homeless man out on the street.
But wait, He could just be a guest tonight without a price.
Perhaps . . . he ran the race of life and won.
Perhaps he's now the honored guest of . . . Christ, God's son.
I pray that it is so . . . I pray the angels sing.
I pray he earned a cherished crown . . . that peace with God will bring.

Barbara Price Burkhardt

A Living Sacrifice

Wretched, wretched death
Is what He experienced at the end,
With no remorseful one around.
It's better in the future, the gifts He shall send.

Though He was whipped
And mocked and beat,
His attitude toward His persecutors was,
"If it's Your will, Father, through death Satan will meet his defeat."

For at that last moment of His earthly life,
Although we crucified Him,
Still blessing us and pleading the blood.
Just as prophesied He left this world without a broken limb.

Daniel Wofford

Vineyard Road

Across time and winding Vineyard Road, I see a pond in summer
filled with croaking frogs. Large turtles inch along the ditches
ending in the neighbor's tubs. During summer's heat, bikers
and walkers dressed to swim followed a dusty lane past an old
tulip tree to Benton Beach. Low tide mud was fun for sliding in.
In biting cold, voices of children echoed over a snow-topped
road, while skaters circled the icy pond. Sometimes a Flexible
Flyer skimmed the nearby hill; waxed sleds made it all the way to
hard stone wall beyond. Once ox carts traveled Vineyard Road.
Holstein cows were bound by ledge, stone walls between. In
later years, "city folks" drove cars to Sachem's Head Hotel, or
rode the trolley, then walked to reach the sound. Time moves
on. A tractor without wheels now rests beside the farmyard
drive. One tall silo has fallen into ruin. Next to it, an empty dairy
barn with faded wood, red and gray. In it, two sons, with
Milton's help, raised Guernsey cows, learning with pitch forks
how to spread manure and hay. Stylish houses line a road once
traveled by a cart. Few stone walls are left. Drivers are warned,
"Slow Down!" No longer does the farmyard pond with croaking
frogs resound. The beach meadow has lost its grazing cows.
The tulip tree drops branches but still remains beside the old
beach lane, its trunk a hollow home to squirrels, birds, and
leaves, hiding tales of what has been.

Barbara Lockerbie Waggoner

Autumn

Autumn came sliding past my window, draped in bold iridescent colors.
Quietly painting the world outside,
Her ancient palette is never consumed;
She never seems to tire.

Autumn came gliding by.
The perfume she leaves in her wake
Draws small creatures from their hiding places
To gather the bountiful harvest.
I inhale this wonderful perfume that immerses me in its warmth.

Autumn came swirling by, dancing with the wind.
The glorious colors sing and dance on the leaves;
They rustle along the ground,
Exploding skyward, displaying Autumn's fireworks.

Autumn came quietly sliding past my view.
The shadows grew long.
Daylight dappled the earth beneath the bright-colored trees
With a priceless treasure of gold.
The birds sang a last farewell as Autumn slipped past my way.

Emily C. Fitch

The Cliff

I look up at the sky to see the sunset's neon colors:
purple, red, orange, blue, pink.
The dry wind whips my face and blows back my hair.
The heavy winds glue my shirt against my skin as
I hear the cars roar by in the distance.
My attention is drawn to the movements
far below the cliff that I rest on.
Jack rabbits move about in search of food.
Many tumbleweeds are being pushed off
the cliff with the grace of the wind.
I watch them fall and wish I was a tumbleweed.
The depression leaves me quiet, gray, numb and empty.
My sweaty palm throws a pebble into the cliff below, as my feet dangle
mockingly on the thin ledge where I sit.
As my eyes follow the falling pebble, I can hear the faint rattle of a
snake between the weeds near a jack rabbit.
I am sitting on top of the world—alone.
I am afraid of life, losing hope, losing my mind.
I try to remember faded friends and memories.
The warmth of the last sun ray hits me and I finally relax.
There is still hope for a better tomorrow.

Cindy Perez

in the beginning

To my loving grandmother, Sylvia Tecosky Brecker
seconds turn to minutes flow seamlessly together,
and here I stay, reality a distant dream, I turn
under the safety handed down to me I remain
the ever-present shrill screaming of that machine
so faint in the distance, so far away
yet it stirs me, fills me with anxiety
of course it will win
it always does
who am I to stop the inevitable?
eyelids flickering, lips stagnant with staleness
that damn machine, why can't it just leave me alone?
the drops of sunlight seeping through glass now
the time is coming, melt back, let me alone! Ahhh . . .
The darkness once again enwraps me, and I fade in with it
(snooze) but it can't possibly remain this way
I must step into the light eventually, be it now
or with a justification. nothing can stay this way, serene dark easy nice
But no! The machine has told me
that this sweet shade will end, and so it will. Now.

Benjami Robert Greenberg

The Nineties

Lack of values in decline, self-respect is all but gone
I need my space a favorite phrase and widely used
Another child will be abused, we're too busy to be bothered
A child will suffer, grow up alone and troubled
There's no street or school that's safe, babies killing just for fame
They don't even feel remorse, I don't know which one is worse
And again we're blaming time, does anyone feel pain
So much at loss and nothing gained
We no longer walk in grace, respect is gone for human race
There's no need to be a wife, there's no price for human life
Are we really so surprised. At such demise
And so much innocence now at loss
Children's lives in such despair, someone has to simply care
It's our duty to reform, but they also have to learn
Life is simple we're complex, and explain it when they ask
Set examples and behave, just remember good or bad you were
The one that set the mold, did you set some solid goals
Spare a minute share a smile to the streets they won't fall prey
And someday they will remember their world you made
A little clear and perhaps life they will hold dear

Maria R. Bruns

Listen to Your Heartbeat

Dedicated to my son, family, friends, and people everywhere
Listen, oh, please listen, to every beat of your precious heart;
For every beat sends a beautiful message of a plan
In which you play a vital and important part.

It tells you how to best prepare yourself for the journey that lies ahead;
For each step that you take is a lesson to be learned,
And each thought conveyed is done at a moment of no return.

First you will cross the streets of love and happiness,
Sometimes followed by the rocky roads of pain and defeat.
Up ahead will be the golden highways of success and prosperity;
Many kindreds, friends, and foes during your challenge
You will meet and greet.

Each intersection you come to triumphant,
  a time for you to stop and rest,
Time to think back on past tests and experiences,
Time to thank God and feel heavenly blessed,
Time to forge forward in your mission to conquer life's quest.

For God, our Father, controls the time on Earth
That you spend in your travel each day;
And it is He who will help you fulfill His will
Until your heartbeat fades away.
Listen, oh, please listen, to every beat of your precious heart.

Patricia E. Reed

What Matters Most

Why is it that we always want the things that we can't have?
Why do we have to lose something important to us,
To make us realize what we've really got?
Why does it have to hurt so much
To make us stronger and to make us learn?
Nobody said that it would be easy,
But in order to make us learn, life has to be so hard.
The funny thing is that it brings us closer together.
And through it all, we stick together and we learn to love each other.
We learn not to take people and things for granted.
We find that life is too short to waste our time fighting with each other.
Eventually, we learn that money isn't everything.
But it's crazy how it can change a person.
Why does Nature have to remind us each year how small we really are?
Why do we destroy everything around us,
In order for us to advance technology and improve our lives?
The sad thing is that people don't realize
In this materialistic world,
that each other are more important than anything.
Why do we seem to ignore what matters most?

Sunshine VanVlerah

The Journey

On this journey of life, there comes those ups and downs,
more in depth than one's imagination
his image of one's destiny,
this vision of ones future.

On this journey, the road is narrow, the road is wide,
the road is never, ever ending. During one's travel in time,
the journey seems short, the journey seems long.
The journey seems to be like a dream.

One travels this journey knowing
not one's destiny, faith, or purpose.
But one knows that one is on a mission,
Standing on one's faith,
Traveling through an unknown destiny searching for one's purpose—
Yet still the mission is incomplete.

To go through this journey not knowing one's reason, or why
one is Even on such death wishes completing this mission.
As this mission is accomplished,
And the journey is complete, what can one say
I accomplished on my journey of life?

Darla Renee Lott

Fish Ranch Road

This is praise of a three mile road where I've walked my life away.
It's a line and a creek in the bowl of a spoon, trickling to the bay.
No one knows when this path began or animals moved up here.
Or Indians gathered and ground their food under a live oak tree.
The Pony Express galloped here, and the clanging 49er's.

Today, you can't guess when the mailman comes,
But your junk mail and letters arrive.
My house is across from a chestnut park, now fragrant in the sun;
Brightly lit with long candles white, a product of El Niño's fun.
Imagine lonely, bobbing buckeyes on Xmas thin leafless limbs.

This morning I heard a bellwether goat, leading-bleating his flock,
Nibbling and tearing the poison oak and thorny undergrowth.
Close by were the herders and dogs, shouting and yipping,
back and forth, talking back and forth in barks and Portuguese.
On the canyon walls of Fish Ranch Road!

Watching over all of this, as the afternoon cars roar by
Is a single madrone of majestic size, with barks as red as clay.
It selected its spot in the middle of the park before its neighbors grew.
So I praise the scents, the sights, the sounds,
and the grounds of Fish Ranch Road!

Robert M. Kubik

Christmas Through the Eyes of a Child

It all started with a star glowing in the east,
Joseph walking and Mary riding on a wretched beast.

Torn and tattered they stop at the Inn, only to be told by the keeper,
There is no room within. Be gone! You must go,
With the child on its way,
    find a cave and bring him into the world today.

Then a marvelous event the shepherds told, the angel Gabriel
Sounded his horn, to tell of the coming King to be born.

He appeared all shining and sparkling with a splendor of light,
Announcing the miracle of a virgin birth that night.

Mary the mother with a halo glowing ever so bright.
Infant Jesus wrapped in swaddling cloths was a wondrous sight.
Joseph keeping watch through that glorious night.
As destiny would be for all eternity to foresee.

Magnificence was all around. The shepherds from the fields
With eyes open wide, the three wise men with gifts of pride.
The ox, the donkey, camel and the sheep,
All laid their heads lazily at the infant's feet.

God opened the heavens to all mankind on this Earth,
Proclaiming glad tidings of a royal birth.

"Blessed are they who see Christmas through the eyes of a child."

Carolyn Daste Hurtado

Hurt for the Last Time

I don't know what to say
Do you still love me? Do you still care?
I can't tell, you don't seem to bother anymore
You don't seem to care, I know you used to love me
And I know you care
But don't you care, but don't you see
What I don't you see
I'm hurting badly and it's your fault
I'm tired of being hurt
I'm tired of being used
You just can't use me anymore
It's not fair, if you're going to love me
Do it right, if you're going to love me, do it right
If you're not going to love me
Then get lost, if you felt my pain
You would want to cry, if you felt my pain
You would want to cry, if you saw my pain in my eyes
You would be there for me, if you are not going to be there for me now
Then don't bother at all!

Kylene O'Connor

One Day

One day . . . I said to myself, pondering alone.
One day can mean so many things, a future still unknown.

I was lost, on my own, not understood
By an entrapping world that never could
Live up to my hopes or fulfill my dreams,
A world being ripped apart at the seams,
Torn to pieces by my unrelenting mind
And frightened by what I could not find,
I was forced to create my isolated world,
Through which its solitary occupant was being hurled.

My simple life divided into decades, years, and months,
But one day can encompass Everything and Nothing all at once.
This lesson learned while dreaming with him, exploring infinity.
He talked of a place similar to mine, sharing his own world with me.
Then, one day I looked into his eyes and said, "Peter, je t'adore,"
Trying to express with sincere words
    something I had never known before:
The happiness he brings to my life, this happiness we share.
The grand ideal found at last in a very unlikely pair.

One day . . . I say to my love, no longer pondering alone.
One day can mean whatever we imagine, a future of our own.

Crystal M. Eubanks

Creation

A breeze blows through this valley, untouched by adversity,
leaving a certain aviance to linger in the air. The white walls
surrounding this serene area are too auspicious. I can feel the
icy snow upon my face and the mystical chill of winter crisping
my bones clean. Bareness falls not on the trees with no leaves,
for they are candy-coated with an icing that holds no flavor,
only emotion. The Earth lay covered by a sheet of frost and still
as the mountains I see before me. As my body turns to leave
this place so filled with richness, I find my mind to be at peace.
My heart holds much joy, for I have become free in one single
moment of ecstasy, created by the bountiful sight I have been
allowed to see, as well as the scent of freedom I have inhaled
with each breath. It is God's brush that has painted this Earth
so white and peaceful. I thank Him for this extraordinary
escapade I have been able to relish in and give great accolades
of endearment to Him for all He has so graciously created for me
to frolic in.

Erin C. Damiani

Welcome to My Home

Though I'm only a person of modest means,
and my home not a castle or mansion,
it is open to all who approach its warm
threshold for either conversation, a home-cooked meal,
or even to bend an ear if troubled.

But this welcome extents beyond my front door.
This I give unselfishly to the sick, the lonely, and the young at heart.

Be it in song, dance, a sweet, or craft, I will bring
my home and its warmth to you.
I do this all from my heart and ask for nothing
more than a smile, a hug, or a sparkle of happiness from one's eyes.

You are always welcome to my home and the love
from within this forever-giving heart.

James H. Glor

Missing You

In memory of my nephew, Shayne Montay Coates
You were my new best friend, with secrets only we knew.
We had conversations with no origin or conclusion.
I was anticipating motherhood for the very first time.

But sadly, the doctors destroyed my heart, telling
me you would not be with me long, saying that once you came,
your life would only be a mist appearing for a little while . . .

The moment unfolded, and the doctors were right.
But I still kept my vow to cradle your innocent body.
You were beautiful. Simply beautiful . . . you had my lips and fair skin,
your daddy's cheeks, and your grandpa's nose.

I watched as my sweet baby emerged and drifted out of my soul.
So, I embraced you close to my bosom as you gurgled your last
good-bye in my ear, in a language only I could comprehend.

Not a day goes by without the thought of you . . .
So now I anxiously await for the day of God to come, the day when
I have a chance to see my son and cradle him in my arms again.

Amber T. Benton

A Special Friend or Best Friend

A special friend or best friend is someone who you really care
much, whom you treat as your real sister, and wherever you go,
you treat her as a friend whom you love and care so much. You
sometimes give her a gift which is precious to her that she kept it
as a remembrance so that she will always remember you, once
she look at that gift that you gave her.

But you'll never know or expect to see each other in a place
where you want to buy something and your friend is also
buying the same thing.

Alicia Mercedes A. Aguinaldo

A Universal Reality

We have been to hell and back.
To hell and back we have come and gone.
We have been the rainbow and the break of dawn,
The night of black, and the evening song.
We have been the friend, the foe, the lover,
The right, the wrong, the child, the mother.

To hell and back we will venture again, and again, until time's end.
Like the delicate wildflower that refuses to bend,
We are one of many in you flower bed.
The daisy, the rose, the sage, the clover,
The perfumed breeze you feel all over.

"To hell and back" historians will write, "singers, poets, brave knights.
Courted by kings and peasants alike,
They were predators and prey. They were birds of flight.
They were known as Meddea, Medusa, and Guenevere
Aphrodite, Mary, Honey, and Dear."

We are all things to all who know.
We are strength, courage, heat, and snow.
We have been both victors and victims throughout time, and then,
Your laughter and warmth at Autumn's end.
We are the women of today, of tomorrow, and of yesterday.
We are a universal reality.

Pauli Rachelle Caruncho

The Quest

The summer winds buffeted the New England bluffs.
Off towards the horizon, the vast, barren,
White-capped, fluid landscape stretched to meet the sky,
Broken only on occasion by the knife-like hulls of race-inspired yachts.
The white sun beat fiercely down on the decks of these mighty
But frail craft;
Wherein men labored to extract every ounce of wind tufts
To propel their craft towards the next buoy.
Above the din of crashing waves and buffeting sail canvas,
One could barely discern the helmsman's gruff barking;
"Ready About", "Hard Alee"
The crews tediously labored, quickly in unison,
As if made of but one.
Each man feverishly strove for one common purpose; Victory.
For today a champion will be heralded.
A conqueror of the winds and the sea,
And all those who would lay claim to his rightful throne.
Nay, no landlubber be he.

Ray Wolfe

My Elusive Daydream

Nights barren of a glint of hope
whose darkness give meaning to camaraderie
Days lacking a single ray of sun
for abduction by rich green foliage
Wind—still as my mind without coherent thoughts—numb

Smiles without faces sincere
frowns cutting my innermost fibers
Alive I am—secluded—feeling for life-ness—as antennae in darkness

Emotions with no occasion to dwell for lack of placid space
Am I not seen—deliberately shunned—spurned—and sidestepped
Distant—as clouds untouchable—lingering—chilled—frosty even

Talking with my inner self
answering from my mold—boldly—truthfully
Conversing—yes, I'm in control now

Visions of scenes emotionally warm exquisitely refined insatiable
as brush-strokes—tangible and deliberate
Fading again—as cool water awaken me—lost?

Listening with delicate ears
elements envisioned—understood—clear distinct
Fitting.   I must go now for some dare acquaintance with reality

Billy E. Worthey

Summer Traces

Summer's on its way, so grab your bonnet
while the birds are singing their favorite sonnet.
Beach towel, swimsuit, and the hot wind blows,
getting red as a beet and freckles on my nose.
Summer traces, like the sparkle in your eye, fade
into winter and a cold gray sky. . . .
Garden seeds peeking out their heads, brilliant reds,
orange, and yellow in the flower beds,
green tobacco plant with its pink bloom,
cattle under the shade tree fighting for room,
from clear, blue skies to thunderstorms,
from long-sleeved sweaters to tan, bare arms,
from hot chili and soups to an ice cream treat,
trading heavy shoes for two bare feet,
a rainbow painted across the sky, such heavenly colors please the eye,
beautiful green grass amid fields of rolled, baled hay,
and breeze-filled nights for sports and play.
From it is too cold, to it's way too hot,
from leaving the sun for a shady spot,
summer traces fill my heart with glee, God's creations for all to see.

Deborah Jones Crump

His Kind of Love

The heat of the day makes tempers short and patience run thin.
The trees are stirred by soft breezes, and if you will be still,
you will feel the stir.
You will feel my cooling touch upon your sweating brow.
My touch will give you sweetness of spirit and
calm among the restless, disquieted ones.
Like a cool, clear lake, I will soothe your soul.
Transport your thoughts to the ocean shore
where the rolling surf serenades the tired body and mind.
Drift out to sea in your imaginings,
far from the cacophony and disturbance of the city.
Look up to me! Adopt the gentle nature of He who died for you.
Is it too much to ask that you not answer meanness in like manner?
What good is it if you only love those who love you?
Even Satan does as much.
No, you are called to do better. You are called to be above pettiness.
Smile and forgive, and you will be blessed for it,
even as others have to forgive you in your impatient moments.
If I held you accountable for every error and failure, what would be your
reward? Now, can you be less forgiving? Dare you to be less
than your best?

Barbara Parkman

Ask the Woman Who Knows

When someone is a recovering alcoholic, they don't look for
answers in a bar. When someone is a recovering drug user, they
don't ask for help from a pusher. When someone is a recovering
gambler, they don't look for sympathy from a Las Vegas card
dealer, but when a woman is deciding what to do with a life,
she'll question adoption, keeping it, or abortion. Every decision
and answer will change her life forever, no matter who she asks
for, where she turns. Adoption, she's giving life a chance that
she could not provide. Keeping it, she will always wonder if she
can support or raise it right. But abortion is very definite. It is a
decision that can't be taken back. Years down the road, she'll
be faced with the question again. But not always because there
is another life, but because there is the past that she can't run
from, so she will continue to ask herself daily: "what if's," "what
about's," and "should have's." Always be wondering why
adoption sounded so bad at the time, or wondering if keeping it
would have been so terrible. But she will always go back to the
decision that was made, so final, and remember the "could have
been's." So before anyone does anything so drastic, please ask
someone who has been there, that has walked in your shoes,
knows the experience . . . but most of all, ask the woman who knows.

De Anza Ferrari

Happiness in a Dreamland, Not a Motherland

A country is called motherland, as it is a place a man is born; of one motherland only, as he is born on one only land of one mother, as by one mother only he can be born. He can be a man of two countries, but not of two motherlands.

This is a land of dreams, of many people, of many motherlands, then becomes their country, but not their motherland. For a brighter future, bring children to this very land to be their country, their motherland for those born in this land. If ever this country fight another, some know whichever one to defend, so hard to imagine what will be the end. Hope it does not disturb not, leader of this country, with other world leaders create everlasting peace on every land.

This is a land of world's most diverse people of racial, ethnic, religious, and tongued origin, but of the same dream. Created equal, life, liberty, pursuit of happiness endowed by their creator, so everlasting peace not a mere dream, despite racism and hatred in violent crimes, those create extreme fear oft deprives them of their freedom and dream.

Abide in this land, be a law abider, speak English only around who does, no malice toward anyone, a ray of inner conscience twinkles on the novel face and heart unveiled in actions with whoever, sensitive to the suffering of others, regardless color of skin, interracial marriage each to get bless.

Perti Sutrisno

The Intelligence of a Man

The intelligence of a man is not his physical features
or the constitution of his preachers,
but of his willingness in times of need to be there and to simply show you he cares.

The intelligence of a man is not physical strength or his bodily length
but the strength of his mind to endure what may be ahead,
and the length of his memory to remember what has been said.

The intelligence of a man is not to care what others may think,
for their thoughts may be dismal and in disarray,
but to carry himself just as a man in his own special way.

The intelligence of a man is not the words that loosely flow from his lips, but the words that come straight from his heart
where many want to be men don't know where to start.

A man is not of brawn but full of spirit and love,
one who will protect you and always respect you,
won't deceive you or ever leave you.

So you see, the intelligence of a man can't be measured by anyone's test, for a man is he who is dedicated and gives his best.

As a man, don't be afraid to cry, but willing to die for what you believe in your heart to be true, striving to be the best, striving to be you.

Felicia Osuley

Why?

We see our world slipping away as a precious baby has died today.
There was no reason for that baby to die, and the criminals who killed that child sit there and lie.
It was only a accident, can't you see?
But it's the baby who won't get to live his dream.
The world we know has somewhat changed
    and many people find it strange
that they can't walk down their street, without being afraid they will be caught in a drive-by.
There are some things in this world I can't understand,
but somewhere, somewhere someone is taking a stand.
Somewhere we will find the faith to cross the line and live day by day.
The truth we will find in ourselves, no matter the riches or wealth.
What it all comes down to, I am sorry to say,
is that we've made mistakes and now the children must pay.
It's not our fault they cry and say, "Why must we have to pay?"
But that baby that died, oh, so soon.
The funeral will be in the middle of June.

Connie Lim

It Hurts So Much

People you love so dearly, somehow someway they always have to go, either they pass away, or they don't have any feelings for you left to show. To lose someone, either which way is an unbearable feeling, that won't go away. You just stand there, unable to move, unable to speak, though you want to run and scream to the highest peak. You want to hold onto those hands that used to touch you so tender, gave you comfort, lead you on a way, so you never had to surrender. But they go, just slipping away, unstoppable, more and more each day. Until they're gone, then there's nothing left but memories, and you? Left behind, alone, broken hearted and nowhere to be.

"What sense does it make, to go through every stage in life? To see and feel the pain, or to say you was once someone's husband or wife? Of course you also get to see the good and happy times, though in today's world, you see less of love, but more and more crimes. Somehow you live through it, cause life goes on, every hour, every day, there'll be someone to sing a new song. So with a little hope left in you heart, it will be your choice, maybe there will be someone else, to hear your voice.

Rovena Harrison

Creation of Love

All things big and small, the Lord God made them all.
Diligently He worked day and night.
He added a little green, a touch of blue,
A sparkle here and there to make his play ground colorful and true,
Along with a touch of water and a bit of fresh air
He made this world beautiful and fair.
He created everything from above for this was the first gift of love.

Little bird flying by who gave you wings to float in the sky.
Big statue on the hill who made you so beautiful and still
Was it God's will?

Green grass low, tall trees high
who gave you such beauty to grace the Earth and sky.
With all the plans that God has given man
on how to care for his beautiful land,
Day after day He must take a stand and touch the land
With His creative hand, thus spreading love
    to every woman, child, and man.

Shirley D. Roundtree

Me and Yesteryear

Travelling down south, I learned to accept the name of "boy";
Chicory drinks, hush puppies and grits taste great, unlike "poi."

We parked at the curb and walked "slowly" down Waikiki Beach;
"Hot" sand forced us to the ocean, our bare feet "had" to reach.

Mariachi music "thrives," under West Coast church gables;
My gringo "hat-dance" partner, crashed into "two" floor-tables.

Storms in the Pacific Ocean could be quite horrendous;
We moved one mile in three days, bucking waves too mountainous.

Goony birds, white beaches and palm trees met us at Midway;
One irate pilot and an engine fire, caused great delay.

Cook Inlet to Anchorage, had testy forty-foot tides;
We dodged icebergs to Point Barrow,
    thanks to our "Blue-Nose" guides.

Yokosuka's "local train" to Tokyo, was full of strife;
I met all kinds of people, who brought my "senses" to life.

Under "Nam" guard, we snaked our way up the Saigon River;
French and "Nam" troops, used our smokes and beer as legal tender.

Why try "atoll softball," when its one-hundred-ten degrees?
Witnessing the Eniwetok "H-bomb," we saw Hades.

The song: "I left my heart in San Francisco," has great rhymes;
My ships sailed "under" that Golden Gate Bridge, twenty-six times.

Sidney Dyer

My Choice

I sit here looking at the wall. It looks so high.
I feel so cut off from the rest of the world.
On this side it seems so dreary and cold.
I could only imagine what is happening on the other side of the wall.

The hurt pierces through my heart like a dagger.
I feel so lonely and abandoned.
My dilemma seems so hopeless and devastating.
I'm at my lowest point in my life.
People have lied to me. They have also abused and cheated me.

I feel so trapped by the wall I have built for myself.
Why don't I just take that step? Why do I hesitate to be part
of something that people say will change my life?
Could it be that I am afraid of what life has to offer me,
or maybe I'm just not good enough, not worthy.
But how will I know if I don't try? So, I decide to take that step.

JESUS, I ACCEPT YOU AS MY LORD AND PERSONAL SAVIOUR!
I SURRENDER IT ALL TO YOU!
Instantly I see rays of hope, peace, and joy on the
other side of the wall. What a glorious day! A new beginning!
THANK YOU, JESUS!

Ursula A. Roberts Gobert

You Can't Own Love

What is love that it is so enchanting,
touching two wandering souls, bringing them together.
The love from one is not owned by the other,
when it is pure, it can not be smothered.

It is not a rose that can be taken possession of,
neither is it a ring that you take ownership of,
merely symbols of the truth of the matter it's an emotion.

It's never saying bye,
tearing heavily as you wipe your eye,
hating the moment when that emotion part,
you feel a rip and a breaking of the heart.

It is daring to search out the one and only one that makes it complete
it's walking five miles in the Hades of heat,
not because you own it, possess it, or demand it against its will
it's the desire to share and ultimately give.

You can't own it like a car
or like a precious diamond ring,
love is bound to the heart
when you give your everything.

David K. Revill

First Light

To my Phantom Man, my love, Wayne Macaulay
First light, a long thin bright line on the edge of the eastern horizon.
At the exact place where the Atlantic meets the sky and land,
I am here once again, standing alone on the sand at dawn.
While warm water is lapping at my toes,
   I'm lost in early morning dreams.
Slowly, lovingly, I speak your name.
Every letter, one by one my tongue lovingly caresses,
As its sweet sound leaves my lips, escapes,
Becomes a whisper on the wind.
It mingles for a moment motionless, then moves, takes wing.
And with it the love in my heart takes flight.

It is done for another day.
One of many days that has come before,
And maybe for endless more to come,
I've again fulfilled the wishes of my heart.
I declared myself to Spirit then,
I asked this of Him, while praying to the vastness of the morning sky:
That He would grant you a day of peace and happiness,
Starting at first light, as it reaches your eastern horizon, to my west.
And I do this in His name,
With all this love for you that lives within my heart

Heather L. Wright

Good-bye, Dear Tree

Dear tree, you stood for centuries in the sunshine and the rain;
With head held high and arms outstretched, you did not stand in vain.
You offered shade to many on the hottest summer day;
The squirrels found your thick branches a delightful place to play.

Hundreds of birds have nested in the safety of your bough,
And raised their little families in the homes that they built there.
In autumn, how you awed us with the beauty of your gown.
And when your leaves began to fall, and fluttered to the ground,

They enriched the soil beneath you while you shivered in the cold.
Yet you never once complained, though the winter winds grew bold.
With the first warm days of spring, you wore your new, green dress,
And to those who walked beneath you, your breath was a caress.

Good-bye, dear tree. We miss you, but your progenies live on
To keep alive your memory, though you yourself are gone.
And in the distant future, maybe our descendents, too,
Will find the joy in them that we have found in you.

Juliette D. Chambliss

Profile

It's dark in there, inside the mind: no peace, no calm, no quiet.
The echoes dance like silhouettes of highlighted, jagged arrows,
charting the torment with clear definition.

A profile of despair and blackness, with shadows to mystify the
bewildered soul residing within—will the sun be led to the
cloven hollow? To light dispassionate space and fuse the severed,
detached thoughts into one enduring nature?

An illusion of unity, untroubled and rational in a world of
insanity, balanced by the unstable. How insidious the treachery
of a reason not fully grown to the wisdom of the ignorant, the
confidence of the naive, the serenity of the foolish.

I long to be one such creature, one who cannot see the danger
masquerading as understanding, the pitfalls of the conceited that
seduce and ensnare. No such blissful complacency for this one.

Helen Franklin

Dream III

To all the believers in Allah and the last days
I had a dream, and in this dream I saw the Earth on fire,
Even the sea as far as the eye could see . . .
But as hot as the fire could be, it didn't burn me,
And in this dream I saw people across the land come together,
Singing a new song, the like never was heard before . . .
Then a light came down from the heavens, and in this light
I saw a man, the like never seen before . . .
He lifted his arms up toward the heavens, and the Earth was new.
And in this dream I saw people across the land come together,
Holding hands until they circled the Earth.
Then I saw the heavens on fire and a light came down from
The heavens, and in this light were three men, the like never seen before.
They lifted their arms up toward the heavens, and all the people across
The land fell on their faces and prayed and the heavens were new . . .
And all the heavens opened up to greet the children of the Earth
And Hell was no more.

Abdul Ali Muhammad

Remember

To my first dedicated pastor, Dennis Spain, God Bless You
We must remember why our Lord and saviour had to die.
Why an innocent man was crucified.
He walked this Earth without wrinkle or spot,
Hoping all would remember what he taught.
He knew among him was betrayal, instead of anger he turned to prayer.
We've all heard the story and we know it quite well,
It is a story we must continue to tell.
As he hung on the cross ready to die, you could hear many faint cries.
He asked his father to forgive you and I, and hung his head and died.
On the first Easter morn'. As many kneeled to pray, the stone was
rolled away. An angel appeared as if in a vision, and said . . .
"He is not here, he is risen."

Lee Ann Thomas

Heaven Imagined

To my friends and family and my Saviour Jesus Christ
Clear blue skies, fresh cool air where birds fly.
Peaceful valleys, quiet mountains, many fruitful trees.
Gardens of colorful flowers that go up to your knees
No more death, sickness, or shedding a tear.
Rivers of water that are crystal clear.
Everything is full of life and everything is Holy.
No sun or moon, for they do not shine brighter than God's glory.
Grace is always felt, love is seen in everyone's eyes.
Imagine! Life in Heaven never dies.
Sitting with God on His throne.
Jesus walking with you up to your new home.
Clear oceans and waterfalls, listening to angels sing.
Friends and loved ones can be seen.
Streets of gold, full of mansions, walls of pearl, rejoicing, and dancing.
Holiness surrounds, for there is no more sin.
Happiness and Joy never leave from within.
Many wearing robes or garments of pure white.
Receiving "The Crown of life."
An eternal place where there is no end.
Brings joy to my heart when the kingdom of "Heaven Imagined."

   Thomas E. Vidaure

Dignity

Tell me who you want me to be,
and maybe I'll come close, or at least closer than most.
Would I make you proud, add to your glad,
or maybe my performance, as usual, would make you mad.
Will it matter if I'm not happy;
will my sadness fall on deaf ears, or will you take me by the hand,
rescuing me, leading me far away from my fears?
Will you lead me on from day to day? Will your faithfulness fall astray?
Will you return to me at night yet sleep another during the day?
Tell me who you want me to be,
   and if it's anything other than what you see,
then take careful note, for I have chosen not to change,
nor compromise my dignity.

   Jacqueline Michael

My Guardian Angel

To my beloved sister, whom I truly miss, Desiree Joint
Her presence is felt even though she is not here
I can feel her in my heart, calming my doubts and fears
She is there in times when I feel all alone
She comforts me at night when I groan and moan
God sent her to watch over me because she was already in my heart
And what God puts together, no one or nothing can tear it apart
It was her time to leave this Earth when she left not long ago
But she came back to be with me because my hurt God knows
God knew we were like one, so he kept us together
Even though she is not here physically, her spirit will be here forever
My guardian angel was sent by God from Heaven like a dove
And Desiree Denise Joint, my angel, will I eternally love

   Catrina Joint

To Brianne

To my special friend, Brianne Barton
I'm so glad that I had a chance to know you.
I just want you to know that you are a very sweet and special person.
I'm so glad that we became friends in high school.
I really appreciate having you as a friend during high school.
You were more than just a good friend,
you were also one of the best artists in the county.
I really got to know you when I viewed your artwork.
You're so talented and I mean that.
It was so sad when I had to say good-bye to you on graduation day,
but, Brianne, I just want you to know
that you've earned a permanent place in my heart.
I will never forget you as long as I live.
I will always remember you, Brianne Barton.

   Austin Simmons

Garden of Flowers

To Vic and Natasha—on Sunday, June 28, 1998—with love, Mom
I imagine your marriage as garden of flowers.
Walk through its paths together every day and celebrate the
many flowers. Stop and talk to them and learn their names. You
will quickly discover that the tallest and the most colorful ones
are the "Love" flowers. If you'll look closer, you will notice that
these magnificent flowers lean and rest their lovely faces on
shorter and less attractive flowers. If you care enough to see
and recognize the lesser flowers, you will get to know their
names, and "Patience," "Loyalty," "Trust," "Tolerance,"
"Friendship," "Understanding," "Compassion," "Gentleness,"
"Tenderness," "Forgiveness," and "Support" will become your
most significant flowers. But, look even closer, and you may
discover the least colorful and yet the smallest flower. You may
actually miss it, but please don't, as this one is my wedding gift
to you—and its name is "Prayer." Hold this flower in your
hands gently, lovingly each day while turning over your worries,
your problems, and your insecurities to the Highest Power. If
you won't forget this little flower and embrace it often, it will grow
above all others and make them bloom in the most astounding
manner. On your wedding day, I pray with love for both of you
and for this simple and, often, the most forgotten little flower.

   Yvonne B. Rek

A Place Called Home

To Spencer Brewer for his music that inspires my creativity
A place called home is everyone's dream.
Like a sweet cologne, like sugar and cream.
Remember the real essence of what life's really all about.
Hopes, dreams, and lessons that guide us through our lives, no doubt.
Follows everywhere we roam—a place called home.

I'm goin' back to a place called home,
Know where I've been, know what I've done.
Success, profits, achievements, come and go like shifting sand
Creates the pain of bereavement, leaves life hanging on a strand.
Keep burning like a fire—home's desire.

I want what I need most, what my heart's desire can boast.
For if a fire came to our house, I'd grab the kids,
The animals, my spouse, and family pictures on the walls.
But I'd leave behind fine things and clutter in the halls,
And hold those who mean the most to me—family.

It's not the things but people, you see,
Who're always in your heart, never to part.
Without them the most beautiful home is just a big ol' empty tomb.
Home's like a big picture mirror that reflects
Who we really are, our place called home.

   Jennie Martin Gall

Poetry

Poetry is undefined,
But through a person's thoughts and words
Can be understood.
It's a flow of raw emotions
And an expression of a thought.

A good poets does not follow the
Rules of the law, but the
Flow of one's hand gliding across the paper.
A good pianist does not follow the notes and chords,
But the rhythm of one's heartbeat
   and the music playing within their soul.

Secrets lie between each line of a poem
And through the reader they are discovered.
Never reveal your secrets until
The end, because a magician
Always has something up their sleeve.

It is the end of my poem and as I said I must reveal my secrets.
Poetry is not judged by the
Words you write, but it is
Remembered by the impression you leave.

   Jonnelly Silva

A Simple Prayer for You

A simple prayer for you . . .
God, has anyone told you "Thank God!" and not just so in jest?
As in "Thank God!" or any slang version
    that slips right out of their mouths?
Has anyone told you to "Take care!" as you have taken care of us?
Who takes care of you when you are sick and lonely?
Who listens to your problems that cause you worry?
Maybe . . . we do!? Maybe you talk to us
In the way we talk to you, like the saying,
"Communication is a two way street."
That is what you do; how you do things!
So, I ask you to help me, help give me courage, build my backbone,
Be my strength, be there when I need you.
This is my simple prayer for you . . . for you to be there with me;
In turn, for me to help others and help the world learn
About the beauty that lies all around them.
Forget those so-called strings attached, that whisper in my head,
For you held none of us . . . for we are yours . . . and likewise.

I don't pray the way other people do or say that they do,
Like kneel, clasp my hands together, or even bow my head. . . .

Belinda D. Daniel

Wagon Tracks, the Trail Overland

For great Grandpa, Michael Fleenan Luark,
Oregon Trail Pioneer (1853)

From the banks of the mighty Missouri, we launched into "the
vast wilderness with nothing guiding us but tracks of those who
had preceded us on this journey." Great-grandad Mike's journal
in hand, we followed those tracks with his words; across the
Nemaha River, the big and little Blue, we traveled with him to
Fort Kearny.

Almost I heard wagons creaking and the sounds of wheels as
they turned, the jingling of harnesses shifting, the oxen hooves
shuffling slowly and wolf voices all blending in concert. My eyes
saw wide open prairies, not fields plowed neatly in rows, and
unfettered streams overflowing, with brave men daring to cross,
knowing full well the chances they took of being grievously hurt.

Twenty long days it took them. We slowly, ambling, took one,
to arrive at Ft. Kearny, Nebraska, where we slept warm and dry
with no fuel to find, no fires to build, and no cattle to guard
through the night. From Kearney to Scott's Bluff was awesome,
and we crossed over the Platte many times, but the mile-wide
giant it once had been, has been tamed and robbed of its might.

We stopped at Ash Hollow and drove up the hills and saw where
ruts from the wagons descended into deep valleys and wound
up grades steeply before us, it was truly a breathtaking view.

Bonita Luark

A Certain Inside

On an edge of despair, the spirit desires not to glide.
Into a lighter setting, fate centers an attentive toward the unknown.
Holding on yet searching closer to the finding of this side.
Might it be the fall is deep and the narrow path has been sewn?
Just to catch a glimpse of this reality is generous to see.
The mask is on and a deep sleep of time has become the mark.
Most do not wish to enter, so they linger in there own decree.
For the sight is more than most can stand: a tree with unmarred bark.
This one countless in the creativeness of a forever world unseen.
To believe in a whisper of fruits to the taste and hold.
A walk is lifting and the torch is filled within and clean.
But some are in the gray stillness of a shadow, motion sold.
In the distance, a winding call sets the unwilling further away.
And then the clay is molded, for the cast has set to form.
Full are the words engraved to few in mind to make the stay.
Come fires swirl and wind surround take way to the storm.
It starts where in a shelter and renders out to all who fear.
Can you trust in self and cleave to the sound of a certain might?
Given to be within from hope afar, yet known in the hand very dear.
Inside of you, the heart has found the soul step into joyous flight.

Susan K. Miller

Love

Love cannot be bought; it does not have a price;
it is a special gift from God.
It can't be mocked; it can be taught, but, oh!
The price we pay for love!

God is love, and God's word expresses that love.
When he died on the cross, He paid our cost;
that's why we can freely live.
No one else, that way would ever give, such
great love that was given to us.

God gave to me, and I freely give and love others
as it was meant to be.

Love is the way God wants it.
Love is the way we need it and is freely accepted.

"Look" at the world now; does it really love?
With all the pain and crime and hate!
So come on, world, don't wait, because it might be too late.
We don't want the world in chaos, but we want the love of Christ for us.

So, dear friends, why don't you try it?
With God's help you won't deny it,
and you will make the world a better place to live.

Mary Catherine Gordon

The Haunting

For those in the shadows, waiting for the light
We met so long ago, two ships colliding in the night
A love that was fire and water all that was you and I
We spent every waking moments together laughing,
talking, holding and making love.
A gift from the God's, so divine, I thought I'd died and gone to Heaven.
A lifetime of longing, dreaming, wishing, even begging finally true.

We ran off and got married, you taught me a thing or two
Strangling to keep my love for you safe inside me,
cutting to show how sharply you ached for me
Burning to demonstrate the fire of your love,
beatings proved your manhood and virility
Rape because as your wife I'm always willing,
Words that degrade so I'm sure to worship you.
Miscarriages my weakness I should have loved you enough to keep
the babies through the beating

This gift from the God's controlled me for 6 years past continues
to Haunt the day's and nights
A psychotic life of fear, doubt and inability to commit
slowly drowning me to insanity or suicide.

Kathy J. Peterson

Listen to the Quiet

Last night, I stood beside the cattail swamp and listened to the quiet . . .
Broken only by the red-winged blackbird's call.
Gazing upward, I saw him perched high on the tip of a dead oak tree,
Reclaiming the quiet that had captured me.

This joyful silence is somewhat sentimental,
The whispering wind nudging ever so gentle . . .
The rustle of leaves brushing in the air
Wind—never seen—yet the feel of presence there.

Soft, gentle sounds repeat the hush that sings,
Reflection of gold from the butterflies' wings . . .
It's simplicity and royalty all gathered in one;
It's ours to embrace when the day's work is done.

With peaceful quiet and serenity of mind,
Surrounded by calmness, it's contentment I find . . .
With the blackbird perched high, I again hear him say:
"Come, listen to the quiet at the end of the day."

God's gifts to us lie closely at hand
To reach out and touch, but we rarely understand
That all we need do is take heed and try it;
Let silence prevail and listen to the quiet.

Marcy Eppers

Struggle Within

For Mom—Mabel Bosley

I walk, I stumble, I lose the way because I did my own thing today.
When I am lost and all alone, why don't I come before your throne?
Why do I neglect the one who listens for my call and holds my hand
when I fall? Why do I hesitate to ask for help? Why do I try to do
things on my own? Why does it seem that I never learn? I am on this
path of life and I continue on a rough and bumpy road. Why do I think
I know the way when all I do is go the wrong way? When will
the road get smooth? When will life be worth living? Haven't I
heard often enough about the one who can lighten my load?
When will I believe you? I pray! I pray! I pray! Why can't I
get through to you? Why do I try to manipulate you? When
will I put off this pseudo? I can't fool you like I do others? Help
me, Lord, to come clean and confess. I have all my life made a
mess. I want to believe you, but I can't let go because, after all
these years, I still hurt so. I know others have suffered, but I
continue to cling to the past. Why can't I let go? Why can't I
be free? I can when I see it is really up to me.

Elizabeth M. Rocovich

February 28th

To Ryan and the loving child we lost

An angel opens her wings, as a new life dies.
Sadness rushes in; a mother closes her eyes.
Not a day goes by that memories fade.
All the dreams that have fallen apart,
what is to be and could have been, has broken her heart.
She will never hold her child, see her baby walk,
share this life with its father, or hear their child talk.
The doctor said everything would be okay, and it wasn't their fault,
that this was a good thing, it was probably growing in the wrong spot.
The lose of a child, a pain no medicine can take away,
a part of their souls gone forever,
for God took their precious baby that day.

Mandy J. Delzer

The Night

Quickly upon us comes the night,
Like a creeping shadow trying to sneak up on its owner.
I rejoiced that night had finally come,
But my brother sat cold and motionless on the bare stone floor.

I looked at him with bloodshot eyes
He was scared, I could tell.
I probed his mind like a bird searching for worms.
The rain began to pour down on my roof like a hammer beating on nails.
My brother's hair stood on end.

His screams broke the silence, and took me out of my dreary
Mood into a panic stricken spin.
My mother would be here in a minute to quiet him.
This brother who was afraid of night, and I, a child of night
With my crooked smile, and horrid grin find delight.

Amber Collins

The Passage of Time

Time passing slowly allows for the making of beautiful memories,
bittersweet memories.
Memories allow for the remembrance of the beginning of a Domain,
the fall of an Empire.
The remembrance of great victories, fame won, and heroes built.
Of the lessons of a great lose, the pain of the underdog.

Time passing slowly allows for the formation of friendship.
Friendship help hold nations together.
Enables people, all races, to get along, to live together.
Fulfills that deep, passionate need to trust,
and gain the trust of others.

Time passing slowly allows for the growth of wonderful love.
The growth of love fills a deep, empty void inside one's soul.
Love gives security, the assurance of a family, no matter your crimes.
Gives that bodily satisfaction we all want, need, and even crave.

Angela Cheatham

Good Morning, Lord

I want to say, "Good morning, Lord," as I start a brand-new day
And pause to think of your goodness, as I hurry on my way
The many things you give each day, are more than I can tell
The quiet peace, just to know that will my soul it's well.

I have eyes to see the sunrise and ears to hear the birds
Lift their voices sweetly, in a chorus without words
Your love is like a river, that flows so smooth, yet strong
It's wide and deep and full of grace, like the chorus of a song

I love the quiet mornings that I can meet with you
And feel your presence in your words, that help to get me through
And gives me strength to bear my cross, whatever it may be
And count it a privilege in this world, that I can live for thee

So I thank you Lord this morning, for the gift of another day
And keep in my mind, all through the day, the price you had to pay
And know it's free, the gifts you give, and I need not repay.
You give me the peace, the sunrise, the birds, and the gift of another day

Kathleen Bash

My Sweet Angel

To my baby, my angel Danielle

I see her almost every day.
At work, in my mind, or in a dream that I'm saving her from
    evil and I'm the hero to portray.
She makes my mind scream and I try to think of something
    smooth to say.
Or witty to think up.
She makes me tremble to the point that I can't hold a cup,
Or what I want to tell her.
When I look into her, I see something in her that I don't see in others,
    I see her soul, a soul that completely glows through her body to
    give her aura that spark that makes me go insane.
My sweet Angel, how far you fly to me,
That I wish you had the key to set me free.
I don't know what to say,
I never know what to do.
Whenever I see my sweet Angel, she sends a ray of light
    in my times of darkness to open a path to get to her happiness.
Only she don't know.

Robert Sanders

My Very Special Angel

Dearest Jan, always an Angel in my heart—Love, Carol

You don't display your wings or your halo made of gold,
And the love that flows from your heart could not have been foretold.
Frequent thoughts of you bring a smile to my face,
And, in this heart of mine, you will always have a place.
A friend like you could not be found
    if I searched the whole world wide,
For together we have laughed and you consoled me when I cried.
I know without a doubt that, for all eternity,
My very special angel in my heart you'll always be.

Caro J. Frey

The Rainy Night

There are raindrops on my window, I watch the soft parade.
The wind, it sneaks up softly blowing its silent aid.
The tree sways back and forth rocking its leafy child.
Silently wishing its child's dreams with this, it secretly smiled.

Lightning crashes, disturbing peace. Thunder booms to join its friend.
Together through the ages, on each other they will depend.
The clouds, they sneak in softly to join the nightly fun.
The new-found friends thundered and boomed
and awaited the rise of the sun.

Clouds of crimson glowed in the sunrise as the sun rose high.
Lightning crashed a good hello and thunder boomed a good-bye.
The clouds, in groups, wondered away as the wind blew by their side
With the wind gone the tree stood still and the rain
went out with the tide.

Christen Morris

Platonic Love

Platonic! What does Plato have to do with this? Do you know him?
Do you know who he is or who he was?
Do you like him? Do you admire him?
Do you reject him? Do you care about who he was?
What do you know about his loves?
Poor Plato! People mention him so often,
And the majority doesn't even know who he was, what he did,
   or what age he lived in.
Could it be said that Plato always had unrequited loves?
He being so idealistic, did he never even touch his beloved?
When I write, do you know if I write from my imagination or from reality?
Lucky Plato! So many beautiful things are attributed to him.
Foolish Plato! Instead of devoting so much of his time to his idealism,
He should have touched and done everything else
   to the women he loved,
So he would not have had "Platonic loves."
Dreamer Plato! If he intended for all of us to believe his doctrine.
Blessed Plato! His name will be known over the centuries.
Do you think that my love is Platonic?
No? Who can tell? I am also idealistic.
Yes? Well, how romantic and passionate Plato must have been.

   Liduvina Vivanco

Outstanding Poets of 1998

We are the Outstanding Poets of 1998;
some might include a Traci, Jason, Bob, or Kate.
We come from all over in this world of so many
to enter a contest and win some prize money.
Some of us are just happy to be published, you see,
because a place in a book is more important to me.
Money isn't everything, though some would be nice,
but it's like taking a chance with a roll of the dice.
We are competing against people we don't even know
   or can't even see,
but we share the same talent—a poet are we.
We are the poets of the future, present, and the past,
and we are the ones who make the memories last.
For we are like authors, who write all the time,
but what some of us write comes out as a rhyme.
Some poems don't always come out as a rhyme,
but it might be a story of a moment in time.
Don't let anyone tell you that poetry's dying,
because, with us in the world, you know we'll keep trying.
So poets out there, wherever you are,
believe in your dreams and you will go far.

   Jim Martin

Tell Me How You Feel

To the man I love, you know who you are
Falling for your mind first and your looks second
Thinking that meeting you is almost equivalent to Heaven
There is only room for you in my heart, there can be no one else
So may I take care of you, like you take care of everyone else?
Perhaps, somehow, make you feel special
I want to hold you in my arms when you've had a rough day
Support any decision you have to make
Make you feel good inside in every possible way
Yes, I have a thing for you, and it has often confused me
To know that I love a man who seems unruly
When we're physically apart, my spirit is always in your presence
And despite what other people try to attempt,
   it doesn't make a difference
I'm not leaving you until you tell me to
I am deeply in love with you
We have a bond no outside forces can break
You know these feelings are real, with you I'm never fake
Baby, come into my world and let me Love You
   like no other woman has
Come let us build a life together that will always last
I am a woman of my word, forever keeping it real
Now it's your turn baby, tell me how you feel . . .

   Carlene A. Wells

Locar's Tale

To the love of my life, Carol
Gaze not upon me with fear fair lady.
For, I am called Locar the prince of the air.
Forsake not your garden for fear of my talons or my stare,
For the great spirit has blessed
Us both with a lair to share.

I am a hawk, a prince of the air and it is whish! as I return to the lair.
Speed and my power that I snare the hare.
Not grand as the eagle
Not wise as the owl
Not loathsome as a vulture
Not small as a sparrow

I am called Locar, the prince of the air,
Yes, my eyes do glare and my talons are sharp
But, if it were otherwise; would I be a hawk.
Like the wolf of the forest and the shark of the sea
The Great Spirit has also created a place for me
Gaze not upon me with fear fair lady.
For I am called Locar, the prince of the air.

   Oliver Sutton

Where Is God

For all God's children everywhere
God is: In the sunrise at the break of day and in the sunset as day
         turns to night. He is in all the twinkling stars that fill the
         evening sky.
God is: In the gentle Spring rain that nourishes the flowers and in the
         Summer sun that warms the grass under our feet.
         He is in the red and gold leaves that fall from the trees in
         Autumn and in the sparkling snowflakes of Winter.
God is: In the wagging tail of a happy puppy and in the contented
         purring of a kitten. He is in the fluttering of the wings of
         butterflies as they dance over the flowers; and in all creatures,
         no matter how small, no matter how big.
God is: In the sound of a newborn baby's cry and in the faces of all
         His children. He is reflected in the eyes of people we love
         and in the smiles of strangers.
God is: In the minister's words during a worship service and in the
         voices of children at play. He is in the healing hands of
         doctors and in all churches, hospitals and homes.
God is: Above us and beneath us. Beside us and inside us.
         God has no limits. He is in Heaven and he is on Earth.
God is: Everywhere and in everything.
         God is love.

   Sharon Mills

Glossy Brevities

Formed from a film, protruding into a profusion of wobble-spheres,
infusing a salient, buoyant breeze, globules zigzag away;
no baggage they bear to burden their weight.

Transparent fragility constrained by frugality,
fearless floaters bob and weave in a drunk-mocking tizzy,
transients soon to be slighted by heretic night.

Superficiality incarnate, insubstantial cocci delight, transfix,
but minuscule endurance precludes their forbearance
(lamentable—it's that their ephemeral looks lacks permanence).

Pray tell, why does a plurality of such delectable delicacies
practice perseverance so ineptly?
Could their inherent weakness predispose prematurity?

Logic says strength portends a life of long length,
but truculent tornados can abduct bony oaks
while sparing puny pansies propped on springy stems which bend.

Yet, inevitably, even these pugnacious beauties
   undergo languishment;
dusky, audacious sundowns always quickly fade,
but must all splendid bubbles break,
   releasing emptiness kept contained?

   Richard E. Smith

Everything and Nothing

It is my will to see the world a better place.
What is it I must do to make this happen?
I can do everything and I can do nothing to change the world.
My actions and my inaction all make the world different.
If I raise one child who has less hate in his heart,
then I have done my job.
If I raise one child with one ounce more kindness in his heart,
then I have done my job.
But then, jobs aren't always what we do best.
Doing what we love is what we do best.
If we raise one child who makes life a little better for any creature
great or small, then we have done what we love.
In doing what we love and raising this child, we will no doubt spread
this same kindness to at least one other human being.
This means we've made a difference in two lives.
If the laws of mathematics works and each of these two lives
impact two other lives, it will not be long before the world is changed.

Make your commitment to change two lives today.

Vicki L. Hicks

Family Ties

When a child growing up, no fancy home to see;
But, wherever Mom and Dad were, that was home to me.
We never owned a real house, that we could call our own
But, always rented our abode, that Mother made a home.
We moved around a lot it seemed, to go where dad could work;
What ever life deemed, Dads work he never shirked!

We struggled through life happily, together just us three;
Seemed it would always stay, just Mom, Dad and, me.
But, years went on and, changes came, which made our lives complete;
I met a man who changed my name and, swept me off my feet!
The year's brought happy times, our children numbered three;
A daughter and two strapping sons, no finer could there be!

Our family's number grew and grew, as years so swiftly passed
Our grandchildren number now to nine,
    and a great-grandson in the cast.
Now, Daddy's gone and, we're retired and,
    many miles are now between;
Our family's scattered here and there, so seldom are they seen—
But, time or miles can't keep us apart for, strong family ties remain
And, we cherish each other in our hearts, love will always reign!

Donna Abell

David

To my son, I am so proud of you
I try to remember the days before
You came into my life, so new.
What joy, what wonder, a boy so small.
What can I teach you? What can I offer?

It's all a blur, that time before you changed my life forever.
You're growing so fast, becoming a man,
Just ten years old, and yet so wise.
What can I teach you? What can I offer?

As I look down the road to the days beyond, to a time we cannot see,
I wonder with hope and excitement and joy: What will you be?
Who will you love? Will you be as proud of me as I am of you?
What can I teach you? What can I offer?

But I realize all I can give you is love,
That very best part of me,
That part which knows no boundaries, no limits.
That's what I can teach you, that's what I can offer.

And I realize as well, it's a two-way street,
For you give so much to me.
It is you who is the teacher, you who gives.
What joy! What wonder! My son!

Frankie M. Garton

Words of Inspiration

Sometimes life seems so hectic and exhausting,
But there's always time for a little revival!
Rejuvenation—to replenish, heal, rest, laugh,
Sing, dance, rejoice, worship, praise, live,
Forgive, learn, give, play, love. Love yourself and others.
See, hear, feel, know, touch, smile, glow, show,
Teach, always practice what you preach.
Freedom of speech, of religion, and of press.
We must reduce our stress and release the negativity
    we so much detest.
We want peace, serenity, and some cosmic, astral divinity!
This will help our hatred cease, causing your inner
Butterfly to be released.

Melissa Kendrick

Factory Floor

I stood upon the factory floor,
the smell of a thousand jobs gone away filled the air,
machines lay idle, cobwebs and dust lined the walls,
echoes of things past shouting through the air,
no need to rush and run about, nothing made nothing to ship out,
once the bedrock of a nation,
now nothing more than this hollow shell, this factory stands no more,
its fabric torn asunder, only echoes of things lost rushing past,
a nation changes its direction,
another factory falls lackadaisically into the crevice of time,
it's swept into the oblivion void,
factory floors can tell much about a nation and its past.

I stand now upon the factory floor,
smelling cutting oil almost everywhere, machines sit idle,
no work today, this very plant was closed ten years ago yesterday,
whatever happened to the American dream,
a full dinner pail and extra pay, it went away this very day,
ten long years since the factory floor.

Bruce J. Edmonds

Winter

Cold, soft snow can do wonders for the mind with its beautiful images,
feelings, and soft sounds of the pitter-patter when it gently,
slowly, quietly falls to the ground.

Trees are hidden in snow, the air is brittle, lakes are iced up,
and the skaters are merrily skating with no worries on their minds.
Pine trees are in the middle of a dark forest,
and if you inhale very deeply,
there will be a wonderful essence of pine drifting in the air.
Animals are quietly sleeping in their nests, waiting for spring to follow.

The fires are extraordinary when they are surrounded
with that magical fine sparkling of the snow.
Children with their sleds are going down icy hills,
with their parents at the bottom waiting for them
to tell their children it's time for bed.
But they don't listen and they run back
up the hill and do it all over again.
Winter is gorgeous with all of its stillness, quietness, and beauty.

Jeffrey Carey

I Will Love You from Afar

Often my arms ache for your gentle touch;
To have you near me, to see and hold you, would mean so much.
I sit and watch as some walk by.
I find myself at times trying not to cry.
I know I have been blessed to know you, as long as I have;
To remember the times we shared makes my heart so glad.
I see you at night as I lay my head down to sleep.
I know the good Lord, your soul he shall keep.
One day, he will give back to me your hand, so I may feel your touch.
I await that day, for our new lives both together, so very much.

Jennifer L. Wells

For There, but by the Grace of God, Go I

God, for my life and talent; family, for love and support
I'm handicapped but shod, as I notice others' feet going bare;
I'm slow, but, oh, so thankful as I still can crest the stair.
My limbs, since being crippled, have a mind quite of their own;
Not mastered now by me, but as time worn they atone.

My eyesight has grown dimmer, but most beauty I still see;
The hands that once were steady seem to shake and tremble free.
I watched the blind and bed-fast with prayer and teary eye;
For there, but by the grace of God, go I.

I'm not alone, but blessed with multitude of friends and family near;
The sounds around me softer, yet still captured by my ear.
Then sweet smells of nature's garden penetrate my dimming sense;
As I inhale breath of precious roses, still bouqueted along the fence.

Soon the laughter of a grandchild warms my heart and thoughts within;
My body's frailties seem so small, I voice a prayer to Him.
Each day I'm humbled as I see the ones who will not try;
For there, but by the grace of God, go I.

Norma Cowart Fisher

The Autumn Flame

Remembering "Joy"—She was that and more, my beautiful Joy.
Because it's such a desperate flame—
dried, brittle, hard—
it will burn momentarily with such intensity,
scorching all who venture near it;
but let it rage.
It has such a little moment of triumph to call its own
before it consumes itself into its own ashes;
and soon enough a stronger force will pick it up and carry it away,
scattering it into the past so that no trace of it remains after this day.
Rather, let us who venture near it
remember it with sadness, too,
that anything so lovely (and it was in its brief span)
must consume itself, then fade away
almost as if it never happened.
So, if an Autumn flame is starting,
and a fascination within there lies,
remember, oh, my warning:
when it starts to live
it begins to die.

Helen L. Groshek

The Vortex

To my lifelong friend, my wife, Maureen
The order is the push of a fallen angel beginning a spinning
descent into Hades itself—my own damnation. In rapid succession, I
concentrate pensively on constant replays of seeming failures,
as the ropes of death surround me in my lamentation. Like a bird
clipped of its wing and let go, with desperate longing for eternal
sleep, my internal spiral journey continues downward into an
underworld of frozen wasteland and darkened concealment. Due
to the quickly spun web of despair, there is a scrambling
through a maze of mayhem; uncertain where I had entered,
whether or not there would ever exist escapement.

Touched as if by my angel of mercy, the cries of a woman implore
me not to sacrifice my soul to the god of forced displacement. Her
own web she spins, the stratagem, to deliver me from the trap of
the bird catcher's hem: A prayer is offered to release this broken
winged creature from its atmospheric cocoon and return it to
light and love's environment.

My inner core burns for freedom from this debasement.
To quench the heat and rid me of these demons of isolation
and worthlessness, does this pen of healing accompany my
angel's gentle prodding and caress. With much groaning and
tears are the internal vehement debates to conquer this hellish
vortex of battle, to invoke refusal to give the God cause to vaunt
concerning its prey. At long last! Free once more to soar!

Paul A. DeGennaro

The Blackballing Experience

To Michelle, Percy, Leila, Steve, Dominique, Natalie, and Antray
The blackballing experience is all of my life tough row to hoe.
Yes, God is my witness. Yes, God is my source of strength. Yes,
I have a personal relationship with God. Yes, God is my director.
Yes, I stand for truth. Yes, I live through faith. Yes, I continue
to make it public knowledge that I am being treated wrong. Yes,
I live the solutions to my problems. My past is my memory not
my clinging vine. Yes, I have forgiven all people that have done
evil against me and continue to do so. Yes, he tried to murder
me. The blackballing experience, the original God is my witness.

Nndra Terry

Trinity: The Mother Church of Savannah Methodism

To my brother, Dr. Ralph S. Bailey, Pastor Trinity UMC
Trinity, O, Trinity, with majesty you stand
Towering old Savannah—a refuge for the land.
Many have come to know Me as you cradled them in your pews.
Many have led from your pulpit bringing My good news
The good news of a Father who has called you by name,
Who kept you during your exile, you are not the same.
Refined by the fire, you are as gold to Me.
I've filled you with My spirit for all the world to see.
What God is like, one can know from you,
The remnant who love me so.
You are those who plant My seeds,
Who share My love, who are called to lead.
The vision of your pastor who was called by Me
Will help you become the best that you can be.
I will equip you for every task,
If only you will come and ask.
Completely refurbished, majestic, you stand,
A beacon of light in a weary land.
Trinity, O, trinity, keep your eyes on Me.
I am the answer—help the world to see.

Rosemary Bailey Short

Cabin in the Woods

Hazy lavender escapes to faraway mountains
as shadows prey on the last stubborn rays of the sun.
Angry clouds battle over distant snowy peaks,
and soon icy fingers impatiently drum on my window.
I seek the comfort of my quilted cocoon.

The muffled fury outside and the cozy crackle and hiss of the fire
assault my senses with nature's soothing music,
yet sleep eludes me.

Life's little burdens take flight,
no longer clawing at my thoughts,
when I hear the comforting sound
of my husband's rhythmic breathing
and feel his warm breath
in soft little puffs against my cheek.
He stirs and gathers me closer.
Only then am I able to sleep.
I will solve the world's problems tomorrow . . . or not.

Lana J. Farley

What Will They Think of Me?

Such peace has come over me—is it visible from the outside?
If, I dare not tell a soul, will they still see a change in me?

Such joy down in my soul; my cup is full. Can it be contained?
If I dare not say a word, will it overflow to the outside that
everyone might see change in me?

Whatever shall my friends say when I tell them I no longer
desire to do the things I used to do or go to places I use to go?
Will they ask what on Earth has come over me?

I dare not tell a soul—whatever shall they think of me?
If I tell them how Jesus came into my life last night, loosed my
shackles and set me free, what will my friends think of me?

Erma Jean Bell

White Roses

White Roses in a bouquet
Was your only desire
To have on your birthday
In place a roses red as fire.

Although your presence I have lost,
Our love remains true,
And, sweetheart, at all costs
I'll preserve the memory of you.

Eighteen roses so white
Have been bound together,
And in each there is a delight
That will shine in all weather.

Eighteen years they represent
And encircle a rose of red;
A fond memory they present
Of my love before we were to be wed.

The Lord took you away,
And I lost my only love,
But I'll be true until the day
I meet you in Heaven above.

Ronnie Lee

More Than I Asked For

When Jesus said, "Come unto Me . . .
I will give you rest to the core,"
I took Him at His word, and came,
And found much more than I asked for.

The rest that He had promised me,
In return for my burdens sore,
Was peaceful and joyful and good,
And so much more than I'd asked for.

He added love to His bounties
And promised there was plenty more,
If I'd only share with others
All the blessings He had in store.

These riches are yours, too, my friend;
He included you in His call.
He wants you to know and believe
That when He gave, He gave His all.

So in my humble way today,
I ask you to open the door
Of your heart and let Him come in.
He'll bring you more than you ask for.

Mary L. Shelton

Trial Run

Stand before the light
And tell what you have done.
Tell how much you loved the Earth
And were enraptured by the sun.

Hope you can say, honestly,
You had hurt not anyone.
But if you did, your sorrow proved
It was never done for fun.

Explain where you went wrong and
From mistakes, a lesson learned.
Show examples of the good you did
And from temptation turned.

Did you make a contribution
To the betterment of man?
Or did you cause destruction
And alter nature's plan?

This trial run will give you
What you need to gain insight
Into what could be your reckoning,
When God holds your soul up to the light.

Joyce Hughes

The Window

As I look out the window,
What do I see?
I see blue skies and white clouds,
Such a peaceful serenity.

As I look out the window,
What do I see?
I see green grass,
Such big, beautiful trees.

As I look out the window,
What do I see?
Gardens with colorful flowers
And a few buzzing bees.

As I look out the window,
What do I see?
I see a reflection.
I see me.

Jeanne K. Watts

I Gave My Heart to a Stranger

I gave my heart to a stranger
And I don't know why!
Sparkling eyes of blue,
I really love you.

I gave my heart to a stranger
And I don't know why!
Your smile really moves me,
Like a whimsical melody.

I gave my heart to a stranger
And I don't know why!
I hope that you'll be my friend
And love me until the end.

Ruth Oppelt

Weaver's Daughter

The weaver's daughter
is beautiful.
The weaver's daughter
is fair.
She spins with her
little spindle,
with her long,
flowing hair.
The weaver's daughter's beauty
is all within,
while outwardly, no one would know
that which lies within.
She spins a thread that's golden,
that will clothe her king.
She works and toils and spins,
that His joy she'll bring.

Jessie M. Combs

Survive

Playing the game,
Not knowing the rules,
Going insane.

Giving all you have to give,
Reaching out,
Just trying to live.

Loving with all your heart and soul,
Holding on,
Feeling out of control.

Playing,
Giving,
Loving,
Things you need to survive.

Annette Duncan

Now That You Are Gone

The birds sit hushed in the trees,
Now that you are gone.
The stars have dimmed their glow,
The moon withholds celestial beams,
Now that you are gone.

And when dawn prepares the scene . . .
Will the sun remain offstage?
Now that you are gone?
Only your return can set the sky ablaze.
Till then the darkened heavens
Will shield a bruised and broken being.

Marion H. Nichols

Lost

Until death do us part
We promised that day
But never did I think
Death would soon come at bay

Life is so hard now
The pain I can't tame
And no matter what I do
It's continuously a game

True love we found
That death cannot take away
Memories I'll cherish
Until we rejoin one day

Your life is over
And lost mine became
With anyone else
It would never feel the same

Marianne J. Decker

A Perfect Rose of Love

When God gave me a sister,
He sent a perfect rose
to give much joy and happiness
to every one she knows.
A gentle heart so tender,
filled with love for those she meets,
old folks or little children,
or a cripple on the street.
A heart full of compassion,
for the sick or those in need,
to her it doesn't matter,
the color, race, or creed.
This is the saintly person
sent to us from God above,
to be my precious adopted sister,
a perfect rose of love.

Mary Lou Cloaninger

Luminescence

Brownish specks adorn my wingspan
And my postured supine torso
Flexes . . . as the night progresses.

Silken yellow velvet wingspread,
Feelers probing for awareness
Once I awaken to day's light.

The day waxes . . . my wings flutter.
The lemon sun repeats itself
In the beauty of my hues.

I reflect its cheerful aura
As I spread my wings and fly . . .
Toward you, then you, then you,
Then you. . . .

Mary Mills

I Used to Believe in Love

I used to believe in love.
When the sun rose,
My heart soared above,
But our time was short.
Like the passing of the day.
When the sun set,
My heart fell to the Earth.

I used to believe in love.
Now I cannot see.
The stars above
Have faded away.

I used to believe in love.
Until you stole my heart,
And took it with you
To your grave.

Jessica Edge

My Brother

I really miss my little brother.
We are so many miles apart.
For me he will never be any further
than right here next to my heart.
Sure, we had our ups and downs,
but this is to be expected.
Many times he was a real clown,
although I never made him feel rejected.
Soon he will come back home,
hopefully with a change in ways.
And when he does come back,
it will be a bright and sunny day.

Lesia Anderson

A Bientot

As I approach my twilight years
I look around in awe
Of beauty I see everywhere
Thankful for every breath I draw
I only wish I had more time
To savor and to keep
The fragrances of this world
To take one more giant leap
But soon I'll take my final trip
When my Father says it's time
So long for now, my dear ones
Until Heaven's stairs I climb

June Samuelson Carroll

My Love, My Life

You picked me up
When I was down
You came into my life
And brought me around
You lifted me up
And held me tight
You have never let me down
You are my everything
My love, my life

Karen Williams

The Game of Time,
or, for My Beloved

In fields where yellow daisies grow
Twilight spreads a golden glow
For my beloved
No matter how near or far apart
I keep a secret hiding place
Within the meadows of my heart

Patricia Panciotti

Let There Be Peace

On the wings of the wind
I whispered a prayer
That peace may cover the world again.
I heard the call of the doves.
As they sang a morning song.
I see the beauty of the Earth.
God's gift to man
I dream of little children
May they never know hunger again.

Stand up, oh! Zion, and pray
Let the weapons of war be no more.
Help them to see the folly of it all.
May they sit to gather, and find peace
For all men are truly brothers
Oh! Wind, spread your wings, as we pray.
Carry this plea to the throne of God.
As I pray for peace, "Let it begin in me."

Thelma Bornes

Childhood Thoughts

No father on Earth to call my own
No hand to clasp when all alone.
No loving eyes to see me grow
Time seemed to me to go so slow.
He went to be with the Lord they said,
So I talked to him kneeling by my bed.
And I told him the day soon would be
When I will look up and his face I see.
We will walk together hand in hand,
Down the golden path in that new land.

Dorothy Mae Evans

Untitled

Your sighs,
Pale yellow,
Your touch,
Vivid green,
Our bodies together,
White hot heat.
Desire in a red, red room,
Our sweat crystal,
Bathing alabaster skin
On midnight blue sheets.
Colors blending, cocooning,
As time stands still.

Shauna Penniston

The Old Homeplace

The old homeplace is deserted
Only silence fills the air
No more happy, childish laughter
No footsteps echo on the stairs

For the last occupant has departed
Now gone on to a higher plane
No more endless days of loneliness
No more sleepless nights of pain

Where long ago dwelled happiness
And a large and loving family
Now there's only gloom and shadows
Dust and cobwebs for the eyes to see

Only small mice now dwell in the attic
Among all the relics of days of yore
Only their tiny feet to scamper
Back and forth across the dusty floor

But alas, their days are numbered
For soon the old house will be no more
Torn down to build a super highway
And a shopping mall with dozens of stores

Ruby Coggins Gordon

Holy Spirit

The whisper of the wind
That echoes in my ears,
It sweeps throughout my soul,
Relieves me of my fears.

The whisper of the wind,
The sweetness in the breeze,
Its calming scent is pure;
It floats along with ease.

The whisper of the wind,
It sings a joyous song,
And unto those who listen,
Bestows a peaceful throng.

The whisper of the wind
That glides beneath my wings,
It takes me far above,
Beyond all other things.

Natalie Jean M. Valdez

The Alpha and Omega

In the beginning was the world.
And the word was God!
From there, theologians, scientists,
Scholars go their own way.

As to their beliefs of the
"Creation-of-the-universe"
How did it begin?
How will it end?

The "mystery of the creation"
Is interpreted in different ways
By different cultures
Around the world.

We watched (on TV) as our astronauts
Walked on the moon!
What's coming up next?
Why, Mars—very soon!

No! I do not believe mankind
Will ever solve this mystery
Of the "Alpha" and "Omega"
Of His divine universe.

Joan M. Dematatis

The Last Train Station

To my wise dad, Meredith Hubbard,
1923 to 1996, train lover
With the passing years of decades gone,
Stubs of destination show:
One ticket in the book remains.
All aboard. This train must go.

A memory of his wife, gold-framed,
Near the window by his bed;
Outside, a world that passes by
Along the railroad of his head.

The roads are made of tile now.
His quiet passing wheelchair
Slows to make its routine turn,
Stops at crossings that are not there.

Old steam engines convalesce
In stations such as these
That cannot hear the wail of trains
Nor their cry on dying knees.

With the passing years of decades gone,
Stubs of destinations show:
One ticket in the book remains.
All aboard this train must go.

Calvin E. Hubbard

Limerick Fun

It was a bright sunny day
When you went away.
Now you're back;
there's no lack
Of sun in our May.

Limericks are such fun;
Just make up a pun.
Tax your brain,
but not in vain,
And let your motor run.

Each is a simple ditty
By a little old biddy
To kill some time
with silly rhyme;
It may make you giddy.

Susan E. Munstedt

To Look Is to Smile

Behold this tiny one
who has so recently
come into the world.

What an awesome sight
is this creation of God!

It matters not,
the color of eyes,
or hair, or skin.
This is God's handiwork.

We cannot help but smile
as we look at this
package from Heaven.

For here is a little person
who invites our love and care.

And for this, Lord,
we thank You.

Stella Edens

Ode to April

April has that certain flair,
Lean and lithe and tall.
With violets plaited in her hair,
You'd think she never had a care,
And only kind words for all.

April's friends view her with delight;
They love to hear her singing.
She never says, "My way is right."
She never says things just for spite.
She's like a gold bell ringing.

A virtuoso at the piano keys,
Her teacher says, "She's super."
Her music swells up to the trees
And then drops down to "nth degrees."
She really is a trouper.

Gladys Loveland

The Moon Tonight

The moon tonight
reminds me
that every
night it is more
beautiful than
the one that came before

And that every day
we together grow
to one more precious
than we were before

M. Joy Bock

Our World

We stayed up till morning
Listening to the night
Telling each other stories
To cause us all a fight

We walked down the railroad tracks
Until we reached our spot
The sign said, "No Trespassing"
But we never did get caught

While lying in my backyard grass
We traveled to the moon
Anytime that we returned
Was always way too soon

We disobeyed our parents
But none of us seemed to care
Our world was just a fantasy
Life, a game of truth or dare

We have all grown up now
And have our separate friends
But for all who made up our world
The fantasy never ends

Sarah Bloedorn

God's Gift

I climbed the rocks
To the icy stream,
Though now that trek
Seems only a dream.

Were the sounds so muted
To the listening ear
As if not allowed
To interfere?

Was the day that warm?
Was the sun that bright
Cutting through the trees
To filter its light?

Though I'll never go
To that place again,
It stays in my mind
Like a long-lost friend.

Throughout the years
As I go my way
I'll always be grateful
For God's gift that day.

Patricia Mexicotte

A Poet's Mind

There's a lot of pages to read
Before you know a book,
But a poet's life is guessed
With just one look.
You scan through the pages,
Only hoping to find
One painful or cheery moment
That shouts the poet's mind.
It's an enjoyment to many
To see what a poet has known.
It brings shadows of life,
So you can forget your own.
Pages of happiness and misery,
Pages you continue to turn,
Pages of someone else's life
That you feel you must learn.
Leaf after leaf,
You need the desire
To see what it's like
To live in someone else's fire.

Lisa M. Cole

Painted Whispers

Crystal waves catch her
by the sparkling hem of her evening gown
tranquil waters kissing barefooted
slippers painted gold.
The wind whispers sweetness
tousling her straw gold hair
with gentle caresses.
The sun rises solemn in her eyes
and a wordless expression of joy
parts the veil of her mystery
as she leaps alone into the waves
disappearing beyond sight
beyond silence.

Joe McSweeney

The Ride

Man he works.
From day to day.
His body gets old.
His hair turns gray.

No time to stop.
You can hear him say.
For I must work.
To earn my pay.

But man is weak.
His body is frail.
When he gets old.
It begins to tell.

There comes a time.
To step aside.
Let someone else work.
Enjoy the ride.

Bobby McCuan

Journey with God in Prayer

Prayer is a journey with God
Faith in Him is your reward
Mind, body, and spirit collected
Unshakable spirit is reflected.

God recognizes prayer's impulse
There's no need for eloquence
Our meager syllables of praise
Are acceptable to Him always.

There's no special time or place,
That's needed to seek God's face,
Thanksgiving and forgiving expressed
The gateway into God's presence

In everything give thanks
And around our Father's Word close ranks
Greater love and compassion for others
Greater patience to discover.

God the eternal source of peace
Thy most precious gift bequeath
To those who believe on thy Son
The eye of faith opens to everyone.

Shirley Brigham

Growth from a Seed

The casting of light,
The casting of shadow,
Two trees that stand beneath
Family heritage that cometh from a seed.
In autumn, trees of red and gold
Engulfing our fears
With tranquility and hope.
Standing together;
But not too near together,
For if one tree over shadows the other
The other will wither and die. . . .

Kim T. Trebing

Comely Bride

Where now my dear? What now?
What frothy brine or deep ravine
Is yet to be explored
around this rugged plane?

No brittle bones nor arid eyes
deny the thrills of magic vistas
that God has left for us
beneath His Christmas tree.

Comely bride, forever mine,
Take my hand, soar with me, love with me.

Derry Sparlin

Love Shines Again

To my knight in shining armor
I have known the injured spirit,
Felt its veil of pain and undertaken healing:
Thin, onion-like film.

Peel away each layer:
Caring
Concern
Encouragement
Faith
Gentleness
Support
Tenderness . . .

Until the core is found:
Love heals.
Love strengthens.
Love shines again.

Gail Valeskie

My Love

I told you how I love you,
But you were not there to hear,
So I told it to a falling star,
And a brook that rippled near.

I told my love to the gentle leaves,
As they rustled 'neath my feet,
Then I breathed it in a prayer God heard
Too sacred to repeat.

I whispered all my love for you
Through storms, and futile tears.

And in one stream they mingled
The flow of endless years.

I told you with my eyes whose depths
Held pools of mirrored pain,
Yet glimpsed through mists each tenderness
The rainbow after rain.

Danis Mandigo

Greetings

As we meet and greet and dine,
We remember January and June 1939.
Fifty-eight years have gone by
Since we graduated from Dunbar High.
We are now a precious few,
But our love is just as true.
Our eyes are dim, our hair is gray.
We don't always kneel as we pray.
Sometimes we lie down, stand, or sit,
But our Precious Lord hears every bit
Of the prayers we utter day by day
For friends we've met along the way.
In Dunbar High School, we were friends.
Friends we'll be, until time ends.

Amanda C. Elliott

Positive, Negative, Yin, Yang

Time: life standing by . . .
Nothing stagnant crawling, why?
Quick something learning high
Positive, doing now, I.
Once lonely, all alone.
Me, one, not clone . . .
Two, turns to too . . .
Because Earth for you
Take, give, live, have.
Cradle arms, hugs crave.
Life, time by, standing
Decision, live loosing faith
Person listens, feelings don't
Give, forgot, forever, thought
Answer, humans lying not
Where love caring death
Trees, steel, concrete, breath
Hate play, enjoy work,
Hear touch, taste feel.
See Earth, be real . . .

Elissa Abbey Keller

Shoeshine Boy

Shoeshine boy, what to do you see?
Is that my image or something else
Deep, almost hidden, inside of me
That takes shape with every stroke
Knowing not whether to stay or flee?

Shoeshine boy, what do you hear?
Is it the sound of your cloth
Or something more, I fear,
That echoes beneath your hands
With resonance both far and near?

Shoeshine boy, what do you touch?
Is it but paste and dye
Or something that hurts too much,
That causes you pain and so is now
Escaping neither wax nor brush?

Shoeshine boy, what do you feel?
Is it the grain of the leather
Or something more toward heel
That drives you to stop and ponder
Whether life itself is but fake or real?

Jim Austin Jr.

My Friendship Quilt

I have a quilt made by friends
their names inscribed thereon,
Stitched lovingly, by lamp light,
when evening chores were done.

Some names are very dear to me,
a cousin, aunt, and grandma, too.
My memories of them will always be
treasures, constant and true.

Other names I cannot place
but dear they must have been
To care enough to make a block
for a little girl just ten.

I see a square that calls to mind
a summer dress and bonnet,
My mother's apron, a sister's smock,
and one with daisies on it.

Many of the colors are faded now,
a sign of passing time,
But love remains within the seams
of this friendship quilt of mine.

Norma Bobbitt

Metamorphosis

Frogs on lily pads,
Looking around in wonder.
Polliwogs swim by.

Lois McIlvoy

Eighteen Wheels and a Prayer

To my husband, CJ, for my inspiration
A key or a button
That starts a truckers life
The rev of the engine,
Whether it be day or night.
As tears in my eyes;
We see him check his load.
Whether heading north, south,
East or west,
Eighteen wheels go rolling
For another weeks work.

We send up a prayers;
So he sees who really cares;
Me, the kids, and the Lord upstairs.
We hear the air brakes come on,
We see that big yellow truck
Came home again
On just eighteen wheels and a prayer.

Willie Sturgis

In the Stillness

In the stillness of dark December
when all of nature is at rest,
I find time to pause and remember
how wonderfully God has blest.

The slowing down at year's end
to reflect on what God has done,
how God cared enough to send
to Earth His most precious son.

In the stillness I come to thee,
as the Magi did at your birth,
I fall on bended knee
and feel at peace with all the Earth.

In the stillness of falling snow
a hush falls over all the Earth,
animals and birds seem to know
that we are celebrating Jesus' birth.

Dean Albritton

Red Geraniums

Life did not bring me silken gowns,
Nor jewels for my hair,
Nor signs of gabled foreign towns
In distant countries fair,
But I can glimpse beyond my pane
A green and friendly hill,
And red geraniums aflame
Upon my windowsill.

The brambled cares of every day,
The tiny humdrum things,
May bind my feet when they would stay,
But still my heart has wings.

And if my dreamings never come true,
The brightest and the best,
Just leave me alone my journey through.
I'll set my heart at rest

And thank God for home-sweet things:
A green and friendly hill,
And red geraniums aflame
Upon my windowsill.

Allen F. Brandon

Right or Wrong?

I don't know when it started.
I only know it did.

I can't say why it happened,
But I wouldn't change a thing.

The way we held each other
Was something very good.

And yet they go on telling us
How very wrong it would be

To go on loving each other
The way that you loved me.

Diana Hodgin Grein

Lifetime

Time, the unreachable goal,
looming before us at the beginning
of our journey,
slipping away gently,
other times whirling, thrashing,
zipping away before we know,
turns into yesterdays,
multiplies into yesteryears.
Down the road, illusions disappear.
Vanities, so vital at the start,
vanish without a trace.
Reality takes on a comfortable patina.
Now the flow of life is smooth.
While horizons are still there,
no longer the rush to reach them,
like the ever returning tides,
horizons and shorelines become one.

Dorothy Hom

The Coming of Dawn

The coming of dawn brings with it
the spirit of the age and a muse
to follow wherever you may go
beneath the harvest moon a tapestry
of thoughts come together
where dawn lingers reminding us
of carvings in stone coming to us
from across the universe
on the ebbing tide like time
through the hourglass that goes on
forever and a day, after the storm.

Kathy Robinson

Prima Donna

Fortune and glory serenade
The washed-up prima donna
As she struts and frets upon the stage
To an old, timeworn sonata.
The lights dim on her passion play;
Her iron will begins to rust;
Time and trial have turned the page
And left her in the dust.

An evil clown awaits backstage
For the final act,
When she will return to her cage,
And the house lights fade to black.

The shadow of what used to be
Lurks behind her eyes,
Of when crowds had come to see
The dancers dressed in white.
The theater is empty, now,
No audience to cheer,
And waiting impatiently, the clown.
But still she dances, every year.

Ripper JAC

The Frosty Night

No scene, I've seen, so keen
As a frosty night.
Light light, on light, frost light
Is my secret sight.

No time, is mine, so fine
For seeing nature right.
I find, to mind, its kind
Means beauty bright.

The state, the rate, the sate
Shows material fate.
The cold, comes bold, to fold
And slow kill its hold.

Such waste, such taste, so chaste
Only mine in dumb haste.
I lad, think sad, yet glad
I can beauty add.

Apart, I chart, in heart
The fine and icy art.
Askew, I view, review
The diamond dew.

Ralph Gregory

She's My Mother

She never owned a palace room
Nor even met the king,
But yet her ways are gentleness,
Her thoughts beyond the queen's.

She never played in a symphony
Or drew upon a canvas,
But in her heart are melodies
A mother ever sings.

She showed her love by little things—
Her smiles meant my successes,
Her tears at night were shed alone
In anguish at my strayings.

She never let me know the burdens
Concealed deep within her heart.
She kept all night the vigil watch
When she herself was ill.

She sacrificed her life for mine
In pain, in joy, in tears.
She gave me all she ever had
Just 'cause she was my mother.

Mabel D. Isgrigg

Give

To March and Renee,
thanks for your endless support
I give you my heart
I give you my hand
I give you my love
I hope you understand

I give you a smile
I give you a kiss
I give you a laugh
I know you love this

I give you my word
I give you my all
I give you everything
You tear down that wall

I give and I give
Want nothing in return
Your compassion and love
For this I yearn

Tonya Harmer

Sharing Our Time

To my one and only, Beverly Bigus
Though our time to gather was short,
The memories we have are long.
The joy and happiness we shared,
The smiles and laughs like a song.

The gentle touching of our hands,
A graceful hug now and then,
Soft sweet lips, a tender kiss,
All things we feel once again.

The love that's within our hearts,
How it must glow once more.
For just to feel our nearness,
Is what were no longing for.

At this point though I'm confused,
I'm sure that you feel the same.
And when we find the answer,
I'm sure you'll call my name.

All though the miles between us,
They are all but a few.
And I'll pass over them again,
Just to tell you "I love you."

Hugh Striker

Father's Day

It's Father's Day once again
How time passed in a jiffy
Is time our friend or foe?
Who can think that quickly?

I think back and recall
When I was just a young lassie
All seems like yesterday
As it passed that quickly

We've shared many things
Some great times and good laughs
There were also some sorrows
But love healed them real fast

I give thanks to you
For your very special ways
And I thank God up above
For our family ties these days

With faith, hope, and love
I've never stood alone
I've been blessed many times
More than can be known

Darlene Lehr

Whisper

He walks with me from dawn
into the stillness of the night,
His presence is never seen, yet
I know I am always within His sight.
He listens to whatever I say
whether it is good or bad;
some days I come away feeling
happy—sometimes sad.
I use to question why things
happen the way they do.
I know now, it's because of
the path we each pursue.
Reach for my soul with gentleness
and your caring hand,
lead me some day, oh Lord, down the
path to your beautiful promised land.
The road of life can bring us
each happiness or fear,
so listen to His words of wisdom,
as a gentle whisper in your ear.

Carolyn S. Shelley

Child Two

To be a child again
with no shield of armour
So secure I'd be,
with no invisible mask to cover me.
So sunny and free
like the wind on a bright hot day,
but confident in knowing
I can be anchored like a tree.

All I need is patience
and for you to be near.
Give me a safe place to talk,
to learn, to grow and to share.
Please hear me;
listen quietly and be a friend.

There is no mask on my face
so don't try to change me;
bring out my deepest feeling
and my reality.

Watch me and praise me
whenever I'm good.

Helen Levatino

There's Life within the Hugging

From living waters of the soul,
To living life where God survives.
To taking love from what we know,
And putting hugs from God in lives.
Knowing life's inside the hugs

Sheltering a tear drop moment,
In the deepness of a prayer.
Believing God's atonement,
Breathe's eternal everywhere,
And we dwell within the deepness

There is love within the hugging,
Of another human being,
There is joy within receiving,
Of the light within the beam,
The hugs prolong the beaming

From the reaching out to people,
To engulf the soul with sun,
Is the everlasting warmth of love,
That hugs bring everyone.
'Cause life's within the hugging.

Jeanne Roberts

Essence of Life

*In memory of my beloved mother,
Peg Hannold*
In the core of the heart
still waters run deep;
it is the essence of life;
the spirit of God sleeps.
In awakening his spirit
it is the water of life;
as a seeker ye shall find
the meaning of strive.
Like a glistening stream
or the tide coming in,
a current runs deep,
the temptation of sin.
Hear the beckoning call
when two forces emerge;
like windswept hair
the evil is purged.
To drink from his cup
a peace ye shall find;
it is the essence of life,
a spirit which binds.

Gwendolyn Hunter White

Truth Itself

Live truth in thought
Words and deeds
Refrain of error
A reality to heed

Of our nature of good
Away to feel
Peace of the heart
Let our love be real

As we train our thoughts
Within our sea of sense
From our great laboratory of mind
Controlling our time well spent

We must always give thanks
And respect to our God
As it honor in our motion
With great rewards of love

So let truth of thought
Within our nature be raised
United with purity
As divine, love give praise

Olivette Moss

My Waitress

My food is cold,
my heart is on fire,
my tongue is tied,
my soul burns with desire,
my glass is empty,
my mind is a blur,
my fork is dirty,
my, my, just look at her,
my stomach feels queasy,
my thoughts are racing,
my wallet feels light,
my lips smile with delight,
my time is short,
my eyes are fixed,
my forehead has become forever
drenched,
my life has changed,
my mouth has fallen apart,
my, oh, my,
good gracious
my waitress has stolen my heart.

Shawn Hutchinson

Where the Pavement
Meets the Green

Running down a vacant lot
Where the pavement meets the green
Reminding me that nothing's
Ever seldom what it seems
You can never run the future
Without a knowledge of the past
You can never, ever hope
That everything will last
You can never expect
To believe what you see
Down along the vacant lot
Where the pavement meets the green
I know the grass is being eaten
By the concrete and steel
In that, I see a mirror
For the way inside I feel
Tell them twenty years ago
What we believe today
They'll just shake their heads
And shrug and say "no way"

R. Durrant Buchanan

WHAT'S IN YOUR HEART

Look into your heart
And What do you see . . .

The control center in action
With all your beliefs . . .

Where all your emotions
Con-verge
To be released . . .

Does it harbor a grudge
Or
Harbor—peace . . .

Only you can examine
The outcome and
What it means . . .

Is it Spiritually Pure
Is it Spiritually Clean
Or
Does it require
A little more of Wisdom
And
A little more of thee. . . .

Nancy Lee Sudziarski

The Loss

They say we don't remember
Beyond a year or so
But I say yes, an emphatic yes,
For after the blow a crater
May remain in the heart
From the loss of someone special
And a voice sound
From a sacred place apart
That one remembers,
For it lingers
Forever!
Love will have it so.

James P. Kelleher

My Brother, My Friend

*In memory of Bill Jenuleson,
April 1953 to September 1997*
Bill, my brother, my friend
You meant the world to me
I looked up to you when we were young
For guidance and advice
As we got older, we drifted apart
But always, you were on my heart
We made many friends
But you were always a part of me
And you always will be
Bill, my brother, my friend

Donna M. Durbin

Somewhere in Time

To Norm Beliveau
I put my pen to paper
Though nothing comes to mind
And think about great poets
So far back into time
All of that about the trees
The lady of the lake
In worlds broad fields of battle
Yes poets they do make
A mind has got to be at peace
To come up with such lines
If only I could be like them
Somewhere ahead in time

Marie A. Lawrence

Epilogue

The skipping of a heartbeat
arrhythmiatic pace
is disturbing.
The painful knees and knuckles,
the edema,
the restless nights,
betray the golden years of life.
The freedom of retirement
is curtailed
by the failings of the body.
The engine skips and balks.
With erosion of youthful vigor
the trek is burdensome with strife.
The memories overwhelm.
The nostalgia brings a sigh.
The time of being
is short and swift.
And soon it all will just pass by.

James A. Todd

Safe in the Arms of Jesus

Our baby, so little and sweet,
Lies silently underneath our feet.
As we look into the heavens above,
We imagine our baby soaring
With the white turtle doves.
Our baby doesn't worry us much,
Because we know he's safe
In the arms of Jesus.

Laurie Williams

Peace

The sound of quiet
Where bombs don't fly,
Where children's laughter
Lights up the sky.
The world's a stage
Where madmen play,
And sanity weaves its thread
Somewhere along the way.
Peace should not be so difficult,
If people would just gather
And hammer out their differences
Instead of kicking up lather.
Sharing and caring
Should replace all these wars.
Find out who your neighbors are
Before you start blowing up their doors.

Linda M. Streng

Come to Build a Bridge

Come to build a bridge.
The bridge that we beheld.
Fall and die away.
Die and fall away.
Come and stay a day.
Smile and hold the day.
The workmen are done resting.

Come to build a bridge.
The workers come to gather.
Their tools gleam in the sun.
We see the blood and sweat of many.
Loyalty and royalty.
Decision and precision.
Unity and humility.

Come to build a bridge.
Come congratulate the bridge. Hurrah.
Until we tear it down.
The workmen are done resting.

DeWayne Hairston

Shoreline

Like wading sea birds,
Seek life's living pleasures
By the water's edge!

Maryanne Bahl Switzer

Respect

It's not easy to tire
Of something we admire,
And so, it does seem,
It's held in highest esteem.

To everyone, it will not fit,
So not everyone does have it.
It's not something to require,
But something we can acquire.

Not something in which to jest,
For he who has it is blest.
It's something all would hope to gain,
And not impossible to obtain.

And now it unfolds.
It's what another holds,
From one to another to come,
Though not from all, but some.

So what is it?
Do I have it one bit?
Considering every aspect,
I find it is respect!

Teresa Hill

Leaving Home

To my parents, Ira and Dora Phelps
The trees are tall and green.
The air is cool and clean.
My car is packed and I must go;
Oh, how I wish it were not so.

My mind is waltzing down memory lane,
Wishing I could be a kid again,
Strong in body, mind, and bone,
And I could run these hills of home.

Like the bird that leaves the nest,
We must try to do our best.
Time goes by, day by day;
Too soon, we are old and gray.

Many of our peers pass on,
And we realize they are gone.
Now we find ourselves alone,
With only sweet memories of home.

Dora Irene Hancock

Crystal Meditation

In dreams, she will send
For those in tune, a lesson,
The crystal's secret.

The crystal rainbow
Light prism is a window
To eternal now,

Where death will meet fate.
The heart of Earth shall erase
Anger, pain, and hate.

One bright star will blast
Through the windowpane . . . at last,
Crystal rays to cast
Light on the future's new past,
When we witness time's last act.

Darla Billington

If

There's many things I would tell
If you would only listen:
The lovely peal of a church bell,
The dewdrops as they glisten,
The sough of the wind in the trees,
The smell of buttercups,
The caress of the summer breeze,
The gay dance of a Johnny-jump-up,
The barefoot joy of squishy dust,
The song of a happy brook,
The sting of an animal's musk,
The startled deer's timid look,
The sun in all its splendor,
The moon and its limpid light,
All the jewels I care for
In a world sparkling and bright.
If by my side you'd stand
And insight seek to capture,
I'd tell of jewels so grand
And my heart's deep rapture.

Evelyn H. Sherman

Eyes of God

Gentle, compassionate
Father watching over us
Full of love and
Devotion . . . eyes so
Tender and loving . . .

Eyes of compassion
And understanding . . .
Eyes of sadness
Seeing us walk our
Own willful way . . .

Eyes of a patient
Loving Father whose
Wisdom is as Infinite
As the universe and
As deep and understanding . . .

Eyes of tenderness
Gentleness, affection
Patience, eyes
Of God . . . Love and
Wisdom . . .

Bonita D. Whitmire

Silence Conspiracy

*To Jimmy Peté USF Oxford educated,
my inspiration*
Black men of self and God renown
But in prison stay forever sundown
Not disposable not throw away
But in prison decay timeless day
Punitive piercing primal pain peak
Wounded spirits healing seek
Longing love eternally speak
Abandoned recesses reach
Universal God chasm breach
Turning tide of passivity and thought
Let people know their worth and want
Their heart soul mind and virgin valor
These men of value beauty color
Once babies pure and precious
Free of prison tyranny cancerous
Let mind and bodies feel their rage
Ravage until active parity engage
Abandon them not in captivity
To majority silence conspiracy
Let true freedom stay black men free today

Angela Kiel Willoughby

Good Night

Good night, good night
Wish we could be together
You by my side
And I by yours
But all we could do
Through the course of time
Is wish that someday
We will be together
Side by side
So for now, I bid you good night
Through the distance that keeps us apart
I silently kiss your lips
And I imagine you
By my side and I, by yours

Elba I. Ocasio

Time to Die

Live for today
Live for the hour
Live for the moment
In just this instant
Live in the now
Please, reach out and
Touch someone with love
From cancer you will
Surely die tomorrow

Lewis C. Alexander

Little Angel

To Allison and Brian,
in loving memory of Brandon
Mama, Daddy . . . please don't cry.
I've passed through Heaven's door.
Now I am being cared for
by the Angels of our Lord.
I know your hearts are aching
and your lives won't be the same,
but God can mend your broken hearts
and help to ease the pain.
I'm warm and safe and happy
in this sacred, holy place.
Mom, I will not forget the look
of love upon your face.
I love you both. That will not change
through all the years to come.
Just know I'll keep watch over you
until each day is done.
Why I was chosen to go first . . .
it cannot be explained.
But with God's grace, one day
I'll be in your embrace again.

Patricia Wall

Lovely Lady

Your hair so lovely,
White as snow,
I wish I had met you
A long time ago.

You are such a joy
To know;
You set my heart
And soul aglow.

You have a twinkle
In your eyes.
You make me laugh;
You make me cry.

My sinking spirit
You do revive.
I want to meet you
Up there in the sky.

Shirley Shuman

Sound Off!

There is a song of victory
In marching with the Lord
Just like the soldiers "sound off"
When the captain gives the word

We're marching to a triumph
That's greater far in scope
Than any earthly army
Here could ever hope

And one day soon, at close of day
The battle won, our feet will stay
And we shall rest and join again
The victor's song—Amen! Amen!

So let us not forget to sing
The victor's song in everything
For we shall triumph at the last
Forget the battles that are past

But sing along and forward go
To battle—conquer every foe
In Jesus' name, at His command
For we are His victorious band

Laura Spencer Silek

Trees of Fleur-De-Lis

As child Fleur entertained the thought
One day she'd surely find
Joy among tall firs. You taught
Her serenity of mind.
America! You have her love
But not for callous rule:
Secrecy in sticky glove
Comforts none save fool.

While Fleur invokes millennium,
Your stewards trespass, peddle dope;
Tax middle class past kingdom come;
Spray saplings with false hope;
Force seniors into HMOs,
Salt banks with monthly check;
Stake elders to a raft of woes
On course for massive wreck.

Configuration of proud elm
Becomes disgraceful joke
When tree is topped to serve as whelm
And yahoos sport the oak!

Judith Pike Boos

Love Myself

Look at this wall.
It's a wall of hate.
It will not fall,
'cause I have no faith.
Look at the tears
run down my face.
I have so many fears.
My life's just a waste.
I love you,
but I don't love me.
If only you knew,
If only you could see.
So much pain
and so much hurt—
I have no one to blame
but myself.
Love me, and I'll love you,
but love myself,
I just can't do.

Sabrina Ragsdale

Snow Flakes

The snow began in the morning
And continued throughout the day
I stood at my doorway
And watched the squirrels at play.
I thought of all the events
In the year—now past
And then I started crying
The tears came freely—at last.
Not tears of sorrow, now,
But tears of joy instead.
And I thought of God's guidance
In His love—we all are led.
My heart was filled with joy
As snowflakes from above
His presence came to me
With His Blessings—and His Love!

Hilda Beltz

Don Juan

With amazing persistence
  and renegade charm,
He fashions a course
  that completely disarms.

He softens the hearts
  of both young and the old
With a cavalier touch
  that's never too bold.

His obsessive drive
  and desire for success
Render him blind
  to the need for redress.

For commitment is never
  a part of his goal;
Only constant pursuit
  mutes the cry from his soul.

Elizabeth Miller Harris

Nowhere to Turn

All doors were shut to me.
Knobs I strained to turn,
Isinglass doors layered in dust,
Corridors running narrower and narrower
As I ventured a hoped for turn,
And when I had shoved
Every push imaginable,
The dawn broke.
The barricaded door was within,
And in this unlit passageway of veins,
Arteries, and heart throbs,
I would have to inflame my own way.

Herman O. Arbeit

Just for a Moment

I close my eyes
And you're holding me
Oh, so tight.

You kiss me tenderly
And make love to me
All through the night.

I suddenly open my eyes
And they become
Full of tears.

I know I can't have you
For your love is hers
All the time.

But just for a moment
In my own little world,
You're mine.

Susy Valenzuela

Brave the Storm

This ship, it sails
Towards the horizon.
The crow's nest reveals
An awesome storm front.
This crew conceals
Their fears in hope.
As we brave the storm
Through the misty air,
Images do form.
Alas, we're overwhelmed;
The wind hinders the helm.
Thus, now in despair,
We abandon ship,
Our fate decided
By murky depths.
From seas of crimson,
Our sins will have risen,
For the assemblage of the skies
To visualize
And reflect upon society.

Salvatore Roseo

Tentatively Seeking

Atop the hill
Whoops a wild wind
A searching breath
Cold and thin

I stand alongside
A denuded tree
And a silent bird
We three surfing eternity.

An ocean of wind
I cannot see surrounds me
I raise my hands, my voice
Seeking chance? Choice?

Or perhaps, I am looking for
Black strap molasses from Parker's
In Prince George county, Virginia?
Your guess? Your choice?

Heey, what? You don't like
Molasses on waffles, my friend?
With butter? Heavy butter?
Aaah, back to the hill, again.

Robert Baker Davis

Vociferous Poem

A Poem Explaining the Need
of Vociferous Speech and
Excessive Explanation
to Prevent Misunderstanding:

So many words from which to choose
that often tend to ramble.
Or if there exists momentum to lose,
I jump in with a gamble.

I cannot say what I must say
in words so simple and sweet.
Everyone seems to confuse it some way,
so I feel I must be complete.

How do others talk so long
and say unlimited things?
Every word they choose belongs
while the overall meaning clings.

Help me learn to speak in brief
and make all my thoughts known,
Then at last there'd be relief,
without the dismissive groan.

Stephen J. Wolf

Let Freedom Ring

All across this great land
God has always had a plan
For men and women to be free
Not held in bondage or captivity

As church bells ring out loud and clear
Let all who hear them far and near
Pay attention to their call
For they are summoning one and all

Quickly now, before it's too late
God will one day close the gate
And all mankind will pay the price
If they don't turn to Jesus Christ.

True freedom comes from deep within
When our hearts are free from sin
Giving up all but not letting go
Of the one who loves us so

We can all shout praises and sing.
To God be the glory, let freedom ring!

Terry Beagle

Castle of Phrases

Tread softly, the writer is at work
Let silence reign in her study
So pure a whisper can be heard
Curve, coin from word clay or putty

Hold closely sweet peace of the bard
Wellspring of her joy of the hour
A test of mettle and metaphor
Builds her castle with word power

Like a spark toward ignition
Subtle humor and contrition
More a have to than ambition
Hardly a master of completion

Beth Sudduth Wills

The Tender Touch of You

I remember back in my youth;
There were hard times
I had to go through.
I wish back then I could have
Had the tender touch of you.
There may not have been as
Many tears to see through,
If only I could have had
The tender touch of you.
All of the years have gone by.
Now, there are less times to cry,
Since I have the tender touch of you.

Robert L. Stowe

Shadows on the Wall

I see shadows on the wall
in my bed at night.
I look at them in fear,
and I recoil from the fright.

Some are small and tiny;
they don't cause me much fear.
Others are big and scary;
seeing them, I want to run from here.

Big ones, small ones,
ones that are distinct or ill-defined—
won't they go away
so I can rest my anxious mind?

Finally, I close my eyes
and I count "one, two, three."
Then, my eyes I open,
and no more shadows do I see.

Elizabeth Meyer

Memories

Heaviness of the downpour
embraces me in arms
of emptiness gone gone

Gone the gentleness
soothing a child's first doubts
gone the compassion
for those less fortunate
gone dedication
to a newly found faith
gone the joys and struggles
of challenged living
gone gone
wrapped in illusive wanderings
of the mind

Tears drop on waves
of loneliness
life snuffed out
in an instant of surrender

No, never gone, only hidden
in a new dimension

Mary Ellen Kapp Allton

Life and Death

To all the Veterans, God be with you!
War is hell,
To be the last and all alone.
To listen to the cries,
Of death and pain
To look into the eyes.
Of the dead, in the rain.
To those of us alive,
Will we ever be the same?
We came back,
But not quite sane
We can't cope,
With civilized pain.
That's why some,
Are still in chains,
We have a wall,
To see all your names.
Whose the lucky one?
They feel no more pain.
Will we ever be the same?
Can we cope with all the change?

Russell C. Peake

Christmas All Glorious

A season of spiritual brightness
immersed with joyous lightness
from stress and every care
with gala events everywhere.

Sparkling windows and decorated stores
invite shoppers entering in galores
to purchase those very special gifts
that bring happiness and spirit lifts.

Our world would be much brighter
and our burdens would become lighter
by praising God in all we do and say
and pleasing Him in every way.

A season with God's love in first place
could change living in the human race
when crime and greed will subside
and harmony between nations abide.

With spiritual morals and less fraud
our nation could be brought back to God
and hearts would overflow with mirth
as we celebrate our dear Savior's birth.

Emma Brinkhous

Kaleidoscope

Life is like a kaleidoscope
Changing all the time
Each one of us a part of it
So many colorful minds

Not everybody thinks alike
Nor feels or is the same
And that just makes the difference
In every human being

So much depends on where you are
What time you're doing what
Listen to your inner voice
And put it on the spot

There are people who really care
And there are some who don't
Make sure you choose above it all
The right side of the road

A smile helps like a kaleidoscope
To brighten up your day
Reminding you of who you are
In a most delightful way

Ilse Roffler

Tortured

Desire mixed with anxiety
nowhere to go, nowhere to hide
Madness creeping from inside out
entombing the soul in solitude
Whatever happened to simplicity?
Confusion masked in silence
afraid to ask, afraid to know
Trust abused with liberty
till wrong feels right
And sin becomes salvation
for just a little while
Whatever happened to morality?
Fantasies come to life
freely given, freely taken
Daydreams suffocate awareness
till truths are forgotten
And nightmares are no longer nameless
Whatever happened to my sanity?
Whatever happened, God, to me?

Janice A. Little

Revelation

'Neath the apple tree stood Adam and Eve
Framed in a cloud of white
A sly old snake, full of deceit
Told them wrong was right
They were so young and innocent
And really not too bright

He said, "You call this Paradise?"
Just you believe in me
You really ain't seem nothing yet
Till you eat from yonder tree

You'll rule the stars of seventh heaven
For the apple is the key
That will make you Lord, a Master
Through all eternity

Now Eve was one to take a chance
So Adam followed suit
The world has never been the same
Since they ate forbidden fruit

'Twas the start of evolution
Corruption and pollution

Jenny Travers Bouza

Blessings

*For Doug, Lakyn, my family
and friends—thank you, God*

'Twas one morning in the spring.
Peace rested in a single
Rose within its bloom.
I captured it in a painting
And hung it in my room.

'Twas midnight in the summer.
I saw moonlight shimmers
Dancing on the sea.
I wondered if I sang a song,
Would they dance in sync with me?

'Twas a sunset in the autumn.
Trees were just beginning
To change their look.
Leaves fell ever so longingly
Into the open arms of the brook.

'Twas in the midst of winter.
Snow cascaded
Gracefully to Earth's floor.
As I gazed upon Heaven's beauty,
I sighed, "Who could want for more?"

Carrie S. Hester

Love

Love is a power greater than no other;
to overcome death and distance;
To wipe away the hate of a generation;
to destroy walls and barriers;
Where love is, nothing else matters,
physical or beyond; all else is trivial.
Because love knows no limits,
and never shall.

Michael S. O'Rourke

Yesterday's Memories

As years go by, we remember
Yesterdays, things that used to be
Fun times spent with loved ones
Never fade from our memory
As we turn life's faded pages
Remembering . . . oh, what joys we knew
Our youth, our times together
Precious days so long ago
Through the years, our sorrows fade
Silver threads among the gold
Tales we share, retold often
Lovelier seem each time they're told
Youth fades, we cannot recapture
Yesterdays filled with smiles and tears
Each day our past grows lovelier
Remembering joys of bygone years
Today our life may be filled with sorrow
With God's help, courage we will find
Knowing that beautiful yesterdays
Will remain forever in our mind

Lillian Kleinfelder Barr

A Bowl of Chrysanthemums

I was out in the autumn musk and
snapped the chrysanthemum stalks.

They are
in a stone bowl
before me now—

Mint white, must color leaf,
yellow stain bud
all snarled
breaking out in shaggy feather.

For me
The warm cool day is mine forever.

Kenneth Marshall Allan

The Tightrope

The ground is far beneath me now;
the sky is ever closer.
The crowd seems to await my fall
as I pirouette and bow.
I kneel and smile and skip along,
never bothering with a beam
and, just for a fleeting
moment, flirt with a fall.
I go forward and backward
and teeter from side to side,
never allowing myself the time
to think of the danger of it all.
What if this time I fall?
What if I lose my nerve?
What happens if I cannot
cross the blink far beneath?

These things I think
each time I prepare for a fresh ascent
upon my rope, my tiny string,
my tightrope I call life.

Gloria S. Coomes

From Ashes to Flame

A life can grow so very stale
That even successes seem to fail,

And the fire that once was bright
Is now but ashes without a light.

Striving, planning, dreaming
Are now but works without a meaning.

But love can blow those ashes cold
To fire again as it was of old,

Give that life a brand-new birth,
With new confidence, esteem, and worth,

Ashes bursting into flame,
Rising anew into life again.

This is what you did to me
When my wife you chose to be.

No more hunger for love and care,
For, with you here, it is always there.

Fire from ashes, burning bright,
With flame and warmth and heat and light.

Haywood K. Cross

Empty

*In loving memory of my brother
and best friend, Wesley Jr.*

Fluid motion, silent and quick
The touch of your hand
The wind in my hair
The feeling of the moment
Your piercing stare
Disappearing in darkness
A mere midnight dream
A tick of the clock
Nothing is what it seems
Flashes of memories
Days gone by
Heartfelt moments
A whispering sigh
Marble set stone—so cold, so hard
A hint of cologne
Your laughter, your tears
Look inside
My heart, my fears
A hole inside my heart, so empty inside
Missing you deeply since the day you died

Margie Merchant

Fastball

Bottom of the ninth,
game won with a late flurry.
Jetstream, world in a hurry.

Packing my suitcase.
Getting ready to go.
Trucking down the road,
hundred miles or so.
Looking on the shelves,
rolling off the counter.
Great curve motion finds
me what I couldn't find.
The after shave lotion.

Short reliever, smokestack,
powder river. Summer heat.
Iced tea or lemonade.
If I don't work,
I don't get paid.
Remember something sweet,
take a seat in the shade.

Charles Morris

Gentle Eyes

To a strong man with gentle eyes,
my son, Taylor
His walk is of quiet strength;
His talk is like his walk.
His laughter gleams gladness
As we glow in his heart.

His smile is a blanket of warmth
Where love is sought.

His heart tenderly embraces us,
His tears purifying the earth
For a new beginning.

His gentle eyes, searching truth
Through one's inner being
With love, not judgement.

His noble spirit soars,
Deeply embedded
In the heart of God.

Jamie L. Arbuckle

My Guide

My guide says,
"Follow my steps,
hold onto my hand.
Come on child,
we're homeward bound."

Rocks and puddles,
can I spot them all?
One can easily slip when near them.
Earthly treasures and pleasures.

He's trod this path before you know.
He knows where the rough spots are.

For strength and support
He's given me his word.
I know I should trust him.

I couldn't have asked
for a better guide;
but my feet still occasionally slide.

Dear guide, please help me,
lest I fall.

Sharon Kay Haggerty

One More

It's tough to sit here dying
And raising not a hand.
There ought to be some way to
Fight it, some way to make a stand.

I think I'll lie upon the floor,
Kick my heels, and make a mighty din.
Maybe the Devil down there
Will give me a pass and never
Let me get in.

Now! I don't think that will
Work so well; they have seen
Too many acts like mine,
So I'm defeated like the rest
Of the world—pardon me, while I
Go stand in line.

Art Williams

When I Think of Beauty

To my sons, Jonathan and Bill
who search for beauty in silver
Why is it when I think of beauty
I think of those who love it
And long for them?
When my longing twists
Within me,
I cry to God, asking for them
Near me. We are as one in mind.
We think on things together.
Sewing in time and space
With a needle of thought,
The fine thread snaps,
Space is endless, time eternity.
I cry again to my God!

Marie W. Inslee

How the Roses Grow

To Sheila and all of my beautiful caretakers
A rose by any other name
Would bloom as sweet, you know.
But, have you ever wondered
How the roses really grow?

Do fairies run beneath the earth
And sprinkle perfume there?
Or do the flower elfins throw
Sweet fragrance in the air?

Does Mother Nature dip her brush
In paints both rare and sweet,
And tint the petals of each rose
That blooms along my street?

I often sit and wonder
How the roses really grow.
But do you think I'll find out?
Do you think I'll ever know?

Jennie T. Gross

Life

Life has its ups
Life has its downs

Life has people who act like clowns
Life is funny and life is tough

Life is sunny and life is rough
Life doesn't give us what we hope for

Life sometimes shuts the door but
Life goes on with a new dawn

Becky Simmons

Cycles

Love, hate, joy, pain.
Cycles of life roll through.
Emote, promote, demote.
I will, I won't, I do.
Crucify, then justify.
Humans cast their lots.
Lessons learned; lessons burned.
The message, they forgot.
Love one another.
Forgive, release.
Vengeance is Mine.
Exist in peace.

Julia C. Alexander

Freedom Is Song

To them on lie Begetter,
Rose and Patrick Higgins
Can poetry survive the shackles of meter
Or do we find to our golden surprise
That freedom melts the cowl of birthing,
And that win this enclosure
As infinite as a womb.
All beginning are.
And your pulse, dear Mother,
Metronomes my measure.
My song is born though I am voiceless
There is surely no labor in our symbioses

Paul V. Higgins

Monster Madness

There was a monster under my bed,
He would scream and howl at my head,
He was grim and grimy,
And slim and slimy,
He was very messy,
And awfully testy,
So finally I did what I had to do,
I put him in a box and I sent him to you!

Ashley R. Stone

In Memoriam

He calls in reverent silence
Like the storm just past,
Even before the Crane returns.
As we file past him, he
Cries the evening dew in rivers
Down his glossed obsidian face.
You almost see him wince
In pain as we touch
The names.
The names of the children
He adopted . . . he loves
Every drop of blood, every
Severed member, every shattered life.
"These are my children," he sobs
For all who came to see him.
"Cry with me, for they will
Never come home."

Joseph M. McCauley

Awakened Serenity

I stood in the storm
And the rain cleansed my soul.
The wind gave breath to my being
And the lightning sight to my pain.

A gentle voice whispered in my ear:
I am here, child.
I no longer felt alone.

Martin R. Higley

Through the Nights

Stillness in the night
Your chest moves against mine;
Every fear forgotten
to every bold breath.

Silence in the night
Your heartbeat pounds in my ears;
Every longing lost
with every tender thud.

Shivers in the night
Your heat radiates through me;
by every torrid touch.

Meghan E. Plumb

Fear

I, oh, fear
Shall dwell with thee
Into the night
Beyond the swelling seas
I shall bond with fright
To bend thee to thine knees
Fringe this flight
Never here
Since divine

Delve in mines
With thine figures
Entwined . . .
Never
Hence be mine
Forever . . .
Death in mind

Jessica L. Corn

Beyond the Stars

Out beyond the stars,
Can it really, really be?
The answer keeps eluding me
That way out beyond the stars,
Life exists on Mercury, Venus, and Mars.

Observing us in all we do,
As we watch animals in a zoo.
A very different type of life,
Free from our stress and strife.
Free from all the violence and war,
From prejudice, hate and much more.

To meet these people some day,
Would be a great honor I would say.
To those people up above,
All I can offer is my true love.
To be a warm and trusted friend,
That's the only message I can send.

Robert J. Long

Monster

To my old friend, Marlena—take it easy
Am I such a monster
that you're afraid to hold my hand?
Why are you afraid of me?
I just don't understand.

Why is it that you shiver
when I touch your face?
As if I were a cruel beast,
that must be kept within his case.

But I am not a monster,
this you must know,
'cause if I were a monster,
I couldn't love you so.

Jon Crouch

So Wonderful

Sad world of mine, what be my fate,
To dwell on greed and live on hate?
My mind is restless, grouping blind;
Perchance I've left myself behind.
For now and then there's the conclusion:
My life is none but an illusion.

Awake! Awake! I heard the call,
So far away my memory crawled
Along the dark and lonely pit
To see what I could make of it.

The light came rustling in the room.
I realized it was almost noon;
I'd been asleep so long, it seemed
As if my life had been redeemed.

I'd closed my eyes for just a bit,
And I but thought I'd dug a pit.
'Twas just a dream; a nightmare sure
Where nothing really did occur.

Mel Magallanes

Daily Blessings

If God would with hold His blessings,
How very weak and frail we'd be.
Heading for complete extinction
Lacking air so pure and free.

We'd have no vegetation
To sustain this mortal life.
As without rain or sunshine.
It'd be a cause for real strife.

There'd be no streams or rivers.
Or oceans so wide and deep
There'd be no stars or moonlight.
Providing time for restful sleep.

Be aware of God's daily blessings
And be content with what He has given;
Praise Him each day and be thankful
For the sacred privilege of living.

Ruth Steinman Sievers

Peace

I would not trade my peace of mind
For material things of any kind
Things of this world, are so fleeting
Contentment and Peace, are HIS greeting
Focus on, The ONE above
Be guided by HIS Divine Love
Then peace in this world, will be yours
And continue to HIS Heavenly Shores.

Jeannette Klee

We Together

As the sun peaks over the horizon
It wakes gently my sleeping soul
I hear the bird of a new promise
That tells my heart it is now whole

Joy skips stones across lake innocence
Rippling undisturbed waters of love
Passions of fire break through the dam
With a peace as gentle as a dove

The honey sweet taste of desire
Lingers on the lips like special wine
Tender and strong is our love
Like morning dew and soft sunshine

Lock me away inside your arms
Free my spirit in the winds of romance
Whether for a moment or forever
We together are worth the chance

Susan Sandell

You

As I sit here thinking
thinking of you
thinking of how to win you over

If I could write a poem
just for you
it would bespeak of simple beauties

If I could offer you happiness
only for you
it would proclaim my thoughts

As I sit here dreaming
dreaming of you
dreaming of how beautiful you are

If only you could love me
only me
I would give you the world

John Sutter

Anniversary Wish

Here we are, there,
there are last,
cresting the summit,
arduous climb where stone
after stone was
an obstacle, no path
to follow, no signposts
telling of the summit,
and near the top,
the air gets thin;
thankfully, we do not,
and so we are ready for more,
perhaps not
a mountain this time,
but something as good
as the first fourteen years.

Richard Lehtinen

Not Knowing

You wake up to get ready
For the day ahead,
Not knowing if it will be your last.

Pleasing everyone around you,
Hiding your true feelings,
Not knowing if they are your
True friend . . .

Being the best you can be,
Doing what ever it takes
To get job done,
Not knowing if it is the best you can do.

Victoria Spade

Cry of Woe

When I was young
A long time ago
Not a star twinkled
In the heavenly skies
The diamonds scattered
Over midnight velvet
Were mere reflections
Of the sparkle in my eyes
As the years pass swiftly by
Dimmer grow the lights
In the darkened skies
A cruel thief is stealing
Diamonds in the night
Where tell me where to keep safe
The sparkle in my eyes
Before tomorrow dawns

Ann Castor

Cote

My special one,
God's gift to me:
My beautiful son.
His hair of gold
And eyes hazel green,
If he were any more perfect,
He would have to be a dream.
When he says, "I love you,"
All words, honest and pure.
His big hugs fill me up inside
And, as I watch him grow smarter,
He builds on my pride.
The closeness and understanding
Is so very true, to think
Of a life without him . . .
I'd be lost without a clue.
So together forever, always side by side,
I'll try to make his life wonderful
For making me feel this way inside.

Carriann MacDonald

Friendship

Many aspects
Many qualities
Many thoughts

Friendship, friendship
Needed, wanted, loved

Lots of love
Lots of laughter
Lots of trust

Friendship, friendship
Needed, wanted, loved

True to the friend
True to the self
True to the friendship

Friendship, friendship
Needed, wanted, loved

Shelley Sorger

Good Friday

On Calvary's mount between two thieves
Behold the Savior hanging dead.
About his head a crown of thorns,
His hands and feet are dripping red.
A gaping wound is in his side.
Oh, torment more than he could bear.
And yet he died upon the cross
That we might all His kingdom share.

May Howden

Can a Person Know

Can a person know at birth
That God is going to call?
Can a person know at birth
That God is all in all?

Can a person want to serve him,
And yet, know the way?
Does a person have to wait
Until a certain day
When the Lord Jesus enters in
And takes his cares away?

The answer is a mystery:
That only those with eyes to see
Can enter into God's good grace
Through Christ's blood;
It's no disgrace.
Then a temple, cleansed, you'll be,
Able to enter eternity.

Ronnie Keirs

Expression of Love

To my oldest great-grandchild,
Cody Allen Clayton
A child's embrace is so sincere,
More than a thousand words
Of comfort to the heart,
Or songs that could be heard.
It tells a story true,
Of love so deep within,
Of love that has been nurtured
And now shines forth again.
A child's embrace is so sincere,
No reservation withheld,
Just honest adoration,
As they sweetly bid farewell.

Dorothy A. Godfrey

Shine

You shine in and out of me
You're everything I wanted you to be
Right now
I wonder if you hear my thoughts
I wonder if I should fear you
Should I fear you because you shine

Me, I am caught up in your web
You're armed and I'm not protected
For fear
You wonder if I can see you
You wonder if I can hide
Should I fear you because you shine

Time, I can't move because I'm blind
I'm blinded by your shine tonight
I can save myself from you
I have no reason to fear you but
Should I fear you because you shine

Annie Walker

On the Composition of Love

My best charter friend, Marlyn
Two fallen stars
From the farthest heavens
So brilliantly blue
The last rays of a
Setting summer sun
All the softer hues of red
Fallen leaves
Coercing the rich brown earth
Is come alive
Gently sloping to grow
The vines and briars
Struggling to grow
From the valley
All of this joined
So perfect, uniquely perfect
And I realize
I have fallen in love.

Micah Myers

Matter

All and gone, a memory
In moments from the sun
As vague as far as eyes can see
As seeing sought for none
A day it seems
Long lost and fought
In between a dream
A drifting thought
Of some said the notion
Revolve is to knowing
Sky over the ocean
The sun should be showing

Jon D. Gemma

Where Is My Smile?

To my grandpa, Daniel Webster Jones,
I Love You
Hey there, mister,
that's a nice smile.
May I borrow it for a while?

The day he laid in the coffin,
right along with my tears,
my smile started falling.

I'm sure it's getting a good use,
but I really would like it back,
even though he has a good excuse.

I've been searching everywhere,
and I haven't found it yet.
Could it be with him up there?

Dear God, is he smiling down at me
when I do something pleasing?
Please tell me, 'cause I can't see.

If it is,
please ask him to drop it down
to me once he has found his.

Danielle Jones

Heretic

Stakes pulled upright
fixed into frozen earth
beneath a scarlet sky
Torches flicker, shadows fall
amid muffled murmurings
hidden, faceless voices cry
"Kyrie eleison . . ."

Wood heaped high, passed
hand to hand, iron men
flank each grim post pointing
toward a pitiless heaven
Halberds glitter, greedy flames
Devour pain and ravage prayers
"Christe eleison . . ."

Embers dying
ashes softly settle
on soulless mantles stilled
briefly by mute agonies
Upon the dark winds, voices
echo in the tomb of night

Edward West

As I Look at You

As I look at you,
I see the sun
And its energy.
I see the darkness
And the mysteries
Of the unknown.

I see children playing—
Running and jumping,
Reaching and climbing.
I see laughing and crying,
Joy and pain.

And now I see
A woman who is free,
Dancing in the rain,
Full of life,
And the music of the
Universe in your smiling lips.

I see you so clear.

Cliff Stone Like

Indian Summer, Wisconsin

Woodland streams are gurgling
and sparkling in the sun.
Nature sends forth warning,
winter's soon to come.

Flocks of geese are winging,
forming V-shaped flight.
October's clear, blue heavens
shine glorious at night.

Aftermaths cease growing.
Frosty crystals chill the air.
A late robin may be seen,
and cobwebs everywhere.

Coloured leaves fall softly.
Waning winds still croon.
Even tide brings Indian summer,
with a harvest moon.

Mabel Hamilton Mueller

Valentine's Day

On this special day
there are so many
ways to say
Happy Valentine's Day

You could say it with
flowers from your own
backyard
or sign your name
on that special Valentine's card

You could say it with candy
shaped like a heart
or say it with words like
"We'll never part'

No matter what you do
or what you may say
it will always be special on
Valentine's Day

Sharon S. Miller

Letting Go

I asked my friend
Who had "let go"
The meaning of the phrase
She said, "Relax, girl—don't sweat it
It's just another phase"
In this game of life we're living
The phases come and go
Sometimes, we think we're ready
Other times, we do not know
So when my son
Moved out last week
I hugged him tight and said
"Dear, I'm going to miss you
But now I'm going to bed"
I "let go"
And I let God
And think I did it right
I know he hasn't left me
He's just out of sight

Josie Haller Teal

Untitled

A leaf has fallen in the trees
I heard the smallest sound
A little flutter falling
Then quiet on the ground

As easy as you please
Just catch a passing breeze
A simple letting go
Then floating down with ease

Lorie White

Forgotten Houses

A fountain of brightness.
Two internal reflections
emerging its intense ray
along a fallen path.
Visible from land
to sea, protecting coastal shores.

Illuminates oceans,
a two ray system
which reaches outer borders.
A bowing light source tracing
its angular radius,
with enough vigor to light a tired city.

White light bends
omnipotent to inner space.
An unbroken, rotating,
ghostly sphere, which leads
the lost, guides others,
and defends its quarters.

Catherine Dunbar

New Set of Keys

I can turn and close the door
That locks the past behind.
There isn't much I'm looking for
Among those memories from my mind.

Here today, I have no use
For some thoughts I had before.
Those misled ways are no excuse,
I'll today accomplish more.

This new day today I make,
Won't leave me sad or sore.
Its dawn reveals a future to take,
And has left an open door.

Life's new times invite me in
To slide across its floor.
I'm welcome in the world again,
But, behind me close the door.

Kevin Manzon

Christ-Like Growth

Grow tall in height of spirit
Grow wide in joy and love
Grow full of running over
Grow quiet to hear above

Grow out in actions and giving
Grow up in fullness of call
Grow well through Christ our savior
Grow in to surrender your all

Grow ready for his coming
Grow steady in giving your best
Grow open to hearing his message
Grow close he'll do the rest

Never better than, but chosen for

Rosalee Robinson

Senses

Seeing you in my dreams,
Hearing you in my head,
Tasting you on my lips,
Smelling your sweet cologne,
Feeling you in my heart,
Wanting you in my arms,
Now I know that it's all true,
This thing I've found
Between me and you.

Rebecca Desjardins

To Show My Love

I've never known such love
As what I feel for you;
I wish this feeling would last forever;
This feeling is so new.
No one has ever cared for me,
The way you have show me;
I wish we could be together,
In love we'd always be.
If I had only one moment,
One moment to show you I care;
I'd write you something beautiful,
Something I could share.
But I don't know where I'd start,
I'm clueless of what I could say;
All I have are the memories,
And the beginning of each day.
We have a weird connection,
Your face I've never seen;
My heart still says it loves you,
Even all the same.

Chandra Xeloures

If Tomorrow Comes

With this generation being evaporated
Before our very eyes
With diseases being widespread
Like the plague resurgence

With no cure for cancer
Which is well past due
When they can put a man
On the moon

But can't cut out destruction
Of mankind
When the politicians preach peace
But hate groups are allowed to pursue

While animals can't roam free
Hunters kill not for food but sport
When we look for signs of hope
In heroes of the past and present

When our parents who gave us life
Are still and always in our corner
Whether they are alive or dead
They shall never leave us inside

Ruby Dee Sheppard

My Grief

My grief is like a wild bird
Captured in its youth,
Imprisoned in a golden cage
Flap, flap, flapping its wings
Against the bars,
Unable to leave,
Unable to sing,
Unable to fly,
Unable to die.

My grief is like a wild bird
Caught in a bush
With a wounded wing,
Weak and weary
Lashing out and
Thrashing about,
Flap, flap, flapping its wings,
Unable to leave,
Unable to sing,
Unable to fly,
Unable to die.

Gwen J. Mathis

Skee

You're the river deep and true
That strengthens me, as we spin through
This labyrinthine
Journey, time

An eagle soaring in the night
My chariot of golden light
With body lean, but tempered steel
So tender was your touch, your feel.

Come, let us drink to what was when
So very much I loved you then
How deeply you fulfilled your vow
And how much more I love you now

Today, tomorrow what care we
Our souls transcend eternity

Lenore Becher

Untitled

Oh castaway, oh castaway,
Thou art a castaway,
Because you're not like me.
Oh castaway, what you believe!
You must follow narrow-mindedness.
Oh castaway, look at your color.
You don't have my subtle shading.
Oh castaway, look at your years.
You're much too old, or is it young?
Oh, no, you're not in any way like me.
God made you a castaway, don't you see?

Johanna Pettit

Away

Away, away and out of sight
As sea gulls taking their wings in flight
As waves pushed onward toward the shores
Are beckoned back o'er sandy floors

Away, away—why is it so?
Where do the smiling faces go?
Yet in our dreams and at our will
Memories remain to help us through
A part of everything we do

Gone from view—away and free!
Soaring high, yet here with me

Sharon Wilson

Our Wedding

Donna, our dear,
Your wedding day is here.
We hope you have peace, joy
And love, my dear.

To Christopher, Matt, and Donna,
We wish the very best,
For from you three
We would expect nothing less.

Matt, today we take you as our son
For the one we couldn't keep.
We know he's in God's loving arms,
Fast, fast asleep.

We wish you three happiness,
But there will be some tears.
We hope your love for each other grows
And grows throughout the coming years.

With this wedding day you three,
We are very glad.
So with our love and prayers,
Good luck from Mom and Dad.

Richard E. Jones

Forbidden

Silently, gently he breathes
I stroke his soft face
Feel the air from his sweet lips
His eyes flutter with pleasure

I long to kiss those lips
To feel his gentle touch
To look deep into those eyes
But he is not mine except in dreams

Our laughs are carefree
Our touches too often
Our words too careless
God, I wish he were mine

But in a far away state
Another lover dreams
As she waits for his return
That is why our knowing smiles
Are forbidden

Christy Maxwell

Outstanding Poets

Outstanding poets, all are we
Uniquely, we write poetry
Timid is how some of us write
Serene be others, some uptight
Translating thoughts, at least in part
And feelings deep within our heart
Nutty ol' poems to make you glad
Depressing ones will make you sad
Inspiring poems, real gifts from God
Nocturnal ones, from heads that nod
Glorious poems, for any age

Perhaps some should be read on stage
Original poems, these all will be
Especially meaningful—you'll see
Themes will vary as ideas roam
Striking! Each and every poem!

Peg Mitchell

Our Red Bird

*To my best friend and loving sister,
Diane Raiford*
Times are hard and sometimes sad.
But I have you, and I'm so glad.
Watch over us, for we are free.
Just like a red bird in a tree.
Silence and laughter are all the same.
Because our anger is so insane.
A tear drop continually begins to fall.
It's time to stand up so tall.
Hurt and guilt can finally stop.
Listen to me and we'll stay on top.
As young sisters, life was tough.
We both felt we had enough.
Parents do what they think is right.
Alcohol made them lose their sight.
Now hold your head up high and fly.
Like our red bird in the sky.

Dreama Szutenbach

Untitled

Porcelain dolls
misleading faces
perfected displays of emotions
pain hidden by painted smiles
fickle happiness
oblivious to their imprisoned souls
the watched become the watcher
placed behind the shadows
to play "dress-up" in a make-believe world

Nadia Heeb

Poet's Reward

Putting together a collection of poems
Is exciting and fun to do,
Though much more involved
Than mere creation.

It's a major undertaking,
Especially when new

To the concept of selecting a topic
Upon which to poetize

Seriously, with humor, or philosophic,
Whimsical, light, or wise.

Thought processes begin,
Hesitating, slow at first.

Words and feelings flow from within
Bubbling forth gently.
The tiniest bubbles burst

Into magical ideas worth writing.
Oh, how majestic, exhilarating,
Rewarding, exciting!

Eve Turkheimer

The Beyond

Every night I see so bright
The stars and moon.
I often ponder to myself—
Am I alone?
Are there things that move
Outside our light?
I see the sky so dark
Yet so very bright.
I watch the constellations
All there at once.
The sky is so silent;
It looks peaceful up there.
As far as I can see
I watch the silent twinkling
Of the midnight stars
As they move through the sky.
I gaze upon the quiet progress
Of the night
As it moves toward tomorrow.

Holly Hughes

Love's Paradise

A fool's lonely dream:
Too far to see,
Too high to reach.

A couple's reality:
Too strong to fight,
Too beautiful to forget.

A widow's sweet memory:
Painfully recurring,
Yet slowly fading.

Christina Felter

Life

Not only for school but for life we learn.
We have heard many wise men say:
Be kind to others and true to yourself;
You will find happiness along your way.

Love your country, help keep it free.
Let the role you play in life
Be one for others to follow,
As they see a loyal American
Sharing love, hope, and charity.

Betty Edwards

Angel's Wing

To my Tyler, you gave me a renewed faith, Meema

An Angel's wing touches my face, as I sit and wonder of God's human races.
A gentle calm comes over me as I wonder
What does this Angel wish for me to see.
All around us throughout God's world destruction exists,
All around humans try to survive on a wish.
Children killing children, hatred everywhere
Mother Earth's fury cleansing out, we need to listen, we need to hear.
Fire, flood, tornados where none have ever gone before.
How we need to see the destruction and death opening its doors,
Angels sent to escort the young and old alike Black, Asian, and White,
It matters not the color of your skin,
It matters that God's fury now begins,
Free will given—free will abused,
It's time to search our hearts, and maybe step into each others shoes,
Hear the Angels shouting out, beware the end is near, see it all about,
The key to God's saving all He created,
Is to end the fighting, to end the hatred.
An Angel's Wing touches my face, what does He wish for me to see,
Love is the answer. Love is the Almighty's Key.

     Dianne Rittenhouse Ritz

Family Gone Astray

Family members—family members—
why can't you behave? You are acting like little children
who don't get their own way.

What happened to that love you all once shared?
What caused you all to distance yourself from one another
and to develop those unnecessary fears?

Well, I guess it must be that greed has taken control of your minds,
and you have left those loving feelings you use to have
for one another so very far behind.

Will money make you happy? Will material things make you whole?
Or have you sold your souls for a few pieces of silver
and let your world and dreams go?

Well, what you really need to do is to rediscover and restore your faith—
Faith in God, faith in family, and faith for the entire human race.
Don't allow yourself to become the devil's pawns because
once you get caught up in his games
you'll loose more than your legs and arms.
So I say: Family members, family members for once and for all
stop acting like little children and grow up and stand tall.

     Robert Hill

What Time Is It?

An old man sits on his porch, rocking on his rocking chair.
The rockers on the rocking chair worn, from many long years of wear.
On the porch some boards are missing while some boards are worn thin,
mostly from the lack of repair, the rain, the snow, and the wind.
"I am retired." The old man says as people go passing by,
steady he rocks and he rocks, while seeming to gaze toward the sky.
"What time is it?" The old man asks so many times a day,
speaking to his neighbors across the street who wish he would move away.
The old man remarked to some children on the street,
"I once was a young boy" then that statement he would again, again repeat.
The old man then explained, "when I was born,
my clock of life began to tick".
Oh, how slowly time seemed to pass with the clock's tick-tock-tick.
When I would ask, "mother what time is it?" her reply to me would be,
"When the sun peeks over the horizon it is morning it is rising,
when the sun shines straight down from high in the sky,
like a big balloon, it is noon and when the sun goes down over
the western horizon it is evening it is hiding.
Now with every tick-tock-tick morning and evening
they come and go so quick.

     Robert L. Yeager

To Touch a Love

I ask of you
Your love inside
To give me love
And never hide
To show me things
So special and dear
To give your love
And stay right here
To hold my hand every day
And give me love
In your very own way
To teach me things
Right and wrong
To have a love
That is so strong
To share true love
From deep inside
To touch that love
We both seem to hide!

     Richard Smith Jr.

The Flame Within

*To Grandmother Edna Brown, Father
Jim Brown, daughter Tiffany and Erie*

A monster lives
within me, deep
striking fear when out
it does creep

This enemy
that lives inside
from others, its fury
I try to hide

I fear myself
its power and strength
for I know not
to what length

It will spew forth its rage
till its flame is spent
when from its dark
chamber it went

To reek havoc or justice
whatever it may
upon those who have summoned
it into the light of day

     Diana L. Cremean

Good-bye

*To my dear friend (brother at heart),
Carey W. Taylor*

Good-bye, one word I thought
I would never say,
Hoping that you could always stay,
A simple word bringing pain.
Tears are falling down like rain.

Time was never on our side.
Painful burning I cannot hide.
We lived a lifetime in few years,
Memories flashing through the tears.

Letting go of childhood dreams,
Trying to absorb what it all means,
Hard to imagine, even now,
Must go on someway, somehow.

Good-bye, one word I thought
I would never say.
Now I must try and find a way.

     Angela R. Linko

Time

The measured step of man through the ages, at times, a "will o the wisp"
that we chase with outstretched, eager hands and nimble feet,
hoping to draw it to our breasts and hang on to it tightly.
Such a long way to go to experience all the mysteries
that life will open up to us.
Each day, a brand new day, filled with play, hope, and happiness,
but bodies must grow, and minds store away all the lessons learned to be
taken out later, scrutinized, and categorized as to worth and importance.
The important things will become permanent,
and the frivolous discarded unconsciously.
Life, evolving from the concentration on "self" to "relationships"
and "interactions" with others of similar and different sex.
But then comes the call to find a soul mate,
to be joined in body and spirit
in the ecstasy of love and fulfillment, bringing forth the seed
to perpetuate
the progress of mankind through the veils of time.
The "river of life" flowing naturally around all obstacles, bridging all
chasms in its headlong race toward the "ocean of life."
How swiftly time flies! If only we could slow it down somehow.

Margaret E. Reed

Life's Changed

Since you've gone, it's my chore to take out the garbage from the kitchen
And lug the trash can to the street every Tuesday, rain or shine.
You always did that, and I never gave it a thought.

Sometimes you puttered in the yard for hours with your hand-powered mower
Clicking away. You'd work a while,
then sit and rest and talk with our neighbor.
Now I hire a handy man to do your work.

And buying groceries! I didn't realize how much time that takes!
You kept our larder filled with never a complaint.
How delightful to discover colorful bouquets of tulips, roses, or mums
Adorning our dining room table, all disheveled in an old Mason jar.

Your surprise, jumbo bear-hugs can never be replaced!
I long to come home to our house wafting with your pot roast aromas.
And how I struggle with the darn vacuum sweeper you always ran and
Replaced the bags when they filled with house dust and Herkie hairs.

Your old, white pickup no longer parks in the driveway. I miss it.

Julia Mattley

Kindred Spirit

I flow within the tranquil waters;
they carry me with gentle hands into the valley and hills beyond.
A kaleidoscope of burnt sienna, ivory, and carnelian shimmers below against
the sun's brilliance, smooth as silk as my feet pass above them.
Softly, the trees whisper,
the wind extending their emerald arms in greeting.
Innocent beauty moves within the cluster of tall giants
as deer chase one another.
Overhead, an eagle soars and eager to join him my hooves
and golden brown skin transforms into a span of opal and ebony feathers
as I stretch my wings, taking to the wind.
A trial beat persuades me to follow its alluring rhythm deep in the hills.
Dancers have joined in the spiral dance in the sacred circle.
The scent of cedar and sage furls into the turquoise sky.
I release my wings and dance with them, unseen,
but my essence surrounds them and lives within each of them.
They respect my many forms and honor me as they always have.
The kindred spirit; Mother Earth, Father Sky.

Julie Michaels

Should I Be Young or Should I Be Old

Should I be young
smooth skin and sure hands
keen bright eyes of blue
darkened hair of my age
free and spirited
quick feet nimble step
time without meaning
carefree confident sure
I grow I learn
Should I be old
fragile skin and gentle hands
wise knowing eyes of blue
silver-white hair of my age
loose and faded
careful feet easy step
time now with meaning
carefree confident sure
I grow I learn

Mardell K. Wood

A Day

It came and it went
With the beat of a heart.

A baby was born,
And an old man died.

With the most welcomed joy
Came the most dreaded pain.

Laughter rang and tears rolled
All in one solitary day

A day of greatness,
And a day of great remorse.

Julie Riley

Seasons

I look on winter's countryside
As down the street the kiddies slide.
The winter's snow hides everything
But, oh! what joy the seasons bring.
The early spring with slush and mud,
But on a tree I see a bud.
Then flowers, grass, and leafy tree,
And thunder clouds of black I see.
With gusty wind, the rain comes down
To bring new life to thirsty ground.
Then harvest time and farmer's fields
Release their full and golden yields.
The autumn smells with leaves that fall,
Air that's brisk with winter's call.
Soon snowy flakes will blow outside
As down the streets the kiddies slide.

Winn Hoefner

Heavenly Destiny

Let this be our destiny:
to live for our Lord,
to love Him more than
anything in this world.

Living and sharing each
new day within Him with
a devotion to His word.

As we adore our Lord
and as our burdens to God
out of our souls pour,
our souls soar toward Heaven,
with Heaven as our eternal life reward,
while we, as Christians, board.

Karen Carpenter

Change?

To my loving husband, William, for all his support
Slippery, shining, swirling leaves blow round the tired weary feet
shuffling back and forth on endless streets that go nowhere.
Starless, empty skies . . . hidden by monolithic canyons in this stark,
gray jungle of concrete beaches and trees of steel
    holding no signs of life.
With military determination, she stalks her fitful prowl of survival.

Alone, the old woman, keeps her head bent, moving fearfully slow . . .
Trying to remember when times were good, different, normal.
Thoughts and memories come fragmented . . . fleeting . . . aching . . .
as she remembers hot coffee and toast on a sunny morning by the
kitchen window, the garden,
    bright with fragrant roses, vegetables and color.

Painful memories . . . the tears roll down the weathered, aged face
into each and every precipice etched deep from neglect and care.
No one to wipe the tears, touch and hug or talk to. Street life is
timeless . . . lonely . . . each day only to scavenge life's basic
existence, no luxuries to bathe or a mirror to comb the once soft,
silver hair, now unkempt . . . kept hidden.

The sorrowful woman mutters . . . whispering as her battered, worn
shoes lift up and down, "You don't know me, who I am or who I
could be. I'm your mother, grandmother, sister. Why be afraid of me?"
The strangers pass, unmoved, untouched. Disdainfully, one pulls a
quarter from his pocket, shoving the token
    in her already forgotten face, "Here!"

Dorothy Forrest

Drawn Away

Moments of strong current taking me far giving
a place to be below shining stars.
During the day I shall have light of day and sparkling lights of night.

Wrapped about creatures of the sea always close to me.
This I choose being close to God because of the love I have all about the
vast ocean strand.   God is the one who truly understands.
My hours lying on the sand.

Enjoyed many days sitting on the beach trying to figure out why I could
not control my mind seemly close of reach. Wondering why all came too an
end lying on my bed to die. My suffering is over for God has given me a bed
beneath the sky—this I wanted after I died. Resting comfortable in a
shell as I sleep. God has given to me—"just for me."

Loved ones brought my remains to the strand. Ocean water carried me out to
my home where I will never be alone. Serenity for me is spending days in
the sun, glad this day has begun. No more worries or pain nor efforts in vain.

Life on Earth was much a living hell, yet now all is well. I shall be
remembered for miles always in my loved ones' minds.

Please do not be saddened for me, for I chose my place here in the sand.
Understand if you can, because this has been a part of God's plan.

Maureen Potts

Night Sky

I look for an answer in the night sky
I search for the meaning low and high
Life's meaning is untold, hidden away from me
Because I know that there are things beyond what I should be
As the questions rush in and no answers roll out
I wonder if I'm taking the right path or if I should choose a different
Route there is no answer for me until the future nears
I tell myself there's no need to worry
Though the pain of the fright still sears
I wish I knew everything so life wouldn't take me through twists and turns
And we wouldn't endeavor pain but only the happiness each of us yearns
I know I will never be able to understand it all
For which rainbow I will climb or which pit I will befall
I wish I knew what danger lurked ahead
Or what people really feel but leave unsaid
I wish I could make up for the faults in my generation
I only wish someone would teach them discipline and cultivation
I pray for all the gunshots that rings out and all the lies that are told
I hope betrayal will unravel and the truth to unfold
I want to live on knowing and learning for yet another day

Robin Ilissa Jacobson

A Promise Broken

A line crossed over,
a promise broken with a kiss.
And with that one kiss
went my heart.
My vision became my handicap.
My feelings became my restraints.
I was promised forever;
I had twenty minutes.
And in that short time
my heart became shackled.
What I took as everything
was regarded as nothing.
As the words were spoken,
I felt the trampling of hopes
in the seed of my heart.
I cried.
Love me; see me; feel me.
But be there for me
and if not;
I ask you, please, let my heart go.

Erica Feldherr

Drugs Aren't a Joke

They tell you to try them,
There's nothing to loose,
But remember one thing:
It's your right to choose.

Drugs may be fun
For two minutes, maybe,
But what is that worth?
Nothing. You'll see.

Think about what you
Want, feel, and need,
And stay on the right path,
Where you're sure you'll succeed.

They damage your body,
They can even kill,
The big drugs, the little drugs,
Even one pill.

Your friends may do drugs,
Drink, and smoke,
But think very seriously—
Drugs aren't a joke!

Denise M. Ontiveros

Making a Move

Our move is just beginning,
So many things to do.
We'll sell the house and start again,
In a place that's strange and new.

Call the movers and pick a date,
For the packers and loading the van.
Then start a list of errands to do,
That yesterday you should have ran.

Finding a place for us to live,
Can't forget this "little detail."
Phone calls to make the address change,
Friends cards to address and mail.

Garage sale dates must be set,
Which item stays or goes?
Then price each one so it will sell,
How much? Oh, God, who knows?

Before you know, it's time to leave.
Family and friends will part.
You take off for an unknown world,
But they're there within your heart.

Gloria Newhouse

A Good Friend

To my boyfriend, Matt, and friends, David and Kim
To have a good friend is to have someone who cares more than anyone else,
Someone who is willing to put you ahead of anything else.
Someone who hates to see you down,
And will do anything to clear a sad frown.
They make you laugh when all you want to do is cry.
You look at them and just sigh,
Because you know you found a true friend.
One who cares more than any other friend.
And you know if life gets rough,
They will stand by you and keep you tough.
They will help you conquer any fear,
And listen until your mind is clear.
They will help you figure out your deepest feelings,
And always try to put themselves in your place to feel those feelings!
A good friend is one to hold on to.
One who will go through anything with you,
And still love you if everything seems to be going wrong.
They will care for you and keep you strong.
And you know no matter what you'll always have at least one good friend!

Holly Midthun

Steal You from the Pain

Baby, I'm leaving, but please don't you cry
You told me you loved me, what you told me was a lie
So baby I'm leaving, it's time to say good-bye

You needed me to tend your wounds, to pamper and to love
You said you loved me far too soon for you to even know
If I could be there to lift you from the blackness that swallows you whole
I'd be there . . . as I breathe to live, my heart is here to hold

I wouldn't turn my back on you when you're too weak to stand your ground
I would lend my strength to empower you, to lift you when you're down
But when you find your strength, I know you're bound to leave
'cause you called on me to fulfill . . . a very painful need

Baby, I'm leaving, but please don't you cry
You told me you loved me, what you told me was a lie
So baby I'm leaving, it's time to say good-bye

Our friendship had been faded, like the jeans crumpled on my floor
But the memory will never fade, for that reason, I offer you more
For if I could steal you from the pain, the pain that you endure
I'd offer a hand to guide you through an open door

But baby now it's time, it's time for me to go
You've chosen a path away from me, It's time we both let go!

Traci Lee Geary

Pancho the Wine-O

He sleeps under the viaducts,
No matter what the weather might be.

With mice, roaches and overhead Mack trucks,
Become tolerant noises he cares less to see.

At dawn he walks the high way with care,
In hopes a few cans he'll find scattered here and there.

They will buy him a cartoon of milk to ease his stomach's hunger pain,
And he'll keep enough for wine to ease whatever other hurts came.

There would be times night would catch him helpless in the medical square.
I've seen him in the waiting room sleeping, some say he's "just taking up a chair."

Yes, his week old beard and smell of wine would always give him away,
But what the heck, what harms been done, and who are we to say?

Can't help but wonder who he is, and what turned him that way,
But we all know he'll be a wine-o until his doomsday.

So should you see him, give him a buck and say, "God Bless You!
They call him "Pancho the Wine-O," by name.

Someday they will find him in an valley with no identification
of whom to notify,
And he'll be buried in Potter's field without a rose or no one to cry.

Sarah Thomas Hendricks

Love

Traveling alone, you and I,
Under a clear blue sky.

From time to time the clouds
Rolled in, but the sun would
Come out again.

Our lives entwined like the
Branches of a grapevine,
And the fruit of the vine made
A wonderful wine.

As in life it mellows.

Slowly sipping the wine of life
Keeps us paired with
The love we share.

Myrtle E. Angle

Hide and Seek

Hide and seek the game,
We all played it in childhood;
My game continues.

Leaving clues, wishing
You would pursue me to
A secluded place.

Making noises to lure
You on, whispering of love
That may await you,

Hidden from your view,
Hoping you'll seek and find me;
Will you come and play?

Betty J. Stewart

I'm Not Dreaming

I want to believe I'm not dreaming
And wake up tomorrow and you'll be gone
I'm afraid of going to sleep at night
And not knowing what might go wrong

I think of you in the morning
And until I go to sleep at night
I can't help but to dream about you
Thinking how I could have done so right

I feel like the world is at my reach
You put the world at my hands for me
When I followed my heart
It lead me straight to you

You make me glad to know you
And to wake up every morning
Just to see your smile

Heather M. Bowser

Fireflies

Fireflies in pattern flight,
searching for their femme fatales,
flashing circles of
glowing illumination
in fields and woods,
which resemble sparks flying
from an autumn bonfire.
I await your coming in the soft,
velvet darkness
and capture you with joy
and exultation;
your diminutive beams flicker
glistens of light in my jar,
but at bedtime
I shall release you.

Faye R. Kauffman

Reflections

I see the face of my future in the mirror
That sends a message to my soul that couldn't be clearer.
The past put behind me now, I reflect the pain.
Images of a new day brighten that road to lead the way.
I've been scared and it's been hard, but I now have control of myself.
This book is done, and my journey has just begun,
So I grab a new one off the shelf; I turn the page to awaken
In a brand-new age where rules could not apply,
No longer held down or a slave to the grind. I have the ability to fly,
With fire in my eyes; I never say die, and I create what I think is art
Through a tiny hole straight from my soul with these words I speak
From the heart, reflections of tomorrow are tapping me on the shoulder.
We start off knowing nothing and learn so much as we get older.
I'm not looking forward to yesterday but what happens today.
Facing the moment of what could be something
You don't want to throw away, cut and paste little pieces
Of yourself together. From the farthest reaches to sandy beaches,
I know I'll take it one step at a time, with my mind as my guide
And my pen at my side, all I have to do is follow the signs.
Every key has the magic to unlock something different behind each door.
As the road got longer, I got stronger
And finally found what I was looking for.

Brandon Pace

The Man within the Dragon

To Michael Karr, whose friendship helped to inspire this piece
One who gazes out into the world, with the immense light of lightning
And possess within himself the spirit of fire and the spirit of life,
Is a man who knows all the enchantments of what reality is truly about
And who dares not to even think of taking anything in immoral strife.

This man is the purest of all human hearts that had forever been created
And deeply within him lies the everlasting magic of the eternal dragon,
With a blaze of fiery glory that shall forever be known,
And never shall any threat, mortal or immortal, over take him.

For within him lies hidden the heart of the dragon and its own immortal soul
Which cherishes him with the strength and bravery
    that has lasted throughout the centuries,
Which has allowed him to take into understanding
    what most creatures, in thought, cannot
And to judge things in life not by face value but by their own grand mortality.

However, there are days even when this great, eternal dragon
    cannot protect him
And in order for him to survive, he must fight with his own heart,
By not giving up the strength of that which comes forth from within
But in taking deep within himself the value of his own struggled hardships.

He is, in himself, his own spirit of fire and life
In fact, he is the immortal soul of his own cherished heart,
For nothing can destroy his faith in the light, of life eternal
And shall forever the Pendragon be his crested symbol of treasured honor.

Alicia R. Wayte

My Flower Garden

To Bonnie, Brooke, Thera, and Krystal
There is a flower garden that blossoms in my heart
These flowers bloom and grow and each one plays a part

The rose is tall and beautiful and shows the others how to grow
The rose has inner strength and courage, but feels no need to boast it so

The daisy is such a special one and has so much to share
One need only look at this beautiful flower to see the worth that's hiding there

The bluebonnet stands tall and true and shows its joy and love
It ties the others together, beauty surpassing the blue sky above

The sunflower spreads the sunshine to warm our very souls
This beautiful little flower touches all and gives us hope to hold

My garden flowers will always stay in that place I call my heart
Because they mean the world to me, that's where true family starts

Anita L. Carroll

A Little Boy

A boy, a baby cried
I picked him up
He laid his soft cheek against my chest
He put his hand in my hair
And began on his slumber
Journey once more
I hope he had dreams
Of love and caring
Of warmth and comfort
In a place he felt really safe
Of twinkling stars and tickling toes
He shows a hint of a smile
And off he goes
I know he is warm
Because it shows
Now he can dream
Be happy little boy

Alice Irene Off

Untitled

Heartbeats walking alone
People stare at each other
Ignoring the titles
They share
Oblivious to their poems
And their treasure
Which is precious enough
To be hidden
But not precious enough
To be shared
For who out there might
Ignore it
Trample dreams
And walk on . . . Oblivious

Barbara McCorkhill

In the Silence

In the silence, my soft tears flow
Remembering the times that hurt me so
Holding your face in my hands
Knowing it was time to let you go

In the silence, my heart breaks
How long will sorrow make it ache
Listening for answers slow to come
Wondering what path my life will take?

In the silence, I feel so alone
Accustomed to it, slowly I've grown
I pray that you are now at peace
For in my silence, I know you've gone home

Shirley A. Nuhfer

Blind Leader

Leave all if's and but's behind you.
Pack away the could's and should-have's.
Walk the path that lies before you;
Do not waste time to look back.
Every single breathing one, now,
Piles regrets beside the door.
If you let the baggage
Follow,
You cannot let yourself explore
What lies ahead, where you
Must travel
Down the road
You do not see.
Take my hand,
And I will lead you.
Where—don't ask.
I do not know.

Amy L. Kurlansky

Because Someone Gave

To Jaci Velasquez for her ministry of love and inspiration
Our lives are so blessed by things we have not,
not so much by things we have sought.
Calamities go unnoticed when you are not the receiver of disease,
sickness, and poverty, and all other attacks of the Deceiver.

Yes, sometimes not getting is getting, when it comes to sickness and debt.
Thank the Lord for your peace and health now, for there are many less fortunate.
When you can stand on your own two feet under guidance of Our Lord,
you can help fight these adversities with the power of His Sword!

With the heart of our Savior, may we selflessly share
our abundance of blessings, concern, time, and care!
At times, just an assuring word, when the Lord's voice is heeded
for someone discouraged, is all that is needed.

Yes, we can make a difference, it this world sees His face;
through the love of His children, this can be a Heavenly Place!
We will overcome, fighting on our knees,
for our Father is the shelter, for He holds life's keys!

God so loved the sinner, He said, "Show you love them, too.
Then also love this child of Mine, from My heart, through you.
Yes, look what love has done through the sacrifice;
one can save, like My Son.
Do ye likewise, so My Love can be known, because someone gave!

Johnson I. Jacob

Yes, I Will

Grandma, you were the one who was always there for me,
and I was always there for you.
Grandma, a big time in my life is approaching quickly; I know you
physically can't be there with me, but you spiritually will be the one
to walk me down that aisle in June.
Grandma, as I will remember you, I will reminisce about your two fluffy
kitties you adored, about the way you would always save those newspaper
clippings for me, and your love for making dolls.
Grandma, but most importantly, when I remember you,
your face and skin will come to mind, for I get to look in the mirror.
I have your brown eyes, brown hair and your dark skin,
we even have the same type of nails, they are thin and weak.
Even the shape of our index finger on the right side shares the same shape.
Grandma, I have agreed with grandpa and mom, they asked if I would help
carry your casket, for it will be one of the last things I'll do for you and myself.
Grandma, I remember you asked long ago, if something ever happened to you,
would I be there for grandpa, to help him around the house and all.
Grandma I have come to answer, "Yes I will, with all of my strength
and all of my power."

Angela Starkey

Imagine Julianne

To my sister's little girl
With my imagination I can be most anything.
A sky diver or a pilot of a ship out on the sea.
There is nothing that I can't do, in my mind perfectly.
With my imagination I am limitless and I am free.
It works for me, it'll work for you. If you want it to, it all comes true.
I can be anywhere I want, you know, or whoever I want to be.
Anytime I decide to become something, it's as new as a sun filled day.
Feeding crocodiles in the jungle or a chimpanzee or two.
Anything I want, no matter what, it always does come true.
Swishing down a fashion runway or becoming a magical Gypsy,
anything I want, anytime I want, whenever I want it to be.
I've been to the moon and I think you should soon
come along maybe just for the ride.
We'll laugh and we'll smile, maybe feed a crocodile but only if we decide.
I've been a squirrel on the telegraph wire, walking gently and taking care.
When I stood before the Olympic stand, I smiled just because I was there.
Did I tell you about all the things I did see,
when I stood on the ledge, just barely on the edge, of another solar galaxy?
Whomever I choose to become one day or whatever I choose to be,
remember that, no matter what, I always will be me.

Frederick J. Ringger

Coming to Face Reality

Wounds of the flesh heal
with an ease unknown
to that of the soul.
Under cushions of pain

The body informs the mind.
Under pins of tears
the mind tells the soul.
And forever do we heal

Wounds that return forever,
through time and memory
and music and charm.
For we know he is gone,
and he won't return to
be the same as anything
was before. So let the
wind light the trees and
allow the ocean to crash the
sand. These things, as
many things in this world,
cannot be changed.

Steve Whitmire

Where Is She Now?

My heart fills with sadness
When I think of her now.

Where is the laughter,
the twinkle, the glow?
Was it really that long ago?

She didn't just leave
to start a new life;
She forgot the past,
closed the door, turned her back.

My heart fills with sadness
at what we have lost.

Oh, she'll still smile,
but from the outside,
from a closed heart.
I miss her, love her, but

My heart fills with sadness
When I think of her now.

Where is my friend?
Where is my daughter?

Beverly J. Rowland

Coal Black

When coal black eyes
gaze at the coal black moon,
the coal black hearts
come shining through.

They know how the game is played,
and they're trying to win;
they're bathed by the masters
in coal black sin.

In the race of life
they're just like we are;
they have no clue
who the masters are.

When the sun goes down
and you can't see the moon,
the coal black souls
come tearing through.

They know how the rules are made,
and they're dying to win;
they thrive in the dark
in coal black sin.

Justin McClain

Young Roy

Dear Nephew Roy,
I hear tell that you want to take up being a cowboy?
As you know, I've been a cowboy as long as I care to remember.
I've ridden herd on cattle in all types of weather,
Through Blue Northerners, thunderstorms, the desert heat of September.
Let's not forget the times I forgot that Christmas is in December.

Oh, yes sir-eee, I'm a true cowboy, through and through.
But I wouldn't recommend this cowboy life, even to a friend like you.
The days are long, the work's hard, pay is short, and things do go wrong.
Then you wake up one morning and find that your life is almost gone.

My young friend, as you can see, the life of a cowboy is never free.
But free men we are, as we are a true breed,
Though the true cowboy is a dying race.
There are very few men that can keep up with our pace.

Well then, my young friend, if it's a cowboy's life that you want to be,
Be the best darn cowboy there ever was to be.
Get out on the range, a'riding and roping and herding them cattle.
It won't take long and you will find yourself asleep in the saddle.

I hear tell that City Folks pay for the fun of herding cattle.
In closing, my young friend, think of being a cowboy as a fee paid.

Jan R. Altman

Crossroads

Before me they lay now, strewn, bittersweet
Permeating my view, as swift as the dust settles on a country crossroad
Bearing my history, invading my private estuary

I could have imagined I'd once been this way, still
Eager to devour a new journey, yet relentless to resurrect ancient crossroads
I have conquered mercilessly

In my youth, I would have likened my crossroads
To a game, laying collected as match sticks, askew
Intertwining, women timelessly now before me
Collected amidst years
Vibrant, visual is this game of life

Unspeakable silence, the epitome of it all
Pools of memories silhouetted endlessly upon the sea of my soul
They taste not of dust now, but of aged saltwater
Anchorless, cast a drift for all eternity

Solemn grows the hour
I ponder, I watch the light of darkness faintly dim, ushering in the sunrise
Time to gather more match sticks
To build more crossroads

Patricia L. Price

Not One More

To all those who have been abused, you are not alone
At the hands of someone you trust, who tells you: I love you so much;
Let me show you how much, and then he begins to touch.
I will not hurt you is what he says; then why are tears falling down my face?
Pain and shame is what I feel. My heart screams when he comes near me!
Day by day I die a little inside.
Scars that are not seen, but scars that stay with me,
I plead with him to stop; this is not what I want.
I guess he didn't hear; he continues to have his way.
I know it's not right; I'm to afraid to fight.
So I pray: Please take him away.
Why can't I tell? Can't anyone see what this man is doing to me?
Is it hidden so well? When will someone help?
Who will wipe away the tears?
Who can understand what has been done to them?
Why are children abused? How can children be blamed?
Why can't adults bare the shame? We can't turn away.
Not one more is what we should say.
Not one more to shed a tear. Not one more to live in fear.
Let out hearts be filled with rage, to stop this insanity that happens every day.
Let our voices speak: No! No! No! Not one more!

Rene M. Sammour

Bittersweet

If I were to take my limb
and extend it toward the sun
If I were to take some metal
and cause a righteous pun

If I were to penetrate that of
my exterior shell
If I were to die, would I
Go to Hell?

If I were to survive and
lead the life I should
If I were to survive, would
I lead the life I could?
But to ones I would have missed
if I had ceased to exist
it was a bittersweet life
that I had once kissed

Amy Letizia

The Last Good-bye

The U.S. Seventh Cavalry rode
out over the desolate plain.
Listening, she could faintly
hear a familiar refrain:
The band was playing
"The Girl I Left Behind Me."

She wanted to be brave,
trying hard not to cry,
never knowing then
it was the last good-bye.

She would remember forever—
some fifty-seven years—
the sights and sounds of that morning
through a veil of tears.
She would remember especially
his last look back,
how he sat on his horse,
the gallant wave of his hat.

Kathy W. Hentschel

The Clock

Why does the clock suddenly cease
Its continuous tick-tock?
When all is going well
And life is its best,
What causes that strange phenomena
That ends all life?
Spontaneous conclusions to all
That we know . . .
Or maybe something more noticeable,
Like a clock slowing down.
Why does the clock suddenly cease
Its continuous tick-tock?

Jennifer Butler

Embracing Eternal Love

Infinite beauty,
Strength and wisdom,
In a breathing universe.
Like a tiny flower
Embracing the power of creation.
Like a white dove
Ascending into the heavens,
Bringing peace into my world.
Like a dream come true.
In the face of the white dove,
I see only you.
Smiling in white and soft blue,
I wish to drown myself
In your eternal love
And become free.

Kevin Lahue

Ten x 4 + 5

I've made life's journey ten times four plus five,
I'm, oh, so thankful to be alive.
Starting over isn't easy to do.
Breaking old habits, each day is new,
and my life on this Earth could be but a few.
Life and love is seen much different in these eyes of forty five.

It's not about passion and heat, or the monetary status we all try to keep
It's about standing on my own two feet or lending a helping
hand to those who I meet.

It's about the simple things in life.
The sound of soft rain on a window pane,
  or a gentle breeze among the trees
The soft grass on my bare feet
  as I walk across a meadow in the summer heat.
Sounds of a morning dove singing in the tree above, or watching
the stars which seem to be in flight, on a moonlit hot August night.

It's about the simple things of love.
Lending an ear to those who are dear,
allowing them to speak those things which they fear.
It's about walking hand in hand as companion and friend,
because you never know when life on this Earth will come to an end.

Connie Cook

The Dream of Paul

He walked a wooded lane one night and saw her standing there;
She stood alone as a falling star lit up her flowing hair.
The wind within a misty glow blew passing clouds away;
She gazed at him with smiling eyes and said, "I'm Ruth of Lai."

The summer passed, and the Autumn gold pleased Paul's Ruth of Lai;
They walked and spoke of many things but his thoughts were far away.
The snow that came upon the land did not help him to know;
The night he saw her standing there beneath that misty glow.

The shining star that lit the night showed on Ruth of Lai;
They walked once more where first they met, remembering the day,
Paul spoke of love and happiness, she gazed up to the sky;
Her smiling face was filled with light as she gave him her reply.

"My home is Lai, Paul, love one another. I will return to help you."

Paul saw the night and the glowing light that carried his friend away;
The air was filled with hope and joy as he bowed his head to pray.
He asked for guidance from above to help him know her way;
He asked our Lord to help him keep his love for Ruth of Lai.

Armard J. Gauthier

The Flute

To Michael Gatto
The alluring meadow felt magical and protected,
  As I entered it's kingdom of beauty.

It's soft pastel of colors circled all around,
  While the morning's sun sparkled of golden light upon me.

Just as all life beings to dance and sing of the dawn's inspirational light,
  My thoughts of you embraced every part of me.

I listened to the animals enjoy every waking moment,
  Being full of fun and love,
    As though a "Flute" was being played of cheerful harmonies and laughter,
      My body was surrounded with warmth and vigorous energy.

The captivating meadow had filled me with such joy and love,
  Allowing me to be free of any possible coldness or sorrows,
    To then secure my every thought of blissful melodies of passions and safeness.

Even when I close my eyes,
  Touching every layer within me,
    There you are, in all those things.

The day be coming to a close,
  But within the valleys of my heart,
    I can still hear the affectionate music Of the Flute
      Of my love,
        For you are always with me.

Jenni Nelson

Life

Life is a strange
And wonderful thing
It changes as it goes
One day we feel one way
And the next nobody knows
So we buckle right in
And we hold on tight
And we brace up for what comes next
And one thing's for certain
Is that it is something
That we won't expect!

Scott Moore

Stock and Trade

must be my stock and trade
like all the silence in the world
is in my head
surrounding me
all at once a pleasure and a pain
feeding me
starving me
how I want is what I want is
a tender heroine for a partner
but all I've got are empty dreams
Jesus is a good friend
Jesus is my best friend
and I'm glad that He made angels
'cause I think that when he made me
he turned loneliness
into flesh and blood

Jack Power

Baby's Eyes

The crystal sparkle of the morning seas
The majestic glimmer of twilight skies
The golden drops on rain touched trees
I see all of these in your eyes

A powder blue Heaven
Emerald kissed
Like pearls shining
In a rainbow's mist

They draw me in
More each day, each week
I'm mystified
With no words to speak

The smile in your eyes
Like sun's first light
A glowing soul
That brightens each night

Shonda Davis

Freedom

Freedom is something we all long for
Freedom we all deserve
Freedom we must work for
For Freedom we must serve

The homeless vet is hungry
The child, forlorn and lost
Just a morsel of compassion
Is Freedom's only cost!

If your neighbor comes a-calling
For something he can't find
If truly you are worthy
Put Freedom on his mind

If Freedom is all you give him
You must fill his pockets well
Freedom is what we all strive for
To ring Freedom's holy bell!

Earlyne M. Simmons

Storms of the Heart

Clouds rolling over the horizon churning and billowing
Great is the crashing of Heaven that echoes throughout the countryside
Energized torrents swirl, continuously growing more gray and bleak
Restlessness that can no longer be held is loosened upon the land
Pouring out its entire being upon the Earth in one swift movement
    of emotional turmoil
Great drops of water break from the sky riding on gusting winds
Racing towards the ground to splatter back up in an ancient dance
Flashing lights rip through the cloud-covered canopy illuminating the darkness
Raging throughout the thirteenth hour, this madness shakes the land
Until gradually the disturbance subsides and dissipates once more
    behind the horizon.

So is the way of love in these times of torment
Great sadness rolls over the soul, as a sudden cloudiness covers the face
Tragically is heard a breaking heart resounding upwards towards the heavens
Tears fall unrelenting from eyes as gray as summer rain
Heavy sighs the heart of mournful romantics, blown by harsh winds of lost love
Wild sobbing erupts, shaking the very depths of the spirit's foundation
Falling into a heap of human vulnerability with a grief that cannot be comforted
Slowly the tears begin to subside, as the sobs grow softer until they fade
Calm settles as concession to loneliness is given, the only fate
    offered the broken hearted
Sadness creeps in where the look of love dwelt for so long,
    a tribute to surviving the pain

   Debra C. Hurd

Ascension

To squeeze head first through the needle's eye, feel the tomb-like embrace
Of God's arms in a manger of stars.
Bleached clean of life's stains, she returned,
The prodigal daughter back to the father she thought had spurned
Her freckled breasts, her sunburnt face,
A father that welcomed the most tarnished daughter back with unflinching grace.
The little things she left on her night table: a bottle of Valium, a
crucifix overturned,
A message in marker on the bedroom door, too smudged to be discerned.
I sought a thread of life among the dead,
A strand of hair, a frayed trace
Of her to roll in my fingers.
But only stillness lasts.
Stillness dumped like fresh dirt
Covers the corpse, smothers its muted cause.
Sheltered now from worldly sorrow,
Her skin unravels in strips of gauze,
Down to a spool of bone which cracks and bares its marrow.
Unwinding, unwinding, death's an unwinding, a loosening of atoms, a pause.
It is dues we pay for the time we borrow.

   Jonathan Lobsenz

Creek of Time

My thanks to Liza Uhlmann for her thoughts and ideas
Calling sad words, despair not!
Creek of time set me down to understanding.
Silent stream whose words call out to deaf ears,
Tell me, what is your song? Tell me why you call upon me!
Driven by wind and rain, no obstacle obstructs your path,
no barrier halts your progress.
On your journey, if you would be forced to cease your endless trek, man
and the universe would end. Like Life, your path branches in many directions
When the road is blocked, you turn and face another.
In the end, you change your state
and fly into the arms of God.
Like Love you embrace the world with your knowledge and teach it to grow,
embrace the soil, and from this love grows the "fetus of spring."
Like Joy, you swell with pride at the coming of spring, and in your
delight share your beauty with the world. Like men and women, you leave your
mother the ocean, and journey, learning, giving and taking.
In the end you return pure and changed into the home of your beginning
where you may at last find love and possess it forever!

   Brian P. Sanker

Winter

My favorite time of the year
Is winter and it's finally here
School is out
So I can go out and about
No school work to be done
Nothing to do but to have fun
Going out on dates
And coming home late
Seeing all the Christmas lights
And the beautiful nights
Going to parties on Christmas Eve
And not really wanting to leave
Celebrating the new year
With lots of cheer
And finally going back to school
Which isn't very cool
But, hey, everyone has a turn
In life to learn
But you can always eat a candy cane
And go down Memory Lane

   Linda Logan

Winter Storm

*To Vivian, Enid, Lisa, and John—
my loving wife and children*
Howling wintry winds
spread arctic
shiver
among dry unfurred
limbs . . .

Of a sudden friendly
static voices
without
assume an ominous death
cacophony . . .

The unwary traveler
juggles life
upon
capricious hostile
wills . . .

As fugitive forebodings
languish into
solitary
requiems of foreshadowed
immortality. . . .

   Manuel U. Blas

The Deadly Host

To smoke or not, aye there's the rub
To breathe in fumes from burning leaf
What pleasure comes to those that do
That we should rule to cause them grief

For not alone they suffer harm
But also those who near do stand
So rule we must to guard against
Not just the main, but second hand

They stand outside in rain and snow
And suck the drug into their blood
The monkey on their back demands
That they pollute their lungs with crud

Alas, no happy ending here
For many young do puff with pride
They choose this stinking social scourge
The Surgeon General's facts aside

Four hundred thousand souls or so
Do every year give up the ghost
The villain is the wicked weed
The cigarette, the deadly host

   James Sabo

Kamushka

For Charlotte

It seems so long ago that we laughed and teased each other,
made silly mistakes, gossiped and such.
Yet . . . when I think of you—it is yesterday and we are thirteen.

It seems so long ago that our children were small,
made us nervous, cranky, not sexy at all.
Yet . . . when I think of this—it is twenty years ago and we are thirty.

It seems so long ago that we shopped,
watched old movies and sold "Char's Creations."
Yet . . . when I think of this—it is ten years ago and we are forty.

It seems so long ago we sat a dusk by your sister's house near the frozen lake,
watched iced trees glimmer, breathed crisp air, dreamt goals and planned gold days.
Yet . . . when I think of it—it is yesterday and not so long ago.

In truth those memories thrill.
Like chords of music from a Celtic rhythm—they stir the sense.
Yet . . . when I think of it—it is yesterday,
and I find myself playing them from time to time.

I wonder . . . shall I wear purple,
or walk in the rain or laugh so hard I cry?
Indeed . . . I will.
For when I think of us—it is always yesterday!

Tarezia Vitale

Monday

Concrete pillows, paper blankets, eyes of stone with endless road,
Destinations unknown, yet, still alone, they roam, they roam, bitter
smiles, calloused lives, savage souls, Cups full of nothing but solitude
and noise, forgotten journeys, Carcass limbs, lonely despair, in a desolate
land; engulfed by malice and greed they dance, to unsung melodies,
Bizarrely swaying to invisible notes, tragic realities, mistaken
practicalities, cascaded rhythms, political examples, unclassified
informalities, Abused, deranged, padded walls, labeled cells, masked
sanity, mirror reflections, translucent eyes, disdainfully hid the horror
behind societies insanities, Carcass frame, still remains, boldly clinging
on to entangled misfortunes of lost destinations, Instilled volition
labeled survival among the muck and the filth, lay the unheard stories
awarded medals of glory, Sanctified engagements, un-ratified dominion,
champagne and caviar at the cost of the starved, Distant whispers,
Intuitive lies, A soldiers lost mind, blasphemous blizzards, explosive
threats, Ignorant, blind fools, Paradoxed impressions at the cost of a
nation, Lays the crystal grain of intricate time, The hands strike four,
all traffic begins, twisted minds, misguided fortunes, as notions decline
riddled charades, haunted hounds, taunting tears, irreplaceable years,
destitute illusions, unbendable fears, as scars lie deep within the corners
  of insanity. . . .

Olga Iris

The Battle of Bannockburn

The English army loomed threateningly before the Scottish hordes,
Soldiers equipped with sharp piercing arrows and shiny mammoth swords.
The Scots' swords were small and rusted, their arrows dull and weak.
Their slender, starving bodies looked so puny, so meek.
The English men were cocky, and expected an extremely easy fight,
Envisioning that most would see their wife and kids that night.
One man yelled confidently, "We'll swallow them whole!"
Another shouted out, "Down to hell we'll send each soul!"
Though the Scots' frail bodies were broken and battered,
Their high spirits were everything but tattered.
With encouragement and hope did the Scots behave.
One was heard to say, "I'd rather die than be a slave."
Shooting arrows lit with fire was how the English started the attack.
The Scots ducked under their shields, then shot some arrows back.
The English were well trained, fighting very well.
But no matter how hard they tried, the Scots they couldn't kill.
Every Scottish man that went out to fight that day,
Had courage, valor, and honor, and seemed to shine in each sun ray.
And before they even knew it, the English men were dead,
The Scottish men let out a cheer, their families would finally be fed.

Brittney Pollard

Two Men

I see a man upon a stage,
Singing from his heart.
He tells of life to be found
And of a brand new start.

I love the man upon the stage;
He brings joy to my life.
He loves me in a special way
And is solace in my strife.

I see a man upon a tree,
Crying from His heart.
He offers life eternally
And wants me to be a part.

I love the man upon the tree
And all He has to give.
He loves me in a special way
And died that I may live.

Aletheia D. Lee

Fly High

Fly high up in the sky
What will I see?
Would it be what I perceived to be
A united world for you and me?

Fly high up in the sky
Undoubtedly, I see beauty
The beauty of every culture's diversity
Diversity with great affinity

Fly high up in the sky
White, brown, black, and yellow race
Finally working together with ease
Unveiling the world, may discover peace

Fly high up in the sky
Should I inhabit up here
Or return down there?
Return to reality with no fear?

Arevel R. Junio

Why?

"Who?" you asked
"Not who . . ." said I, "Why"
"Why?" you, the confused one
"The affection, it was not there,
Nor was the love, only you,
The naive one, the one who does
Not know how to love,
How to give affection . . .
I gave, you took
But you never once gave me love
Never once did you show affection
You took from me
The only thing I can ever give
You never gave
You never thought about me
This is why"

Alison Heberling

Showed a Love

God sent you across my path
Never thought I would find real love
Honey, you have lighted my life up
In more ways than you'll ever know
The sparks had gone
The flames had died down
I thought my life had no return
It seemed beyond repair
Only you knew how
To get the sparks rekindled
You showed a love
That I never knew

Frances L. Walters

Certainty

My cup is full of all kinds of fears
Of events that could happen at any time.
Aside from disasters to me unthinkable,
Today may prove the day that. . . .

I fall down the stairs and break a toe;
Little Jennifer catches German measles;
Her pink and blue birthday bike is stolen;
Rover develops an aging dog ailment;

I find my tall pine tree starting to brown;
Leaks show the roof in need of repairs;
Burglars make off with the new television;
A reckless young driver mangles my car.

If even one thing were free from all doubts!
But we're told only death and taxes are certain.
Still, some succeed in escaping taxes,
And others are sure there's life after life.

Where then can I find my peace of mind?
In faith! That after walking a path
Sometimes surprising, its length unknown,
All will come out well in the end.

   Roger Mather

Rain Colors

Tonight I sat by window and watched
the rain; the rain sang a sweet story then called my name.

Mirror, mirror, where can you be?
I'm looking for a friend to dance with me.
I'm pouring down past from the sky—
take a look at my drops as you sit and sigh.

I'm full of color as you can see your
reflections of lights are the same as me.
Come dance, mirrors, come dance with me.
For, tomorrow I'll bring all the colors you see.

Do remember our dance, my story of the night,
My song to you in early twilight.
My colors, your colors, shimmering in the rain,
I do believe, mirror! It was you
Who called my name rain. . . .

   Mary Kathenne Nolan

Clock with No Hands

The number are burning on the clock with no hands,
and knows no sound of ticking.
A music box sings a lullaby that swells my soul with sorrow.
Observing empty spaces I have little to offer.
The numbers are burning on the clock with no hands,
and knows no sound of ticking.
Seconds run into minutes and hours are passing.
No one should feel so alone.

   Marilyn Mullins

For the Price of a Meal

Wrestle the notion of vagrancy
To become a forgotten glance of hidden faces
Listen to the voices measure your box
That poor lost soul on Melrose Avenue
Picture the suit, a stretched-out hand of porridge
Just another vagrant soul with lavish taste
He knows your forte of gin and tonic
A shot of courage for some uncomplicated pleasure
You play the game of repercussion
A paltry expense for autonomy
But watch the hand pass you by
To leave you starving from the hunger
Only a fool would follow suit
For Wednesday comes around like clockwork!

   Joseph Kirkpatrick

My Son

I remember the day you were born:
Those tiny little parts of your body were so precious
I knew that you'd be my last child, and a precious gift from God.
As you grew up, there was nothing you didn't have.
You gave me joy, love, understanding, and the opportunity to
see you grow into a fine young man.
Then tragedy struck, and your life ended on the cold December
day shortly after Christmas,
for God had called you home
When that day happened, a part of me died, but the love
and memories will live on forever.
Some day my dear son, I will see you again.

   Sara Bonnett

The Elusive Valley

This is my life long journey's quest,
To survey beyond from a hilltop crest;
To find a vale where peace abides,
And nature's elusive valley hides.

One day I will discover this dale,
While hiking along some hidden trail.
The valley will open before my eyes,
Green rolling hills will reach the skies.

High against blue sky eagles soar,
Their shadows will drift on valley floor.
The morning sun will dip its face,
And caress the Earth with warm embrace.

I'll hear a brook's cascading sound,
As it meanders over rocky ground.
A whisper echoes on the wind,
"Come, let your spirit be free again."

When I find this peaceful glade,
My quiet retreat 'neath oak trees' shade
I'll rest on cool moss-covered sod,
And feel ever secure and close to God.

   LaVerne Moss

Rememberings

Long ago rememberings
Still echo in my ear.
Calls of the driver hauling junk,
"Old rags, old iron,"
"Old rags, old iron,"
Today sound just as clear in my ear.

A peddler came and
Called his wares;
He sold fresh fruits and veggies.
But the calls of the driver hauling junk,
"Old rags, old iron,"
Remain forever clear in my ear.

   Eve Schultz

The Tears

To Carol, Kenneth, Roy—with love, Mom
I cried today for all the things,
That I could never do.
To give my children so many things,
That only money could buy.
I gave them love, and dreams to dream,
And hopes to replace the fears and tears.
But the things I couldn't give them,
Were such costly ones to buy.
A steak, perhaps a pot roast, a dress, or shirt,
Or shoes, or socks, were not the things,
I gave my little tots.
Just love and hope and dreams to dream,
Because they were free.
I paid for them with love, that I had plenty of.

   Vanna Marberry

A Siren's Song Was Sung

To my Siren and love, Mara Kelley
A Siren's song was sung
Capturing the focus of my stare
Revealing a woman without compare
Perhaps a mythic dance has begun

Just notes, yet an affinity
I must fight, cannot submit
Myself alone I commit
Against this sense of infinity

The song inspires, yet defeats
Within me, around me
Close enough to be free
Yet near enough to retreat

I can resist with all my might
Yet the song still consumes
A feeling of myself resumes
Perhaps there is no reason to fight

No rope thick enough to restrain my fear
A separate form, but one
I am beaten, yet undone
The song becomes clear

David K. Morse

Don't Cramp My Style

You can't blame it on the song
When things go wrong.
You can't blame it on the rhymes
When it's a sign of the times.

Music is a reflection, you see,
Of the world around you and me.
To censure my thoughts and feelings is wrong.
It's makin' it hard to write this song.

There's no denying evil exists in this life,
But so do love and anger and strife.
From this panorama of creativity,
Here's my message for humanity.

In a free society,
We must honor creativity.
If you silence one voice,
There's no free choice.

In writing this I'm reaching out.
I'm trying to tell you what I'm about.
I desperately want my voice to be heard,
And I don't want you to cut a single word.

Rita Siermala-Hanley

Kudos for Gefilte Fish

The four-year-old arrived at his grandparents
Apartment and nature called.
He was about to sit on the commode when he was
Distracted by a fish leaping in the bathtub.

He scampered off the seat and leaned on the
Wall of the tub, only to be greeted by an
Armada of open-mouthed fish hustling for manna.
He ran to his mother and announced, "Bubby
Has an 'acarion' loaded with great fishees."

The woman was well aware of her son's experience,
Since it was an indulged ritual, for the thirty
Years of her life span, in preparation for the
Passover Holidays. She reached for the boy's hand
And said, "Lead me to the aquarium, Jacob."

Once there, she saw the wonderful Pikes, Carps,
Mullets, and White fish. She was certain this
Champion array would elicit raves as prepared
Gefilte Fish for the Seder dinner.

Willoughby Albin

Witness

Above me billowing, bold, and bright,
A luminous cloud grows in my sight.
The wonder, mastery, changeling spreads
Above our thoughts and trees and heads.

I wonder what that mystery sees
As he climbs higher, contrary to breeze
Or bird or flash of coming storm,
Changing color, changing form.

Below the brilliant crown that glows
Lies a darkening heart predicting woes,
And a shadowy form that takes the shape
Of a silent watcher we can't escape.

Does he know of what is to come;
Does he see storms greater than some
Would ever imagine, so far from here
On a green isle divided by fear?

Three young, sleeping candles' innocent flames
Will be snuffed out . . . an act that shames.
Whatever reason, if any there be,
To continue holy hate and disharmony.

Delores Meder

Tender Feelings I Feel for You

To my husband, for his love and support
Here you go again, with your soft, easy lines,
And all these lines become lies.
Because of the lies, I don't want any ties.
You try to put me up there in the skies because of my
"Tender feeling I feel for you."

You make me feel like I really belong,
But now it seems to be so wrong.
Years back I did belong,
For I felt our love could be strong because of my
"Tender feeling I feel for you."

You say that you want to try again.
How much would we gain?
For I cried so many tears in vain.
All my tears sound like the rain because of my
"Tender feelings I feel for you."

You said you love me; I was so happy I could scream.
Pictures of us linger, eyes full of gleam.
Now it's all gone; it's come apart at the seams.
What does this mean, like a forgotten dream because of my
"Tender feelings I feel for you."

Sharon K. Burke

Two Bibles

Two bibles were seen by me.
One still looked like new and,
Not one well-worn page could I see.
On a beautiful table this bible was used as
A lovely centerpiece.
It was surrounded by candles and lace.
What a honored position was this place.
All those who entered the room saw this lovely sight.
But no one, not even the owner, saw the true "Light."
The second bible I saw was torn and tattered.
I could tell this bible was used for more than show.
Well-worn pages opened to scriptures that mattered.
The owner loved the living words within, I know.
Looking closer, I could almost see fingerprints,
As page after page had been turned.
The pages had been caressed with tears and love.
Words of comfort flowed easily, as if guided from above.
Tears stains from many battles, marked many a verse.
So I now ask, which bible resembles yours?

Terri McElhaney

Man of My Dreams

One day, I hope to find
A man whose heart will be totally mine,
Someone whom I've known in past lives,
Heart of my heart, soul of my soul.

I've only seen him in my dreams,
A man so wonderful and so dear.
My soul is connected to his soul,
With a love that stretches to Heaven's shore.

I search daily each man's face,
Hoping to find my dream love.
Heart of my heart, soul of my soul,
How much longer must I wait?

Days go by and still I wait;
My dreams are becoming quite real.
I see him, he is here . . .
But then I awake.

Lucy Baca Catano

Screwdrivers, Scissors, and Knives

Screwdrivers, scissors, and knives, you know,
can be very dangerous tools.
Old people need to carry them,
but it's against the rules.

The kid-proof caps and bottle tops
keep children safe, I'm told.
But screwdrivers, scissors, and knives
are the tools of the old.

With old and stiff arthritic hands,
the caps get pretty tough.
Those foil tops are something else—
I've really had enough.

A screwdriver can poke holes,
the knives will make a slot,
and scissors will help with anything
that aged hands cannot.

Old people really need these things;
they just might save their lives.
That's why the tools of the old
are screwdrivers, scissors, and knives.

Carol Meier

Twin Pins

To my loving twin, Ernestine I. Nelson Hyland
Daddy's worried frown became a very joyous grin
As doc announced, "Your wife delivered twins!"

Two individuals entered life, unique as they could be;
Different bodies, size, looks, but same personality!
Thus began our role in life, divided now by two—
Unison loving trust, sharing of everything we do.

Outsiders are astonished, much to our delight.
Loving words on our lips, we never seem to fight!
Whenever one's in crisis, the other feels it all;
Before they get to the phone, the other one will call!

Through diapers, teenage fads, and adulthood alike,
We shared work, play, and things like a long hike!
We shared dreams, schemes, activities like skates,
And there were times in life we even shared our dates!

People say we laugh, think, and even act the same.
They look at us in wonder; to us, it's just a game!
Our plans get interwoven; most of them do succeed.
Whenever one's in crisis, the other feels their need.

Although life's path has led us, in distance, miles apart;
Thoughts and love in unison are shared—within our heart!

Emmalene I. Nelson

I Remember

I don't want to lose them, you see.
They are seeping away.
Slowly, slowly, sweet memories.

Do I want to remember the pain?
How can the joy remain?
So very tightly, closely woven.

Roses have thorns, bees sting with honey
I listen for the sound of
Words that were softly spoken.

Maureen A. Radle

Homeless Angel

Sitting in the corridor, there by the subway.
A filthy face with tattered clothes,
yet you stood out among the rest.
There seemed a glow about you,
which attracted my curiosity.
You were a homeless angel.
As I listened, your words encouraged me.
I learned more about life
in a few moments from your pain,
then an education could ever supply me.
At the end of my lesson,
I paid my respects as I turned to walk away.
Once more, I looked to see your glow.
Vanished, you were gone.
Truly a homeless angel.

Tanya L. Wells

My Solid Friend

I've always claimed you as my best friend.
There are countless ways you have proven so.
You'll probably be here at my very end,
For I will never say, "you have to go."

There are times on you I bare to God my soul.
Other times I put you through abuse.
Many times you've helped me reach my goal,
And when need be help me pen a good excuse.

With your support I pay my bills on time.
With your support I keep in touch with friends.
With your support I compose my little rhymes.
With your support I give instead of lend.

On you runs rampant my imagination.
On you I close my eyes to rest.
On you I gather information.
On you I strive to give my best, my solid friend,
   my desk.

W. Anna D. Kamas

Daddy

Adrift and alone amid turmoil and strife
With naught to anchor my wayward life
I miss the rock that kept me stable
My leaning post, always there, always able.
I yearn for the strength that billowed my sails,
The unconditional love by which all else pales.
So many the years gone so swiftly by
Still deep in the night I sit and cry,
Naught I have found to replace what you gave
Nor anything that would this emptiness stave.
Love, hate and anger . . . hand in hand
Before a cold marble stone now stand.
Memories echo without a sound.
A body . . . a box . . . a plot of ground . . .
My mind becomes a swirling tormented sea,
Had only that body laid to rest have been me.

B. J. McKee

Are You Involved?

Hello there!
Have you gotten involved in anything or anyone?
What about marriage?
Before getting involved did you think about your baby carriage?
How many you might see in your home?
Did you think about expenses and all kinds of difficult problems
you may not be able to solve?
But regardless, you just wanted to get involved.
What about credits, loans, buying a new house?
You may receive bills so often which might scare you
  like a scary mouse.
What about a new car?
When you receive your bills, don't get drunk at a bar.
Are you involved with a lot of friends?
How fortunate you are!
Loving, trustworthy, and kind,
These folks are hard to find.
What about your neighbors?
If a devastating storm would occur,
  would our neighbor say, stay with me.
I love you and her.
Involvement means displaying discernment and love.

  A. V. Little

A Tear Falls

Staring into the pale, lit sky
As the colors begin to show,
I think of the times I had with you.
Thinking of the times we had,
A tear comes to my eye,
Knowing now, that there will never be
a "we" once more.
While a tear falls down my cheek,
I wonder of what went wrong.
From all the happy moments to all the dark ones,
We were always one.
Now it can never be.
For you have left me alone,
in this cold, dark world.
A tear falls to the ground.

  Maria De Los Angeles Santiago

Alonelinest

A fresh blanket of snow untrod upon except by one;
No trail forward, just back where your journey's begun.

A table with place setting, not for two, but for one;
The chores of the household, by you daily are done.

At the theatre you wait and embrace the dark;
Misty-eyed, watching others' children play in the park.

Watching couples laughing, and smiling, as they walk hand-in-hand;
Or the waves as they eat away your castle of sand.

Thoughts and dreams, that never are said;
As there's no one to share with, just echo in your head.

  Ronald C. Brown

Gaia's Symphony

Night settles in and darkness envelops me like a shroud.
Silver white whispers beam down from Hecate as she grins
her contented menace in the murky black of eve.
As conductor of Gaia's earthly orchestra, she marks a downbeat
and the coyote's howls sing across the distance of a continent
to grip the hearts of weak mortals with alarm.
Fear is not the intent of these natural predators,
so unappreciated by spineless wastrels of humanity.
Their howls bear unearthly sadness to their mother on the wind,
And she responds in kind.
The breeze shifts and the waters murmur the quiet conversations
of the Earth mother and the goddess of the moon,
Breath for breath the keepers of life.

  Brooke Gilman

Vieve

With merely words at our command to tell our thoughts today,
We find they do not measure up for what we want to say.

We want to say we like Vieve Gore; she's high in our esteem.
She's been with us for forty years, a leader of the team.

We marvel at her grace and charm, her purpose, strength, and poise,
Her way of getting at the task without a lot of noise.

We treasure most her helping hand to make a job well done,
And many hearts will skip a beat among the friends she's won.

These things we say of Veive today in words that are sincere,
But words alone can never tell how much we like her here.

  Robert Lyall

Winter Snow

Wouldn't it be beautiful if snow came down
Till it was deep all over town?
If cars and buses could not move,
We would have a holiday from school.
Wouldn't it be great if it began to sleet,
And we could slide all over the street?
If we saw our postman sliding down the hill,
And he brought our mail to the window sill?
All this might happen very soon,
And we could play all afternoon.
If we woke tomorrow and this had begun,
What a wonderful day to have fun.

  Grace S. Pick

Peace

While walking down a trail thinking about peace
I heard music, wondering if it would ever cease
I gazed upward to the sky and felt a gentle breeze
I could feel a presence amidst the swaying trees
The birds were singing, I knew I was not alone
The river was flowing, I felt a peace I had never known
My heart was beating fast as I fell to my knees
As I knelt in silence, an eagle soared with ease
Then I heard a voice as I closed my eyes in prayer
It said, "Fear not, my child, I am near, I am everywhere
You are a lamb amidst my flock, I will not lead you astray
Just believe in me, I will guide you on life's highway
If your love is true and your faith in me is strong
I will walk with you, talk with you all day long
No more sorrow or strife will be, just peace and unity
There will be joy, happiness, and glory in eternity"

  Jeanette M. Johnson

Walking through the Darkness

To my greatest blessings: George, Kenny, my grandchildren, family
I know there's many out there
Who can testify with me;
The journey seems forever
As we take down tree by tree.
I feel I'm in the center
Of a forest with no light;
I panic and I stumble,
For worthless is my sight.
I beg, I pray, "Lord, help me."
Feel your presence with me here.
Send a sign, touch my heart.
Please take away my fear.
When I allow the doubts to come,
Fears follow close behind.
Next, my faith gets challenged;
Now fear controls my mind.
Then, suddenly, a voice not mine
Consumes my every thought;
It says, "I've never, ever left you yet."
Stop! . . .
"Let me be, God."

  Constance L. Horner

I Send You These Things

I send you happiness, your day to start
I send you roses, straight from my heart

I send you the best songs anyone can sing
The memory of nature's songs in early spring

I send the warmth of a sunny day
The sweetness of the air after the rain's gone away

I send the beauty of the prettiest flowers
The contentment of seeing nature's powers

I send you the wonder of an innocent child
That unquestioning faith when everything is wild

But, most of all, because you're my mother
I send you the love that I have for no other

Bonnie Jean Hern

Jonny

In loving memory of Jonathan Daddona
The days pass one by one,
each just as hard as the other one.
Some days I struggle to make sense,
others I wonder why such a mess?
I miss you Jonny every day, especially while I pray.
Many years have passed since the day you left,
back to God you are now.
Forever you shall be close to the hearts of all your family.
God gave you to us to love and inspire,
you made us laugh you made us cry, you taught us how to smile.
I miss you Jonny now and forever, someday
I'll see you again in Heaven we'll be together forever.

Amber Rose Ferratto

My Punishment

What have I done so very wrong
To deserve such a harsh punishment?
To feel as though I am cursed.
To give so much and yet receive so little.
To love yet feel unloved.
To hurt and feel so many things,
To have so much to say and yet
be at a loss for words.
No threat, physical, or verbal abuse
Can pain as badly as when one feels abandoned.

Maria Nargi

Daddy's Girl

To my Daddy, Jack Warcup
It came as no surprise to me
When I decided on my man,
He would have the grace and charm
Like my dear daddy has.

He'd have large hands with a gentle touch
That would wipe away my tears.
He'd always have the tender words
To quiet all my fears.

He'd have the twinkle in his eye
And the joy in every smile.
He'd hold me close yet give me room
And love me all the while.

He'd whisper secrets in my ear
That only we would share.
And never would I wonder
How much he really cared.

Daddy, I have found a man
Who's given me his world.
He loves me now as you did then
When I was Daddy's Girl.

Sandra W. Graves

Mamika, Timeless Love

My mother, when she was a child she was a strange little person
Didn't like her hands dirty or grit of sand on her feet
As a teenager was sent away from her poor house
to live with her mothers friend, to become what she already was
Prissy and a lover of "fine things." Married as a young woman, she
went through tribulations of children war and escape
A real beauty in flesh and soul,
Helping not only us but other poor souls
As a mature woman, gentleness caressed her once more,
She was carrying a boy. Now winter approaches
    with aches, pain, and more
Still beautiful and gentle, I love my mother, her life is a glow.
A Gyerekeid magyon szeretnek.

Susana E. Bereczky

Bosnia

Once beautiful streets
are spattered with the blood of thousands,
dumped into open graves,
forgotten by the world.

My grandfather walked here
where the blood drips into my own heart
and oozes out again.

Spirits huddle in doorways
as the bullets rain down
on rows of brown suitcases
waiting to leave Srebrenica.

Deborah Kalain-Spears

An Olympic Queen

A tribute to Miss Dominique Dawes, U.S. Olympic team
She's known the world over
With style and grace
An athletic performance
With sophisticated taste

She flies, tumbles, rolls, and jumps
The peoples are amazed at the performance she gives
I would guess but to think the frustration it seems
For a woman of color to aspire to be queen

Her name will ring out through the history of time
Of a beautiful black woman
Who's etched deeply in our minds
And though we may crave for the Olympic queens of our day
We wish them all good fortune and good will for being brave

You've been an inspiration . . . congratulations

Elmer J. Wilson

Injured Child

God gives us many trials, and though you may protest,
It's He who controls the waves and when we reach the crest.
When we scale those mountains, struggling all along the way,
The top provides a better view of this, our new day.
When we descend the valleys and seek the depths so low,
Then our perspective changes, and so we come to know.
Whether you are high or low, each has its special place.
Each different situation requires another pace.
Perhaps before you hadn't found that you had the time
Or lacked the energy necessary for the climb.
Comes the opportunity to stop and show you care
And the need to let your feelings out and so laid bare.
Perhaps you needed this chance just to sit and talk
Or stay in silence and hold your hands as you walk.
As you sit, heart in hand, beside his hospital bed,
Seeing your broken child and feeling so much dread,
Come to know some pure thankfulness as it all is well.
He is alive, you both are there, the rest time will tell.
Friends and family gather 'round to lend support and love,
And we're sure God and Angels, too, are watching from above.

Phoebe W. Abbott

Remember When

Dear ones, I hear you're on your way
To catch up a plane to Vegas today;
And I wouldn't object if, while you're there,
You'd win a mil' and return and share.
But, my dears, while money's always nice,
Here's just a bit of a mother's advice;
Take each minute, while you're there,
To please each other and each moment share.
Your love means more than wealth and fame,
So touch each other's heart—that's the rules of the game;
And later in the day, when it's time to dine,
Find a romantic spot that's quiet and divine,
Order a glass of wine, so as to toast
The one that each of you love the most.
When looking into each other's eyes,
The love looking back will be no surprise;
Cherish that moment to press in your mind,
To look back on, at another time.
And down the road, when hurt feeling move in,
You can say to each other, "Remember When?"

Dean L. Jones

Last Good-byes

He turned to say his last good-byes,
Then left us for awhile.
But I will see him on that day
When Jesus comes to take me home,
When all my tears will be swept away,
And I will not have to hear anymore last good-byes.

Laura Egli

Dragon Flight

The dragon soaring in the full moon light
In search of the demon to defeat in a fight
To bring on the angel of death and stir the four winds
To carry out a prophesy of old
The coming together of two foes
The light against the darkness
A fight 'til the end.

Wings spread, the search goes on
The demon in wait for the right place and when
To snatch a soul unaware
Through lies and deceit to lure that soul
To Hell's fire where there's no escape to burn through eternity.
The eye of the dragon focused on the demon's snare
Dived to face the demon in the air
The demon took to flight to face the dragon with all his might
The dragon drawing his power from the most high
Struck down the demon and sent him back below
No foe can face the dragon of light and win
Because he's filled with eternal light from above.

Rev. Jerry Wenger

Release

Frost hangs heavily upon the trees,
Coated in ice on branches and leaves.
Majestic they stand in thin white array,
As twilight moves in at the end of day.
Silently they stand watch over the night,
Groaning with their burden until daylight.
As the sun rises and warmth appears,
The trees shed their coats with big drops of tears.
As the ice melts, and the trees come to life,
They shed their burden, as well as their strife.
Is this a lesson we all should know,
Are our burdens as heavy as the ice and the snow?
When despair hangs heavily and one wants to flee,
We should go to our Father on bended knee.
As we groan with problems and many fears,
Our Father sees our big drops of tears.
And as the ice breaks from our very soul,
The love of our Father makes us whole.

Phyllis Wagoner

The Good Old Days

The good old days, what were they really like?
A mystery to me, I've heard it from my dad and he from his.
When I was very young, I tried to learn
What they were about but never could.
I did as I was bid.
So the thought became dormant; hibernating
in my silent brain. But as I moved along
to become husband, father, and grandfather,
each day was a candidate.
As fate proscribed most were good, better, or best.
Some were bad, not worth the time or a thin dime.
Tragedy stalked out its post, bending mind some, but spirit most.
These days don't qualify; we throw them out,
for the injuries cause wounds that forever hurt.
The good old days come from the better and best,
recalled in memory's easy test.
They were happy; we learn that good days are both new and old.
The mind discards the bad and we live the good new days,
until they become the old.

Jean Howard Webster

Kaddish

Time since the first Adonai you have been
Even here in these barracks, so grim
Concrete buildings loom in the distance ahead
To our deaths we are all being led
Surrounded by panic, gasping with fear
In a trancelike state, my words ring clear
Who will say Kaddish for me when I am dead?
No passage from Torah for us to be read
Another's hand slips into mine
A lever sounds the metal chime
Gas forms a mist between our eyes
Regardless, though, our lights still shine
Our last few breaths in Adonai we trust
We speak you here to be with us
Now traveling forward in space and time
Decades beyond this hellacious crime
Every year, on one spring day
Sometime during the month of May
Hear Kaddish, my child, for you
Being spoken by one million Jews

Kathryn Kauffman

For My Darling

My darling, please don't sit and weep over me,
For I'm still here, in your heart.
Just remember that I love you!

Shawna Kristine Wagner

Wondering Why

So long ago I wondered why you loved me,
I'm as stubborn as I can be!
You keep telling me to be good
As if I never would or could.
Now I'm wondering why.

The night you gave me your class ring
I thought I heard an angel sing.
The love for you so deep in my soul,
I was afraid to let go
Now I'm wondering why.

You came home over the holiday.
I wished that you could forever stay.
You gave me the sweetest gift
It gave my heart quite a lift.
Now I'm wondering why.

I wear your rings, but not in heart
Our quarreling ways are tearing me apart.
Since you say I don't love you
And claim I'm being untrue.
Still, I'm wondering why.

Jannell Howell

The Spit Suckin' Blues

What do I do, now that my job makes me sick and
I've never done anything else?
For twenty years now, I've had this career
it's how I identify myself
I know that I'm at a fork in the road
But I don't know which path I should take
I've loved helping people take care of their teeth
and to lose that old dental chair shake.
I've given my hand, my smile and my trust
this career and I really did fit
The only good thing about leaving it now is,
I'll no longer have to suck spit!

Beverly M. H. Kremer

Sharing Life with You

To my wonderful husband, Peter
Time has passed
And our love is still strong
Our lives have changed
But our hearts will always belong

Life can bring many surprises
Along the road to where?
No one really knows, but
I know with me, you'll be there

Our love has grown
Through good times and bad,
We've built lots of memories
Of special times we've had.

A husband so unique and talented
Doesn't come along every day
I don't know where life's path will take us
But our hearts will show us the way.

Liz Fumo II

The Midst

What I've given thee 'tis all of me
And there is nothing left to lay wayside.
Like a newborn's faith do I wait decision,
Grieving words to balance the truth and lies.
The simple place I once felt safe
Mocks my weakness to know thee there.
Even I speak fool when my reflection's cast,
But speak thy name I do not dare.
If it is indeed by Heaven
That I have come to seek thee out,
Then by Hell shall I have rendered
Desperate tears that felt my doubt.
Struggles gaze upon questions asked
And deeper still no answers lie.
That thou hast not even spared my heart
To know if thou hast given thine.
Know this then, forever I'll love
Not one so completely as thee.
For, to or not is neither life nor death.
Yet in both shall this love burn within me.

Robin Sunde

Moods

A disheartening mood settled on my brow
Like the weight of a ship, settling on its bow
A myriad of thoughts running hither thither
Some heavy as anvils, others light as a feather
All the thoughts spread wide from left to right
Leaving me with no clue of an opinion for tonight
My wants and needs are caught in a jumble
A wholly unhindered stumbling tumble
When my thoughts return upright
I wonder what's on your mind tonight

Edward Lynch

The Sea of Living Waters

To my loving parents, Harden Green and Mary Etta Rorrer Cochran
In the beginning was a tiny spring head
That formed at the Mountain's peak,
So cool and fresh, clean and pure,
As it flows on down to the sea,

As it finds its way,
Through trees, slopes, and terrains,
And begins to widen as it travels
From other springs, creeks, and rains.

Its use is great for people to take
As is needed for many chores;
The water picks up many things;
That's not useful for any shores.

But it keeps on traveling
As it gets meander, deeper, and wider
And sometimes finds some fallen travelers
And picks them up along the by ways.

Soon it gets to be a river
With a sandy bottom to filter the matter
As it goes to the sea "For fishers of men"
In the "Sea of living waters."

Addie C. Hartkopf

Is It Hopeless?

"Help me," those words came from my mouth and my heart,
but no one was around to assist me.

"Provide for me," I said,
but it seemed no hand was there to care for me.

"Answer me today," but really,
I did not need to hear anything today.

I rested in silence, my mind thinking of all
the issues that grieved my heart.

Around me it was quiet, only the outside
sounds came in from my bedroom window.

At that moment it came to me . . . love is all
I really need.

The love from the One above is when all help,
providence, and answers will be fulfilled.

I didn't understand it all,
but a peace now became real.

Lorrie M. Schasiepen

My Hero

To my dad, who has always cared, Don Merchant
I once saw a man frantically jump fences
To warn a neighbor of a threatening fire.
I saw that same man give a woman in need
More than the help that she asked.
I again heard of that man traveling to another country
To help others in the best way he could.
I have also seen that man love his family,
Asking nothing in return.
That man once frightened me when he lay on the ground
And I thought of losing him.
Was this man a hero?
Or a famous figure?
Fame was not his goal.
Only to care for those around him . . . and far away.
As for a hero? Yes . . .
He is mine.
I know the man who did these things.
Yes, I know this man . . .

He's my dad!

Matthew P. Merchant

Melody of Verse Praise—One

I love the Lord, what can I say?
He's blessed me yet—another day.
This bonus day has not been used,
An excellent opportunity to share the "Good News."

When I was sick, bound by sin,
My precious Savior took me in—
Forgave my sins and cleansed my soul.
One day I'll walk on streets of gold.

I love the Lord, I do indeed!
He gives me everything I need.
When Satan tries to spoil my mood,
My Lord offers me a new attitude:
When he attempts to steal my happy thunder,
I take God's Word and ground him under.

I love the Lord, indeed I do!
If you knew the Savior, you'd love Him, too.
Why not try Him, friend, just taste and see.
His love and grace will set you free!

He gave His life on Calvary's tree—
For sin-sick souls—like you, like me.

Priscilla D. Washington-Davis

I'll Be Back

Although, my dear, I'm far away,
I will be back to you some day.
So count the days and please don't cry,
'Cause I'll be back by and by.

I think of you both night and day.
I love you more than words can say.
And to you, my darling, whom I love so dear—
Although I'm far away, your heart is here.

I came here, dear, to help them win.
I've learned to take it on the chin.
I've trained until I have got tough.
I'm not afraid when things get rough.

And through it all you helped me out.
You gave me the courage when I got in doubt.
So put aside your grief and woes,
I'll get back safe from these wicked foes.

And cheer up, dear, it won't be long.
I know we'll win and right the wrong.
So remember, my darling, there's always a way,
And I'll be back some sunny day.

E. James Toliver

Dry

The rain falls,
Drip drip.

Why are you crying?
This I would like to know.

Did I do something wrong?
Why are you upset?
Did I make you angry?

I know I have sinned,
But, God, please don't cry.

I am sorry for anything I have done,
And anything anyone else has done.

The rain falls,
Drip drip.

I shall know that you have forgiven us when the rain stops
and the sun is up,
shining above to dry our tears.

The rainfall stops,
Drip by drip.

Christine Neto

Laughter-Filled Halls

When you're still and you listen quietly,
you can hear the laughter of the children.
What a joy it brings to your heart.
You can hear Tommy, Billy, Susie, and Donnie as they play.
The years have gone by, and the children have all left.
Sometimes when you are quiet and listen with your heart,
you can hear the laughter that filled these halls,
with the shouts of joy from excited children as they run and play.
Tomorrow is a new day, and the grand children will be here.
Once again laughter will fill these halls,
with young children at play.
If you listen quietly with your heart,
you can hear the laughter that filled these halls.

Gary D. Buck

Matt

I told you I loved you and you said the same.
My heart soars every time you whisper my name.
I've loved you since the first time we met.
Our love is something I will never regret.
I love you more than words can say.
I love you more and more every day.
I love your eyes, your smile, your face.
Nobody in the world could ever take your place.

I'll love you forever,
I'll think of you my whole life.
Every moment of every day.
I love you.

Jennifer Olsen

Ultimate Act of Love

As I looked up at Him
with a back drop of the sky,
As I saw Him in pain,
tears fell from my eyes.
As I looked up and saw this man,
a chill went down my spine.
As I saw the nails in His hands,
I clinched mine.
As I looked up at Him against the blackened sky,
I fell to my knees
as I heard him cry:
"Father forgive them;
they know not what they do."
As I watched him,
He breathed his last breath.
Somehow I knew
the son of God would not be bound by death.
As I remember the love in his eyes,
I turn my eyes above; I look to the sky
and thank God for His ultimate act of love.

Daniel Mason

Berth

Sailor
Bytes rotate area inside noggin.
Bells ring as integrals nag.
Bright room awake instinctive nature.
Brilliant rainbows arc interior nest.
Bommer rebels at intense nail.
Brief rest activate intense node.
Bawling roar animate inactive nanny.
Brief reach acquire interesting node.
Bean roam around inky network.
Bright realm atop intense nose.
Bouquet restore animal instinctive need.
Balls rotate around ingenuous nook.
Big retainer assays increasing numbers.
Bits reveal an intriguing net.
Bubble retains articles insuring navigation,
Sail her.

Roger K. Morris

The Umbrella Prayer

Longing to cover humankind,
Divide myself, grant all a part.
Needy, ill, abused, all I find,
Offer a benevolent heart.

Looking through the wretched windows.
Read obituaries and grieve.
Anguished, struggling, and filled with woes,
The endless crying I perceive.

My wallet funds a poor man's bank.
My house gives the homeless shelter.
My time restores the elder's rank.
Pouring compassion, a swelter.

Overwhelming, a tiresome toll,
Earnestly craving to touch all.
I realize with a bleeding soul,
My vast intentions are too small.

Dear Lord, open your umbrella, please.
There are drenched sheep in despair.
Call more troops 'til the torrents ease.
Many are in need of your care.

Nancy A. Cunningham

Passing Scene of a Day in the Garden

Flowers in the Garden
Nod and gently sway.
Glad morning breaks across the lawn;
It is the dawn of a new-made day.

A splash of golden sunshine
Steals its way to the heart of a bower,
Where rustling brown and russet birds
Chirp a greeting to the early hour.

There's evidence of scurryings
Among vines and rocky cover,
As small creatures nibble and munch
In verdant even clover.

Straightforward passes noontime;
Onward saunters the day;
While beneath the leaves of ancient trees
An arising of errant breezes invites the shadows to play.

The garden's evening movements grow still
Like a dream that has come to an end.
Dawn's return is awaited in the garden's soul
Like a longed-for, expected friend.

Catherine M. Piper

The Perfect Man

If I had a baby boy, I'd proudly name him after you.
The first time you held me in your arms,
I knew right then you were the one.
'Cause, you are all and everything that a man should be.
You are all and everything in a man I need to see.
You're the perfect man for me.

You make this woman proud when you enter my room.
You are magic, ooh, pure magic,
A magician can't touch you.
You're like three good men wrapped up into one.
My leader, My overseer
And I wanna, wanna be the one.

You make this woman proud.
I'm on a throne, I'm on a cloud.
'Cause you're God's plan in motion,
Inviting me to stay awhile.
You're the perfect man, the perfect man,
The Perfect Man for me.

Sylvia Gordon

Chrysalis

I walked along that tarmac of leafy greenness,
knowing that all along while others were there
Hovering around me, dancing and loving life,
I was alone in my journey, oblivious to fan fare.

The warm arms of morning sun chased away the dew
Which threatened the very womb for which I spun and toiled.
For each fragile thread covered a piece of my lonely sordid past;
Suspended in time and place, purgatory unspoiled.

God created another road for my restless spirit,
When songs of life seeped through my fabric of death.
Faith tugged the sleeve of courage to break me from contentment;
The sabbatical of self pity ended in bated breath.

I broke loose from those sticky old walls of what was,
Imagine my surprise when I reached out to the sky,
And basked in the glow of a gallant new heart.
I had wings! I found freedom! I was able to fly!

I met others who journeyed as I once did from below.
Now full of color, and dancing, and living our best.
Gathering for the great exodus flight, southward, smarter,
Winking at chrysalises, knowing each is unaware they too are blessed.

Angela Tretina Loda

Other Eyes

I see through eyes of many shapes,
set in the faces of rainbows.
I drift from one world to the next,
never stopping to take a rest.
My mind moves always without a break,
taking risks that were never mine to take.
I lose myself in a world of dragons
and find myself riding on a caravan wagon.
I soar across the sky on wings,
and see both wonderful and horrible things.
I pass through portals of distance and time,
living in worlds that were never mine.
I am a soldier on a battle front.
I am an actor doing a stunt.
I am a unicorn prancing with glee.
I am a magical pixie.
I've fought on both sides of every war.
I've listened to tales of every lore.
I have been the dragon, and I have been the knight.
I've been the hunter and the bird in flight.

Heather Weeks

Flying (Above the Courtyard)

For my muse, Lee Diane, who has inspired me always
Urgency overcomes me
Run, run, run
Huffing, puffing, aimlessly
Cardiac arrest
Circle the boundaries of the courtyard
You can get in easily, but you can never leave
Spirits stir the cauldron—Monsters, all
Only wings will save me now
It's a labyrinth of energy
With no release and no reprieve
Climb, climb, climb
But the footing is much too shaky and unstable
Let it slide, for the moment
And try again, another time, another place
Escape is imminent, but impossible in this dimension
This courtyard has no entrance
And the price you pay to exit is much too high
Hungry wolves know exactly how to survive
. . . I've found my way around the maze
Now it's time for me to fly!

Jim Barker

Hooray for Birthdays

Birthdays come and birthdays go;
gray hair and wrinkles start to show.
Gravity begins to exact its tolls,
turning our tummies into jelly rolls.

Middles get bigger and bigger around.
Bottoms get closer and closer to the ground.
Shoulders get stooped, legs get looped;
other things get drooped and everything gets pooped.

Slim and Trim become Grim and Dim.
Brag and Stag become Bag and Sag.
Chic and Slick become Crick and Hick.
Sleek and Unique become Creak and Antique.

And the list could just go on and on
'til it would make us moan and groan.
But enough of this gloom and doom.
Let's look for some plume and bloom.

Onward and upward may our birthdays climb,
onward and upward for a long, long time.
Hooray for birthdays! Let's cheer them on!
For without them, we would all be gone.

James Rex Sowell

Dreams and Beaches

To Ann Evridge, an education in the Arts is priceless
Walking on a warm beach
In the soft rain, yet, the sky is blue,
As if it were about to end . . .

Wearing long, soft gauze
That feels like a caress
When the ocean breeze blows it against my skin . . .

Turning my face toward the clouds
When the sun appears
Now and then, a pink, gray, or purple ray . . .

Vanishing as my eyes catch them,
Then, reflected in water,
Appearing to dance as if in play . . .

Moving clouds and the drops on my cheeks
Roll down my face.
In surf and sand, they are swept away.

Shivering a little,
But not with cold . . . the dream, the beach:
They are a lie.

Aging now . . . too many dreams, beaches . . . and clouds
I can not tell rain from tears . . . No strength to try.

Linda Evridge

To Dominique with Love

To Dominique, for inspiring the poet within me
She is like a painting you cannot buy with cash.
Worthless, I think not; Her value is unmatched.
Like a family keepsake, passed down for generations,
Her beauty is timeless; it exceeds expectations.
She's like that dress in your attic that you couldn't bare to sell,
Because it fits you just right and has a story to tell.
She's like a memory from your past, burned into your eyes,
Like your very first kiss, or seeing the sun rise.
She's like that feeling you got when you knew it was true love.
Like Cinderella's glass slipper, she fits me like a glove.
She's like mother's intuition, when mom knows something is wrong.
Her face is like poetry, her voice like sweet song.
These are all moments in time, perhaps natural selection.
She's that thing you can't pay for, priceless perfection.
Whether it's a feeling, a memory, or an antique,
There's nothing you could give me, worth my Dominique. . . .

Jeremy R. McSorley

Godsend

Dear God, I hope you hear my song
What have I done that's so terribly wrong?
I'm so scared of dying this way—I can't sleep at night
I'm so tired and stressed, I can't even fight
Please God, hear my prayers
I'm getting so weak, I can't climb stairs
I need You to tell me it will be all right
I need You to hug me and hold me tight
I pray to You to send me a sign
Come into my body and my mind
Sometimes, I just want to jump out of this skin
But I know You will come, I can't give in
I believe in You and the Heaven above
But my place is here with the ones I love
Life is taken for granted, this I am seeing
Just a prayer from one human being

Richard Berntson

Ode to the Lord, My God

Because of the beauty of Thy love
I lift my voice to You above.
My Lord to Thee I pray, show me the way,
I want to follow You.

Because of the beauty of Thy wisdom,
I have decided to serve You, not to roam.
In Thee do I trust, for I will be lost,
In this sinful world.

Because of the beauty of Thy compassion
I thank Thee for Your own submission
You died for me to set me free,
So I can live forever.

Because of the beauty of Thy promise
My life is filled with joy and peace.
You arose from death and spread the mercy net,
Over a sinner like me.

Because of the beauty of Thy holy face
I turn my heart towards Thy throne of grace.
Where my soul found the goal,
To be with Thee, in blessed eternity.

Nada Gavrilovic

My Mother

My mother was my best friend
How I loved her to the end
I was the second of six girls
When we buried her with pearls
Of wisdom that she learned
Wed at sixteen, what a degree she must have earned
When I awakened, she was up
She brought me coffee in a dainty cup
It was such a little chore
Oh, how I loved it, now—no more!
Our last visit, I longed to hold her in my arms
As I sang about the charms of the everlasting arms
Just a closer walk with thee
Take my hand, precious Lord, lead me home
Peace in the valley for me, I pray
There was peace in the coma from which she passed away
I think of her in Heaven, where I hope to go someday

Evelyn G. Miles

The Gift of Gifts

Surrounded by miracles on every side:
To watch the birds that fly,
To see the sun light up the sky,
To enjoy another day under His watchful eye,
To see the unseen yet to be,
For now and all eternity.
What a gift to humanity!

Ruth E. Brokate

Life's Race

Sometimes it seems daily life is too much
With children and work and bills and such.
Never-ending problems and endless stress.
Always so weary, never stopping to rest.

Day to day living at such a fast pace.
Constantly running to stay in the race.
No time to enjoy all the things that we see.
Never thinking of others, thinking only of me.

Such a vicious circle we find ourselves in.
Slowing your pace is considered a sin.
People always wanting, never satisfied.
Relationships falter, too soon tossed aside.

Children are forced to grow up too fast.
Childhood and dreams a thing of the past.
Heartache and suffering are what most know.
Taught never to allow emotions to show.

Taught to be strong and prey on the weak.
Take what you want, to Hell with the meek!
This is the message our children have heard.
Instead of loving kindness, instead of God's word.

Donna Washburn

I Remember Mama's Prayers

James, Amin, John, Gene, and my sister Patricia
I don't know what prayers Mama prayed
But my loving God, my Father, my Redeemer
You kept all six of us
I used to look at Mama kneel down on her knees to pray
And say Lord, have mercy on my children
I use to hear Mama plead with God for her children
And my God was at the mercy seat and he
Would have mercy on anyone's name she would call out
Because he was her God and Savior
And she said I will fly away but I won't stay
I will be back one day
And he heard her cry and she waved good-bye
And this is what my Mama would say
Lord, I am weak, but Thou art strong
My Lord, my Redeemer, my Sustainer
Whom I trust with my whole heart
And this is what Mama would say
When I leave this place I will have a brand new start
Where I am free to worship my God for eternity
And I will see my Mama after a while
When my work is finished down here

Marian C. Wilson

Feelings Shine Bright

Break it down, tear it apart,
looking inside you'll know where to start.
Seeing yourself, feeling your heartbeat you will
know who you are and who to be.

That feeling can get so strong, it'll burn from
deep inside, it'll light up and make that color in your eyes.
It can take you along for quite a ride, you'll
feel it in your veins, it will make you tall and
walk with pride, so everyone can see the glow of your eyes.

You'll have the feelings others only dream about,
it will be good, it will be real.
Many things will come many will go.
These feeling will go straight through the body
and hit your soul.

Now that you realize this is for real,
follow your instincts, follow your heart.
This is just the beginning with no end in sight.
Let these feelings flow and all will see you shine
as bright as a star in the darkened night.

Steven Pettit Jr.

Another Sunset

We celebrate a place somewhere in the past
We try to find for the future to last
Another sunset
To begin again the start of a new day
Same old memories that won't go away
As they fade to surface once
More, I wake up lonely, the same as before
Another sunset
It's so easy to let time slip on by
Waiting for something that never arrives
Can we move on or is it the same?
We found a new way
Same life, different game
Another sunset
Another sunset falls from the sky
The distance has aged
Between you and I
Forget the ending
Remember the start
To last forever, this time apart

Mark Culbertson

The New Hampshire Pine Tree

The New Hampshire pine is regal, there is no other word
It is the home of the crow and many another bird
It stands in the valleys and on the hills
It withstands the summer heat and the winter chills

It can be short or tall or any height
As it sways in the breeze, either day or night
In winter, something happens that isn't very nice
Some tree limbs are broken under the burden of ice

When spring comes after the long winter freeze
You see all the damage that's been done to the trees
After spring cleaning up, it looks better than before
Then the birds come to them by the score

Then all summer you hear the crows call
It continues right on through the fall
Some people think the crow is a pest
But it is nice to hear the little ones in the crow's nest

The pine tree is different and has needles and the cone
For these two things the pine tree is well known
I'm glad we have the pine tree and living here was my fate
For New Hampshire is called the "Pine Tree State"

Lena Watts

The Darkness of Day

The days continue to become even more slow,
This fear inside me continues to grow,
The purpose of life I don't yet know.

As each day passes me by,
Another tear I sit and cry,
And a deep breath I take in and sigh.

Getting up everyday is such a strain,
It doesn't seem to be worth all this pain,
With everyday, this life feels more mundane.

My life I now feel I must take,
This move only I can make,
No longer this smile can I fake.

I cannot deal with my shrinking hope,
With this life I cannot cope,
I'm at the end of a fraying rope.

I think it's time for this life to end,
I'll leave this world with only one friend,
Especially to him my prayers I will send.

Erin Kane

My Mom

Born with beautiful, blue eyes and lovely, blonde hair
Whenever I need her, she'll always be there

Growing up for her, times were hard and somewhat a quirk
Her mother took sick, and she was forced to go to work

She met a handsome, young man, a Prince Charming, you see
He said, "What a beautiful lady, will you marry me?"

They raised all little girls, and I'm one of the six
With parents so intelligent, there's nothing they couldn't fix

Taking care of her garden in the day and, sometimes, night
Making sure that her flowers and vegetables grew just right

Our holiday dinners wouldn't be special
Without her homemade bread and pies
Smelling the aroma of something so wonderful just opens your eyes

So loving and caring, so dear to my heart
I think of her always, even when we're apart

She may not be famous, or even a star
All the goodness inside her helped to make us what we are

Now I know there are many wonderful mothers out there
But the soul love for my mother cannot be compared
For she is, oh, so special to me and will always be my mom
        Mary Anne Ventimiglia

Candlelight

The flame flickered
Beside the old woman's bed
Memories flashed with each new dance of the wick

A child's secrecy brought her misery
School activities were a welcomed escape
Bouncing a ball, no cares at all
But weekends held a different fate

Marriage was a good escape for her
Children brought new distractions
Life now had laughter, yet the darkness was always there

Prayer helped for awhile
But she never felt worthy
Old thoughts of youth banished her from happiness
As life went on the sadness deepened
But her eyes never gave her secrets away

Growing old and feeling very alone
Time ticked away along with her self worth
Growing tired of the life she'd lived
She ended it all in the flicker of the candlelight
        Sherri A. Moore

Feelings Set Free

In trials we learn so much,
We learn to keep in better touch,
In better touch with our Heavenly Father,
As we run to the throne to gather our strength.

I've discovered how marvelous our Lord really is,
That no matter how lost; Yet we still are truly His.
We wonder and go astray, and yet He is always there,
Ready and willing to forgive us, no matter when and where.

The word of God is so simple; Yet so powerful,
If we apply it to our lives; Let's remember His word,
He wants the best for us, and praise Him as our Lord.

Thank You, Lord, for all that You are.
You are ever so perfect; With not even one mar.
All Your love is everything to behold,
For God is love and love is God; This is once what I was told.

So, as we turn from our sinful ways,
Please take a moment to look and gaze,
At the marvels of God and His righteousness,
And all of His love and perfectness.
        Jeanne May Cash

Duck Feather Lane

To my husband, Mark, who is my greatest inspiration
Take a right on to duck feather lane
Follow the road to the dead end
Look to your left and what do you see?
A big sad figure in need of a friend.
The weeds grow wild on her overgrown lawn
Where children once loved to blissfully play
Her fence is rotting and falling apart
It once kept the dog from running away.
The ducks still swim in her murky pond
It doesn't seem to bother them at all
They keep her company when she feels lonely
They give her the strength to stand and not fall.
Yes, right now she is just a house
She stands there empty and alone
A family can come and make her whole
Until then only memories can make her a home.
        Rachael McRonald

The Phoenix

Rising swiftly, graceful wings
Burning cosmos, dreamlike things
Consumed yourself with burning light
Lying an ash heap through the night
Morning dawns and you awake
And once again to wing you take
The cycle begins yet again
Further defying Death's leering grin
Each day consuming yourself with your own fire
You rise everyday from the ashes of your own pyre
Immortal legend, living still
All our dreams at one time fill
Thoughts of the mighty Phoenix bird
Stories shared through music and word
Rise yet again to live your dreams
As your fiery plumage once again gleams
        Jennifer M. Bird

Action Requested

Hometowns were first established to supply folks' varied needs,
But God created country, where workers sowed the seeds.
If nourishment were provided, the weakest plants could be
Abundant, and the healthiest at their maturity.
Compare this growth to children for, with the gift of love,
Their roots are firmly planted as they breathe fresh air above.
We observe our close surroundings and assume that all is well.
We gain cars, big homes, and riches to enjoy, our neighbors tell.

"What happened to priorities?" we ask ourselves each day.
"Was the heritage that was passed to us deferred or thrown away?
Did faith and honor disappear? Did residents loose their worth?
Have virtues been discarded for luxuries here on Earth?"
We know that something's lacking; our future is not bright.
We stumble through the darkness, as we search to find the light.
Our ways prove inefficient; we have shown our spirit's weak.
God has promised to accept us, if forgiving grace we seek.

We must learn to work together for a better world to see.
It's the privilege of existence that is shared by you and me.
        Blanche Campbell Pinion

If There Were a Chance

I feel something special when I look into your eyes
I can't explain the feeling; I just don't know why
I wake up every morning with the thought of seeing you
You're always on my mind; yes, I'm talking about you
I picture us dancing to a romantic kind of band
We hold each other so closely; we take each other's hand
Every time I'm with you, my mind drifts away
Where are you and I are together far, far away
I see a chance between us, because I can see it in your eyes
I'm hopelessly falling for you; Baby, this isn't a lie
        Jose Flores

First Kiss

We sat talking on a starlit night.
It was if something had gone off inside your head.
You stopped talking, your mind seemed to go blank.
You sat looking at me.
Though it was but a few brief moments.
It seemed like an eternity to me.
Your eyes met with mine, locking together,
I could feel my heart racing, my body began to tremble.
You kissed me for the first time with intense passion.

Such a long time ago, and yet it feels like yesterday.
Many, many more kisses have been exchanged over the years.
And still, that intense passion lives.
That desire to feel your lips upon mine lives deep within me.
Even after all this time.

Tammy Coatney

I Have Survived

Dedicated to my father, Allen A. (Toby) Tobias, after the rare
chance of surviving two open heart surgeries two weeks apart
I have gone into the black abyss, my eyes were shut tight.
Angel wings fluttered by, I was going toward the light.

Someone was softly calling my name, saying,
   "We love you, we need you so!"
The Reaper was standing there so grim, saying, "C'Mon, just let go."

The pain shot through my body, I was more dead than alive.
But love and prayers pulled me through, thank God I had survived.

Death came knocking once again, His grip around me was tight.
He tried every way to get in, the darkness was engulfing the light.

My will to live was very strong, Faith once again stepped in.
My Angels held fast their post, I would not be one of Death's kin.

Yes, I have lots of scars, my recovery will take some time.
But here I am once again, by God's grace I have survived.

Ginger Tobias Holland

Eternal Rain

To my Pap
You sit alone; no one is around.
The thunder pounds; it's sound is like a beating heart.
You hear the sound of the falling rain
on your roof, and you start to slip away.
You go into a daze, and you start to dream.
The sound of the rain grasps your soul, and you can not escape.
Your imagination starts running wild;
You start to reminisce about the mistakes of your life.
The thunder is now rolling.
It's no longer like a beating heart,
but is now like a sorrowful cry of pain.
One loud clap of thunder wakes you from your dream.
The rain no longer falls,
But you remain to hear the eternal rain forever.

Brandi Kemplin

Our April Time of Life

My heart soars with the birds in the sky,
My heart sings as I read those sweet words
In your letter, that came from a seaside town.

Maestro Robin sings his songs, while raindrops waltz.
A blue jay chatters among the tender leaves.
I'll paint the words "I love you" across the April sky.
Every flower curtsies in the April breeze.

Now I'm sure that I could win, if I raced the filly
Across the meadow's rolling green.
For, this is our April time, our April time of life.
We're so full of living we'll dissolve in April moonlight.

And reappear with the waning moon in the morning sunlight.

Doris A. McClanahan

Stars

A valley of stars on a dark night
Is a river of souls with a glimmer of light.
Oh, so bright, so bright.
Oh, what a light in the night.
They look down upon the Earth
With only good thoughts in mind,
The little souls overlooking mankind,
Watching out for our spirits and hearts.
Oh, so bright, so bright.
Oh, what a light in the night
To create a path of light in a world of darkness,
To shine through all the bad, like a sword cutting through evil.
They shine so bright, like they can never die out,
To be the head light in the night,
And the steering wheel of hope and life.
Oh, so bright, so bright.
Oh, what a light in the night.

Tammy Farris

To My Grandma

Grandma's always been sweeter than any red rose.
She's always known more than anyone knows.

She's been there to talk with, to love, and to hold.
And she'll be in my thoughts, even as I grow old.

She loved me so dearly, and has cared, oh, so much.
She has made me grow together with her gentle touch.

The memories we've shared will stay in my heart.
And I'll think of them often while we are apart.

Until the day comes, I can see Heaven's door,
She'll be in my heart, soul, and mind, each day more and more.

Alissa Olsen

The Moon

Does the moon feel?
Does she look upon the Earth
with love or disgust?
Does she see how we destroy our home,
and silently hope we will learn
or simply disappear?
Is she just another rock orbiting
endlessly around us, waiting?
Waiting for what? Or is she perhaps our protector,
someone to watch over us?
Will she pick up the pieces when we self-destruct?
Or will she turn her grand head
and search for something new?
Will the Earth have another chance to begin again?
Clean the slate?
Does the moon feel?
Or will she too someday self-destruct?

Angela Nelson

Away to the Stars

When you close your eyes at the end of the day
Your mind reviews the world that surrounds you
The visions of pain burn through so clear
Let your mind lift you up and away

To the stars where their beauty can ease your pain
An innocent world that warms the heart
You can travel to a place of tranquility
Then return prepared for reality

Make your way through each and every day
Enjoy the wonders you uncover
Anticipate the time when you close your eyes
Let your mind lift you up and away

You're not ready to reside in this state
But use its powers of rejuvenation
Cleanse your thoughts, fix your soul; become whole
Make reasons for tomorrow . . .

J. L. Lang

Time

Dedicated with love to my friend Mama P., Willene Paschal
What is time?
Is it something to tax our mind,
Or merely draw the line?
Is it something that's for us,
or something to destroy us?
Is it something that we waste,
that can never be replaced?
Or something that we spend, that never, never ends?
Is it something we can measure, perhaps in our favor?
Is time a stolen moment that can never be recaptured?
Or a merely a term of laughter
to get just what we're after?
We waste time, spend time, keep time,
lose time, have periods of time.
We use it, abuse it.
We even "do time" when committing a crime.
So, at this "point of time," I'll bear in mind
as I draw attention to these last lines and again
I'll ask, "What is time?"

Dee Williams

Grandma's Kitchen

To grandmas whose hearts are as warm as their kitchens
Grandma's kitchen was full of life
at Easter, Thanksgiving, and Christmas time.
In Grandma's kitchen there was lots to do,
and there was always room for me and you.

We opened pods to remove the peas;
we used our fingers for snapping beans.
We skinned the carrots and shucked the corn;
my Grandma's ways I did adore.

Mixing batter and licking spoons,
little girl things that end too soon.
We whipped up brownies while having fun;
the gingerbread cookies were already done.

Kneading bread and baking pies,
and we iced the cakes
that I helped to make.

The fragrance of spices filled the room,
blackberries, raspberries, and cranberries, too.
Baking turkey and its dressing,
Grandma's kitchen is such a blessing.

Angela Willis

A Mother's Love

To my mom, Ruth Senter, my inspiration for this poem
It doesn't take long
For a mother's love to begin
As soon as she knows she is with child
She begins to love from within

From the moment of your birth
And continuing your whole life through
There isn't anything she wouldn't do
To keep all harm at bay from you

She will try to instruct you
In what is wrong and what is right
And she'll rush to be at your side
To give comfort in the dead of the night

She will rejoice in your happiness
She will cry with you in your sorrows
Then she'll tenderly take you in her arms
And remind you there will be brighter tomorrows

For her eyes of compassion
For her gentle touch
For her unselfish giving
Mom, I honor you, and I love you so much

Terry Jean Glenn

Understanding Nothing

To my mom and sister, thanks for everything
I don't know why I'm here.
I don't know why I can't leave.
I don't know how to trust.
I don't know what to believe.

I don't know why I still love.
I don't know why I still hate.
I don't know where I belong.
I don't know how to escape.

I don't know why I'm still with him.
I don't know why I can't move on.
I don't know how to be happy.
I don't know why I need to be strong.

I don't know why I can't worry.
I don't know what is real.
I don't know how to stop confusion.
I don't know what to feel.

I don't know why the stars shine bright.
I don't know why the sky is blue.
I don't know how to be perfect
But what I do know is . . . I still love you!

Andrea Stenseth

The Long Road Home

While making our way down the road we call life.
We often hit valleys and mountains of strife.

In not always knowing which way we should turn.
At times we seek guidance for knowledge we yearn.

It may be direction from the Lord above.
Or in family and friends for whom we do love.

Sometimes we feel lost like we've hit a dead end.
In picking up people we thought we'd be friend.

But we learn from mistakes we pass on the way.
And grow with the wisdom of each precious day.

All the miles traveled and the things we have seen.
The closer we get what does life really mean.

Up peaks and down hills all the roads they do wind.
Like heartache and passion can be so unkind.

But we forge ahead sometimes looking behind.
Hopeful for happiness, true love we will find.

Though the landscapes change every place that we go.
There is one thing we wish that we all want to know.

That at the end of it all we'll turn out fine.
Following the path of that man made white line. To Home.

Denette Krpan Palmer

Memories

To my mother and grandmother, whom I love very much
I think, as I lie here listening to the echo of thunder,
Evidence of the storm brewing outside,
I think of my family and of old friends.
Memories, as clear and bright as a shiny new penny,
Flood my mind and fill my eyes with familiar scenes.
Memories from my best friend to my first date,
Births to deaths, tears of joy and sadness.
But my most vivid are those of my mother and grandmother
I think of how much I love them
As I pull out each memory of them and examine it.
From birthdays to Christmases to summer vacations
God teaches each of my eyes and urges me to sleep now.
As I obey His command and drift off to a peaceful slumber,
I realized that, not for the first time and certainly not the last,
How much my God must love me to bless me with
Such a loving and caring family and a magnificent group of friends,
Especially such a loving mother.

Amanda Lynch

My Rose, My Love

I have delivered myself
all this time incoherently
picking weeds when initially
I had sun roses
so enthralled in finding the
one rose that lust complements
everything it represents
How long must I search through the fields?
When will I breathe in that
enticing scent?
How long must I wait to hold
my idea of perfection?

Eda Mosteller

All About You

I remember that first night we met.
You appeared by my side without warning.
It was winter and I was frozen at heart
. . . when you found me.
I couldn't see you then for who you really are,
but (thank God) you saw through me,
(with my backward fixation on the mirrors of time.)

Lost in a world of unrealized dreams,
where little is cogently what it seems,
an idealist, cast into the wilderness of
. . . Fallen Expectations.
(Driftwood in the beating desert sun,
refusing to believe it is no longer growing.)

Fear, more than arrogance, made me turn
. . . away from you then.
But your persistence shattered the mirror
and released me from my past—
To dare believe what you told me is true:
To see that my future is
All About You!

Leah S. Deming

Falling

When the spinning stops
Where will we stand?
Far apart, still hand in hand
Daylight's shifting into gear
My head is unsettled
I say the words over and over in my mind
They don't make sense to me when I say them out loud
Hoping that you might understand
Knowing that your mind might twist them around
So I carefully step around you
Blocking my thoughts with my hand
Pretending to believe
When I didn't even understand

Sarah Harper

Perpetual Adoration

By the power of the Holy Spirit, Jesus came to be.
To all priests who gave their celibate life, to humanity.
Our Almighty God dwells in the Eucharist for all to see.
Awesome Presence; of Jesus' Body, Blood, Soul, Divinity.
The Presence of our Lord Jesus, fills our hearts, with Divine grace.
For all who gaze at our Lord, in this Holy of Holy place.
Majestic Presence, of our Creator and eternity.
Sacred Heart fountain of love, overflowing infinitely.
Radiant love encompasses, our mind and soul.
Reparation for all offenses, against God's law and goals.
We pray for all souls, in the human race, living and deceased.
To accept the greatest treasure, God's love and mercy released.
"Glory be to Father, Son and Holy Spirit," my heart sings,
"Praise the Lord, for an audience, with my Supreme Royal King!"
Gift of the Holy Spirit!

Helen M. Deckler

Another World

To my family and friends for their support and inspiration
I know a place where butterflies drink the morning dew,
A place where, each and every day, life begins anew.
Here the plants and animals never hunger or thirst,
And, no matter how often I visit, each time is like the first.
Here there lives a magic creature who flies on golden wings,
And few are blessed to ever see him or hear the song he sings.
"O', King of the Pegasi, please tell me of your task!"
"I am here to bring love and joy to all who may ask.
But there's a price for such a gift—and only he or she who pays
May enjoy what I bestow for all remaining days.
My price is fair, although some may consider it too high.
I ask of them that receive to share with all who happen by.
If you agree to what I ask, I'll grant your gift today.
But heed my words, for if you fail, my gift will fade away."
"I accept your terms, fair King; on me your gift please bestow."
And over me came a peace that very few will ever know.
That was very long ago, and I'll tell you true:
The tale I tell is my way to share my gift with you.
I know a place where, every day, life gets a fresh, new start.
And to get there, you only need to open up your heart.

Alex A. Robertson

Sleepless Night

As I lie here in my bed, the night is silent,
not a sound to be heard, everyone's fast asleep except for me.
Desperately struggling to sleep, but my thoughts stroll
into never land, visualizing the day to come.
Toss and turn, no sleep to come.
As the sun rises, day comes quickly.
Tired and weary, my body, in a nervously, edgy daze.
My day of toiling is lengthy and tedious.
Hands on clock slowly tick tock.
Day is over and I visualize another sleepless night.

Betty J. Graham

Steps

Dancing by candlelight in days of old,
Holding hands with a whirl, a kick, and a hug
Now and then made hearts glow.
The fiddler with a nip from a jug at times,
Others having a good time upon a floor of pine,
A few behind in steps have left age out of view.
The young have plenty of time to step.
Still the night thrives to stay young,
Surrenders to a golden rose-tint sky.
Farewell words are spoken; only steps left
Are home, my dear.

Nicholas A. Nastasi

Party Life

Life of parties all the time,
never matters if you spend your last dime.

It's fun staying high, so they say!
Fun? Not realizing today is now yesterday.

Does it solve problems, remove inner fears?
cure all your hurt, heart break, tears?

Dope, parties, what's reality? What's a dream?
The high life, simple, carefree? So it seems.

Ever stop, let reality hit?
Is this truly you? Is life good or the pits?

Is this the life you sought?
A question you should give deep thought.

No one rules what you do, except you!
In your life, is a change overdue?

Live life the way you decide.
"True happiness," only you can provide.

Lisa Payne

Thank You, Mom

Thanks for being a special part of me, Mom
How do I begin to thank you
for everything you have ever done for me.
From the time I was young until today
by my side is where you'd always be.
You took me by my hand when I was lost
and comforted me when I was down
Somehow you had that touch to make a smile
out of my biggest frown
Now that I'm grown I appreciate you
even more than I did before.
And with everything you've ever done for me
I could never ask for more.
I'll always need you mom to guide me,
to help me, and most of all your love.
I treasure you in my heart
because your love comes from above.
"You only get one mother so take care of her"
grandma told me that when I was young.
I'll never forget all you've done for me mom
our journey has only just begun.

Cheryl Henderson

Granddaughter's Heart

Special dedication to my grandmother, Angela, always in my heart
So special a place held deep in my heart,
my grandmother will always stay.
Your love carries on forevermore,
even though you are faraway.
Though the years pass by without you now,
your memories remain . . . forever mine.
A grandmother's love held deep in my soul,
knowing she was thoughtful and kind.
As time passes on, my heart can feel
what it has never felt before:
A grandmother's love secured away,
so to be felt once more.

Victoria C. Dovie

A Fixed Mind on Jesus

Just remember, God first!
He's the head and not the tail,
For He's the beginning and the end!

The first and the last,
Keep Him in your mind and your heart!
Worship Him and Him only,
For all other things will be added unto you.

For we must rejoice
Praise Him and all instruments!
Make a joyful noise
For our trials and tribulations are minor things,
We must keep on fasting and praying.

Francie H. Sanders

Night's Mystiques

The sky is overcast at the midnight hour
As millions of stars explode with accord.
They illuminate the darkness with supreme power
And the atmosphere awakens with monotonous discord.

Birds hover in the trees so tall
Rocking and chirping with weary delight.
Far away wolves emit a menacing call
Forewarning others of the oncoming light.

The sky is overcast at the midnight hour
As millions of stars explode with accord.
An impetuous wind blows with sinister power,
Keeping the woods' mystiques again restored.

W. Hamby

Sunday, July 12, 1998

What a perfect summer day
With deep blue high in the sky for a brave heart
With dark green brooding under the sun uttering hay
White clouds overlook the world's silver linings apart

As if no reason to whine
At pink oleanders flirting with the breeze
At my Wilde t-shirt laughing away the clothesline
At last the sun is setting off her last glees

Light in the sky is now the thin moon
Light blue overhangs her mystic loom
Quiet now is the day's colorful tune
Quiet loneliness as if holding a plume

What a perfect summer night
After fireflies rekindle a world in vain
Let sweet tuberoses perfume no bite
Quite patiently is the meteor to shower again

Tien-yi Lee

You Fool

The strangers eyes that rest upon me
Belong to you
Knowing you at first glance
Yet not knowing you
Not knowing that look in your eyes
Not knowing the sound of your laugh
Yet filled with love for you just the same
Feeling as if
You are not the stranger that you are
Seeing you in the recesses of my mind
Dreaming of running toward you
Finding countless obstacles in my way
Every sigh in the night brings me closer
To realizing what kind of fool I can be
To wait for you to scorn me
My name could be transformed to almost any name
The letters always rearrange themselves to spell "You Fool"

Laura Morgan

The Gift

To Davidee, thank you for touching my soul, love always
Love is manifested in many forms.
In all of them, God's name is silently spoken.
In solitude, we feel the presence of the sound . . .

Davidee . . . a gift from God,
a gift of Hope,
a gift of Love . . .

To touch, to see, to hear, to know.
To nurture, care for, feel, and love.

Davidee . . . warmly beautiful,
beautifully warm . . .
God's sweet gift in the form . . .
of Davidee.

Robin Dover

Can Love Love Me?

Aimlessly I walk through the minutes of the day
Trying to stay strong while finding my way.
I look at this face, I look at that face
Hoping to find someone who'll know my face.

I want them to look through the skin and the flesh
And to see all the bad instead of the best.
I want them to know all the pain that I feel
I want them to know it's what makes me real.

But more than anything I want them to know
For me to live, the walls they must show.
But with all the walls that surround all of me
I would give anything if I could be free.

Cheryl L. Pendl

Believing Is Having

What Right do We Have in Asking for Life?
    Why Should we Live in Freedom of Strife?
Why Should our Lives so Radiantly Glow,
    And Why our Sins be made Whiter than Snow?

What Gives the Right to Share His Great Love?
    And Blessings of Truth Showered from Above?
Why Should We not Die, and be Buried in Sin?
    While We Reject His Will with Our Will Within!

How Much of God's Truth are We Willing to Live?
    How Much of His Love are We Willing to Give?
How Much do We Want . . . while He Offers His Best?
    Are We Willing to Believe in Entering His REST?

What Kind of a Prayer are We Willing to Pray?
    And will We Give Him All that We Say?
Now, honestly speaking, Are We Still Seeking—
    The Life that He's Willing to GIVE!

Stephen Fetchko

Legacy

They left your shores once, long ago, and sailed across the sea.
They brought a legacy of love and passed it on to me.
Though the tides go rolling on, your shores I've never seen.
Every year, my legacy grows with love for your land of green.
Gone now the folk to the heavens . . . still, their tales I can hear
Of the Castle Blackrock and a cottage on a road so far from here.

Pauline Lane

The Moon's Watch

This moon is the same moon
That watched and saw me in New Jersey,
As it looked down upon me
And saw me in misery.

Then I looked up in its mighty light,
So gleaming from above,
And asked it to keep you safe
And give you my real love.

If I was looking at it, maybe
You'd be watching sometimes that night.
And the same light that was watching me
Would be watching you and keep everything all right . . .

The one thing we both could look upon,
Even though miles apart,
Hoping this celestial being would
Transmit the thoughts racing in my heart.

But I'm sure it was the same moon
That shined on Jersey's Atlantic ocean,
Then shined over California,
Transferring a mighty potion.

Kathryn Asbury

I Hear Eden Calling

Inspired by the Sawtooth Mt. Wolf Pack and Isiah 11:6
I hear Eden calling, in the solitary howl of
her daughter mourning the death of perfect innocence
and the lonely separation of paradise.
As the sun fades behind the wilderness
She licks the blood of her prey from her face
driven by a hunger she cannot deny.
And at night she cries
for the grievous injustice of man's law
at the full moon of time.
But one day, he will play and dance again
when the alpha returns exposing our sin
and leads the way for both beast and man
and all the world will see a day
when the wolf shall lay down with the lamb.

Susan Dye

Dew Drops

I awoke one morn' and peered through my window
To behold a most beautiful sight;
It was the sight of the radiant sunlight
Reflecting from the crystal dew drops
Nestling on shrubberies nearby.

The beauty of the warm sunlight
Radiating through the crystal dew drops
Was like sparking diamonds rear.
I gasped in wonder at nature's beauty
And how elegantly she adorns the Earth.

I then lift my eyes to the heavens above
And give praise to the Great One
Who has adorned the Earth and sky
With such splendor and beauty
That moves my heart to adoration and praise.

Joycemin M. Levy

Saul Revisited

To Caleb
Any given morning as usual I'll see
The young, the old, and those in-between.
Each one I greet much the same as the other but,
with those in-between sometimes I wonder.
"Did I see him already?" I'm sorry, you see
most of them look quite alike to me.
Later viewing from my pew I spied a fresh look, something new.
Kind of like what God must have seen
when the children of Israel demanded a King.
Of course Saul was not chosen by looks solely.
God's decisions are based on that which is holy.
The physical, though, was what Samuel could see and
what's on the inside the outside will be.
Saul's outward appearance was his alone;
Valiant, mature, and leadership-prone.
The young man I saw, his character not told.
Of course character is not judged by one's look nor
quality of content by the cover of books.
Should all books on the outside appear the same,
we would read only one, then give all one name.

Monica Walton

Gone

The dreaming still lingers on,
Even though you are gone.
My dreams of you keep going flooding down on me.
I thought, deep down in my heart, that we were meant to be,
But I guess you didn't quite think so, my love.
I used to think that you were sent to me from up above.
I still love you so dearly.
I know you can tell it quite clearly.
My dreaming of you still lingers on,
Even though now you are clearly gone.

John S. Stone

Iago Resurrected

We smiled into each other's eyes,
Supposedly calm and serene,
Thinking the other in disguise,
And watching Othello turn green.

Accusations of telling lies,
Eyes covered with a mirror's sheen,
Snapping shut my once open eyes,
And watching Othello turn green.

I felt my mind go lifeless, dead;
I watched him move through a veiled screen.
I watched my love turn bitter red
On the day Othello turned green.

Deborah Craft

Quicken

Shadows that lurk behind the scenes
prey upon the unconscious dreams
Dealt a hand of life to spare, but fate to feel no one to care
Crimson blood or an array of hope
Till the end, forced to cope
Embodied by the black masses of fear
Conjuring little strength, for death feels near
Is it a cloud, a haze, or a crystal glaze that watches?
You feel its overwhelming strength
but know you must fight
Then, in your imprisoned mind, you begin to understand
that you must run from the darkness and
speed towards the light

Michael A. Crain

Just Another Day

One of life's challenges was standing in the road
It welcomed me with open arms
Then would not let me go
The more I struggled to be free
The tighter it's embrace on me
Until I felt I couldn't breath
And that is when it said to me

You silly man, are you so blind
Instead of ahead, you looked behind
The only thing you will find
Is what led you to me at this point in time
And if you truly want to fell at ease
You'll endeavor to get past me

As it's words resounded in my ears
I swallowed my pride and suppressed my fears
Lifting one leg up high
I stepped on through to the other side
Of life's challenge for today

Michael W. Peck

Love Never Ends

Though I in tongues of men and angels speak,
but have not love, what more than noise am I?
And, but for holy love, patient and meek,
what meaning has the gift to prophesy?
Or even faith with strength to mountains move,
and understanding of all mystery—
without Christ's love, these virtues nothing prove;
apart from love no goodness can there be.
True love is kind, not arrogant or rude.
It is not lightly vexed, nor makes demands;
love bears all things, believes with hope imbued.
Love, never ending, all things else outstands.
And so faith, hope and love abide, these three—
the greatest: love, most Sacred Heart, to Thee.

Lynn Roberson

Between Darkness and Death

I fly through the dark and unforgiving night,
On a carpet made of purest white,
Dancing in the shadows of the full golden moon—
Death will come to you soon.
Maiming all of the undeserving hearts,
Midnight is a glorious time to start.
Racing through the dark, guided only by the stars,
Dreaming dreams of erasing the scars,
The scars from the flames that ruin your soul,
The flames from the fire, your heart they stole.
The flames that will burn you, burn you all down
As I fly on my carpet, over the town,
Striking a match, unlocking a latch,
And throw the flame in, as you are sleeping,
And as you are dying, you will be weeping.

Kimberly Wallace

World's View

Life is what we see it to be.
We don't see the empty places.
We don't look around us to see what is wrong.
When we do it is to late.
You gradually walk through life without seeing the life
you want pass you by.
The dreams and goals become memories and regrets.
The travel plans become posters on the wall and the passport
collects dust.
Every day you think "just one more" or "this will be the last one."
Every day it is the same thing. Always just one more.
Then one day death takes you out of the "one more club" the world
walks over you with no more thought than a speed bump.
You are not judged for the pain and sweat of a lifetime.
You are judged for the balance of your stock portfolio.
The car you drive and the house you live in.
The world is a cold and empty place.
The soul has gone out of the world.
This is the truth of the world whether we admit to it or not.
The world is what we all have made it.

Chad Lynn

Violets

To my son, Alexander, in memory of his Grandmother
The festivities of life enchanted our souls.
Birthdays, holidays, weddings did show.
Little girls pranced in halos of ribbons and sweet peas.
Radiant brides leagued in trails of gardenias and peonies.
Handsome grooms sport bashful
boutonnieres, knowing their fate was true.

"Water the flowers, my friend." I heard it again.
This day of days, life seemed to stand still.

Violets still heart her dressing table.
Hydrangea for Easter flourish her yard.
Last night she left like a shooting star.

By late afternoon in the midst of a crowd,
the flowers were art, vibrant and strong.
Hybrid blue delphinium for the strength in her eyes,
Dozens of pale peach roses for her name that was high,
Cascades of ivy draped her long and delicate life.
Pure, white orchids pave the way for everlasting light.

From heavens above we were a team.
Little did I know, flowers were her dream.

Patricia A. Rizzo

Our Lives

Born one day we are but children, innocent, helpless, and carefree.
Full of love, comfort, and joy for those to whom we were born.
Finding comfort in the nurturing of a loved one.

Then one by one the years fly by
   and we become teenagers awakening
to a world of technology and machines.
Where decisions must be made,
and we must learn the technicalities behind it.

Finding it hard to cope with reality,
   we sit down to take in the knowledge
of our society only to find we'll never know it all.
We awaken to a harshness of pollution and smog
caused by our technology and machines.
In the middle of our lives we realize we must do
something to stop the harshness of our society.

Again we let the years fly by only to find we're not young anymore,
but on the last leg of our lives.
We awaken only to learn we spent half of our lives trying
to learn what society had to teach us, and half
trying to change it, only to realize we learned too little too late.

Mandy Newton

Snowflakes

To my loving husband, George Doolittle
I gazed out of the window as I lay in my bed.
The moon displayed snowflakes turning to ice.
Clusters twinkled as they spread,
Slowly melting through the night.

The lace of the snowflakes
Brought forth a pattern on the ground,
As the ice mingled in numerous shapes.
By tomorrow, none shall be found.

As I snuggled against the pillow,
My feet warmed slowly under the sheet.
While gazing out of the window,
I soon fell quietly asleep.

Lois E. Doolittle

Surfacing

My physical being has lost its flavor.
My mental state is frustrated and constantly battling.
I watch the clock as time dreadfully passes,
Laughing in my face, making me shameful.
The hours slipped like so many years behind me.
Sluggishly, I let fate take its place in my yielding life,
Hoping only happiness will surface
From the dark and dangered waters,
Pain slowly fading into the past,
Bursting bright and powerful colors in view now,
Casting out all the dark like sin,
Lovely tunes tickling my ears.
Joyfully I do skipping dances as I rejoice joyfully,
Rainbows crowding my surroundings, yet making life easier,
Animals prancing all around like talented ballerinas.
It is all so joyful and pleasant.
How life can do such a turn around is superb in your thoughts.
Once again you shall stand.

Jennifer Owens

Mother's Flowers

Bleeding hearts and peonies in the front yard,
Yellow roses and phlox by the fence,
Forget-me-not and lilies in the back yard—
But best of all, there was the fragrance.

Walking with mother, seeing her flowers,
Is now only in our memory.
She is by the pine tree that towers
Over the artificial ones in the cemetery.

Dolores Peek

You Never Looked Back

As you float away, sun setting on our tryst,
The scent of your departing kiss lingers.
Cafe conversations just past mingle,
Drifting through deep fields of philosophy,
While gossip chattered in the darkening skies,
And childhood tales rustled the autumn leaves.
Dreams and memories strolled to and fro,
Desires played hide and seek
Between sips of coffee and furtive glances,
Fingers, palms touched and made love.

Are these recollections only mine?
This desire simply my imagination?

As you float away, moon rising over passion,
Oceans of passion, rising flowing with each step.
I wait for a look that will answer, yes or no?
I long for a glance that will requite, all or nothing?

But you never looked back as you walked away.
And still I ponder.

Andrew Jaffray

Divine Frustration

Will My children ever understand that I am the perfect Father?
Of all the creatures on My Earth, the humans are My favorites.
They drown Me in pride and in sorrow as well.

Why do they fight, IN MY NAME?
Why do they kill each other, IN MY NAME?
I should have told Moses, "Thou shalt not fight over Me!"

I am in the heart of the Jew in a temple in Israel.
And in the eyes of the Moslem in a mosque in Palestine.
I'm on the faces of the children in a Catholic church in Ireland.
And in the thoughts and prayers of the Anglicans in the North.
My hands are big enough to hold Everyone.

When you stand on a mountain top above the world, alone,
I am with you.
When you watch the sun sink into the ocean with someone special,
I am on that beach with you.

So you have different skin colors.
And you've all been to Babel.
You all have two eyes and two ears and two arms and two hands
And two legs and two feet and ten fingers and ten toes.
And you all LOVE!

Robert Levesque

Coming Home

In memory of Paul A. Rankin
I know I'll never see you again until that wonderful day
When the Lord almighty takes me away.

To me it seems just like yesterday,
But it's been four weeks since you passed away.

Oh, you are missed so much,
Because you had that special touch.

You were a friend to everyone
No matter what they may or may not have done.

You never judged,
You always loved.

You talked about living a life without sin.
There was no doubt that Christ lived within.

You did so much and you did it well,
God had blessed you, we could tell.

If we only learned one thing it would be,
Live for Christ and you will have life eternally.

So this is good-bye until we meet at God's throne,
Singing and shouting, "We have come home."

Grant Williams

Blazing Mastery

My parents, they inspire my poetry
The flame rises higher and higher
encasing everything in its path
Its power is unstoppable
The raging flame knows
knows its strength as it grows reaching for the sky
The objects in its way feed the flame
as it turns a brighter even more vivid orange
If one looks close there is a touch of blue to the flame
Its ambition is unbelievable as it continue its
desperate try to touch the sky
Its frustration grows as it
realize that it is trapped
trapped with a small brick place
The black from its anger marks the walls.
This time the anger grows
grows stronger when it realizes its no longer in control.
You, you have control
You control how much power it gets
You, control when it lives and when it dies.

Victoria Pasciuto

Abandoned

I lay here on my bed so mad.
I think of all the times we've had,
Of all the times you'd pick me up.
I've always hated it when our time was done.
I've always loved you very much,
And I always will, for time to come.
I feel so bad because you're far away;
When I go to see you, I feel I can't stay.
You never ever left me alone,
Not even when I was sick and cold.
You always told me that you would stay with me,
So why did you move so far away from me?
You're missing the most important years of my life;
You are my father and you should be my side.
Eleven months without you is hard enough,
But when you don't come and see me, it feels like I'm not loved.
I feel so mad, you see,
Because I feel you abandoned me.
As you lay their in the Florida sun,
Remember your daughters that miss you a ton.

Roxanne Ruiz

A Reaction to Eternity: As Projected, Felt

I go to the city
for scattering multiplied cacophony, the noise
to lose myself in the crowding
a form of distraction really, diversion
a deliberate unintention.
For from where I was, so rustic, to flee
that singular hum
that pervading quietness of the deafening
silence of eternity
the weight of extended time
of blown up passing scenes of millions and millions
staggered magnitudes, of comings and goings
starts and ends
sunsets and sunrises
round and round its orbit of repetition.
Season for season, finite quantities
unending, flowing, hurtling endlessly on.

Michael F. Franco

Nothing Seems as Precious as You

I've sat here in the evening shadows, night after night,
Trying to describe the love I feel toward you.
Sometimes, it feels like white, dream-enchanting clouds,
So soft, so pure, and so true,
Maybe like a sweet tender song of joy,
Or the tender finger touch on a baby's cheek,
Or the glee coming from the innocent laughter
Of a child playing with its toy.
Or a gentle noise from two tender lips
Releasing after a gentle kiss.
I've found out there is nothing more
Depressing than to lose something you love,
and something you would forever miss.

Johnny L. Espenschied

Regrets

She looks at her hands, calloused and scarred,
Rough from the work of a life that's been hard.
She feels of her hair, now thinning and gray,
And her mind wanders back to a long-ago day.
She wishes that things were different somehow,
But the past can't be changed by things we do now.
So she thinks of her youth and the prime of her years,
Before there were heartaches, before there were tears.
And she cries for all the time that has passed,
As she wonders how life could go by so fast.
And as the sun sets and the memories fade,
She closes her eyes on the coming new day.

Molly Burgan

Only You

To Charles, Godspeed, I love you for all my life
You strayed into my life,
Cut into my heart like a knife.

So strong you hold me at night,
So much lover when we turn out the light.

When you leave,
Only your love my heart will research.

Only memories of you,
My mind will retrieve.

Only your touch,
My soul will miss so much.

And till the end of eternity,
You will see.

We're a Bind,
of heart, soul, and mind.

Jessica Ross

Tender Nights

Walking through the veldts on this sunset day
I seek to discover anything new,
A pond and thicket lie straight ahead
So I ask myself, where shall I go to?
The sun slowly hides behind the mountains
And nighttime envelops the sky,
The moon and stars are suspended above
Throwing soft light into my eye.
I resume my walk to the waters
Where the wind becomes breezy,
Glistening moonlight dances in the waves
And the sight of this is really pleasing.
I begin walking back to my cabin
While the crickets chirp and snakes slither,
Experiencing all this can be rewarding
Because the fashion of nature is sweet, never bitter.
Tomorrow is another day to enjoy the scenery
For it is all a soothing sight,
My love for peace exists in this form
The remarkable form of tender nights.

Efren Rodriguez

A Winter's Night

The whispering, gently-falling snow,
A crackling fireplace, all aglow,
Lends beauty to a winter's night.
Where can be found a more wondrous sight?

The lure to venture into the storm
Confronts our will to stay in and warm.
Our need to go out and play
Soon overrides the will to stay.

Like overgrown kids, we venture out,
Singing, playing, running about.
And after all is said and done,
It's hard to remember when we had such fun.

Returning home to our warm fire,
All our play has made us tire.
Off to sleep we're sure to go,
Listening to the whispering, gently-falling snow.

Robert G. Lumpkin

Our Freedom in Christ

Our American flag tells it all in its colors,
The red strips for the blood of Jesus Christ,
White for purity, blue for the color of the heavens,
Stars shining for freedom in our country,
As well as in Jesus Christ,
Forever and ever.

Sylvia M. Stevenson

Just

What do you think that you have been given?
And will you do what is best?
How many times will you close your eyes
before you're allowed to rest?
How many times have you given all that you had
and spent every ounce of your soul?
Yet, it's just not enough to keep the prize,
not quite far enough to dig you out of the hole.
In life, it's not whether you win or lose,
whether you produce or idly watch life drift by.
It's just a matter of what you do.
Are people going to miss you after you die?
How many souls will stand the test of time
After their lively bodies diminish?
What they've given to the world lives on in their friends,
And that work is never finished.
Just what do you think about this world?
Have you made your God proud by what you've done?
Death is always right outside your door.
Until I die, I'm going to keep struggling on.

    Keith Stall

Thankful for Robin

To God and my loving husband, Robin M. Reece
Thank you Father God, for my husband Robin.
Thank you for his kind, gentle and peaceful spirit.
Thank you for his helpfulness to me when I need help.
Thank you for his listening to me when I talk to much.
Thank you for his loving me and me loving him.
Thank you for the hugs and kisses he gives me.
Thank you for this dark black hair and dark brown eyes.
Thank you for his golden skin and nice looking frame.
Thank you for his gentle eyes and warm smile.
Thank you Father God for I truly love him.
He is a very precious gift in my life.
Thank you Father God for your gift to me, my husband Robin.

    Nancy Lynne Reece

Full Moon

There are many stars in the sky tonight
The moon has never been so bright
The Milky Way gleams across the sky
Lights of a plane, ever so high

In the distance, the hoot of an owl
Near, you can hear the bawl of a cow
Coyotes can be heard once in a while
Boats in the river from about a mile

These are the peaceful sounds you can hear
Nothing here to cause you fear
The sweet fragrant air of the night
Comes from the honeysuckle on the right

    Agnes K. Edmond

These Are the Things

Love from children is not easily lost,
their laughter and smiles do not have a cost.
They feel our love, they feel our pain.
All they ask is that we do the same.
When children say they can't,
they must be told they can.
When they are older, they must be able
to get up and take a stand.
They must be nurtured and cared for,
so they know life is an open door.
Children should know they have someone to trust,
someone who cares about their concerns and disgusts.
When they do right they must be cheered;
they must be encouraged and revered.
These are the things that children should know.
These are the things that help them grow.

    Leandra M. Flores

A Love for Two

She was lovely and radiant in youth,
And he was good through and through,
Gently persuading her with "I love you."
Slowly, like two magnets, masculine and
    feminine,
They were drawn together and joined.
They danced in the fiery dance of temperaments
    and passions,
Pulled apart and reconciled until they finally
    realized
They shared a need for this to last.
The tender strains of love that remained,
Became the foundation of their relationship
    and the contentment of their days,
As they matured in the knowledge that this
    was not a passing phase.
Now, mellow and gray, hand-in-hand they stand,
Testimony to their love that does not fade.

    Joyce G. James

Pickles in My Driveway

While out driving one fine day,
I returned to discover . . . Pickles, in my driveway.

Quality Kosher, Garlic Dills, they were,
The pickles in my driveway.

There they sat near my neighbor's cat,
Those pickles in my driveway.

My husband had nothing whatsoever to say
About the pickles in my driveway.

The kids I stopped and asked, ran away
From the pickles in my driveway.

So the mystery remains as to the true origin of
The pickles in my driveway.

    Deborah L. McEnery

Slayer

Walking through the forest with only fear in mind,
Not knowing what could be lurking too far behind.
I am prepared to fight any battle, win any war,
But that is not of what my quest is for.

From what I was told of this beast, I call no man a liar.
But fight such a beast that breathes of fire?
You could see monstrous tracks across the land.
Losing my fear, I make my stand.

I raise my sword and suddenly feel weak.
Trembling with fear, I can hardly speak.
Here with the beast, I shall fight;
I have struck him with blows of all my might.

I have lost my strength and feel my heart
Has missed a beat.
Killing that dragon, this slayer
Knows no defeat.

    Darrel Zietek

Forlorn Black Rose

In my heart, a black rosebud, its stem has rooted fast;
Its briars their piercing wreath round my heart have cast.
In fury, I've spat upon it, trampling it with scorn.
My dark bloody fingers have crushed it, leaf and thorn.

But it will not wither, my forlorn black rose;
Undaunted, it blooms and in proud defiance grows.

In the grim agony of my heart's ease,
I shall raise it high, the moonlight to seize.
On the salt of my tears itself to nourish,
And watch it, in bitter blossom, flourish.

    James Dunning

October

The drifting autumn smell in the air
Tastes better than any wine;
Blazing leaves upon the trees are dying in colored glory.
You can feel the coldness creeping,
Coming to bury the King of October.

He wears a crown of copper.
A festival mood prevails.
Geese crying up above see
Revelers harvesting wild apples
And hunting deer for woodland feasts.
Fall flowers lie in merry maidens' hair.
Elfish laughter echoes as faery subjects dance
Around a wood fire, sending up smoke
Into a sky that will crash upon the head of the King of October.

For now, sunshine will fall on the goldenrod and thistles.
But when the waiting snowflakes
Take on a murderous mood,
They drift down in the night and
Mysteriously kill the King of October.

Julianne Irene Day

It's Christmas, Once Again

It's Christmas, once again,
and soon I'll see old friends and hear
the sleigh bells in the snow.
While the fireside is slowly burning,
inside children will be yearning for a bright
early Christmas morning, once again.

Oh, the sleigh bells gaily ring,
while the children sleep and dream
of the morning it will bring, all
through the night, while their parents are a'sleeping,
The children were a'peeking—that's how they caught
old Santa in the house.

He was dressed in funny red clothes
from his head down to his toes,
with a sack upon his back full with toys.

Granmaw, Granpaw are on their way;
they will be here on Christmas day
to make it a bright and merry
Christmas, once again.

June D. Barefoot

Whispers of Spirit

When I arise in His presence at early morning daybreak,
My first words are, "Thank you, Father, for precious life."
Then I begin scheduling meditation for His sacred namesake,
And the mental race rapidly progresses away from all strife
As I am being instructed by whispers of spirit.

When the glow of life comes quickly into lovely unexpected play,
Scenic flicks of untitled beauty seem to reach for a goal
That tries to match historic, natural epics of transpired days.
And as varied eventualities appear to take their untimely toll,
I continue listening to soft whispers of spirit.

Now I go on composing superlative phrases for His holy name
In order to share these unspoken emotions with all humankind.
So I become solemnly aware that nothing is rarely ever the same,
While I ponder al realities imaged in my inquisitive mind.
This can only be inspired by whispers of spirit.

Finally, I gather together thoughts from prophetic dreams,
In my quest for answers to questions about growing and living.
Then I'm apprised, once again, that life is never what it may seem,
'Til one learns the deep truths about loving and generously giving.
So I never stop learning from whispers of spirit.

Marie Wright

My Special Hill

As I stand alone on a treeless hill
and deeply breathe a long, trembling thrill,
I can see afar the beauty of new, sparkling Spring
and know majesty that only Persephone can bring.

Brambles grow in the bottoms and along the ditches,
redbuds, cherries, plums, berries, and willows
that flash billowing wonder of Persephone's riches,
the redbuds, yellow pussy willows with soft grey pillows,
creamy white plum and berry blooms tucked in cliffs and niches.

From my every day world I am transported with ease.
The fragrant whiffs of blooms flow gently to me,
wafting at leisure on the soft, soothing breeze,
and clear my mind of all worries, leaving me free.

I wander to that special hill often as I can
to seek the powerful magic for my heart,
to calm my cares, dream, and quietly plan
a contented future with a bright, new start.

June Jamison

Continuity

To my daughter Alia and memories of my mother Trish
Her life force proclaimed its birthing hour,
the very moment to begin.
I supported, my labor assisting
the efforts of the unborn within.
The lifeline still united two as one
as I held her for the first time.

Our eyes met.
And in those eyes not yet burdened by time,
I witnessed the continuity in love found and defined,
eternity captured in a single moment.

Her life force declared its homecoming hour,
the very moment to let go.
I supported, releasing and departing
from hopes and efforts to postpone
her body's shutdown process, already in progress.
I held her for the last time.

Our eyes met.
And in those eyes no longer burdened by time,
I witnessed the continuity in love found and defined,
eternity captured in a single moment.

Karen Ann Ostranger

Super Wishbone

If I could be your wishbone
I'd snap myself in two
And give to you my bigger half
Then make your wish come true

Or let me be a penny
And toss me from your hand
I'll drown down to the bottom of the well
And grant your one demand

I could be your lucky trophy
A lamp with a golden gleam
But instead of three, I'll give you one
To make reality of your dream

I could be a four-leaf clover
See me as your shooting star
I could be a birthday candle
If you see things as they are

You've made your little wish
But I would not make it so
When you asked me to stay with you
Instead, I let you go

Kyler Wilson

Drowning

Violent waves of blue and green
thrashing in a sea of sorrow
a suffering soul drowns
yearning to reach the surface
for one last breath of cleanliness
choking on its rage and anger
strength is minimal, so close
yet so far away
kicking and screaming
painfully swallowing the filth it created
forever living in its own hate

Heidi Irwin

Tears Left Behind

How are words spoken
So long overdue?
When does one's heart mend
And never again pretend?
When do tears stop longing
To fit in and belong?
When does one stop running
Toward that so far away?

How does one find courage
To leave with time undone?

These are things I've wondered
So often along the way,
The answers I've searched for
Were already within my mind,
Things I once feared so
No longer have control.

Like the tears of time
That long to touch my pillow,
To give of oneself so freely could not be,
Till destiny set me free.

Joan Karen Sides

Assata's Theme

The sun is arising; it's a brand-new day
All my cares and worries have been slept away
The positives are out there, all that joy and cheer
Believe in myself, have faith, my time is near
Put one foot in front of the other, do what's there to be done
I'm alive, the potential is mine, already, I've won
I have everything I need, some of the things I want will come
Whatever anyone else can think, feel, or do
I'm no more nor less, I can accomplish that, too
Diligence, commitment, goals are achieved one by one
Smile, there's nothing but goodness ahead for me
Sometimes I might not understand, but if I just be still, I'll see
Let me enjoy this life, that's what I was put here for
Only I can hold me back, and there's just so much more

Eugene Thomas

Dawn

The light so soft and warm through window breaks
The dew's light fingers touch upon the land
The land with holiness this hour makes
The time that fills one hourglass with sand

As all the creatures stir and lift their heads
And gently lift their bodies off the ground
They take a step and move out of their beds
All is a hush, they dare not make a sound

Before the busyness of all the bees
The softness of the light brings a new day
It dances through the shadows of the trees
It is the time of prayer ere work or play

And so we start this day that's just begun
As we awake for dancing with the sun

Rachel McRoberts

God's Awesomeness

I believe in God's Awesomeness   He sent a white pigeon
To this humble farm woman who was painting the sheep barn
Friends said, "It was a Blessing."   I have been truly blessed
I would like to pass my blessing on to you

God gave me the gift to write a poem about this Miracle Messenger
My daughter encouraged me to enter a poetry contest
The poetry people like what I did and encouraged me to write more
Only God can give this gift   I believe in His Awesomeness

God loves and blesses all of us if we just know and accept
In days of old He gave His inspired word, the Bible
And sent His Son, Jesus Christ, to show us the perfect way
Jesus said, "Follow Me," and died for the forgiveness of our sins

God loves us all and is a magnificent provider
I want for nothing   I am content   I love you, God
You are good to us   You protect and care for us
I believe in your awesomeness, God.   Thank you

Jane Ann Moody

Thoughts

Thoughts that are banned from every day life
secluded to be kept in your mind
You don't have the right
to think what you wanted
without being questioned
or asked what you thought
Ideas are already pushed in your head
whether they're right or wrong nobody says
It's just expected that you will believe
what you're taught, and what it means
so no longer are you one in your own
You're the same as the others a twin, a clone
Don't listen to what they teach you
Instead listen to what you believe and know

Jennifer Zimmer

The Finish Product

When tears run down our faces,
Tears run down the face of Jesus.
He too knows rejection, abandonment, and loneliness.
He feels our pain, our deepest sorrow.
He knows the future, the tomorrows.
He sees the whole, the finished product.
Amidst the trials and temptations we face
He covers us with His everlasting grace.
He sees the strengthening of our inner being.
He knows deliverance is not always best
Because we grow stronger through the test.
He, Himself, has suffered much.
He prayed that the cup might pass.
But He did hot try to run away.
He let God have His way.

Karen Austin

Does Anyone Care?

To Michelle, my very best friend, I love you
As I walk through the halls of strife
I wonder: What is there to life?
I dare to ask why am I here
Does anyone care and is the creator near?
The Earth was once a beautiful place
But now I look—it's such a disgrace
The world is full of death and turmoil
We destroy our plant life and ruin our soil
We pollute our rivers and smell up the air
And I wonder: Does anyone care?
All natures creatures great and small
Will we be happy when we kill them all
Will we ever stop destroying the land, sea, and air?
And I wonder: Does anyone care?

Raleigh Rush

Rain

To my loving husband, Richard Swinyer
I love it when it rains;
We have so much to gain.
It wets the flowers and trees;
We see such dark green leaves.
The birds sing a happy song;
Spring will be here in not too long.

The patter of rain has a rhythmic sound;
It dances up and down, as it
Falls to the ground.
Umbrella's line the streets;
A parade of colors where everyone meets.

The rain makes me happy
And I prance.
The children laugh,
As they watch me dance.
When it pours, don't complain;
Thank Mother Nature for the rain.

Theresa Swinyer

For My Mark

Brave and strong, proud and true,
My own hero,
I know you will get through this.
"Pain comes and pain goes," yet you endure.

You try to convince me that this physical pain is nothing,
but even one as strong as you is soon worn down by this throbbing.

No medicine, no relief . . . no hope?
Ah, but hope does not shirk from pain.
Hope flourishes and grows.

I have seen your hope and your courage.
I am sure you will live on . . .

But even hope needs help once in a while.

Abby Lowe

He Is

He is everything.
He is my strength and my weakness.
He is the light, as He is the dark.
He is my rock and my confidant.
He is my Father, as He is my Mother,
    my brother and my sister.
He is my best friend and soul mate.
He is the greatest love of all.
He allows me to shine in His light.
He forgives me of my sins,
    and helps me to become a better person.
He blesses me with His love.
He is always there in my time of need.
He is my happiness.
He is my Savior.
He is GOD.

Allison Trotter

The Library

A man walks into the library.
All freeze in mid-step, fear etched, hyper-vigilant.
Three a table, heads shaved, shout lewd jokes.
Librarians chatter and gnaw, then elect an appeaser.
Sent forth, her plaintive squeaks go unheard
Until security scatters the table-like chaff.

Turmoiled appeaser, thus appeased,
Still battles the slaps and assaults of her past,
Unable to feel relief even in the zest of youth.

A grid of demons laid on every moment.

Nick Merola

Humble

I am still learning to the humble yet proud.
Dare I to compare myself with a cloud.
But surely these feelings that I feel
are down so deep they can make me real.
The learning of the humble bring feelings that are rich.
And learning to be proud enriches me more.
It's the knowledge that keeps me from being poor.
To compare me with a cloud is an open declaration,
of how we thrive and share in this creation.
Having felt like one with all, I know now how it feels.
Having known all, I have so much more to learn.
Having been all, I tenderly show concern.
Yes, I can feel the humbleness of the greatness that surrounds me.
And I can enrich my life by being proud.
To share in the knowledge,
of that which makes me the same as a cloud.

Rosemarie Sere

To Wonder

When the fog lifts
The sun cuts through what we call the night
The sky becomes the most wondrous sight
With the colors red, blue, and purple
Waves crash on the sharp and jagged rocks below.

I sit and look out on the sea
Think of what might lie at the bottom
Maybe an old pirate ship or even a lost city
To wonder what might be out there
Beyond what one can see
But when to be brought back to reality

After the fog rolls back in
The glow of the full moon shows me the way home
As I look behind for one last look to never forget
What may lie ahead is something not to know
If I knew yesterday of today, would I change it?
I hope not

Melissa Buttram

Together

My love grows stronger with each passing day,
Missing you, wanting you, when you are away.
I feel your strength within your embrace,
With your love around me, helps me feel safe.
I feel your warmth when holding me near.
And your gentle touch erases all fear.
We will walk life's path discovering new roads.
Living and loving, as our world unfolds.
For our love grows stronger each passing day.
When we are together, or you are away.

Stacey Lynn McDaniel

Freefalling Faith

To my God, Savior, and friend, Jesus Christ
I'm holding onto the rock above
I'm ready to fly like a dove
Soar through the air with my wings spread out
But I still have just one doubt
I can't be sure what lies below
But I know I must let go
Hanging there I say good-bye
To my past, my former life
Now I have another chance
To go to a place to sing and dance
He is calling so I must depart
'Cause He's given a fresh start
Now that I've heard His call
I know I'm ready to fall

Carl Grant

Fallen Heroes, Wasted Dreams

Where have all our heroes gone?
They have fallen from grace.
Those whom we worshipped
In our childhood have fallen
Off their pedestals.

What happened to our dreams?
Have they been forsaken?
Did we leave them behind
To be thrown out on pavement
And forgotten forever?

I know you have lost some heroes,
But so have I my friend.
We kept dreaming through their fall,
Knowing we would find a better world.
How did you get lost along the way?

I'll leave my fallen heroes,
For they have let me down.
But, unlike you, I'll cling to my dreams forever.
They give me hope in my darkest hour,
And they give me a place to call home.

Cynthia R. Rowe

Green

Where have you gone my friend.
Where have you led yourself,
On a path of excess and greed
Where is your son, when will you learn
What does this mean
The never ending walk into the green.
Your arms they bleed from the spixes.
A heart beats no more, the inhale
has risen you home too soon.
You've left us all bewildered,
Where is the sun, when will you learn.
What could all this possibly mean
As all of you slip from tender to obscene.
And stroll the path, that lead's to the green
I would join you my friend,
but I've got to live for me.
I'll hold fast to the memory,
The lapse in time we shared
The dark and golden hair
To many times I've seen them there.

Joseph R. Spencer

Like the Snowflake

Like the snowflake that falls upon us on a winter's day,
each of us is a possessor of an unique beauty

This beauty lies in the core of your heart
Its content is wise and true
Its quality is pure and fine
Its purpose is just and kind

One touch can awaken a heart in slumber
And open an eye closed to the world
One look can bring a smile out from hibernation
And give water to a mind living in a dry well
One impact can add light to a darkened place
And freshen the serenity smothered by confusion

This uniqueness lives in the center of your being
Its body is firm and strong
Its mind is sure and bold
Its soul is full and rich

And like the snowflake that exists only for a short time,
Each of us is a possessor of a precious moment

Sabrina L. Jahn

Ode to Halloween

Ghosts and skeletons, all bleach of white
Grave markers in the distant moonlight
Hearts beating rapidly with an occasional whisper
As we pass the cemetery tonight

Lonely crypts in need of repairs
Ghosts and goblins hidin' in there
A Chilling finger in every breeze
Dust so thick it makes you sneeze

Whose trick will we treat
When the black cat crosses our feet?
An unhallowed sight full of creatures of fright
Converge upon the world tonight.

Monsters and ghouls, spiders and bats,
Even witches with pointed hats.
Burning lights shine through distorted pumpkin faces
A myriad of aliens from different places.

The clock struck one and we had our fun
All on a Halloween night.

James Davis Ward

Poor Little Grace

Innocence was her only friend
in her dry, lonely hours:
a slave of games, candy, toys
that filled her empty void.
She would sleep the dawn away,
and at sundown she would cry,
gripping the teddy bear to her chest
as she would stare out the window,
not a child, merely purity,
nothing vile in her being.

While she gazed through glistening glass,
she would muse about the birds:
forever free and so content,
never seeming to fear the death,
and she would wish beyond any wish
that she could have those immortal wings.
Thirsting escape from her shackling nest,
she lifted her arms to embrace the sky.
None seemed to notice her quick descent;
nobody mourned her innocence passed.

Andrea Krantz

Eyes into Eternity

I looked into the eyes of eternity once,
I was only ten-years-old.
Mortality unveiled its sombre cloak,
Clutched my heart and turned it cold.

I aged more than nature wished that year,
The world had changed its hue.
Each person appeared more precious and frail,
The universe more fragile than the one I knew.

I learned days are far less kinder,
When one holds the passing of your life.
And time becomes a major foe,
Who gnaws at your success, and magnifies your strife.

The years wear on, and teach you much,
When eyes, compelled, must view the fray.
Strewn yesterdays carry far less worth
Than each gift that is today.

There are too few days, too little praise,
The world is too unknowing of the virtues we bring.
Finally, we see, it's love, friends, and family,
That make living a worthwhile thing.

R. Vincent Riccio

What to Do

I don't know why I stay with you,
Praying that you love me too.
As I look into your eyes,
It makes me ask myself why
I even care—
You never are there.
You just come and go,
No love you ever show.
You expect me to always be
There for you.
After all that you have put me through,
When you look at me, I know
It's her you really see.
You played a foolish game
With my heart,
Right from the very start.
I try to make you mine.
I just need to quit trying.
You don't care and you will never be there.

Kim Lane

Where Has the Time Gone?

Inside a future born of a shattered past,
nothing is immortal, nothing is built to last.
Everything changes and goes away—
even the world's greatest trice goes astray.
If you build it, they will tear it down again.
Time will heal, but parts of a soul will never mend.
I thought you were my best friend,
and you treated me as a passing trend.
Prepare the spikes to break my fall.
No one will hear my helpless call.
Will anyone read this poem?
Will I remember where I came from?
My time has neither come nor gone,
it just slips by when I yawn.
In this world, everybody gets replaced;
time is best known for its ability to erase.

Lucas V. Lindon

God's Gentle Touch

When I see a baby wave a good-bye
When I see a bluebird start to fly
When I see a smile on someone's face
Which neither doubt nor trouble can erase
I feel God's Gentle Touch

When I see snowflakes falling all around
And soon a blanket on the ground
A home where the fire is burning bright
And reading the good book is my delight
I feel God's Gentle Touch

When I go to worship Thee in church
And sing the hymns I love so much
And hear the pastor's message to all
To keep us, so we do not fall
I feel Thy gentle touch

Helen O. Ridenhour

The Flight of Life

In loving memory of my grandpa, Tommy Lance
Beyond the depth of life, a raging, senseless need is to possess,
bewildered in the midst of the progression of endless life.
A desire to endeavor the very breath of awe
meanwhile evoking the wonder of anticipation and acceptance.
Perched upon a fine line of insecurity, awaiting a chance
for the melody, granted by God, to be heard.
Watching intently for the opportunity to fly beyond
the realm of worry and pessimism.
Insecurity is banished and pain is soared through.
Mountains are flown over with ease.
Oceans of tears, once devastating to life, are overcome,
sparkling in the magnificence of the sun.

Tonia C. Lance

Don't Show Me a Poet

Don't show me a poet
Whose heart has never been broken,
One who has never lost hope,
To whom despair has never spoken.
Don't show me a poet
Who has never shed a tear,
One who has never known grief,
Who has never been ruled by fear.
Don't show me a poet
Who has never felt the pain
Of searching endless years for love,
Then offering their love in vain.
But show me a poet who has done this
And still can give you a smile,
One who still searches for love
And knows that quest is still worthwhile.
Show me this poet,
Then and there we will see
Someone who looks very much
Like me.

Paul Hoefling

He's Sweet

To my son, Victor, family, Maurice, and Peace Temple COGIC
To all I love and who love me,
let this be a time of growth, change, healing, and unity.
Remember me as a child of God.
Do not mourn but rejoice for me.
Rejoice and love one another unconditionally
as I through Christ loved you.
Jesus knows the life I lived,
let Him comfort you.
There is one way,
travel that path without hesitation and delay.
Let Him be your source and strength.
I am happy now because I started my new life. This reward is great!
The God of peace will keep your hearts and minds,
He's just that sweet.
May God also be glorified in your life.
Come and meet me at the appointed time.
To God be all the glory and praise,
Hallelujah.

Damita Lucas

The Loner

To all who live, and wish to continue forever
I don't know what it's like to really be loved.
I've just recently learned that I really can love.
It's such a wonderful feeling, an enchanting thought
To hold in my heart that I'm the one sought.

I've written and said all the words in my head,
And sometimes I've wished I were dead.
But that never happens; I suppose that is good.
Since I can neither have nor replace you, I will not brood.
But instead I will look, not hard, mind you,
For someone like me, of a different color and hue.
Someone to talk to, someone to hold,
Someone to love and who loves back
(I'm told there are people who actually can,
But I've never seen this breed of woman).

No, I've spent much of my life alone.
I don't know if I can go on.
The days are beautiful, the nights full of fun,
With sunshine at dusk and rain at dawn.
But these are not enough reasons to live.
What I need, want, is someone so I won't have to live . . . alone.

Daryl A. Marcus

Without Warning

No one warned me,
Least of all you two.

How tiny paws,
Pointed ears,
Liquid eyes could

Brush aside deep pangs of isolation,
Hear faint stirrings of a wounded soul,
See flickering rays of a rising spirit,

No one warned
Me, least of all

You cats! Charlatans for pets!
Independent, suspicious, conceited, cunning,
You deluding imposters for pets!
Whose one deceit lay in stealing my
Unsuspecting heart without warning.

Joan M. Schumack

Daisies

Surrounded by daisies, I thought.
Regard for nature I was taught.
So much beauty to behold—
Purely white petals, eyes of gold.

Mingling, wiggling, giggling in the breeze,
May I pick one of you, please?
Into my hand, you obediently came.
Your life I could not claim.

I hoped to pick a beautiful bouquet.
Now, each one of you must stay.
I leave with an empty hand,
The way nature had it planned.

I looked back at the daisies and smiled.
I'm glad I left them wild.
My heart was full of pride.
In my hand, they would have died.

Karen Cody

We Had a Son Who Was Lost Very Young

We had a son who was lost very young
Here just a short time, then the storm, the silence
Few pictures, memories, his name, and the long, long
Silence, the long, long lifetime of silence

We wondered often what he'd be like
Would he have grown tall with a song in his heart
Would he have run deep with a song in his heart
Would he look like us with a song in his heart

We had a son who was lost very young
Then, in an instant, the call, his voice
No longer lost, soon no longer denied
And the warm, warm joy, pure and simplified

We have a son who was found, who is back
Here is the great thing—the love is intact
We have a son who was found, who is back
Here is the great thing—the love is intact

Claire Arnold

Diamonds

Diamonds are by far a girl's best friend.
I'm reminded of this more and more, each time I stretch out my hand.

Such exquisite beauty, precious and, oh, so rare . . .
Friends often wonder why I just sit and stare.

There you are—constant, unyielding, yet never changing.
Just like my love—far enduring and forever sustaining.

In you, I've found a bond which can't be measured.
Timeless and flawless, so I call this my impeccable treasure.
Now you understand why
  Steve, Reece, Karen, Vincent, Jamie, Eric and Kevin
are the diamonds of my hand.

Kevin L. Waller

Because of You

Have you ever been the victim of a moonbeam attack,
Felt drawn into its glow and then not wanted to come back,
Ascended toward the heavens as your lungs filled with moonlight,
And wiped stardust from your eyes as they twinkled their good night?

Ever had a dream that made you want to sleep forever
Thoughts that made you smile and wish you'd set the clock for never
The type of dream that made you pull the blankets to your chest
And curl up to the empty space where your lover should rest?

Has the wind ever kissed your cheek and told you should smile,
Dried teardrops from your eyes to let you focus for a while,
So you could see with clarity your loneliness was fear,
And made you feel with its soft breeze a new strength would appear?

Have you ever felt that you didn't want something to end,
Felt a gift given to you was better than pretend,
Known that you would die inside to lose what's given to few?
Have you felt any of these things? I have, because of you.

Leigh Anne Sutter

I Need

I need to find a dream to believe in,
I need to warm this heart grown cold,
My bridge is burned, but I can rebuild it,
One by one, I'll place a stepping stone,

I need to look beyond what's known as living,
I need to touch the heartbeat of my soul,
All my life, I've lived within the shadows,
The path I've walked, I traveled alone,

I need to close the door to self destruction,
I need to see, and read between the lines,
For what seems real, may need another answer,
From what I learn, I'll build and then believe,

I need to know that love is still within me,
I need to feel what I've felt before,
Take back my life, and see my own reflection,
Then tell myself, I am me once more.

Bill Billington

Remember

I walk through these mirrors, I carry these days,
I see myself in the glass, in something whole different ways.

Swaying along, the careless wind blows about,
Taking to the trees and carrying the dead leaves out.

The dead leaves, the worriless child with her hands
whipping in the air, and as she catches those dead leaves,
she knows they're cracked and lifeless,
but still handles them with care.

The tender, small child, I see her soft white skin,
it beams with her soft, painless eyes,
and the eyes have such confidence, as if any battle she could win.

She holds her head high, but I hold my head down,
and as my eyes meet hers, she gives one a confused frown.

For, know you are happy, child, but in the future you will see
life is not all beauty, so savor your happy times,
and remember these words within me.

Christina McKinney

Failure

2 Lose all your dreams, U would build your life on
Feelin' bitter with a hint of scorn
Losin' the hope that U had 2 accomplish your dreams
CONFIDENCE!! in yourself gone down the tubes
Every day, becomin' more & more Lazy
Not even carin' 2 try again
Slowly, Becomin' a . . . Failure

Xzavier

I Tried

To my love, Katie Clock,
for her love and support
I took my thoughts
And laid them down,
So I could see
My reflection on the ground.

I took my thoughts
And placed them on a page,
So I could see
If I were a sage.

I took my pages
And threw them in the sea,
So the world could
Come to understand me.

The sea took my words
And swallowed them up,
So all that was left
Was my broken cup.

Mark W. Fields

Yashiro

In loving memory, Yashiro Robert
Inukai—I miss you, Bob
The badge was only worn
In the shadow of the rising sun
The badge is worn more proudly now
But time has run out

In touch with a past
Close at hand yet a world away
Enigmatic yet tangible
Brought closer by departure
I'll sit another vigil for you

The badge worn in the past
At this vigil will last
As these regret filled words
Are lost to the night:

I wish I could have been with you
To say good-bye together
Just to say good-bye to you
As you said good-bye forever

As I focus again on a blur or tears
I wonder can I take you home . . .
Or are you already there

Michael A. Homisak

If Ever Would I Leave

If ever would I leave you,
Shall you not be filled with sorrow.
To bear to part with you
Takes a lot of courage.

I must leave you,
For I do not feel the same as you.
When I am gone,
Do not mourn for me,
For I will always have you
As a precious memory.

You were the only person
Who truly cared for me,
Who loved me,
Who would die for me.

I thought I loved you,
But I did not.
I am truly sorry for the sorrow
That I will cause you.
But please forget me not.

Aimee A. Aimers

The American Cowboy

The American cowboy
Rides the cattle trails no more.
He can only be found in
Our tales of western folklore.

Like the rolling tumbleweed,
Or a dust cloud in the wind,
They roamed across the prairie
Never to be seen again.

Their time was short and lonely.
They were wild, reckless, and lean,
Driving the herds from Texas
To the rails at Abilene.

Their home was in the saddle,
Sleeping on the cold, damp ground,
And nowhere else in history
Can such a story be found.

Robert Rayburn

Southern Summer

All the colors to see
As the copperhead strikes out at me.

In a flash, I take flight,
Striking back with a mighty blow.

Missing and wishing
That it would go.

"No," "no,"
It won't go.

Got to take another blow.
It retreats, and the day is won.
For I had "no" copperhead on my mind.

Life is sweet, just like a beat.
Can't you hear the birds,
"Tweet," "tweet."

Now summer is for all,
Even the friends
We don't like to meet.

So have fun, and mind your feet,
Because you don't know
Who you might meet, just toe deep.

Jamie Lynn Stinde

Hope

Thanks, Mom . . . I love you
Hope is the open field
Where hearts are free to roam,
Where size and shape and color
No longer tie us down.

Hope is the rainbow of color
That brightens all of our dreams
And heals the wounds inflicted
By the heartless of the world.

Hope is the wind of change
That fills the sails of ships
And gently rustles the treetops
Where we rest our weary heads.

Hope is the softest blanket
That cuddled us as children
And, as the world goes on,
Will soon comfort our own.

Hope is the place in which
Our souls go for serenity.
And while the world crumbles,
Hope remains within us.

Matthew D. Ficarelli

My Father's Hands

One day I noticed,
For the first time,
The strength and the nurturing
Of an awesome kind.

The power they exuded
From the years gone by,
And the yet the gentle touch
When they stood at my side.

They brought tears to my eyes
As the life they unfolded,
And my heart filled with hurt
From my lack of holding.

I pray they have time
To now enjoy,
For this life they've struggled
Since a young boy.

My father's hands,
Full of much love,
May we now embrace hand in hand
Till life says last touch.

Patricia S. Taylor

Hidden

Light brown, dark brown,
Sometimes even white.
I just don't understand
Why they keep it outta sight.

Formed in many different shapes,
It comes in any size.
Oh, how I truly love it.
It puts a twinkle in my eyes.

I've searched through the cupboard,
Even through the drawer.
Where did they hide it?
I gotta have some more.

Maybe I'll just pick some up
My next time at the store.
Darn! Where did they put it?
Wow! There's another drawer!

Eureka! I have found it.
They can't keep it hidden from me.
I truly love my chocolate;
I think you will agree.

Edward Stiner Sr.

Birthday

In remembrance: SLM, 1959, Perry
Soon enough time
For the Bird-at-Hand,
Now, I am away after
Any and all on the wing,
For this day,
I am One-and-Twenty!

Ah Youth!
Tho' no tomorrow
I shall live forever!
—tho' Forever be
But Forever lack-a-day!

O Youth!
Never a moment's joy have you known
But before the verymost moment is come
You have mourned the passing!

Too soon! Too soon gone to Earth!
Too long! O Forever too long, shall,
Having gone—stay gone!
O Youth! O Youth!

R. C. Pope

A Mother's Prayer

A word softly spoken
To the Father up above,
Each one carefully chosen,
Each word spoken with love.

From the very beginning
When first I was conceived,
A prayer was softly uttered
For the life that was received.

Each day my mother breathed
She spoke a prayer for me,
Thanking God in advance
For the life I was to be.

My mother's prayers have carried me
Safely through the years,
Each one spoken with reverence
And sprinkled with her tears.

I thank God for my mother
And her willingness to pray,
So a lost and dying soul like mine
Could be forever saved.

Gail Sutton Wolfskill

To Marina

It's no doubt that we will miss you;
There's an empty place on Earth.
But your journey here among us
Taught us lessons of great worth.
With your quiet strength of spirit,
You made Earth a better place.
Love for friends and sense of humor—
Blessings death cannot erase.
There are those whose years are many,
Yet those years are empty shells.
Your short life will be remembered;
You have lived it full and well.
So, Marina, we will miss you.
Thought and illness cannot touch you;
Peace and joy are your reward.
Now, the only fitting tribute,
Is for us to follow through,
Sharing love and strength of spirit,
Blessing others, as you'd do.

Carole Giles

Distant Hearts

To Cathy and Scott,
may your hearts grow ever closer
Once near . . . now far.
      Although distant,
         Ever closer
            My aching heart.

Tender fingers
      Through golden locks.
         Wisps of presence
            Pervade my thoughts.

A gentle touch
      Warm, yet sublime
         Evermore seared
            Into my mind.

Laced with passion,
      A loving kiss,
         Forever etched
            Upon these lips.

Spirits reach out
      To meld o'er miles.
         I close my eyes.
            Please . . . stay a while.

Raymond D. Miller Jr.

My Dear Friend

Many are the friends I've known
Some young, some old, and yet
There are those who touch so deep
The ones we can't forget

Your eyes portray a gentleness
You cherish deep inside
Of the love and affection
For friends you cannot hide

God is ever present
In everything you do
How fortunate we are
The friends who know you

"He" can feel your tenderness
As you kneel to pray
Others know your gentleness
Your friends along life's way

I will thank the Lord above
When I begin to pray
For knowing my dear friend Ellen
She too has passed my way

Janis L. Krepp

The End of Hope

To my friends and family, especially
Grandma Terry, for encouragement
For want of Comfort
For a Reason for our
Senseless Destruction,
We strike out in
Hate and Greed.
A pitter patter
drip drop drip of rain.
Of our own blood
on the cold cold ground
That rushes up to greet the warm
Lifeblood of our Mother's wounds.
Of our own Wounds.
Made by the Wanton Rape of our
Own Twisted Souls.
Forcing Ourselves into
Bodies far too small to contain the
Helpless Rage we feel.
Released in Words, Deeds, Names—
Fear. Death. Panic.
The End of Hope.

Becca Manzak

Lost in Time

In the pale gray sky,
tiny clouds dance by.
Lost in time,
she shuts her eyes.
Lost in her mind, her thoughts fly,
not understanding why
she runs into the night.
Holding back tears, she gently smiles.
Lost in time,
her heart slowly dies,
wondering if it has ever been loved,
perhaps, but now it cries,
cries for him, who is lost from time.
She tries to make sense of a crazy life
that he left behind.
So young at heart, never even tired,
never said a good-bye.
Now there is nothing left to do but cry
of a love that took his life.
So young at heart, never even tried.

Jacob Allen Kuhnle

Past Times

As I look out the window
   Raindrops fall before me,
I wonder why I'm in this place?
   Yet I do not seem to see
   Why am I locked up in here
      With nowhere to go.
   Yet I have to stay here
   Because they tell me so.
   My life is based on things
      I wish not to repeat;
   I wish to fight the system
      Yet I can't compete.
I train my mind to handle it
   Things no one else could;
Why will they not let me out
      I wish they would.
I will be here for a time
   Don't expect me soon,
      I have to stay here
      and pray to the moon.

David Harmon

Papa

To the greatest father, Marcial Gough
Some people say,
That a Father is a Sperm Donor.

But not my father.
He donates more then that,
Time, Love & Patience.

Time—To raise three kids
and no time for himself.

Love—To love all three equal
and don't let us feel any different.

Patience—To stay with all three
kids without help from anyone
and not abandon either of us.

Can I call my Papa a sperm donor
I think not.

But I do call him the Best Father
in the world.

If he was your Papa you'll be
saying the same thing too.

But you can't because he is my, (Papa)

Jannett Gough

A Long Lost Friend

His eyes were always filled
with such wonderment

His soul no one seemed
to ever understand

He felt alone or so
it seemed in his mind

He was loved by many
many he didn't even know

His mind and thoughts
weren't understood

His only mistake was
taking his life

He will be cherished and always
appreciated deep in the hearts of many

He will be missed for
eternity and a day

Michelle Herrmann

Sea Scapes

I sat beside the sea today
To watch the waves roll in.
The sea gulls squabbled over food,
Oh, What an awful din!

The pelicans went gliding by
Between the breakers high,
Searching for a hapless fish.
I hear their mournful cry.

The porpoises were playing tag.
Oh, what a wondrous sight!
It was my pleasure to behold,
And view with sheer delight.

A little girl sat in the sand,
Her houses row on row,
She came and took me by the hand
And said, "It's time to go."

I bid good-bye to sand and sea,
To pelicans and such.
I must return to reality
And make my girl some lunch.

Dorothy A. Paulson

If I Were an Artist

I would sketch my childhood
Way back in the hills
With farmers and log cutters
Camps and saw mills

The little white school house
The church next door
Children playing by the roadside
None were wealthy, but none were poor

I'd sketch the sweet memories
I'd leave out all the bad
I'd never sketch the death of a friend
Nor the face of the lonely and sad

I'd sketch a thousand sun sets
At the closing of a day
The beautiful sparkling stars
Out near the milky way

I'd sketch a little cemetery
Angels hopping from tomb to tomb
In the twilight of the evening
In the light of a silvery moon.

Bernice Howard

A Sense of Strength

My shadow is not
My own, it has belonged
To every other shadow it
Passes by
My shadow does not sit on
Your wall; it crawls in your bed
Where it bleeds with pain
Soothing is its soul
Clever is its mind
Uncontrollable is its heart
Its eyes spill like waterfalls
Hands of despair, time and anger
Love is a word my shadow
Does not understand for
My shadow has never been loved
Only hated by the person to whom
It belongs to, my shadow is naive
But willing to change
For my shadow has the desire to
Live

Jessica Stuart

Heart and Soul

I have yet to see the
beauty of a sunset or a sunrise
atop a rugged mountain.
I haven't seen the Seven Wonders
of the World yet either.
What I have seen is the beauty of
your heart and soul.
Also the Seven Wonders of
"Your Love of Me."
As long as I have you,
I will be content with the beauty
and the wonders you have
brought to me!

Kathy Hanson

Dark Night

I can't do this again
I fresh start, a new try
As I sit here in tears
Asking myself why?

I deserve to be happy
What's wrong with me?
Is there a black cloud
That I just don't see?

There's no silver lining
At least, not in my sight
Is it just hidden
In this dark, deserted night?

When does the sun rise?
Shall I hear the birds sing?
If there's a new day coming
What exactly will it bring?

New hopes, new dreams
Dare I hope for light?
With just a glimmer of hope
I escape from this long, dark night!

Alicia H. Smith

Indian Sue

Who is that
With teeth like pearl
Kissed by the sun
As an Indian girl
With dusky skin
In suntan hue
Hair and eyes that match
Brown
In love, "all fresh," "all new"
Why, she's the prettiest little girl
In town
My granddaughter
Maura Brooke
She's Indian Sue
All dressed up in love
She's brand-new

Edith Guillotte

Love Is Hate

Only with joy
can one open the door to pain.
With each step we take
up that ladder of happiness,
we only increase the distance
of the fall into depression.
Though a life without love
is hardly worth living,
it is a regretful reality
that only through that gift of love
can we experience the most horrid
of emotional agony.

Matt Thompson

Beloved

My soul is filled with music,
My heart is filled with joy.
I'm happy we're here together,
With so much of life to enjoy.

We wonder where the time went,
Being busy it passed us by.
Yet, we took some time
To watch sunsets in the sky.

We look at our loving families,
The gray in our children's hair.
So many ways they show us,
That they truly care.

Tho our backs are bent,
Time was so worthwhile spent.
On bended knees we planted seeds,
A bountiful harvest for our deeds.

Our life has been blessed,
With grace from above.
We can look back on our days,
Filled with happiness and love.

Dorothy Schenck

There by the Gates

Crystal clear
the lake was
the naked tissue
of a Siamese heart

August assents
everything sacred
untimely Caribbean sun
hot over Scandinavia
in the shrouds of the winter

Inside survival
we built the fire of our dreams
a light house of a thousand years
a sign made to inspire
this embryonic fluid
to the understanding only
flaming doves can decree

When I see the flowing curtain
my hand reaches out
and I almost touch you
outside this galaxy's borders.

Kymberly Brown Valenzuela

Ripen Up Right

Learn your lessons;
Learn them well.
Of the destiny of well-gotten lore
Time will tell.
So when opportunities come,
Just expel
Doubts and grab on
For a chance to excel.
Life is yours to
Push forward; don't fail.
Keep trusting;
Work hard—prevail.
Be a model,
Leave a trail
Of aspirations
That can fulfill
The need to keep
The cycle going and foretell
The youth of 2000
Renaissance compelled.

Bobbie Jean Mack Duhe

Great Aunt Teggie

Born to the role
Of a Capricorn soul—
Daughter, sister,
And tomboy, heard told.
Niece, aunt, a lover,
Then wife;
These are the main springs
Of her long life.

Impelled by the stars,
This mother of three—
Now singer, dancer,
Role model she;
Great Aunt Teg
Writes poetry
Rich in rhyme, yet faithful
To reality.

Margaret M. Rugg

Our Lake

Our lake is full of diamonds,
Of this I'm very sure.
How else could the sun's rays
Dance in light so pure?

And then sometimes at bedtime
I stand at my window in prayer
And find that even the moonbeams
Are reflecting their presence there.

The sight is so wondrous!
I wonder why God would take
A chest of His crown jewels
And empty them in our lake.

Norma Hubbard

Scented Candle

To my friend Cody Haas,
a little girl with attitude
Life is a scented candle
Which burns very brief,
Giving off a heavenly scent
Before quickly burning away.
And as the candle burns,
Take heed of it with no delay,
For rushing winds and heavy rains
Can come with no forewarning.
So, enjoy the light and scent life gives
While the scented candle burns away.

Douglas Alan Pratt

Armistice Day Remembered

Far in the distance we hear
A wistful melody loud and clear.
Twenty-one shots from guns on a hill
Gives our hearts a tug and a chill.
— Remembering armistice day
In an old fashion way
American legion and VFW vets
Selling poppies to help us not to forget
Why we celebrate with pride
And rising patriotism deep inside.
The veterans of today
Share in a personal way
The pride and honor of World War I
And the war we really won.
There was no question why
They went to Europe to do and die.
Honor to all veterans this day
As we recall who paved the way.
From world war I to desert storm
Kept the USA safe and warm.

Marilyn C. Luce

Untitled

A caption of a time soon to be a memory.
A day lived a year gone.
What to do? Just stay strong!
Live each day as if your last,
For everything becomes our past.
Only you know all the contrast
And format of your film.
A caption of a time soon to be a memory.

Angela Marsala

Darkness

Darkness
Envelopes
Me like
A tomb.
It surrounds,
Penetrates,
And sustains me.
Its presence
Comforts me;
I lie in its
Warmth,
Sinking deeper
Into its
Loving arms.
I will not fear
In its embrace.

Carla Ballard

Life with You

You make me smile.
You make me laugh.
With you beside me,
Life's journey is an easy path.

The way that I feel is simple.
I love you, and I will not deny
The fact that you make my
Feelings go crazy inside.

When I am feeling low,
You know just what to say
To cure all the sadness I feel
And make my tears go away.

When I am happy,
I hope that you know
It is because life with you
Makes my outsides glow.

Kathy Mains

Woman

Womanish will of the wistful
Nude thoughts cascade
Rampant saying hello
Then self-examine's disease
Roaming own mind
With clairvoyance finding
Something never before seen
Great intuition clothed word emotions
Luminary pristine feelings revealed
Learning discernment hard nut to crack
Inner being exposing controlled command
Femininity only allowed
To illuminate false modesty
Woman lust released to track
One moment at a time she's
Disaffection with electricity
Choosing mater final crowning
Woman is woman

Sandra Jeanne Myers

A Message for Mom

You held me when I cried,
Wiped the tears from my eyes.

You taught me how to sit and walk,
You taught me how to laugh and talk.

Stood beside me,
Though right or wrong.

Showed me the ways,
Both short and long.

Through my journeys there you stood,
All the happiness the joys and worries.

At times I've seemed so far away,
Yet, in my heart you've always stayed,

My mother, my friend,
With you beside me,
Always, I will win.

Bobbie L. Murray

Trying to Soothe the Wounds Inside

As I sit alone all by myself
My thoughts and dreams with me
I am searching for some happiness
But happiness to my eyes I cannot see
Right know my mind is all confused
I don't know where to go
I close my eyes to ease my mind
But it won't help I know
As I sit alone, I concentrate
I pray for peaceful thoughts
But all I see is darkness
All good things that I have lost
And then I want to say good-bye
I want to leave this place behind
Feeling as if I don't belong
These thoughts won't leave my mind
The road that leads my way is winding
It seems there's no end in sight
I try to find a light that's shining
Was my life wrong, or can I make it right?

Christopher Bigger

On My Way

When I die in this world today
please lay me to rest
where the children play,
where laughter is heard
instead of tears,
where people live without any fears,
where the sun shines down
through the years.
"For it is here"
I shall find comfort
In all these things,
just sitting back
taking A ride on
an angel's wings.

Rebecca McKenzie

Younger

Can't wait to be older.
Acting just like mommy,
wearing high-heels and make up.
You begin to feel old.
Regressing to the childlike ways,
which you swore you'd never do,
becoming so much younger
than ever thought possible,
and realizing that we are all
children playing house.

Aimee Larraga

To Me

To me
He is an angel
sent to me by some higher force
He is an inspiration
that my heart will sing
He is an enigma
in which my heart is entangled
He is the passion
where my heart longs to be

To me
With a mystical smile
He can make the sun shine
With a magical stare
He could make the saddest tear
turn into a tear of joy
With enchanting eyes
He could open my heart

Diane Sargent

When Your Dream Dies

My daughter, Tina M. Ray,
and my sister, Joyce A. Pauley
When I could not see anymore,
You were my eyes; when my heart
Was wounded, you said hang on,
My heart beats for you.
When my back was to the wall,
You went there with me.
Stand up, walk with me,
Hang on until you can see.
Let your heart beat for me.
Come, we can share a dream you and I,
Our hearts can learn to fly.
No false pride, our dream is alive.

Helen M. Henderson

My Angel

Last night, I had an angel
Sitting next to me;
She told me of the future,
Of things that someday will be.

She told me of the world beyond,
Just past the pearly gates.
It made me feel so anxious
That I can hardly wait.

She told me to be ready
To meet some of my old friends.
She told me of the other world,
The one that has no end.

Then suddenly I woke up,
But I still can't forget,
'Cause she is the very first angel
That I have ever met.
She is "My Angel."

Vincent Pizzi

Izzy

Izzy does chocolate
with garage doors wide and open,
August melting down like tiny dancers.

Calendar girlie
(twenty years up on the wall)
still smirks, as always.

An old friend
curls up with dreaming paws
that twitch with every moan.

Out back a cigar box is in sync . . .
a yellowed road map, a lock of hair,
a pebble long forgotten.

Charles Davidson

A Prayer for You

I feel the need for prayer tonight,
So I'm sending up this one.

I ask you, Lord, to touch my friend,
And heal the loss of her son.

Only you can comfort her,
In your very special way.

Hold her close and help her through
Each and every day.

Show her as you've shown me,
That if we seek your face,

There is where our loved ones are,
Resting in your grace.

I lift my friend to you, Lord,
Walk her every mile,

Give to her a happy heart,
Followed by a smile.

She really hasn't lost him,
He's never far away,

For you hold him in your arms
And you're with us every day.

Betty Ann Bowerman

My Only One

To the one I'll never forget, Clint Agnew
You are not the only one
My heart has ever known
Yours are not the only lips
That have ever touched my own
Yours are not the only eyes
That whispered tenderly
And yours are not the only arms
That held me lovingly
But no one else in all my life
Has ever meant so much
And no one else could ever have
Your soft and endearing touch
No one else could ever match
The magic in your eyes
Your character and all the ways
In which you are so wise
The others are forgotten
And without least regret
I only wish you had been
The first I ever met

Jennifer Loeffler

Children in the Pool

Raucous cries echo,
Little girls splash
As if swimming in the tears of God.
A blue rectangle,
Deep end,
No diving,
How their faces rise and sink.
Their eyes closed,
Lifted as if in prayer,
Their voices shrill,
No lifeguard on duty,
My eyes watch in apprehension.
They sink
And rise.
Such little, slippery forms,
As if they had already
Been worn smooth
By lives they never had.

M. Klosner

Remnants of the Day

Against a sky
Cold and gray
Broken clouds
Peel away
Shafts of gold
Breaking forth
Painting their limbs
Russet orange
From ashen gray
Golden green
From evergreen
Wind whistles
Dying embers glow
Remnants of the day

Sara Blue

Holidays

Hear the children's laughter
As happy snow men they make,
So sure that, soon after,
There is hot chocolate and cake.

Wintery winds steadily blowing,
Christmas bells merrily ringing,
Colored lights cheerfully glowing,
And carolers softly singing.

Shoppers bustling in merriment;
Another year is almost spent.
Soon, the new year will begin,
Ushering in the flowers of spring.

Janet Tyrrell Kimmons

The Master's Touch

As I sat staring at an empty canvas
With the brush and paints in my hands
Wondering what stokes to paint
An idea came to my command

It was the master's touch
The strokes fell heavy on the canvas
An image began to appear
Taking away my despondency and fear

Bright colors flowed from my brush
In many shades and hues
Ideas came faster and faster in a rush
Red, green, purple, and blue

At last, the picture was finished
The paints and brush fell at my side
Inside, I felt satisfied
As the master's touch had passed on by

Jacqueline Atkins

Tiny Tears

Tiny tears, tiny tears
filled with frustration full of fears
tumbling down a pale sad cheek
to the depths below

Gone is joy from the soul
a smile to grace the face
no more twinkle in the eye
just pity in its place

The sounds of sobbing can be felt
sadness fills the air
sorrow does surround the moment
for all of us that's here

Despair ruptured in the heart
triumphant in this fate
grief is eased by this emotion
Tiny tears, tiny tears.

Rodney P. Wrinkle

Marilyn

To the memory of Marilyn Hesse
A friend is gone.
We're full of grief.

We feel a sadness
Beyond belief.

Her years so brief,
Only sixty two.

We look, but her smile
We do not see.

Only in our hearts
Will she ever be.

Until someday
When our spirits flee,

Will we again in Heaven
Her face to see.

Dorothy Hadad

Seeing Is Believing

Seeing is believing
Is not necessarily so,
For some things are so tiny
That they're there, but you don't know.

Yes, I think there are flying saucers,
Though I have not seen one,
But I haven't seen a lot of things
That I have heard of done.

I've never seen a tornado,
And I hope I never do,
But I know from seeing pictures
That they too exist and brew.

I've never seen my Creator,
But I know that He exists,
And if I keep an open mind,
That He will be my guest.

Arlene Windom

I Didn't Know

*In loving memory of Kris Hansen—
see you when I get there*
I didn't know
About the pain he wouldn't show
He needed to realize
Love never dies
No one can visualize
All the lies
Being told
So we can be bold
All along
We've tried to be strong
When our hearts ache
We continually shake
Kris, we'll never know
What made you go
Why, oh, why
Did my big brother die?

Shelly Ingle

Little Anna

Little Anna has no fears.
I myself have shed a few tears.

Little Anna had big, blue eyes.
We now would like to say our good-byes.

I ask her now to pray for me,
And I understand why God made me.

Melissa Parmiter

No Second Chance

Sometimes you meet the love of your life
When you're just too young to know.
Too immature to realize,
And so you let them go.

You're frightened by these feelings,
Afraid of what they bring.
But true love doesn't tie you down,
In fact, it gives you wings.

If you knew then what you know now,
Would you have walked away?
No one could have changed your mind,
Free will comes into play.

If fate is kind, a second chance
May someday come your way.
This is often not the case,
A price you have to pay.

Cheryl I. Metz

Cats

Cats, cats, cats.
Small cats,
big cats, fast cats,
slow cats, skinny cats,
fat cats.
Most of all, I love furry cats.

Brittany Clisso

Who Are You? Inside of My Brain

I cannot see you,
Don't even know your name,
But I can hear you,
Your voice, a whisper in the wind.

Who are you? What do you want?
Why don't you get out of my head?
I don't want you around here no more.
Why don't you just go away?

You tell me things that I ,
don't want to hear,
You tell me things that I,
Don't want to know.

Who are you to take up residence
Inside of my brain?
Why can't you at least
Tell me your name?

Brett Hawks

My Little Girl

I love to touch your tiny fingers
Play with your tiny toes
I think you're really beautiful
Bet you'll have a lot of beaus
It really is amazing
To see the things you do
I always get excited
When you're trying something new
The first time you tried standing up
You thought you were so smart
Instead, you looked so funny
'Cause your legs were far apart
Then you started walking
And getting into things
Sometimes you were too fast for me
I thought you had grown wings
That is part of growing up
A woman someday you'll be
You'll marry and have a baby
And know how much you mean to me

Evelyn Ferrari

Corey, My Guardian

*For Corey, my knight in shining armour,
forever yours, Denise*
Lying here beside you,
And whispering your name,
Telling you I love you and,
I hope you feel the same.

With you beside me,
The pain is gone,
You hold my hand,
So I can carry on.

You take my fears,
Of all that is dark,
And light the way,
You are my spark.

For any dragons,
That dare to come my way,
You are my knight,
And always ready to slay.

I have never known,
A love like this,
With constant harmony,
And magical bliss. . . .

Denise Rios

The Christmas Season

Artificial trees with blue lights
Blinking computer games. What a sight!
We have moving and talking toys
Instead of playing with girls and boys.

We should have pine trees
With red and green, lights
Making such a beautiful sight.
The holly, the fire, the mistletoe,
The songs and cards bestowed.
The cookies and the pies a-baking
Remind us of the joy in making.

When the star shown above the Earth
The shepherds went to see the birth.
The wise men then came from afar
All of these set our hearts ajar.
For the baby Jesus was born in a stall
And now shows us his love for all.
Remember the joys of Christmas
And friends of yore
With peace and joy forever more.

Frances Ann Flory

A Child Lost

*To my loving husband, Ken, son Keith,
and Mr. Baker*
I look at the child,
And what do I see?
Confusion, pain and turmoil,
Yet he reaches out to me.

And I can't help but wonder
What madness made him this way;
What can I do to help him;
What is there I can say?

He seems a million miles away;
His soul seems truly lost,
Yet he is sent from place to place
To "help" him, at what cost?

Will he ever have a happy life
With someone who really cares,
Or will he be forever lost,
Wandering alone somewhere?

Norma E. Ackerman

The Prophecy

Out
She sprang
I am Alive
Hold me, love me
for what I now know
so will the world.
Please
Embrace
Our new life
so that we may know
our true purpose.

I ache for your touch
Don't shut me out in a room
with a door
I cannot open

Kathryn McGlynn

Unwanted

My egg donor, biological mother
Your eyes looked so loving,
like you wouldn't hurt a soul.
Then, one day, everything changed
as your heart turned into coal.
You said you'd never hurt me.
Maybe you didn't in a physical way,
but you've scared me for life
and now I'm paying with pain.
All I ever wanted was to be
loved by someone like you, but
now I'll never want it, because
your love could never be true.

Carmella Trimarchi

Wind Spirit

To anyone who has lost a loved one
The breeze drifts by.
Was that a slight sigh?
The trees wave their branches.
Could voices be chancing?
The leaves dance to and fro.
Was that a groan or moan of woe?
The flag flutters on the pole.
Was that someone's broken soul?
The wind whips through one's hair.
Was that meant to scare?
The whispers of air wisp along.
Was that a heartfelt song?
When you sit outside,
Think of all the spirits passing by.
One never knows . . .
It maybe someone of old.

Elizabeth Talley

Lycanthropy

Autumn's breath blows colors of death,
Shades of winter's birth.
Transformation seizes.
Lunar rays grasp the limbs,
Forest cries out and finds the wind,
Which shakes it of its fear.
Winter wind, graveyard friend,
Sing to the forests of icing.
Tomb's chill fills the air,
It will not be much longer.
Coarse hair seeps through flesh,
Fangs are born in screams of agony.
Milky, yellow, sleepless eyes
See through distorted light.
The harvest is ripe,
Night is dark and heavy
With the breathing of the werewolf.

David Durham

I Wish I'd Said I Love You

I wish I'd said I love you
When I had the chance,
You did everything for me,
Swimming, basketball, and dance.

I wish I'd said I love you,
I argued with you instead,
You were always there for me,
Listened to everything I said.

I wish I'd said I love you,
You could've been a friend,
Though it will be hard,
I'd like to try again.

I wish I'd said I love you,
After all, you are my mother,
Even though I've said otherwise,
I'd never want another.

Heather Sieben

Emotion?

Frightened beyond continued remorse
Chastise my morals within due course
Nothing to fear, service withdrawn
Abolished issues harboring my pawn

Scoot Dekruif

Thank You, Firefighters

The fires looked more grim
as they ate our home state,
spreading at the wind's whim,
the rains are way too late.

We celebrated the Fourth,
but with some sorrow,
for those evacuated north,
and we prayed for tomorrow.

Hurricanes have spared us most,
now fire hit us in the belt,
turning crops and home to toast,
nationwide the sorrow is heartfelt.

We hoped that rain would soon fall,
and drench our home and crop,
but there was almost none at all,
so you fought and didn't stop.

We thank all who came to the rescue,
now the future looks brighter,
and all because of people like you,
who became a firefighter.

Todd Pickin

The Watchman

I only would say,
in thought of mind,
not a sound be heard,
as if to find
the silence as I unwind
into the night.
The watchman keeps time
with the souls
that sleep, not unkind,
for all the dreams
that free, not bind,
the spirits, colors, and rhymes,
our dreams, the mind's eyes
and awaking into the biggest dream
with all the questions
of what's and why's.
Are we still dreaming, watchman?

Howard Wayne Cousland

Leaving Home

My loved and dear little girl,
Now that you leave me
And other doors open to you
I will always think of you.
My missing you will surround you.

And in the late evening hours
When silence descends on the house,
I will bless Destiny
That I lived
To see you as a Bride.

May God give you luck in life,
And may everything around you
Blossom like the morning.
Now, when you go far away,
May joy always be your part.

And don't forget
In your thoughts of many things
With how much love
I raised you and loved you.

Iancu T. Carp

The Bell

At the sound of a bell
It all came to an end,
No more teachers or tests
Or calls from my friend.

We just split up and left;
We all went different ways;
That bell meant the end
To our high school days.

As I think back in time,
I once wanted to be free;
I used to reach for the days
When they'd just let me be.

But now the last bell has rung,
Telling me to go,
But I stand here and wait
Because to where, I don't know.

All I need is some direction
Of how to get around.
So now I'm listening and waiting
For the next bell to sound.

Julie Chernavsky

A Message to Sonny Bono

In your lifetime,
Not only did you help yourself,
You helped everyone around you,
Never remained on the shelf.

In your lifetime,
Your hidden wisdom fooled those snobs.
Everyone felt joy around you,
Never disinclined your jobs.

In your lifetime,
You've emerged to the highest point.
Hidden evil was around you,
Almost made it to the coin.

Heaven took you away
From the politician's ring.
Heaven took you away
To serve their only king.

Everyone felt joy around you.
You helped everyone around you.
Hidden evil was around you
When Heaven took you away.

Kim Soli

Castles in the Sky

Last night I fell asleep and dreamed
Of castles in the sky.
I dreamed of all the wonders
And the magic there on high.
I caught a glimpse of all the things
I've longed for all my days,
And there they were, before me
In a hundred different ways.
I found that I could wave a wand
And make a wish come true.
Then suddenly I saw your face
And there, my dear, were you.
But then, alas! I came awake
And found, to my dismay
That all my dreams were fantasies
That drift along the way.
I could forgo those wondrous things
That faded in the blue
If only I could wave a wand
And know your love is true.

Dorothy Keaveney

For Michael

In loving memory of Michael 1970–1992
I shed a tear for you today
Amongst the misty rain
My heart bled for you today
The scars always remain
I kissed the air for you today
The scent of wildflowers was true
With each new day, I still miss you

Tara M. Benton

Time

Time will ease your pain
But is that true?
Will it take away your scars
And your bruises too?

Can a wounded heart heal
And become whole again?
Or does it stay in pieces
Becoming worn and thin?

Time will ease your pain
That's what they say
Time will dry your eyes
As you count the days

Jessica Banta

Memories

Memories are haunting visions,
of the past.
That are always with us.
Memories slip in, when we least
expect them,
bitter and sweet, dark and bright,
always we
feel their presence near.

Memories are the dust of our lives,
from the beginning
to the end
the good, the bad, and the ugly,
that dwells, with us,
day and night

Memories are held close to the heart.
They are the
hidden blessings
and griefs of our lives.

Mary Overcash

Tempestivity

When The Reaper claims his harvest,
Tarry not, for what's to gain?
A life that lives beyond its purpose
Is a life that's lived in vain.
For the virtue's not in living,
It's the cause for which we die.
In the treasure there's no value,
Save the good that it can buy.
And the grain that's cut when golden,
Through sacrifice to man, serves God,
But the chaff that lingers longer
Is but buried beneath the sod.

Robert K. Edson

Sparrow's Fall

To Junie Moon, a small, sweet warrior
Long houses painted midnight
With eons until down.
Steep path up the mountain,
Hope just eking on.

Sparse breath, day and brittle,
Seared as winter's hay.
Demon's fire flung spittle,
Will power burns away.

Scattered rags of yearning,
Strobe lit sorrows pall.
Earth keeps right on turning
Love mourns sparrow's fall.

Doris J. Stevens

You

To Wendi, my heaven
The love I feel, it burns inside
It leaves no room for it to hide
The passion's rage has grown so strong
It breaks me down when you are gone

My love for you, I let it show
Like the candle's fiery glow
I must do things I've never done
To show my love has just begun

I've never felt this way before
To feel so loved, yet feel so sore
I feel your pain with every breath
To you, what's sadness, to me is death

I pray your feelings never fade
I try to pray away the shade
So I will do all I can do
To prove that all I want is you

Kyle S. Doan

Eve

Adam took her hand and led
Her to his firelight-warmed bed

But she gave to him apple fair
And clothed him with more than hair

From the garden, him she'd steal
Yet helped him to create the wheel

King of beasts, the man she made
Standing quietly in his shade

Sons and daughters from her torn
He knew but pleasure when were born

A life of penance, Eve has lived
So, like good Adam
Did God forgive?

Donna Duell

Windows

Windows, windows everywhere
What do they mean to me?
An open space, a pane of glass
Through which I look and see
A flying bird with wings outstretched
Against a clear blue sky
An airplane that glides along
Miles and miles on high
God guides them both along their way
With His loving hand
He made the bird so it could fly
The plane designed by man
God gave the man a mind to think
And try to figure out
The ways to make things work
And know without a doubt
That He is always there
Just a prayer away
If we but only call on Him
His love will make our day

Dorothy Fisher

Time

I took my time
    as if it were mine.
 All the time in the world was mine.
Spend time? Save time?
    Who—
        to the nearest dollar,
            can round off time?

As if . . .
    knowledge of time can expand
    grains of sand,
        slowly shifting
            &
    fiercely forming,
in tide-pools of time.

When I seek time, I waste time.
If I find time, I've lost time.
The time I share was hardly there.
So little is time. So little time.

Though never undone is the past,
    we may borrow a bit of time.
Some time to learn is time to grow.
    (the hour-glass will never know)

A little time to be is ours . . .
never to be undone by time.

Troy Christopher Saulters

Lovers

To Nancy, with all of my love
More than need . . .
I want to share
All of me with all of you,
With all my tender loving care.

More than want . . .
I choose to give
My loyalty, devotion, and love.
Our growth together forever will live.

More than life . . .
Our love means to me,
Of destiny, of time and beauty,
Where our spirits soar free.

More than me . . .
I am with you,
A thought that caresses,
I am, I will, and I do.

Terry J. McElmurry

A Real Man

A real man is meek
A real man is loving
Without these, there is no man

A real man is peaceful
A real man is unselfish
Without these, there is no man

A real man is long suffering
A real man is trustworthy
Without these, there is no man

A real man is helpful
A real man is loyal
Without these, there is no man

A real man is kind
A real man is cheerful
Without these, there is no man

Matthew Johanan Wilkins

Waiting for the Right Time

Dedicated to my one and only true love,
Thomas J. Lundy
I've wanted to tell you
For a long time.
I finally got
Up enough nerve.
One night we took a walk
And sat on a curb.
I finally said
Everything I wanted to
How I've liked you
For a long time.
Let's just say
Things went well.
You're the best guy
I've ever known.
My soul mate
Has finally been found.
I love when you're around
You make me feel complete.
I'm just glad I finally
Told you I love you!

Jenny L. Deeds

"Love"

To my family
Love finds its way
through the misery in
this world like a
rainbow in the sky

Love never fails
as it gives itself
Love brightens your
darkest moments

Love is a way of living
presenting pleasantly
yourself as you seek
not your own

And you are not
easily provoked
but dressed
with the light of kindness

Love is divinely
inspired and earthly
portrayed because
of the Master of all times

Carmem M. Cruz

Stand For

Why are you straddling the fence?
Don't stand there all day
You must make a stand
Are you with our Lord?

Christ died for you and me
He took a stand for us
Don't turn one way or another
Unless it is following God

We must take our stand for Jesus
Without Him, we are nothing
Jesus took a stand for us
He showed how much He loved

L. Orveline Buckner

All She Needed

Looking at her sorrow-filled face,
How could she be so sad?
I wondered what her memories were
And what kind of life she had had.

People thought she needed money
Or some sort of help.
She loved everyone,
But was loved by only herself.

So much love she had to give,
Yet no one to give it to.
I couldn't just pass her by,
Yet I knew not what to do.

I wished I could make her happy,
I wished I could find a way.
I just smiled with all my heart,
And her frown faded fast away.

No one had ever done this,
She'd been sad for quiet a while.
She needed one thing—from anyone.
All she needed was a smile.

Jyll Collins

A Fire Burning

Their is joy on this Earth
Give it time and it will surf
It's not easy from day to day
But I rise and am on my way
I pray to the person up above
That I find someone to love
I've been lonely for so long
Looking for love, but I go on
The fire in heart wants to be free
For that special person who wants me
Time goes slow when an all alone
To find that someone to bring home
I wonder what I've done to deserve this
To carry around that emptiness
The fire still burns, what can I say
For that special love to come my way

Ray Steils

Tiganca Fromasa

For all the Romaniacs here and there,
I love you
O, beautiful gypsy,
Eyes enchanted, dazzling
Skirt spun of silk,
Dance through midnight's sky.
Each blue hue blending perfectly,
And only your bright smile
Guiding me through the night.

Carrie Carlson

My Guardian Angel

It really wasn't that long ago
When we both knew you had to go.

My eyes were filled with tears that day
As I watched you drift away.

You fought so hard, longing to stay,
Yet, cancer won again that day.

But your presence I could feel
With me now, my sister dear.

Am I right? Are you near?
Show a sign so I could hear.

There is so much I need to say,
And it gets harder every day.

I wish this was just a dream
And you were back the way you've been,

Loving and protecting me,
A Guardian Angel to set me free.

Helen Michniak

Beauty of a Sunset

The people in the walls
As sunset lights an evening sky
The magic of it all
For there you find a quietude
And peace within oneself

To dream beneath this sky above
Will send your spirit soaring
For each sunset has an awesome show
To be set before your eyes

So as gentle dark approaches
Before the stars appear
Now's the time to look
For at least just even one

For a sunset is a gift of beauty
And, oh, how beautiful it is
A gift given to all
If one takes the time to look

So as the day comes to an end
Gaze upwards at the skies
And be grateful for this day
Yet another given you

Marion McLain

Missing You

To the loves of life, and my darling Debia
Like a heart without a beat
I feel so incomplete
until the day we meet
I'm missing you

Like a name without a face
a memory without a place
or gone without a trace
I'm missing you

I feel the freedom of the eagle
the peace within the dove
the calmness of the ocean shore
beside the one I love

The soft caress of your touch
a passion I shan't ignore
to this world we give so much
when we should give each other more

So this vow that I dispense
will forever remain intense
because from my heart it represents
that I'll always be missing you

Marty J. Fetch

Friend (Affection)

Yesterday you made me smile
Today I'm not so sure

I never thought I'd have
The strength to abuse you
But I found it . . .
(Unsecured)

And yet . . . you shrug
Forgiving . . .
(Forgiven)

Jared N. Kunath

God's Children, Your Children, Their Children, Our Children

*Family: Richard, Eva Lee, Noah,
Cristina, Freedom, and Alex*
Angels of mercy
rescue these forlorn
neglected children
hungry and ragged
sleeping out on streets
in public places
some with families
others abandoned

We pray and beg you
to give them comfort
lift up the spirits
of men and women
show them how to care
to shower on these
human sympathy
the blessings of love
angels of mercy
your compassion
protects and saves

Dr. Eleanor Otto

Shadows

I sit silent in the dark.
Amongst the shadows of the night.
They creep across the walls
like a spider toward its web.
And my mind, writhes in pain,
scorched with agony, singed with fear.
Images flash in front of me
like moments of genius
or signs of madness.
Surrounded by the world
and yet, I am alone.

Stephanie Teixerio

Walking Through the Garden

I'm walking through the garden
on this brisk, fine day
thinking of my youth
and my carefree way
savoring this peaceful feeling
smiling to myself simple, pure thoughts
as I enjoy nature's wealth

I'm walking through the garden
of serenity, wonder, and dreams
high on the fragrant breeze
and light of my feet
enveloped in remarkable feeling
that I never wish to leave
if only I could remain blind
to what I truly see . . .

Catherine Povloski

Euphoria

I know I am human,
And yet I try.
My instincts pull me.
It's them I defy.
So many horrors,
We all share the blame.
I fear similarity
For I know I'm the same.
Hatred for the people,
Disgusted by my own,
To find euphoria
I must search alone.

Carolyn Sharp

Pain

I see the pain you feel
I hear the hurt you know
Wishing the world were different
Somehow knowing it won't get better
You see the pain I feel
You hear the hurt I know
Wishing there was no pain
Feeling only that

Cherie Carpenter

One Last Wish

Can you see me peaking through
With eyes now lacking shine?
Can you hear me calling out
With a voice no longer mine?

I am more than a shell
Now lying listless in this bed
With all of this technology
I'm being drained, breathed, and fed

There is much more to the man I am
The man I used to be
Look beyond your guilt and fear
With compassion—just see me

As someone who has lived his life
With love, hopes, and dreams
And now is being called back home
Life here is done, it seems

If these machines could go away
What is meant to be will be
I lived my life with courage and pride
Please let me die with dignity

Chris Fischer

The Violin Sings

Listening to the soulful strains
flowing from the violin,
tears trickle down
those cheeks so fine and frail.
Her mind softly treading . . .
down that cherished
memory lane.
Tired and alone,
she closes her eyes;
a tender face hovers over her
with a gentle smile.
Sweet love strains
pour from the violin,
as her spirit soars from the cage
and the rain stops within.
The violin sings on
as two souls join in love
unfulfilled in life . . .
but reunited in the heavens above.

Piyali Ganguly

Vision

Oh, what a beautiful sight I saw.
The heavens rolled back so lovely.

I saw Gabriel, a horn he was a blowin'.
And there stood Michael the Archangel.

One foot on land and one on sea.
He was telling all that Jesus was here.

It was now time for all believers,
To take their long awaited journey.

But, my, what a terrible sight
As I looked back to see.

Total destruction on every hand.
Brother fighting brother.

But then I sat up and looked about
What a disappointment I felt.

Tho' I rejoiced for the lost,
For what I saw was just a vision.

A vision for all to come.
The time was not yet.

Debora K. Asbury

Saint Clare of Assisi

Dear holy Clare, fair of face,
Sister of Agnes, virgin of grace.
Followed Father Francis
With much suffering to endure,
To live the Gospel Life,
To be faithful and pure.

Devotion to the Blessed Sacrament,
Your sweetest delight.
As you knelt in adoration,
Your heart took flight.
In God's plan, a very special soul,
One of beauty and goodness,
With Heaven your goal.

All brothers and sisters pray
For your guidance each day,
Dear Clare, that your seraphic spirit
Will lead the way, to the kingdom of God
Where our joy will never cease,
And we all will live forever
In harmony and peace.

Elizabeth Ondroczky SFO

Paths

Where are you?
The direction is the same
The path is equivalent
Destination's are not

How will I know?
Am I right?
Did I do right?
Where did I go wrong?

How do I get to you?
We were the same
Now we are different
Yet we did not vary

The paths we took
Like railroad tracks
Yet I am east
And you south

Where is the middle?
How do we find each other?
Back together
Were we belong

Charlie Griffin

Stranger

I need to know,
from where I came.
To the path I follow
where now I am.

Like a fish
that swims down stream.
Must turn around
to see where he has been.

I never know
what's just ahead.
I only can feel
what I once had.

So I'll not judge you
for what you may do.
'Cause like me
you are a stranger
of what's ahead.

I need to know just who I am
from which I came
from wherefore I am going.

Georgina J. Robinson

Wisdom Is Faith

I only know that I know nothing,
Once a wise man said.
But, I thought and said,
We know it all if we have faith.

Faith is the magic wand
That reaches for the impossible;
It is peace within ourselves,
And a true promise in our hearts.

When we know, we are confident.
Although we never know how much we know,
Faith is the answer to all questions.
We know it all if we have faith.

Faith leads ourselves to the hope road.
While we are on the hope road,
Peace and happiness impulse us.
We know it all if we have faith.

Before and after, yesterday and today,
Who were first and who were last.
What does it matter after all?
We know it all if we have faith.

Edys Coro

My Father

Who blessed the day that I was born,
And walked with me from dusk to morn,
And taught me not to be forlorn?
My father.

Who kissed me ere I was tucked in bed,
And laughed at the inane I said,
And went to work to earn my bread?
My father.

Who cheered me up when I was sad,
And spanked me hard when I was bad,
And gave me part of all he had?
My father.

Who called the doc for my cracked head,
And dried the tears my mother shed,
And greatly feared lest I were dead?
My father.

Who leads me onward yet today,
And hears everything that I say,
And keeps me on the righteous way?
My father.

Betty Neeb Ihde

Amy

In her eyes,
The light of blue sky . . .
In her smile,
The glow of summer sun . . .
In her touch,
The caring of an angel . . .
In her words,
The wisdom of passing years . . .
In her thoughts,
The lifetime yet to transpire . . .
In her laughter,
The song of a bird . . .
In their tears,
The despair of suffering . . .
No, not a vision, not a dream:
It's my niece.

Julian Hansen

Opportunities Abound

dreams danced
opportunities knocked
life was good

but . . . (there is always a but)
had a problem
was an introvert
can't do this
can't do that
too shy
must remain in comfort zone
dreams faded
opportunities dwindled
life was sad

but . . . (there is always a but)
by the grace of God Almighty
no more mr. shy
dreams are dancing
opportunities are knocking
life is good
i have decided

James Hartman Moore

The Masses

Through the masses of people I walk
Never looking at anyone's face

I walk only looking down
Toward the ground.

To no one I speak
To no one I smile nor frown

Programmed robots just going
Around and around.

To jobs we all go
Grinding ourselves down.

Leaving at the end of the day
To endure the masses of people
All with their heads
Hanging down staring at the ground.

Through the masses of people I walk
In the city as the lights fill
Our dark Surround.

Melody Morris

Pen Pal

Sunshine Clan
A warm hello and special message
Across the miles to you
That someone is thinking of you
With best wishes and good thoughts for you

Dorothy Harris

Longing

I love someone
Who likes me
But loves me? I don't know
I want to see you
I want to hear your voice
I want your kisses
I want your embrace
I think about you
All the time
But my way to you
I can't find
So I sit back
I watch with longing
My desire grows
I reach out to you
But I can never touch
I wish you could love me
As much as I love you
I want you
I only wish you knew

Tina Kline

Letting Go

The time is soon approaching
When we'll go our separate ways;
We'll say good-bye forever
And only hope to meet again one day.
I've held you in my heart
For as long as I now know,
And you'll always be a part of me,
No matter where I go.
Our differences I've put aside,
The memories I hold true,
But as these tears fall from my eyes,
I realize I must let go of you.
I held on for the longest time
And, with each day, I grew strong.
So as I turn and walk away,
I'll know I've not done wrong.
And if, someday, down the road
Our paths should cross and meet again,
I'd hope that you would take my hand
And say you're still my friend.

Shanna Lynn Yurewick

You

*To the man who completes me,
Bob Malaguti Jr.*
On the cloudiest days
Your smile shines so brightly
On the coldest nights
Your love warms me
You give me the strength
To conquer my fears
You are a masterpiece
With your beauty and grace
Like a carousel horse
Revolving around me
Hold your head up high
And proudly and let me
Ride through life with you

Kathyann Coon

Hopeful Thoughts

Today is here!
Tomorrow will be.

Yesterday was,
has been, and will
never be again!

Martha Wells Soto

The 800 Meter Run

My stomach rumbles
The first call for the 800
Then the second
I go down to the bullpen
They line us up
I'm in lane three
It was 50 degrees
I was in shorts and a tank
On your mark, get set, bang
The first lap I ran my hardest
I was in first the whole lap
After the first lap I was getting tired
But I kept ahead
I could hear her footsteps coming
The final 100 meter
Your supposed to run your hardest
I tried so hard but it wasn't hard enough

Tracy Matlock

The Nestling's Plight

Passion's pain and lover's folly
Exuberated melancholy
Responsibility unknown
Placed upon one not quite grown

The fear of future and the past
Life's loom weaving, ever fast
How may a soul set straight the way?
Curved and wandering paths belay

Lose hope, never glance abreast
Let family love provide the nest
A love intense and always ever
The nestling's plight we feel together

Alone is then a distant place
And happiness consumes the space

Lane Watts

Her Heart

Shattered beyond repair, it fell,
Scarred and marred with marks of wear,
Dumped into the depths of Hell,
To burn with pain; I cannot bear.
An idle thought, a passing lie,
Enough to crush the trust of years,
Although it tries, it will not die,
But beats throughout the flood of tears.

Strength of soul, comprised of faith
Possessed by few, there's no compare,
Of which without, this wretched wraith
Would live a life so cold and bare.
I look to her for love, and so,
Begin again; to never part,
To comfort and begin to show,
I'll never break, again, her heart.

Jerry Kendrick

Perspective

Weak, fragile, power.
The insignificance of millions . . .
How important is one?
Satan, evil, fun.
Hearts shattered by broken promises.
Our goals achieved: friendship,
Life, energy, love.
Small object, its match an abundance.
A toy with no purpose.
The prize to be won, completely unique,
Shows the fate of our future.
God, purpose, curious.
What is the fate of my soul?

Steve Wandel

My Heart

I lost it
Somewhere along the way.
I don't know
What could have happened;
I haven't seen it
Since the day I first saw you!
Did you hear it?
Maybe it fell and shattered.
I wonder
Could it have been stolen?
If you find it,
Please take good care of it.
It's precious to me.
It's been broken too often.
If you see it,
Please keep it close to you.

Deborah Underhill

Adolescence

I know not my path,
though the path might seem clear;
my intentions and deeds
are overshadowed by fear.
My decisions are based
on artificial laws;
my actions are enacted,
though I can't explain their cause.
Unanswered questions
number many in my mind;
though I strive to find their answers,
the task has left me quiet and resigned.
Though I have knowledge of self
and what may be right,
I find myself tormented
and haunted at night
by misjudgments during day,
and what I know lies not far away:
the day when innocence fades
and maturity is the order of the day.

Geoffrey Pusung

Thanking God

Thanking God is good.
It's also kind and thoughtful.

If you thank Him enough
He will accept it;
If you thank Him in prayer
He will appreciate it.

So, thank Him everyday
whenever you can
and always have the strength
and courage He did,
when He died for Us.

For we all have a little bit
of Jesus, the Lord, God,
(whatever you want to call Him)
inside of all of us.

Stephanie Needle

Oasis

In a desert of despair
I escape into your arms.
Kisses, like showers of rain drops,
Wash away the pain
And fill the empty corners of my soul.

Hold me.
Hold me until
I know the green horizon of hope.

Jo Ellen DeVilbiss

Spool of Life

The spool of life
just keeps on spinning
filling—each day
its new beginning.
Threads get tangled,
sometimes are broken,
causing heartaches
when anger spoken.
Weaving in and out our lives,
sewing up good with bad,
allowing all the distance
for happiness along with sad—
never knowing how long
this thread may be,
we go from day to day
with worries free.
For each spool of life is different,
as we all well know.
So stitch carefully, my friend.
Only include what you want to sew.

Cheri A. Heydman Jackson

A Year Ago Today, You Died

A years ago today, you died
And broke my heart forever.
You had your life all figured out.
You thought you were so clever.

I didn't know how much I loved you
Until the day you said good-bye.
I miss you so much now.
Why did you have to die?

I think of you every day
And miss the way you smile.
Life goes on without you,
But you're with me all the while.

And every day that passes
Is another day without you.
Sometimes I can't bear to go on,
But I always make it through.

A years ago today, you died
And stole my love forever,
Until we meet again,
And then I'll leave you never.

Rachel Thompson

The Rings

On a pond,
So short lived.
On one's finger,
a love gives.

For a tree,
means long years.
Given back,
brings forth tears.

The rings . . .
From melodic bell
our hearts may swell,
Another time, all laughter quell.

Once more in water,
These same rings, like our lives
constant changes bring.

The rings,
Ere outward bound
but, like our smiles
they come around.

Robert Jay Coyle

Eternity

I am drawn deep
into your slate blue/green eyes

And although the color
is mesmerizing . . .

It is the intensity
that captures me

Drawing me from here
to forever. . . .

Kelly Angela Stavely

The Comforter

To my loving husband, Sunny Wilson
Jesus reached down and touched my soul.
With His love and heart did overflow.
For the Spirit took me so high,
My soul just went up to the sky.
I lift my hand to praise His name.
When in my soul the Spirit came,
Down my face the tears did flow,
For the Spirit in my heart and soul.
So for this reason His blood was shed,
And by the Holy Spirit we are fed.
Jesus died so that we might live,
And a comforter He did give,
Of the Holy Spirit within our heart,
Now and always, never to part.

Jo Ann Wilson

Separate Souls

Dream of love
never promised, received
Days and nights
mystified, not believed

Gifts of moments
tangled two are shared
Time slowly speeds
unnoticed, not cared

Gone in a breath
sharing now a past
Unleashed tears
a painful task

Two souls met as one
for a portion of time
Separated by fantasy
a new love to find

Diane Price

Untarnished

To place my feet upon a spot
No other man has trod
Helps me feel alive and whole
And one step nearer God

To drink my fill from virgin stream
And know that I'm the first
Quenches deep within my soul
Another kind of thirst

To feast my eyes on beauty
Unseen by other eyes
Tells me of God's power
And helps me realize

That man is really nothing much
But rather very small
Why God even bothered
That's the wonder of it all

Gordon Bouskill

Preconception

I hear the warmth of infancy
it whispers softly
in it's mindless form
dipping and swelling
like the sea at dawn
you slept I listened
I felt your love
Distant as night
and smelled your honey breath
in the dampness of morning
who called you to dance
in the sufferings of men
and hollow out footsteps
in the attics of fools
did you wish for the light
from the depths of your wound
that sting of surprise
for all mortals to feel

M. Billings

Untitled

The darkness yields to newborn light.
The eyes return from the surreal.
The creatures that pursue the light
Make ready to live through the day.

The fast of dark ends with the light.
The yearning heart feasts on the day.
But souls entrapped by Beauty's strength
Find sustenance in days long past.

Transpires much in light of day,
Enough to hold one's fancy captive.
But minds engrossed in Beauty's grandeur
Find impetus in memory.

In aging day, the light subsides.
Creatures of light flee from the dark.
But beauty's slave finds solace when
The eyes return to the surreal.

Kenneth Patrick

My Pen

Me and my pen
Are best of friends.
We have been through thick,
And we have been through thin.

Sometimes we meet early.
Then, sometimes it is late.
We don't have any problems
Making a date.

There are times we agree,
And there are times that we don't.
And in the final analysis
It gives me what I want.

Sometimes, I am surprised
When the outcome is revealed.
Whatever it is,
My desires are always filled.

Karen Hardin

Frosty Birds

Frosty birds
fly over lemon trees
of blue knotted wood

Sitting under the empty
shadow of the sun
tree limb bugs
freeze and fall off
into the wind

John Svehla

New Beginnings

To breathe, to love
To grace the sky above

Walk, run
Hide from what's
Been left undone

From a child grows the
Adult with the undefined
Memory of a life unknown

Accept, live on
Walk with the
Aid of a caring hand

Live into
Eternal bliss
Sorrow buried beneath
The grass

A new life begins
With new memories stored
Not beneath the grass
But in the mind to be
Adored

Kristi Massey

Night

A lamp clicks
Blackness
Distorting familiar shapes
Descends on the mind
Leaving little
For the morning sun
To find

Sometimes
The blackness of the mind
Far exceeds
The darkness of the night
And sometimes
The morning light
Never warms
The corners of the soul

For the soul always questions
The Why's and the Wherefore's
While the sun rises and falls
Each day
Questioning nothing

Grace A. Meyer

A Task

*In loving memory of my departed
husband, Samuel Hogencamp*
Tears flowed like rain
From eyes of brown
As mother and daughter
Upon the ground did kneel.

With nothing but their hands,
They set about a task,
Straightening out the dirt
That covered you last.

When all was done,
A silent prayer was said;
Then they placed
Wreaths upon your head.

Two hearts broke that day;
For they both knew,
Never again would they see
The beauty that was you.

Sandra Hogencamp

The Violin Concerto

Guns mute, goriest war over;
Brabant fog in Brussels.
Dark night, concert hall lights beckon
To hear his mighty song.

Beethoven violin solo
People's victory hails.
Melancholy malaise dispelled,
Great Titan liberates.

Heiligenstadt ordeal, no more.
Deafness challenged, conquered.
Eroica heralds new spring:
Art and courage exult!

Heavenly violin begins,
Timpani resonate,
Glorious themes repeat throughout—
Haunting drama, sad joy.

Blend of power and of beauty,
Fresh, new rhythms, slow and fast.
Victor! King of musical light,
Olympus majesty!

John Devlin

The Gallant Ghost

You deem yourself invisible,
an apparition at most;
Others esteem you invincible,
Never wavering at your post.

Being sought out for favors
Rarely makes you feel used,
Like a pack of lifesavers,
Keeping taste buds amused.

Some folks dub you "buddy,"
'Cause on you they depend,
But they melt down to putty
Whenever you need a friend.

You accept putty kindly,
Molding it to fair form,
Rather than chasing blindly
For the perfect or the norm.

As ghosts go, you're a Casper,
The friendly one people know
Will free them from disaster,
Leaving the credit to Joe Blow.

Jeanne Gaskell

Memories Must Fade

I recall her anguished cry,
"It is hard to choose
Between the man you love dearly,
And the God you worship truly."

She gently explained in a letter.
"You are not a believer.
Light wedded to light is better.
Please think of me as a little sister."

Almost thirty years later,
I decided to be her big brother
And attend her mother's funeral,
While I kept wondering why.

But then, when I saw her,
I felt my pulses quicken.
Her startled, anxious look
Told me that she did remember.

Although I am now a believer,
We each have married another.
It is sad to think of what might
Have been, but memories must fade.

Ava L. Russel Benn

Fathomless Faith

How far can my word go?
How high can it reach?
Will it travel alone?
Will it whisper or screech?

I'll package it gently,
Its message intact.
Will it buffet its cynics?
Will it bounce back unscathed?

Will its strength be elusive?
Will it heal; will it shatter?
Will its truth be conclusive?
Will it spread—will it scatter?

How far can my word go?
How high can it aim?
Its horizons are boundless.
My word is your name.

R. Elaine Frawley

LIFE'S BATTLEFIELD

Dear HEAVENLY FATHER,
bless my mind, body and Spirit—
That they all might work for YOU
and others hear it!

Bless the words
that I might write,
So as, to give the world
a better insight!

Therefore, what we
all should feel,
As we march through
Life's Battlefield.

Bring our heart
close to mind,
What we all
left behind!

Touch these feeble,
but loving hands
As they stretch
throughout the land!!!

Rev. James E. Culley

It Could Happen to You

Reality has its edges
Be careful not to fall
Some will cut you deeply
Your one last curtain call

Thin line stretches tautly
The borders seem to fade
That is when it all goes south
Spent choices that were made

The truth—you're just a passenger
The trip—not what you think
You've been taken for a ride
And driven to the brink

Cruelty in the making
No realization gleaned
Deep end calls you sweetly
In sheep's clothes is a fiend

Some have a chance at freedom
For others, salvation missed
They stumble, reaching blindly
And fall in the abyss

Cherie K. Johnston

Emergence

I reached deep down inside of me
To let my very soul be free,
To wander through eternal light,
To guide me through my special plight,
To find some answers to my quest,
To help me do my very best.

Now knowing all I need to know,
My journey will be far from slow.
A new emergence I now can see
With such increasing urgency,
And crashing through the waves will be
A new and wondrous person—
Me!

Mary Turenne

Mother

Mother, when I look
Deep within your eyes,
I can see
Everything that describes beauty
Looking back at me,
For true beauty
Comes from the heart.
Mother, when I look
Deep within your eyes,
I can see
The woman I can only hope to be,
Because your beauty
Is your love
That you share so graciously.
And every time
I think of beauty,
I will know it's you, mother,
Looking back at me.

Linda Lou Carter

Intrusion

Desperately seeking; quietly speaking.
The floor beneath is creaking.
Heard. They won't find us weeping.

Armed they are, an easy par.
Interested took at the bar.
To our home for a war.

Hand in hand, to be a man.
Let us not be damned.
Ask not—demand.

Bullets fly, a bloody eye.
Damn this guy to the grave, I lie.

Why, oh, why must I die?
Watch my wife start to cry.
My silent kisses sigh good-bye.

Salomon M. Chavez

Angel

When light fades and oceans dry
And the wind in stillness lies
To sleep with the creatures,
There will be you;
With radiance you give
Illuminating joy,
With soulful touch
You bring the breath of angels,
A haven of delight;
Ecstasy it is to be
In your arms;
Forever I will stay in humble awe,
A servant of love

Micah Marin

My Friend, the Tree

So sad to see
My friend the tree
No limbs or leaves
No place for birds
To stop and rest
No place for squirrels
To build their nest

Speak to me
I'm here beside you
Tell me
Who did this to you?

See the man
With the saw in his hand
He did this to me

So sad to see
My friend the tree
Nancy Steele

True Blue, This Is You

Can you tell me
why I try so hard
to see this romance through
Everyday becomes a lifetime
in deciding what to do
I can't remember
when I tried so hard to mend
a relationship I love
to keep it till the end
You must try your darndest
to make your dreams come true
But only two together
will make these dreams "True Blue"
Marilyn Tschopp

On Prejudice

In my sin, their colors viewed
A multitude of less redeeming
Souls of equal value, hued,
And counted thus with lesser meaning.

With blinded eye, I saw their faces
Marked by years of guarded trust
With deafened ear, I heard their cases
And kept my pent feelings just.

Then beneath the cross, I glanced,
My blinded eye made clear
Their faces seen from grace enhanced
Left not a trace of fear.

I heard a thousand voices calling,
Their tongues in one accord,
Embraced the souls I'd found appealing
And gathered them unto my Lord.
Tom Ermish

The Eagle

I am the poetry of the heart.
In prayer and praise
I impart the Light of Love.
I travel on wings of Grace
beyond time and space.
Through nature's fold
I behold the law of cycles.
I commune with God's Being
In everyone and everything
I am seeing
with the "eye" of love—
"Perfection" of the sphere above
Marguerite Roosen

Marriage

Marriage is a lot of work
More work sometimes than "work"
Knowing when to speak your mind
Or play deaf, dumb, and blind

Decisions that were yours alone
Now take a different tone
You no longer make them on your own
Now see how much you've grown?

If marriage were much more like play
It would be a lot more fun
Not caring what you do or say
Or even who has won

In marriage you're supposed to share
That is the golden rule
Showing your spouse how much you care
Now that is really cool!

When everything is said and done
Of this you can be sure
Marriage can be a lot of fun
If only you can endure!
Denise Ann Martorano

My Secret Garden

Early in the morning
When the air is crisp and fresh,
I have a little garden
That I call my secret place.

The birds are sweetly singing
As their music fills the air,
And the brightly blooming flowers
Spread, gather their beauty everywhere.

A tiny little fountain
Hums a merry little tune,
Little chimes that tinkle softly
Every evening, morn', and noon.

And when the day is over
And I want to meditate,
I leave the weeds of life outside
Before I enter through the gate.
Helen Marang Gafford

It's within You

Have you ever wondered what
Is life's reward to me?
Might be right in front of you
Yet somehow you don't see

Do you ever think about
How life just passes by?
But inside our soul, you yearn
To spread your wings and fly

Could you ever find the strength
To take this thought to heart?
You may then give life the chance
To help you make your start

Will you ever realize
Excuses just get old?
Take responsibility
And life will fit your mold

Can you ever figure out
It's you who has to show 'em?
When you do, you'll understand
How I just wrote this poem
Russell L. Foss Jr.

The Tree

There was a tree
Standing in the meadow
Alone.
I went and touched the tree.
We were both alone and isolated.

Birds came
And nested in the tree.
The sun lay golden
On the leaves.
The tree was not alone.

I stood
And heard the birds sing.
The sun warmed me.
Again I went and touched the tree.
We were not alone; we belonged.
Joan Gordan

Does It Even Seem Like Poetry

Now-a-days, or Is It Just Me?

Poetry sure has changed
Often I read over the oldies

Donne
Shelley
Byron
Dickinson
Whitman
Browning
Blake
etc., etc.

And notice that
They never wrote
Poetry like this
Eric Hryb

Meditation

To my Aunt Judy, for all her love and support
Cultivate self-reliance;
Grab hold of all your fears.

The decisions made today
Should still profit come twenty years.

Lend caution when impulsive,
But grasp patience and endure.

Observe and let experience guide.
Look in your rear view mirror.

Let the drift of life float by;
Don't mistake it for the stream.

Grab yourself a good direction.
Cut to the chase; get to your dreams.
Jean Finlinson

Hope

No matter how you feel inside,
I will always be by your side.
Hold your head and chin up high,
Admiring God's beauty in the sky.
You will never have to fear;
I am always very near.
I will cradle you in My arms,
Keeping you safe from hurt and harm.
Stretch forth your hands and talk to me,
While you are bending on your knees.
On My word continue to stand,
And on your feet you will always land.
Robin L. Oliver

Barfly Blues

The bartender grinned about me not getting the joke.
Distracted, gullible me didn't have the faintest clue.
I was breathing in a femme fatale's teasing smoke.
She said, "A little kiss might chase your blues."

I mistook her sexy presence for an obvious answer.
A bold knight could win sweet petite's love sure and true.
The brazen b**** slammed me as I moved to romance her.
My heart became a piece of meat in a boiling stew.

You get loads of laughs in a barroom battle zone.
A home run swing may not erase a strikeout or two.
Booze generates charisma until the covers are blown.
Desires and dreams dissolve into a nightmarish hue.

Why must I always be the lonely, tormented man?
Why do endless miles of effort reap inches of gain?
Witness a dejected barfly lacking a winning plan,
Ensnared in a time warp of devastation and pain.

Another whiskey to anesthetize me before sleeping bartender.
No women were left to care or make a one-nighter click.
I couldn't bear a dream encounter with myself sans this bender.
Soon a swatted barfly staggered away, blue and sick.

Ken Miller

The Worm

I see the white, repulsive slug, as it slides across the dirt;
I watch its color change to black, and my head begins to hurt.
I see it covered now with filth, as it leaves a slimly trail
And feel like I am truly trapped, behind the bars of jail.

I see the sick, disgusting worm, as it wiggles through the gate
And far inside the depths of me, my despair is very great.
It slides across a fallen leaf, then squirms along a brick.
I feel as though it's on my skin. It makes me very sick.

But I was just a child then, with no means of control;
No way to stop your roaming hands, nor keep them from their goal;
No way to turn them from the path, down which they chose to stroll.
It hurts to know I'll never find, those parts of me you stole.

I can't erase my anguish deep, with it's never ending pain;
Nor forget the nights I cried aloud—and no one ever came.
So the ugliness spread downward, through my body and my soul
And left me with the knowledge that I never will be whole.

And because you were a man yourself, you took away my faith.
You smashed it with a hammer, then sliced it with a lathe.
For how can I believe in God, as a father kind and wise;
When the only father I have known, is the devil in disguise?

Karen M. Johnson

Physically She Was Never Raped

My queen, please! Don't corner your heart from me.
Why are you so frightened by the past?
Do you still hear the dragon's cold echoes
Ringing inside your head? Do you feel the heat
Of his hands around your heart
As if the memories were asphyxiating your purpose,
Leaving you jaded and without reason to love me!

Lonely, empty, woman . . .
Exquisite is the shadow that precedes
Such physical beauty.
Wishing for a chance to hold you
In my arms again.
My queen! These four walls will not give life back to you.
This ragged chair of oak that holds your fragile body
Has soaked up lives and tear-filled palms of everyone who has
Allowed it's rocking comfort to perpetrate them!

A diamond in the rough I found in you.
Just as rare as you are blue . . . helpless a man I will remain
In my life, if to breathe means—gasping for air until the dragon
Inside your memory lets go of you.

Khrystan Page Renfro

Breathing Milk

I'm breathing milk. Little droplets of sweat
careen down the slopes of my body. I squirm
in the itchy office chair, on the wrong side
of the oak desk. Awaiting one's Fate is a little
slice of Hell pie with soggy crust.

From all four walls, gilded diplomas gloat.
Whether I'll ever get one is anybody's guess.
I say it over and over, to practice.
I Cheated I Cheated I Cheated
He'll ask me why. Stress? Get used to it.
Parental Pressure? They want what's best.

No sir, the elephants made me do it, sir.
The elephants? Eyebrows raised.
Yes sir, the chartreuse ones that are
always looking over my shoulder.
Know-it-all b*******, sir.

I won't get suspended; the test will be tossed.
I'll have to see Dr. Sigman every week
just like when the puce rhinos told me
to put a cherry bomb in the lunch lady's car.

Caroline Lee Sheppard Springer

Christian

He's been gone for only a few minutes,
and, already, my skin reaches out
towards the door, through the windows
into the open air.

My senses pick up a faint trace of the man who just left,
who loved me for hours . . . an eternity.
One night. Was it a dream?

No. He has left a mark. I feel him. I smell him.
I know him.

        I love him.

I miss him, yet he is still in my room, my body,
my bed . . . in my sheets,
woven into the fabric of my life.

I look up into the grays of night.
His eyes are deeply hidden in a mass of hair hanging over me.
His hands are on me . . . in me . . . releasing me.
Holding me.

He is in me. He is so into me.
How else could I be so feverish,
and so free?

Deborah Stambaugh

As One

To Cesar, something we once shared, but lost
I love to love, sharing my heart and soul.
Giving him my love that not only he needs, but wants and desires.
Letting him feel the warmth and compassion that I have for him.

When we wrap our arms around each other, we
exchange this unbelievable tingle-like sensation,
and knowing that all I am giving is exactly what I get back.
No greater or less.

Neither of us having to speak a single word,
Just looking into each others' eyes says
Everything that is needed to be said,
and that I am his everything as he is mine.
Having a bond that is so strong
It could never be broken.

Giving ourselves to each other again and again,
Having every time feel so powerful,
it's like a burst of pure heaven rushing through our bodies.

Teasing each other, as we're pleasuring each other,
As we're loving each other.

Melanie Schouwenaars

Real Illusion

Making love to him I think of you,
and it becomes your hand caressing my thigh.
He speaks.
I silence him with one finger across his lips.
My eyes close. His face fades into your gentle stare,
and a sob escapes my lips.
Feigning love, I stop his questions with a kiss
and slowly roll away.
His breathing is as shallow as my love,
and he is far more likely to be wakened.
I wrap my arms around a bear You once used as a football.
His brown furry paws catch my tears.
His soft, gentle love soothes me to sleep
with a dream that spans the oceans that separates us.
And I dream I watch you pause, between sips of laughter,
and silently stare into your pint glass where
you see my face in the foam of your Irish beer.

Kerrie Saraceno

Stone Cathedral

For my wife, who made this a night to remember
You wore the night like a velvet gown.
It whispered with your movement
like a river to its audience of stones like a pearl;
between your breasts the moon swayed
on a diamond chain. Your hair flowed
like a cataract at night brushed by the
wood-scented wind. Your moon-sculpted
shadow danced in a stone cathedral
music spun by nature in hollows of
timeless solitude. My heart joined a
silent ovation, joy unspoken.
Gratitude clung silently like sequins on my cheeks.
Reluctantly you returned the night
with a vow to wear it again.
Paradise may continue to elude us
but we'll always have Yosemite.

David Coombs

Veritas* [L.]

For humanity and the Dario Salas for Hermetic Science
The tools of self-creation are conscious thought, word, and deed
By these shall you define yourself
You work at your own speed
You are not your name, the clothes you wear
your possessions, or what you can buy
Your sole purpose is to remember your Soul's purpose
when you ponder "Who am I?"
You are far greater than is dreamt of in your philosophy
A lovingly wrought, intricately stellar design
of powerful Divine Energy
Be still and know these words as Truth*
Set your internally-bound Spirit free
and use your tools expressively
to create yourself as whomever you choose "To be". . . .

Cydya Smith

Your Room

The haziness of the morning light
shines through the window, cracked
for the escape of old cigarettes'
stale scent. I awaken to find your arm,
limp from sleep, wrapped around my waist.

We've been here before.

I search your room for my shoes,
my shirt that somehow found their way
to the floor the night before.

You remain silent.

Only the sound of your breathing
fills the room as I silently
close the door behind me.

Cynthia Grace

Blessed by the Sea

The lore of the down-hearted
my wish to thee implore
A waning gift the tide doth bring
its promise to restore

When head bends pity to thyself
a groan to humble b****** whelp
As humility and faith to he is health
in windswept waves bring ocean merchant's wealth

Love in its nourishing embrace
cannot the ill-of-soul replace
As to great shores life's chain revived
a love to feed the soul survived

Far below sea's countenance amiss
thrust thy life circle's genesis
Thee having bade, thy debt repaid
mother nature's value is seldom remiss

Thus her benevolence settles the score
and alters faint-of-spirit's lore
From matron waters here-to-fore raising sustenance upon the shore
Her nourishment abounds! Thy need never more

Philip Moleski

Tainted Dove

Why do I love thee; let me drown in sorrow,
Tormented in despair, trapped within, within,
Tears and pain, love and hurt, longing for nothing,
Dreaming for romance standing alone, loving the dark,
Swimming in dirt, dying from pity,
Falling behind, old footsteps crumble apart,
Swallowing fear the butterflies f***
Frightening with a passion for pleasure,
Regrets too high to count beyond the horizon.
Let it be known my love lives forever; whether in vain,
Or in purest virtue, thou has no limitations,
No boundaries of such; in the sky, all of my pink clouds
Have turned to gray consumed damnation, living unto whenever.
Why should this horoscope of mine lie,
Fire within begging to be let free, one too many denied feelings of hurt.
I live for no reason, a confusing thing in its own
Always to question, to live in fault,
An existence of never knowing just why this,
Hardly any difference in this life I live and this death,
This imminent ending.

Brian Cole

Joint Custody

Wrenched from loving arms,
The child, a scream torn
Deep inside the soul, is silent.

Her eyes grow huge.
She pants short breaths to
Numb her body and her mind.

Each week she knows she will be
Forced from mother's safety
to her father's beer-stained breath.

Each week she makes
The sick'ning plunge from
Heaven down to hell.

A judge, a judgment, brings that sword
The cut the child in half. One half is sane.
The other waits for footsteps in the night.

The child is made a woman, premature.
Her small and private part made known
To him who calls it love.

Her scream will never end.

Anne Hart

Mistrust

It happened one Thursday night in June.
I wonder did she arrive just a little bit too soon.
He took her to the movies then back to his place.
And what he did was really a disgrace.
He took her and laid her in his bed.
I wonder what things went through her head.
She is only a teen and he is a grown man.
I wonder if when he first saw her, did he
Then begin to make plans.
How will she explain this to her husband
When she becomes his wife?
She will also have to live with this nightmare
For the rest of her life.
This man is evil and full of lust.
Unfortunately, he is her cousin and someone she used to trust.
Will this be all over once he is in jail?
I doubt it, because before he goes, he will probably put her through hell.

Evonne Myers

Sebaraitas' Bonita

You wrapped your Self exquisitely about me
Like a peel of tender banana over the strangeness of my sweet pulpy flesh
Consuming my selfishness with open arms of vulnera-peel-ity
Covering my fruit with your sunshine-dangerous safety
Brilliant yellow in the Golden Starbeams of True Love
Wanting . . . now I'm naked in the open rain of your tropical mouth
Devouring the tasty wholeness of myself
Once barred from its own splendid ache

Stacey Roll Dillon

Shattered Dreams

Ignitable, your shattered dreams haven't your childliness.
You wonder why the world is discontented while you barter illegally.
Your games will do no good for he knows your methods.
Too often you b***** of unimportant matters but
lack the sight of wisdom to prevent madness.
You want it all, you want them both, but you'll end up with nothing.
Your gamble will not pay.
I beseech to all that remains good and innocent,
attempt no futility and accept the loss.
You are entitled to your knowledge, but miss distinction.
Intangible ethnicity is a prison . . . entrapped,
encamped, denial that history frightens.
Insecurities run deep like the river wild.
Acknowledgement of friendship is no sin,
yet you disregard him with no thought to his feelings.
Respect above all, respect is the law.
Your thoughts are tangles, a labyrinth to be lost in.
I wish I could advise but my disgust is strong,
my anger unsurpassable. Meekness is no excuse.
Hiding behind a lawyer image releases no pain.

Aurora Matthews

Code 9

Dime, dime, please give me a dime.
You see my cup on a stick.
For your convenience,
Don't come too close fearing I will make you sick.
If you give me a dime,
And she gives me a dime,
Well, then maybe
I won't die in winter as I sleep outside
Over a grate so not to shiver.
Oh! What was that it just flew by.
Not another of those damn pigeons.
Alas, I got in my cup on a stick
Only another pile of s***.
Dime, dime, please give me a dime.
Thank you.

Dolores Kitzer

Whirlybird Cowboy

With a tobacco chaw and a swagger,
The Cowboy mounts his Helicopter.
Above the cactus and the brush,
He dashes all about
Looking for the cattle,
To Round 'em up and Head 'em out.
One old long-horned cow stood to fight,
Pawing the ground and snorting
When the "Chopper" came in sight.
The Cowboy brought his "Chopper" close,
To give the cow a scare.
The cow came charging,
Jumping into the air.
She caught the "Chopper" with her horns.
Then, flipping down into the thorns,
The wounded "Chopper" fell.
The Cowboy, crawling from the wreck,
Said, "My pony hit the dust."
He told the cow, "You go to hell!"
Then spat his chaw and cussed.

Florine Nolen Hollan

Last Words

Her hair was blond.
Her body long.
Her face so hurt and pale,
She never spoke a single word,
Except words of love and care.
She never stole a thing or lied,
Until the night she died.
He was tall, dark, and wide.
His face he did not hide.
He hit and yelled until she fell,
And punched till she cried.
He stabbed her flesh,
But then he wept,
And held her limp body in his arms.
He yelled he was sorry,
And kissed, then lied,
But all that he heard were her last words:
Goodbye.

Natalie Carrion

Ecstasy

Take the dare of the odyssey.
Climb the ladder into mystery.
Feed the fire of the instinct
And taste the rage at its peak.

Kiss the night and stain the day,
Images of a child at play.
Razor's edge of truth and dream,
Thing's are never, but always as they seem.

Sweat a breath of exotic strife,
Scream, beg, and cry for more.
Smell the line and lick the knife,
Taste the essence and close the door.

Kiss the night and stain the day,
Images of a child at play.
Razor's edge of truth and dream,
Thing's are never, but always as they seem.

Take the stairway to desire.
Destiny carries you to the height.
Find yourself in too far.
Battle for ecstasy, the eternal fight!

Jesse Marshall

Wanton Waste

Shimmering desolate desert plains
Where masked men stalk and blood rains
Monkey man dances to throbbing drums
Echoing dragging and spilling crumbs
Of ruin and cremating heat
With syncopated rhythmic beat
In poisoned clouds while phantoms float
Round and through malevolent gloat
And greedy buzzards gorge on eyes
Filled and stilled in wide surprise
With horror etched and burned at core
In wanton waste waged by war
Fueled from a chemical pile
Of weapons to destroy defile
Destruct and point with senseless aim
To random target kill or maim
Obedient boots with trusting air
Saluting marching smell of fear
Who follow senseless high commands
For sheep to sleep in foreign lands

Marcelle A. Slaven

Untitled

I was lost
a strange swirling sea
of emotions
common sense
abandoning me

Womanly desires
now fully awakened
I leaned
heavily against him
allowing him
to part my lips
his tongue
gently nudged me
creating
sensations
that amazed me

Caroline E. Huches

Silent Desire

To my angel, Elizabeth Cook
Erotic desires clear and gray
In the autumn tint of may
Flirting among the silent quest
Love and truth are at their best
Whispering in thy majestic court
Evil love of compassion sort
Eyes to touch and hands to see
Aroused by all but beloved by me
Fiery beauty became thy name
When sex and love became the same
Desired looks and deepest dreams
Innocent to the world of which she seems
Yet hidden darkness lies within
As hands and eyes behold her sin
I long to sleep and touch her face
In my mind her gown of lace
Black and sheer with lust I stare
Upon my love through breathless air
Finally real within dreams great hall
Mystique undone and the gown doth fall

John Egner

Survivor

To the victims of rape and violence
She struggled!
She lamented, but she rose
From bushes of thorns
Bruised, scratched, disheveled,
Bloodied, and worn!
Where she had been
Beaten, deflowered,
Thrown, and left to die!
She rose with a secret smile
And glint in her eye,
With all the thanks she could give,
Raised her arms and face to the sky,
In a foreign body, determined to live.
She rose with courage,
A painful dignity in her walk,
Sway to her battered hips,
And limped toward tomorrow,
A vow on her knowing and telling lips.

Arlienshia Shaffer

Untitled

To my old friend, Jim
You and me
caught in something dirty
try to get ourselves undone

You take a shower
I take a bath
washing with the TV on
Suddenly the news comes on

You're in the shower
I'm in the tub
I get spilled out on the floor

I'm slipping farther
out to the street
into the gutter and more
My washing got me into more!

Denise Lowe

Chocoladesia

Have you ever realized
how deeply sensual chocolate is
I mean it's almost sexual in nature
I'm tellin' ya', do without for a while
then eat some chocolate, wow, you won't believe
what this can do to your g-spots
man, you should've been there
the last time I did that
but then of course
I wouldn't have needed
the chocolate would I
well maybe for play

Shaddoe T. Wines

Shadows of the Moonlight

I have intimate knowledge of the upheaval of the sidewalks
they have been hard on my a** I have seen the blue blown out
of the sky by the stiffening wind or at least the sky seems
less blue than when I was young and saw bigfoot or so
I thought lost in my reveries until I was startled by
a falling star glinting through the black and white TV
eye night sight a sprite slight bright light glimpsed
while riding right handed bike in the shadows of the moonlight
after midnight

Greg DeMarco

Provoking Images

I'm not here to make sense I'm here to provoke images
   within your mind.
It is the reason for ink on this paper.
We are putting one of Santa's helpers into the ground today.
It still amazes me how the silvery liquid works so well
to keep his body preserved in this heat of June.
The sudden rise in temperature has brought to life the last
of the mosquito hatch which was now laying claim
to this particular section of the yard.
He knew of his demise prior to this engagement
and had been planning his departure for quite sometime.
Disease, cancer, you know the story.
Fading footsteps seem to be crowding my memory-riddled mind.
Have I been here before? He found pleasure in picking
out his final resting place. As far as pleasure is concerned
I find that the physical is a much more forgiving feature.
It's strange as I view the body, he doesn't appear
to be wearing the clothes of a dead man.
As the roar of the wind through the pines seems to mark his passing,
I am now left with a soul full of sorrow and grief to work with.
Until we meet again, farewell.

William H. Fort

Love, The Power of Creation

Dear Jesus,
"Love," the power of creation!
You are the "Love," flowing freely from above,
Touching all to Your presence, Your Being. . . .
Without "Love," a great vastness would become void,
A darkness of nothingness, a rapture of blackness caressing the land.
No breath would be spoken, only broken in the darkness
Of nothingness spread vast. But behold! Your light shines bright,
Lifting the hearts of man, mending in "Love"
Spread, perfuming Your Greatness seen and held in Your Majesty,
Your Plan, called "creation!"
Yes, fellow man, exploit "Love," turn loose, hear the words
Spoken, fulfill them in the pleasure of the "Lord,"
And all will remain in a light, as a "halo,"
Caressing from the Heaven floor, flowing freely over the land,
Gifted indeed from Your Hand, drawing all to "Life Anew in Your Plan!"
Without "Love," there is a nothingness, a darkness of the heart!

Donna Struble

How Do You Say Good-bye

How do you say good-bye
to someone who's always been there,
to the one who always held your hand when you were small?

How do you say good-bye
to the one you've loved and hated all your life,
to the one who made you feel so small no matter how big you were?

How do you say good-bye
to the controller, the manipulator, now that he's so small and frail?

I'll love you and hate you and care for you till you're smaller still,
and as you fold inward, this butterfly will unfurl
and kiss your unseeing eyes, saying I love you,
though you did not know how.

That's how I'll say good-bye.

Georgene Messina

Loyal Companion

On a cold grey day the mist swirls as it rolls over the land.

Out from the darkness stride four strangers.

Strangers from different wars, clad in pristine uniforms, standing tall in
the face of danger.

Their gallant companions standing alert at their sides.

Protecting, loving, loyal to the end.

Tina A. Booton

Strength

Shhh, don't laugh too loud,
You might know joy.

Don't hold on too tightly,
You might feel the need.

Don't talk too much,
Someone might understand.

Don't touch too feverishly,
You could start a raging fire.

Don't let down your guard,
You could be loved.

Is this what makes you strong?

For my strength laughs wholeheartedly, and leaves my stomach aching.
My strength clutches one so fierce, the need stabs the soul.
My strength speaks until it's sure you understand.
My strength's caress sears the flesh with every touch.
My strength has no guards as to be loved without restraint.

You see, my strength allows me to sleep with a clear conscience
at night and fulfills my mind, body,
and most importantly my soul, with incomprehensible
satisfaction with self.

Heather L. McWalter

African Mama

I passed her many times, that poor emaciated woman,
lying on the fragment of a concrete utility pole,
beside a busy city street.
At times, her clothes barely cover her nakedness.
Her body mirror the effects of inadequate food.
By her side, on the ground, sits an enamel bowl,
Sometimes empty, sometimes partially filled with a bit of dirty water.

Down the street, sits another beggar,
protected from the sun by a large umbrella.
He calls greetings to those who pass,
hoping someone will give him a "dash." (a gift)
His body is sleek and well fed;
His strong legs carry him to his "work,"
sitting beside the busy city street, begging for a "dash."

Meanwhile, the poor demented woman lies in the broiling sun,
stretched out on the fragment of a flat, concrete utility pole.

At first, I passed her by, occasionally giving her a glance of pity,
Then, I noticed how like a living skeleton she looks.
Now, I cannot pass her without giving her a small bit of money.
And I wonder, "Is she really somebody's mother?"

John H. Tullock

This Lady Knows the Blues as True Blessings

This lady knows the deep down blues
That God gives through his unexpected clues
Those small things we may not understand
That makes us question, why am I on Earth, my man?
That makes us scream and holler, I'm being used
Even makes us sometimes take off our hallelujah shoes

These things sometimes come when we're all alone
But there's a bright side on this Earth, I've been shown

Thank God he saw fit to let me take the test
By sparing my life, so I can tell the rest
That Jesus lives and he will use
All those who call upon his name, you don't have an excuse

This lady knows too well, the mighty blessings
That God gives through his tough lessons
Those big things that we would rather escape
But he sends them to make us strong as a slate
That has endured the winds of time, not leaning, but standing
That prepares us for the next level of life's meaning and understanding
Knowing that by faith, we will resurface ever new
Never doubting God's goodness and purpose, our life he will renew

Marion L. Newton

What Is Beauty?

To my beloved mother, Beatrice (Raver Zimmerman)
Beauty can be anything or everything.
If you truly seek it, you will find it.
We are surrounded by beauty,
But our business sometimes blinds us to its awareness:
The splendor of a sunrise at dawn,
A spectacular sunset coloring the sky,
In winter, the sunlight casting iridescent fairyland shimmers on sleet
And snow-covered shrubs and trees,
In summer, a sunbeam highlighting a dew-kissed rose,
Birds on the wing or nest building.
The seasons paint many pictures:
The first daffodils and tulips,
A carpet of violets around a tree,
Fields of bluebonnets, clover, daisies and poppies,
Vivid autumnal colors of flowers and trees,
Blue skies and fleecy white clouds,
The wonder of the heavens at night,
   rising of moon and twinkling of stars,
Smiling faces of our children and devotion of our pets,
The spiritual beauty of people who are kind and loving,
All these things remind us of God, our Creator.

Edna Zimmerman Prentis

My Church in the Woods

To my grandparents, Bea and Lloyd, and Pat and Woody
My dog is glad to be out. I drop his leash hesitantly and go to
the empty lots. A few trees, as if dropped in delightful abandon
by the wind, form a small, boundary-less shrine.

I walk between them, hands shoved deep in pockets, as if I were
among old friends. We are silent, though content, in each other's
company. I weave in between them, like the wind through their
ungiving trunks, like a ribbon woven through a broom's bristles.

The light from the branches is my stained glass window. It falls
on the ground in shapes and figures, my religious icons. There
is a spot, just through the branches of the tallest tree. At its
trunk, where I stand, the sun can see me now, like an eye looking
through a peephole. I must be seen. In that spot, a single flower
grows, my offering. I take it up under the sun's beaming face,
where I am in full view. I strip it of its roots, like mankind. I
remove its gaudy leaves, like our outward appearance. It is a
single flower, no more, no less. It is equal to all others—no
leaves to hide behind, no roots to lean on, like a tiny child when
it enters the world.

I lay it down before God, under the shadowy tree, so He will see
me and know I am here.

Alexia Underwood

Jamie's Poem

There were days I thought no one cared,
I thought no one loved me, my life I did not want spared.
I wanted to be buried, just to live no more
Wouldn't it be great just to go to the beach
And be washed away with the shore?
Then through all the toil and snare of this uncaring place
I saw through the sea of people one single caring face.
Suddenly upon my shoulder I felt a warm touching hand.
That's the only time you've ever looked down
On me it was just to help me stand.
You picked me up gently and patiently taught me to walk
You gave me a hug and said you'd be there if I ever needed to talk.
Slowly and gradually I learned that people cared
I saw my life was meaningful and worthy to be spared.
Still, sometimes I feel people hate me and I sometimes want to die
When I'm upset you feel my pain and I see a tear in your eye.
But you have the strength to pull yourself together
   and give me that loving
Smile that gives me the strength to walk that extra mile.
Now I think I have the strength to take you by the hand
And when you've fallen I can gently help you stand.

Catherine Ann Sink

Untitled

To my daughter, Gage Brooke Marie Gibson
I know where you are now is a better place
But the pain I feel is agony not being able to see your precious face.
My heart is always with you, this you already know
But how do I move on in life if I have to let you go?
I know I will never let you go but I will have to move on
No matter what this world brings to me,
I will never forget what the Lord has given me
   in the late October dawn.
You were very special to everyone even before you were born
I know the Lord is watching over you and those of us who mourn.
I'm trying to be brave just like I know you would want me to be
But every day without you, my heart cries for you to be here with me.
Maybe I'm being selfish-the Lord knows what is best
And now I should feel peace knowing you are with Him
   and laid to rest.
Someday when the Lord decides, I know we'll be together again
And from now until that day arrives in my heart is where you remain.

Robin L. Yarger

Land of the "R"

The land I see so blind with color
is the land I wish to share with you.
From afar you could not captivate
The beauty of this land.
Without you not being in this breathtaking view.
The land is different like your hairs'
images captured with everyday movements.
The forest is at most green without sunshine or rain.
For it's growing greener and stronger
as it's being captivated by your smile.
This land's beauty is indulged with your eyes.
That on a rainy darkened day the raindrops light-up from a spectacular
display of lights dancing as darkness looms over your land.
All moving to your every command, which is never played out of key.
This land is you and you are this land.
The land I lay my body on is the land I'll call home.

Jessie H. Preciado

Precious Memories

Oh, the many, many pictures on the wall
How sweet, how kind, and yet so simple were they
They meant a lot and yet not
The memories of the past, present and future
Still hang—do they not many realize the value of them all?
Yet each one stands for a priceless worth
None can compare to the other and besides many are
Words of praise compared to one another
Words of wisdom, thoughts of kindness, yet many words to live by
Heaven for delight, hell if no praise
So look at each and see memories of a fond land and people of no past
Each stand for grace, God, liberty, and freedom of a special kind
God, our Lord Jesus, creation in
Thought, word, and deed if you please!

Doris C. Downey

God Gave Me Life

No, I'd never raised my hands so high to Heaven
in the hopes to see the glory of tomorrow's Golden light.

Nor to deal with all the trials and tribulations or all the strife
that flows with the still pastel colors of the twilight
against the dark canvas of the night sky.

Until I saw the purity of the innocent in your eyes.
No, I'd never raise my voice so hard to give great thanks, my true God.

Before that day of exultation.
For that you where, born my dear Daughter, God gave me life.
Yes, God gave me life.

Frederick L. Newkirk

Chaos

We all live in an incredible world of unpredictable situations
Where we witness many controlled and uncontrolled mishaps.
Whether those unforeseen mishaps affect us personally or indirectly,
Our internal emotions may be filled with disappointment or hatred.

Witnessing more war amongst the human race instead of love,
By seeing it through our eyes or listening through our ears,
The unraveling of order throughout our glorious mother land,
A land once of purity now tainted with unforgettable animosity,

All human beings are victims of each other's hands and crimes.
Marveling on whether you will be the next forgotten statistic
From the likes of irresponsible and irrational menaces to society
Who stir up, disturb, and damage the contents in the melting pot,

How is it that our land full of God's loving heart-filled children
Could turn out to be a land full of unloving heartless children
Who dislike others and their ways for no valid reason whatsoever
And feel or show no remorse towards those who are afflicted?

Martyrs of this shared world must change their unappreciative ways
To allow it to blossom and grow for the better and rise to the very top
Of its challenging set game and achieve what should have been before
They came into play and cheated us out of something rational . . . order!

Gena M. Baxter-Connelley

Two Hearts Living in Two Separate Worlds

As one looks out the door
one sees across the street
Two hearts living in two individual houses
keeping a steady beat.

One can grasp the scenery of two houses two cars
And much greenery possessed by each of these two dwelling places
Yet one is left to wonder what lies within
these dwellings as two separate cases

These houses each probably possess furniture
   within their dwelling places
And the cars are their way of taking possession
Of things that will enliven them as single cases
As they proceed down the road of life
Wanting to enhance the good in their individual lives
They fail to view one another
As potential helpers building each other's hives

They are decided upon as two hearts
Living in two separate worlds on an individual basis
As they exist next to each other in these two separate oases

Kathleen A. Guenther

Was It You

Were you the one that was there living all the pain?
Were you the one that passed on by not showing any shame?
Or was it you, the evil one, which we all should blame?

When in the night, you hear a scream and you wish it was only a dream,
who do they want, this evil thing; discrimination is its name.

Maybe it will take the girl down the street,
or even the boy you never got to meet.

The night is filled with so much fright; when will you begin to fight?
Fight for one, maybe more, what will it take to stop this score?
You feel their pain, but in the morning it's still the same.

So, try on their shoes, whether big or small,
and see if you can still ignore.
I say "no," if you know me well, and I will be sure to tell.
For you should know as well as I,
the past, the future, and today will die.

To save one soul you save the world
So, take a stand for one and all or our world shall crumble and fall.
Now come with me to this old willow tree
and thank the Lord that we are free!

Ronda Johnson

Whispers of My Prayers

To my parents, Leo and Vicky Agdigos
I pray to myself silently at night,
that I can continue on with this fight.
I pray and dream that my sleep doesn't come with tears,
I pray that I have the courage to face my fears.
That I have to courage and strength, the will to survive, instead of
staying here in the lonely shadows waiting for death to arrive.
I pray that my head doesn't look down at my feet,
suffering the agony defeat.
I pray that someday that I have a lover to caress,
I pray that someday amidst these struggles will come success.
I'm down on my knees, begging God, "Oh, please."
Guide me in my fight,
against the nightmare I suffer from at night.
I pray to you that I can survive my greatest enemy,
it's the reflection in the mirror I see before me.

Alexei Agdigos

The Chieftain's Daughter

With breathless awe, I watched your ship
Drop anchor near my rock-bound shore.
I trembled to call out to you,
To welcome you in peace, and more.

I saw you stumble, tired and ill;
You kissed the ground and said a prayer.
My heart made drumbeats as I thought:
"Someone to teach, to love, to share."

My brothers taught you to survive;
Our Massasoit was at your feast.
Brave Squanto helped you plant the corn
And, gradually, your tribe increased.

But somewhere between then and now, my dreams of camaraderie
Were trampled into prairie dust like broken Indian pottery.

The future holds no shining hope; my pride lies dormant in my breast.
My eyes are dimmed by poverty; my native spirit is oppressed.

Perhaps before the race is won, we'll meet, in essence, heart to heart,
And you will watch with breathless awe: full circle, still a world apart!

Mildred S. Morrish

Dream Realized

To a very special woman in my life, Margaret
Early in my manhood I sought out womanly perfection.
This princess of mine was endowed with all the virtues of her sex.
She possess beauty, grace, understanding,
and her tenderness encompassed my being.

And late at night when my mind became drowsy,
   she suddenly appeared
At the door of my imagination radiantly beautiful,
   her understanding smile
Subdued all my fears and frustrations.
All at once, I was completely at peace.

As hours serenely passed and dawn crept into my room,
Suddenly this gorgeous princess of mine
began to fade from my fertile imagination,
Until she disappeared into the fuzzy corridors of my memory!

Years have passed and this imaginary princess
was just a blurred image in my mind now.
I knew what I sought was some fleeting, nonexistent, shapeless form!
Such despair and desolation!

Then one day this obsessive dream of mine suddenly came into focus,
This elusive image I had been fruitlessly chasing for years
   came into view!
Her enchanting smile, warm personality,
and queenly bearing were there to greet me!

Carl John Marko

Love Mourn for Me No More

She came to me in the morning of my life. And I took her for my
wife. Upon the winds of love we rode to a land we did not know.
Into one soul and one love we grew. The stars from Heaven
would fall if I were ever untrue. The oceans would turn away
and the sun would never rise. If I caused a teardrop to fall from
her eyes. The mourning dove would forever weep, if my promise
of love for her I could not keep. The evenings of time slipped by
unto the ending of my life. Held in the arms of death's last
breath. Oh, again to let my head rest upon her tender breast.
For the Angels come to carry me on silver wings unto my eternal
rest. How can I tell her a tear must fall? And the morning dove
shall forever cry it is my time to die.

Tears fell upon scarlet ribbons and satin pillows. Silver moon
beams shyly touched her golden hair. Sleep come swiftly collect
my tears least my soul over flows. Upon thy wings bear my
bleeding heart to the winds of forgetfulness. Rest my heart.
Never to see the sunrise lay its beams against the misty hill
sides again. Never to enter the garden of dreams caressed in
evening shadows, nor to hear his whispers of love come to me
beside the garden gate. Shall I forever remember the fragrance of
Lilac as we lay on tender grass? Oh love, mourn for me no more.
Sleep closed her eyes and stole away into the silent night. On
the wings of sleepless dreams she fled to remember his love no more.

Dorothy Shockey

Trials in Life

In life so many a trials come our way,
His way to cause our faith to grow each day.
We say, "When will this end and we rise above?"
And in it all see God's wondrous hand of love?

'Tis such an easy thing "we think" it is to believe.
But somehow doubt in our mind is what we sometimes weave.
The Savior knows this weakness we so easily fall to,
But thanks to His grace, for it's always there to uphold you.

For He wants all things be entrusted in Him,
And not carried out by our small thoughts and whims.
For if we do, it is in our flesh we end up with the glory,
And not telling of the beautiful gift of grace in God's gospel story.

In Him we are blessed and can be most encouraged and assured.
That He truly loves us, cares for us, and for us He will endure.
For, He knows the pain and sorrow of all our daily cares,
And, yes, He is ever so mindful of all the burdens we bear.

He is faithful to make a way, where there is no possible way.
And, He will watch over us and keep us each and every day.
As we age we'll look back over the years with restful delight,
And see how He always remained faithful to us in all trials of life.

Gisele J. Bowman

To Berkeley

Road cars vroom! Vroom! Digestion beasts, sidewalk city,
Raccoons with jittery eyes, kick-stand hearts, and palm-frond fingertips
Saunter down straight, lit, narrow pavement paths.

Dotted and clotted with moonbeam sentiment, police badge pertinence,
Tuesday music masters burn books under drip drop candles
(Because it gets to them under their crawling skin), as delirium hate
Poems pass street signs unheard, like odes to irrelevancy.

Lash crash emergency siren surrealism
With flickering trip lights—red spin brake yellow craft,
The midnight flash,
The end and the slow, a symphony of the blinking fanciful.
Backpack elite 3 AM till dawn move along melt into morning
With a will against the wall. Leaves still like trash and rags;
Trees blown over.

Tick, tock, tock, tock, the clock strikes no tick after the first:
Watches are wound backward and inside-out here.
We don't know why. All is awry.

M. T. Wilkens

Mother Theresa

I cared for those who couldn't care for themselves.
I guided those who wanted to find the right path.
I believed in those who had the force to live.
I clothed those who lacked clothes.
I helped all of those who needed me,
but who did not posses the voice to cry for aid.
These people are the ones that I have given my life to.

I prayed for those who needed my prayers.
I fed those who lacked food.
I nourished those whose soul hungered for love.
I loved those who weren't capable of loving.
I left the world knowing that I had made a difference in someone's life.

The gift of giving has no limitations and
only brings about the soothing of the soul.
Don't ever turn your back on someone who is in need of you,
for one day you will yearn and you will be left to find that they have
all turned their backs on you.

Daniela Henriques

My Story

When our soul died I cried and cried and tried to run and hide.
I wanted to run away, but found my heart ran
Along with me and won't let me be.
I searched to find a reason. Why? Why? None could settle me.

You see, he was only 21, you know.
He could act and sing and "Wow" smile like a King!
He was handsome and kind. Why? I cried, Why?

I searched for a new beginning a reason to live again.
I tried to act and sing but it wasn't the real me. You see
What to do, where to turn, it all seemed so mean.

Then a path unknown to me began to make its way
Storyteller, Storyteller, what is that you say?
Stories with legends and myths, stories with words abound.

Stories touched my soul and began to make it sound.
Stories became a magic bridge that bound my son to me.
I can feel our hearts singing as one, when our stories are told to thee

Stories share a moment, stories bring us tears.
Stories shower us like a soft rain bringing freshness to our ears.
Stories can heal the broken and has made me almost new.

Storyteller, Storyteller I call myself. Adieu. Adieu. Adieu.

Sandra J. Coyer

A Picture of a Cross

To my loving wife, Mary Francis
I have a picture of the empty cross on which Jesus died,
And when I have looked at it, I have almost cried.
For it shows the bloodstains of my Lord and Friend,
Who gave His life on the cross, and suffered a terrible end.
He died for all men and women, so they could be free,
Of the bondage of Sin, which kept them in slavery.
He laid down His life for His friends and enemies, too;
Jesus said on the cross, "Father, forgive them, for they know not what
    they do."
But Jesus rose from the dead and His wounds showed to many,
And His resurrection is priceless, worth more than a diamond or rare
    penny.
For the Price Jesus paid was His life, and for us bought,
The Heavenly Jerusalem, which Christians have always sought.
The suffering on that Cross I cannot imagine,
But I know that what put Him up there was my sin.
Thank you, Jesus, for suffering and dying for me,
Because now Your love is manifested so clearly.
"For God so loved the world that He gave His only son,"
Thank you, Lord Jesus, for us Heaven You won.
I have a picture of the empty Cross on which Jesus died,
I could never repay that debt, no matter how hard I tried.

T. Michael Francis

Outcast

He labored up the sidewalk
a meager covering of white flesh stretched taut
concealing bone, muscle, sinew that held together his six-foot frame,
head shaven, downcast eyes,
lesions on his neck and face,
a stubbled chin, shoulders hunched toward his ears,
arms held close, hands thrust deep into his pockets,
traversing space,
one city block, then another,
stopping only for a racking cough,
the sound emitted traveling up from deep within,
falling upon deaf ears of people jostling nearby,
who looked but did not see
this most noticeable of humanity,
drifting aimlessly,
uncertain when he'll meet death's sweet embrace.

Meanwhile, city people pile their plastic twist-tied bags of garbage
on the sidewalk containing items of no value,
stacked up high as a full-grown man,
waiting for the monstrous, groaning trucks to discard this unsightly mess.

B. J. Brown

Fulfillment

Emotions are mixed as a child moves away
to fulfill their life's dreams and wishes.
A mother's amazed at how fast years have gone
and wonders if she's said all she should . . .
taught all she could . . . prepared her child for this day to the fullest.

There's a stirring in her heart,
a lump in her throat,
and she does her best not to weep.

Then suddenly she realizes that the tears in her eyes
come from knowing that the love she has shown
has nurtured and grown into a lovely adult
with caring and passion for others.

A calmness sets in, and she knows in her heart
that the child will do well in life's quest.

It's a mother's dream to raise a wonderful adult,
and alas . . .
she knows she's fulfilled it!

Connie Gray

Steer Your Own Course!

I have reached beyond year number seventy-seven
And am certainly glad I am alive and not in Heaven.
At this point in time and for the past several years
Loneliness and depression have been my two main fears.
Generally, I am happy go lucky, handle trouble with minor strain
But the loss of my wife and daughter gave me considerable pain.
Alone with hardly anyone to turn to for therapeutic assistance
Many times, recently, I have questioned by continued existence.
Advice from all sources seems to come to one very cheap
And all the while I am trying hard my sanity to keep.
Nostradamus, I am not, the future I definitely cannot foresee
The major question I ponder is exactly what is the best for me?
A son, his family including a new grandson
    have goals they must pursue
His sage advice to me, stay active, have fun,
    and do what you have to do.
Whatever the source of advice, I know they all mean well
As far as I am concerned, what happens only time can tell.
For the rest of my years, my outlook will not be too great
And that is one aspect of life that I do truly hate.
So if you are old and lonely and are in somewhat of a stew
Please steer your own course, whatever you decide to do.

William B. Booth Jr.

Night Angels

Whispers in the darkened sky, to where cries the golden whippoorwill.
Where the recent sun has set, and all the Earth beneath is still.
The storm clouds roll across the deep,
Of Heaven's door while all now sleep.
The winds calm down and now in sight,
Are all the blanketing stars of night.
If you listen close you may hear,
The sound of angels hovering near.
In morning's light when babes awake,
And the light rolls away the darkened sky,
Those lulled to sleep by the whippoorwill,
And the dews of night set the evenings chill.
These know not that in Heaven's door just out of sight,
Are the guardian angels of the night.

Wilma D. Mueller

Special Sister

To a spiritually special sister, Robin S. Hall
You're a special sister, you're blessed beyond the world.
You have a lot more value than treasures of Gold and pearls.
A lady more radiant than the sun,
You have a Christ-like spirit, so giving to everyone.
Special sister, you mean the world to me,
Perhaps more than I show, or what others may see.
You're a special woman who's busy night and day.
One with trials and tribulations, but with faith that victory's on the way,
Special sister I write this poem to you whispered from my heart.
You're on my mind, you're in my thoughts,
    but we're never too far apart.
Roses are red, violets are blue,
When God needed special, he created you.

Mike E. Quinn

I Got My Life Back

It's like you saw the light on and all the sudden the lights went out.
You have been taken away from your life and society.
My world was like I was in a flat box
And trying so hard to get out.
I hoped and prayed to God to pull my spirits up and to put in my mind
The will to live, even though I was not treated too well at all.
And I was drugged, but I always thought, deep in my heart, I wanted
To see my friends again, and I wanted to see the trees, birds,
And breathe fresh air. My mind was so out of it, but after a year,
They finally found me, and the light came back on.
My mind and soul was so happy, but scared, but now I can recover
And now I have my life back.
I would tell anyone:
Never take advantage of what they have in their life,
Because they never know when it will end.

Zina S. Ference

Blackfoot Maiden

The little Indian maiden stood quietly by the stream,
her heart was pounding for she had just waken from a dream.

In her dream she had met him, walking through the trees,
he was badly wounded, and fell slowly to his knees.

Where was this brave warrior she must bring to her medicine lodge, quickly she must find him or death he could not dodge.

Looking toward the morning sky she raised her arms in prayer,
and then she heard the wild bird song floating in the air.

She followed the birds song and found him lying on his side,
with pain he rose, smiling at her with brave warrior pride.

Together they walked slowly to her medicine lodge where she could make him whole, and this story was many times retold.

The Blackfoot were a happy people and their life was good,
horses were their wealth and they believed in brotherhood.

The warrior and the maiden lived many happy years,
until the white traders and trappers came and left a black rain of tears.

Doris Winkleman

Graphing a Point

each person
        a line
condemned to wander
through the one-dimensional space
alone
        until x meets y
I am the x   you are the y
        we meet . . .   here
together,
each part of one point
                half of the whole
we are unable to move,   to be separated
but by love, or math?

no one will ever know
        each as strong as the other

our point is graphed . . .   forever

Julia Greene

Precious as a Rose: A Mother's Love

I know a rose by another name: This rose is named "My Mother."
Of all the flowers in my garden of life, she's sweeter than any other.
Her seed of love has fertilized my present and my future.
Her stem of patience left petals for my children's seed to nurture.
When the storms and winds of life had beaten
    upon her within my garden,
Her leaves of perseverance taught my flower how to pardon.
When life's storms are over for me, bringing final peace and calming,
Knowing that she's at rest will be enough for my embalming.

Janet M. Gant Graham

Like Sienna Spilled

Silhouette of a giant oak tree against a night sky,
like sienna spilled from a tube upon a willing canvas,
a transforming image that will do to relate the less familiar to the more.
For what if I said, "I saw the hand of God, just the other night?"
Better to borrow from one frame of reference to explain another.

The birth of a child is such a frame.
When I was young and I felt small,
I thought, "my fear is bigger than I am; as big as this tree."
Instead, I think how big is my progress at
leaning on present moment to present moment,
as though moments were thoughts and the future, my mind.
It is better to be in love; and, vouchsafing this, it is better to be.

Nancy Runion

Please, My Love!

Please, my Love, meet me in the orchard 'neath the pomegranate trees?
There, let me look into the pools of your lovely eyes,
Seeing into your very soul.

Please, my Love, come to me in the shade of the whispering leaves,
And let me touch my love, let me sing unto you the love
That is in my heart.

Please, my Love, run to me with the speed of the hind,
Enwrap me with your golden arms, kiss me with your lips of softness,
Tell me of your sweet wine of love for me, yes?

Please, my Love, hurry to me, for my heart is cold without you,
I shiver with desire for your touch.
Please, my Love, be swift, be running to me,
Hurry, hurry to me. Oh, I can hardly breathe without you,
My heart cries your name constantly.

Please, my Love, rush swiftly to
Me, for my life depends on your being near me,
Within my arms of love, within my soft embrace,
Partaking of the nectar which is awaiting thee.

Please, my Love, be swift as lightning, for you are my love.

Jean Gordon

Ransom

The greatest! Most awesome! Ransom ever paid,
Was when Jesus in his tomb was laid.

Death, the grave, the tomb wouldn't and couldn't hold him down.
He was succinctly shortly, very briefly, back in town.

Not the first, nor the second, but on the third day, He arose
Heavy hearted but not morose.

Business yet to attend to, his presence he had to make known,
His countenance it had to be shown.
To those who were very close to him who believed,
He was the chosen one,
Jesus the Holy King, for these people
He had a special love and deep esteem.

His disciples and loved ones could not believe that it was He,
Who died nailed to a tree, the cross on calvary.

His wounds and scars he had to let be felt and expose,
To doubting Thomas one of those.
He had to show the puncture holes of feet and hand,
Before to Heaven He could ascend.

His task finished here on Earth He goes forth to prepare a table for us,
His new eternal reign just beginning, on the upper berth.

Work well done, our Master, Savior, King J-e-s-u-s.

Amy P. Juarez

Upon up High

Amidst the stones of dragon bones,
I found my love today.
Not a moment away nor a day to pray did I find my love this day.

Upon up high, where the eagles do fly, did I find my love this day.
No pardon to pay or a word to say when I saw my love her way.
The way I saw a dove, some say, did I see my love that day.

For a day away did my love not say she would leave some day.
Like the dove, she could not stay.

Yet for what seemed a day, she surely did stay, before she flew up high
Where the eagles did fly. Yet no more do the eagles fly through those
Lonesome skies, where deepening pain forever will lie.

For no more can I adore these feelings that lay outside these skies,
Only a heartbeat away from a once more open sky,
Where the eagles did fly.

Eric Croswell

Yes, I Love You

I love you, and you asked my why . . . you said you really
wanted to know. There's so much I want to tell you. I know just
saying it doesn't make it so. When we first met I was drawn to
you. I really love to be touched and to touch. Your hands are
so strong and so gentle; but it was more than that, so much.
Your touch created a magnetic force, while the sparks permeated
and flew . . . throughout my body and into my soul, while the
desire for more of you grew. When we first embraced if felt so
right . . . like it was really meant to be. I never had any fear or
regret, only this feeling of tranquility. I love the way you look at
me. Your eyes are so loving and kind. They are so warm and
inviting . . . the windows to your soul and mind. I love the
sound of your voice as you speak to me soft and low. I feel like
melting into your arms, as the fires within me grow. I love the
fact you understand; I am an individual with my own mind. I
don't need to be anyone else to obtain any goal or happiness
find. I love your sensitivity and your ability to openly express
joy and pain. It clearly shows you are "in touch." You can
deeply feel sunshine and rain. I love the fact you "are you" . . . I
love your attitude about life. I love your way of tackling
obstacles and how you handle strife. Yes . . . I love you and
everything about you. You are beautiful inside and out.
Ultimately, I will be with you . . . I know you are my destiny . . .
There's no doubt.

Margie Gamger

Another Year Has Passed

As I contemplate my poem in the county jail Oklahoma City,
I remember the bombing of April 19, 1995, oh, what a pity.

Had it not been by an angel of the Lord to save me from that blast,
I would not be here writing this poem, "Another Year Has Passed."

You see my poem exonerates me
   from what I should have been a part of,
But by the mercy of God, He sent an advocate to protect me in love.

Oh, when I think of the many lives taken by such a devastating blow,
At first there is anger, then sadness, and finally my tears show.

You can't see me, as I wipe away the sorrow from my eyes,
But I can assure you, I am one who can relate with eternal ties.

So as I remember those of our loved ones taken from us so fast,
My poem is not a reminder to those who hurt,
   since "Another Year Has Passed!"

The people of this great land came out in full force.
Not knowing what to expect during that time, love was our source.

Men, women, and, yes, even children gave up their life,
Not freely you see, it was taken by one living in strife.

How can I express such devastation sown against our society?
With the mere essence of a Poet's pen, I claim not this piety.

In remembrance to those who perished so gallantly,
I pray continually that this never happen again, speaking blatantly.

   Wilkie L. Sanders

Newcomer

He struggles to stand on his wobbly new feet;
Searching intently for a cozy place to eat.
With gentle nudges and lashing licks of love,
He finds a four star diner hanging up above.
Stumbling and fumbling as he gets his first taste.
He samples all four entree's leaving none to waste.
With his belly now full and an urging to roam,
He convinces his mom he's a big boy and she should stay home.
But after who steps and staggering with the third.
He figures mom should probably introduce him to the rest of the herd.
As they mosey on over to the rest of the lot,
A horse from the adjoining pasture runs over and slides 'er to a stop.
She lets out a neigh in recognition of the newly arrived calf.
All of the cows move aside and form a makeshift path.
Each taking their turn bellowing and sniffing the calf as he walks by.
It's kinda the bovine version of a sports player's high five.
At the end of the path he sees a group of older calves just ready to play.
And so ended in jubilation the newcomer's first day.

   Rob Underhill

Friends in Exile

Hello, my friend. It's good to hear your voice again. I feared
you had left as you did before, with the passing of my innocence. It's odd that I knew you not gone then, but I suppose
you, a friend to all in the spring of their life and far through the
summer, know well the sorrow of being cast aside. It is fortu-
itous for I that you chose to seek me out again. Before you
came back to me I wanted so badly to die. I was so lonely, even
though many came to call. Although I can feel the slightest
touch, I cannot respond. For me, the outside world is a blur of
sounds, and I can smell the stark, sterile walls that surround me.
Within my shell, I used to long for the end, but try as I might, I
could not stop my life's blood from pumping through my veins
in precisely measured beats. Then, in my darkest moment of
despair, you came to end my dreary exile. I love you for that as I
can love no other. I needed you so much and you came. I know
that you will stay with me until time takes me back into the never
ending circle of life. I have been talking ever so much since you
returned. I haven't let you get a word in edgewise. Come, my
friend, make yourself comfortable. Let's remember the days
when we were young. Let's talk about the time I was five and
pretended I was a knight and you were a fire breathing dragon.

   Rederick D. Lewis

In Tears I Cry

They say a man isn't supposed to shed tears and cry. He
should be strong, grit his teeth, and never ask why. But have
you ever loved someone way down deep in your soul; and try
as you might, it's so hard to control. You wake up in the
morning with them on your mind. You go to bed at night and try
to leave it behind. I love the times we spend together; it's so
hard to say good-bye. The pain hurts so much. In tears I cry. I
want to hold your hand as we walk down the street. But we
have to look around at the people we might meet. They don't
understand about the love we share. They can't comprehend;
this kind of love is so rare. I want to take you in my arms and
hold you all night. But you belong to someone else, and it
wouldn't be right. Why didn't we meet long ago, before the
commitments in our life? I'd make you so happy as my darling
wife. This question I ask always comes back to why. Princess,
it hurts so much. In tears I cry; so I try to be strong and pray for
strength to go on. Lord, you put me through a lot, but that's
why Jesus was born. He's our ship in troubled waters. He's our
Saviour in close quarters, to love someone with all your heart
and know one day you will soon be apart. With your help, my
love, we can enjoy each day. I hope and pray you love me in the
same way. Maybe one day, if it's in God's plan, you will become
my wife as I become your man. But until that day, I'll pray to get
by. The pain hurts so much. In tears I Cry.

   Craig R. Smith

My Mother's Arms

My mother's arms are the best place on Earth.
Her arms are big and strong, yet gentle and loving.
They are the color of a Hershey's candy bar,
and have the sweet scent of brown sugar and cinnamon mixed together.
Her arms feel smooth as silk as she wraps them,
protectively around me.
Her arms are always open, and ready to surround me
with the warmth of her love.
While she rocks me in her melted chocolate arms,
nothing in the world can cause me any harm.

My mother's arms are where I learned life's best lessons.
It was in her arms that I learned the peace of being loved,
the warmth of being compassionate, the joy of being kind,
the sweetness of being caring, and the beauty of being a friend.

I have been many places,
   but none were as beautiful as my mother's arms.
Her arms shall forever remain the best place on Earth to me.

   Jequetta Bellard

That Special Girl

You're on a boat at sea, gathering oysters to search for a pearl.
You have looked through dozens of oysters, looking for the best
pearl. You looked and looked and looked and looked, until all of
a sudden, you find the ideal pearl. You're pleased, overjoyed
with your find. So you take it home for it to be polished and
mounted. The pearl is mounted and you begin to wear it with a
measure of pride, receiving compliment after compliment. You're
happy with this pearl you've found. You cherish it and care for
it. But after some time, the joy that was associated with the pearl
isn't there anymore. You begin to lose interest and no longer
care for or cherish the pearl. So one day, you walk to the
seashore. Unhappy with the pearl, you throw it into the sea.
You walk away from the shore and go on with life, with no
regrets of throwing the pearl away. But as time passes, as you
try on different stones and the like, you realize that nothing
compares to that pearl. So one day, you go back to the sea,
determined to find the pearl. You swim as deep as you can,
desperately looking for the pearl, but to no avail. You return to
the shore, exhausted and disappointed. As you fall to your
knees, your head sinks into your chest, as low as it can go—you
couldn't find the pearl. But then you hear the happiness of
another swimmer. You look up and see the pearl that was once
loved and cherished but thrown away, in another person's hand.
You rise and slowly walk as the sun sets.

   Clayton M. Crumell

Ship at Sea

Many days spent adrift on these trenching, lonely waters,
Years I watch fade into the sunset as did the travelers;
Ports that were found were interesting,
Yet always intrigued to what the others may bring;
There were many days that the waters were rough, yet I dredged on.
This ship I traveled upon was strong,
But throughout the storms only grew weak,
On those days where the water ran cool and gentle,
I swam within lavishing in the place;
Often I thought of those passing travelers of which I met along the way,
There were those of mystery, some filled with laughter,
One was a soldier who carried me through a rough storm,
They were interesting, yet never to stay;
In my dreams I could intertwine them into one,
One in which to assist in my journey;
Growing tired of this long journey,
It was time to draw this ship to its final port,
I could always look up to the heavens for God was my trusting guide,
It was time to walk on land, loneliness was left at sea.

Diane M. Steele

The Memory

You used to take my fears away,
and with that you would say:

"I'll always be here for you,
no matter what you may go through.
Sometimes life treats you wrong,
but remember you must always stay strong.
Someday the day will come and I'll be gone,
but in your heart I can live on."

That I have always remembered when times seem rough.
I just look deep in my heart to find the strength I need to remain tough.

Sammie Purtee

Once Again

Once again we met,
Once again we loved,
Once again we are separated,
Alone. I live for our measure reunions.
I memorize your total being.
Your warm eyes, your broad smile, your deep laughter and . . .
Your penetrating love.
I replay our conversations over and over again.
It's as if . . . they are the only records my mind recognizes
Or . . . my ears elect to hear.
I write letters and poems to you.
Which, more often than not,
   find themselves rejected by my own censorship.
They seem too shallow or to deep, too weak or too strong,
Not acceptable in my own mind for your eyes to read . . .
Or for your soul to digest.
Once again the depression of separation sets in,
Leaving me painfully sad. Fighting the tears that force themselves
Down the hollows of my aging cheeks.
Once again I think of you.
Once again I smile.

Sarah Kirk Oden

Passion

One day, an old, frail man asked me, "What is it that makes you glow?"
I said, "It's passion, passion for life that makes me so."
The man, bewildered with my answer, asked me to explain.
And I said . . .
"It makes my stomach warm, like a hot bowl of soup,
It makes my skin burn, like a fire's flame,
It makes my hair moist, like the morning's dew,
And it voluminously fills my whole body.
You see, passion is everywhere.
Just search within yourself, and you shall find
that glow which has enlightened me."

Roopa R. Batni

Reflections after Key West

While the gods were out for recess, we headed off into the light.
A great heron, misjudging his timing, was shattered early in his flight.

So we began our hopeful journey with golden rapture all around
unaware that to the gods our dreams are heron on the ground.

Though we walked the streets with laughter
dreaded shadows stalked the bay,
for beneath the sparkling turquoise sharks were circling their prey.

Was this really an emotional wasteland, abundant life without a soul
or just an unwitting instrument assigned to play a role?

Perhaps the gods resumed their watch to set the stage and cast a part
in the relentless and deliberate destruction
of an already fractured heart.

They like to trick us into dreaming dreams
and then they wake us with a start.

Dorothy W. Rack

A Daughter's Love

The love for a mother from a child is something that we all know;
We give this love to our mother in different ways,
So that this love will always show.

I have seen the love for a mother from a daughter's love-filled heart,
A love shared by each other, whether near or far apart.

I have watched this daughter's love
and compassion as she cares for her mother, so dear.
She always touches and kisses her mother, each time that she is near.

I know this daughter with so much love and compassion in her life:
This daughter is the person that I love . . . this daughter is my wife.

Bob Travin

Opening the Door Again

The heart is a place of many doors;
some doors must close before another can be opened.

Some doors are closed softly, some with a bang,
some with a by-golly, some with a dang!

Some close so softly, I wasn't even aware.
Some close so harshly, I can only sit and stare.

I pray each day that the door to my heart won't stay closed,
that I can open it again, even if only slowly.

Thank you for showing me how to open the door again,
even if only for a short time; the joy was mine, and that was just fine.

Sometimes I am afraid I might not be good enough for
what knocks at my door.
Afraid to open the door again and afraid to keep it closed,

I know I can be sweet, loving and kind,
if only I can remember to let this part of me shine.

I know I can be giving and forgiving, sharing and caring;
when I can find these things in me, then I know I will be free
to really be me, and then I can open the door again.

Mary E. Johnson

Hope

In memory of all those who died in the Holocaust
A body falls. A stomach rumbles. A woman cries, "No more!"
The smell of corpses fills the air. An officer's whip leaves a sore.
All around me is death and pain. Maggots are our friends.
Word is Americans will come, come and make this end.
Death's cold hand is on my shoulder. He's telling me to come.
I know when I go the pain will stop. My hunger will be done.
But I really don't want to leave, and this is my reason why . . .
"I have to stay here, and keep all of our hope alive!"
Death nods his head, and walks away,
   though I know I'll see him again.
I look at a worker whose eyes are dead and say,
   "Don't worry; we will survive, my friend."

Sharon Dillenburg

The Love of Wonder

Stirring fragrant sizzling onions and reading, Olive Pomace Oil,
with an Italian flair, from the can on the shelf, brings thoughts of
a long ago friend, Gina, and the funny Lucy episode when she
crushed grapes between her toes. I remember the excitement of
wondering, what's it like, "Gina, what's this in Italian?", as I
point to a dewy-wet rose. Don't you love how memories come
quickly, not seeming invasive at all? Blarney Stone, bet you see
the impish elf! The love of Wonder was an exciting gift to a farm
girl in a small Texas town; yes, the love of Wonder did abound.
Wonder can be troublesome at times . . . you read how Huck and
his friends built an incredible raft, lashed and launched it into a
riveting adventure. Then . . . when you drag yourself and two
wet siblings "shipwrecked" from the pond, you fervently say
prayers that bargains can be struck and no one utters a word to
a "landlubber" Mom, who would likely "make you pay."
Heartbreaking Wonderment of "Why?" upon hearing the words
"Grandpa died." You feel like your ears have been hit! Love of
Wonder returns as you envision Gramps teaching young
Angels how to whistle and spit . . . yes, Wonder does abound!
Many folks describe love as an abstract form of vaporous-
fleeting tangibility, and feign amazement at simple explanations
of wondrous feelings of love while watching a puppy wiggle its
feet when dreaming of chasing its tail or a laughing child.

Leta Koch

Grandpa's Rocking Chair

There's an old rocking chair, casting memories everywhere
On that old front porch across from the general store.
You can see where the arm is worn,
From where my grandfather rested his arm
On that old rocking chair that don't rock no more.

I came from a broken home, I was blinded by a faith gone wrong
I had no vision of what the future held in store.
Just a baby at the end of three, when we came to
Grandpa, my sister and me
So he could rock us in that rocking chair that don't rock no more.

Grandpa lived the Christian way, out of goodness he would pray
He would sit and gather his thoughts as he rocked
  on the hard wood floor.
Well, he loved just to sit and rock,
  pay no attention to the time on the clock
As he rocked me in that rocking chair that don't rock no more.

If a rocking chair could read the thoughts from people's minds
The stories that it would tell after time.
Stories that others never hear, of the thoughts one hold so dear
Oh how I wish I could of read my grandpa's mind.
As he rocked me in that rocking chair that don't rock no more.

Archie R. Pairadee III

Encroachment

Continuous loft frontages, walkout basements,
Creek-side town-houses, bustling meadow villages,
Panoramic views with every lot.
A new community at the spring
Shopping malls at every intersection
Will you please, help avoid the squeeze
  from population and construction?
Let space therapy prevail on the open range
Unfenced, unfettered, unscheduled,
Where sunshine, rainbows, and moonbeams are in reverence held.
There is opportunity to see wildlife, sage brush, and cactus,
To smell the fragrances of milkweed and clover,
To hear the sounds of silence mingled with bird song,
To touch the short grass blades of the prairie,
And to feel the expanding freedom produced by space.
Space therapy bespeaks of the quiet, elevating place
That permits the mind, heart, and soul to entwine, to embrace.
Help keep the knolls, meadows, ridges, and the orchards in the valley.
Please, therapy bespeaks of the quiet, elevating place
That permits the mind, heart, and soul to entwine, to embrace.
Help keep the knolls, meadows, ridges, and the orchards in the valley.

A. Sandstead

Broken Hearted

To David Glen Windham
You said you would be eternal friends, always be together
be honest amongst one another but . . .
An Alaskan Dark Cloud has entered this region of sincerity
your true heart has shown its unsavory colors
Wow, can we cease this string of deception,
the pain it causes it unwarranted
For gain of self gratification? A selfish heart appeared, the reason
An uninformed innocent "other-half," waiting in the wings.
What causes this?
A broken heart, if shattered in some areas, is beyond repair
but the hurt one should not despair
thou that breaketh a heart, shall forever reap the heartbreak
they have sowed
boomerang . . . do you hear me
glen dale in the heights that cast between win and a throp
Look at me, look at you
you entered knowing its legacy of sorrow
Entering with an agenda and insincere selfish intentions
for self gratifications?
Crushed I am; I will live
but in my garden I will forever have a legacy
you left me . . . a Broken heart.

Janeese M. Bland

Sarah Fey

Hey, Sarah Fey—
your desperation is the tears that scrambled from my eyes last night
tears heavy enough and salty enough
to force their way through this scrubby beard
quenching the pillow that you so carefully placed the day before
I could not hold them; I could not control them for either you or me
and sleep, although I had a firm grasp on its reins
always stayed at its farthest point
tugging around the corner or under the bed
perhaps worrying that our union would leave us amiss
  of your condition,
so safe, I cannot sleep from the condition you are in

Hey, Sarah Fey—
your desperation is like these vision spawn rivulets
in that it seeks out and settles into the fabric of those things
I prefer to conceal, among the papers and the photos
and the other assemblages
it seeks a target like a fist seeks a jaw
or a single shard of glass seems to seek the bare foot
sometimes, one cannot relish the flavor of grace
until it is stirred by sin

Dam Graham Jr.

Who's at My Door?

To my papa, Jack Pacent
I'm special in my own kind of way.
Let me tell you about this strange encounter I had the other day.
I was relaxing, thinking of all the memories of my life.
And felt a pain in my heart like a piercing knife.
All of a sudden there was a knock at my door.
It was the grim reaper dressed in black velour.
The pain in my heart got stronger as he floated over to me.
My feet were planted as I tried to flee.
I've been close to death before,
But now death itself was coming in the door.
He told me he had come for my soul.
The aroma from his breath smelt like burnt coal.
He said that I've been wanting to die for so long,
That he's here now to take me to where I belong.
He was so right, I had wanted to die, that's one thing I can't deny.
Now that death was in front of me, I wanted to live so I copped this plea.
"Grim reaper, please spare my soul for many years to come,
I don't know what I was thinking—I was really, really dumb.
I want my life—I'm just a troubled teen,
I want to start new, I want to start off clean."

Adrienne Ann Barnes

Open Your Eyes

Your neighborhood, your barrio, that isn't anything to be fighting for, but if you think it is can you tell me why you fight for something that'll never be yours? Now, eternal life is your gift from the Lord. So, you should "Be strong not in yourself but in the Lord, in the power of his boundless strength." Eph. 6:10. And you should do this at any length. You need to "Put on God's complete armor so that you can successfully resist all the devils craftiness." Eph. 6:11. Just live right and follow the word and to Heaven is where you'll surely progress. Don't let the devil keep you so blind that you can't see there's no reason for all this killing. "For our fight is against no physical enemy" Eph. 6:12. And now I understand the devil and his evil from the other side is why one of you enjoys watching the other die. But all caught up in gang banging that thought never crosses your mind that he wants to watch you die too. And the pain your victim's family feels and the tears they cry will be the same your family feels and cries when it's your time. Don't you realize, our fight, "It's against organizations and powers that are spiritual. We are up against the unseen power that controls the dark world and spiritual agents from the very headquarters of evil." Eph. 6:13. And by doing the bad things you do you're actually opening for him the door to your life, and if you keep going the way you are you're going to die twice.
Please, open your eyes.

Connie Melendez

A Candle Unlit

Take my hand and lead me from these days of fire, to any place of quiet retire and soothing comfort. This grinding life of hastiness leaves me feverish and stolen; all my vicious disputes sear my exigent heart. I know my sins, but cannot just toss all our hopes upon another impetuous pyre.

How quickly my senses have flown apart from my desires, yet even as my discretions have ceased, your trust, so dearly needed, has exposed me. I am blistering from my own despotic behavior, breaking me apart. I am tired; lead me from my incontinence.

Fear has been disguising itself as need, conspiring against us, trying to sever the course of our fidelity, sinking our affections under its ichor. All of my crimes and indiscretions, even these words are prone to bloated, egocentric schemes. So now I am alone, naked and ashamed, begging for a glimpse of my dignity undone.

Even though my propriety has kept me from your reach, I extinguish it now and reach for you because your touch can still appease, perhaps even release me from my blunders. My sense of myself has expired; I seek absolution and forgiveness so as to begin again. Light a votive candle near my former place, I want to remember a once happy, compassionate man. Take my hand and lead me back to you, only you. I may find myself there, too!

Fr. Patrick J. Russell

Song at the Caged Bird

The obscure image gallantly strides across the lonely desert, creating vague footprints that will never be followed, disappearing with the wind, rushing toward the sky. The mirage is not seen by others, only known by itself, like illusory twists in the still air. The blurry figure traveling in the wind, unable to see the light vigorously pounding on her crippled body, just as a delicate rose begins to wither in the great luminary light—she is trapped, surrounded by the blows of humanity, like a caged bird, only bars separating the free and the condemned. Her voice miraculously evolves into a sweet aroma of ginger, singing— determined to be heard, like the ringing sound triggering the denying ears of the world. A bitter cloth of hatred is thrown over her cage, capturing the truth, intertwining among its threads, as treacherous thunderclouds cover up the radiant sunshine. When will the song bird be free to sing her melody? "Never," the world protests, but the obscure image continues to pound against the bars that have confined her, like a beast with a fierce soul that will eventually destroy the walls in order to escape. Her courage is a blazing lion ready to devour animosity. The pious, yet caged, bird will soon fly away without the strangling, black scarf that twists around its joyous voice to suppress the righteous candor. The blithe will shine through the darkness, like electrifying eyes that will see and tell all.

Sarah Ramsay

Life

What is it? Does it have a meaning?
The truth must be let out
But the answer is nonexistent
If the answer is not there, what do the questions mean?
Are they real? Are we real?
If there is no beginning and no end, why are we here?
Life had a start and it will end
Is life a fraud, a thought, or just one big dream?
Am I in that dream or am I the dreamer?
Does life have a purpose or just separate ones?
Is everyone's life combined like one huge mind
With multiple personalities or are we all separate?
The one's mind who had thought us all up
Left us thinking and making questions
That we are smart enough to know
They will never be answered without a missing link
Not ever knowing or being able to explain
What is life?

Diamond K. Foley

Desiree

Anything beautiful you can see or say
comes in a package called Desiree.

Her eyes are blue as the deepest sea,
and they smile and laugh when they look at me.

As straight as a arrow, as gentle as a dove,
both strong and sweet, and easy to love.

There are four seasons so they say, but
I know a fifth named Desiree.

She is sometimes hot and sometimes
cold, but sometimes a little out of control.

Flowers in December and snow in May—
but there never will be another like Desiree.

Carol A. Gatewood

Silence

Oh, secret siren's seductive sound
rewarded with felicitous gain,
silence panders the harmonious song
attention is your bane.

Injustice inspires impassioned cries,
intellectual arguments flow;
trapped within boundaries rigid and tight
anchored close to the soul.

For midnight scoundrels drool with delight
scavenging sensitive pray,
fictitious critics discredit on sight;
demons in every way.

Oh, secret siren's seductive sound
rewarded with felicitous gain,
what strength it takes to break the bond
when attention is one's bane.

John C. Keppel

The Swordfish

A swordfish is an incredible creature,
extraordinarily unique and remarkable feature.
If it was to give you a poke from behind,
the pain would drive you out of your mind!

With a built-in sword on the tip of his face,
even the sharks keep away from his space!
But I'm sorry to say, on my platter today
is the swordfish who plundered the seas.
Even though he was caught he still has a chance—
he's going to set up a feast!

Richard Ammel

The Legacy

Sándor, only sixteen, kissed his mother good-bye.
Weeks later he gazed in awe at the majestic Lady
and her torch in the harbor.
Her torch signaled that he now had a secure foothold in life.
In his new homeland, he met, years later, his life partner, Tilda.
Tilda, at eleven, had entered through the same freedom gate.

As "Papa" and "Mama," they toiled for the family's "daily bread."
The harvest of their work, love, song, prayers, and charity during
the Great Depression reinforced the Lady's promise though
Mama and Papa were "white-collared" only at church.
There Papa's tenor rang out, and there the two were known for
sharing their home and Mama's delicious chicken and pastry.
The beggar who asked for "a little food" enjoyed a meal at the family
table, a bath, and left wearing a clean shirt.

Papa's and Mama's "secret votes," their son's and daughter's
educations and being able to pass on the Lady's legacy to their "gyönyörü"
(beautiful) grandchildren—all manifestations of their country's blessings.

Still flying is a flag on "Grandpa and Grandma's
    one-hundred-foot flagpole,"
and their/her beacon still lights the way.
        Tillie Atkins

Fleeting Starr

And then I wept, expressing passion as grief by shedding assonant tears
Aching to point the finger at anyone but him
The lies, his wicked betrayal of all I trusted to be real
Tell me that truth and I'll tell you how happy I am
Can you, if only for myself, redeem for your oblivion
The sound of a breaking heart; voices, breath and sunflower seeds . . . crash.
All turned black and white on that fateful day, that mutual day
The inevitableness of it makes me laugh
Then you took such a sorry plight downward
In saying you cared, and I believed
I'm defeated in love; 8779 rings apathetic in my ears
But you have the Devil to pay and yourself to wrestle
I think though, we are forgiven for our ignorant ways;
for blinding ourselves
Even in denying me, darling, in the midst of your selfish pride
I have learned more than I ever thought attainable
From the landslide of our 14 months of,
Heaven only knows what we had . . . love?
I, ten thousand times mine. You, in which I will never lose hope
I smile now for you, you David, who stole so much.
        Lai Gaylean Ferreira

Love Like Snow

Love is like snow coming down on a cold winter's night.
Love covers a multitude of sins.

The snow, wherever it falls, on a clean-cut yard in an upper
Class neighborhood or the dirty, filthy grounds of the ghetto,
It makes everything look so clean and white!

Just watch it as it falls on beer cans, bottles, broken glass,
Sticks, mud, and rocks, slowly making the ugly look pure and beautiful.

Snow makes a ghetto look just as beautiful as an upper class
neighborhood.

Love covers the beer cans of hate and the bottles of despair.
It covers the broken glass of hope and the sticks of malice.
It covers the mud of prejudice and the rocks of discrimination,
Slowly making the ugly look pure and beautiful.

It does not matter who you are or how bad your situation.
If you will just let some love fall into your life, like snow on
A cold winter's night, the snow of love will lighten up your darkest
Night and cover your worst faults and shortcomings, so that no one
Would be rich and no one would be poor, the word race would have
No meaning, no black, no white, for all the world would be as one!
        Wintrell Pittman

Highways in the Wood

The allure of the wood
Is special to me
The serenity and beauty
Down and highways lined with trees

The creators of these roads
Are wild and free
Streets ancient and well traveled
Full of wonder and mystery

Make a left make a right
Travel slowly look around
Perceptions keen senses aware
Moving with hardly a sound

Imagine the travelers
Over these bridges and down those lanes
Some hopping some scurrying
Some feathered some maned

Next time you're in the wood
On a crisp fall day
Take a little journey
Down a miniature highway
        Thomas M. Walker

Regeneration

The leaves turn brown
When winter comes.
The cows shiver in the wind,
And God spreads a blanket
Of heavy fur over them.

The leaves fall down
When winter comes.
The gopher goes underground,
And the wind blows fallen leaves
Over his doorway.

The leaves form mulch
In the winter time,
And a tiny seed slithers on a breeze.
The mulch seals it from the snow.

The mulch layer cracks
As the winter goes.
A tiny sprout peeks out,
And a sunflower grows
Toward Heaven.
        Claudia B. Williams

Taking the Time

Take time to care and
Time to share
Your life and love that's
Sent from Heaven above

Take time to see and
Time to listen
Time to feel and to
Know each season

Take time to grow and
Time to reason
Just what you're doing with
Precious time that's fleeting

Take time to pray for
Guidance to know
The one true way
Each and every day

Take time to forgive other's and
Your own mistakes
Take the time, take the time
While there's still time to take
        Grace Paschal Wheeler

There's Not a Day

There's not a day that goes by when a thought of you
doesn't pass through my mind.
No matter what's happened between us in the past,
the memories of time we shared will never be left behind.
I love you in various and uncountable ways.
I love you as a sister does brother, as mother does child,
as girlfriend does boyfriend, as wife does husband,
as best friend does best friend.
All of these loves will live within my heart until my dying day,
but will live in my soul far past my last days.
Everyone says leave him where he's at—he's obviously done you wrong.
I hear what they're saying, but that's something I can't do,
because of the fact every feeling I proclaim to have for you
will live beyond lifelong.
I always told you how much I care for you and wanted to protect you.
After all we've seen one another through, you probably stopped
believing all I said has still held true.
To clarify and reassure you,
I want you to know, in my mind, you'll never stop
being my Baby Boy and My Boo.

Jamarah Botley

Wagon Wheel

A wagon wheel leaned against a tree, covered with a mantle of snow.
Its mission ended, its journey done; it had no where else to go.

Time was when America needed wagon wheels for it was young in age.
It had men and materials to move, over mountains, through valleys and sage.

The track was long from the east to the west; the country was wild and new;
And often the way was rough and steep, but there was a job to do.

Young men, with a purpose, drove their teams over the winding track;
They faced the future with a prayer and a song, never thinking of turning back.

They carved a nation out of the wilds because God willed it so.
And youth is still eager to do its part if we give them a place to go.

It won't matter if the way be rough and steep or leads over desert sand;
If we give them a purpose and help them know that God will hold their hand.

There are wilds to conquer, just as real, as our forefathers ever knew,
And youth is just as eager to travel life's trail-ways, too.

Don't lower the standards marked out by God along the wagon track;
For if we do, our youth will go where there'll be no turning back!

The wagon wheel rolled through the grandest time America will ever know.
Now it stands idle, its mission done, rotting under its mantle of snow.

Our youth too will know decay unless they are helped to see;
God wants to mark out their course to keep America free!

Elva P. McQue

Saying Good-bye

As I sat holding onto my child,
Never did I think it would be for a short while.
I wish each day that my little angel could stay,
As enough time wasn't made and on that very day I had so much to say.
Only a short time to do so but I just didn't know how long.
It was God that knew but he allowed us some time before saying good-bye.
I asked to be alone as I cried holding my angel,
Not knowing when he was leaving me but there was a moment that I
Felt so alone and also a feeling of this special touch.
The very look in my angels eyes, I could do nothing more than cry.
To see my child looking at me and knowing it was his mother that he could
see. Deep down I felt that he was telling me in the only way possible that
he was hurting so. During the moment when I felt alone and empty inside,
it was a moment when all things went dim except for my child.
That was the time that I had sensed to send my love so he could be free
from any more pain and sorrow. Prayers for my little angel were done night
and day but it was in God's nature to take him away and wipe away all the
agony. I couldn't help not to ask, "Why?" Why my child? It didn't seem fair
that my angel was leaving me for a little while till God chooses me
for me to go so at this moment I must be saying my good-bye. . . .

Jamie A. Sims

Confusion

*In honor of my parents
and my grandmothers*
Eyes staring
rapid breathing
hot under the collar
panic
Searching, fumbling with papers
quickly—clean the desk
Lift papers for the third time
scan, survey the surface
like a vulture looking for food
getting hotter
sitting, staring
wondering
Where could it be?
Glance upward
Duhhh
Where it belongs, but never is

Mary K. Mongan

Thinking of You

To the love of my life, William Walker
Thinking of you,
I pause for a while,
Remembering your laughter,
I quietly smile.

Thinking of you,
Deep inside I quiver,
Remembering your touch,
I start to shiver.

Thinking of you,
I wonder about when,
Remembering your heart,
We'll be together again.

Darla Feldman

Words

Precious your words
I long to hear.
Your radiance glistens;
I feel you near.

Pure loving voice
Of wisdom drips
Like honey from
Your magnificent lips.

"I long to taste
Your sweetness, dear,"
I wish to hear
Whispered in my ear.

Show the way
Eager hearts do lead;
Fulfilling and nourished,
They long to feed.

Debra Balmer

Saoirse

I sat inside anonymity
At a table of ambiguity
Embraced by my own serenity.
Now I stand on obscurity,
Amazed at my own commodity,
And focus on how fairly
I spit on my own grave
Specifically, because, oh, no,
It shall not be.
Once Written, Death cannot become me.

Jennifer Melone

This Old House

Once this old house beamed with life; babies cried into the night.
The stove glowed hot because back then,
you cooked and cooked and cooked again.
The kids ran in and the kids ran out.
We thought they'd wear the hinges off the door of this old house.
Laundry piled up knee deep; that poor old washer ran all week.
We didn't have a dryer way back then;
we hung the laundry with clothespins.
Then before sunset, you'd get it off the line.
And, if you held it to your face, you could smell the sunshine.
And, at night, when the kids tried to sleep,
that old house would begin to creak.
It made them think of a movie they saw,
about a monster with great big claws.
So, before long, they'd be knocking at your door,
saying they couldn't sleep anymore.
And, in the morning, once again, the sunshine would come beaming in.
Another day would start to begin for this old house and the people within.
Well, we sold our old house today, 'cause all the kids have moved away.
We thought we'd get a smaller place; we really don't need all that space.

Donald J. Schoenberger

God's Master Plan

We have an immutable heavenly father, by him all things are conceived
The master planner made Adam, then from his rib made Eve
The garden of Eden was a paradise, for pleasure and delight
But the two transgressed, and put out, their spiritual light;

Now Noah was sent to build an ark, and save a remnant for rebirth
For God would destroy such evil, with a flood upon the Earth
When the children of Israel cried to God, from Egypt for relief
Then God called Moses to lead them, out of their grief

Moses led, and gave laws, saw the pass-over, and Red sea victory
After this Christ was born, our Saviour born of flesh and deity
And most of thirty years, he taught salvation, that we might understand
He brought his great love to us, but many rejectors cried, "Crucify Him"

From the cross he prayed, forgive them Father, they know not what they
do; Death, hell, and the grave are conquered, I will come back to you
The Master's plan, was costly, many martyrs, paid a great price
Stephen's vision of Christ standing on the right, relates divine sacrifice

And the Shekinah glory shone to prove, Christ had rose up above them
Which angered the objectors, for this proved, They killed an innocent man
Apostle Ananise was called to pray for blind Apostle Paul
When he touched Paul, he was sanctified, and given a gentile call

Mary Nettie Hinshaw

Missing You

I still remember the day, when I first came to you
Afraid at first, but you gave me the strength to make it through
Peace in my heart is what I have felt ever since
It was at that beginning stage that I knew I was Heaven sent
Not to do what my flesh would have, but instead the things of God
But father I have slipped out of you will, and now things seem so odd
That's why I say I miss you Father God, especially the peace that you
gave me. For now I just wander around not realizing the truth inside me
I miss the talks we had when I was down and out
And the way you calmed the storms, is what it was all about
For I had to realize all over again that you are the truth, the way,
and the light. But you know the way I feel, for I tell you each and every
night. So missing you isn't the words to use anymore
But there are still some places in my heart that you and I need to explore
For you already know, but I need to see
That what lies inside of me is only the truth that you taught me.
And now Father God I pray that you open our eyes wide, so that we all
may believe. That we shouldn't worry, but instead be of good cheer
For you said that you would never leave

Allen L. Hill

Momma

Hold me Momma,
For I need
That nurturing touch
That only you can give me.
Put your arms around me tight.
Hold me close with all your might.
No one can hurt me,
Because you are there.
There is no fear,
For I am against your breast,
Safe within your loving fortress.
If you should ever leave,
Leave me with that feeling of safety
To carry me through
Life's ups and downs without you.

Pattie Hardin Nichols

Elizabeth

Coordination of beauty,
harmonizing the expressions
tell the tale of an inward peace.

Tapestry of colors flow with elegance,
weaving the wonder of a moment,
painting a picture of femininity.

Stars in the sky seem
to be reaching out to the jewels,
moving others through time and space,
serving notice to a outward grace.

Refinement of Elizabeth's Charm,
electric current of her ways,
generate the sensations of a tour,
experiencing the magnetism
of Queen Elizabeth's Grandeur.

Demps Pettway

Living Life's Adventure

Life wouldn't hold much meaning
If in life we had no end.
For if life went on forever,
There'd be no Earth to Heaven transcend.

Soon days would lose their beauty.
Would a year still be a year?
With a guaranteed tomorrow
There'd be nothing to hold, dear.

The uncertainty of living
Is a treasure we should hold.
Not knowing when God's Heaven will come
Becomes the adventure of growing old.

Phillip Warren Olson

Children

To all of our children
Daughters and sons:
dreams of our dreams,
loves of our loves,
and desires of our desires,

angels and monkeys,
dolls with genius,
and homunculi with flesh.

Dharma,
start with pats and breath,
continue with pats and breath,
and finish with pats and breath.

Neoteny,
we are all children.

Joseph William Oliver

Loose Sand

To my children, Rodger Jr., Crystal, Tonya, Rachel, and Christopher
Do you ever feel life is like loose sand beneath your feet?
Sometimes it feels good but sometimes it burns from the heat.
Loose sand under our wheels can help us go through the ice and snow.
But stuck on the beach with wheels spinning—nowhere is where we go.

Sometimes it tells us the time in our lives as the hour glass will display;
Used to make castings of things which endure—molding changes day by day.
Found in heavy weights sometimes too difficult for us to handle,
Placed on a flame can extinguish the brightest of all the brightest candles.

Loose sand known as life can put out the flame of love.
It can make us hard as iron castings where we once were soft as doves.
Life can stop us from breathing as the candle flames that flicker.
Making as bitter and cold, knowing only how to complain and bicker.

Let's use the hourglass sand to show us the time when not to walk
   in life's hottest hour.
So pain and sadness will never turn us bitter, cold, and sour.
To wear the casting of iron protecting us known as our will;
Let our treasures of love be safe—so the dove, we will never kill.

Let's put a fence and a gate around our treasures in our lives,
So we can share the good and not let in the bad to assure love survives.
At the end of each day when we pray, kneel and fold the hand,
Say a prayer so the treasures of life will never be buried in loose sand.

   Rodger H. Reed

The Eyes Are the Soul

Staring, gazing deep into space
Imaginings of a splendor time and place
Yet, who really knows what's behind that view
I really know and maybe so do you
For I'm holding on to that "real" part of me
Scared to let anyone see me be free
'Cause that part's been hurt, it's been out there before
That's why I keep it behind this closed door
The door to my soul, my most inner me
I once shared this soul, the same it'll never be
So think for a minute when you look into one's soul
Does she feel what I'm thinking? Does he think I'm losing control?
For the eyes are the soul of you, which reveal
All of the things you wish to conceal
Falling in love, baring fruit, hating having to face these truths
Drying my own tears, laughing within, makes me question this life I'm in
Now the next time you gaze into these eyes, you'll think of things you
Secure inside and just maybe we will realize; there's a place we both have
Reached to confide. So stop for a minute, 'cause maybe you see, your eyes
May help these eyes break free.

   Aliscia R. Ramsey

Dawn

The world stood still and silent in the dawn.
Not a sound was heard, except the still small sound of God's
Great love in the voices of the awakening little creatures.

The solitude of love where there is no fear,
The gentleness of having all God's love given freely and taken
With no doubt is why they sing with happiness.

If you and I were to love Him as faithfully as the birds in the sky,
Then we'd never have a doubt of fear that Heaven's gates we would not see.
If we would but believe as the small creatures do,
That His love is freely given, if we would but do as He says,
Heaven's portals would open wide and His love protect us from all else.

The trials He gives are to test the strength of all who love and honor His Name.
But no test is more than we can bear, for all we need to remember,
Is to whisper His great name and the Strength of His Legions will be ours.

We all need the quietness of the dawn to remember Him.

   Misty J. Hammerbacker

Hidden Pond

To Jean sweet Witty Irish
A whole different world
Pristine, at a glance
There wasn't a road
We found it by chance

A place of our own
Past towns and beyond
It was secret and quiet
And called, "Hidden Pond"

We walked in the woods
Held hands and sang
Cuddled and whispered
A distant bell rang

We lay on a blanket
And looked up at the sky
Listened to the stillness
Watched clouds drifting by

You're gone, and I miss you
Many fires have I lit
But the joy of Hidden Pond
I shall never forget

   Ronald M. Gifford

Fading Flowers

Fading flowers in the garden
Fading flowers down the lane
Petals slowly drifting downward
Like sweet melodies refrain

They as aged ones departing
Bow to nature's way of life
Lived their portion of abundance
Lived their times of trials and strife

But the stems which bore their blooming
Are not reft of all that's fare
Look, and you will see the seedlings
Which in other years may bare

So like aged ones in leaving
Leave a melody to chant
Leave some seedlings on their life stem
For the younger ones to plant

   Edna Pinkerton Hirons

Mary

To my special friend, Mary Beth Goehl
In the dark she sat there,
One little corner of the room.
Her eyes were miles away in thought.
She felt so alone.

The noises from beyond the room
Were muffled in her mind.
Unaware of her surroundings,
Her heart was breaking deep inside.

Her tear-stained cheeks, they glistened
When Mary began to sigh.
She sat with her feeble hand in hers,
Watching her mother die.

The darkness was interrupted
By a tiny shaft of light,
Like the light of hope
That brightens the darkest of nights.

Riddled with exhaustion,
She sat and slept right there.
God took her mother home with Him
While she was unaware.

   Kathy Abernathy

A Lesson in Life

What tomorrow might bring, are what yesterday meant?
If we only knew. In our life we need to learn from what the past
has told us, and what tomorrow will tell us.
If we all use our past as a ladder to tomorrow we would all
understand that in climbing the ladder it will take us all that much
closer to what our lesson in life and our goal really is.
(For in our climb it will take us that much closer to Heaven).
God's will is (we can not know are destiny), we can only know
right from wrong. In choosing what is right we open the doors to our soul
and are able to learn from ourselves, and to what yesterday, has taught
us and tomorrow will teach us. If you choose to do wrong, you will wrong
yourself and close all the doors to your life. Being wrong cannot allow
you to grow enough inside to climb the ladder to a better understanding
to what God is trying to teach you. In order to know what we need to in
life and to climb above the wrong and learn from all the right, we need
to always look behind us and never forget what we learned from yesterday.
Always look ahead to tomorrow, with an open mind in knowing you will
learn something then to. Now you are one step closer to all the answers
in your life.

Toni Ernst

September Winds

September winds sweep across the land, swirling upward through the trees
and down enticing each painted leaf to soar, "Come fly away with me in the
morning sun," the chilling wind seems to hum.

What a colorful display as the leaves obey, flying away with the restless
wind. Swirling and twirling high in the sky around and around they go red,
gold, crimson and brown the leaves soon drift freely to the ground.

Again the leaves are touched by the playful winds. Together they go
dancing up the lane across the yard and back again.

The colorful leaves now lie around every bush and twig laid low. Soon to
be covered by the first snow fall.

In the spring, no longer shall they be red, crimson, brown and gold but
rather crinkled, crushed and old. All their beauty washed away by wind,
rain and snow.

Like memories pressed between the pages of time, so are the memories of
once colorful fall pressed upon the back roads of my mind, forever to recall.

Juanita Jones Lunsford

Fear of Death

Why does man so greatly fear death's knock upon the door to hear
If, as we are often told by the learned men of old,
Life will so much sweeter be when "Streets of Gold" we finally see?

Is it that our faith is weak or our dread of the grave so bleak?
Is it fear of the great unknown; maybe guilt for wild seeds we've sown?
Whatever it be, it's always there; fear of death is a burden we share.

The answer seems to be that God knows our nature better than we.
We're greedy and want only the best.
We'd misuse the gift with which we're blest.
Our life on Earth would be ignored without the fear of death's mighty sword.

We wouldn't see His lovely flowers, or seek the rainbow in the showers,
Or stand in awe on a mountain high, or listen for a baby's sigh,
Or sweat to plant the wheat in the field,
Or work so hard to harvest its yield.

We wouldn't watch a bird on the wing, or listen at evening to him sing.
We'd be discontented to here abide; we'd strive instead for the other side.
So fear of death is the only way to make us cherish the gift of today.

But comes the time for us to go, He'll lift the veil so we will know
The long, dark trip down a path so hidden
is but a few short steps already taken.

Norma Coble

Untitled

Life became a magic show
when first I looked into your eyes.
Time was all but forgotten,
for in you a full future lies.

The mystery of your bosom
is something I long to know,
to touch your woman's heart
with feelings that forever grow.

Never-ending emotions
in the mystic bonds of time,
always changing together
till you're forever mine.

The knowledge of all life
can be found in your gentle smile.
When I'm lost, hurt, or lonely,
I find rest in your arms awhile.

M. Phillip Brown

Snowy Christmas

It's Christmas time and all is aglow.
Our world is clean with driven snow.
The children's eyes, though ever bright,
Enlarge and shine with each new sight.

Our Christmas tree stands very tall
Against the darkly paneled wall.
The ornaments and lights do glow,
Reflecting on packages below.

The birds keep flying in to feed,
Hoping our feeders are filled with seed.
The chickadees just flit about,
And cardinals pop the seed right out.

Our yard is a sight to behold.
The grass is white and looking cold.
Little rabbit tracks all around,
Adding interest to the ground.

The silent snow came in last night,
And we awoke to a beautiful sight.
The evergreens are gently bent
Wearing white garments, Heaven sent.

Margaret Carey

Red

To my muse, love, and friend,
Joshua, you complete me
Women have red blood,
Cry as angels and are weak too,
But soar high with broken wings.

Tanya Dugree

Emily

To my husband, Jim, with love
A charming smile,
Big, beautiful blue eyes,
A little pug nose,
And a look that's wise.
Full of pepper and ginger spice,
A personality that can melt the ice
Of the frostiest heart
When she bats her eyes.
And her sunny laugh seems to hypnotize
Anyone she deems to favor
And allows to sample the special flavor
Of Emily's cheerful disposition.
She seems to have an intuition
Of knowing how to touch one's heart.
For a girl so young, she's very smart.

Beatrice A. Engels

Mother, Another Word for Love

A mother is someone near and dear to our heart.
No matter what troubles we get into she will always lend a helping hand.
When life seems to bring us down
She will be there to put a smile on our face.
She will support our dreams big or small,
She will wipe away our tears with each warm smile that she gives.
A mother is another word for the sensitivity and care she gives every day.
The softness of her voice and tender touch will help take away the pain.
She makes sure I have the best life has to offer.
As I look at my mother I can now see all the wisdom
And joy she has brought into my life.

A mother is a teacher, a caretaker, and a best friend,
We will laugh, cry, and argue together.
You took my dark and made it light, you took my fear and made me smile,
You took my pain and helped me heal.
You made me believe in the good times,
And you allowed me to forget the bad times.

A mother never gives up on her strength and loyalty towards her family.
I would like to give thanks, because having a mother like you
Has made me into the woman you see before you.

    Ronnie Sanchez

Jealousy and Envy

The Crystal bedecked banquet room teemed with excitement and anticipation.
The audience, sated with food an drink, leisured in trivial conversation.
The Emcee slowly approached the dais, then tapped a glass for attention
and silence rolled across the hall like the misty fog of the moors.

Beautiful gifts and prestigious awards were among the presentations,
amidst eloquent toasts, amusing roasts and glowing accolades.

The Green Eyed monster lounged in the crowd,
feigning an air of disinterest. He yawned and stretched;
he looked around, then reared his ugly head.

"Your gift is brown and mine is blue; why must all of the good things
come to you? I think your box is larger than mine; you got the lion's
share of everything, the very best kind! The audience raised their
glasses and sang your praises as you were toasted. They clapped and
cheered when you made your speech, but laughed when I was roasted."

The Monster always compares his gifts and blessings to those of others,
and his never quite measures up to those of his sisters and brothers.

Jealousy and envy, surpassing sibling rivalry,
feeds on living organisms like parasitic growths.
A fungus-like thallophyte grows suddenly and rapidly,
becoming a part of its own life source until it engulfs its host!

    Shirley J. Parker McCoy

A Woman

A woman dreams; a woman seems so ready to give to her.
All she knows and all that shows is how much a woman dreams.
A woman loves; a woman hopes to live a life of happiness.
But too often a woman hurts and feels the emptiness, when a woman loves.
A woman cares; a woman shares a lifetime with the children she bares,
Yet there are times even they don't understand how much a woman cares.
A woman tries; a woman cries to please the one she loves,
Still too many times love goes wrong no matter how much a woman tries.
A woman gives; a woman lives to cherish the love she vowed to take.
But one can only ask so much of what a woman gives.
A woman can without a man be so much more than she was before
She gave her heart away, as only a woman can.
A woman is so much more than meets the eye, soars so much higher
Than the sky; to honor a woman is to honor you and honor me.
For without a woman, a man would never be.

    Janie Almaguer Diaz

Stephen

To my sweet nephew,
Stephen Blake Cookenour
When around you
I became content, fearless
Protective of you
I feel whole
As if nothing is missing
You become the most
important thing to me.
Life becomes carefree and simple
Full of laughter and games
You always fill the empty space
that lies deep inside my heart
In your sweet and gentle way
With love and affection
That only you can give
Taking me away
To an innocent place.

    Sharon Cookenour

Two Loves

It's flowing; it's gushing,
Bullet wound to the head.
Close your eyes;
The pain will be gone.
Your friends are crying.
The gun's still in your hand.
Your boyfriend stands over you,
Sad, not knowing what to do.
He goes for the gun.
His friend stops him.
He gets away.
He does it anyway.
He loves you too much,
But didn't show it.
He cares too much,
But didn't act it.
He's lying by your side,
Gushing, too, flowing, too,
No heartbeat, eyes shut,
Two loves, together forever.

    Michele Breau

Keep the Mind of a Child

Keep on dreaming,
I tell everyone.
Keep the mind of a child,
And let your mind run wild.
Keep on hoping;
Have lots of faith.
My hopes come true,
And I'm sure yours will, too.
Keep on wishing;
Don't have a doubt.
I have the mind of a child.
My mind runs wild.

    Amy Besser

I Wonder

To my father, Clenty Smith
I often wonder why you left;
is it something I did?
Or something I didn't do?
I miss your smile, your voice,
and the way you smell.
I miss the sound of your feet
walking through the house.
I miss everything about you,
but I must go on and just think
about the good and some of the bad.

    Clennetha Smith

Senior English

Josh's 295 pounds are molded into the creaking desk
as he sits towering over the outline of the pallid, little duckling.
With his tongue balancing his head against the air in Michael Jordan style,
he struggles to keep the tattered, yellow stub pinched between his huge
fingers and inside the black lines, just like twelve years
before on his first day of school when he colored life into a baby bunny
using each stroke to cover the uncertainties
of crowded halls and lunchrooms and making new friends.
Now with each yellow streak, he muffles the nagging possibilities
of bungled football tryouts, broken scholarships, and lost friends.
As Josh struggles, Joe reaches across the aisle
with a pale blue crayon announcing, "I'll do the background!"
and Kylee turns around with an understanding smile and draws a big,
bright, radiant sun, just like they did twelve years before.

Thomas J. Miller Jr.

The Birth

The angels sang of his birth on the night Jesus came to Earth
and the glory of the lord shone all around in the City of David
(Little Bethlehem Town).
Creation sprang alive, the wind blew, the trees danced, the
oceans roared and not by chance.
It's a wonderful, marvelous, magnificent story . . .
The whole blessed Earth was full of God's glory.
God Almighty in the form of a babe had come to Earth, his people to save.
Oh! You know the rest, it's oft been told. How he astounded the priests in
the temple of old.
How he turned water into wine at the wedding in Cana—don't you know?
It was Jesus' first miracle and not for show.
He taught us to love one another, to love our fellow man, believe in God,
and take a stand.
He cast out demons and healed the sick. He caused the lame to walk and
the blind to see. He performed many miracles, this man from Galilee.
Jesus had a mission; it came from God.
He was to go where the angels had not trod.
This Christmas, when you celebrate His birth, remember the Christ
who came to Earth.

Ray D. Nixon

The Gift

He gave the greatest gift of love the world would ever know,
When God, the father, sent his only son to us so long ago,
A gentle man whose name was Jesus with loving heart and healing hands,
Soul heavy with the burden he would later bear for man,
He came to touch our darkened hearts, to teach of faith and love untold,
To heal once twisted bodies, to release tormented souls,
But we turned away our faces, believing not because of ignorance or fear,
That he was our Lord and savior why his father sent him here,
As he said, "Father forgive them, for they know not what they do,"
He left to join his father for his mission here was through,
Taking all the sins of mankind, every sorrow, pain, and strife,
His promise left behind for us: forgiveness and eternal life.

Roxanne Hale

A Voice Set Free

I sit calm as the sea. I remember the old me.
Shy as a kitten, cute as a mitten.
Struggled and trapped in dismay, ripped on, picked on in every way.
Mom was fat, Dad a joke, and me silent, who never spoke.
As I grew, so did my pain, stricken with poverty and no domain.
Inch by inch, year by year, my face was smothered, my heart with fear.
Beaten by boys of nonsense, trapped behind that fence.
And then I moved to a boring town, for it was I who would no longer frown.
But then again things aren't they seem, for it, was only a dream.
My junior year, hard as hell, a sleep deprived turtle crawling in his shell
That summer I changed because of some boys,
who taught me I had to make some noise.
And so I did, proud as can be, speaking my mind to extremity.
Not too far to cause despair, just a silent fellow trying to be fair.
It's me, I'm here, No longer silent, No more fear.
My smile is etched through my heart and soul,
for I am a man living his goal.

Chris Maki

I Am

I am me
I wonder how come
I hear sounds
I see creatures
I want nothing
I am me

I pretend to be others
I feel alone
I touch a tear
I worry about life
I cry about home
I am me

I understand little
I say someday
I dream to know more
I try to be me
I hope that someday I will be
I am me

Sofia Oberg

Knowing

I stared reality in the face
Just the other day.
The more I looked, the more it changed,
And then I looked away.
I couldn't believe before my eyes,
Such a painful sight to see,
My perception of an illusion
Staring back at me.
How could I be erroneous?
I know what I just saw.
Was it only an interpretation,
An image, after all?
How does one know the difference
Between truth and reality?
Is our vision so selective
That we see what we want to see?
I stared some more in disbelief.
It really can't be so.
The more I looked, the more I knew
That truly, I don't know.

Rhonda S. Henderson

I Made My Choice

I left my Washington state homeland
where I had sisters so dear to me,
for the grandmother role in Indiana
to my son and his family.
A loving son, a daughter for me,
grandchildren I just could not refuse,
for I can always visit my homeland
and live where my heart is used.

Martha L. Kady

Al

My precious brother, where can you be?
I seek you out so desperately.
I hear your voice inside my mind,
The one I've heard a thousand times.
I walk up and down your dwelling place,
But of my brother there is no trace.
I think of all the times we shared;
In joy and sorrow, you were there.
Together, we stood tall and strong.
You always taught me to carry on.
And now it finally comes to me . . .
My brother sleeps in restful peace,
Until that day when all abounds,
When life and love are worn as crowns.

David Ganci

Suggestions

To whomever much is given, much is expected
That's why with my talent, I choose to share, to show people
There are still some of us left who really do care
I always make time and I'm open to any and all suggestions
Poetry to me is just like school, you must study your lessons and analyze
What you've been through, so count on me and expect me
To give my all in my poetry
My writings are my creations, I hope by reading my poetry
Your brain gains stimulation, food for thought
Teaching the masses and all those who read my poetry, attend my classes
At the end of each semester, there's a test
To see how far you've progressed
Retention is the key
I hope you're able to trigger your memory
If much is expected from me
I expect the same in return from everybody
Much is given to me continually, that's understood so
I give back plenty, it makes me feel good!

Romuald L. Evertsz

Life

Life is a gift of flight which is fueled from a very warm light.
The light many may say is God, yet others tend to nod.
Whether this nod means a yes or a no life is still around us
wherever we go.
Each day is a new beginning with a spirit of our energy is never ending.
We take life for granted, as if it's just a simple thing
but when time of death, we try so hard to cling.
I suggest we all consider where would we be without life.
Without life there is no joy, no toys, no sadness, no happiness,
no love from above.
We need to take our time and enjoy what we have
and show our appreciation
in many ways if we have the pleasure to stay.
For, one day we will miss this wonderful wonder that we tend
to blunder and sometimes fall under.
So, I say be happy for each and every day, whether it's bad or good
you should still take time to say thank you to the one above.
For, he is a dove and will always shower you with love.

Saundra L. McCain

First Love

As I sat alone that day, the hot sultry wind seemed to whisper his name.
How was I to know our paths would cross and I would never be the same?
I definitely knew his name, but how could he ever possibly know mine?
For he was two years older and all the girls thought he was so divine.

Suddenly, he was standing there above me with a smile I could not resist.
My heart was beating faster now and I was filled with wondrous bliss.
And then he softly spoke my name and his voice was like music to my ears.
Somehow, I instinctively knew we would be together for many, many years.

Yes, many years have passed since our encounter that summer long ago,
And tomorrow we will be celebrating our golden anniversary, you know.
What a perfect time to share our lives with family and friends this way,
For neither time nor age can dim the love my husband brought that day.

Wanda Gerland

Brave Little Indian Boy

On a crisp, autumn morning, as first light peeped over the Grand Canyon rim,
A little Havasupai Indian boy of eight years began a survival test, his bravery to win.
He took his sharp knife, dried meat, and special moccasins of soft, tanned leather.
The elders had challenged him to find clues of a tribe mysteriously vanished forever.
As he passed through dense areas, he pondered the elder's strong but kindly warning
Of possible danger from sly, hidden creatures during the autumn's early morning.
He knew he must concentrate all of his efforts and actions upon this bravery test.
As hours passed, he grew weary, and stopped to sip stream water, but no time for rest.
His sharp eyes surveyed the rocky cliffs, the scrubby trees, the flowing stream,
And, scurrying from rock to rock, were scaly, long-tailed creatures best unseen.
Then—at first he did not see it—the most beautiful of butterflies. . . .

Maryoleta Bauman Diel

Across the Street

Across the street
roaring flames arose from
two Chevys tangled
into each other
as if they were welded together.
Fire-fog engulfed the sidewalk
erasing the ability to focus
arm's length ahead.
Crimson, beaming lights
ripped through
the pandemonium.
And the smoke
continued to creep slowly,
across the street.

Victoria A. Ohanna

Change My World Around

The wind has blown autumn away
And all the colors have turned gray
But it won't get me down
I will change my world around

I'll be alone again today
Friends come and go but seldom stay
But it won't get me down
I will change my world around

I love you but you don't love me
Nothing I can do but set you free
But it won't get me down
I will change my world around

I sometimes laugh sometimes cry
The seasons change and so do I
But it won't get me down
I will change my world around
I will change my world around

Michael L. Denniston

Dreams Are Not Black or White

In the old days, the black women
Brought up white children.
Today, I, a white girl,
Baby-sit a black child,
My little curly Cherub.
Her eyes are bright like May sunshine.
Her skin is soft as silk.
When she smiles,
Violet roses flush her cheeks.
She dreams of becoming a pianist,
And I . . . a surgeon.
(Dreams are not black or white.)
Little brown fingers close
Over my pink ones, creating
A butterfly with striped wings.
By our command,
The butterfly begins to fly
And with it . . . our dreams.

Rozi Theohari

Surfboard Love

I never rode
A surfboard
Gliding on
The waves or through
The tunnel of the great
Bonzazi pipeline
Looking for the ultimate wine
But how can
You measure the waves
And keep yourself upright
On the surf board
On the ultimate love?

Jamie June Bartson

A Stranger

Sometimes we see a stranger, and look at him and wonder why
He is dressed in torn and tattered clothing, not like you or I
With worn out shoes, that has no soles, and a worn out coat full of holes
A smile he tries to muster up, as he holds out his tin cup
He looks at us with hope inside, only to see us hurry by, closing our ears
to the strangers cry
Occasionally we will stop, and drop some money in, thinking this makes us a
better a better human being
What if the Lord had done us this way?
When we were in the miry clay
What if when we looked up in hope
He would have looked away, leaving us alone to cope
We would be no different then the stranger, going our own way
With no direction, just trying to make it through another day
So, tell me if you may
Where would that leave us on judgement day?

    Olivia Michaels

The Secret of a Happy Marriage

And the two shall be one . . .
There's more, much more in the ocean than what the eye can see
And there's more, much more in marriage, than what you dream there'll be.
Marriage is a mathematical conundrum, a puzzle that "two" can be "one"
And this "oneness" is the fountain of blessing where the battles of life can be won.
Marriage rules out a winner, in problems that face the two.
Both must win in the hassles, for this gives marriage its glue.
It's one in a goal for the family, one in a walk with the Lord.
One in daily communion, one in joyous accord.
It's one in pulling together the loads along the way.
And one in playing together that holds the stress at bay.
It's one in talking together, in feuds where fear holds sway
And it's one in confessing, forgiving, that brightens and heightens the day.
It's one in the art of coping with problems that loom so vile.
And it's humor and laughing together that oft-times sparks the smile.
Good marriage has joy in sharing a life that is well secure.
Breeds life with a taste of heaven, and a life that will long endure.

    C. Wilson Shultz

Imaginary Illusions

Time drifts through a black vacuum, it has no meaning to human intellect,
yet it pries at your bewilderment of this phenomenon.

You temporarily reside in another dimension.
Nothing has feeling and nothing exists.
You run but cannot, you scream but only a whisper,
you are naked with fright yet you feel secure.

Confusion has taken its toll, chaos is spread worldwide.
There is mixed emotions welling up inside, a burning desire to kill and
hate, sensations of peace, love, and devotion.
Everything is misinterpreted and scribbled upon the wall.

Your head swims into the clouds, dizzy with pandemonium.
Space suddenly surrounds you, stars tickle your nose as you flash back
through your nightmare, awake, instead of sleep and sound.

    Heather Urban

Shadowed Leaves

Shadowed leaves . . . I break into your arms in the night cinema on my feather
pillow . . . seeps, sinks in through skin as silk sensitive to water
My heart skips over your shoulders and through your vertebrae;
I'm buzzing on the thoughts as riding bareback nude on a steed racing through
voluptuous fields . . . I'm moving sitting still . . . ebbing
flowing the animal and I the sea
Your hair snow crystals in my blood stream flurrying in my head;
all crystallized gems of yearning shining fluid glass . . . your essence in every facet;
floating serene birds, velvety animals all along crisp tree branches in lucid winter
You reach me in slumber; paint pictures in my eyes;
sit there innocently at the easel with beautiful muted hues
subtly blending as clouds merging; cream in milk
The door leading to the studio where you paint is of see-through crepe
You flood my canvas with color from your fire which smolders in coals undercover
heats me like a furnace; glowing on the edges infinite Fahrenheit within
to create another planet, another world
But it's all shadowed under the canvas; under the leaves . . .

    Laurie A. Sulman

Have You Ever Watched the Ocean

Have you ever watched the ocean
As its breakers rolled ashore,
Sending each wave even higher
Than the one that came before?
Have you seen the ocean
At night when waves were stilled
And the surface of its waters,
Like the sky, with stars were filled?
Have you seen the angry waves
Throw themselves against the shore,
Tearing loose a bit of shoreline
And then coming back for more?
How much our life is like the ocean,
Filled with anger and with pain.
But still we must remember
That the joy will come again.
For as Jesus stilled the waters
In far off Galilee,
He will calm life's angry ocean
As He one time calmed the sea.

    Gertrude L. Tandy

Unanswered Prayers

To the memory of Ken Hofer and Eric Kayl
Kenny was kind and generous
And he touched so many lives.
"Lord, I wish I knew
Why my best friend had to die."

Lord, you have your reasons,
And there is nothing anybody can do,
But may I ask,
"What did Kenny do to you?"

He was young and bright
And had his whole life ahead
Why did he get lost that night?
"Lord, why is he dead?"

I already lost one best friend,
And I never wanted to lose another.
"Lord, why did you take Kenny?"
He was like my brother.

I know someday I will meet them again
In the glory of Heaven,
But I'd give anything to have them back.
I'll miss you both forever!

    Mathew Haynes

I Have No Quarrel with Death

I have no quarrel with death
My quarrel is with life
That makes of me a woeful wreck
'Ere it takes away my breath

God knows I loved this life
And gave it all I had
I tried to check its wanton ways
And sought to make it glad

I parried a while with death
As the gathering darkness loomed
It stalked me a long, long time
'Til finally we met

Was there any doubt of the outcome
When life gave up on me?
But I . . . I have overcome
And now, I am truly free

I had no quarrel with death
My quarrel was with life
For life deserted me . . . just when
I stopped to catch my breath

    Lynden S. Martin

Nova

I know that I should stop this as soon as I can because
Last time this hit me from behind I became lost inside of myself.
I'm scared of more than I let on, and
I know that I can't draw pictures of these nightmarish dreams any longer.
I've got to be strong, only if this fit wouldn't last any more than
I can handle. Live my stay, only for one day . . .
Can I shrink back into a Young star?
Because my hands are melting from dangerously hot tears
But I will wipe them all away anyhow.
I borrow what I can and the rest I throw away over our great divide.
I can't trust my words anymore and I'll just ignore the restless laughs
That they surround me with. I wasn't always ready for all of this hair to
Fall from my head onto my wrinkling hands.
I guess I am growing old through all of this,
Although the wise of me that should be alive isn't included.

Jenny Kalota

Us

This very fragile thing between us can be dropped and then would burst in a million pieces.
Shattered and separated, the memory would stand like a mirror broken, leaving only a twisted image.
It could still be beautiful I might say, but that reality bars,
and so fate takes another petal from the rose of life and slips away into the night.
What could have been such a rare gift thrown aside to rot alone.
"I should've prevented it" you could say, but then again, maybe I couldn't have.
So we go along, we humans in this game of life, unaware how close the time
will come when regrets cannot be dealt with, and it's over, and we live above.

Shell Bobo

A Sister's Prayer

May a child's smile warm your heart and give you hope along the way
May a hug from someone you know give you strength to begin each day

May peaceful places surround you and mother nature reach out her hand
To bring you a sense of calmness from the beauty of this land

May laughter by your shadow, and rainbow skies appear
Anytime you're feeling blue, to dry away your tear

May love always be near you, though at times may seem far away
Like the moon and the stars and the sunshine
Love will always be here to stay

May your journey through life be enlightened and shower you with joy
If not from life itself, most certainly, from your little boy

Diana Balogh

May I Help?

The song is silent in your soul
A great sorrow muffles the melody and withholds the voice
The streams of life that bring heaven from the mountains
Flood your spirit and wash away your happiness
And the sun in your smile can't shine through the clouds in your eyes

Invite me to shelter you from the rain
Permit me to open the music box of your heart and bring harmony back to you
I can polish the diamonds in your eyes and return the beauty of life to you
I can love you and you can sing again

Lee A. Butts Jr.

Escape on Horseback

To New River Riding Stable, my inspiration, my escape
For a moment I went away, so very far away.
I felt the splendor of running wild, spacious plains and open sky.
My spirit was my beauty, break it, watch me slowly die.
My strength was my majesty . . . I ran for speed, I raced the wind,
I frolicked playfully in disarray.

For a moment I went away, a moment I won't soon forget.
I found myself in the old wild West.
Dusty and proud was this hunter, his drifter, this cowgirl at her best.
My horse and guns, my only friends, as I rode into the sunset.

For a moment troubles went away, lulled by my horse's steady sway.
We stopped . . . hugged the beauty of a tranquil mountain's peak.
We stopped . . . watched a brazen sun and opal moon play hide and seek.
I smile, a peaceful smile, for a horse had lightened the heart he stole today.

Amelia M. Fox

Her Last Day in Jamaica

My last day in Jamaica,
and you're still sweeping;
he's still cleaning;
she's still cooking;
I'm still sleeping
and promising lightly:
"We'll be back soon.
We expect you to be here in June
in best of health.
I with my wealth
enjoying the heat
staying off the street."
Maybe then I'll know your name
and all will be the same.
Until then remember me.
For now so long, Jamaica!
My memory 'tis of thee.

Helen G. Smith

Dying Love

In a way such as every day
    I lay
Amidst the persisting of a thought
    Being caught
In the trap of my very own
    All alone
With no more than her on my mind
    In a bind
Facing reality of my worst fears
    Bring tears
Feeling with such a force the heart
    Torn apart

Shane Hoover

Night Encounters

For Patty
Diamonds and black satin,
Barefoot,
On a warm summer's night,

Dark, shimmering streams,
Fire burning hot,
Amber coals glowing bright,

Gentle winds caressing the long grass,
Cool touches in the air,
A scent of roses,

A symphony of sounds,
Calm and soothing,
Heaven around us closes.

Matthew Billapando

Booty.com

I turn on my computer.
I get on-line.
I get e-mail,
and what do I find?
Ads, ads, ads,
about porn, porn, porn.
I never did ask for it.
This is what I've sworn.
Soft-core, hard-core, apple core,
I'm not that kind of man.
E-mail coming from every seashore,
I'd rather see buried in the sand
What can I do;
What can I do?
I have reported it,
but it keeps coming back.
Anytime this is sent,
I delete it, throw it in the sack.

Timothy B. Gunter

Thoughtful Branches

Upon the thoughtful branches of my soul,
my heart sings like a bird.
I'm digging myself a lonely hole,
deeper and deeper on your every word,
making myself suffer to be admired,
overflowing with love no more.
Oh, how I long to be desired.
My heart is now at war.
I do imagine our footsteps in the sand,
for this day was dark and cold.
I reach but I can't grab your hand;
I'm too deep in this hole.
Everyone throws the dirt in on me
and I scream and shout.
Once upon a life, I struggle to be free,
but no one will help me out.
Is life a myth? I care not to be told.
My lost self changes as I wait for the day,
upon the thoughtful branches of my soul,
that my heart will sing away.

Cloudy Ann Walton

The Art of Simplicity

To my loving family who always had faith in me
How do I find my central core
To achieve what I must be,
Without living like a hermit
In search of simplicity?

Modernization creates complications,
Involving countless demands,
Trying to achieve this ultimate goal of
Security and for all which it stands.

What do I really need to obtain,
What is it that I don't see?
Could it be that I have overlooked
The art of simplicity?

The sizing down of material possessions
Is a technique that is good for the soul,
Finding out how to keep life simple
Should be my ultimate goal.

I do not talk of shedding or
Discarding obligations on a fling,
I seek for freedom from luxuries
And the hypocrisy they bring.

Phyllis Seeley Burroughs

Little House of Prayer

Down a narrow, dusty country road
That winds its way through a forest green
Near where crystal water gently flows
Down a sandy-bottomed stream

There stands a little country church
Beneath the shade of old oak trees
Nestled in the hollow that father made
And cooled by the beating of Angel's wings

A ray of sunlight shines upon her door
She bids me to come in
And sit with her in quiet stillness
Where once the praise of saints had been

I walk across her creaking wooden floor
To an old upright piano in the corner of the room
And as my fingers touch its yellowed ivory keys
I smell the lovely fragrance of, "The rose of Sharon's bloom"

Father, thank you for, "Mt. Pisgah Baptist Church"
Little house of prayer
Where I can come and talk with you
And leave my burdens there

Paula Middleton

Eight Second Ride

To Jerome Davis, Professional Bull Rider
The news came out across the radio waves,
And our minds were paralyzed with fear.
We listened for details, but they were few,
So we prayed as we cried uneasy tears.

The lights were bright; the air was thick
As you pulled your rigging four-finger tight.
With a nod of the head, the gate swung out.
It was you, the bull, and an eight-second fight.

It had been a real bad weekend all around.
Some of the best had been taken down.
The bulls were leading in the scoring match
As the Wranglers hit the hard, dusty ground.

A deafening silence fell over the startled crowd
As the Justin Healers ran out to your side.
You didn't move but said as you looked up with a grin,
"Hey boys, not one of my better rides!"

Lane Frost must have been looking out for you,
Another cowboy who came and tried,
Whose dreams went up in a cloud of dust
All for an eight-second ride.

Bobbie Ward

Memory Lane

To my wonderful husband, Ed Sherrill, of 44 years
Down a winding country road, up a shady lane
To the old Mill Pond my mind returns again.
Things were much slower then, it seemed time stood still
When I visited Grandma's house and watched the old grist mill.

As the wheel so slowly turned grinding out the corn
From which came the meal for flapjacks in the morn'.
So lonely now, the Old Mill stands, filled with decay
Useless and helpless, it's weathered a silvery grey.

Many fond memories now quickly flood my mind
Thinking of those good folks who were to me so kind.
I see a young small girl with flaxen flowing hair
Playing in the sunlight without a single care.

Gone now are those folks who were to me so dear
And as I view this scene, I suddenly shed a tear.
It seems to me I faintly hear the creaking of a wheel
As I turn and walk away from that old grist mill.

Thelma H. Sherrill

La Wanda's Song

The smell of honeysuckle permeates my senses.
Pastel trumpets intertwining the old and the new.
Envelope me in a quiet place in my mind.
There is a peaceful calm that I once knew.

Cars quickly rush by unaware of my presence.
As the road reaches up to grip the forward moving mass
A quiet, numbing noise hums me to sleep.
Perched in my lone slumber atop a bed I've not known hence.

Gently the brush peels away the tangles of the night,
To reveal a plucky white face framed in brown braids.
The chimes of a merry-go-round ring true.
So many glimpses of love clutch my heart with all their might.

Little Joe the wrangler don't wrangler here no more.
The sad tune of yesteryear a common lullaby,
Reaches into my hearts door to places almost forgotten.
Wandering Star how far have you gone? What is your lore?

In this life you may not know how far reaching your touch.
You listened, you cared, you prayed and you taught me.
You wandered far enough to be real, yet stayed close enough.
But know this now, it was more than enough.

Winona Pennels Eichner

Children of the Living God

To my family and the children of the living God
Sometimes we will have problems,
But don't despair.
We are in this world, but we are not of it.
God hears our prays.
He sees us when we cry.
He dries all our tears,
For He has always loved us.

We may be beaten, but we will not die.
We may lose some battles, but the war is won.
Persecuted, but not defeated,
Hurt, but not destroyed,
Passed over, but not forgotten,
In your trials, count it all joy.
For by Jesus' blood, we have been redeemed.
We have the victory!
For we are
CHILDREN OF THE LIVING GOD;
Our war is already won.

Wanda M. Lawson

With or Without

With or without the wants of this world
My life will not become unfurled.
With a heavy tear I've loved and lost.
My heart has been broken and double-crossed
But I won't give up. I will trudge on.
I'll leave the night to see the dawn.
And when my head is stricken with fear
I know, in my heart, that God is near.
He erases the hurt and relieves the pain
And leaves a feeling that I can't explain.
So, with or without these worldly things
All that I need is what God brings.

Kevin Marsh

Mother to Sons

Upon my passing, dearest sons, cry no tears for me
When you notice the blue sky up above
The ocean waves, or the flowers in the spring, think of me
And if too busy you become in life, I ask, take time
And have a cheerful heart
You came into this world when I was but a youth
My heart swelled up with love
Love, I would need more than love . . . life, I did not understand
I could not give you wealth (money) but I gave you lots of love
And tried to teach you about joy
I taught you how to catch a fish, I taught you to prepare a meal
I taught you simple things in life
But best of all was in being a family, and then I learned
This was love, life, and joy

Anita Elliott

Soul

I am a lost soul waiting to be free.
I am locked away, I cannot see light,
And it is quite sad when it comes to me
That—no matter what I do—I lose the fight.
I am alone, waiting to come alive.
I feel like I shall fade away and die,
And I wonder if this I can survive.
I think of death, and I begin to cry,
Closed from everyone who lives or breathes.
I cannot see one who will help me,
For myself I always seem to deceive.
I have been blinded, my eyes cannot see,
So I wait for death to come upon me.
And I indeed know, I cannot be free.

Loretta Lovin

Can You Feel My Pain?

Dedicated to God, my wife, and my seven children
Try and try as you might,
Unless you see and feel the light,

You cannot feel my pain.

Twice I have visited the warmth of the light,
Now, unequivocally, know what's right.

Yes, I can feel your pain.

I feel the pains of the whole world!
My being screams its thoughts unfurled.

Venting the whole world's pain,

A scream that warbles 'cross the Universe,
Shaking the soul of every being, yet terse,

Yes, you too can feel this pain.

You who feel the light, can feel such pain.
Can you, really, can you feel my pain?

John Wesley

Beach Retreat

Languid, hot summer creeps into my very soul
Feeling as eternal as the roaring surf's roll

The whirring ceiling fan cuts through the thick air
As I swirl and pin up my long, dampened hair

My bare feet welcome the cool, soothing wooden floor
Of my summer retreat on this far Southern shore

The golden seething sun, that glowing sphere
Unrelentingly heats the atmosphere

Floating in crystal bowls, magnolia blooms
Decorate and sweetly scent my summer rooms

Collected colored shells, my treasures from the sea
Embellish a tray, all of them special to me

Through the open window, hung with transparent lace
Blows the aroma of salty air, just a trace

I prepare a cold dinner of grilled fish and rice
Then make tart lemonade, pouring it over ice

The breeze through the lace curtains is now very slight
As another sultry day oozes into night

Paula K. Henson

Reflections of Love

For my two absent children, I searched the trunk through.
Jeremy and Jennifer, I dearly love you.
My empty heart feels happy as I reminisce.
Those precious years I have grown to miss.

Photos, report cards, letters and such.
Those little things that mean so much.
Never did it ever occur
That God would take our Jennifer.

Loss of his sister really tore him apart.
Along beside her, Jeremy buried his heart.
To this very day he has not cried.
Sadness, confusion, and anger bottled up inside.

He shuts me out, pushes me away.
Conversations are few for he has nothing to say.
Spells of anger surface once in a while.
Oh, how I miss his genuine smile.

Dear Lord, how I long to hold them so tight.
I pray that our lives will turn out all right.
I hope my prayers are ones that you hear;
To restore our love from yesteryear.

Pamela Sue Keville

Heart, Mind, and Soul

In memory of my late wife, Joyce
When I speak of my heart, mind, and soul,
You'll see all of them have taken their toll.
But I took in stride one day at a time.
Out of every problem I found I could climb.

There were times that I could've come apart,
But was always saved by that reliable heart.
On occasion, it might've skipped a beat.
But with its help, I'd admit no defeat.

With His help, I remained sound of mind:
One day at a time through that daily grind.
I didn't worry about what might be on the morrow.
Today alone has enough of its sorrow.

What I hope is forever is the saving of soul.
Through the Golden Gate is my final goal.
My final line in this, my life's story,
Is I'll find my way to eternal glory. Amen.

   Walt Larson

Eternal Love

Eternal love, you said, when you were young.
Why is it that we are more in tune with eternity
When we are far away from death?
The closer we get to death through the passage to mature years,
We receive glimpses of the everlasting
And just know, it is not human's territory.

Eternal love is just a young lover's dream,
Optimism of youth.
In our winter of time we realize
Life brings many turns to the bicycle rider.
We need to adjust speed, repair tires, switch chains.

And eternal love is just a promise of youth and thus hardly doable.
But why is it that it still hurts?

   Teresa Gonzalve Lee

Untitled

The greenery of the willow sprout
The things in me that cannot unwind
The unbearable locks of space and time
The other entities within my mind
Will all come together in the end of time

With the terror that comes from being without
The kind of beauty that flows throughout
The greenery of the willow sprout

So let the circle be unbroken
And let not the destructive words be spoken
And let it serve as a token
Of my hate and despair

And come with me to Scarborough Fair
And let the ribbons dangle from your hair
To another place that we can share
Where I'll always know you love me
And I'll always know you care

   James Ray Trent

You Left Too Soon

In memory of Norma Sanchez, 1954–1995
There's not a day that goes by that I don't think of you
Reminiscing on the days you were there for me, far from a few
I not only lost my Mom, you were my best friend
Would give anything in the world to see you again
Sometimes I feel cheated out of life because you left too soon
Braking that chain, leaving me empty, someday it will be renewed
One thing I know you're in Gods' hands forever
But I still wonder, why me! My dear sweet mother I'll always remember

   Tosha Denise Jenkins

What Is Christmas?

Does Christmas mean working extra shifts
So we can buy more gifts?
Does it mean working extra hard
To remember everyone with a card?

Is Christmas a time of gathering with our kin
And each and every friend?
Is it a time spent hoping for snow
Or listening to the cold wind blow?

No, you don't have to spend a dime
To know that Christmas is the time
That God send His Son to Earth
To make a way for our new birth.

Jesus came as a tiny baby
Born to a virgin lady.
He was laid in an animal's manger.
Even then, His life was in danger.

What is Christmas—is it things?
Toys, balls, cars, and golden rings?
No, Christmas is love,
Sent from God above.

   Roberta N. Williams

Collisions

Colliding with myself, I feel abash
For in forgetting how to love, I now am old
As I wake another new day
I ask the sun forgiveness
Don't let me shrivel to a neglected mound of dust
Rather, let my soul be free
To take in each day with wonder
About this vast universe of ours
As when I was a child
And each day a new day
Would fill my heart with song
To know there was a purpose
A key to my existence
At dusk, the sun bids farewell
And I am left with me
My soul begins to reflect this stranger
Who I never gave a chance
And, once again, I remember how to love
Myself as well as others
And I am young once more

   Sandra Jacobucci Miles

Lovely You

When I saw you first, absolute stunning green eyes,
I know it's not right telling you this, I can tell no lies,
That smile, positively sweet, you too made my day,
If I'd have met you sooner, I would have sent all I am your way.

You are, in my eyes, incredibly beautiful, I was left dazed,
I was dancing inside, just to be talking to you. Amazed,
Without a doubt I will always remember, those eyes, your smiles,
You have been blessed with complete elegance, "wow" what style.

Leaving me with perfect thoughts of your utter charm,
Hoping you know I mean well, not to cause you any harm,
You deserve the complete best, to match the flawless you,
For you to know silently that I think of you this way in all you do.

I do know for you I'd travel many miles, climb high mountains tops,
With me, the day will never come, where this will stop.
The wrong idea is what I don't want you to get.
I know it was a gift of Heaven sent, when we met.

In the end I didn't want to tell you this, but I will,
Meeting you, my heart skipped a beat, even days later, still,
The Lord has been above fair, with your loveliness.
I hope this will brighten your life with total completeness.

   David J. Polpstein

God's Tears, Gave Them Wings

As in Heaven and on Earth,
There are mothers who have no lies.
Conceiving seeds for immortal worth,
Of a newborn baby filled with pride.

All darkness stands still to hear them cry!
Only fading when a new baby dies.

Through sadness, tears, and
Blaming perhaps.
To a "God Almighty" for a hellish act!

Eternal babies, they do not die.
They came to be little Angels,
From Mothers' wombs, deep inside.

Gregory Mayhew

Ardent Beauty

To my sister, Vesta Carter
Beauty is always in the beholder's most critical eye,
And may be found from the inmost depths of the Earth,
Through the black holes that we've found in the sky.
Everything is beautiful to us at the moment of birth;
Natural beauty never fades away, only makes changes.
Gothic cathedrals are structures that glorify God;
Their beauty, like towers, enhances the image of a city.
We see beautiful little churches where people trod,
And small stores, stands, and homes that are so pretty.
Beauty bursts out from the seas to the wide open ranges.

There is much beauty in the arrangement of the word,
Whether the words are written, telegraphed, or spoken.
Pleasing sounds are beautiful music when they're heard,
And a touch can be beautiful to a heart that's broken.
Beauty, natural or synthetic, gives much inspiration,
And soothes our souls and hearts awed in admiration.

Lester W. Boyd Jr.

There Is a Place for Me

When there's not a one to whom you can relate,
No fitting place to settle to this date,
No place for me!
No place to belong!
No place for which love can be fulfilled,
In the most ultimate form,
I'll retreat to His Realm; there is an ultimate loving arm,
There is a place for me.

When you feel you're on the outside just looking in,
You don't feel you're of any connective part,
God will be there to embrace your lonely heart,
When your spirit is broken beyond repair,
Don't be discouraged, Jesus won't let you despair,
When you feel all alone, alone then alone again,
When you've fallen into the deepest of despair,
Be encouraged, it's Jesus to whom you cast your greatest care,
Whether I go to my Realm in this present world,
Whether I dwell beyond in the most sacred paradise entwined,
I'll always know that there does exist, a place for me.

Janice R. Watson

Rainbows to Remember

Rushing through time, such agony and pain,
I ran with you, nothing we seem to lose.
Being brave with our openness and weakened only by the past,
We chased yesterdays with no regard for tomorrows.
Time now rushes through us, only leaving us with what we took.
Now I ride the storms alone, just memories of misguided takings.
Growing and learning through grief, the calm sets in,
And now my yesterday are past rain, and my todays
Are rainbow to remember for all my new tomorrows

Nilsa Lugo

The Rake's Tale

"Aharumsh, aharumsh," my big rake on the ground
Said repeatedly to me. I swirled it around
As it gathered with fingers of spring steel, like thieves.
"Aharumsh," the rake told me, "the Imp of Dry Leaves."

"First, he colors them brightly with tints like a torch
And we view them all over, from garden to porch.
He the formula carries at hand, in his cup;
Then, he makes the leaves fall just for us to rake up."

"Aharumsh? Aharumsh." I raked leaves up in piles!
They were all we could see here, for miles upon miles.
Next, he sent a strong wind to bring more from afar,
And they got in the buildings with doors blown ajar.

There were other men putting their leaves in large bags;
They were laughing and chatting, the carefree young wags.
But he got in among them, turned bags upside down—
Not the least of his tricks, but it has some renown.

Then, he hoisted their work to the roof and the eaves,
Aharumsh, yes, that little known Imp of Dry Leaves;
In the winter, he sleeps out there, under the snow.
Now I've told you his story. I thought you should know.

James G. Billson Jr.

One Precious Moment

To my mother, Ramona
In the light of eternity
everything else matters.
If only for one brief shining moment,
we are alive.
Life is such a precious gift,
an opportunity so distinctly unique.
Discovering the moment,
enjoying the moment.
To be alive in a fleeting second of time,
is a miracle indeed.

I am precious, just the way I am:
I am worth it.
That I exist, that I breathe,
that I am alive, counts most.
To be born is a great privilege,
to be what we can become.
Whatever challenges experienced
make life worth living.
For one brief moment in time I matter.
For one brief, shining moment I am alive.

Regina Pleno

The Love of My Heart Bourne on the Wish of a Star

Sunny days bring unforeseen smiles
As jackets are shed and sandals are donned
My capricious feelings take deference
In light of the ubiquitous seasonal tides
Sunglasses black replace worries recurring
Lifting my spirits so high
Eyes slowly fade shut, a celebration of
Her soothing warmth and silent reverie, with
Stolen smiles enervating the stress of the world
Where, then, do hopes go when she sets in the western
Horizon? When grey clouds pepper afternoon skies
Hiding her brilliant countenance? When raindrops
Scurry down cheek and neck, and hair is blown back
Like sand in the desert? Where? I plead with you
Do not dissemble my happiness

The answers elude me, but I do not care
To relieve my ignorance, for I still
Feel her warmth, her touch still lingers
And I grieve not when Night strips her colors
But live for these moments when she grants serenity

Jeffrey J. DeSando

Words from a Dying Woman

Please, my loved ones, do not weep
as I close my eyes for eternal sleep.
Strength, I have none left in store,
for this cancer has finally won the war.

Years of treatment I have endured,
in hope that they would find a cure.
A surgeon's blade was used to begin
a battle I truly believed I could win.

Chemotherapy was the next step,
and I wasn't quite sure what to expect.
Anorexia, fatigue, and the loss of my hair,
was just about all I thought I could bear.

This disease, like wildfire, has spread,
and I am now confined to this bed.
A morphine drip pumps through my veins,
in order to relieve this unbearable pain.

The end of my suffering is almost here,
and death's embrace I do not fear.
Angels are coming for me from above
to lead me to a place of undying love.

Lorine Seyffarth

When You Still Loved Me in Your Dreams

If I could stop the march of time and take us back again,
Turn the clock back to a simpler day
When life was sweet and we were young and you were mine to love,
We would be in love forever and always.

In your sleep, you'd pull me close, whispering my name
As our bodies touched and kindled that sweet flame.
Desire was sweet and left no doubt what passion was about.
When you still loved me, you still loved me in your dreams.

We'd sing those old familiar songs and we knew every word
As the music played and we would sing along.
"Dream Lover' and "Come Softly to Me" . . . those are just a few
That filled our mind with thoughts of love so strong.

Oh, Time, please stop and turn around; take us back again
To when our love was once so strong and true.
Let us love as we loved then for all the world to see
When you still loved me, and I still loved you in my dreams.

Hold me close as you did then and kiss away the pain;
Sing those love songs sweet and tenderly.
Let us feel that flush of sweet desire again,
Like when you loved me, as I still love you in my dreams.

Sara O. Collins

Taps for the Soldier

"Fire!" Elevated to the western sky,
Seven guns cracked with a loud, single shot.
For the flag-draped coffin waiting nearby,
For the soldier, claiming his burial plot,
In honor, again the Leader's command:
"Ready! Fire!" Seven muzzles spouted flame,
Saluting one who had fought for his land
In the "good war" for peace that never came.

Then with final volley of their salute,
The honor guard came to rest with their arms,
And over our assemblage, still and mute,
Wafting out across the neighboring farms,
Came the measured, reverent bugle call
Of ending, of blessing: for day, for life.
Our country's flag was lifted from the pall,
Folded, presented to the soldier's wife.

Long were the years he mourned over the war.
Myriad, profound, the good he'd begun,
Always preparing to face that last door!
We know he has heard our God say, "Well done!"

Emmit H. Lehman

Mother Ellen

To my mother, Ellen Alexander Hamblen, with eternal love
"Mother Ellen," is the rose of my heart,
Blossom of rare, and beautiful art.

Babe of thy womb, I cuddled near,
Beat of your heart, I still can hear.

Spring of virtue, you are with love,
A spiritual fountain, from above.

Guarding your lamb from wolves of prey,
My tutor, you were for God each day.

"The Sculptor," with His Finger did write,
Honor thy parents will all thy might.

That your days be, long on the Earth,
And you shall have good health and worth.

Loving care, from you did I learn,
You cared for me . . . now it's my turn.

When rose bud petals weep and fall,
Prepare to hear your Master's call.

The time, the place, we do not know,
Our FATHER calls, and we must go.

My rose, to God in peace did pass, . . .
My heart bleeds tears, on grave yards grass.

Aubrey E. Hamblen

Memories on My Mind

To my wonderful Family and in memory of my Dad
Sometimes, and especially at night,
Just as the sun goes down—
Yes, I can see it! The sun!
There! Behind the lilacs
As it slowly sinks from sight.

And I can hear! Yes, I hear the
Screech owl across the way,
Up in the old hickory tree.
He is singing to his lady love:
"O', come rest till light of day with me?"

Now, it's sunrise! Do you hear
Those soft, soft sparrow sounds
And a pigeon's morning "coos?"
Bright gold across the emerald grass,
Making diamonds in the dew.

Myra Holycross Canaday

Thoughts about Christmas

What do people think of the word "Christmas" today?
What thought came to your mind first, on this holiday?
Christmas is more than a day—it is a season.
How many of you first thought of the true reason?

It is Jesus Christ's birthday that we celebrate,
It's for our savior that we love to decorate.
Something is missing! I think it's a birthday cake.
Could we ever give Jesus the wish that he would make?

Christ wants us to be happy, feeling love and joy,
Children opening their presents, each girl and boy.
Teach your child why we celebrate on Christmas day,
Singing "Happy Birthday" to Jesus is a way.

I would not dare write X-Mas, leaving out Christ's name.
How that must hurt Christ's feelings you should feel shame.
I think Christ deserves a gift on his birthday;
A promise that you keep, and a prayer to him say.

I thank you God for our savior, your only son.
Christ is our best friend, he cares and loves everyone.
There are so many things that money cannot buy,
Money can't buy our way to Heaven when we die.

Linda Anne Garver

Humanity

The flesh of life
Continues to rot
The awful stench of circumstance
So nauseously overwhelming
Taking in a generous breath of filthy air
Attempting to subside the sickness
Life pours upon us
Corrosion of the heart and soul
Defeats the ever-so-popular love
Love within oneself
Spreading the disease of hatred
We all turn on one another
Causing the death of many hearts
Selflessness is lost
Every man for himself, so sad
It all comes down to this?

Rebecca Hook

A Message to Heaven

Stamped and fully paid with love
This is a special Mother's Day message
Sent to Heaven above.

Dear Lord, I thank you dearly
For such a wonderful gift.
Sincerely from my heart and soul
There is no way to dismiss
This powerful feeling of peace and joy
That fills my entire being
When I for a moment pause and reflect
On my life, future, past, and present.
Memories my mind can see
Dreams my heart can hope
My mother's love is eternally everlasting
And dear Lord the greatest present was mine to receive
In my mother's hugs and kisses.

Debra Thomas

Voices Beckon

I listen, as past voices beckon
calling deep from within my soul
Reminders of distant treasures
of memories that won't let go

Resurface now to encase thy thoughts
of what once was, but now can never be
Yet tucked away desires awaken
a longed for belief in destiny

Timidly I embrace this abandoned quest to be
Yielding to awareness, a quiet stillness unfolds
What once was thought to have long since died
I find in my hands I still tenderly hold

What was meant to be through eternity
the promised hopes of so long ago
Yes, I hear the voices ever so clearly
Beckoning now from within my soul

Elizabeth Papp

Interpretations

See the young girl, as happy as can be.
It's hard to believe that girl once was me.

See the young boy, always wanting something to do.
It's hard to believe that boy once was you.

See the young birds learning to fly.
It seems all the answers are in the sky.

Feel the wind whistle through the air.
It coaxes you to believe the end is near.

Feel your eyes close as an acceptance to the fight.
It's hard to believe you got through one more night.

Patrice Grimes Miller

Bits from a Scrapbook

Having been a landlocked lass
Used to cozy mountain streams
And lazy rivers winding,
Caught my breath, could scarcely breathe
To gaze upon the ocean . . .
Tropical waters of Prussian blue,
With sparkling waves of turquoise hue.

Good-bye.
It's too soon to say good-bye,
The sun is high upon us,
And there's naught but time ahead,
Deceiving and besotting.

Pressed
Fragrant peachy posy, fluffy powder puffy,
Pressed into my memory . . . Mimosa . . . ahh.

Meeting
Is that sunshine upon my face?
I feel it there gently embrace
Of light and flesh . . . my eyes adjust and in a while
I know I'm basking in your smile.

Dorothy Shepard Nazzaro

You Are the Love of My Life

Just as the grass grows green in the spring
My love for you will always bring
Joy and laughter that clings when the church bell rings.
I thought I would never be able to give my heart again
because of a past love grown sour from beginning to end.
When I met you I thought you were only a dream
I said, oh God, Please! Don't let this happen again.
But as time went on and we became friends
I knew you were "The True Love Of My Life" only Heaven could send.

Sadie L. Hines

Escape Artist Down Under

In Hershey's cage, his life is fair.
His hamster license keeps him there.
His needs are met without much strife.
Hershey lives an easy life.

One night, he nosed the door aside.
He dropped to the floor and set astride.
On his haunches, Hershey stood,
And then did what he knew he could.

Hershey embarked on the kitchen trail.
His cabinet colony would not fail.
He left very little for us to track:
A subtle scent trail and a midnight snack.

We searched where we knew he could be,
And then we smelled what we couldn't see.
We found "Houdini" in his keep,
A small brown fur-ball, fast asleep.

Jonathan Jacobs

Wastelands

To my wife, Peg (deceased), who still inspires me
No one to share, to talk or listen to.
The Sahara in summer is greener.
Talking and talking and listening
And listening . . . to yourself.

Isolation is ear-splitting
And depression has surrendered.
Feelings have fled to woebegone,
And energy and spirit are satellites of Pluto.

Nothingness is a state of euphoria.
Except for dreams of water lilies,
Blue butterflies, and reincarnation,
Sea and sky are the only intimates.

Gerald M. Cawley

The Conversation

The Lord and I had a talk one day
I said, "Lord I'm a sinner; I've lost my way"
The Lord looked down and said to me
"If you want to be saved, believe in me"
I picked up the bible that I'd never read
Stories of miracles ran through my head
The Lord looked down and kinda smiled
I must have looked like a little lost child
"Where's this place called paradise?"
Be the light unto my eyes"
Then an angel took my hand
"I'll take you to the promised land
At a fork in the road appeared a sign
To "Satan's Greed" or "Lord's Paradise"
I knew the choice was mine, all mine
I'll take the road to paradise
'Cause I believe in you, Lord, indeed I do
And when I get to the pearly gates
I'll be seeing you

Lorice C. Rivest

The Picture of Life

My husband, Roland Wayne, and Sandy for being the best
The picture of life is all around us.
You have to look and have to find it
because it is the small things
like the wind blowing through
the trees. Little creatures such
as bees and grasshoppers and others
laying in the sun kicking back with ease.
The picture of life is seeing the bright
blue sky and planes flying by way up high.
The picture of lie is seeing the birds flying
in formation for everyone down here
to see their relaxation.
The picture of life is to be creative
and have an imagination.

Kathleen Wolstenholme

Good Morning

Just the other day a Robin flew my way.
Good morning, good morning he said seeming to be wise.
How do you know I said, as the sun has yet to rise?
He cocked his head to the side and answered with a chirp.
I woke up this morning and didn't have a hurt.
I laughed but begin to think.
Life will pass you by fast as a wink.
So enjoy what good you have left,
About the bad don't even whisper to yourself.
As I walked away I turned and had to say, Good morning,
Good morning.

James Edward Honeycutt

To the Man of My Dreams

Guys like this
Run once in a lifetime
Another one of my daydreams maybe
No more like a dream come true
Do you have to look or search?
Papa, what more can be said?
Always tell that man you love him

Going gets tough
Run behind this man
Any man you ask
No way
Dad, that's what he was like to me
Papa is what I liked to call him
And I need his love more than anything in the world

Kimberly Phillips

Impression

To April, thanks for the memories
Memories haunting me from the past,
Memories haunting me, how long will they last?
At night, they invade my dreams,
Torturing me heart and soul.
Suddenly, my life is a surreal movie scene
Watching myself play the role.
Are they dreams of what could have happened,
Or what is yet to come?
My feelings for Her, this has not dampened,
For every night, to me She comes.
How can I be faithful to another,
When I am faithful to another,
Trying to give my Love to some other,
When I don't know what's wrong or right.
This is the battle that constantly tortures me,
Being so close to her, but yet so far,
Hoping someday, somehow I will be free
But never completely healing the scar.

Shane M. Brooks

Growing Old

The other night I had a dream,
An old lady was watching me,
I turned my head; she turned hers,
Why was this old lady copying me.

The very next morning I looked in the mirror,
I was really started to see,
The old lady I saw in my dreams,
That old lady looked exactly like me!

What do you do when you look in the mirror,
And an old lady stares back at you,
A little old lady with wrinkled skin,
Could this old lady really be me.

What happened to the pretty young girl,
The girl with eyes of blue,
With skin so fair and silky smooth,
What happened to the young girl of twenty-two.

I didn't know I was growing old,
Until I had that dream,
How in the world was I supposed to know,
Growing old was happening to me.

Marvel Dodd

Destiny

To my mother, Dorothy Boyer, who led me to Jesus
There will come a time and place
In eternity
When we will meet the Master
Face to face
Either clothed with His glory
Or sackclothed in disgrace
Do you know, my friend, on which side
You will stand?
Now is the time of decision
For every mortal man

The time is soon approaching
When the mighty trumpet shall sound
And those who have received Jesus as Savior
Shall in His arms be found
If you do not know this King
Who paid the price for sin
Let me introduce you to Jesus
My Lord and Savior
You, too, can invite Him in

Nanette M. Boyer

Kindred Souls

With love to Patrick Joseph Ramirez
Let us share a communion of Yin and Yang.
To destroy our walls of alienation.
My incarnate Aztec can blow smoke rings to Orion.
Once more, let me taste your latté skin under neon lights.

To destroy our walls of alienation.
May our kindred souls whisper in the darkness.
Let me taste your latté skin, once more, under neon lights.
Weave our sacred vows in webs of cotton candy.

May our kindreds souls whisper in the darkness.
My incarnate Aztec can blow smoke rings to Orion.
Weave our sacred vows in webs of cotton candy.
Let us share a communion of Yin and Yang.

Susan Backus Samit

Man's Plight

Where'er o'er this great land I wander,
I find Nature's beauty torn asunder.
For in his thoughtless quest for power,
Man is destroying Mother Nature's tower.

With brick and mortar, steel and beam,
He covers Nature, destroys a dream.
When will he realize his blunder?
When will he cease to destroy and plunder?

Where once were great forests, majestic towers,
Now stands naught—not even flowers.
For with his quest for power and gain,
Man will destroy even the smallest grain.

Forthwith, I say that all men should heed:
He must conserve, he must concede.
Do not succumb to force and greed;
Save this Earth for man's future seed.

All hark, all men should heed . . .
Or future man will have no seed.

Goodrich Hall

Untitled

Here within I lie not dead
Just my shell whose soul has fled
A life of thorns has drawn to a close
No more heart, no more woes
Our earthly lives hold not a candle to
The unfathomable things, after death, we do
So place no flowers where, underground, my body lies
For a poet's soul never dies

Kylie James

A Trek to Grandma's House

The summer sun, so hot
Bore relentlessly down upon me
My shirt felt as though it had been glued on
As though I had carelessly forgotten
To remove it before taking my shower
My burning feet could hardly endure the heat
That penetrated my floppy old tennis shoes
Causing me to walk as though
I were treading on a bed of burning embers
I espied a lazy lizard sunning himself on a rock
And the trill of locusts serenaded me
As I trudged slowly along
I absentmindedly hummed quietly to myself
As I made my way through fields of flowers
My every step carrying me closer to my destination
My Grandma smiled, gave me a hug as I drank the ice cold tea
And devoured freshly baked cookies as I rested
How well I remember those hot summer days
And the long trek I so often made to grandma's house
Oh, it seems just like yesterday

Jewell Castro

Be the Best

Be the best that you can be
That's what has been told to me
In all you do—every day
Be all that you can be

While growing up and searching
For what brought happiness to me,
I found happiness the days I knew
I was the best that I could be.

We are many things to many people,
At home, work and on the friendship tree
However, one constant will remain with us
Our drive to be all that we can be.

I now give guidance to those in need
I advise what has been told to me
Success will always come to you
When you've been the best you can be.

Carol Warner

Ponies

They are cute in every way,
With their velvety soft noses,
And their hooves just a little bigger than my fists.
Their mouth is just the size of my mouth.
They have small halters just like baby horses.
In the shows, they do well.
Some love baths, some do not.

Miranda Downing

It Is a Dream I Have

I have a dream of love, unknown
I have a dream of life, remains

I have a dream of love, fantasy
I have a dream of life, fool's paradise

I have a fear of love, trapped in a cage
I have a fear of life, bound in chains

I have a dream of love, on fire
I have a dream of life, impassioned

I have a dream of love, in ruins
I have a dream of life, in smoke and ash

I have a dream of love, unfulfilled
I have a dream of life, unlived

More's the pity, I fear
The fault lies within me, here

Lisa M. Yancey

True Love through the Test of Time

Love . . .
I have heard that word many times before.
It seems to be a casual word.
It is used that way very often.
It is used so much that I think that people forget the true
meaning of the word. . . .
Most people do.
Love to me means the deepest bond that two people can share.
It means that unconditionally I will be there.
When one is weak the other provides strength.
That is a great test of endurance.
When one is sad, the other will not get mad.
In times of sorrow, happiness might I borrow.
Partners are we, together and through eternity.
So make no mistake when I tell you I Love You.
Straight from my heart it comes,
My heart and no other,
Today, tomorrow, and forever.

Shellini Dianand

Roses of Truth

I shed a tear for a long lost lover
Who mangled my soul like a rose undercover
As beauty struck my eyes like gold
And the aroma of ignorance grew far too bold

Petals of tragedy engulfed a weeping floor
While thorns of hatred stabbed all the dreams I bore
Deeper and deeper my heart bled tears
And an ocean of blood swallowed all my fears

Vines tightly grasped my soft red lips
Suppressing the power beneath my finger tips
Slowly, so slowly my innocence deceased
While I raised my head up high and my wisdom increased

With no sorrow or regret I watched it harshly die
And realized that all heartless demons live within a lie
Every night it rains and petals fall, I see it as they cry
Ignorant souls and narrow minds, helpless roses and trembling vines

Gena Mangiacapra

Do You Believe in Tomorrow?

Do you believe in tomorrow?
Today leads there, you know.
Though each "today" has a way of
Slipping into "yesterday" still like
The center strips on a highway;
They've been there.

Do you believe in tomorrow?
Enough, perhaps, to build something into it
So it will grow into the next tomorrow?
Do you believe that by doing so
You will benefit your fellow man?

Will people look and say, when your
Tomorrows no longer are,
This is because that person was?
Or will they go on down their own highways
Of "yesterdays," "todays," and "tomorrows"
Without knowing that yours has ever been?

Donna Stumlin

Subway Rhythm——

Wishes—Wishes—Wishes—
How they run like Sand—
through the narrow time clock—
into wasted Land——
Dreamer—Dreamer—Dreamer—
Do wake up and see—
Day by Day escaping to Eternity——
Rugged Work and Travel—
Sickness—Sweat—and Gloom—
from the dewy Morning—
to the early Moon—
O', the daily burdens heavy Road to see—
Stay, O' lonely Dreamer—
let me dream with Thee———

Kaethe M. Mahon

XIV

you humble yourself
to offer conversation
and feign interest
in what moves me
(she massages her hand from 3 hours practice)
so I become the poet
who carpes every diem
knowing her arms can't reach the sky
but reaches,
reaches
anyway

Aydrea Diahann

What Makes You So Different

What makes you so different?
How come you put me down?
Is it my race or my religion?
Am I from the wrong side of town?

What makes you so different?
When you bleed, isn't your blood red?
How can you criticize someone
When in their shoes you've never tread?

Take time and get to know me.
Don't judge a pictures by its frame.
You may find, we have lots in common;
In many ways, we may be the same.

For I'm sure you've felt pain and sorrow
And shared love and happiness, too.
And you have hopes and dreams for tomorrow—
Can't you see that all of us do?

What makes you so different?
Could it be your point of view?
Don't you realize God made all of us
And I'm human, just like you?

Gertrude Murt

Little Girl with Brown, Curled-up Hair

There was an old house in much disrepair
With many, many rooms and a rickety stair.

If you're not afraid, go up the winding stair. . . .
It's just a little room with plaster 'bout bare.

The room appears empty. (No furniture is there.)
Except for the little girl with brown curled-up hair.

Her dress is light blue with crinoline slips.
Her shoes are shiny with bright patent black tips.

She stands in the emptiness as if waiting—alone,
Just waiting for someone to make it a home.

She yearns for the dolly and the chair she rocked in.
She yearns for the laughter the family brought in.

She fades away as the warm sun settles in.
Her spirit is friendly, but her energy thin.

Will someone notice or feel her near?
Will someone bring back the joy and the cheer?

Barbara A. Youngert

How Do I Stop Loving You

At first meeting, I gave my heart away
Hoping its void would be replaced with love
Perhaps her heart would come my way
And could our love be blessed from above

When a heart is given to another for sure
The excitement and passion is sometimes shortly put aside
Through time love appears to have been simply a lure
Then leaves us hollow inside

Why attitudes change and struggles come about
To cover that once smoldering passion now with ice
Spoken words once turned our heads and caused us to shout
Now we simply shy away from paying the price

The battles we endure to simply keep our place
Are fought many a time and again
Battle scars mount as frustration on our aging face
It goes on and on and nobody wins

I loved her then, I still love her now
Though love is not always returned
Going on in a life without her, I know not how
So maybe if I stay, loving me she may learn

William J. Fry

You

I believe in the power of laughter—
in its ability to divert one from dark thoughts
and lighten burdens . . . in its ability to bring
moments of peace in times of turmoil.

I believe in the power of compassion—
in its ability to bring one comfort
and to calm fears . . . in its ability to inspire hope
and healing amid drowning waves of despair.

I believe in the power of touch—
in its ability to bond two souls, to bring warmth
and security . . . in its ability to spark fresh life
within, dispelling loneliness.

I believe in the power of friendship—
in its ability to understand where one has traveled . . .
in its ability to accept that which is,
with a gentle challenge to grow beyond.

I believe in the power of you—
in your ability to offer both laughter and compassion . . .
in your ability to touch body and soul,
accept who I am, and yet be my friend.

Pat Yongue

Autumn Glory

To my loving husband of fifty-four years, Kenneth Johnson
A leaf fell, flitting as a butterfly
With wings spread out to catch the autumn sun
Its brilliant colors magically displayed
A silhouette against the blue beyond

The soft breeze whispered, gently kissing leaves
With breath of summer past and winter yet to be
And changed their green to amber laced with red
Then held them cradled, floating from the tree

A squirrel ran busily from its nest
To hurriedly look for nuts beneath a tree
A raccoon stopped, then went on its way
A cardinal lit upon a branch to sing his melody

The cry of blue jays, high above, sounded an alarm
As if to warn the creatures there of anything unknown
And still the autumn breeze did blow
With scent of leaves, a fragrance of their own

While nature sang its song in perfect harmony
As if to say don't wait—it's brief, the sun's warm glow
The croak of frogs beside a lazy stream
That soon will still beneath the white of snow

Jewell Johnson

Never Give Up

The Cliff swallows are industrious and persistent,
busy building their homes.
They don't really care where as long
as it's high off the ground.
Be it a barn, or the side of a house,
they carry their mud quite as a mouse.
Beak full by beak full they pack mud on the edge,
hopeful to soon nestle in and lay their eggs.
In teams of two the couples do fly,
all day long packing mud on the side.
When evening falls, once again I aim the garden hose
and in a few minutes a days work I destroy.
Angry they swoop and chatter down toward my head,
they don't get the hint, but rebuilt instead.
Day after day who is going to win this war?
They never give up, just come back for more.
In life's journey so often we give up
When persistence could carry us to the top.
There's a lesson to learn from the little Swallow,
never give up, there's a brighter tomorrow!

Pamela J. Krause

Forever You

Life begins with love.
What is love?
Are we defining it?
Guiding you into my arms
And holding you tight,
A thousand dreams come and go,
But don't leave me behind.
Many tears fall from my brown eyes,
And that's part of love . . .
I love you and I'll never let go.

A thought of love is forever.
Destiny is what we are meant,
Am I so wrong?
Has my fate died with love of you?
Love within me may turn to lethal.
What is love?
Isn't love supposed to give us
That special strength?
If it's wrong to love you sweetly,
Then I'd give my love to you for eternity.

Katherine B. Sripipatana

Day by Day

Day by day I sit alone,
Not caring what I do.
My thoughts run over little things
Things that make me blue.

The frequent times that you stopped by
And rapped upon my door,
The sun that shone within my heart
I know will shine no more.

All the love held in your heart,
With me you no more share.
Life could be a sweet embrace,
If only you would care.

So once again, the memories
Within my heart will dwell.
The longing of the passing years
Will hold me in its spell.

All these joys have gone away
Because you went from me.
I guess for you and I to part
Was always meant to be.

Alberta Miller

First Birthday

Today is my granddaughter's first birthday,
A miniature angel sent our way
God has carried you in his hand
For your life, I know, he has a plan.

The first time I touched your little hand,
I called you, "Granny Pooh's Baby," Makala Ann
I love you so much, words can't say,
You're a little miracle sent my way.

I love you more each and every day,
I wish with me you could stay.
You have a mom and a dad
But you're the first grandchild I ever had.

God sent you here for a reason, I know,
But Makala Ann, I love you so,
Where ever you go, what ever you do,
Always remember your Granny Pooh.

One little candle gleaming so bright,
To Jesus we owe your life.
One miniature angel, sent our way
We are so thankful for this first birthday.

Anna Flatt

Apocalyptic Sunrise

A brilliant sunrise occurred today.
Clouds of radiation finally parted,
rays of sunlight showered me.
Winds blow for days on end
but no one is around to feel
the vast emptiness replacing man's work.
Tundra begins to thaw,
rivers will resume flowing,
time will heal the errors of man's ignorance.
Mountains still stand tall and solid
but stripped naked,
lifeless mounds of rock
awaiting new seeds to be sown.
Million of years destroyed in hours
all because of some political stance.
Life will return,
but man has lost its opportunity.

James F. Moore

In the Meadow

The grass in the meadow,
Have all turned yellow,
And the river had run shallow,
But the deer stayed mellow.

Here in the meadow,
Stood a lonely willow.
With its leaves all turned brown and yellow,
It bows its head, in despair, like a weeping widow.

Although it's dying, the willow,
The shade it casts, its shadow,
provided shelter for the exhausted deer who stayed mellow,
Even though it has lost its mate and was made a widow.

It's natural in the meadow,
Where the river that had run shallow
May, suddenly, rise again tomorrow,
And turn the grass green, once more, from yellow.

Life in the meadow is;
Fragile like the flower of the yarrow,
Happy like the sparrow,
Sad like the willow, and busy like a squirrel.

Kelly Khoo

Daylight

The woman's bitter beauty
lay near my hometown.
The drunken summer never still.
Ed was born in a bathtub.
His mother panting honey sweat,
lured the neighbors in for a closer look.
They trudge through the garden
with their rain boots on.
Peering into the bathroom window
at the woman's raw skin.
I was born into tears.

Lucy Bell

Nature's Event

From the safety of a branch, leaves steadfast hold
With brilliant colors of reds and golds

A whisper of wind security is lost
As through midair they are tossed

Falling to the ground
Back to earth homeward bound

Cycle of nature's event
Man cannot prevent

Nola Kinziger

The Cabin in the Woods

To my family
There is a log cabin in the woods,
upon a mountain high.
As you drive up to the cabin,
you want to touch the sky.
As you sit upon the porch
and smell the clean, mountain air,
the chipmunks, squirrels,
wild turkey, deer, and even bears
are the visitors that stroll by here and there.
The cabin in the woods,
with the stars and the moon
guiding the way at night.
With the cool mountain breeze
and the deep, white snow.
The wood stove heats the cabin
with its warm, cozy glow.
A secluded, quiet family nest,
as the family goes there to rest
at the cabin in the woods.

Sandy Byerly

I Want To Be Poet

Like so many marionettes dangling from a string
are the rhymes of this would be troubadour
One touches the waiting page with a lighthearted refrain
Another darts into the "ode zone" to be remembered no more
And while a Poet Laureate I will never become
I'll keep on rhyming because it is so much fun

Some rhymes would be ridiculed by a man grown
so I will share them with children alone
There was a little man who lived in a pocket
and he shot out in a matchbox rocket

When it comes to writing a poem of love to show
the words that come to mind are never right
for keeping the love light in his eyes aglow
If I had kissed Freddie one more time
I might not have married Joe

There is a place with paper scraps, yellow with age
and some brand new ones, but all with lines
meant to be a part of some poetic page
Whether free verse or perfect rhythm and rhyme
they will wait for another poem and another time

Shirley H. Baldwin

Rollercoaster

Excitement and anticipation at the start,
My body feels a rush in every part;
Electrifying ascent of the trolley car,
The momentum in our life is on the rise;
Gusts of wind drown the euphoric cries.
Up.

The landscape passes by in a hurry.
Squinted eyes scan the blur with worry;
Perilous descent of the trolley car,
Overwhelming difficulties are seen by all;
Melancholy thoughts fill the fall.
Down.

Every now and then the directions change.
It feels a little familiar and a little strange;
Such are the vicissitudes of the trolley car;
The cycle continues day after day;
People adapt, change, and pray.

Rise with the crest; bounce off the through.
Harness the smooth; smooth out the rough.
Such is life: a little peace and a little strife.

Puneet Sharma

Soul Mate

To my loving husband, Warren F. Cearfoss
I love you so much that I can't even say
What you've meant to me each and every day.
It's hard to believe time has gone by so fast,
And I wouldn't trade a minute for that which has passed.
You have given me so much over the years.
The days that I hurt you bring me to tears.
I know there were times when I've been so wrong,
But it never stopped you with your love that is strong.

I cherish the children we both have raised;
They are a gift from God and will always be praised.
Together, we've shared our joys and our sorrows,
And we promise to continue with every tomorrow.
Our walk through life has been my greatest treasure;
It has filled my heart with nothing but pleasure.
This destiny I chose is forever my fate.
Our love will eternally prove . . . you are my soul mate.

Julie M. Cearfoss

What a Wonderful Day

Today is a wonderful day
When March's weather is more like May.

My Jasmine is now in full bloom;
Its scent permeates every room.

The birds wake me gently every morn',
How could I ever have felt so forlorn?

This glorious feeling I hope will not pass;
I'd like this wonderfulness to last.

The trees are budding and soon will have shade;
It will be nice for the flowers who'd been displayed.

Right now I must say I don't appreciate the heat
But if I was at the beach, the weather'd be sweet.

So for now I will dream of sweet summer days,
Of watermelon, ice cream, the beach, and waves.

Mary Ann Roser

I Said a Prayer

I said a prayer, no answer came.
I prayed again, the answer the same.
I asked, "Lord, when?"
The Lord said, "Be patient. Maybe one year, maybe ten."
I said, "Lord, I don't understand."
He said, "There are other problems throughout the land.
Continue to pray and your answer will come your way,
Maybe not tomorrow, but someday.
I hear your prayers day and night.
Be assured, all will turn out right.
It may seem your problems will never end,
But on me," says the lord, "you can depend."

Denise Merritt

Man and Tree

The different tribe and species inhabit earthly domain,
Making merriment, dance a worldly sight,
Become dependent of the rain,
Hunger and thirst gather to different appetite,
Besting the body in the cool of night,
Like stoic sentries grow in strength and stature,
Bowing still to the supremacy of God and nature.
The numbered hair and leaf shed
With tired limb and aged—
The buttle branch dread—
Lay earthly and decay;
Bestowing the remnant to nature's array.
Though hope, a worldly quest,
Finds eternity lingering to reach its best.

George Thomas

Dream Catcher

Webs of light and articulate dreams
Weave the patterns of life's schemes,
As souls collide in the meshing
Of eternal wants and needs.

Darkened clouds of lover's toil
Brings unwanted fears to claim the spoil.
A moment gained, an hour lost,
Defeating dreams, to steal the cost.

In broken lives, the masquerade unfolds
Silken strands loosening the hold
As darkened nights conquer endless days
And all hopes fade away.

Yet through the dark, a ray appears,
A sliver through the tortured fears,
And with it's dawning, hope breaks free
To endless possibilities.

Dream catcher reaches through the dark
To hold on to the tiny spark.
The future lies within her reach,
The truth of life for her to keep.

Linda Vasconcelos

The Saguaro

Magnificent giant of the desert.
Keeping watch high above all else.
Watchtower of the hawk and eagle.
Nesting place of the desert wren and woodpecker.
Fierce and untouchable, yet clothed in spring,
With the most delicate of blossoms.
Living many times mans life span,
Growing numerous arms that reach
Towards the sky.
In a worshipful pose.
The dry blistering sands about her feet,
Disturb her not at all.
Nor the lack of moisture, as she has
Stored far ahead for this time.
Sharing her moisture with those that
Can avoid her bulwark of thorns.
Withstanding sand storms, flash floods.
And most of man's efforts to contain them
They flourish without man's assistance,
And often fail with his tender care.

Mildred Hyatt McLoud

Forget Not, My Love

Forget me never, wherever you go.
Perchance, recall with fondness

Some smiles, some word, some timid touch.
Then, by some means, as you consider fit,

A word to confirm, with you all is well.
And why should I ask of you this task?
Must I speak the words that say I care;

For care, I do, and curse the doubts, I love.
In some way and somehow.

Yet time is here and opportune now.
There is a bud, of this much it's certain,
But to weather a harsh season, fraught with confusion,
So tender the blossom could not bear the brunt
To come full bloom.

So, if someday you pass this way again,
Let not your thoughts of me fly away with the wind,
But bring them back fully, safely to me,
And in that direction, you will see,
The tender twig shall surely bend.

Paula Foster West

Neon Eon

Long live the "neon eon," I'll never let it go,
The florescence of real value does, and does not show;
Too vivid for the passing World, I never heard the drum,
To toe the mark, and walk the line is not my rule of thumb!
I've lived my life, forever, in one old the dye shirt,
Every time I wore it, their sense of style would hurt;
The finest silk and satin can't hold my shirt a light,
I wear it when I ride my horse, sleep in it at night.
A black light makes it neon, hints dreamer's elusive goal,
Squint your eyes, you can glimpse my "wild child neon soul!"
Just bury me in my old shirt, made now of holes and thread,
Don't weep for me, just on a trip, I really won't be dead.
What you see is what you get, myself, from sun to sun,
I sure can tell it like it is, but never skip the fun;
My feet have made ten million steps, in boots and faded jeans,
Pity those who wore the hats, still are clueless what life means!
My spirit wanders psychedelic paths, in search of rainbow's gold,
"Neon Eon" has a haunting lilt, "nevermore grow old;"
Long live the "neon eon," I'll never let it go,
I own the love of freedom's rush most others never know!

Patsy Jo Reed Sircy

The Crusader's Son

To my loving daughters, Mary Bonne and Louise Watters
Upon my return from England's wars,
while I had hoped for good news,
I still held a silent prayer that all would be well with him,
the youngest, the fairest, the most beautiful.
But, with the dawn of a dark day
as I rode my horse that had taken me safely
through the heaviest battles,
I knew somehow that a light was failing
in the castle where my loved ones spent their days
and nights and where news is long in reaching them.
The fever smote him like a viper's tongue
while I held him close so that his bare
breast shone bright like the eternal sun.
All glory is of naught when a loved one's soul
has flown into the vast unknown.
And so I had to let him go, while I, myself,
would gladly part this world, instead.

Dorothy Stevens Berentsen

The Power of Music

Music can satisfy the soul
And quickly banish each fear,
It can change our mood at will,
Inviting a laugh or a tear.
Play me a tender ballad today,
Transport my thoughts to romance,
Tomorrow an exciting rock tune
Will lure me into a lively dance.
When we travel on vacation
To countries quite far away,
Music is our common language
Sharing friendship and joy every day.
Classical, country, jazz, rhythm and blues,
Or those great songs from Broadway shows,
Music brings long lasting happiness,
With its beauty the whole world glows.

Gail Ruth Stewart

The Sun in the Dark

One may be in the dark about the sun.
One may not be enlightened in the dark.

Art is the light that keeps the dark at bay.
Darkness encroaches where lore is forgotten or lost.

Light is like the consciousness that expands our paradigm.
Lightlessness is lack of color given by the artist of life.

David Greeley

The Open Line

There is a power that is free
In answer to folks like you and me
That if we lay our problems bare
On our knees in solemn prayer

With the Holy Spirit in our hearts
Letting the sinful ways depart
There will be no charge to switch the call
The line is constantly open to all

It is message with sure contact
If confessing all the sinful acts
There is no place to hide the faults
Our records are in the heavenly vaults

Great rewards return for earnest pleas
To the ruler of the land and seas
What a joy that will be, just to hear
"Sins erased, the sound, all clear!"

William T. Kimberlin

Sincere

You took care of me
When I needed most love.
When I needed most care,
You looked after me
Like a little girl,
Like a rose that falls.
How can I forget?
How true you are!
Guiding me, advising me
Helping me, all the way.
You are truly sincere
I feel it in my heart
In my bones and in my soul.
Oh, what a pain it has been!
Losing my best friend and my greatest love.
I wanted to give back to you that tender care
But I didn't have the chance.
Suddenly, you left into eternity.

Mary Di Salvo

I'll Teach You to Read (Ps. 139:16)

To Bob, indelibly written in the book of my life
Your eyes saw my unformed body.
All the days ordained for me were written
in your book before one of them came to be.

Your life is a book, and I've written each page.
Seek me at daybreak, I'll reveal my way.
I'll teach you to read this book of your life.
I'll unveil my plan for each new day.

I caution you don't dwell on yesterday's page.
Let me guide you forward along your way
I have carefully authored this book of your life
Each page of this book is a fresh new day

Never trouble yourself about tomorrow's page.
I will shepherd you along your way.
Skip no page as you read this book of your life.
Don't miss the glory of each new day!

Rebecca Harwerth Beste

Flexible Vessels

He used to smile with a wink and say,
"Woman was made to be a vessel for man."
I never really understood the term.
Later I read, "Don't put new wine in old vessels."
Now that made sense to me.
But a wise man said, "Wisdom, like love,
is best preserved in flexible vessels."
Is that what I was meant to be?

Bettie Lou Stewart

Tomorrow, Today Will Be Yesterday

Inspired by my brother, Stanley
When I was young I frittered my time away
My hours were filled with pretty pictures and frivolous play

Why work and think and cogitate?
When one could flirt and frolic and fornicate?

Thoughts of pretty clothes and fancy dances
sweet sad songs and yearning romances
Filled my head

I had many years to spend, many miles to travel
Before I'd be dead

My days and nights were filled with excesses
I chuckled and giggled and tossed my tresses

Too many eager men came knocking at my door
Too many novel experiences teasing me to explore
This girl child clutched at life and cried for more

There was no time for somber thought, contemplation, or sorrow
"I'll think about that tomorrow," trouble I will not borrow
No tears will these blue eyes shed

What was that you said?
Today is yesterday's tomorrow. Oh!
        Sheila Byers

Loving You

To the only person who truly showed me how to love.
I will always love you, Scott.

I will never stop loving you.
You showed me how to love again
When I thought it was hopeless.
You always see the brighter side in things
When I am feeling down.
At times I have wondered
Why you are still with me
But when you smile,
I know the answer.
I feel such love from you
When I look in your eyes that
I know everything will be all right
With you by my side.
You are my light in the dark,
And my comforter when I'm sad.
I love you for the person that you are,
Sweet and tender all the time,
Stern and hard when I need to see the truth.
That's why I will never stop loving you!
        Jennifer Lyn Woodworth

Naked Singularity

I most dread those days the world collapses;
When I stand at the center of a dark and dying universe
And feel the boundaries begin to cool and contract.
Caught within the deflating balloon of existence,
The sky falling under the horrible weight of stars,
I am forced to stoop, then bow, then drop to my knees;
Finally to lie curled in a whimpering ball,
Struggling to breathe with dense conglomeration
Of all the Cosmos sitting on my chest.

I made you the Atlas that bestrode my narrow world;
That stood high above me, arms and legs wide,
Holding back the circle of the universe.
But you were never born the Titan,
And stepping out of my sphere
You allow reality to recede
Until I am crushed out
In that infinitely
Unimaginable
Point

        Dong Thomas

Enemy from Within

Charles, your faith in me has made the difference
Self-doubt and self-recrimination
weaken the foundations of our ideas.
Giving in and giving up instead of moving forward
weakens the cornerstones of our creativity,
sabotaging our efforts with fear and apathy
instead of using our resolve to press forward,
allowing uncertainties to cloud our desires instead of
building a wall of successes on which our dreams can rest,
listening to that voice in our head that urges caution
instead of following our heart and daring to dream,
accepting the advice of hostile foes that would have
our dreams dissipate into a river of nothingness.
Instead of loudly declaring that our rights to succeed
are paramount to our existence,
getting rid of the most powerful enemy that we will ever encounter,
the one who knows all of our fears and feeds on them one by one,
You, and only you alone, can stop the enemy from within.
        Bernetta Thorne-Williams

The Butterfly

Born among the most forlorn of butterflies
Caught between two disagreeable wings

He was made to be an apprentice of harmony
But instead flying about in a slumber

His hypocritical flight assured praying for forgiveness
His wing of affliction has fallen away

Replaced by a wing of prudence
He has placed his harmonic wings together
His hope of flight now certain
For flying among willows has made him humble

His flight has become a song, one that the most plain spoken
Of butterflies can sing between two agreeable wings
        Eugene F. Wiesner

New Mexico Daydreams

Afternoons of creeping, white cotton clouds
Sliding over the crystal blue sky
And a cool, gray hue pulling around the sky's edge
Tree limbs shaking softly as the wind blows kisses
Into the sun before it goes down behind the mountain
Raindrops fall gently with a rhythmic pulse into the
Once cracked ground of red clay and sand
If you stand quietly, you can hear lonesome coyotes
Calling out into the night for companionship
And scouting for a place to rest
Elk and doe jump over broken tree limbs dotting
The forest floor and then bounce off onto the field below
Come and see jackrabbits playing tag
And rattlesnakes carving S's into the muddy arroyo
In the early morning rain
New Mexico daydreams and realities
Colliding on mountain tops in the snow
        Dawn Vision

I Know Right Now

I know right now she's leaving, yet she is still with me,
For I can feel her love; with me she'll always be.
I know right now she's looking every time I see a bird or flower.
She'll be there with me, watching, no matter what the hour.
I know right now she's smiling; she likes us all together.
She will laugh along when we do; she'll be hugging us forever.
I know right now she's crying; she's sad to see our pain.
She knows she's truly loved, just as sure as clouds do rain.
I know right now she's happy; Paradise has taken her in.
She is now with her Father; she'll be all right with him.
I know right now she's leaving, but forever in my heart,
As long as I remember, we will never be apart.
        Chuck Hilsenbeck

Pathopoeia: "The Inner Mirror"

(The "Illusion of Truth" is when you became blind to the
Dark Side Within) . . .
    Thus, remorsefully I sense the distant, drifting passions that
have become translucent emotions venturing as if, but obscure
shadows streaming across the labyrinthine of mine own Immortal
Soul, losing their selves within the depths of mine own Mortal's
Heart, as, one by one, they opaquely lose their glow. . . .

When, only, as the iridescent dew drops glisten upon an
open spring bloomed meadow, and the light rain brushes
fondnessly upon my flushed cheeks, will I allow my betraying
tears to shed, to ebb, to flow. . . .

       Tell Me
    Could it be that, "You" are, but the Reflected Echo, faintly
resonating myriad images from the obscured corners of my Illusive
Mind . . .

    Kaleidoscopically distorted distant memories, of the
       "" WAY WE WERE ""
Fading, transcendently silhouetted, into~
. . . "" ONCE UPON A TIME "" . . .

      ~ TELL ME ~

       . . . finis . . .

M. L. Raymer

Growing Older

Granddaughter, Renee D. Jones, with love
Dear God, as I commence to grow older,
With fewer temptations, but more understanding,
Let the twinkle in my fading eyes
Be not a reflection of hate,
But a shining glimmer of Love
For God, myself, and man.

Dear God, as I commence to grow older,
With less to do, and time on my hands
At the fireside of friendship
Receiving joy and giving joy
To God, myself, and man.

Dear God, as I commence to grow older,
With more life behind me
Than there is in front of me,
Let the good in my life be a lighted path,
The not-so-good a warning to avoid,
So that someone will follow
For God, himself, and man.
My prayer is that as I grow older,
I grow to be kinder and have more love for my fellowman!

Rausie V. C. Jones

Wanting . . .

Another chance at love,
before I lose sight, at what love is. . . .
Catching glimpses as strangers kiss,
desperately wanting a taste.

Entering my own fantasy,
finishing where I always leave off,
Getting emptier by the hour . . .
(Insider, screaming to get out!!)

Hoping for some relief,
Just hoping for one last time . . .

Kidding myself? Just maybe.
Lust or love? The great debate.
Me versus myself;
"Ponder that one, if you will."

No one really seems to care;
they only seem to judge.
Once . . . just once . . . I'd like to experience
compassion and true understanding from another. . . .

Kristie Cameron Christiansen

Satin Dreams

In perfect clarity, like a giant sheet it unfolds,
Across the limitless expanse of my imagination.
Unfettered by time, or space, or man made restrictions.
Determined to play itself out and find its destination.
Luminous at the first, opaque in its murky scenes,
With a shiny sky against the foreground of pearlesque colors.
Dancing, darting, teasing mysteries to me and no others.
Hypnotically watching, mesmerized by moonlit beams,
Constantly changing, shifting with subtle themes.
Like the wind which causes rippling waves,
They crest and lead me to darkened caves.
Then upon awakening, I search to know their obtuse schemes,
And the meaning of these transient, elusive, satiny dreams.

Timothy Johnson

Blessed

To Mom and Dad, my most cherished gift
August 31st, 1968, a child was born.
This child was destined for pain and unhappiness.
God looked down and saw two people
Who were unable to have a child of their own,
But their faith remained strong.
So when the time had come, God looked to the East.
He saw that child cold and alone
And reached down and touched the face
Of that tiny little soul.
At that moment the heavens opened
And filled with the voices of Angels singing.
For, this child had just been blessed,
Blessed by God's very own hand.
This was the child He would give to them.

Kimberly L. Klinge

Mourning

I have looked into the eyes of death
And embraced the painful emptiness
Of a tormented soul whose body burgeons
With agony and struggles to let go.
Too weak to say the words, never able to whisper
Feelings of love, remorse, forgiveness . . . good-bye.

An anguished mother, torn between life and death
Of her precious child, whose tear-stained face
Reveals the hollow. Questioning how she could live
To have to bury her child.

Death.
A reminder to the living
To seize opportunities, be content with one's soul,
To express tenderness, and continually dance the dance of life.

Shannon D. Richter

The Wise Old Owl

A wondrous giant oak stood
In the denseness of the wood.
All alone, for a century, was she,
And greater in wisdom than any other tree.

Many creatures were sheltered by her branches
As the rains came pouring in avalanches.
And thousands of diamonds sparkled like dew,
Encompassed with beauty as the sun shone through.

Big ripe acorns she would drop for the squirrel,
Watching him leap as his tail he'd unfurl.
She could sense the approach (by the song that he sang)
Of the dear whippoorwill and his notes as they rang;
      "Chip the widow's red oak!"

Who knows how many rings are in this great tree?
Or what age, in years, she is meant to be?
The wise old owl, usually so mute;
Replied, when asked, that he didn't give a hoot!

Eva McLelland

My Miracle Life

With each breath
With each kiss
with each word
With each waking moments
With each dream
You are in my heart on my mind and in my thoughts
My world consist of you and the knowledge that
I accomplish something that was not suppose to be
For you are my miracle child
For you are my soul
With all my being and all that I am I will give to you
All that you have given me
You have given me happiness love joy and moments
That forever will be cherished and dear to my heart
With all the memories I have with all that I have experienced
I thank the day and moment you were born
For you are my miracle child

Darlene Bridgman

January Thaw

January thaw and weather so warm.
Since the first snowfall and every storm.
Skies mostly cloudy and sometimes fair.
These hard, crusty snow banks returns to soft.
Unlike the fresh blanket of snow,
So smooth and light.
These snow banks are slushy and rough,
Throughout the night.
While these last months will certainly fly.
With some snow and some early rain.
It'll stop and do it again!
Windy skies and blowing snow,
Starts the cycle of the fallen snow.

Lana Wakefield

Intimacy Lost

Intimacy lost
Lost in the perils of everyday life
Forgotten amongst the ruins of fights
Holding on to yesterday
Not realizing there is no tomorrow
Each day passes, another the same
Bad out weigh the good
Eyes begin to stray
When two joined as one forget what to say
Intimacy lost
The gentle caress and movement of bodies
Turn into libido driven forces
Minds wondering in between
Who will end this repetitious cycle
Can they both stand the pain
To carry on would hurt even more
But who's at fault when Intimacy's lost

Wendy O'Brien

Prayer Answered

The angels in Heaven don't want us blue.
They joined our hearts to build a love this true.
Two lonely people in need of the other.
God heard our prayers and put us together.
We were out of place in a smoky Bar Room.
When we first met our thoughts were filled with doom.
There was a bond right from the start.
We held each other and vowed not to part,
Making promises to be there to comfort the other.
With this support we could ride through stormy weather.
With you in my arms day became night.
You told of your pain the dawn of light.
You laid down beside me, and when asleep you call my name.
Our arms reached for the other; there was no shame.

Barbara Jean Olson

A Psalm for Today

Technology is my Shepherd,
I shall not want.
It leadeth me in the paths of the Network,
And teacheth my children also.

It leadeth me beside the still waters for enjoyable surfing.
It maketh me lie down in the green pastures
Of lassitude and false security.
Its TV invadeth my home
And filleth the evenings of my family
With violence and the tawdry.

Yea, though I walk through the valley of the shadow of death,
And though a thousand warheads be aimed straight at me,
I will fear no evil,
For the legislation and the precepts of my Congress,
They comfort me.

It preparest a table before me in the presence of mine enemies:
Global warming and Toxic Pollution.
So with a Sound Economy and a good Ecology;
I will dwell in the House of Technology forever.

Wendell Vaughan

All That I Am

I am not all that I appear to be
There's so much more
More than what's before you
What you see

I am not all that I appear to be
There's much more love
Enough to last through eternity
Therefore, I am not all that I appear to be

I am not all that I appear to be
There's much more life contained within me
I am not and will not seem all that I appear to be

You will not know all that I contain within myself
You will not know of all life's harassments
In which I've dealt

You will never know of all my love
And caring generosity
For you will never know of all that I am

Just what I appear to be

Sonya R. Garcia

Peachtree Street, Atlanta, Georgia

It's 6:00 a.m.. The Atlanta alarm clocks start to ring.
Peachtree wakes beneath her joggers' shoe strings.
Condo coffee makers begin their black bean brews,
While Caribu celebrates with cappuccinos,
Espressos, and dog biscuits, too.

Silver rims on sports car wheels
Are detailed and polished, ready for weekday deals.
Three piece suits are all office-bound,
While Hartsfield International holds its business class,
Who are all leaving town.

It's 8:00 a.m.. Atlanta is alive—humidity rising.
Peachtree is covered with the population driving.
Sidewalks shake with social confrontation.
Four and a half million people look ahead with great expectations.

City store fronts open; merchants are really, willing, and able,
While Peachtree patios bloom beneath umbrella tables.
Culinary cuisines abounds upon pottery plates, hot and hard,
All paid for in full on corporate American Express cards.

Evening settles in—gyms start to bustle.
Atlanta works hard on its bodies and muscle.
Buckheard waits with glasses of chilled anticipation;
Now Peachtree, dressed in cocktail attire,
Is vibrant with social participation.

Chevonne Tiana Siusa

A New Day

As the morn is slowly approaching, God's
grandeur is unfolding before us.

The wind rustles soothingly in the trees;
the parched falling leaves magnify the
footfalls of passersby.

The majesty of the Father is shouting
forth the day!

Birds caressingly sing His praises. . . .
The flowers bow their newly-opened buds
in worshipping homage.

The Earth speaks triumphantly as the sun
takes its place in the sky!

Once again, God's nature has conquered
the darkness . . . another day is now beginning!

    K. Erin King

Perfectionist Personality

Each glance she takes reminds her of herself,
That every day she wakes she's doomed to die.
Her sallow look portrays her fading health
And she continues, though her insides cry.
The phobia persists, distortion grows;
Emaciation lets her feel success.
All healing hands at once become her foes,
For fear they'll know she's weighing less and less.
The lithium can't cure her self-esteem.
Depression tears away at her young soul.
To stay below the norm's her lifelong dream
And she'll proceed until death takes its toll.
    The pressures all around society
    Cause all her illness and anxiety.

    Jill Turanski

Sweet Dreams

I see your face; you make me smile.
You look at me, and I wonder for a while.

What do you feel? What do you see?
When you are looking, looking back at me.

Can you see what I try to hide?
Can you see so deep inside?

You are good, kind, and sent from above.
I wished you knew how easy you are for me to love.

I can't hold you or say this aloud.
If you were mine, I would be so proud.

I wish I could show you right now,
And say I love you right out loud.

The secret of you is mine, to hold and to keep.
I'll be with you in my dreams, when I sleep.

    S. A. Rice

Wonder

So where do we go from here?
Where do the lilies bloom on a lonely tear. . . .
What happens now in the black of night?
Where are you at—where do you go with your light?
I am here waiting for your countenance to shine.
I wish you would appear; I wish you were all mine.
My doubts begin to show; my sadness enters.
You are my all. Around you my world centers.
Be alone. Be alone with me. I'm your only;
Without you, I am unhappy; I am sad and lonely.
I wish you felt the same, but your flowers are blooming.
Mine are dying; slowly but surely, shadows are looming.
Come to me, my love; be with me, my friend.
Be with me, breathe me, love me, 'til the end.

    Jason Milholin

Rocking Chair Cowboy

I often dreamed of being a cowboy,
And round up doggies on the dusty trail.
I somehow missed my chance to be a cowboy,
The years flew by, and now I'm much too frail.

So I sit on my rocking chair pretending,
And flip a Western on my R.C.A.
And with my cowboy boots and hat I manage,
To ride my favorite Pinto every day.

A trusty six-shooter is in my holster,
It's oiled and loaded for the bad man's dare.
With lightning draw, I plug him in the forehead,
A shooting from my squeaky rocking chair.

And as he falls in anguish from his saddle,
I toss my Stetson high into the air,
As I give out a "Yippity-Yip" in triumph
I dismount from my favorite rocking chair.

Then I reach out and grab my pretty lady,
And flip her on "Old Faithful" with a flare.
And then I ride with gratitude behind her,
Into the sunset on my rocking chair.

    John W. Hyndman

Summer's Breeze

I remember the year of 1998
when I encountered summer's breeze.
The gentle wind coursed through my veins
and put my mind at ease.

It made me think of old days past
when summer was still for fun;
the summer toys, the bratty boys,
the laughter, and the fun.

It made me think of future days
when summer would be for love;
the relaxing walks, the tender talks,
the stars hovering up above.

The careless wind then shifted
and brought me closer to today;
the changing times, life's endless rhymes,
the place I longed to stay.

I shifted my position
and looked up at the sky.
Right then and there I knew,
the summer's breeze would never die.

    Autumn Nicole Cross

Journey into Finality

They came for you when your short time with us had ended.
Farewells were said.
Stillness enveloped the room.
Darkness descended.
All things seemed empty.

Like death.

They came for my loved one when his short time
on Earth had ended.
Farewells went unsaid.
Stillness enveloped the room.
Darkness descended.
All things seemed empty.

Yet life
continues.
We say good-bye here.
Someone waits there,
with gladdened heart and open arms, to call:
Welcome home! I'm glad you've come!
I've been waiting for you!

    Lola V. Gilbert

Lessons

Lessons have been taught, but few seem to learn.
Just think of the statement . . .
Those who play with fire ofttimes get burned.

The lesson may seem silly and a total waste of time,
But by not learning the lesson . . .
Have you committed a crime?

If there is a lesson you already know,
Teach it to someone else, think of your knowledge as money
And share your wealth.
Because the lesson you learn today, tomorrow maybe lost . . .
Someone else will not learn it and then, think of the cost.

The lesson you teach doesn't have to be long . . .
It can be taught through music, writings, games and songs.
Believe in this lesson and others will too,
Then your lesson will be carried on to many from a few.

I end my lesson now in hopes you understand that this message
will travel to many but it started from this one man.

O'Nee D. Fowlkes

Untitled

Sitting on my bed, the realities around me
seem to fall away with each content
that take from this box.
Memories, disturbed from their quiet resting place
dance in my place, dance in my head to the throbbing beat
of distant mental drums . . .
All of the emotion that I thought I let go
plays here now, fresh in my mind—
Like it never left.
Tears fill my eyes as I see the dreams
that I'll never realize.
And the others around me matter not;
For here I sit . . . alone.
Just me and the memories in this box.

Anathea D. Carrick

The Littlest Brave

To my grandson, John Sewell Parker
Oh littlest Brave, what does the future hold?
How many batters will you face so bold?
No other southpaw throws the way you do.
Just what does the future hold for you?

At the year two thousand eight you are so tall,
With perfect stance you swing the bat and hit the ball.
With great speed you beat the throw to first base,
In the stand there are smiles on each grandparent's face.

Each batter dreads to see him on the mound.
He adjusts his cap and stares with a frown.
The catcher signals, he shakes his head once more,
It was the fast ball that fanned this guy before.

At year two thousand twenty you are twenty-two,
Called up from the minors, rookie of the year for you.
Twenty game winner who knows what you will do,
Oh littlest Brave, we wish the best for you.

Neil Sewell

Perceptions

Frail memories and relationships intertwine in your reality
perceptions of the heart are masked with ambiguity
as reflections in your mind are mirrored with your image
what soul you envision in me will secure my rest in peace

What perceptions you would need in me to capture
while you search for solace in your loneliness
as you witness what my eyes cannot envision
I will forgive your unquestionable lack of perception

John Bradley

Butterfly's Eyes

Butterfly is her given name.
She is very sweet and tame.
Her hair is long, silky and blonde—
Of which her master is quite fond.

She curls up like a ball in her master's lap,
Enjoying and purring while taking a nap.
Her master's soft caresses send her into ecstasy,
Playing with her catnip is her favorite fantasy.

But the most mysterious and beautiful feature
Are the emerald-green eyes of this creature.
In the dark, deep, emerald-green, pools of light
Are secrets unknown for her love of the night.

As her master sits and stars at her eyes,
She blinks and throws a look which is quite shy.
But if he could read those eyes and what is hidden
He would find answers of thoughts forbidden.
But the truth of it all, it is not strange or taboo
But only Butterfly's feelings and her master's, too.

The feelings of love and tenderness abound—
The gentle touch of emotions that surround.

Denise Nichols

You Are Me

To my Native American family I never knew, Cherokee
I am your enemy if you so chose to have.
I am your God if you so chose to pray to.
I am the sun in your eyes.
I am the moon at night that shines on your face.
I am the cricket that plays you music while you sleep.
I am the wolf that cries to warn you.
I am the fish that feeds you and your people.
I am the back you ride so often in battle.
I am the arrow that strikes down your enemy.
I am the blood that you will carry.
I am the eyes of the guardian eagle that visions your danger
And gives you strength and courage.
I am the water that quenches your thirst.
I am the fear you will never fall beneath.
I am the grizzly that covers your back.
I am the buffalo that feeds you meat.
I am the drum that beats in your heart.
I am the medicine that heals your pain.
I am the Creator that gives you visions.
I am the fire that lightens your night.
I am the leader you so long to be. I am all, for you are me.

Johnny A. Ray

Loving Husband and Best Dad

As we grow older from year to year,
I can't but help shed a few tears.
Every minute we're together is so precious to share.
I want you to know how much I care.

No matter where we go or what we do,
I want you to know I care for you.
The moments I've spent by your side,
I've loved you so, and I'm filled with pride.

Always and forever,
As we walk through life together,
Hand in hand we inch our way
To the very end of this lovely day.

As I sit here with you on my mind,
And look back over the years in time,
You really are my pride and joy.
A wonderful father to our four boys,

A dad so faithful to our sons you've been.
They, like you, are wonderful men.
The best of husbands you've been to me.
I will walk by your side through eternity.

Eloise Callin

Beginning to End

With this ring, I thee Wed.
Why do these words echo in my head?
Until death do us part.
Why do these words tear at my heart?

Just a small simple ceremony
Us, a Notary, friends, and music on a Sony.
A best man, a maid of honor,
No more time to stop and ponder.

A happy day full of sunshine,
Smiling faces, everything just fine.
A lot to drink, a lot to eat,
Waiting for the sunset to start its feat.

No ceremony.
No Sony,
Two lawyers, and a judge,
Silence, no one wanting to budge.

With this ring, I thee Wed.
Why do these words echo in my head?
Until death us do part.
Why do these words tear at my heart?

Sheryl Ann Kelly

Depiction of Silence

Silence;
Whether the deepest hollows of nature, the darkest depths of night,
A narrow wooden hallway, or seclusion at last light.
It is indifferent.

Silence;
The absence of all laughter, the callous void without sorrow,
Yearning for one tranquil moment, out of reach like past morrows.
It knows not privacy.

Silence;
Hectic confusion of days stresses, with college, career and life,
Managing with decayed composure, for household, children, wife.
It shows no compassion.

Silence;
Although insane my life may seem, alas the silence comforts me,
Knowing it's there in time of need, ageless, eternal apathy.
It does not proclaim judgement, it is absolute.

Chad R. Sedo

Miracle Child

To my son, Joshua, the miracle of my life
Not everyone gets miracles in life
But my life has a few
And every single one of them
Has to do with you

The first of these miracles, is the miracle of life
That is when God gave me you
Though the hours were long and rough on us both
God let you live, that is miracle number two

The third miracle I will never forget
It is still very fresh in my mind
You were 4 months old with only 3 months to live
If the surgery did not happen in time

With no money and no insurance to pay for it all
I was growing very ill
But thanks to God and his miracles of life
Today I have you still

So, always remember how special you are
And a miracle you will always be
Also remember you have miracles of your own
Your first is when God gave you me.

Julie Kay Stewart

Prisoner of Your Love

Behind these walls stands a man in his lonely world.
Looking out over the horizon and wondering if you are his girl.

Although the monotony sometimes is overwhelming
With nothing much to do, so guys play cards and handball.

But I often think of you!
Behind these bars there's nothing much to see,
So I find myself chasing a fantasy.

I fantasize that I am with you and holding you tight.
In reality just being without you makes me feel uptight.

Though I'm behind these bars and you are there,
We can still have a life of love that we can share.

Be patient, my love, it won't be long, before I am out,
Then I can show you what loving you is all about.

Surely you must have been sent from "God above"
Because now my heart is a prisoner of your love.

Richard Rousseau II

IF

If in the future you see a falling star,
make one wish for me.
If in the future you embrace a child,
embrace that child for me.
If in the future you say a little prayer,
say a little prayer for me.
If in the future you hear a soft melody,
think of me.
If in the future you can say, I love you,
say one I love you for me.

Toni M. Berthold

Buried Love

Lay me down now, cover me.
A grave so shallow, I still see the sun.
It hurts my eyes; I beg for night to come.
And so, condemned,
I'll search for you.
You have a shallow grave here, too.
Or visit me today, my love,
Here at my shallow grave above.
The other dead sleep content beneath me.

Shawna L. Hunt

I'll Remember Dad

He got married while in college to his sweetheart Natalie
He spent his life working for his wife and family
He helped others when he could and set the example for me
That's how I'll remember my dad

He provided for his loved ones and not one did he neglect
He was skilled with his hands and a developed intellect
He earned a teacher's salary and he earned my respect
That's how I'll remember my dad

As years rolled by, he instilled the value of truth
He wasn't hypocritical as friends offer up proof
He loved an intrigue novel and a satirical spoof
That's how I'll remember my dad

He sculpted people's characters with various disciplines
He demonstrated courage through some trials from within
He overcame many challenges that tried to weaken him
That's how I'll remember my dad

He communicated wisdom like a telling photograph
He was understanding even through any checkered aftermath
He rarely cried in public but how loud he loved to laugh
That's how I'll remember my dad . . . I love you, Dad

Tom Russell

Untitled

This world and these industries and those economics
A symbiotic relationship, we work for each other and hate it
Asteroids and egocentocrasticopolis, self made
Million! of dollars of starving pictures, babies!
Gaping mouths, distended stomachs, greed infested "ironics"
Who can feed on gold? Who can live on fossil fuel?
Who can synthesize life from a major elixir
    and call themselves a creator?
Is life a financial means or is life a value for living?
And woe to us who would crowd together
    to make money from tragedy,
To turn a blind eye to degradation and evil, safely removed
From the carnage, but in a way a remote accessory to murder.
And before our very eyes, a Christian God has been bastardized,
A demanding father, replaced by a smiling, unisexed face
Whose front men and women are building living colonies
And swallowing the bitter pill of commercialism
With painful regret
Too despondent to teach, too smart to learn.

Mark F. Obran

Child of Dreams

Hope, newborn,
Struggles against the night,
Forsakes the chambered womb,
and dares believe to soar.
Suddenly, takes flight,
Anew! Snatching breath—it captures air!

Unconfined,
done with narrow, timid things,
seeks largely of the unseen skies,
Child of dreams on liberated wings,
views higher realms to prize.

Janice Laird

I Need a Friend

I need a friend, not a sister or a brother.
I need a friend who is not like any other—
One who will listen to my tales of woe,
Or who on short notice will take off and go
To a movie, a game, or something like that,
Or perhaps just sit down for a nice, long chat;
One who laughs a lot from stories we tell,
Laughter, you know, keeps us all well;
A friend who shares tears of joy and of sorrow,
One you can depend on today and tomorrow;
Someone who cares a lot, but never does judge,
Yet not afraid to give a gentle little nudge
If a decision you are about to make is wrong;
Willing to share a book, a recipe, or an old song.

Where can I find a friend of this kind?
Right now several good people come to my mind.
Many friends I have, not just two or three;
I have been truly blessed, don't you see?

Margaret Scheider

Roaming

I've flown, like soaring eagles, in skies of ethereal blue,
And down on Earth, I've seen the bloom of desert cacti, too.

I've left my print on the ocean floor, with sea life far below,
Time has lapsed and tides have gone, the tracks no longer show.

I've trod the fabled treasure trails, to sate the wayward soul,
But the treasure in my heart is the beauty, not the gold.

I've used my hands for labor, to till the dark rich loam,
And plant and grow and harvest, to make this Earth my home.

These things so extra special, not everyone can see,
And when I say my prayer at night, I thank my God, I'm me!

William Kizziar

Passions of the Wind

Sometimes the wind is reckless,
Tearing at houses and ripping up trees.
It shows its violent nature,
Throughout the land and across the seas.

Sometimes the wind is saddened,
Raining tears upon the ground.
Torrents of water blowing futilely,
Pounding at everything all around.

Sometimes the wind is very cold,
Fingers gripping of ice and snow,
Tugging and pulling with a blustery grasp
At the trembling Earth down below.

Sometimes the winds blow hot and dry,
Licking and lapping at the swirling dust,
Burning with a heat that none could match,
Except perhaps the devil's own lust.

So, the wind has many passions,
Ever-changing from day to day.
Like a woman that is filled with emotion,
Who knows how she'll feel today?

Judie A. Shull

Resonance

To my husband, Terry A. Thompson, with love and appreciation
You cast the most brilliant light
into the darkest corridors of my heart,
allowing hope to escape from the shadows.

Effortlessly, you loosed my spirit
from the bonds of uncertainty
to fly undaunted into the wonders of tomorrow.

The silent, harmonic melody of you
resounds ever vibrantly in my ears,
etching notes in my mind for eternity.

Belle Poe

Americans Beware

Beware the counterfeit patriots
And the drastic methods they may use;
They will punish some indiscretions,
And important freedoms you may lose.

Under the threat of communism,
We created "Old-tail-gunner Joe."
Now with a special prosecutor
We've made voyeurism a national show.

Gnawing fear can weaken or even wreck
What we fought for, since 75, to protect.

A cold house can be heated
By burning it to the ground.
Many freedoms will be lost
If zealot's powers abound.

Robert L. Laumeyer

Country Field Hockey

Oh! The freshness of the country air . . .
All our teams were in pairs.
With stick in hand . . . the fun began.

Sticks swung earnestly through the air.
Newcomers could only stare!
To run . . . was sure defeat.
This was not a game for "the elite."

In "Country Field Hockey," "winner" took all.
You had to be lucky, to fling far and wide . . .
What is commonly known as . . .
"Cow pucky."

Colleen A. Barker

4 And 2 Is 8

My momma done tole me
As I went out the gate
God is never, ever too early
And He's never ever too late.

He's always and forever on time.
On that you can bet your last dime.

My time on this Earth is in His hands.
And by grace I live by His commands.

So I try to be anxious and try to do His will.
I even thank him for my daddy named Bill.

My daddy done tole me that 4 and 2 is 8.
I'm praying that he got through Heaven's gate.
God's never too early and never too late.

I'm not going to fret nor fear,
'Cause both of them done tole me
That God was always near.

Phyllis Rawlings

Friends Forever

Friends are forever and marriages are too.
When friendship turns to marriage,
those are the best marriages to have.
Because, when you can be friends together, you can be friends apart.

So when friendship turns to marriage, the marriage will last.
Friendship in a marriage means a lot of trust.

So when friendship turns to love, then marriage,
you must never lie.

Because once you break the sacred trust,
you break the friendship chain.

It's a chain that holds your marriage
and it must never break.

For broken chains get lost,
lost friendships never mend.

So when friendship turns to marriage,
remember to never lie.

Because friendships born of trust, they will never die,
and when friendships turn to love,
the marriages born from this love will never die.

Karen E. Oosterhof

Flight of Time

To my loving wife, Juanita Virtue McGill
A minute flight passed overhead;
Hours followed in fast pursuit;
I killed them all with great delight,
Hour by hour, flight by flight.

Days, months, then years flew by in turn;
There seemed no end of time to kill,
Until one day, I realized
That I was growing old and ill.

"Too late! Too late!" is my heart's cry,
"Too late to live but time to die!"
These haunting thoughts occur to me
As I face, now, eternity.

Yet, still on this departing day,
Another flight is on its way.
Against life's sunset red I see
A flight of moments left for me.

As twilight fades and night draws night,
Not many moments cross the sky,
And I can feel the darkness fall . . .
Life's day is gone beyond recall.

Leslie D. McGill

Is This Love?

When I look into those wonderful eyes
I myself become lost in your world
Full of so many hopes and dreams
Yet knowing they never come true
I think to myself, why does it have to be you
Still asking myself that same question
I keep hoping someone will come along
But then I compare them to you
And to you no one compares
I wonder why I keep sticking around
When my heart always ends up on the ground
Still, there always seems to be a chance
But that chance I won't take again
As long as you'll always be my friend
My happiness will never end

Lynessa L. Walters

Infinite Love

To my dearest love, Jennifer Fabian
With blood for tears, tears for lies,
and lies that flow like a river of wine,
the demons devour the heart and soul
of all who are left open for the ridicule.
Love is the only sure, strong survivor
with eternal happiness as it grows and transpires.
Like an angel with wings of silver and gold,
love comes to us like a savior strong and bold.
It fills us inside with every touch and kiss,
And every word spoken brings us endless bliss.
With all this love growing deep inside,
I know I'll love you till the end of time.

John Kuhn

A Picture of the Prairie

I'd like to paint a picture of the prairie just for you.
No artist yet has caught that grandeur rare.
It's just a perfect mixture of color, tint, and hue,
With a touch of Heaven added here and there.

A flaming sun is setting, and skies are azure blue.
Fleecy clouds are drifting slowly by.
The air is strongly scented by a cactus plant in bloom,
And hills are rising high against the sky.

A little band of cattle, grazing on a green hillside,
Rocks and boulders dot the rolling plain.
A rider in his saddle, silhouetted against the sky
As the sun is slowly setting on the range.

This picture of the prairie that I've painted here in words
Of a bit of God's own handwork at its best.
If you think it necessary, I can add the deer and birds
To my true portrayal of the golden west.

Kenneth Schofield

An Ozark River

Like a silver ribbon tossed askew,
She meanders with flashes of gray and blue,
Periodic frothing like unraveled thread
Interrupts the view of her rocky bed.

Concentric rings rippling out
Providing food for circling trout.
Muskrat traffic disturbs the flow,
A misty splash reveals a bow.

Spring has arrived with power and strength,
No man can imagine its depth or length,
Summer brings calm and quiet reprieve,
Announcing new life with each floating seed.

The autumnal chore to carry the leaves,
And winter brings ice with each little breeze.
Seasonal change like the aging of man,
In an ozark river that also ran.

F. Chris Nelson

Laments of the Lamenter

When the hours seem hopeless and dark
And despair reaches the very depth of my heart . . .
When frustration and fears take the place
Of the sight of his wondrous grace . . .

What then?
If yesterday passed—and without much change—
How can I look for tomorrow? Will it be the same?
Why the worry, despair, and care,
When you said my burdens you'd bear?

What then?
Maybe, on my shoulders, I'm laying it all,
Just butting my head against the wall.
Yet I know my strength comes from your word,
Aware that, in your timing, I'll be heard.

What then?
What then, when I reach the Heavenly Shore
And time for me shall be no more?
Will I be able to enjoy my eternal years,
Forgetting Earth's sorrow and its tears?

What then?

Virginia Greening

Mr. Woodchuck, I'm Here

To Miss Kitty, my first pet, who taught me love
Pondering, aching, feeling tears coming,
I witness torture in the evilest manner.
Those who are cruel to the small and the weak
Are revealing abyss in their lives through others.

He wanted to get across the road;
He took two steps before it showed;
The beast that flies on four round wheels
Came along, cares not, impels him over.

Before my eyes the woodchuck fell;
The driver flew, and there he stalled;
We all knew that he didn't belong;
He's running, will be, safe places no longer.

I wish it could be just a dream,
A dream so I'd forget the pain.
He's one of wild life's gentle creatures;
It's not a dream; he's injured; save him.

To all who read these words on page
This isn't a story that comes from my head.
Before you know it all life could be gone,
Please be humane, their existence does matter.

Mary E. Pollara

Spring Memoirs

All my poems are dedicated to mankind
The joys of spring are here again.
The air is clear, the sun shines like a dream,
The birds are singing, and we beam.
With a song in our heart,
We are awakened from the white winter dream.
The charming wild flower scent of spring
Is here again: forget-me-not, violets,
Daffodils beneath the hill,
The iris and pansies in the garden.
Every morning they greet me
With their shy little heads,
Reaching something beyond.
In compassion, we are given
The drink for the soul,
So broken spirits are made whole
As we wander deep in the forest
And watch the sun shining through.

Elsa R. Irom

The Angelic Visit

To the woman who always believed, I love you, cutie
I have wandered an eternity alone.
Its presence has been felt, but never seen.
One night, while asleep in the midst of a dream,
I danced with an invisible maiden.

The silence within my soul was smashed with emotions,
Emotions I have never felt before.
I heard the welcomed words of nectar and wine.
I felt the meaning of true love.

I reached out to feel, to caress,
But as my fingers were licked by the dancing candlelight,
I became embraced by the flame.

I have never seen Heaven, but in her eyes . . .
Eyes that sparkle like stars when we see each other.
A voice as soft and gentle as a kitten's purr.
Beauty as radiant as the sun after a spring shower.

After an eternity of searching,
I have leaned the meaning of true love.
And, I love her as an angel might.

David Shaffer

A Mother So Sweet

This one's for woman, Hattie B. Powell
Who can compare to a mother so sweet,
Holding fast to the end and never accepting defeat?

Who can imagine a mother so strong,
Giving the weight of her love with the reassurance that you belong?

Who can picture a mother so great,
Never framing herself and knowing that Jesus holds her fate?
Who can sculpture a mother with such masterpiece,
Showing a mind of wisdom and a ray of beauty, to say the least?

Who can hope for a mother with such elegance,
Chastising you through the years
and still holding a heart of pure countenance?

Who can ever want a mother constantly praying for their life,
Knowing when to spoil you in the misty times of sacrifice?

Who can ever fulfill her position in your heart?
Even though the physical cord was cut,
   the spiritual can never be torn apart.

And who can remember the overflowing of her aspirations,
Always standing proud, watching your life flourish
with astounding dedication?

And who can deserve a mother so unique,
A mother of love, kindness, and so sweet?

Wendell J. Powell I

A Christmas Prayer

To my loving family, Ken, Jillian, and William
Christmas is coming, with its trimmings and presents.
Some will have dinners with turkeys or pheasants.
All the gifts are delightful; their beauty is grand.
There's peace and there's love all over the land.
So when your joy turns to laughter and your day fills with fun,
Remember that on Christmas God gave us His Son,
That today is Christ's birthday, this day in December,
So heed this small prayer and soon you'll remember. . . .

God give me strength, give me all Your love.
Send me courage and truth, send them down from above,
For these are the gifts I need most while I'm here.
I need them at Christmas and all through the year.
So as I lay me to sleep on Christmas Eve night,
With the hope of arising to the sun's golden light,
I whisper this prayer, and I hope it comes true,
That I live on in eternity with the love sent from You. . . .

Deborah Davidson

Gifts of Love

As I looked from my window, all I could see
Was the beautiful world God gave you and me:
The sky up above, so blue and so bright,
The clouds, how majestic, so fluffy and white.
A butterfly flutters its dainty wings.
The birds building nests—that's a sure sign of spring.
A soft gentle breeze causes the trees to sway;
They reach to the sky, as if to pray.
The gardens are aglow with delightful color,
As a hummingbird dips, and sways, and hovers.
The lawns are lush and a beautiful green,
Making a carpet to add to the scene.
The morning dew sparkles everywhere,
As if tiny angels placed diamonds there.
Our Heavenly Father from Heaven above
Sends us these gifts with all of His love.

Mildred L. Galvin

Trees

Our children ask, will there always be trees
If you cut them, and they cut these
Children have now, started to ask
How can we live?, like we lived in the past?
People must now, learn to preserve
Now is the time, we must learn to conserve
If the world, that we live, cease to exist
Think of all, our children, will miss
If all the animals, must live in the zoo
How will our children, ever know what they do?
Life in a cage, just doesn't seem fair
Not for a bird, much less a bear
So on this Earth, we must learn to exist
We must find a way, cause we can't do it like this
So as we build, a new ten area mall
How many more trees will have to fall?
I just wonder, as we continue to build,
What we'll we leave, just over that hill?

Mavis A. Castleberry

Aeolian Kings

To my daughter, Su Yim Hoeber, I love you
Out of Troy and homeward bound
Aeolian kings Odysseus found,
Tossed on seas of gold; fish boats
Dance beneath smoke trees; Stromboli grows;
Obsidian hills guard cobblestone lines
Above turquoise waters bleached by pumice mines.
Liparian vendors ply their trade
While volcanic pools of mud tourists raid.
Hydrofoils rise to pay tribute there
To Aeolis, Poseidon and Vulcan's lair,
Like Etna who upon Trinacria reigns
Magnificent Aeolian kings,
Prerogative wrought,
Do much the same.

James W. Hoeber

Things You Can't Buy

You can't buy the sunshine at twilight.
You can't buy the moonlight at dawn.
When you're are old, you can't buy your youth
Or your life when the heartbeat's gone.

You can't buy your way into Heaven,
Though you'd be a welcome guest.
You can't buy a friend when you need one
Nor safe guarantees for your quest.

You can't buy the smile of a baby
Nor a word that's already been told.
It's just like your mother, you can't buy another,
Though you own the whole world and its gold.

LaVey Adams Alexander

My Personal Mark

To my best friend and husband, Mark Levine
Once I was soft spoken, made with satin and lace.
Now I am all broken, a total mental case.

I used to sing a lovely song, all delicate with grace.
Now it seems all wrong; I've completely lost my place.

What has happened to me; where has the time gone?
Can you tell me; it just goes on and on.

Don't leave me alone; won't you help me please?
Call me on the phone; I'm down on my knees.

It's my fate, so be my hero; be my savior.
Set me straight; do me this favor.

Change is good; situations aren't bleak
I know it's understood, so don't be weak.

You're the one I count on; only you can pull me through this.
With you is where I belong; with your lips so gently do you kiss.

Through your strength and guidance, I know I will find my way.
With all certainly I confide this, sweet; again dare I say?

Barbara Levine

Love Is Affliction

To a beautiful young woman whom I met during Xmas of 1997
I just realized that I wasn't sleeping in the night
It's a beautiful sunny day, and I'm dreaming you in my sight
I look around, and I see you in every piece
It seems like you are leaving in my eyes

It's the magic of your eyes; I feel like hypnotized
The way you talk, the way you walk, I need not to memorize
I feel you in my blood; you can't be that apart
Every cell of my body says you leaving in my heart.

Was it a really little time?
Or, I couldn't express my love to you
If I could, I would have hold the time
Just to say you that I love you

There'd be no reason for things I'll do, if I couldn't find you
Don't left me in mysterious boat baby, should I forget you?
You are not a dream, how can I forget you?
I would have forgotten breathing, if I would forget you

Love is enigmatic feelings; I'm keep saying to my reflection
The man in the mirror keeps saying that love is affliction

Jignesh Mehta

Path to Love

Love enters our life as a silent whisper
Only our hearts and souls can hear
We hold that whisper, oh, so close
But with many doubts and also fear

We are not quite sure just what we feel
Or what our hearts are telling us
As days go on so does the whisper
Hoping what we hear, we can truly trust

Since meeting again after many years
We tell our hearts it cannot be
He also has those rustlings deep within
But we hold those whispers each privately

We go about our separate lives
But take some time for just a call
Now each time we talk, the whispers grow more persistent
Slowly in our hearts, we are letting down those hidden walls

We now have shared our inner feelings
Shyly, not quite knowing what the other hears
Overwhelming disbelief and joy embrace us
As two whispers becomes a blend of loving words and loving tears

Edna Backhaus

The Song of Love

In a world that enhances the sound of violence
I still hear the sound of love's sweet silence
It tinkles and moves with the westerly breeze
As the sun sinks into the rolling sea
It scatters dark and weighted clouds
And chimes through the sullen crowd
It plays in a tune that's soft and sweet
As the sun finds a spot in the eastern sky
Perhaps a magical time will arrive
When I hear it ring out, strong and alive
Then I will know the sound that I hear
Is the song of love replacing fear

Vicki Gleason

A Walk in the Dark

The cave is dark and cannot see
the rough rock walls that grow inside,
nor meet the dwellers such as we,
who grope and feel for light not spied.

The cool, damp air is tears not cried,
though echoed steps reveal its voice,
and draw the two from fear beside
that their bright world was not a choice.

They know their plight but stand with poise,
the man and cave can have no eyes.
This blind respect sees no rejoice,
but will not look for help or cries;

Alone, each question the "how's" and the "why's,"
All caves possess the earthly dark
Their inner strength solid and wise,
And walk with man whose eyes are marked.

Tracie L. Davidson

Shall I Go?

Like a robot, I walk through this day
Wondering: Do I walk away?
We've been together for so long. I love him so.
Do I have the courage to let him go?
He loves me, he tells me I'm his life.
For twenty years, I've been his wife.
Along the way, we've grown apart,
Not within our spiritual heart.
All the "what if's" come into play.
Shall I go or shall I stay?
I feel he could not survive;
Only I will come out alive.
My courage for life is stronger today.
Have I the right to destroy him this way?
Then again, I say:
Shall I go or shall I stay?

Christy Falk

Dear Mom

Although you will not be "England's Rose,"
You are and always will be "Our Rose."
Time is soon to be gone as you are fading fast.
I'll always remember when we were young and going places.
You were always the center of attention
    when you danced the "Charleston."
I never could get the hang of that dance.
You always took us to Sunday School and Church.
We never had much money, but love was always there.
Out of feed sacks you'd make beautiful clothes for us to wear.
There were nine of us kids; however, you never seemed to tire.
At times, I know, you felt like pulling out your hair.
As I look at you now, lying in the bed, not able to walk,
Sure makes my heart hurt to see you that way.
I know, soon God will call your name.
I shall always remember "Your Smile and Caring Ways."
So, you see, Mom, you will always be "Our Special Rose."

Anna Ruth Davis Karner

The Little Red Wagon

Daddy, do you remember when I was nine?
The little red wagon and the mountain we must climb?
You have always been there for me no matter what I've done.
I know it wasn't an easy road,
Nor seldom any fun. But Daddy, I am older now,
Lessons learned along the way
Like respect and how to accept
Not always getting my own say.
Now the down slope we must go from this mountain we have climbed.
Separate but together we will be from time to time.
We will make it through these up coming rough and bumpy years,
Through the happy and the sad, the laughter and the tears.
Never will I leave your side, Daddy.
You never did leave mine. Even when I thought you had,
You were never far behind. I'm proud to be your daughter.
I'm proud to be your friend. And if I ever had a choice,
You're the choice that would have been.
I want to tell you thank you, happy birthday, too,
That I love you very much,
And Daddy, God Bless you.

Peggy Ann Owens

In Gratitude I Give

I gave my vows to be a wife
But to you, God, I surrender my very life
It was you who gave me this wondrous gift
When I give it back, my spirit you do lift

You are my life
You are my guide
To know and feel your love
I need only go inside

I have gone through life
And taken for granted
The fact that you have given me
Everything I have really wanted

I wanted to be a wife and mother
You gave me that and even more
You gave me family, friends, and loved ones
All of whom I do adore

You gave me eyes to see your face
In all I behold, I see your grace
I know the real meaning of joy by knowing you
In gratitude, I can start each day anew

Mary Anne McCubbin

Everything and Nothing

I can hear the rain falling on a metal roof;
It kindly puts me in a state of dreams.
I see it and I feel it—and yet remain aloof.
Everything and nothing join at the seams.
This easy high has always done me good.
Naturally, spiritually, in touch . . .
Well, that's the way I came, and I understood
Everything and nothing mean so much.
I can't see the clouds for the rain that's in my eyes;
Still, I know they're out there in the haze.
And I know that, just beyond them, there are sunny skies.
This is one of those days.
Now I believe my eyes, I think, and most of what I feel,
Some of what I read and what I hear.
I try to be prepared for life, to know what's really real—
Sure as I am that I am not as I appear.
Everything and nothing, blending themes.
Strong silent facts contain the loudest screams.
Reveling in theoretical extremes,
Everything and nothing is what it seems.

W. C. Wampler

Michael David

Michael David came to visit
And he imparted his angelic touch
Our hearts, our souls, our lives he blessed
In so little time he gave so much
Michael: Big and beautiful like God's Archangel
David: A human being after God's own heart
The proper name for this newborn baby
Who fought to stay but had to depart
Grieved and pierced were mother and father
But not beyond repair and hope
For they entrusted their son to his Creator
When in their arms he slept, in God's arms he awoke
Michael David came to visit
Forever touching our innermost
Five days he came to live for us
But now eternally with the Heavenly Host

Edmundo Oranday

A Glimmer of Hope

I scanned one night the nebulous sea
To sample the brilliance of our galaxy.
No star twinkled, no cluster blazed
Because of city lights, the glare, air hazed.

Since we've no heroes wisdomed and brave
Our overcast planet from ourselves to save,
Are we died in lots to self-implode
Polluting Earth in quest of alchemied gold?

Then wondered I from whence inspiration came
To flesh our visions, our dreams to frame.
We've ignorantly gambled possibilities away
Exploiting generations in the foray.

If one by one Earth's species extinction face
Survival of the fittest hollows as saving grace.
A glimmer of hope sparks our darkened plight
In prophetic whispers imploring vision of starlight.

Henry P. Mucha

Complete Freedom

If we are really free, then why do we still have racism?
Why do we still have homeless people, people who are starving?
If we are free, then why do children die of starvation?
Why do mothers bury their young children?
And why are kids killing kids?

Will we ever be completely free?
I believe that we may never be completely free.
There is too much greed, hate, and vengeance
In this world for us to be completely free.

Go ahead and celebrate, celebrate our freedom this Fourth of July.
Just remember we haven't reached complete freedom.
But it can start with you—you can make a difference
If only you are willing to try.

Ginger Larene Burgess

That Beautiful Rose

I stumbled upon a beautiful rose growing on a lonely roadside.
The most beautiful rose I've ever seen, so tall and stately.
The rose was so delicate and beautiful with character all its own.
I wanted to reach out and pluck the rose—
Instead, I stood in awe of the beautiful rose.
Each day I returned to look at the beautiful rose standing there.
But this day I returned, and the rose was not there.
Why didn't I capture that beautiful rose
That I look for granted would always be there?
Now I find myself in search of that beautiful rose.
I will somehow, some way find that beautiful, tall, stately rose
Which stood on that lonely roadside and make her mine.

Athielene Tillman Wolf

Nereus

I can be whatever I want to be.
I have no limitations.
My mind is an ocean of possibilities,
Deep and blue . . .
Each thought saturated and soaking with power.

I am a protean, immutable and ever-changing.
Sheer will transforms me, molds me, and will break me.
Careful, lest I prick you
For today I am rose, beautiful and eternal,
Sharp and withered . . .
Hindered only by my thorns,
But patient and growing.

Christina H. Sanchez

To Thomas, My Son

Here it is your wedding day.
Well Son, you've come a long, long way.
When you were three you said, "I'll make!"
What was, in your mind, a birthday cake.
With flour and butter smeared through the house,
Was our baker that night a midnight mouse?
But in your quest you did not waiver.
For a mixer you used an electric shaver!
One day at school when you were a teen,
You threw the main power switch, but you were seen!
Instead of getting an honorable mention,
All you got for that effort was more detention.
But from all this, your curious obsession,
A concrete-mixer driver became your profession.
All through your life I watched you grow;
I wondered of your future, but now I know.
Your bride to be, a girl ever-so-sweet,
I know in my heart, God meant you to meet.
And why did it take me so long to see,
My son, my son, why you're just like me!

Joseph L. Pisz

We Sing

"America! America! Crown thy good with brotherhood"
So why are we killing one another?
"Our Father's God to Thee, author of Liberty"
So why are we chained to "rights?"
"Thy love divine hath led us in the past"
So why are we so confused?
"Let our rulers even be men that love and know Thee"
So why do we not trust our leadership?
"God bless America . . . Stand beside her and guide her"
So why do we refuse His guidance?
"Blessed be the nation whose God is the Lord"
So why do we leave Him out of our government?
This is our motto: "In God is our trust"
So why do we ignore Him?
"When the wild tempests rave, Ruler of winds and wave,
Do thou our country save by thy great might"
O' Lord God, forgive us for being so foolish
As to think we can save ourselves!

Sylvia Bray

Life

A journey that we all must go through,
perhaps a challenging adventure too.

We have many choices that we have to face,
many problems that occur in this race.

A race called life, very rough,
very hard, but there're always pleasant
moments that help up survive.

All of us claim to know what life really is,
but none of us think that it's a breeze.

Maja Stevanovich

Master's Clay

I know not what I've done for You,
But know what You've done for me.

You've changed my heart and shown me that
I'm becoming what I ought to be.

I trust you, Lord, with heart, soul, and being
And know you'll not leave me alone, cold, or bleeding.

You suffer my losses by taking my hand
And guiding me through them with Your understanding.

I have not yet arrived and will continue to become
A workable clay for the Master to form.

Then to hear You one day finally say,
"Well done, my child, and welcome home."

Carol A. Ross

Why I Think of You Often

The laughter that you bring when I'm feeling down and out.
The joy to my heart when it's broken and I feel it can't be mended.
The warmth of your hands when you're holding me;
Along with your kisses that caress me.
My days are long, and empty but you're constantly on my mind.
Our lives are like different kinds of spices
And flavors seasoned just right.
When you need me, and I you we're there for each other.
Hanging on to each other's words in such a reality, and pleasure.
The tars of sadness are all forgotten and washed away with love.
"That's why I think of you often."

Damita Robinson

Man upon the Sea

I remember the day you set the sail
and headed into the westward gale.
To see in your eyes, anticipation and glee
Of a man going to sea.

I dream of the breeze caressing your face,
strong arms grasping the rig of the fore and aft.
And pray that you're safe within the lee
as you stand on the bow of your craft.
My man upon the sea.

I wonder what you are thinking
when you wake to a golden aurora.
Do you dream of our little island
with all of its beautiful flora?
Oh lonely man at sea.

You've finally come to the water's edge,
the day looks bright as the vessel is kedged.
I tremble as you swing lo' to me.
For the look in your eyes, anticipation and glee.
My man returning from sea.

Sheryl Wehr Barker

Life

Sadly alone, against the world I stand
No one is here to lend me a hand
No one is here to offer any advice
No one to help me in this game called life
Night after night, I pray for hope
Living with myself it is so hard to cope
I strive for something better to fall into my path
I just sit and wonder how long I can last
Was I ever strong? Was I ever proud?
Everywhere I go, there follows a black cloud
Wherever I go, there's a dead end waiting
Hope for me is quickly fading
Forever locked in this circle of hate
Has this hell become my fate?
From miles away, I can hear the rain
If it did any good, it would wash away my pain

Jason Highfill

Wasted Chance

To Marie, you have touched my heart and soul
It's Saturday night, and I'm staying in.
Don't understand why, it's been a while.
All I can think of is you; your beauty
Has overpowered my train of thought.
I guess I lost that rambling urge when I met you.
It really threw me for a loop.
I thought those days would go on forever.
I just got used to you being there (the dog too).
Then you got lost, and you were gone along with my chance.
I should have told you instead of being so coy,
After three bad relationships, I think I know why.
I should have tried to keep you, but
I think they call that kidnapping.
I thought I was so slick, a free spirit,
Then I met you and fell in love.
So why am I sitting home watching the X-files
Instead of being with you?
I long for one more chance to be with you,
My door and heart will always be open for you.

Frank F. Lewis

A Lighter Shade of Brown

Since the day I realized you were divine,
I could not keep my hands off you.
You became the center of my universe.
I wanted you for better or for worse,
But I kept playing with you and didn't appreciate your finesse.
The way your figure looks makes me try to guess
If I do deserve you, because I hope I really do.
Every step you take has a sensuous bounce.
When I touched you, there were no words I could pronounce,
Because your silky body was perfect, ounce for ounce.

Joaquin Hernandez

Runners

From the sky I see little figures bouncing under me

From a distance I can see shining faces full of
eagerness awaiting for the final hour

From the sides I can see flashing colors passing
by with a thunderous roar

Finally the hour is the minute and the winner
has won the race!

Elizabeth J. Boone

Kisha

Who's glad to see me when I get home
And when I'm out never roams
Kisha

Who sleeps with me on lonely nights
And comforts me through all life's fight
Kisha

Who's there for me when the world's too much
And constantly desires only my touch
Kisha

Who tries to protect me from all the world
My sweet and cuddly Maltese little girl
Kisha

Who loves me and needs me each and every day
And shows affections she just can't say
Kisha

Without her I don't know what I'd do
She's all I got to help me make it through
Kisha
I love you

Wynona Douglas

thy love

for my soul mate
blackness of night
illuminated only
by moon, white and shiny
reflecting off ripples
of thy blue midnight sea
dusted breeze carrying
soft silken touch
warm scent enveloping
purple of a rose
intent on flame burning
imagery so real to eyes
passion stirring every emotion
beginning in very center
of other worldly wisdom
loving thy spirit, loving thyself
delicately viewed, intense through nature
mesmerizing deeply-felt attraction
bringing love, bringing union
peacefully, securely remembering thy soul
motionless moment, feel my dream . . . forever

Danielle H. McBride

Beyond Survival

I am a bird without wings
And yet I fly high in the sky
And when I fly over our land
A rain of tears pours out of my eye.

I am a bird that flew astray
I am a bird caught in a cage
I am a bird that cannot sing
Tied up in helpless, hopeless silence
Watching our children being killed.

You have cut off my wings, torn up my feathers,
Cracked my bones, burned my eyes,
And against the rocks, time after time,
Smashed my head.

And now, with bloody hands, proud you stand,
Doomed never to wake up from you sleep.
Unable to dream, you feel no pain;
Only rage, wrapped in a sheet of surprise,
Each time you look up at the sky
And in spite of everything you try
Still see me fly!

Nadia Hava-Robbins

Elegant Violence

I may be sweet and soft,
But only on the outside.
Inside, I feel raw and hurt.
I am ready to fire at anything,
Anything at all that stands in my way.
But then I'm meek and turn away,
And watch the flames fire up around me, all of me,
My face, my heart, and my soul.

I am a white girl in a white man's world.
I laugh, cry, hate, dream, flirt, love, yell.
I want to hit and lash out.
I want to love, I want to be loved.
I am beautiful, I'm as ugly as hell.
I want to be me, whoever I am.
I am just another pretty face, but in the devil's body.
I cry for peace and cause all hell to break out.
I'm trapped inside my head between what I want and can't have.

I am silently painful, rudely polite.
I am calm craziness, I am peacefully restless.
I am elegant violence.

Antonia Brouillette

Still Free

The best things in life are free
That's the way it's meant to be
Special moments spent with friends
Things we never want to end

Smiles and laughter, love and cheer
Remain with us throughout the years
Times change, and so do we
That's the way it will always be

These are the things that mean so much
A kiss, a hug, a tender touch
No money or power needed you see
'Cause the best things in life will always be free

Carol Sterzinger

For the Love of a Trucker

I sit here alone every night;
the one I love is out of sight.
I wish I could tell him what is in my heart
every day we are apart.
I wonder what he thinks about night and day,
rolling down those lonely roads, miles away.
He chose the highway;
I chose to stay, so every night I pray:
"Please, Dear Lord, return him safely to me,
for this is the man I love, you see."
When we said "I do," many years ago,
we took that step too few will make,
a life commitment, everything to forsake.
I'll love you, "Candyman," forever in my heart,
Together or miles apart.

Mary Toolan Clarke

Hospitals

To my caring family, Barbara Howard and Katarsha
Hospitals are shelters that accept anyone who is sickly
Regardless if it's sunny, rainy, or snowy
People come here to be healed
And then are nourished with good meals
They endow patients with a phone to call love ones
Who have permission to bring gifts and sing songs
Hospitals keep the insects out of the air conditioned rooms
Thus, prohibiting mosquitos from irritating any open wounds
Rest rooms are being cleaned throughout the day
As a result, its cleanliness welcomes visitors to stay
Police are on guard to protect patients day and night
So patients will no longer be filled with fright
Placing a curtain between patients is its policy
So each individual is given his/her privacy
This place is filled with machines that monitored my mother's health
Alerting doctors to come immediately to prevent her death
Going to this place when you're sick is truly wise
Because this temple is truly a paradise

Howard Deland Coleman Jr.

Those, Oh, Kentucky Days

Old rocking chair creaks; wond'rin' mind slowly retreats
To a place in those hills far away,
Biscuits baking there, Momma's silvery-graying hair;
Sweet the memories of those, oh, Kentucky days,
But sad, so sad the memories of the day I went away.
And Patty Sue was sayin', Billy Joe, I'll be a-prayin'
That someday you'll come back home to my arms.
But through her tears of sorrow, she knew that, come tomorrow,
I'd be gone, and we'd never meet again.
And Momma said, "Son, don't go." I said, "Momma, I've got to know
Where the river goes on the far side of those hills."
I can see her standing there, wind in her hair.
Then she beckoned, "Oh, son, I love you so!"
Kentucky river flow on down, down to my old hometown.
Sometimes I wish I'd kept those simple ways,
The food, the fun, and the frolic of those, oh, Kentucky days.

William J. M. Wallace III

Virtue

Awoke this morning with my face in my hands
Another day, one more chance to understand
Open my eyes and cross the line
Try to gather my peace of mind

Step into my stride and begin my journey
Throw back the curtain and just be
A man whose masks all look the same
He whose insight is souls, not a name

My never-ending search for love without despise
One to look upon me with simple eyes
A beating heart in my side for evermore
The healing hand for the wounds life bore

And as the day gives way to the shadows
Whether the shallow depths will consume me, God knows
Foreseeing daybreak, I ask, "Love, give me wisdom to know
Wrong from right"
And I pray, "Lord, grant me the strength to fight"

   Joseph J. Daiker II

Bits of Beauty

A pristine white bloodroot . . .
Pick one and see why it's named.
Hold a yellow buttercup under your chin
To see if you like butter.
A purple violet growing in the crutch of a dogwood tree,
A most unlikely place to find one!
A humming bird feasting on honeysuckle,
The only bird able to remain in the air to feed.
A red cardinal and a blue jay,
Alighted on a snow-covered tree.
A doe with twin fawns,
Right nearby on the lawn.
A big Brittany Spaniel,
Cuddling a toy poodle.
Flying 39,000 feet above the Earth,
Seeing fantastic cloud formations.
Flying at sunrise towards the Alps,
Glorious gem-like gleams.
All samples of God's gracious goodness!

   Lois M. Steele

Be a Father

To my darling stepdaughter, Barbie
It's easy for a man to father a child
But to be a "Father" can take a little while
A father is the head of a Christian home
To lead his family to the foot of Jesus' throne
A father is to love with all of his heart
With unceasing love from the very start
A father gives protection and a sense of security
Teaching through example the importance of purity
Purity of the spirit and trusting in the Lord
It's taught by both parents who are in one accord
A father teaches patience, responsibility, and more
But disappointments and sacrifices he must endure
He must be an example, roll model, and friend
Giving correction and direction until the bitter end
With God's help, God's word, and God's love in your heart
You can be a father till death do you part
Our Father in Heaven is the example we need
And he gives us the Bible, if only we'll read
He teaches us the secret, and that is to pray
For our children are worth it. Happy Father's Day

   Thomas Ridgway

Independence Day, 1998

Here, 1998 was an unusually cool Fourth of July
To celebrate over 200 years of independence
Because our forefathers heard the cry—
Men of social and economic prominence.

They fought the British lords
Who had proposed many taxes
To try to keep them as their wards
But colonists were ready with their axes.

Enduring hardships in a new land
To show their tormentors they meant business
The colonists grouped to take a stand
With lofty aims they did profess.

Picnics, parades and political addresses,
Fireworks, ball games and sunning
Today, keep the holiday with a gala class
While others work to keep things running.

   Dorothy Stephenson

The Lord's Powers

To my beautiful wife, Helen, for thirty-five wonderful years
He created brown rocks in the mountain sides
and green growths of trees,
grasses and flowers gently swaying in the breeze.

We see God sending his rainfall to assure
that all his creations can live.
The black and gray clouds interspersed with
blue skies in the heavens he also does give

The lightning, thunder, and strong heavy rains
he does loose with all of his might,
on his creations below—what on ominous sight!

As we all cross through our lifetimes
and watch hour by hour,
we should be truly in awe of our
Lord God's remarkable powers.

   Scott M. Wilson Sr.

When Night Comes to the Mountains

When night comes to the mountains
there's a hush comes over the hills.
You can feel the magic of the stillness,
as the moon beams on the fields.
The whippoorwill starts his calling
separating night from day,
and you can hear the hooting of the owl
as he searches for his prey.
There's an affinity with our maker,
listening to the sounds of the night.
You can actually feel his presence,
as you sit there in the quiet.
The darkness mesmerizes the mind,
changing reality to a dream,
and life takes on a new dimension,
enlarging the meaning of paradise, like a ream.
Though the physical beauty of the hills is hidden
by the black of the night,
there's a beauty not equaled in the solitude
and sounds, the mind the only sight.

   Paul C. Preston

A Gift for You

The birds sang as the morning dew dried.
The breeze blew gently through the trees in the sky.
The warmth, you could feel as the sun began to rise.
Below, I stood seeking eagerly with my eyes.
For in distance, you had appeared, and such a surprise.
From me to you, this Valentine's Day gift will soon arrive.

   Gary E. Casto

Heaven's Touch

In loving memory of my papa,
John Mozden Sr.

His eyes so bright
like Heaven's blue skies,
he always knew when to smile,
he always knew when to cry.

His smile would light up
a room full of frowns,
and his laugh, with no doubt,
was the perfection of sounds.

Now all his tears
turn into rain,
and his laugh, a bird's chirp
on a warm, sunny day.

He was a wonderful man
and wise to the core,
but he is not in our reach—
he walked his path to the Lord.

He's still here by my side,
for I know when I sleep,
because he will reach out his hand
and crawl into my dreams.

Trisha Mozden Smith

You and Me

I jumped on my horse
One dark day
It was beginning to storm
In a terrible way

It wasn't the weather
I was talking about
It was my heart
Just wanting to shout

I gave you love
I gave you me
But somehow, baby
You were too blind to see

I rode all day
And I rode all night
Looking for something
To make me feel all right

I finally found it
While sitting under a tree
I couldn't believe it
The answer was me

Angie Whitney

Looks Can Be Deceiving

This is how the world ends
This is how the world ends
Not with a bang
But with a whimper
The masses will flock
To the one they call savior
Only to find
He's no savior
But another evil in a world
Full of sin
And that he is the one
Who orchestrated the whole ordeal
In the first place
And this tin God will cause
The downfall of them all
And when he comes again
No one will realize that
This is how the world ends
This is how the world ends

James Pillow

You're Gone, Now GO

She's moving out now.
The house has only
My furniture here.
Where is all her stuff?

Having this roommate—
My dead mother—makes
It unbearable
For me to go on.

I have become her
And lost myself. I've
Changed into an old
Lady staying home.

Trusting in no one.
Just watching TV,
The bright, talking lamp,
My only friend.

She has to leave here.
It's my turn to live.
I want my life back:
Men, danger and all.

Sheryl K. Erickson

For Martie

When you did leave me,
It was as if I too did die!
For you made me see
That our love was not just a lie.

To love you as I did
Keeps me on my lonely way,
With sweet thoughts only of you
When temptation makes its play.

It is you alone that I do love
No matter what our fate may be.
Our souls were mated from above
And only God can set us free.

I think about our life together,
What wondrous joy it did bring,
When we could have each other
Joined in life's brief fling.

There is no other in my life,
Nor could there ever be,
Whom I could love for a wife
For all the world to see.

William H. Lamkin

Life's Too Short

Life is good, life is great
Why do people want to hate?
Hate is neither good nor great
Unless you're anxious for
The pearly gate
Hate causes stress which
Leads to pain and could cause
A tumor in the brain and
Heart attacks can lead to death
From living in total stress
So try real hard not to get
Upset or wear a frown
Whenever people or things
Sorta get you down
Stop and think how serious
The situation is for it
'Cause anything to smile or
Grin and makes your body
Heather within
Life's too short

Oscar F. Stroene Jr.

I Imagine

I imagine my life unfolding
I see the things I wish to do
The hand that mine is holding
I hope will always belong to you

Our beginning starts out sweet
As most beginning are
I never think once of retreat
From you, I can't be far

But then it gets a little rough
I guess that's to be expected
If we can only hang on tough
We can fix what's been neglected

It's good between us, for a while
But then it starts falling apart
Inside, it seems, we're apart by a mile
So much for the brand new start

I imagine my life unfolding
I see the things I wish to do
In the image, my mind is holding
I can't seem to find a place for you

Gregory J. Middleton

I Only Want To Show You

I wish that I could tell you
How happy I feel today,
But you are afraid to listen to
The words I want to say.

I know I must be dreaming
To think I could make you mine.
I guess I can't stop wishing
To be with you all the time.

My nights are long and lonely,
Except when I'm with you—
Then they pass so quickly.
It's just too good to be true.

I'm not trying to scare you
Or make you say kind things.
I want very much to be with you
And tell you of my feelings.

Please don't run away from me;
It's the one thing I cannot bear.
I only want to show you
That I really, truly care.

Robert I. Stupplebeen

Whispers

Whispers, whispers evil hush,
That lie dormant within her touch
Abound, abound deep in her soul,
Does likely make her that of cold!

Whispers, whispers evil hush,
No one dare or she may crush
No man shall have a softened hand,
For she will blow his soul to sand!

Whispers, whispers evil hush,
For her to change would be a rush
Upon the brow of man she sees,
That she wishes for eternity!

Whispers, whispers evil hush,
Does she wish that gentle touch?
As she sees him at the gate,
In her lifetime it's too late!

Come, come as we do play,
To hear her whispers on this day!

Terri Frey-Simi

God, Why Today?

God, why today?
Why do I feel so lonely?
Why do I hurt so much?
Why do the tears insist on falling?

Today is no different
From any other day
When I miss him so . . .
Except, the nurse told me

That when I called him today,
His eyes were shining
And he tried to kiss the phone
When he heard my voice.

Marguerite H. Atkins

Stürzen

Sixteen candles burn in the rain—
Ten to mark her path,
Six more to show for pain.
An angel walks among us,
Weeping while we smile.
An angel talks among us,
Unwary of her wiles.
Innocence . . .
Gentle eyes and lips and soul.
Dark thoughts . . .
Trapped inside with no place to go.
Catch a tiger by her tail.
One, two, three . . .
Set her free.
The broken clouds were an open door—
Should the world split open
An angel falls once more.

Bounphone Chanthavong

We Can Make If—If We Try

Not so very long ago
At least that's how it seems
We both had loves that went astray
And shattered all our dreams!

Our worlds were gone—the ones we knew
We both made brand new starts
We would never ever love again
Or give away our hearts!

But then we met and fell in love
And as the days went by
I knew without a doubt dear
That we would make it—if we try

We can make it—if we try—love
You don't have to run and hide
With love and understanding
I'll be there by your side!

I hope you won't be sorry
And that I'll never make you cry
But I know down deep inside my heart
We can make it—if we try

Robert L. Slater

In Days of Old

In days of old
When knights got cold
The ladies came a running
With furs and such
To keep them satisfied
But, in days of old
When the ladies got cold
All they got was
The shaft

Pam Skiles

The Deep End

To all the daughters missing fathers,
and mine, Ron Fietsom
Black lives in front of me,
as I mourn for thee.
My pupils swallow my eyes,
as I watch the living souls cry.
The clouds seem to feel my pain,
for they spill an endless rain.
How death drains the breathing,
selfishly jealous of Heaven's receiving.
The falling red sun
spreads like things undone.
I ponder the mystery,
why take you instead of me?
Violet hair hangs down,
this face is a lonely frown.
Lost in white water,
drowning this homeless daughter.

Julie Fietsam

The Green

"I miss the green," she said,
As she bent her knee and bowed her head,
To take the tender, slender shaft
As though it was blessed.
Trembling fingers gently caress,
A teary eye beholds.
Memories unfold
Feelings untold.
In silent reverie, reunited,
A newness in the old,
The old forever new.
The circle in the cycle
Completing me and you.
Joyful reunion to see this sea of green,
Framed by boughs abundant.
Could this be but a dream?
Knees bent to savour,
Head bowed to pray,
"I thank you, Lord," she whispers,
"For this truly special day!"

Magaret Kist

One at Last

Come to me, my precious one.
Come stay with me, I pray.
I long to hold you closer
And love you night and day.

There was nothing I could do.
Sorry you did not live.
So you chose to visit me,
Love and support to give.

Never knew I missed you so.
But now we're one at last,
Holding close and keeping dear
The future with the past.

Mary B. Wadzinski

Cookie

It was my birthday.
Headed for the doorway,
Was in a state of disarray,
My olfactory
Mechanisms drew me
to the Pizza Factory,
And I'm not telling you a story.
While eating my pizza,
An angel appeared with a cookie,
Wishing me Happy Birthday.
And with that memory,
I will always savory
The Birthday spent at the Pizza Factory.

Frank Van Dusen

Special of the Day

Waitresses hustle,
Serving the day's special,
Plates and silverware clanging
Echoes from the kitchen.

It's room rush.
Chatter of bust!
As patrons discuss
News about town.

Each group secluded,
Every table quite individual,
As the latest gossip spills
About some group across the room.

Then, one by one, the groups disperse.
As men and women search pocket and purse
For loosed coins and bills
To lie on their table of spills.

As each group leaves
With individual thoughts,
Whether of news or food,
Each had the special of the day.

Brenda S. Ball

My Kitty Cat

Do not know what to write
I am kinda uptight,
My Kitty cat broke
My glasses!
I forgive her, this is true
Now so good I cannot see
To type poetry.
One day, new glasses I will get
And this I will forget.

Arlene F. Wiley

Peace

My children are safe
All tucked into bed
I turn out their light
I kiss them on their foreheads

I will see them in the morning
And will sit by their sides
Look at their joyous faces
And see the smiles in their eyes

Our time is so precious
Our days are so few
Another parting will come sooner
And, once again, I'll have to miss you

But for now, my angels
You are here with me
And tomorrow is a new day
I will set your spirits free

Christine Miner-Brown

Bittersweet

Lying here almost asleep
Tear-stains on my eyes that weep
Hope, I can no longer keep
Pain has gnawed its way too deep
What was sown that I so reap
Such cruel burdens on me heap'd

Life, your pain, I thee now cheat
Ending with my heart's last beat
Filled with lies and foul deceit
Cold as death that I'll soon meet
Caving in against defeat
Brings peace that is bittersweet

Carla Hobaugh

Brinkmanship

In the breeze that blows the bubbles
quietly resting on the plane
the light shapes hang
across the oscillating stems
vibrant like slender shuttles
turning
first to the right then to the left
repeating the attempts to stir
the forms staring the tree
far yonder.
Listen to the rumble of their murmurs!
The muffled sounds
were often thought
as flourishes
on azure sheets
that flutter and return to rest
pausing again on the nodding stems
teasing the captive creatures
creeping on their padded knees
to the brink of the furrow.

Piero Braggiotti

Precious Angels

To Joey, with all my love forever
Life is so precious;
So many take it for granted,
So unaware
Of those so less fortunate,
To care for and love
No matter how they are born.
Only God shall decide
For each and every one.
A child shouldn't bear this,
Yet they're born all the time;
It's amazing how they accept it.
They're all one of a kind:
So dependent with care,
Helpless and small,
So unknowing they stare,
Some not even loved at all.
But for the ones who are,
So happy they feel,
Knowing in someone's heart
Their heart fills.

Dana Sparks

Orpheus Mine

To my forever love, Paul A. Gigl
You read me
Like an open book
Word by word
And page by page

You sing me
Like a symphony
Of notes and chores and melody

You play me
Like a silver bell
Suspended from a golden string

You shake me
Like a storm-torn tree
And wrench the over-ripened fruit
From out my arms
That I may bloom anew

You love me
With the perfect love
Of time and space and harmony
You read my soul and play my song
Upon the woodwinds of your heart

D. Lynn Ackerman

The Creation

In the beginning, all was night,
God changed the darkness into light.
The air we breathe, all things in sight;
God made everything!

The waters parting, formed the seas;
On dry land grew the grass and trees.
The sun, the moon, the stars we see;
God made everything!

Next he placed, abundantly;
All creatures moving in the sea.
And fowls above, to fly so free;
God made everything!

The cattle, beast, and creeping things;
His labor the sixth day did bring.
All these he made fit for a king;
God made everything!

And God said, "Everything looks grand;
Now all that's needed is a man.
In my own image, he will stand."
God made everything!

Eva J. Hines

If This Means That

If the soft touch of your hand
means I'll have to stay,
Then keep your graceful hand
away from me today
If your gentle kiss
means for me to love you more
Then let your sultry lips miss
and walk straight out the door
If your kind words
mean for me to believe what you say,
Then I shall give you scornful verbs
to make you go astray
If your probing eyes
mean to intrigue my deepest soul,
Then I'll show you the world's lies
that make it seem unwhole
If your heart that loves
means to do me wrong,
Then I'll show you the white doves
that always fly away strong.

M. Birden

Helen

Helen is my little wren
A flitting here and there
At first she's cooking breakfast
And then she's on the stair

There are ten flowers to water
Kitty Kat to be let in
And Murphy's scratching at the door
She's calm amid the din

She's shopping by the cat log
Eddie Bauer and L. L. Bean
Christmas is a-comin'
Soon old Santa makes the scene

Our Helen's a grand nurse maid
She has a gentle touch.
A cleaning all her animals
And PA from such and such

We couldn't do without her
We're lucky that she's here
She's affable, she's lovely
And filled with great good cheer.

Nathan Z. Bridwell

Under the Wings of a Dove

The very first time we met,
it was under the wings of a dove.
We looked at each other,
then looked at the sky above.
The first time we touched,
it was under the wings of a dove.
Each time we met,
we always looked above.
We always hurried from the pier
then . . .
Lying in my lover's arms,
under the eaves, I saw the silvery dove.
No dove in winter.
In spring, we walked the wet sand.
As we embraced, we saw, really saw
we were under the wings of the dove.

Mary T. Price

Never Mind, Little Girl

Never mind the shadows,
Never mind the rain.
Just keep on, little girl
Living just the same,
The sun will shine tomorrow,
It will be a better day,
The rain that falls is borrowed
From rivers far away!
Even though your hopes may fade,
Like the setting sun,
Keep on smiling, little girl,
Till your life's work is done.
Shed not tears of sorrow,
If you must walk alone,
Others have gone on before you,
And they like you have roamed.
When you have failed just smile once,
The clouds will all roll by,
And take up where you left off,
No use to sit and sigh!

Martha Serbu

Mirrored Eyes

Your hazel eyes like moon beams shined
Your hazel eyes once mirrored mine
You looked at me with the purest love
As pure as heavenly angels above
Their glimmer shined as did the sun
Their glimmer shined, I was the one
I watched the spark diminish and die
The spark went out, you said good-bye
Your eyes turned into empty cores
My eyes turned and mirrored yours

Athena Papavlo

Sometimes I Need You

Sometimes you're like a child,
so innocent and small.
I hold you in my arms at night,
and to sleep you fall.
Sometimes you're a lover,
so passionate and true.
Holding me in your arms is all
I ever knew.
Sometimes you're like a beast,
flashing your angry eyes,
holding me in your gaze;
I want to run and hide.
Sometimes you're like my father,
guiding me out of the wrong,
holding my heart in your hands so strong.

Shellie Waite

Don't Go

Hold me closer.
Kiss me longer.
Do the things
That make love stronger.

Show me things.
Take me places.
Hold me in
Your strong embraces.

Tell me what
I long to hear,
Instead of wandering
My biggest fear.

Don't go so much.
I want you to stay.
Stop leaving my heart
In such dismay.

I want to be loved.
I want you to care.
You are the one
I always want there.

Elizabeth Walker

Deep as Water

Grandma's salt and pepper head
lolls sideways as she drifts
into the damp lands where
the ghosts of Hawaii beckon
The soft pillow of her neck
dangles a deflated balloon
The rise and fall of her breath,
deep as the waters she dreams

She floats somewhere safe
between the ones remembered
They save a place for her,
the ripe throbbing Earth's beat
envelopes her brief visit,
a contracting uterus for birth

As she sleeps in her rocking chair,
her skin sheds cells for the birth
called death, and freedom for
waters that wait to bathe her there

Kim Brashears

Untitled

How much I want you
There's nothing in my way
But I always hide my battered heart
I rarely hear one word you say
I've loved and lost before
But this seems so real

How do I convince my heart
Of everything I feel
And you're everything my heart desires
But all I seem to think of is the past
Why can't I forget and start anew
It's so clear you're nothing like the last

Melissa Bushnell

The Wonder of the World

The only wonder of the world
Should be to know what love really is
To look in someone's eyes,
And know what there soul was like,
But we may never know that's why
It's called a wonder of the world.

Niki Wilson

Dimensions

Coffee, hot fudge and brownies,
Fried chicken, heavy cream,
Twenty and one hundred pounds,
What a delightful dream!

Decaf tea and carrots sticks,
Tofu, skim milk and rice,
Two laps down and portly,
Reality is not nice!

Droopy blobs and wrinkles,
A gut that's here to stay,
Hair dyed blond and cellulite,
Can this be me? No way!

How did I get here?
When did I grow old?
What about the smart part?
That's what I was told!

Pick yourself up girl.
There's lots more life to live.
Make peace with that mirror.
Read, teach, love and give!

Sandra Ann Nadean

Just Look for Tomorrow

To Barbara and Tom Gelow,
Frank and Carol Pool
When I have told this world good-bye
To be around no more,
Now don't feel bad or shed your tears
For I'll be on that distant shore.

I know that you will miss me
When I'm no longer here.
But just remember the happy times—
That one always holds dear.

I've lived a long and happy life,
To that you'll all agree.
So there's no reason to feel blue,
Or even weep for me.

So just always remember:
When all of this is done—
We'll have a happier future—
Under the rule of God's Son.

Velma R. Pool

What You Have Become

You've become the sunshine.
You've become a star.
One is very close.
One is very far.

You've become the water.
You've become the drink.
More than you imagine.
More than you might think.

You've become the morning.
You've become the light.
With you comes the freshness.
With you ends the night.

You've become a feeling.
You've become a thought.
One that keeps repeating.
One that's never fought.

You've become a symbol.
You've become a thing.
You've become undoubtedly.
You've become . . . my everything.

Maricela Gonzalez

Cry Down

I may never see a sunrise
I may never see the moonlight
But I will always feel the rain
Soft and cool
It falls around me
Dancing to the ground
Cry down
I may never feel the shadow
Of a love that haunts me
But I will always feel the rain
Jagged and pained
It crashes down
To my angry ground
Oh . . . cry down
Show me all your sorrow
I may never see you again
Teach me of your secrets
I may dance in the truth
No, I may never understand
But I will always have the rain

Rachel Kowalsky

A Day

Moonlight shines from up above
Gazing down on one I love
Singing softly of my longing
Touching him tears are falling

Sunlight shines even brighter
Transforming hearts a shade lighter
Holding faces helping us stand
Shouting love as only it can

Dusk paints skies a million colors
Showing truth to two lovers
Coloring the sky in golden hues
Painting a portrait only for you

Dawn peaks over the horizon
Kisses you bringing teary eyes
Reminding you the newness of life
Whispers that I'm to be your wife

Deborah Miller

The End

Can it be the end of life,
or the end of a story?
Maybe it's the end of the world,
but I don't think so.
Is this the end of a love life,
or the end of everything.
I do believe it's the end
of a new beginning.

Jesse Ceuteno

What You Have Taught Me

From the moment you entered my life
Nothing has remained the same
A feeling of everlasting bliss
Has overcome my pain
My world was once so empty
And there were no stars above
But then you came into my life
And taught me how to love
With your caring words and warm embrace
You've opened up my eyes
I can appreciate the beauty of the night
And the simplicity of a sunrise
As much as the oceans are deep
And as much as the skies are blue
That is how very much that I love you

Alaina Van Breen

Void

In the absence of what has been,
For many years,
The only thing to help me win
Is tears.

And rage,
Uncontrollable and destructive,
Like a wizard-mage
That is counterproductive.

Listening to ones
Who think they know,
The ones that won,
Maybe I shall give them a blow.

Especially her,
For things I plan,
Who now causes me to stir
Into the frying pan.

That all point and laugh
Are not the goons,
Destroy the riff-raff,
Soon. . . .

John V. Chmielowiec

Put All Your Trust in God

While on this tedious journey
Down the road of life,
We are often encountered
With trouble and with strife.

If there were no troubles
We wouldn't know how to pray,
For prayers are our communion with God
That help us along the way.

So when trials and tribulations
Seem too much for you to bear,
Just put all your trust in God
And your burdens He will share.

Start each and every morning
With a fervent, sincere prayer,
Your day will be much brighter
Because God is always there.

Be not weary nor dismayed,
Just remember that God cares.
Whatever your daily problems may be
Can be answered through your prayers.

Alice Webb

Going Home

My father used to say to me,
Don't wait too long to come home.
I only thought he missed me.
Not that he'd go alone.

When I think about his promise
To always be my dad,
I'm confused by the emptiness,
And then I guess I'm mad.

Beware of the day he calls you
To say he's taken ill.
Don't think it's only temporary,
And he will be there for you still.

The days of your life go by quickly;
You can't stop them, so don't even try.
My dad is gone, though he was young,
And I didn't say good-bye.

My father used to say to me,
Don't wait too long to come home.
I didn't listen, and now I miss him.
Momma lives there all alone.

Gloria Schevers

Shattered Dreams

To Kelly Cusick, I love you
Contemplating my life
I ask every question except "Why,"
I see myself in the mirror
The last star falls out of the sky.
In the mist of this confusion
I wonder if anything really matters,
Every dream I have
I personally see to it that it shatters.
Shed a tear for myself
'Cause there won't be any time to cry,
When my opportunity arises to die.
I take the spoon
Pour in the rest of my sack,
'Cause I don't wanna be here
When the sun comes back.

Brian Dailey

A Woman Who Gives

I came in hysterical
Crying was the name of the game
Years spent and lost
By a sickness that never was

Instead of passing judgement
Hope was the middle name
She gave me
Direction and a future
Were now seen

She spends her life giving
With or without acknowledgment
Because of her oath

I wish to say thank you to her
Somehow, someway
Her name is Dr. Mary T. Kennedy
I call her angel

My tears became rainbows
And now I welcome my future
Thank you.

Marguerite Mariani

Empty Bookshelves

Empty shelves, empty lives;
A river of lives flows to the sea.
Where have the children gone?
To find their tomorrow—westwardly.

The shelves have held the books,
Dr. Spock, Pooh, and Montessori,
Hemingway, Shakespeare, Freud,
Chemistry, Physics, Biology.

The shelves are empty now,
No more cookbooks, no more needlepoint.
New books will fill the space,
Our lives now free to find a fresh place.

Virginia Dickey McCreary

Life's Sorrows

Standing in puddles
Of life's sorrows

Shivering from the cold of
Loneliness and despair

Seeing through
Aching, weary eyes

Wondering
How did I get here?

Angela M. Diaz

If

To Suzanne
Were you to pass away
Unexpectedly, I fear
I should be caught smiling.
Then, perhaps a dance
With a bit of pantomime.
I have no doubt that I would
Fill the air with laughter.
There would, of course, be endless
One-sided conversations while
Walking in your flower garden.
This would all be repeated
Over and over . . .
There would be time enough
Later for grieving.

Randolph Allen Hughes

Key Keeper

To Meredith,
just one glimpse through the steel
The clock strikes three.
The ring of the bell.
What is fate today?
Heaven or hell?

Time is an enemy.
There is no shield.
No strong barrier,
Too weak to build.

Lock the soul.
Swallow the key.
Eyes of steel
Imprison me.

Keys at the door.
Don't come in!
Until I know:
Foe or friend?

D. Renee Mitchem

Letting Go

It remains to be seen
from within the heart,
Sure of a chance to grow.
Feeling the pain
whenever we're apart.
Right or wrong;
We may never know.
Comfort and love we share
With the will to go on.
In turn sadness appeared,
Now all seems so far gone.
Together we will never be
Even though it's wanted so.
Since happiness we lack,
Pain is what we show.
Apart
Our lives would be much
Better,
If we could just start
By letting go!

Tammy S. Bauer

The Rose

The red color of the rose
reminds me of God's love,
His never ending mercy,
And grace from up above.
Each petal with its tenderness
Says patience will endure.
Every fold of petal one to the
other, says God forevermore.

Delores Nocchi

Beyond the Shadows

Beyond the shadows of the tomb
There waits a day so bright,
Where loved ones watch, and bid me come,
Where there will be no night.

Love, peace, and joy await me there,
And it will not be long
'Til I shall enter Heaven fair
And join that happy throng.

I'll see my Saviour there at last,
My Lord who died for me,
Where earthly sorrows all are past,
No parting there will be.

Oh, meet me in that happy place.
Get ready, friend, I pray.
Come, join me in this Christian race.
Christ Jesus is the way.

Lila Knight

My Friend

Tall, tan,
Sandy hair,
Broad shoulders,
Very fair,
Long arms
Reaching round the waist,
Should I have slapped a face?
Could be Bob, Dave,
Or maybe Jim.
But wait!
Bill!
I remember him!

Evelyn Hodgdon

Loneliness:　What Could This Be?

Staring off into the great distance
between me and my destiny,
Drifting off the precious memories,
of my past adventures,
Crying my tears of sadness,
within my heart and soul,
Drowning in this sea of tears,
not knowing which way to go,
Reaching for hands
that long ago disappeared,
Holding myself tight at night
when I should be sleeping,
Hoping that someone will keep
me from drowning,
Waking to a new morning,
finding myself all alone!
What could this be?
Is this loneliness?

Charlie N. Lee

Chapter Seven

A child of eleven,
ridiculed by her peers,

She cries at night,
flooding her pillow with tears.

A girl of fifteen,
finding something new,

She found renewed religion
sitting in God's pew.

A young woman of seventeen,
full of a new confidence,

Matthew's Chapter Seven—
let it rest on their conscience.

Shannon Tracy

The Wind in My Hair

Riding through the night
With the wind in my hair
All I see are the stars
All I feel is the air
The vibration beneath me
Stirring my soul
As we cut through the darkness
Just us two, alone
We ride for the place
That we've made for our own
To make love in the grass
And bring our hearts home
Is there anything better
Than this freedom I feel?
Life pulsing through me
As these hours we steal
All I can think of
When I look at you there
Is our love and the stars
And the wind in my hair

Debra M. B. Jarvis-Ferguson

So Strong My Love

To my loving wife, Mildred Warfield Austin
Nothing on Earth could take away
The love I have for you.
Not even anything, my dear,
That you might ever do.
Not even if you told me that
You cared for me no more.
And if you turned away and tried
To close and seal the door.
Not even if you laughed at me
And struck me on the face.
Or slandered me most viciously
In every public place.
Yes, you could really hurt my heart
And you could make me cry.
And cause me suffering until
I wished that I could die.
And bombs could blast the Earth and sky
And every ocean blue.
But nothing, darling, could destroy
The Love I have for you.

William C. Austin

Pathway

I walk the path of no man,
My secrets to reveal;
I walk the path of no man,
My knowledge deemed unreal.

I walk the path of no man,
Learning lessons of defilement,
Brought about through innocence,
Intelligence, or beguilement.

I walk the path of no man,
Secrets held in heart and soul,
Gleaning age and wisdom,
They one day will unfold.

And though this wisdom was denied
As I was once denied myself;
Realizations of who I am
My being do engulf.

Tho' I walk the path of no man,
I do not walk alone.
I walk beside my sisters;
One day our wisdom will atone.

Barbara S. Newell

The Kiss

To my loving husband, Gary Vogelsong
But an innocent kiss,
in the middle of the day.
What would I have missed,
had you not come that way.
The pin upon my chest,
my heritage to declare.
I had stopped for a rest,
turned and you were there.
"Kiss me I'm Irish",
my pin did boldly state.
Though your kiss was not my wish,
it was truly great.
The years have come and gone,
nineteen since my heart you did win.
The two of us became one,
and now our daughter wears the pin.
So much we would have missed,
if the pin I did not wear.
If that day we had not kissed,
and our lives we did not share.

Joanne A. Vogelsong

When I Grow Up

When I was just a young lad,
My father asked of me,
Someday, when you are grown up,
What do you want to be?

When he received no answer,
He turned and walked away.
Not that I hadn't listened,
But what was I to say?

My thoughts weren't of the future,
Nor were they on that day.
I don't know where my mind was,
But it seemed far away.

What once seemed unimportant
Now means the world to me,
Since, now that I have grown some,
I see things differently.

Now fifty, I still ask myself
That question he asked me,
Someday, when I am grown up,
What do I want to be?

Thomas E. Vincett Jr.

Thoughtfulness Is

Saying you're sorry, even though
you're hurt, crying inside.

Sharing your belongings,
hoping they will treat
them with respect.

Smiling outside,
yet knowing
in your heart
you are sensing
deep regret.

Visiting the sick
with outward joy,
sadly feeling
that tomorrow
they may die.

Holding hands,
kissing, hugging
those you truly love
because you never
want to lose them.

Juliana R. Underwood

Look to the Sky

As we look to the sky,
We see all the past.
Of all of the people,
In our history a last.
Of those that for took,
To make this our land.
Who worked e'er so hard,
With their time on hand.
To make this a better,
Place to service.
With things that they done,
While they were alive.
But it's up to us now,
To keep it a going.
In the right way,
To keep it a growing.
So the moral is clear,
As a bell it does ring.
We must put out best foot forward,
For the future it'll bring.

Donald Ray Mashburn

Baby Dolphins

To my parents
Baby Dolphins, in the sea,
Won't you come and play with me?

Around your home, out in the ocean,
you swim with grace poetry in motion.

Boy, we could cause a big commotion;
Hey, do you wear sun block lotion?

Well I have to, out in the sun,
While we're having all this fun.

Say, you could teach me how to dive,
Over loaves, to jump real high.

Why, I could teach you different ways
To use your fins, hello—you'd say.

Then, side by side we'll swim along
Teaching one another songs.

Next, we'll float among the foam
Until our mommies called us home.

So, won't you come and play with me?
Baby Dolphins in the sea.

Ralph Koelling

My Sister

To my big sister, Shelli Spor
My sister, so sweet and so kind,
She'll always be there by my side.
If I fell and scraped my knee,
She would be there, comforting me.

My sister, so cute and so nice,
She is made of sugar and spice.
Sometimes we fight,
But we always wind up telling secrets
Later that night.

My sister, so awesome and so cool,
We'll always have fun times
Playing basketball, baseball,
Or walking home from school.

My Shelli, sister so sweet and so kind,
We'll be together for all time.
We will always be close,
No matter how far apart,
Because I'll forever love her
Within my heart.

Samantha Jo Spor

Take These Tears Away

*To my loving girlfriend,
and soon to be my wife, Andrea*
Come to me
Love me forever
Never leave me
Take these tears away
Hold me close
Speak to me
Touch my hand
Kiss my lips
Take these tears away

David J. Strickler

Rain

Dreamlike rhythms
amid the thunder and the rain.
Windswept visions
flow across the window pane.
Exotic storm is unleashed,
as the powers that reign
in my mind when I think of you.
Each time, I but think of you.

And as the shadows dance
to the strains of light,
elusive specter,
sweet, compulsive delight.
Within the softly muted
waters of time,
my love has always been
and will always be thine.

Terence P. Daniels

Grandma

Grandma,
When I was a young boy,
You'd read a book with me
And do so many other things
That have so much influenced me.

As the years went by
And slowly faded away,
Your love overwhelmed me,
And in my heart,
And in my mind,
Your love will always be.

Through the green grass
And the blue skies,
You shall never die,
Because in my heart,
Clear as day,
You'll always be alive.

Mark Lookingbill

Haunting

Haunting themes of you
Crept from my radio
Beside me, half asleep

As pillow talks and frantic frustration
Changing roles and stolen champagne
Reminded me and fled

And though we couldn't find
The right time
To forget fear, before

May it suffice to say
If we had it over
It would be nice the same, again

Carl W. Chamberlin

It All Happens

It all
Happens:
Snow,
Rain,
Fire,
Icicles,
Wind,
Storms
Coming
On down
The tracks
Like a
Freight
Train.
It all
Happens
To our
Lives.

Brian Bailey

A Date with Gunfire

*With love, to all the students,
Somerville Charter School*
Westside Middle School
in a rural Arkansas town.

I never thought it could happen
everyone was heartbroken.

Tears were born in our hearts
nobody could imagine from which hands.

Dressed in camouflage, two students
who destroyed lives, brought suffering.

Everything is different now,
I really don't know how.

Oh, my God, that's not fair!
Do these people even care?

I don't want to be here,
I don't want to be there.

All I want is to sit alone and pray,
All I want is to scream one day,
that everybody has the same wish.

KEEP GUNS OUT OF CHILDREN'S REACH.
Liliam Gema Alvarez

Wandering Dog

The dog that wandered
with one seeing eye
out a'sniffin' at the
ground.

Smelling the air
a breeze somewhere
and frogs croak
lazy on the pond.

I'm alone
looking for my bone.
There's a master
out there somewhere.

There's nice lady,
give her a sniff.
She screamed
and ran instead!

Water in the gutter
think I'll have a swaller
and go take a nap
somewhere.

Penelope Parrish

Untitled

The touch of your hand,
The look in your eyes—
Whenever you're near me,
I feel so alive.

We talk for hours
Of this and of that;
The sound of your voice
Brings such joy to my heart.

Wish you could be here
Every day of the year.
But we're miles apart
And there's an ache in my heart.

So hurry back to me, dearest;
I'm waiting right here.
'Til once again we're together,
I'll always love you, my dear.

Tina Strange

To You and Only You

If this is true,
I will listen to you
And know how you feel
About this thrill,
Which cuts like a knife
Through our life.
I realize now
And wonder how
This happened to you
And made you so untrue.
Only if you could have known
How I loved your tone
That whispered in my ear:
I love you, so dear.

Scotti Shay Daw

Together, Forever as One

All it took was just one look
For him to see the sign
I met him and my world was shook
I knew he'd soon be mine

Looking for our soul mates
For all these years of past
In a world that's full of hate
We've found a love that would last

In him I found my best friend
And a happiness I'd never known
I feel this love will never end
And I will no longer be alone

He asked me to marry him
To be his soul mate, his wife
To stay with him through thick and thin
Together, the rest of our lives

I married my best friend, you see
Because of all he means to me
And all that we will ever become
We'll be there together, forever as one.

Michele L. McNulty

In the Rain

To the one I love, Carla Isabel Pereira
You and me touch in space
velvet dream floating forever
in love floating
in the clear sky
kiss of fire
darkness fades

David deAssumpcao

Acceptance

Here, today, I am
Wishing for something to be
That can never be.
Life is here tomorrow
But never stays for long.
We must strive to accept
What is and learn to love
All things as they are.
I will be complete and whole
For all the rest of my life.

Shelia D. Michaud

The Lonely Life

*In loving memory of our mom
who passed away on June 28, 1998*
Aboard the old and sea-worn ship
Across the rotting planks.
To memories of lonely years
of silly, stupid pranks.
Beyond the dark and misty sea
past green and slimy reefs.
Throughout the pages of a book
Like sad and lost beliefs
Underneath a cloudless sky
within a broken soul
upon a pile of shredded wood
without a single goal
above the wet and tangled sails
behind the twisted flags
around the lifeless, empty craft
over dirty rags
Beneath the ripped up magazines
under dirty clothes
toward the far and distant shore
with just a single rose

Leigh Corey

True Empathy

Eyes are ocean
Tears in eyes
Tears are pearls
Pupils are like ships
The water of ocean is salty
Tears are salty
Eyes are ocean
Same shore, same longing
Same thirst, same nuances
Same silence, same turbulence
Same stillness, same solitude
Same depth, same profoundness
Same tide and sinking ships
How much they are alike
Eyes and ocean
Those who plunge in the eyes
never survive
As those who drown in the ocean
never survive.

S. Imrana Nahstar

A Single Bud

Give me not a big bouquet
but rather a single bud
chosen with care
and thought and love
filled with you
and not your riches
apart not from you
but rather of you
a gift to share
and not to own.

Lou Ellyn Edens

Before You Blink

I walk the line,
I seek the gold,
my dream attainable
before I'm old.
Look to the stars,
God's eye to wink,
the future's upon you
before you blink.
Each moment a wonder,
every day is a miracle,
look all around you . . .
it's all quite spiritual.
Share all your love,
make prayers sweet,
enlighten your children
before heavens meet.
Look to the stars,
God's eye to wink,
the future is upon you
before you blink.

Frank J. Maldonado

Heartache

Silence fills the room;
angry words left unsaid
grew deep within,
bursting forth as molten lava,
leaving a trail of destruction.
It was too late . . .
the damage was done.
Hearts cry in their mute voices;
pained eyes mirror their hurt;
tears fall silently; love surely hurts.

J. Martin

Shattered

I've been up, I've been down
I've been twisted 'n turned around
I've been in, I've been out
I've been shattered, spread about
What it comes down to, my friend
When we come down to the end
I am me and you are you
To ourselves we must be true

It doesn't matter what we say
Life will go on anyway
It's not what we say we feel
But what we think we are that's real
We can run; we can hide
We can shut down from inside
Or we can stand and we can fight
And we can make it to the light

Frances Abemathy

With All My Heart

We'll be forever
Together spending time
Our hearts locked, guards two keys
With a golden shine, and
When you hear the love lock click,
We mend, with affection.
The Lord's Baby angels
Made a love connection.
Be merry and toast wine.
A wedding it shall be, for
forever I will cherish
The love you share
With me . . .
By accepting the key to my heart.

William Hoppe

The Leaf

Traveling through its era of time
the innocent leaf hangs on
while watching others fall
and laughing all the while

He begins to dry and brittle
and yet he stays in place
hoping all have noticed
his change of style and grace

Slowly his hold loosens
but he manages to survive
just that little while longer
stating he is alive

Lasting to the very end
he begins to slowly let go
proving to everyone himself
but no one seems to know

Jennifer Mooney

Because of You

Because of you I know that I
Will never settle less.
You're all I ever wanted,
The best—I must confess.

You give me feelings that I never,
Ever had before.
For now I know true happiness
And joy and much, much more.

Now you say that I'm the one,
That gave these gifts to you.
But I think what you really see,
Is your reflection—yes I do.

Of all those feelings bouncing back,
The ones you gave to me.
Oh, wait—perhaps it's both of us,
That's it—it has to be.

I finally found true happiness,
True joy, true peace and such.
I found it in your gentle arms,
And in your tender touch.

Warren Good

To Me You Are . . .

To me you are my bright candle
a light unto my path.

To me you are my funny bone
one to make me laugh.

To me you are my security
I'll never worry again.

To me you are my jewel chest
not held by other men.

To me you are my pure water
with a sip I thirst no more.

To me you are life's beauty
one I can truly adore.

To me you are Talent's talent
a step above the rest.

To me you are a poem's verse
from Longfellow or none the less.

To me you are ecstatic joy
and I could go on and on.

But to me you are worth it
forever from dusk to dawn.

Darrell L. Smith

Silent Friend

Who are you, my silent friend?
I think of you often
I feel I know you
Maybe I don't
Maybe it's just a dream
I will wake up, you will be gone
My heart may hurt
I don't know!
Who could think of me
So much to call and only hear my voice?
Thank you, my friend

Sherry Gail Grindstoff

Weight Loss Waiters

Here's to my peers, all good hams
Trying to lose weight by grams
We count the fat and calories in pounds
But round silhouettes are still around

We can exercise, that's true
Will it shed inches, just for you?
Although we are earnest and clever
Dieting is our best endeavor

When it's over in just four classes
We mere mortals join the masses
So, are we wiser now? Oh, well!
Can we hack it? Only time will tell

When we meet in later years
I expect to hear you're trying!
What you've gained be clear
Pounds and pounds, maybe inches, no lyin'!

Robert Waltsak

The Regulator

I spoke to no one
And none to me
As I strolled
On the sands by the sea
When a pelican lighted
With ponderous grace
Assuming and solemn
Sober face
Then I paused for moment
Then slowed my pace
As I strolled on the sands
By the sea

William J. Byrne

The Real Meaning of Christmas

For my sons, Joe, John, Jason Kinder
It's Christmas Time again my sons,
and everywhere you go,
There are twinkling lights, presents,
and Christmas Trees aglow.
These things are very pretty
they bring you lots of joy, but
The Real Meaning of Christmas lies,
in the birth of a baby boy.
The baby's name is Jesus,
He was sent from God above
to show His understanding
and His everlasting love.
The baby grew to be a man
and then was Crucified,
To save our souls and give us peace
Our Blessed Savior died.
So on this Christmas Morn, my sons,
think not of just your toys,
But of God, who gave His only Son,
for your eternal joys.

Nancy C. Keough

Of Humankind

Realistically thinking . . .
if the world were of freedom
and there were no doors made
to lock a man in, unruly,
to cage him from others who love him.

If one man of words would decide
to take the labels and bad names
off a man to tell about humans
being inhuman, pretending they are God,
to forgive when they see
the consideration to forgive.

To find a power
or opposition, to use as power
and debate himself,
so unconsciously in other men.

Yvonne M. Hampden

Memories

Look into my eyes and see
A window to my soul.
My life and loves are written there
And each one took its toll.
The years that pass leave memories,
Some sweet, some hard to bear.
And as you look into my depths,
You'll find that you are there.
As each day dawns it adds
Another line upon the page.
And when my book is done,
I'll just walk off the darkened stage.
The memories I'll leave behind
Of all that I once knew,
Will wear the colors of the love
That I once knew with you.

Bonnie Krampert

Lost Love

The distance between us grows longer
We're a thousand miles apart
Even though that we are separated
You still are in my heart
It's been forever since we talked
I miss the sound of your voice
We'd be friends again forever
If I had my choice
The times, they've made us different
We've gone our separate ways
But every day my heart tells me
I will love you always
Yes, I know it's over now
What love we had is gone
I've found my life—myself again
And yet, this feeling lingers on
You've taken a piece of my soul
And made a place in my mind
With everything I do in life
A memory of you follows close behind

Wendy Cass Gaarder

Help Me Find the Way

I wandered through the woods one day,
from north to south and east to west,
and wondered to what purpose I was born.

What could I do, what could I say
to make a difference in the world?
What was it I was meant to do?

On bended knee I prayed to God,
Please help me find the way.

Audrey F. Evans

Untitled

When first I lay eyes
On your beautiful face,
I knew I would long
For your sweet embrace.

And as I looked in your eyes,
I knew from that day.
Your thought from my mind
Would never far stray.

I knew then that I love you,
So I'll know right from the start
That if I ever lose you
I'll forever lose my heart.

James T. Chambers

Arizona Moonlight

Arizona moonlight
Cactus in bloom
Cool, enchanted evening
Day breaking soon

Holding you so closely
Not a care in the world
Tell me you love tonight

I have always cherished
Your bright, sunny smile
Wish I could persuade you
To linger awhile

My heart grew so anxious
It was so hard to wait
Until you said yes
I'll be your soul mate

John . Steadman

Puzzled

From whence did I come;
From whence will I go?
My travels while here
Have been happy and not slow,
Reaching heights I would've never
Dreamed I could go.
And now having traveled thus far,
From whence did I come,
And from whence will I go?
The distant stars, the heavens vast,
Is that my future; was that my past?
I've been here many years,
Yet it seems so short.
Just a few more winks of my eyes,
I will know at last.

Hazel S. Green

Debra Joe

When sound is silent
And human activities cease
The still of the evening
In constant defeat
There waits a beckoning call
Come here, come to me
An addiction to an addiction
Where in the heat
Men in one-tenth of their glory
Move with swift feet
Although filled to the brim
They will not eat
They will not eat during
The sacrifice of dement and time
A twist of spirit
A twist of lime
Sweet to taste, bitter to the soul
A washed-out feeling of self-control

D. Dragon Moon

The Pilgrim's Thanksgiving Prayer

Father, as we bow before Thee,
Please hear us as we pray;
We ask Thee for Thy blessing
On this Thanksgiving Day.

We thank Thee for our daily bread,
For this table before us spread,
For family and friends who gather here;
We ask Thee to be very near.

We thank Thee for the sun and rain,
And for this harvest of golden grain,
For strength to till this fertile land,
For mighty trees, like sentinels stand.

We have wondrous visions, Father,
Builder of all creations,
Of a land that stretches far beyond;
Help us build a mighty nation.

May we ever look to Thee, Father,
As our ruler in every way,
And may we ever keep in our hearts
The spirit of this Thanksgiving Day.

Anna Maxine Holt Leak

In the Light

In all the hurt and pain,
There is a hope that still remains.

In all the greed and lust,
There is a fairness that is just.

In all the hunger and despair,
There is a faith beyond compare.

In all the prejudice and pride,
There is a love that will abide.

In all the hate and war we see,
There is a peace for you and me.

In all the fear and horror around,
There is a calm that abounds.

In all the sadness and the sorrow,
There is a strength to find tomorrow.

In all the anger and cruelty,
There is a kindness that can be.

For if we look beyond our plight,
We will see God's heavenly light.

Joan Huffman

Snowflakes

I think there is
no stillness
Quieter than falling snow.

Tiny crystals
drift the sky.
Flakes that twist
and twist and twirl,
Drift the hills
in fields of white.
Blanch the trees.
Frost the grass.
Twirling, silent,
Waiting the dawn
to bring the light.

Twirling, twirling.
  Snowflakes
twisting, turning
  In the night.

Clarence Bates

Unnoticed

I sit there in the shadows,
darkness, hoping you would see me.
To my dismay, you pass.
Me unnoticed.

You then give me
attention for a moment in time.
In that instant, you leave.
Me unnoticed.

At night I pray
that soon you would realize me.
But it is still
Me unnoticed.

Finally, you see the light
at the end of the tunnel.
You love me.
Me no longer unnoticed.

LaShire Hull

Treasured Miracles

More precious than
Gold, rubies, and pearls
Close to my heart I keep.

Each loving friend
Treasured miracles
Any loss they have, I weep.

Life's burdens and joys
And shared with each
Great happiness I reap.

Unknown paths await me
I plunge into tomorrow
Spirit guides
Friends calm my fears

A s
Into the future
I leap.

Doris Smith Nath

Tracks in the Snow

Tracks in the snow
Are like marks made on the mind
Of an innocent child.
Some are crooked and
Some are straight.
Some are deep and some are faint.
Some are fresh and some are old.
Each has its meaning as it unfolds.
A teacher can, with a little care,
Imprint upon the child's open mind
Lasting tracks of right and wrong
That he will use his whole life long.
So teachers, take care you impress
That child with the best that you possess.

Louise K. Salyer

Consequence

Echoes of pain ring through the streets.
Endless gloom and disenchanted repeat.
The hidden embers of burning love,
We try to defeat.
Pretending fools are different
Than who we meet.
Drain and disconnection we create.
Nowhere is everywhere.
We build kingdoms of insecurity.
The Consequence is,
Forgetting our Childhood Dreams.

Jamie Pease

What? Me, Write a Poem?

You asked me for a new poem.
Now? This minute is all
racketty-tack, or maybe,
it is really snacketty-click?
Everyone is pulling at me
this way and over there.
Don't look at the clock!
Suddenly yesterday is three
days ago last month! I need
to go quietly out early to
hug a tree, find some green,
look at cool delicate ferns,
so the words can come with laughter,
winging to you!

Jean Pitts

A Rose Blossoms into the Night

A rose blossoms into the night,
With peace and tranquility;
Her soul's soared into flight,
To meet the trinity.

A rose blossoms into the night,
No more pain to suffer;
God's made it all right,
She's taken what's offered.

A rose blossoms into the night,
God's taken her home;
Leads her the light
To sit beside the thrown.

A rose blossoms into the night,
She'll never be awakening;
From restful sleep tonight,
'Cause of God's beckoning.

Jeannie Kincaid

Strangers

I feel him,
Though I cannot see him.
We talk through our letters,
Though we have never talked.
We live in a different time,
Still I know him.
We may never meet,
For a thousand years to come.
But I know him,
And he knows me.
Still, we are strangers
In a different world,
In a different time.
But I'll wait for him always.

Amy E. Zacek

To Whom I Love

When the sun rises,
I think of him.
I eat and sleep
With him on my mind.
He's in my thoughts,
No matter what.
Harsh words are spoken,
But the love we share is greater.
When I watch a movie,
He is the hero,
When I am the damsel in distress.
When I close my eyes at night,
He is all I see.
This is to whom I love,
My husband.

Rhonda Smith

Golden Rings and Silver Threads

The golden rings upon their hands
Symbols of the golden years just past
Golden rings for heartfelt pledges
Beginning lives of a love to last

The silver threads of faith in God
Of seeking diving direction
Of working together, side by side
Silver threads giving love perfection

Laughter, love, forgiveness, prayer
Thoughtfully, carefully used as tools
Blended with respect and honor
Gathering days into a strands of jewels

Sons and wives, now grandchildren, too
Gems of a life of love they've led
Beauty given freely to all
From golden rings and silver threads

Pat Franklin

Loving You

Loving you has been the best thing
    in my life.

Loving you is the best thing
    in my life.

Loving you and knowing you
    has made me complete.

You speak to me in ways
    I never knew I could hear.

] love resonates
    in the very core of me.

Loving you,
    just loving you,
        has helped me be me.

Lorrie Serrao

The Great Wall

The vultures came to gnaw at my chest
as the last one left I wished him best
The great wall of me
The Lord had said I passed his test
when asked the answers I said I guessed
The great wall of me
The Devil invited me to be his guest
as I left his hell I made a mess
The great wall of me
The woman came in loves fine dress
as she left my heart she left it blessed
The great wall of me
The eagle came to build his nest
as he reached my wall I gave his quest
The great wall of me

Robert E. Skiff II

Childhood Lost

Why do some children fail to know
How to enjoy the simple life?
They're constantly craving action,
Violent and cruel in their strife.

True joy and laughter are missing;
Just cruelty and hatred abound.
To them life holds no real future;
They live for now, to astound!

It's sad to have lost childhood.
The teen years of life are lost, too.
It's time for parents—to be parents!
Giving love that's long overdue.

Ruth Enid Walter

Welcome Wondrous Light

Welcome, welcome
Wondrous light.
Surround me with delight
So astonishing bright
You are just so right
You are wisdom
You are understanding
You are warm
You are healing
You are just so marvelous
Welcome wondrous light.

Misery has no place
Complaining to complain
Treat yourself
Chase your dreams
Join up with the right team
God will provide the means
He's merciful
He's righteous
Welcome wondrous light.

Tesha A. Vinson

The Last Word

Remember, when I die,
Bury me at Dongnai,
Kept guard, a grasshopper,
Covered, a dragonfly!

Why? Where's your concubine?
Oh! She can't no more wait.
She has to get married
To enjoy her green age!

And, where's now your wife.
Is she still in your house?
Yes, but she's very tired
Of waiting day and night!

At last, she recognizes
It's time to say good-bye.
Therefore, I die or I live.
She doesn't really mind!

So, in cold ground I'll lie,
Deserved for a lady-killer.
Joy, anger, love and hate
Becomes nothing after life!

Sum Duong

True Dream

The way I wrote by candlelight
Was God's greatest gift to me,
Resting on a windowsill,
Watching the full moon so bright.

I dreamed an awesome destiny—
Perhaps God would help me through,
To see the world with greatest joy
And tell my lovely story.

One cannot be pessimistic
To let all the joy go by.
Meet the folks who love you so;
Return your love more kindly.

See the world in different ways,
The sunrise so awesome, too;
Write by candlelight no more,
And I see the happy days.

I hope this poem someday
Will be read with joyfulness,
For I had a dream elsewhere,
And made it to the U.S.A.

Béla Ambrus

Head over Heels

My body heavy
with sleep
and my mind
submerged in your eyes,
falling deep
into the blue pools
that reflect our
two worlds,
slowly becoming one.
Moonlight strikes
and refracts,
casting desires and dreams
onto my soul,
like a blank sheet
of innocence . . .
waiting for a heart like yours
to take control.

Scott Thompson

He Loves To Hate Her

He loves to hate her
He loves tears streaming
He loves wife beatings
He loves hysterical screaming
He loves nightmarish feelings
He loves the wretched mess
He ends and begets
Thriving deep within his soul
His heart so ruthlessly cold
This little tale unfolds
At crime scene number ninety-nine

Brenda Thurmond

Dawn

The air is sweet and soft and still.
Gentle wavelets bathe the shore.
Not long ago the birds went south
To warmer lands to chant their love.

Here, 'neath autumn's paling sun,
In pensive silence, I recall
A stirring promise came to me
When night had hardly gone.

'Twas not a voice, no, not a song
But just a thought, a dream, perhaps,
Awakened me at dawn.

"Thy heart is not alone," it said.
"Nor is it without art."
 I could not sleep, I rose instead,
To see new life, a rising sun
More glorious than I had ever known.

Elizabeth Bishop Gilmore

Your Pillow

If I could relive each moment
lying in your arms,
melting with your kisses,
it would be exactly the same
as the pearls of thought
I have stored away
in a crystal with your name on it.
Each tender caress lingers there,
wrapped in sweet emotions
that flow when lover's touch.
How I long for you already
as I cling to the pillow
wrapped in your scent.
I drift in sweetness.

Phyllis Ann Parker Di Nardo

One Drop

One drop of deep, dark red
From the thorns upon his head
One drop from his striped back
Where the whip cut with a crack
One drop from his hands or feet
Where nails were driven in so deep
One drop when they pierced his side
My savior bled for me and died
One drop saved me from death and sin
One drop gave me peace within
One drop bought me and set me free
One drop was shed just for me

Jolene Goss

Those Days

Those days I remember well
The curse that haunts me
Straight from Hell
The obsession just to see your face
No matter what the cost
The bitter sweet sting of love's wasp
The jubilant joy the driving pain
The languish that still remains
All others they still pale
Against the magic of your spell

Brenda K. Markgraf

A Bond To Create

There is a closeness
I hold deep inside
A feeling of love
That I will never hide
A special tenderness
In my heart is held
A fragile emotion
And an undying devotion

There is a seriousness
A sensation meant for heart
Without the sad tears
And the pain of departing
There's something vital
That hearts can gain
With every breath of life inhaled
Like the chances all promises take
Inside our hearts we'd never fail
And a bond we would create!

Richard H. Smith

You

How your hair sparkles.
How your smile brightens my day.
I love you so much.
I wish you loved me like I love you.
So, forever I keep this secret
Hidden in my heart,
Hoping that, someday,
You will find my feelings out.

Emery Taylor

The Beach

I feel the cool sand
Cover my feet and toes
I hear the rumbling waves
And the smell of salt fills my nose

It's almost as if
I'm one with the ocean
It's so special and quiet
Kind of like a magic potion

Shannon Jones

Foghorn

Muted moaning far from shore,
It lingers in the air,
A rocking sound that comforts one
Who's safe and snug a bed.
It wraps its tone around the mind,
And gently lulls all thoughts.
Secure in sense of days gone by,
It is the adult's lullaby.

Nanette Currie

Lightning Bug Thoughts

Thoughts go fluttering through my brain
Like lightning bugs they don't remain;
If I can't catch them when they light,
They vanish in the summer night.

Dorothy Allen Nicholson

If a Cow Says Moo

Oh, what can I do
If a cow says moo
In the middle of a night in June;
Or if she eats hay
In the middle of May,
And drinks water from the blue lagoon;
Or if in July
She makes me cry
Because she demolished a fence;
Causing eyes to blink
Before I can think
If she really is worth six pence;
But reflecting once more
While in the barn door
How haunting her big brown eyes;
For only bites of bran
She gives milk for this man
And she really is quite some prize.

Randolph F. Simon

Good-bye

As I walked away, I said, "Good-bye."
I didn't hear you reply.
I know I let you down,
And you broke my heart,
Even with the wall around!
I wish it hadn't ended that way.
The torment with me will stay.
I wish I had heard you say,
"Good-bye."

Virginia E. Vey

Fall to Pieces

To all who support me
A loved one falls
And with them, my heart
Slowly that's when
I fall apart
God takes them at will
Or we simply lose touch
Sometimes the far distance
Is simply too much
We take for granted
When we know they are there
It's when they go
That we see why we care
I guess then we'll notice
Just what life teaches
But until then
I'll just fall to pieces

Christina Shields

Time

This vast expanse of time we bide
Is just a changing, moving tide
With many beginnings and an end
That we may yet again ascend
To the better life we often sought
A life to live the way we ought

Anthony Wyant

Life

Oh, what is life
But a mere existence,
Full of laughter and despair,
A never ending illusion
Performed for all to see.
It is a thing of immense delight,
But also of great sadness.
Life can be an empty shell,
Impossible to fill,
Or a happy shrine
Full of love and joy.
It continues through the ages,
Like a long-standing tree.
But it can end in a silent moment,
Only to repeat.

Peg DeVeny

Michael Valore

Michael Valore is his name,
The City of Cleveland his place of fame.
And on this you can rely:
His vodka martinis dry
Have the strongest taste
Since the first toothpaste
Our ancestors once did buy.

Whenever a customer weeps,
That confidence he keeps.
He's ever forgiving to all,
Even to those who fall.
Legions of friends has he,
The likes you never did see.
So courteous and skillful
And never a bit willful
He quenches all thirst with glee.

Rush P. Webb

Breathe

For Greg
Let me breathe you into my soul
I'll be anything you want me to
I'd give up everything I have
Forever just to be with you

I'm everything you've wanted
In a dream that has come true
I'm the hope you breathe when all
The pain that you have felt is through

I love you every way you've been
And every way you ever will
You'll hear me whisper in our time
The words I breathe, I love you still

The wish I breathe will be for you
And in it everything I feel
A silver glimmer in the dark
Is just to know that you are real

If it came down to just one life
And one of us was bound to leave
I'd give you my life in your hand
With all the love that I will breathe

Elaine Appelhanz

Your Child

There is wonder in his eyes
as he sees the world anew.
He asks so many questions
and believes the answers from you.

So, do not be so casual about
those remarks you make,
for this young mind of innocence
is being formed for the path he'll take.

For whatever kind of character
in you he sees today,
shapes and encourages the actions,
he'll do along his way.

A child will see your example,
even if you're unaware,
for he watches every action
and hears your words of care.

So, in your daily living,
be mindful of the things you do.
Be careful of each thing you say,
for your child will mimic you!

Doris Christian

In Heaven Above

I never could have imagined
How in such a short time
Someone could touch my heart so deep
All with pantomime

There were no words spoken
Our eyes, they did not meet
But our love was being shared
In our every heartbeat

So young and so tiny
His chances were slim
He struggled for life
I struggled for him

I held him so close
In my arms when he died
I couldn't let go
I just sat there and cried

Someday I may have the answers
About my tiny love
And why God chose to keep him
In Heaven above

Cindie Suders

Love's Serenade

*To my husband and children, Norman,
Sybil, Inez, Arnold, Courtney*
Let's serenade in the moonlight
Let's serenade tonight
All through the day
I always pray,
Sweetheart, for you
Let's sing our own peaceful love song
Let's chant it all along
Darling, I'm yours
All through those hours,
Sweetheart so true.

Come serenade in the moonlight
Come serenade tonight
My days are blue
I long for you
Sweetheart, be mine
Let's call together the moment
Of love, which Cupid sent,
Darling, I'm yours
All through those hours,
Sweetheart so true.

Ivy Constable Richards

My Mother

For all the love you've given
When the day was bright and fair,
When there were special times
And lots of happiness to share,
And for all the love you've given,
Even when the day was long,
When you felt very tired,
But your love was warm and strong,
For the love so sure and constant,
That your heart has always shown,
This brings a world of grateful love
Meant just for you alone.

Melvin Van Zeeland

Wayward Exodus

As you embark on a voyage
Stormy seas await
Over the horizon
Carrying cargo so precious
Navigating so blindly
Taken this journey
Once before
The lightning struck
And you turned for familiar shore
Planning to return
Willing to pay the price
Clinging to the hope
That lightning
Won't strike twice

Eric L. Synder

Drifting Dreams

Thoughts wasted on dreams,
Dreams to far away to come true,
Wasted with every puff you take
Drowned in every sip you make
Hiding deep inside of you,
I see all that you don't.
The life wasted to early
for your dreams to catch up,
Doing stupid things to fit in,
Or maybe just to wasted time.
They say life goes on,
but only time goes on.
You only live once . . . live it well.
Time is used.
Life is wasted.

April Constable

Reflections

I muse of days gone by,
Of friends, kin, and beloved ones,
Then end with a sigh.
They are gone, as water that runs.

So much has been lived
And now is in the past.
Today and tomorrow are ahead,
Yet only the past will last.

Thank Heaven for memories.
I can think only of the good.
The bad recedes into a darkness
That is there and now understood

To look ahead to a life fulfilled,
Overlooking the mishaps that could befall
And hoping for guidance
For one, yet for all.

And so I turn to Heaven above
To fulfill cherished dreams,
Happy days with fond friends,
Utopia, or so it seems.

L. Ryder Park

Thirty-Nine Plus Forty

Today as I've reached this 39 plus 40,
Look back—it's been one continued sortie.
Been dive-bombed by self-righteous majority.
It's really a wonder how I got past 40.

As boy was to receive wisdom from old sage,
Those that double talk—beware of their page.
Past middle age, valuable gift was given me.
Yes, poetry, that gave me a heart that's free.

Oh, I have things go wrong like my old car.
It seems I cannot stretch nearly as far.
The plumbing every once in a while fouls up,
Get it in order with water, cup after cup.

My headlights seem to perform in good shape,
But my elephant ears, words seem to escape.
And my get-along isn't the worst yet,
But this computer seems to foul up and forget.

Never, ever tried to be man's pleaser that I know,
Once tried to be woman's, was impossibly so.
Now that I've got to this, 39 plus 40 today,
I'll take it easy, and play it day to day.

    Lee Wells

The Inn by the Sea

In half sleep, she whispers, the storm has passed,
golden rays of early morning sun pierce the dark room of
the Inn, then we remembered the storm last night.

Rain mist, rising from washed shores and driftwood, appears
like silver dust, slowly falling from rainbows to wash
the face of the sea, comber silent ripples marking the sand,
shimmering waves carry yellow sand from ancient sea beds as
the gulls' loud call breaks the silence again.

So soon, again—dark clouds bank across the horizon
chasing gulls to safe haven in dark coves on shore and the
wind-song returning to play ancient music in twisted pine
and washed shag—whistling shrill chords across the roof of
the Inn, swiftly dancing across the surf by changing galaxy
and pull of the moon, to sing and play for us again.

Hear the wind-song leaving? Rain mist appears once more
like silver dust in rainbows, slowly failing to wash
the face of the sea, and gulls' loud call breaks the silence
once more. Hear the wind-song leaving? It will come
back another time, to sing and play for me.

    J. H. Honeycutt

The Seasons

The spring brings buds with colors bright
And singing birds sail on the wing.
Gentle rains bring season's flowers
As nature wakes to lovely spring.

Summer pushes spring aside.
The dreaded heat will soon begin.
Maturing crops for winter's needs
Are stored in basements, jars, and bins.

Fall comes along on lazy feet.
Trees don their colors, warm and bold;
All dressed in yellows, browns, and greens,
And dazzling reds and burnished gold.

Winter bristles, sharp and raw,
With ice and snow and bitter cold.
Men seek the shelter of their homes
And beasts, the shelter of the fold.

Seasons come and seasons go.
They're all a part of the Master's plan
Who, in His wisdom, rules the Earth
That feeds and clothes both beast and man.

    Marjorie Carpenter

My Guardian Angel

I can not see you, but I know you are there.
You protect me in my home, outside, and everywhere.
No matter what I do, I can not get rid of you.
But why would I want to?
For God sent you to me.
That way He always has someone to watch over me,
To help me do right not wrong,
And with God's word keep me strong.
My guardian angel, I love you,
For all that I do not know, you do.
Please stay with me tell the end of my time,
Even though I will not see you at any one time.

    Tony J. Tummons

A Unicorn

My granddaughters sat talking with me the other day,
As they told me a story of their dreams far away.
As I listened closely, a unicorn came by,
Caught in their spell, with love in his eyes.

I watched him listen as their story unfold.
So intent was he, no fears to behold.
Only love he felt as their words sang a song,
And I felt it grow as they continued along.

He stood there so long, as I looked on amazed,
Caught in their song, with the magic it made.
And his love filled the air that surround us three.
My two granddaughters, a unicorn, and me.

    Claudia Kosinski

Seasons the Taste of Life

To Sister Marion and family general (love—peace always), Lloyd
Seasons are the taste of life, in them
they can bring the spirit in spices in lives
exciting all the senses, dulled by life's
unfavorable and untasteful circumstances.

June and summer most say are their favorite first,
like a savored beverage on one's taste buds it bursts;
as the sands and salt of the Earth, it saturates with
sunshine our moods and acrid smells, with appetizing taste.

Fall, then comes deliciously relished still by others.
Sweet fermenting scents of dampened leaves and soil,
become a constant reminder around us all through
moistened bark and leaves which fall—fall, yes, oh, lovely fall.

That winter shall come soon with its nutmeg flavor
atmosphere along with its snow cone mountain tops
and ice cream lane and meadows, festive dreamy states in
kind, along with exciting party taste and sober thoughts of mind.

Once again then spring arrives where its fragrances
of cool lakes and streams replenished our beings
and refresh our senses in taste with newness of life it brings,
the past year now gone ahead—
mouth-watering, ardent taste of seasons.

    Lloyd Puckett

Dante's De'tente

To my children, Mary, Faye, Jeff, and Dave
Dante, today your timeless grandeur holds
Valid reminder of our trampled years;
Still towering firm against vain, selfish goals.

Faith over malice guides man to the heights;
A measured living aims for paradise.
Courageous souls hold through their daunting nights.

No temples have been built to honor doubt;
Lofty cathedrals rise to hope and prayer.
Out of the flaming vortex comes a shout:

"Abandoned—all who wallow in despair!"

    Myrtle D. Zimmerman

The Sailor's Widow

Here romantically on this beach they stand
With bare foot toe, and hand in hand.
They vow this will be their special place
As ocean spray christens their loving embrace.

Sad the day they learned that he must be
That sailor who, duty calls back to the sea.
He will sail forth to another patriot's war
And she will wait as she has done before.

He smiled and said, "Wait and be brave,
For soon I will return on the breaking wave."
But now she stands on that same shore
And this beach is not what it was before.

It has become for her a lonely place
Where never again will she feel his embrace.
Yes, the sea gull calls and soars as before
And the wave chases the sandpipers on the shore.

The wind whips spray upon her face and hair.
She stands and sighs and is lonely there.
Her heart is heavy and her face is wet with tear.
She waits and looks, knowing he will never appear.

Leon Peter Wren

Reality

To Bamboo, will miss and love you, hugs and kisses!
There are only two ways you can lead your life
You can lead it in a dream
Or . . .
You can lead it in reality
I used to lead my life in reality
When you were around
Now I lead my life in a dream, a dream with you in it
The sweetest dream that he dreamed
Realizing how I took advantage of your preserves
I drifted into this sweet dream
Filled with the smell of roses
Filled with the happiness we used to share
That wasn't my reality
I have no way to say how sorry I am,
To you in my reality nor in my dream
But, I can say sorry in every prayer
In every prayer I pray in my dream and reality
I'll be waiting for a sign from you
Telling me you have forgiven me
And my welcome to reality!

Cintia Dacosta

Dream Quest

Follow your dreams
Wherever they take you;
Follow your dreams
Dreams are what make you.

Dreams are your wishes,
Your thoughts and your hopes
They keep you going
Through all of your slopes.

A dream is an ongoing path,
Where only the dreamer can go;
A twisted and tortuous road,
But, the map is concealed in your soul.

A dream is a promise of all you can be,
A promise that is hard to fulfill,
But through all the times, the good and the bad,
Always keep your strong will.

A dream is a beautiful sunset
Which only that dreamer can view
It is rewarding to work towards, and hard to achieve
But in the end it's an honor to you.

Colleen Katana

Progress

To my beloved father, Vincent Kursweil, Conservationist of Mother
In the beginning,
God created Heaven and Earth.
It was about this time that
Father Time took Mother Earth
As his beautiful bride.
As in all marriages, there were
Mountain, peaks, and valleys,
But in this union, for many centuries,
There really weren't any major problems—
Until Father Time went galloping off,
Off with Progress, about
The middle of the twentieth century.
Progress, then, really made an onslaught
On Mother Earth, whether it be
Her atmosphere, water, land—
Unless Father Time wakes up now!
Right now! Make Progress stop this abuse.
Mother Earth will collapse,
Father Time and Man, with this Progress,
Will be no more!

Anna B. Kursweil

Evolution of Self

I feel myself evolving—changing
Going in a direction that is unfamiliar to me
I am curious but apprehensive
A place of unknown origins
Looking, exploring, absorbing all that is around me
I exit this place of unknown origins
I continue on this journey, wondering
Continuing with questions unanswered. . . .

Rachel Edwards

No Mystery to Him, but Indeed for Us

When we lay down our heads
At the closing of day,
We know not whether this will be
The final, closing chapters to our lives;
Only He and He alone has those answers.

So each night, we sledge through the depth of darkness,
A replication of a sign of death;
And according to His schedule for our lives,
He carries us through to that other side
Then back to the wakening of another day.
And still, we know nothing of the coming hours
Nor the outcome for the closing of day;
Only He and He alone can fill that blank;
As the way it's supposed to be!

Joan E. Gettry

Too Early for Roses

In love for my dear mother, from your daughter, Inez
Mother died early in the spring, daffodils,
crocus, tulips, were only joys to bring.
Mother loved my flower garden especially roses,
they brought her happiness, to see them bloom
with color so bright in the moth of June.
Time came for her funeral and no roses to
bring to lay on her coffin.
I sent my love in remembrance to Mother dear,
I wouldn't forget, I hope the road mother
took in the glory land; her and God have met.
I brought tulips and kissed them, the best
I could find, and said, "Here is my love and best
memories to Mother Dear," as if my lips have touched
her lips in divine, my thoughts of remembrance to
leave Mother with pretty tulips to give her my love
and hope God in Heaven above, created her sleep
in a garden of roses.

Inez Kobus

Stolen Virtue

As I look around my world,
The pictures I see frighten me.

They tug at memories from the past,
Remind me of horrors and night haunts.

Things creeping up on me in my sleep
As my nightmares come to life.

Images of things I'd rather not know of,
And images I have always known.

My life is entangled in a web of disgrace.
It holds me to my despair like cement.

This world sucks dry all of my self-respect.
It pulls from me all of my desire for life.

To describe these places I know of and have been
Would be too horrific for anyone to bear.

All the people who try to get close to me
Lose themselves in the emptiness that my soul holds as its own.

People become victims of my psychotic tendencies.
My darkness enfolds them as they come into my life.

As I sleep, my soul carries them to my world of torment
To become a part of the horror we see around us every day.

Pamela S. Adkins

A Christmas Tree

We put a Christmas tree up once a year, to honor
Jesus' birthday for this time of the year.

When we take it down we often forget,
Why we put it up and what it really meant.

He stood for goodwill to men and peace on
Earth and often we do forget.

If you leave it up for one year maybe you will
Remember why Jesus is so dear.

When you come home feeling blue and sad look at the
Tree and I promise you will feel good and glad.

The tree stands for Gods' love, who will always
Care and teaches us to always share.

Leave it up for one year,
maybe your worries will disappear

Look at it every night and see how Gods' love
will always shine so bright.

Gaetano Ibelli

Golden Leaves

Golden leaves are falling, and remind me of you
Last Autumn when our great friendship, loyal and true
Grew closer. With joy, it happened! We fell in love!
Our romance seemed filled with sweet blessings from above.
As I watched the lovely leaves dropping down so fast
I thought; the fine perfect things never seem to last.
You wrote! We cannot marry. I do not love you.
That is not so. Why? To find truth I will pursue!
This changes my life. My heart aches. I feel bereft
Our cherished dreams vanished. Not one of them is left.
We planned to begin soon, sharing life together,
I had no reason to doubt your love or whether
You were sincere. All mine! Everything was sublime,
Fortunately, you revealed your feelings in time.
I never could bear being hurt like this again
In the light of "Honesty" obviously then.
I must think of myself, wisely, and say "Farewell!"
And hope some day we find new love, and "Peace" as well.
Loved ones and good friends know our love affair is through.
But dear girl, I am still, yes "still!" in love with you.

Laura E. Miller

Remember

I see the anguish in your eyes,
the paleness of your face.

I hear your call to me for help,
a plea you've never made.

I feel—and know—
the torture you are going through,
the self recrimination.
Oh, yes!

I'll give my hand to you—a fraction of my soul.
I only ask that you remember,

I reached the same dense mountain top
so very long ago, fell into the deep,
dark abyss below and never found my way again.
Remember.

L. Gwen Shirah

Siege

In memory of my loving mother, Edna Savadsky
I sit here in my apartment cocoon
protected from sounds external
with my white noise shield

While I elect to fight the demons within
the pain of suffering tastes so real
like licking a piece of metal

As I swallow the sour taste of strangeness
I'm aware that whipped cream is also bad
I can die from sweet tasting saturated fat
or watch the beauty of the solar eclipse
rapidly strip my sight if I don't protect it

I can place myself under siege
If I choose to ignore reality

Richard Savadsky

Why's and Wherefore's

My thoughts this day
And not to my dismay
Centered on why's and wherefore's for me—
How did I become so devoted to composing poetry?
There was a genetic factor.
My mother had poetic ability,
So finally in my retirement
I latched onto this facility.
As a fellow in the U. U. religion,
I know that few of us are utterly divine or Stygian.
We seek truth, we focus above
On all we can categorize
As justice and love.
Unlike fundamentalists,
We do not espouse rigid dogmas or creeds.
The essence of it all
Emanates from humanist seeds!
Doing for others
Heads our list of druthers!

Bert A. Kanwitt

Grandmother's Garden

The sun grows long across her furrows
shadowing leaf and silvering hair
Grandmother tears sink deep
into the lives planted there
salting each heart with her memory

Her springs were as harsh as her winters
time kept its heartless vow
If she could but see the handsome bouquet
we gather on each fertile bough
grafted and nursed with her life

Anne Wilson

Untitled

Earth defiled
Man gone wild
Nothing here for the little child

Blood in the streets
Scraps and rap
Listen to the beat, hear the devil tap

Bubbled minds
Eyes stone-cold
A twisted mass of dust and bone

Evil romps
On a fierce black horse
Death plays a tune on a rusty harp

Broken hearts
In a bleeding bowl
The hourglass cracked the sand stands low

Withered souls
Hang upside down
Still
The sun comes up
The Earth whirls round

Frances Reynolds

Unique Star

Ode to Sr. M. Eustella, age 95
The whisper came softly in her ear
The time is near to take leave on here
A new kind of life you shall begin
Away you must go from hearth and kin

To ease their pain
Your brother's anguish from sheer neglect
From poverty he did not expect
Indifferent love, even abuse
The years of sickness he did not choose

To ease their fear
Your brother's great pangs of loneliness
You shine the light of togetherness
Dread of what's in store from up above
You give him comfort from God's deep love

To ease her soul

The whisper now is louder call
Farewell, beloved, I must leave you all
Away I must go from hearth and kin
God's service I will, I must, enter in
To ease my soul

Marie L. Postel

Foquita (Little Seal)

To my friend and partner, Victor Cornejo
With summer spent, fall had come
When the moon rode high in the hazy sky
When raindrops fell to cloud your face
And silence surrounded us in that ethereal place

The water caressed me back and forth
As clouds rolled in from the North
You gently scooped me from the sea
In your arms, you carried me

From the gulf on the eve of morn
At the start of a wondrous storm
The sun broke through and rose
Even as you lightly pressed my nose

For times to come and those that have passed
With fortunes told in the looking glass
Through high elation and etched sadness
Travelling within life's ultimate madness

Rita L. Rawson

Heart and Soul

That good-loving man makes me feel so warm.
Even in my dreams at night, I'm in his arms.
When he says "I love you," my heart begins to melt.
He makes me feel more emotions than I've ever felt.
His love is priceless and could never be bought,
But if it could, I wouldn't give the money a second thought.
He lets me know that I'm safe and wanted,
And it's with his tender words of love I'm haunted.
He brings me tears of joy, and never tears of pain.
His love's forever falling down on me like rain.
Not a day goes by that I'm not reminded that he cares,
But sometimes his sweetness still catches me unaware.
I would give up my world if that's what he asked,
For to give him my love is a precious task.
I can't get him out of my head or my heart,
And I know I would die if we were apart.
Now I hand him my heart on a silver platter,
For nothing else in this world could possibly matter.
I know that without him I could never be whole.
This is why I am his, my heart and my soul.

Lacey Irvin

Doin' the Best I Can

I'm doin' the best I can, man,
But where do I fit in God's ultimate plan?

I try hard to do that which is right,
To stay out of trouble and not pick a fight.

But while the spirit is willing, the flesh is weak,
And the wrong that I do is not what I seek.

Don't judge me too harshly though, you without sin,
Who never seems to lose and who it comes natural to win.

How can you understand the life that I've had
When you don't even know what it's like to be sad?

Raised in a family where it has always been well,
How can you possibly visualize a life that's been hell?

So please don't judge me by your way of life,
Where harmony prevails and there is no strife.

Just help me up and point me the right way,
For it's actions that count and not what you say.

While you seem to know where you fit in God's great plan,
Are you sure you are doin' all you can, man?

Harry Butts

A Work in Progress

Even before the beginning there was Spirit,
    Supreme Being, the Prime Mover—GOD
Love, Law, Timelessness filled that incredible
    vastness of unbounded space, time, and energy

Movement, change, and creativity without ceasing
    are the benchmarks of this colossus—infinitesimal
atoms, microscopic organisms, light traveling for billions
    of years at 186,000 miles per second

Earth encircles one of the 100 billion stars in the Milky Way—
    that sparkling galactic band in the midnight sky where
galaxies meet, pass, collide, cannibalize, and even light
    cannot escape the magnetic power of the Black Holes

Love, law, and spirit continue to create perpetually—"Blue Stars"
    are new suns aborning, babies arrive with 100 billion
neurons awaiting tender loving care to systematize that wondrous
    complex of vision, language, and motor skills

Created in the image of the Creator, that same Divine Spirit
    is the core of our spiritual nature, all religions and
the revelations given through God-Realized messengers
    But only one time in all Earth's millions of years?

G. Calvin Tooker

Retrospect

How can I make you understand
That my words are from my heart and soul
And not just ramblings of other men?
How can I make you understand that the life of this man
Will be spent in retrospect
For not having been able to make you understand?

Wilson F. Machin Jr.

Reminiscences of a Lost One

In loving memory of Violet and Chap Moore and Gerry Roderick
Just because someone loses their physical being,
Nothing can chase away the spirit.
You'll see them everywhere and in everything!
All those little things you took for granted,
The phone calls when you least expected them,
And those words that just seemed to be right.
Remembering will surprise you in the day
And comfort you in the night.

The mind and its memory will serve you well.
The sky will be blue again and the birds will sing.
Sometimes, you will be melancholy and sad.
Then you will remember and your heart will swell.
All the good times . . . the hugs . . . and the love.
And without . . . you'd have no sense of being!
Never would I ask to have missed any of the times we
Shared . . . pain mellows . . . after time.
The love and caring are forever mine.

Patricia A. See

Phantom Oaks

Many mighty oaks graced that space,
Where now you see a concrete sea of grey.
Those who only see the good in life as money
Determined their fate and concluded they could not stay.
So uprooted was everyone and heartlessly hauled away.
They developed the land, then turned it to stone.
Not an image remain to hint that this place
Was where an oak tree forest had grown.
But those oaks have a secret, their spirits did linger,
For those with special hearts to enjoy.
For if you look close, when the moon is hung right,
Or the sun placed just so, a miracle one can behold.
All the trees, just where they were, gently swaying in the breeze.
And when the wind blows just the right way
One can hear the rustling leaves, and the birds among the branches.
Can you see the phantom trees living on despite their absence?
Can you hear them living on in today's fast world?
Remember them and see with your heart
That those mighty oaks have yet to depart,
But remain to remind us of the way things used to be.

Starsha Truesdale

Self Study

This is my face; know it well.

Hard-staring charcoal eyes peering out,
with a certain intensity, from a sun-browned face
narrowly calculating the distance from youth to
old age while observing all that strips me of naivete.

Lips that curl downward and grow taut
with the difficulty of reconciling yesteryears
with the present, then pull back, revealing a
snarling grimace and eager teeth.

Thick black hair tousled by wind,
made brittle by harsh sunlight, flowing
over a pockmarked yet unwrinkled visage like a
tarantula's slender leg.

This is my face—caught between a wish to remain innocent
as a child and a great lust to face adulthood.

Dennis Jolis

A Message

To my loving boyfriend, Matt Bell, who's always been there
I stand alone on this hill of rolling grass,
The light green grass that seems to go on forever,
The wind blowing softly around me,
It embraces me like a blanket;
I stand silent and listen,
Listen to the trees swaying ever so slightly from side to side,
Then I see the purplish flowers that splotch the never-ending green,
Their smell filling the air with their soft scent;
They all seem to be sending me a message,
A message only meant for me;
The birds chirp and fill the area with song,
The bees hum along; they all are a piece of the message,
The message meant for me;
They all are reminding me,
Reminding me of you!

Rochelle Almonte

She Said

Walk in the quiet night's mist.
Float across the moon-washed earth.
Fly with the nightingale.
Step into the shadows of the unknown.
"Forever, forever."

Wear the cloak of darkness.
Surround yourself in the Elbe.
Bathe your spirit in the Starlight.
Drink the cool waters of the Milky Way.
"Forever, forever, forever."

Red Wine of life flows warm.
Fires, so hot, burn bright in mystery.
Chants from midnight rituals whisper the wind.
Caresses from dark figures send icy shivers.
"Forever, forever, forever, forever."

Swirls of ebony breathe.
Showers of night tears.
Wails of dark lost souls.
Nightmares from Passion's Child.
"Forever," she said.

Kelvin D. McCoy

Epoch of Love

A path was laid before us since before time began.
Where it will lead is the destiny of man.
There are so many things I do not know,
But this, I know, is very true:
My life is for nothing but loving you.
I have known you forever, although we've just met.
There is somehow a past between us my soul cannot forget.
I have reached for you in anguish, in sorrow, and in pain,
And somehow you've been there, again and again.
In a whisper that's eternal, my love for you cries out,
Like a transpiercing light awakening the night.
Loving you is what my life is about.

Jodi Mason

Virtual Reality

I was never square nor well-rounded in a world
Shaped by pictures and people who cry out
From their separate corners for brighter
Color and sharper sound overloading
Their minds as they point to each
Perfect image trying to parallel
Fantasy with reality circling
Phantoms pierced by fame
Flat screens of ghosts
Functioning without
Lives as lines
Form

Alina Lingenhelter

The Touch of an Angel

To all the teachers who touch the souls of children
You were my eyes when I did not see
But your eyes were open and you saw his plea.

You were my ears when I did not hear
But you took his hand and calmed his fear.

You cared enough to look inside the heart of a child
You were his guide.

To stand in the shadow is a hard thing to do
But you gave me peace, my son was safe with you.

This race we run has got to cease
Our children need us more is my belief.

Never question the path that you have taken
For, the touch of an angel cannot be mistaken.

You touched a child and guided a mother
A gift such as this is like no other.

As you go through life, find peace in your heart
The love that you give sets you apart.

The wings of angels will guide you along the way
For parents to treasure you is what we will pray.

People and places are forgotten in the strife . . .
But you we'll remember for the rest of our lives.

Ginny Anderson

Thoughts of Adornment

"A folly really," I do surmise,
"Of man and woman."

With boundaries of tears and
Emotional exuberance.
But no avail I am just one
Of these persons to which
My taste buds are nubs.
My nose works not as if
I'll with a common cold.

To discover these dimensions of ecstasy and emotion,
Of sweat dribbling from our pore-entrapping bodies.

"I do so wish for an explanation?"
I cry. So does the babe from the cradle
That cannot and will not rock.

All are but meanderings of a mindless but happy . . .
Blind poet . . .

Robert D. Martin

Is It Really Me?

The world crashing down on me, it's raining inside.
Feelings immeasurable, toy with foolish pride.

Love taken from me, what a price to pay,
Stubbornness and stupidity, look what it cost today.

Blind eyes don't know; they can't think or see.
Happiness taken for granted, look what it's done to me.

Dreams into nightmares, Heaven turns to Hell,
Life into confusion, reality to sell.

Visions running rapid, reeling in my mind.
Desires forged from myths, stolen from another time.

A veil of indecision, my sanity spins on by.
Knowing how to love, learning how to cry.

Rebirth comes about, leaving pain behind.
Gonna give it all, making it this time.

For if I fall again, will I surely see.
Was it only circumstances, or is it really me . . .

Paul C. Devlin

The Big Lioness

Whether or not it is in the early morning light,
Or the stillness of the dark night,

There roams on the Island of Indian Creek
Something that is not so meek.

She is a big lioness with finesse,
Who moves about like a regal princess.

You will often see her on the prowl here
And frequently on the prowl there,

But when you see her in her favorite mink,
It will no doubt be the color pink.

Even when she sounds her proud roar,
She is a feline who is seldom a bore.

For those who can keep pace,
This is a big lioness with much grace.

Nina A. Giambalvo

Wagon Trails West

To the courage of the Oregon trail pioneers
As I stand and study these old wagon ruts
Worn by the wheels of a long-ago time
When the country was young, unspoiled, unfilled,
There was room to roam and roam they must
As they headed west in wagons and dust
To travel the uncharted way
Over rivers, great prairies, and barrier mountains.
What a glorious, primitive landscape was theirs
What dangers, what storms, what hardships they bore
As they joyously followed their dreams and
As I gaze at this segment of the Oregon Trail
Near the western edge of Nebraska
So close to the state of Wyoming
Do I hear their voices in the evening air?
Smell their campfires, the coffee, the food?
Know their spirits, hear them sing?
What a wonderful thing for me to be here.

Helen Hofman

A Tribe Who Lives on Mindanao in the Philippines

In dreams I've drifted to your tribal land.
Black-tinged teeth behind native smiles I see.
Brown-skinned children dressed in nudity
Encircle me, each clamoring for my hand.
Then lead me to their humble hut so poor.
Men loitering, with belted swords, do stare.
The Datu, with his many wives, is there
To greet me, as so many times before.
Then guides me to his small and simple room
And from a chest displays some antique ware
In hopes that I will buy some I presume.
The strum of faglongs I hear in the air.
And the sound of agongs in the distance booms.
Night creeps in and a sense of mystery looms.

Janet L. Ryman

Angels from Heaven

Gently assuming souls of delightful winged things,
placing in your path some of the joys that life brings.
Like butterflies and birds; colorful and bright,
sharing their beauty even as they take flight.

Softly invading your suffering and tired mind;
relaxing inner thoughts with those loving and kind.
Just when you're feeling there's no sleep in sight,
they gracefully steal your dreams for the night.

Guarding over you throughout each and every day,
becoming anyone with the right things to say.
Trust your Angel to always guide you right,
with promises of a future that's bright.

Sherry Blanchard

Mom and Dad

For Mom . . . June 1932 to September 1997
You're there whenever I need you,
Whether they're good times or bad.
You're two of the best friends I have.
The two I call Mom and Dad.

You watched me pick a career
You may have not wanted me to do,
But you encouraged me to do my best
And hold my head high whether I win or lose.

You taught me not to be afraid,
To show me who I really am,
To stand tall and help myself,
And to help others when I can.

You gave me a sense of humor,
To laugh when everyone else wants to cry,
Not to quit cause it looks too hard,
But rather say, "I'll give it a try."

So, for all these things you've given me,
I want you to always know
That the lessons you taught me when I was younger,
I take them whenever I go.

Daniel R. Lothamer

The Crucified One

I care not for a gold gilded cross
Suspended high from a chancel truss
Or one of rare mahogany, polished smooth—
Our Savior was nailed to one so crude;

Or vestments of velvet or satin brocade,
That are sacred and hallowed and skillfully made—
But he hung shamefully naked upon a tree
For all the mocking world to see.

Nor do I care for stained glass hues
Playing a dazzle of color on altar and pews.
My Lord bore it all in darkness and chill
Amid the roar of thunder and a quaking hill.

Don't give me a porcelain Jesus—Dresden cast
And expect any artist, whether present or past
To paint suffering, anguish, pain and grief—
He suffered it all between two thieves;

But give me Jesus, the Crucified One,
With all the ugliness sin had done—
His visage and form so marred in depth,
That Mary, his mother, turned and wept.

Deborah G. Kenney

The Illusionist

I am an illusionist. I have created me.
You think you know me? You think you can see me?
As an illusionist, I only allow you to see the me I have created.
Just when you think you know me, it is only a shadow you see.
I have many shadows.
Each one is created to keep the illusion in perfect order.
I have created the me you think you know.
And you don't even know it is an illusion.
I am not a magician, I am a shadow, I am invisible.
As the illusionist, I also have lost who I am.
I am buried beneath distrust, betrayal and loneliness.
The walls are secure and unmovable.
They are buried so deep within my psyche,
Sometimes they cry out to be released.
However, the pain will not release them.
Now you see that the illusionist is trapped.
Unable to release herself.
I am an illusionist. I have created me.
I have many shadows; no one can really see me.
I am an illusionist, I have created my illusion of shadows.

Mary C. Halfmoon

Bitter Sweet

My memory flows back to when life was kind
Then I was yours and you were mine
Your touch, a kiss, your love around me
Express the passion for the world to see

Seasons change and time goes by
Search down deep for reasons why
For the younger days now are gone
Bring back our love, turned to stone

Walk past me now, all through the day
No touching for us, nor much to say
A trip to town, the doctor, and such
In all that we do, it doesn't mean much

Now, time for bed, and watching him dream
To put out the light, how sweet it seems
A touch on his face and holding his hand
I still thank God for the love of this man

Claire Ledford

Always

Don't mourn for me when I am gone,
for I'll be the warm summer breeze
in the morning of a cool dawn.
I'll be sunlight that dances as it shines upon your hair.
I'll be in raindrops that kiss your skin so fair.
I'll be in rainbows after the storm in the sunlit sky,
in stars that twinkle like diamonds to light the heavens on high.
I'll be in a stranger's smile in a day that seems so long.
I'll be melody in the harmonizing music of a song.
I'll be shadows, thoughts, and even footsteps
when no one else is there,
for it is you, and no one else, who I gave my heart to share.
So remember me with a kind thought and a smile,
for I am with you always, forever,
not just a while.

Lisa R. Schmidt

Grandma D

I felt her hand like a command,
Pushing me on the narrow way.
I didn't understand, like shifting sand,
How she kept temptation away.

She loved A.R. in times near and far,
But she gave God her very soul.
She was Grandpa's wife, but she knew all her life
That God was in control.

Wise beyond her years, through shadows and tears,
She lived a Christian life.
She showed me the way, at work and at play,
To live without eternal strife.

Now she's gone, but not for long;
We'll all be together one day.
Her faith was strong her whole life long;
Heaven has one more grandma today.

Steve DePriest

Diana

Sadness descended upon the world as you were placed to rest.
Glory unto Heaven, for our princess did her best,
A purity remembered for the depth of her true love.
God chose our dearest Angel Face to be with him above,
For all the good deeds finished or undone.
You are now as you were then, forever number one.
We will miss everything about you for a long, long while.
Diana, do you look upon us with your charming smile?
Your portrait will always be of beauty, style, and grace,
As precious as the painting of Mona Lisa's face.

Marquita M. Doshier

Porcelain Angel Dolls

To my friend Serena McGregor
I look around the room
At all the little angel dolls
With wings and golden crowns upon their heads
I listen and my collection calls

What are you going to do with us
All porcelain so beautifully made?
I knock my brain and think
If moved how much they weighed

And then I knew exactly
Just what I would do
Leave them where they are
To look at just like you.

L. Mila Warn

Saved

Little tears have slipped away
For a wounded heart that I once gained.
Then I got a call one day,
From a man who said he'd wipe my tears away.
He said all the tears in the world
Could never stop the love you feel.
The hurt will go away one day,
But I am the love that you can gain.
Please take my heart and ease your pain,
For my love will heal your heart today.

Tonya Smith

Performance

I am one more player on
a vast stage in a large arena.

Only I can play this part . . .
No substitutes, no understudies.

I perform as best I can,
tho the critics are not always kind . . .
and there is only occasional applause.

The acts cannot be rehearsed
or replayed . . .
they are final.

Tho the stage in temporary,
my role is eternal.

When the acts are complete,
the curtain does not close.
Those with whom I share this stage
continue their performances.

Diane T. Miller

Beauty as I Say

Who knew what a flower could do
Only those that were exposed to thee
Its presence was as much as you could see
If you were precious enough to believe

I passed this flower day after day
This flower changed my life, made my world tilt
But over the years the pedals began to wilt
Only God could destroy an object of beauty, he alone had built

Gone for so long, I hadn't seen the petals fall
I stood searching, as tears rolled down my face
Hitting the ground, in the flower's place
Lost and alone in its space

Only then I realized my memory of the flower was its beauty
This flower was not one you could pass by
Its inner beauty made me cry
But its beauty can still be seen in my eyes

Jamie L. Seaman

Paired Rockets

Like rockets fighting Earth's scorching "pull," we blast away.
Like light-attracted nighttime moths, we attempt to flee.
Amidst mindless confusion; too close to flame we stay,
Igniting our future at our moment of folly!

Like goddesses we watch from refuge safe and distant.
We refuse to touch our dying embers' stinging heat,
Disabling us from sharing tears that should flow constant,
While the terror of tomorrow with today does meet.

Ignoring the reasons we continuously burn:
We hiss over anger at allegations of shame;
From pride, mistrust and ignorance, we refuse to turn;
We fault the other rather than our own faults proclaim.

Therefore, the roaring flames are inflicted to devour
All reminders of embers from our doomed history
While in the hearth, the bones of our ancestors cower.
Embers . . . love . . . disappearing into fire's mystery.

Will the goddesses allow a new destination
For us to choose to improve or to repeat the past?
Will goddesses again watch us in fascination
While they sit and warm their feet at our hot, fiery blast?

Florence Rebecca Wenske

A Lyric of My Thoughts
(A Tribute to the U.S.A. in the 1940's)

To my wonderful teacher, Gloria Roka
This is my poem to a country I used to know . . .
To the people that my father taught me to understand and love:
The honest and hard-working men, noble, clean, and dedicated,
The merry, kind, and optimistic, wise and ambitious people,
To the thousands of Americans who glorified their land
And made it renowned as America, the Beautiful, the Great!

To these fine and humane people the world over so admired,
I sing, salute, and pray for, and humbly ask our Lord
To guide those who still are true and loyal to their beliefs
And keep them brave and free to guard the incomparable image
Of a fair and unique nation in its singular motto, which reads:
"IN GOD WE TRUST."

Oh, precious, oh, wonderful America,
Clear example of freedom and democracy . . .
Your patriots' hopes and all my prayers are with Thee!

Beatriz Arriola de Astiazarán

Love on the Internet

To an incredibly loving and special husband, Richard Kelso
Let me tell you a story with a twist,
of two people who met and kissed . . .

But I'm amiss in jumping ahead
of their honeymoon that took them to . . .

Well, it's a difficult story you see;
she wanted children, but did he?

All right, so first a courtship, then marriage
with a starlit ride in a carriage,
this, however, is where tradition did end,
and their new life together
went around its own little bend.

"Five children," said she.
"A computer? Maybe?" Said he.

So here is their story, short and sweet,
printed on a computer, to make it neat. . . .
There once was a cute little she-male,
who married a handsome young he-male.
But sex went out the door,
when the computer consul on the floor.
Gave birth to a little, E-Mail!

Jean Kelso

Golden Harvest

Glenn and Jammie Parker work from sun to sun
To make sure all of us have a place to work that's fun

We each arrive to work with a mission in mind;
We offer each customer the best service they can find.

Although the work is hard and the hours are long,
It's so nice to work where you feel you belong.

I may not be a doctor, or a lawyer, or the such,
But I wouldn't trade this job just to have that much.

It's nice to offer coffee to a customer who calls me by name;
This is the closest I may ever come to fame.

I remember searching years ago for the best job around,
And at Golden Harvest, it was a family I found.

Vivian Wilson

I Love You

I loved you for your honesty when you told me
you would never leave her for me.
I hated you because your honesty had to be so brutal.

I loved you because you took me to her bed.
I hated you for being so willing to hurt another woman.

I love you more than I have loved anyone else,
but I hate you for not being mine.

Do I love you so much that I hate you?
Or do I hate you so much that I love you?
I don't know.

Patty LaRae Taylor

My Wandering Mind

To my dear husband, Richard
Sometimes I let my mind just wander
And fly from star to star.
I let it glide through the clouds
And wander near and far.

I let it walk on the rocks of life
And fall from treetops to the ground,
And soar away on the wings of birds,
And then again come around.

I let it peek into the future
And hope for sunshine future brings,
And smile in anticipation,
Or weep when sadness rings.

I let it touch the frost on the windowpane
And catch the raindrops from the sky,
And paint a sunset in glowing light,
And wipe a tear from a child's eye.

And building a castle in the sand,
Though knowing tide is near and soon,
I let it catch the fireflies in the dusk
And swing upon the crescent moon.

Antonina D. Marsh

Embers

Bone grey branches, crooked limbs,
some leaves falling;
on stone steps I looked into owl's eyes.
Wine in my mouth, deep breaths, suppressed cries
I saw my soul separate, with wings fly.
"Where is my answer?" I scream.
It's over now, you have taken her sleeping,
but here I am left with human weeping.
A wordless silent room is left me, mourning;
I watch them raise your dark house,
the words I want to say lost in my mouth.

Elizabeth M. Ernst

One More Chance

I wonder what the Lord would say
If He were here on Earth today
Would God let His only son give up
His life again? Would He give up and say
The devil's had his way?
Would He be so full of pain to see
What is left to remain?
Would He be able to give us one more chance,
Or turn His head and cry?
Would the devil then laugh and dance
To see us all fail and die?
Would God feel so betrayed that
His children hadn't tried?
That all of mankind strayed
And let His only son die?
Maybe He would give us one more chance
And not feel so betrayed.
Maybe we could stop the devil's laughing or His merry dance,
If all of us would try to thank Him
And pray for one more chance.

Shirley Bridgett

Am I To Only Dream

As darkness has fallen and all is still,
I'm to dream this night of thoughts of broken
dreams, and I'm unable to sleep, bewildered by
thoughts of what could be, so the pain of sorrow runs about free.
For I have yet to see the flowers
of spring that bloom in open air.
My heart has carried the burden of lonely days of sight
of yet better tomorrows.

For such a man as I dreams are but dreams for a man
who sees no sight of day, where dreams kept
will ever have wings of its own to take flight.
Yet as I dream this night I pray I may find wings
of flight this night in hope I too,
may find sight through this night that will lead me out to be
free of faded dreams, am I to only dream.

Kenneth Saunders

On Listening to Beethoven's Pastorale

I have gardened my Soul
With the beautiful flowers of Music,
A vast array of melodious notes
Spread out upon the utmost reaches of the ear,
In fulsome bloom and fit to brighten
The darkest corners of the spirit,
To give one hope anew
That life is not the daily grind alone,
But rises higher than a lonely mortal can conceive,
When viewed and heard through the works
Of a specially gifted mind,
From whom a talent flows that is
Nothing short of magic.

Virginia A. Tomlin

Untitled

Will you dream of me when you close your eyes,
Will you open your heart for whom it cries?
Will you open your arms to hold and protect,
From a painful world from far to much neglect.

Will you ease the pain that burns inside,
Will you trust in us and learn to confide?
Will you look at me from across the way
Thinking only of love and wanting to stay.

Will you dry the tears that burn my skin,
Will you learn to love from deep within?
Will you take my heart and my soul forever,
Leaving, hurting nor forgetting me ever.

Tara K. Verhaaren

The Prayer

Lord, Lord, hear my prayer.
Let me know you are there.

Lord, Lord, help me pray.
Let my heart know what to say.

Lord, Lord, guide my way.
Let me feel your presence today.

Lord, Lord, show me the light.
Let me know everything is all right.

Lord, Lord, up above.
Let me feel the angel's love.

Lord, Lord, the one I love the most.
Let me feel the holy ghost.

Lord, Lord, you gave your son for sin.
Let me witness—through Christ all are forgiven.

Lord, Lord, bless my walk through life.
Let my walk be free of strife.

Lord, Lord, teach me to serve your cause.
Let me know when to act and when to pause.

Lord, Lord hear my prayer.
Let me know you are there.

Barbara C. Wallace

My Little Angel

To Jamey Oliver Smith
As I look back, I think of how you use to act.
You were so sweet, and how you loved to eat!
When you were born everyone could see
How much you looked like me.
I miss you so, no one could ever know.
I remember how you love to swim,
And Jeremy, as you played with him.
I can see why I just want to cry.
You're still my son, I'll love you forever, hon.
I wish you were here, I just want you to be near.
You're a part of me, I wish you could see,
How much you mean to me.
Please, Lord, take care of my baby
And maybe, just maybe, one day,
I'll be blessed with another little one.
No one could ever take your place,
My dear little one, your sweet little face.
You're in God's hands now . . .
Please, Lord, can't you give him back to me?
For, I can't stand it, I'm so lonely, for my baby, Jamey.

Marie Christman

Untitled

To life, death, and adversity
I know you see before you the Reef, light from the moon,
By sands where you stood as Midnight's wind blew
I know you wish to dance again the way you danced that time
When you sped across the Ocean, as Red and Dark as wine.
Billowed were your sails as you left the Spanish Coast,
And fierce were the Tales your sailors could fold.
The foam that's so white—the Snow of the Sea—
Just helps to remind of the years you were free.
The taste of the salt and the clank of the Wind
Still bring to your mind the bloodshed and skin,
Which made your hands rough and turned your voice to a cough
As you fought in Triumph the war you had lost.
The Swords you survived, Betrayers betrayed;
Now safe with your life, you wish you had stayed.
You wish to return to the land you so loved—
To the Midnight winds of Magnificent Spain,
To the moon on the reefs, and to Wine-darkened blood,
To Die and be free and to dance once again.

Amanda G. Mabey

A Painful Needle

Words are said to warm the heart
It is painless at the start
If kind words were easy to say
Then there would not be so much struggle every day

Words can really shatter, they can really hurt,
But it is the river for our dying thirst
If words sparkle the lives all around us
Then why isn't it easy to ever trust?

People say, "Actions speak louder than words,"
But if actions speak louder, then why are words more often heard?
Words can be painful, if ever said,
It is a needle with a sharp head.

This needle brings us happiness and sometimes fear
It can be an unexpected illness, or a sudden cure,
Some say "Just let the hands of time heal,"
It may heal the pain, but the cut we still feel.

Some like to feel from this needle of pain
What do they get from it? What do they gain?
Others fear the silence of this painful needle
They fear the cravings of a deadly beetle.

Ai Vy Kim Nguyen

Women in Marriage

To my wife
Women who remain married for twenty-five
Years are very special women, because they know
What they want, and they are receiving it in terms
Of years and hard work to get it done completely.

Each one realizes that one is all they want,
And when each of the women finds that one man,
They are very pleased, and they realize that
They will stay with him for the rest of their lives.

Women who are average and who are happy
Will do everything within their power
To remain happy and keep their marriage
Going on forever and forever.

Women who want to remember why they
Are happy will see that their destiny
Is changed, and they can do it through religion
To make sure they are right.

The average women do not want a divorce,
But they are forced to take it, because their
Husbands want to meet new women and learn
To live with them for the rest of their lives.

Michael Swartwood

Golden Leaves

Pieces scattered everywhere
And teardrops floating in the air;
Broken dreams, like broken hearts
Always have their scattered parts.
Golden leaves upon the ground
That the wind has torn and blown around
Finally find a place to rest;
Against the earth, they make their nest.
The world seems barren—cold and gray;
The trees and flowers have passed away.
The sunshine's gone, I don't know where.
Life seems hopeless this time of year,
But no one seems to care. . . .
Days are shorter, but seem to have no end;
They drift like loners without a friend.
Where is the answer to a happy day?
Somehow, I must find it in myself to pray.
Pieces scattered everywhere
And teardrops floating in the air,
Broken dreams like broken hearts.

Andrea F. Lorah

My Island Cephallonia

I miss you, lovely island;
I want to swim again in your
beautiful blue waters.
I want so much to see your seashore.

My father's house is there, and my
Mother is waiting for me, to see me
"after all those years, being away."

I hope to see you soon, my Cephallonia,
to share my joy with you
and with all you there.

Oh, blessing land, of my fathers,
with the wide fields and the high mountains.
Famous of Homers' Odyssey and historian Thoucidedes.
Oh, my dear island, how much I miss you.

Dionysia N. Garbi

Rest

In loving memory, may you be happy among Heaven's fields
Dear baby, sleep well.
You shall know no more hell.
Now you can play
The whole day away.
We will never know what you might have been
Someday when . . .
And you have missed, so much to see
But you are luckier then we,
For you shall feel no pain.
That is to be our bane.

Jennifer Michele Dean

Sincerity

To Connie Krell and Debbie Diller, sincere good friends
Sincerity shown by another,
may just be the uplifting words the one who receives them
needs to hear.

Sincerity, we look for it in our friendships,
or from those we love; it has been that we look for
in dealing with each other.

Sincerity, let us show it when we mean it,
never use it to deceive;
sincerity can show our kindness to each other,
when our kindness means so much.

I have known both sincerity and kindness from one who is a friend,
so I can say first hand, my appreciation is sincere.

Margaret H. Taylor

Spirit in Flight

In the early dawn, as you leave my side.
Star shares his lonely hours; loving me,
in his special way. Until you return!
That part of me, goes with you; the warm
golden . . . golden glow that is my spirit.
My love flies along, holding and cradling your spirit.
Giving reason and meaning, to each day and tender dreams;
each and every night.
Distance cannot change, my need to hold you!
Feel the touch of your hand, in mine.
Hear your voice in the night, whispering; come into my arms.
We have been joined as one, since we met.
Two lost and lonely spirits, searching threw time and space.
Our spirits touched, eyes met; we both knew.
Without a word, our love came rushing through.
Surrounding and flooding every part of our worlds.
Until you and me, became us; for the whole
universe to see! Two spirit, shinning in the golden light,
that is love.
My spirit, is in flight; with you always day or night!

Mary A. Myers

Edd A Good Man

Edd my brother
Like no other
Was a good man
Did the best of everything one can
Was a good farmer
Was quite a charmer
To his family and clan
Good-hearted as he could be
And as busy as a bee.
Always would be working
And at anyone never smirking
He passed away
The day before Valentines Day
I'll never ever want a valentine
To remind me of the time
He and his wife and I would sometimes dine
In a special cafe or place
He always had a happy face
Although he never did embrace
No one can never, ever take his place

Florence D. Schmalko

Sixteen

Age sixteen.
I'm dreaming upstream.
A pulsing desire that taunts me.
A desire to unite with someone unlike myself,
an innocence that haunts me.
My senses keep urging these feelings of virgins
that we dream about in depth.
An aunt who adored me, said,
"Tread lightly on the brink of inept."

H. H. Rutledge

Faith (Verse One)

A resonance of sound
A vibration from a force deep underground
Retrospect through a phase of life
A deep consciousness grasped through the
Essence of shadows by the candlelight
Which one has done or will become
A hesitation . . . fear of success
Images repressed by a mist of negativity
That's consumed by the fog of one's society
Clouded the mind and reigned on the pasture of time
As we know it, forthcomes the seed of greed for which the
Average man cultivates and sows it
The night has fallen on individuality
A condescending image of darkness in the reality
Take notice to what has begun
The countdown three, two, increments of one

Blaise Adza

Good Things All Look Different

If you were a coward and I were but a rose
And the morning's dew was there to impose
Would you the yoke then swallow and hold out your hand?
Open up your senses, or just let love demand?
Would you pluck me from my bush, or look the other way?
Would I stand there looking lovely, or would you want to play?
Clip me at my bottom and walk me down the path
Pass down through the meadow and set me near the bath
So lovely is the stream there, I sure would love to see
Lined with pebble stones near
You'd prance into the house with me
You'd have the vase all ready and not gaze at me for a while
Then, when I wilt and whither, you'd give me a fragile smile
Remembering my beauty and how I bade you come
When you were the lonely coward
Who thought so dear your thumb

Tiffany Tetidrick

The Concert (Peter's Poem)

They came from all around, some near, some far
Drawn together by the sound of his guitar
Some of us waited forever for this day
We could sit at his feet and watch him play

He picked up his guitar and began to sing
We left behind our worries, cares, everything
Want a joy, how it thrilled our hearts on that day
Just to sit at his feet and watch him play

When we looked upon his face and his gentle smile
We let go of our sorrows for a little while
Listening to his songs, laughing at things he'd say
As we sat at his feet and heard him play

Many were crying "We love you!" that night
With our outstretched hands to his left and right
And we dreamed of things we would love to say
As we sat at his feet and watched him play

We came from all around, some near, some far
Drawn together by the sound of his guitar
And we knew we'd wait forever for the day
We could sit at his feet and watch him play

Denise Rymer

Gott Mit Uns

My father brought it to my mother at the close of World War One,
A belt buckle taken from a fallen German foe.
Some fifteen years passed by and I, a lad of ten,
Walked with my daddy wherever he went,
And he opened his heart and told me the story.

Well, most of the story, that is,
Up to the unspeakable point—he could not tell his son
That he had killed a man.
But he talked about the soldier in German uniform,
A manly youth, just like one of us, he said,
Promising, and full of plans for his future.

And dad's eyes filled and voice failed,
I never heard the rest.
Like one possessed by a dark sorrow,
Like one who pleads for forgiveness,
He must have been praying that his son somehow
Would fulfill the dream of brotherhood which bound him
To that noble youth forever dying in his arms.

Always I keep the belt buckle and treasure the words inscribed:
"Gott Mit Uns."

William Hinchman

Unconscious

A whispering wind rolls along the lonely shelf,
Casually riding seas of sublime sheen skin
As the sun cries in the eyes of lost images,
A diamond-like panic from yesterday's shores.

Shot through a window to cavernous balconies,
Shuttered thoughts sleep in the twilight of shadow worlds
While a sensualized paralysis seizes with ease
The forbidden armies charging electrical lust.

The cardinal-colored angel spreads her feathered wings
As messenger glances dance with illusions.
Soft garrisons caress the mind without a touch,
Bathing sub-realms in a gentle hue of jewel.

Showers of heat drown the loose mind in ecstasy,
Subversive hearts conspiring against their jailer
As rosy rain floods the fingers with divine madness,
Flashing moments that tell the conversations of souls.

Along her thorny strands of scarlet betrayal
Reside our secrets and all their severed ways,
Alluring the skies that were stolen from her eyes,
Our violet scandal blinded by another.

Damon Ross

A Sense of an Ending

The slow-footed and slouching wanderer,
with his gray and black speckled cap pulled low
and dusk-colored trench coat collar turned up,
shuffles his cold-cracked secondhand boots
through damp, leaf covered paths
that wind through the dark forest
like a slowworm slithers
through the blackheart cherry bushes.

Alongside, a sluggish stream prepares to freeze
and above, the millennium suspends
its bare and lifeless skeleton limbs.
Through his black-frost covered whiskers
the traveler exhales a visible sigh
that joins the mixture of falling rain, sleet and tears.

This lone straggler endures the dawdling century,
the gray, color-drained winter skies,
the dreary rainbows long faded,
and the smiles long exhausted.
His reluctant steps cease, and he stands motionless.
And sinks into a second stony sleep.

Cyle Stowe

American Legacy in War

It was a "war to end all war," in 1918.
"We'll git the Kaiser soon!" Tom wrote from France.
A church was bombed, that soldier died.
He had no chance . . .

The "Day of Infamy" denounced by F.D.R.
Brought us to war with "Nipon" and "Nazi"
In 1942 . . . Tom Junior got a shattered knee at Normandy . . .

Grandson Tom lost his eye and innocence in 'Nam in '65.
His Buddy is "MIA" in some secret place.
In a rotting jungle war they grappled Mars
With tortured face.

Tom Thomas, last of the line, grown in prosperous days,
Now stands a U.N. troop in Asian space.
He missed the Gulf War. Is the world now
A safer place?

The echoes of these wars drum, drum, drum down
Our generations' lines. Youth are killed—or maimed.
Peace, fragile peace, a tender, fainting victim
Of Mars is shamed.

Arvella Stokke

Eight Years after That Miscarriage

We couldn't even arrive to give you a name,
or to know whether you were a boy or a girl.
But we love you forever all the same,
and forever you'll be part of our world.

Although friends may tell you to just move along,
a miscarriage means tears, bereavement, and loss,
even if faith remains firm and strong,
and all the family together bears such terrible cross.

Now, as years went by, the pain healed somehow,
with three wonderful children to give joy to our days.
But from time to time up to Heaven we raise our eyebrows,
and scrutinize the skies in all possible ways

Until we find you there, whether it's sunny or starry,
next to God and still next to us,
tiny little angel that in my womb I carried
even if only for less than three months.

We wish at our table we had one more seat.
But you're not just gone as some people think.
From Heaven above you watch our sleep,
little angel dressed in light, whether blue or pink.

Lillian Godone Maresca

Final Good-Bye

I wanted to call you as soon as I heard
As they told me I hung on every word

They said that you were getting married again
Do you think this one will last till the end

I don't understand and am really confused
I feel hurt and used

Our marriage was like a game to you
Do you really think that you can say "I do"

And really mean it from your heart
Or are you going to tear someone else's world apart

Whether you ever believed it or not, I loved you so much
And thought I felt love too in your touch

On that day when I became your wife
I honestly thought I would be for the rest of my life

But now there is someone else that you've chosen instead
You can't imagine all of the thoughts and questions in my head

Marriage again has been there farthest thing from my mind
Getting over you and learning to trust again has taken time

I am now finally doing what others said I should
I'm saying "good-bye" to you and this time it's for good
        Leslie N. Puckett

Summer's Ending

White, billowing, fluffy clouds
Dancing across the sky of blue
Children hopping across the lawn
Searching anxiously for lost shoes.

Lovers strolling hand in hand
Oblivious to others, enjoying contentment in this moment
"Senior Citizens" enjoying the music of the band
Remembering their own young "first-love" enjoyment.

Infants, toddlers, children by the numbers
Fascinated by activities, butterflies and flowers
Fathers pitching horseshoes or swimming wisely
Enjoying the coolness of a sudden summer shower.

Mothers quiet, but alert as their children
Toddle nearby picking flowers
Gifts of wilted bouquets held by children,
Ignoring the showers, to gift to mothers.

To soon the day is over, sun sinking in the west
The last day at the park quietly ending
Summer is almost gone, parks prepare for rest
Autumn is sending early warning of winters' coming.
        Dorothy L. Crum Wagner

See You in Southampton

They stood upon the sloping deck that evening;
A gentleman and his bride;
Although he was offered a seat,
He stayed in gallant pride.

She protested, "Come with, don't leave me alone!"
But still he stayed with strength of will . . .

No time for boastful farewells;
No tolerance for bawling theatrics;
Just a few words;
That made the bride feel calm at heart,
Just a gentle kiss and, "See you in Southampton"
Was all she needed to calm her panic . . .

And though the North Atlantic has long washed over Titanic decks,
In the waves you hear the whisper . . .

"See you in Southampton . . ."
        Brent Koenes

Sadness

Sadness is a hawk circling in a summer sky,
And no one cares to share it.

The simple joy of a shoreline sunset.
And no one cares to dream it.

When the dark of night surrounds you . . .
And there is no one to reach out for.

When your heart is open for the giving
But none trust enough to take it.

Sadness is when you must walk your path.

Alone.
        Scott W. Kniss

Rock Bottom

I finally made it
I hate to say it
But it's the truth
I'm the proof
Where do I go from here?
Everything seems so unclear,
Open your eyes and look around
The answer is there, it needs to be found.
Search for that reason
For living and breathing,
And in time you'll surely find
It's never so easy, but its
Rewards are so divine.
        Calvin Grove

Contention

Thundering over dark clouds
He swore visions of past and present
Gleaming orbs that reveal every secret
A monster in blue and gold
He stood gloating
A voice chilled the air
"Michael!"
But he merely struck open Ararat
Thousands of novas shone down past Ezekiel
And he waited
A young man struck a match
While the past slid away
Frozen souvenirs collided under the surface
His beating wings aroused the oceans
And it all began to fall
A feather tumbled to the ground
For a child to find
        Amy S. Hall

An Ode to a Napkin:

When words of poems come to my head,
all I seem to have to write them down on are napkins.

I am usually in my car, a restaurant,
or, you guessed it, in bed.

If the words aren't written right down,
they are lost or forgotten.
Napkins are such handy things.

The obvious use for a napkin is to wipe your mouth while you are
eating and put it on your clothes
to catch the spills.

You can also clean your glasses, the windows on your car,
or wipe away your tears.

Other uses for napkins are to write notes on,
telephone and Lotto numbers and addresses.

Napkins, I don't know what I would do without them.
        Shirley J. Ward-Shields

For Mine, Was My Father

In memory of William J. Wallen Sr.
Everyone has special person in their life.
Whether it be your mother, father, sister, brother, husband or wife.

As time ticks away, the one thing I regret I didn't say.
That is I didn't tell you I love you at least once a day.

There is so much I still have to say, so I say it in my prayers.
For you had to go to Heaven now, and it just isn't fair.

You are one of two who created me.
Making sure that I would have a life that would make me happy.

For times we had laughing, and the times we spent crying.
And for the saddest time I've had was when I had to watch you dying.

As I seen you dying, and they started pumping your chest.
God yells down to me "It is time for him to come,"
so we must go and put him to rest.

I am sorry, Dad, for not saying it so very often.
For now your soul is upstairs looking down at me
while your body rests in a coffin.

Father, please come back or at least show me a sign.
So that I will know that in the days to come I will be fine.

For every day goes by I know we must go on.
Having to face the truth that you are gone.

Michael A. Wallen

My Testimony

Dedicated to my Lord and Savior, Jesus Christ
I have a testimony and it's all mine.
Very dear and special to me, it's one of a kind.
I will carry it with me, until the end of time.
It's not just precious words, it's something special
From deep within my heart, about the love I share with God.

I have a testimony of the Lord Jesus Christ.
And how it strengthens me and enriches my life.
I shared my testimony with others I know.
I carry it with me, everywhere I go.

I have a testimony, of how good God is to me.
How He has delivered, sanctified, and set me free.
And of all the blessings he's bestowed on me.
Miracles, signs, and wonders, I've seen with my own eyes.

If you want love, peace, happiness,
Joy, and comfort in your heart,
I challenge you to try Jesus for yourself.
As the praises go up, the blessings will come down.
From a true woman of God.

Barbara Akins

How Shall It Be Spoken?

How shall it be spoken
When loveliness dying
Carries with it all the beauty
One may gather in one's hand?

Beneath these feathers beats a small heart gallantly.
Beneath these feathers wrought with blue
Was the manufacture of the ages
Caught in a tender body.

What brought the mourning dove to ground
Is not known. It was found
Fluttering helplessly, and died
Before frost had dried,
Before tulips in green rows unfurled.

Sigh, wind, and in your sighing
Let the world hear sorrow
For one so lovely dying.

Florence B. Palmer

The Trail

There is a power greater than us
that starts us on a journey.

We are alone on this adventure,
travelling to places unknown.

The road is not paved
and offers us several directions.
At times we struggle with what road to take,
or whether we should even continue.

As we wander aimlessly trying to make our choice,
we are suddenly embraced by a new dimension.

A traveller has joined our path;
we invite them to travel with us.
The traveller listens and consoles
but never picks our direction.
Instead they give us courage to continue
and hope of a better course.

As the traveller bids us farewell,
to head off on their chosen path,
we no longer walk as one
on this unpaved road.

Jacqueline M. Brosius

Destinations

To my future wife, dearest love, and friend, Kathy
I once spoke with God and he said
Fear not, my son, but stand instead
Walk tall, be strong, travel often and long
and I'll be at your destinations
Oh, how I did seek, while reaching each peak
but never heard you speak?
As God again said, as I lay fearful in bed
I was all the right places and faces
and when your heart races
the eagle, the raven, and the spirit to fly
all the right rhymes and the comforting pines
each the water, the ties, and her beautiful eyes
the stories, the measures, the treasures
and beautiful pleasures
the endeavors, perseverance, and pride
the ability to stand
and her wonderful hand
a mate for your soul
and all without toll

Bryan F. White

Dear Ms. Emser

Although you're asleep in a garden of peace
Where you have no more pain and your worries have ceased,
I just thought perhaps when the Earth is made new
That your Guardian Angel might read this to you.

I found the three boys you raised while on Earth,
The ones who were crippled and unloved at birth.
They've had such a struggle but turned out quite well;
They tell me the stories you often would tell.

You told them of love God had for them all
And there must be a reason why Wayne cannot walk.
Their sufferings were why Jesus came and He died;
There must have been nights you just knelt down and cried.

They miss you so much and can't wait to see
Your sweet smiling face and hug 'til you squeeze!
And then they'll run off in their bodies so free;
Wayne will run like the wind and Norman will see.

I try to go visit whenever I'm free
And remind them this Earth is just temporary.
You've changed three men's lives in a wonderful way
And our Heavenly Father will thank you someday.

Kendell Greene

Mississippi Summer

The winter has come and gone.
The spring, we just left behind.
Our farmer's seed is sown
and we're waiting now for harvest time.
So with a straw hat on our head
to hide our eyes from the sun,
we grab a can of worms,
a fishing pole, and old sport,
and away we go to have some fun.
Down a dusty country road,
past the cotton fields that soon will be white,
until our favorite fishing hole is coming into sight.
There beneath the giant water oaks and old magnolia trees,
we sit upon the banks, with the cool water up to our knees.
Our corks go bobbing as our hearts go throbbing,
for there is a fish on the end of the line.
It's not long now till supper-time
Yes, the days are long and lazy as we sit and slumber
amidst a hot and humid Mississippi summer.

Ronald D. Thomas

We Are the Men of the Future

We are the earners of time plagued with vulgar
Traditions and disdain.
We are the yesterday that left our souls
Shattered with its disillusions and defeats.
We are the time without end of humanity
That struggles after it for ideals and empty and vain
Philosophies of iron tasks proposed by the minorities
That dominate the majorities by trying to impose mandates, laws,
And borders by force, power, and the force of the courageous
That will die thinking he offered his life for peace and justice.
We are the future we cultivate today . . .
And who knows if the future generations will thank us for it?

Alejandro Bonilla

Amy's Day

Pride in your parents' eyes, joy expressed by siblings.
A tear drops to the ground.
Beautiful, vibrant flowers grow from the soil.
A new life begins.

Today is the dawn
Not only of the rest of your life,
But that of a dream.
You have worked so hard and made many proud.
It can be seen in your father's smile
And your mother's tear.
They realize you are no longer a child but now teaching them.

Knowledge.
You have found it and used it well.
No one deserves it more than you.
Now your life has truly started.
Take this knowledge and make your life great.
Teaching is the noblest of careers.
Without great ones like you,
Our world's children would be lost.
Inspire them all!

Jodi Bachim

God Is an Artist

God is an artist.
God is an artist, a painter supreme,
Refreshes our land with color so clean.
Winter-white snow came in flakes from above,
While plant life is sleeping, to be 'wakened by his love
Along with the warm breath of springtime.
Crops bursting forth from underground,
A shower of green growing all around.
God is an artist, a painter supreme,
Refreshes our land with color so clean.
With color so clean, so clean.

Romano Margaret

Break the Habit to Bury the Past

In uniform style, I wait and I run
And do so only as you beckon
As if somehow I live with tradition at hand
Bringing archaic customs to a new foreign land
Never raised my eyes out of distorted respect
Never speak nor question and never expect
A masquerade that follows to wherever you lead
Assuming it's only you whom I must please
Don't demand freedom, don't fight for anything
Just simply exist to become your nothing
Can't escape the haunting of a familiar past
To conquer this battle, to make my love last
No more, I protest, old habits must die
To only my heart must I comply
Scratch the surface, dig deeper, I can
I will not remain in the palm of your hand
My triumph is to follow only where my heart leads
No longer shall I question who I must please
Breaking the chains of subservience, at last
For I am in control of burying the past

Hylda M. Fenton

The Cycle of Life

The sun rises over the hilltops
Giving warmth to the morning air
Children hurry off to school
With not a care in the world
As I sit
I hear the steady rhythm of the ticking clock
My heart begins to beat
Almost in unison
I watch as the hands continue to move slowly
Yet the rocking chair is empty
As empty as I feel inside
Soon there will be a crispness in the air
For darkness will be upon us

Cynthia Dummick

Woe to My Heart

To Ebony, I will always love you
My winding path has been trampled on,
Explored and exposed! Oh! Woe to my heart. . . .

The long, slender, silver key to my soul
Has been stolen by a single word! Oh! Woe to my heart. . . .

My imagination, challenged by a lean, sleek panther—
(We wrestle like two lovers, arms, legs everywhere,
ecstasy a moan away, finally, gasping for breath, we call a truce)!
Oh! Woe to my heart. . . .

My soul weeps into the great amazon, the waters of forgiven sins
("Toss in a few" it mocks, "For the sins of the world are many!")
Oh! Woe to my heart. . . .

My salvation, kept in a crystal vase, helps my heart to mend,
But my soul will forever mourn, "Oh! Where has my lover gone?"
Woe to my heart.

Barbara Valerio

Faith

In darkness a candle is lit
Burning darkness away
Burning evil away

It creates passion . . .
And out of passion we get everything
We get love for things we adore and cherish
We get faith and hope for things we don't really see . . .
Out of darkness those are the most important things

It creates everything we see and feel
And sometimes the people that don't see it and feel it
Are still trapped in darkness
But out of darkness . . . hope is born

Michael Nowicki

Begin Again

I surrender to these thoughts,
as the tears well up within my heart;
they spill out through this pen.

My mind is full of thoughts,
my heart aches stronger with each one;
finally breaking out into this world.

I have been destroyed by these thoughts,
'cause of that, a stone replaces my heart;
I am no longer willing to be in this life.

Good-bye, 'til we meet again.

Tina R. Garcia

Listen and Hear

Can't hear the squirrels chatter
Nor hear the birds sing
Can't hear the grass growing
Nor flowers as they blossom in spring

Can't hear the wind gently blow
Nor a leaf floating as it lightly falls
Don't hear wild life scurrying, storing
Preparing as old man winter calls

Can't hear my heart loudly beating
When you're far, nor when you're near
From within, tune and listen
A rhythm so sweetly, love you my dear

Life and joy from you slipped, oh, so far away
Take down your barriers, release your fears
All these sounds surround you, believe me
It's not that you're deaf, it's just you will not hear

Ashley B. Burch

God's Stars

What guided the wise men to Jesus was His Star;
It brought them to Jerusalem from countries afar.

The Star shone before them, oh, so bright;
They continued to travel by day and by night.

The Star glowed from Heaven, so distantly high;
It covered the world through a night-darkened sky.

To say to God's saints, while they live here on Earth,
"Born again stars, follow Him in your rebirth!"

My life will glow brightly for others to see
That the love of Jesus is shining through me.
Each day, I will pray for the Lord's renewal,
To keep my love for Him a bright, shining jewel.

I'll tell the world of the Infant, our Lord's true Son.
I'll worship Him, praise Him, for he is the One.

Who will light my pathway to Heaven's own door
When my own long journey here on Earth is over?

Rosebud Elliott Bonar

The Bottomless Pit

Oh, deep bottomless pit, you keep calling to me.
Like the abyss between my conscious and my external
world which I try to reconcile.
However, my attempts appear to be in vain.
Alas, I am drawing closer to the bottomless pit.
Won't someone or something rescue me?
Suddenly I hear a loud voice speaking to me.
It is the voice of truth speaking in tones that
I cannot escape.
The truth speaks loudly and I hear every word.
I understand what he is saying.
The bottomless pit has vanished and it no longer calls to me.
The voice of truth has saved me from the bottomless pit!

Glenda Colleen Gambill

Gilbert

To my soul mate, my Harley Man
I often wonder
how a man I never met
can know me so thoroughly.
He claims to have
his own self doubts and imperfections.
Still "finding" himself
has led him near and far.
He has explored much,
but says he has found little.
If only he would take a step back from life
would he understand
he had "found" himself
and by doing so,
has aided me in my "finding"
so much wisdom at a young age.
Sharing it with all,
but only the clever know to listen.
I am grateful that our "findings" crossed,
for I cannot see my life
not knowing him.

Jobynne C. Prazak

Jealousy or Kindness

There is nothing to ever get jealous about,
No, not a thing.
God made everyone beautiful,
No, He did not forget one thing.
Everyone is special,
Yes, in every way.
God did not say, Be jealous,
And hurt that person that way.
Jealousy is frivolous; besides,
It does waste time.
Instead of hurting others,
You could have done something kind.
Jealousy is ugly, right down
To the core.
Kindness is so beautiful,
It rates a higher score.
So take a look deep inside
And tell me what you see—
That wonderful, beautiful kindness,
Or that ugly jealousy.

Judy D. Stephens

The Criminal

He lives in that second homeland
Not quite in sync with sun and sand
Where insidious act is done innocently
Where foul-play is glamorized cavalierly
Where murder, arson, rape are strategized
To be means to an end, by the end justified.

To the hurt of others, he is apoplectic
In his dealing with others, very sadistic.
Autistic and self absorbed, to virtue averse,
A psychopath at the center of his universe.
An undertaker who digs a grave inside himself
There to bury conscience and the nobility of the self.

His habitat is subterranean and dank
Into human abasement by choice he sank.
Connection, compassion, sublime indexes of humanity
As foreign materials rest on his individual psyche

The law, the courts, the prisons do not him deter,
Negating institutions he should rather revere
Still he be afraid of light, of truth, of justice
Why, the deuce, are we afraid of him.

Chudi Conleth Anya

Who Borrowed My American Flag

Thank you, Mother Ireland, for sending my mother to Chicago
Who borrowed my American flag as I laid asleep
in my little cabin in County Donegal
Someone did creep—
was it John, James, or Paul

Suppose it ended up in Croke Park
When Donegal beat Dublin for the All-Ireland
After 1000 years my American flag brought
Good luck and the spark,
So let bygones be bygones and I'll shake
your hand.

I am coming to Ireland this coming May
to that little cabin in County Donegal
And whoever borrowed my American flag
I want to say
Return the stars and stripes and I will
feel 10 feet tall.

Edward Bonner

Just a Touch of the Master's Hand

To Jesus for the gift He gave me of writing poems
Just a touch of the Master's hand
Heals and lifts me where I stand.
A touch of the Master's hand
Shows me I am His to command.
I am flesh and weak at best,
Yet in His hand I can out do the rest.
The touch of the Master's hand
Oh, how grand, Lord, oh, how grand.
To feel that scar-pierced hand
Touch and heal me as you've always planned.
Saviour Jesus, Lord of life,
Help me cease this stress and strife.
Completely healed by Thee,
Spirit and soul set free,
Cleansed, oh Lord, by Thee.
All by just "the" touch,
The touch of the Savior sweet.
Touch of the Master's hand.

Margaret Ann Dwyer

The Hopeful Romantic

So here I
Am, upon this mount of those yearning for amore,
No quiet sure whether fate will
Decide to allot my fragile heart from those shattered here before.
Rhetorical questions of sort hidden in the things I say to you,
Asking "Do you love me?" Or will you show me the door?"

Whelmed by my feeling of love
I hope you are not, because the intensity of your
Loveliness pierced my soul with Eros' arrow, deeply.
Luster glowing so illustrious that
I long to be with you night and day
And now I've found that I've come to the peak of my affections
My mind has now been made, I know what I must do
So I leap from this cliff with full faint in you!

William Feoster

Love Is Like a Rose

Love that is nourished flourishes
and grows like the flower and the seed it sows,
the bud becomes a lovely rose.

By late summer, the flower weathered and worn,
a forgotten rose is tattered and torn,
clinging to a vine of thorn.

Whence, it withers, hence,
it dies, into the womb of earth
it crumbles, in ash it lies.

Anne R. Burkholder

Shawn—How and Why

How,
How can I let him go?
That little boy, who never met a stranger.
Although I know he's here no longer,
How is it still, I miss him so?

Why,
Dear Lord, why is he gone?
I know that he was yours and mine
But he called our place his own.
His passing left a grief so deep.
The years between have been so long,
That only now, can I relax and weep.
But, Dear Lord, why is he gone?

Robert G. Dunford

A Cry for Help

Here I sit, all by myself,
In turmoil and in need of help.
My life seems like an empty shell.
I feel that I'm in a living Hell.

I am truly lost, and I know not why.
My feelings are numb, and some have died.
My mind is a tunnel without an end.
I'm so confused; oh, God, be my friend.

I need your help, now more than ever before.
Please open your heart and open your door.
I am like a child, a frightened dove.
Please open your arms and show me your love.

Seeing the love shining down from your face
Will help me get over my feeling of disgrace,
And maybe again I will walk, head held high,
And be able to know what person am "I."

Donna D. Tietjen

My Flower Garden

Welcome to my flower garden (Summer 1998)
Come walk with me along its paths
And enjoy the many wonders of nature
Through the rose arbor with roses in bloom
Dropping their petals in the breeze
Impatience, snap dragons, and blue bells
Surround the Japonica bush
The Rose of Sharon shelters a bird's nest in its branches
Marigolds, zinnias and asters are a beautiful sight to behold

A bird bath stands in the midst of a circle of flowers
where birds come to drink and splash
Bright yellow calendulas, red and
white geraniums, white alyssum
Two pink flamingos stand guard at the scene
Oh, there is so much more, but let us sit on the rustic bench
While humming birds whiz over our heads
As they dart among honey suckle, trumpet creeper and then to
feeders on a pole
Entwined with heavenly blue morning glories

Virginia Guthrie

Little Autistic Child

Little child, you once called my name.
But now your silence is not to blame.
Little child all locked inside,
I know your love for me has not died.
I know your silence is not by choice.
Why are you different from other girls and boys?
Little child I once knew,
Little child who laughed and smiled,
Where are you?

Catherine V. Godone-Maresca

My Very Best Friend

To my very best friend, Kaila Carter
Many have come and gone,
A friendship not real strong.

But you, my friend, have come to stay
And help me through my not-so-good days.

You're a sister I always prayed for
And the best friend I always searched for,

The friend to listen when things go wrong.
When I am weak, you help me be strong.

I cannot thank you enough for the time you give.
You're my very best friend for as long as I live.

Sarah E.R. Prindl

Wipe Those Feet

Each American city evaporating
into the clean cool dusk
experience sends tapping nervous patients
on suspicious knees, devoid of grassy knolls,
brokering unabridged entropy, fixated
on last hope expense checks electronically mailed,
and yet without fair warning.

We laugh out of sheer geometry,
absorbed in a crackling worth, our capacity
for sweet shock stilled for camera shots
and misfitted shoes of fortune gaping at the naked
grizzled flesh, shoving it across in public
bodies of waters and wine and mud. . . .

We drop our coin
into each inverting slot,
pulling a bag behind the bushes,
a bag actively malevolent, still cruising
our crusted minds like a decade
we forget to peel.

Gabriel Thy

The Stone Rolled Away

To my loving husband, Jack Ashmore, Jacquelin, my sister
I was at the tomb where my master's body was placed,
we gently kissed him as tears ran down our face.
When we left the tomb the stone was rolled into place.

The next morning the stone was rolled away,
as I looked around I saw a man walking in the garden.
Please sir? Where have you taken my master's body?
Why did you take him away?

He turned to me and in a gentle voice said,
look at my hands and feet.
When I saw his nail scared hands and feet,
I cried master and fell on my knees.

My master said peace be upon thee,
I'm with all my children through all of eternity.

Cheryl Ashmore

Spring

Of molt and crumbled edges, lay
leaves of fall with time decay,
while slender white swords for freedom fight
the last of winter's days.

While crumbled earth hither
falls, like time takes toll with river,
and life filled air floods hidden roots
blind shoots aversely shiver.

New life springs from earthen dun,
slow as Sol's march south is from,
and buds like spears from twigs they fight,
then battle is joined with the sun.

Tim Chard

That's Reciprocity

One day, I came across an old, old, saying
That has been around for a long, long time.
It says, in effect, "I'll scratch your back
If only you would scratch mine." That's reciprocity.

So bear this in mind, because one day
You may meet a friend in dire need.
Oh, what wonderful satisfaction you will derive
From doing this friend a good deed. That's reciprocity.

Should your fellowman be at a crossroad,
Not knowing which way to turn,
Give freely your help to set him right.
What a wonderful warm feeling you'll earn. That's reciprocity.

Even if someday you may be called upon
To help some sad person who is cursed,
Remember, should you fail to respond to this call,
You'll not be making things better, but worse. That's reciprocity.

So always strive to be helpful
And make sure that your acts are kind.
By so doing, you'll reap a bountiful reward,
A feeling of satisfaction and peace of mind. That's reciprocity.

Fred G. Bennett

Rainy Countryside

The constant hum of a country rain
Falls steadily o'er the meadows wide.
You can almost hear the blades of grass
Inching upward o'er the greening side.

The graveled road is full of rain,
And ditches run while the creek beside
Fills up from the ditches full,
Until water runs almost double wide.

Country rain falling on the slated roof
Of the cottage house, as the lane ends,
Quiet and peaceful from the city's noise,
Soothing the soul which God intends.

Peaceful, soothing country rain . . .
It takes one back to memories lost,
As a child sat on a country porch
Dreaming dreams, knowing not the cost.

The years pass swiftly and they are gone
Into the vapor as a steamy mist.
One sets quietly on a rainy day,
Realizing the life that they have missed.

Wilma Spaur Wood

Mixed Blessings

We count our blessings on the
    loose feathers of Guardian Angels
And ask Cupid to blow kisses
    to warm our cheeks at night

We pray for strength, kindness, and patience
    from One whom we cannot see
And trust that earthly miracles
    are forced by His hand indeed

We beg Lady Luck to be charitable
    when we seek a quick fortune in the lottery
And thank Mother Earth for showering us
    with rose petals and autumn leaves

We dance to the music of Gabriel's trumpet
    regardless of his tempo or beat
And ask Father Time's pardon
    in the hours we feel sick or weak

No matter the comfort
    or how great the need
There is a cure for all that ails us
    if we truly believe

Angie Clark

After the Shadows

After the color bleeds out
I can gaze behind the stained figures
entrapped inside elaborate panes of sand

To free the silhouettes with my finger
until the first rays creep
across an earthen floor
diffusing amidst yellowed pages
to leave arms and teeth and eyeballs and
the birthmark stolen from your mother

Tear masks the dream
and descends into a desolate respite
as the breakers retreat into oblivion
a pink lattice creeps across malachite striations
twisted in marbles

Behind the broken shadows, an eye peers
into a cackle
and somewhere
a house of sticks
collapse

Bill Banks

Soothe

To my loving friend, Larry Dean Mann
What is wrong with darkness
Why can you not abide silence.

Does peace frighten you
Do you hide at the calm before the storm.

Listen to the voices of the dark
They will soothe your tortured soul.

Blackness is all encompassing—it is the dark the light
     And everything therein

Light is chaos—
How can you heal in only light

Close your eyes—what do you see
When you sleep you are encompassed in a blackness that
     Heals you; when too much light invades that
     Blackness chaos erupts and you do not heal

What do you have to fear of darkness
So much fear can only hurt you, that fear in itself can
     Paralyze

Respect the darkness, for it will refresh you

Listen to the voices of the dark—let them soothe your
     Tortured soul.

Misty Dawn McCray

Inner War

Built on a mountain with fire below.
Everyone walking with shackles in tow.
Soldiers with weapons are all around.
The only safe place is underground.
Death all around, you can hear a faint chant,
Why enslave and kill people over a plant.
God has spoken, "Thou shalt not kill."
But this doesn't stop them, they do it still.
It's getting so hard to go to the store.
As America crumbles in the inner war . . .
     Changing the rules, their finances meet.
Forcing and tossing the poor in the street.
God made all things good and all people free.
But the man with the dollar says this can't be.
He hires some people with badges and guns.
A legal war on the chosen ones.
Heartache and torture for the man with the seed.
Brother against Brother, they pay for a lead.
Killing their own because they are poor.
No Love, no Peace, just inner war. . . .

William Newhouse

What Now, My Bitter?

O' you of darkling mood
Who sees only negatives,
Who utters pejoratives,
Who blames, belittles, belabors,
Who denigrates, deflates, demeans,
Who criticizes, curses, condemns,
Who curdles joy and crushes hope,
What makes the grudging, gritty growl
And the sour, smirking smile that claims loving concern?

Love it cannot be that chills the soul into a deep despair.
Am I a punching bag?
A dumping ground for hostile memories?
Is it revenge for hurts endured before my time?
Misplaced revenge is not sweet;
It roils the heart, enrages the mind, and kills innocent love.

Faith B. Willis

Forever

To my Princess Diane with much love
My Princess

My love, you succor my desires
Oh, the morphine passion burning inside!
My princess, I need and want you so!
For your flesh, your heart, your soul!
Oh, the pain of endless wanting!

I thirst for you with such craving hunger pains
Let me drink your passion, for
Will it quench this endless fire inside?
So that I may now smolder from your touch?
No!
Never!
It is endless, forever encircling me

Oh, the sweet pain of wanting you so!
You are my rapture, my feelings!
While my soul sings sweet ecstasy!
My never ending desire for you

I love you, Princess, forever . . . oh, what you do to me

Kevin J. Rondles

Dragon's Gold

For my Scotty Joe—thank you for being my knight
On the nights when the loneliness finds the chink in my armor
and my shoulders sag at the burdens they bare and bare alone
the tears flow freely to wash away the worries of the day
and my arms hug my knees
This is when I miss being in love
someone to hold while I sleep
to give my body to
to escape the world and its skepticism
finding peace beneath your skin
to get lost in your embrace
to be saved by your desire
gaining strength to slay the dragons of the morrow

Keo Cummings

Dividend of Reality

Dreams intertwined
     tightly into a bundled
          mass,
     An infinite celebration of molecules
          dance to the pulsating
               sound of our heart's
                    magic.
               As we grow wisely old,
          the fluidity of the waltz
     spins recklessly off course
to an insignificant dividend of reality.

Keith Campana

A Gentle Autumn Breeze

Up the path and over the hill
Across the creek below the ol' water mill
Barefooted and knickers to my knees
How I enjoyed a gentle autumn breeze

Me and my friends ambled off to school
Mary, Claude, and Beattie—to name a few
With the bright, golden hue of the chestnut leaves
How I enjoyed a gentle autumn breeze

When leaves tumbled to the ground
And sprinkled the school yard all around
Where we played hide and seek, catch me if you please
How I enjoyed a gentle autumn breeze

The shadows are growing longer each day
And covering the school yard where once I did play
Leaves are curled from the December freeze
But I still enjoy a gentle autumn breeze

Time has brought a blanket of snow
A velvet soft sheet wherever you go
I am no longer barefooted with knickers to my knees
I still enjoy a gentle autumn breeze.

Maxwell B. Williams

Day Dream

Time in a mirror looking back at me,
lost and gone, faded old memories.
The sun through the window shines
as the ice in my glass crackles and whines.
Funny how life is . . . what you want is what you've already got.
The sweet smell of summer has come.
Oh, how I missed it a lot.
Destiny is when the wind blows,
and the magnolia grows.
The leaves, the trees, the sweet, sweet breeze.
Soft touches on my leg, little hands embrace with such ease.
Feelings of tumbling in my tummy as you toss and turn.
So much she will teach you, so much you will learn.
Be careful what you wish for, be careful what you do.
You see . . . some dreams come true.

Jennifer Fowler

The Cup

It was my fathers cup
He drank the daily brew as did his father
The Cup waited for me to live out a reckless life

I sipped the muddy medley of flavors
Swirling inside the Cup
It passed through my soul as if it were light
searching for darkness
the light was inside of me

My senses capture the light
causing tears, laughter, and love

The heart of the cup is a powerful elixir
causing an echo to resound upon my mirror
the sound was my fathers words
saying the Cup now belongs to me

Sandra Hawkins

Journey

There are voices that don't want to be heard,
hands in the darkness passing whispers like shadows
in places where light hides in the darkness
and people walk the cities searching,
pressing their heads against walls,
waiting to feel something other than pain,
waiting for the things they remember, but can't describe;
with dreams underfoot and eyes toward the sky,
problems dissipate and contentment inhabits the horizon
as a ghost to be chased.

Eric Buth

May the World See You as I See You

Remembering those who were killed simply because they were Jewish

I see you in life's richest things:
In the clearest of mornings,
In the stormiest of nights,
In the endless rolling of the ocean,
In the calming stillness of the forest,
And in great symphonies.
I see you there,
All you who did not survive the Holocaust,
You whose lives were unfulfilled:
Your songs not sung,
Your games not played,
Your books not written,
Your weddings not celebrated,
Your babies not born,
Your laughter not heard.

Everyone should see you reflected in life
And remember, and mourn
And remember, and mourn.

Jennie Saben

Don't Be a Heartbreak

You told me you loved me only
That you were so lonely
But you love someone else too
And he loves you, too, I've found out

Why you wanna be
With two guys at the same time?
Who you gonna love more, baby?
Him or me, honey?

I don't want you to love him less
I don't want you to love me less
But how can you love me more
If you love him more?

It just isn't right
Even if you love me more
'Cuz I can't share you with another lover
And don't say you'll ditch him for me

No, don't be a heartbreak
You wanna break my heart
You know that's foul
So, keep your man and I'll keep my heart safe

Ekow Asmah

Brotherly Love

If brotherly love flowed in sincerity
Haters were not upon this beautiful Earth
O', the peace we would have in daily living,
With harmony, instead of haughtiness.

If brotherly love spinned in serenity
Terrors were not upon this wonderful Earth
O', the rest we could see in brave survivity,
With courtesy, instead of calamities.

If brotherly love beamed in supremity
Thieves were not upon this plentiful Earth
O', the height we could aim in bold heroity,
With great victory, instead of vicery.

If brotherly flashed in security
Murderers were not upon this bountiful Earth
O', the glory we would have in broad longevity,
With pleasures, instead of pressures.

God says "Love one another as I have love you
Make brotherly love your heart's desire,
But haters, terrorists, thieves and murderers
Will burn forever in the lake of fire."

Jean Lomax Jackson

Me, Myself, and I

I don't understand.
That's because you don't want to understand . . .
I try to understand, though.
No, you don't, because once you understand, you have to do it . . .
Not necessarily.
Yes, it is, you are just running away . . .
No, I am not.
Who said running away was something bad . . .
I am not running away.
You can run away if you get scared . . .
I am not scared.
Yes, you are, you are scared of yourself . . .
What is there to be scared about myself?
You are just scared of rejecting . . .
You are just scared of being rejected . . .
You are just scared of being lonely . . .
You are just scared of knowing who you really are . . .
But you'll feel good once you learn to accept and forgive . . .
You'll see the beauty—the moment you realize it . . .

Reimi Sasaki

Dreams

Reachable visions,
Big and small . . .
I know that they're reachable, almost all.
Several key factors to keep spirits high:
"High faith in yourself and reach for the sky!"
"America" holds the secret to all.
"I can" is the key to unlock all doors.
So keep in mind that dreams do come true.
I can do it . . .
So can you.

Tammy Cirksena

A Pet

I have a pet cat.
She is, oh, so very nice!
She is so clean and has no lice!
Nor does she even try to catch my nice!
If I have had to stop, raise my voice,
and speak to her twice,
The cat's meow is then as sharp as ice.
She looks at me as if to say,
"This day is dull.
It needs some vinegar and spice.
This is the reason I'm not always so very nice!"

Sharon Daniels

Crossing Over

For Ron, who taught me to name my poems
Listening to the radio in the car on a
Bridge over the East River, I hear a Southern
Black prisoner work chant called "Rosie."

It's about the woman who should be waiting
For every man to get out of jail: beautiful,
Faithful, full of grace at Sunday meeting and
Dollar-in-your-pocket thoughts that give power
To strokes of chopping wood and smashing rocks.

Announcer says researcher dating the song
Walks into a Mississippi bar full of black
Ex-cons, asks if anyone knows the work
Chant, "Rosie." Nearly every hand goes up.

A surge of electrical energy ignites the center
Of my torso. In a Mississippi bar, chain gangs and
Slaves from the past are calling me to attention.

Hand manacled, foot shackled to thousands
I didn't know I knew, I am in tears.
My tears flow into the river below me.
The Subaru crosses the Williamsburg Bridge.

Audrey St. Mark

Untitled

Close your eyes and hear the cry.
Listen to the lullabies.
Edgy and restless, try to sleep,
Kicking and crumbling twisted sheets.
Racing and running through your brain,
Turn over, flip the pillow to keep things sane.
Clench your fists, quarantine from the clock,
Getting restless, was that a knock?
Waiting for what is already known,
For once again he won't be home.
Hear your heart as it screams pain.
Humiliation travels in your veins.
A believer you've become once again,
As he said, I'll be home at ten.
Dozing off, hear a car.
Nothing near and nothing far.
Self-esteem leaks out my eyes,
By now I should have realized.
Four thirty six and still no one.
Who's he having that much fun?

Lisa Pezza

Friendship

Finding true Friendship is a Spirit finding the perfect body:
   A Miracle of Life witnessed with awe and envy,
A continuing renewal of Hope and Encouragement,
   A mystical source of Joy and Energy.
So much Promise is offered by no other event;
As Universal is no other event.

From the smallest grain of sand to the largest star,
I long to announce the most profound reflection:
An unending sound and deep Affection—
It is my hallowed honor and sweet bless
To call you dearly, the Soul of my flesh.

For the years of Caring and special Sharing,
For years of wise Counsel and Support to Me,
For your years of Confidence and Faith in Me,
I offer the most valuable Gift I have to You:
I offer my continued and faithful Life to You.

The brightest sunlight is but a dim glow in the Cold
Compared to the very Touch of your heavenly Soul.

Cleo Evans

City Cowboy

To my wife, Nelli, the best days will come in
When my life is boring
When my body is soaring
I'm going to bar with country band
Where I'm shaking the cowboy's hand

Oh, man! take me away from the city
Here I'm as a dog on a chain
I don't need somebody's pity
I want to ride the horse again

A wise man speaks of joy
A free man speaks of fun
I just like to be a cowboy
I just want to enjoy the sun

Give me a lasso and saddle
Give a me rifle and salt
And look how runs my colt

The steppe will be my bed, my saddle will be my pillow
Oh, Lord! I never seen so beautiful a sunset!

Oh, man! Don't kill my dream, and take me away from the city
Where I'm as a dog on chain, I don't need somebody's pity
I want to ride the horse again.

Komanetsky Alex

Special

To Gregg, friend, lover, husband, fantastic father of five
Special is such a wonderful word,
And a wonderful way of being.
It's a way of looking at many things,
And believing what you're seeing.

It's made of the presence of God in your life,
And the people closest to you.
It's the thoughts you think and the words you say,
And everything you do.

It concerns your strengths and weaknesses.
It's what makes you so unique.
In all the world, there is just one you,
No matter how hard we might seek.

Every person in all of time
Is different from all the rest.
Isn't it great that the special you
Is one of the very best?

Ann Haney

To a Kindergarten Graduate

All my children and grandchildren
You have not travelled far through childhood,
Or sailed life's troubled seas,
Yet, oh! what joy you have given,
With simple childlike ease.
Right from birth, until this present day,
Your little hands busy strewing
Forget-me-nots all along the way.
To be a little person is something very special,
Just the way you were meant to be . . .
Allowed to romp in your merry ways apart
Or shout in freedom wild,
That parents—or grandparents—who, like me,
Will remember we were once a little child.
God must have given childhood,
With its laughter and its tears,
Thus to prepare parents for His children,
In all the future years.

Eulah G. DeMatties

Inspiration

Wandering the trial,
Passing the wonderment of nature's growth,
The stopping, slow, methodical steps, and a silence,
There is not one sound.
A breeze, yet no singing through the pines,
What an unbelievable moment of quietness.

As standing on a slight knoll,
The sight as far as the eyes could see
Are trees upon trees of green delight,
Falling to a valley then up the mountain's rise to sky.
Ever was a chance to be swept away
From sheer beauty,
This would be the time.

This moment,
One small infinite speck
Of what life's lesson has to show,
Before wandering to another spot of time on this trail,
A path showed only through imagination.

Albert L. Wade Jr.

Grandmas

Grandmas are special in every way.
They're loving and kind every day.
Their smile warms you like the sun,
And they're as sweet as chocolate chip cookies when they're done.
They grow sweeter and sweeter everyday,
And that's why I love my grandma in every way.

Sherria Lynn

Wandering Mind

If you let your mind wander you can go many places
You can be in the big city or in the wide open spaces

You can travel to other countries, you can travel far and wide
It's all in your mind so you don't even need a guide

You can go to exotic places that are very far away
You can stay a long time or just spend the day

You can also be anyone that you wish to be
You can be rich and famous or you could even be me

You could be in the circus, perhaps you'd be a clown
You could be a queen and wear a jeweled crown

When all is said and done the best thing you can do
Is be happy with yourself and just be you

Ruth McKenzle

The Piano

dinto
The keys of a piano are white,
black, shades of brown and yellow.
Press them a certain way . . .
they produce different tunes.
Some are loud, some are soft.
All together, they make beautiful music.
Sometimes, only sometimes,
when you press them all at once,
they make a very uncomfortable sound.
The search for that right sound
has not yet been found.

The piano has beautiful stories
behind its making.
The love for it is there for the taking.
The cracks in the piano prove there is aching,
waiting to sing melodies of love and romance,
waiting to sing beautiful notes of peace,
once again.

Brandon Durousseau

Stuck

Working in a factory, in a room where only elites flare,
voices at a distance and darkness everywhere.
It seems out of proportion like a mixed-up movie
in time, scenes of mole people in a different world
with someone's sick mind.
Noisy machines running, trying to soothe the air
and such a loneliness and yet it comes from everywhere.
Voices in the distance raging, I'll go to school
you'll see and I'll be somebody, maybe have a family.
Five years later the voices are still the same,
they never did anything, it was all in vain.
As I shake my head, it's all so sad to me,
how the voices still talk of what they wanted to be.
Are these people so controlled that escape they would never see.
I feel they need answers,
direction and faith will set them free.

Michael Medina

Untitled

The stars in the sky
Could never compare to the stars in your eyes
As I lay alone looking at the sky
I wish that you were here to lay by
The stars are bright and beautiful
But not as beautiful as you
You are always on my mind
And there always you will stay
As well as in my heart and soul
Someday fate will bring us together
And nothing will pull us apart

JoAnn M. Martindale

To Do List

I'm a dot that must become a line
Must create myself by being me
Fast-forward from this point in time
For tomorrow arrives belatedly

I'm a line that must become a square
Must single out my singleness of purpose
Accept the truth but take a dare
For lies do life a great disservice

I'm a square that must become a cube
Must find depth else risk the depths of Hell
Define new dimensions to improve
For shallow graves leave no tale to tell

I'm a cube that must become a sphere
Must smooth the edges of my ways
Sing in a voice the world can hear
For talk is cheap and rarely pays

I'm a sphere that must outweigh the world
Must strengthen the character I display
Sidestep the demons that are unfurled
For straight paths lead to disarray

James C. Crooks

Today Is Yesterday's Tomorrow

Today was yesterday, and today is its tomorrow.
It was full of joy and gladness, without sorrow.
Tomorrow will come, as long as there is
A day after today, if not, in Heaven we will stay.

When we do as much as we can in one day as there is to do,
Tomorrow may come to fulfill another stay.
Yesterday was here the day after, and on and on is the way.

Live each day as if it were your last.
All stress and strife, you can cast.
Enjoy yourself all you can, and the day will be in the past.

Life is short, we all know, a year full of days.
Make the most of it because there may not be another year.
Jesus may come, and fill your heart with cheer.

Yes, today is yesterday's tomorrow, hopefully no more sorrow.
Life is full of days, as He shows the ways.
Come to a stop, when you fulfill your days.
When you do, and when life is complete, Jesus will show you the way.

Thomas E. Mullett

If God Has Taken Him

If God has taken him, then we've lost and he's won.
Without my man with me each day, then I'll be only one.
The thoughts that have gone through my mind, make me stop and say,
Please, God, don't take my man, for this to you, I pray.

He's been my life and love since I just turned thirteen.
To spend my life with him has been my lifelong dream.
We have three kids we have to raise, it takes a mom and dad.
Without him in our lives to love, our world will be so sad.

Our friends and family are here right now, praying, same as me.
Without him in our lives to love, an empty space there'll be.
He teases and he jokes around, he keeps us on our toes.
Don't get me wrong, 'cause he's no Saint, as you very well know.

The Doc just came out through the door,
   the news does not sound good.
But I know you'll give him back to us, if you feel you should.
It's been eleven days since we were sure that he would die,
But our God has decided to give him another try.

God has not taken him, he's not lost, but yet we've won.
He gave me back my man, now we together will be one.
The thoughts that have gone through my mind, make me stop and say,
Oh, thank you, God, You saved my man; for this to you I pray.

J. Tichy

For Carrie

Every night I bow my head,
Take a knee, and pray.
I thank the Lord for each blessing
Given me that day.
Then I pause for a moment
When I come to you,
And then I thank Him one more time
That my search is through.
You are my queen, my everything . . .
You make my life complete.
I could search the world a thousand times,
And not find one as sweet.
You are my inspiration,
The icing on my cake.
You're the dreams I dream when deep in sleep . . .
You're my dreams when I'm awake.
I love you to the deepest depths
Into my heart's abyss.
I die each time we say good-bye.
I'm born each time we kiss.

Matthew Sullins

Day by Day . . . HIS WAY

The sun is bright as gold today,
Showers of yesterday all dripped away.

The sky is a beautiful "true blue" all around,
Not a dark cloud in the sky to be found.

Sometimes the days seem dark and dreary,
Maybe an illness, a sorrow, or just too weary . . .

But the Lord knows our every need,
Is eager to hear our prayerful plead,

To drive the darkness of night away,
To fill our hearts with Jesus' love and peace each day.

Doris De Vault

Waking

I still feel warm from your touch, sleepy from your caress,
Your scent lingering on my flesh.
Snuggling up to the mass of tumbled warmth,
I sigh remembering my musky heater.
We try to hold ourselves in check, but the magic has gone
As well as warmth.
A true old time with us awaits
We try to hold the passion, yet my moods and skin
Convince us otherwise.
The memories flood through me
With a warm rush, descending me to sleep's edge.
I curl catlike into the warmth and drift in memory.

Jennifer L. Nelson

The Masque

A masque of painted horrors forced upon a face
A masque not chosen but willingly worn
Fear of the beast has made this masque
The beast is gentle
Yet the masque projects a monster
They made this masque
They fear the truth
Yet never have they known it
I embrace the beast and find comfort
And so a masque is made for me
A masque of painted horror forced upon my face
A masque not chosen but willingly worn
I fear not the beast
I fear nothing, save their masque
And so I gasp as it is affixed upon my face
And so I live the masquerade

Sabastienne Illyra Brighton

Walk with Jesus

Give God the glory
"Come to me," I hear him say
"Follow me . . . I am the way"
The circle of love cannot be broken
Jesus' words so clearly spoken

Along the path, do not despair
The patient Jesus awaits us there
Jesus, so firmly strong
When we are wrong

To do His will, we shall overcome
All sin and sorrow with God's Son
He leads us on through the night
Heaven is Our Home, "Heavenly delight"

The path with Jesus leads to eternity and home
Nevermore to roam
Walk with Jesus, He will lead you to yonder shore
Home with Jesus, forevermore

Grace M. Stuffle

A Passing Dream

All I'll ever love is this passing dream
It's taken me over body and soul
With a passion that's so out of control
That it's left me without any esteem

All I'll ever love is this passing dream
In my heart it's taken more than its toll
In fact it has created a deep hole
A passing dream is far more than it seems

To me it has become a part of life
To not have everything go as it should
But a passing dream is more than it seems

A passing dream has took over my life
You don't have to tell me that that's no good
But a passing dream is more than it seems

Laurie Susen

Night in Manhattan

I'm alone, and it's night
In the city open to a winter blizzard.

Frosty wind blows the snowflakes
Tarnished with the patina of abrasive desolation
Along the narrow passages of the marketplace
Flourishing with the trade of phantoms,
Covering the crowds busy making coffins for desire
With the blanket of eternal oblivion.

The reality breaks into tiny fragments
Dizzying and overlapping one upon the other
Until clarity is lost in the world of black foam,
Where shadows meet shadows
Clinging to the fear of passing time.

Julio J. Ferreira

Our Faith

To my great God who lives above
Faith is a gift that we can't see;
It comes from God for you and me.

We can use this gift both night and day.
It also helps if we learn to pray.

We pray to God and then believe
That, what we have asked, we will receive.

We stand on words of God that are pure,
And, in return, we are secure.

We see from the past, the beginning to the last,
That having faith in God makes us strong as a rod.

Richard E. Gant Jr.

Seeing Tomorrow

Vision, like life is confounded, different from your eyes to mine.
The future like the past compromised, compounded by untruths.

This way, that way, your way, their way, my way, our way.
Life endangered, life empowered, life changed, life left as it was.
He is, he might be, he could be, he couldn't be, he shall be.
She was, she wasn't she wants to be, she is not sure if she is.

What they want, what they need, what they have, what they take.
Where I'm going, where you've been, where we need to be.
I will see what you see, when you are me and I am what you want.
You will see what I see, when there is nothing left to see but me.

Life expands with each waking thought, vision is life awakening.
Seeking yesterday, living for today, seeing tomorrow

Patrick A. Carney

I Could Give to You

I could give to you all of my love
everything under my opened sky
I could give to you all of me, at times
these notes, for now, get me by

Sometimes, I can feel you are here
not just an old picture of who you once were
but who you are for a moment of thought
and how it might be with you near

Then, times come again where you're far
Simply to pick up a phone, I could do
and feel this face that I wear
mirror my joy in talking with you

Is not love, my most special friend
always here when all else goes away
reminding me from now to the end
how lucky am I on this day?

To have you living here in my heart
peaceful and warm and gentle, too
reminding me that I am a part
of some of the things that are you

Robert J. Cooper

My Love

For Russell, who has given me an eternity of love in a short time
My love is as real as you or I
With eyes so clear they show all that has been or will be
A face that shows all that is being felt
A soul so bright it shines with a bright light
Love so honest, pure, and chaste
It holds the magic of eternal grace
With a laughter as loud as a choir on Christmas Day
A smile so vibrant it begins to spread on all that is around
Hands that are calloused from hard, honest work
Yet tender enough to tend to a small child with a gentle embrace
Along with a heart so full of caring it must be Heaven sent
My love is as real as you or I
Your life and your love is gift for all from above

Teresa E. Townsend

Mothers Can and Are

Mothers are so gentle.
Mothers are so kind.
Mothers can get moody, only in your mind.
Mothers try to understand and kiss your fears away.
Mothers try to do the best for you, each and every day.
Mothers can have hearts of gold.
Mothers can have hands of wool.
Mothers can wipe your tears.
Mothers can touch your hearts so dear.
Mothers are the only ones that can do all these things.
Mothers can also peak inside your mind and hold your many dreams.

Kimberly Elliott

The Magic in You

Discover the magic within you
The ability to love and give
The drive to dream and then to do
The best that you can while you live

The magic that sets your aim on a star
While keeping your feet on the ground
The faith that helps to see visions afar
For this is the plateau where success is found

Discover the beauty that is you
And always stay humble and sweet
Remember old friends and seek for new
Be the same with each person you meet

Be loving, kind, gentle, sweet
Do all things both honest and true
Leave a good impression with those you meet
And they will see the magic in you

Hazel Bungardner

Creator

To my loving husband, Deacon Hays

Who is this one whose birds early in the morning sing,
whose stones would shout if our praises we didn't bring?
Deep in our souls is He slumbering, this Creator, God?

They say He loves us unto folly, each and every one of us.
Without fear we must trust; this King so supreme does love us,
you and me. Oh, what a King have we; oh, what a King have we.

The lonely worm does his job in your garden and mine,
doing what his Creator has created.
Can we do less in our own interior gardens?
Oh, Creator, hear our pleas; may we love you
as you love us, without much fuss.
Oh, what a King have we; oh, what a King have we.

Oh, Creator, help us along our paths with stepping stones of thee,
all the people you have created and especially little me.
Oh, what a King have we; oh, what a King have we.

Rosalyn Hays

Sara

She comes up like a fresh sunflower in a bed of weeds
each morning stretching to the sun
extending her beautiful, golden petals to all ends of the Earth
shining her happiness on whoever passed by
Suddenly, one day, the weeds raged with jealousy
tearing her petal by petal
She faints, withers, death is creeping up
Could this be it?
Fear not
for one true love will save her
As I nursed her back to health
she became stronger and more beautiful than ever
Now she has become the sunshine of my life
I will love her always and forever
A one eternity is forever
So forever it shall be.

Matt LaBerta

Think Thus

Think thus
If someone makes your path thorny
Then, you too, make his path thorny
If this pattern goes on
Someday the world will become a "thorny place"
No flowers will bloom
There will be no fragrance
No birds will sing
There will be no melodious notes
Who knows then what will become of this world.

S. Suhela Nashtar

Laisy Dazy Cloud Trip

angry blackened fury sanctity of a cloud
Sanctuary of its mind
Asylum for those wanting to scream
at all ills and peculiar frustrations

but look up—concrete faces look-alike mutating
fall apart to dissembled nothingness upon wisps
arabesque harmonies cumulus so phallus
circus animal cirrus; crumbling, like stale angel food cake-men
A filter to consciousness looking up
the lazy long puffs and mean streaks
generation after generation
water never dies is only reborn
as thunderbanks gray mists . . .

. . . for if sky was a River
clouds would be Stones
if sky was a Body
clouds would be Bones
and lazy daisy is always high
looking at the sky
even when he's Down . . .

Dennis Koski Jr.

Love's Story

It is a song sung throughout the ages;
it is timeless in its course,
but it dances around in my soul
and strangles my heart with its force.
It has lived centuries without fail,
but died an infinity of death
while coursing through the gasp in a lover's final breath.
It has tortured the bravest heroes;
it has conquered dying souls.
It has softened the darkest of hearts and
played a thousand different roles.
So why do I feel I am the first
that love has taken prisoner and claimed
with its obsessive, flaming fury
that has never yet been tamed.
It has branded those before me
with its unbroken seal of need,
and still it holds the strength of a passion to be freed.
But it cannot cease existence, for neither time nor age nor death
can suppress this purest love that lies within the lover's breath.

Melanie Wilderman

I Reverence You, Lord

I reverence you, Lord.
Oh, my soul
From depths untold,
With mysteries to be unfold.
I reverence you, Lord.

I reverence you, Lord,
More than I can bear.
From the depth of my soul
None can ever see
How much of you I behold.

I reverence you, Lord.
What more can I say?
No joy can compare
To the love that I bear.
Oh, Lord, what more can I say?

I reverence you, Lord.
With all that I hold,
Singing and praising you, Lord,
My joy just overflows.
To you, Lord, my love just grows and grows.

Jean Ray

Life

Here I stand, alone,
A madman adrift in a turbulent sea,
Always searching,
Yet never finding,
Forever dying,
Yet never having truly lived.
I hear the cry of the thunder,
And the lightning sears my soul.
Onward I look and see my hopes;
An island stands where calm abounds.
Is it reality or illusion?
Truth or lie?
And what is the cost to purchase this land?
The wishes of my heart at the damnation of my soul?
Is this not truly the curse of life?
The only destiny of this shell they call . . . me.

Merle Leslie Kinder III

Revenge

We have come a long, long way
I guess it's the end today
We have memories we laid by the way
Guess they didn't matter anyway
We went down many roads together
It's over, I guess it's better
Sometimes at night I have sweet dreams
Can't sleep at all, at all, it seems
Shouldn't have told you to leave
It was my foolish pride
I loved you more, more than I thought
It was revenge that you sought
You really hurt me, I guess you meant to
I hurt you bad, I didn't mean to
Payback is Hell, look what I've been through
And now you say we are through

John West Sr.

A New Birth

Sittin' on a park bench to rest
Watchin' a robin building a nest
While I sat there for a while
A man came by with a smile
I looked up at him, full of joy
He said that he was a new father of a boy
I bent my head down to pray
Only to hear him say, "He's okay!"
I asked, "What did he mean by that?"
He took hold of my hand and sat.
See, the Lord gave me a boy today,
but when I reached out for Joey,
I gained the Son of God in my heart
and He is there now, never to depart.

Sequeeta Potter

I Loved You Then

"Love," she murmured, "is so fleeting.
My first glimpse of your face retreating
into the shadows of childhood time
is forever etched in the niches of my mind."

"I loved you then; you couldn't know.
We seemed worlds apart even though
our desks were separated by the narrow aisle
that I easily measured as more than a mile."

Touching his hand after so many years,
The lovely lady hoped behind her tears,
Searching for a glimmer of the passion past.
"You couldn't know," she whispered, alas!

Jettie M. McWilliams

Tribute to My Mother

To my loving mother, Lena Mauchk
Mother, all during my growing up years,
You were there for me whether laughter or tears;

Family was your greatest concern,
You gave your all and asked nothing in return;

You were the strength of our home, a lady with class,
Whatever hardship life dealt, you would smile
and say, "This too shall pass";

My heart is full of gratitude for your unselfish way,
And how you brought sunshine to each and every day;

You were a lady with unending duties to fill,
Always striving to please and to do God's will;

I thank Him for you, who with all of your strife,
Taught me faith and gave me wisdom to face life;

That's why it's so easy for me to see,
You're the perfect example of what a Mother should be;

God's most beautiful creation is no other,
Than His masterpiece, a loving mother.

Sharon L. Coleman

On Angel Wings

In memory of Mel: You know no bounds
On angel wings you fly away
to discover a brand new journey
leaving all behind to miss your
presence and await our reunion.

We mourn in sorrow our loss
and hope one day to find you
filled with the love and life
that clearly eluded you.

In the mistily shrouded start of
tomorrow we remember our love for you
our loss so deeply instilled
we shed our tears at every whim.

None can comfort us through this time
as we wander through the days aimlessly
when on angel wings you've taken flight.

We say good-bye and wish you joy
we mark the days and count the hours
for when life will rejoins us
And as you travel on Angel wings may there
be no boundaries before you.

Sheila Devere

Gargoyle

I sit like stone with a crooked backbone,
My nails carved sharp upon the top of an arch.
My wings spread high, three feet in the sky.
With a scorpion's tail, my eyes remain stale,
Focused on the sun down by the horizon.
But I speak not a word, nor a murmur, nor a sound,
As I guard my castle and watch over the town.
Cold yet still, my body without a shiver,
The water begins to flow within me like a river.
Perched upon my shoulders is the blackest of all birds,
Whispering into my ear, "knowledge," but not "words."
Suddenly, I feel a rush, the water begins to shout,
Showering on the streets beneath this water spout.
Leap upon my head, the raven nods instead.
Drink from out my mouth, the raven screams, "No doubt!"
A screech and then a flutter—I'd like to greet another.
Time too short, the night my mother,
A new crack has formed upon my horn—that for which I'm scorned.
I sit upon this tower, listening hour to hour,
Hearing hopes and dreams that flower under moonlight power.

Anthony Di Crosta Jr.

Shiver

Quivering under your hands
Is a shivering body next to you.
No fire could warm these limbs,
Nor could any blanket or warmth you provide,
Even though you try so hard
To embrace and warm her soul.

She looks to you, and you see in her eyes
A broken heart bared and bleeding,
Trembling from the pain of another,
Unforgiving, unrelenting, and unprotected,
From your gentle touch.
Open your heart and give over a piece of your soul.
Kiss her lips, caress her skin,
And tell her she is beautiful over and over again.
She might just believe you for an instant.

Pull her in close; just do not let go.
And as she tangles her fingers in your dark hair,
Kiss her blue eyes shut and tell her you love her.
But before you doze off in the safety of her arms, look down man.
She is not shivering anymore.
        Michelle Ewing

The Keeper

I enter the ancient door
an old question I must explore
the keeper listens with doubtful eyes
then slowly begins his reply:

"The answer is written in time
travel the eternal vine
your eyes you will not need
with them you will not see"

Through darkness the visions come clear
hate, war, betrayal, and fear
it seems darkness is all I see
the horrific result of selfish needs

In light I saw the keeper weep
ashamed, I turned to take my leave
from a distance I heard the keeper say
"The question of a lifetime cannot be found in a day"

As tears of frustration escaped my eyes
I vowed to return, for another try
        Nichelle Y. Williams

I Think of You

To my big teddy bear, Joe Campbell
When the moon rises in the sky,
I think of you,
and from my lips escapes a sigh,
A sigh of pain, pleasure, joy, or sorrow,
I know not which,
I just know I can't wait to see you tomorrow.

When I stare into the darkness of the night,
I think of you
and I sometimes begin to cry,
To cry because you make me complete.
I know not how,
I just know you are the other half of me.

When I lay my head down to sleep,
I think of you
and pray the Lord you're mine to keep,
To keep beside me forever.
I know not why,
I just know I love our being together.
        Melissa Kay Frizzell

Twilight Lowing

Take a look in the orchard where the apples are hung.
Listen to the brook with its sparkling tongue.
Underneath the bridge with its pertinent arch,
See the boy and the girl by a sugarloaf larch.
It treefully reaches with its arms to the sky,
Trying not to hear each inexorable sigh.
The breeze trips along, ruffles grass, ruffles hair,
While love quickly blossoms in the bosoms of the pair.
A dog trots his course with his nose to the ground,
Then stops his sniffy-snuffering at what he has found.
The two had stopped embracing at the animal's approach,
For they thought the look he gave them was an animal reproach.
But he was just a dog with a doggy daring-do,
So he lifted his best leg as he stared down at the two.
The world will never know what went through that canine head
As he trotted by the couple on their beside-the-water bed
The sun was next to setting and the moon not far behind.
To leave them where we found them is to be (at least) most kind.
        S. Dunham Wilson

My God

My God, my God is the God of all Gods.
He is the Father of the Savior.
He is my God.
He helps me through life.
He shows me the way.
He is my God, Jehovah,
or some may call Him Yahweh.

God is there when there is no one else.
He answers my prayers when they're not selfish.
I see His love time after time, and I know
while God is close to me, everything will be fine.
I realize now why I am here,
and words cannot describe the happiness I feel.
I want to share my whole life with my God.
He has been there from the beginning
and I hope until my end.
God's not only my God, He's my best friend.
        Tonya Cashion-Watson

Dirty Ole Man

Don't you come home tonight
Don't you even knock my door
'Cause this is not your home now
And you don't live here anymore
Your clothes are all packed sitting
Outside in the cold, cold rain
Just get them and leave, don't you
Ever come back here again
I saw you with that sorry ole
Jezzie Bell last night
Drinking your booze and
Hugging her with your all might
Grinning from ear to ear like
A young sixteen-year-ole boy
Who had just found himself
A brand new toy
If I should ever see you again
You'd better turn and run as fast as you can
'Cause I hate you
You ain't nothing but a Dirty Ole Man
        Nell Lorraine Brawley

Meeting You

The first time I ever laid eyes on you,
The only thing I thought about was meeting you.
Your voice—something so special, something so sweet—
Every time I thought about you, my heart would skip a beat.
Your smile, your sparkling eyes told me you were going to be mine.

Finally, at last we meet. . . .
        Christina Tenorio

Drowning

Drowning in his sorrows, a boy left all alone
A nameless face in a crowd of many, no place to call his home
Abandoned one day, and left for dead
He sleeps on the streets, he has no bed
Drowning in his sorrows, starting to get gray hair
Living all the pains and sorrows, no person deserves to bear
A nameless face in a crowd of many, does anybody care?
With ragged clothes and battered feet
He looks for food left on the street
He has not eaten, only God knows why
A soul so beaten, you want to cry
Drowning in his sorrows, wondering how he survived
And why the cruel streets, kept him alive
He lays in an alley, waiting to die
Nobody in sight to hear his cry
A tortured soul, he has no more life
Wishing that death had not taken his wife
Drowning in his sorrows, a boy left all alone
A nameless face in a crowd of many
No longer needs a home.

Aaron Givens

The Sunset for Tomorrow

When the sun retires at night beyond
The shore and waves so bright,

Announcing in orange and then in red
It's portents for the days ahead,

I calculate its dramatic fall
In the special beauty of it all

And think of the closing out to night
As another beginning of a night in flight.

How can the sun so brightly shine?
See how the waves the rays refine!

See how the breeze in its gentle way
Stars the night which pursues the day.

Kenneth A. Friou Sr.

Will It Matter

Before letting anyone ruin your day,
Ask yourself . . . will it matter ten years from today?
How much will it matter?
What costs are at stake?
Will it change someone's life?
Or whose heart could it break?
We all have our moments,
The strong and the meek,
When it seems as though Monday
Lasts eight days a week.
Before losing control,
Before ruining your day,
Ask yourself . . .
Will it matter ten years from today?

Judith Hamilton

Once upon a Dream

Once upon a dream, I thought I saw you standing
Once, within the clouds, I dreamed I danced with you
The music that was played was so entrancing
There among the stars we danced the whole night through
We gaze as other dancers surround us in graceful motion of their own
To the beat of the heavenly music we swing and we sway
These precious moments we are in each other's arms to stay
As other dancers fade, we're dancing all alone again
As other dancers fade, we're dancing on our own again
Once, within the clouds, I dreamed I danced with you
The music that was played was so entrancing
There among the stars we danced the whole night through

Rae Ann Barton

Family Is Forever

On that day of the year,
I hold it so very dear.

Through years of good and bad weather,
We grow in life together.

The trust we give is felt in return;
Love is deep, not having to yearn.

The laughter is so strong,
Nothing can be done wrong.

Volleyball, euchre, horseshoes, or croquet—
a few of the games we play.

We do enjoy our time to reminisce,
Honoring each other and those we miss.

All are welcome with open arms;
We show off our inherited charms.

Yes, we are so clever,
Because family is forever.

Mari Pratt

Observation

Climbing to the top of the world,
I take a snapshot of what my journey will entail.
I see the large obstacles, the goal, and the people—
and yet, obscured is my trail.

Setting out, alone and determined,
I forge a path through the sand and the crowd.
I realize people are watching, observing
My silent trek, though all is loud.

But certainly I intrigue no one so much
as to cause them to watch me beginning to end.
As life passes by and the journey goes on,
there may be just One who is truly my friend.

J. D. Sutherland

Silent Voices

To be a strong soul is not to die but to live on in the bright
memories left in the hearts of those who were touched by the
radiance of their existence.

What's the point of living, dying, and/or suffering
if it can't change another life beyond your own?

To feel another's pain and to be able to see into their sorrow
inclines us to be stronger people—more insightful, more in tune
to listen to what life and the blessed are whispering

Take the time. Listen to the soft breeze in and around yourself;
you'll feel the energy and hear the voices of angels.

Rebecca Noelle Anderson

Aberrant Forms

Where to, O' celestial beacon?
What shore draws thy
          Ethereal glow?
Is it from I which thou flee?
Or dost thou, too, seek without knowing?
Pass not by without divulging
          Thy secrets, for
They must be deep from all thou hast seen.
Stay! And we shall dance together, for
My eyes have also distant gazed.
But alas! Our moment has passed, and
          Thou art gone.
Whence shall we meet again? Over
Which horizon will the wayward paths of
          Vagabonds
Dimidiate? Thou knowest only.
Between then and now, farewell.

Michael F. Mallette

An Anched Calum

Upon shrines of bones rise apostles from their rest.
The clouds shed their tears to dry the soil.
An old crafter peers into what once used to be mist.
A fog now swallows the belt in its black coils.
The sky rolls like the lion,
Thundering, shattering the parliament.

Is that freedom dripping from the beehives?
Sweeter, is that honor blooming on the highlands?
Better, it was once a promise,
Then a lie, it was once a whisper, now a cry,
A thought revolution.
A new bearn in the cradle of
Ingenuities, a flood of imagery,
And finally, a break from the shackles
And a long anticipated run . . .

The path is worn,
Sweet tears of sweat beading on the brow.
Hearts suspended, hung clenched by their time
Hands . . . aghast white hands stuck to cavernous mouths,
"It only come to take what is ours and mine."

Robert Keane

Little Girl Lost

In the middle of the night you ran away
Every moment that passes someone does pray
Please do come back, whatever the cost
We all know you're a little girl lost

The questions are many
And your answers are sure to be plenty
Was it really that bad; were you really that sad

To whom, little one, did you manage to run
Did it start as a lark; you wanted more fun
Was it worth all of this? For you, we all surely do miss

Oh, where will they find you, and what then when they do
Every lead your parents have combed
Just wanting their daughter back home

Where have you gone, and what have you done
Found you will be, and when you are found
Will your mind, body, and soul still be sound

For a journey you've taken
But never think you're forsaken
Please do come back, whatever the cost
We all know you're a little girl lost

Gloria Elliott

It Calls

It calls me when I sleep
And in my dreams of distance
When I'm awake it lingers in my thoughts
Though in a mist of untouchable comprehension
It is there
Uncontrollable awakenings for a new escape
It sets me free of anger, sorrow and hate
And when touched, frustration will arouse
For don't touch the unlimited, uncontrollable
Non-feeling world, unallowed
Because it sets me free . . . free

It calls me uncontrollably in the still, night air
And whispers a freedom to my mind

Set me free; set me free!
I am calling, hear my plea
Let me escape to your wonderful world
Calm my anger
Tell them to let me be

Truly, devoted and unwittingly there,
It is there for me in the still night air.

Brooke Leigh Fonfara

Ulysses Southbound

My skin's too loose, too tight.
It always gets this way when the scratching
starts inside my skull.

Looking past the reflection in the bus window that isn't me,
climbing into the bed of night,
searching for a laugh or tear;
I can only recall that fish's face, its eyes,
as it twitched undecidedly
between the shore and the sea.

The men have loosed the mad north winds from their prison-flesh,
untied the silver knot as I lay
dreaming of a hand of clouds,
that ravaged the naked sky.
The field fell silent, sound was fled—
bruised fingers stretched out overhead.

Waking from my distant sleep,
ankle deep in a river-street, I blink—
my stop was miles back and years ago.

David Kendrick Ware

Passing the Flowers of Time

For my little flower that healed and for other flowers
River waters come and go.
It be so like love
Which blooms in the ambiance of the night
Then languishes in the blanket of snow that lies upon.
Love is to be the flower.
You become one, but to return then again to another day.
Love is the petal in one's eye;
It dilates with one's true compromise.
Love is the stem of the flower,
Which would support the whole other.
But you are the soil
From which the flower grew,
Holding all that love 'til it grew into the flower.
Beauty is not the sight, but true beauty.

At times, some do not see that beauty,
And soon the wind shall come,
Blowing all the petals away,
Flowing with the wind until it ceases to take them.
Through time you shall heal,
And the flower shall grow once again. . . .

Andre M. Agraviador

In the Eye of the Beholder

Beautiful and green,
Tightly fixed to its outstretched limb,
Dancing with each gust of wind,
That's how it all begins.

Food and water surging through my veins,
Some is from the sun, strained.

Admired by all 'cause I signal the beginning,
But soon, too soon, the ending.

New life nursed in my arms
Now fill the skies with a swarm.

Cold,
So cold now.
My green to gold then brown,
Beautiful brown.

Dancing downward with a blast of air;
Landing, I don't know where.

A child lifts me up and takes me home.
Tells her friend "I got the best one,"
Beautiful and very brown.

Teresa A. Brown

The Unforgettable Event of 1986, "The Torch"

Our Lady Statue of Liberty . . . to look
at her standing on the star shaped wall,
she's a big doll who will never fall—
for her gravity of strength has given
justice to all.

She is like a Greek Goddess who stands
tall holding the golden lit torch which
represents freedom for all.

As the Lady closed her 100th Birthday,
she will always hold the harbor,
a landmark she is!

Her spectacular event has brought forth
flags and with glorious spirit the singing
of the American Anthem that has always
made America beautiful as we saluted her.

The Lady has given many people the right
feeling and that is . . .
"LIBERTY ENLIGHTENS THE WORLD."

　　　Evangeline Katranis

Mirror

As I looked in the mirror to check my hair,
I faced a man with a piercing stare.

As I tried to get a closer look,
My life became an open book.

The form I saw was one of me
Standing bare—how could this be!

No garb to hide what I could see,
The deep and inner man call me.

I used my hand to hide my face;
This image I could not erase.

So plain it stood for me to see,
What I hide deep inside of me.

The heart that schemed for personal gain
Was now exposed, with me to blame.

And though I held it deep within,
I now was forced to face my sin.

And what I saw was living proof
That, though one tries to hide the truth,

That which we are we cannot hide
When we peer in the mirror at the man inside.

　　　Glory D. Slyton

Final Thoughts from Living

I wish I had more to give
But we all know how much it costs to live.
I am sure that if I could make wealth and class
My love would have last
Life and love comes and goes
I am just glad that God knows.
Always believe in yourself and pray
No matter what others may say.
God is our true judge
And surely he will not hold a grudge.
Live each day as if you have to face many tomorrows
We never know what may be our sorrows.
When you have friends, learn how to trust only a few
You will find out later that this is the best thing to do.
Maturity and growth will let you go beyond the past
Remember, only eternity will hold blessings that will last.
Live right, do right, be right, and think right.
Then hopefully you will be favored in God's sight.
Always think about and plan for Heaven and tomorrow.
For then we can somehow find joy in our time of sorrow.

　　　Ms. Loretta Williams

The Sound

Sitting here all alone, I realized the world has a distinct sound.
So many people hustling about, each one avoiding the sound:

The sound of the beggars, homeless, and hungry;
The sound of the elderly whose money was lost to some scam;
The sound of the youth who rob, steal, and kill for attention;
The sound of the family who just laid a loved one to rest; and
The sound of the woman crying because her husband
　　has just left her.

So many people all over the world,
But no one seems to care about the sound.

　　　T. M. Park-Frederick

Divine Glory

Divine Glory I beseech,
Glowing lamp-lit holy seat,
You are the creator of all
Whose presence was given Divine call.
I bless the ground you walk on,
Day in and day out.
Sermons Christian life is beckoned;
Angels rest upon your holy feet.
Dancing with bells that declare your Divine seat,
We call upon you night and day,
With scriptures of the lay.
The warm glow pronounced in the clouds
Speaks of Heavenly bodies all in a row.
Glorious rainbow amongst the clouds
Depicts the Father, the Don, the Holy Spirit endowed.
Your presence sings beyond the peaks,
Hills, mountains, valleys, clouds of whom we seek.
God bless you who sits on the Divine Seat.

　　　Dians M. Newman Gregerson

Carcinomically Speaking!

When the tears arrived,
it was signed "Carcinomically yours."
That's not a word
I said to myself.

But the message was clear
and, characteristically speaking,
reflected a time drawing near.

Desperate times ignite
desperate thoughts
that spread like only
a wildfire can . . .
the very same way
carcinoma moves when
oxygen sets it free
to take a life . . . carcinomically speaking.

　　　Melissa B. Graves

Each Day

I live beyond the paling of each day
Throughout each night and the days of gray
Which bring the beauty of spring
And the glory of summer
That take us right into fall
We then pass summer when skies become over cast
And leaves of summer begin to fall
The leaves of autumn turn copper and brown
And cascade their beauty all over the ground
Then old man winter begins his trek to our land
And touch our faces with his cold hands
With snowy flecks of snow he has cast down
Then, with the icy milk of winter, all become still
With winter in its full dress and frills
All of these days and nights given us, one day at a time
Should give us the supreme understanding of
A spirituality of great divine

　　　Willie D. Cooper

Dog Tags

I finally got the courage to go through all your things.
It hurt to touch each item, and the memories they bring.
But as I sorted through a box, I found something from your past:
Your army dogs tags on a chain, a lost part of you—at last.
I held them tightly in my hand, a heat began to swell.
I felt your presence with me then, first time since we bid farewell.
I wear them now around my neck, along with your wedding ring.
They lie nestled between my breasts, and they mean everything.
When I'm scared and lonely, I hold them in my hand,
And I'm comforted in a way only you could understand.
Somehow, I feel you're with me, morning, noon, and night,
And when I hear the metals clink, I know that you're all right.

Jo Medlin Meyer

Search in Cyberspace

I followed you out to Cyberspace,
Lord High Executioner.
I, a punching bag,
Waiting for the next blow, the old puncheroo.
And I say—look here—
I like to imagine I am free.
Then the long arm of the government reaches out again
And I try to stand, weaving my way, bobbing the darts,
But in spite of all, despite the little people gods,
The self-worshippers,
There is time alone—the perfect peace,
Time for changing the clocks back
After they stopped in the storm,
Time for remembering
The privilege and obligation of age.
Dear departed friends,
Oh, how long will it be?
Have you looked into those white billows in the sky?
I would fly into them and find rest—peace in the storm—
The peace of music and flowers, and the peace of love.

Alene Jones McNamara

Ode to a Grandma

Down in Virginia and all alone
No TV, radio, nor telephone

Three kids she left to show she was known
The age upon her surely was shown

With her spring house, pastures and fields
She never stopped, tired or yield

When the government came to take her away
She looked at them and said "Please let me stay"

Now she knew those days were gone
How wrong we were to leave her alone

If she was here, She'd surely say
I lived to the fullest each and every day
So let me go and live your own way

Patty Anderson Olson

Dear Daughter

We just talked on the telephone;
It is next best if you can't be at home.
You are beautiful, sweet, thoughtful, and kind,
So far away, yet so close in my mind.
I worry about you living alone,
Then I think how much you have grown.
You are responsible, a good mother and friend
With deep compassion, on whom many depend.
I treasure the time we have spent together;
It is part of my heart forever and ever.
Life is not easy; sometimes it is tough.
Just being your mom, the reward is enough.
I am proud of you and all you do . . .
The need overwhelmed me to say "I love you."

Donna M. Ochs

The Day of the Golden Eagle

It seemed the road stretched far too long,
with space and time in between.
A world of life we passed by,
the sun gave way to gleam.
Insignificance deemed the theme,
of the brazen day,
until I saw the beauty of the Lord,
high upon the land.
His golden wings illuminate,
take hold, he has your hand.
That road we thought, oh, so long,
that voice we did not hear,
it took us to a special place,
a gift of peace so rare.

Sharon Hanna

Time Out

Everyone needs to take time out
From the noise, from the crowd,
Even from our children.
Take time out to listen to
The birds, smell the air,
And look at the green grass.
No more running around.
Take time out
To kick your feet up,
Relax yourself,
No matter how busy we seem to make ourselves.
Take time out
To thank God above
For giving us love.

Barbara Blackmon

Just Like You

Someone that you can tell your deepest, darkest secrets to
To be used against you at any given time
Someone that you can trust and depend on when you are blue
To keep you blue, but doesn't figure it's a crime
Someone that will be there for you when your spirit is low
So you'll always be depressed and never try to leave
Someone that will brighten your day and help you feel aglow
So they can lie and you'll never know you're being deceived
Someone that can help you forget all about your sorrow
As long as they can always make you cry
Someone that can help you look forward to tomorrow
Of more abuse and wishing you would die
Someone that is as funny as a clown
That takes great joy in laughing at your fears
Someone that will never let you down
Until you break, so they can see your tears
Someone that with time, a friendship can grow
Or with time, you can really learn to hate
Someone that is just like you. Doesn't it show
You thrive on suffering? So is it just your trait?

Cindy Boyd

Hate

Invisible walls of this twisted hell
hold me prisoner of worldwide pain
helplessly I lay in the arms of defeat
blood red tears blur my vision
darkness forms an unforgiving way
everything I've lived for or loved is destroyed
I'm too far to reach and too tired of trying
fading into nothing, I slip away. The winds pick up
and reveal hidden pictures to my mind I realized:
"this is the end of my world and the star of theirs"
drifting on the current of despair
mute witnesses don't show emotion . . .
don't try to help pretend nothing's wrong
then everything's Gone

Jessica Bell

Earth

Earth and Heaven
Around us roll us
With love and faith in God
No matter how hardship that we encounter,
Like thunderstorm or tornados,
Earthquake and war of all nation,
We are still divided in true love in our heart.
So even that winds, the rains,
and the brightest sunshines,
The flowers, the trees, the birds, that flying by.
The Eagle look like sparrow in the eyes of God,
He is always there up above the sky
To granted our wishes like a million star.
When it come to money the root of all evil.
Jesus Christ our Lord, the Savior of mankind.

Letty F. Mendoza

Rose

Oh, glorious form, your scent perfumes the air.
The brilliant colors you display
Dance playfully in our eyes.
Rose of summer, you transform the mundane
Into the magnificent!

Lynn Owen

Secret World

A secret world exists
Where force becomes form;
There, creation takes place.

When autumn scarlet sets trees afire,
This force moves snow geese
To trace their calligraphy in the sky.

As the first rays of the sun
Illuminated the great pillars
Of the temple of Amen-Ra at Thebes,
The singers who raised clear maiden voices
Praised this force.

Galileo, rebuked, sensed this force,
Muttered under his breath,
"And still it moves."

The formula E=MC2 describes this force:
Mushroom clouds, the cloning of genes
Reveal it—
The matrix of creation.

J. Wallace Bastian

Pure Golden Words

"Lord, let thy word penetrate in my soul as an arrow
so thy word be alive in me, and I'll be strong in thy word!
Let thy hands touch my lips so my mouth speak up only thy word,
and let thy word be in me as Pure Golden Words!"

Mercy Marbella Pedone

My Soul and My Heart

Do you see my soul?
It is the part of me you cannot see.
Can you see my heart?
It is hidden inside my body, but the heart
I mean is another part of me you cannot see.
I can't see them either.
But I can feel them inside me.

Don't look for my soul, or my heart.
You will not find them.
Close your eyes, you may feel one of them.
You may experience their purity and depth.
They're there, I know.

Louisa Slappery

A Mother's Love

A mother's love is divine
A mother's love is caring
A mother's love is loving
A mother's love is sorrowful
A mother's love is happiness
A mother's love is hopeful
A mother's love is greatness
A mother's love is powerful
A mother's love is sadness
A mother's love is peaceful

Divine wants her child, youths, adults to be divine
Cares for offspring, while not forgetting self
Loving always whether family is good or bad
Sorrowful when things goes wrong in life
Happiness when they are happy and successful
Hopeful that they future will be brighter, than her's
Greatness when they achieves their life goals
Powerful when they solve their life goals
Sadness in the time of problems or great loss
Peaceful and serenity for their accomplishments

Bettye Russell

Love and You

Roses aren't always the color of red.
This poem represents them, by your sick bed.
Scientists can change violets' color of blue.
So, let these words express my love for you.

You've been more than family, yes, a good friend.
This is not a lie, because I don't pretend.
With loving kindness, you've always been there.
Indeed, you treated me more than just fair.

The parties you gave made many happy and cheer.
The delight you rendered happened more than a year.
Don't think your actions, no one did not care,
For the attention and love you so freely did share.

Then you left, in another state, you did relocate.
Your old house has an unwelcome looking gate.
No more entertaining, no more parties, no more fun,
The house didn't provide all of that, you were the one.

You always read my written words with such glee.
You really knew how to pamper and cater to me.
Always remember these words I express to you.
God always loves you, and I do too.

Joyce Kelly

The Night That Jake Soared

My Jake seemed content, from what I could gauge
Then again, maybe not, spending life in a cage?
I wasn't aware he was restless and bored
But I found out that night, that night that Jake soared

He'd spent many hours gazing out at the trees
Where the birds on the outside flew free as the breeze
I wondered what other signals I had ignored
That led to that night, that night that Jake soared

Coming home one cold evening, with Jake in the car
I thought "I'll leave his cage here; I don't have to go far"
I'd carry him in through the rain that just poured
And that's how it happened, that night that Jake soared

Off he went, flying high, up and into the night
I'd tried to hang on but he put up a fight
The sound of my heartbeat, so loud it now roared
With the fear that I felt, that night that Jake soared

Through that endless night I searched, waited, and prayed
A moment of carelessness, was this the price to be paid?
Then at first light I did find him, that small bird I adored
and thanked God Jake survived, that night that he soared

Donna and Eve Shavatt

The Day of Gloom

What is this incredulous life
That comes to us in all solemnity,
Fallacious 'er without one moment's warning,
And steals o'er us so silently we hear not
A single tread?

Bursting relentlessly it thrusts forth
Its shadows and gloom
To entail us, inveigh us,
Beleaguer us until we feel life's lost thread.

Ah! It is but the night that
Enshrouds us, enfolds us in its shadowy mist
And lingers on as a poison to torment the soul.
No rest will come, but verily we feel
The devils, tentacles to taunt and daunt us.

But there is a light, a shimmering light.
It reveals a new day in dawning—
And hope again yearns anew.

Anita Saladen

Deepest Realms of Our Age

Age goes deeper than one might think
our souls, minds, and desires, one's past life
is another's dream while the other's nightmare.

Spinning around in one's misty muck
is another's misty rich
whether the other is real or not.

Mysterious, yet true one thought to be dead
still exists in dreams, the subconscious, or in a new body.

Answers to one's questions go unanswered.
The reason is to be unknown, for the unknown
is to stay unknown.

Curiosity wells inside of me—
who, where, when, and why?

Laura Rousseau

Day by Day

Each and every day, we learn by our past mistakes.
My eyes are open to a new direction:
I see a road of new experiences . . . most of all,
A challenging life ahead for me.
Knowing that I will have many faults to learn by,
I can't go wrong willing there is always tomorrow.

Odette De La Torre

The Cat Sent by God

I found him! Here he is!
My intent was a rescue.
He sprawled full length,
Absorbing the autumn sun.
He stood
He yawned
He stretched
He allowed himself to be rescued.
I took him into my house
My intent was to protect
He prowled
He spied
He sniffed
He settled into the protection
Of the hand-carved Queen Anne's chair.
Those days I felt so sick
My intent was to sleep
He curled. He snuggled
He purred. He never left my side
I allowed myself to be rescued and protected.

Betty Kay Rebeck

When Life Was Sweet

We pierced the tranquility of the velvet night
With our frantic laughter
Creating a haven of brilliance for ourselves
In the middle of the darkness
We ripped through the blazing freshness
Of the morning with our sheer excitement
Enjoying the first blush of dawn as it healed our fatigue
We were like goddesses, so naive yet so sage
Youth lingering on our faces
Of all the tangible things in the world
This experience was far better
A cloud of joy was our only endeavor
And life was sweet

Tara Riccelli

The Greatest Man I Ever Knew

When I was small.
He say us play ball.
After working hard all day.
He always had time for us to play.
He liked to tease his wife
But he loved her all of his life.
I was the oldest of ten.
He see that the little one would win.
He was always a hard worker very wise.
He taught me how to use an axe and scythe.
Mornings when you heard the alarm.
You knew there was work to be done on farm.
Milk the cows slop the hogs
And don't forget to feed the dogs.
You had to know how.
To hitch the horses to the plow,
He wanted you to have fun.
So you didn't have to go in a run.
I am very glad.
That this man was my dad.

Walter A. Sandy

Boundless Love

My family is so dear to me.
Their love shines through for all to see.
When times are bad I breathe a sigh,
As I look around and they're close by.
At times my patience becomes very thin.
A helping hand they freely lend.
They caress my shoulder and quietly say,
"I love you, Mom, rest today."
My beloved partner, steady and strong,
Gently tells me when I'm wrong.
Respect and honor to me they give.
I'll treasure this as long as I live.
My family is my strength and pride.
My love for them I cannot hide.
I thank the Lord for a life of bliss
In giving me a family just like this.

Louise Webster

Happiness

All the things you do,
No matter large or small,
My heart beats with gladness too,
But did I say "thank you;"
I don't recall.

There are no words that can say
That in my heart there is a song
Which feeble words can never convey;
My wish for your happiness every day.

Happiness is in every place,
Even by the silent countenance of your face.
This happiness fills within me that empty space,
With a heavenly embrace.

Irene C. Haberer

RUSH

The beach was beautiful last night.
The moon flashing, sparkling light on the water
highlighted his face as if it were painted white on canvas.
The wind gently blowing, whistling off the ocean
and running up, kissing him like a child,
pushing his hair back off of his staring face.
An image of the moonlight on the ocean reflected in his eyes
as I looked into them, filling me with warmth.
He reached his hand up to touch my face,
and as his fingers dance on my skin
my head is filled with the imagination of what could happen
on this beautiful, starry, moonlit night.
I am awakened from my haze by the gentle sweep of his lips onto mine
sending chills deep into my soul.
Slowly he pulls away, brushing my cheek delicately
with the tips of his fingers.
He takes my hand as we walk together
into the rolling waves of the breaking tide and slip
Back into the ocean.

Sherah Krista Manley

My Love Is Everywhere

My love is in the rising sun
And fills my day with loving care
And I will know when day is done
That my love is everywhere

I see her in the beauty of spring
Across the meadows resplendent with flowers
I hear her when the meadowlarks sing
And feel her presence in my lonely hours

My love is in the gentle winds
That fluff the clouds on dreamy days
My love is an angel who sends
Messages of her love in countless ways

She is among the stars twinkling so bright
Like sequins flickering in brilliant light
She is in each wafting snowflake
Drifting down for my soul's sake

Oh! My love is in the setting sun
With colorful hues beyond compare
And I will know when day is done
That my love is everywhere

W. L. Allen Jr.

Angel Baby

Every now and then I wonder,
wonder who you would be.
I wonder who was the little boy,
the world will never see.

You were cute as a button,
and small as a dime.
I wanted to tell you,
but there wasn't enough time.

Nine months I waited.
For what? I will never know.
I don't understand,
why so fast you had to go.

I never said good-bye,
yet I never said hello.
You left me so quick,
before our brother, sister bond could grow.

But I got the chance of life
that you never would.
And I have a love for you,
that you never could.

Nicole J. Rankin

Silence

Most thirty years have come and gone
since the lady tried in vain to warn
of a world who's birds would disappear
if her advice was left but to scorn

How right she was in what she said
of the way we have abused our land
how many creatures must vanish forever
before we address the problems at hand

We have little time to correct our ways
and must work with the utmost concern
before our planet goes the very same way
of our songbirds who shall never return

Once something precious leaves our sight
and we realize just how wrong we were
can we not now awaken our minds
and make our world a better place for sure

Let us now heed the advice of that lady
who was so caring about all these things
and wanted for us all to never hear
the lonely sounds of the silent spring

Joe E. Huffman

The Liar

No one wants to be alone;
people were made to live together.
So why is it so hard for me to not feel so alone?
As I sit here, so a part of this grand design
yet isolated unto myself,
this glass surrounds me at all times,
never allowing anyone to pass too close to me.
Why? So what do I do
When I've lost everyone I thought I cared about?
So I run my hands over the glass and frame,
dying inside 'cause it's all in vain.
Anger, darkness are all that I see—
no more, no less in misery.
So where do I go now?
Here I stay, never looking back—or do I?
I'm a liar.
I need people more than they need me.
Why can't they see my pain and sorrow?
'Cause I hide so well?
No, 'cause I push so hard that they just can't help me.

Monet K. Sanchez

Mother Mary Litumbe Remembered

As death claims your earthly body,
God, the Creator, recalls your heavenly soul.
Your life now resides
In our feeble and weak minds.

When understanding and closeness
Eluded us, you were always a friend,
And when the absence of a voice
Created emptiness, you were heard.

When tears had no solution
To bear the depth of the pains
In this cruel, sinful world,
You provided shoulders for us to cry on.

When the brightness of the rising sun
Blinded us not to see beyond us,
You shaded our eyes without a price.

When the heat of Douala seemed infernal, you fanned it off,
And when the coolness of the nights by the Mount Fako
Chilled the children's body, you provided the needed warmth.

In your children and grandchildren, their "Storyteller" lives.
In the memories of time, in your friends and foes, you live.

Gahlia Njongoh Gwangwaa

His Hands

One look and they are dirty,
The hands of a working man,
But look and they are sturdy
For they built this life that can
House all our needs,
And it's not out of greed
That these hands work, but of love,
For they could easily wear gloves
Of protection, for "the way always scars,"
But those are what makes these hands what they are,
Rough and yet gentle when they create,
Callous but humble for they know their fate
And reward for their labor,
In the sound of a student, a woman, or neighbor
Saying plainly two words,
Or a simple smile inferred
To say thank you,
There lies the power for all that they do,
These hands in themselves need no fame,
But I know that the Father's look just the same.

  Richard Cassford

Closer Than Most

To Tresa, with love, for all my life
Thinking of you has become such a delight,
that I often sit and wonder with all of my might.
Having visions of us becoming much closer than most,
are they just simply dreams that I'm tempted to boast?
You are far more than someone I've merely dreamed,
you are my life choice with whom I want to be teamed.
Together we can build a most prosperous life,
together we can overcome both pain and strife.
How can this be possible in a world sickened with doubt,
could such a promise even be mentioned, let alone come about?
The answer may not be all too easy to see at first,
but once it is realized it'll almost make your heart burst.
Simply trust in the Lord and believe in His way,
as you awaken in the morning and as you go about the day.
Never forget that God's grace is sufficient for us;
if we are to truly prosper, then believe this we must.
Yes, thinking of you is indeed my delight,
no more must I wonder as I've accepted outright.
These visions are real so there's no need to boast,
you and I together, much closer than most.

  Bill J. Dunbar

Sunrise

Cherished dream languished in a lonely heart,
Yearning for daybreak, end of the sinister spell,
Radiating glow at the distant mountain crest,
Ultramarine slowly revealing in contrast to excel.

Solitary soul in listless labyrinth of erudition,
Celestial luminaries twinkling away uncanny codes;
Hovered awhile, oblivious of the mission ultimate:
Opportune navigation towards climactic episodes.

Wondrous spirit in incessant pursuit of progress,
Determined with lofty ideals for pure perfection,
Heralded the glorious era of hopes and happiness,
Ushering a blissful, bountiful century of civilization.

Rejuvenating joy, celebration in healing hearts;
Youthful courage wins over the demon of dismays;
Hilarious magnolias dancing with charming smiles:
Astounding display of life in vivid, vivacious arrays.

Perfumes of sublime scents, appeasing the sentience,
Permeate every entity, transforming to a precious gem,
Yielding gifts of golden grace and gracious grandeur;
Begins thus a marvellous sunrise aflame of fame!

  Jerry Chowdhury

Also-Ran's

There is much to be said for the also-ran's
The guy on the team who is not number 1

And maybe a cheer should be raised for the soul
Who falters and stumbles but gets the job done

"All hail to the chief," to be sure this is true
But a little hail's needed for the plain me and you

Because we do our job and obey every rule
We complete every task and sometimes play the fool

And we keep this world going, you know this is true
So hail and best wishes, 'cause we're needed here too.

  Margaret Kritikos

Answer

I reach for my thoughts as they run away,
But time hasn't given me the words to say.
A face of pleasure, but a heart of pain,
The soul of Peter with the mind of Cain.
I've found myself in an all too familiar scene,
Subtle clues are given, I never know what they mean.
It seems that every time I was deserted,
It was certain that with death I flirted.
What fears did I always hold inside?
I tried to run but, from my mind, I couldn't hide.
I hear noises comin' from things I know don't exist,
Expecting shots around the corner from a man who won't miss.
I looked for a way out, but I had no choice.
When I began to step closer, I heard your voice.
While I was talking with you, I found a reason to care.
So I walked around the corner and only you were there.
I saw there was no reason to run and hide,
And realized I had no fears inside.
You are the answer to the questions I couldn't understand.
And the thoughts I couldn't catch, you hold in your hand.

  Sean Mele Bowen

Words, Words, Words

Words of rhymes and reason, that can be pleasing, yet tongue
teasing, that bring with them the golden splendor of the day
to give way to rhymes and reason, can make or break the day,
as many can do with silly little words of nonsense.
Since happiness is found in our silly little words, here starts
the day that we can pave, as the day goes on, in tales of
bats that chase the cat who now sits on a mat, with a funny
little bunny who can spin money into honey, as the sunny
day will drink in the splendor of golden streams.
As a twinkle in the sky, milk and cookies, can turn into pies,
in turn lies, the little miner who dreams of riches,
in streams of gold and silver that can make you quiver
with sure delight, as the stride of the happiness, will
always keep you and delight you, as pride.
In a moment you change from rhyme to a reason of
seriousness of life, words of the day bring time
to the shear moments of the knowledge to change;
in an instant, silly words come to mind, such as
willy dilly come fly a kite into the night sky.

  Marie E. McKerlie

Moment in Time

The hands of time march to a steady drum beat,
while the winds of the east blow . . . gusting . . . the
snow falls with a steady rhythm . . . the hills look
like Angel's white wings . . . dipping and
dancing . . . performing one of God's miracles.

Angel snow puffs lie on the hills, while
no footprints mark the movement of the morning,
transcending peace marks this moment in time . . .
feeling the beauty of the inner stillness of the
spirit within . . . harmony and grace . . . bless this moment in time.

  Sharon Dunn

Barbara

When I realized that I loved you
It was as if time stood still
I looked at you
And my eyes took a picture
And stored it in my heart
You are my heart's delight
In my darkness
You are my daylight
You radiate a sparkling kind of joy
You see a rainbow where there should be clouds
Just the thought of you
Makes my heart with rapture sing
My love for you is purer than the whitest rose
Deeper than the deepest ocean
You are the one who has taken my heart
And made it soar to new heights
You are a woman
So rare and beautiful and precious
You take my breath away
I will forever love you

Paula V. Galvez

Silent Dream

A silent dream surrounds me
unfolding my deepest thoughts.
It is filled with scattered seeds
of pains and sorrow of my heart.
There in my dream I behold
the mighty secrets of your mind,
I contemplate the sinful virtues
which brought the two of us apart.
A silent dream is killing me
revealing emotions long ago
from my soul gone,
I can feel and see you like before . . . at last,
It is a dream of love forgotten
with sweet desires of my mind.
I am drowning slowly because I love you
but even in dreams, I wonder why.

Vielka E. Rollins

My Dream

I dream of walking through the clouds someday,
With the man who created it all
Where I wouldn't have any fears to hide away,
And I'd always have him close to call
The only reason I dream this dream
Is because right now he's so far away
But my hope is for this to come true,
On some distant day

To some my dream is lame
'Cause they say if I went right now
I wouldn't want to be
And I understand everyone I love
Would now be gone from me
But someday we'd all meet again
Along with the man that loves us all

Jessica Johnson

Death and an Old Man

My friends are dying, falling like ripe fruit from the trees.
Yes, death is claiming all my friends.
Now, like a wanton whore she beckons to me.
"Hello there! Yeah you, death, surprised I know you, huh?
Oh, I've known you for a long time,
of course not like I am going to know you now,
but I was there when you visited so many others,
just standing around watching you.
Oh, yeah, I know you, come in,
sit for a spell, I'll be right with you."

Phillande C. Jackson

Ethereal Devotion

you ask why, do i
use the heavens to describe your beauty
your celestial body
is the one i hold exalted above me

like the firmament hangs over the earth
so does your aura hang over me
your eyes are like stars
that dance in the evening
and when you smile, you shine like the moon
breaking from behind the dark clouds of midnight

you are the earth
the fruit you bear feeds my soul
from you comes everything needed for life

my soul is the sun, you are the moon nurtured by me

your beauty transcends all of space
the birth of stars, the life and light of the nebula

your personality mapped out like constellations
yet difficult to understand like ancient astronomy

an endless existence, unbound by time or volume
but trapped by me, me trapped by you. . . .

Cole W. Brenize

Princess

A princess, I'm sure you are
with eyes that gaze afar
Long dark hair and eyes to match
all can find the beauty in that
But can they see your inner self
the one that causes my heart to melt?
The fragile soul that lies within
that makes your choices whether to sin
Then flashes red when your anger flares?
no one would approach, no one would dare
Or the gentle side that shows you care
and the worry over whether it's fair?
The tears that come when life's not right
are not always kept just for the night
Beware of the jealousy you hold so close
a lesser amount would destroy most
Your love, acquired in generous portions
is far more precious then any lotion
A princess, I'm sure you are
Truly in life, you'll go far

Nancy D. Wells

My Trudy

To my late wife with love, Trudy Louise Martin (Nylin)
Our Trudy walks those golden streets
With jewels in her golden hair
Her smile would melt the devil's heart
Even he would stop and stare

She went to our heavenly mansion
Where soon she will sit on a heavenly throne
She tells me not to be down hearted
That she hasn't left me here alone

I'm up here with our Savior
We're in your hearts I know
I know you'll never forget our love
Or that I still love you so

God saw Trudy was, oh, so tired
And a cure was not to be
So he put his arms around her
And whispered, come with me, with tearful eyes
We watched her pass away
Even though we love her dearly
We could not make her stay

Harold Roy Martin

Which Way Now

So many years gone by, to get you to this place.
Choices made, working plans, to get you in the race.
So many years of changes, still fighting to keep the pace.
To keep your wits about you, you often seek out space.

Feelings seem to worsen, as the days glide by.
Could there be fresh options, or has the well gone dry.
Where stagnant dreams and empty
Hopes leave you wondering why.
This was the way, at that time, no one can deny.

So many years gone by, what will be your fate.
Other interests abound you now, but feelings of too late.
Self-induced changes, what difficult decisions to make.
No one else has an answer, for it is your happiness which is at stake.

Pamela J. Stein

Too Many Years

Too many years have passed and gone.
Inside of me I wonder what went wrong.
My heart is yearning, my eyes filled with tears,
Just because of wasted years.
No love, no laughs, no strolls in the park,
No hugs, no kisses, no passion in the dark.
My dreams haven't come my way.
So often I think I was led astray.
The dawn of a new day has passed,
But precious moments still do last.
What can I do, where can I go?
I'm tired of being tossed to and fro.
A brighter day is awaiting untold.
I'm waiting for that mystery to unfold.
One day I will soar to the sky
Without a doubt, a whimper, or a sigh.
I'll land on the top of the hill.
There I'll never regret too many years.

Dorothy J. Johnson

Was It Me?

Please hold your tongue,
until I am done.
Why not try something new:
You let me speak until I am through.
My words, thoughts, and feelings are worth the wait,
but, instead, you always have to spew your hate.

Bitter and angry is your soul,
slowly and surely consuming my goal.
Happiness, peace, and love
slip through my fingers like removing a glove.
I've watched you evolve from happy to bad.
My being the cause is, oh, so sad.

Laura A. Simmons

To Fill the Emptiness

There's a hole inside my heart
that's longing to be filled
It's gnawing at my insides
and tearing me apart

I have tried to fill it
with parties, toys, and fun
but though they worked for a time
I really haven't won

I've prepared myself for living in the gray
for being unhappy, bummed, and blue
when my eyes found my bible
and I began to pray

And now my life is better than ever before
My heart is light and free
I've asked Jesus to be my friend
and there's no emptiness anymore

Desi Gottfried

Why the Birds Sing

The wind whips
as you boldly plant your feet.
You pray to the clouds
as you grip the steely strut.

Slide to the edge, hang suspended in midair,
look to the cockpit with eyes of trusting fear.
Receive the thumbs up sign, release your fragile hold,
arch to the heavens as you fall towards fields of gold.

Jerk of the harness
as the cloth of life unfolds.
Sigh of relief
as the twisting cord unbinds.
Silently soaring
as you gently drift through space.
Realizing, as you tiptoe back to Earth,
this is why the birds sing their daily song of mirth.

Fran Williams

Long Ago

There was a boy I used to know, one I miss so much.
I remember his sweet smile, his gentle touch,
The way the wind blew through his hair,
His showing off 'cause I was there.
Our first meeting, just by chance,
The first date, our high school dance,
Sometimes I see him in my dreams,
In wayward places and far-out schemes.
I hear him laugh, see him smile,
Hold out my hand, and beg, stay awhile.
Then I awaken and know he's gone;
I become aware that it's all wrong;
to see his smile, to feel his touch,
that would just be too much.
For he has his life and I have mine,
We are in another place, another time.

Roxie McGaughy

You Are My Love

You are my one and only love,
My sun and moon and stars above.

Our hearts and souls are intertwined
Like grapes turned into vintage wine.

Your happiness is my desire.
You light the match that starts my fire.

My entire world will start to sing
When on my hand you place your ring.

We'll trust, we'll hope, and share our love
And ask God's guidance from above.

Like when our love had first begun,
I pray that we are always one.

Pat Huffman

Acceptance

Echoing thoughts of my dismay
I live my life day to day
A peaceful death for which I pray
Why must you stand in the way?

The pain within shatters my mind
Slivered shards of my own kind
Searching for something I will never find
My tainted soul you try to bind

You seek to control that which is mine
Never ever will you walk that line
Wherever you look you see the sign
Don't worry about me I'll be just fine

Gavin Meyers

The Bum

Approaching, a man I thought was a bum;
Of my possessions, would he want some?
He stood out, unlike many.
I have nothing for him, not even a penny!

This bum stuck out like a sore thumb.
Praying he'd not ask me for a crumb.
He has his now sorry life to live;
Why should I, to him, anything give?

"Who is this degenerate?", pompously, I said.
Judgmental thoughts, appearance convicted him in my head.
The closer he got, the better I could see his face.
Yes! He was a refugee from the human race!

He now was upon me and I could plainly see . . .
Apparently, this bum wanted nothing from me.
"Silver and gold have I none,
But such as I have, I'll give you some!"

These words proceeded from the bum's mouth,
Arrested my judgment from heading south.
Offering of life, he halted my heart for a while . . .
"Jesus loves you," he added with a smile!

Victor Baskett

What Do I Know?

I'm a kite flying by the seat of my pants
Down the international, interracial, intergender,
Across-the-ages highway . . . of Depression.

It's my favorite place. It's my most hated place.
I know it so well; so familiar is it to me that I must love it,
But so barren and terrible is the landscape that I must hate it.

Oh, God, get me out; oh, Heaven, let me be!
My confusion leads me here and keeps me wandering
'Round and 'round this nothingness,
But my vast storage of knowledge gets nowhere . . . fast!
What do I do? How do I get out?
This mind-set is driving me crazy,
Or was I mad to begin with?
I don't know. I don't know! I Don't Know!

I think I need help,
But where do I get it?
Will it hurt; I hate the pain.
Will it help; I am unfamiliar with the feeling.
Can the outside world help? It scares me.
My world helps and hinders, but it's familiar to me.
I know it.

Wendy Nicole Lane

The Sacrament

She feels the weight, vision blurred . . . the litany continues.
Standing in a daze, she watches as
They all move forward, seeking His body and blood.

She aimlessly follows, her broken heart beating furiously.
Chords of terror strike the child within.
The Celebration has become a sword, a test.
They come as children, she as a shell of the woman she once was.
Unconsciously reaching out her hands . . . the world stops.

The offering hands do not hold the bread of life . . .
In His mercy, God is ever-present.
For the hands which took her soul and faith have nothing to give.

Another guides her with unknowingly kind eyes.
The bread of life, His body, is given and received.
Tasting of the blood of Christ, her hands shake
While entranced by the crucifix.

"Yaweh, I Know You Are Near" echoes through her soul.
Maybe she too can be resurrected from this man-made crucifixion.

Ann E. Fairbairn

A Loving Mother's Faith

Each day she asked for guidance
To be directed and shown the way
Never veered from the straight and narrow
Never forgot to pray

She struggled each day of her life time
Worked so hard at what she did
With three mouths to feed
There wasn't much time to kid

The faith that she lived by each day
Was beautiful to see
It was always put into practice
Wherever she might be

Holidays were what we lived for
Going places together
When we had her all to ourselves
In all kinds of weather

My best friend, my mother, left me
For a happier home on high
No one can ever replace her
Nor her faith that I live by

Mary E. Ewachiw

Joy

My parents, Gillan and Rosetta Whyte, fourteen brothers and sisters
Sitting at the edge of another day,
I looked to hills that God hath made.
What strength transcends from God's awesome landscape.
I'd give anything for a moment's escape.

The trees stand tall, fresh, and clean,
Humbly bowing and swaying in the breeze,
Bathed from the heavy showers of the day,
Giving thanks and praise in their own sweet way.

Birds singing their various tunes,
Flittering from tree to tree,
Happily drinking from the leaves,
Leftover drops from the showers of blessing.
Grey sky from overcast clouds,
Awaiting to descend as rain.

May God grant me wisdom, knowledge, understanding,
Love, and peace of mind
To discern and appreciate God's given beauty,
To know that in every leaf, tree,
Rock, mountain, or stream.
There lies "A message."

Hyacinth E. Silvera

Drink to Drown

You're a little late,
And I'm all little gone.
All I want is to feel this way
To always feel the same.
Not feeling life's accusations and blame.
Where was I going without knowing the way!
I try to calm down to reason out,
Come to terms with what it's all about.
Sorry, no happy endings here!
Bartender pour me another beer.
Even when you have nothing to say,
You just go ahead and say it anyway.
I hear you talking but I don't care what you think,
You're just a fly in my drink.
Last call! Good night!
Last one turn out the light.
There is no more laughter,
And my face turns to plaster.
I'm holding on to a feather expecting to fly,
I feel to the ground, my third time down, drink to drown.

Paula A. Kobel

Nikki

Another branch is added to the family tree . . .
Christened Ashley Nicole by loving family.
Born February tenth, nineteen ninety-seven,
Unplanned for Mom, but still a gift from Heaven.

As we celebrate your birth,
As we celebrate you now,
We'll be careful to give thanks to God above,
For when He gave us you, 'twas a blessing undisguised,
For He gave us all a portion of His love.

Cathy E. Wright

Victor's Garden

Some people search long and hard
To find truth that transcends their yard
Others let someone else do the thinking
Or hold to a lie, even while sinking

To have a nice garden, plant seeds with care
Good soil, sun, and water bring crops to share
At times, weeds may choke, gaining control
Likewise, we need to tend spirit and soul

Flowers, trees, fruits, and vegetables
Come in quite an expansive variety
Those who think God loves only certain peoples
Are sadly mistaken in their false piety

People are so fascinatingly unique
There are more born as we speak
We are image bearers, free to choose
Some win the race, others do lose

Water is essential for plants to thrive
Sunshine is needed to keep them alive
We hunger and thirst for various things
"Sonshine" is needed to heal hurts that sting

Rebecca Frainey

On My Own

My heart will still be broken, yet hidden deep inside
My face shall smile again, my tears will soon be dried
I'll find some way to never show the pain held inside
No one ever really knows what's hid behind one's eyes

Since you left, I have been alone, trying to find a way
To get through life on my own, I've learned to face each day
I've found I'm stronger than I've ever known
I can put the past away

Though I miss you still and love you so
I know somehow, somehow I know
I'll make my gray skies blue again
It's time to start over, those old wounds to mend

My face shall smile again, my tears they will be dry
The pain will never show what's tucked away inside
For no one ever really knows what's hid behind one's eyes

Liz Y. Nelson Swick

The Town

A small breeze will lead flowers to kiss
As the morning sets and leaves a mist.
The mushrooms will pop their heads up;
They are shaded by a tree's giant trunk.
A butterfly will pass all of this by
As the toad from the pond eats a fly.
All is well in this small, little place
As the morning sun brightens its face.
But soon, all of this will be gone:
The flowers, the trees, even the pond.
Fate's evil hand will strike all of it down
And, in nature's place, there will be a town.

Amanda Beal

Not Earthly Bound

Not tied to the things that are here on Earth
Having gone through an awakening, a rebirth.
Not pondering over what I can have
No cheating, stealing, nor anything bad.

Not after the material things of lust
Learning more and more to have trust.
No big Cadillac, Sedan, or Seville
No rolls Royce, parties, or cheap thrills.

Not bound to the things or ways of man
Nor trying to be any other, than what I am.
Just standing here in the presence of Light
Away from all those earthly plights.

Craig D. Watson

I Awoke

To my loving mother, Lois Martin
I awoke this morning to the sweet smell of flowers;
The aroma, it lasts for hours and hours.
Then came the rain, and then the rainbow;
It lit up the sky with colors all aglow.
Then came the night, all peaceful and gay;
That's when I knelt by my bedside to pray.
I thanked the Lord, my Savior, my King;
I asked Him for strength to do the right things.
I asked Him to guide, to show me the way.
And I thanked Him most for His beautiful day.

Judy Martin

Morning Mist Rising

It was one of those misty river mornings . . .
When angels have cried the night before
For the wrongs that men have done
But saddened hearts
Resolve to cheer
With the dawning of the sun!

It was one of those misty river mornings,
A lonely walk to the river's edge, she wept . . .
A man whose life, full of love, was gone
Her eyes glance up
Her joy uncontained
And a promise made is kept!

It was one of those misty river mornings . . .
I had vowed to you, "Never Again!"
I was so tired of choosing the wrong paths
Your forgiving spirit
My desire to love
Let beauty rise, and left my sin!

Jennifer Lehner

Out Standing

I was out standing in a world of sin.
I was down and out without a friend.

I was out standing in the cold.
I had nowhere to turn to, nowhere to go.

I was out standing, lost and confused.
Controlled by Satan, he blew my fuse.

I was out standing when Jesus called my name.
He told me that He loved me, that He was my friend.

He received me with understanding, unfeigned love.
He gave me His strength to help me move forward.

Now I am out standing, happy and free,
Because I have a Saviour whose name is Jesus.

I am out standing with God's whole armor on.
I am able to withstand evil and having done all—
I stand.

Lela Pendergrass

Just a Friend

I am the blood that pumps through your veins.
I am the food that nourishes your soul.
Come unto me, and you shall not be lonely.
Come unto me, and you shall be saved.

I am the darkness, the light,
The night, the day.
I shall be anything and everything
You want me to be.

I am the air you breathe,
The solid ground you walk upon.
I will never abandon you.
I will never leave you empty.

Put your head on my shoulder
And let it all out.
Cry to me;
I understand.

I'll be by your side
Until the end.
I am not God,
I'm just a friend.

Brianne Rider

As Nature Sings

I look into the deep blue sky.
As large white clouds float gently by,
I ask of him the question, "Why does
He loves me so?"

I see his carpet on gentle slopes.
Dry leaves on streams below me float.
Hear woodland music from feathered throat
And ask him, "Why?"

Proud mountains raise their snow-capped peaks.
Wild flowers around, his sunshine seeks.
Small creatures come so shy and meek
And I ask, "Why?"

Each blade of grass, each mighty tree,
From highest peak to rolling sea,
Are there each day anew for me,
But I ask, "Why?"

His sunshine warms the crisp blue air;
I see his spirit everywhere.
For each of these, God knows he cares.
He loves me so.

Diane Dalum Groth

Senses of Love

Let's eat a meal of a passionate flavor
Let me taste the rhythm of ecstasy
My mouth tingles in anticipation of embrace
Lips of mine moisten as ours meet softly
Touch me as the night is upon us
Make me feel alive as only you can
Caress me away to a forbidden life
I'll hold your body gently as our journey ascends
The gentle fragrance you wear shows me you are here
Scents of eroticism abound as you approach me
Your body exudes its own mystical scent
This natural fragrance is what draws me to you
I look at you, and I am in amazement
Seeing the ideal woman standing by me
Your perfect form enhances an angelic face
Flowing hair drapes down, caressing your back
Silence fills the heavy air of the night
I hear you calling me to yourself
Sounds of gentle footsteps mark a wooden floor
In a seductive voice you whisper, "I love you"

Jason A. Mann

Heartbreak Hill

I walk the street of loneliness
With heartache and despair.
Looking for someone to love me,
But no one seems to care.

I walk and talk with loneliness
And cry my heart out at night.
I cry out to God for help,
To end my lonely plight.

At night, I sleep with loneliness,
With teardrops in my eyes.
My heart cries out for love,
But no one hears my cries.

One day, I'll leave the street of loneliness,
And if it is God's will,
I'll meet someone who loves me,
And say good-bye To Heartbreak Hill

Jack Dominy

God's Sweetest Angel

In memory of my beloved, severely disabled brother, Bubby
God's love is not found in gold crowned kings
Nor in fancy worldly things
Nor in a darkened heart grown cold
Without love to brighten the soul
His love is found in the helpless, the meek and the mild.
And in the eyes of His sweetest angel, the special child.
We do not know, we ask not why
A child is born unable to cry
When another born can speak and play
But God's sweetest angel can show us the way
The words in his eyes, the smile on his face
Show God's love to the whole human race
From eyes that speak love with words never spoken
With a smile that can heal hearts that are broken
For God's love is merciful and kind
And only through love can we truly find
That God's sweetest angel, so pure and sweet
Is God's greatest gift, with love that's complete.

Betty Dean Myers

Running with Me

Running with me, running with joy,
slowly and constantly is leading to love.
Running with me again and with fun,
brings togetherness and stressless time.
Weekend is here, so are our hearts.
Fireplace is open, so is my heart.
Increasing the friendship and each word of yours,
therefore we can chatter honestly to overflow,
setting up schedule and making lists of spare time.
I feel warmed, attracted considering the respect from you,
contributing greatly to this long-lasting love.
Your sense of responsibility remains in my life,
accepting the consequences when problems do arise.
Your attitude has changed through willingness to accompany more
and more my soul, my heart and mind.
You overworked your feelings proving the impossible.
Rewarding and challenging is my true heart to you.
Yet is love really the magic? Or you who makes it happen?
Bringing the affection through the desire of spending time together.
The growing relationship is fulfilled with friendliness.

Nina Chilargi

Windy Day

The nascent wind begins his rolling day.
Complacently, he throws his life away.
The clouds swing through the sky on roller blades
And fling their tattered scarves and streaming braids.
The pallor of their raiment, grey and dun,
Will soon be brightened by a scrambled sun.

Shirley Rice Lewis

Rick Derby, from Death to Life (1996)

My friend, you are a treasure in God's keeping.
Jewel of light you sparkled in my life
Laughter from your eyes was never ending
Wisdom from your lips could straighten strife.
Always, like a beacon, you were standing,
Pointing to the Lord and showing how
To live within the kingdom without bending
And in the kingdom you're residing now.

God also gives me treasures for the keeping:
Like precious gold I add your smiling face,
And tears to soothe the sadness of your passing
Well knowing you are in a finer place.
But you remain a beacon, ever standing.
Pointing to the Lord, now at His side.
What a gift from Jesus to have known you,
To keep within my heart with grace and pride.

Pennee Struckman

To My Mother-In-Law

If I would have known, if I could have saw,
that you'd be in my life as my mother-in-law . . .

The decisions I've made, I'd change not a thing,
'cause I know in my heart the joy your friendship can bring.

Thank you so much for all the things that you do,
to give me your son and these grandchildren, too.

I think of you often, with all of my heart;
without you and your family, my life would fall apart.

I go through each day without ever a care,
'cause I know in my heart you will always be there.

I love you so much and it's easy to see
that I really love you and you truly love me.

I will be happy till life's at an end,
'cause you're not only my mom, but also my friend.

Donna Kirkness

"Dearest Daughter"

I looked down and thought I saw
a dewdrop fall from the sky,
but it was a teardrop from mom's eye
There was sadness in my heart
a numbness I could not feel,
what was happening was it real?
The pain, the sorrow, would this be gone tomorrow!
The unknown how long would it last
would it soon all be in the past.
I have faith, maybe this happening is a test?
Mom's prayers will have been answered
my faith will have been restored
and I can lay this to rest.
In mom's heart she knows daughter
will be fine, and,
Mother's and daughter's love
will forever be entwined.

Janet E. LaRue

The Rose Beside the Wall

The rose that grows beside the wall has become
The most cherished one of all.
This year it bloomed so bright and fair
(In memory of mother who planted it there.)

She left us to tend the Lord's garden where his roses
Never shall die.
We know she is at home in his garden
That is way beyond the sky.

I still have that rose beside the wall, for it
Has grown since she planted it there.
You know it almost seems eternal with its beautiful roses
So rare!

Virginia Morton Ross

Immortality at Birth and Forever

Face childhood with a zest for life
As the fawn, just minutes old;
Determined, struggles to get up.
Or as the human infant drawing breath
Exhales it in a wail of hope!
Neither perceives a future more
Than sustenance from its mother's breasts.

Then weaned, human and beast alike,
Set out a larger world to know
Through practice, intuition and will
They gain maturity of courage and fear,
Which through the odyssey of our lives,
Govern our attitude and coping choice.

Maturity attained, the value guests
For immortality. And it looks
Into a future, distant, out of sight!
Oh, flaw of nature, to ignore
The truth we should have learned:
Immortality. And it looks
Into a future, distant, out of sight!

Dr. George O. Phillips Sr.

The Looking Glass

Come look in my mirror
and tell me what you see
There's reflections and remnants
of our past history

We laughed through childhood periods
struggled through our adult years
This looking glass brought births and smiles
it also brought us tears

Now if we could, or if we should
change a moment or a day
Were the good old days really all that good
would we bring them back today?

If by chance we could look ahead
see our future in his glass
Would we really change a day or year
and be left without a past?

Come look in my mirror
now what do you foresee?
A future waiting to be lived
with great expectancy

Jean March Beckmann

Am I Alone?

Sitting pensively in the piercing dark
Wondering . . . What day is it?
Or is it . . . What night is it?
Will I, this day, leave my mark?

Where is my Mommy? Will she come home?
Will my reluctant Daddy work late?
Will my tasteless, frozen dinner be late?
One more question, Lord . . . Am I alone?

Trapped unwillingly inside my confused mind
Listening closely to my timeless thoughts
Watching my colorful, wandering thoughts
There's one, my Love thought, it's wonderful to find

I walk alone in a confused, dark fog
My thoughts are fearful—get them away!
I run from the ever-changing sounds of life, far away
Stopping to listen, I stand on my spiritual log

Finding my creator, asking . . . Am I alone?
Why the dark colors and fearful thoughts?
Will there always be darkness and dark thoughts?
Watching the unconditional purity of love, I know, I am not alone!

Lucia A. Weisman

The Love between Them

To my loving family, Dad, Mom, and Kelsey Bolin
We are very good friends
And I hope this won't end our friendship.
"I like you," I say in the mirror every day.
Then I finally get the nerve to tell you and
Blurt out, "Lyon, I like those shorts."
Someday I'll tell you.
The thing I'm afraid of most
Is that it will run our friendship.
The other thing is
That you'll say no and I'll never be able to
Talk to you again.
The day is today that I'm going to ask you
And make my life a little easier.
I'm getting closer to you . . .
And I still can't believe that
You came up to me
And asked me out.

Abby L. Bolin

At the Boys Training Camp

Off the express around the ramp . . .

I went to visit my sister's son
and saw the expression on everyone.
It's a beautiful place out there,
boys, boys from everywhere.

Mothers and fathers looking sad,
wondering what made their boys go bad.

Many boys could've had fun,
but got mixed up with the wrong one.

It's nice out there, air free as a dove,
but so many boys out there need love.

Mothers and fathers, for goodness sake,
we need less boys at Whitmore Lake.

Anna L. Wilson

Life's Dreams

She grew up as a child
Having dreams of life, and for a while
It looked as though they might come true
Then the shades of white turned to blue
But she never forgot her dreams and goals
Even though she was growing old
Then one day she realized, quite to her surprise
The only thing that had kept her sound
Through her life of ups and downs
Was not what she had done
Or things she considered to be fun
It was her dreams
That gave her wings
To fly above the clouds so bright
And keep her heart warm at night

Steve Brookins

The Gallery

A painting is a life; not one is like another
Each canvas is a different life; each has its own color
Paintings give to some a feeling of radiance of life within
And I saw and listened to a painting that made my life begin
I captured the colors of warmth and hope
With insight into this painting's wisdom, I could somehow cope
The colors at first seemed so harsh and so bold
Then the shades took to life and formed a new mold
The memory of this painting will always be in my mind
Its aura and its purpose have always been so kind
It gives strength to others and it will always be
Embellished in my mind for myself to be
The person one should be to love and to live
And maybe like this beautiful portrait I can somehow give

Lynne Baker Topakoglu

In Every Human Heart

In every human heart, there is a sacred duty
to return to the memory of who and what we are,
for we have forgotten we are loved.

We are one people on one Earth
and we have the power to protect
Mother Earth, Father Sky, and sacred oceans below.
We made that journey to live on Earth,
in alignment with the Great Mystery and Energy,
to live in harmony with all living things
and all races of humankind.

In every human heart, we have the power
to abolish weapons of war.
We must raise leaders of peace,
unite the religions of the world,
so spiritual forces can prevail in love
and there is no war in every human heart.

That, my friend, is where peace begins;
then—and only then—can one truly walk
the native Indian beauty path.

Nancy A. Myers

All of Me

To my family for encouraging me to write poems
My essence has never felt the rush of your lips against mine
Or the rush of your hand in mine.
My eyes have never seen the sunrise against the blue ocean
Or the sunset fall behind a mountain.
However, I know the sight is majestic.
My ears have never heard the roar of
The waves as they crash on the beach.
Yet, I know it is amazing.
My lips have never tasted snow as it drifts across the sky.
However, the image alone sends chills through my body.
My legs have never walked along the sandy beach.
I have yet to leave footprints in the sand.
My dreams have not become reality.
I still dream.
My spirit has not yet flown free.
Inside it's trapped, yearning to totally be free.
My soul has never felt united with another.
I yearn for the feeling.
My heart has never felt love.
I must be free.
I must love myself before I can begin to love others.

Jessica Marie Belzner

Pinnacle

A vision without a cause
Soul to soul, mouth to mouth
Illuminating the path of our lives together

Nakedly we ache for each other's arms
Not knowing completely however yearning for more
How easily I have come to you and you to me
Obviously meant to be

Blinded by your beauty
Longing for your caress
We dive into the world holding hands
Never letting go . . .
Grasping tighter with each passing second

We flow with the tide, side by side
Indescribable, a miracle thrust in front
How dost thou love thee?

Fate
Soul to soul, mouth to mouth
Illuminating the path of our lives together,
Forever

Karen Dyer

Timid Touch

Contemplating the moisture of a raindrop
And the texture of a tear,
The sun and the rain
Have joined their pained hands.
They have looked into each other's awkward eyes,
Unsure of what is unknown.
Another sweet seduction,
Imagination, inspiration only an issue
For their air that surrounds the planets.
For the moon will gaze upon this match
And his hope for the Earth will strengthen,
For the sun and the rain have joined hands
And a prism has filled the eyes and skies
Of its atmosphere.

Michelle Franzwa

Could It Be You?

Eternity in darkness have I waited.
Waited for Eros' bolt from gilded bow be loosed.
Song of Venus, fill my ears, my heart.
Banishing time's shadows with your sweet melody.
Leading me down Iris' path, to a brighter sunrise.
Is this love?

Your behavior, an enigma to me.
The playful teasing, bashful sidelong glances . . .
The subterranean river, erupting in spectacular display.
Caressing your immortal beauty, watching . . .
Inviting my lusty azure orbs to do the same.
Is that an arrow I hear whistling?

Perhaps You are the one.
Pursuing me through verdant Spring of dreams.
Where Eros' aim is true and never failing.
Two lovers lying tangled in each other.
I ask myself and pray,
Could it be you?

William Fahnestock

Fiction

Heat waves radiate through my face
As my flesh trembles from the cold.
Emotions run wild through my body
While my eyes show the emptiness of my soul.
Feelings don't exist, I don't know them
Carelessness runs freely from my mouth.
By the light of day I stumble my way through the necessary
By the dark of night I live as much as an empty shell can.
Colors are muted to almost match each other
Blackness is my domain.
My life is like a surrealistic painting
Reality has no meaning, no texture.
There is no escape from this kind of life
Survival is not an option.

Andrea Bragdon

House of Ice

December descended upon the house in June
Halls no longer ring with laughter
Ceremonial bells tolled within the empty tomb
Tarnished rings and promises of ever after

Shattered souls knocking on the barren floors
Unshielded tears go on forgotten
Vows go like demons locking all the doors
Unyielding fears here so newly begotten

Ideals and passion washed down with blood
This empty heart no longer can suffice
Lifeless hope and pain drowned within this flood
Not ever to escape this house of ice

Heather Moyer

Entertaining My Friend's Friend
from Montreal on a Saturday Night

She asked if she could wait here
until Wendy got back from the dressmaker.
So I stepped aside and let her through the door.
She was tall, very tall. She wasn't this tall before,
but, last time, I was so busy trying to get Judy
that I probably ignored her and her height.
So I offered her a drink
and asked about the drive from Canada
and about all the snow there.
Twenty centimeters worth, she said.
She was hungry but all I had were
three bags of pretzels I stole from my Mom's house.
She wanted dinner, but she didn't want Chinese food,
so I took her to Shimon's Pizza and we talked about tattoos
and Walker, Texas Ranger,
if she'll ever move to New York.
Then Wendy walked in
and they went back to her place
and I got on the train and went to work.

Samuel Davidowitz

No Quarrel in Me

You can smell the grinding in their spirits,
See the upset in their eyes,
Murmurs from the side of their mouths,
Others a depression so black it clothes them.

I look to God again and say:
"Please, let there be no quarrel in me."
I am tired of crossing thin lines of
Despite, hearing lies—we care.

My tools of trade being taken, gone,
My worthless roues that roam.
"Please," I say, "let there be no quarrel in me."

For my life five
Times I've had to fight; with God's help
I've made it right.
Through these steps, let there be no
Quarrel in me.
To my life, whatever the future holds,
Let it be easy, no quarrel in me.

Phil Welborn

Beautiful

Oh my goodness, you are so beautiful.
With lovely hazel eyes
With tender lips and fingertips
For days of lonely sighs.

Blessed my eyes for seeing such beauty
With flowing chocolate brown hair
With precious legs and tender feet
To take you here and there.

Beauty is a virtue which lasts forever
In the mind, the body, and the soul.
Intellectual mind can calm anytime
A spirit of fire hot coals.

You are the angel of love and grace
With those inviting, puppy-love eyes.
Warmer and cuter than Winnie the Pooh.
Your essence will never die.

Oh my goodness, you are so beautiful.
You deserve the royalty of a queen.
Your goodness, charm, intelligence and love,
Could make all the angels sing.

Jesse Davis

Grandmother's Heart

Where are you?
Your children growing up without you,
You are missing so many things.
What are you doing?

Young son don't even know you're that sad too.
Someday he wonder where you are why you left him, too.

Your son's playing baseball.
He's growing into nice young man.
His eyes are sad, learning all he can.

Your daughter is so pretty.
She's got your eyes,
A heart of gold, but many of your ways, see it in her eyes.

Where are you, daughter?
Trying help raise the grandchildren, doing the best I can,
With the help of the Lord, be good children.

Some day we will met again.
Hope it not to late,
Because we are kin.
Letha I. Graham

The Streets of St. Paul

Children walking in the night with painted faces,
Mimes with jet-black, tousled hair,
eyes glazed by drugs
to hide and numb the children
from the insidious pain
lurking in the depths
of their aching souls.

Fathers, long gone to
meet their depraved needs.
Mothers, work worn, trying
desperately to keep families
together when father deserts.
Mothers, too exhausted to see
their children's pain.

Children walking the dark street of the night,
Looking . . . groping for something
they won't find in needles, sex, pot, or a bottle.
Looking for love and acceptance.
Mothers wait at home
Wondering, wondering: Where are the children?
Ardeth Anderson Davidson

The Twenty-Century Hope from Despair

The twentieth century is slowly ebbing away
Bringing unusual chaos, violence, and destruction;
Places that once were havens of protection—
Schools and churches are now places of corruption.

Unpresented moral decay has eroded human values;
This disparity has bombarded every segment
Of humanity children's committing violent crimes,
Teens having little or no regards for God's Divine Law,

Mass confusion in everywhere no pleasurable solution.
Avenues for eradicating this immoral pollution.

Evangelist are calling for the church and repentance;
Taking prayer out of schools brought negative reactions,
Politicians are conspiring to bring down the presidency,
While the Nation is sinking deeper in destruction.

What then can eradicate this immoral pollution
And give this Nation a spiritual/ethical solution?
America must renew its faith-Blessed Hope in God.
Then our motto—"In God We Trust" will combat the odds.
Dr. Bessye Tobias-Turner Ph.D.

The Muse

Who are you my little white sea gull
when you flow in my dreams like in the past times.
Now you are here in my present,
and I would give my life to have you in my future.

With a million tears I would make an ocean
where your spirit can sail
in the torrent of my existence.

Do not run away from me . . . sublime muse
do not cure the wound from which my inspiration feeds.
do not mitigate my suffering with your breath
because in each and every respiration the sublimes
and delight of your essence is pronounced
and the enchantment of a remote time adhere to you.

My beloved muse, I will care for your spirit
until your flesh of wind grows old, I will care for your soul,
until your sparkling eyes never blink, again.

I will alleviate your pain, making it my own
because in your every moan I die
in the uncertainly of not having you . . .
please . . . let me abandon myself in you my adorable muse.
Aurora G.

Untitled

I'm married to a situation
That patience condescends
The tension in inspiration
Often leads to painful ends

I open the glass box of denial
And take a peek outside
The innocence is bewildering
There exists no place to hide

The sentiments can never compliment me
As they dance in the hands of provision
The ego of intimate limitations
Represents a common null decision

The sensitive June turns its back on me
Leaving me to survive by a lie
While compelling to introduce the season
It evokes more distance to the sky

The sense of attainment carries atonement
And the position of relevance sighs
The centripetal thoughts of a sentinel
Bring a vision of peace to the eyes
Michael McCray

Soul's Handshake

Words escape me, as I thought they would
My mind's eye screaming for an ear to hear
Knowing these words exist
But the feeling that is meant
Doesn't translate from pen to paper
Yet I need her soul to feel
What it truly means if it is ever revealed
When the words
"We can be friends"
Are asked, said, maybe led
From my feelings inside
For her beauty is deep
Revealed in the sorrow behind her eyes
What I would give
To simply see all smiles deep inside
For this is my handshake
Or maybe a kiss on the cheek
And I can dream
That we will hold hands as the sun sets on a new day
Mark E. Camire

World

A strange man waits
Alongside a dirty street,
For what?
Who knows;
Is he crazy?
People walk away from him,
Scared they might catch his disease.

The sky is gray.
Several dirty cars pass.

The man's eyes are open,
Staring at the violence and death.
A cry from a child is neglected, forgotten;
A blast from a gun is fed.

But we still have each other,
For now.

Brian D. Buckley

Nature's Dissension

Trees on a hill bow to the Earth like servants to the wind
Their leaves like hair and limbs like arms flow
With the raging wind while flowers,
Along with the trees, struggle to stay erect.
But the wind won't give in to them.
He is much stronger than they;
And, like the servants, they serve the wind,
Until he tires of the their services,
Stops his breathing, and subsides . . .
Only until he needs them again.

Terry Ann Edwards

My Very Special Ina

As on the porch I viewed the sun
Feeling that warmth deep inside
For Ina has touched me
In a very loving way

Through my life had searched for
But never could find
Or ever dared to try
What, each day, my Ina gives me

Ina is that rare, beautiful, blossomed flower
That brings to all of my days
That very special reason
For me to keep on going

I find that with Ina's love
That I am able to face that old world
That I have been so running from
Now I need not face it alone

Stanley Arthur Marquette

Wire Ball

I have a wire ball
that's not a ball at all.

Red, blue, black, and green beads,
it is very pretty; they are what it needs.

If you so should choose,
make something that you can use.

Make a nice flower;
you can also make a large tower.

Make a bowl or cup,
or make a spaceship that goes up.

You can make a crown,
guaranteed you'll never frown.

Almost anything's possible with a wire ball
that's really not a ball at all.

Joel Alex

May God Be Found

Make the time to stop and pray
Feel his love from day to day
If your heart has been torn in two
Whether or not the sky is fair blue
It is in His will to make you strong
But the road is narrow and very long
May His hand guide your path, through thick and thin
Never looking back, knowing He is within.
The Bible says we are to live by His word
Even when we feel that it is absurd
Whether you take the challenge to live for Him
It is all up to you to let Christ in
When the road you are treading becomes too hard
Remember that Christ has dealt you the card
It will make you strong or make you stray
But if you believe God is there, either way
Christ hung on a cross with bleeding sores
So we may see Him in Heaven forevermore
As we stop to look at what is around
May God be seen and always found

William D. Corbitt

Hugo the Hurricane

Well, what do you know?
It was the hurricane Hugo.
Hugo! Hugo! Where did he come from?
And where did he go?
The answers to those questions, we will never know.
With terrific winds, Hugo really did blow.

Have you heard of the great Hugo?
He left the Atlantic Ocean and came ashore.
He blew down houses, uprooted trees,
And left us able to bow on our knees.

Hugo was not the will of man,
But was controlled by an Almighty hand.
Let us be thankful unto God
That Hugo did not bury us under the sod.

Henry B. Heath

My Brother

My brother Corey plays a lot of sports
As in Hockey, baseball, and other sorts
He wants to become famous
But most of all, rich
The talent he's got
Is such a great gift
My brother's liked Hockey all of his life
But baseball comes through
Like a shining knife
He likes Hockey, and baseball
And other things too
That's my brother for you
So for all of you who have the same wants
Rich and famous you all hunt
Remember it's all in hard work
But fun is the best perk

Wendy Dotzler

I Have a Friend

I have a friend,
A very dear friend.
Every other day he invites me over.
Can't find that luck in a four leaf clover.
He'd never leave me out,
No doubt about.
He still cares
When everyone points and stares.
This is my friend,
My very dear friend.

Johnny Pillips

Good Night Precious One

To Beth and Bill who unfortunately lost their unborn child
A tragedy unspoken, with a magnitude not to believe.
A life given, yet not conceived, a love tendered, yet not received.
An heir to the throne, which will inherit not,
the toils and troubles that humanity's got.
But nay shall we bow our heads to the sorrow of life's passing,
for the soul knowest no bounds of love everlasting.
Rejoice in the knowledge of knowing,
'tis a much better place he is going.
Shed a tear for our sorrow,
and remember the morrow,
how precious this love you hold dear.
And sing but a song of love to this one,
in hopes that this day may hear
a lullaby, a lullaby.
Good night Precious One,
Good night!

Don E. Rondo

My Knighthood

I'm knighted in an army, in service to my King;
With joy, all the victories to Him I gladly bring.
I keep my armor polished; I keep my weapon near.
I know that, as I trust Him, He wipes away my tears.
I turn to Him for guidance; I listen to His voice.
I'm so glad that He found me, yet gave to me a choice!

I choose to walk beside Him, to fight with all His might;
Together we can conquer, chase the devil into flight.
I praise Him for His blessings He so richly does bestow;
I know that where He leads me, my heart will surely go.
Yes, I'm knighted in God's army, in service to my King;
With joy, all the victories to Him I gladly bring!

Lee Lautenschleger

Full Love

I love you in the morning, when you first awake.
I love to watch you stretch out your arms and see
The first deep breath you take.
I love you more when you look at me, and a smile
Forms deep inside of you, and comes bursting out, too,
And for me.
I love to hear your voice when you first speak to me,
And hang on to every word as you say,
"Hello dear, I love you"
And I love you even more for the glow that lights up
Your face, when I in turn say, "I love you too, my love."
I love you so much and in so many ways.
It took me days; trying to discover, just how much
Do I love you.
And then it came, it is there for you and all to see.
For I discovered that I love you, just as much; as I love me.

James Carter

Frustration in Ink

Empty pages, white, endless, to fill
With words from deepest places unseen.
What a scar the wound retains
From the pondering endured that fools jest
At knowledge they know not of.
My words, to you, are clear as glass
Unseen, unfelt, where from they come
You cannot tell.
So what holds their meaning but me?
To make you understand is a forsakeable task,
Bringing the world to rest in your palm
Is more foreseeable than this.
Therefore, the ink stained forms that do rest
Here stay within only me
With the wanton wish that some soul
Somewhere would catch them in their prime.

Robin Bunnell

Poems Everywhere

Poems, poems everywhere
Some of them good and
Some of them bad?
Some poems take priority
Some are giddy—others are sad!

Some say—reach out and touch someone
Others say—stay away or else
Never know ahead of time
What each poem will bring out!

But when they come—oh, the beauty they have
Bestowed upon a human race
Never knowing what the mind will think next!

Yeah, poems, poems everywhere
Some of them good
Who knows what the poet will write next!

Sharon G. Phillips

September 9, 1995

Holding just one finger, my daughter orbits my body,
Then lets go and walks a comet's tail, spiraling out.

She is one year old today.
This is the beginning.
Her orbit will increase with the passing years.
The being my body encircled now circles me,
In motion, gleeful and utterly alive.

Dana Gaskin Wenig

Discovery

To Jeff, the love of my life
What does it mean to be happy?
Does it mean a nice sunny day?
Does it mean becoming all sappy?
Does it mean sitting by the bay?

What's it like not to be sad?
Enjoying every moment of life?
Knowing for sure what's good and bad?
Never having to endure the strife?

I never knew how happy I could be
Until one man changed my whole way of thinking
Everything is so clear and now I see
Now I no longer feel like I am sinking

Life is so much better now
I learned to love me
Before, I never knew how
But I soon found the key

Jamie Hudson

Polly Maude

She sat in a chair, her purse on her arm,
a walker beside her to keep her from harm.
Her belongings, packed in boxes, sat on the floor,
ready to be carried out the front door.
As she looked around the room, sadness filled her eyes,
she can't change things, no matter how hard she tries.
In a few short minutes her life here would end,
as she moved to a new place, far from her best friend.
Her body had failed her and her mind slipped a lot,
now she must move in with family, like it or not.
She had never married or had children of her own,
but she helped raise a brother till he was grown.
She would be welcome in his home, of this she was sure,
there she would be cared for and her future secure.
She sat there, shoulders dropped and head bowed down,
on her face was the beginning of a small frown.
As she wondered how the time could have passed so fast,
they told her all was packed, it was time to go at last.
She stopped for one last look before she stepped out the door,
then turned her back on a life that existed no more.

Pamela G. Smith

Almost Me

It was almost me he spoke to that day.
It was almost me he loved right away.
It was almost me he loved at first sight.
It was almost me he kissed by moonlight.
It was almost me he asked to wed.
It was almost me, so everyone said.
It was almost me he reached for at night.
It was almost me he held so tight.
It was almost me he grew tired of.
It was almost me he no longer loved.
It was almost me who cried all night.
It was almost me couldn't face the light.
It was almost me he cheated on.
It was almost me waiting up 'til dawn.
It was almost me who begged him to stay.
It was almost me watched him drive away.
It was almost me he left alone.
It was almost me he shook to the bone.
It was almost me who took the pills that day.
It was almost me who went away.
It was almost me and, now, I am free.

Cretia Cooper

Evening Peace

When the golden sun is sinking
'Neath the mountains in the west
And you're feeling kind of lonely
But your soul's at peace and rest

Just let your thoughts dwell slowly
On the blessed Lord above
Just think of all the blessings
You've received from His great love

There's the ocean filled with white caps
Just tumbling here and there
The grass so green beneath your feet
And flowers everywhere

With the sunset soft and glorious
The sky so blue and clear
O', we see so many wonders
Of God's great love and care

It's a time to count your blessings
Ere the peaceful moment flies
And you're wafted home to Heaven
With our Father in the skies

Georgia Poe

This Door

Our hearts aren't in this anymore
As we're slowly diminishing.
Further everyday we shut the door
To this not-so-happy ending.
We used to share our laughter
As well as our point of view,
Yet somehow our lives are separating,
And we are becoming two.
Many times I've tried to talk to you,
But things remain the same.
How can I share my life with you
If you're not willing to share your name?
We just cannot see eye to eye
Because now we only disagree,
We both know we love each other
But are we really meant to be?
This door we are closing upon us
Is the only life we've come to know,
So the only question left is
Hold on or just let go?

Stephanie Verity

The Awakening

The sun is on the rise this day,
with cool winds blowing over the Earth

Trees are opening their eyes this morn',
stretching their arms into God's blue Heaven

Flowers are robed in colors bright,
singing forth praises after their long winter rest

Days are getting longer,
the sun putting forth its warmth

The brooks are reaching forward,
never to return to their winter place of rest

Nature has come alive this day,
once again to proclaim God's power and glory

Sherry L. Christensen

The Price

Living with Dad
Was so very sad
Mama was always black and blue
For us, there was nothing she wouldn't do
Mama doesn't laugh or sing
She doesn't do much of anything
Since she had to put an end
To seeing her best friend
He begged her to go
Mama stood there and said, "No"
He done like she asked, even through he doesn't understand
He will always be there if she needs a hand
As we watch Mama cry
We all understood why
Mama stayed to keep us safe every day
That's the price Mama paid
To keep Daddy from taking us away

Rosalie Allgood

The One I Love

As the morning light enters the window,
I lay and watch the dreams escape her,
As her eyes open I then know it's real,
And I wonder, why me? What did I do to deserve her?
As I watch one of God's finest miracles,
Doing the simplest everyday routines,
Not sure of my intentions,
Not even sure of my thoughts,
As the sun starts to set
And the day comes to an end,
I lay beside her in silence,
With skin like a rose, a heart like a gold trumpet,
Her eyes of wonder close as her dreams reenter,
My thoughts and intentions become clear,
As I whisper, "A love that's too deep for tears."

M. F. Walton Sr.

Through a Daughter's Eyes

My throat is sore. I am weak.
What say you about this foreign matter growing inside me?
Tests and more tests, always out of breath.
Pretty nurses in white uniforms don a smile.
I see rooftops with chimneys;
At dark, they resemble people, ready to take flight
Against the cold, black sky.
My mind is wavering. The treatments I can bare.
Her caring hands and sad heart cradle me,
Four pairs of eyes staring blankly.
A wreath of smoke circling my head,
Nearly half a century.
My halo is made of tar, and not the sky.
Another breath I take,
Another day I make. I smile.

Tammy Durant

When a Good-bye Is

Maybe we can hold hands forever
and kiss good-bye,
but hopefully
you'll come back this time.
"Come back"
I asked,
but with a kiss hello
and without that nervous look in your face,
the feeling of bad news
throbbing
in the back of my head.

I only wish one day,
a foolish wish,
that you'll be mine,
 and I can wake up
  to your breathing,
   naked legs touching—

  and then I could go back to sleep
feeling okay,
for once.

     George Tsolekas

A Letter to Heaven

Dear Dad, I do remember well
Mother summoned us with the bell.
We'd hear it echo over the hill
And answer it against our will.
We would always scamper away
And leave the other kids at play.
We dared not tell Mom how we felt,
Because we feared the leather belt.
Yet, when I think how hard she tried,
The many things she did provide,
I feel that we were greatly blessed
Because of riches we possessed.
I don't forget support you gave.
You were the best; you tried to save.
You made easy Mom's daily chores
By painting the walls and staining the floors.
You tended the garden, grew flowers and fruits.
From the catalogs you ordered suits.
These are sweet memories I'll never forget.
The jobs you did were perfect, you bet.

     L. E. Broadus

A Gift of Destruction

Why are we purchasing weapons for our children to kill?
This certainly was not in God's will.
What are the obligations of a husband and wife
When children are snuffing out their classmate's and parent's life?
What are children learning here at home?
Is it a will to kill with a gift made of metal and steel?
Why are we saying, that's no big deal?
Don't give your children a gift of guns and slugs.
I suggest to you, given them a hug. A hug is free, a kiss is too.
It will cost you money to give a .22.
A gift that hurts, a gift that kills.
Are you aware of how that feels?
When you purchase a gun for your child and your pride,
You are buying a gift for your own suicide.
Get rid of the guns or leave them in stores.
We might live with peace and killings no more.
A gift of a .38 or a magnum .45
Will lessen your chances of staying alive.
Some say it's TV and our learning in school.
I say it's the guns that are killing tools.

     Vera Norman Butler

A Talk with the Lord

Thanks, Grandma, for giving me a religious foundation
I have so many questions to ask,
So many things I need to know.
How do I find the right path?
The one that's straight and narrow?

All of my prayers are answered
Though he doesn't always say, "Yes."
When my life is tempted and tampered,
His voice rings out, "This is only a test."

But will I hear angels sing
Or be surrounded by ghoulish things?
Will I fly with heavenly wings
Or dance with the devil in tight blue jeans?

Too many different religions, different versions
He chimes, "My child, the answer is easy."
How do I choose, how can I be certain?
Then he asks, "Have you read a GOOD BOOK lately?"

     Shirlynn Baldwin

Awaken the Dream

Awaken the dream, latent deep within,
With a burning desire to achieve.
For life's reward, do stake your claim.
Success will eventually come about,
If only you believe.

Pursue your passion with unyielding faith,
And set your vision vivid and clear.
Don't give up or the dream forsake.

Persistence is the key
To all that one can have
And all that one can be.

So begin with action to all your fears allay.
With determination and a committed will,
The fruit thereof will soon come to bear.

Life will step aside and bow to let you in,
Because success is the reward for those who try.
Do follow your heart and vow to win.
Victory is yours—just dare to dream.

     Kalimah M. Walid

If I Had a Million Dollars

I wish I had a million dollars
to share around the world
I wish I had a million dollars
to give with love and care

I wish I had a million dollars
to help bring peace and joy
I wish I had a million dollars
to share the love I have
to every girl and boy

To see the tears of sadness
of hunger, strife, and despair
I would spread it all around
the world to every girl and boy
Then I would see peace, love, and tears of joy
on the faces of every little girl and boy
With tears of joy and eyes aglow
I shared the love of God to all
the girls and boys

     Eloise I. Budd

A Love Gone Wrong

In a time not long ago,
We loved each other, oh, so well!
At time passed on, we had a few despairs.
Now, it seems as if he just doesn't care.
Unaware of how I feel, he continues to think of himself.

With every night that passes by,
I feel as though I need to cry.
And as I sleep, I have a vision . . .
Two people, one being me, fighting . . .
And the next thing I know, I'm crying.
As he walks away from me, he says but yet again, "Good-bye."

Now that he's gone, I'm left wondering if I'll survive.
When I wake each morning, I feel as if something is missing.
An instant replay of him leaving me runs through my mind.

Oh! How I pray that one day he'll
Come back to mend my broken heart
And tell me that we'll never part.

Cheree Almeida

Childhood Dreams

When I was a child, I used to have dreams,
Dragons, unicorns, of many things.
Why do dreams leave us as we get older?
The memories in my mind seem to grow colder.
But I hold on to the ones I remember still.
There were unicorns and elves playing on a hill.
Mighty dragons blowing smoke rings in the sky.
Tiny fairies flying by.
The clouds were the color of pink and blue,
There were puppies and kittens too!
Beautiful flowers smelled so sweet.
Lots of candy for me to eat.
There was no pain or tears to shed,
Only good thoughts inside my head.
Now I am married and I am grown
I have children of my own.
How I wish I could be a child once more.
So I could go back through that imaginary door,
Seeing the things I have long forgot,
I really miss my childhood dreams a lot.

Grace Lethcoe

Sandy

The saddened look in your eyes
Gives away the deceptions of your heart.
Pools of hurt reach up through the murkiness
Like icy fingers, wanting claim on your soul.
Try not to give in to their hunger;
You must live!
Learn to embrace life again.
In time,
The shadows of haunting sorrow
Will leave your eyes.
Your inner light will shine anew,
As those you love
Will always stand by you.
Leaning shoulders, lending ears,
Family and friends
Will always be near.
Draw strength from them
Where it need be.
You will get through.

Tammy Lee Szczygiel

The Hurt

You have suffered a great hurt,
One I may never know.
You share your thoughts
And some of the pain with me,
Yet I cannot relate to it.

I try to help you put this past,
But how can you?
Looking back into time,
It hurts you that all those special moments are forgotten.
You are left wondering why.

I hate seeing this hurt on you,
Yet I cringe on losing you,
Your friendship and your kindness.
These things mean a lot to me,
Yet it pains me that someone can give you such a hurt
That it may never heal.

Frederick Earp

It's O.K. To Be Afraid

What do I do when I am afraid?
Do I walk through my shadow of fear?
Do I stay in my circle of safety?
What adventures in life am I denying myself
With my net of insecurities.
I must reach out and feel the power of life.
Allow mistakes to be made and remade.
Say to myself, it's O.K. to change my course.
It's O.K. to follow others sometimes; and
It's O.K. to lead others to their dreams.
It's when we don't sail on our dreams.
That fear holds back our lives.
The safety net closes our path to the future.
Walk forward and grow with knowledge.
Step sideways to make adjustments and changes.
Review the past for the wisdom it brings.
And know it's O.K. to be afraid.

Doreen Hill

Return Postage Due

He came in the mail today,
Smaller than I remember,

In a box, no larger than a pair of ballet slippers.
His voice was faint, but his laugh distinct.
We walked to the park, him in my hand,
My hand on the bottom, his on the top,

Divided by the lifeless steel urn.
I settled him in the child safety swing
And began to push.

I envisioned the wind in his blonde hair
And the glimmer of hope in his eyes.

By sunset, his laughter had dissipated,
And the urn was empty.

He came in the mail today;
I set him free.

Abra Layne Stanley

Angel

I have an Angel in my living room
She sings to me all day
While she pecks and grooms
With nothing much to say.

She laughs for me when I'm sad
She spreads her wings
And whistles when I've been bad
Then she sings.

At night she chirps in sorrow,
Because the day is gone,
She just can't wait to see the morning sun.

Amanda D. Bushey

A Prayer for My Children

To my children of the womb
And to those who have touched my life,
I love you intensely.

To my children of the womb
And to those who have touched my life,
I celebrate you immensely.

To my children of the womb
And to those who have touched my life,
I praise you lovingly

For your ability to live in this turbulent world with dignity
And remain inspired, focused, imbued, and dedicated.

To my children of the womb
And to those who have touched my life,

May the Supreme Being above
Tenderly keep you embraced in His love!

Gayle V. Dancy Benjamin

Love Me

Shy . . .
"Snob," someone says.
"Thinks she's better than us."
Loud, outgoing . . .
"Rude," they say.
"Just being rebellious, hogging the spotlight."
They never ask,
Always assuming.

Quiet, crying within,
Pain so overwhelming . . .
Where do they turn?
Does anyone understand,
Is anyone listening?
Who can they reach out to
Family, friends, strangers?

Listen to the tears.
"Love me," is what they say.
Love me.

Sommer L. Sorenson

My Forever Friend

Your energy gives me strength.
Your support brings courage,
a trust for sharing,
and wisdom for learning and growing.

Your honesty is my faith,
your hope . . . my ambition,
truth for understanding
and confidence for
winning and succeeding.

Your gentle words of comfort
and the softness of your soul
touched my heart with fullness
and made it whole.

A thought, a fantasy, a dream came true
with joy and happiness the day I met you.
The memories we share will never end
You are truly my forever friend!

Debra J. Ellis

During the Long Winter Drought

Outside the lone east window of my dining room, I see
In the twilight gleam the leafy top of a redwood tree;
It rises majestically into the darkened rain-less sky,
Silhouetted by patches of white clouds, floating idly.

Wu-Chi Liu

A Day in the Woods

As the sun peeks over the horizon
The lake's water shimmers like glass
Trees cast a soft shadow
On the dew-laden grass

As I walk through the woods
Towering trees filter the sunlight
Leaving patterns on the forest floor
Nature can be a visual delight

An afternoon storm blows in from the east
The dry landscape is blanketed with rain
Steam rises from the foliage
A sign of relief for the forest and plain

As the sun fades in the west
The sunset lights the sky ablaze
The many wonders of nature
Never cease to amaze

James R. Alberts

Charlie Brown

A boy I knew from long ago
has shown his face again
And thought I knew as a child
I'm happy he's still my friend

He has the laugh of a smile on cool summer night
I can hear it now if I shut my eyes tight
He's wise for his years, though still a child deep down
with the magic to make a smile from a frown

He possesses strength in both body and mind
but a gentler person you'll never find
You can see his soul beneath the depths of dark eyes
showing kindness without so much as a try

I can tell him my secrets without worries or fears
for I know he'll accept all that he hears
He's a gentlemen through and through from his kiss to his toe
a childhood sweetheart from long ago

Heidi White

A Lark's Song

To my husband, Edward George Kaleck

How a lark ascends
From where its song emanates.
On a clear day the liquid song gives
Heat and splendor indicative of God.

 Franz Schubert wrote
His "Trout quintet"
Wolfgang Amadeus Mozart, too, his "Magic Flute"
accompanied by Liquid melodies to heavenly conclusion.

Like the lark's song sparkling
Behind suspended clouds;
Just due North of Heaven's vault,
Beauteous to hear and spiritually a joy forever.

Susanna W. G. Kaleck

In Thought of Love

Your thoughts, of course, are but your own.
And, as are mine to yours, are to me unknown.
Passionate emotions within thee burn.
From whence and why, 'tis my desire to learn.
'Fore, our minds are living mysteries,
Bound only by eternity.
Within these realms our spirits yearn,
For answer, to questions of most concern.
So when our quest's for common friends.
Bring these concerns to common ends,
Then when in truth, we come to find,
Kindred hearts, of common mind.
And if, or when, before all else,
'Tis this our thoughts are of,
Alas, my friend,
What we've found is love!

Edwin C. Welch II

The Wall

Entombed within the sightless wall
A place I choose to be
I stand protected
Your eyes' daggers will no longer penetrate
The ringing of the shrills shall no longer dismay
I shall stand protected
As the palming anger soars to strike
The wall shall catch the fall
Within my own I shall reside
Gaining strength to overcome
I shall stand protected
No longer at the will of thine
Besieging all to only you
The wall shall set me free
I shall stand protected

Barbara L. Jackson

Untitled

Yesterday, I died for the thousandth time.

A green-eyed, warty monster so bold,
Knocked me down and trampled on my soul.
As I looked up at the creature despised
It was laughing at my demise.

Then big, black, gossipy birds in a stream
Swooped down to peck away at my self-esteem.
And what was left of my reputation,
Nothing remaining but seeds of speculation.

The best of my intentions fared no better.
Sat on by an elephant, they were squashed flatter
Than flat, two dimensions shy of their former selves.
Beyond recognition, they were mistaken for something else.

Yet today out of the ashes I rise.
You cannot stamp out the fire in my eyes
Or quench the flames in my heart.

Kirsten O'Connor

Wishing You Could

I wish you could feel me,
Feel my heart, feel my soul, feel my tears.
Tears that I cry because I've never felt like this before,
So full of alive, so happy.
I watch you, I wish that if I stared at you long enough
You could feel, feel my heart
Feel my soul, feel my love.
I look into your dark, mystic eyes
And I wonder what it would be like to
Feel your heart, feel your soul, feel your love.

Melissa A. Berrly

Carousel

Time will not stop to hold on to today
As it dashes on to tomorrow,
Speeding along to next week, next year,
Leaving no moment to select or borrow.

Ah, now is soon gone; hope springs anew
Here where the plans and dreams dwell,
And tomorrow rushes in to start over again
To speed on the cycle as well.

Around in the pattern of every day's chances
Looking back, starting over, spinnin' out all the dreams
We circle, move on, as time disappears
Leaving us counting no answers it seems.

But here is today, and yesterday's gone
Tomorrow will come in its time.
Each day with its shadows sets its own light
We can live in the now with our future in sight.

Doris Barton

Love E'er Thine

Unlike the beauty rose doth bloom
From stem to root the air perfume
For swiftly moot the gentle plume
As by its duty hastens doom.

Nay not akin my love to rose
Bud, harlequin wryly in pose
For love has been nigh flame and snows
And there within dying depose

More as the oaken mighty tree
Hence tiny token seed bursts free
E'er fights death's yoke, in slavery
Essence provoke instinctively

Still heart, like wood, to death resign
And youth's manhood rue withered vine
And yet love would through sleep still shine
Conceive then could you love e'er thine.

John Walker

Mind Fishing

My intricate, numbed mind is a morning vagueness
topped with testing mountains spread back, over, and some ahead
Every colored day is another tiring shadow or exciting, radiant ride
around this amusement park
And sometimes when my penciled in shoes fit,
I can take a Scantron journey
into the night of free love, the sunrise of realization,
the afternoon of integrity, or the dawn of experience
These pictures aren't ever erased
Some show their masked face in my incoherent dreams.
But my frame of relaxation and my natural emptiness
brings that same numbness coming up from the underwater
underneath the mountains, the tests, the rides.
Unable to subside any longer
I climb, silently reaching the light, the surface
the cool air filling into my lungs.
And I awake

John Kernla

She Is in Heaven

When you lose someone you care
about cherish the memories
watch out for one any, remember all
The good times we all shared
with her, she in Heaven, she's happy, no more pain
and suffering, she's watching over us.
Now she is an angel, she's with God and He will
watch out for her now
Just remember that she cares and it was her time to go
Her warmest heart was there with us and
life she was special to all.
We will all miss her and all of the memories.
Happy in Heaven and waiting for her family.
She'll say I've been waiting for you.

Joyce Lum

Brilliant

Brilliant is he who made man, with his bare hands.
Brilliant is he who, put the stars in place.
Brilliant is he who hung the world in space.
Brilliant was he when my soul, he saved.

A second chance, my life he gave.
The straight and narrow is the way he paved.
Brilliant, is the trail he left, for us to follow.
Many know, but refuse to go.
Broad is the way to destruction, which many will find.
Brilliant, is he who refuse to be led, by the blind.
Lean not to their own understanding, but to
Every word, that proceeds out of the mouth of God.

Carrie Vaughan

Our Children

Our kids wear baggy jeans and braids in their hair
They have no respect, and they don't seem to care
But don't they know, and shouldn't they be aware
That to survive in this country, we all must share

Our parents are working for their own material gain
They're neglecting the children, it causes much pain
If we could all sit down around a long, long table
We can work out the plans to make our world stable

The nations are fighting, without and even within
Our families are not turning, against their own kin
It's important that we teach others always to forgive
Hug a sister or a brother, and help them learn to live

The kids are emulating what they see on the TV
But what it doesn't teach them is how to be set free
Love starts in the home, and spreads to our Churches
It changes the Hearts and Souls of everyone it touches

Jesus loves our children, and it pains Him to see
The way we have, by our neglect, caused them to be
If our children are not trained to used new information
Farther on down the road, who will lead our Nation?

Lois Johnson

Our World Today

To my other parents, Margaret and Bob Beaver
The pain and suffering I witness in our world today,
   is harder to overcome, harder to look the other way!
I recall the Oklahoma City bombing that interrupted the U.S.A.,
   shocked the Nation; we didn't know what to think or say!
Pictures on the TV told us our country is no longer free;
   we looked for excuses while dealing with humility!
There was not explanation, just the guilty plea,
   a man in handcuffs, losing his freedom and liberties!
My memory of the student creating a shooting spree,
   killing fellow students and a teacher with a family!
What is the answer to the violence of our society today;
   can we foresee a troubled neighbor along our way?
Maybe we need to return to what I call the good ol' days,
   family and neighbors watched out for us in the same way!
Children attended school feeling safe and free from harm,
   there were rules to follow and lessons to be learned!
We said our daily prayer and the allegiance to our flag,
   proud of our accomplishments, praises from Mom and Dad!
Go ahead, voice your opinion in the land of the free;
   remember, many lost their lives just for you and me!

Deborah Roche

Unforgettable

The words of love are beautiful
But we shared a quiet love
That filled us with the joy of each other and made us a one.
A smile as we reached the altar
Where we promise silently that, "Today is forever."
Arms that held me and needed no explanation.
The soft brush of his lips on my cheek
That said quietly, "I understand."
The soft squeeze of my hand in his
As we walked together assured me he was happy.
His strong but gentle hand holding my weakened one
and saying without a sound, "Don't be afraid. I'm here with you."
His bright blue eyes that told me, "I'm glad you're with me."
A sudden unexpected hug, "Just because."
A kiss that exulted, "Aren't we lucky to have each other?"
Beautiful years of love and togetherness
But then he was taken from me
And it was dark and still and I was afraid.
But then I felt a warmth and I could almost hear him say,
"Don't be afraid. I'm here with you. You will never be alone."

Dowling Gordens

The Eaching

Decisiveness leads you on to emotion
Nourishment of truth dies out slowly
The Receptive ground gives no pardon

Pleasing stimulants let you forget dying
Conformity is out so you fight the breeze
Persistence of the wind breaks you trying

Abundance of the sun in youth, collides with
Gathering clouds that fill your mind tonight
Increase the dose exponentially 'til you hide

Reduction of brain-cells leads to sleepwalking
Returning in dream to your mother's heartbeat
Following the sounds of your father's talking

Innocence is ignorance for your trials
Exhaustion wears you for a tribal-mask
Happiness comes to you with more vials

Contention stalks you like a starving kid
Rising from a polluted river of bad dreams
Thunder awakens you from your haunted head

Travel back to your Eden like Christ
Treading the water of his own guilts

Robert Conner

The Man from the Sea

Washed ashore by the white cliffs of Dover
Came the man from the sea
Of his destination he thought not
of as he set foot into a land of mystery

With the foam from the waves still upon his shoulders
he was a strange sight to any soul
yet he continued on with a steady trod
into a valley below

To a small village he came
but spoke not a word to anyone
nor took his sight from the road ahead
trailing off into the distant horizon

Just once did this man stop
when he came to a beautiful meadow
roaming his eyes across the vast bouquet before him
of flowers with every color of the rainbow

Through rain and lightning this man did endure
without a single blink of an eye
his mind remained empty, his destination unknown
as loud cries thundered from the sky

Kristi Shypknowski

Angel on High

As moonbeams dance throughout night sky
O, where are you, "Angel on High"
Gazing from my balcony, waves crash along the beach
Only in my dreams, can you my arms reach.
Remembering your touch, your soft and gentle kiss
Your flowing hair so shiny, O, how much do I miss.
My thoughts of you cut through my heart
Desire sets me burning while we're apart
As stars begin to show their face
All thoughts drift off to a tranquil place,
Foamy white caps burst on the ocean blue
Creating a burning image of the Angel in you,
My footprints lead from water's edge
Walking aimlessly to your heart's ledge
Shivering palms in snow white sand
Let me be your guide and take you by the hand.
As an ocean's breeze
Begins to form a high
Here I am forever yours
My love "Angel on High."

Alan J. Miccia

Soul Mate

It all started simply asking you for a date
After exploding the deep inner feeling be my soul mate
I searched the inner parts of you
Seeking feelings, trust, helper, these things are true
I showed you my feelings, told my desires will that do?
You know I care wanting you my everywhere
Even my heart and eyes can't deny the feelings, my dear
I long for your presence every moment of the day
You being there sends troublesome thoughts on their way
Your love and compassion keep me wanting you
I'm not ashamed to ask will you love me too!
Be part of me, continue setting my soul on fire
Where love will grow between us with many desires

Doris Elizabeth Taylor

Shadow of the Heart

I sit alone and I think,
of how my life is complete.
The heart has love, the heart has hate,
and what I feel I can't mistake.
I know the heart can feel much pain,
but my love will stay the same.
My heart is filled with joy and laughter,
when your body's next to mine.
I see our life, I see our love,
and this I keep within my heart,
for our love will never part.
Late at night I stay awake,
and wonder how you are?
I sit and think about or love,
and if it will go far?
The shadow of the heart will say,
I know we'll stay forever this way.

Amber Keefe

Dubbonet

"Pledges not to chase women with it.
The bit about the amount of it."

The hour that already came
Is about to be revealed anew
In another way!

All comfortures and fortunes delivering
The tidy confusion of unadulterated passion,
Fruit and comfort veiled
In the hypothesis of
Counter entertainment.

The device of men wheeling
In the wind awaiting
Sure turn.

The tide steps and cloud loop chime.
Dealing over again,
Away from the corridor of false impregnation.

Christopher J. Lizza

Thrift Shop

What is a thrift shop?
Is it a place of castoffs and rejections
Where poor folks buy their clothes
and the workers get no pay?
Some people think so
but they don't know much.
Just take a look at this one.
A mother with three children finds
three fresh-washed toys;
another gets the party dress her daughter needs,
teenagers grab old jeans.
And so things move as shoppers come and go.

Yet—all the time the biggest winners
are those pay-less workers who once more can find
friends to talk with and exchange ideas,
and even more, the chance to make
a difference in the lives of people
who are not just customers.

Anne L. New

The Poet's Pose

Is to strike accord
Linking themselves with
The heartbeat of the reader
To Paint with words
Igniting the canvas with
Strokes of strength and subtle hints
Caressing the reader with sensual sounds
And visions of foreplay
Of words that give
Taste, touch, sight, and sound
Inflaming that spiritual hunger
With titillation in abstract
Leaving the reader gasping in orgasmic wonder,
But unsated in their hunger
Hands shaking, to quickly turn the page
Ravenous eyes seeking those
Words of stimulation
Senses Heightened,
They reach for more
This is the poet's pose

Frances S. Houston

To Mine

So precious and soft
one of life's joys
But only at my cost
passing up many of life's toys.
Fragile in the ears
and encumbered by sight
There will be no fears as long as I'm the light.
But I'm not really to support your cry
Or powder your rump and dry your eyes.
As much as I want you by my side
I know I'm not ready
So in longing I confide.
Gold is needed for future's bright
I'm trying now,
With all my might.
Just you wait
I'll have you someday
I've already a mate
And where there's a will
There's a way.

Jodi Aboad

The Saddest Good-bye

The saddest good-bye is in departing.
From the friend you've had so long.
Yet there comes a time when each must
Go a separate way of his own.
Yet the saddest good-bye is not in leaving
But it's when you realize you're left alone

You're left alone to cherish
The memories that you have so dear
And to think of all the ups and downs
That you've had through many years.
You see a friend departing
Then there comes the drop of one sad tear.

A handkerchief is handed
To wipe the tear from your eye;
And a smile comes on your face
In order to hide that sad sigh.
But nothing can erase
The memory of the saddest good-bye.

Angelee Coleman Grider

Retrospect

How can I make you understand
That my words are from my heart and soul
And not just ramblings of other men?
How can I make you understand that the life of this man
Will be spent in retrospect
For not having been able to make you understand?

Wilson F. Machin Jr.

The Most Precious Thing of All

"I wish I may, I wish I might, have the goal I strive tonight,
and if I stumble and go astray, Lord, please help me and show me the way."

God heard this man's silent prayer, and granted him his wish,
therefore picking out a star for him, and enclosing it in his fist.
The man awoke one day from a restless, long night's sleep,
and he noticed the creak of his bones and shrivel of his feet.
His once youthful back had bent over with age . . .
the now old man with gray, thinning hair screamed at God in rage.

"Why didn't you help me? You let the time go by too fast.
All my goals and dreams . . . they are all left in the past!"

God responded with empathy toward the man on the brink of death.
"My promise was kept. I would surely help you on your way, but, my child,
your laziness took hold of you—therefore having no chance to go astray.
I sent opportunities along your way, surely you must know.
It's like going to plow the fields, but having nothing worth to grow."

The old man watched as God opened his now-loosened fist,
and there was that star that was chosen for the wish.
The man watched sadly as he watched his star fall to the Earth
in a straight, narrow line, and in the middle was engraved:
You lost the most precious thing of all—time.

Rashana Mims

The Growing Need

Mankind is like a great-tree that started out as a seed and grew up
little at a time, to learn about the likable, needed, and dislikable
needed things around about them. Learning how to grow and their
needs for the fullness of growth. "One day" looking upward into the
skies of Heaven. They decided to spread out their seeds of
knowledge, the life of growth.

Many different branches of one's own-self that is within one's own self!
They seen growing old and some of the young branches grew old
before their time of growing up has come. Still human branches of
Old Mankind continue on toward the skies of Heaven, push by
growing needs to grow, and learn to live, and to hate, and to find a place of their own.

Oh Little human needs, when will you grow up?! How will you stand
within your life? Remembering that human learning has grown from a
seed upward like a great tree. Oh Great Human-Tree, that has seen
many things likable and unloveliness, things around their learning to
grow up to the needs, to grow for the things in life. Continuing the
growth of life with love!

When understand about life and all that is around them, they grew
with understanding of self and fellowship with self in love for life.
"Have we all forgotten how to grow?! Has there ever been a time that
we all have forgotten how to learn, the need to grow spiritually?!"

Michael M. McCarthy

Summer Rain

The rain was a calming effect on me.
Soft, gentle breezes, cool, wet rain.
Harder, faster, don't break the flow.
Come down on me, let me know what you're here for.
Is it to cleanse my soul or is it to punish me for not being a part of it?
Lightning flicks. Rolls of thunder. Is it any wonder why I love you so?
You come in so quiet, I can hardly tell you're there.
Your crescendo is deafening.
You wreak havoc on my inner being because I wasn't prepared for your arrival.
Don't go. But you told me to have to move on to let others know.
Why does it have to be that way?
What can I do to make you stay? Cry with me, feel my pain! He said.
So I did. We have a forever bond now. No one understands the rain like I do.
Ride on, my cool breeze lady soul, tonight I take over. Calm down, it
won't hurt a bit. I just want to kiss you. It hurts too much to do.
You'll be gone tomorrow to make someone else feel this way today!

Monica T. Ward

My True Love, Roy

There aren't enough words
In this world to express
The feelings that weigh
Heavily on my chest

Love is a profound
Emotion and feeling
With every day
It's my heart you're stealing

I agree, there is a different
Feeling about this with you
It's something so strong
I know you feel it too

My heart can't stand
To be without you
I'm not sure which way
To turn or what to do

I am still amazed
By how you knew
How much my soul longed for
And my heart ached for you

Mary Norgaard

The Colorful Sky

The sky is pink and gray
Blue and golden,
And all the colors
Look like they're molding.

You can't see the clouds moving
But the shapes and colors
Are constantly changing.

Some are puffy and fluffy
Some are long and some are short.
Some are nothing but streaks in the sky.

It's as if God took a paintbrush
And touched the colors here and there.
Not quite sure what He wanted.
He kept changing them everywhere.
It's a prelude to a spectacular sunset.

Alice Piotrowske

Transcendence

The future holds your key
And fortune unfolds your destiny
The ocean's ominous waves sing
With the spirit of the wind
Strange calls from far-away lands
Voice in harmony to flow
through the sands
Only to show you what is in life's plan
Can you call a fortune teller?
Or do your memories lend a hand
Full of doubts our dreams we must mend
For those of us who see
Will find a moment and understand
The world's new song of peace
Is for all who love,
Listen, and transcend.

Howard Lowe II

Infinity Expands

My soul immortality
Flies and flies.
My life eternity
Cries and cries.
My heart infinity
Expands and expands.
My mind stupidity
Everything disbands.

Sri Chimoy

A Special Miracle

To my beautiful daughter, Sanarah Renee
On this particular March morning
the sun was shining extra bright.
Making the glow through the window
a beautiful sight.

For this day a miracle was going to happen.
One that took nine months of preparation,
but was worth the whole duration.

She came perfect as can be
so perfect that I could not
stop thanking Thee.
He gave her a little round face
with a button nose.
And ten wonderful fingers and toes.

I thank Him each and every day
for my miracle child that day.

Marcellina Renee Missouri

Trying to Soothe the Wounds Inside

As I sit alone all by myself
My thoughts and dreams with me
I am searching for some happiness
But happiness to my eyes I cannot see
Right know my mind is all confused
I don't know where to go
I close my eyes to ease my mind
But it won't help I know
As I sit alone, I concentrate
I pray for peaceful thoughts
But all I see is darkness
All good things that I have lost
And then I want to say good-bye
I want to leave this place behind
Feeling as if I don't belong
These thoughts won't leave my mind
The road that leads my way is winding
It seems there's no end in sight
I try to find a light that's shining
Was my life wrong, or can I make it right?

Christopher Bigger

On My Way

When I die in this world today
please lay me to rest
where the children play,
where laughter is heard
instead of tears,
where people live without any fears,
where the sun shines down
through the years.
"For it is here"
I shall find comfort
In all these things,
just sitting back
taking A ride on
an angel's wings.

Rebecca McKenzie

Younger

Can't wait to be older.
Acting just like mommy,
wearing high-heels and make up.
You begin to feel old.
Regressing to the childlike ways,
which you swore you'd never do,
becoming so much younger
than ever thought possible,
and realizing that we are all
children playing house.

Aimee Larraga

The Violin Concerto

Guns mute, goriest war over;
Brabant fog in Brussels.
Dark night, concert hall lights beckon
To hear his mighty song.

Beethoven violin solo
People's victory hails.
Melancholy malaise dispelled,
Great Titan liberates.

Heiligenstadt ordeal, no more.
Deafness challenged, conquered.
Eroica heralds new spring:
Art and courage exult!

Heavenly violin begins,
Timpani resonate,
Glorious themes repeat throughout—
Haunting drama, sad joy.

Blend of power and of beauty,
Fresh, new rhythms, slow and fast.
Victor! King of musical light,
Olympus majesty!

John Devlin

The Gallant Ghost

You deem yourself invisible,
an apparition at most;
Others esteem you invincible,
Never wavering at your post.

Being sought out for favors
Rarely makes you feel used,
Like a pack of lifesavers,
Keeping taste buds amused.

Some folks dub you "buddy,"
'Cause on you they depend,
But they melt down to putty
Whenever you need a friend.

You accept putty kindly,
Molding it to fair form,
Rather than chasing blindly
For the perfect or the norm.

As ghosts go, you're a Casper,
The friendly one people know
Will free them from disaster,
Leaving the credit to Joe Blow.

Jeanne Gaskell

Memories Must Fade

I recall her anguished cry,
"It is hard to choose
Between the man you love dearly,
And the God you worship truly."

She gently explained in a letter.
"You are not a believer,
Light wedded to light is better.
Please think of me as a little sister."

Almost thirty years later,
I decided to be her big brother
And attend her mother's funeral,
While I kept wondering why.

But then, when I saw her,
I felt my pulses quicken.
Her startled, anxious look
Told me that she did remember.

Although I am now a believer,
We each have married another.
It is sad to think of what might
Have been, but memories must fade.

Ava L. Russel Benn

Under the Wings of a Dove

The very first time we met,
it was under the wings of a dove.
We looked at each other,
then looked at the sky above.
The first time we touched,
it was under the wings of a dove.
Each time we met,
we always looked above.
We always hurried from the pier
then . . .
Lying in my lover's arms,
under the eaves, I saw the silvery dove.
No dove in winter.
In spring, we walked the wet sand.
As we embraced, we saw, really saw
we were under the wings of the dove.

Mary T. Price

Never Mind, Little Girl

Never mind the shadows,
Never mind the rain.
Just keep on, little girl
Living just the same,
The sun will shine tomorrow,
It will be a better day,
The rain that falls is borrowed
From rivers far away!
Even though your hopes may fade,
Like the setting sun,
Keep on smiling, little girl,
Till your life's work is done.
Shed not tears of sorrow,
If you must walk alone,
Others have gone on before you,
And they like you have roamed.
When you have failed just smile once,
The clouds will all roll by,
And take up where you left off,
No use to sit and sigh!

Martha Serbu

Mirrored Eyes

Your hazel eyes like moon beams shined
Your hazel eyes once mirrored mine
You looked at me with the purest love
As pure as heavenly angels above
Their glimmer shined as did the sun
Their glimmer shined, I was the one
I watched the spark diminish and die
The spark went out, you said good-bye
Your eyes turned into empty cores
My eyes turned and mirrored yours

Athena Papavlo

Sometimes I Need You

Sometimes you're like a child,
so innocent and small.
I hold you in my arms at night,
and to sleep you fall.
Sometimes you're a lover,
so passionate and true.
Holding me in your arms is all
I ever knew.
Sometimes you're like a beast,
flashing your angry eyes,
holding me in your gaze;
I want to run and hide.
Sometimes you're like my father,
guiding me out of the wrong,
holding my heart in your hands so strong.

Shellie Waite

Biographies
of
Poets

ABERNATHY, KATHY JO
[pen.] Quiet Dawning; [b.] December 27, 1959; St. Paul, MN; [p.] Gerald and Marcia LaMotte; [m.] Darrell W. Abernathy; September 10, 1978; [ch.] David and Nicole; [ed.] Associate Degree in Applied Science Major, Clinical Laboratory Technology, Forest Park College, Fox High and Joliet West High School; [occ.] Medical Laboratory Technician; [memb.] American Society of Clinical Pathologists, Clinical Lab Tech. Club, Cave Club, Bible Club and Band; [hon.] President of Clinical Lab Tech. Club from 1986-1988; [oth. writ.] Poem, "Forever Pain," in Essence of a Dream, and "God's Voice" in Best Poems of 1998. Various unpublished poems; [pers.] My hope for my lifetime is that my gift to write will be used and expressed in a way that will open others' minds and hearts to the limitless love of my father, the great spirit who gave me this gift.; [a.] Barnhart, MO

ACKERMAN, NORMA E.
[b.] December 18, 1946; Lancaster, PA; [p.] Edith Fair Robinson, Lloyd M. Fair; [m.] Kenneth; October 7, 1966; [ch.] Keith; [ed.] J.P. McCaskey High School; [occ.] Cafeteria/ Playground Aide, Bucher Elem. School, Lancaster, PA; [memb.] National Honor Society; [oth. writ.] Poems published by The National Library of Poetry in The Lasting Joy and A Pleasant Reverie; [a.] Lancaster, PA

ADAMS, FRANCES E.
[pen.] Frances E. Adams; [b.] July 11, 1911; Effingham, KS; [p.] Arthur and Rillie Craise; [m.] Walton W. Adams; October 10, 1931; [ch.] Patricia; [ed.] ACC High School Effingham Del Rio Business College, TX; [memb.] Morning Glory Garden Club, Eastern Star Chapter 204 AARP Local and National; [hon.] Certificate of Appreciation, forty years of service to Del Rio S.P. Credit Union and Beautiful Clock; [oth. writ.] Correspondent to S.P. Bulletin Houston, 1950's Newsletter for S.P. Employees, garden into Local Newspaper 1987; [pers.] I am the master of my fate, I am the captain of my soul.; [a.] Del Rio, TX

AGDIGOS, ALEXEI
[pen.] Alexie Agdigos; [b.] October 31, 1979; Clark AFB, Philippines; [p.] Leo and Vicky Agdigos; [ed.] Sophomore at California State, San Bernardino; [occ.] San Manuel Indian Bingo and Casino Pulltab Cashier; [pers.] I'm a young Filipino whose struggles in life have become my success.; [a.] Highland, CA

ALBERTS, JAMES R.
[pen.] James R. Alberts; [b.] October 18, 1948; Dearborn, MI; [p.] Ervin and Carol; [ed.] BA Communications—Michigan State University; [occ.] Sales Manager; [memb.] Sierra Club; [hon.] Academic Scholarship—Michigan State University; [oth. writ.] "Christmas Alone"; [pers.] My poetry has been inspired by two of my dearest friends, Earl and Ruth Coons.; [a.] Clarkston, MI

ALCARAZ, BRINDICY T.
[b.] May 30, 1981; San Francisco, CA; [p.] Moises and Griselda Maciel; [ed.] Jane L. Stanford Middle School, Gunn High, McAteer High; [occ.] High School Student Intern for S.F. Mayor's Youth Works Program; [memb.] Girl Scouts USA; [hon.] Student of The Month and Honor Roll Awards; [oth. writ.] Songs, Short Stories; [pers.] Although I'm physically challenged, I'm going to try to reach my dreams and achieve something new every day. I want to thank everyone, especially my English teacher, Mr. Lunt, for seeing the true writer inside of me.; [a.] San Francisco, CA

ALEXANDER, JULIA C.
[m.] Thomas Nelson Alexander; [ch.] Joseph Allen Holt; [occ.] Writer; [oth. writ.] "It Takes Two," "Now and Then," "Somewhere," "Guardian Angel"

ALMEIDA, CHEREE
[pen.] Cheree Almeida; [b.] September 30, 1978;

Escondido, CA; [p.] Kenny and Vickie Almeida; [ed.] Currently getting ready to sign up for fall semester at Maysville Community College; Going to major in Business, Sales and Marketing; [occ.] Sales Representative for a major company; [memb.] Was in Band while attending Harrison Co. High. Now active in sports (softball) and fitness clubs; [hon.] Honor Roll while attending Harrison Co. High., Received an All-Star Award for softball, The President's Club Award for fitness; [pers.] Don't let people live your life for you. Go out into the world and be yourself, only then can you do what you want.; [a.] Cynthiana, KY

ALMONTE, ROCHELLE
[b.] June 19, 1983; [p.] Gilbert C. Almonte Jr. and Sharon Rocha; [ed.] Currently a Sophomore at Granada High School; [occ.] Work as a T.A.; [oth. writ.] Written imagination and other writings not yet published; [pers.] If you live through this with me, I swear I'll die for you!

ALVAREZ, LILIAM GEMA
[pen.] Gema (Hemma); [b.] March 27, 1949; Havana, Cuba; [p.] Pablo and Onelia; [m.] Manuel; September 8, 1982; [ch.] Alejandro, Rebecca and Samuel; [ed.] Spanish Teacher Certificate (Havana Cuba 1968-70), GED 1981, USA; [occ.] Spanish Teacher—Somerville Charter School; [memb.] Ciculo de Lectores, International Society of Poets, Guild Memberships, Amherst Society, Sparrowgrass Poetry Forum, National Library of Poetry; [hon.] AIDS Action Committee 1993, Boston City Council (The Cuban Woman), Certificate of Official Resolution 1994, Blackstone Elem. School (Parent of the Month) 1995-1996, AIDS-HIV-PLENA-CASA Iris 1996, Poet of Merit; [oth. writ.] "Oklahoma Cry" (a poem contributed to the Oklahoma City Disaster, appears on a cassette, Together We Stand, 1996; [pers.] Poetry is a gift. It's always survival. God created the heavens and the earth, and also the muse that adorns our lives.; [a.] Boston, MA

AMMEL, RICHARD
[b.] May 2, 1987; Leavenworth, KS; [p.] Harvey, Deeanna Ammel; [ed.] Entering 6th grade; [memb.] Christian Church; [hon.] Honor Roll; [oth. writ.] "Tyrannosaurus" in Spirit of the Age; [pers.] Have enjoyed writing stories and poems since I was in 2nd grade. My favorite poet is Shel Silverstein.; [a.] Canon City, CO

ANDERSON, ALAN
[pen.] Alan Anderson; [b.] June 18, 1941; Moline, IL; [p.] Glenn and Verda Anderson; [ed.] Graduate of Rock Falls High Schools, graduate of Bailey Tech. in St. Louis; [memb.] North American Fishing Club/Handy Man-of-America Club; [hon.] High School National Honor Society, Several Awards and Trophies for poetry; [oth. writ.] Several Poems and a couple of short stories; [pers.] There is much more to life than technology and money.; [a.] Rock Falls, IL

ANDREATTA, MARY RUBINO
[b.] April 19, 1924; Omaha, NE; [p.] Alfio and Ninfa Rubino; [m.] Alfred O. Andreatta; July 10, 1949; [ch.] Steven David, Lawrence, Dennis and Gina; [occ.] Mother; [memb.] International Society of Poetry, National Library of Poetry, Verdiettes of S.F. Verdi Club; [pers.] Poetry offers happiness and laughter, sadness and tears. Poetry also offers imagination to take one where otherwise could not go. Poetry can be called "Life."; [a.] San Francisco, CA

ARBUCKLE, JAMIE LEE
[pen.] Jamie L. Arbuckle; [b.] September 1, 1958; West Palm Beach, FL; [p.] Nancy A. Taylor and Elwood V. Taylor; [m.] Robert L. Arbuckle; October 31, 1977; [ch.] Taylor James Arbuckle; [ed.] G.E.D., Lenawee Vo-Tech, 2 years Commercial Printing. The Covey Training Program, The seven habits of Highly Effective people; [occ.]

Folder Operator at Braun-Brumfield Inc.; [oth. writ.] Two poems published in The National Library of Poetry: "Unsung Hero" and "Children Agony"; [pers.] "Gentle Eyes" is a poem specially written about a young man, Taylor, whose love and insights gave courage when I felt afraid and alone. Thank you son.; [a.] Dexter, MI

ASBURY, KATHRYN
[pen.] Kathryn Asbury; [b.] April 26, 1948; Christiansburg VA; [p.] Harley Asbury, Mary Asbury; [ch.] Julia Hamada; [ed.] Woodbridge High, NJ, New York Phoenix School of Design, NY city NY; [occ.] Disabled from stroke; [oth. writ.] "Obsessive Depression Facts," Beliefs and the Occult Life's Maize," "The Discreet Kiss of Queens"; [pers.] Keep folklore alive, and nothing beats a true story.; [a.] Moorpark, CA

ASHMORE, CHERYL ANN
[pen.] Cheryl Ann; [b.] May 15, 1951; New Jersey; [m.] Jack M. Ashmore; February 25; [ch.] Jessica; [ed.] Completed high school, graduated with an A-B average—worked with special children while there; [occ.] Housewife and Country singer; [memb.] International Society of Poetry was elected into the International Hall of Fame, Boystown; [hon.] Won the Editor's Choice Award, several awards from Precious People Daycare, honored member of Boystown for neglected children; [oth. writ.] "The Stone Rolled Away," "My Heart Shaped Angel Box," not yet published; [pers.] I always pray and ask God to use my poetry to help others, to see and feel God's love and beauty.; [a.] Greer, SC

AUSTIN, JIM, JR.
[b.] October 19, 1938; Ft. Worth, TX; [p.] James Barbara L. Austin; January 1, 1983; [ch.] Marne Leigh (13) daughter, Seth Allyn (10) son; [ed.] B.A., Texas A and M University, History, 1961; M.A., St. Mary's University; S.A.T., TX, History, 1966, Ed.S. Education Administration, Troy State University, AL 1981; Ed.D. Adult, Voc. Education, Auburn University, 1986; Elementary Certification, Brigham Young University, HI, 1996; [occ.] Professor, Graduate Education, Northern AZ University, Phoenix, AZ; [memb.] American Historical Association, National Education Association, International Society of Poets, Retired Officers Association; [hon.] Who's Who Among America's Teachers (1996, 1997), National Dean's List 1996; [oth. writ.] Poems published by The National Library of Poetry, 1996 and 1997; [pers.] I enjoy the mental release and surge of enjoyment writing poetry permits and its ability to express the human soul.; [a.] Gilbert, AZ

BACKHAUS, EDNA
[pen.] Eydie; [b.] June 7, 1936; Marytown, WI; [p.] Claude and Anna Weber; [m.] Roman Backhaus; May 7, 1960; [ch.] Mark, Ann and David; [ed.] Kiel High, Various Schools for art; [occ.] Art Work for resale; [memb.] GAP (Guild of American Paper Cutters), Member of The National Library of Poetry; [hon.] Medals, plaques and a publication in a German newspaper and radio station; [oth. writ.] A special poem written for addictions and for mental health; [pers.] Since my attending The National Poetry symposium in D.C. in 1997, my conversing with such talented poets were a great influence on my writings now.; [a.] St. Nazianz, WI

BADIANG, REMEDIOS H.
[pen.] Mer Barn; [b.] August 13, 1949; Philippines; [p.] Eusebio Badiang (deceased) and Salvacion Hermosura; [m.] Wellmore C. Barnacha; [ed.] Saint Mary's College, Bayombong, Philippines; B.A.-B.S.E. (English History), M.A. units; [memb.] Distinguished member of The International Society of Poets; [hon.] 1996 Editor's Choice Awards for Outstanding Achievement in Poetry presented by The National Library of Poetry for poems "Beyond the Cries of Life" in A Tapestry of Thoughts, "Hope Lingers On" in Memories of

Tomorrow, "Beyond The Horizon" in Best Poems of the 90's, all NLP anthologies; [oth. writ.] Poems published in order NLP anthologies like "The Carpenter's Kids" in Best Poems of 1998, "A Glimpse of Dawn" in A Picture of Elegance, and "Star Of Destiny" in Outstanding Poets of 1998. Poems selected for recording in NLP The Sound Of Poetry, several unpublished, "The Heart: A Poetic Pursuit", a reflective article published in a local church paper, unpublished essays and oratorical pieces used in secondary schools, and an unpublished personal reflective analysis on depression; [pers.] Through this God-given poetic talent, my inspiration comes foremost from Him above, from my loving husband, Wellmore, and from my family. My pieces of poetry reflect myself within and my grateful appreciation of life. I write to express what life is to me with the hope to be remembered and to help others to understand that life is precious. This poem is written in memory of my most loved niece, Roxanne, whose short life of 25 years has left much reason to live on with stronger faith and more love.; [a.] Glendale, AZ

BAGLEY, MARY
[a.] Kemp, TX

BAILEY, BRIAN
[pen.] Skippy; [b.] March 3, 1977; Ravera, NY; [p.] Kathy and Bill Bailey; [ed.] One and half years of College in Fish and Wildlife Management; [occ.] Cooking at Joey's Pizza (Ravena); [oth. writ.] Write poems all the time. Have an unpublished book written; [pers.] I write for the people and hope someday lots of people will read what I have to say.; [a.] Ravena, NY

BALDWIN, ANNA SHIRLYNN
[b.] January 25, 1974; Brock, TX; [p.] Gene and Keen; [m.] Cody A. Baldwin; January 8, 1994; [ch.] Levi and Zachary; [ed.] Brock High School, Diploma of Veterinary Science, Associate of Arts in Theater; [occ.] Substitute Teacher; [hon.] Highest Awards Honored in TX Jr. College Competitions for acting and costume design, Dean's List; [oth. writ.] "More Than A Memory," published in Etches Of Time; [pers.] Since birth, life and God have tested me. My marriage and my children have been my rewards for following my heart and my Lord.; [a.] Weatherford, TX

BALLARD, CARLA M.
[b.] November 15, 1954; New Port, NV; [p.] Mr. and Mrs. Dave Tolbert; [occ.] Illustrator; [memb.] International Society of Poets; [hon.] National Library of Poetry Editor's Choice Award, 1997; [oth. writ.] "Dream," "Choice," "Peace"; [pers.] I write what I feel.; [a.] High Point, NC

BANKS, SHALAINA A. PINKNEY
[pen.] Shai; [b.] September 11, 1972; Bessemer, AL; [p.] Shirley A. Pinkney; [m.] Nickalus W. Banks; August 14, 1997; [ed.] Augsburg American High School and Bachelor's in Psychology, Tuskegee University; [occ.] Executive Secretary, Medical Records Supervisor; [memb.] African American Association, NCOA, National Society of Poets; [oth. writ.] Poems published in The Voice Within and The Best Poems of 1997; had a short story published in a newspaper at age 15 years; [pers.] Go forward and never lose sight of your dreams. Keep on keeping on, keep on doing on through whatever strife, keep a hold of your life.; [a.] Fairview Heights, IL

BANKS, WILLIAM F.
[b.] September 4, 1971; Knoxville, TN; [m.] Leah McMahan; [ed.] Bachelor of Arts English, M.S. English Education; [occ.] St. Catherine College, Regional Assessment and Resource Center Co-Director, and Instructor. English, Computer Science, ESL; [memb.] Assistant Basketball Coach SCCI Lady Patrols. American Career Society, National Council of Teaching of English, Knox-

ville Writer's Guild, other education related organizations, Washington County Literacy Council; [hon.] American Cancer Society, State Courage Award, Finalist (State of TN), American Cancer Society Board of Directors (1989-1990) Knoxvile, TN, published writer; [oth. writ.] "Two Hint Of Nightshade," (1994), two collection of 40 poems rooted in the underside of human experience, "Two Little Color" (1998) fiction, "Something Elastic" (1998), fictional work in progress; [pers.] Always in pursuit of tigers in red weather.; [a.] Springfield, KY

BAREFOOT, JUNE D.
[pen.] My Shadow My Soul; [b.] June 2, 1927; Tennessee; [p.] Dorothy and Herman Camp; [m.] Harold Barefoot; December 17, 1942; [ch.] Sherelyn Davis; [ed.] Jefferson High, Washington, DC, Dennison Vol, Washington, DC, Tompson Vol, St. Petersburg, FL, School of Bible Prophecy Atlanta, GA; [occ.] Volunteer work—collect and clean animals for all children's hospital; [memb.] Served as President for St. Pete Grand Mother's Club, Coin Club, St. Petersburg's Hall of Fame Senior Award; [hon.] St. Pete Grandmother's Club Award, School of Bible Prophecy Award, Received Key to the City of St. Petersburg by major Fisher in 1996 for outstanding volunteer work, Hall of Fame 1996 Senior winner; [oth. writ.] Song, "Hold Back The Dawn," Copyright 1968, several poems published in St. Petersburg Times unpublished songs, gospel, and poems; [pers.] To bring joy into other's lives with reading and singing my songs and poetry.; [a.] St. Petersburg, FL

BARKER, JIM
[a.] King City, CA

BARNES, ADREINNE ANN
[pen.] A.D.; [b.] September 20, 1981; Medford, NY; [p.] Catherine Pacent and Frank Barnes; [ed.] G.E.D.; [occ.] Student; [hon.] Invited to Washington, DC, for the Eighth Annual International Society of Poets Convention and Symposium; [oth. writ.] Several poems published with Iliad Press and National Library of Poetry; [pers.] Always believe in yourself.; [a.] St. Petersburg, FL

BARSTOW, RUTH E.
[pen.] Ruth Elizabeth; [b.] February 22, 1927; Tampa, FL; [p.] Glidden J., Mabel West Barstow; [ch.] Cairn Terriers: Scarlet, Sandy, Tara and Candy; [ed.] B.S.N., University of Iowa 1949; M.S.N., UCLA 1962; D.N.S., UCSF 1973; [occ.] Retired R.N. Educator; [memb.] Sigma Theta Tau, National League for Nursing, International Soc. of Poets; [hon.] Sigma Theta Tau is nursing honor, Research awards during doctoral program; [oth. writ.] Several poems published in newsletters, Nursing journals, Articles in nursing journals re: care of patients with heart/lung disorder; [pers.] My poetry reflects the life around me and my feelings toward life, both personal and universal.; [a.] San Rafael, CA

BASH, KATHLEEN
[pen.] Kathleen Lefebure Bash; [b.] September 27, 1934; Indiana Co., PA; [p.] Allen J. and Oneta King; [m.] Lyle C. Bash; August 15, 1992; [ch.] Bernice Lefebure, Ronald J. Lefebure and Lilian F. Bash; [occ.] Homemaker; [memb.] National Reamer Collector Association, Pine Flats church of God; [oth. writ.] Over 100 poems, also songs; [pers.] The talent I have of poetry is a gift of God and I am inspired many times by the Bible and my knowledge of it. My desire is to help encourage others.; [a.] Cherry Tree, PA

BASKETT, VICTOR
[b.] October 17; Louisville, KY; [ch.] Khatina Sheree and Zerric Allen; [ed.] Thomas Jefferson High, Sullivan College; [memb.] Newburg Church of Christ; [pers.] This poem changed my life!; [a.] Louisville, KY

BAUER, TAMMY SUE
[pen.] Tammy Sue Smith, Bauer; [b.] May 11, 1966; Phoenix, AZ; [p.] Tom and Susan Smith; [m.] James Michael Bauer; November 12, 1994; [occ.] Singer; [oth. writ.] The poetry writing is strictly inspired, by the true unknown passionate feelings possess in the depths of heart and soul.; [a.] La Jolla, CA

BEAL, AMANDA
[b.] July 24, 1998; Methodist Hospital, IN; [p.] Michael and Marion Beal; [ed.] Graduated from Southwestern high school in May of 1998. I will be attending Indiana University of Bloomington in August.; [occ.] I work at O'Malia Food Markets.; [memb.] National Honor Society; [hon.] Delta Theta Tau Scholarship, Presidential Honor, Governor's Honor, Midwest Grocer's Scholarship, I Alumni Scholarship; [oth. writ.] "On Being A Flower," "Where Am I", [pers.] Let your weakness make you stronger, your fight make you wiser, and your fears make you human.; [a.] Shelbyville, IN

BECKMAN, ANDY
[pen.] Ranger Andy; [b.] November 21, 1946; Fort Wayne, IN; [p.] Wally, Ruth Beckman; [occ.] Interpretive Park Ranger Georgia: Hofwyl Plantation State Historic Site; [pers.] Colossians 1:15-17 "Who (Christ) is the image of the invisible God, the firstborn of every creature. For by Him we're all things created, that able in Heaven, and that are in Earth, visible and invisible. And he is before all things, and by Him all things consist."; [a.] Brunswick, GA

BELL, R. SCOTT
[pen.] R. Scott Bell; [b.] September 30, 1969; Minneapolis, MN; [p.] Ray and Kathy; [ch.] Elizabeth Ashley; [ed.] Osseo Sr. Osseo, MN, Natic, Memphis, Bethel College, Brown Institute, North Hennepin Community College; [occ.] Rentalz Coordinator; [hon.] National Honor Society, Academic Achievement (4.0 GPA) Brown Institute, Editor's Choice for last submission; [oth. writ.] "A Little Older," "Through Sun and Shower"; [pers.] Writing frees you to look at areas of your life you wouldn't normally see.; [a.] Brooklyn Center, MN

BELLARD, JEQUETTA
[b.] May 16, 1965; El Campo, TX; [p.] Rita Moore and Lloyd Bellard Sr.; [m.] Keith Crowder; March 28, 1992; [ed.] Presently attending El Camino College; [occ.] Office Manager, Surviving in Recovery Inc.; [hon.] The National Library of Poetry Editor's Choice Award; [oth. writ.] "This Beautiful Queen," "Lie Lovers," "Blessed"; [pers.] No human being is disposable.; [a.] Los Angeles, CA

BELZNER, JESSICA MARIE
[pen.] Jessica Marie Belzner; [b.] May 12, 1981; Mercy Hospital, Baltimore, MD; [p.] Suzanne Marie Belzner; [ch.] Michael Anthony Belzner; [ed.] High School; [occ.] Student; [memb.] National Geographic; [hon.] Music, Editor's Choice Award, S.A.D.D., Good Citizen, Drug Poster Contest, Chorus Award, Principles Award, D.A.R.E; Art Award, passed all county tests; [oth. writ.] "A Right To Remember," "Your Gentle Voice," "A Woman's Hands"; [pers.] If you really want to achieve something, all you got to do is try, and believe in Jesus.; [a.] Baltimore, MD

BENJAMIN, GAYLE V. DANCY
[b.] December 23, 1946; New York City; [p.] Isaiah and Essie Dancy; [m.] Bishop Kenneth M. Benjamin Sr.; May 20; [ch.] Michelle, Michael and Marc; [ed.] Julia Richman H.S., University of the Virgin Islands; [occ.] English Teacher, Charlotte Amalie H.S.; [memb.] Church of God of Prophecy, National Alliance of Black School Educators, International Society of Poets; [hon.] Graduated Magna Cum Laude University of the Virgin Islands; [oth. writ.] Linkages: The Contributions of Virgin Islanders to the Harlem Renaissance, "We Are

Family" (Newspaper Article) published poetry; [pers.] My love for teaching and assisting young minds in discovering the joys of learning permeates my being.; [a.] St. Thomas, VI

BENN, AVA L. RUSSELL
[pen.] Ava L. Russell-Benn (Ava Benn); [b.] January 15, 1914; Aid, OH; [p.] P. G. and Nettie Phillips Russell; [m.] David H. Benn; June 5, 1943; [ch.] Adoptees Yong Newsome and Lee Soon; [ed.] Aid H.S. Capital U, Ohio State (B.S.) Miami U. (Masters); [occ.] Retired Ohio Former Business Ed. teacher and missionary, Brainerd Indian School, SD; [memb.] Stonecroft Consulting Coordinator for Friendship Bible Coffeess, United Methodist Church, The International Poetry Hall of Fame; [hon.] Rio Grande Scholarship, Pi Omega Pi (honorary Fraternity) Distinguished Member of International Society of poets; [oth. writ.] News reporter for Ironton Tribune, Poems published in Ironton Tribune, Oxford Press, Miami Student, Bristol Banner Books, IN; [pers.] Writing for enjoyment, benefit to others, and to honor God and Christ "in whom are hid all the treasures of wisdom and knowledge."; [a.] Oxford, OH

BENTON, TARA M.
[b.] March 23, 1972; Myrtle Beach, SC; [p.] Betty and Bobby Benton; [ed.] Myrtle Beach High, Carson-Newman College; [occ.] Manager, Palm Crest Motel, Myrtle Beach, SC; [memb.] National Wildlife Federation, Greenpeace; [pers.] If you let it, life will pass you by.; [a.] Myrtle Beach, SC

BERENTSEN, DOROTHY STEVENS
[pen.] Haryott Stevens; [b.] Toronto, ON; [p.] Fred and Edith Stevens; [m.] Lambert Berentsen; [ch.] Albert, Mary, Louise, Henry and Lambert; [ed.] Gledhill Public School (Toronto), Two years High School (Toronto), Graduate Famous Writer's School Community; [occ.] Composing a book about angels; [memb.] Academy of American Poets; [oth. writ.] Four books of poetry: Sleeping Lady At Sunrise (New York), Adoration (Mexico), My Love . . . The Sea (California), A Book of Love Poems (Texas); [pers.] I have lived under three flags: Canada, Mexico and U.S.A. I am now a widow and have written my memories.; [a.] Glendale, CA

BERNSTON, RICHARD
[pen.] Richard Bernston; [b.] January 3, 1958; Hollis Queens, NY; [p.] Caresse and Richard Sr.; [m.] Kelly Wells Bernston; June 13, 1994; [ed.] Graduated from Freeport High Freeport, NY, took limited music lessons, learned mostly by ear, learned to write by true life experiences; [occ.] Ritchie Dagger Band, Lead Vocalist, Guitarist, Lyrics; [hon.] Have won several poetry contests also was a runner-up in Battle of the Bands contest with my band "The Ritchie Dagger Band"; [oth. writ.] Have written many songs, one called "Some Son" was a top ten hit on college radio stations, also "Beloved Memory," and many poems, "Parade of Tears," "Remember Forget Kelly Green," and "The Park"; [pers.] I'm currently working on a poetry book, also solo music project. Remember, there is no failure in art of music, as long as the artist is happy with this work. Take chances, don't fear the critic.; [a.] Ft. Pierce, FL

BESSER, AMY MARIE
[pen.] Ame; [b.] October 9, 1985; Tulsa, OK; [p.] Gordon Besser, Cheryl Besser; [ed.] Claremore Elementary; [occ.] Student; [memb.] Ministry of Puppets M.O.P. Squad; [oth. writ.] Only the ones wrote in free time; [pers.] My poems are usually based on my hopes, dreams, and wishes; although, only a few I have written down on paper.; [a.] Claremore, OK

BESTE, REBECCA HARWERTH
[pen.] Rebecca Harwerth Beste; [b.] May 1, 1949; St. Louis, MO; [p.] Leonardo and Agnes Harwerth; [m.] Robert C. Beste; August 9, 1987; [ch.] Amy Beste; [ed.] Ascension Grade School, Mercy High

School, Florissant Valley Community College, National Academy of Beauty Arts; [occ.] Hairdresser, Computer Imaging Tech.; [memb.] Lemay Democratic Organization; [hon.] Outstanding Young Women of America; [oth. writ.] "I've Been Called Home"; [a.] St. Louis, MO

BIRDSONG, KAREN WILKERSON
[pen.] Karen Birdsong; [b.] April 13, 1953; Muncie, IN; [p.] Shirley Simmons; [m.] Alex Birdsong; September 19, 1987; [ch.] Carlos, Carletta, Feather and Ocean; [ed.] Roosevelt High School Dayton, OH; [occ.] Housewife, poet; [memb.] International Society of Poets; [hon.] National Library of Poetry, Editor's Choice awards; [oth. writ.] Several poems published in National Library of Poetry, The poetry guild, area news, local newspaper daily Xenia Gazette; [pers.] "And God said, let there be light . . ." Genesis, Chapter 1:3. My sister, Linda Bolton, thanks for the many prayers. Without them this would not have been possible. You're a treasure to be displayed.; [a.] Beavercreek, OH

BLAKE, OSBOURNE C.
[pen.] Osbourne C. Blake; [b.] September 16, 1932; Darliston JA, WI; [p.] Hezekiah and Florence Blake; [m.] Hermin M. Blake; June 26, 1982; [ed.] Elementary School and High School, Trade School England; [occ.] Carpenter; [memb.] International member of Society of Poets, and of the Salvation Army; [hon.] Editor's Choice Award for poems published in River of Dreams, Best Poems of 1997 and of Sound of Poetry, and National Award of Merit from the NCT for serving the public (Eng); [oth. writ.] Writing life story in poetry, also writing short stories. Few poems published in local papers and own book: Belly of Reason (Watermark Publisher); [pers.] My poems comes to me like stories I've known before, some I can repeat immediately after writing without looking. I would say my gift from a Divine friend.; [a.] Hartford, CT

BLAKE MOSS, LA VERNE R.
[pen.] La Verne Moss, L. R. Moss; [b.] September 9, 1929; St. Louis, MO; [p.] Donald A., Ruth Wilson Blake (Deceased); [m.] Wayne C. Moss (Deceased); February 7, 1953; [ch.] Timothy Blake Moss; [ed.] Festus High School (Festus, Missouri), Photography and Laboratory Tech, USAF Schools (Denver, CO); [memb.] Charter Member of WIMSA (Women in Military Service of America), International Society of Poets, Our Savior Lutheran Church, Branson, MI (Art Fellowship Group, Bible Class, Inhouse Artist); [hon.] Service Ribbons/Medals, (Korean, Vietnam, Cuban Conflicts), ACIC Service Outstanding United Award May 1961 through March 1963, Who's Who in Missouri 1974; [oth. writ.] Travel short stories; poems on nature, personal and family; talent shows, skits and inspirational narrations; Women's National Day of Prayer—commentary and prayers; The Rose (about Christ); 23rd Psalm explanation; skits: Patriotic Tribute to To Desert Storm, Casey at Bat, Hillbilly Woodcarver, and Rose Tells All (Friends 50th wedding anniversary); soon to be published poem—"Love Revisited," in A Pleasant Reverie (December 1998); [pers.] "Writing poetry, to me, is like composing music, having its own mood, rhyme, beat and meter, painting a mental picture of my inner feelings, expressed through words and language especially when I combine Christ and nature into a poem. It reflects my love, faith and hope in the Lord Jesus, plus explains my existence in God's natural world."; [a.] Pt. Lookout, MO

BLANC, DONNA
[pen.] Donna Blanc; [b.] June 1, 1995, CA; [ed.] Graduate of Holy Names College; [occ.] Classical Musician (Cellist); [oth. writ.] Published in The Ebbing Tide and Best Poems of 1997, by The National Library of Poetry; [pers.] As a musician, I found great success with the nonverbal communication of music. After bridging nonverbal and verbal communi-

cation, I experience written expression equal to musical expression. Using a pen or my cello changes only the texture of my statement.; [a.] Oakland, CA

BLAS, MANUEL U.
[b.] August 22, 1934; Agana, Guam; [p.] Mr. and Mrs. Jose Santos Blas; [m.] Vivian Pizzicara Blas; February 27, 1965; [ch.] Enid Turner, Lisa Ann Kellerhous and Johen Paul Blas B.A. LLD; [occ.] Lawyer/Arbitrator; [memb.] State Bar of California Patrons of Italian Culture—currently president of the club; [oth. writ.] Plays and essays, including "An Encounter in the Sistine Chapel" (One Act Play) and two full length plays entitled "Saran Out Post" and "An Incident at Villa Mysteria." Essays on Michelangelo as a poet; [pers.] I'm a traditionalist in literature and in religion as a Catholic, greatly influenced by the classics—Virgil, Horace, Dante, Petrarch, and Shakespeare—the romantic poets—Keats, Byron and Shelley—and in the modern era, T.S. Eliot.; [a.] Burbank, CA

BOCA, LUCY
[b.] August 1, 1946; Roswell, NM; [p.] Mike Y. and Sostena Boca (deceased); [ch.] Teri, Cuki, John and Robert; [ed.] High school graduate, some college; [occ.] Part-time Manager, Wildwood Gailey, Demonstrator-Demo. Ltd.; [memb.] WASA (Willcox Against Substance Abuse) Friends of the Library, writer's block; [hon.] City of Willcox, for poems, "Diana," "Jackie," "First Knight," "Faded Rose," Honorable Mention for "Thug The Caveman"; [oth. writ.] Children's stories, Joke AZ Highways, poems published in several newspapers, high school class reunion year book; [pers.] I never give up.; [a.] Willcox, AZ

BOCCALINO, DENISE NICHOLS
[pen.] Dee, Butterfly, Dee Rice; [b.] January 24, 1947; New York City; [p.] Jacqueline and Nicholai Nichols; [ch.] Joseph James and Christopher Anthony; [ed.] Executive Secretarial/Liberal Arts Degree - Dean's List, Nassau Community College, Garden City New York; [occ.] Administrative Asst.; [hon.] Editor's Choice Award for "The Loving Word," written under the pen name Dee; [pers.] All my poems are written with deep emotions, reflecting all the feelings that touch my heart.; [a.] Freeport, NY

BONILLA, ALEJANDRO
[pen.] Alex Bonilla; [b.] April 24, 1962; El Salvador; [m.] Lizley Marisol Arellano; February 10, 1995; [ed.] York College, Government and Public Administration; [occ.] Cashier at La Guardia Airport; [memb.] Seventh Day Adventist Church in Queens; [oth. writ.] Many poems to the greatest God, "Love Affair," and I would like to write a novel; [pers.] Nothing in this world has meaning without God.; [a.] Queens, NY

BONNER, EDWARD
[a.] Cicero, IL

BOOTH, WILLIAM B., JR.
[b.] March 19, 1921; Belleville, IL; [p.] William B. Booth Sr. and Grace; [m.] JoAnn Wiest (both deceased); July 7, 1946; [ch.] Cynthia James booth (deceased) and William Bennett Booth; [ed.] Belleville Township City Jr.-Sr. High School, 1938; University of Maryland, College Park, M.D. B.S.; Southern Illinois, Edwardsville, IL, M.S.Ed.; [occ.] Retired USAF, November 23, 1966, 23 years. Retired Teacher of Jr. High, Mascoutah, IL, 1984; [memb.] Moose and Legion of Moose, VFW. WW II, Korea, Vietnam, Masons 50 years pin, 1996. Honorable mention, World of Poetry, Sacramento, CA, December 1990; [hon.] Several Decorations including Legion of Merit; [oth. writ.] Have written between 100-200 assorted poems fishing or golf, take your pick, published in With Flute and Drum and Pen and many others. Several published in Local papers in America.; [pers.] Write to inform and entertain.; [a.] Henderson, NV

BOWERMAN, BETTY ANN
[pen.] Pinky Pardue Bowerman; [b.] November 29, 1953; Victorville, CA; [p.] Edward James, Patricia Pardue; [m.] Benjamin M. Bowerman; May 9, 1995; [ch.] Patrick (Deceased), Jennifer and Jesse; [ed.] Apple Valley, Senior High School; [occ.] Musician, Housewife, Crafter; [oth. writ.] Poem published in local paper, and in the book entitled The Lasting Joy; [pers.] Music, and poetry have been a blessed gift from God in my life, and a pleasure to share with others.; [a.] Columbia Falls, MI

BOWIE, EDMUND C.
[b.] Washington, D.C.; [m.] Margaret S. Bowie; [ch.] Edmund C. Bowie Jr. and Ellen M. Bowie; [memb.] Bars of District Court of US, US Supreme Court, Ninth Generation Marylander; [hon.] Captain US Army, World War II, Retired US Navy Reserve Major, Former Legal Analyst, Legal Examiner and Attorney Advisor, US Government; [pers.] May peace prevail, and happiness fill all hearts.; [a.] Temple Hills, MD

BOYD, LESTER W., JR.
[b.] January 18, 1931; Hamlin, TX; [p.] Mr. and Mrs. L.W. Boyd Sr. [ed.] B.S., M.Ed., North Texas University, Forestburg High School; [occ.] D.J. KRJT, Bowie, Texas and a Rawchen; [memb.] Texas retired Teacher's Association; [oth. writ.] Several poems published in National Library of Poetry books, and some in local Newspaper; [pers.] Each person is on Earth for a purpose. We must constantly re-assess ourselves, with The Guidance of God, in order to achieve that purpose.; [a.] Forestruna, TX

BOYER, NANETTE M.
[b.] September 10, 1973; Pittsburgh, PA; [p.] Dorothy and Richard Boyer; [ed.] Christian Liberty Academy, Florida Southern College; [occ.] Teacher and performer in the Fine Arts; [memb.] Who's Who in American Colleges and Universities, Albert Key Award for Outstanding Senior Artist, graduated Valedictorian Florida Southern College; [oth. writ.] "Impression" in The Promise of Dawn, published in Cantilevers, the Florida Southern Literary publications; [pers.] Only what's done for Christ will last.; [a.] Lakeland, FL

BOYKO, ANDREW W.
[b.] January 13, 1947; Gainsburg, Germany; [p.] William and Maria Boyko; [ed.] South Park High, Buffalo, NY; Electronic Computer Programming Institute, San Diego, CA; Control Data Institute, Anaheim, CA; [occ.] Field service engineer;[memb.] Marine Corps League, American Legion, VFW, 1st Marine Division Assn., Disabled American Veterans, NRA; [oth. writ.] "Brand," The Isle of View, "1st Marine Division"; [pers.] The horror and trauma of war is branded in every warrior's mind. Survival is not determined by the experience, but how one chooses to deal with it.; [a.] Riverside, CA

BRADBURN, JAIM
[pen.] Jaimi Bradburn; [b.] February 25, 1981; Henderson, KY; [p.] Pat and Wes Bradburn; [ed.] Sturgis Elementary Union County Middle School, currently a senior at Union County High; [memb.] ASPCA - American Society for the Prevention of Cruelty to Animals, Wildlife Mag.; [hon.] Softball, Pep Club, Bike Showing/Racing, being published by The National Library of Poetry; [pers.] When born, we are given a deck of cards, how we play it is up to us. Sometimes we get the jokers, other times, we get the ace's.; [a.] Sturgis, KY

BRADY, LOUISE
[pen.] Lou; [b.] April 16, 1964; St. Ann, Jamaica; [p.] Mr. and Mrs. Lovelle Brady; [ch.] Racquel (deceased) and Frank; [ed.] High School, some college; [occ.] Poet, mother and song writer; [hon.] Two Editor's Choice Awards for "Time For The Power Within You" and "Don't Have Be No Begger Man," a Plaque for "Time For The Power Within You" from The National Library of Poetry; [pers.] These Awards - Poems are from the collection. I think this is the best work I have ever done. Rave review from American Literary services: "Poems for Poets is one of the best collections of Poems I have read in some time. It is marvelous. You have written an exceptional book, Ms. Brady, a creative and well written book."; [a.] New Rochelle, NY

BRAY, ROBERT L.
[b.] Oklahoma; [m.] Verdia; [ch.] Robert Jr. and Billee Jansen; [occ.] Maxcor Inc. as a Teflon Coating Specialist; [oth. writ.] His poetry has been published in Local Papers and The National Library of Poetry.; [pers.] I would like to reach as many people as possible through my poetry and tidbits of writing.; [a.] Colorado Springs., CO

BRAY, SYLVIA
[b.] October 2, 1913; Ft. Wordom, WA; [p.] George and Pearl Bray; [ed.] Pacific Arode High School, Child Evangelism Institute Fellowship; [occ.] Retired Missionary, was in Alaska 1949-67, Bible Teacher to children; [memb.] First Baptist Church of Monterey Co.; [hon.] Certificate of Achievement from Defense Language School, President Monterey (for teaching Sunday school, children's chapel and Vacation Bible School, 18 years.) Certificate of appreciation from CEF of Monterey County, CA for 25 years of service; [oth. writ.] "Far, Far Away" 1996, "Someday He's Coming" 1997, "Words" 1998; [pers.] Sew, crochet, knit clothing for needy children.; [a.] Pacific Grove, CA

BRIDGES, LAURA
[pen.] Laura Bridges; [b.] May 29, 1976; Shelby, NC; [p.] Kent and Linda Bridges; [ed.] Shelby High, East Carolina University; [memb.] Central United Methodist Church; [hon.] Dean's List; [pers.] I write from my own personal experiences. The feelings expressed are true and very dear to me.; [a.] Greenville, NC

BRITT, MAISHA DORRAH
[pen.] Peggi Dorrah; [b.] October 22, 1944; Laurens, SC; [p.] Charles J. Britt and Versena Kennedy-Dorrah; [m.] Divorced; [ch.] Terri Rochelle, Trina Michelle; [ed.] Bachelor of Science, Associate in Science, Philadelphia College of Textiles and Science Master of Arts, Antioch University Murrell Dobbins Vocational Technical High School; [occ.] Organizational Development Consultant, Entertainment Management; [memb.] American Association of University Women, International Police Association; [hon.] National Library of Poetry Editor's Choice Award, International Association of Women Police Officer of the Year Award, County and State Detectives Association of Pennsylvania, Leadership Award, Women of the Year, Business and Professional Women of Pennsylvania; [oth. writ.] Several published poems and a book on the story of past experiences; [pers.] I write through pain and things that I don't understand. The conclusion lifts me up and is usually poetic. It is my hope to give light to others in despair and lift them up.; [a.] Dover, DE

BROADUS, LILLIAN E.
[pen.] Lilyan B; [b.] December 12, 1919; Bermuda; [p.] Samuel Kirton and Elizabeth Jane; [m.] Cleo Broadus; December 24, 1943; [ch.] Daughter Claudette - Deceased; [ed.] Excelsior Secondary Berkeley, Institute (B.D.A.), Dress designing, 12 years pianoforte Voice - Graduated in Beauty Culture and Aesthetics. (religion) Baptist; [occ.] (Ret.) Beauty Consultant, Distinguished Poet; [memb.] International Society of Poets; [oth. writ.] Short stories

BROWN, B. J.
[pen.] Barbara Jean; [b.] November 29, 1949; Newcastle, NE; [p.] James M. Brown and Faye M. Brown-Ripper; [ed.] Wichita East High, Kansas State Teachers College; [occ.] Trial Court Technician, 3rd Judicial District, State of Iowa; [memb.] Lifespring, Los Angeles 121; [oth. writ.] Poems, short stories; [pers.] To consciously embrace and co-create a future of love, peace and spiritual purpose every day for everyone.; [a.] Sioux City, IA

BROWN, BARRINGTON
[pen.] Tiger, Dr. Sud; [b.] May 30, 1967; Clarendon, Jamaica; [p.] Adella and Eustace Campbell; [m.] Jenice Ambey Brown; April 10, 1997; [ch.] Tafari, Daniel and Falola Brown; [ed.] Effortville and May Pen Primary, Cross All Age and Vere Technical High School; [occ.] Cook; [oth. writ.] Several ooems and songs, all unpublished; [pers.] I was born in the Ghetto, but the Ghetto wasn't born in me. It's not where you live, but how you live.; [a.] Miami, FL

BROWN, RONALD C.
[pen.] R. Carlyle; [b.] January 11, 1950; Philadelphia, PA; [p.] Nash and Nancy Brown; [ch.] Douglas DeShields and Patricia Brown; [ed.] Halifax Area High; [occ.] Cashier, Central Parking Systems; [oth. writ.] Numerous published by The National Library of Poetry; [pers.] Life has forced me to look inside myself for the happiness and satisfaction that I could not find elsewhere; I am content.; [a.] Philadelphia, PA

BUCHANAN, R. DURRANT
[pen.] Buchanan R. Durrant; [b.] April 21, 1979; Hungtington Valley, PA; [p.] Cecelia and Don Irby; [ed.] Uppatinas High, acting classes people light plus theatre, Wyomissing Fine Arts, Encore; [occ.] Custodian, Songwriters, Screenplay writer; [hon.] National Library of Poetry, United States Copyright Award; [oth. writ.] Screenplay, Spokesman for a dying mind, Six hours to morning, Cates/Newspaper articles Mercury Newspapers. Poetry Of Love's Demise; [pers.] Pop Culture and Entertainment has replaced religion as the opium of the masses.; [a.] Elverson, PA

BUDD, ELOISE I.
[b.] October 5, 1917; Washington, DC; [p.] James and Gertrude Mason; [m.] Richard Edward Budd; October 9, 1939; [ch.] Edward, Mildred, Roy and Dolly; [ed.] Seventh Grade; [memb.] Ambassador Temple Holiness Church of Christ; [hon.] Outstanding member of the church, member also of Mothers Board, President Overseers of Mothers Board; [oth. writ.] "Great Is He," "Lost In Space," "Height's Of A Man," "The Mysteries Of Life," "If I Had A Million Dollars," "Yesterday and Today"; [pers.] If I can help somebody as I travel along, if I can help somebody with a word or song, then my living shall not be in vain.; [a.] Lanham, MD

BULLOCK, JOIE L.
[pen.] Joie L. Bullock; [b.] August 22, 1931; East-Kentucky; [p.] Glen and Lela Helton; [m.] Clyde Bullock Jr.; May 15; [ch.] Pete and Pamela; [ed.] 10th grade; [memb.] International Pen Friend Club, Independent Baptist Church; [pers.] I love teaching mankind the truth of the holy bible, because God created all mankind.; [a.] Lake City, TN

BUNNELL, ROBIN FRITH
[pen.] Robin Bunnell; [b.] February 3, 1971; IN; [p.] Richard and Patricia Bunnell; [m.] Michael G. Grith II; September 28, 1990; [ch.] Stephanie, Erick, Elissa and Viktorea; [occ.] Writer, full time mother of four; [memb.] International Society of Poets; [hon.] Editor's Choice Award 1998, International Poet of Merit Award 1998; [oth. writ.] Pieces include: "Untitled" in The Rustling Leaves anthology, "A Lover's Ransom" in Of Time and Tide anthology; [pers.] Have faith my good fellow poets, the world is still in great need of the poet's tranquil light! May God inspire us all.; [a.] Indianapolis, IN

BURCH, ASHLEY B.
[pen.] Ashley B. Burch; [b.] March 21, 1943; Tift Co., GA; [p.] Ashley and Nell Burch; June 20, 1968;

[ch.] James and William; [ed.] High School; [occ.] Disabled Truck Driver; [memb.] The National Library of Poetry; [oth. writ.] Three poems published by The National Library of Poetry; [pers.] I love writing both poems and songs and would like to have a song recorded by a top star.; [a.] Orlando, FL

BURKE, SHARON K.
[pen.] Sharon K. Burke; [b.] July 30, 1956; Wise, VA; [p.] Owen and Irene Caudill; [m.] Charles Martin Burke; July 15, 1977; [ch.] Charles Jason, Robert Benjamin; [ed.] Castlewood High School; [occ.] Housewife; [memb.] Mountain Empire Arthritis Association, Rings Chapel Church; [hon.] Editor's Choice Award; [oth. writ.] "Treasures Of The Heart" published in Soaring With the Wind; [pers.] The great gift a person can give is of himself or herself.; [a.] Nickelsville, VA

BURROUGHS, PHYLLIS SEELEY
[pen.] Phyllis Seeley Burroughs; [b.] March 13, 1939; Glasgow, MT; [p.] Albert and Beatrice Seeley; [m.] Tom L. Burroughs; September 7, 1964; [ch.] Victoria Hoffman and James Thomas; [ed.] B.A. Degree from University of Utah, (Major in Theater, Minor in English); [occ.] Sales in golf USA store; [memb.] Bigfork Community Theater, Music Ministry (Piano) at St. Catherine's Catholic Church, and Alpha Phi Sorority; [oth. writ.] Local newspaper, two poems in Mystic Montana Magazine; [pers.] Most of my writings are based on personal and lifelong experiences.; [a.] Bigfork, MT

BUTLER, JENNIFER
[pen.] Guinevere; [b.] October 15, 1978; Tuscaloosa, AL; [p.] Don and Allison Butler; [ed.] Robert E. Lee High; [occ.] Writer; [oth. writ.] Several poems published in school paper; [pers.] "The world is but a stage, and I am but actress playing a role." I write what I see in life and what I feel.; [a.] Ridgeland, MS

BUTLER, VERA NORMAN
[b.] August 25, 1940; Corinth, MI; [p.] Lathan and Zealia Norman; [m.] James Butler; July 17, 1965; [ch.] Andre' R. Norman; [ed.] Easom High, MI College, Drakes Business School, NYC, Fashion Institute of Technology, NYC, John Jay Law School, NYC; [occ.] Retired Claims Adjudicator; [hon.] Scholarship in Drama, Jackson, TN, Academic Scholarship, MIC; Award and Certificate to Perform at Shakespeare Theatre, NYC, Music Scholarship, Itabena, MI; [pers.] My writing is due to experiences, thought and with the hope of helping others re-shape their lives.; [a.] Slidell, LA

BUTTS, LEE A., JR.
[b.] December 26, 1970; Compton, CA; [ed.] B.S. Biology, USC, 1997, Ph.D. Neuroscience, 2000; [occ.] Graduate Student; [oth. writ.] One poem published by The National Library of Poetry in Morning Song; [pers.] I write so that people will feel the same as I. There's a song associated with every poem I write. I want people to hear that song.; [a.] Los Angeles, CA

BYERLY, SANDY POOL
[pen.] Sandy Pool Byerly; [b.] July 9, 1951; MD; [p.] Norris and Marie Pool; [m.] Ken; November 6, 1971; [ch.] David, Nicole and Kenny; [ed.] College; [occ.] Educator; [hon.] Editor's Choice Award; [oth. writ.] Mary Jane, Mother Pool and numerous children books and poems; [pers.] All my love to Ken and my children.; [a.] Elkridge, MD

BYRNE, WILLIAM J.
[b.] August 21, 1909; Auburn, NY; [p.] Mr. and Mrs. Edward Byrne; [m.] Patricia Donovan Bryne; June 2, 1948; [ed.] Graduated St. Mary's Parochial School, Auburn, NY, 1925; [occ.] Retired; [memb.] Knights of Columbus, International Brotherhood of Electrical Workers-Aoo Hibernians; [hon.] Excel in English upon graduating, St. Mary's; [oth. writ.] Newspaper articles; [pers.] Strive for perfection in all things.; [a.] Dunedin, FL

CAMIRE, MARK E.
[b.] November 18, 1965; Bennington, VT; [p.] Russel (deceased), Elizabeth; [ed.] B.S. in Social Sciences and Psychology; [occ.] Restaurant worker, part-time writer; [memb.] Beta Sigma Delta Social Fraternity; [hon.] Nominated as Poet of The Year, 1997; [oth. writ.] "Empty Pages" in Memories of Tomorrow; [pers.] Motivation comes from within, yet inspiration is external. Hope to connect both into greatness soon.; [a.] Burlington, VT

CANADAY, MYRA HOLYCROSS
[pen.] Myra Holycross Canaday; [b.] July 15, 1926; Plain City; [p.] Clifton and Christine Holycross; [m.] Read Burton Canaday Jr.; January 12, 1946; [ch.] Barry B. '46, Craig H. '48, C. Star '50 and Cliffton R. (Riff) 1954; [ed.] Grad. Chuckery Darb HI, Unionville C. Ohio, Ohio State U., Indiana U., Purdue Ex, U. of west Florida (Short time in each); [occ.] Housewife, Mother to four, great grandmother to three, volunteer at hospital; [memb.] West Florida Literary Federation, Gulf Breeze Hospital Volunteers, National Genealogical Soc., G.B. Presbyterian Church, Wally Byam Int. Caravan Club (41 years); [hon.] 1st in Union County, O. Declamation Contest (1943), tied for Salutatorian (1943), scholarship to Ohio State, recent recipient of Rotary's Paul Harris Fellowship; [oth. writ.] Poems accepted by Sparrowgrass Poetry Forum: "Dance Of The Fall Flowers," "Dogwoods," '98, and The National Library of Poetry: "Gift at Twilight," '98; [pers.] Wildflowers and birds, rocks and shells and people are all collectibles to me. I love beautiful scenery, far away places, my husband and family, poetry and love stories.; [a.] Gulf Breeze, FL

CANGUREL, DR. SUSAN
[b.] September 11, 1946; Madison, WI; [p.] Mr. and Mrs. John Mather Murray; [m.] Mel Cangurel; April 8, 1985; [ch.] Lora Rae Quezada and Julie Lynn Colorusso; [ed.] Ph.D. with honors, Century University, Albuquerque, NM; [occ.] Corporate Vice President, Human Resources at Peppermill Casinos; [memb.] National Society Human Resource Management, Northern Nevada Human Resource Managers; [hon.] Who's Who in America, Who's Who in American Women, Women of Achievement Award, Reno; [oth. writ.] Many poems and short stories; [a.] Reno, NV

CANNON, YVONNE H.
[pen.] Yvonne D. Head Cannon; [b.] January 20, 1950; Atlanta, GA; [p.] Robert L. and Helen Daniel (deceased); [m.] Herman Cannon Sr.; January 1, 1988; [ch.] Arkos D'Andre' Head and Herman Cannon Jr.; [ed.] Booker T. Washington High, Morris Brown College, Atlanta University; [occ.] Behavior Disorders Teacher; [memb.] Central United Methodist Church, Zeta Phi Beta Sorority, Council on Exceptional Children, National Teachers of English, Coordinator of School's Beautification Committee; [hon.] Steller Teacher 1997 and 1998, Nominated as a 1998 Honor Teacher of Washington High School, Editor's Choice Award 1997, Special Recognition Award for Commitment to the Students of Washington High School; [oth. writ.] "Walking Along the Shores of Sands," published in Sketches of the Soul, currently developing a book of poems and short stories; [pers.] We have all been bestowed with precious gifts; however, it is up to us to cultivate our "diamonds in the rough" and allow their brilliance to illuminate for the good of mankind.; [a.] Atlanta, GA

CARP, IAN T.
[b.] April 18, 1913; Husi, Romania; [p.] Maria and Toader Carp; [m.] Achilina Gheorghitescu; July 16, 1945; [ch.] Sorin Carp; [ed.] Academy of Advanced Commercial and Industrial Studies, Bucharest M.B.A. 1944; [memb.] Member of the Literary Cenacle "George Calinescu" of The Romanian Academy, Member of The Association for

Accountants, Expert Witness Council; [oth. writ.] 1937- Poems published Gheorghe Lazar High School magazine, "Youth," 1941 Book Review of History of Commerce in Romania, published in The Bulletin of Commercial Academy, Romania, 1947, Poems published in "Iasul" Review, Bucharest, 1987-1996, Thoughts, Essays on Everyday Life, Radio Bucharest, 1991-present Epigrams for Romanian celebrities. Screen and stage actors, Minister of Justice, Minister of Culture, Foreign Minister. Published in TV Guide and Weekly Magazine, Broadcast on Radio Bucharest; [pers.] I believe in Love and Peace.; [a.] Newark, NJ

CARPENTER, VELMA
[pen.] Lady V; [b.] July 14, 1965; Columbus; [p.] Roger and Carolyn Long; [ch.] Daniel and Angel Carpenter; [ed.] Licking Heights School and Licking Country Joint Vocational School; [occ.] Hairstylist, Aerobic Instructor and a strength trainer; [memb.] Distinguished Member of the International Society of Poets; [hon.] Editor's Choice Award for "A Special Prayer" published in Where Dawn Lingers, "God's Words For You" in Best Poems of the 90's, "Be On Your Guard" in In Dappled Sunlight, "All Are Children Of God" in Best Poems of 1997, "He Choose Me" in Days Gone By, and "A True Friend" in Best Poems of 1998; [oth. writ.] A few poems written about brother in the Columbus Dispatch; [pers.] Live your life for God and give unto others so you can receive God's blessings and the meaning of true happiness.; [a.] Johnstown, OH

CARUNCHO, PAULI RACHELLE
[pen.] Pauli Rachelle Caruncho; [b.] December 30, 1952; New York City; [p.] Gladys Marcconi and Marco Caruncho; [ch.] Fabio and Paul Napoleoni; [ed.] B.A. from: University of Maine, M.A. student: University of Phoenix; [occ.] Assistant Dean of Students and Director of Admissions at Washington County Technical College in Calais, Maine; [memb.] National Council for Marketing and Public Relations: New England Association of College Administrators and Counselors; Maine Counselor's Association; [oth. writ.] Articles published: Machias Valley News, Calais Advertiser, Kennebeck Journal and the Bangor Daily; [pers.] Colors are for decoration, not discrimination; for beautification, not separation.; [a.] Calais, ME

CASSFORD, RICHARD
[b.] December 26, 1976; Long Beach, CA; [p.] Miriam Keere and David Cassford; [m.] Heidi Helene; March 16, 1998; [ed.] West Texas A and M University; [occ.] Student, theatrical carpenter, electrician; [memb.] International Thespian Society, Alpha Psi Omega, United States Institute of Technical Theatre, Phi Mu Alpha Sinfonia; [hon.] Best Actor Hobbs Community players, 1995, Irene Ryan Nomination, 1996, Brarding Iron Theatre Award, 1996 and 1997, Liberace Scholarship Recipient; [oth. writ.] Several poem and songs, a few short theatrical pieces, "Casted Off" a musical, and currently a musical waiting for a title; [pers.] I write with talent and inspiration on loan from the Heavenly Father. I attempt in writing, to reveal to others the truths I have discovered through my own experiences.; [a.] Canyon, TX

CEARFOSS, JULIE M.
[b.] April 9, 1960; St. Paul, MN; [p.] Richard and Carol Erlandsen; [m.] Warren F. Cearfoss; August 28, 1982; [ch.] Rebecca Sarah and Rianna Leigh; [ed.] Henry Sibley High School; [occ.] Homemaker; [memb.] The International Society of Poets; [oth. writ.] "The Child" (The Music of Silence anthology); [pers.] I am greatly inspired to write about my children, family, friends, experiences and love.; [a.] Apple Valley, MN

CHEATHAM, ANGELA
[b.] August 20, 1983; Galveston, TX; [p.] James

and Betty Cheatham; [ed.] Homeschool, currently beginning Junior Year; [occ.] Volunteering at the Library, Youth and Family Counseling Service, and the Museum; [memb.] Volunteer Program of United Way; [hon.] Honor Star, Ranked fourth at the Texas Star of Star Competition; [oth. writ.] Have many poems published in other National Library of Poetry books, also working on a novel; [pers.] I believe that as a teenager, (while I may not show it) I should listen to what my parents teach me, as they are older and wiser than me. I do not believe sleeping late or driving too fast is the best way to live life.; [a.] Angleton, TX

CHENIER, PAULA
[pen.] D. Dragon Moon; [b.] Escanaba, MI; [p.] Clint and Micki Marenger; [m.] Donald Chenier; [ch.] Jen and Amy Chenier; [ed.] Graduated Gladstone High School and Bay de Noc Community College; [occ.] Nurse, Artist; [pers.] To go where the Monet is; [a.] Lincoln Park, MI

CHILARGI, NINA
[b.] December 4, 1958; Bucharest, Romania; [p.] Maria and Constantin Cruceru; [m.] Gabriel Chilargi; March 26, 1979; [ch.] Francesca and Victor Chilargi; [ed.] Nutrition High School, Gastronomy 2 years, Technical School, and ESL school 2 years in Romania; [occ.] Teaching ESL, housewife; [memb.] St. George Cathedral Orthodox Church, Certificate of Outstanding in Poetry in 1997; [hon.] Honorable Mention from Romania, Award of Singing Soprano in choir, Award for performing excellently in a play during elementary school; [oth. writ.] Poem in Promise of Tomorrow, "Bring Me" Romania; [pers.] I get inspired by my imagination and by life itself that's around me.; [a.] Wichita, KS

CHIMOY, SRI
[b.] August 27, 1931; Chittagong, East Bengal (now Bangladesh); [ed.] Sri Aurobindo Ashram, Pondicherry 1944-64; [occ.] International peace advocate, poet, author, musician and artist; [hon.] Nehru Medallion 1995, Gandhi Peace Award 1994, Medaille d'Or 1993, Order of Balboa 1981; [oth. writ.] Has authored 1,218 published works in English. Has composed over 13,000 songs in Bengali and English. Has painted 135,000 paintings as well as 7 million drawings on the theme of the Soul-Bird.; [pers.] Our philosophy is the acceptance of life and also for the manifestation of God's Light here on Earth at God's choice Hour in God's own way.; [a.] Jamaica Estates, NY

CHOWDHURY, JERRY
[b.] July 12, 1938; India; [p.] Azharul H. and Maliha K. Chaudhri; [m.] Sara Chowdhury; August 8, 1965; [ed.] University of Calcutta (I.S.C.) and Jadavpur U (B.S.C.-I), Degree in Mechanical Engineering (Germany), Research engineer at University Stuttgart/RWTH Aachen, Germany, Graduate studies in Aerospace Engineering (University of Toronto); [occ.] Senior Engineering Specialist, Allied Signal Aerospace, Engines Division; [memb.] National Society of Professional Engineers, American Institute of Aeronautics and Astronautics, American Society for Quality, Board of Certified Safety Professionals, Professional Engineers Ontario, International Society of Poets; [hon.] International Poet of Merit and cash awards by International Society of Poets, Numerous Editor's Choice Awards by Allied Signal Aerospace, many other awards for Composition, Recitation, and Drama Performances; [oth. writ.] Poems published in The National Library of Poetry Anthologies. "The Search," Best Poems of 1995, "Heartache," Between the Raindrops, "Wake Me Not," Dark Side of the Moon, "Palais De Versailes," Best Poems of 1996, "Poetry," Best Poems of the 1990's; [pers.] With poetry, we communicate our thoughts, express our perceptions and feelings, share our dreams and hopes, and unwittingly create new visions for life. Poetry, though not always

expressible, is uniquely inherent in every natural entity; it is dramatically displayed in the harmony and beauties of nature and spontaneously generated by the human mind. I believe it is the quintessence of creation, of life and love.; [a.] Mesa, AZ

CHRISTENSEN, SHERRY L.
[pen.] S.L.C.; [b.] September 29, 1955; Kenosha, WI; [p.] Mr. and Mrs. Eugene Richter; [m.] William; May 14, 1983; [ed.] Diploma R.N., B.S.N. - Mt. Scenario College, Masters Health Care Administration, St. Joseph's College, Maine; [occ.] Director of Med.-Surg. and ICU; [memb.] AMSN, Community Church; [hon.] Graduated Magna Cum Laude, Honor Society; [oth. writ.] Poetry published in High School "Driftwood" was Associate Editor; [pers.] Matt: 5-6; [a.] Bailey Harbor, WI

CHRISTMAN PARKER, MARIE
[pen.] Sugar Sweet; [b.] August 6, 1957, Hammond, IN; [p.] Dozier and Doris Parker; [m.] Harry Christman III; July 11, 1989; [ch.] Jeremy Smith, Fayth Michael and Justine Christman; [ed.] Morton High, International Correspondence School, Master Art Cartooning Class, Purdue Calumet College, Hammond, IN; [occ.] Cashier Walgreen's, Oil Paintings, Poetry in spare time; [memb.] Hobart Arts League, profit share Walgreen's; [hon.] Award of Merit World of Poetry April 1990; [oth. writ.] "When One Dreams Of Yesterday," in A Tapestry of Thoughts, December 1995; [pers.] My mother has been a great inspiration in my life. I've loved poetry since I was a child, reading, and later writing poetry.; [a.] Hammond, IN

CHUBA, MARY
[pen.] Bola; [b.] March 28, 1941; [p.] Mack Thurman and Sarh Barton; [ch.] Marlon Stevens, Sharon and Kim Angela; [ed.] 10th grade; [hon.] Editor's Choice Award, The International Poetry Hall of Fame; [oth. writ.] "Love Sometime Can Be Pain," "Past Present And Then The Future"; [pers.] I am hoping soon I will be able to write better poetry. I would like to mention my brother, James Thurman, his wife is Jeane.; [a.] Columbus, OH

CICAIROS, LOIS A.
[pen.] Lois Tarski Cicairos; [b.] May 6, 1953; Oakland, CA; [p.] Bill and Betty Tarski; [m.] Albert Cicairos; September 21, 1976; [ch.] Justin, Kim, Kelly, Kris, Alex and Jake; [ed.] Pacific High, San Leandro Beauty College of California; [occ.] Housewife and Mother; [memb.] Prader-Willi-Syndrome Association Foundation; [hon.] Editor's Choice Award of 1997, Honorable Mention Award of 1998; [oth. writ.] Published Poems in: Iliad Press, Crossroads, Treasured Poems of America; [pers.] I would like to further my writing accomplishments by successfully becoming a short story writer.; [a.] Coulterville, CA

CIRKSENA, TAMMY
[ed.] 11th grade student at Severn School; [hon.] Will be inducted into the International Society of Poets and compete for Poet of the Year Award 9/98, Editor's Choice Award—National Library of Poetry, Poet of Merit Award—International Society of Poets, Won photography Award of Merit and Certificate of Excellence, Honor Roll student, Modeled for seventeen magazine.

CODY, KAREN
[b.] May 14, 1964; Youngstown, OH; [m.] Joseph T.; March 31, 1990; [ch.] John Paul and Kara Elizabeth; [ed.] UNC at Chapel Hill School of Pharmacy, Currently Student at the Institute of Children's Literature, West Redding, CT; [occ.] Pharmacist; [oth. writ.] Published poem "My Mother and I"; [pers.] My poems are the physical expression of my heart and mind.; [a.] Newton, NC

COHEN, KAREN D.
[pen.] Karen Cohen; [b.] November 28, 1954; New Brunswick, NJ; [p.] Marcia and Irwin Mirkin; [ed.]

Grant H.S., California State University, Northridge, Mt. St. Mary College, Los Angeles, CA; [occ.] Pshychotherapist Program, Director Santa Anita Family Services; [memb.] California Association Marriage Family child Therapists, Monvovia Kiwains and Chamber of Commerce; [hon.] National Dean's List, City of Monvovia, California School of Professional Psychology; [oth. writ.] "Family Land," in The Hand of Destiny" 1998; [pers.] Poetry is a wonderful tool to heal the human heart and mind.; [a.] Sherman Oaks, CA

COLEMAN, HOWARD D., JR.
[b.] September 30, 1980; Fort Pierce, FL; [p.] Howard and Barbara Coleman; [ed.] Morgan Educational Center (pre-school) currently a senior at Lincoln Park Academy; [memb.] Mount Olive Missionary, Baptist Church, Youth Nursing Ministry, National Honor Society; [hon.] Honor Roll, First place winner in the Omega's Psi Phi Fraternity Talent Hunt Competition in 1997; [pers.] Thank you, Jesus.; [a.] Fort Pierce, FL

COLLIER, ANDREW T.
[b.] January 30, 1975; Pierre, SD; [p.] James (d.1990) and Sandra Collier; [ed.] B.A., American University, M.B.A., University of Maryland; [occ.] Business Manager and Consultant; [hon.] Pi Sigma Alpha, Golden Key, National Mortar Board Society, Golden Gloves, American Legion, National Honor Society, National Eagle Scout Association, Society of Professional Journalists, Optimists International; [pers.] "Show me a good and gracious loser and I'll show you a failure."—Vince Lombardi; [a.] Bethesda, MD

CONNOLLY, AURELIA C.
[pen.] Aurelia C. Connolly; [b.] December 11, 1941; Salinas, CA; [m.] Victor Connolly; August 6, 1983; [ch.] Kim Berko; [pers.] Painting with words. That's what writing poetry means to me. From A-Z, it never ceases to amaze me how many different ways things can be expressed.; [a.] Seaside, CA

CONWAY, KEMMIE L.
[pen.] Kenny Neasom; [b.] December 22, 1953; St. Louis, MO; [p.] Samuel and Maudie Conway; [ed.] Associate Degree Management, University of Maryland; [occ.] Medical Records Technician; [hon.] Outstanding Leadership Award, Business Computer Training Institute, Tacoma, WA; [oth. writ.] Numerous poems published in hometown newspapers; [pers.] If you don't stand for something in life, you will fall for anything.; [a.] Tacoma, WA

COOK, HERBERT N.
[pen.] Herbert N. Cook; [b.] June 14, 1923; Indainapolis; [p.] Albert B. and Elsie B.; [m.] Miriam (Deceased); January 21, 1946; [ch.] Eight; [ed.] Degree Electronic; [occ.] Retired Electrical Consultant; [memb.] Life, rebuilt and flew antique airplane for forty years; [hon.] Give a poem each year to Communicate the dead of Army unit for Army Division; [oth. writ.] Cook Book of Poetry, Shemyz Island, Life Is a Joke (mini Autobiography to be out soon; [pers.] I wrote this poem when my mother died and she have been using it since.; [a.] Philadelphia, PA

COOK, TERRY ROY
[b.] April 19, 1959; Dodge City, KS; [p.] Larry and Marlene Cook; [ch.] Evan Ray Clark; [ed.] John F. Kennedy; [occ.] Structure Construction; [oth. writ.] Why Do I Feel Like a Stranger When it Comes to Writing; [pers.] I write to feel the truth from my writing when it comes from my heart or The Passion of the moment.; [a.] Englewood, CO

COOK, TINA MARIE
[b.] December 4, 1982; Chicago, IL; [p.] Shirley and Alan Cook; [ed.] Theodore Roosevelt High School; [occ.] Student; [hon.] Roosevelt's Merit Award, Miss Geris School of Dance, Perfect Atten-

dance; [pers.] Being active in life can carry you far, it can also bring excitement along the way.; [a.] Chicago, IL

COOPER, CRETIA
[b.] March 30, 1959; Stuttgart, Germany; [p.] Daniel Lewis Boone, Carolyn V. Frary; [ch.] Clarissa, Tara, A. Erin, Jenna, Reginald and Ariel; [ed.] Army Base Elementary Schools - Italy, Virginia, Vermont (civilian), Alaska, South Hagerstown High School, Maryland, South Florida Comm. College, University of Florida, College of Dentistry, Community College of Vermont; [occ.] Dental Assistant; [memb.] State of Vermont Early Childhood Work Group for Professional Preparation and Development Committee, Church of Jesus Christ of Latter Day Saints, Frary Family Association; [hon.] FFA Honorary Degree, DAR Outstanding History Award, Scholarship Activities Award, Athletic Award in Track, Young Womanhood Recognition; [oth. writ.] "Flower Fairy" stories of age six, biographical/historical profiles for local newspapers, published poetry in Tracing Shadow, published "The Vermont Guide To Early Childhood Careers"; [pers.] Live in the present, for the past is only a perception developed over time and the future is but a space in time that is forever beyond reality.; [a.] Brandon, VT

COOPER, WILLIE D.
[pen.] James Edgehill; [b.] January 8, 1925; Kingstree, SC; [p.] Thomas Cooper; [ch.] Three; [ed.] High School Graduate; [occ.] Owner of Car Service; [a.] Westbury, NY

COREY, HAROLD
[m.] June 29, 1965; [ch.] Ian G. Corey; [occ.] Colonel, US Army, Retired as Volunteer, do community service; [pers.] I have two major advocacies: 1. Proper reaching and education of our children. They are our greatest asset. 2. Tolerance of all nationalities and ethnic, also of all religions. We are all human beings and most of us are good.; [a.] San Diego, CA

CORTEZ, DIANA
[b.] September 14, 1967; Los Angeles, CA; [p.] Gloria Ybarra and Luis Cortez; [m.] Jesse Hernandez IV; [ch.] Arron, Alexandria, Jesse and Tuesday; [memb.] International Society of Poets; [hon.] Editor's Choice Award—1996, 1997 and 1998; [oth. writ.] Several poems published by The National Library of Poetry, "Enchanted Dreams," "Highland Promise," "A Vampire's Lullaby"; [pers.] Deep within one's soul lies a poet waiting to be heard.; [a.] N. Hollywood, CA

CORTEZ, SARAH
[pen.] Sarah Cortez; [b.] May 17, 1984; Phoenix, AZ; [p.] Diane, Ernest Cortez; [ed.] O.L.P.H., Our Lady of Perpetual Help, Scottsdale, Eighth Grade; [occ.] Student at O.L.P.H.; [memb.] Dance, Cheer leading, flutist, and alter server for the church, student council secretary; [hon.] Perfect attendance for seven years, high honors student; [oth. writ.] Numerous poems published in The National Library of Poetry; [pers.] I believe that every individual looks at a poem in a different way than someone else may see it. One poem may mean numerous things to different people.; [a.] Scottsdale, AZ

COWLES, LAVERNE E.
[b.] August 12, 1928; Johnstown, PA; [p.] Ralph K. and Della M. Keiper; [m.] Eugene J. Cowles; June 21, 1958; [ch.] James, Jeffrey and Jonathan; [ed.] Johnstown Central High; [occ.] Retired Secretary; [memb.] Bedford United Methodist Church, American Red Cross; [oth. writ.] "Disappointment And Delight," page 346 - Where Dawn Lingers; [pers.] This poem was written for our youngest son, Jonathan.; [a.] Bedford, PA

CRAIN, MICHAEL A.
[pen.] Michael A. Crain; [b.] November 1, 1970; Elizabethtown, KY; [p.] George H. Crain Sr. and Agnes Corrine Crain; [m.] Deborah L. Crain; [ch.] Jennifer N. Cruse and Bradley J. Cruse; [ed.] 12th Grade Graduate of Larue County High School, Computerized Small Business Management Degree, five Belts in Songham Style Taekwondo, three diplomas in world wide Bible studies; [occ.] Lot Maintenance Management Ancir Reynolds Cars and R.V. Sales Campbellsville, KY; [hon.] Several Military Awards, Editor's Choice Award, Elected into National Library of Poetry's Hall of Fame; [oth. writ.] "Our Salvation Plan," "Quicken" and other unpublished works at this time; [pers.] Life is concealed by a cloak, but often uncovered as a dagger. Never surrender to someone else's destiny, hold close your own journey.; [a.] Buffalo, KY

CRAWFORD, JUDITH ANN
[a.] Winter Park, FL

CRAWFORD, WANDAMARIE B.
[b.] November 8, 1953; Chicago, IL; [p.] Maurice Sr. (deceased) and Eugenia Bailey; [ed.] Masters in Marketing, Roosevelt University 1986, B.S. in Management - Eastern Illinois University, 1975, Harper High School, 1971; [occ.] Loan Officer, Mortage Broker, Minister - Living Word Christian Center, Forest Park, IL; [memb.] Living Word Christian Center, Asst. Teacher in Intercessory Faith; [oth. writ.] Previously published "The Holy Spirit," a poem in the 1998 Passages of Light publication; [pers.] Anyone who reads this poem, believing in faith that God hears you, you will be set free.; [a.] Chicago, IL

CREMEAN, DIANA LYNN
[pen.] Diana Lynn Cremean; [b.] March 2, 1958; Ft. Worth, TX; [p.] Jimmy Louis Brown and Alice Rae Price; [m.] Kenneth L. Cremean Sr.; September 20, 1991; [ch.] Tiffany and Rachel M. Steger; [ed.] High School, Nurse Training, not completed; [memb.] National Wildlife Assn., American Indian Relief Council; [oth. writ.] 25 Year Collection, starting in school; [pers.] She loves all animals and birds, outdoors action, climbing, underwater exploration.; [a.] Fort Worth, TX

CROOKS, JAMES C.
[pen.] J. Coulter Crooks; [b.] February 4, 1972; Warwick, RI; [p.] Bruce and Jennie Crooks; [ed.] B.B.A., Finance College of William and Marcy Class of 1994; [occ.] Regional Sales and Mktg. Manager, Nantucket Nectars; [hon.] National Honor Society, Merit Scholar Warwick Veterans Memorial High School, All Division and All City Soccer and Baseball; [oth. writ.] "Contention of One," "Moonlight And Wishes," "Agoraphobic and Epilogue," "Long and Winding Road," "Reservations," "The Confluence," "Quicksand"; [pers.] My writings are fairly egocentric because my thoughts, feelings, and beliefs are the only subjects that I know more about than anyone else.; [a.] Arlington, VA

CROSBY, DOROTHY B.
[b.] May 21, 1927; Chester, SC; [p.] Alberta C. and Edgar A. Barrett; [m.] Joe I. Crosby Jr.; October 22, 1949; [ch.] Marcia, Connie and Joe III; [ed.] Harding High and Oakhurst High Charlotte, Business Course; [occ.] Homemaker; [memb.] Active member, First Baptist Church, Charlotte, NC (since childhood), National Alliance for Mentally Ill because of my great interest in mental health issues; [oth. writ.] Inspirational booklet, "My Healing God's Timing" (self-published), hundreds of original poems which are shared with friends as well as strangers. I feel these poems are a gift from God which I must share to encourage others. Published in National Library books Between The Raindrops, Best Poems of 1996, Best Poems of 1997; [a.] Charlotte, NC

CROUCH, JON D.
[pen.] Janus McLoud; [b.] September 29, 1981; Aurora, MO; [p.] Sam and Dottie Crouch; [ed.] Monett High School; [memb.] NFL; [hon.] 1998 Lettered in Debate and Choir, District Choir Section Leader, International Society of Poetry, Internet Museum; [pers.] I believe time is a companion that goes with you on the journey, reminding you to savor each moment for it will never come again.; [a.] Verona, MO

CRUMP, DEBORAH JONES
[b.] July 25, 1948; Cynthiana, KY; [p.] Williard Hartley and Blanche Garrison Jones; [m.] Thomas Edward Crump; June 30, 1990; [oth. writ.] Other poems and letters to the editor of the local paper; [pers.] I was very lucky to have been born out in the country on a farm, because all I write about I have experienced, and if someone can experience this through my words, then my whole mission will have been accomplished and that will make me very happy.; [a.] Cynthiana, KY

CULBERTSON, MARK
[b.] August 1, 1963; Chicago, IL; [p.] Wes and Mary; [memb.] Catholic Church; [pers.] My words breathe life's breath once forgotten.; [a.] Covington, GA

CUMMINGS, KEO
[pen.] Keo Cummings; [b.] June 16, 1960; Colorado Springs, CO; [p.] L.G. Snyder Glenn Kensinger; [m.] Scott Cummings; December 20, 1997; [ch.] Travis, Daniel and Stasha; [ed.] Kingman Union High, Plaza III Modeling School; [occ.] Muralist, Sales Associate; [memb.] Children's Miracle Network; [hon.] Nominated poet of the year 1997; [oth. writ.] "Of Salt and Sand," published 1997, several other poems appearing in local publications; [pers.] I believe in fairy tales and refuse to let the negativity of society change me.; [a.] Las Vegas, NV

CURRIE, NANETTE
[pen.] Nanette Currie; [b.] April 18, 1922; New York City, NY; [p.] Wm. and Juanita Currie; [m.] Richard S. Cunliffe; May 22, 1943; [ch.] Spencer and Thurlow Cunliffe; [ed.] Bradford College, Music Major; [occ.] Artist; [memb.] Rehoboth Art League, Brush and Pencil, International Garden Club, Manor Club; [hon.] Judge's Choice Award for poem in memory of Howard S. Schroeder, several one woman shows, group shows, developer and choir 20 years R.A.H. fine arts outdoors show; [oth. writ.] Works in progress, published in Through The Hour Glass; [pers.] Through my poetry and painting I hope to reach people and increase their sensitivity towards all living creatures.; [a.] Southbury, CT

DAIKER, JOSEPH J., II
[pen.] Higher Love; [b.] July 9, 1976; Abert Lea, MN; [p.] Barb and Bernie Daiker; [ed.] Junior at the University of Northern Iowa Studying Psychology; [occ.] Student; [hon.] Honorable Mention from Iliad Press, Editor's Choice from The National Library of Poetry, Diamond Homer trophy from Famous Poets Society; [oth. writ.] "Introspect," "Within," and "For All I've Lost," also many unpublished poems; [pers.] In solitude we are least alone.; [a.] Cedar Falls, IA

DALY, TRACEY
[b.] November 16, 1962; Morristown, TN; [p.] Sharon McCrady and Vernon Ross; [m.] Bryen; [ch.] Daniel and John; [ed.] Graduated from Mt. Bake High School in 1981 in Deming, Washington; [occ.] Mother/Retired; [memb.] (WIGS) Whidbey Island Genelogical Searchers; [oth. writ.] Poem, "You Are The Sweetest Thing In My Memories"; [pers.] Poetry is the Heart and Soul poured out onto paper; [a.] Oak Harbor, WA

DANIEL, BELINDA D.
[pen.] Georgia B.; [b.] August 9, 1976; Chattahoochee, GA; [p.] Gary and Delores Daniel; [ed.] East Rowan High Pfeiffer University; [memb.] Student National Education Association; [hon.] Dean's List, National Dean's List; [oth. writ.] One

poem in Embrace the Morning; [pers.] I wish to thank Ginger Miller, Mrs. Barringer, Beth Teat, Sheila Smith, Mary Jones, and Terry Holt for reminding me about the love for learning and in different ways.; [a.] Rockwell, NC

DANIELS, TERENCE
[pen.] Terry Daniels; [b.] June 2, 1955; Ft. Bragg, NC; [p.] Robert Spencer and Mary Jo Daniels; [ch.] Jonathan Ashley Daniels; [ed.] Self-taught in Philosophy, Theology, Physics, The Poetry of Science, Astronomy, History and Art; [occ.] Architectural Cadd Technician, Computer Graphics; [oth. writ.] "Words," in Embrace The Morning; [pers.] I got a little black box with no poems in it.; [a.] Dallas, TX

DANIELSON, J. DAVID
[b.] September 2, 1926; Manistique, MI; [m.] Carmen Elena Galvagno; November 12, 1965; [ch.] Nicolas, Dan-Alan; [ed.] M.A., Ph.D., University of Michigan, B.A., Northern University; [occ.] Retired Professor, Emeritus; [memb.] Linguistic Society of America (em.) American Association of Teachers of Spanish and Portuguese (em.); [hon.] Fullbrights to France (1954-5) and Argentina (1991), several grants, two Third prize medals from National Library of Poetry; [oth. writ.] As translator, The Exiles, and other stories, by Horacio Quiroga (Austin, UTP, 1987), poems in a few literary mags., professional articles and reviews, other published translations; [pers.] I favor poetry as song, assonantal rime, avoidance of poetry and archaisma, staying close to the rhythms of American English everyday speech, concreteness, syntactic clarity, lexical precision, and banishment of obscurity, though not.; [a.] Bloomfield, CT

DAVIDSON, DEBORAH
[pen.] Debbie Davidson; [b.] August 16, 1957; Sharon, CT; [p.] Curtis and Gloria Irish; [m.] Kenneth R. Davidson; October 12, 1991; [ch.] Jillian and William; [ed.] AAS Criminal Justice; [occ.] Firefighter and Paramedic

DAY, JULIANNE IRENE
[pen.] Julianne Irene Day; [b.] February 22, 1984; Grand Rapids, MI; [p.] Margaret Irene Albee Day, James Sheffield Day; [oth. writ.] "Windows," in Adrift on the Breeze, "African Night," in Peninsula Writers Student Anthology, "Those Anonymous," in Kaleidoscope 1998; [a.] Grand Rapids, MI

DE GENNARO, PAUL A.
[pen.] Opie; [b.] July 31, 1958; Brooklyn, NY; [p.] Anthony and Marjorie De Gennaro; [m.] Maureen Maher-De Gennaro; September 21, 1985; [ed.] Fort Hamilton High, Long Island University, Mercer County Community College; [occ.] Software Analyst; [hon.] Merit Award, 1997, National Library of Poetry; [oth. writ.] "The Portrait Of A Lady," published in a Prism of Thoughts, National Library of Poetry, 1997; [pers.] Only by constant cultivation throughout its growing season will the creative process, once planted within the fertile heart, grow to maturity and bear fruitage.; [a.] Cranbury, NJ

DE LA TORRE, ODETTE
[b.] January 19, 1964; Los Angeles, CA; [p.] Martha Caceres; [ed.] Bishop Conaty Memorial High School, Los Angeles City College, Santa Monica City College; [hon.] Service Awards Volunteer, AIDS Walk Dance-a-thon 1990-1993, United States Olympic Festival 1991, Coaching Award For Basketball-Volleyball High School Students 1989-1991; [pers.] What goes around will defiantly come back to us. Be kind to ourselves.; [a.] Los Angeles, CA

DE MATTIES, EULAH G.
[pen.] Eulah G. De Matties; [b.] January 19, 1911; Oneonta, NY; [p.] Irving and Florence Harvey; [m.] Joseph De Matties; August 31, 1933; [ch.] Seven children; [ed.] High School Equivalency

Diploma, School for Practical Nurses, Albany, NY; [occ.] Nurse 20 years Glens Falls, NY Hospital, retired March, 1988; [oth. writ.] Poetry, "Childhood in the Adirondacks," May 24, 1989, "Our Hands," September 1984, "To a Kindergarten Graduate," May 1975, all in Warrensburg news "The Imaginary Winky Form," and "The Stars Tell the Story," in American Poetry anthology; [pers.] Likes to write about special people we should remember, children and their wonderful ways, and things of beauty. Special people, a few were, town Doctor, Priest, an Inventor, Mom and Dad.; [a.] Warrensburg, NY

DELZER, MANDY J.
[pen.] Mandi J. Delzer, Miranda Jo; [b.] June 22, 1976; Fond Du Lac; WI; [p.] Gary and Sandra Delzey; [ed.] Goodrich High; [hon.] Editor's Choice Award from The National Library of Poetry; [oth. writ.] Poem published in The National Library of Poetry's publication Winds of Freedom; [pers.] All my poems are inspired by my life experiences and emotions created by them, from finding my true love then losing it, to the loss of my unborn child and more. I believe everyone should keep a diary. The daily thoughts we reflect on may be the beginnings to great poetry.; [a.] Appleton, WI

DEMARCO, GREG
[pen.] G. T. DeMarco, Pentagonal Antagonist; [b.] October 7, 1964; Bridgeport, CT; [p.] Ralph and Judith DeMarco; [ed.] Graduated High School Venice, FL 1982, two years college Belmont Nashville, TN, continuing in self-ed; [occ.] Vigilant doubter; [memb.] Eagle Scout, Order of the Arrow, Bum Club; [oth. writ.] "Reflections," printed in National Library of Poetry anthologies, "Blind Man's Rainbow," Chapbook; [pers.] Attempt a stream of consciousness style of word play as social criticism as catalyst for social change influenced by John Coltrane.; [a.] Nokomis; FL

DESANDO, JEFFREY
[b.] November 18, 1976; Chicago, IL; [ed.] University of Illinois, Champaign Urbana; [occ.] Computer engineer; [pers.] Laughter is the sun that drives winter from the human face.; [a.] Bolingbrook, IL

DEVAULT, DORIS
[b.] June 10, 1917; Oak Grove, TN; [p.] Robert M. DeVault Sr., Bess Moulton DeVault [ed.] Watauga (Baptist High School), Butler TN; Carson Newman College (2 years) Meredith College B.A. WMU Training School; [memb.] Dawson Memorial Baptist Church, Watauga Association of Genealogist, E. TN, Washington Co. Historical Society, TN; [hon.] Sophomore in High School a Medal for essay on "Music," Senior yr. Best All Round Student Medal; Valedictorian of class, wrote and delivered a talk, "Floating or Rowing" in College Caslliopean Literary Society was Miss Freshman and Miss Sophomore; [oth. writ.] Ten yrs., articles for WMU Missionary magazines The Window and Royal Service, Features in Vol. 1,2,3,4, Southern Baptist Encyclopedia, Family genealogy in Washington Co. and Sullivan Co. Histories, East TN; [pers.] Since becoming a christian at age ten, my desires have been to follow and serve Christ. My home provided guidance and encouragement. We were not rich financially, but wealthy in terms of love, books, music, and biblical teaching.; [a.] Birmingham, AL

DEVLIN, JOHN J.
[pen.] John Devlin; [b.] November 15, 1920; Newton, MA; [p.] Mr. and Mrs. Edward R. Devlin; [m.] Nancy; May 31, 1948; [ch.] John, Charles, Teresa, Ginny, Peter, Chris and Pat; [ed.] A.B. Harvard, M.A. Turts Graduate School, Columbia; [pers.] Truth, beauty, love, freedom always.; [a.] Vienna, VA

DICROSTA, ANTHONY, JR.
[b.] June 28, 1978; Philadelphia, PA; [p.] Anthony

Di Crosta Sr., Debbie Weir; [ed.] St. John Neuman High School, Penn State University, DPT Business School; [occ.] Lock Box, Processor, First Union; [oth. writ.] "Loneliness," in The Rustling Leaves; [pers.] One moment can last for an eternity and totally affect the Universe. Eternity can only be a few moments and be totally meaningless.; [a.] Philadelphia, PA

DILLENBURG, SHARON
[b.] April 3, 1984; Alexandria, LA; [p.] Ronald and Dorothy Dillenburg; [occ.] Student; [oth. writ.] "Arizona," in anthology of poetry by young Americans, 1996 and "Hero," National Library of Poetry, Priceless Treasures, 1997; [a.] Tucson, AZ

DILLON, IRIS B.
[pen.] Iris Dillon; [b.] September 20, 1924; New Orleans, LA; [p.] Deceased; [m.] Deceased; May 10, 1939; [ed.] Bus. College, New Orleans, Tulane U. Nola, Denver U. Denver, CO, School of Grapnology, San Diego, CA, Chaplaincy Pro-Christ Church, San Diego, CA; [occ.] Financial Asst. and Case Mgr. San Diego Home Care; [memb.] Numerous Service Organizations including Alcoholics Award, Animal Leagues, Christ Church Unity; [hon.] Hospital Chaplaincy Degree, Certification in graphology, various service awards through working with the elderly and through serv. Center for the blind; [oth. writ.] Tributes and greetings cards (as well as sympathy and encouragement) for use by friends and businesses, my personal birthday, anniversary and holidays, won radio contest comm. flight contest, published in local newspaper; [pers.] To do the will of God in my life and express His love in all my endeavors and relationships.; [a.] San Diego, CA

DINARDO, PHYLLIS ANN PARKER
[b.] April 29, 1954; Tenaha, TX; [p.] Donald F. Parker, Jean Beard Parker; [m.] John P. DiNardo; November 15, 1985; [ch.] Angela and Anthony; [ed.] Tenaha High, Stephen F. Austin State University; [occ.] Arrow Custom Plastics, Bedford, TX, Plastics Press Operator; [memb.] Distinguished Member, International Society of Poets; [hon.] Two Editor's Choice Awards, elected into International Poetry Hall of Fame; [oth. writ.] "Soulmates," "Verdant Lands of Spring," and "My Sweet Hands" in A Picture of Elegance; [pers.] The Journey to heaven on earth is the path of self-realization. Walk gently.; [a.] Newark, TX

DOAN, KYLE S.
[b.] June 8, 1981; [p.] Claude and Deborah Doan; [pers.] Throughout your life, things will happen. But, no matter what else you remember, you will remember love.; [a.] Cincinnati, OH

DOLERHIE, BERT D.
[b.] April 2, 1927; Cincinnati, OH; [p.] Bert and Catherine; [m.] Paulina Dolerhie; December 24, 1949; [ch.] Bert Jr., Jacqueline, Jill and Dawn; [ed.] Riverside Elementary, Central High School, University of Cincinnati; [memb.] Western Hills Church of Christ Green Township, Bowling League; [hon.] High Individual bowling average, selected as Roast Master for many retirement; [oth. writ.] Numerous poems and songs, also joke writer, directed two musical videos for public television station in Cincinnati; [pers.] Always tried to set a good example to lead others to Jesus Christ. Put God first in my life, always praising Him.; [a.] Cincinnati, OH

DOOLITTLE, LOIS E.
[b.] October 29, 1936; Canton, OH; [p.] L. W. and Ruth Helmick; [m.] George W. Doolittle; November 21, 1976; [ch.] Kenneth, Susan, Dennis, Holly, Michelle and Robert; [ed.] Massillon, Cleveland, Ohio and Long Beach, CA, Speedwriting Inst., Institute of Children's Literature, Crawford, Modeling School; [occ.] Computer, Typist, LAT retired December 1993; [memb.] Protestant, Baptized 1949, Massillon, OH; [hon.] Ohio, H.S.

Drama, Clarinetist 1952, 1954; [oth. writ.] Poetry, Short Stories, Journals, Novels; [pers.] I come from a family of philosophers. The men were conservatives. As a woman, I am known as compassionate, intelligent, loyal and loving.; [a.] Long Beach, CA

DOSHIER, MARQUITTA M.
[pen.] Marquita M. Doshier; [b.] August 7, 1950; Kingman, AZ; [p.] Mr. and Mrs. E. S. Torres; [m.] Melvin M. Doshier; December 27, 1995; [ch.] Rene Martin, Jason Arnold, Michael and Nicholas Gibson; [ed.] Graduate Mohave County Union High School; [occ.] Collector of 1960's Memorabilia, Homemaker and mom; [oth. writ.] Have kept a personal diary of the most emotional traumatic and unjustifiable marriage left behind; [pers.] Free yourself with a pen as often as allowed, you will feel solace, once again, review and resolve.; [a.] Kingman, AZ

DOUGLAS, WYNONA
[b.] Spartanburg, SC; [p.] Dr. and Mrs. J. M. Douglas; [ed.] B.S. and M.A. from Ohio State University, Licensed Professional Clinical Counselor (LPCC), Degrees in Criminal Psychology; [occ.] Psychology assistant and used to sing professionally; [oth. writ.] Two articles published on Retin, Ohio Psychologist Magazine, Other Poems, Songs, Recorded Song, written; [pers.] Creativity is a gift shared by all and given to a few.; [a.] Reynoldsburg, OH

DOWNEY, DORIS C.
[pen.] Don C; [b] November 2, 1942; Austin, TX; [p.] Ruby and Carroll Downey; [ch.] Nita Fay Glenda, Kay Gordon, Wayne Andrew and James Roger Lynn; [hon.] Picture in Austin Statesman in Art class Fulmore Jr. High, Picture in Paper Highlander for cake decoration and best cake, 31 poems entered in a contest, 12 selected and all printed in nine books, Received nine Editor's Choice Awards; [oth. writ.] "Trumpet Sounding," "Calvery's Hill," "Tribute to Grannie Old Leaning Past," "Do Friends Ever Cross Your Mind?"; [pers.] See the ages roll, roll for times untold, all for one, one for all, yet there's that rainbow and a true soul for that search of words of wisdom still.; [a.] Marble Falls, TX

DRINNON, JANIS BOLTON
[b.] July 28, 1922; Pineville, KY; [p.] Clyde Herman and Violet Hendrickson Bolton; [m.] Kenneth C. Drinnon; [m.] June 13, 1948; First Baptist Church, Middlesboro, KY; [ch.] Dena D. Drinnon; [ed.] Middlesboro, KY High School, 1943, Journalism classes at Lincoln Memorial University, Harrogate, TN, 1947-1948, Commercial Art Certificate from Art Instruction School, 1968, Correspondence courses with Newspaper Institute of American, Drama Instruction and singing lessons with private teachers; [occ.] Homemaker; [memb.] New Hopewell Baptist Church, Knoxville, TN, Distinguished Member of International Society of Poets; [hon.] Editor's Choice Awards by The National Library of Poetry for 11 poems, "When Our Purpose Here Is Done," published in the Dark Side of The Moon, 1994, "Blessing," published in the Best Poems of 1995, "My Daily Best," published in Windows of The Soul, 1995, "Going Home," published in The Best Poems of 1996, "On Call," published in Through the Hourglass, 1996, "He Is Real," published in Best Poems of The 90's, 1996; [oth. writ.] Wrote articles for local newspapers. Recently had poems published in anthologies. Author. In His Care, a book of inspirational poetry published by Watermark Press, 1998; [pers.] I have always enjoyed the finer things of life and nature, especially those that are spiritually uplifting and bring beauty to the soul. My family has always come first in my life. I have never been much for organizations, preferring to be a doer rather than a participant.; [a.] Knoxville, TN

DUGREE, TANYA MARIE
[pen.] Albertina Seppa; [b.] March 12, 1977; Iron Mountain; [p.] Valerie and Victor Dugree; [ed.] Soon to be completed Bachelor of Political Science from Lake State University; [occ.] Student; [memb.] LASA and Lake State Theater Company; [hon.] Editor's Choice Award,1997 (The National Library of Poetry), and numerous poems published; [oth. writ.] "Bleeding," "Why Ask Why," "Untitled," and many other poems written but not yet published; [pers.] When I feel like no one will understand or listen, I turn to a piece of paper for comfort. A piece of paper will always listen.; [a.] Sault Ste. Marie; MI

DUHE, BOBBIE JEAN MACK
[b.] December 23, 1943; Rt. 1, Falls, OK; [p.] Neola Parrish and Roosevelt Mack Sr.; [m.] Albert A. Duhe III; October 5, 1965; [ch.] Helen and Ursula; [ed.] Guthrie High, Langston University, UMKC, M.A. Degree; [occ.] Art Teacher, Pointe Coupee Central High, New Roads, LA; [oth. writ.] Poems and other writings for later punishment; [pers.] My poems usually center on man in relationships with others or on nature.; [a.] New Roads, LA

DUNBAR, BILL J.
[b.] August 7, 1959; High Springs, FL; [p.] Willie and Idella Dunbar; [ch.] Caleb Jemar and DeiAndre Jamall; [ed.] Associate Arts, Pikes Peak Community College; [occ.] United States Army; [oth. writ.] "About Last Night"; [pers.] I strive to always be kind and considerate of the feelings of others, and to leave this world in a little better condition than when I first entered it.; [a.] High Springs, FL

DUNCAN, ANNETTE
[b.] September 16, 1962; AL; [p.] Jessie and Lillie Duncan; [ed.] J.O. Johnson High School, International Career Institute, Institute of Children's Literature; [occ.] Nanny; [hon.] Editor's Choice Award, 1995; [pers.] I believe that my writing is a precious gift from God.; [a.] Huntsville, AL

DUNNING, JAMES
[b.] February 7, 1950; Onslow, Co, NC; [p.] James W. and Laura S. Dunning; [m.] Gertrud E. Schweizer; June 1, 1976; [ch.] Eva L. Laura K.; [ed.] A.B., B.S., Ph.D. Pharmacy; [occ.] Scientist; [pers.] I discover, wonder at, and seek to express the sanctity in everyday things. I admire the work of Pushkin and Lermontov, W.B. Yeats and Christy Moore.; [a.] Marietta, GA

DUONG, SUM
[pen.] Sum Duong and Duong Tu; [b.] July 28, 1935; Bienhoa, Vietnam; [p.] Hinh Duong and Chinh Do; [m.] Hiepho; October 31, 1961; [ch.] Hoa D., Nhu D., Giao D. and Lam Duong; [ed.] Petrus KY H.S. (Vietnam), Teacher Training College (VN), University of Saigon (Vietnam), Rancho Santiago College (USA); [occ.] Chemist Lab Technician, Cosmetic Specialist (R and D Lab); [memb.] Petrusky H.S. Foundation Former Teachers' Association, International Society of Poets; [hon.] Education Order of 2nd Class (1973) by The Vietnamese Ministry of Education, Editor's Choice Award (1998) by The National Library of Poetry; [oth. writ.] Many poems and prose writings published in local magazines and some Social Associations' Magazines; [pers.] Have been greatly influenced by French Romantic Poets of XIX Century, strive to be more and more social, humoristic and satiric.; [a.] Garden Grove, CA

DWYER, MARGARET ANN
[pen.] Margaret Ann Rees-Manley; [b.] January 25, 1936; Mt. Ash, South Wales, United Kingdom; [p.] William Charles and Dwynwen Manley; [m.] Charles William Dwyer; February 21, 1959; [ch.] Karen Keturah Ann and Curtis Duan William Charles; [ed.] Educated in Great Britain, graduated April 1951 with honors; [occ.] Retired Women's Royal Air Force (WRAF); [memb.] The King's

Harvest Foursquare Gospel Church, The King's Harvest Praise and Worship Team Vocalist, AARP, International Society of Poets; [hon.] The World Poetry 1987 Honorable mention Award of Merit, 1988 Golden Poet Award, 1989 Silver Poet Award, 1990 Golden Poet Award, 1992 Golden Poet Award; [oth. writ.] Poems "Helping Hands" published by New American World of Poetry Press, "At Calvary," National Library of Poetry's Best Poems of 1995, "God's Love Is Always With Me," National Library of Poetry's Best Poems of 1996, others yet unpublished; [pers.] It's time for USA and worldwide nations to return to their basics. Let us mean it when we say, as on our currency, "In God We Trust." Put God back in our families and classrooms again. Restore America to the place our foundling Father's Labored in God and through God to place her and in God we will trust and shall overcome.; [a.] Terre Haute, IN

DYE, SUSAN K.
[b.] August 31, 1969; Painstville, KY; [p.] Morris and Willodean Caudill; [m.] Henry Lee Dye; April 2, 1994; [ch.] Harrison Dye; [ed.] B.A. Degree in Psychology; [occ.] Housewife; [oth. writ.] "Hands Of Clay" in The Soft Parade; [pers.] I need to learn to be more patient and forgiving of myself as God is with me.; [a.] Carrie, KY

DYER, SIDNEY
[pen.] Sidney Dyer; [b.] July 14, 1932; Kansas City, MO; [p.] Carmen Floyd, Sid Dyer, Frank Pope and Frank Roush; [m.] Barbara, Jeanne Stubbs Dyer; May 4, 1957; [ch.] Peter Michael, Pam Marie, Camilla Ann, Janene Louise and Allan Joseph; [ed.] St. Stephens, Elementary, KS, MO, Dela Salle Military Academy, High, KCMO, Rockhurst College, KC, MO; [occ.] Used Car Sales, Hot Wheels Auto Sales of Jonesboro, GA; [memb.] Knights of Columbus, VFW, St. Philip Benizi, Catholic Church; [hon.] Eagle Scout, Veteran of Foreign Wars (Korea and Vietnam), Operation Ivy, (1st H-bomb Test), US Navy Sk-1 (honorable discharge four ships in four years), Neptune, Golden Dragon, International Dateline (equator crossing), Blue Nose (Arctic Circle Crossing); [oth. writ.] Many poems (20), several songs and one book; [pers.] Through him, with him and in him, I am all things and all things are possible. I love God and I love my neighbor.; [a.] Jonesboro, GA

EARGLE, LIZZI
[pen.] Lizzi; [b.] March 30, 1982; Newberry, SC; [p.] Mr. and Mrs. Dale Eargle; [ed.] Jr. at Newberry High School; [occ.] Student; [memb.] NHS Beta Club, NHS Spanish Club, NHS Concert Choir, Church Youth Group, Woodmen of the World; [hon.] All State 1998 SATB Choir, 1998 Southern Regional ACDA Choir, United States Achievement Academy—1996, All American Scholar—1996; [oth. writ.] Poems published in The Best Poems of 1998 and Dance Upon The Shore; [a.] Newberry, SC

EARP, FREDERICK
[b.] January 9, 1971; Los Angeles, CA; [p.] Thomas and Josefina Earp; [ed.] Antelope Valley High School; [occ.] Engineering Tech. for Injection Molding, Special Device Inc.; [pers.] "If my being here can make a difference, then I will do my best to make that difference."; [a.] Lancaster, CA

EASTMAN, JENNIFER M.
[pen.] Sunshine; [b.] August 13, 1978; Fort Collins, CO; [ed.] Completing B.A. in Marketing and Management, will be complete in December of 1998; [occ.] Work in photography studio owned by my father; [oth. writ.] "Sweet Dreams" published in Amidst the Splendor; [a.] Bend, OR

EDENS, LOU ELLYN T.
[b.] August 8, 1941; Ruffin, SC; [p.] Llewellyn B. and Francis B. Thomas; [ch.] John E. Edens II, James G. Edens; [ed.] B.A. University of SC (1962) Sociology; [occ.] Retail Merchant, Inn Keeper,

Real Estate Developer, Farmer; [hon.] Phi Beta Kappa, Charleston Metro Top Award, SC Blue Chip Enterprise Award, Mt. Pleasant Community Service Award, San Walton Business Leader Award; [oth. writ.] "Imagination," in Whispers at Dusk; [a.] Mt. Pleasant, SC

EGLI, LAURA
[pen.] Roo; [p.] Steve and Anne Egli; [ed.] High School; [pers.] I believe you should never allow age or physical appearance to hinder you or any one else.; [a.] Squaw Valley, CA

EGNER, JOHN
[pen.] Polar L.J.; [b.] February 11, 1983; Albuquerque, NM; [p.] John and Debi Egner; [ed.] Just started Tenth Grade; [hon.] Editor's Choice Award given by The National Library of Poetry; [oth. writ.] "Midnight summer" and "Secrets Beheld"; [pers.] Life goes on . . .; [a.] Murrieta, CA

EICHNER, WINONA PENNELS
[pen.] Winona Pennels Eichner; [b.] March 17, 1954; Riverside, CA; [p.] La Wanda and Don Pennels; [m.] Rodney Dean Eichner; May 31; [ch.] Michael, Christopher and Cheri; [ed.] Master of Nursing Education; [occ.] Nursing Manager and Educator; [memb.] Association of Rehabilitation Nurses; [hon.] Who's Who 1998, 1997 Nursing Exemplar winner, 1998 Employee of the month, University of Phoenix, So Cal Ontario Campus; [oth. writ.] "Michael's Ride," "Dad's Autumn's Hands," "April's Love"; [pers.] With God's love you can be the best you can be.; [a.] San Bernardino, CA

ELFOND, VIRGINIA
[b.] October 19, 1921; Detroit, MI; [p.] Hilda Zimmermon and Joseph Hennic; [m.] July 28, 1949; [ch.] 5; [ed.] Graduate Major Piano, Univ. of Det., Det. Institute and Musical Arts, Post-grad at Boston Conservatory of Music; [occ.] Retired Management, do much volunteer work, and Trainee; [memb.] Sisterhood of Temple and Emanu El Board Member - Life's Disabled Vets of WW II, The international Society of Poets, won a Book for Interacting with People - Read of very Paes on Cable TV15, gives the honor of writing for the current book; [oth. writ.] "The Walls," "Rose in Hand," "Through Blind Eyes," "The Spinner," "No Busy Lines," "Hi Grandpa," "Memories," "Light in Window," etc.; [pers.] I agree with Einstein: "Imagination is more important than education, but to be blessed with both, you have everything in this God-given world we can ask for."; [a.] Southfield, MI

ELLIS, DEBRA J.
[b.] January 7, 1953; Casper, Wyoming; [p.] Harold Hitshew (Father), Bernice Boranich (Mother); [ch.] Jeremy D. and Clayton D. Ellis; [ed.] Graduated from Newcastle High School in 1971 and Graduated from Butte Academy of Beauty Culture, February, 1988; [occ.] Cosmetologist/Nail Tech. at Bei Capelli; [oth. writ.] "Reflections," published in 1996, was my first poem to be published; [pers.] My friends are always an inspiration to me and I wanted to in some way show them how special they are to me.; [a.] Butte, MT

EMRY, SUZANNE J.
[b.] March 25, 1974; Van Nuys, CA; [p.] David L. and Janice L. Emry; [ed.] Two years at Multnomah Bible College, two years at Warner Pacific College; [occ.] Customer Service Representative at Soloflex, Incorporated; [oth. writ.] 570 Christian Lyrics, approximately 20 secular lyrics; [pers.] Psalms 27:13 "I am still confident of this, I will see the goodness of the Lord in the land of the living."; [a.] Portland, OR

ENGELS, BEATRICE A.
[a.] Ft. Lauderdale, FL

EPPERS, MARCY
[b.] April 24, 1930; Marshfield, WI; [p.] Louis and

Julie Beck; [m.] Glen Eppers (deceased); May 1, 1951; [ch.] Linda, Cheryl, Renee', Julie and David; [ed.] Parochial School Home Correspondence courses, self-taught; [occ.] Retired homemaker, antique dealer; [memb.] Red Cross, St. Vincent De Paul, St. Mary Catholic Church, International Society of Poets; [hon.] World of Poetry—Silver Poet Award, Honorable Mention, International Society of Poets Editor's Choice Award; [oth. writ.] Poems published in local newspapers, Dick E. Bird News, and a short story book, Back To The Farm, of my childhood; [pers.] Feelings triggered by God's gifts of nature that surrounds us, inspire me to write and share my vision.; [a.] Sheboygan Falls, WI

ESPENSCHIED, JOHNNY L.
[pen.] Johnny L. Espenschied; [b.] July 22, 1944; Dover, OH; [m.] Shirley Ann, July 4, 1991; [ch.] Three; [ed.] High School; [occ.] Steel Worker (Forklift Operator); [memb.] Sugarcreek Chapter of Archeology—Ohio Archeological Society, International Society of Poets; [hon.] Twice Editor's Choice Award, The National Library of Poetry, Nominated 1997, International Society of Poets, Twice—Reader's Choice Award (Lines-N-Rhymes); [oth. writ.] Published poems in Seen Newspaper, Lines-N-Rhymes, Wey Farers Guilford Poets Press, Sparrowgrass Poetry Forum, The National Library of Poetry, Poetry Guild; [pers.] I'm grateful I have an ability to express feelings of compassion, happiness, sadness and feelings that are part of life, that one can feel and understand.; [a.] Dover, OH

EVRIDGE, LINDA DELONE
[pen.] Lin; [b.] December 3, 1957; Odessa, TX; [p.] Ann Evridge; [ed.] Ball High School, Galveston, TX, Sam Houston State University, B.S. Psychology, University of Texas Medial Branch at Galveston, B.S. Nursing; [occ.] Critical Care Registered Nurse at Orlando Regional Health System, FL; [memb.] AACN (American Association of Critical Care Nurse); [hon.] CCRN Certification (Certified Critical Care Nurse); [oth. writ.] Previously published poem in A Sun-Filled Dream, published by the National Library or Poetry; [pers.] There are those who would see education in the arts removed from our schools. They claim it is not practical or financially beneficial. Art reflects the beauty and life in a world growing colder and harder before our eyes, it is our only escape.; [a.] Longwood, FL

FARRIS, TAMMY
[pen.] Tammy Farris; [b.] February 1, 1962; Westminster, CA; [p.] Kenneth and Lena Harrison; [m.] Ronald Farris; October 15, 1988; [ch.] Crystal Farris, Sean King and Ronnie Farris; [ed.] Westminster High School; [occ.] Floor Person, Golden Nugget, Laughlin; [pers.] I would like to hit the Powerball and buy a home on a small lakefront and live as close to nature as possible.

FELDHERR, ERICA
[pen.] Erica Feldherr; [b.] August 25, 1983; New York, NY; [p.] Linda and Jerome Feldherr; [ed.] Fiorello H. LaGuardian High School of Music and Art, and Performing Arts Vocal Major, five years bullet and tap dance dynamics, four years violin (Concert mistress) Louis Armstrong Middle School, NY; [memb.] Apaloosa Horse Club, 4H Scenic Valley, Onondaga, NY, World Wild Life Federation, LaGuardian H.S. student Organization; [oth. writ.] Several articles published in Newsday (NY Newspaper), Kidsday reporter, "Anger," in The National Library of Poetry's Tracing Shadows; [a.] Jackson Heights, NY

FELDMAN, DARLA MARIE
[b.] December 17, 1966; Meade, KS; [p.] Kathy Hawke and Glen Feldman; [ch.] Jessica Irvin and Megan Feldman; [ed.] Wheatridge High, Red Rocks College; [occ.] Information Management Project Manager; [oth. writ.] Several poems published locally; [pers.] Life is but an adventure, live every day to the fullest.; [a.] Arvada, CO

FERRISS, ERIC
[b.] April 10, 1980; Des Moines, IA; [p.] Rick and Cindy Ferriss; [ed.] Urbandale High School, Des. Moines Area Community College; [occ.] Assistant Manager at Embers Restaurant; [hon.] Editor's Choice Award for "Power of Earth," and six Martial Arts Open Tournament Trophies for six events, black belt in Kenpo Tae Kwon Do, several poems published by The National Library of Poetry; [oth. writ.] "Power Of Earth," "Sickness," "The Fire, Rain, Sun, And Wind," "Petals," "Ignorance of Man"; [pers.] "Saru mo ki kosa ochiru," which is Japanese for "Even monkeys fall from trees."; [a.] Urbandale, IA

FICARELLI, MATTHEW D.
[pen.] M. David Ficarelli; [b.] January 15, 1978; Brunswick, GA; [p.] Vallarie E. Ficarelli; [ed.] Benedictine Military School [occ.] Writer and Puppeteer; [memb.] International Society of Poets, PETA; [oth. writ.] "Clouds," "Serenity," and "Wings," all published by The National Library of Poetry; [a.] Ponciana; FL

FIELDS, MARK W.
[b.] October 3, 1979; Levitown, PA; [p.] Wayne and Peggy Field; [ed.] Marple Newtown High, Delaware County Community College; [occ.] Student and Computer System Analyst, Fastech Inc.; [memb.] Spruce Street Baptist Church, International Society of Poets; [hon.] Dean's List, President's First, Phi Theta Kappa, Pegasus Poetry Contest, third place; [oth. writ.] Several poems published in Pegasus, spring of 1998 and in The National Library of Poetry's The Innocence of Time; [pers.] Throughout life I've strived to increase my wisdom and understanding of life and my Lord—He gives me the strength to do so.; [a.] Broomall, PA

FIELDS, SUSAN LAUREN
[pen.] SLF, pronounced "Sluf"; [b.] February 20, 1943; New York City, NY; [p.] Leon Epstein and Mildred Morse; [m.] Sedrach Eugene Diaz; June 24, 1986; [ch.] Roberto Sedrach Diaz; [occ.] Wife and Mother; [hon.] The National Library of Poetry Editor's Choice Award for "All Along," poem published in The Scenic Route anthology in 1997; [oth. writ.] As mentioned, "All Along" in The Scenic Route, 1997, "Diamonds and Lullabies" in The Best Poets of 1998 anthology, in 1998; [pers.] The pieces and the Gemini are real people who live at my house. I write to tell of the love we've shared and of the great admiration I feel for the man who changed my lonely life into an epic adventure. We are the copper pieces that love turned into God, and hold that truth to be self evident.; [a.] Bronx, NY

FILES, LISA P.
[pen.] Lisa P. Files; [b.] November 25, 1932; Rouses Point, NY; [p.] Alfred J. and Mary Elizabeth Perkins; [m.] Douglas D. Files Sr.; December 1, 1951; [ch.] Douglas D. Files Jr. and Denise D. Files; [ed.] Rouses Point H., Women's Army Corp Courses, Misc. College Credit Courses, E.S.A., International Seminars, Misc. Self-Improvement Seminars; [occ.] Retired Active Southeastern Regional International ESA OFC's (Volunteer); [memb.] ISP Distinguished Membership, 28 1/2 year ESA International Leadership Local and National Philanthropic War; [hon.] Two NLP Editor's Choice Awards, 1997 Poet of Year Nomination, many ESA Honors (Local chapter, district, State Southeastern Regional and International Areas); [oth. writ.] Published "Echoes Of Him," "Arrivals And Departures," "Life Well Spent,"; unpublished, "Full Circle," "Empty Rooms," "The Woman Across The Room," "Special Touches"; [pers.] Each has something of value to contribute and should never complete the process of becoming or fail to encourage others to accompany us.; [a.] Stuarts Drafy, VA

FINLINSON, JEAN
[pen.] Jean Finlinson; [b.] October 3, 1970; UT; [p.] Vance and Helen Finlinson; [ed.] Bachelors of

Science, 1992, UT State University, Masters of Education, 1997, Brigham Young University; [occ.] Elementary Teacher and Consultant; [memb.] Church of Jesus Christ of Latter-Day Saints, International Reading Association, National Council Teacher's of Mathematics; [hon.] Teacher of the Year, Alpine's Outstanding Educator, Dean's List; [oth. writ.] "Tears Blind Cars," "Developing and Implementing a Balanced Approach to Teaching," "Writing in the Elementary," "Math and Literature"; [pers.] My writing always reflects my life. That's one way in making meaning out of experience.; [a.] Oak, UT

FISHER, NORMA C.
[a.] Bluffdale, UT

FLANIGAN, TAMMY
[b.] November 19, 1971; Aransas Pass, TX; [p.] Buster and Linda Flanigan; [ed.] High School; [memb.] The International Poetry Hall of Fame and The International Society of Poets; [hon.] Five Editor's Choice Awards for Outstanding Achievement in Poetry; [oth. writ.] Eight Poems are published in eight different Anthologies; [pers.] To all of the sad, lonely and broken-hearted: Hang in there, we will all have someone soon. Just Don't give up on love and trust.; [a.] Aransas Pass, TX

FLORY, FRANCES ANN
[b.] July 9, 1942; Appleton, WI; [p.] Mary and Charles Flory (deceased); [ed.] Edgemont High School, De Pauw University, Boston University, University of Southern California; [occ.] Teacher (retired); [oth. writ.] "Clouds," poem for High School Poetry Contest, poems in International Hall of Fame, Poet's Choice, The Poetry Guild titles "Jelly Beans," "The Personality of Jesus," "The Christmas Season," "My Perennial Garden"; [pers.] I try to stress the beauty of the environment in verse.

FOGLE, MISTY DAWN
[pen.] Mystic, Foggy Morn, Misty, Myst; [b.] December 15, 1977; Takoma Park, MD; [p.] Sam and Brenda Fogle; [ed.] Parkadale High School-Riverdale, MD, graduated May 1995, attending Shippensburg Univ., Shippensburg, PA Double Major Biology and Computer Science; [occ.] Full-time student, co-op with Raytheon Systems in Falls Church, VA; [memb.] ACM, IEEE Computer Society, Shippensburg's NRHH and Hall Council; [hon.] Shippensburg's National Residence Hall Honorary; [oth. writ.] "The Night Man," published in The National Library of Poetry's Through The Hourglass, and "I'm Going," published in The National Library of Poetry's A Picture of Elegance; [pers.] I believe that you can tell a lot about the type of person that you are, based on what sort of name you'd come up with for a band. If I had a band, I'd call it "Poke me in the age . . . ow!" What about you?; [a.] Ijamsville, MD

FORREST, DOROTHY
[b.] Yakima, WA; [p.] Ida M. and James Marvin; [m.] William Peter; May 10, 1995; [ch.] Ian, Leslie, Gabriella, Noelle, Shaun, Amber, Jennifer, and Billy; [ed.] Palo Alto High, Santa Rosa Junior College; [occ.] Sp. Ed. Program Director; [memb.] Int'l. Society of Poets, Distinguished Member; [pers.] Through words and poetry we honor and make tribute to life.; [a.] Dixon, CA

FRANCIS, T. MICHAEL
[m.] Mary Francis; [ed.] Degree in Finance from large, major university; [occ.] Mortgage Broker; [memb.] Distinguished Member of the International Society of Poets; [hon.] Dean's List in college, also member of The International Poetry Hall of Fame, Museum At WWW.Poets.Com, UNDM The Last Memer "Francis"; [oth. writ.] Come Closer To God, a book of poetry to be in bookstores February 1998. In Love With God, a book of poetry to be in bookstores July 1999; [pers.] I am a humble servant of Jesus Christ. I

strive to serve Him as best as I can in this life, to be happy with Him forever in Heaven.

FRANCO, MICHAEL
[b.] November 29, 1941; Romblon, Phil; [p.] Col. and Mrs. Luis M. Franco; [m.] Edith S. McClean; July 28, 1995; [ed.] Liberal arts courses, certificate in Computer Programming, Cobol, RP GIII, and Assembler Language; [occ.] Feelance writing and chess; [hon.] 1st Hon. Mention, Elementary Grades, Most Outstanding Boys Scout of Misamis Oriental, Philippines, Silver Medalist, Declamation Contest, Champion Chess Guard, Trophy Captain Ball, SUHS, Basketball Team; [pers.] Sometimes one needs to starve deliberately. For it is hunger that causes us to want fulfillment and stretches our will to live till we fall ripen and to the ground.; [a.] Long Branch, NJ

FRANKLIN, JOHN C.
[pen.] Rod N. Berry, John Jefferson; [b.] July 6, 1961; Oakland, CA; [ed.] Diablo Valley Junior College, San Francisco State University; [occ.] Gardener; [oth. writ.] Have written a EEW; poems such as "Faith Forevermore," "Days of Yore," "Dark Horse," "Renaissance Man," and "Arbitrary Truth;" now processing of writing a couple of books, but poetry will always be the main focus; [pers.] A poet's greatest challenge is to shed light on the hidden truths and to unearth as well as decipher life's subliminal messages. A poet's greatest responsibility is to translate feelings, observations, and perceptions into a universal language that all walks of life can easily identify with. A poet is also like a barometer that signals out the winds of change while change is still in embryonic stage.; [a.] Lafayette, CA

FRANKLIN, PAT
[b.] February 6, 1948; Chicago, IL; [p.] Mathias and Ethel Scherer; [m.] Rick Franklin; June 15, 1996; [ch.] Peter Janeczko and Erik Janeczko; [ed.] Resurrection High School, University of Illinois Chicago Campus, Southwest Missouri State University; [occ.] Self-Employed; [memb.] Psy Chi; [oth. writ.] Several poems published in national anthologies, article for local magazine; [a.] Springfield, MO

FRAZIER, OSCAR
[b.] January 21, 1956; Bluffton, SC; [p.] Oscar B. Frazier and Daisy P. Frazier; [m.] Marcia R. Frazier; July 16, 1995; [ch.] James, Bridgette, and Joshua; [ed.] M.C. Riley Elementary; H.E. McCracken High School, Bluffton, SC; three years U.S. Army; 1 1/2 years Beaufort Technical College, Beaufort, SC; [occ.] Assistant Operations Manager and Shipping/Receiving Clerk, Grayco Home Center, Bluffton, SC; [memb.] Deacon, St. Johns Baptist Church; Board Member, Bluffton Community Center; [hon.] Bronze Medal Poet of Merit, Poetry Convention and Symposium, Washington, D.C. August 1997; May 28, 1997, selected as a Distinguished Member of The International Society of Poets; March 19, 1997, received the Editor's Choice Award; [pers.] Through my writing I've inspirited a lot of people, young and old, spiritually and satisfying to all through this gift that I've been blessed with. I'm quite sure that the Lord wants me to share it with others.; [a.] Bluffton, SC

FREDERICK, TAMARA M. PARK
[pen.] T.M. Park; [b.] July 10, 1971; New Castle, PA; [p.] Gary K. Park, Susan M. Weschke; [m.] C.A. Frederick; July 4, 1998; [ed.] Quakertown Comm. Sr. High, Upper Bucks Vo-tech School, Del Val College; [occ.] Administrative Assistant; [hon.] Editor's Choice Award for "For Pedro" 1998; [oth. writ.] "For Pedro" published in Winds of Freedom, "Time After Time" published in Edge of Twilight; other poems; [a.] Sellersville, PA

FREEMAN, VERNA
[pen.] Dean; [b.] September 1, 1927; Sapulpa, OK; [p.] Clarence and Edna York; [m.] Ottis Freeman

(deceased); January 17, 1946; [ch.] Four; [ed.] 8th grade; [hon.] Two Editor's Choice, two Golden Poet Awards, two Merit Certificates, tapes Sounds of Poetry, member First Society of Poets; [oth. writ.] Poem published, "Desert Sun," Best Poems of '90.; [pers.] I reflect on my feelings and write it; if i feel it or live it, it's my emotions letting go; I feel blessed I can be able to do this;. [a.] Eureka, CA

FRIEDMAN, DAISY
[a.] Thomaston, CT

FRIZZELL, MELISSA KAY
[b.] November 25, 1980; Michigan City, IN; [p.] Katherine Kenworthy and John Frizzell; [ed.] Westfield Washington High School; [oth. writ.] Several poems that I hope to publish someday, "Innocence" in The Fabric of Life; [pers.] I want to thank my dad for my writing gift, for without him being a poet I wouldn't have it. I also want to thank my mom for all the support she's given me.; [a.] Westfield, IN

FUTRELL, FRANKIE P.
[pen.] Frankie Pittman; [b.] February 15, 1942; Germantown, TN; [p.] Henry and Willie Mae Pittman; [m.] James Willie Futrell; May 31, 1963; [ch.] Faye DeRochelle Futrell and Sonja Rene Futrell; [ed.] Lambuth College, Tennessee State University, Memphis State University, Mt. Pisgah High School, Wells Elementary School, Cotton Plant Arkansas Vocational School; [occ.] Eligibility Counselor, Hardeman County Dept. of Human Services; [memb.] Member and bible class teacher, Tate Rd. Church of Christ; volunteer with the Church at local nursing home; member Searey, Nannie Scholarship Fund; member Tennessee State Employees Assn.; [hon.] Salutatorian Mt. Pisgah High School class of 1960; Alpha Kappa Mu, P. Delta Phi honor societies while at TSU; certified bible teacher through Fishers of Men; [oth. writ.] Malcolm X Parts 1,2,3, and 4: Part 1 published in NLP's Walk Through Paradise, part 2 published in NLP's Best Poems of the 90's; [pers.] I read the article about the woman in London who had one of her twins killed before. The child could be born. Reading this article touched me deeply and brought tears to my eyes. I visualized in my mind what the innocent victim would say if he or she could speak.; [a.] Bolivar, TN

GAFFNEY, IMOGENE ADKINS
[pen.] Jean Jeannie Jeanbaby; [b.] July 6; Elmo, TX; [p.] Earl and Louisa Adkins; [m.] Edward O. Gaffney; July 30, 1955; [ch.] Theresa, Edward Jr., Orlando Cyernard, Regina, and Darrell; [ed.] Booker T. Washington High School, two years Prairie View A and M College; [occ.] Retired Nurse, takes care of Disabled Veterans; [memb.] International Society of Poets, inducted into the National Museum Poets Hall of Fame; [hon.] Several Editor's Choice awards, Newsday Merit Award, several more poems in The National Library of Poetry's anthologies, local paper, church bulletin; [oth. writ.] Songs and poems lost years ago due to relocating; [pers.] I hope and try show love through my writing. I would like for love to be so contagious that when one touches another's head, he, or she, would become infected with same.; [a.] N. Babylon, NY

GAFFORD, HELEN MARANG
[pen.] Helen Marang, Helen Marang Gafford; [b.] April 26, 1924; Columbus, KS; [p.] Edward Horine and Belle (Frost) Horine; [m.] Floyd Marang; 1942-1986; remarried Dee Gafford; 1989; [ch.] William Bill Marang, Jeannie Walker, Donald Marang, and C. Dale Marang; [ed.] Shell City, MO, Elementary and High School; North Idaho College; [memb.] Pen and Quill Writing Club, North Idaho Christian Writer's Assoc., International Society of Poets; [hon.] Several Golden Poet Awards, Lifetime Member of International Society of Poets, The International Poetry Hall of Fame; [pers.] I

feel I am truly blessed for the gift from God to write from my heart.; [a.] Pinehurst, ID

GALL, JENNIE MARTIN
[pen.] Jen; [b.] August 12, 1958; CA; [p.] Don Martin and Mickie LaDelle; [m.] Ed Gall; November 19, 1982; [ch.] Jonathan and Jennifer; [ed.] A.S. Child Development, Family Relations; A.A. Liberal Studies; Certified Medical Transcriptionist; best grade in English, creative writing, and music; [occ.] Song and Creative Writer, Medical/ Legal Transcription Service, Business Owner; [memb.] American Association for Medical Transcription, National Association for Female Executives; [hon.] Editor's Choice award for NLP's The Peace We Knew book in which I entered my poem, "Where Have All the Years Gone to Now?" written to music; [oth. writ.] "Earthquakes," "A Shaking Experience" (short story published in He's Alive), "Where Have All the Years Gone to Now?" (NLP Spring 1998), written to music, "A Place Called Home," lyrics; [pers.] To music, to combine words with music is my obsession.; [a.] Ukiah, CA

GALLEDGE, KATHY D.
[pen.] Kathy Pippins-Gulledge; [b.] May 15, 1961; Temple, TX; [p.] Mr. and Mrs. Eugene Pippins; [m.] Grant L. Gulledge; June 11, 1988; [ch.] Gary, Charles, and Kevin; [ed.] Twin Cities Baptist School; [occ.] Accounts Payable—Administrative Public Relations; [memb.] International Society of Poets; [oth. writ.] Several poems published in National Library of Poetry, articles in Troy Sun Newspaper; [pers.] I write of God's beauty and of His love. He guides my pen from Heavens alone. It is He who inspires me.; [a.] Troy, TX

GALVEZ, PAULA V.
[b.] September 12, 1961; Dallas, TX; [p.] Pablo P. Galvez and Filiberta Galvez; [ch.] Jackalyn April Galvez Ruiz; [pers.] The inspiration for all my poems has always been my mother and three other very special women.; [a.] Los Angeles, CA

GANT, RICHARD E., JR.
[b.] December 23, 1943; Frederick, MD; [p.] Richard E. Gants Sr. and Ada G. Gant; [m.] Kay L. Gant; January 2, 1965; [ch.] Daphnie Fossett and Lesley Goines; [ed.] Grade school, Lincoln High School, St. John's Institute at Prospect Hall, Loyola Evening College, Argerstown Junior College, Devry Institute; [memb.] Frederick Worship Center, U.S. Karate Assoc., Local 305 Mail Handlers Union; [hon.] Big Brotmen of the Year, Shop Steward of the Year; [oth. writ.] Many poems; [pers.] The Bible is the greatest book you see; this, along with my God, has greatly influenced me.; [a.] Frederick, MD

GARCIA, MINERVA A.
[b.] November 1, 1959; Dom. Republic; [p.] Lydia and Seterino Frias; [m.] Jose Garcia; August 25, 1985; [ch.] James S.; [ed.] B.S. Biology, St. Francis College; M.S. Bacteriology, Wagner College; [occ.] Laboratory Technologist Cls (NCA); [memb.] American Society of Turoviology ASM NYC Branch, American Chemical Society, American Association for the Advancement of Science; [hon.] Mayor's Scholarship, Anaerobic Bacteriology certification, New York Academy of Sciences judge, Editor's Choice awards (1994, 1996, 1997), Outstanding Achievement in Poetry, The International Poet Merit award; [oth. writ.] Ice Cream in the Sun, Local 1199 News, The National Library of Poetry and chosen for anthology, A Far-Off Place, 1994; "Depression and Paper Frog," published in The National Library of Poetry, 2nd chosen for anthology Best of 1996; [pers.] An individualist through my writings, I've found enormous creativity and passion for many splendid things. I feel very less that God has given me this gift to express myself freely and completely. I love to convey a language that is expressive to understand and spread it like a seed for peace. I write a

lot for my husband and my son, for they are my rainbow in my life. God is the focus in all my writings. I respond to the surrounding, and I do seek peace and liberty through this. For me, poetry is a childhood passion that has transcended into a living language that is meaningful and compassionate to the hearts. I started writing at 9, but in reality the artistry was seen by me by age 12. Now, I am confident with my work. I was greatly inspired by Elizabeth Barrett Browning, William Shakespeare, Emily Dickinson, and Cervantes.; [a.] Staten Island, NY

GARTON, FRANKIE
[b.] November 17, 1953; Vallejo, CA; [p.] Arnold and Joretta Garton; [ch.] Five; [ed.] B.A. from Greensboro College, Masters Degree (M.DIV.) from Duke Divinity School, Duke University; [occ.] Pastor; [memb.] Alpha Chi, International Society of Poets; [hon.] Alpha Chi Awards, Who's Who in American Colleges, Greek awards, Religion awards; [oth. writ.] "From Papa" and "Cause I Want You To, Daddy"; [pers.] My children are my inspiration.; [a.] Chapel Hill, NC

GASSERT, GEORGE B.
[pen.] Double (G) The Edge Walker; [b.] October 20, 1949; Harrisburg; PA; [ch.] Dan, Danielle, and Dena; [ed.] High school graduate; [occ.] Hourly employee; [oth. writ.] At My Moment, I Am A Journeyman—on the Pathway of Life, I Will Rise Above You; [pers.] Life is existence before death, most chosen for it to be good, some may conspire to ruin yours, stream lane thought patterns are defense.; [a.] Harrisburg, PA

GATEWOOD, CAROL
[b.] June 24, 1936; Independence, MO; [p.] Boyd and Etta England; [m.] Jim; April 20 1973; [ch.] Kandi, John, Jesse, and Vivian; [ed.] Mike High School; [memb.] Assemble of God Church; [hon.] Three poems, National Poetry, one Poet's Guild, one Editor's Choice, one Outstanding Poetry, one Outstanding Poets 1998; [oth. writ.] Brown Eyed Child, Diamond in the Rough, A Falling Star, Golden Child, My Mother Saving, Time, many more; [pers.] I love life and my children, and grandchildren, flower and animals; Jesus is center of my life; be kind and forgiving, and it will come back.; [a.] KC, MO

GAUTHIER, ARMAND J.
[pen.] Armand J. Gauthier; [b.] Willow City, ND; [p.] Lucien and Petroneline Grant Gauthier; [ed.] Graduate St. Cecilia High, Hastings NE; graduate Central Community College, Hastings, NE; (Communication Radio Broadcasting); [occ.] Retired; [hon.] Awarded U.S. Paten, published in Popular Science Magazine, poems published in National Library of Poetry anthologies; [a.] Hastings, NE

GEARY, TRACI
[pen.] Traci Lee Geary; [b.] March 10, 1966; NJ; [p.] Daniel and Katharine Geary; [ed.] Bachelor of Arts—University of Pennsylvannia; Associate Applied Science—Burlington Country College; Certificate—Intro. to Claims and Small Business Mgmt; [occ.] Executive Assistant; [oth. writ.] Through the Looking Glass, 97, The National Library of Poetry, pg. 260 "Winter In The City"; [pers.] Lets not let the steps we've taken to create a unified Nation perish in the flames of a backfire. In our quest for freedom, we must remember that our actions touch the lives of other living beings.; [a.] Cherry Hill, NY

GELINEAU, KIMBERLY
[b.] August 8, 1962; Austin, TX; [ed.] Clark High School, San Antonio, TX; [memb.] Distinguished Member of the International Society of Poets; [hon.] Editor's Choice Awards 1995, '96, '97; [oth. writ.] Poetic Voices of America—three times; Treasured Poems of America—two times; Best Poems 1996, '97, '98; Best Poems Of 90's; Tomorrow Never Knows; Moments of Reflection;

American Poetry Anthology, Ten Years of Excellence; [pers.] Writing has always been therapy for me. I hope my writing will inspire others to express themselves or help them thru a difficult time in their life.; [a.] San Antonio, TX

GERSTENBERGER, LISA A.
[b.] February 8, 1964; Coco Beach, FL; [ch.] Meghan and Julianne; [ed.] High school; [occ.] Aircraft Electrical Inspector; [memb.] International Thespians Society, US Naval Reserves; [oth. writ.] Several poems published in scholastic magazines during school years, "Strength," a poem published in a previous collection of writing by amateur poets; [a.] Venice, FL

GETTRY, JOAN E.
[b.] Jamaica, WI; [m.] Martin D. Gettry (deceased); [ch.] 10 1/2 year old English Springer Spaniel Dog; [ed.] LaGuardia Community College; [occ.] Homemaker; [memb.] Women's Auxilliary, NY Medical Center, The International Poetry Hall of Fame; [hon.] Dean's List; [oth. writ.] Published book of poems in 1996; [pers.] I came this way in life not of my own choosing, but if I had to do it on my own all over again, the choices would remain the same. I've been blessed and have been loved by all those who have touched my life.; [a.] Beechhurst, NY

GIFFORD, RONALD M.
[pen.] Ron Gifford; [b.] November 28, 1923; Rockford, IA; [p.] Ray Gifford and Darlene Gifford; [m.] Geraldine Rose; January 21, 1950; [ch.] Jill Diane and Mark Raymond; [ed.] Lindblom High, Wilson Jr. College, Chicago, IL; [occ.] Retired Loco Engineer; [oth. writ.] Short stories, fiction, and non-fiction; [pers.] I like to write about the past, sometimes with humor. I like my readers to think.; [a.] Mimbres, NM

GILBERT, LOLA V.
[pen.] Me; [b.] December 20, 1918; Omaha, NE; [p.] Marshall and Esther Nelson; [m.] Clarence W. Gilbert; November 21, 1939; [ch.] Meg, Ted, and Linnea; [ed.] High School Omaha NE; [memb.] Midwest Cheparral Poets Clubs, NE; [hon.] Voted Best Child's Poem, "Baby Thoughts," also it was read on Joan Gray's TV program in California; several articles and poems in Cappers, and Kingman AZ, Miner; [oth. writ.] "He will Shoot," "We Will Rise," song, have a book of poems entitled "My Efforts, My Roverios, My Gosh!" several by Dines; had columns in Heedles Desert Star, Mohave News, Shopper for five years; had two poems read Kila FM Radio; [pers.] Christian; [a.] Mohave Valley, AZ

GLEASON, VICKI
[pen.] Alicia Frost; [b.] May 13, 1967, OH; [ed.] Northern Kentucky Technical College, Edgewood Campus Medical Office Technology, EMT Training, EMT—D (Defibrillator); [occ.] Student; [hon.] Editor's Choice Award, National Library of Poetry, 1998, In Recognition—for 50 Hours of Hospice Volunteer Service; [oth. writ.] "Your Smiling Face," in The Soft Parade, by The National Library of Poetry; [pers.] Because of my background and experience as an EMT, I enjoy jobs that most people find "Difficult." Examples: Hospice Patients and Homeless Children.; [a.] Cincinnati, OH

GLINSKI, FRANK Z.
[pen.] Zdzislaw F. Glinski; [b.] October 17, 1928; Poland; [p.] Mawa, Stanislaw; [m.] Eupeina; September 2, 1950; [ch.] Lech, Evon; [ed.] P. German College, (Rutgers Univ. Newark, NY); [a.] West Orange, NY

GODFREY, DOROTHY A.
[b.] November 25, 1926; Verona, MS; [p.] William L. and Christine H. Jenkins; [m.] Joe Allen Godfrey; December 31, 1944; [ch.] Clyde, Gene, and Marion Godfrey; [ed.] High school graduate—one sem. college; [occ.] Housewife; [memb.] Brewer U.

Methodist Church, Peale Center; N.E. Miss. Writer's Forum; [occ.] Poem published in "The Breeze," (college publication); [pers.] I am hoping to portray the love and beauty of God in my poetry. It is such a blessing.; [a.] Tupelo, MS

GOMEZ, DORA ELVA
[b.] May 30, 1963; Uralde, TX; [p.] Luis H. Gomez and Herminia G. Gomez; [ed.] Batesville Elementary School, Uralde, TX; Southwest Texas State University, San Marcos, TX; [occ.] English/ESL teacher at the 6th-7th grade levels at Sterling H. Fly Jr. High School, Crystal City, TX; [memb.] American Federation of Teachers; [hon.] Who's Who Among American teachers (1996 and 1998); [oth. writ.] Who Am I? Mentor/Teacher, Twins, which have all been published through The National Library of Poetry; [pers.] Poetry lets us express a variety of emotions that most of us can't express otherwise. Let's continue to celebrate our true selves through poetry for it allows others to see who we really are.; [a.] Batesville, TX

GORDON, SYLVIA
[b.] March 20, 1957; Detroit, MI; [p.] David and Annie Gordon; [ch.] Lakeisha Gordon and Gloria Walker; [ed.] Wayne County Comm. College; [occ.] Asst. Buyer for Blue Cross and Blue Shield of MI; [memb.] Word of Faith Int'l Christian Center, Nat'l Assoc, of Purchasing Mgt, Metro Detroit Songwriter's Assoc.; [hon.] Who's Who among Students in American Tech and Vocational Schools, 1975-76, The Great Ideal Award (BCBSM) 1995; Pride in Excellence Award 9 (BCBSM) 1998, 1989, 1995, 1996, 1998; [oth. writ.] Impromptu song for TV commercial for BCBSM (August 1997); Play: "The Charmin Kelly Show" copywright 1979; Songs: Gospel, R and B, Jazz; [pers.] With my songwriting I have two personal goals: first I will write a mega hit song, a song that will never go ot of style because of its message, such as: "We Are the World" or "The Greatest Love of All;" second, I will write a jingle for a radio and a television commercial that the whole world will be singing.; [a.] Detroit, MI

GOUGH, JANETT
[pen.] Bibi; [b.] January 28, 1965; Panama; [p.] Marcial Gough; [m.] Single; [ch.] Elijah and Denzel; [ed.] SCS Business and Tech. Inst. for computer operator, State University of NY in Brooklyn for Nursing Assistant, GED; [occ.] Nursing Assistant; [oth. writ.] Why? Why her? in Embrace the Morning, The National Library of Poetry; [pers.] I thank God in Heaven for every day, my Tia Olga, and niece Anita for all their help in life, and good friend Ann.; [a.] Brooklyn, NY

GRANT, CARL S.
[b.] November 7, 1981; Santa Cruz; [p.] Carl and Susan Grant; [ed.] Justin Siena High School; [occ.] Full Time Disciple of Christ; [pers.] In my life, I try to do three things: learn, laugh, and love; these three combined equal happiness and contentment.; [a.] Napa, CA

GRAVES, SANDRA W.
[b.] August 16, 1965; Utica, NY; [p.] Jack and Elaine Warcup; [m.] Christopher Graves; May 12, 1995; [ch.] Nathan James and Austin John; [ed.] Holland Patent Central High, Oneida County Boces, Regents College of Albany; [occ.] Nurse; [oth. writ.] Poems published: Miracles, Mother's Love, and Loving a Memory; [pers.] Writing has been a way for me to express myself and reflect on past experiences—happy and sad. Writing is a vent for my emotions.; [a.] Remsen, NY

GRAY, CAROLYN
[pen.] Cerise; [b.] Trowell Nottingham, England; [ed.] Some years in a British boarding school; [pers.] As an essence I was educated esoterically since I was three weeks old, under the care of "The angel of his presence" Isaiah: 63:9; [a.] Indianapolis, IN

GRISET, DONNA L.
[pen.] D. Lynn Ackerman; [b.] June 30, 1949; Merced, CA; [ed.] B.A. English, M.A. Education, M.A. English Literature; [occ.] English Instuctor, Merced College; [memb.] American Assoc. of University Women, National Council of Teachers of English, Phi Delta Kappa, International Society of Poets; [oth. writ.] Several poems; [pers.] I do not write my poems, but rather they write me, haunt me.; [a.] Atwater, CA

GROSS, LE ETTA
[b.] August 18, 1979; St. Pete, FL; [p.] Margie Doyle and Richard Gross; [ed.] A year at the University of South Florida; [occ.] Student; [hon.] Dean's List; [oth. writ.] Few in prior Library of Poetry volumes; [pers.] Through my writing I spill myself onto the page.; [a.] St. Petersburg, FL

GROTH, DIANE DALUM
[pen.] Diane Dalum Groth; [b.] August 23, 1948; Clintonville, WI; [p.] Herbet and Dorothea Dalum; [ed.] Marion High, Metropolitan College of Bus. and Tech, U. of WI, Alverno College; [memb.] International Society of Poets; [hon.] Editor's Choice Award; [oth. writ.] Several pieces published in various church bulletins and papers, Marion Advertiser, National Library of Poetry anthologies; [pers.] With poetry I attempt to paint pictures of ordinary events in ordinary lives. Hopefully my legacy will be a body of work all can identify with.; [a.] Marion, WI

GROVE, CALVIN
[pen.] Cal; [b.] June 30, 1968; Homestead, PA; [ed.] High school graduate; [hon.] Editor's Choice Award, National Library of Poetry; [pers.] Life is the hardest to endure but it's the most for its rewards.; [a.] Dayton, OH

GUNTER, TIMOTHY B.
[pen.] Timothy B. Gunter; [b.] August 12, 1964; Fort Smith, [p.] Leonard and Martha Gunter; [ed.] Southside High School, Westark Community College (A.A.), University of Central Arkansas, (B.A.), Instituto de Filologia Hispanica (M.A.), Mexico; [occ.] Manufacturing, Whirlpool Corp.; [memb.] Haven Heights Baptist Church, Heritage Foundation, Libertarian Party, Future of Freedom Foundation; [hon.] (Atesto) Certificate from ELNA, an Esperanto Association, degrees from colleges and universities; [oth. writ.] Several articles published in state and local newspapers, and several unpublished poems; [pers.] I write based on the feelings we as human beings possess. I am influenced by L. American writers like Octavio Paz.; [a.] Fort Smith, AR

GUPTA, PHYLLIS DATTA
[a.] Dallas, TX

HAGGERTY, SHARON
[b.] May 21, 1964; Pineville, KY; [p.] Howard and Dorothy Hensley; [ch.] Charity Ann; [ed.] Fairmont East H.S., Wright State Univ., Miami Valley, and Dayton Practical; [occ.] Geriatric Nurse; [memb.] Adult Choir—Baptist Church; [oth. writ.] "This Too Shall Past," Vol., Where Dawn Lingers, 1998, "Suffering" poems by the fireside (Infinity Pub. Co.); [pers.] Praise the Son; [a.] Kettering, OH

HAILU, IRIS
[pen.] Iris Hailu; [b.] August 9, 1958; LA; [p.] Queen Esther Fraise; [m.] Tesfaye Hailu; November 23, 1976; [ch.] Xenia and Netsanet Hailu; [ed.] Dorsey High, Trade Tech. College; [occ.] Pastor of, Walk With Cathedral; [hon.] Many music awards, pastorial/evangelicalawards, major's office; [oth. writ.] Plays, (drama), skits, songs, many other poems; [pers.] By His word, I believe God.; [a.] Los Angeles, CA

HALFMOON, MARY C.
[pen.] Mary Celeste Halfmoon; [b.] November 12, 1954; Los Angeles, CA; [p.] Connie Skanen; [ch.]

Ilia Rose, Blair Ellen, and Harrison Howard Brown; [ed.] High school graduate, attending college now; [occ.] Observer; [oth. writ.] "Him," National Library of Poetry; [pers.] When I write, I hear music, and the words express the music. My soul rejoices with each poem I write.

HAMBLIN, LINDA
[b.] August 28, 1962; Worcester, MA; [p.] Shirley Billington and Ronald Pong; [ed.] Don Antonio Lugo High School; [occ.] Print Shop Coordinator—Pomona Valley Hospital Medical Center; [hon.] High School Bank of America, Drama Award; [oth. writ.] Poem published in the anthology book "Through Sun and Shower"; [pers.] Writing has always been a passion; however, poetry is still rather a new medium for me.; [a.] San Bernardino, CA

HAMPDEN, YVONNE M.
[pen.] Astariam; [b.] July 9, 1959; New York City; [p.] Ivan Hampden Sr. and Jean E. Hampden; [m.] Michael Rivera; November 28, 1987; [ch.] Melanie M. Moe; [ed.] Cuny Health Education, Transfer student towards LPN Degree; [occ.] Housewife; [memb.] F.O.C.U.S. Bible Studies Class; [hon.] Phi Theta Kappa; [oth. writ.] The Reaquaintance of Love, and Between Silence and Sound, looking for publication; [a.] Yonkers, NY

HANCOCK, DORA IRENE
[b.] October 26, 1924; Caddo, OK; [p.] Ira and Dora Phelps; [m.] Marion M. Hancock; July 7, 1951; [ed.] 1943, Grad. Haileyville High, OK; 3 1/2 years college, Southeastern, Durant and Obu, Shawnee, OK; [occ.] Retired U.S. Treasurer; [oth. writ.] Poems; [pers.] Greatest Loves are God, Poetry, and my Fox Terrier.; [a.] Garland, TX

HANEY, ANN
[b.] May 16, 1927; Bronx, NY; [p.] Jack and Lea Bannan; [m.] Gregg Haney; February 11, 1950; [ch.] Peg, Lea, Gregg, Heather, and Kathy; [ed.] Univ. Of Cincinnati, two years; [occ.] Write personalized poems, Fund Raising mysteries; [memb.] BPW/VSA, Marriage Encounter, Stephen Ministers; [oth. writ.] Speeches, Eulogies, Ideas; [pers.] Life is learning, enjoying, anticipating, and mostly loving.; [a.] West Chicago, IL

HANSON, KATHY
[b.] September 26, 1952; Omaha, NE; [p.] Frank and Joann Krimmel; [ch.] Dawn Alida, Lance Jason, and Shana Rebecca; [ed.] South High School, Metro Tech Community College; [occ.] CSA, US West Communications; [pers.] I write to help me find myself. I am always amazed, when someone reads my sayings, that they really enjoy them.; [a.] Omaha, NE

HARDY, AGNES
[a.] Huntington Beach, CA

HARMER, TONYA
[b.] September 28, 1981; Port Huron, MI; [p.] Jon and Debbie Harmer; [ed.] Yale High School; [occ.] Student; [oth. writ.] Two poems in The National Library of Poetry, church published a poem; [a.] Emmett, MI

HARRIS, DOROTHY
[b.] September 6, 1957; Detroit, MI; [ed.] Grosse Pointe South High School; [occ.] Nurse's Aide; [hon.] Foundation for Exceptional Children Certificate Award, Pearl S. Buck Foundation Certificate Award; [oth. writ.] Some poems published in some anthology books; [pers.] It is nice to be able to share a thought inspiration or viewpoint with others.; [a.] Grosse Pointe Park, MI

HARTKOPF, ADDIE COCHRAN J.
[b.] October 4, 1912; Stuart, VA; [p.] Harden Green and Mary Etta Cochran; [m.] Rudolph H. Hartkopf; February 16, 1991; [ch.] Two step children, five

step grandchildren and four step great grandchildren; [ed.] Victoria High School, Victoria, Virginia; John Marshal Night High Business, Richmond, VA; Oil Painting, Calligraphy Writing, Seamstress, Photography, Music; [memb.] First Baptist Church, Beverly Hills, FL; Women's Mission Union; Senior Citizen's clubs; Senior Citizen Bowling League; Ashcake Rescue Squad Auxillary Hanover, VA; Historian for Work Related; Naomi Chapter No.4 Order of the Eastern Star; [hon.] Bowling trophies and certificates, calligraphy writing certificate, photography certification, Fifty-Year-Member Pin Award from Eastern Star Naomi Chapter No.4, December 1995; [oth. writ.] Newspaper and magazines articles, poems for "The National Library of Poetry"; [pers.] I strive to reflect emotion and love and interest in the Subjects I write about. I was inspired by my mother, who wrote poems, and also by other poets.; [a.] Crystal River, FL

HAWKINS, SANDRA
[pen.] Louise Jay; [b.] November 18, 1950; Lagrande, OR; [p.] Betty and William Pistorius; [ch.] Will Hawkins and Jennifer Taylor; [ed.] some college; [occ.] Directory operator; [memb.] International Poetry Hall of Fame; [hon.] Various awards at work, public safety from West Jordan City; [oth. writ.] Published a book for teens "Speaking Softly"; [a.] Midvale, UT

HEATON, AUDA M.
[b.] February 20, 1931; Diamond, WA; [p.] Edwell J. and I. Blanche Berg; [m.] Wayned L. Heaton, deceased; October 9, 1948; [ch.] Jennifer Jean, Sheila Rene, Becky Anne, and Sandra Louella; [ed.] Pullman High School, Big Bend Community College; [occ.] Door Greeter, Walmart Store, Moses Lake, WA; [memb.] Past member of Ladies Auxiliary of Fraternal Order of Eagles; National Society of the Daughters of the American Revolution; Emmanuel Lutheran Church, Tabatha Circle, of which served as president, vice president, and secretary; [hon.] Editor's Choice Award in "Tomorrow's Dream"; [oth. writ.] Best poems of 1997, Best Poems of the 1990's, Tomorrow's Dream , two books published, several in church monthly newsletter; [pers.] I intend to have all my poems in one book someday. I have read my poems to others twice at readings and published in two books.; [a.] Moses Lake, WA

HEBERLING, ALISON
[b.] May 9, 1981; Denver; [p.] Colleen and Richard Heberling; [ed.] Greeley West High School; [memb.] Member of The International Society of Poets; [hon.] 1997 Editor's Choice Awards; [oth. writ.] Two other poems in a couple of anthologies; [a.] Greeley, CO

HELFERICH, DIANE
[pen.] Diane Balog-Di, Diane HelFerich, Annie; [b.] November 19, 1951; Chicago, IL; [m.] Dr. O.K. Helferich; [ch.] Jessica Balog Combs, Jasm Balog, Joshua Balog, and Abby Balog; [occ.] State of Michigan; [memb.] Hospice of Lansing, Michigan Athletic Club; [hon.] Semi-Finalist, International Poetry Guild, ISP Merit Award, Several Editor's Choice Awards, many personal inner rewards; [oth. writ.] Several anthologies, Flying Solo Newsletter, personal portfolio; [pers.] To give the reader the gift of seeing into the window of my soul; [a.] Haslett, MI

HERRICK, TIM
[pen.] Herrick, Timothy; [b.] June 17, 1947; Hamilton, OH; [p.] Howard Herrick, Jackie Herrick; [ch.] Lukas Howard Herrick; [ed.] Mansfield Senior High Ashland University, The Ohio State University; [occ.] Defense Logistics Technician, Columbus; [memb.] American Heart Assoc., American Legion, First Methodist Church; [hon.] President's Nat'l Medal of Patriotism, Kappa Sigma Scholarship Committee Ashland Univ., Dean's List; [oth. writ.] Several poems in local newspapers, articles

for the Stars and Stripes newspaper; [pers.] "It's not always the greatest things that make the biggest show, rather it's the little things that people do that makes this old world go."; [a.] Dickerington, OH

HEYDMAN JACKSON, CHERI A.
[b.] August 23, 1957; Oklahoma City, OK; [p.] Blayne And Aline Heydman; [m.] Jack R. Jackson; September 9, 1994; [ch.] Kylie; [ed.] Nortwest Classen High School, State Barber College; [occ.] Barber/Hair Stylist; [hon.] Editor's Choice Award 1998 by The National Library of Poetry; [oth.wit.] (Poem) "Loving Wings" published in back The Peace We Knew by The National Library of Poetry; [pers.] I learn through life's experiences, be they good or bad, happy or sad. Therefore, the encouragement of my writing, with the desire to be published. Love life to its fullest . . . Strive to fulfill every dream.; [a.] Oklahoma City, OK

HIGGINS, PAUL V.
[b.] October 30, 1919; New York City, NY; [p.] Rose Degnan and Patrick Higgins; [m.] Richard N. Eastwood; April 15, 1950; [ed.] B.S.—Fordham, 1941 and M.A.—New York University, 1948; [occ.] Retired; [hon.] AAAA Award: Writer and Director "Religion in American Life"; [oth. writ.] "Book of Haiku: Musings By the Sea"; [pers.] We must love our differences; tolerate our sameness. Peace and joy are one.; [a.] New York City, NY

HIGLEY, MARTIN R.
[pen.] Greg Wolf; [b.] February 10, 1947; Tiffin, OH; [p.] Perry M. and Sarah J. Higley; [m.] Colleen M. Higley; [ch.] Erik S. Swansun; [ed.] Some College; [occ.] Respiratory Therapist; [memb.] AARC, VHMS; [oth. writ.] Numerous poems and ramblings; [pers.] God has given you a face and you have made yourself another; go in search of the original.; [a.] Toledo, OH

HINSHAW, MARY NETTIE
[pen.] Mary Nettie Hinshaw; [b.] March 24, 1916; Randolph, CO; [p.] Roy and Effie Mosier; [m.] Cecil B. Hinshaw; [ch.] Franklin Potter, Rodric and Paul Hinshaw; [ed.] High School graduate and a Bible Course and Cross Road Bible College; [occ.] Housewife; [memb.] Mr. and Mrs. or two at home members of Dunkirk Friends Church; [hon.] Won about six or seven semi-finalist awards on the poems; [oth. writ.] Three small books of other poems; [pers.] I enjoy reading and studying. Later, many thoughts are sifted out of another poem. It is hard to sort out the best thoughts to write.; [a.] Winchester, IN

HINTOCHEL, KATHY W.
[b.] March 18, 1940; Boone, NC; [m.] Glen Hentschel; [ch.] Ernest Hentschel II; [ed.] B.S. degree, Library Science, Appalachian State University, Boone, NC; [occ.] Housewife; [memb.] Custer Battlefield Historical and Museum Association, Inc.; [hon.] Dean's List; [oth. writ.] Poem, Poems of the Twentieth Century, poem, View From Afar, National Library of Poetry; [a.] Fleetwood, NC

HOFMAN, HELEN
[b.] Brookfield, IL; [p.] Joachim P. and Karoline Braun Cohrs; [ch.] Wanda M. Lauderdale and Gwendolyn J. Meythaler; [oth. writ.] Have always written—nothing earth-shaking, just a constant urge to write; [pers.] All of us, young and old, need courage and adventure in our lives.; [a.] Salida, CO

HOGENCAMP, SANDRA
[b.] September 23, 1951; Suffern, NY; [p.] Rose and Kenneth Conklin; [m.] Samuel Hogencamp (Deceased); November 1969; [ch.] Sandra A. Morris, John G. Hogencam; [ed.] GED 1 1/2 years Delhi Tech; [hon.] Just the honors received through NLP, never tried to pusblish any material; [oth. writ.] Just a collection of poems written over the years; [pers.] I write what I feel in my heart at the

time. I hope to pass on to others something that they too can relate to.; [a.] Roscoe, NY

HOLLAND, GINGER TOBIAS
[b.] 1954; PA; [p.] Allen Tobias; [m.] Robert Holland; 1992; [ch.] Toby Holland; [ed.] Bonita Vista High School, Southwestern College; [occ.] Homemaker, Writer, Retired after 17 years of Banking; [memb.] El Dorado Community Church, International Society of Poets; [hon.] Poetry Awards, The Diamond Homer Trophy and Poetic Merit Medallion, Numerous Awards for Croched Items in State and Local Fairs; [oth. writ.] House of Many Rooms, Wales G.B., Secrets of the Soul, Soaring with the Wind, A Starlit Night, The Peace We Knew, A Pleasant Reverie, Poetic Voices of America, Summer 1998, Rhymes of Greatness; [pers.] I write my poems from the heart and thank God for my talent and my three boys, (my husband, our five-year-old son, and my father).; [a.] Somerset, CA

HOLOWINKO, ETANA
[pen.] Satana, Juniper; [b.] March 28, 1981; Norwalk, CT; [p.] Marsha, Ed Holowinko; [ed.] Hillel Academy, Colonel White High School for the Arts; [occ.] Artist, Writer; [hon.] First place for The Mental Retardation Theme Poster in Elementary, 2 years in Who's Who Among American High School Students, 3rd place in Holocust Awareness June 1997; [oth. writ.] Spark, Let's Pretend, To: The Death of Pure Thought, Society Breed, Child of Reflection, Bottled Life, Wardrobe Walkers; [pers.] Lustful need of broken passion, destroyed faith in an invisible God, whom no one found; [a.] Dayton, OH

HONEYCUTT, J.H.
[pen.] J.H. Honeycutt; [b.] February 23, 1927; North Carolina; [p.] Gnover and Julia Honeycutt; [m.] Lean June Street Honeycutt; July 28, 1951; [ch.] John, Stephen, Susan, Manie; [ed.] Tipton Hill High School, Special Training in Bible History, Ancient Poetry, special studies of Romantic Poets, past and present; [occ.] Retired Missionary Evangelist, Musician, Songwriter and Poet; [memb.] United Christian Fellowship and Ministerial Asso., Cleveland, Tenn, IAF, Christian Org., Oklahoma City, OK, Fifty years of Ministry, World Traveler; [hon.] Local display of capative sewing, ink drawing on fabric, depicting history of things, places and events, "Gulf War on Fabric" and others; [oth. writ.] Weaping Trees Spoken Words, WW2 Morning Clouds DD 677 Shadows in the Night, When the World Became Sick, 200 Poems unpublished; [pers.] My songs and poetry are designed and written from my heart, to heal the Troubled Spirit And to present Christ to a troubled world, And to be a better man than I was yesterday.; [a.] TX

HUBBARD, NORMA
[b.] January 21, 1932; Laurel, MS; [p.] Annie Jones Davidson; [m.] J.C. Hubbard; December 27, 1951; [ch.] Linda Little, Judy Flanagan, Terry Hubbard; [ed.] West Point, MS High School, High School Valedictorian, graduate—Wood Jr. College, Mathiston, MS, further hours at Delta State Univ. Cleveland, MS, Bible course at Jerusalem Center for Biblical Studies, Jerusalem, Israel; [occ.] Secretary in Greenwood District, United Methodist Church office; [memb.] Grenada First United Methodist Church; [hon.] H.S. Valedictorian, Wood Jr. College "Wood Lady"; [oth.pers.] Poems and stories for my own enjoyment and for expressing my thoughts; [pers.] Growing up under the influence of caring, loving parents, grandparents and aunts and uncles provided me with a foundation of faith and family values that have served me well as the wife of a United Methodist Minister and the mother of four precious children. My writings are expression of these values and rich experiences.; [a.] Grenada, MS

HUDSON, CAROLYN ROGERS
[pen.] Carolyn Rogers Hudson; [b.] September 23,

1931; North Little Rock, AR; [p.] Odessa and Elbert Rogers; [m.] Robert Byars Hudson; October 18, 1947; [ch.] Michael, Craig, Darryl and Elizabeth; [memb.] Munsey Memorial United Methodist Church, Administrative Board, Care Committee, National Honor Society, Y's Minette of the Year, United Methodist Women Life Membership; [oth. writ.] The Gifts of Night, Tethered or Free; [a.] Johnson City, TN

HUFFMAN, PATRICIA J.
[pen.] Pat; [b.] March 29, 1941; Elmira, NY; [p.] F. John Garbay and Alice E. Garbay; [m.] Edward L. Huffman; May 28, 1960; [ch.] Debra Palmer, Thomas Huffman, Matthew Huffman; [ed.] Corning Community College, B.S.—Elmira College; [memb.] Ladies of Charity, International Society of Poets, St. Mary Our Mother Church, Nocturnal Adoration Society; [hon.] Dean's Llist, manpower awards; [oth. writ.] Several poems published in National Library of Poetry's "Best Poems" books; [pers.] My writing reflects the love I share with others, and deep emotions that I or my loved ones feel. I believe that we were put on this earth by God to help each other and those less fortunate than we are.; [a.] Horseheads, NY

HUGHES, HOLLY
[pen.] Holly Hughes; [b.] May 18, 1986; Dallas, TX; [p.] David A. Hughes, Constance Hughes; [ed.] Country Day School of Arlington, The Oakridge School; [occ.] Actress, singer, entertainer, student; [memb.] National Fraternity of Student Musicians, Jazz Elite Dance Company; [hon.] Principals honor roll, 1st place winner—Optimist Club oratorical contest, dance company Dancer of the Year, Miss Spirit of Arlington, Editor's Choice Award—poetry, International Poetry Hall of Fame; [pers.] I strive to care about the earth and all nature to help others.; [a.] Keller, TX

HUGHES, RANDOLPH ALLEN
[pen.] Randolph Allen Hughes; [b.] July 2, 1946; San Francisco, CA; [p.] Tryge and Dee Allen; [ch.] Jesse and Heather Hughes; [ed.] 52 years of life; [occ.] Designer; [hon.] Editor's Choice Award; [oth. writ.] Currently working on a novel; [pers.] Sometimes the shortest distance between two points is the long way around.; [a.] San Clemente, CA

HUNT, SHAWNA L.
[b.] May 23, 1977; San Luis Obispo, CA; [p.] Frances K. Hunt and John W. Hunt; [occ.] Military Police, U.S. Army; [oth. writ.] "Cold Love" in The Nightfall of Diamonds; [pers.] If God gives you a gift share your gift with others and as I do in my poetry and as my father has done before me.; [a.] APO, AE

HURTADO, CAROLYN
[pen.] Carolyn Daste Hurtado; [b.] March 10, 1941; [p.] Harold and Marion Daste (deceased); [ch.] Claude, Roberto, and Catalina; [oth. writ.] Poems and songs—never published; [pers.] When I write poetry I feel my poems are a spiritual and inspiration to reach out and touch the souls and hearts of mankind. The harvest begins with us.; [a.] Brentwood, CA

HUTCHINSON, SHAWN MICHAEL
[b.] July 30, 1976; Shawnee, KS; [p.] Jim and Margaret Hutchinson; [ed.] Saint Thomas Aquinas High School, Johnson County (KS) Community College, University of KS; [occ.] Journalism Student at the University of KS; [hon.] 10-times Kansas Associated Collegiate Press award-winning sports writer; [pers.] "Ad Astra Per Aspera" (A rough road leads to the stars.); [a.] Overland Park, KS

HYMAN, MARJORIE WEIGEL
[pen.] Marjorie Weigel Hyman; [b.] February 28, 1925; San Francisco; [p.] Garnet and Wiegel; [m.] Alan William Hyman; September 1, 1946; [ch.] Jill Edith, and William Alan; [ed.] Calif. School of Fine Arts, S.F., Arts Institute—Art Major, Stanford University, Minored in speech and drama; [occ.] Artist; [memb.] "Vision Twenty"; [hon.] Poetry Awards in past four years, Distinguished Member—International Society of Poets, Past Juried Awards for Portraits and Paintings; [oth. writ.] Writing goes back to the early childhood days. The need for written self-expression is excessive.; [pers.] If I can project on paper, in verse, or words, feelings others can relate to—if I can express true feelings in any creative form of the arts, there lies my joy in life.; [a.] San Mateo, CA

IACCHEI, NICOLE
[b.] February 8, 1983; Philadelphia, PA; [p.] Jack and Marcia Iacchei; [ed.] Sophomore at Nazareth Academy High School; [occ.] Student; [memb.] School (JV) Soccer and Softball (Varsity) Teams, and YMS Travel Soccer Team; [oth. writ.] Several poems for my grandfather, who passed away, and to family and friends who have inspired me; [pers.] Get your mind set, confidence will lead you on.; [a.] Yardley, PA

INGLE, SHELLY
[pen.] Gremlin; [b.] November 30, 1983; Galesburg, IL; [p.] Janet Ingle, Louis Ingle; [ed.] ROWUA Junior High; [memb.] Oneida Softball, ROWUA Valleyball; [oth. writ.] The poem "Run" published in an anthology; [pers.] My poems are written with nothing but true feelings.; [a.] Oneida, IL

INSLEE, MARIE W.
[pen.] Marie W. Inslee; [b.] November 2, 1920; North Wales, PA; [p.] Mae Dowlin Waldron, Won K. Waldron; [m.] Joseph Won. Inslee; June 30, 1945; [ch.] J. Wm. and Jonathan Dowlin Inslee; [ed.] North Wales High School, Wilson Teacher College, M.S. Westchester U., Doctoral Program Univ. of PA, Art School—Corcoran Gallery of Art, Washington; [occ.] Retired Teacher; [memb.] Member Friends Meeting and Downingtown 333 Honorary Sorority, Sierra Club, Wilderness Society, Amnesty Int., Defenders of Wildlife; [hon.] Scholarship for 6 week workshop on Early Childhood in Phila., having scored highest on admissions questionaire to be eligible; [oth. writ.] Poems; [pers.] Goals: In meditation and action to seek unity with the natural world and humans, and to work for betterment of us all.; [a.] Downingtown, PA

IROM, ELSA R.
[pen.] Elizabeth Knub; [b.] January 1, 1927; South Tyrol, Austria-Italy; [p.] Franz Knub and Frida Reiehegger; [m.] Abraham Irom; December 24, 1953; [ch.] Sylvia C. and Billy Irom; [ed.] Three years Commercial School, Diploma, Medical Assistant, attending Medical Transcriptionist School; [hon.] Honorary Mentions for poetry and Golden Poet Award, with the Precious Poetry Collections

IRVIN, LACEY
[b.] December 8, 1982; Kansas City, MO; [p.] Mike, Linda Irvin; [ed.] Cass-Midway High School; [occ.] Student; [memb.] Choir; [hon.] Editor's Choice Award for "Alone," Principal's Honor Roll; [oth. writ.] "Alone," In Memory of Jason Bergstrand, many unpublished poems for friends and family; [pers.] Savor every moment, take joy in every day.; [a.] Cleveland, MO

ISENMAN, PATRICIA
[b.] September 3, 1952; BenneTerre, MO; [p.] Walter, Virginia Weiler; [m.] Charles Isenman; June 13, 1970; [ch.] Brian, Grey, Tom, Christy and Barb; [ed.] Farmington High School, Mac for awhile, Some nursing, several years of Christian Education; [occ.] Disabled, not completely, can still write; [oth. writ.] Started writing when fourteen, altogether have written close to 1500 poems, lyrics and short stories; have written "Wedding Prayer" which was published in Lyrical Heritage; [pers.] God gives us many talents; if we do not use them we will not receive any more. I thank God for all the talents He's given me and for my wonderful family.; [a.] Ste. Genevieve, MO

JACKSON, JEAN LOMAX
[b.] October 15, 1939; Greenville, SC; [p.] David and Annie Mae Lomax; [m.] Jesse Jackson; [ch.] Kathy, Michelle, Camala, Nicole and LaPrentice; [oth. writ.] "Practice Makes Perfect, Perfect Makes Pleasant" now I recite all around, published in local newspaper, The National Library of Poetry, and chosen by the International Poetry Hall of Fame to be on the Internet worldwide; [pers.] I thank God for the gift of writing poetry, which is inspiring, edifying and most pleasant.; [a.] Orlando, FL

JACOB, JOHNSON I.
[pen.] Johnson I. Jacob; [b.] April 7, 1960; Honolulu, HI; [p.] Rachel and Celestino Jacob Sr.; [ed.] Kamehameha High School 1978, Honolulu Police Department 78th Recruit Class, on-going Music and Related Technical Studies; [occ.] Security Officer-Alamoana Center, Honolulu, HI; [memb.] Ekklesia Christian Center, International Society of Poets; [hon.] Two Editor's Choice Awards for previously published poems (The National Library of Poetry); [oth. writ.] "I Seek You Now" from The Nightfall of Diamonds and "The Light" from Best Poems of 1997 (National Library of Poetry); [pers.] As a Christian Musician, songwriter and poet I strive to encourage others through writings, music and personal interaction.; [a.] Honolulu, HI

JAFFRAY, ANDREW
[b.] March 22, 1967; South Africa; [occ.] Computer Programmer; [pers.] "Live, love and find joy in each note of the symphony of life."; [a.] Mountain View, CA

JEN, ALYX
[hon.] 1997 Critics Choice Award, Member of the International Poetry Society; [oth. writ.] Published in Sparrowgrass 1990, Amherst Poetry Society 1990, Quill Books 1996, Watermark Press 1990, National Library of Poetry award 1997; [pers.] She works as a clerk in federal government agency and ontinues to write about human events in the environment in which she lives and works.

JENKINS, TOSHA D.
[b.] April 3, 1975; West Jersey Hosp., Vorchees; [p.] Ruby Jenkins, Curtis Jenkins; [ch.] Tahj Bolden; [ed.] Graduated from Camden High School in 1993; [occ.] Assistant Teacher at Leaps and Bounds Daycare Center; [hon.] Editor's Choice Award, Honorable Mention from Iliad Press; [oth. writ.] Other poems published in anthologies; [pers.] Many poems that I write are feelings from my heart, from the experiences that I've been through.; [a.] Lindenwold, NJ

JOHNSON, JANE B.
[a.] Gilead, OH

JOHNSON, JEANETTE M.
[pen.] Jeanette M. Johnson; [b.] August 15, 1938; Batavia, NY; [p.] Avis Farewell; [m.] Deceased; September 30, 1967; [ed.] 9th Grade; [occ.] Housewife; [oth. writ.] A Bible and a Rose, So Sad and Stages of Life, plus several others; [pers.] No matter how many problems we incur, have faith and above all wear a smile.; [a.] Batavia, NY

JOHNSON, JEWELL
[b.] June 3, 1927; Sturgeon, MO; [p.] Charles H. and Katie Leonard; [m.] Kenneth Johnson; October 28, 1944; [ch.] Kenneth Jr., Tom, Larry, David; [ed.] Two years of college, Degree in Interior Decorating and Drapery. Real Estate Brooker, currently in school at Institute of Childrens Literature; [occ.] Retired, writing; [memb.] Baptist Church; [hon.] Editor's Choice Award (The Nat'l Library of poetry) Honorable mention (Illiad Press), Outstanding Poets of 1998 (The National Library of Poetry); [oth. writ.] Many poems—

poems published in several anthologies, songs, 2 books, many short childrens stories; [pers.] My greatest love is writing especially for children, and I like writing songs. My greatest influence was the guidance of my mother.; [a.] Benton City, MO

JOHNSON, LAWRENCE A.
[pen.] L.A.J.; [b.] June 5, 1948; Durham, NC; [p.] Lawrence and Pearl Johnson; [ch.] Lawrence Jr., Shanti Callender and DeAnte McQuaig; [ed.] Merrick Moore H.S.; [occ.] Retired, U.S. Army, U.S.M.C.; [memb.] Red Cross, Disabled Veterans of America, Paralyzed Veterans of America; [hon.] Exceptional Volunteer service award (Red Cross) Driver of the Year (Red Cross) Two Purple Hearts (Vietnam); [oth. writ.] Sweet 16 Shanti; [pers.] Being on many search and destroy missions, I want to heal my wounds and hearts of others.; [a.] Durham, NC

JOHNSON, TIMOTHY
[pen.] Timothy Johnson; [b.] April 13, 1955; Pontiac, MI; [p.] William and Carolyn Johnson; [m.] Gloria; October 15, 1988; [ed.] Diploma in Ministerial Studies, Berean School of the Bible Springfield MO, currently attending Trinity Theological Seminary, Newburgh, IN; [occ.] Pastor of Hillcrest Church of the Nazarene, Edinboro, PA; [memb.] Distinguished Member, International Society of Poets; [hon.] Editor's Choice Award 93, 94, 95, 96; [pers.] Poetry is more than words on a page; it is life painted on a page, an artistry more beautiful than a Rembrandt or a Dali or a DaVinci.; [a.] Edinboro, PA

JONES, MELINDA
[b.] June 20, 1969; Monticello, KY; [ed.] Bachelor of Health Science University of Kentucky; [occ.] Medical Technologist, Laboratory Corporation of America, Lexington, KY; [pers.] I simply put into words that which can be no longer contained in thought.; [a.] Lexington, KY

JONES, RAUSIE V. CARTWRIGHT
[b.] June 9, 1923; Voth, TX; [p.] Rev. and Mrs. S. J. Cartwright; [m.] May 10, 1943; [ch.] James; [ed.] B.A. Degree; [occ.] Editor of a Monthly Newsletter, eight published books; [memb.] International Black Writers, New Friendship Baptist Church, Support Diabetes Group, The American Diabetes Association; [hon.] Poems published in Who's Who in New Poets 1996, Honored June 9, 1998 for 15 years as Editor of a monthly newsletter. Received $1000,00 and two plaques, also celebrated 75th Birthday June 9, 1998; [oth. writ.] Eight published books, three hardbacks and five paperbacks; my latest paperback is entitled "How You Live with Diabetes"; [pers.] What you do for others always returns to bless you!; [a.] Chicago, IL

JORDAN, GLENDA
[pen.] Glenda Jordan; [b.] October 5, 1947; Columbus, GA; [p.] Clara and Robert Barron; [m.] Randy Jordan; December 31, 1979; [ch.] Tammy Lynn Grande; [ed.] Keith Dawayne Lowden Daleville, AL, Wallace College and Manpower Technology, College, AL. University of Maryland Overseas, Europe Majored Forenzics, Anthropology, and Certified Welder; [occ.] Working on Ph.D. and studying (Interior Decorating) Imports and Sales; [memb.] Garden Club; [hon.] Was in Daleville Beta Club, on honor roll, dean's list, welding certificate; [oth. writ.] Poem published in Portraits of Life, also in process of writing a book; [pers.] I thank God every day for my writing skills and I strive to awaken people's imaginations with my poetry. Edgar Allan Poe is my favorite poet.; [a.] Farrell, PA

JOSEPHSEN, RONALD A.
[b.] July 18, 1951; Hammonton, NJ; [m.] Leslie Jean (Miller) Josephen; [m.] August 18, 1979; [ch.] Jeremiah, Jamie, Damon, Tara; [ed.] Pleasantville High School, Pleasantville N.J. Class of 1969; [occ.] Facilities Technician Bell Atlantic/NJ; [memb.] Chestnut Assembly of God, Royal Rangers, Frontier Camping Fellowship, VFW; [hon.] Honorable Discharge, USAF; [oth. writ.] The National Library of Poetry—Tracing Shadows, Various Assorted Poems and Writings About Life; [pers.] I want to praise my Lord and Savior, Jesus Christ, in word and in deed. To God be the glory.; [a.] Vineland, NJ

KADY, MARTHA L.
[pen.] Lynn B. Kadimar, Martha Bevens; [b.] February 22, 1932; Seattle, WA; [p.] William Bevens, Hazel V. Mannon; [m.] Ernest R. Kady (deceased); September 12, 1966; [ch.] Mark A. Kady; [ed.] Franklin High graduate and additional training and courses; [memb.] Church of Christ; [hon.] Editor's Choice Award for Outstanding Achievement in Poetry presented by The National Library of Poetry in 1997; [oth. writ.] Children's poems and other books in process; [pers.] I believe in positive thinking and moral upbringing. I am a great nature lover. Our earth's beauty still astounds me.; [a.] Kokomo, IN

KALECK, SUSANNA
[pen.] Susanna Kaleck; [b.] October 27, 1939; New Haron, CT; [p.] Mr and Mrs. A. Whitney, Griswold; [m.] Mr. Edward G. Kaleck; June 12, 1976; [ed.] A Liberal Arts education, but still pursuing a bachelor's degree at Albertus Magnuc College; [occ.] Housewife, Student; [oth. writ.] Have been published by Arcadia Poetry Press and with NLP a total of five poems; [pers.] I hope to express an idea in my poems equivalent to "Strive to be happy compassionate and to work in justice, peace and contentment."; [a.] Hamden, CT

KAMSCHROEDER, HELEN
[pen.] Helen Kampschroeder; [b.] July 26, 1934; Beloit, KS; [p.] Perry and Mary Spurlock Betz; [m.] Walter Kampschroeder Jr.; July 4, 1959; [ch.] Karlin and Daryl; [ed.] Glen Elder, KS, High School, 3 years at University of Kansas, NIA (Newspaper Institute of America) writing course; [occ.] Proofreader of scholarly and scientific journals; [memb.] International Society of Poets; [hon.] 1st Prize among hometown correspondents while a freshman at KU; [oth. writ.] Poems in The Colors of Thought, With Flute and Drum and Pen, Best Poems of 1997; [pers.] We are expecting our first grandbaby, due date Valentine's Day, 1999! How conductive that should be to writing more poetry.; [a.] Lawrence, KS

KANWIT, BERT A.
[pen.] Bert A. Kanwit; [b.] October 8, 1916; Lynbrook, NY; [p.] Harris and Dorothy Kanwit; [m.] Jane; 1970; [ch.] Glen, John, Betsy, Marianna, Thomas and Dana; [ed.] AB—U. of Michigan—'37, MD; Harvard Med. School—'41, Board Certified Surgeon—'51; [occ.] Retired Surgeon; [memb.] Fellow Amer. Coll. of Surgeons, Fellow Unitarian Universalist Church, Poughkeepsie YMCA, Fellow American Legion; [hon.] Chief of Surgery—Vassar Hospital (1964-'69), Pres. Med. Staff—Vassar Hospirtal (1969-'71), Pres. Upstate Chapter of Surgeons; [pers.] The pluses have far exceeded the minuses in my life, a very fine professional career six wonderful kids. Still go to the "Y" exhale and this keeps me in great shape physically, mentally and spiritually.; [a.] Poughkeepsie, NY

KASELNAK, JOHN R.
[pen.] Jack Kaselnak; [b.] March 2, 1928; Minneapolis, MN; [p.] Andrew and Lillian Kaselnak; [m.] Joann Mary Kaselnak; [b.] August 27, 1952; [ch.] Patrick, Michelle, Michael, Robert; [ed.] Edison High School, many service schools, U.S. Navy; [occ.] Retired CPO—U.S. Navy and American Red Cross; [memb.] Pastoral and Eucharistic Minister, Mary Mother of the Church, Fleet Reserve Assnt.; [hon.] Two Editor's Choice Awards, Veteran's Hospital Volunteer Award; [oth. writ.] Several poems in other poetry publications; [pers.] Try to reflect true events, thoughts or humor.; [a.] Eagan, MN

KELLEY, DOROTHY M.
[pen.] Dorothy M. Kelley; [b.] March 5, 1923; Crockett, TX; [p.] Burton and Dessie Munsinger; [m.] Herbert Eugene Kelley; November 24, 1941; [ch.] Herbert Jr., Vivian, Stephen; [ed.] High School, did volunteer work, also training through AARP in Medicare, Medicare Assistant; [occ.] Joske's, Foleys Department Stores; [memb.] Air Line Manor Baptist Church, North Freeway Chapter 1094 of AARP; [hon.] Past president North Free Way Chapter 1094 AARP, AARP Volunteer of the Year, AARP Oustanding Service of Community three times; [oth. writ.] Short story, How the Tiger Got His Stripes, I Remember Mama, In the Valley of Ferry, God Not Only Made the Canary, He Also Made the Crow, Old Glory Press, others unpublished poems; [pers.] I found the work as a volunteer rewarding, even wrote A Volunteer to be used in the work. I've written poems since I was twelve years old and I get many blessings for what I call a gift from God.; [a.] Houston, TX

KELSO, JEAN
[b.] February 3, 1962; Bismarck, ND; [p.] Marian Sorenson, LeRoy Sorenson; [m.] Richard Kelso; December 12, 1992; [ed.] Bachelor of Science, Child Institute of UT—ongoing; [oth. writ.] Pub. in 1996, "The Soldier" pub. in 1997 [pers.] I live and deal with two chronic diseases. The praise from my husband, on top of seeing my verses in print, oftentimes negates the pain and expenses of my life. Writing verse is a fantastic outlet.; [a.] Mesa, AZ

KIMMONS, JANET N.
[pen.] Janet Tyrrell Kimmons; [b.] April 21, 1937; Proctosville, VT; [m.] Harry Tyrrell, Dorris Tyrell; [m.] Roger M. Kimmons; June 20, 1969; [ch.] Caren, James, Jon, Teri, Tami, Kathi; [ed.] Chester High School, Springfield Community College and Southern Vermont College; [occ.] Domestic Engineer; [oth. writ.] Poem published in Melodies of the Soul; [pers.] My poetry is an expression of my thoughts and feelings.; [a.] Springfield, VT

KLINGE, KIMBERLY L.
[b.] August 31, 1968; Cincinnati, OH; [p.] Denver and Carolyn Klinge; [occ.] Artist; [pers.] Money is not the root of all evil. Fear is. And once we know fear as an illusion, we are no longer bound and it is powerless.; [a.] Crothersville, IN

KOCH, LETA
[b.] January 12, 1945; Denton, TX; [p.] Mary B. Foster Cross, J. M. Cross; [m.] Steven Robert Koch; November 23, 1977; [ch.] Dee and Mary Lisa; [ed.] California, Oregon and Texas; [occ.] Executive Director, Crisis Center—shelter and services for victims of domestic and sexual assault; [oth. writ.] Poetry, songs and short stories since childhood; [pers.] Never take yourself or life too seriously.; [a.] Pottsboro, TX

KOELLING, RALPH M.
[pen.] Ralph M. Koelling; August, 1955; Germany; [p.] Martin and Lilian Koelling; [memb.] International NS of Poetry; [oth. writ.] With National Library of Poetry—Father, Son, Dad, The Sparkling Diamond; [b.] Corona, CA

KOWALSKY, RACHEL
[pen.] Wolfmoon Dancer; [b.] September 11, 1972; Malden, MA; [p.] Jim and Ruth Kowalsky; [ed.] Lyndon State College, Lyndonville, UT; [occ.] Radio Producer and Announcer; [oth. writ.] Cherished Poems of the Western World, Treasured Poems of America, A Picture of Elegance; [pers.] Stand out in the Quiet of night. There is poetry all around you. Watch and listen to people. There is poetry there. My inspiration is life.; [a.] Monomet, MA

KREMER, BEVERLY M.H.
[b.] March 22, 1961; Santa Monica, CA; [p.] Berry Winton Hildebrand; Bonita Luark; [m.] Vic Kremer; May 18, 1985; [occ.] Bartender—Outlaw Saloon,

Afton, WY; [oth. writ.] Several poems published by The National Library of Poetry; [pers.] I try to write about life as I see it, usually from a slightly "twisted" point of view.; [a.] Etna, WY

KRUPA, DONNA MARIE
[b.] August 25, 1955; Derby, CT; [p.] Clara and The Late Walter Krupa; [ed.] Ansonia High—1974, Naugatuck College—received an A.S. Degree in Human Services in 1998; [occ.] Writer of Poetry; [memb.] In the International Society of Poets; [hon.] Editor's choice Awards for 1997 and 1998, Dean's list spring of 1997, International Poetry Hall of Fame in 1997; [oth. writ.] "The Seed of Life," "What a Tear," "Torn Apart," "Out of Sequence"; [pers.] "For I know the plans I have for you, declares the Lord, plans to give you hope and a future . . . You will seek me and find me when you seek me with all your heart."—Jeremiah 29:11-13; [a.] Ansonia, CT

KUHN, JOHN
[pen.] Johnny Love; [b.] May 4, 1980; Washington, PA; [p.] The late John M. Kuhn Sr., Paula J. Wright; [ed.] Burgettstown High, Weir High; [oth. writ.] "The Psycho" and many other unpublished works; [pers.] I used to write from anger and pain, but now I write for my dearest love, Jennifer.; [a.] Weirton, WV

KURSWEIL, ANNA B.
[pen.] Joy Ann Peace; Grandview, MO; [p.] Vincent and Bertha Kursweil; [ed.] Grandview High, SHLTC from Warrensburg State Teachers College, B.S. from Avila College, MA. from University of MO at KC, enough graduate hours equivalent to a doctorate, spent nine weeks at St. Benedict House of Study, Wurzburg, Germany, doing Contemplative Practice. Travel—"Globe Trotter; [occ.] Retired Teacher; [memb.] Rockhurst Literary Guild, CWC, MRTA, KCTA; [hon.] The International Poetry Hall of Fame, a member of good standing in the International Society of Poets, recognition of good and faithful service for 25 years in KC Public School System; [oth. writ.] Poems in American Poetry Anthology, "The Roll," "Pin Cushion Single"; poems in several anthologies by The National Library of Poetry, and an article in Fellowship in Prayer; [pers.] Although a Christian, white and American, my ecumenical interest reaches out to other religions, races and nationalities, when we celebrate in a contemplative matter our common understandings, not our differences. In this atmosphere, Peace and Love reign supreme.; [a.] Kansas City, MO

LAMKIN, WILLIAM H.
[pen.] William H. Lamkin; [b.] August 12, 1914; Downey, CA; [p.] Jerome and Gladys Lamkin; [m.] Jessie Meers Lamkin; March 25, 1977; [ed.] University of Alabama—B.A., Jones Law School—L.L.B.; [memb.] Kiwanis Club, American Philatelic Society, Scandinavian Collection Club; [hon.] Honorary Member of Scandinavian Collection Club; [oth. writ.] Numerous articles on stamp collecting, having been a stamp collector for 70 years; [a.] Lawrenceville, GA

LANCE, TONIA C.
[pen.] Tonia C. Lance; [b.] October 8, 1979; Lubbock, TX; [p.] Eddie and Margie Lance; [a.] Sundown, TX

LARSON, WALT
[pen.] Wolf and Walt Larson; [b.] August 16, 1926; Milton, MA; [p.] Henry J. Larson and Mildred Louise; [m.] September 29, 1946; [ch.] Walter E. Larson; [ed.] Tucker School, Milton, MA; Milton High School, Milton, MA; Navy Radio School, Bedford Spring, PA; LaFrance College, Los Angeles (Accounting); [occ.] Retired from Teledyne Camera Systems, Arcadia, CA; [memb.] American Legion, International Society of Poets, Knights of Columbus, AARP, served in U.S. Navy 1944 to

1951; [oth. writ.] Romantic Vignettes, Column of Poetry in "Senior Script"; poetry in a number of anthologies; [pers.] If at first you don't succeed write and write again.; [a.] So. El Monte, CA

LASSICK, LORNA
[b.] June 9, 1930; Homer City, PA; [p.] Elmer and Alice Cravener; [m.] June 25, 1947; [ch.] Marlenea, Michael; [ed.] Graduated from Horace Mann (1941); graduated jr. high school (1943); graduated senior high (1947); graduated technical (1951); classes at Indiana University, Indiana, PA; graudated Philadelphia, PA, School of Nursing (1958); [occ.] Retired from Indiana University, Indiana, PA, 1991; [memb.] Byzantine (Greek) Catholic Church, Charter Member of Indiana County Practical Nurse (license), Director for number of years; [hon.] Given recognition for outstanding Voluntary Contributions to various organizations, also Achievement Award for writings, for community, Golden Poet Award; [oth. writ.] Freelance poems published in magazines and pamplets; in the process of writing a novel; [pers.] I try to be the best that I can be in all walks of life. I'm inspired by my father Elmer W. Cravener (a teacher).; [a.] Indiana, PA

LAUMEYER, ROBERT L.
[b.] August 31, 1932; Wolf Point, MT; [p.] Joe and Rose Laumeyer (deceased); [m.] Kathleen McGlynn Laumeyer; August 31, 1953; [ch.] Mary Runkel, Barbi Miner, Jean O'Leary and Robert A. Laumeyer; [ed.] High school, Nashua, MT; jr. college, Havre, MT, University B.A. and Masters Degree, Missoula, MT; post-graduate work, AZ State University; [occ.] Retired Educator—30 years MT, five years AZ; [hon.] Elected into The International Poetry Hall of Fame in 1996; [oth. writ.] Book: Song of the Hunter and Other Poems (1998), New Voices in American Poetry 1980 and 1987, poems on Internet's World Wide Web, others by National Library of Poetry—Best Poems of 1996, Soaring with the Wind, and others; [pers.] Patriots: We should protect our government, and help ensure that it survives. Even though it is not perfect, it's been the best man can devise.; [a.] Boulder, MT

LAUTENSCHLEGER, LEE
[b.] December 7, 1944; Asheboro, NC; [p.] Rev. and Mrs. Allen Thompson; [m.] Jerry Lautenschleger; September 28, 1961; [ch.] Loretta Rivera, Samuel Lautenschleger; [ed.] Asheboro High Sch. graduate 1964 Rhema Bible Corress. School; [occ.] President—Prayer Warrior Inc., Pastor—Gospel Missionary Baptist Church, Column—Area Newspaper—The Randolph Guide (weekly); [hon.] Who's Who Plat. Edition Outstand Business Person; [oth. writ.] Weekly Randolph Guide, The National Library of Poetry; [pers.] My greatest desire is to show my Heavenly Father, His Son Jesus, and The Holy Spirit in my walk through this life to all I meet!; [a.] Asheboro, NC

LAWRENCE, MARIE
[a.] Manchester, NH

LAWSON, WANDA M.
[b.] April 16, 1965; Washington, DC; [p.] Claudine E. Lawson; [ch.] Dwayne S.E. Lawson-Brown; [ed.] Spingarn S.T.A.Y. High school, Southeastern University, Northern Virginia Community College, Marymount University; [occ.] Legal Instrument Examiner, U.S. Patent and Trademark Office; [memb.] Children of the Living God Ministries, Delta Sigma Theta Sorority, Inc. and Phi Chi Theta Fraternity of Business and Economics, Inc; [hon.] Assistant Church Clerk, Emmanuel Baptist Church, Washington, DC, Vice-President, Delta Sigma Theta Sorority, Xi Zeta Chapter, President Phi Chi Theta Fraternity, Inc, Epsilon Xi Chapter; [oth. writ.] Have written several poems—one was previously printed in Of Summer's Passing.; [pers.] In everything you do, let God lead you. Trust God; He is in control.; [a.] Washington, D.C.

LEAK, ANNA MARIE HOLT
[b.] February 28, 1928; Madison Jefferson Co, IN; [p.] Allen L. and Leah V. Barber Holt; [m.] Ralph Bauer Leak; June 9; 1968; [ch.] Three step-daughters; [ed.] Graduated from North Madison High School, Madison Indiana and one year at Dwyer Business School in Indianapolis; [occ.] Retired after 43 1/2 years from National Heardquarters of The American Legion, Executive Secretary Legal; [memb.] Victory Memorial United Methodist Church, Member and Teacher of Christian Builders Sunday School Class, V.M. Choir Director, United Methodist Women, American Legion Auxilliary, International Society of Poets; [hon.] Several through the years with regard to my work, and through my poetry; [oth. writ.] Several poems through the years—when a poem or citation was needed I usuallly provided what was needed.; [pers.] I am a dedicated, joyous Christian and I always try to live my life so as to show my faith, and I think a promise is a sacred thing and should always be kept.; [a.] Franklin, IN

LEE, ALETHEIA D.
[b.] October 30, 1977; Normal, IL; [p.] Gary and Catherine Lee; [ed.] Central Gwinnett High, Lawrenceville, Georgia, Currently attending Atlanta Christian College, East Point, GA; [occ.] Full-time student, part-time pharmacy tech with Eckerd; [memb.] National Thespian Society, Delta Theta, National Dean's List, International Society of Poets; [oth. writ.] "Silently Loving You" in the Nightfall of Diamonds, "Wings To Fly" in the Best Poems of 1997; [pers.] I use my writing to express my inner self and to show the world how much God loves us.; [a.] Lawrenceville, GA

LEE, TRUDY A.
[b.] February 5, 1951; Hartford, CT; [p.] William J. and Melva S. Lee; [ch.] Amy Montague, Brian Montague; [ed.] Bloomfield High School, Hartford Community College; [occ.] Self-Employed, Small Business; [memb.] St. Judes, American Red Cross; [hon.] National Library of Poetry Editor's Choice Award, Service Appreciacian Award, Leo Club International; [oth. writ.] The National Library of Poetry—Of Moonlight and Wishes, The Poetry Guild—Dreams Gone By, local newspaper articles; [pers.] There is so much beauty in life that is often overlooked or taken for granted. My writing simply expresses the love that my heart feels inside.; [a.] Bloomfield, CT

LEE, YUKWOR
[b.] January 6, 1924; Burma; [p.] Ping Cheung and Liu-che; [m.] Shui-Ming; [ch.] Wendy; [ed.] North Cote College of Education, Dip, Hong Kong, Hwu Kui College of Commerce of Engineering B.A., Hong Kong, Biology Teachers Course, Cert. University of Hong Kong, Insitute of Education, University of London Associateship; [memb.] International Poety Hall of Fame Distinguished Member of the International Society of Poets; [hon.] Hong Kong Government Civil Servants Scholarship, British Common Wealth Education Fellowship, 1973, Editor's Choice Award by the National Library of Poets, 1996, International Poet of Merit Award by the International Society of Poets, 1997 and 1998; [oth. writ.] Hong Kong in Blossom a documentary film in flowers of the four seasons, In the Land of the Midnight Sun, Iceland, English version of a Selection of fifty Chinese poems of the Tang Dynasty, 918-906, Award Winning poems, Midnight Sun, Hong Kong, The Pearl of the Orient Forever Prospers, The Dawn of a New Bright Morn; [a.] San Francisco, CA

LEHFELDT, HAROLD E.
[pen.] Harold E. Lehfeldt; [b.] July 18, 1931; Helena, MT; [p.] B.H. Lehfeldt; [m.] Marla R.; September 1, 1950; [ch.] Brend, Amy, Paul, Lisa; [ed.] Collage of Hard Rocks and Big Rocks; [oth. writ.] Several poems unpublished; [pers.] My po-

ems are mostly combined with photos, that are memory makers for family and friends. "Dancing Water" was written for my son, at Glancier Park, going to the sun highway.; [a.] Longmont, CO

LEVY, JOYCEMIN M.
[b.] June 20, 1943; Manchester, WI; [p.] Gladstone and Wilhel Levy (deceased); [ch.] Melbourne and Andrew Edwards; [ed.] St. Martin's High School, Durham College, Institute of Management and Production-Jamaica, WI, Jackson Mem. Hospital-Miami, FL; [occ.] Retail Sales Associate; [memb.] Calvary Gospel Assembly, American Heart Association; [oth. writ.] Several poems published and unpublished; [pers.] In my writings I strive to draw attention to the beauty of creation, the power of God and to uncover the beauty of the human spirit.; [a.] Hollywood, FL

LEWIS, FRANK F.
[pen.] Frankielew; [b.] November 22, 1955; PA; [p.] Frank and Audrey Lewis; [m.] Divorced; [ch.] Daryl, Richard, Frank Jr., and Danielle; [ed.] Thomas Jefferson; [occ.] Chemical Worker; [hon.] Editor's Choice Award from The National Library of Poetry—1988; [oth. writ.] If You Only Knew, published in Above the Clouds, 1988; working on a book of poetry; [pers.] Life's too short—go for your dreams!; [a.] West Elizabeth, PA

LICKING, TERRI ANN
[b.] December 9, 1954; Omaha, NE; [p.] Jim and Bonnie Sturtz; June 19, 1976; [ch.] Nadene Marie, Clarine Rae, Russell James; [ed.] Salutatorian, Stapleton High School Class of '73, Registered Nurse (diploma), Mary Lanning School of Nursing—Hastings, NE; [occ.] Rancher, Part-time R.N.; [memb.] NNA-ANA, Sandhills Cattle Association, NE Cattlewoman, UCC Church of Thedford, NE; [hon.] NNA-AIN 1982, Excellence in Writing Award; [oth. writ.] Other poems, beef articles in local papers; [pers.] The Lord has blessed me with family, life in the wide open spaces. He is my inspiration; my words are for gratitude to life's many blessings.; [a.] Thedford, NE

LINDON, LUCAS V.
[b.] January 6, 1982; Dennison, OH; [p.] Sherry Lindon; [ed.] Tuscarawas Central Catholic High School; [occ.] Student; [memb.] Boy Scouts of America, Yearbook, Saints Basketball Team, Nicole's Fan Club; [hon.] Editor's Choice Award From National Library of Poetry, State Championship Power of the Pen, Who's Who Among High School Students; [oth. writ.] "Future Warrior" found in An Eternal Flame, Who's Who; [pers.] "Had I not know that I was dead already I would have mourned my loss of life."—Ota Doken (1486); [a.] Dennison, OH

LINGENHELTER, ALINA
[pen.] Alina Lingenhelter; [b.] January 4, 1964; Peoria, IL; [p.] James and Genevieve Lingenhelter; [ed.] Bachelor of Science in Education, attending Bradley University for Masters in English; [occ.] Owner of Knights - a computer service; [hon.] The National Library of Poetry, Editor's Choice Award; [oth. writ.] Several poems published in anthologies; [a.] Pekin, IL

LINKO, ANGELA R.
[pen.] Angela Renea Linko [b.] May 10, 1971; Jacksonville, FL; [p.] John and Bonnie Linko; [ed.] Englewood Senior High; [occ.] Customer Service Rep. for Pearle Vision for nine years; [oth. writ.] Had my first poem published in 1996; [a.] Jacksonville, FL

LODD, LEOTA
[pen.] Leota Todd; [b.] February 12, 1910; OH; [p.] Frank and Cora Moyer; [m.] George Edward Todd; July 28, 1931; [ed.] High school; [hon.] Two in high school singing; [pers.] A Sunday School Teacher for ten years, I worked and raised my family with my husband of 58 years.; [a.] Sandusky, OH

LOWRY CURRY, MARY EARLE
[pen.] Mary Earle Lowry Curry; [b.] Seneca, SC; [p.] Ullin Sidney and Mary Sloan/Earle Lowry; [m.] Reverend Peden Gene Curry; December 25, 1941; [ch.] Eugene Lowry and Mary Earle Curry; [ed.] Attended Furman University; [memb.] United Methodist Church; [oth. writ.] "Looking Within" (1981), "Looking Up" (1949), Anthologies and Newspapers, Poetry Goals; [a.] Seneca, SC

LUARK, BONITA
[b.] October 21, 1942; San Mateo, CA; [p.] Truman D. and Bernice Luark; [m.] Karl M. Dreihaupt; November 11, 1992; [ch.] Beverly, Christine, Lenore and Sam; [ed.] High School—San Mateo, CA, Mohave Community Coll., Bullhead City, AZ; [memb.] Soc. of Decorative Painters, Chaporral Women's Golf Assoc.; [oth. writ.] 1st poem—Nat'l Library of Poetry; [pers.] My daughter Beverly Kremer sent her poems to the Nat'l. Lib. of Poetry; she's my hero. I always loved words, painting; now I'm painting with words.; [a.] Bullhead City, AZ

LUCAS, DANITA JOE
[pen.] Mita/DJ; [b.] July 13, 1967; Newark, NJ; [p.] Juanita and Scottie Lee; [ch.] Victor Colter Jr.; [ed.] Vailsburg HS, American Business Institute, Bloomfield College; [occ.] Office Manager, A/G Christian Schools, Newark; [memb.] Peace Temple COGIC, Worldwide COGIC Auxilaries, Mary Kay; [hon.] NJ State Youth, President's Chosen Generation Award, Dean's List, Star Consultant, Employee Recognition, Editor's Choice Award; [oth. writ.] Poems published in Bloomfield College Newspaper, Dusk and Dawn Christian Fiction Magazine, Christian Souvenir Journals; [pers.] My poems reflet closure to experiences applying Biblical principles to my life.; [a.] Newark, NJ

LUKREC, SHULAMITH
[pen.] Shelly Lukrec; February 13, 1930; [p.] Jacob and Freda Waid; [m.] Aron Lukrec; May 15, 1960; [ch.] Charles, Samuel; [ed.] B.A. from Roosevelt Univ., Coursework towards M.A. in Music Therapy at NY Univ.; [occ.] Retired Elem. Teacher, still on file with Board of Educ. for Substitute teaching; [memb.] NAMI NYC SI (National Alliance for the Mentally Ill, NY City, Staten Island. Active from 1990-96 in Toastmasters International Staten Island Branch UFT (United Federation of Teachers), Recording Secretary of SI Alliance for the Mentally Ill; [hon.] Past president of AAUW (American Association of University Women 1963-64), Past president of Staten Island [oth. writ.] Regular contributions to The National Library of Poetry; [pers.] For me, the fullest expression of life lies in creative endeavors: music, dance, poetry.; [a.] Staten Island, NY

LUNA, JILL
[b.] March 15, 1982; Nashville, TN; [p.] Johnnie and Janice; [ed.] Park Avenue Christian School (K-4 and K-5), Gower Elementary, Head Middle School, Duponts Hadley Hume-Fogg High School; [occ.] Arhitect's Assistant; [hon.] Who's Who Among American High School Students, Beta Club, Honor Roll; [oth. writ.] One Thoughts, Frost at Midnight (book published); [pers.] Poetry is a great pasttime; keep writing and thinking.; [a.] Old Hickory, TN

LUNSFORD, JUANITA JONES
[b.] November 26, 1932; Rock Island, IL; [p.] Rev. John Jones and Rebecca Jones; [m.] Cecil Lunsford; December 24, 1951; [ch.] Wanda, Alan, Michael, Janice, Tenna and Tim, also 14 grandchildren; [ed.] Rocky High; [memb.] Distinguished Member of International Society of Poets, 1996-1997; [hon.] Editor's Choice Awards for Outstanding Achievement in Poetry presented by National Library of Poetry; [oth. writ.] International Society of Poets, (I.S.P.), Poem for Peace "Sweet Peace and Victory", The National Library of Poetry, (N.L.P.) anthology—Beneath the Harvest Moon, poem "Blackberry Delight", N.L.P.

anthology Best Poems of the 90's Poem "Lessons of Love", N.L.P. anthology Daybreak on the Land, poem "These I Like the Most" also N.L.P. anthology of Moonlight and Wishes, poem "Seasons", N.L.P. anthology of Isle of View, poem "A Special Place to Pray", N.L.P. anthology Best Poems of 1998, poem "Just Like Yesterday", N.L.P. anthology Outstanding Poets of 1998 poem "September Winds"; [pers.] Juanita is inspired by nature, love of life, God, family, friends and childhood memories. May the poetic light within us all continue to shine and our spiritual light shine even brighter.; [a.] Brazil, IN

LYNCH, AMANDA
[a.] Columbus, OH

LYNCH, EDWARD R.
[b.] September 11, 1966; Holyoke, MA; [p.] Richard, Dianne Lynch; [ed.] Holyoke High School; [occ.] Software Developer; [pers.] Laugh at those who say you can't.; [a.] Holyoke, MA

MABEY, AMANDA G.
[b.] December 21, 1980; Salt Lake City, UT; [p.] Edward and Gun Mabey; [ed.] 3 years high school—starting 4th year in the fall of 1998 (17 years old); [occ.] Student; [memb.] International Soc. of Poets; [hon.] 3 National Library of Poetry Editor's Choice Awards and various merit publications; [oth. writ.] Poems published in print and cassettes for The National Library of Poetry and International Soc. of poets and Iliad Press; [a.] Scottsdale, AZ

MACDONALD, CARRIANN
[b.] December 18, 1969; Lowell, MA; [m.] September 16, 1995; [ch.] Cote MacDonald; [occ.] Real Estate, Book Keeper, Housewife; [memb.] International Society of Poets; [hon.] 4 Editor's Choice Awards; [pers.] This poem was written by me along time ago, and you certainly live up to it. Thank you for giving me so many smiles and so much laughter—I love you, Cote.

MANN, JASON AARON
[b.] August 9, 1971; Milwaukee, WI; [p.] James Mann, Kathleen Mann; [m.] Nichole Theresa Mann; June 20, 1998; [ed.] Northland Pines High, Waukesha County Technical College; [occ.] Assistant Office Manager; [memb.] Business Professionals of America; [oth. writ.] "Pat's Vision" published in Chambers of Time; [pers.] My beautiful bride inspires my romantic writings.; [a.] New Berlin, WI

MANNING, JEAN
[pen.] Jean Manning; [b.] Atlanta, GA; [p.] Emma Kate and Mack H. Thomas; [m.] Dr. Willie James Manning; [ch.] Zario Laurenz Manning; [ed.] David T. Howard High, Morris Brown College, Atlanta University, The University of Oklahoma; [occ.] College Professor; [memb.] National Federation / State Poetry Societies: Georgia State Poetry Society, Georgia Writters Poetry Society, Inc., International Society of Poets; [hon.] Editor's Choice Award, published in Distinguished Poets of America, 3rd prize winner (Best Poems of 1995); [oth. writ.] Visions of Kate, Love Impressions, Golden Years, The Faithful Two, Guest Divine, Of golden boy; [pers.] I write to portray beauty and to cheer and inspire mankind.; [a.] Decatur, GA

MARCUS, DARYL A.
[b.] May 17, 1979; Clanton, AL; [p.] Thomas and Glenda Marcus; [ed.] Advanced diploma from Chilton County High and currently attending the University of South Alabama—majoring in Computer Science; [occ.] Student; [memb.] International Brotherhood of Magicians; [oth. writ.] "I Saw the Tears as You Began to Cry" published in An Eternal Flame; [pers.] My philosophy is simple: If someone says you can't, do it just for spite.; [a.] Clanton, AL

MARESCA, CATHERINE V. GODONE
[b.] April 26, 1986; [p.] Paul A. Maresca Lowell

(Deceased) and Lillian A. Godone Maresca; [ed.] Currently in intermediate school; [occ.] Student; [memb.] St. Michael's Parish, Poway CA, International Society of Poets, Independent Writer's Assn., San Diego CA; [hon.] Achievement Award, National Library of Poetry; [oth. writ.] "Murder in Disguise" (ProLife Article), in St. Michael's Parish Bulletin, November '97, and in Youth Voice (The Youth Ministry Newsletter), other poems published by The National Library of Poetry and in the Independent Writer's Association's Newsletter; [pers.] My writings praise God, talk about my family and my feelings, defend the right of life, and speak against racism and injustice in the world. My family has also taught me to be sensitive to other people's pain, even in situations which are not my own, like in this poem.; [a.] San Diego, CA

MARESCA, LILLIAN A. GODONE
[b.] June 9, 1958; [p.] Armand C.E. Godone Signanini (Deceased), E. Nydia Soracco Godone; [m.] Paul A. Maresca Lowell (Deceased); [ch.] Catherine, Gerard, Warren Godone Maresca; [ed.] J.D., Catholic University of Buenos Aires, Post Graduate Teaching Training Course, same university; [occ.] Attorney at Law (private practice) in CA.; [memb.] State Bar of California, St. Michael's Parish, Poway CA, International Society of Poets, Independent Writer's Assn., San Diego CA; [oth. writ.] Other poems published by The National Library of Poetry, in the Mothers of Twins Club Newsletter, and in The Independent Writer's Association Newsletter; some papers submitted in professional conferences; [pers.] My poems are inspired by my unusually loving and devoted family, and by my Catholic faith, and are committed to protect the right to life and to denounce racism.; [a.] San Diego, CA

MARIANO, PORFIRIO A.
[pen.] Porfirio A. Mariano; [b.] March 27, 1922; San Mateo, Rizal, Philippines; [p.] Lorenzo and Apolonia A. Mariano; [m.] Eugenio B. Mariano; June 30, 1947; [ch.] Nini, Evelyn and Arthur Mariano; [ed.] 2nd year College of Philosophy and Letters; Course—Journalism, University of St. Thomas, Manila, Philippines; [occ.] Retired Gov't Records Officer V, Republic of the Philippines; [memb.] Philippine Veteran Association and Philippine Records Management Association, Inc; [hon.] Service Award Certificate with Silver Long Service Pin for having completed 30 years of continuous and satisfactory service in the Gov'.t of the Republic of the Philippines; Editor's Choice Award for outstanding achievement in Poetry, Presented by The National Library of Poetry (1997); [oth. writ.] Service Not Connected—published in Into the Unknown—The National Library of Poetry; Vernacular Stories, novels published in local magazines at Mla.; Radio Script Writer—DZBB; Script Radio Director over DZEC, QC, Philippines; [pers.] The pen is the brain, heart and blood life of the people to express the truth and honest opinion.; [a.] Kilauea, Kauai, HI

MARSH, ANTONINA D.
[pen.] Tony; [b.] November 5, 1913; Lurkutsk, Siberia; [p.] Deceased; [m.] Richard H. Marsh; December 3, 1949; [ch.] Douglas, Edwin, Carol; [ed.] Raised and studied in China, know four languages; [occ.] Retired—an artist, painter, was a teacher for 22 years; [oth. writ.] Plan to write my autobiography; [a.] Fayettteville, AR

MARTIN, HAROLD ROY
[pen.] Hugh Clifford MarRoy; [b.] December 19, 1923; Ottumwa, IA; [p.] Martin Hugh Clifford, Mildred Elizabeth; [m.] Trudy Louise Martin (Nylin); July 7, 1982; [ch.] David Lee Martin; [ed.] 8th grade; [occ.] Hotel Restaurant Worker at Holiday Inn—Moline, IL; [oth. writ.] Have written hundreds of poems since eight years old, around one hundred unpublished poems; [pers.] Poetry is

one of the oldest ways of recording and passing on events of the past and present. Without poetry there would be no songs.; [a.] Moline, IL

MARTIN, JANICE M.
[pen.] J. Mattson Martin; [b.] 1945; OR; [m.] Frank S. Martin; 1961; [ch.] Two daughters; [ed.] AHS, GC College; [hon.] Several Editor's Choice Awards from National Library of Poetry; [oth. writ.] Desires, Reality, Memories, No Identity, Far Away, My Love, Children from a Distant Land, Lost, Children's Stories; [a.] Astoria, OR

MASON, DANIEL
[pen.] Daniel Mason; [b.] July 30, 1975; San Diego, CA; [p.] Albert and Lorane Mason; [ed.] Mira Mesa High, Mesa College; [occ.] Manager of Higher Grounds Coffee House; [memb.] Young Life, Grace Chapel; [oth. writ.] Several other poems published in other publications; [pers.] "Faith, hope, and love . . . the greatest of these is love."—1 Cor. 13:13; [a.] San Diego, CA

MATHIS, CHERYL DIANNE
[b.] November 21, 1951; Atlanta, GA; [p.] Howard and Ruth Green; [m.] Norman Clayton Mathis; January 10, 1970; [ch.] Clay Mathis, David Mathis; [ed.] South Hall High School, Lanier Tech; [occ.] Housewife, mother; [memb.] Calvary Baptist Church, Fairburn, GA; [oth. writ.] Several poems published in newspaper and magazine, have written several short stories and songs; [pers.] God has richly blessed my life with wonderful parents, a loving husband, and two fantastic sons. All my writing comes from a loving God.; [a.] Fairburn, GA

MATHIS, GWEN J.
[b.] February 20, 1929; Milwaukee, WI; [p.] Chester and Sola Melke; [ch.] Two daughters; [ed.] B.F.A. University of Wisconsin at Milwaukee, M.A.—Thebster College; [occ.] Customer Survey at a Car Dealership; [memb.] American Evangelical Lutheran Church, AARP; [hon.] Past President of Artists' Equity Association, have had my art work shown in many juried art shows; [oth. writ.] Have had several poems published; [pers.] This has been an interesting journey.; [a.] Phoenix, AZ

MAXWELL, JENNIE
[pen.] Jennie Maxwell; [b.] January 11; MS; [p.] Sip and Katherine Terry; [ch.] Four; [occ.] Kitchen Help; [hon.] 21 Rewards; [a.] Bristol, IN

MAYER, TAWNIE L.
[pen.] T.K.; [b.] May 13, 1960; Denver, CO; [p.] Robert Mayer, Nancy Swanson; [m.] Jerry Hemphill; January 10, 1997; [ed.] Northglenn High School; [occ.] Data Entry and Small Business Accounting; [memb.] International Society of Poets; [oth. writ.] Poem published in Fields of Gold—The National Library of Poetry; [pers.] For those who go before us, let them give us guidance and support, to maintain the best that life has to offer us.; [a.] Federal Heights, CO

MCBRIDE, DANIELLE H.
[b.] March 10, 1975; Woodbury, NJ; [oth. writ.] Two poems previously published in other volumes with The National Library of Poetry; [pers.] I owe everything to God; His many blessings continue to rain upon me.; [a.] Stratford, NJ

MCCRAY, MISTY DAWN
[b.] February 4, 1975; Oklahoma City, OK; [p.] Julie Clark, Rick McCray; [ch.] Charles Donovan Nichols; [ed.] Currently attending University of Oklahoma, Norman; [memb.] United States Army Reserve; [pers.] We all make discoveries about ourselves all the time. Are the things we find out anything we want to know?; [a.] Norman, OK

MCCUBBIN, MARY ANNE
[b.] October 24, 1938; Denver, CO; [p.] H.P. (Mac) and A Macauley; [m.] Donald G. McCubbin;

June 2, 1962; [ch.] Sheryl Anne and Dona Lynn; [ed.] Wheatridge High School, University of Colorado, Unity School of Christianity, Real Estate Prep; [occ.] Spiritual Teacher, Realtor and Mortgage Broker; [memb.] High Country Unity Church, Sales Professionals USA (President) SCUCA So. Central Unity Churches Assoc.; [oth. writ.] Poem in Above the Clouds; [pers.] My purpose in life is to let God love through me and to teach about our loving God.; [a.] Littleton, CO

MCELHANEY, TERRI
[b.] September 10, 1946; Corsicana, TX; [p.] Jack and Virginia Gibbs; [m.] Paul McElhaney; October 19, 1996; [ch.] Bart Gable; [ed.] 4 years of College Associate Degree in Nursing; [occ.] Director of Nursing at A Nursing Home; [oth. writ.] Images of Our Princess, Face in the Mirror, Goodbye to the Yellow Brick Road; [pers.] Try to help someone each day. I have always been a caregiver, even as a child.; [a.] Palestine, TX

MCELMURRY, TERRY J.
[b.] June 18, 1947; Wichita, KS; [m.] Nancy L. McElmurry; [ch.] Erin T.; [occ.] Management Consultant; [oth. writ.] Poems of Love, Life and Liberty; [pers.] Challenging the human spirit to look past trials and tribulations, and experience a world unlimited, fresh, and new; [a.] Elkhart, IN

MCENERY, DEBORAH L.
[pen.] Leigh McEnery; [b.] July 2, 1955; Millington, TN; [p.] Dwight and Anieta J. Hauser; [m.] William Patrick McEnery; February 27, 1993; [ch.] Tanya Leigh Moring; [ed.] Havelock High School, Knapp College of Business, Southwestern College, Washington Tech.; [occ.] Clerical for National City Fire Dept.; [memb.] San Diego Lapidary Society, National Geographic Society, Parrot Rehabilitation Society; [hon.] Two certificates of Achievement for Outstanding Taxpayer Service by the California State Board of Equalization; [oth. writ.] The Lollipop Song, published in Traces of Yesterday. Several short stories—unpublished; [pers.] I enjoy writing amusing subjects for kids. I think "Pickles" would make a great kid's book.; [a.] National City, CA

MCGILL, LESLIE DALE JOLLY
[pen.] Jolly; [b.] March 17, 1919; Williston, ND; [p.] Donald and Anna McGill; [m.] Juanita Virtue McGill; [ch.] Dale D., Ralph A., Glenn E.; [ed.] Central High, University of Minnesota; [occ.] Retired Carpenter; [memb.] Arrowhead Poetry Society, Calvary Temple Church; [hon.] Numerous Honorable Mentions by Arrowhead Poetry Society, The National Library of Poetry; [oth. writ.] Several poems published in North Country Cadence, poems for church bulletin; [pers.] Much of my work reflects my faith in God and my love of my family. I am inspired often during sermons.; [a.] Duluth, MN

MCHANEY, MEGHAN
[pen.] Meghan A. McHaney; [b.] April 6, 1984; [p.] Jill and Jim McHaney; [ed.] Hartford Elementary, Bogle Jr. High School, Hamilton High School; [hon.] Reading, Principle's List, honor roll, citizenship, Student of the Month; [oth. writ.] Published in Frost at Midnight, A Walk on a Summer's Night; [pers.] Those who influence me are my teachers and parents to further my artistic talent. I'm unique because I'm me.; [a.] Chandler, AZ

MCILVOY, LOIS
[pen.] Lois McIlvoy (née Sanders); [b.] September 25, 1912; Fennville, MI; [p.] John and Rebecca Holton; [m.] Walter McIlvoy; August 25, 1994; [ed.] South Haven High, MI, Associate Degree in Liberal Arts, FL, Bachelor Degree in English, FL, correspondence courses in various forms of writing—newspaper, fiction, poetry; [occ.] Retired; [memb.] National League of American Pen Women, Ocala Branch, St. John Lutheran Church, FL Telephone Pioneers, MI International Society

of Poets, Business and Professional Women's Club, South Haven, MI; [oth. writ.] Column in Ocala Star Banner, Ocala, Fl, A column "Woman's World" in MI General News; a general telephone company publication for its employees—it came out once a month—wrote in it for 20 years for GTE and its predecessors; children's stories, hobby, travel, news items for several newspapers and magazines, for various publications, put together a book of poems; [a.] Belleview, FL

MCINTYRE, DONALD M.
[b.] January 19, 1940; Winnipeg, MB; [ed.] Villanova Preparatory School, Ojai, CA, B.A. (Philosophy), 1963, St. John's College, Camarillo, CA, M.A. (English) 1968, Loyola University of LA, Los Angeles, CA; [memb.] The International Poetry Hall of Fame, Owings Mills, MD; [hon.] Winner of the Golden Poet Award, 1985-1992, from World of Poetry; [oth. writ.] Published in numerous anthologies and listed in "Who's Who in Poetry" by World of Poetry, and published in several anthologies by The National Library of Poetry; [pers.] The art of poetry, as expressed by this author in his writings, is an illustration of modern existentialist philosophical theories coupled with the contemporary psychological technique of stream of consciousness.; [a.] Santa Barbara, CA

MCKERLIE, MARIE E.
[b.] February 2, 1965; Tacoma, WA; [p.] Rita Mary and Georgie Houchens; [m.] Russell D. McKerlie; April 11, 1980; [ch.] Rusty, Micheal, Ryan, Ashely, Marie; [ed.] G.E.D., Studies in Cosmetology—several degrees in Trichology; [occ.] Office Supervisor for a Distributor Company; [memb.] P.T.A. in children school, also new member of International Poet Society GPPA; [hon.] Best in Sales of Products, Second Places in Arts and Crafts, mostly in painting, honor in writing poetry; [oth. writ.] Several poems published in The National Library of Poetry and some local papers, other contests; [pers.] A pen with paper can be immortal for your heart and soul, your life forever.; [a.] Phoenix, AZ

MCKINSTRY, JEANNIE L.
[b.] February 26, 1935; Howard City, MI; [p.] Harold and Margaret Hewitt; [m.] Deceased; [ch.] Kimberly, Cary, Brian; [ed.] Owosso High School Graduate 1953; [pers.] I was raised in beautiful Curwood Country of Owosso, MI, home of author James Oliver Curwood.; [a.] Lansing, MI

MCLAIN, JUSTIN
[pen.] Jud McClain; [b.] January 7, 1978; Paducha, KY; [p.] Ronnie and Donna McClain; [ed.] High School Graduate—Graves Co. High School; [occ.] Parts Counter Man at Wheeler-McClain Ford—Mayfield, KY; [oth. writ.] Several poems published by The National Library of Poetry, and in the local newspaper; [pers.] Don't wish.; [a.] Mayfield, KY

MCLAMB, CHRISTOPHER MICHAEL
[b.] July 2, 1979; Harrisburg, PA; [p.] Bonnie Ann McLamb, D. E. McLamb; [ed.] John Harris High School, Harrisburg Arts Magnet School, Susquehanna University; [occ.] Private Voice Instructor and Student; [memb.] Phi Mu Alpha Sinfonia, Students Promoting AIDS Awareness, Dance Team, Improvable; [hon.] NATS Champion, Vocal, Freshman division, President and song leader of the spring 1988, Phi Mu Alpha Pledge Class, Lambda Beta Chapter; [oth. writ.] Poems published in various magazines, anthologies and newspapers; [pers.] One of my main goals in life is to make people laugh because of the times when I had no reason to.; [a.] Selingrove, PA

MCPHERSON, IRMA CLAIRE
[b.] February 25, 1921; Leipers Fork, TN; [p.] John and Vivian Overhey; [m.] James W. McPherson; June 12, 1943; [ch.] James W. Thett, Jerry Lee, John Clair and Jeffrey Allen McPherson;

[ed.] Diploma Nurse, Diploma in Photography, Diploma in Art; [memb.] Tennessee Art League, Madison Association of Retired Persons; [hon.] Two Awards in Photography; sold my first oil painting—was an honor for me; Salutatorian of High School Graduating Class; President of Freshman School of Nursing; [oth. writ.] Two other poems published. "Seasons of the South," "An Anniversary"; [pers.] My inspiration to write poetry, in art and photography, is in nature and God's Holy Word, in children and grandchildren.; [a.] Nashville, TN

MCRONALD, RACHAEL
[b.] June 28, 1974; Paget, Bermuda; [p.] Raymond and Helen Medeiros; [m.] Mark A. McRonald; October 14, 1995; [ch.] Jordan, Daniel; [ed.] Mt. St. Agnes Academy; [occ.] Homemaker

MCSORLEY, JEREMY R.
[pen.] J.R.; [b.] June 29, 1979; Lakewood, WA; [p.] Kathleen T. McSorley, Eric McSorley; [ed.] Graduated with honors, from School of Hard Knochs; [occ.] Songwriter; [hon.] National Library of Poetry, Editor's Choice Award, published in The Spirit of Song, a poetry anthology; [oth. writ.] Dominique; [pers.] Today is tomorrow's yesterday, make it count, it could be your last.; [a.] Lakewood, WA

MEIER, CAROL
[b.] November 6, 1931; Freeport, IL; [m.] Harold Meier; June 7, 1952; [ch.] Catherine, Donna, Diana, Patricia; [ed.] Freeport Senior High School Graduate, Institute of Children's Literature, West Redding, CT; [occ.] Retired—Insurance Administration; [memb.] Ladies Auxillary of Eagles Aerie 679, International Society of Poets; [hon.] Editor's Choice Award—1998; [oth. writ.] "A Shapely Tree" in Aspirations of Pen and Thought published by The Poetry Guild, "I'm Going Fishing" in Soaring with the Wind by The National Library of Poetry, also, "Oh To Be a Mother"; [pers.] I try to give my all at whatever I do and throw in a little humor along the way. If you spread enough happiness, some is bound to fall on yourself.; [a.] Freeport, IL

MELENDEZ, ELYSIA IRENA
[pen.] Lee; [b.] December 28, 1980; New Haven; [p.] Pedro Melendez and Bohdanna Banias; [ed.] Senior in High School; [occ.] Cashier and Waitress; [memb.] Blue Coffee, SADD; [hon.] Award for participation R.J. Julia, Honors through high school; [oth. writ.] School books; [pers.] This world is but canvas to our imagination.; [a.] Branford, CT

MENDOZA, LETTY F.
[pen.] Letty F. Mendoza; [b.] October 21, 1945; Philippines; [p.] Lucia and Benigno Ferrer; [m.] Eduardo Mendoza (deceased); January 22, 1975; [ch.] Carol, Edwin and Earl; [ed.] Graduate of Vocational Teacher; [occ.] Care-giver for Elderly; [memb.] American Heart Association; [pers.] "Measure people by the size of their heart, not the size of their bank account." Be a good person always and be humble of what you're doing.; [a.] National City, CA

MEYER, GRACE A.
[b.] August 21, 1952; Weymouth, MA; [p.] Gilbert and Lucille Meyer; [m.] Andrew Williams; June 21, 1998; [ed.] B.F.A. in Design and Illustration, Southeastern Mass. University Certification; [occ.] Artist, gardener; [hon.] Dean's list high honors; [oth. writ.] Dance upon the Shore, Parnassus; [pers.] I do not write; poetry "rights" me. I often draw first, then write an accompanying poem. I have the gift of being able to express myself either way and have presented my illustrated poems as gifts for friends.

MICHEL, EUGENE C.
[pen.] Eugene C. Michel; [b.] October 7, 1913; Savannah, GA; [p.] Leon, Ann Michel; [ed.] St.

Ann's High School Poughkeepsie, NY, Fordham University, B.S., M.A. Fordham University, endless seminars and workshops; [memb.] Marist Brothers, a teaching society of the Catholic Church, Schools around the world; [hon.] The thousands of students have thought (1933-1986). The last five poems submitted to the Library of Poetry have been chosen for anthology, for that contest; numerous editorial letters and guest columns published in newspapers, interest in poetry, reading and creating is that poetry provides in part the beauty mankind hungers after more that it hungers after food; [pers.] The multiplication of loaves and fishes; [a.] Augusta, GA

MILES, EVELYN G.
[pen.] Evelyn G. Miles; [b.] April 24, 1918; Queens, WV; [p.] John and Merle Marple; [m.] Deceased; April 28, 1936; [ch.] David L. and Mary Louise; [ed.] G.E.D., L.P.N., Writer's Certificate from Famous Writer's School, [occ.] Physical Therapist—10 years, Nursing—21 years; [memb.] Ft. McKinley United Methodist Church, Natt Garden and Prayer Power; [oth. writ.] First poem published, few newspaper items, school items and one true story: "Sheep Killer"; [pers.] Do what is right because it is the right thing to do. No regrets. Love God and your fellowman.; [a.] Dayton, OH

MILLEN, ELAINE P.
[pen.] Lainey Millen; [b.] January 23, 1951; Johnson City, TN: [p.] Vera and Louis Millen; [ed.] B.A., News-Editorial Journalism, Memphis State University; [occ.] Production Manager—Giordano Advertising; [memb.] Charlotte Club of Printing House Craftsman, Hadassan, Temple Israel, Chavurah Tikrah; [hon.] Poet of Merit for Carvings in Stone, Essence of a Dream, and Best Poems of 1997; International Bulletin Competion, 1st place category; [pers.] Poetry is my comfort and my ally. It allows me to express through the written word what I can't do verbally.; [a.] Charlotte, NC

MILLER, ALBERTA
[pen.] Allie; [b.] December 13, 1924; Bloomville, NY; [p.] Silas and Maude Cleveland; [m.] Ellsworth W. Miller (deceased); October 27, 1949; [ed.] Graduate of DLI and Franklin Central School, Franklin, New York, University of State of New York, Delhi, NY; [memb.] Christ Community, Church of Carman, American Center for Law and Justice, National Associations of Evangelicals, President Club, General Electric Quarter Century Club, The Rutherford Council; [hon.] Merit Award, National Association of Evangelical Certificate of Appreciation, Moody Bible Institute, City Mission of Schdy. Christian Coalition; [oth. writ.] Short story; [pers.] Any talent I may have is a gift from my Lord.; [a.] Schenectady, NY

MILLER, DIANE T.
[pen.] Diane T. Miller; [b.] October 29, 1948; Palatka, FL; [ed.] U. of Tampa, U. of S. Florida; [occ.] Nurse; [memb.] World Vision; Red Cross; Friends of the Forest; Sierra; [oth. writ.] Other writings only published: "Love" in With Flute and Drum and Pen; [pers.] We must realize that all life is connected. It is impossible for us to live without touching the life of another.; [a.] Marietta, GA

MILLER, HANNAH
[b.] August 29, 1983; [p.] Terry and Joann Miller; [ed.] Just entering High School at ACCHS; [oth. writ.] Written many poems and short stories, currently writing a story with best friend; [pers.] I usually write about sad things such as death. I guess it comes easily to me since I've endured three losses.; [a.] Atchison, KS

MILLER, KEN
[b.] July 30, 1949; Morgantown, WV; [p.] Bill Miller (deceased), Louise Wright; [m.] Sheryl L. Miller; February 12, 1972; [ch.] Kristin L. Miller; [ed.] DuVal High, Prince George's Community

College, The American University; [occ.] Grocery Store Dairy Stocker/Checker, Safeway, Dunkirk, MD; [memb.] US Congressional Staff Member (1970-1992) Distinguished member of the National Author's Registry; [hon.] A third prize in the NLP's North American Open Poetry Contest (1998). Seven NLP's Editor's Choice Awards, Eight poems selected for the NLP's "Sound of Poetry" series, Honorable Mention, Fall 1997 Iliad Literary Awards Program; [oth. writ.] Ten poems in NLP anthologies, a poem in The Poetry Guild's Anthology, By the Light of the Moon, a poem in the Iliad Press anthology, Moments; [pers.] "Barfly Blues," my poem in this anthology, came from bar visits and people I knew in 1993, a time when I was unemployed. I hope anyone who reads something I have written will, at the very least, not be bored.; [a.] Port Republic, MD

MISSOURI, MARCELLINA RENEE
[b.] January 29, 1962; Washington, D.C.; [p.] William D. Missouri, Sandra W. Missouri; [ch.] Sanarah Renee Missouri; [ed.] University of the District of Columbia, William McKinley High School; [occ.] Records Control Clerk, U.S. Department of Commerce; [oth. writ.] Poem published in the book, The Hourglass; [pers.] Most of my poems come from my strong belief in God.; [a.] Washington, D.C.

MITCHELL, KATTIA
[b.] May 19, 1985; Redlands, CA; [p.] Jason Mitchel and Elizabeth Lewis; [ed.] Student at Serrano Middle School in Highland, CA; [ed.] Student at Serrano Middle School in Highland, CA; [occ.] Student; [hon.] Honor Roll, Honor Society Student Council, many writing Awards and presentations at Author's Teas at my school; [oth. writ.] "An Emotional Poem," "If I Could Fly," "If I Had Wings"; [pers.] I express myself more in writing than in words and I try to show that in my poetry.; [a.] Highland, CA

MITCHELL, NORMA JEAN
[b.] August 28, 1942; St. Augustine, FL; [p.] Jeffie L., Willie Mae Mitchell; [ed.] R.J. Murray High, Florida Memorial College; [occ.] Disabled—retired Pre-Kindergarden Teacher; [memb.] Rogers Memorial United Methodist Church; [pers.] I hope to help people think about the facts of life.; [a.] Bradenton, FL

MIXELL, GEORGE S.
[b.] June 13, 1921; Enola, PA; [p.] Foster; [m.] Miriam M. Mixell; November 20, 1997; [ed.] 11 years and 4 years 7 months in Army and Civil Service tests for many positions such as Packer, Chemical, Storage; [memb.] VFW Lifetime; [hon.] Too many to mention—art awards, safety awards and govt. cost-saving awards; [oth. writ.] Book of life from age 5-75—Close Encounter, A True Story; [pers.] I have not published my book as it would cost too much; Vantage Press, NY, wanted to published it—8000.00-some dollars to put it on the market worldwide.; [a.] Carlisle, PA

MOLESKI, PHILIP ALLEN
[b.] February 4, 1962; MI; [p.] Joe, Mary Moleski; [m.] Dawn Moleski; February 23, 1996; [ch.] Jessica, Jenna, Nolan; [ed.] Galsburg High School, Associate in Arts with Honors at Kalamazoo Valley Community College; [oth. writ.] Many poems, some short stories and songs—nothing published; [pers.] Words lacking benefit to the intended's ear should be sheared off like sheep's wool, stockpiled until used purposefully at a later date; language properly used can be made into a colorful quilt.; [a.] Plainwell, MI

MONGAN, MARY K.
[pen.] Mongan, Mary Katharine; [b.] May 8, 1967; Milwaukee, WI; [p.] Marilyn and Dennis Mongan; [ed.] Mount Mary College, B.A. in Education/ Communications, a minor in History; [occ.] Data Entry, Mount Mary College, Fund Raising Department; [pers.] I saw it a bumper sticker—"Very Funny Scotty, Now Beam Down My Clothes!"; [a.] Wauwatosa, WI

MOODY, JANE ANN
[pen.] Jenny Wren; [b.] August 27, 1935; Galesburg, IL; [p.] Wallace Chadwick and Georgia June (Kincaid) Behringer; [ch.] Steffanie Ann Brown and Tepe Rench Hamilton; [ed.] University of Illinois—Bachelor of Science, Satisfactorily completed Dietic Internship—University of Michigan; [occ.] Raise Sheep; [memb.] Wataga Congregational Church Galesburg Chapter Order of Eastern Star 3 times past matron; [oth. writ.] Poem "God's Blessings of the Miracle Messenger" published in Above the Clouds; [pers.] "With God all things are possible."—Matthew 19:2 and my mother's favorite saying: "This above all: To thine own self be true—thou canst not then be false to anyone," from Shakespeare's Hamlet—Scene 3, Act 1; [a.] Galesburg, IL

MORRIS, MELODY
[pen.] Melmor. Melody Littlefield; [b.] May 2, 1972; Portland, ME; [p.] Vera Wajerski; [ch.] Paige Littlefield; [ed.] Computer Learning Center—Studying to be a Network Administrator; [oc.] Cashier at Dominick's Food Store; [hon.] Editor's Choice Award from The National Library of Poetry for the poem "Mother"; [oth. writ.] "Mother"; [pers.] Every day can be a new discovery.; [a.] Streamwood, IL

MORROW, RUSH T.
[b.] February 25, 1897; Topeka, IN; [p.] Frank D. and Laura (Morrel) Morrow; [m.] Violet E. Morrow; March 26, 1959; [ch.] R. Conrad Morrow and Mel Morrow; [ed.] H.S. Charlotte, MI, Argubright Business College, Battle MI, Creek Real Estate Course and Appraisal Writing Courses; [occ.] Retired, former Corporate Pay Master and Real Estate; [memb.] First Baptist Church, American Legion, VFW, Nat'l. Assn. of Realtors, served in Michigan Nat'l. Grand under Pershing to "tame" Poncho Villa in `17; [hon.] World War 1 Veteran; [oth. writ.] Collection of 300 poems published in NLP and in several papers and magazines; [pers.] What you put into your head, no one ever take away from you. "Trust in the Lord with all your heart, and lean not to your own understanding."—Proverbs 3:5; [a.] Charlotte, NY

MOSS, BILLIE LOU PIKE
[pen.] Billie Lou Pike Moss; [b.] July 4, 1939; St. Joseph, MO; [p.] Jerva Mae and Amos William Pike; [m.] Selig Moss; [m.] September 15, 1978; [ch.] Bob, Tuesday, Robin, Billie Jo; [ed.] Bellermine Jefferson Catholic High, Ventura College and Oxnard College; [occ.] Social Worker; [memb.] National Kidney Foundation, Ventura Doll Club; [hon.] First Place at country fair for hecktie quilts; [oth. writ.] Fraudulent Friend, Sweet Deceiver, Tear of Jewels and Pain a Grown, Billie's Angel, Rainbows and Rain, and Profound Sound; [pers.] Perseverance, Passion and Patience along with love of God and country will most certainly see us thru life's trials, but we need to pratice generosity of soul.; [a.] Eugene, OR

MOSS, LOIS N.
[b.] July 11, 1930; Hampton, AR; [p.] Jessie, Sally Ware; [m.] Ardie V. Moss; September 4, 1956; [ch.] Larry D., Anthony G., Ardine Y., Ardie Jr.; [memb.] Providence M.B. Church, S.S. Student Missionary Worker, Sanctuary Choir, Golden Agers Christ and G.M.W.A. Choir Member; [hon.] The R.M. Hospital V.S.P, The Ann Helloway Award of G.M.W.A.; [oth. writ.] Three poems published in The National Library of Poetry; [pers.] Life is about love, hatred and eternal desire. For this cause I have to give total control to God, in whom I believe. I enjoy writing expressions of all mankind, trying to bring out good in all subjects.; [a.] Rockford, IL

MUHAMMAD, ABDUL ALI
[pen.] Charles Brown; [b.] March 2, 1952; BPT; [p.] William A. Brown and Hazel E. Brown; [ch.] Keyshea, Termaine, Tawana, Mary Kay; [ed.] Trumball High, New Haven Academy of Business; [memb.] Life Member of Vietnam Veterans of America, Distinguished Member of the International Society of Poets; [hon.] The International Poetry Hall of Fame, Golden Poet Award, Merit Awards, Outstanding Achievement in Poetry and Editor's Choice Awards; [oth. writ.] Golden Treasury of Great Poems, New American Poetry Anthology, Who's Who in Poetry, Searching for Soft Voices, Thoughts by Candlelight, Best Poems of 1998; [a.] Westhaven, CT

MURPHY, MARION
[a.] Mastic Beach, NY

MYERS, BETTY DEAN
[pen.] Betty Dean Myers; [b.] November 11, 1946; Tampa, FL; [p.] Chester Olin and Nadine Ruth Myers; [ch.] Wren Wade (son), Amanda Wade (daughter); [pers.] My brother Chester Olin Myers Jr. ("Bubby")—I surely miss him and look with anticipation to that time in eternity when we will see each other again and this time we'll talk. How much richer is my life because he lived, how much richer is my soul because I knew him.; [a.] Winter Park, FL

MYERS, EVONNE
[b.] January 14, 1977; Joliet, IL; [p.] Mary and Harold Myers; [ed.] Graduated from Joliet Junior College on May 15, 1998 with an A.A .Degree; [occ.] Cashier at a local beauty supply store; [pers.] "It's better to try and fail than to not try at all."; [a.] Joliet, IL

NASHTAR, DR. SYEDA SUHELA
[pen.] Suhela Nashtar; [b.] Gwaliar U.P., India; [ed.] Ph.D. in Languistics, Aligarh M. University, Aligarh, India; [memb.] Member of Aligarli Association, Atlanta; [pers.] Poetry is the powerful expression of sensitive heart and reflection of thoughtful mind.; [a.] Lawrenceville, GA

NASTASI, NICHOLAS A.
[b.] July 22, 1932; Paulsboro, NJ; [p.] Joseph and Angeline Nastasi; [ch.] Nicholas Jr. and William; [ed.] Paulsboro High, Rutgers S.J College, Franklin Penna. Medical School of Laboratory Technology; [occ.] Medical Technology and U.S. Postal Service; [memb.] AMT, AOPA Pilots Assoc, DAV, 4 time commander VFW, Knights of Columbus, NJ Hall of Fame Pilots Assoc. Poets International; [oth. writ.] The National Library of Poetry's Winds f Freedom; [pers.] I enjoy writing about life, family, nature and romantic feelings in life.; [a.] Lindenwold, NJ

NATH, DORIS SMITH
[pen.] Doris Smith Nath, Doris Leroy Bennet; [b.] 1919; Tacoma, WA; [m.] Nathan Budd Nath; [ch.] Terry Patricia Christine; [ed.] Child Actor—Stage, Screen and Radio Art and Music Pierce College Ministerial Graduate Science of mind; [occ.] Miraculous Finger Print publisher CO, flight into infinity; [memb.] Owner of Child Haven Preschool in Reseda (10 yrs.); [hon.] Computer Analyst—First Interstate Bank—17 years, WH letter of commendation and Merit; [oth. writ.] Flight into Infinity, The Empyreans, Beyond Time, Historical Novel, Tapestry of Love, poetry books; [pers.] My vision for mankind is one of constant evolving growth towards perfection. Courageous is my way of life.; [a.] Desert Hot Springs, CA

NATHAN WOODS, XZAVIER ASHANT TREDDIE
[pen.] Xzavier; [b.] August 13; [ed.] Western Alamance High; [hon.] Principal Award, Editor's Choice Award; [pers.] If you truly care or love for an individual you must accept their many different individualities.; [a.] Altamahaw, NC

NELSON, ANGELA
[b.] August 24, 1973; Cleveland, OH; [ed.] Westerville North High, Miami University in Oxford, OH; [a.] Westerville, OH

NELSON, CHRISTINA
[pen.] Christina M. Nelson; [b.] February 11, 1949; Baunade, Germany; [p.] Margareta Ekstrand; [ch.] Melissa Sharpling, Shawn J. Nelson; [ed.] Grade School and Private Business College in Germany, High School, Business College, EPCC, El Paso, TX; [occ.] Accountant; [memb.] Hayashis Martial Arts Academy, ElPaso, TX; [hon.] Am. Bus. Womens Assoc., Women of the Year 1986, Very Involved in Martial Arts such as Kendo, Kickboxing, Kali, Jeet Kune Do, Wing Chum, Aikido, Judo and Tai Chi; [oth. writ.] Published by Nat'l. Lib. of Poetry 1997 and 1998, Participated in first Poetry Reading at EPCC, El Paso, TX, Preparing a book with poetry for publishing; [pers.] Studying martial arts has made a tremendous difference in my life— even after a really hard and exhausting workout or sparing session, I feel renewed with energy and ready for a new day. What is the next challenge that I have to overcome?; [a.] El Paso, TX

NELSON, JENNE
[pen.] Jenni Nelson; [b.] March 22, 1970; Fontana, CA; [p.] Jack and Sue Vermillion; [occ.] Telecommunications; [memb.] Moo Gong Do Martial Arts School in Laguna Hills, CA; [hon.] Black Belt, several Most Valuable and Inspirational Player Awards in the 15 years of soccer played growing up; [oth.writ,] Midnight, Gift, Moonlight, My Sea, Sunset, Shadows, Timeless—all poems; [pers.] Vulnerability is one's biggest strength; our naked self is who we are, the essence of our purity and creative being.; [a.] Laguna Hills, CA

NEWELL, BARBARA S.
[pen.] Barbara S. Newell; [b.] February 14, 1949; St. Louis, MO; [memb.] Humanity; [hon.] Resiliency and Humility, Endurance; [pers.] Believe that through art, moments of Transedence may be shared, personally sustained by Margaret Mead, Carl G. Jung, and Robert Zimmeman; background— Anthropology and gnostic Christianity.; [a.] Kiekwood, MO

NEWHOUSE, GLORIA
[b.] August 6, 1946; Ansted, WV; [p.] Hechert and Vivian Buckland; [m.] Paul, March 17, 1987; [ch.] Donna Nottingham, Brenda Jager, April Highstrom; [occ.] Homemaker; [memb.] Grange, U.S. Chess Federation; [hon.] Tiffany Award, Manpower Temp Serv.; [oth. writ.] Chess, National Library of Poetry; [pers.] Writing poetry provides comfort and helps deal with everyday life, whether good or bad.; [a.] Cupertino, CA

NEWTON, MANDY
[b.] July 23, 1979; Benton Hospital; [p.] Homer and Marilyn Newton; [ed.] Received High School Diploma in May of 1998; [hon.] Recognized as one of many students in Who's Who Among American High School Students; [oth. writ.] "Loneliness" published in Traces of Yesterday; [pers.] I strive to write poems that get in touch with everyone's loving yet serious side.; [a.] Benton, KY

NOEL, DEANNA
[pen.] Deanna Noel; [b.] September 6, 1962; Concord, CA; [p.] Howard and Roberta Bisek; [ed.] Pinole Valley High School, Pinole, CA, A.A. Degree from Contra Costa College, San Pablo, CA in dramatic Arts, currently studying for B.S. degree in Psych. at CSU Hayward; [occ.] Student at California State Hayward; [memb.] Rollingwood Baptist Church; [hon.] Editor's Choice Award for my poem titled "Aftermath"; [oth. writ.] "The Beating," published in Memories of Tomorrow; "Aftermath," published in Best Poems of 1997; [pers.] If our society lived by the golden rule, the world would be a much better and safer place.; [a.] San Pablo, CA

NORMAN, ELAINA
[pen.] Lena Love; [b.] April 12, 1983; Flint, MI; [p.] Keith Norman, Nanci Norman; [ed.] Currently a student at Flint Central High School; [occ.] Student; [memb.] Superintendant's Student Advisory Board, Student Congress; [oth. writ.] Previously published only twice, once in 1995 and again in 1997; [pers.] I strive for success and happiness in everything I do.; [a.] Flint, MI

NORRELL, GENEVA STOCKTON
[pen.] Geneva Stockton Norrell; [b.] July 18, 1928; Okolona, AR; [p.] Alfred and Gertie Stockton; [m.] John C. Norrell; December 16, 1978; [ch.] Charuly and Wade Williams; [ed.] Okolona High School, C and H Modeling and Fashion Display, Hot Springs, AR, National Institute, for Residence Exterior and Interior Design, Dallas, TX; [occ.] Retired Home Builder; [memb.] Wesleyan Service Guild, Baptist Church, American Cancer Society; [hon.] National Homes, Poet Laureate Plaques; [oth. writ.] Poems and articles printed in various newspapers and magazines, poems written and read in public appearances for special occassions; [pers.] I have no major educational degrees. My genealogy is undistinguished. What you read in my poems reflects what I have to say about God, Jesus, The Holy Spirit, my loved ones and friends, also about the wonderful world God created for mankind to live in. May God get the glory for the words in rhyme that He places on my heart to write.; [a.] DeSoto, TX

ODEN, SARAH
[pen.] Kirk; [b.] December 30, 1942; Athens, TN; [p.] Mignon-NB Kirk; [m.] December 21, 1963; [ed.] B.S.—University of TN, M.A.—University of DC; [memb.] Phi Beta Phi, Int. Soc. of Poets, NEA, Saint Pauls UMC; [hon.] Published numerous times, Phi Beta Kappa; [oth. writ.] Time Was, Spring with You, Spring, Summer Clouds, Night Now; [a.] Etowah, TN

OHANNA, VICTORIA ANGELINE
[b.] November 17, 1983; Brazil; [p.] Isaac Ohanna, Carol Ohanna; [ed.] Sophomore at Oldfields School, Glenoe, MD; St. Johns University program for gifted students, Queens, NY; [occ.] Student; [memb.] Permanent Press newspaper, Environmental Awareness; [hon.] Lacrosse Coaches Award; [oth. writ.] "Soar" published in A Whispering Silence; [a.] Rego Park, NY

OHRENSCALL, JOHN C.
[b.] September 16, 1935; Wichita, KS; [p.] Robert and Dorothy Ohrenschall; [ch.] Mark Alan, James Edward; [ed.] Sacramento High School, Reed College, University of Colorado, University of WI; [occ.] Interpreter; [memb.] Atlanta Israeli Dance Group; [hon.] California Scholastic Federation. Dean's List, University of Colorado School of Law; [oth. writ.] Previously published by The National Library of Poetry, Co-authored article in University of Poetry, Land and Water Law Review, Contributed to University of Colorado Law Review and Nevada State Bar Journal; [pers.] Amid the duality of good and evil, I seek to emphasize joyful energy as the essence, braCha, of life. I have been greatly influenced by writers as diverse as Dante Alighieri, Jack London, and Peter Hoeg.; [a.] Decatur, GA

OLIVER, JOSEPH WILLIAM
[pen.] Joe Oliver; [b.] August 18, 1936; Grants Pass, OR; [p.] Joseph and Vesta Oliver; [m.] Divorced; [ch.] Joseph Karl Oliver and Margaret Joan Olivers; [ed.] M.S.—Applied Physics, 6-60, U.C.C.A; [occ.] Parking Attendant; [memb.] The Planetary Society and National Audubon Society; [hon.] Editor's Choice; [oth. writ.] River; [pers.] I am happy to be continuing in the arts.; [a.] Pasadena, CA

OLSEN, DAVID
[pen.] David Olsen; [b.] December 31, 1928; Floral

Park, L.I, NY; [p.] Sverre E. and Hilda Marion; [m.] Penelope; September 12, 1965; [ed.] Florida Southern College, Lakeland, FL, B.S./Magna Cum Laude, L.L.B. Blackstone School of Law Chicago, IL, J.D. Blaries; [occ.] Patent Prosecution; [memb.] US Patent Office Bar, District of Columbia Bar Association; [oth. writ.] Textbook, "Two Wrongs Don't Make a Writer"; Full Length Novel, "Pacific Memories"; three poems Nova Aryas, four poems Cymru.

OPAL, MAUREEN
[a.] Fountain Hills, AZ

ORTIZ, BETTY
[b.] August 5, 1968; Chicago, IL; [p.] Miguela and Betty Ortiz; [ed.] Lane Tech H.S. Malcolmx EMT certified S. Francis Paramedic program; [occ.] Licensed Paramedic, Medical Express Ambulance Co., Chicago, IL; [oth. writ.] Many publishings in other anthologies and poems to special friends; [pers.] I write to express my emotions in my life and maybe to help others understand theirs. No one is alone in life; someone is by your side.; [a.] Chicago, IL

OSHER, REGINA LYNN
[pen.] Gina Osher; [b.] February 11, 1951; Topeka, KS; [p.] Stanley Osher, MD and Shirley Minor Osher; [ed.] El Cerritos High School, El Cerrito, CA; University of Oregon, Eugene, Oregon, graduated 1973, Bachelor Degree: CSPA, Community Service and Public Affairs; [occ.] Employment Counselor, Welfare Work Program, Alameda County Social Services Agency, Oakland, CA; [oth. writ.] Approximately 100 poems to date, also have written four children's stories: "The Legend of Greenhorn," "The Barefoot Boys," "Sky And Cloud Together," and "The Little Plum Tree"; also written an article: "Journal of a Californian" about experiences, observations, thoughts and afterthoughts in regard to the October 17, 1989 Bay Earthquake; taken the first step toward writing for the first novel; [pers.] I believe that people should be connected by the down-to-earth aspects of life and I revere Mother Earth. I try to reflect this in my poetry. I try to create poetry that will promote peace on earth and peace of mind, which is timeless and enjoyable to all. My poems are dedicated to The World: May it flourish, May peace reign, may peace endure.; [a.] Alameda, CA

OSTRANGER, KAREN ANN
[pen.] Kate Garrett; [b.] March 6, 1955; Milwaukee, WI; [p.] Ronald and Maryann Ostranger; [ch.] Alia; [ed.] West Allis Central High School, Denver Metro Community College, Auraria Community College; [occ.] Consultant/Speaker, Raven's Heart; [memb.] International Society of Poets, Religious Science of the Mind; [hon.] Numerous Award for public speaking, Original Oratory, writing and singing and performance, 18 Editor's Choice Awards, The National Library of Poetry [oth. writ.] "Promise" published in The Peace We Knew; [pers.] "It's a funny thing about past experience— it can be our reason to overcome any obstacle and live the life of our dreams or our excuse not to."; [a.] Port Angeles, WA

OTTO, ELEANOR
[ed.] B.A. University of Rochester (1 year), postgraduate studies in Political Science, Columbia University, various special courses in music: voice, opera, music history at the Julliard School of Music, etc.; [occ.] Poet, musician, composer and artist (frequent appearances in the opera "La Boheme"); [hon.] Numerous prizes for poetry; [oth. writ.] Seven songs recorded (lyrics and music), four published books of poetry, two plays, paintings exhibited in various galleries.

OWENS, PEGGY ANN
[pen.] March 17, 1965; Springfield, MO; [p.] Luther Deckard, Doris Deckard; [m.] Robert Lee Owens; July 1, 1995; [ch.] Jason Lee, Chad Ray,

Jamie Lynn, Linsie Michelle; [ed.] Kickapoo High School Spfd. MO; [occ.] Full-time Mother, Bookkeeper, also Bobcat Operator; [hon.] Editor's Choice Award, Poetry Hall of Fame; [oth. writ.] Elected into Poetry Hall of Fame, also poem published through The National Library of Poetry; [pers.] I have been blessed in my life! I feel the Lord has given me a very unique talent—I like to share my blessings for others to read.; [a.] Macks Creek, MO

PAES, JOYCE MARIA
[occ.] Management Consultant; [hon.] Editor's Choice Award, The National Library of Poetry, 1997, In Dappled Sunlight; [oth. writ.] Several poems published in various anthologies, numerous business articles and manuals; [pers.] The ability to write has come as a gift from my creator. He alone is worthy of any recognition give to this talent.; [a.] San Antonio, TX

PALMER, DENETTE
[pen.] Denette Krpan Palmer; [b.] September 27, 1965; Alton, IL; [p.] Judith Spiess Krpan, Anthony Krpan; [m.] Paul Palmer; July 19, 1986; [ch.] Jason Thomas, Nicholas Anthony; [ed.] Alton Senior High School, Lewis and Clark Comm. College; [a.] Cottage Hills, IL

PALMER, FLORENCE B.
[pen.] Loren Palmer; [b.] 1908; Winsted, CT; [ed.] Elmira College, Elmira NY, B.A.—English Literature; [memb.] American Association of University Women; [hon.] AAUW Education Foundation; [a.] Elgin, IL

PANCRAZI, PIERRETTE
[b.] November 8, 1926; France; [p.] Alois, Marie Greff; [m.] Ernest; November 19, 1955; [ch.] Peter, Katie, Andy; [ed.] Graduated N.Y. State University at Buffalo. Majored in Education and English; [occ.] Retired Teacher; [memb.] Assistance League Volunteer; [hon.] Raiceda family and husband; [oth. writ.] Presently working on a book of short stories; [pers.] I hope my writings will reflect why I am here and hope through them I will not be forgotten.; [a.] Yuma, AZ

PARKARD, ALAN H.
[b.] August 24, 1938; Huron, SD; [p.] Bruce and Ruth Packard; [m.] Judith; November 24, 1962; [ch.] Melissa, Michael; [ed.] York Comm. HS—Elmhurst, IL; B.A.—Elmhurst College; M.A.—Rockford College Rockford, IL; [occ.] Teacher (English)—St. Mary's Spring HS, Fond du Lac; [memb.] National Council of Teachers of English, Kettle Moraine Press Assoc.—Bd. of Directors; [hon.] Who's Who Among American Teachers, Silver Beaver Award—Bay Lakes Council, BSA; [a.] Fond du Lac, WI

PARKER, THELMA JO
[pen.] Thella Griff; [b.] November 12, 1915; Rogers Bell, TX; [p.] Jordan Simeon Griffin; [m.] LaNora Fredricka Moeller; December 11, 1954; [ch.] William Dennis, Paul, Sherly, and Karen; [ed.] Tahoka High School, Draughon's Business College, Long Beach City, Machine Shop, Various Courses in many adult courses; [occ.] Housewife and writer; [memb.] Church of Jesus Christ of Latter Day Saints, no other current memberships—too busy; [hon.] High School Salutatorian, and several others, including Teaching Certificate, Poetry Awards, etc.; [oth. writ.] Words and Music; "Leave Me Your Heart," "Uh Huh," "Babbling Brook," "Welcome, Little Angel," and story: "This Is My Life," plus: poems, greeting cards—have not attempted publication (seemed egotistical of me!); [pers.] Number eleven has some significance for me; therefore, as much as possible, each line of my poetry contains 11 syllables. My desire is not only to be entertaining in my writing but in some way help my reader friend.; [a.] Placerville, CA

PARRISH, PENELOPE
[pen.] Penelope Parrish; [b.] Palo Alto, CA; [p.] Col. and Mrs. Richard L. Temple; [m.] Richard Wolfe; July 29, 1991; [ch.] Lori Ann and John Patrick; [ed.] Bethesda Elementary, American School of Beirut, Bellevue Main and Rantoul Township High, Santa Barbara City College; [occ.] Telephone Communications Operator; [memb.] American Dowser Association, Self-Realization Fellowship (SRF), Good Sam Full-time RVER; [oth. writ.] Published in Tracing Shadows and Best Poems of 1997; [pers.] To me, poems are like looking at paintings in a gallery: One must stand there and take it all in to be really enjoying the vision.; [a.] Las Cruces, NM

PASCIUTO, VICTORIA
[b.] June 2, 1982; [p.] Frank and Margaret Pasciuto; [ed.] High School; [occ.] Retail Sales Clerk; [hon.] Editor's Choice Award from National Library of Poetry, honor roll in school; [pers.] I am inspired by the breathtakingly beautiful and simple things in life.; [a.] Lynnfield, MA

PATE, GEORGIA ELIZABETH
[pen.] Georgia Elizabeth Pate; [b.] August 28, 1933; Ross Co., OH; [p.] Martin and Carrie Miller Ralston; [m.] James M. Pate (deceased); August 6, 1955; [ch.] James Jude, Carrie Elizabeth, Mary Kathryn, Amy Theresa, Martha Ann; [ed.] Huntington HS, Ross Co. Lay Pastoral Ministry Program at the Athenaeum of Ohio Mt. St. Mary Seminary, Cincinnati, Ohio; [occ.] Coordinator of Religious Education—St. Julie Billiart Church; [memb.] St. Vincent DePaul Society, Member of the International Society of Poets; [oth. writ.] Holding Time, Simple Childhood, Life Deemed Worthless; [pers.] All gifts come from God. The greatest of gifts are life and the ability to love.; [a.] Hamilton, OH

PEAKE, RUSSELL C.
[b.] May 20, 1949; Highland Park; [p.] Russel and Geraldine; [m.] Christine A. Peake; June 18, 1988; [ch.] Jessica and Cynthia Peare; [ed.] Lincoln Park High School; [occ.] Inventory Control Clerk, Ford Motor Co.; [oth. writ.] Several poems in other anthologies; [pers.] I've seen the world with all of its good and bad.; [a.] Taylor, MI

PECK, MICHAEL W.
[b.] February 12, 1955; Rapid City SD; [p.] Herbert A. and Eflet E. Peck; [ch.] Krystle Lee Edsberg Peck; [ed.] University of Alaska, Tanana Valley Community College Folks; [occ.] Service Manager, North Bay Copier, Santa Rosa, CA; [a.] Santa Rosa, CA

PENN, ODELLA JONES
[pen.] Dell Penn; [b.] July 15, 1930; West, VA; [p.] Nathan and Alice Jones; [m.] James W. Penn; December 23, 1958; [ch.] Kim, Sandy and James; [ed.] Excelsion High School, Community College, Kindergarten projects; [memb.] Public School Retirement System, PA Association of School Retires; [oth. writ.] I Am Women, Save Our Children. God's Country; [pers.] My poems are from experience, passion for others and a life of hope and dreams that anyone can accomplish.; [a.] Philadelphia, PA

PERALTA, ISMAEL O.
[b.] December 14, 1936; [p.] Blas T. Peralta, Alberta Ortiz Peralta; [m.] Esther Miguel Peralta; April 21, 1961; [ch.] Edmund, Demler and Imelda; [ed.] Northern Luzon Adventist College Academy Dept. 1955, Blackstone School of Law Inc., Management Consultant-Harvard Business Pasadena Unified School District 1984; [occ.] Certified Nurse Assistant; [memb.] International Society of Poets, Distinguished Member, Republican National Committee, S.D.A. Church, Highlander Club; [hon.] CNA of the Year 1998, Most Punctual CNA 1998, International Poetry Hall of Fame, GOP/TV Founder Washington D.C., FDR Memorial Registry, Washington, D.C., Editor's Choice Award 1997, Capital Award 1997; [oth. writ.] Reflection of a Poet, The Scenic Route 1997, The Death of a Princess, A City on a Plateau, High Landen Club Information Panacea—Inter. Poetry Hall of Fame Museum; [pers.] "If you have done it, to the least of my brethren, you have done it unto me," saith the Lord—Matthew 25:40; [a.] Pasadena, CA

PEREZ, CINDY
[b.] July 9, 1973; McAllen, TX; [p.] Robert and Lucy Perez; [m.] Adrian A. Aniceto; November 7, 1998; [ed.] McAllen High School, University of Texas—Pan American, South Texas Community College; [occ.] Billing Clerk at Van Burkleo Motors, McAllen, Co-Owner K.C. and Co. Bookkeeping Service; [hon.] Poetry published in high school and college literary magazines and previously published in The National Library of Poetry Awards from Duke University for UIL Writing and a Presidential Award for Academic Acheivement; [oth. writ.] The Circle, I See, Hear, And Feel, Finding Myself; [pers.] Through the love and patience from my mother and fiance, I can achieve my most difficult goals in life.; [a.] McAllen, TX

PETTIT, JOHANNA
[b.] July 18, 1934; New London, CT; [p.] Silvestro Grasso, Frances Pescatello Grasso; [m.] Melvin Pettit; June 12, 1954; [ch.] Duane and Craig; [ed.] High school graduate; [occ.] Pettit Plumbing and Heating partner; [memb.] Rosicrucian Order; [a.] Ledyard, CT

PHILLIPS, DR. GEORGE O., SR.
[pen.] George O. Phillips Sr.; [b.] May 9, 1916; Tobago, WI; [p.] H.A., Helena Phillips; [m.] Sadie C. Phillips; June 1948; [ch.] William, George, Gaylord, Lloyd, Linda; [ed.] Elementary/Secondary, T and T, W.I. B.Sc., 1953, M.Sc., 1955, Nebraska U. Ed.D., 1969, U. of Pennsylvania; [occ.] Retired, Founder/President, Non-profit Association, TPA; [memb.] International Reading Association, Kappa Delta Pi 1978, International Society of Poets; [hon.] Delta Kappa Pi-Education, International Reading Association, Tobago Progressive Association of the U.S. Inc., Several Church Awards and Momentos; [oth. writ.] "Study Habits and Attitudes of College Freshmen, Leaders In Education 1974, Several Publications In Educational Literature; [pers.] Have faith in yourself and move mountains.; [a.] Laurelton, NY

PICKIN, TODD EMIL
[b.] December 19, 1978; Anapolis, MD; [p.] Kathy and William Pickin Jr.; [ed.] Sandalwood HS, University of North Florida; [occ.] Computer Consultant; [hon.] Who's Who of American High School Students; [oth. writ.] "Teacher" and "The Hand of Destiny"; [pers.] Don't just educate your children, enlighten them.—Todd Dockingbay;[a.] Jacksonville, FL

PINSON, REBECCA ANN
[b.] August 12, 1978; [memb.] International Society of Poets and American Auxiliary; [hon.] Poetry Award from Central High School, Two Editor's Choice Awards from The National Library of Poetry; [oth. writ.] Six poems with The National Library of Poetry, one poem with The Poetry Guild; [pers.] Throughout my life I have been picked on. I say, they were all jealous. Besides, where are they now, the ones that were so "good" with the spoken words?—On skidrow!; [a.] Glendale, AZ

PISZ, JOSEPH L.
[b.] October 4, 1930; Detroit, MI; [p.] Louis, Regina; [m.] Greta; December 12, 1970; [ch.] Tina, Thomas; [ed.] AS degree in General Education, Olympic College; [occ.] U.S. Army Retired; [memb.] Reserve Officer's Association; [hon.] Bronze Star, Combat Infantry Badge; [oth. writ.] Children's Stories, Sampson The Clumsy Cat, Wildwind, Bat Bear, Varoom, King of the Jungle,

Charger, Duel in the Sand Box, A Bird Comes A-Calling; [pers.] I believe that children's stories should uplifting in a philosophical sense as well as entertaining.; [a.] Poulsbo, WA

POE, BELLE
[pen.] Lesa K. Bledsoe-Thompson and Belle Poe; [b.] September 4, 1958; Kansas City, MO; [p.] Ronald D. and Laura B. Schroll; [m.] Terry A. Thompson; January 26, 1987; [ch.] Tammy-Cherie, Heather; [ed.] 1982 Iowa G.E.D. at Western Iowa Tech. Sioux City IA 1986 writing and literature courses at Morningside College, Sioux City, IA; [occ.] Housewife; [memb.] Distinguished Member of the International Society of Poets and SIGB (Siouxland Information Group for the Blind); [hon.] 1989 Merit Award for "Rights of Passage" from World of Poetry—Sacramento, CA; 1998 Editor's Choice Award for "Sublime" "Moonlit" Invitation "Wayward Son" "Love Among Friends" from The National Library of Poetry in Owings Mills, MD; [oth. writ.] "Into Me" American Poetry anthology. "Moonlit" Invitation "Traces of Yesterday"; "Sublime" Adrift of the breeze. "Wayward Son" Above the Clouds; "Love Among Friends" The Glistening Stars; "Everlasting" The Poetry Guild; several editorials in local newspaper; [pers.] Poetry speaks of and to the hearts and souls of all that is living. It chronicles the past and embraces the future.; [a.] Sioux City, IA

POLLARA, MARY E.
[b.] September 16, 1962; Albuquerque, NM; [p.] Victor G. Pollara and Aldona Gloria Wayler; [ed.] Passaic High School graduate; William Patterson College, B.A. in Music; [occ.] Bank teller; [oth. writ.] Have written many poems on and off in my life, but none has been published except one with The National Library of Poetry; [pers.] The poem I wrote was written after witnessing a driver run over a woodchuck. That person had no regard for life. I rushed him to the hospital; he could be saved, but he did not make it. I wanted to send the message to those who read my poem that whether or not you love animals, they are our balance in our world and nature. It's time we respect them and stop abusing them.; [a.] Eatontown, NJ

POOL, VELMA R.
[b.] June 5, 1920; Garden, KS; [p.] Eli E. Gift and Rose C. Gift (both deceased); [m.] Frank E. Pool Sr. (deceased); October 26, 1938; [ch.] Barbara, L. Gelow, Rank E. Pool Jr., and Mary A. Green (deceased); [ed.] High school and advanced College Education Degree; [memb.] Charter Member Gateway Elkettes, Records Control Little League Baseball Team, Assistant Leader Campfire Girls and Blue Birds; [hon.] Midwest Tri-State Mathematics Champion, Midwest Tri-State Spelling Champion; [oth. writ.] Write farewells to departing and greetings to incoming people, otherwise just for family and friends, until recently have had two poems published; [pers.] I try to put in words my thoughts and feelings regarding the person I'm writing to and about. Started writing pre-school, but later I was influenced by James W. Riley, Henry W., Longfellow, and J.G. Whittier; [a.] Portland, OR

POWELL, ANDREA
[pen.] Andrea Thomas-Powell; [b.] December 19, 1966; Yonkers, NY; [p.] Oliver and Susie Thomas; [ch.] Dayna Marie and Heather Lee; [ed.] Tucumcari High, Barnes Business College; [occ.] Receptionist—Coldwell Banker—Everitt and Williams, Ft. Collins, CO; [oth. writ.] Tumbling Walls (boo-Olympus), various poems with National Library of Poetry; [pers.] Strive every day to compete with end and surpass your expectations of yesterday.; [a.] Ft. Collins, CO

POWELL I., WENDELL J.
[b.] September 26, 1969; Neptune, NJ; [p.] Charlie W. Powell Sr., Hattie B. Powell; [m.] Arnesia N.

Powell; August 19, 1989; [ch.] Anthony A. Powell and Wendell J. Powell II; [ed.] Trenton Central High; [occ.] Independent Driver; [memb.] International Society of Poets, Community Bible Fellowship; [oth. writ.] 12 Spiritual Voices, New Revelation in Creation, The 1st Seven Days; [pers.] There is no greater mystery than love. Even though unexplainable, it will never go unknown.; [a.] Trenton, NJ

PRATT, DOUGLAS ALAN
[pen.] The Dougster; [b.] June 27, 1980; Springfield, MO; [p.] Ray and Janet Pratt; [ed.] Graduated from Derby High School, May 24, 1998; [occ.] Freshman College Student and JC Penney Sales Clerk; [oth. writ.] A Sight to See; [pers.] My inspirations to write come from many places: nature, children, God, and the ungraspable concepts of life, but my favorite ones come from beautiful female friends.; [a.] Wichita, KS

PRENTIS, EDNA ZIMMERMAN
[pen.] Edna Zimmerman Prentis; [b.] November 15, 1915; Welcome, NC; [p.] E. J. and Beatrice Zimmerman; [m.] October 23, 1934; [ch.] Linda; [ed.] Welcome High School, attended Duke University two years, studied Music and Art for years private and classes; [occ.] Musician, Artist, Poet, Newspaper Columnist; [memb.] Have belonged to garden clubs, book clubs, and civic clubs through the years, also music groups; [hon.] Twice won "Citizen of the Year" from local Civitan Club, Jefferson Honorable Mention from Winston-Salem; [oth. writ.] Have written songs lyrics and music; [pers.] My philosophy of life: to make the world better and more beautiful. That includes safety environment.; [a.] Welcome, NC

PRICE, PATRICIA L.
[b.] July 16, 1949; Kansas City, KS; [p.] Wayne Francis Price and Helen Lorraine Price; [ed.] Van Horn High, Central Missouri State University; [memb.] National Geographic, Kera Public TV; [hon.] National Honor Society, Regent's Scholarship, Dean's List; [oth. writ.] Non-published travel articles, non-published songwritings; [pers.] Self-styled, independent, my works emanate not from influence by other works, although I admire romantic, naturalist works. I have desire to interpret life's ultimate pursuits through reflections of life in mankind's intangible relationships and passionate struggle for essence of truth, destiny, through mankind's own perceptions.; [a.] Dallas, TX

PRIDDY, BOBBY LINDON
[pen.] Bobby Lindon Priddy; [b.] April 28, 1935; Tobyth Co, NC; [p.] Silas A. and Gladys P. Priddy; [ed.] Stoneville H.S. 1955; U.S.A.F. Tachnihawa, Japan 1957, 58, 59; Air Police; member of O.C.S. through ECI; [occ.] Retired from Kale Copper Products; [memb.] 32 Seattle Rite Mason Member of Southern Bapt. Church; [hon.] Certificate from Military Law School, play violin, records several recordings, still playing, love all good music; [oth. writ.] Several poems, two published; [pers.] O' powerful death, you in all your glory of swiftners and haste can only, even if you strive, visit but once.; [a.] Stoneville, NC

PUCKETT, LLOYD HAROLD
[pen.] Harold Hunley; [b.] Brooklyn, NY: September 2, 1947; [p.] Naoni Puckett and Lloyd Hurley Sr.; [ed.] Franklin Elementary Hempiteal LS; Franklin High Brooklyn, NY; New York State High School Equidiploma 1996; Bren Community College Bronx, NY; [occ.] Artist, photography student, commercial artist; [memb.] American Legion, Democratic Parking—also—International Society of Poets, member; [hon.] International Society of Poets, Distinguished Member and Hall of Fame; Editors Choice Award—1997, several anthologies; [oth. writ.] "Pharoah Gold," "Revelens," "Songs of Praise and Have Forever,"

"Faces"; [pers.] "Playing the game of life is important."; [a.] New York, NY

PULKOWSKI, MARGARET J.
[pen.] P. J. Marks; [b.] June 21, 1944; Queens, NY; [p.] Joseph and Catherine Shepard; [m.] Stephen Pulkowski; February 28, 1976; [ch.] Laurie and Stephen; [ed.] Flushing High School, American School of Chicago; [occ.] Retired Motel Owner and Entrepreneur; [memb.] Perinton Community Center, Various Animal Rights Associations; [hon.] Republican Committee Awards from Reagan/Bush Admins., elected into International Poetry Hall of Fame December 30, 1996; [oth. writ.] National Library of Poetry anthology series: (In Dappled Sunlight) "Books," (Priceless Treasures) "Poets," (Best Poems of 1997) "Peace of Mind," (Best Poems of 1998) "The Sun"; [pers.] I've always wanted to write a "love song." I feel this poem included in this book is a beginning! I also wanted to mention the fact that I absolutely love silk flowers.; [a.] Fairport, NY

PURPEL, RACHAEL REBEKAH E.
[pen.] Rachael-Rebekah E. Purpel; [b.] October 1, 1961; Asheboro, NC; [p.] Jack Henderson and Clara Nance; [m.] Mark A. Purple; April 3, 1992; [ch.] Scott Allen Leonard; [ed.] Randolph Community College, International Correspondence School of Scranton Penn (for Journalism), Institute of Children's Literature; [occ.] Poet, Short Story Writer, and Housewife; [memb.] I am a distinguished member of the International Society of Poets.; [hon.] I received an Editor's Choice Award from The National Library of Poetry.; [oth. writ.] I have had several poems published by Sparrowgrass, Poetry Guild, National Library of Poetry, A teen magazine, and a local newspaper.; [pers.] I write with great sensitivity—revealing things about my inner self—hoping to bond with my readers—to somehow find a common link in a world of differences.; [a.] Asheboro, NC

PURTEE, SAMMIE
[b.] August 5, 1983; Adams, County, OH; [p.] Sam and Diana Purtee; [occ.] Student; [memb.] Varsity Soccer Team; [hon.] Honorable mention Daughters of the American Revolution Award, first place SWCD Conservation contest, first, second and third places in Youth Rally, principals award, various honor roll awards, athletic awards, Science awards, Clogging awards, and Editor's Choice award; [oth. writ.] Goodbye, Graveside Goodbye, The Memory, Someday, and others in local papers; [pers.] This poem is a memory of my Pappy, whom I miss and love very much; I'm trying to let his memories live on through my writings.; [a.] West Union, OH

PUSUNG, GEOFFREY
[pen.] GP, Anomaly; [b.] May 25, 1982; New York, NY; [occ.] Student; [a.] Queens, NY

QUIMBLEY, W. PEARL
[b.] November 13, 1946; Baconton, GA; [p.] Sylvester and Jessie Bell Quimbley; [ch.] Shawana Edison and Sigmand Thomas; [ed.] Middle Grades Education, School Counselling; [occ.] Teacher (Math) Mitchell Co. Middle School Camilla GA; [pers.] My writing is healing to the heart and illuminates joy to those that read it.; [a.] Camilla, GA

QUINN, MIKE E.
[pen.] Akai; [b.] February 17, 1961; Hartford, CT; [p.] Charles and Elain Quinn; [ch.] Barrington D. Hall; [ed.] Bloomfield High (1979) G.H.C.C.; [occ.] Loss Prevention and Safety Specialist; [memb.] International Churches of Chirst Discipling Team; [oth. writ.] Waiting to Excel; [pers.] Do your best to make every effort, and great things are going to be achieved.; [a.] East Hartford, CT

RAFFERTY, CAROL
[pen.] Doc; [b.] February 12, 1947; Philadelphia, PA; [p.] Grace and Harry Vevle; [m.] Thomas;

January 27, 1968; [ch.] Carol Ann Ace, and Wendy; [ed.] Completed high school, top 1/3 of my class; [oth. writ.] Trying to Get to You; [pers.] I love to write, but then I got hit with one poem after another, because of my family's experiences.; [a.] Philadelphia, PA

RAMSAY, SARAH
[b.] November; Tehran, Iran; [p.] Abraham Ramsay and Sue Ramsey; [ed.] Lake Oswego High School; [occ.] Student; [hon.] John's Hopkins Talent Search Awards, IPSU Award; [oth. writ.] Poem published in "An Eternal Flame"; [pers.] I strive to reflect the power and love of God in my writing.; [a.] Lake Oswego, OR

RAND, CHRISTY M.
[b.] January 3, 1979; Portland, OR; [p.] Dennis and Jane; [ed.] HS Diploma, enrolled in Community College; [occ.] Childcare, Student; [oth. writ.] Ode to My New Step Sister, Clegy to My Grandpa, Love, Elegy of My Life, Today's World, A Wish for the Future, and many more; [pers.] I would enjoy hearing what others have to say about my writing.; [a.] Portland, OR

RANDLES, KEVIN J., JR.
[pen.] Moses, Black Moses; [b.] February 17, 1956; Chicago, IL; [ed.] Double B.S. Engineering, St. Louis University, Class of '84; [occ.] Engineer for a Telecommunications Corp.; [memb.] SAE, LSC, ICA; [oth. writ.] There's a Place, Black Man's Love for a Black Princess; [pers.] "A man needs a focal point in life . . . and that is usually God, and a woman! That which makes him great! Cuz, God and she are greater and if you take a way that which makes that man great, you effectively blind him, and he will be lost.; [a.] Chicago, IL

RANKIN, NICOLE JOANNA
[pen.] Daria Storm; [b.] June 30, 1983; [p.] Catherine Lloyd and Scott Rankin; [ed.] Indian Rocks, Christian School; [memb.] Student at John Casablancas Modelling and Acting School, True Vine Ministry; [hon.] 1998 Editor's Choice Award (National Library of Poetry) Florida Vocal Association (Superior); [oth. writ.] "Believe"—Passages of Light; [pers.] Around every dark cloud there is a silver lining. Do not grow weary in well doing.; [a.] Largo, FL

RAY, JEAN
[m.] Frank Ray; [ch.] Evene H. Gar, Byron, Ernest Courtney, Brooke, and Trank; [occ.] Radiology Technologist; [oth. writ.] Poem published in contest, Brooke; [pers.] I try to live a life of giving, not only of myself but financial as well. I try to live in peace with all.

RAY, JOHNNY A.
[b.] April 2, 1969; Los Angeles, CA; [p.] Gloria A. Morales; [ed.] Venice High, Grossmont College, Mesa College; [occ.] G and K Uniform Service Team Leader, Sales Representative; [memb.] International Society Of Poets; [hon.] Editor's Choice Award, Military Decorations: Navy Commendation Medal, Four Navy Achievement Medals, and Combat Action Award; [oth. writ.] "Yours" and "The Gifted Family" were both published by The National Library of Poetry; [pers.] To accomplish your goal to success, you must have a dream and then making that dream a reality. Never fear failure, for it will only make you wiser.; [a.] San Diego, CA

REDMAN, ANGELA D.
[pen.] Morning Star; [b.] January 16, 1951; Big Spring, TX; [p.] H.C. and Bernice Tidwell; [m.] Justin Redman; August 2, 1986; [ch.] Shawn Maderer; [ed.] Forsan High School, courses at Southeast OK in Durant, OK; [occ.] Homemaker; [memb.] International and National Society of Poets, Interstitial Cystitus Association; [oth. writ.] Poems published in local newspaper and by National Library of Poetry; [pers.] I strive to reflect

on personal emotions in relation of nature's beauty and healing power.; [a.] Wright City, OK

REECE, NANCY LYNNE
[pen.] Nancy Lynne Reece; [b.] March 28, 1954; Sumter SC; [p.] William Q. Jeffords, Hazel M. Jeffords; [m.] Robin M. Reece; September 12, 1987; [ed.] Lakes High School, Clover Park Voc Tech., Accountant; [occ.] Disabled Accountant; [memb.] TBN, World Vision, Gospel for Asia, Bethany Christian Assembly, Roots Messianic Congregation; [hon.] Editor's Choice Award by The National Library of Poetry; [oth. writ.] Poem in The Rustling Leaves; poems given as gifts to family, friends, and a church; letters to the editor published in the Tacoma News Tribune; [pers.] I strive to project God's truth, love, peace, and beauty in my writings. I am greatly influenced by God the father, Jesus his son, and the Holy Spirit.; [a.] Everett, WA

REED, MARGARET E.
[b.] November 13, 1930; Waco, TX; [p.] N.M. and Ruby Lee Calfee; [m.] Alvin Morris Reed; May 27, 1950; [ch.] Daniel, David, Ray, and Paul; [ed.] Mosheim High; Mary Hardin Baylor College, Belton, TX; Clifton Jr. College, Clifton, TX; [occ.] Housewife; [memb.] Playhouse of design art organization, Kingsville, TX; [hon.] Valedictorian of 1948 Senior Class, Mosheim, TX, received a scholarship to Mary Hardin Baylor College, Belton, TX; [pers.] Poetry is a vast, untapped source of inspiration that springs into life when triggered by strong emotions, such as the loss of a loved one in death, the joy of being with family and friends. It is an unearned gift from God that is deeply satisfying and very mysterious. I thank God. He has given me this outlet for my life's experience.; [a.] Valley Mills, TX

REED, PATRICIA E.
[pen.] Trish, Red Bird; [b.] December 17, 1952; Charleston, SC; [p.] Mr. and Mrs. David Reed; [ch.] Akeem Kalil Reed; [ed.] Masters plus 30, Winthrop College, Rock Hill, SC; [occ.] Teacher of Children with Learning Disabilities; [memb.] Smithsonian Institute and Flower of the Month Club; [hon.] Who's Who in the World, Who's Who in Education, American Biographical Institute's Medal of Honor and Distinguish Service Awards; [oth. writ.] Poems—I Am, Who Said, and Expressing of Freedom; [pers.] As thoughts come into my head, I write them down immediately because I know that writing will retain my thoughts forever, thoughts that will be reflected now and throughout my life, and in some ways will touch the lives of others.; [a.] Summerville, SC

REED, RODGER H.
[b.] Mary 6, 1949; Lebanon, TN; [p.] Estle B. (Mann) and Dorothy Mae Reed; [ch.] Rodger Jr., Crystal Rene, and Tonya Mae; [ed.] Trousdale Co. High, TN, Tech. University Volunteer State University; [occ.] Business Owner; [memb.] Hartsville, TN Masonic Lodge 113 PM, Knob Springs Baptist Church; [oth. writ.] "Search for Half a Soul," Isle of View 1997; "You are Souly Mine," Treasured Poems of America, Winter 1998; [pers.] A man can have no greater treasure than his child.; [a.] Hartsville, TN

RENFRO, KHRYSTAN PAGE
[pen.] Panther Moon, Thestream; [b.] April 14, 1967; Springfield, IL; [p.] Doris E. Renfro and Maurice E. Renfro; [m.] Michael J. Stella; October 18, 1997; [ed.] 1985 graduate of Sacred Heart Academy; continuing education, 1998, in Holistic Nutrition in a correspondence degree program at Clayton College of Natural Health; [occ.] My own independent "Angel Girl" Handcrafted Jewelry Business; [memb.] World Natural Body Building Federation (WNBF); Professional Body Builder; [hon.] 1997 Editor's Choice Award from The National Library of Poetry; 1997 Top-ten finisher—Ms. International Pro-Body Building Com-

petition; 1995 Top-ten finisher in the World Natural Body Building Pro Championships; [oth. writ.] Sunday's Pain, The Oracle of a Woman's Soul, The Abyss; [pers.] The beauty of being a poet is . . . you can be any color you wish to be. Race is only a category, not a defining moment.; [a.] Marlborough, MA

REUTER, ALOLA J.
[pen.] Alola J. Reuter; [b.] June 23, 1940; Phillipsburg, NJ; [p.] Gladys and George Berry; [m.] Alfred William Bowers; June, 1959; [ch.] Alfred, Kevin, and David; [occ.] Respic Workers for handicapped children; [memb.] Women of the Moose; [hon.] Art Award in Washington High and Place Bowling Award on open League for score of 230; [oth. writ.] Wrote poem for Morning Song number 45; [pers.] Be honest and work hard for what you want in life.; [a.] Gulfport, FL

REVILL, DAVID K.
[b.] December 12, 1963; Moultrie, GA; [ch.] Yvonne, Chris, and Kiesha; [ed.] Graduated from State University of New York, Albany, B.S. Bus. Acct.; Colquitt Co. HS; [occ.] Financial Analyst; [memb.] Rotary, Republican Party; [hon.] Poet of the Year; [oth. writ.] Several anthologies have published my poetry.; [pers.] "Unto thine self be true, thus never be afraid to face the world."; [a.] Dallas, TX

RHODES, HARRISON
[pen.] Harrison Rhodes; [b.] January 8, 1982; Dallas, TX; [p.] Sam and Judy Rhodes; [occ.] Life Guard; [oth. writ.] I Am a Man; [pers.] I have no boundaries, no limits, no barriers, as long as I believe in my abilities.

RICHARDS, IVY CONSTABLE
[b.] January 6, 1921; Hope Bay, Portland,; [p.] Isaac Samuel Constable and Mary Constable; [m.] Wilfred Richards, Deceased; February 25, 1950; [ch.] Seven children, one deceased; [ed.] At James Hill Primary School, Clavenders College, and Caenwood Junior College, after which taught at various primary schools; [occ.] Housewife; [memb.] Tabernacle Congregational Church, was an organist for various churches in Jamaica, W. Indies; [hon.] Two Gold awards and one silver from World of Poetry, CA; two honorary awards from International Society of Poets; Bronze Awards and Certificates of Merit for Music in Jamaica; [pers.] I pray for those who love me, whose hearts are kind and true, for the heaven that smiles above me and awaits my spirit too, for all human ties that bind me, for the task God has assigned me, for the bright hopes yet to find me, and for the good that I can do.; [a.] St. Albans, NY

RIDGWAY, THOMAS J.
[b.] August 13, 1945; Bridgeton, NJ; [p.] Tilghman D. and Hester Ann; [m.] Barbara Ann; December 12, 1997; [ch.] Robert and Norman; [ed.] Bridgeton High; [occ.] Maintenance Journeyman Owens-Brockway, Williamsburg, VA; [memb.] Williamsburg New Testiment Church, American Legion; [hon.] "Father of the Year" by his family, "Husband of the Year" by his wife, Vietnam Veteran; [oth. writ.] Some local churches and for special occasions, also published in National Library of Poetry, poems of love to my wife and children; [pers.] I am a husband and father first. I am a friend to all who need a friend. I am a romantic and live life to the fullest.; [a.] Williamsburg, VA

RIDLEY, ELAINE
[b.] March 17, 1946; Lewiston, ME; [p.] Carroll and Emma Webster; [ch.] Mary Ann Martel Carrie McCoy Clayton Tenney II, Michael Ridley, and Paul Smith II; [ed.] Mon Mouth Academy University of Maine Lew/Aub.; [occ.] Mother; [memb.] First United Pentecostal Church, Friends of the Light; [hon.] Dean's List, Phi Theta Kappa; [oth. writ.] Hooked, Friends of The Light, short stories, personal testimony stories, numerous poems for

friends and family; [pers.] I strive to write in a way to touch people's hearts, to bring an awareness of the love of God, to let them know He is real and there is hope no matter how bleak things may look.; [a.] Sabattus, ME

RINGGER, FREDERICK J.
[b.] May 1, 1954; Baltimore, MD; [ed.] Eastern Vocational Technical/Graphic Communications; [hon.] Editor's Choice Award, 1998, National Library of Poetry; [oth. writ.] Published in The Music of Silence; recorded on The Sound of Poetry (1998); [pers.] My poetry reflects life's vicissitudes.; [a.] Timonium, MD

RIOS, RICHARD
[b.] March 16, 1966; Orange; [m.] Cheryl; [ch.] Brandon Rios and Richard J. Rios Jr. III; [ed.] Ontario High, UCLA; [occ.] Screenwriter; [memb.] The Writer's Guild of America; [oth. writ.] Freelance writer for television and motion pictures; [pers.] Is there a heart that a poem cannot melt?; [a.] Fontana, CA

RITZ, DIANNE RITTENHOUSE
[pen.] D.R. Ritz; [b.] September 5, 1946; Brooklyn, NY; [p.] Helen and Bill Rittenhouse; [m.] Norma; October 23, 1966; [ch.] Dana and Jason; [pers.] Listen to your heartbeat, within it lies the sound of courage, strength, and love.; [a.] New Port Richey, FL

RIVERA, GEORGE
[pen.] Messenger G. (MSG); [b.] May 1, 1963; [memb.] The covenant of Godly men; [oth. writ.] Up-coming trilogy: I, The Last Wizard of Terragon; II, A New Beginning; The Return of Jesus Christ, III in the International Year of the World, Assault from Nicoliasha; [pers.] 39.3.1 Each book contains poetry incorporated into the story line and cryptogrammiz puzzle contests.

RIVEST, LORICE C.
[b.] November 12, 1922; Liberia L, KS; [p.] Mart Y. Baker and Esther I. Baker; [m.] Omer E. Rivest; August 20, 1973; [ch.] Mona, Cheryl, and Gregory; [ed.] Edler School of Dance High School; East High, Wichita, Kansas; Wenton Stages how at 16, singer, dancer, comedian; [memb.] W.O.T.M; American Legion Puppets, Southern CA; Motion Picture Council; [hon.] Most recent? National Library of Poetry; [oth. writ.] Commercials (radio), not active now; show material— songs, parodies, poems; [pers.] I love people; they are my inspiration, my feelings, can reflect like a mirror. I'm a happy person, but I love to sing blues. I'm still a child.; [a.] San Diego, CA

ROACH, JOHN W.
[pen.] John W. Roach; [b.] October 14, 1917; Thompson Falls, MT; [p.] Moses and Dona Pallett Roach; [ch.] John Jr., David, Edith, and Vincent; [ed.] Polytechnic College of Engineering (Draftsman); Stockton College, A.A. Poly Science and History; [occ.] Sheethetal worker—29 years; [memb.] Christianville Foundation; City of Hope; Skills Applied for Evangelism 1994, 95, 96, 97; National Library of Poetry; Sparrowgrass Poetry Forum 1996-97; [pers.] I try to express my love of God and His care for humankind as well as my love for others while observing the world around me.; [a.] Sonora, CA

ROBERTS GOBERT, URSULA A.
[b.] January 18, 1966; St. Martinville, LA; [p.] Harry and Geraldine Roberts; [occ.] Secretary/ Retail Associate; [oth. writ.] Admiring You from Afar; [pers.] With my writing, I strive to bring out the personal feelings that some are afraid to express or share. You should share your feelings, thoughts, and dreams with others, because someone may benefit from hearing you talk about it. You never know what a person might be going through in their life. So your personal experiences

may bless that person's life, and in turn you will be blessed.; [a.] Lafayette, LA

ROCHE, DEBORAH
[pen.] Squirt; [b.] August 11, 1951; [p.] James and Lee Roche; [ed.] High school; one year jr. college; [occ.] Circuit Assembler for Major Communications Company; [memb.] The National Library of Poetry, Distinguished Member of International Society of Poets, Daughters of Foreign Wars; [hon.] Best of Show Award in the Charles County Fair and 1st Place Award; Silver Poet Award, 1989, from World of Poetry; Golden Poet Award, 1987, from World of Poetry; [oth. writ.] Published in Great American Poetry Anthology, Silence of Yesterday, Best Poems of 1995; [pers.] I enjoy writing about family and friends as they add so much to my daily life.; [a.] Waldorf, MD

ROCOWICH, ELIZABETH M.
[pen.] Missy; [b.] August 16, 1930; Brets, WV; [p.] Lance and Mabel Bosley; [m.] William; September 16, 1950; [ch.] Paula, William, Lisa Ann, and Ronald; [ed.] High School; [occ.] Retired from WVU; [memb.] St. Mary's Church, Choir Morgantown Senior Center; [oth. writ.] I Come to You, Hear Me, Intercessor, We Care; [pers.] Since I came to know the Lord, He has given me a beautiful song and several poems. Put God first, and you will never be lost.; [a.] Morgantown, WV

RODRIGUEZ, EFREN
[b.] February 6, 1980; San Gabriel Valley, CA; [p.] Efren E. Rodriguez and Amalia Rodriguez; [ed.] Moreno Valley High School; [hon.] Honor Roll, Editor's Choice Award for Achievement in Poetry, received eight first-place awards for mechanical drawing entries at the Riverside County Industrial Educational Exposition in 1997 and 1998; [oth. writ.] "Where Is The Light?", a poem published in the book Traces of Yesterday; Cavern Voyager (unpublished novelette); several other poems and short stories; [pers.] My goal to try to inspire the reader's mind for the good in my writings. I have been influenced by many 19th century authors.; [a.] Moreno Valley, CA

ROFFLER, ILSE
[b.] February 28, 1940; Switzerland; [p.] Hans and Ida Schoedler; [m.] Hans Roffler; June 24, 1961; [ch.] Kathrin, Robert, and Jean; [ed.] College and Trade School in Switzerland; [memb.] International Society of Poets, San Pedro Writer's Guild; [hon.] Editor's choice awards; [oth. writ.] Articles in newspapers, poems in different anthologies; [pers.] I like to express myself through poetry about topics I am concerned about.; [a.] San Pedro

ROGERS, DIANA LYNN
[pen.] Diana Lynn Rogers; [b.] May 7, 1947; Kokomo, IN; [ch.] Michelle Robertson and Jarrett Jones; [ed.] Western High School; Lasalle University; [occ.] Federal Emergency Management Agency; [memb.] The International Poetry Society; [oth. writ.] Modern Poetry—The Poetry Guild, other collections of National Library of Poetry, and two song releases; [pers.] It is my desire to let the love of God shine thru me and encourage those who need to see God's love in my writings.; [a.] Denton, TX

ROLLINS, VIELKA E.
[b.] May 28, 1955; Panama; [p.] Genera and Ellis Williams; [m.] Julian Rollins; March 6, 1976; [ch.] Nadia Rollins; [ed.] B.A. Spanish; [occ.] Spanish teacher; [memb.] Association de Literation Femenina; [hon.] Pipeline Diamond fellowship for Ph.D. studies, Association of Language of Excellence in Spanish, CSI Auxilliary Service Corporation award for Academic Excellence in Spanish; [a.] Staten Island, NY

ROSE, CAROL
[b.] June 7, 1940; Oakland, CA; [m.] William R.

Rose; February 6, 1965; [ed.] B.A., University of Oregon; graduate work, University of Oregon, S. OR., University of Colorado; [occ.] Former High School Teacher; presently: Artist, Writer, Poet; [oth. writ.] Autobiography, other poetry; [pers.] The Cultural arts are one of the leading avenues for enlightenment and understanding. Art in all its wide-ranging aspects is the province of every human being. It is simply a matter of beginning and doing. When the artist inside of us is nurtured and alive, whatever the effort or work may be, that special person becomes an inventive, searching, caring, self-expressive creature.; [a.] Medford, OR

ROSS, CAROL A.
[b.] May 28, 1949; Grove City, PA; [p.] Annabel (Blom) and Charles E. Morrow; [m.] Richard Ross; July 13, 1970; [ch.] Twins, Richard Robert, Renee, and Randall; [ed.] 12 years, nine months college; [occ.] Housewife; [memb.] Institute of Children's Literature; [oth. writ.] Poem "Truth" featured in Tracing Shadows, anthology; [pers.] I take the relationship with my Lord in heaven very seriously; after all, He's the reason I'm here and willing to do His call on my life.; [a.] New Castle, PA

ROSS, VIRGINIA MORTON
[pen.] Virginia Morton Ross; [b.] April 29, 1927; Petersburg, IN; [p.] Clyde and Merle Morton; [m.] Adrian Ross; September 22, 1946; [ch.] Dewayne Ross; [ed.] Petersburg High School; [occ.] Wife, mother, artist, and poet; [memb.] The International Society of Poets; [hon.] Several Awards from my painting and writing; [oth. writ.] Two poetry books: Just Beyond the Bend, Thru Sunshine and Shadow; [pers.] If my poems can help to raise the spirit in a person who has given up, then I will feel that I have written something worth more than money.; [a.] Petersburg, IN

ROSSA, ISABELL G.
[pen.] Greer; [b.] March 28, 1928; Pasadena, CA; [p.] Josephine and Isabell Jarewicz; [m.] Lawrence R.; November 11, 1946; [ch.] Two sons, three daughters; [occ.] Retired Manager of costume shop; [memb.] American Legion Aux.; [hon.] National Library of Poetry; [oth. writ.] Epitaph of Age; [pers.] Enjoy life; a "good morning" or a smile to a stranger makes me feel great, hopefully the stranger, too; love your family; life is sometimes too short.; [a.] Hobart, IN

ROUSSEAU, LAURA
[pen.] Laura Rouseau; [b.] July 8, 1972; Tucson, AZ; [p.] Philip and Nell Rousseai; [m.] Rick Bouna, Fiance; October 24, 1998; [ed.] Sahuaro High School, Northern Arizona University; [occ.] Bookkeeper, Accounting Assistant; [oth. writ.] "Web of Death," published in Flagstaff, AZ, local paper; "The Noise," "My Little Friend," published by NLP; [a.] Phoenix, AZ

ROWLAND KEENAN, BEVERLY J.
[pen.] Beverly J. Rowland; [b.] October 3, 1945; Lincoln, NE; [p.] Russ and Virginia Rowland; [m.] Michael Brill Keenan; July 18, 1998; [ch.] Lisa and Ron; [ed.] Upper Moreland High School, Willow Grove, PA; [occ.] Administrative Assistant, private school, St. Mary's Academy; [memb.] Englewood, CO CNA—State of Colorado; [oth. writ.] "The Bricklayer," anthology Days Gone By, 1997; "My Hunter," anthology Best Poems of 1998; [pers.] Oh, the mountains we climb! Thank you, Brill, for wiping my knees off and picking me up.; [a.] Lakewood, CO

RUSSELL, BETTYE
[pen.] Princess Bea; [b.] Inverness, MI; [p.] Mr and Mrs. G. and Odell Russell; [ch.] Shon, Shonna, and Pamela Russell; [ed.] Mackenzie High School; Wayne County College, 1980's; [occ.] Self-employed and Child Care, communication field; [memb.] Community Coalition, YWCA; [oth. writ.] Poems to be set to music which is my passion from

earlier in life. This is one of several poems published in a small town.; [pers.] Songs and poems reflect the memory of my grandmother, mother, father, and love for my grandsons. A special poem which in the poetry book for my father burial "90" I love and miss now and forever; [a.] Detroit, MI

RUSSELL, PATRICK
[b.] May 10, 1959; Boise, ID; [p.] Glenn and Dolly Russell; [ed.] Bishop Kelly High School 1977, Boise State University: Communications and English Literature (B.A. 1982), St. Patrick's Seminary, Menlo Park, CA (Master of Divinity 1986); [occ.] Roman Catholic Priest (1986); Chaplain, Chateau de Boise Retirement; Chaplain, Bishop Kelly High School (1993); [memb.] Amnesty International, Special Olympics, National Catholic Office for Persons with Disabilities, Sigma Phi Epsilon Fraternity, Founder-Director Fr. Russell Charity Golf Scramble for Persons with Chronic illness (1986); [hon.] International Man of the Year 1995 (Campbridge, UK); Who's Who in the World 1995; Who's Who in the West 1998-99; Honorary member of the International Biographical Centre Advisory Council (Cambridge, UK 1995); Outstanding Young Man of America: 1983, 84, 86, 87; The American Biographical Institute's Honorary Appointment to the Research Board of Advisors; Most Admired Man of the Decade by the Board of International Research, American Biographical Institute 1996; Who's Who in the West 2000-0221; Who's Who . . . World, 1999; [oth. writ.] Poems and articles published in University anthologies, professional newspapers, and other poetry collections; three poetry volumes have been published by the author's friends: 1996 "Just Some Thoughts," "Dancing Between the Blades" in 1987, "The Stanford Poems" in 1985.; [pers.] It is vital to not only nurture the arts, but contribute in them as artists in order to bring joy to every human soul. Imagination, like prayer, embraces our communities and God.; [a.] Boise, ID

RYDEN, ALICE GMITEREK
[b.] January 30, 1951; Chicago, IL; [p.] Michael and Stephanie Gmiterek; [ed.] B.S. in Physical Education from the University of Illinois in Chicago; [occ.] Physical Education Teacher in elementary school; [memb.] International Society of Poets; [hon.] Editor's Choice Award for poem "Impressions of Scotland" for Outstanding Achievement in Poetry; published in the Best Poems of the 90's by The National Library of Poetry, 1998; President's Award for Literary Excellence for poem "Winterstorm" from the National Author's Registry, Iliad Literary Awards; [oth. writ.] "Impressions of Scotland" published in Best Poems of the 90's by The National Library of Poetry; "Winterstorm" published in Keepsakes Anthology by Iliad Press; and "Commemorating Excellence" to be published in 12/98; poem "Peace will Come" published in Poetic Voices of America.

SALADEN, ANITA R.
[pen.] Anita Saladen, Anita Von Ende; [b.] September 21, 1913; Berlin, Germany; [p.] Martin and Martha Rehtus; [m.] Deceased; August 16, 1934; [ed.] Lincoln High of Lincoln NE, University of NE, Lincoln NE—student; [occ.] Homemaker; [memb.] International Society of Poets; [hon.] National Essay Award 1933; Two Gold, Two Silver Awards from World of Poetry, 86-89; Acclaimed by John Frost '85; [pers.] "Life Is Love."; [a.] Lompoc, CA

SAMER, BILL
[pen.] Billy C. Bayway, Sammy Nut-Out but with hair; [ed.] Kean University, M.A., Age of Reform, Lutheran College, Union College, A.A., Liberal Arts—Urban Studies; [memb.] American Museum of Natural History, The Library of Congress, The International Society of Poets, Garden Club; [hon.] Who's Who, First Place, Dean's List, Telephone Crisis Hot-Line, VBS; [oth. writ.] "Romance," a modern ballad starring Zeke, the carpet-tramp clown from Arrow Funpapers, "Fun-O-Rama," "Mermaid Seas," a short story starring Sammy Nut-Out from "Arrow," "Morning of the Fog," registered and filled by my town; [pers.] Lectured to art class about Russian plays; I studied Great Britain's Age of Reform, as a history major and appreciate the fantasies of Lewis Carroll and earlier works of Jonathan Swift. Batty, you're good.; [a.] Union, NJ

SAMMOUR, RENEE M.
[pen.] Renee M. Sammour; [b.] October 28, 1966; Cincinnati, OH; [p.] Frank Phillips and Donna Darling; [m.] Nader D. Sammour; October 19, 1985; [ch.] David, Nadia, and Naseem; [occ.] Housewife; [oth. writ.] Many poems written but haven't been published except for, in TNLOP's anthology The Peace We Knew, "Bye Bye Birdie"; [pers.] I hope that my writings will bring forth truth and understanding in a world of confusion to let people know there is hope and the greater good will be.; [a.] Savannah, GA

SANDERS, ROBERT
[pen.] Rob Fresh; [b.] March 22, 1977; Paris, TX; [p.] Jacqueline Sanders and Robert Limerson; [ed.] Belle, Chassetligh, Delgado Community College; [occ.] Bagger; [oth. writ.] Second poem sent in; [pers.] Many of my writings strive on the good and bad of my life, like Yin and Yang. But, if you set your mind and heart to it, you can accomplish anything.; [a.] Belle Chasse, CA

SANDSTEAD, AURIEL J.
[b.] High Plains of NE Colorado; [p.] Charles F. and Fae Stanley Oram; [m.] Willard N. Sandstead; March 16, 1946; [ch.] Three daughters; [memb.] Alpha Delta Kappa, teacher honorary; [hon.] Charter president of Colorado Quilting Council, 1978; first quilter inducted into C. 2C. Hall of Fame; lifetime honorary memberships, High Plains Heritage Quilters 1992; [oth. writ.] Contributor to "Leaning into the Mind, Home, Write from the Heart," 1997; [a.] Sterling, CO

SANKER, BRIAN P.
[b.] November 1949; New York, NY; [p.] Margaret Corrigan; [ch.] Aaron J. Sanker; [ed.] B.A. English, St. Francis College, Loretto, PA; [occ.] Private Investigator; [oth. writ.] Love's Critiques, 1973; [pers.] One must cultivate their garden.—Voltaire Candide; [a.] Los Gatos, CA

SAPSER, FRAN
[pen.] Fran Sapser; [b.] April 8; Wilkis-Barre; [p.] Mary and Michael Kasminsky; [m.] February 7, 1958; [ch.] Tom; [ed.] Graduated from St. Ami's Academy, W-B General Hospital, attended Marywood College and Pratt Institute in New York; [occ.] Regular Nurse and a Business Manager; [memb.] Dean's List at schools, belong to Sacred Heart Church and Astrological Associations, etc.; [hon.] Best writing awards—Best Latin Award in Pennsylvania, best dressed awards, scholarships awards; [oth. writ.] Poetry awards, short story award, spelling bees; [pers.] Someday I will write that best "seller." And it will be a mystery who done it.; [a.] Wilkis-Barre, PA

SAVADSKY, RICHARD
[b.] February 28, 1942; Brooklyn, NY; [p.] Edna and Moe Savadsky; [ch.] Jena Gaye, Sheryl Rae, and Glenn Paron; [ed.] B.S. Aerospace Engineering, Polytechnic Institute of Brooklyn; M.B.A. Business, Adelphi University; [oth. writ.] Poems basis on heritage, personal growth, and observations; [pers.] I am, like you, a unique member of the human race.; [a.] Williston Park, NY

SCHICK, BARBARA ANN
[b.] August 25; Bakersfield, CA; [p.] Adolph and Flora Schwartz; [m.] Doyle Preston Schick (deceased); [ch.] Christy, Donna, Leila, Shem, Brian, and Nobi; [ed.] B.S. California State San Bernardino; graduate courses, Long Beach State University and Loma Linda University; [occ.] Ret. Medical Record Analyst; [memb.] Armed Forces Writers League, National Authors Registry; [hon.] various poetry honors and awards; [oth. writ.] Local Newsletters; [pers.] "You Don't Find Happiness; You Cause It."; [a.] Calimesa, CA

SCHMALKE, FLORENCE
[pen.] Flo; [b.] July 14, 1923; Ramey, MN; [p.] Paul and Rose Gorecki; [m.] Divorced; February 7, 1942; [ch.] Diane, Ray, Elaine, Patricia, Jim and David; [ed.] High School; [occ.] Cook for board and care home retarded people; [memb.] Senior Clubs Rosary Solidarity Club 4-H Leader of Gromac non club; [hon.] Award for song "America is beautiful land of Liberty," certificate of achievement song "Gentle People," 1991 KFC Billboard song contest write songs for records, Cos hill top, Nash Co., Rainbow and Majestic records; [oth. writ.] Do oil painting of landscapes, gardening, write songs, sing at luncheons play card games; [pers.] Love people young or old around me.; [a.] Brooklyn Center, MN

SCHOUWENAARS, MELANIE
[pen.] Melanie Schouwenaars; [p.] Peter and Patricia Schouwenaars; [ch.] Andrew Rene Escobar; [oth. writ.] I have a notebook full of poems that I have written. One other poem, besides this one, has been published in a book named An Evolving Secret.; [pers.] This is how being in love feels like to me, and how it should mean to one another.

SCHULTZ, INGRID
[b.] December 16, 1978; Arlington, VA; [p.] Guillermo Schultz and Cecelia Schultz; [ed.] Stone Ridge 14 years, Catholic University of America, one year; [occ.] Student; [memb.] National Author Registry; [hon.] Editor's Choice Award, Outstanding Volunteer 1994-1995 and 1995-1996; [a.] Great Falls, VA

SEGAWA, RICHARD Y.
[pen.] Dick Segawa; [b.] August 23, 1927; Hilo, HI; [p.] Riichi and Fukuyo Segawa; [m.] Ethel S.; [ch.] Richard Jr., Whitney, and Leslie Leilant; [ed.] B.S.C.E. and M.S. University of Missouri; advanced graduate studies, Univ. of Minnesota; [occ.] Professional Civil Engineer registered in CA, HI, MO, and MN; [memb.] National Society of Prof. Engineers, Soc. of American Military Engrs., American Legion, Shriners, Scottish Rite; [hon.] Outstanding Executive Award, City of Glendale, CA; Research Assistant Fellowship Award, U. of MO.; Outstanding Performance Supervisory General Engineer; Commander US Naval Forces, Vietnam; US Air Defense Command Commendation; Honor Student Medal, Hilo, HI; commissioned Second Lt. US Army; commissioned Captain, US Air Force; GS-15 Pearl Harbor US Civil Service Board; US Air Defense Commendation for Meritorious Achievement in Engineering; [oth. writ.] Editor, Shriners' Bugle Notes and Office Publications on Poetry; [pers.] Strive for excellence in enfranchisement of humanitarian thoughts to enhance our daily lives.; [a.] Gardena, CA

SERE, ROSEMARIE
[pen.] Rosemarie Sere; [b.] September 30, 1937; Brooklyn, NY; [ch.] Rosemarie, Elizabeth, Jeannie, and Victor; [ed.] Associate Degree in Liberal Arts, still attending college to achieve B.S. of Arts and a minor in Philosophy; [occ.] Paraprofessional in a special education program at public school; [oth. writ.] Article published in Science of Mind magazine entitled "Navigating Mid-Life Crisis," poem published in Adrift on a Breeze entitled "I," and many unpublished works; [pers.] Love is the core of the universe, and the lack of love is where evil and corruption are hatched.; [a.] Staten Island, NY

SEWELL, NEIL
[a.] Lexington, AL

SEYFFERLE, BETTY
[pen.] Betty Seyfferle; [p.] Ernest and Gladys White; [m.] John Richard Seyfferle; December 19, 1970; [ch.] Michael Zornes, Steven Zornes, and Chris Seyfferle; [ed.] Wilkinson High School, Apex Beauty College, Bill Miller College RE; [memb.] Kappa Delta Phi, PSI IOta XI; [hon.] Past President, Knightstown Business and Professional Womens Organization; [oth. writ.] Several poems and songs; [pers.] In addition to my personal feelings and experiences, I try to capture the emotions of family, friends, and also those I read about. I then try to reflect these feelings of happiness, sadness, triumph, and accomplishments in my poems and the lyrics of my songs; [a.] Knightstown, IN

SHAFFER, ARLIENSHIA
[b.] May 7; Lafayetteville, NC; [p.] Mr. and Mrs. C.H. Carver; [m.] LTC Clarence E. Shaffer; December 6, 1969; [ch.] Steven and Catita; [ed.] University of Hawaii, Nursing Major; Presbyterian St. Luke, Rush; University, Chicago, IL; [occ.] Marketing Consultant, Association Executives International; [memb.] International Society of Poets, CAP, North Atlanta Band Parents, Continental Colony Comm. Association, and other organizations; [hon.] Honored as President of The Chairmettes, Inc., Atlanta Chapter; Charmette of The Year; Red Cross volunteer; Vice President of Continental Colony PTA, and others too numerous to mention; [oth. writ.] 1992, "A Touch of Class;" "All Too Soon," Recollection of Yesterday, National Library of Poetry; "Dream Exaltation," Color of Thought; "Unconditional Love," Best Poems of 1996, National Library of Poetry; received two Editor's Choice Awards; [pers.] I am a positive person who believes we can all make a difference, "If we open up our eyes, and not be too blind to see beyond our noses, nor too deaf to hear the cries of another."; [a.] Atlanta, GA

SHAFFER, DAVID
[b.] October 2, 1972; Clifton Springs, NY; [p.] Gloria Shaffer and Anthony Shaffer; [ed.] Cazenovia College; [occ.] U.S. Army—Infantry; [pers.] Writing expresses the thoughts I can't put in the correct words to say.; [a.] Fort Clayton, Panama

SHARMA, PUNEET
[pen.] Clark Brown; [b.] March 27, 1969; Chandigarh, IN; [p.] Dr. B.K. Sharma and Dr. Sarot Sharma; [m.] Vandana Sharma; June 4, 1996; [ch.] V. Sharma; [ed.] Guru Nanak Public School, D.A.V. College, Christian Medical College, MA General Hospital; [occ.] Doctor; [memb.] International Society of Poets; [a.] New York, NY

SHERRILL, THELMA H.
[b.] August 4, 1934; Old Hickory, TN; [p.] Delia and Walter R. Hackney; [m.] Edward Sherrill; May 22, 1954; [ch.] Barry and Jeff Sherrill; [ed.] Graduate of Mt. Juliet High School, Mt. Juliet, TN; [occ.] Retired, Metro Davidson County Division of Assessments Administrative Assistant; [hon.] Received many certificates of merits, "World of Poetry;" Editors Choice Award, "When Life Tumbles In," National Library of Poetry, 1998; [oth. writ.] Book, Moments of Meditations; many poems published in other anthologies; [pers.] I write poetry for the sheer joy of uplifting others; I like to encourage others with my poems.; [a.] Old Hickory, TN

SHERROD, RONALD E.
[pen.] Harl Sherrah; [b] November 16, 1947; Knoxville, TN; [p.] Harllee Sherrod and Harriet Sherrod; [m.] Sue Sherrod; July 11, 1986; [ch.] Tom, Jerry, and Paul; [ed.] Central High, Wheaton College, University of Tennessee; [occ.] Soil Scientist and Professional Conversationalist; [oth. writ.] Co-author of several publications in scientific journals; [pers.] Reading and writing poetry

keeps me in touch with the heart of the universe; I find peace and joy in that beautiful rhythm of reality deep inside, the part of us that is eternal.; [a.] Strawberry Plains, TN

SHIELDS, CHRISTINA ANN
[pen.] Christina Ann Shields; [b.] August 5, 1982; Del Rio, TX; [p.] William and Rosie Shields; [ed.] Starting college in fall of 1999, Central High; [occ.] Student, Data Entry, Web Design; [hon.] Editors Choice Award in Poetry, 1998; [oth. writ.] Poem published in A Piece Of Elegance; [pers.] Even when you feel like the world is against you, remember that God will love you no matter what.; [a.] San Angelo, TX

SHORT, NANCY C.
[pen.] Courage; [b.] January 9, 1959; Fayette, CO; [p.] Betty and Harold Greene; [m.] Howard Short Jr.; June 16, 1995; [ch.] Carrie, Billy, and Howard III; [ed.] 12th Grade Henry Clay High School, Eastside Center; [occ.] N.C. Towing, President of this Company; [oth. writ.] Children of the World, My Feeling Too, Flood Waters of Heaven; [a.] Lexington, KY

SHORT, ROSEMARY B.
[b.] December 28, 1942; Charleston, SC; [p.] Mr. and Mrs. Ralph S. Bailey Sr.; [m.] Jordan P. Short IV; December 22, 1964; [ch.] Jay Short, Linda S. Reed; [ed.] B.S. Ed., minor in Music, GA. Southern Univ., Statesboro, GA; [occ.] Homemaker, Older Adult Co. Ord. Func, Tifton and for S. Ga. Conf; [memb.] Arts Council, FUMC; [hon.] Golden Deeds Award, Exchange Clark, Distinguished Memb. ISP; [oth. writ.] Several poems published in anthologies, working on a collection of poems, Through Eyes of Love; [pers.] Writing helps me to slow my hurried pace and to reflect on the beauty and blessings that surround me, as well as giving me an opportunity to motivate others by sharing the spirit of the living Christ, who can open one's eyes to a life of purpose, hope, and heart's peace.; [pa.] Tifton, GA

SHUMAN, SHIRLEY
[pen.] Shirley Shuman; [b.] December 23, 1935; Newell, WV; [p.] Harry and Katherine Simmons; [m.] Robert Shuman; August 3, 1951; [ch.] Roberta, Patsy, Kathy, Randy, Harry, and Robert Jr.; [ed.] Wells High School, Newell, WV; [occ.] Homemaker; [memb.] Church of the Nazarene, The International Society of Poets; [hon.] Editor's Choice Awards from The National Library of Poetry; [oth. writ.] Poems published by The Poetry Guild and by The National Library of Poetry; [pers.] Poetry is a means of self-expression.; [a.] New Cumberland, WV

SILVERA, HYACINTH E.
[pen.] Hya; [b.] May 20, 1939; Jamaica; [p.] Gillan and Rosetta Whyte; [m.] Arnold Silvera; March 23, 1963; [ch.] Rachel A. Silvera; [ed.] Registered Nurse, State Certified Midwife, Public Health Nurse, Home Health Quality Assurance Nurse; [occ.] Registered Nurse, Quality Assurance Department; [memb.] Jamaica Nurses Association of South Florida, Miami Oratorio Society, Jamaican Folk Review, Norland United Methodist Church, Board of Directors for JNAF; [hon.] Jamaican Folk Review for Devoted Service and Contribution since 1975 as Treasurer and founding member JNAF for service and dedication, 1985; Outstanding Service and Dedication Toward the Growth and Future of JNAF, 1989; for service and selfless dedication to JNAF, 1996; [oth. writ.] Poem "Nurses Nurses," published by National Library of Poetry; "Embrace the Morning" [pers.] "Love for God, self, and others. We are all God's creation."; [a.] Miami Lakes, FL

SIMMONS, LAURA A.
[b.] January 22, 1962; Maquoketa, IA; [p.] Arnold and Darla Mangler; [ch.] Whittley, Kay, and Morgan; [ed.] Delwood High School; Lena Clinton Community College, Clinton, IA; [occ.] Accoun-

tant; [hon.] Editor's Choice Award (National Library of Poetry), Award of Recognition (The Famous Poets Society); [oth. writ.] Withered Heart, Forever Wonder, among others, not yet published; [pers.] I write poetry simply from experiences of the heart and day to day observations.; [a.] Delmar, IA

SIMON, RANDOLPH F.
[b.] March 14, 1914; Converse, TX; [p.] Walter and Clara Simon; [m.] Betty Cobb Simon; August 9, 1938; [ch.] Gayle Jensen and Joy Eric Simon; [ed.] B.S.E.E. Univ. of Texas; graduate studies, Univ. of Texas, UCLA, UCSB, Bakersfield College, Venture College; [occ.] Manager of LAAP, which produces greeting cards sold to public; [memb.] Tau Beta Pi, Eta Copper No, Phi Eta Sigma; [hon.] Distinguished Paper Award from SEG, Golden Poet Award from World of Poetry; [oth. writ.] Technical Papers for SEG, review of Scientific Instruments, American Geographical Union, geeting cards marketed by LAAP; [a.] Ventura, CA

SINGLETON, ROSEMARY
[b.] Southport, England; [p.] Mr. and Mrs. Nathan John Singleton; [occ.] Dress Designer; [pers.] A transplant from England to Palm Reach County, Florida, Rosemary has hands on with romantic stories when she designs and fashions brides at her bridal salon.; [a.] West Palm Beach, FL

SIRCY, PATSY JO REED
[pen.] Pattijo rainbow, JaDoM, Rastus, Screaming Eagle, Sista; [b.] February 8, 1944; Gainesboro, TN; [p.] Lester G. Reed and Eliza Jo Lynn Reed; [ch.] Jason Shawn Sircy; [ed.] Gainesboro Elem.; Jackson Co. High, Gainesboro, TN; St. Thomas School of Nursing; and Aquinas Jr. College, Nashville, TN; [occ.] Retired Registered Nurse for 29 years, (ret. due to M.S. in 1991); [memb.] F.U. Meth. Church, Gainesboro; Cub Scout Leader; Red Cross Nurse; NAACP; INS Poets; N&IN Poetry Hof F; MADD; Prev. Beta; 4-H; Science Cl.; "J" Athletic CL, HS; Yearbook St., HS and Col; News P St; Honor St. for 95.18 ave. 4 years; basketball, ES, HS, NS & Col. (Capt.); volleyball, Col; cheerleader, HS; majorette, HS; ten., Col.; JDMFC; [hon.] 8 Ath. Letters, HS—4 Basketball, 3 Maj., 1 Chl., Wolf P in Golden Poet Award 1988 (first year in WC) and IN Awards each year since including National Library Poetry, IN Poetry Museum, Poetry Today Radio IV, Incl. Broadcast IV Source YB of Experts, Authorities, and Spokepersons; [oth. writ.] Several poems published in local newspapers, magazines, and anthologies; published each year since 1988, but some written as early as 1954 at age 10; articles in several magazines, incl. article in TN Conservationist Mag. at age 16, which helped bring attention and action to flood control in TN; also stories, both fiction and non, some children; [pers.] Gap is different in what you know and what you think you know. Advice: don't let your gap get too wide! I have M.S., but nobody is promised a day and mine are well-spent, with no prejudicial thoughts or judgments. Capturing in words the elusive beauties that only exist in the realm of evoked emotions, my rush comes from again setting them free when I share the words with others in love. I am rich! I'm never bored.; [a.] Hartsville, TN

SKILES, PAM
[pen.] Pam K. or Lady P; [b.] June 5, 1953; Chicago, IL; [p.] Richard and Patricia Irelan; [ch.] Gennuie and Nathan Winters, Niaomi and Effie Skiles; [ed.] Phoenix College, Business; Glendale Community College, Social Work; Arizona State University West, Social Work; [occ.] Full-time student getting a degree in Social Work; [memb.] Spectrum, Society for Creative Anachronism (SCA), Social Work Club at Asu West Campus; [hon.] An award from the Phoenix Urban League, awards for poems from SCA; [oth. writ.] Several stories, two plays, tons of poems, and working on two books;

[pers.] We are all related in this world no matter what color our skin, our religion, sex, sexual preference. Therefore we must and should love one another as we love ourselves.; [a.] Phoenix, AZ

SMITH, CRAIG R.
[pen.] Craig R. Smith; [b.] July 24, 1961; Miami, FL; [p.] Enmon Smith and Catherine Smith; [m.] Sharon D. Smith; February 14, 1991; [ch.] Latoya, Tony, T.J., and Azriele; [ed.] Miami Northwestern High, Nova College; [occ.] System Administrator ASA—Ussouthcom—Miami, FL; [memb.] Koninia Worship Center; [hon.] Retired Veteran—United States Army; [oth. writ.] "If, Best Friend," published by The National Library of Poetry

SMITH, CYDYA
[pen.] Sekhmet; [b.] August 25, 1946; Detroit, MI; [p.] Charlie and Edna Ruth Smith; [ed.] Ph.D. in experience from the "University of Life" and a Master's Degree in continuing education; [memb.] Dario Salas Institute for Hermetic Science, International Society of Poets; [hon.] Distinguished Service Award, American Airlines; Golden Poet Award for 1986, World of Poetry; Editor's Choice Award for 1998, National Library of Poetry; [oth. writ.] American Poetry Anthology, 1994; A touch of Elegance, 1998; [pers.] I seek to share the Creator's gifts . . . all of the insights, recollections, and feelings I can capture within the most provocative, evocative combination of words I possess.; [a.] New York, NY

SMITH, ELLEN M.
[pen.] El Lion!; [b.] January 3, 1934; Guymon, OK; [p.] Mary Frances and Carl A. Smith; [ed.] Received Doctorate of Education in Curriculum and Instruction in 1998; [occ.] Educator, Author; [memb.] Phi Delta Kappa, The Delta Kappa Gamma Society, [memb.] International Membership in National Poetry, scholarship from the Delta Kappa Society International, membership in National Poetry Ass., Leader in Elementary Education 1968; [pers.] I have worked in a school for at-risk students in high school in South Carolina. I've learned we need to impose the power of love.; [a.] Notlingham, PA

SODERQUIST, GEORGE WILLIAM
[b.] April 17, 1962; Germany; [p.] Richard and Marlene Soderquist; [occ.] Delivery Driver; [oth. writ.] Have other poem published "Mother Earth Cries" which can be found in the book Chasing The Wind, have also written an unpublished book of poems entitled "Unfinished Songs"; [pers.] I write my poems as songs. I would love to see my poems put to music.; [a.] San Antonio, TX

SOLI, KIM
[pen.] Kim Soli; [b.] July 26, 1973; Philadelphia, PA; [p.] Samuel and Carmela Soli; [ed.] South Philadelphia High 1991 graduate Business Academy (I've taught myself to write poetry.); [memb.] International Society of Poets 1998 (member in good standing); [hon.] The National Honors Society (1990-1991), Four years of excellence in general Business (1991), Editor's Choice Award (1998); [oth. writ.] "A Thank You Condolence to Mother Teresa," published in an anthology called Beyond the Horizon and three unpublished manuscripts; [pers.] "In order to resilience from a personal disaster, evade the evil forces and follow your intuition."; [a.] Philadelphia, PA

SORENSON, SOMMER L.
[pen.] Sommer L. Sorenson; [p.] Michael and Katherine Harrison; [m.] Daniel Sorenson; March 21, 1998; [ed.] Graduate from high school—Half-Moon Bay High; [occ.] Manager at Pet Supply Grooming Shop; [memb.] International Society of Poets; [hon.] Editor's Choice Award for "Close Your Eyes," The Poetry Guild, and Editor's Choice Award, The National Library of Poetry, for "Sunrise," 1997; [a.] San Carlos, CA

SOWELL, JAMES REX
[pen.] J. R. Sowell; [b.] January 18, 1942; Chipley, FL; [p.] Charlie B. Sowell and Ruby Benefield Sowell; [m.] Louise Stone Sowell; [ch.] Patricia, Michael, Jason, and Jacob; [ed.] Chipley High School, Chipley, FL.; Gulf Coast Community College, Panama City, FL; [occ.] Captain (retired), Panama City Police Dept.; currently Deputy Sheriff, Bay County SO Auxiliary; [memb.] Member, International Society of Poets; member, Fraternal Order of Police; member, Central Baptist Church; treasurer, Retired Panama City Police Officers Assoc; [hon.] Received various honors and awards during police career including Optimist Club Policeman of the Year; [oth. writ.] Hobby song writer; [pers.] It's easy to be tough, but it's tough to be easy.; [a.] Panama City, FL

SPADE, VICTORIA
[pen.] Ace, Tori; [b.] June 10, 1983; Franklin, IN; [p.] Julia Spade Scott and Mike Spade; [ed.] Wauconda High; [occ.] Baby Sitter; [memb.] United States Soccer Federation, Swarouski, Umbro Preferred Player Club, and Dreamsicles; [hon.] Many awards in sports and school spirit awards; [oth. writ.] Several poems written, some in school paper and other National Library of Poetry books; [pers.] The poems I write have to do with what I see going on in this world.

SPARKS, DANA
[b.] July 7, 1973; Wayne, MI; [p.] Charles Sparks and Patricia Sparks; [ed.] Wayne Memorial High, Voc. Tech. Registered Nurse's Aide; [oth. writ.] "Their Baby" poem published in Portraits of Life; [pers.] Dana died in 1992 of Cystic Fibrosis, a genetic lung disease. She was only nineteen. She began writing poetry the last year of her life. She dedicated "Precious Angels" to her handicapped nephew, Joey.; [a.] Westland, MI

SPENCER, JOSEPH R.
[pen.] Joseph R. Spencer; [b.] December 3, 1971; Watertown, NY; [p.] Betty Angus, Ronald Spencer; [ch.] Lexa Rain Spencer; [ed.] Watertown High School; [occ.] Poet; [hon.] Outstanding Poets; [oth. writ.] Several poems unpublished; [pers.] "I believe we are here, to enlighten one another."; [a.] Lafanquill, NY

ST. MARK, AUDREY
[b.] October 16, 1942; Worcester, MA; [p.] Edith and Harvey Rayner; [ed.] B.A. University of Mass. at Amherst; M.Ed. Lewis and Clark College Portland, OR; [occ.] Bilingual (Spanish) Public School Teacher, NYC; [memb.] St. Mary's (Episcopal) Church, Editor's "Magnificent" literary publication; [hon.] Who's Who Among Students in American Colleges and Universities, Editor's Choice Award; [oth. writ.] Groping toward Grace, Up from Under, various local publications, former journalist with Association Press; [pers.] My poems are expressions of points along the continuum of human experience. They alight on my shoulder like butterflies; if I don't catch them, they flit away.; [a.] New York City, NY

STANLEY, MARY R.
[b.] June 4, 1930; Burlington, NJ; [p.] Noel A. and Katie Sampson; [m.] Glenn A. Stanley; [ch.] Joanne Mae, Linda Joyce, Donna June, and Lisa Ellen; [ed.] Graduate of Wilbur Watts High School, Burlington, NJ; [occ.] Retired cashier; [memb.] Burlington chapter of Deborah Foundation; [hon.] Received several awards of merit for poetry; [pers.] Poetry reflects my belief in God, my love of country, strong family ties, and hope for the world we live in.; [a.] Burlington, NJ

STEELE, LOIS M.
[b.] May 3, 1913; Newburgh, NY; [p.] Mr. and Mrs. H. S. MacNary, Sr.; [ch.] Dr. Lois Musmann and Richard A. Steele; [ed.] Normal School 1933; Bachelors Degree 1952; Masters Degree 1954;

[occ.] Retired Teacher; [memb.] New York State Retired Teacher, Newburgh Retired Teachers, The Mother Church—Boston; [hon.] Certificate of Appreciation from the N.Y.S. Retired Teacher's Association S.E. Zone, The National Library of Poetry; [pers.] Sharing, helping others, and church activity bring health and happiness.; [a.] Newburgh, NY

STEELE, NANCY
[b.] August 7, 1916; Currituck, NC; [p.] Marvin Leigh and Emily Leigh; [m.] Alexander Steele; April 15, 1933; [ch.] Linda Lee and Alex Ray; [ed.] 7th grade; [occ.] Housewife; [pers.] I love nature.; [a.] Woodville, FL

STEINBRECHER, CHRISTINA
[pen.] Yellow Hat Ramie; [b.] May 3, 1983; Syracuse, NY; [p.] Charles and Wanda Steinbrecher; [ed.] 10th grade student of Cicero North Syracuse High School; [occ.] I currently work with special education children on my free time during school.; [memb.] I am currently a member of the NSTRK Softball Team and have a red belt in Karate at Steve Lavallee's Studio (1998 all-star).; [hon.] I have won awards and many school awards including Outstanding Students.; [oth. writ.] I have written many poems and have had the honor of five publications.; [pers.] I believe that you've never failed or lost, because if you're tried you've already won.; [a.] Syracuse, NY

STEVANOVICH, MAJA
[b.] October 6, 1984; Serbia, Yugoslavia; [p.] Zivomir and Stoja Stevanovich; [ed.] Elm Dale Elementary School, Greenfield Middle School, and four years (1st-4th grades) in Serbia; [occ.] Student; [memb.] National Junior Honor Society, Kidz Biz—Warner Cable's TV Show, forensics, band, chorus, and school newspaper; [hon.] Honor diplomas, 4.00 GPA award, top 0.05 percent of class, speaking club's trophies, band medals, writing contest trophies, math awards, editor of school newspaper; [oth. writ.] Poem, "Science of Future," a couple of other stories and essays, also articles for the school newspaper; [pers.] I always tried to improve, throughout my years so far. I owe most of my accomplishments to my Uncle Steve Stevanovich and my teacher Mrs. Tosic.; [a.] Milwaukee, WI

STONE, ASHLEY RHIANNON
[b.] August 13, 1986; Akron City Hospital; [p.] Robert Stone and Peggy Stone; [ed.] 7th Grade at Miller South School; [occ.] Student; [memb.] Fan Club for the WNBA Cleveland Rockers; [hon.] Scholarships; [oth. writ.] Shiloh, My Cat; [pers.] I have two black cats named Shiloh (boy) and Getty (girl). I also have a goldfish named Blackie. I am very honored to have my poems published; [a.] Akron, OH

STOWE, CYLE
[pen.] C.T. Sekulski; [oth. writ.] "Endure": a poem; [pers.] While we may call it progress that the end has lost its naive sense of imminence, I fear it has also lust its sense of immanence. Mankind needs origins and ends to make meaning of his life and world, even if that order is constructed, provisional, and temporary.

STREETMAN, ROBERT O.
[b.] September 22, 1940; Columbus, GA; [p.] Ruth N. Streetman and Walter H.; [m.] Nancy G.; January 23, 1959; [ch.] Robert Jr., Nancy, and Jennifer; [ed.] Columbus High School; [occ.] Maintenance Supervisor, Tom's Foods Inc; [memb.] St. Mark United Methodist Church, Proactive Evangelism Ministries, lay evangelism and discipleship ministries, Promise Keepers; [oth. writ.] Poems and Thoughts (Unpublished), "People Of Loving Heart" in '97 National Library of Poetry anthology, "Love Songs" in '98 National Library of Poetry anthology; [pers.] The one things that is a constant of life is love. He was there in the

beginning and will be there when all else is gone. The alpha and omega is love, and we would not be here without him, for God is love.; [a.] Cusseta, GA

STRICKLER, DAVID J.
[a.] Ft. Polk, LA

STRIKER, HUGH
[pen.] Hugh Striker; [b.] January 22, 1947; Jackson, MI; [p.] James Hugh and Helen Minney Striker; [ch.] Christopher Lee and Melody Ann Striker; [ed.] 7th grade; [oth. writ.] Spirits of the Eagles, A Chance, Sweet Little Sis., and many more, like Two Its My Time, Simple Things, and others; [pers.] I love the works of Helen Steiner Rice—she is great. I write about the spirits, death, and life, for I am half Indian and have been dead and know what the other side is like.; [a.] Interlachen, FL

STUFFLE, GRACE M.
[b.] January 21, 1922; Martin, CO; [p.] Wilbert and Belma Dove; [m.] Calvin H. Stuffle; January 4, 1941; [ch.] Loren, Nancy, Marilyn, Joe, and Johnny; [ed.] High School; [memb.] Catholic Church; [hon.] Certificate of Talent Cactus Flower 1984; Honorable Mention, 1989-1990 by World Of Poetry; Award of Merit, 1998; Golden Poet Award 1989, 1990-1991 from World of Poetry; [oth. writ.] Several songs over the years; International Poetry Hall of Fame, certificate; [pers.] I thought I would quit writing when I recognize my Hall of Fame Certificate. "No way," thank you; [a.] Loodootee, IN

SULMAN, LAURIE A.
[b.] New York; [p.] Lois M. Sulman and Michael Sulman; [ed.] Tallahassee Community College, State University of New York; [hon.] Dean's List, "The Eyrie Award for Distinctive Service," specifying the free verse "Foreward" and "Afterword" to "The Eyrie," annually published humanities magazines of Tallahassee Community College, award for a poetic contribution to another issue of "The Eyrie;" appointed to editorial staff of said magazine, other honors include (partial listing) early recognition in a Canadian-based youth competition at eleven years of age: awarded first prize in poetry, and first prize in art; [a.] Lynbrook, NY

SUSEN, LAURIE
[b.] August 15, 1983; NJ; [p.] Allan and Ruth Susen; [ed.] Eastern Christian High School as a Sophomore in September 1998; [oth. writ.] Many other unpublished poems and musical lyrics; [pers.] I would like again to thank three special brothers from Tulsa, OK. These are a couple of quotes I value: "Each of us wages a private battle each day between the grand fantasies we have for ourselves and what actually happens."—Cathy Guisewite. "Young people have an almost biological destiny to be hopeful."—Marshall Ganz. "Volunteering and giving should not be honored or admired, it should be expected."; [a.] Haledon, NJ

SUTTON, OLIVER
[pen.] "All of a sudden"; [b.] March 3, 1951; [ch.] Omar (son), Iyana (daughter); [ed.] San Francisco State; [occ.] Security officer; [memb.] Pro Arts theater group, Polk and Bean poetry club; [hon.] Editor's Choice Award, The National Library of Poetry; headliner, Polk and Bean Poetry Mc; "Spoken Word," Fisherman's Wharf, SF; [oth. writ.] "The Alley," "Wings of freedom"; [pers.] "Life is motion, motion is life; if you never go, you'll never know."; [a.] Oakland, CA

SWARTWOOD, MICHAEL
[b.] September 24, 1937; Omaha, NE; [p.] Mr. and Mrs. Merril Swartwood; [m.] Kathy Swartwood; April 17, 1973; [ed.] Junior college; [memb.] Odd Fellows; [a.] San Mateo, CA

SWINYER, THERESA
[pen.] Theresa Swinyer; [b.] September 9, 1938;

Claremon, NH; [p.] Edmund Lavoie and Annabell Lavoie; [m.] Richard Swinyer; May 23, 1959; [ch.] Karen Ray and Jodi Herrera; [ed.] Saint Mary's High; Los Angeles Mission College, the Degree of Associate in Arts; [occ.] Special Education Assistant, Beachy Elementary School, Arleta, CA; [memb.] Paralyzed Veterans of America, American Heart Association, National Foundation for Cancer Research; [hon.] PTA Honorary Service Certificate, Los Angeles Mission College, Certificate in Child Development, Award, Exceptional Children Teachers Assistant; [oth. writ.] Precious Daughter; [pers.] I love to write poerty, and I love that my poems are inspirational and meaningful to the people who read them.; [a.] Sylmar, CA

SZUTENBACH, DREAMA
[pen.] Dreama Szutenbach; [b.] August 5, 1954; Bainbridge, MD; [p.] David and Joyce Dishman; [m.] Richard; July 2, 1983; [ch.] Chris, Richard, and Bryan; [ed.] St. John's High, some college; [occ.] United States Air Force; [memb.] Air Force Sergeants' Association; [oth. writ.] The Colors of Thought, The National Library of Poetry, 1996; [pers.] Thank you, God, for giving me such a special sister and the encouragement I get from her.; [a.] Dover, DE

TALLEY, ELIZABETH
[pen.] Caticah Erosia; [b.] June 20, 1070; Little Rock, AR; [p.] Stanley P. and Lela Talley; [ch.] Megan Farnum; [ed.] Conway Schools and The University of Central Arkansas; [occ.] Workstudy; [memb.] American Red Cross and The International Society of Poets; [oth. writ.] Various newspapers, magazines, vortex, many National Library of Poetry anthologies; [pers.] If you do something and you don't like it, then try something different. Trying is what makes a person better.; [a.] Conway, AR

TAYLOR, MARGARET H.
[pen.] Margaret H. Taylor; [b.] October 22, 1933; Paisley, Scotland; [p.] Ben and Sarah Hamilton; [m.] Joe Ben Taylor; March 25, 1953; [ch.] Joanne, Tracy, and Craig; [ed.] High school, college soph.; [memb.] IS of P, Sadia Presbyterian Church Women, UNMH Auxiliary; [hon.] Distinguished Poet 97, Poet of Merit, President's Award 1998 NAR, and several other awards; [oth. writ.] A Helping Hand, The Season of Loving and Giving, Past, Present, Future, Seasons Coming and Going; [pers.] My poetry comes from my schooling in Scotland and a very special teacher; I try to have a point that is understandable in my poems.

TAYLOR, MARGARET H.
[b.] October 22, 1933; Paisley, Scotland; [p.] Ben and Sarah Hamilton; [m.] Joe B. Taylor; March 28, 1953; [ch.] Joanne, Tracy, and Craig; [ed.] High school, soph. college; [occ.] Housewife; [memb.] Sandia Presbyterian Church and Sandia P.W. Group, member Aux., UNMH, International Society of Poets; [hon.] Poet of Merit, Honorable Mention (2) Editor's Choice Award, Honorable Mention, National Author's Registry; [oth. writ.] Mountains, Peace, Time, Houses That Become Homes, Seasons Coming and Going, My Garden of Flowers, Teacups, Winter Blessings, Just Think, When Night Comes, Angels Everywhere, The Misplaced Book; [pers.] My poetry writing was greatly influenced by an English teacher in junior high level in school; this was at Barrhead, Scotland. My writing is varied. We have three children, all College graduates. I've been published seven times.; [a.] Albuquerque, NM

TAYLOR, PATTY LARAE
[b.] September 3, 1969; Tulsa, OK; [p.] Barbara and Russell Shipley; [ch.] Marshall; [ed.] Graduated from Tulsa Central High School in 1988; [occ.] Imaging Associate with Danka Services International; [oth. writ.] Previously published in the Between the Raindrops anthology; [pers.] Live every day as if it were your last.; [a.] Olathe, KS

TEAL, JOSIE HALLER
[b.] August 15, 1936; Houston, TX; [p.] Walter and Viola Haller; [m.] Dr. James S. Teal; August 7, 1960; [ch.] James S. Teal II; [ed.] Jack Yates High, Wiley College, San Francisco State University, Texas Southern University, University of San Francisco; [occ.] Recently Retired Educator; [memb.] Jones Memorial (UMC, CACD, Alpha Delta Kappa Sorority for Women Educators, NAACP, cascos martial Arts; [hon.] CACD Human Rights Award; [oth. writ.] Black History Is No Mystery, Strange Happenings, Families, My Gifts, I Write, My Story; [pers.] It's a joy, to me, that my simple writing brings pleasure to so many.; [a.] San Francisco, CA

TERRY, NNDRA
[pen.] Nndra Terry; [b.] January 11, 1935; AR; [p.] Dave Terry and Arlene Terry (deceased); [ch.] Michelle, Percy, Steve, Natalie, Leila, Dominique, and Antray; [ed.] Lincoln High School, Fort Smith, AR; Arkansas A.M. and N. College (incomplete), Pine Bluff, AR; [hon.] Editor's Choice Award for Outstanding Achievement in Poetry, presented by The National Library of Poetry, 1997; [oth. writ.] My Books; When Push Comes to Shove; Where I Am in My Life; Do the Best That I Can Do, God Will Do the Rest; Expose; My Truth; [pers.] Do the best that I can do. God will do the rest. Do not worry about anything ever.; [a.] Portland, OR

THAYER, MILDRED N.
[b.] September 12, 1918; Brewen, ME; [p.] John Craig and Natalie Mae Thayer; [ed.] Brewer High School; Machias Normal School at Machias, ME; B.S., University of Maine; Med. University of Maine; [occ.] Retired; [memb.] Nat' Honor Society, Delta Kappa Gamma, Magna Cum Laude, Machias; [hon.] Leader in American Secondary Ed., chosen as typical of the best in church school teachers; [oth. writ.] History at Brewen, ME, 1962; book, Patch Work and Plough Shares, 1994; articles in Down East, The Maine Teacher, Nat'l Science Teacher, other educational magazines; [pers.] Briefly—I believe my personal feelings are the love of God, people, and nature, as are reflected in my poetry.; [a.] Hampden, ME

THEOHARI, ROZI
[b.] April 9, 1939; Albania; [p.] Pandi and Alexandra Cheque; [m.] Viktor Theohari; December 28, 1959; [ch.] Diana Sommer Theori and Akil Theori; [ed.] University of Freiburg, Germany and University and Tirana, Albania; [occ.] Student in NSCC, Lynn; [memb.] Community Minority Cultural Center, nc. in Lynn, MA; member of Lynn Arts, Inc. in Lynn, MA; member of International Poetry Hall of Fame; [hon.] Phi Theta Kappa, The National Dean's List; [oth. writ.] Several books in Native Country, publishes constantly in the local newspapers and in "Illyria," the Albanian American Newspaper in New York; [pers.] A poem is just a fragile flower which can flourish only with the care of a skillful poet.; [a.] Lynn, MA

THOMAS, BARBARA
[pen.] Barbara Thomas; [b.] February 5, 1936; Ft. Yuma, CA; [p.] Melvin and Geneva Stanley; [m.] Marvin D. Thomas; April 4, 1976; [ch.] Five; [ed.] 12th, self-taught, have ten songs published by Hilltop Records, hope to have first manuscript published for poetry; [occ.] Mining and Construction; [memb.] Private Property Nia Mining; [hon.] Music, poetry, Hilltop Records, The National Library of Poetry, Motorcyle Riding Award; [oth. writ.] Otoe Missourian Indian, have been writing for 15 years, National Library of Poetry—have 15 poems published in anthology books; [pers.] If I can touch person's heart with one word, what a wonderful world is sharing of poetry and music. She welcomes hearing from you.; [a.] Downieville, CA

THOMAS, EUGENE
[b.] June 14, 1942; SC; [ch.] Gary, Shawn, Chris-

topher, Phaedra, and Bruce; [ed.] Some college; [occ.] Disabled Back Injury; [pers.] I'm a pretty good example of "You can take the boy out of the country, but you can't take the country out of the boy."; [a.] Brooklyn, NY

THOMAS, LEE ANN
[pen.] Sparky; [b.] October 7, 1976; Jamestown, NY; [p.] Lee E. Jones and Ruby L. Farrally; [m.] Gavis V. Thomas; June 25, 1996; [ch.] Lee Robert, Sterling Gavic-Von, and CY Joshua; [ed.] Adult Learning Programs of Alaska High School; [occ.] Cab Driver, Homemaker, Floks, AK; [memb.] Greater New Hope Baptist Church; [hon.] Poetry awards given since 3rd grade, Mental Toughness Award, Youth Build; [oth. writ.] Several poems published in newspapers, two poems published by National Library of Poetry; [pers.] I write most of my poetry by experience, some by thought, but all of my poems are blessed by God.; [a.] Floks, AK

THOMPSON, MATT
[pen.] Dick Williams; [b.] December 22, 1978; Indianapolis; [p.] Madonna Thompson and Wayne Thompson; [ed.] Graduated from Center Grove High School, attending Indiana University's School of Journalism; [occ.] Co-host of "The Really Really Big Show" on WIUS Radio; [hon.] Two time winner of Academic Academy of University Women's free verse poetry award, National Library of Poetry's Editor's Choice Award; [oth. writ.] Several published poems, two screen plays, two novels, long narrative Christmas poem, three award-winning poems: "Would A Baby Walk," "Testing Troubles," "Mr. Question"; [pers.] My writings are only as good as my readers proclaim them to be. (Unless I disagree with them.); [a.] Indianapolis, IN

THRASHER, ELISE
[b.] May 3, 1935; Germany; [p.] Johanna Wonderlehr, Furst Kies; [m.] William A. Thrasher; July 8, 1983; [ch.] Three; [ed.] School of life, skill living and learning; [occ.] Retired from Sales; [memb.] Covenant Presbyterian, Kennestone Volunteer Services; [hon.] Sales Award, Award for poetry written; [oth. writ.] Many other poems and short stories; [pers.] I bring my life's path to my writing in the hope it can benefit others.; [a.] Marietta, GA

TIBBITTS, JOSIE
[b.] August 16, 1979; Alexandria, VA; [p.] Thomas and Linda Tibbitts; [ed.] Hemet H.S., Brigham Young University; [occ.] Student BYU; [memb.] International Society of Poets, The Church of Jesus Christ of Laller-Day Saints; [oth. writ.] Several other poems published by The National Library of Poetry; [pers.] It is our responsibility to preserve our beliefs, but we must be careful that in doing so, we are not nullifying the freedom of others.; [a.] Hemet, CA

TIETJEN, DONNA D.
[pen.] Donna D. Tietjen; [b.] March 27, 1948; Rockville, Ct; [p.] Donald J. and Marion J. Donegan; [m.] William J. Tietjen Jr.; November 7, 1970; [ch.] William D., Janet L., and Siobhan E.; [ed.] Twelve years, high school; [occ.] Bank Teller, American Savings Bank; [memb.] Church of the Open Door; [oth. writ.] The Tragedy of Fun E.T.; [pers.] I thank the Lord my God for the gift that He has bestowed on me, and I wish that my poetry is enjoyed by others.; [a.] Clinton, CT

TOWNSEND, TERESA E.
[pen.] Tet; [b.] June 3, 1954; Lincoln, NE; [p.] Helen L. Rustermier White and Thomas L. Townsend Sr.; [ch.] Michael, Robert, John, Chris, and Clara Mae; [ed.] Some college and a degree in Truck Driving; [occ.] Homemaker; [memb.] St. Mary's Catholic Church; [hon.] Navy Wives Club; [oth. writ.] Unseen Gifts; Elvis's Story in His Songs, published in Letters to Elvis from His Fans; [pers.] Writing comes from God and your heart.; [a.] Lincoln, NE

TRACY, SHANNON
[b.] September 6, 1981; [p.] Ginny and Jeff; [ed.] 10th grade, East Paulding Middle School; [occ.] Student; [memb.] Girls Scouts, Band, The National Beta Club; [hon.] Silver Award, GS Honor Roll; [oth. writ.] Other poems in books, personal writing, and one new print; [pers.] Matthew's chapter seven: judge not, that ye be not judged.; [a.] Dallas, GA

TRIMARCHI, CARMELLA
[pen.] Candi Merideth; [b.] February 6, 1982; West Palm Beach, FL; [p.] James and Jerilyn Merideth; [ed.] 10th grade; [memb.] International Society of Poets; [hon.] Editor's Choice Award; [oth. writ.] "Gone in the Night," published in Anthology of Poetry by Young Americans; "Dreams," published in Soaring with the Wind; [pers.] Don't ever say things will get worse; keep your head up and things will go your way. Don't lose faith.

TSCHOPP, MARILYN
[pen.] Marilyn Tschopp; [b.] February 6, 1939; [p.] Helen and Bill Sargent; [ch.] Warner Jr., Aimee, Wendy, and Heidi; [occ.] Handicapped, owned a florist and garden business; [memb.] Milford Garden Club; [hon.] National Library of Poetry—poem, "Loving You, My Brother, My Friend,"—Editor's Choice Award 1998; [pers.] My love was to listen to my mother's poems, and I feel I have been greatly inspired by them. She now has passed away.; [a.] Milford, PA

TULLOCK, JOHN H.
[b.] April 24, 1928; Delano, TN; [p.] W. R. and Ollie Grace Tullock; [m.] Helen Curtis Tullock; June 21, 1946; [ch.] Sharon E. and John Laurens; [ed.] B.A., Carson-Newman; B.D. Southeastern Baptist Theol. Sem.; Ph. D. Vanderbilt; [occ.] Retired, Prof. Emeritus of Religion, Belmont University; [memb.] Soc. of Biblical Lit., National Assoc. of Bapt. Profs. of Rel.; [hon.] Teacher of the Year, Belmont College, 1993; [oth. writ.] The Old Testament Story, Sepren. Hall; "Deuteronomy," Mercer Comm. on the Bible, Mercer Press; Numerous dictionary articles, Sunday school lessons; [pers.] I have been happily married to my high school English teacher for two years. I never worry about the past; I just look to the future.; [a.] Delano, TN

TYSON, JUDY
[pen.] Judy Tyson; [b.] January 4, 1950, Denver, CO; [ed.] B.F.A., University of Tennessee; [occ.] Artist, Reiki Practitioner; [memb.] Tennessee Artist Association; [oth. writ.] Poems published in other books of The National Library of Poetry; [pers.] I hope that my poetry reflects the beauty and honesty of the human situation.; [a.] Maryville, TN

UNDERWOOD, ALEXIA
[b.] October 29, 1982; Kuwait City; [p.] Carmel and Robert Underwood; [ed.] Edward Douglas White High School, Bear Creek High School; [hon.] Attended FL State Young Author's Conference, was invited to attend International Poetry Conference, two years; [oth. writ.] Have had four poems published; [pers.] Live each day to its fullest.; [a.] Stockton, CA

UNDERWOOD, JULIANA R., PH.D
[pen.] Juliana R. Underwood Ph.D; [b.] February 8, 1938; San Bernardino, CA; [p.] Wm. Pittand and Lilah D. Hand; [m.] Arthur; widow; [ch.] One—Christopher; [ed.] B.A. in Music, Ph.D in Psychology; [occ.] Retired, some counselling; [memb.] Treasure of the Poetry Society of CO, Inc., Evergreen's Women's Club, AAUW, Christian Women's Club, Secretary of Ridge Runners; [hon.] Square Dance Club, Gifted in the International Who's Who in Poetry, International Biographical Centre, Cambridge England; [oth. writ.] Poems in: Spirit of the Age, Best Poems of 1996, 1997, and 1998, Of Summer's Passing—National Library of Poetry; poems in Parnassus of World Poets 1996, 97, and 98; [pers.] I started writing poetry in 1986.

I like to incorporate my psychological and musical background into my writing.; [a.] Evergreen, CO

VALENZUELA, KYMBERLY BROWN
[pen.] Kymberly Brown; [b.] May 4, 1968; Montclair, NJ; [p.] Edward W. Brown and Ethel M. Brown; [ch.] Cornelia Adelita and Virginia Charlotte; [ed.] B.A. Douglass College, Rutgers University, studied with Miguel Algarin, English Dept., and Stephen Bronner, Political Theory; [occ.] Teacher; [memb.] Bittman J. Rivas Theatre Ensemble, C.H.A.R.A.S., NY, NY; [hon.] Edna Herzog Prize for Short Fiction, Douglas College, 1988; 3rd Place, The National Library of Poetry, Verdant Lands of Spring edition; [oth. writ.] Novel in progress, The Electric Zip; poems in Aloud, Voices from the Nuyorican Poets Cafe, and Long Shot Magazine, Hoboken, NJ; [pers.] "A poem bridges the loneliness of the soul and the imperfect world, pulls out the bits of glory, and destroys false sentimentality."; [a.] Jersey, NJ

VAN ZEELAND, MELVIN
[pen.] Melvin Van Zeeland; [b.] March 29, 1932; Little Chute, WI; [p.] George and Josephine Van Zeeland; [m.] Doris Jean; September 8, 1956; [ch.] Julie, Larry, Karen, and Bruce; [ed.] High school and many years at Fox Valley Tech, Appleton, WI; [occ.] Pipe Fitter; [memb.] Wisconsin Orchestra Association; [hon.] Leading Salesman all four years for magazines, Best Grandpa Award, upper third of my class; [oth. writ.] "Song of My Heart," also "My Friend," also "My Mother"; [pers.] Put a little fun in your life, go dancing.; [a.] Kaukauna, WI

VANBREEN, ALAINA
[pen.] Destiny Marie; [b.] February 14, 1980; San Jose, CA; [ed.] Graduate of Presentation High School; [occ.] Sales; [memb.] National Arts Honor Society; [hon.] Editor's Choice Award, International Poet of Merit; [oth. writ.] Silence published in Above the Clouds, other poems published in school paper, The Muse; [pers.] I write feelings that come from my heart.; [a.] San Jose, CA

VANOORD, LISA
[pen.] Lisa VanNoord; [b.] July 22, 1979; Grand Rapids, MI; [p.] Craig and Mary VanNoord; [ed.] Calvin Christian High School, attending Calvin College; [oth. writ.] My poem "Grandpa" published in A View from Afar; [pers.] I use my talents to glorify my Lord and savior Jesus Christ. I strive to live my life for Him.; [a.] Grandville, MI

VASCONCELOS, LINDA
[b.] September 27, 1947; Omaha, NE; [p.] Trygue, Lilian Vie; [ch.] Alejandro, Amanda, and Jennifer; [ed.] A.A. in Science; [occ.] Vocational Nurse; [memb.] Girl Scouts, Writer's Progress, Good Shepherd Lutheran Church; [hon.] Golden Poetry Award, Award of Achievement—Amherst Society, Editor's Choice—The National Library of Poetry, Poetry Hall of Fame, Dean's List in college; [oth. writ.] Poems published in various anthologies since 1989; book of poetry Between Laughter and Tears; short stories, A Tale Spinner; [pers.] "Creativity and logic combine to fire life."; [a.] Joshua Tree, CA

VAUGHAN, WENDELL L.
[b.] May 8, 1921; Iberia, MO; [p.] Samuel and Mellie Vaughan; [m.] Vivian R. Vaughan; December 28, 1941; [ch.] Victor Vaughan and Debbie Bellew; [ed.] Iberia Academy, Iberia, MO; (AB) Drury College Springfield, MO; (BD) Brite Divinity School TCU, Ft. Worth, TX; [pers.] My writing has done much for me in obtaining additional insight and perspective into self, others, and life in general.; [a.] Lakewood, CO

VERNON, EMILY
[pen.] Emily; [b.] May 30, 1986; Pasadena, CA; [p.] Fran Vernon and Steve Vernon; [ed.] 7th grade; [hon.] Medals and trophies from dance and gymnastics; [a.] La Canada, CA

VIDAURE, THOMAS E.
[pen.] Tommy Vidaure; [b.] October 7, 1973; Phoenix, AZ; [p.] Thomas S. Vidaure Sr. and Mercedes G. Lopez; [ed.] Maryvale High, Metro Tech, Maricopa Skill Center; [occ.] Cook (at the Olive Garden); [hon.] Editor's Choice Award (Presented by The National Library of Poetry); [oth. writ.] Written 80 other poems, one poem in Thoughts by Candlelight book; [pers.] My love and my poetry have something in common: I have a lot of it, and I'm always willing to share it. Poetry is also a good way to serve God. And the talent should not be wasted.; [a.] Phoenix, AZ

VINSON, TESHA A.
[occ.] Retired white-collar worker; [memb.] Mount Horeb Baptist Church N.C., N.W. and K.H.S.A.A., and Local 153, Langston Hughes Library Community Center, Ladies Aux. to V.F.W. Post 5298; [hon.] Have appeared on TV twice, Deoconess in my church, Church Announcer, Public Speaker, received certificate for religious writings, recite and write plays and stories; [oth. writ.] In Dorie Miller Housing History Book, "Tillie, the Homeless Mother," co-editor—Dorie Miller, News Golden Poet, Queensboro Public Library System Award; [pers.] I love to treat. I wish to be treated, provide opportunities and involve others' love, sharing.; [a.] Corona, NY

WAGGONER, BARBARA
[b.] November 29, 1922; Milwaukee, WI; [p.] Ethel Williams and Robert Laderlie; [m.] Paul E. Waggoner; November 3, 1945; [ch.] Von and Daniel Waggoner; [ed.] B.S. University of Wisconsin—Madison, WI, 1941-45, majors in Speech and English, minor in History; [occ.] English Teacher, Juneau, WI, 1945-46; Proofreader, Iowa State University Press 1950-51; Substitute Teacher, Guilford, CT, Junior High School 1960; Teacher, Community Nursery School, Guilford, CT, 1964-71; Transcriber, Tape Guide, Guilford, CT, 1984-85; Salesperson, Zimmerman and Fink, Guilford, CT, 1986-87; Customer Service Representative, Audio Forum, Guilford, CT, 1987-88; [hon.] Volunteer Recognition Program Award, Hartford Courant 1983-84; Coalition of Connecticut Bicyclist Recognition 1988, Pequot Cyclists; John Fletcher Award 1988; [oth. writ.] Story of the The Mile Course Bike Race in Guilford, CT; "Biking Day" poem in the Connecticut Bicycle Book; "Deserted," The National Library of Poetry, Chambers of Time, 1997; "The Attic," The National Library of Poetry, The Fabric of Life, 1988; [pers.] I have always observed the world around me. Most of my writing expresses those observations.; [a.] Guilford, CT

WAGNER, DOROTHY CRUM
[b.] December 20, 1923; Wilmore, PA; [p.] William and Meta Crum; [m.] Frank W. Wagner; October 24, 1943; [ch.] Kenneth Wayne, Eileen Marie; [ed.] Conemaugh Twp. High School, American School, 2 years in College (Business). Secretary, St. Luke's Luth. Church, Breakthrough Intercessors, Esther Circle, Past Publicity Chairman; [memb.] Member of Bowling League, Rifle Club, Who's Who in Executives; [oth. writ.] Mostly poems, prayers, short story for children; Two poems previously published by National Library of Poetry, two prayers published; [pers.] I like to encourage people, still believe in themselves, convince them they can achieve if they are willing to try and not give in to doubts. I have been influenced by people who achieved their goals through hardships and struggles and determination.; [a.] Cuyahoga Falls, OH

WAGNER, TERESA
[pen.] Teresa Wagner; July 29, 1966; Tucker, GA; [p.] Jerald Venson Bryson and Bobbie Ann Pligrim; [m.] Donald Jay Wagner; February 7, 1997; [oth. writ.] Several poems have been sent to The Na-

tional Library of Poetry. "Surrender" was published in the book Whispers at Dusk.; [a.] Covington, GA

WAITE, SHELLIE
[pen.] Shellie Marie Waite; [b.] October 14, 1975; Denton, TX; [p.] Patricia Stone, Gil Waite; [m.] Paul A. Howard; June 6, 1998; [ed.] Mission Blvd. Christian High, Fayetteville Beauty College; [occ.] Hairdresser, Nanny; [oth. writ.] On the Other Side?, Hero's Never Forgotten, a book called Passion for Poetry; [pers.] Never regret the trials in your life, for that is when we truly grow.; [a.] Springdale, AR

WAKEFIELD, LANA
[pen.] Bright Eye and Bushy Tail, The Poet; [b.] August 17, 1963; Ogden, Weber, UT; [p.] Dennis and Louise Wakefield; [ed.] High school graduate and four years of Seminary of the Church of Jesus Christ of Latter Day Saints; [memb.] The Church of Jesus Christ of Latter Day Saints; [hon.] Nominated Poet of the Year in 1997 and 1998, 4th place Editor's Choice Awards, seven of the poems writer; [oth. writ.] About five poems are written a year; [pers.] This is to the families of the ill-fated Titanic disaster. I haven't been able to see the movie and may never; parts of the excerpts of the movie I have seen. The parts that I have seen tell me a lot of how tragic it was. I am sorry for your loss.; [a.] South Ogden, UT

WALLACE, WILLIAM J. M., III
[pen.] B. DuBua; [b.] December 5, 1934; Louisville, KY; [p.] William II and Martha E. Wallace; [m.] Harriet Frances James Wallace; October 10, 1959; [ch.] Matt and Will IV; [ed.] Graduate of Bexley High, OH, 1952; graduate of Universal Heavy Equipment, Beaumont, CA, 1962; [occ.] Security Officer; [oth. writ.] "Your Favorite Car, Your Favorite Job," influenced by Stephen Collins Foster and O. Henry, "A Vocational Synopsis, W.V. M.W. III"; [pers.] I am but I ain't; I would but I won't; I was but I wasn't; I did but I don't.; [a.] Columbus, OH

WALTERS, FRANCES L.
[b.] Magnolia, MS; [p.] Arthur and Dollie Walters; [ed.] Magnolia High School LPN Nursing School; [oth. writ.] Have had three poems published, one each in three different anthology books; [pers.] I like for my poems to have words about God in them. Maybe someone's life will be touched.; [a.] Magnolia, MS

WALTSAK, ROBERT
[pen.] Bob Waltsak; [b.] May 31, 1921; Newark, NJ; [p.] Wiliam and Regina Waltsak; [ch.] Robert, William, Carol, June, Richard, Mary Ann, Mark, Monica, Julia, and George Waltsak; [ed.] United States Merchant Marine Academy, Kings Point, LI, NY, class of 1943; Seton Hall University, South Orange, NJ class of 1949; [occ.] Retired (Poet and Artist); [memb.] Annapolis Water Color Club, Knights of Columbus; [hon.] International Poetry Hall of Fame, Albert Galletin Award, US Treasury Department; [oth. writ.] The National Library of Poetry: Man's Dilemma, 1993; My Destiny, 1995; Choice, 1994; and Due Response, 1997; [a.] Annapolis, MD

WAMPLER, W. C.
[pen.] W. C. Wampler, Aka Wild Bill; [m.] Dianne M. Lynch; [ch.] W.C.W. Jr.; [occ.] Songwriter/Musician; [memb.] J-Bird Records Inc., Witton, Ct., Wilton, Conn.; M.U.S.I.C. Coalition, Springfield, Mass.; [hon.] Piano Player of the Year in the Berkshires 1993, Berkshire Eagle Newspaper; [oth. writ.] Four poems published, 21 songs copyrighted, 100 songs written; [pers.] I am Wild Bill, songwriter, musician. I write what I play. I mean what I say. They can like it, or they can don't.; [a.] Otis, MA

WANDEL, LAURA DIANE
[b.] February 28, 1984; Fort Worth, TX; [p.] Warren and Dara Wandel; [ed.] High school at All

Saint's Episcopal School; [occ.] Student; [memb.] National Junior Honor Society; [hon.] Daughters of the American Revolution Essay Award, Silver Medal Short Story Award, published previously in National Library of Poetry; [oth. writ.] Several other poems and short stories; [a.] Ft. Worth, TX

WARD, BOBBIE
[b.] August 25, 1951; San Angelo, TX; [p.] Marshall and Inez Rackley; [ch.] Tommy and Tammy; [ed.] High school plus come college; [occ.] Legal Secretary; [hon.] A certified professional legal secretary, I have another poem coming out in The Glistening Stars this fall.; [oth. writ.] Profile of West TX; [a.] Midland, TX

WARE, DAWN P.
[a.] Independence, MO

WARN, L. MILA
[pen.] L. Mila Warn; [b.] March 23, 1913; Goose Hollow in Portland, OR; [p.] Harold and Rena Warn; [ed.] Graduate of Gregory Heights Elementary School; Grant High School, Portland, OR; and University of OR, Portland State University to teach; [occ.] Retired Fashion Coordinator, Minister, and Teacher; [memb.] Orea, AARP; [hon.] After studying the ministry and being ordained, filled the pulpit 13 1/2 years at Christ Church Universal where became a Doctor of Divinity before leaving the church to teach it; [oth. writ.] Poems Eugene, OR, ESL at Lincoln H.S. 1970 to 1980; [pers.] After teaching ten years at Lincoln H.S., I was transferred to Madison H.S., taught there 1980-1982. At 65 years old I had to retire; now I have been a volunteer tutor 16 years at Cleveland and Madison High School each day; [a.] Portland, OR

WATSON, JANICE R.
[b.] June 24, 1960; Marion County; [p.] Milton Reaves and Martha Bethea Reaves; [m.] Eddie D. Watson; June 23, 1979; [ch.] Kristi Lee Watson; [ed.] Mullins High School—1979, Florence Darlington Technical College, Associate in Business, 1989; [occ.] Art Director for "Different Strokes Art Gallery," Legal/Medical Transcriptionist; [memb.] Dillon County Museum Volunteer, Atta Revitalization Sub-Committee, Alumni Association; [hon.] National Dean's List, Scholastic All-American Award, Voice of Democracy Speech Contest Winner, Good Citizenship Award, Editor's Choice Award 1998, International Poetry Hall of Fame; [oth. writ.] Local articles for Different Strokes Public Relation Dept., inspirational poetry plaques; [pers.] I enjoy sharing life experiences through poetry writing, relating positive feelings and solutions from my personal experiences.; [a.] Latta, SC

WATTS, LANE
[pen.] Lane Watts; [b.] July 21, 1961; Midland, TX; [p.] Lynwood and Shirley Watts; [m.] Maureen Watts; December 31, 1990; [ch.] Georgia, John, and Reid; [ed.] Robert E. Lee High School, IBEW Electrical Apprenticeship, Brazosport College; [occ.] Projects Manager, Hensley's Computer Cabling; [memb.] National Rifle Association; [hon.] Phi Theta Kappa—National Honor Fraternity, Deans List; [oth. writ.] "Desert Nights," published in The Peace We Knew, several unpublished; [a.] Midland, TX

WATTS, LENA
[pen.] Lena Watts; [b.] December 31, 1917; Kensington, NH; [p.] George and Ada Beckman; [m.] Stephen Watts (deceased); October 31, 1959; [ch.] Frank Watts; [ed.] high school; [hon.] Have six poems published, no awards; [oth. writ.] Published my state of New Hampshire policeman's song, Human City, Life and How It Is, Save the Rain Forest; [pers.] I love to write, believe in helping others, was a shoe worker; I am 80 years old now.; [a.] Manchester, NH

WAYTE, ALICIA R.
[pen.] A.R. Wayte/Solice Black-Raven; [b.] June 23, 1979; Riverdale; [p.] Rosa and Donald Wayte; [ed.] Graduate of Jonesboro High, current student of Clayton College and State University; [occ.] Student; [oth. writ.] Published in Etches in Time, Best Poems 1997, Best poems 1998; [pers.] Life is the greatest mystery, but once it has been discovered it becomes the most cherished treasure of all time.; [a.] Riverdale, GA

WEBB, JACKIE
[pen.] Jackie Webb; [b.] May 4, 1942; Minneapolis, MN; [m.] Clayton Webb; August 19, 1998; [ch.] Alita, Marjorie, and David; [ed.] Robbinsdale High School, University of Minnesota; [occ.] Retired, Disabled Student; [memb.] Minnesota Woodcarvers Assn. (President), Praise Assembly Church; [oth. writ.] Several poems published, articles in small, local newsletters; [pers.] Life happens, and I want to be there to record it.; [a.] St. Louis Park, MN

WELBORN, PHIL
[pen.] Phil Easy Welborn; [b.] October 8, 1952; High Point, NC; [p.] Dale and Nora Welborn; [ch.] Rachel and Jenny; [ed.] Grade 12; [occ.] Heat and AC Contractor; [oth. writ.] Lady Glow, Budwiser ExWife, Boarding House Blues, 1/2 of the 400-Ft Picture; [pers.] Like my daddy and grandaddies, I am a greasy working man! Some women know me as a man of poetry and roses; I thank God every day for breath and ability to work.; [a.] High Point, NC

WELLS, CARLENE
[b.] July 4, 1975; Washington, DC; [p.] James and Anita Jones; [ed.] Currently a student at Howard University, Elizabeth Seton High School; [occ.] Assistant Manager, Jones Transportation Services, Inc; [pers.] Through my family's support, I have been able to hold on to my dreams of becoming a poet; [a.] Oxon Hill, MD

WELLS, NANCY D.
[b.] June 8, 1948; Tacoma, WA; [p.] Louise and Dale Ball; [m.] Gary D. Wells; November 12, 1966; [ch.] Amy Wells and Karen Turning Robe; [ed.] Wilson High, Tac, Voc. School, Life; [occ.] Wife, mother, grandmother; [hon.] Several Editor's Choice awards; [oth. writ.] Spirit Dance, Sun's Rays, Void, Silent Communication, and many more, also, published in the News Tribune; [a.] Tacoma, WA

WENGER, JERRY
[b.] September 18, 1952; Harrisonburg, VA; [p.] Mr. and Mrs. Joe O. Wenger; [m.] Linda; November 16, 1973; [ch.] Five; [occ.] Walt Disney World; [memb.] Poetry Hall of Fame; [oth. writ.] Dragon of Light, Angel of Light, Walt Disney Resort Design, The Way Home; [a.] Dundee, FL

WESTON, SHIRLEY
[pen.] Shirley Weston; [b.] September 19, 1934; Pueblo, CO; [p.] Charles and Georgia Scoleri; [m.] Herbert J. Weston; [ch.] John, Mark, Matthew, and David; [ed.] B.A., M.A., Secondary Education in History, Am. Govt., and English; [occ.] Artist, Writer; [pers.] Poetry is the ultimate medium for the individual expressions of the soul.; [a.] Chino Hills, CA

WHITE, ELGA HAYMAN
[b.] L.A.; [p.] Rev. and Mrs. William C. Haymond; [m.] Rev. Nedgel J. White; October 23, 1971; [ed.] Attended Denver University and University of Colorado; [memb.] American Poetry Assn.; Distinguished Member, International Society of Poets; The Poetry Guild; [hon.] Permanent Display on the World-Wide Internet's Web-International Poetry Hall of Fame Museum; [oth. writ.] "Living It Up . . . On Your Income" (a self-help booklet on budgeting), a series of children's books (elementary age), writing two novels: Return To Eden, an adventure novel; Vermont, My Vermont, a religious book; [pers.] Life-line between a short story

and a full-fledged novel . . . spanning a life-time in a few short phrases; [a.] Denver, CO

WHITE, TIMOTHY L.
[pen.] T. Lawrence White; [b.] April 21, 1950; St. Paul, MN; [p.] Eva White Stokes and Al White; [m.] Kimaka Ashanti White; August 22, 1975; [ed.] B.A., Metro State University, St. Paul, MN; [occ.] Social Worker for path; [memb.] Children's Cancer Society; [hon.] Outstanding Poet of The International Poet Society, World of Poetry Outstanding Poet 1985, 1989; [oth. writ.] Prayer for the Poor, The Ultimate Force, A Prayer for a Saint, The Secret of Forever; [pers.] Knowledge comes from the gold print of Yahweh God's power: use it to heal, not to steal.; [a.] St. Paul, MN

WIDDER, SHAREEN
[b.] January 13, 1972; Sullivan, MO; [p.] Don Lahmann and Nat Anderson; [m.] Jim Hixon; August 23, '98; [ch.] Scott Allen Widder (4 years); [ed.] High school graduate; [occ.] Lyson Foods in Berryville, AR; [memb.] International Society of Poets; [oth. writ.] Several poems published in many anthologies; [pers.] Never give up on your dreams, 'cause you'll never know how anything will turn out unless you give it a try.; [a.] Berrryville, AR

WILKINS, MATTHEW JOHANAN
[pen.] Matthew Johanan Wilkins; [b.] June 19, 1985; Richmond, VA; [p.] Virginia P. Wilkins; [ed.] Eighth-grade honor student at Chandlee Middle School; [memb.] Providence Park Baptist Church, Boy Scout Troop 476, J. Sargent Reynolds Community College Talent Search Program; [hon.] Science and Technology, Art Crime Prevention Award and Citizenship Award; [pers.] I try to inspire others, to stimulate positive thought. Hoping for positive action; [a.] Richmond, VA

WILKINSON, MARQUERITE I.
[pen.] Marguerite I. Wilkinson; [b.] December 12, 1922; Pasadena, CA; [p.] Robert A. and Margaret I. Roberts; [m.] Vernon R. Wilkinson; December 6, 1943; [ch.] Mitchell R. Wilkinson, D.D.S., M.S.; [ed.] Pasadena College, Pasadena Business College; [occ.] Homemaker, Rancher, Writer; [memb.] Farm Bureau of Texas, Riverside and Landowners Protection Coalition, Inc., Distinguished Member International Society of Poets; [hon.] Many Editor's Choice Awards from The National Library of Poetry, winner of the Diamond Homer Trophy from the Famous Poets Society of Hollywood, CA, 1998, for my poem, "Sail the Blue Sea, Oh, Cumulus"; [oth. writ.] "Love Granny, a Gift for Allison," Books I and II, as yet unpublished; [pers.] Most of us in ranching have been good stewards of the land, but restrictive legislation is infringing on our private property rights. This is very frightening to us who ranch for a living.; [a.] San Angelo, TX

WILLIAM, SUZY
[pen.] Suzy Williams; [b.] September 11, 1947; Fort Worth, TX; [p.] Tiney and James F. Williams; [ch.] One; [ed.] Baylor University, Waco, TX, graduated in Biology with a minor in English, June 1969; Post Grad Work, Baylor University, graduated; [occ.] Physical Therapist 27 yrs; [memb.] APTA/VPTA, AARP, ROA (Reserve Officers Assoc.); [hon.] Editor High School Yearbook May '65; numerous awards, Army Reserve; two previous publications through The National Library of Poetry; [oth. writ.] "A Rainbow in Disguise" (Chambers of Time), "Just Yesterday" (Best Poets of '98); [pers.] To share my love of others through my health-care occupation and my army reserve unit as well as being blessed, through my family; [a.] Roanoke, VA

WILLIAMS, BERNETTA THORNE
[pen.] Bernetta Thorn-Williams; [b.] May 6, 1961; Washington, DC; [p.] Tempie R. and Thomas Thorne; [m.] Charles; December 15, 1984; [ch.]

Wesley and Brandon; [ed.] B.A., English; B.S., Criminal Justice; [occ.] Foster Care Consultant; [memb.] National Poetry Society, TFA, Alpha Kappa Alpha, Children's Defense Fund; [oth. writ.] Several poems including "If Our Children Only Knew," "Queens and Twilight," short story "The Bulldozer, the Teapot, and Me," novel Remembrance; [pers.] Strength comes from within. This concept should be instilled in our children while they are young.; [a.] Raleigh, NC

WILLIAMS, CLAUDIA B.
[pen.] Cee Bee Williams; [b.] March 12, 1930; Houston Co, AL; [p.] L. J. and Ilene Baxter; [m.] Henry Williams Jr.; July 8, 1953; [ch.] Michael, Yul, and Karen; [ed.] AL State University, Auburn University, Indiana University; [occ.] Retired Media Specialist; [memb.] Genealogical Society, NEA and Locals, Nat'l. Association of Women's Club; [hon.] City Centennial Award; [oth. writ.] Unpublished essays, poems, short stories; [pers.] I look for good in everything and believe that a divine Providence guides my life.; [a.] Dothan, AL

WILLIAMS, DEE
[pen.] Byrdie; [b.] September 14, 1950; Columbus, Oh; [p.] Betty and Johnie B. Ellis; [ch.] Charles "Tiger" Ellis; [ed.] East High School; Columbus State College, Child Development Associate Degree; [occ.] Retired school teacher and writer for young children and teens; [memb.] New Covenant Believer's Church, Hospitality Committee, American Cancer Society; [hon.] CMACAO Headstart, Teacher of the Year—2 years, Dean's List at Columbus State, Parent Volunteer of the Year at CMACAO Headstart, Volunteer Receptionist for CMACAO Headstart, CDA Award; [oth. writ.] "Suddenly" other stories written for children, not yet published; [pers.] Live each day to the fullest, because tomorrow is not promised to you.; [a.] Columbus, OH

WILLIAMS, DONALD O.
[b.] March 20, 1923; Salt Lake, UT; [p.] August O. and Alice C. Williams; [m.] Janice E. Williams; October 20, 1945; [ch.] Susan Hopper, Robert Williams, Stephen Williams; [ed.] Marshall High School, Los Angeles City College, University of Southern California, BFA, MS; [occ.] Retired Teacher and Administrator, LA Unified School District; [memb.] United Methodist Church CRTA, Educare, AALA, Whittier Art Assn. NAEA; [hon.] Marquis Who's Who in the West 1980/81 publication, numerous art awards, International Society of Poets; [oth. writ.] Art education articles for national publications, poems in Sparrowgrass Poetry Forum, National Library of Poetry, and Famous Poets Society publications; [pers.] I explore thoughts and ideas and develop them through creative expression as I observe life in daily relationships.; [a.] Whittier, CA

WILLIAMS, FRAN
[b.] Brockport, NY; [p.] Peter and Patricia A. Williams; [ch.] Shannon, David, and Alena Rae Pattee; [occ.] Office Manager for Specialty Distribution Fortune 500 Company; [memb.] Distinguished Member ISP, NAFE (National Association of Female Executives), Licensed Real Estate Agent; [hon.] 1989 Award of Merit and Golden Poets Award, 1990 Who's Who In Poetry, Honorable Mention, Award of Merit, and Golden Poets Award Editor's Choice Award 1996 and nomination to Poet of the Year; [pers.] "Don't follow where the path may lead. Go instead where there is no path and leave a trail."; [a.] Indianapolis, IN

WILLIAMS, NICHELLE YARINES
[pen.] Nici; [b.] January 31, 1971; CA; [a.] West Covina, CA

WILLIAMS, RAY
[pen.] Ray William; [b.] August 30, 1964; Midland, TX; [p.] Bill and Jean Williams; [m.] Cindy Wil-

liams; September 30, 1981; [ch.] Richard; [ed.] Life; [occ.] Owner and Operator of The Rose Studio; [hon.] International Poet of Merit Award, Editor's Choice Awards (7 different ones); [oth. writ.] Love to Mom Six-Feet Dead and Gone if Tear Drops Were Silver in the Shadows of my Mind; [pers.] The Rose where life is sweet; [a.] Memphis, TN

WILLIS, ANGELA
[pen.] Angela Willis; [b.] October 12, 1964; Springfield, IL; [p.] Sylvan Smith and Ernest Miller; [m.] Richard Willis; January 4, 1994; [ch.] Rachel, Rebecca, and Brittany Miller; [ed.] Pleasant Plains High, GED; [occ.] Housewife; [memb.] Harvard Park Baptist Church; [hon.] William B. MacKenzie Jr. Distinguished Community Service Award, Jaycee of the Month 1986-87; [oth. writ.] "An Angel's Wings" in Traces Of Yesterday, many other unpublished poems; [pers.] Poetry is the vision many writers use to remind themselves and others of the realities of this life, beauty of the world, and the unconditional love of God; [a.] Springfield, IL

WILLOUGHBX, ANGELA KIEL
[pen.] Angela Kiel Willoughby; [b.] January 8, 1936; Brussels, IL; [p.] William C. Kiel and Dorothy Schmidt Kiel; [m.] Joseph Victor Willoughby; March 9, 1957; [ch.] Mary Kay Willoughby Donnally, Jeanne Marie Cory; [ed.] Graduated nursing program, completed studies as real estate broker, worked Multiple Specialist in health profession, currently working as labor and delivery nurse; [memb.] With environmental, animal, and other humane causes; [oth. writ.] My personal collection of writings, McLude articles, letters, poems, and tributes to family and friends; [pers.] Born of soul-wealthy parents, I have awakened to the intrinsic worth of every living human and animal kingdom and love eternal for my family.; [a.] Burlington, CO

WILSON, ELMER J.
[b.] December 4, 1947; Tulsa, OK; [p.] Jessie L. Wilson, Minerva Wilson; [ed.] GED, some junior college; [occ.] Wal-Mart Associate, Wal-Mart Stores Inc.; [hon.] Billboard Music Acknowlegment, Editor's choice award; [oth. writ.] Inspiration at the Masters (published), The Poetry Guild—New York; The Rush of Fall (published), The National Library of Poetry—Owings Mills, MD; [pers.] With my poetry, as in my music, I'm inspired by the circumstances in life, whether it be human or animal.; [a.] Kansas City, MO

WILSON, JO ANN
[b.] March 12, 1949; Morgantown, KY; [p.] Roy Snodgrass, Lora Snodgrass; [m.] Oscar Wilson; February 1, 1966; [ed.] Butler County High School, Morgantown, KY; [occ.] Kellwood Co. Clothing Industry, Morgantown, KY; [memb.] Active member and Clerk of the Wilson Home General Baptist Church, a member of the International Society of Poets; [oth. writ.] Written several poems and also Christmas plays; poems published in local newspaper, in an anthology for The National Library of Poetry; plays were performed by our church; [pers.] I strive to give an insight of our inner feelings and of God's love as He guides each of us through the good and bad times of life.; [a.] Caneyville, KY

WILSON, MARIAN C.
[pen.] Chris; [b.] December 4, 1947; Tallahasse, FL; [p.] James and Jeanette Wilson; [ch.] Three; [ed.] 11th Grade; [occ.] Writer; [memb.] National Library of Poetry; [hon.] Editor's Award—One Book, Merit Award—Two Poems; [oth. writ.] A Book of Poetry, How to Have Faith In God, In the Middle of a Storm; [pers.] I am a volunteer at a local hospital. I love reading magazines and books of poetry; a voice started to speak my heart 2 years ago, and I started writing, and I love it.; [a.] Trenton, NJ

WILSON, VIVIAN
[pen.] Vivian Wilson; [b.] May 4, 1964;

Lawrenceburg, TN; [p.] Margaret E. and Wayne Harrison; [m.] Harold Dean Wilson; August 14, 1987; [ch.] Jay Wilson and Charlie McMullins; [ed.] West Limestone K-10; National Career College Business School, Aug. '92 through Feb. '93; completed GED at Calhoun in 1990; [occ.] Server at Golden Harvest Country Buffet six years; [memb.] Member of Central Baptist Church of Decatur, AL; [oth. writ.] "Just a Housewife" was written for and published in The Traces of Yesterday in 1998, was honored as "Editors Choice"; [pers.] No matter what we do for a living, there is dignity as long as your work is decent.

WILSON, SCOTT M., SR.
[pen.] Scott M. Wilson Sr.; [b.] August 26, 1943; San Bernardino, CA; [p.] Everett P (deceased) and Leanora K.; [m.] Helen B. Wilson; December 5, 1964; [ch.] Scott M. Jr. and Michelle Renee; [ed.] Weber High School and some college Ogden, Utah; [occ.] Retired, September 13, 1997, after 24 years, Federal Bureau of Prisons, Department of Justice; [memb.] Fraternal Order of Police, Vietnam Veterans of America, AARP, American Legion, South Ashland Lion's Club, F and A Masons, Aetna Hosg, Hook and Ladder Co. Volunteer First Dept; [hon.] Elected to the International Poetry Honor Society in February 1998; [oth. writ.] I Saw God's Gifts—1997, This Angel Was a Princess—1998, both published by National Library of Poetry; [pers.] This poem was written as my wife and I drove through a thunderstorm that stretched from Cumberland, Maryland to Charleston, West VA.; [a.] Ashland, KY

WINTERS, WALTER L.
[b.] November 16, 1972; New London, WI; [p.] Debra Franski, John Joseph; [ch.] Brett E. Kolstad and Cassandra M. Gostas; [ed.] High School drop out, HSED Moraine Park Technical College; [occ.] Interior Systems Inc; [hon.] First Place 4H Drawing Contest, 4th grade; 4th place, 8th Grade Wrestling Invitationals; [oth. writ.] Savage Dreams (published), Gypsy Life, Confined, Wrongful Death, Tar Bender, Little Fussy Kitty, and True Love; [pers.] Love your partner, love your kids, love your family and strive to succeed in life and everything you do.; [a.] Fonddulac, WI

WISE, DOROTHY
[a.] Irving, TX

WITHEE, BEVERLY
[b.] December 26, 1967; St. Thomas, Virginia Islands; [p.] David Frederick Withee Sr. and Pamela Brackett Withee; [occ.] Insurance Verification Consultant for Liberty Medical Supply, Inc.; [memb.] Member of First United Methodist Church of Stuart, FL; [hon.] Member of the International Society of Poets, published in 10 anthologies through The National Library of Poetry, 10-time Editor's Choice Award winner; [oth. writ.] A Tapestry of Thoughts, 1996; Tomorrow's Dream, 1996; Best Poems of the 90's; Best Poems of 1997; Chasing the Wind, 1997; Whispers in the Wind, 1993; Outstanding Poets of 1994; Best Poems of 1995; Walk through Paradise, 1995; At Water's Edge, 1995; [pers.] A friend is there before you know it, to lend a hand before you ask for it, and give you love when you need it most.; [a.] Port St. Lucie, FL

WOLSTENHOLME, KATHLEEN M.
[pen.] Kathleen Gilmour Wolstenholme; [b.] November 24, 1972; New Haven, CT; [p.] Doug and Judy Gilmour; [m.] Roland Wolstenholme; June 6, 1997; [ed.] Platt Tech, Milford, CT; took four years of Culinary Arts, one year track, three years cheerleading; [occ.] Walmart Store Sarasota, FL; [hon.] Most improved Cheerleader, Certificate of Appreciation for Monday night Depression Dinner at Elks; [oth. writ.] "Calm," place to be being published 1000, 1995 in the Music of Silence Anthology; [pers.] I always try to show that people can be happy with the simple things in life.; [a.] Sarasota, FL

WOOD HOLLAND, WILMA L.
[pen.] Wilma Spaur Wood; [b.] February 26, 1933; Braxton, CO; [p.] Perry H. and Gertrude Spaur; [m.] James R. Holland; March 6, 1998; [ch.] Jayne Harris, Stephen Wood, and Jeffrey Wood; [ed.] Sutton High School, Mountain State College, credits through Glenville State College; [occ.] Retired Dept. of Health and Human Resources; [memb.] International Society of Poets, Gassaway Baptist Church Choir, Treasurer for Church; [hon.] Blue, Red, and White Ribbons from Arts and Crafts Fair; on Poetry, poems published in A Moment to Reflect, Best Poems of 1997 and 1998, and The Other Side of Midnight; [oth. writ.] Book of poetry entitled Through The Looking Glass unsubmitted, first section for Mother's Life "Early Years: 1892-1915" (A Book) writing on 1915-1968; [pers.] To honor God and to bring encouragement to others; [a.] Gassaway, WV

WRIGHT, LOUISE
[b.] August 31, 1931; Morgantown, WV; [p.] George and Helen Wood; [ch.] William Kenneth Miller and Sherry Wright; [ed.] Morgantown High, Business College-Stenotype Institute Washington, DC; [occ.] Secretary, Government Relations, Communications Workers of America-Headquarters, retired after more than 39 yrs. on Capitol Hill; [memb.] Charter Member of National Museum of Women in the Arts and Distinguished Member of International Society of Poets; [hon.] Editor's Choice Award, National Library Of Poetry, 1995, 1996, and 1997; Semi-finalist Winner of 1995 International Society Of Poets Symposium and Convention Poetry Contest; [oth. writ.] Nine poems published or accepted for publication in various National Library Of Poetry anthologies and one poem published in The Poet's Corner Magazine; [pers.] I strive to blend words much like an artist blends paint to create mental images of people, places, and the beauty of nature. I also enjoy the challenges of telling short stories in poetry form.; [a.] Alexandria, VA

WYMAN, PAMELA
[pen.] Pamey; [b.] December 8, 1983; Saratoga; [p.] Patrick and Maria Wyman; [ed.] Entering my first year in High School, a ninth-grade freshman, Hadley-Luzerne High School; [memb.] Troll Book Club, D.A.R.E., Contact Kids; [hon.] Special Recognition, Special Achievement, Honor Roll, High Honors, 2nd place in Essay Contest, 2nd place in Spelling Bee, Society of Poets, Student of the Quarter, Editor's Choice Award in Poetry, Artist of the Year on Honorable Mention, Perfect Attendance, Spanish on Honorable Mention, President's Education Award of Outstanding Improvement; [oth. writ.] Friends, I Love You . . ., A Man Known as My Grandfather, Daddy's Little Girl; [pers.] I love to write short stories and poetry. I wish to make my career in writing and hope to become a teacher or singer.; [a.] Corinth, NY

XELOURES, CHANDRA
[pen.] Cat; [b.] September 5, 1982; Canton, OH; [p.] Donna Xeloures; [ed.] Tenth grade student at Jackson High School; [hon.] Honor Roll Student, Student of the Week, Several "Outstanding Writer" Awards, published before; [oth. writ.] "The Enchanted Unicorn," published in A Moment To Reflect and "Liar, Liar," published in Embedded Dreams; [pers.] I dedicate my poem "To Show My Love" to my very dear best friend Jerry Fletcher.; [a.] N. Canton, OH

YANCEY, LISA M.
[b.] January 27, 1965; New York, NY; [p.] Joseph and Miriam Yancey; [ed.] New York University; New York Restaurant School; [occ.] Cook; [memb.] International Society of Poets; [hon.] Regents' Scholarship, Certificate in Culinary Skills, Highest Honors; [oth. writ.] Three other poems published by The National Library of Poetry; [pers.] I am

deeply influenced by the works of Emily Dickinson, and I am an admirer of the passionate writing of John Keats and Pablo Neruda.; [a.] Bronx, NY

YANCEY, PAMELA FAYE
[pen.] Charisse Marcell; [b.] April 11, 1963; Joliet, IL; [p.] Simon Jones, Mary Mones; [m.] Henry L. Yancey Jr.; June 14, 1986; [ch.] Adriene Marcel, Marquis LaVell; [ed.] Joliet West High, Paul Quinn College; [memb.] Alpha Kappa Alpha Sorority, International Society of Poets, Brown Chapel A.M.E. Church, Youth Coordinator, Poetry Club; [hon.] Editor's Choice Award, Community Service award, Dean's List, Magna Cum Laude college graduate, Distributive Education Award of Excellence certificate of achievement in music; [oth. writ.] "Christopher My Son (My Heart Cries For You)" published in A Moment To Reflect, "Heal Our Hearts"; [pers.] I was inspired by the writings of Maya Angelou. My poems are based on personal experiences in helping me to deal with the tragic loss of my two infant sons. I dedicate my poem to my parents who gave me life, my kids who bring joy to my life, and my husband who brought love into my life—also to my faithful dog, Pierre, who is the light of my life.; [a.] Overland Park, KS

YONGUE, PAT
[b.] April 30, 1948; Muroc, CA; [p.] Mavis C. Nichols, James D. Nichols; [m.] Divorced; [ch.] Jana Jones; [occ.] Disabled—attempted murder by ex-husband; [memb.] Distinguished member of The International Society of Poets; [hon.] Outstanding Young Educator 1980 Distinguished Educational Services, International Poet of Merit Zodiac, Summa Cum Laude; [oth. writ.] God Bless the Child, Wherever Is Your Treasure, The Last Dance Is the Hardest, Home, Shadows, He Cares, The Beach; [pers.] I use poetry to share the human state heart, soul, mind with those who "feel" but cannot express.; [a.] Cedartown, GA

YOUNG, LINDA M.
[pen.] Jessica Yvonne Milton; [b.] September 27, 1954; St. Louis, MO; [p.] Chester and Theola Williams; [m.] March 21, 1975; [ch.] Derrick Avery and Brian Kristian Young; [ed.] Northern Va. Criminal Justice Academy; Associate Degree in Human Services; Masters Study in Non-Profit Agency Management; [occ.] Collection Assistant with Mercantile Bank; [memb.] Nation Sheriffs' Association, Nation School Board Association, Missouri School Board Association, Citizens for Missouri's Children, John E. Nance Scholarship Committee, The June Teenth Historical Commemoration Association; [hon.] I create original poems for family and friends, Advanced Boardmanship Award, Community Volunteer of The Year Award; [oth. writ.] Have poems published in the Harvest Moon Anthology, The Book Cowboy Caravan; [pers.] Writing allows me the opportunity to please, interpret, and learn.; [a.] St. Louis, MO

YOUNGERT, BARBARA A.
[b.] January 1, 1938; [p.] Marie Francis and Hector Achiel; [m.] George Youngert; February 27, 1960; [ch.] Four children; [ed.] St. David's grade and high school in Detroit; [occ.] Currently serving as a program manager for a major automotive trade association where have been employed for the past 15 years; [hon.] Received an Associate Degree in Computer Science from Henry Ford Community College in 1993 and will receive a B.A. in Business from the Detroit College of Business in 1999; [oth. writ.] "Together Alone" and 83-page booklet of verse on personal feelings of living and dealing with alcoholism in the family, also had several poems published in various anthologies

ZIETEK, DARREL
[pen.] Ace 2000; [b.] December 16, 1968; Campbell River, BC; [m.] Marion; September 30, 1991; [ch.] Christopher; [ed.] Tide Water Community College, going for A.A.S. in Acquisition and Procurement; [occ.] Purchasing Agent for the United States Navy; [memb.] National Contract Management Association; [hon.] Dean's List; [oth. writ.] Society's Reality, Slayer, Quest for Power, Unwanted Wish; [a.] Virginia Beach, VA

ZIMMER, JENNIFER
[b.] June 11, 1984; Beaumont Hospital; [p.] David and Donna Zimmer; [ed.] Midvale Elementary School, Derby Middle School, Alexander Middle School, Cabarrus Academy; [occ.] Student; [oth. writ.] Poems published in two other books; [a.] Cornelius, NC

ZIMMERMAN, MYRTLE D.
[b.] March 25, 1924; Edmore, MI; [p.] Alonzo and Rose Thompson; [m.] Hollis P. Zimmerman; [ch.] Mary, Faye, Jeff, and Dave; [ed.] Jr. college, Spring Arbor, MI; B.A. Greenville College, IL; M.A. Wayne St. University, Detroit, MI; [memb.] Republican Woman Selby Gardens Supporter (Sarasota), St. James V. McHurch; [hon.] Wrote words and music for high school sing, wrote centennial operetta for Spring Arbor Jr. College, "The Flame; The Spring," was appointed to promotion of International Theatre Festival Olympiad, 1983; [oth. writ.] A few published poems through the years; my M.A. thesis; a collection of poems, Running Night Meadows; [pers.] Get a goal and head for it, at the same time minding Emerson's admonition: "A foolish consistency is the hobgoblin of little minds."; [a.] Sarasota, FL

Index
of
Poets

Index

Noel, Deanna 70
Noisette, Vivian 39
Nolan, Mary Kathenne 132
Norgaard, Mary 292
Norman, Elaina 1
Norrell, Geneva Stockton 32
Norris, Daniella 51
Norton, Nile B. 48
Nosker, Sue 57
Nottestad, Sharon 5
Nowicki, Michael 253
Nuhfer, Shirley A. 126
Nunn, Patricia Dian 86

O

Oberg, Sofia 194
Obran, Mark F. 217
O'Brien, Colleen 24
O'Brien, Wendy 213
Ocasio, Elba I. 114
Ochs, Donna M. 269
O'Connor, Kirsten 289
O'Connor, Kylene 97
Oden, Sarah Kirk 4
O'Donnell, Elizabeth E. 3
Off, Alice Irene 126
Ohanna, Victoria A. 195
Ohrenschall, John C. 61
Oliver, Joseph William 190
Oliver, Robin L. 173
Olsen, Alissa 144
Olsen, David 37
Olsen, Jennifer 139
Olson, Barbara Jean 213
Olson, Patty Anderson 269
Olson, Phillip Warren 190
Ondroczky, Elizabeth SFO 168
O'Neal, Judy L. 44
Ontiveros, Denise M. 124
Oosterhof, Karen E. 218
Opal, Maureen E. 65
Oppelt, Ruth 107
Oranday, Edmundo 222
O'Rourke, Michael S. 116
Ortiz, Betty 42
Orveline, L. Buckner 167
Osher, Gina 83
Ostrander, Sharon 62
Ostranger, Karen Ann 153
Osuley, Felicia 99
Otto, Dr. Eleanor 168
Ouellette, Nancy 48
Overcash, Mary 166
Owen, Lynn 270
Owens, Jennifer 150
Owens, Peggy Ann 221

P

Pace, Brandon 126
Packard, Alan H. 58
Paes, Joyce Maria 47
Page, Jack C. 25
Painter, Barbara L. 35
Pairadee, Archie R., III 186
Palmer, Denette Krpan 145
Palmer, Florence B. 252
Panciotti, Patricia 108
Pancrazi, Pierrette 26
Papavlo, Athena 228
Papp, Elizabeth 203
Park, L. Ryder 238

Park-Frederick, T. M. 268
Parker, Thelma Jo 17
Parkman, Barbara 98
Parmiter, Melissa 164
Parrish, Penelope 232
Partanen, John E. 95
Pasciuto, Victoria 150
Pate, Georgia Elizabeth 12
Patrick, Kenneth 171
Paulson, Dorothy A. 161
Payne, Lisa 146
Peake, Russell C. 115
Pease, Jamie 235
Peck, Michael W. 149
Pedone, Mercy Marbella 270
Peek, Dolores 150
Pendergraph, Millard G. 16
Pendergrass, Lela 277
Pendl, Cheryl L. 147
Penn, Odella Jones 64
Penniston, Shauna 108
Peralta, Ismael O. 71
Perez, Cindy 95
Pernorio, Josephine 71
Pernorio, Mary 46
Peterson, Kathy J. 102
Pettit, Johanna 121
Pettit, Steven, Jr. 142
Pettway, Demps 190
Pezza, Lisa 259
Phifer, Hoyte, Jr. 72
Phillips, Dr. George O., Sr. 279
Phillips, Kimberly 204
Phillips, Ruth 19
Phillips, Sharon G. 284
Pick, Grace S. 135
Pickin, Todd 165
Pike-Moss, Billie Lou 34
Pillips, Johnny 283
Pillow, James 226
Pinet, Michele 54
Pinion, Blanche Campbell 143
Pinkney, Shalaina A. 6
Pinson, Rebecca Ann 24
Pinto, Rosalind 7
Piotrowske, Alice 292
Piper, Catherine M. 140
Pisz, Joseph L. 222
Pittman, Wintrell 188
Pitts, Jean 236
Pizzi, Vincent 163
Platt, Louise 15
Pleno, Regina 201
Plumb, Meghan E. 118
Poe, Belle 217
Poe, Georgia 285
Poindexter, Ophelia 54
Politis, Elaine B. 86
Pollara, Mary E. 219
Pollard, Brittney 131
Pollock, Constance 15
Polpstein, David J. 200
Pool, Velma R. 229
Pope, R. C. 159
Porfirio, Mariano A. 41
Porter, Joyce Matlock 36
Post, James W. 63
Postel, Marie L. 242
Potter, Sequeeta 264
Potts, Maureen 124
Poulos, Misti 79
Povloski, Catherine 168
Powell, Wendell J. I 219

Power, Jack 129
Pratt, Douglas Alan 162
Pratt, Mari 266
Prazak, Jobynne C. 254
Preciado, Jessie H. 179
Prentis, Edna Zimmerman 179
Preston, Paul C. 225
Pretekin, Jodi E. 40
Price, Diane 171
Price, Mary T. 228
Price, Patricia L. 128
Priddy, Bobby Lindon 73
Primmer, Philena 74
Prindl, Sarah E.R. 256
Privett, Marjorie Marie 80
Privitt, Gary L. 66
Puckett, Leslie N. 251
Puckett, Lloyd 239
Puglia, Dublin M. 91
Pulkowski, Margaret J. 43
Purpel, Rachael-Rebekah E. 58
Purrett, Patricia L. 9
Purtee, Sammie 185
Pusung, Geoffrey 170

Q

Quimbley, Pearl 39
Quinn, Mike E. 182

R

Rack, Dorothy W. 185
Radle, Maureen A. 134
Raduziner, Peggy 8
Raffa, Thomas G. 80
Rafferty, Carol 76
Rafferty, Jeanne 29
Ragan, Ronald "Tosie" 56
Ragsdale, Sabrina 114
Ramsay, Sarah 187
Ramsey, Aliscia R. 191
Ramsey, Robin 16
Rand, Christy M. 7
Rankin, Nicole J. 272
Rawlings, Lillian M. 33
Rawlings, Phyllis 218
Rawson, Rita L. 242
Ray, Jean 263
Ray, Johnny A. 215
Rayburn, Robert 159
Raymer, M. L. 212
Rebeck, Betty Kay 271
Redder, Kim 67
Redding, Deborah J. 4
Redman, Angela D. 88
Reece, Nancy Lynne 152
Reed, Emma Noon 1
Reed, Margaret E. 123
Reed, Patricia E. 96
Reed, Rodger H. 191
Rees, Christine 40
Regalla, Dawn M. 38
Rek, Yvonne B. 101
Renfro, Khrystan Page 174
Reuter, Alola J. 55
Revill, David K. 100
Reynolds, Frances 242
Rhodes, Harrison 17
Rhodes, Virginia 85
Riccelli, Tara 271
Riccio, R. Vincent 156
Rice, Dorothy S. 13

Rice, S. A. 214
Richards, Donald A. 85
Richards, Ivy Constable 238
Richter, Shannon D. 212
Ridenhour, Helen O. 157
Rider, Brianne 278
Ridgway, Thomas 225
Ridlen, Lillian Heigle 16
Ridley, Elaine 86
Riley, Julie 123
Ringger, Frederick J. 127
Rinker, Richard G. 3
Rios, Denise 164
Rios, Richard 27
Ritchie, Pamela 68
Ritz, Dianne Rittenhouse 122
Rivera, George 40
Rivest, Lorice C. 204
Rivett, Anne 11
Rizzo, Patricia A. 149
Roach, John W. 60
Roberson, Lynn 149
Roberts Gobert, Ursula A. 100
Roberts, Jeanne 112
Robertson, Alex A. 146
Robinette, Rebecca 14
Robinson, Charles 85
Robinson, Damita 223
Robinson, Georgina J. 169
Robinson, Kathy 111
Robinson, Rosalee 120
Roche, Deborah 290
Rocovich, Elizabeth M. 103
Rodrigues, Mila 93
Rodriguez, Efren 151
Roffler, Ilse 116
Rogers, Diana 62
Rollins, Vielka E. 274
Rondles, Kevin J. 257
Rondo, Don E. 284
Roosen, Marguerite 173
Roper, Michael K. 37
Rose, Carol 73
Rosenman, Sarah 72
Roseo, Salvatore 115
Roser, Mary Ann 209
Ross, Carol A. 223
Ross, Damon 250
Ross, Jessica 151
Ross, Virginia Morton 279
Rossa, Isabell G. 64
Rossi, Philomena 6
Roundtree, Shirley D. 99
Rousseau, Laura 271
Rousseau, Richard, II 216
Rowe, Cynthia R. 156
Rowland, Beverly J. 127
Rugg, Margaret M. 162
Ruiz, Madelein 49
Ruiz, Roxanne 151
Rule, Eva Darrington 8
Runion, Nancy 183
Rush, Raleigh 154
Russell, Bettye 270
Russell, Fr. Patrick J. 187
Russell, Tom 216
Rutledge, H. H. 249
Ryden, Alice Gmiterek 16
Ryder, Esther T. 69
Ryman, Janet L. 244
Rymer, Denise 250

S

Sabata, Milan F.   87
Saben, Jennie   258
Sabo, James   130
Saladen, Anita   271
Salyer, Louise K.   235
Samer, Billy C.   38
Samit, Susan Backus   205
Sammour, Rene M.   128
Sampson, DeAnna Drake   3
Sanchez, Christina H.   222
Sanchez, Cristita Mae   68
Sanchez, Monet K.   272
Sanchez, Ronnie   193
Sand, Phyllis Sue Newnam   7
Sandell, Susan   118
Sanders, Francie H.   147
Sanders, Robert   103
Sanders, Wilkie L.   184
Sandstead, A.   186
Sandy, Walter A.   271
Sanker, Brian P.   130
Sankey, Maegan J.   30
Santiago, Kamylle   74
Santiago, Maria De Los Angeles   135
Santos, Edward   5
Santos, Shannon   48
Sapser, Fran   43
Saraceno, Kerrie   175
Sargent, Diane   163
Sargent, Shirley E.   32
Sasaki, Reimi   259
Saulters, Troy Christopher   166
Saunders, Kenneth   247
Savadsky, Richard   241
Sax, Carolyn S.   59
Schasiepen, Lorrie M.   138
Scheider, Margaret   217
Schenck, Dorothy   161
Schevers, Gloria   230
Schick, Barbara Ann   19
Schmalko, Florence D.   249
Schmidt, Lisa R.   245
Schmidt, Mason W., III   77
Schmiege, Diane Doris   53
Schmitt, Eugene A.   32
Schoenberger, Donald J.   190
Schofield, Kenneth   218
Schouwenaars, Melanie   174
Schriver, Kimberly   63
Schuchard, Tammi S.   51
Schuepbach, Lynnette   23
Schultz, Eve   132
Schultz, Ingrid   2
Schumack, Joan M.   158
Scranton, Deborah L.   75
Seaman, Jamie L.   246
Sedlak, Amanda   21
Sedo, Chad R.   216
See, Patricia A.   243
Segawa, Richard Y.   45
Segit, Louise   40
Seidl, Adam   44
Sellers, Dean   71
Senkbeil, Irma Blase   34
Serbu, Martha   228
Sere, Rosemarie   155
Serrao, Lorrie   236
Serviss, June   20
Sewell, Neil   215
Seyffarth, Lorine   202

Seyfferle, Betty   76
Shabazz, Tonia J.   70
Shaffer, Arlienshia   177
Shaffer, David   219
Sharma, Anubha   29
Sharma, Puneet   208
Sharp, Carolyn   168
Shavatt, Donna and Eve   270
Shaver, Claude   69
Shaw, Rosemary   41
Shelley, Carolyn S.   111
Shelton, Mary L.   107
Shelton, Samantha   80
Shepherd, Robert E.   59
Sheppard, Ruby Dee   120
Sherman, Christen   88
Sherman, Evelyn H.   113
Sherrill, Thelma H.   198
Sherrod, Ronald   62
Shields, Christina   237
Shirah, L. Gwen   241
Shockey, Dorothy   181
Short, Nancy Carol   61
Short, Rosemary Bailey   106
Shull, Judie A.   217
Shultz, C. Wilson   196
Shuman, Shirley   114
Shypknowski, Kristi   290
Sides, Joan Karen   154
Sieben, Heather   165
Siermala-Hanley, Rita   133
Sievers, Ruth Steinman   118
Sigler, Wanda   30
Silek, Laura Spencer   114
Silva, Jonnelly   101
Silvera, Hyacinth E.   276
Simmons, Austin   101
Simmons, Becky   117
Simmons, Earlyne M.   129
Simmons, Laura A.   275
Simon, Randolph F.   237
Simpson, Wanda   24
Sims, Jamie A.   189
Singletary, Pamela Denise   91
Singleton, Jennifer   54
Singleton, Muriel G.   23
Singleton, Rosemary   35
Sink, Catherine Ann   179
Sircy, Patsy Jo Reed   210
Sirois, Monique   3
Siscoe, Jason   78
Siusa, Chevonne Tiana   213
Skiff, Robert E., II   236
Skiles, Pam   227
Slappery, Louisa   270
Slater, Robert L.   227
Slaven, Marcelle A.   177
Slyton, Glory D.   268
Smith, Alicia H.   161
Smith, Clennetha   193
Smith, Craig R.   184
Smith, Cydya   175
Smith, Dana D.   76
Smith, Darrell L.   234
Smith, Helen G.   197
Smith, Linda   12
Smith, Pamela G.   284
Smith, Rhonda   236
Smith, Richard E.   104
Smith, Richard H.   237
Smith, Richard, Jr.   122
Smith, Tonya   246
Smith, Trisha Mozden   226

Soderquist, George   75
Sohm, Ann Trinita   24
Soli, Kim   165
Sonnenberg, Annette K.   81
Sorenson, Sommer L.   288
Sorger, Shelley   119
Sorrell, Angela P.   42
Soto, Martha Wells   169
Sowell, James Rex   141
Spade, Victoria   118
Spanier, Stuart L.   83
Sparks, Dana   228
Sparlin, Derry   110
Spencer, Joseph R.   156
Spencer, Larry   58
Spor, Samantha Jo   232
Springer, Caroline Lee Sheppard   174
Sripipatana, Katherine B.   207
St. Mark, Audrey   259
Stall, Keith   152
Stambaugh, Deborah   174
Stanley, Abra Layne   287
Stanley, Mary R.   1
Starkey, Angela   127
Stavely, Kelly Angela   171
Steadman, John .   235
Steele, Diane M.   185
Steele, Lois M.   225
Steele, Nancy   173
Steils, Ray   167
Stein, Pamela J.   275
Steinbrecher, Christina   88
Stenseth, Andrea   145
Stephens, Judy D.   254
Stephenson, Dorothy   225
Stepney, Lillian   76
Sterzinger, Carol   224
Stevanovich, Maja   222
Stevens, Doris J.   166
Stevenson, Brent   70
Stevenson, Sylvia M.   151
Stewart, Bettie Lou   210
Stewart, Betty J.   125
Stewart, Bianca C.   24
Stewart, Gail Ruth   210
Stewart, Julie Kay   216
Stinde, Jamie Lynn   159
Stiner, Edward, Sr.   159
Stokke, Arvella   250
Stone, Ashley R.   117
Stone, John S.   148
Stowe, Cyle   250
Stowe, Robert L.   115
Stowell, Jason   15
Strange, Tina   233
Streetman, Robert O.   52
Streng, Linda M.   113
Strickler, David J.   232
Striker, Hugh   111
Stroene, Oscar F., Jr.   226
Strom, Evelyn M.   28
Struble, Donna   178
Struckman, Pennee   279
Stuart, Jessica   161
Stuffle, Grace M.   262
Stumlin, Donna   206
Stupplebeen, Robert I.   226
Sturgis, Willie   110
Suders, Cindie   238
Sudziarski, Nancy Lee   112
Sullins, Matthew   261
Sulman, Laurie A.   196
Sunde, Robin   138

Susen, Laurie   262
Sutherland, J. D.   266
Sutherland, William   89
Sutrisno, Perti   99
Sutter, John   118
Sutter, Leigh Anne   158
Sutton, Oliver   104
Svehla, John   171
Swain, Sharon M.   18
Swann, Janet Nicholson   41
Swartwood, Michael   248
Sweeting, Moira   21
Swick, Liz Y. Nelson   277
Swinyer, Theresa   155
Switzer, Maryanne Bahl   113
Synder, Eric L.   238
Szczygiel, Tammy Lee   287
Szerzo, Louise E.   30
Szutenbach, Dreama   121

T

Taitano, Anthony   64
Takata, Janice   87
Talley, Elizabeth   165
Tandy, Gertrude L.   196
T'ang, Meng   76
Tatum, Jimmy James   59
Taulbee, Amanda Rose   66
Taylor, Doris Elizabeth   291
Taylor, Emery   237
Taylor, Harvey   14
Taylor, Margaret H.   249
Taylor, Mary B.   23
Taylor, Patricia S.   159
Taylor, Patty LaRae   247
Teal, Josie Haller   120
Teixerio, Stephanie   168
Tenney, Jessica   75
Tenorio, Christina   265
Terry, Candi   46
Terry, Nndra   106
Tetidrick, Tiffany   249
Thayer, Mildred N.   28
Theohari, Rozi   195
Thomas, Barbara   13
Thomas, Debra   203
Thomas, Dong   211
Thomas, Eugene   154
Thomas, George   209
Thomas, Janet K.   84
Thomas, Lee Ann   100
Thomas, Mandee   2
Thomas, Ronald D.   253
Thomas-Powell, Andrea   77
Thompson, Catherine K.   20
Thompson, Matt   161
Thompson, Rachel   170
Thompson, Scott   237
Thorne-Williams, Bernetta   211
Thrasher, Elise   68
Thurmond, Brenda   237
Thy, Gabriel   256
Tibbitts, Josie   26
Tichy, J.   261
Tietjen, Donna D.   255
Tingelstad, Anthony   55
Tobacman, Jessica   37
Tobias, Ginger Holland   144
Tobias-Turner, Dr. Bessye, Ph.D.   282
Toczko, Craig   57
Todd, James A.   113
Todd, Leota   11